Math Expressions

Teacher Edition • Volume 2

Developed by
The Children's Math Worlds Research Project

PROJECT DIRECTOR AND AUTHOR
Dr. Karen C. Fuson

This material is based upon work supported by the
National Science Foundation
under Grant Numbers
ESI-9816320, REC-9806020, and RED-935373.

Any opinions, findings, and conclusions, or recommendations expressed in this material are those of the author and do not necessarily reflect the views of the National Science Foundation.

 HOUGHTON MIFFLIN HARCOURT

Teacher Reviewers

Kindergarten
Patricia Stroh Sugiyama
Wilmette, Illinois

Barbara Wahle
Evanston, Illinois

Grade 1
Sandra Budson
Newton, Massachusetts

Janet Pecci
Chicago, Illinois

Megan Rees
Chicago, Illinois

Grade 2
Molly Dunn
Danvers, Massachusetts

Agnes Lesnick
Hillside, Illinois

Rita Soto
Chicago, Illinois

Grade 3
Jane Curran
Honesdale, Pennsylvania

Sandra Tucker
Chicago, Illinois

Grade 4
Sara Stoneberg Llibre
Chicago, Illinois

Sheri Roedel
Chicago, Illinois

Grade 5
Todd Atler
Chicago, Illinois

Leah Barry
Norfolk, Massachusetts

Special Thanks
Special thanks to the many teachers, students, parents, principals, writers, researchers, and work-study students who participated in the Children's Math Worlds Research Project over the years.

Credits
© Kerstin Layer/Age Fotostock

Illustrative art: Robin Boyer/Deborah Wolfe, LTD; Dave Clegg, Geoff Smith, John Kurtz, Tim Johnson
Technical art: Nesbitt Graphics, Inc.
Photos: Nesbitt Graphics, Inc.; Page 93 © C Squared Studios/Photodisc/Getty Images; Page 455 © Nick Green/Jupiterimages

Printed in China

ISBN: 978-0-547-06041-5

4 5 6 7 8 9 NPC 17 16 15 14 13 12 11 10 09

Introducing

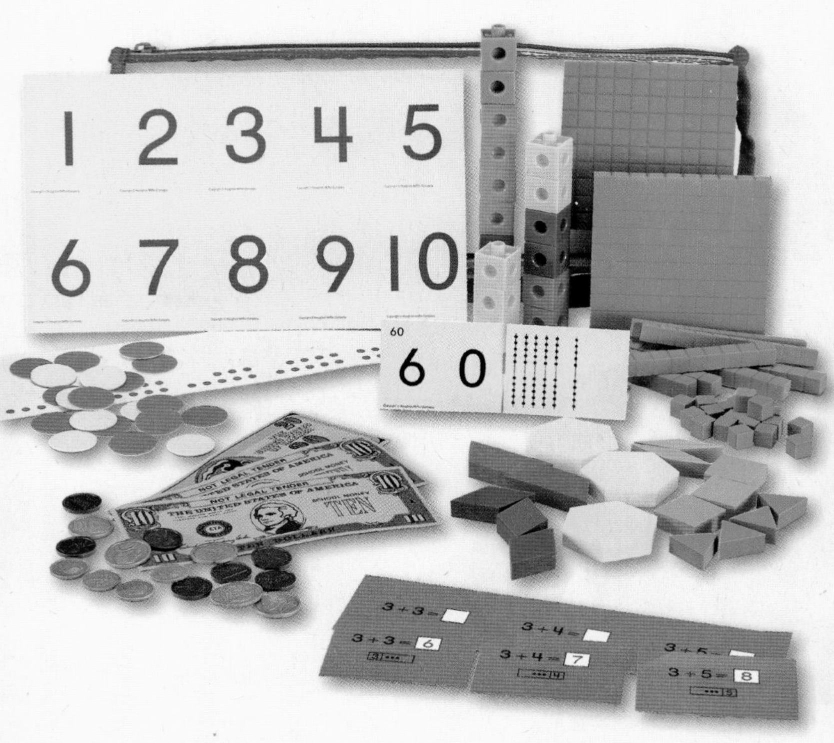

A Fresh Approach to

Math Expressions is a comprehensive Kindergarten–Grade 5 mathematics curriculum that offers new ways to teach and learn mathematics. Combining the most powerful

Standards-Based Instruction

elements of standards-based instruction with the best of traditional approaches, ***Math Expressions*** uses objects, drawings, conceptual language, and real-world situations to help students build mathematical ideas that make sense to them.

Math Expressions implements state standards as well as the recommendations and findings from recent reports on math learning:

Curriculum Focal Points (NCTM, 2007)

Principles and Standards for School Mathematics (NCTM, 2000)

Adding It Up
(National Research Council, 2001)

How Students Learn Mathematics in the Classroom
(National Research Council, 2005)

Focused on Understanding

In ***Math Expressions,*** teachers create an inquiry environment and encourage constructive discussion. Students invent, question, and explore, but also learn

and Fluency

and practice important math strategies. Through daily Math Talk students explain their methods and, in turn, become more fluent in them.

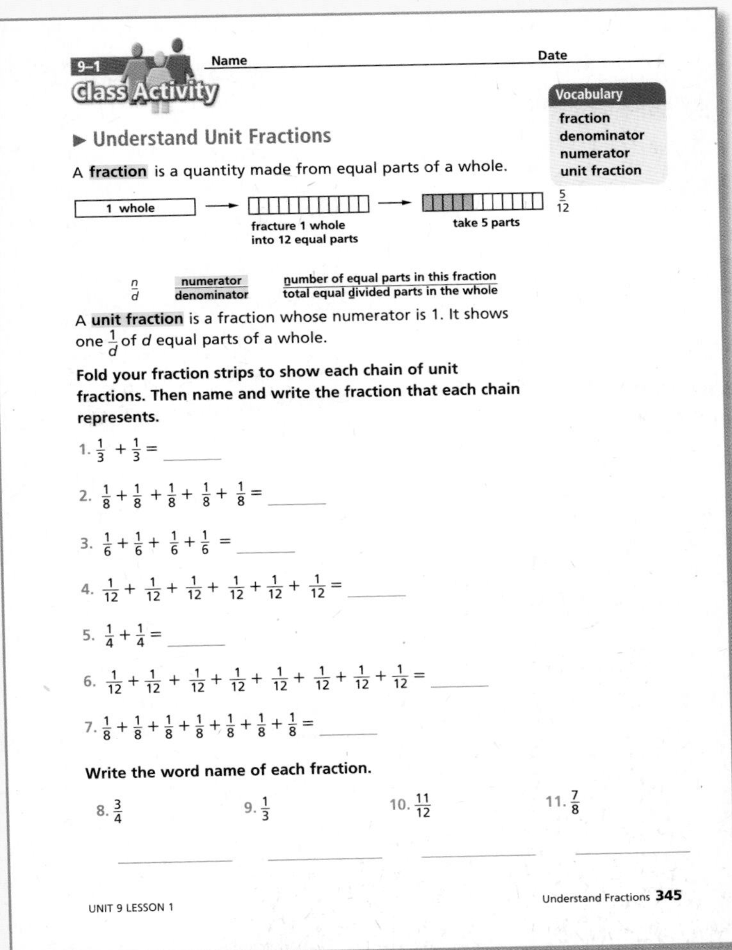

9–1 **Class Activity** Name ____________ Date ____________

Vocabulary
fraction
denominator
numerator
unit fraction

▶ **Understand Unit Fractions**

A **fraction** is a quantity made from equal parts of a whole.

1 whole → fracture 1 whole into 12 equal parts → take 5 parts $\frac{5}{12}$

$\frac{n}{d}$ $\frac{\text{numerator}}{\text{denominator}}$ $\frac{\text{number of equal parts in this fraction}}{\text{total equal divided parts in the whole}}$

A **unit fraction** is a fraction whose numerator is 1. It shows one $\frac{1}{d}$ of d equal parts of a whole.

Fold your fraction strips to show each chain of unit fractions. Then name and write the fraction that each chain represents.

1. $\frac{1}{3} + \frac{1}{3} =$ ______
2. $\frac{1}{8} + \frac{1}{8} + \frac{1}{8} + \frac{1}{8} + \frac{1}{8} =$ ______
3. $\frac{1}{6} + \frac{1}{6} + \frac{1}{6} + \frac{1}{6} =$ ______
4. $\frac{1}{12} + \frac{1}{12} + \frac{1}{12} + \frac{1}{12} + \frac{1}{12} + \frac{1}{12} =$ ______
5. $\frac{1}{4} + \frac{1}{4} =$ ______
6. $\frac{1}{12} + \frac{1}{12} + \frac{1}{12} + \frac{1}{12} + \frac{1}{12} + \frac{1}{12} + \frac{1}{12} + \frac{1}{12} =$ ______
7. $\frac{1}{8} + \frac{1}{8} + \frac{1}{8} + \frac{1}{8} + \frac{1}{8} + \frac{1}{8} + \frac{1}{8} =$ ______

Write the word name of each fraction.

8. $\frac{3}{4}$ ______ 9. $\frac{1}{3}$ ______ 10. $\frac{11}{12}$ ______ 11. $\frac{7}{8}$ ______

UNIT 9 LESSON 1 Understand Fractions **345**

"As students are asked to communicate about the mathematics they are studying ... they gain insights into their thinking to others, students naturally reflect on their learning and organize and consolidate their thinking about mathematics."

- Principles and Standards for School Mathematics, **National Council of Teachers of Mathematics (2000), p. 12**

Organized for

Math Expressions **is organized around five crucial classroom structures that allow children to develop deep conceptual**

Quick Practice

Routines involve whole-class responses or individual partner practice.

Math Talk

Students share strategies and solutions orally and through proof drawings.

Building Concepts

Objects, drawings, conceptu language, and real-world situations strengthen mathematical ideas and understanding.

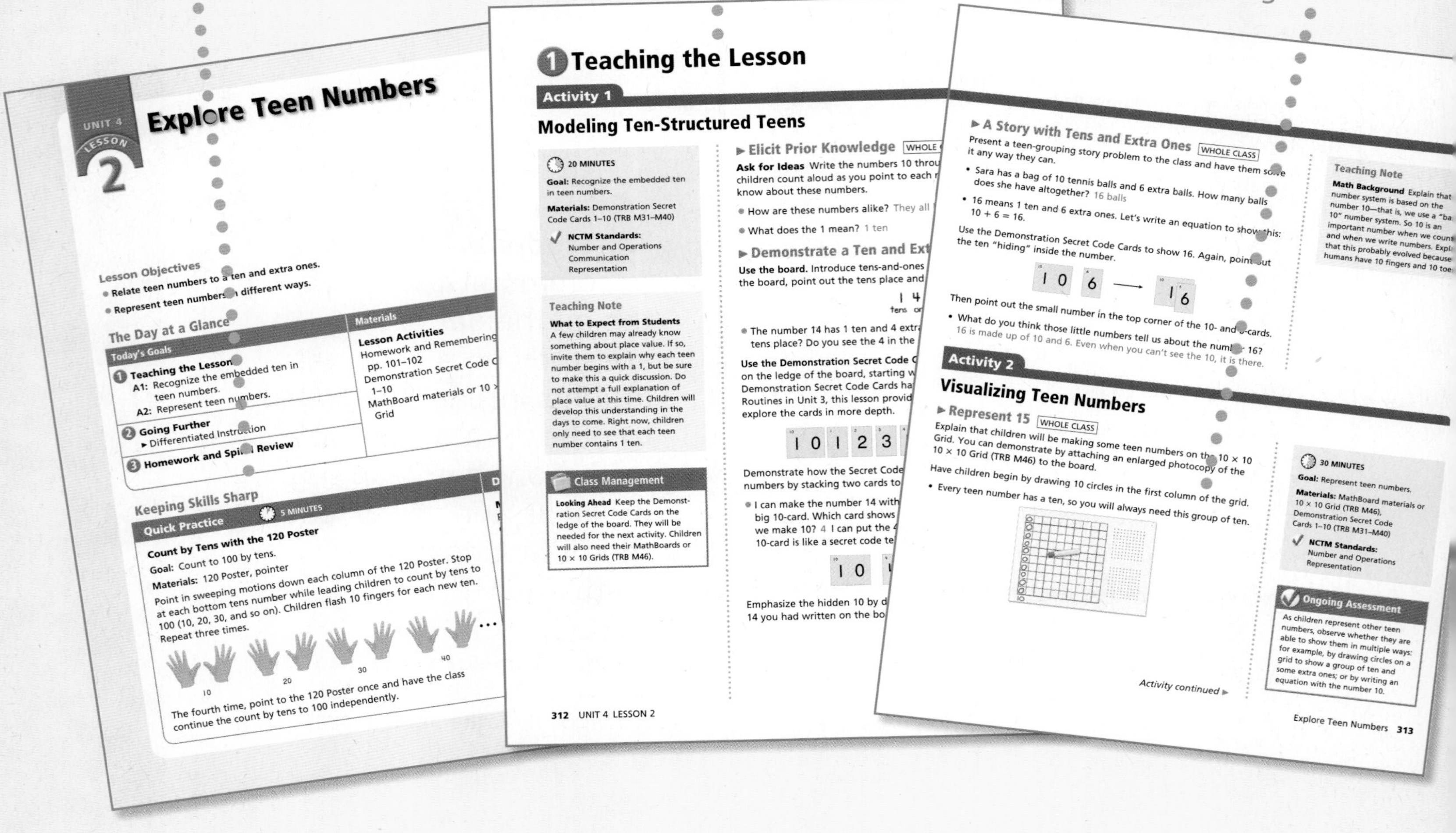

UNIT 4 LESSON 2

Explore Teen Numbers

Lesson Objectives

- Relate teen numbers to a ten and extra ones.
- Represent teen numbers in different ways.

The Day at a Glance

Today's Goals	Materials
1 Teaching the Lesson A1: Recognize the embedded ten in teen numbers. A2: Represent teen numbers.	Lesson Activities Homework and Remembering pp. 101–102 Demonstration Secret Code C 1–10 MathBoard materials or 10 × Grid
2 Going Further ▸ Differentiated Instruction	
3 Homework and Spiral Review	

Keeping Skills Sharp

Quick Practice 5 MINUTES

Count by Tens with the 120 Poster

Goal: Count to 100 by tens.

Materials: 120 Poster, pointer

Point in sweeping motions down each column of the 120 Poster. Stop at each bottom tens number while leading children to count by tens to 100 (10, 20, 30, and so on). Children flash 10 fingers for each new ten. Repeat three times.

10 20 30 40 ...

The fourth time, point to the 120 Poster once and have the class continue the count by tens to 100 independently.

1 Teaching the Lesson

Activity 1

Modeling Ten-Structured Teens

20 MINUTES

Goal: Recognize the embedded ten in teen numbers.

Materials: Demonstration Secret Code Cards 1–10 (TRB M31–M40)

NCTM Standards: Number and Operations, Communication, Representation

Teaching Note

What to Expect from Students A few children may already know something about place value. If so, invite them to explain why each teen number begins with a 1, but be sure to make this a quick discussion. Do not attempt a full explanation of place value at this time. Children will develop this understanding in the days to come. Right now, children only need to see that each teen number contains 1 ten.

Class Management

Looking Ahead Keep the Demonstration Secret Code Cards on the ledge of the board. They will be needed for the next activity. Children will also need their MathBoards or 10 × 10 Grids (TRB M46).

▸ **Elicit Prior Knowledge** WHOLE

Ask for Ideas Write the numbers 10 throu children count aloud as you point to each n know about these numbers.

- How are these numbers alike? They all
- What does the 1 mean? 1 ten

▸ **Demonstrate a Ten and Ext**

Use the board. Introduce tens-and-ones the board, point out the tens place and

1 4 tens o

- The number 14 has 1 ten and 4 extra tens place? Do you see the 4 in the

Use the Demonstration Secret Code C on the ledge of the board, starting w Demonstration Secret Code Cards ha Routines in Unit 3, this lesson provid explore the cards in more depth.

1 0 1 2 3

Demonstrate how the Secret Code numbers by stacking two cards to

- I can make the number 14 with big 10-card. Which card shows we make 10? 4 I can put the 4 10-card is like a secret code te

1 0

Emphasize the hidden 10 by d 14 you had written on the bo

312 UNIT 4 LESSON 2

▸ **A Story with Tens and Extra Ones** WHOLE CLASS

Present a teen-grouping story problem to the class and have them solve it any way they can.

- Sara has a bag of 10 tennis balls and 6 extra balls. How many balls does she have altogether? 16 balls
- 16 means 1 ten and 6 extra ones. Let's write an equation to show this: 10 + 6 = 16.

Use the Demonstration Secret Code Cards to show 16. Again, point out the ten "hiding" inside the number.

1 0 6 → 1 6

Then point out the small number in the top corner of the 10- and 6-cards.

- What do you think those little numbers tell us about the number 16? 16 is made up of 10 and 6. Even when you can't see the 10, it is there.

Teaching Note

Math Background Explain that number system is based on the number 10—that is, we use a "ba 10" number system. So 10 is an important number when we count and when we write numbers. Expl that this probably evolved because humans have 10 fingers and 10 toe

Activity 2

Visualizing Teen Numbers

▸ **Represent 15** WHOLE CLASS

Explain that children will be making some teen numbers on the 10 × 10 Grid. You can demonstrate by attaching an enlarged photocopy of the 10 × 10 Grid (TRB M46) to the board.

Have children begin by drawing 10 circles in the first column of the grid.

- Every teen number has a ten, so you will always need this group of ten.

30 MINUTES

Goal: Represent teen numbers.

Materials: MathBoard materials or 10 × 10 Grid (TRB M46), Demonstration Secret Code Cards 1–10 (TRB M31–M40)

NCTM Standards: Number and Operations, Representation

Ongoing Assessment

As children represent other teen numbers, observe whether they are able to show them in multiple ways: for example, by drawing circles on a grid to show a group of ten and some extra ones; or by writing an equation with the number 10.

Activity continued ▸

Explore Teen Numbers 313

Classroom Success

understanding, and then practice, apply, and discuss what they know with skill and confidence.

Helping Community

A classroom in which everyone is both a teacher and a learner enhances mathematical understanding, competence, and confidence.

Student Leaders

Teachers facilitate students' growth by helping them learn to lead practice and discussion routines.

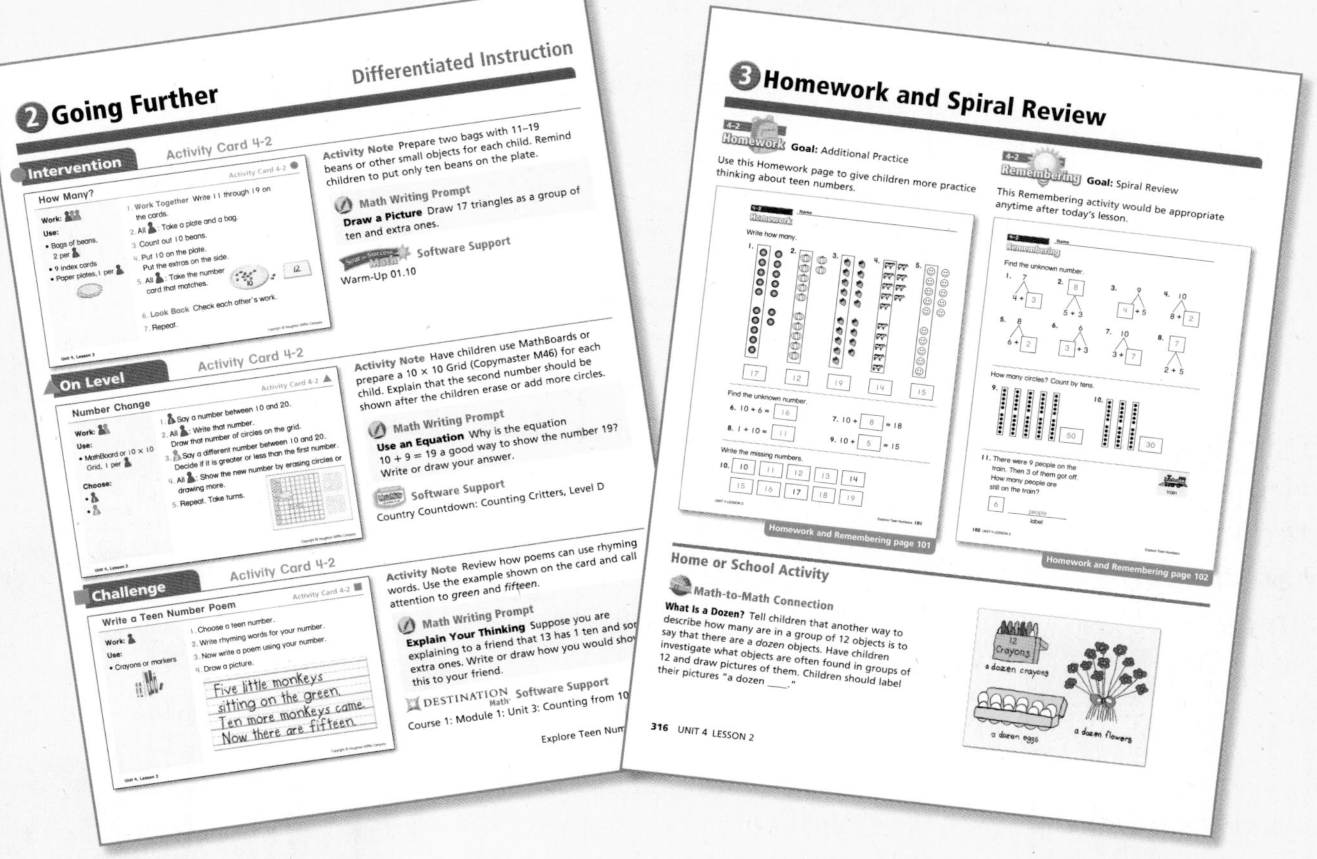

2 Going Further — Differentiated Instruction

Intervention — Activity Card 4-2

How Many?

Work: Use: • Bags of beans, 2 per • 9 index cards • Paper plates, 1 per

1. Work Together Write 11 through 19 on the cards.
2. All: Take a plate and a bag.
3. Count out 10 beans.
4. Put 10 on the plate. Put the extras on the side.
5. All: Take the number card that matches.
6. Look Back Check each other's work.
7. Repeat.

Activity Note Prepare two bags with 11–19 beans or other small objects for each child. Remind children to put only ten beans on the plate.

Math Writing Prompt
Draw a Picture Draw 17 triangles as a group of ten and extra ones.

Software Support
Warm-Up 01.10

On Level — Activity Card 4-2

Number Change

Work: Use: • MathBoard or 10 × 10 Grid, 1 per
Choose:

1. Say a number between 10 and 20.
2. All: Write that number. Draw that number of circles on the grid.
3. Say a different number between 10 and 20. Decide if it is greater or less than the first number.
4. All: Show the new number by erasing circles or drawing more.
5. Repeat. Take turns.

Activity Note Have children use MathBoards or prepare a 10 × 10 Grid (Copymaster M46) for each child. Explain that the second number should be shown after the children erase or add more circles.

Math Writing Prompt
Use an Equation Why is the equation 10 + 9 = 19 a good way to show the number 19? Write or draw your answer.

Software Support
Country Countdown: Counting Critters, Level D

Challenge — Activity Card 4-2

Write a Teen Number Poem

Work: Use: • Crayons or markers

1. Choose a teen number.
2. Write rhyming words for your number.
3. Now write a poem using your number.
4. Draw a picture.

Five little monkeys
sitting on the green.
Ten more monkeys came.
Now there are fifteen.

Activity Note Review how poems can use rhyming words. Use the example shown on the card and call attention to *green* and *fifteen*.

Math Writing Prompt
Explain Your Thinking Suppose you are explaining to a friend that 13 has 1 ten and so[me] extra ones. Write or draw how you would sho[w] this to your friend.

DESTINATION Math Software Support
Course 1: Module 1: Unit 3: Counting from 10

Explore Teen Num[bers]

3 Homework and Spiral Review

4-2 Homework — Goal: Additional Practice

Use this Homework page to give children more practice thinking about teen numbers.

Homework and Remembering page 101

4-2 Remembering — Goal: Spiral Review

This Remembering activity would be appropriate anytime after today's lesson.

Homework and Remembering page 102

Home or School Activity

Math-to-Math Connection

What Is a Dozen? Tell children that another way to describe how many are in a group of 12 objects is to say that there are a *dozen* objects. Have children investigate what objects are often found in groups of 12 and draw pictures of them. Children should label their pictures "a dozen ___."

316 UNIT 4 LESSON 2

Differentiated for

Every ***Math Expressions*** lesson includes intervention, on level, and challenge differentiation to support classroom needs. Leveled Math Writing Prompts provide opportunities for in–depth thinking and analysis, and help prepare students for high-stakes tests.

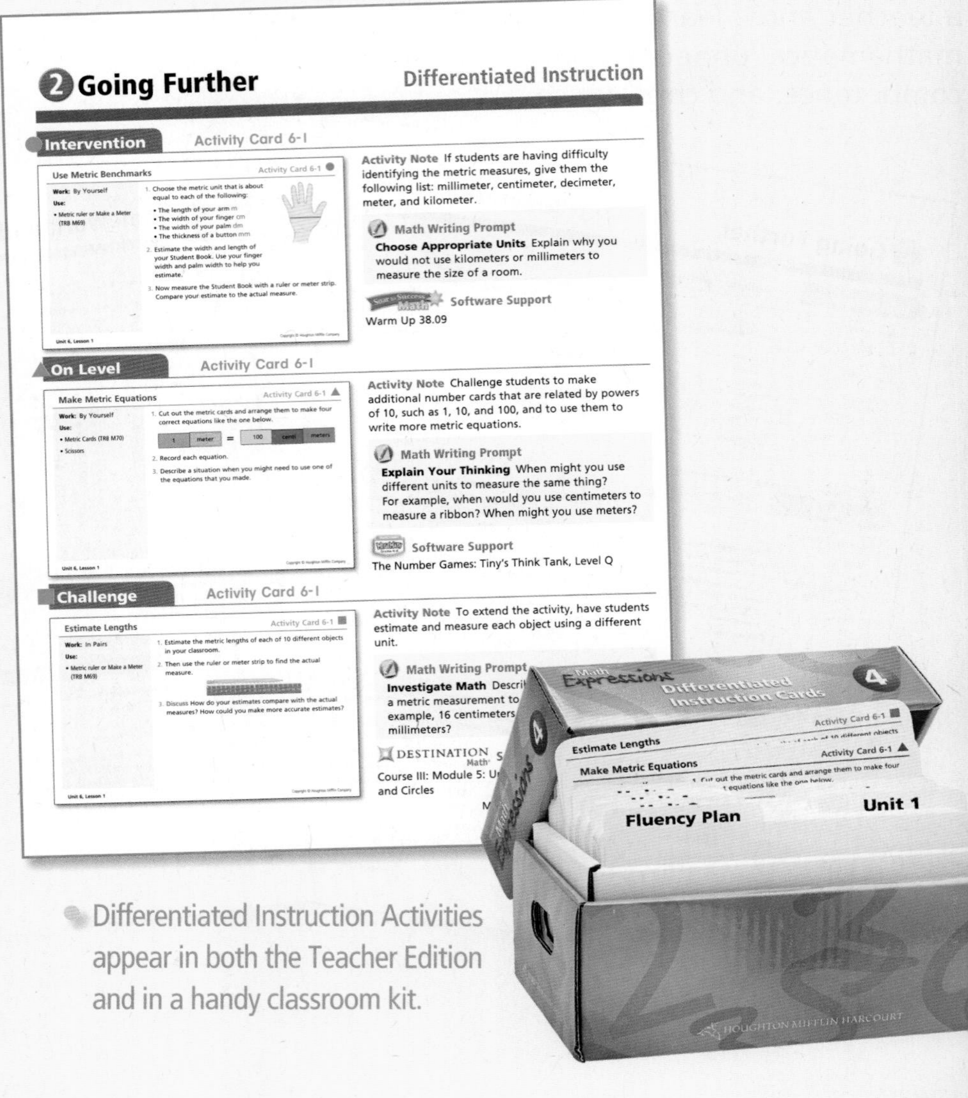

2 Going Further — Differentiated Instruction

Intervention — Activity Card 6-1

Use Metric Benchmarks

Activity Note If students are having difficulty identifying the metric measures, give them the following list: millimeter, centimeter, decimeter, meter, and kilometer.

Math Writing Prompt
Choose Appropriate Units Explain why you would not use kilometers or millimeters to measure the size of a room.

Software Support
Warm Up 38.09

On Level — Activity Card 6-1

Make Metric Equations

Activity Note Challenge students to make additional number cards that are related by powers of 10, such as 1, 10, and 100, and to use them to write more metric equations.

Math Writing Prompt
Explain Your Thinking When might you use different units to measure the same thing? For example, when would you use centimeters to measure a ribbon? When might you use meters?

Software Support
The Number Games: Tiny's Think Tank, Level Q

Challenge — Activity Card 6-1

Estimate Lengths

Activity Note To extend the activity, have students estimate and measure each object using a different unit.

Math Writing Prompt
Investigate Math Descri… a metric measurement to… example, 16 centimeters… millimeters?

DESTINATION Math
Course III: Module 5: U… and Circles

Differentiated Instruction Activities appear in both the Teacher Edition and in a handy classroom kit.

"Activities and strategies should be developed and incorporated into instructional materials to assist teachers in helping all students become proficient in mathematics."

- *Adding It Up: Helping Children Learn Mathematics*, National Research Council (2001), p. 421

All Learners

Support for English Language Learners is included in each lesson. A special Math Center Challenge Easel with activities, projects, and puzzlers helps the highest math achievers reach their potential.

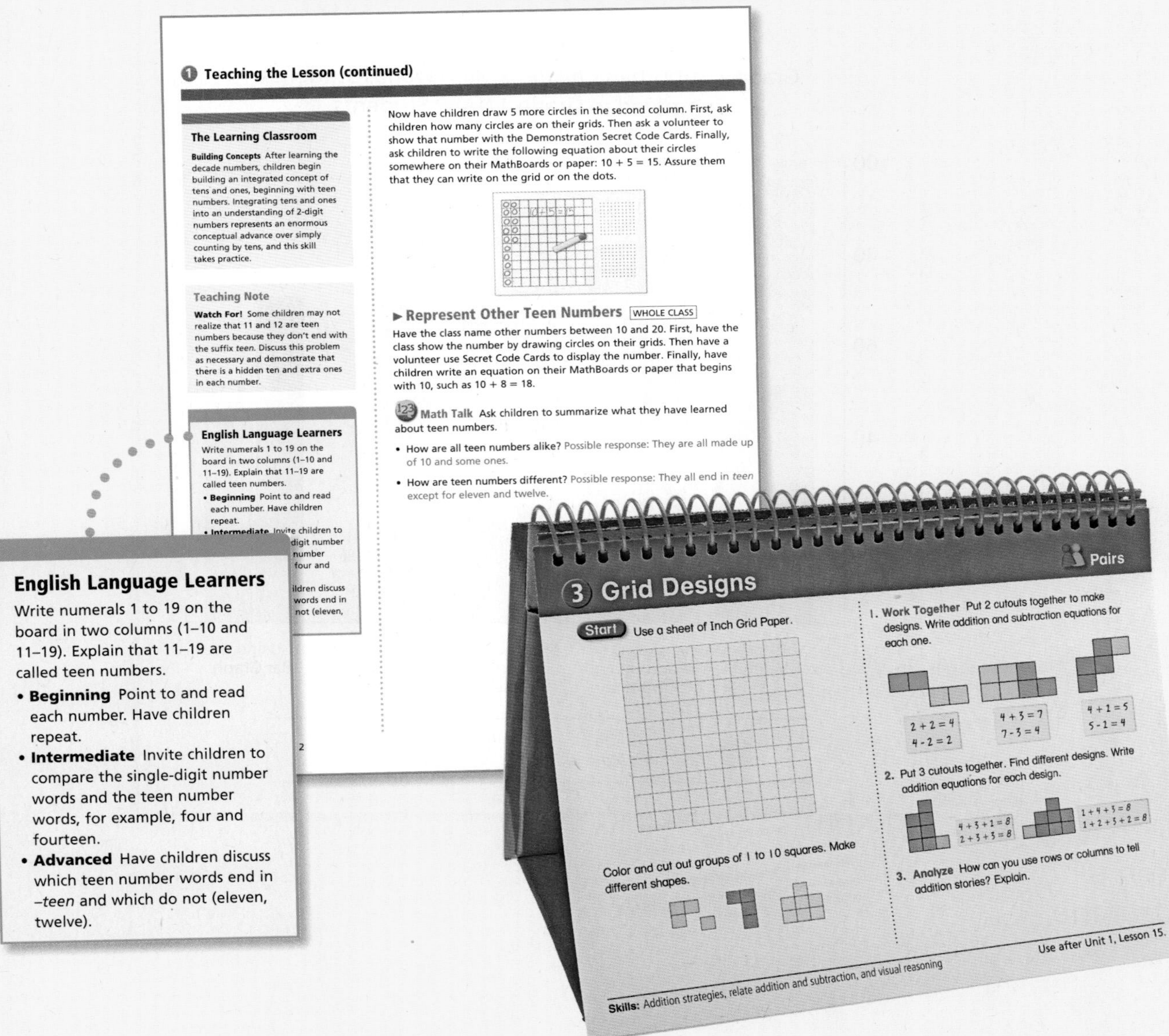

Validated Through Ten

For twenty-five years, Dr. Karen Fuson, Professor Emeritus of Education and Psychology at Northwestern University, researched effective methods of teaching and learning mathematics.

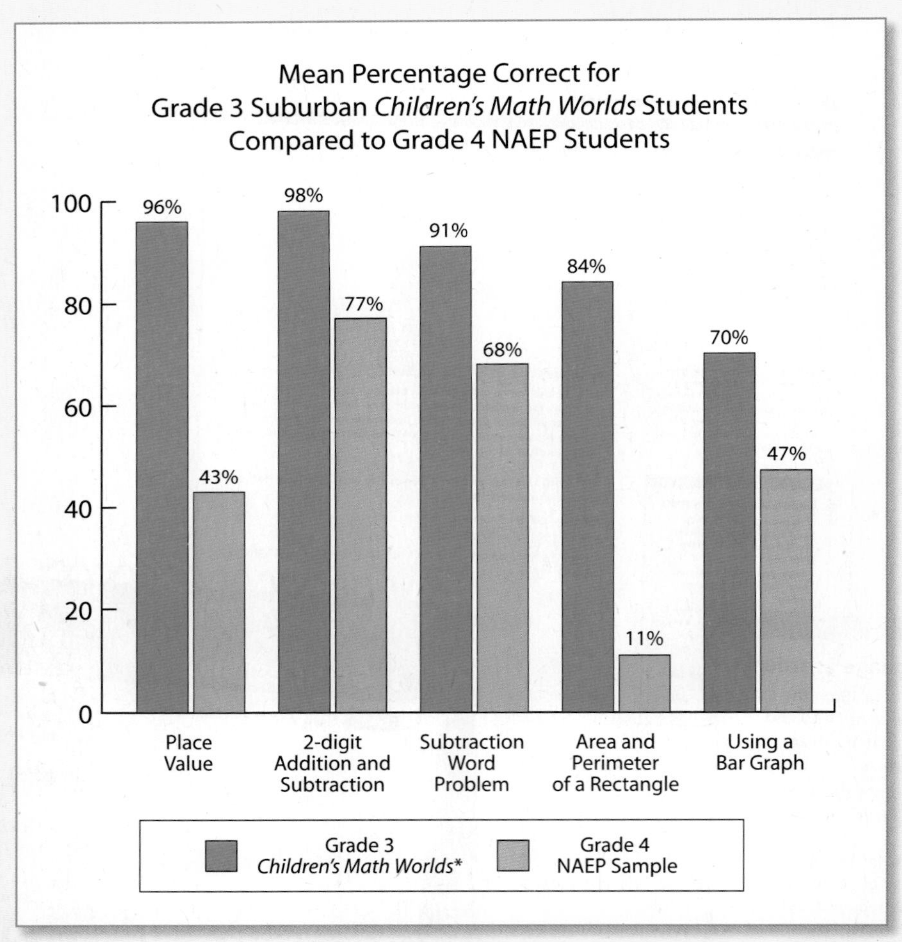

"I have many children who cheer when it's math time."
- Grade 2 Teacher

Years of Research

During the last ten years, with the support of the National Science Foundation for the Children's Math Worlds research Project, Dr. Fuson began development of what is now the ***Math Expressions*** curriculum in real classrooms across the country.

Powered by

Math Expressions is highly accessible by all teachers. To ensure the program gets off to the right start, our educational consultants are available to support districts implementing ***Math Expressions.*** Unique Teacher Edition support and professional development options are also provided.

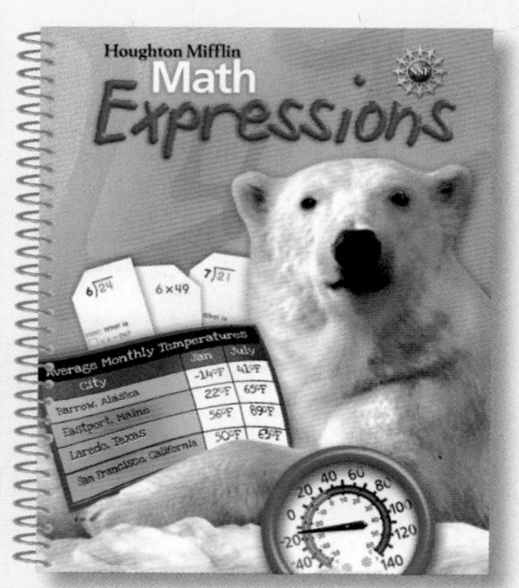

Teacher Edition

Written in a learn while teaching style, math background and learning in the classroom resources are embedded at point of use in the Teacher Edition.

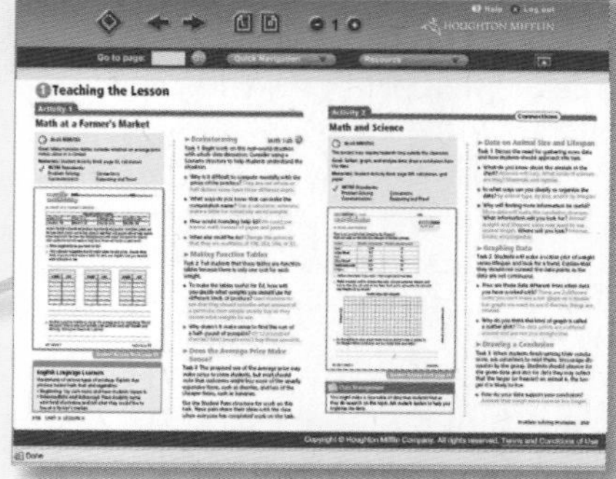

eTeacher Edition

Offers on-demand professional development

- Available 24/7
- Direct links in the eTE
- Math background, author talks, and classroom videos
- Relates to content being taught

Professional Development

Special in depth ***Math Expressions*** seminars are also available.

Administrator Institute
For administrators with school-based curriculum responsibilities

Level I Institute
For teachers who are new to *Math Expressions*

Level II Institute
For teachers who have at least 6 months' experience teaching *Math Expressions*

Components

New Hardcover Version Grades 3–5

	K	1	2	3	4	5
Core Components						
Teacher Edition	•	•	•	•	•	•
Student Activity Book*	•	•	•	•	•	•
Homework and Remembering	•	•	•	•	•	•
Assessment Guide	•	•	•	•	•	•
Teacher's Resource Book	•	•	•	•	•	•
MathBoards		•	•	•	•	•
Ready-Made Classroom Resources						
Individual Student Manipulatives Kit	•	•	•	•	•	•
Materials and Manipulatives Kit	•	•	•	•	•	•
Custom Manipulatives Kit	•	•	•	•	•	•
Math Center Challenge Easel	•	•	•	•	•	•
Differentiated Instruction Activities Kit	•	•	•	•	•	•
Literature Library	•	•	•	•	•	•
Anno's Counting Book Big Book	•					
Technology						
eTeacher Edition	•	•	•	•	•	•
eStudent Activity Book	•	•	•	•	•	•
Lesson Planner CD-ROM	•	•	•	•	•	•
ExamView Ways to Assess	•	•	•	•	•	•
Houghton Mifflin Harcourt Online Assessment System	•	•	•	•	•	•
MegaMath	•	•	•	•	•	•
Destination Math®	•	•	•	•	•	•
Soar to Success Math		•	•	•	•	•
Education Place	•	•	•	•	•	•

*Grades K–5 available as consumable workbook; Grades 3–5 available as Hardcover book with companion Activity Workbook.

Materials and Manipulatives for Grade 3

The essential materials needed for teaching *Math Expressions* are provided in the Student Activity Book and/or can be made from copymasters in the Teacher's Resource Book. However, many teachers prefer to use the more sturdy materials from the materials and manipulatives kits. This allows the students to take home the paper materials (from the Student Activity Book) or the cardstock materials (made from the copymasters) to facilitate the connection between home and school.

Material or Manipulative in Grade 3	Pages in Student Activity Book	Copymasters in Teacher's Resource Book
Demonstration Secret Code Cards*		M3–M18
Secret Code Cards*	8A–8D	M19–M22
Strategy Cards*	244A–244Z	M63–M88
120 Poster*		M60
Time Poster*		
Geometry and Measurement Poster*		
Class Multiplication Table Poster*		M50
Pointer		
Inch/Centimeter Ruler		M26
Play Coins (pennies, nickels, dimes, and quarters)		M40
Play Bills (1-dollar, 5-dollar, 10-dollar)		
2-Color Counters		
Connecting Cubes		
Number Cubes		
Base Ten Blocks		
Pattern Blocks		M27
3-D Shapes		
MathBoards		M1, M39

* These materials were developed specifically for this program under the leadership of Dr. Karen C. Fuson, director of the Children's Math Worlds Research Project and author of *Math Expressions*.

Using Materials and Manipulatives for Each Unit

Material or Manipulative in Grade 3 Kit	Unit													
	1	2	3	4	5	6	7	8	9	10	11	12	13	14
Demonstration Secret Code Cards	●				●									
Secret Code Cards	●				●									
Strategy Cards							●		●					
120 Poster							●							
Time Poster										●				
Geometry and Measurement Poster														
Class Multiplication Table Poster							●		●					
Pointer	●	●	●	●	●	●	●	●	●	●	●	●	●	●
Inch/Centimeter Ruler		●		●				●					●	
Play Coins (pennies, nickels, dimes, and quarters)	●				●		●				●			
Play Bills (1-dollar, 5-dollar, 10-dollar)	●				●						●			
Two-Color Counters	●		●			●	●		●		●			●
Connecting Cubes					●		●		●		●	●		
Number Cubes	●		●		●				●			●		●
Base Ten Blocks	●				●		●					●	●	
Pattern Blocks		●		●		●					●			
3-D Shapes												●		
MathBoards	●	●	●	●	●		●	●	●		●		●	

All materials for each unit (including those not in the kits) are listed in the planning chart for that unit.

Introduction

History and Development

Math Expressions is a K–5 mathematics program, developed from the Children's Math Worlds (CMW) Research Project conducted by Dr. Karen Fuson, Professor Emeritus at Northwestern University. This project was funded in part by the National Science Foundation.

The Research Project

The project studied the ways children around the world understand mathematical concepts, approach problem solving, and learn to do computation; it included ten years of classroom research and incorporated the ideas of participating students and teachers into the developing curriculum.

The research focused on building conceptual supports that include special language, drawings, manipulatives, and classroom communication methods that facilitate mathematical competence.

Curriculum Design

Within the curriculum, a series of learning progressions reflect recent research regarding children's natural stages when mastering concepts such as addition, subtraction, multiplication, and problem solving. These learning stages help determine the order of concepts, the sequence of units, and the positioning of topics.

The curriculum is designed to help teachers apply the most effective conceptual supports so that each child progresses as rapidly as possible.

During the research, students showed increases in standardized test scores as well as in broader measures of student understanding. These results were found for a wide range of both urban and suburban students from a variety of socio-economic groups.

Philosophy

Math Expressions incorporates the best practices of both traditional and reform mathematics curricula. The program strikes a balance between promoting children's natural solution methods and introducing effective procedures.

Building on Children's Knowledge

Because research has demonstrated that premature instruction in formalized procedures can lead to mechanical, unthinking behavior, established procedures for solving problems are not introduced until students have developed a solid conceptual foundation. Children begin by using their own knowledge to solve problems and then are introduced to research-based accessible methods.

In order to promote children's natural solution methods, as well as to encourage students to become reflective and resourceful problem solvers, teachers need to develop a helping and explaining culture in their classrooms.

Student Interactions

Collaboration and peer helping deepen children's commitment to values such as responsibility and respect for others. *Math Expressions* offers opportunities for students to interact in pairs, small groups, whole-class activities, and special scenarios.

As students collaboratively investigate math situations, they develop communication skills, sharpen their mathematical reasoning, and enhance their social awareness. Integrating students' social and cultural worlds into their emerging math worlds helps them to find their own voices and to connect real-world experiences to math concepts.

Main Concept Streams

Math Expressions focuses on crucially important core concepts. These core topics are placed at grade levels that enable students to do well on standardized tests. The main related concept streams at all grade levels are number concepts and an algebraic approach to word problems.

Breaking apart numbers, or finding the embedded numbers, is a key concept running through the number concept units.

- Kindergartners and first-graders find the numbers embedded within single-digit numbers and find the tens and ones in multi-digit numbers.
- Second- and third-graders continue breaking apart multi-digit numbers into ones and groups of tens, hundreds, and thousands. This activity facilitates their understanding of multi-digit addition and subtraction as well as solving word problems.
- Second-, third-, and fourth-graders work on seeing the repeated groups within numbers, and this awareness helps them to master multiplication and division.
- Fourth- and fifth-graders approach fractions as sums of unit fractions using length models. This permits them to see and comprehend operations on fractions.

Students work with story problems early in kindergarten and continue throughout the other grades. They not only solve but also construct word problems. As a result, they become comfortable and flexible with mathematical language and can connect concepts and terminology with meaningful referents from their own lives. As part of this process, students learn to make math drawings that enable teachers to see student thinking and facilitate communication.

Concepts and skills in algebra, geometry, measurement, and graphing are woven in between these two main streams throughout the grades. In grades two through five, geometry and measurement mini-units follow each regular unit.

Program Features

Many special features and approaches contribute to the effectiveness of ***Math Expressions.***

Quick Practice

The opening 5 minutes of each math period are dedicated to activities (often student-led) that allow students to practice newly acquired knowledge. These *consolidating activities* help students to become faster and more accurate with the concepts. Occasionally, *leading activities* prepare the ground for new concepts before they are introduced. Quick Practice activities are repeated so that they become familiar routines that students can do quickly and confidently.

Drawn Models

Special manipulatives are used at key points. However, students move toward math drawings as rapidly as possible.

These drawn models help students relate to the math situation, facilitate students' explanations of the steps they took to solve the problem, and help listeners comprehend these explanations.

The drawings also give teachers insight into students' mathematical thinking, and leave a durable record of student work.

Language Development

Math Expressions offers a wealth of learning activities that directly support language development. In addition to verbalizing procedures and explanations, students are encouraged to write their own problems and describe their problem-solving strategies in writing as soon as they are able.

Homework Assignments

To help students achieve a high level of mathematical performance, students complete homework assignments every night. Families are expected to identify a homework helper to be responsible for monitoring the student's homework completion and to help if necessary.

Remembering Activities

Remembering Activities provide practice with the important concepts covered in all the units to date. They are ideal for spare classroom moments when students need a quick refresher of what they have learned so far. These pages are also valuable as extra homework pages that promote cumulative review as an ongoing synthesis of concepts.

Student Leaders

Student Leaders lead Quick Practice activities and can help as needed during the solving phase of Solve and Discuss. Such experiences build independence and confidence.

Math Talk

A significant part of the collaborative classroom culture is the frequent exchange of mathematical ideas and problem-solving strategies, or Math Talk. There are multiple benefits of Math Talk:

- Describing one's methods to another person can clarify one's own thinking as well as clarify the matter for others.
- Another person's approach can supply a new perspective, and frequent exposure to different approaches tends to engender flexible thinking.
- In the collaborative Math Talk classroom, students can ask for and receive help, and errors can be identified, discussed, and corrected.
- Student math drawings accompany early explanations in all domains, so that all students can understand and participate in the discussion.
- Math Talk permits teachers to assess students' understanding on an ongoing basis. It encourages students to develop their language skills, both in math and in everyday English.
- Math Talk enables students to become active helpers and questioners, creating student-to-student talk that stimulates engagement and community.

The key supports for Math Talk are the various participant structures, or ways of organizing class members as they interact. The teacher always guides the activity to help students to work both as a community and also independently. Descriptions of the most common participant structures follow.

Math Talk Participant Structures

Solve and Discuss (Solve, Explain, Question, and Justify) at the Board

The teacher selects 4 to 5 students (or as many as space allows) to go to the classroom board and solve a problem, using any method they choose. Their classmates work on the same problem at their desks. Then the teacher picks 2 or 3 students to explain their methods. Students at their desks are encouraged to ask questions and to assist their classmates in understanding.

Benefits: Board work reveals multiple methods of solving a problem, making comparisons possible and communicating to students that different methods are acceptable. The teacher can select methods to highlight in subsequent discussions. Spontaneous helping occurs frequently by students working next to each other at the board. Time is used efficiently because everyone in the class is working. In addition, errors can be identified in a supportive way and corrected and understood by students.

Student Pairs

Two students work together to solve a problem, to explain a solution method to each other, to role play within a mathematical situation (for example, buying and selling), to play a math game, or to help a partner having difficulties. They are called helping pairs when more advanced students are matched with students who are struggling. Pairs may be organized formally, or they may occur spontaneously as help is needed. Initially, it is useful to model pair activities, contrasting effective and ineffective helping.

Benefits: Pair work supports students in learning from each other, particularly in applying and practicing concepts introduced

Math Talk (continued)

Student Pairs (continued)

applying and practicing concepts introduced in whole-class discussion. Helping pairs often foster learning by both students as the helper strives to adopt the perspective of the novice. Helping almost always enables the helper to understand more deeply.

Whole-Class Practice and Student Leaders

This structure can be either teacher-led or student-led. When students lead it, it is usually at the consolidation stage, when children understand the concept and are beginning to achieve speed and automaticity. It is an excellent way for students to work together and learn from each other.

Benefits: Whole-class practice lets the less advanced students benefit from the knowledge of the more advanced students without having to ask for help directly. It also provides the teacher with a quick and easy means of assessing the progress of the class as a whole.

Scenarios

The main purpose of scenarios is to demonstrate mathematical relationships in a visual and memorable way. In scenario-based activities, a group of students is called to the front of the classroom to act out a particular situation. Scenarios are useful when a new concept is being introduced for the first time. They are especially valuable for demonstrating the physical reality that underlies such math concepts as embedded numbers (break-aparts) and regrouping.

Benefits: Because of its active and dramatic nature, the scenario structure often fosters a sense of intense involvement among children. In addition, scenarios create meaningful contexts in which students can reason about numbers and relate math to their everyday lives.

Step-by-Step at the Board

This is a variation of the Solve and Discuss structure. Again, several children go to the board to solve a problem. This time, however, a different student performs each step of the problem, describing the step before everyone does it. Everyone else at the board and at their desks carries out that step. This approach is particularly useful in learning multi-digit addition, subtraction, multiplication, and division. It assists the least-advanced students the most, providing them with accessible, systematic methods.

Benefits: This structure is especially effective when students are having trouble solving certain kinds of problems. The step-by-step structure allows students to grasp a method more easily than doing the whole method at once. It also helps students learn to verbalize their methods more clearly, as they can focus on describing just their own step.

Small Groups

Unstructured groups can form spontaneously if physical arrangements allow (for example, desks arranged in groups of four or children working at tables). Spontaneous helping between and among students as they work on problems individually can be encouraged.

For more structured projects, assign students to specific groups. It is usually a good idea to include a range of students and to have a strong reader in each group. Explain the problem or project and guide the groups as necessary. When students have finished, call a pair from each group to present and explain the results of their work or have the entire group present the results, with each member explaining one part of the solution or project. Having lower-performing students present first allows them to contribute, while higher-performing students expand on their efforts and give the fuller presentation.

Benefits: Students learn different strategies from each other for approaching a problem or task. They are invested in their classmates' learning because the presentation will be on behalf of the whole group.

Volume 1 Contents

Basic Facts Fluency Plan Basic Additions and Subtractions

Unit 1 Place Value and Multi-Digit Addition and Subtraction

Big Idea Group to Add

REAL WORLD Problem Solving

Big Idea Ungroup to Subtract

REAL WORLD Problem Solving

Unit 2 Lines, Line Segments, and Quadrilaterals

Unit 3 Addition and Subtraction Word Problems

Big Idea Solve Multi-Digit Word Problems

REAL WORLD Problem Solving

MINI UNIT Unit 4 Figures, Angles, and Triangles

Big Idea Properties of Quadrilaterals and Triangles

Unit 5 Use Addition and Subtraction

Big Idea Round, Estimate, and Compare

Big Idea Use Money

Big Idea Tables

Big Idea Complex Word Problems

REAL WORLD Problem Solving

Big Idea Pictographs, Bar Graphs, and Line Plots

REAL WORLD Problem Solving

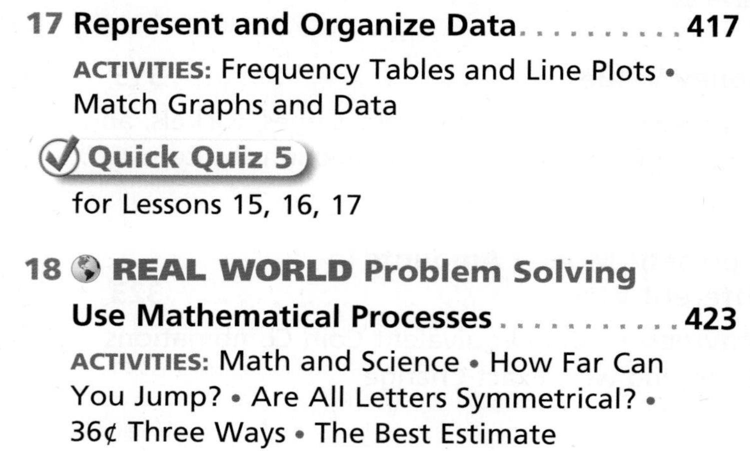

Unit 6 Patterns

Unit 7 Multiplication and Division with 0–5, 9, and 10

Big Idea Meanings of Multiplication and Division

Big Idea Patterns and Strategies

Big Idea Strategies for Products and Factors

Volume 2 Contents

MINI UNIT Unit 8 Area and Perimeter

Unit 9 Multiplication and Division with 6, 7, and 8 and Problem Solving

Big Idea Multiplication Comparisons and Square Numbers

Big Idea Word Problems

REAL WORLD Problem Solving

Unit 10 Time

Unit 11 Exploring Fractions, Decimals, Probability, and Division with Remainders

REAL WORLD Problem Solving

Big Idea Mixed Numbers and Division with Remainders

MINI UNIT

Unit 12 Three-Dimensional Figures

Big Idea Properties of Three-Dimensional Figures

Unit 13 Measurement

Big Idea Length

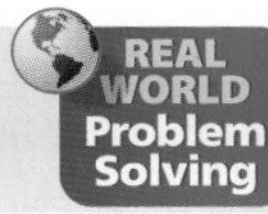

Big Idea Capacity, Weight, Mass, and Temperature

Unit 14 Directions and Locations

Extension Lessons

Pacing Guide

Unit 1 is designed as a review of topics from Grade 2 but extends multi-digit addition and subtraction to larger numbers. Unit 11 builds strong conceptual development and skill fluency at a level often seen in the curricula of other countries that rank high in math performance. In the first year many classes may not cover all of the content of the later unit(s). But as more students experience *Math Expressions* in the previous grade(s) and teachers become familiar with *Math Expressions*, movement through the earlier units is more rapid and classes are able to do more of the later material in greater depth. Some lessons in every unit, but especially the geometry and measurement mini-units, can be omitted if they do not focus on important state or district goals.

Be sure to do the Quick Practice activities with student leaders that begin each lesson, as they provide needed practice on core grade-level skills as well as supporting the growth of students as they lead these activities.

	First Year		Later Years	
Unit	**Pacing Suggestions**	**Days**	**Pacing Suggestions**	**Days**
1	Elicit student ideas and build community. Develop place value and grouping concepts. Mastery can build throughout Units 3 and 5, so move along quickly.	25	Many ideas are review for students who had Grade 2 *Math Expressions.* Move as quickly as you can while eliciting student ideas and building community.	17
2	Be sure that students understand these ideas.	9	These are central Grade 3 ideas.	7
3	The multi-digit word problems will be challenging. Unit 5 will continue to develop understanding, so continue on without mastery.	16	The multi-digit word problems will be challenging. Unit 3 will continue to develop understanding, so continue on without mastery.	12
4	Be sure that students understand these ideas.	7	These are central Grade 3 ideas.	6
5	Two-step word problems are difficult for some. Continue on and build fluency in multi-digit addition and subtraction.	28	Continue to move more quickly as fluency in multi-digit addition and subtraction builds.	20
6	Teach only important district and state goals.	3	Teach only important district and state goals.	4
7	Spend time on patterns, word problem situations, and building fluency in multiplication and division. Most ideas will continue into Unit 9.	26	Move more quickly than in Year 1. In Unit 6, target word problems and basic multiplication and division fluency for individual students.	18
8	Area and perimeter are key Grade 3 topics.	6	Area and perimeter are key Grade 3 topics.	4
9	Fluency with 6s, 7s, and 8s can continue to build all year. Two-step word problems will remain difficult for some. All students should be mastering single-step (but not multi-step) word problems with all 4 operations.	26	Fluency with all numbers can build in Units 6 and 7 where basic multiplication and division are used, so go on. All students should be mastering single-step (but not multi-step) problems with all 4 operations.	21
10	Unit 10 extends the skills in telling time that students developed in Grade 2.	4	Do only important district and state goals.	4
11	Lessons 1 through 5 are a nice introduction. The ideas in this unit will be built in depth in Grade 4.	5	This unit provides experiences to support earlier ideas and will provide a strong basis for Grade 4 fractions.	20
12	Teach the important goals and content of the lessons.	2	This unit is good for building students' spatial visualization.	6
13	Concentrate on important district and state goals. Lessons 7 and 8 continue Unit 11 fraction ideas.	2	Concentrate on important district and state goals. Lessons 7 and 8 continue Unit 11 fraction ideas.	11
14	Maps and directions relate to other subject areas.	1	Explore coordinate graphing if these are part of your state goals.	4
All Units	**Total Days**	**160**	**Total Days**	**154**

Correlation to NCTM Curriculum Focal Points and Connections for Grade 3

Grade 3 Curriculum Focal Points

1 *Number and Operations* and *Algebra:* Developing understandings of multiplication and division and strategies for basic multiplication facts and related division facts
Students understand the meanings of multiplication and division of whole numbers through the use of representations (e.g., equal-sized groups, arrays, area models, and equal "jumps" on number lines for multiplication, and successive subtraction, partitioning, and sharing for division). They use properties of addition and multiplication (e.g., commutativity, associativity, and the distributive property) to multiply whole numbers and apply increasingly sophisticated strategies based on these properties to solve multiplication and division problems involving basic facts. By comparing a variety of solution strategies, students relate multiplication and division as inverse operations.

1.1 understand multiplication of whole numbers through the use of equal-sized groups	U7 L1–3; U9 L3–5
1.2 understand multiplication of whole numbers through the use of arrays	U7 L3, L7, L8, L12, L13; U9 L3–5, L11, L14; Extension L2
1.3 understand multiplication of whole numbers through the use of area models	U7 L10, L12; U9 L1, L3, L4, L8, L11; Extension L4, L5, L7
1.4 understand multiplication of whole numbers through the use of equal "jumps" on number lines	U7 L1, L5; U7 L5
1.5 understand division of whole numbers through the use of successive subtraction	Extension L11
1.6 understand division of whole numbers through the use of sharing	U7 L4; U11 L20
1.7 use properties of multiplication (e.g., commutativity, associativity) to multiply whole numbers	U7 L3, L9, L12, L14
1.8 use the distributive property to multiply whole numbers	U7 L7; U9 L3, L5, L9; Extension L4–8
1.9 solve multiplication and division problems involving basic facts	U7 L5, L8, L11, L15, L16; U9 L2, L6, L7, L10–13; U11 L19; U13 L6, L11
1.10 relate multiplication and division as inverse operations	U7 L4–7, L9, L12–14; U9 L1, L3, L5; U11 L21; Extension L9

2 *Number and Operations:* Developing an understanding of fractions and fraction equivalence
Students develop an understanding of the meanings and uses of fractions to represent parts of a whole, parts of a set, or points or distances on a number line. They understand that the size of a fractional part is relative to the size of the whole, and they use fractions to represent numbers that are equal to, less than, or greater than 1. They solve problems that involve comparing and ordering fractions by using models, benchmark fractions, or common numerators or denominators. They understand and use models, including the number line, to identify equivalent fractions.

2.1 understand fractions as parts of a whole	U11 L1, L7, L10, L22
2.2 understand fractions as parts of a set	U11 L2, L3, L6, L8, L22
2.3 understand fractions as points or distances on a number line	U11 L16, L18

Grade 3 Curriculum Focal Points (cont.)	
2.4 understand that the size of a fractional part is relative to the size of the whole	U11 L1, L17
2.5 use fractions to represent numbers that are equal to, less than, or greater than 1	U11 L1–5, L7, L9–16, L18; U13 L7
2.6 compare and order fractions by using models	U11 L15, L16
2.7 compare and order fractions by using benchmark fractions	U11 L16
2.8 compare and order fractions by using common numerators or denominators	U11 L15
2.9 use models, including the number line, to identify equivalent fractions	U11 L9–13

3 *Geometry:* Describing and analyzing properties of two-dimensional shapes
Students describe, analyze, compare, and classify two-dimensional shapes by their sides and angles and connect these attributes to definitions of shapes. Students investigate, describe, and reason about decomposing, combining, and transforming polygons to make other polygons. Through building, drawing, and analyzing two-dimensional shapes, students understand attributes and properties of two-dimensional space and the use of those attributes and properties in solving problems, including applications involving congruence and symmetry.

3.1 describe, analyze, compare, and classify two-dimensional shapes by their sides and angles	U2 L2–5; U4 L1, L3; U13 L11; U14 L3
3.2 connect attributes to definitions of shapes	U2 L2–5; U4 L1, L3; U12 L1, L3–5; U14 L3
3.3 decompose polygons to make other polygons	U2 L3, L4
3.4 combine polygons to make other polygons	U2 L3; U4 L1, L3; U11 L22
3.5 transform polygons to make other polygons	U6 L1
3.6 use attributes and properties to solve problems, including applications involving congruence and symmetry	U4 L1, L2; U5 L18; U11 L22

Connections to the Focal Points

4 *Algebra:* Understanding properties of multiplication and the relationship between multiplication and division is a part of algebra readiness that develops at grade 3. The creation and analysis of patterns and relationships involving multiplication and division should occur at this grade level. Students build a foundation for later understanding of functional relationships by describing relationships in context with such statements as, "The number of legs is 4 times the number of chairs."

4.1 understand properties of multiplication	U7 L3, L7, L9, L12, L14; U9 L1, L3, L5; Extension L4–8
4.2 understand the relationship between multiplication and division	U7 L4–9, L12, L14; U9 L1, L3, L5; Extension L9
4.3 create and analyze patterns and relationships involving multiplication	U7 L1, L2, L5–9, L11, L12, L14; U9 L1, L3, L5, L8, L9

Correlation to NCTM Curriculum Focal Points and Connections for Grade 3 (cont.)

Connections to the Focal Points (cont.)	
4.4 create and analyze patterns and relationships involving division	U7 L5–7, L9, L12, L14; U9 L1, L3, L5
4.5 describe relationships in context	U7 L1, L2, L12; U9 L6, L7
5 *Measurement:* Students in grade 3 strengthen their understanding of fractions as they confront problems in linear measurement that call for more precision than the whole unit allowed them in their work in grade 2. They develop their facility in measuring with fractional parts of linear units. Students develop measurement concepts and skills through experiences in analyzing attributes and properties of two-dimensional objects. They form an understanding of perimeter as a measurable attribute and select appropriate units, strategies, and tools to solve problems involving perimeter.	
5.1 measure with fractional parts of linear units	U13 L1, L2, L4, L11
5.2 develop measurement concepts and skills by analyzing attributes and properties of two-dimensional objects	U2 L1, L3–5; U4 L3, L4; U8 L1–3; U9 L14
5.3 understand perimeter as a measurable attribute	U2 L1, L3, L4; U8 L1–3; U13 L2
5.4 select appropriate units, strategies, and tools to solve problems involving perimeter	U2 L1, L3, L4; U8 L1–3; U13 L2
6 *Data Analysis:* Addition, subtraction, multiplication, and division of whole numbers come into play as students construct and analyze frequency tables, bar graphs, picture graphs, and line plots and use them to solve problems.	
6.1 construct and analyze frequency tables and use them to solve problems	U5 L9, L10, L17, L18
6.2 construct and analyze bar graphs and use them to solve problems	U5 L15–L18; U9 L7, L14; U13 L11
6.3 construct and analyze picture graphs and use them to solve problems	U5 L17
6.4 construct and analyze line plots and use them to solve problems	U5 L17
7 *Number and Operations:* Building on their work in grade 2, students extend their understanding of place value to numbers up to 10,000 in various contexts. Students also apply this understanding to the task of representing numbers in different equivalent forms (e.g., expanded notation). They develop their understanding of numbers by building their facility with mental computation (addition and subtraction in special cases, such as 2,500 + 6,000 and 9,000 – 5,000), by using computational estimation, and by performing paper-and-pencil computations.	
7.1 understand place value of numbers up to 10,000	U1 L1–4; U5 L1–3; Extension L1
7.2 represent numbers in different equivalent forms (e.g., expanded notation)	U1 L1–4; Extension L1
7.3 use mental math to add and subtract	U1 L8, L11, L13, L15; U5 L7
7.4 use estimation to add and subtract	U5 L1, L2, L7, L18
7.5 use paper-and-pencil to add and subtract	U1 L5–15; U3 L6–8; U5 L8–10; U13 L3

NCTM Standards and Expectations Correlation for Grade 3

Number and Operations Standard	
Understand numbers, ways of representing numbers, relationships among numbers, and number systems	
• understand the place-value structure of the base-ten number system and be able to represent and compare whole numbers and decimals;	Unit 1, Lesson 1–Lesson 4; Unit 5, Lesson 3
• recognize equivalent representations for the same number and generate them by decomposing and composing numbers;	Unit 1, Lesson 1–Lesson 4; Unit 5, Lesson 4–Lesson 5
• develop understanding of fractions as parts of unit wholes, as parts of a collection, as locations on number lines, and as divisions of whole numbers;	Unit 9, Lesson 6–Lesson 7; Lesson 12; Unit 11, Lesson 1–Lesson 7; Unit 13, Lesson 7
• use models, benchmarks, and equivalent forms to judge the size of fractions;	Unit 11, Lesson 1–Lesson 3; Lesson 7; Lesson 9–Lesson 13
• recognize and generate equivalent forms of commonly used fractions, decimals, and percents;	Unit 11, Lesson 7; Lesson 9–Lesson 13; Lesson 16
• explore numbers less than 0 by extending the number line and through familiar applications;	Unit 13, Lesson 10
• describe classes of numbers according to characteristics such as the nature of their factors.	Unit 9, Lesson 6
Understand meanings of operations and how they relate to one another	
• understand various meanings of multiplication and division;	Unit 7, Lesson 1–Lesson 16; Unit 9, Lesson 1–Lesson 14
• understand the effects of multiplying and dividing whole numbers;	Unit 7, Lesson 1–Lesson 16; Unit 9, Lesson 1–Lesson 14
• identify and use relationships between operations, such as division as the inverse of multiplication, to solve problems;	Unit 3, Lesson 1–Lesson 3; Unit 7, Lesson 5–Lesson 16; Unit 9, Lesson 1–Lesson 14
• understand and use properties of operations, such as the distributivity of multiplication over addition.	Unit 7, Lesson 3; Unit 9, Lesson 9

NCTM Standards and Expectations Correlation for Grade 3 (cont.)

Number and Operations Standard (cont.)	
Compute fluently and make reasonable estimates	
• develop fluency with basic number combinations for multiplication and division and use these combinations to mentally compute related problems, such as 30 × 50;	Unit 7, Lesson 1–Lesson 16; Unit 9, Lesson 1–Lesson 14
• develop fluency in adding, subtracting, multiplying, and dividing whole numbers;	Unit 1, Lesson 5–Lesson 15; Unit 3, Lesson 1–Lesson 8; Unit 7, Lesson 1–Lesson 16; Unit 9, Lesson 1–Lesson 14; Unit 11, Lesson 18–Lesson 20
• develop and use strategies to estimate the results of whole-number computations and to judge the reasonableness of such results;	Unit 5, Lesson 1–Lesson 3
• develop and use strategies to estimate computations involving fractions and decimals in situations relevant to students' experience;	Unit 5, Lesson 7
• use visual models, benchmarks, and equivalent forms to add and subtract commonly used fractions and decimals;	Unit 11, Lesson 14–Lesson 17; Unit 13, Lesson 4
• select appropriate methods and tools for computing with whole numbers from among mental computation, estimation, calculators, and paper and pencil according to the context and nature of the computation and use the selected method or tool.	Unit 1, Lesson 8; Lesson 9; Lesson 14; Lesson 15; Unit 5, Lesson 7

Algebra Standard	
Understand patterns, relations, and functions	
• describe, extend, and make generalizations about geometric and numeric patterns;	Unit 6, Lesson 1, Lesson 3; Unit 7, Lesson 14; Unit 9, Lesson 3; Lesson 5; Lesson 8
• represent and analyze patterns and functions, using words, tables, and graphs.	Unit 5, Lesson 8; Unit 6, Lesson 3; Unit 7, Lesson 5; Lesson 12; Unit 9, Lesson 1; Lesson 8; Lesson 13; Unit 13, Lesson 8–Lesson 9
Represent and analyze mathematical situations and structures using algebraic symbols	
• identify such properties as commutativity, associativity, and distributivity and use them to compute with whole numbers;	Unit 7, Lesson 3, Lesson 14; Unit 9, Lesson 11–Lesson 12
• represent the idea of a variable as an unknown quantity using a letter or a symbol;	Unit 3, Lesson 1–Lesson 3; Lesson 6; Unit 8, Lesson 3; Unit 9, Lesson 2
• express mathematical relationships using equations.	Unit 3, Lesson 1–Lesson 3; Lesson 6; Lesson 8; Unit 5, Lesson 13; Unit 8, Lesson 3; Unit 9, Lesson 8; Lesson 11–Lesson 12; Lesson 14

Algebra Standard (cont.)	
Use mathematical models to represent and understand quantitative relationships	
• model problem situations with objects and use representations such as graphs, tables, and equations to draw conclusions.	Unit 3, Lesson 1–Lesson 3; Unit 5, Lesson 8; Lesson 10; Lesson 16; Unit 6, Lesson 3; Unit 9, Lesson 1–Lesson 2; Lesson 7; Lesson 11–Lesson 12; Unit 11, Lesson 7; Unit 13, Lesson 8
Analyze change in various contexts	
• investigate how a change in one variable relates to a change in a second variable;	Unit 9, Lesson 1; Lesson 7–Lesson 8; Lesson 13; Unit 13, Lesson 8–Lesson 9
• identify and describe situations with constant or varying rates of change and compare them.	Unit 9, Lesson 7; Unit 13, Lesson 8–Lesson 9

Geometry Standard	
Analyze characteristics and properties of two- and three-dimensional geometric shapes and develop mathematical arguments about geometric relationships	
• identify, compare, and analyze attributes of two- and three-dimensional shapes and develop vocabulary to describe the attributes;	Unit 2, Lesson 3–Lesson 5; Unit 4, Lesson 1; Lesson 3; Lesson 4; Unit 12, Lesson 1–Lesson 5
• classify two- and three-dimensional shapes according to their properties and develop definitions of classes of shapes such as triangles and pyramids;	Unit 2, Lesson 3–Lesson 5; Unit 4, Lesson 1–Lesson 3; Unit 12, Lesson 3–Lesson 5
• investigate and predict the results of putting together and taking apart two- and three-dimensional shapes.	Unit 2, Lesson 3; Lesson 4; Unit 4, Lesson 1–Lesson 3 Unit 12, Lesson 1; Lesson 2
• investigate, describe, and reason about the results of subdividing, combining, and transforming shapes;	Unit 2, Lesson 3; Lesson 4, Unit 4, Lesson 1; Lesson 2; Unit 6, Lesson 1
• explore congruence and similarity;	Unit 4, Lesson 1; Lesson 2
• make and test conjectures about geometric properties and relationships and develop logical arguments to justify conclusions.	Unit 2, Lesson 4; Lesson 5; Unit 4, Lesson 1; Lesson 3; Unit 8, Lesson 2; Unit 12, Lesson 1

NCTM Standards and Expectations Correlation for Grade 3 (cont.)

Geometry Standard (cont.)	
Specify locations and describe spatial relationships using coordinate geometry and other representational systems	
• describe location and movement using common language and geometric vocabulary;	Unit 14, Lesson 1–Lesson 3
• make and use coordinate systems to specify locations and to describe paths;	Unit 14, Lesson 1–Lesson 3
• find the distance between points along horizontal and vertical lines of a coordinate system.	Unit 14, Lesson 1–Lesson 3
Apply transformations and use symmetry to analyze mathematical situations	
• predict and describe the results of sliding, flipping, and turning two-dimensional shapes;	Unit 4, Lesson 1; Lesson 2, Unit 6, Lesson 1–Lesson 3
• describe a motion or a series of motions that will show that two shapes are congruent;	Unit 4, Lesson 1; Lesson 2; Unit 6, Lesson 1
• identify and describe line and rotational symmetry in two- and three-dimensional shapes and designs.	Unit 4, Lesson 1; Lesson 2; Unit 6, Lesson 1
Use visualization, spatial reasoning, and geometric modeling to solve problems	
• build and draw geometric objects;	Unit 2, Lesson 4; Lesson 5; Unit 4, Lesson 1; Lesson 2; Unit 6, Lesson 1–Lesson 3; Unit 8, Lesson 1–Lesson 3; Unit 12, Lesson 1–Lesson 5; Unit 14, Lesson 1–Lesson 3
• create and describe mental images of objects, patterns, and paths;	Unit 2, Lesson 2; Lesson 3; Unit 6, Lesson 1; Lesson 3; Unit 8, Lesson 1; Unit 12, Lesson 1
• identify and build a three-dimensional object from two-dimensional representations of that object;	Unit 12, Lesson 1–Lesson 4
• identify and build a two-dimensional representation of a three-dimensional object;	Unit 12, Lesson 2–Lesson 4
• use geometric models to solve problems in other areas of mathematics, such as number and measurement;	Unit 6, Lesson 3; Unit 7, Lesson 10; Unit 8, Lesson 1–Lesson 3; Unit 12, Lesson 2
• recognize geometric ideas and relationships and apply them to other disciplines and to problems that arise in the classroom or in everyday life.	Unit 6, Lesson 3; Unit 8, Lesson 1; Unit 12, Lesson 2, Unit 14, Lesson 2

Measurement Standard	
Understand measurable attributes of objects and the units, systems, and processes of measurement	
• understand such attributes as length, area, weight, volume, and size of angle and select the appropriate type of unit for measuring each attribute;	Unit 2, Lesson 1–Lesson 4; Unit 4, Lesson 1; Lesson 2; Lesson 4; Unit 7, Lesson 10; Unit 8, Lesson 1–Lesson 3; Unit 9, Lesson 2; Lesson 4; Lesson 8; Unit 10, Lesson 1–Lesson 3; Unit 12, Lesson 5; Unit 13, Lesson 1; Lesson 3–Lesson 6; Lesson 9; Unit 14, Lesson 1; Lesson 3
• understand the need for measuring with standard units and become familiar with standard units in the customary and metric systems;	Unit 2, Lesson l; Unit 13, Lesson 1–Lesson 3; Lesson 5–Lesson 6; Lesson 9–Lesson 10; Unit 10, Lesson 1–Lesson 3
• carry out simple unit conversions, such as from centimeters to meters, within a system of measurement;	Unit 13, Lesson 2–Lesson 3; Lesson 5–Lesson 9
• understand that measurements are approximations and how differences in units affect precision;	Unit 2, Lesson 1; Unit 13, Lesson 1; Lesson 4
• explore what happens to measurements of a two-dimensional shape such as its perimeter and area when the shape is changed in some way.	Unit 2, Lesson 4; Unit 8, Lesson 1; Lesson 2
Apply appropriate techniques, tools, and formulas to determine measurements	
• develop strategies for estimating the perimeters, areas, and volumes of irregular shapes;	Unit 8, Lesson 1; Unit 12, Lesson 5
• select and apply appropriate standard units and tools to measure length, area, volume, weight, time, temperature, and the size of angles;	Unit 2, Lesson 1–Lesson 4; Unit 4, Lesson 2; Lesson 3; Unit 8, Lesson 1–Lesson 3; Unit 10, Lesson 1–Lesson 3; Unit 12, Lesson 5; Unit 13, Lesson 1–Lesson 5; Lesson 9–Lesson 10; Unit 14, Lesson 1–Lesson 3
• select and use benchmarks to estimate measurements;	Unit 13, Lesson 2–Lesson 3; Lesson 5; Lesson 9–Lesson 10
• develop, understand, and use formulas to find the area of rectangles and related triangles and parallelograms;	Unit 8, Lesson 2; Lesson 3
• develop strategies to determine the surface areas and volumes of rectangular solids.	Unit 12, Lesson 2

NCTM Standards and Expectations Correlation for Grade 3 (cont.)

Data Analysis and Probability Standard	
Formulate questions that can be addressed with data and collect, organize, and display relevant data to answer them	
• design investigations to address a question and consider how data-collection methods affect the nature of the data set;	Unit 5, Lesson 15; Lesson 17
• collect data using observations, surveys, and experiments;	Unit 5, Lesson 10; Lesson 15; Lesson 17
• represent data using tables and graphs such as line plots, bar graphs, and line graphs;	Unit 5, Lesson 8–Lesson 10; Lesson 15; Lesson 16; Lesson 17; Unit 7, Lesson 5
• recognize the differences in representing categorical and numerical data.	Unit 5, Lesson 17; Unit 11, Lesson 8
Select and use appropriate statistical methods to analyze data	
• describe the shape and important features of a set of data and compare related data sets, with an emphasis on how the data are distributed;	Unit 5, Lesson 10; Lesson 15; Lesson 17
• use measures of center, focusing on the median, and understand what each does and does not indicate about the data set;	Unit 5, Lesson 17
• compare different representations of the same data and evaluate how well each representation shows important aspects of the data.	Unit 5, Lesson 16–Lesson 17
Develop and evaluate inferences and predictions that are based on data	
• propose and justify conclusions and predictions that are based on data and design studies to further investigate the conclusions or predictions.	Unit 5, Lesson 15–Lesson 17; Unit 7, Lesson 5; Unit 9, Lesson 7; Unit 11, Lesson 3–Lesson 5; Lesson 7; Lesson 8
Understand and apply basic concepts of probability	
• describe events as likely or unlikely and discuss the degree of likelihood using such words as *certain, equally likely,* and *impossible;*	Unit 11, Lesson 8
• predict the probability of outcomes of simple experiments and test the predictions;	Unit 11, Lesson 8
• understand that the measure of the likelihood of an event can be represented by a number from 0 to 1.	Unit 11, Lesson 8

Problem Solving Standard	
• build new mathematical knowledge through problem solving;	Unit 1, Lesson 5; Lesson 10; Unit 3, Lesson 3–Lesson 4; Unit 5, Lesson 4–Lesson 6; Lesson 10; Lesson 13–Lesson 14; Lesson 17; Unit 7, Lesson 3–Lesson 4; Lesson 10; Lesson 12; Unit 9, Lesson 2; Lesson 6–Lesson 7; Lesson 10–Lesson 11; Lesson 14; Unit 11, Lesson 3; Lesson 6; Lesson 11; Lesson 14–Lesson 15; Lesson 17–Lesson 20; Unit 13, Lesson 5
• solve problems that arise in mathematics and in other contexts;	Unit 1, Lesson 3–Lesson 7; Lesson 10–Lesson 15; Unit 3, Lesson 1–Lesson 8; Unit 5, Lesson 4–Lesson 7; Lesson 9–Lesson 15; Unit 7, Lesson 1; Lesson 3–Lesson 6; Lesson 8; Lesson 10–Lesson 11; Unit 9, Lesson 2; Lesson 4; Lesson 6–Lesson 7; Lesson 10–Lesson 14; Unit 11, Lesson 3; Lesson 5–Lesson 6; Lesson 11–Lesson 13; Unit 13, Lesson 6–Lesson 7
• apply and adapt a variety of appropriate strategies to solve problems;	Unit 1, Lesson 3–Lesson 7; Lesson 10–Lesson 15; Unit 3, Lesson 1; Unit 5, Lesson 4–Lesson 7; Lesson 9–Lesson 15; Lesson 17; Unit 7, Lesson 1; Lesson 3–Lesson 4; Lesson 6; Lesson 8; Lesson 10–Lesson 12; Lesson 16; Unit 9, Lesson 4; Lesson 6–Lesson 7; Lesson 10–Lesson 14; Unit 11, Lesson 3; Lesson 5–Lesson 6; Lesson 11–Lesson 15; Lesson 17–Lesson 20
• monitor and reflect on the process of mathematical problem solving.	Unit 1, Lesson 3–Lesson 7; Lesson 10–Lesson 15; Unit 3, Lesson 1–Lesson 8; Unit 5, Lesson 4–Lesson 7; Lesson 9–Lesson 15; Unit 7, Lesson 3–Lesson 4; Lesson 6; Lesson 10–Lesson 11; Lesson 16; Unit 9, Lesson 3; Lesson 6; Lesson 7; Lesson 10–Lesson 14; Unit 11, Lesson 3; Lesson 5–Lesson 6; Lesson 11–Lesson 15; Lesson 17–Lesson 20; Unit 13, Lesson 5–Lesson 7
Reasoning and Proof Standard	
• recognize reasoning and proof as fundamental aspects of mathematics;	Unit 5, Lesson 1–Lesson 2; Lesson 9; Unit 9, Lesson 10
• make and investigate mathematical conjectures;	Unit 4, Lesson 1–Lesson 3; Unit 5, Lesson 1–Lesson 2; Unit 6, Lesson 2, Lesson 3; Lesson 5; Lesson 10; Unit 13, Lesson 5; Lesson 7
• develop and evaluate mathematical arguments and proofs;	Unit 5, Lesson 1–Lesson 2; Unit 6, Lesson 3; Lesson 5; Lesson 10; Unit 13, Lesson 5; Lesson 7
• select and use various types of reasoning and methods of proof.	Unit 3, Lesson 7; Unit 5, Lesson 1–Lesson 2; Lesson 9, Unit 6, Lesson 3; Lesson 4; Lesson 10–Lesson 11; Lesson 13–Lesson 14; Unit 9, Lesson 10; Unit 13, Lesson 5; Lesson 7

NCTM Standards and Expectations Correlation for Grade 3 (cont.)

Communication Standard	
• organize and consolidate their mathematical thinking through communication;	Unit 1, Lesson 3–Lesson 4; Unit 3, Lesson 1–Lesson 5; Unit 4, Lesson 4; Lesson 6; Lesson 12–Lesson 15; Unit 5, Lesson 3–Lesson 6; Lesson 8–Lesson 12; Lesson 15–Lesson 16; Unit 7, Lesson 11; Unit 9, Lesson 10; Unit 11, Lesson 15–Lesson 16; Unit 13, Lesson 1–Lesson 4; Lesson 9–Lesson 10
• communicate their mathematical thinking coherently and clearly to peers, teachers, and others;	Unit 1, Lesson 3–Lesson 4; Unit 3, Lesson 1–Lesson 5; Unit 4, Lesson 4; Lesson 6; Lesson 12–Lesson 15; Unit 5, Lesson 4–Lesson 6; Lesson 8–Lesson 9; Lesson 11–Lesson 12; Lesson 14; Lesson 16; Unit 7, Lesson 11; Lesson 13; Lesson 16; Unit 9, Lesson 6; Lesson 10; Unit 11, Lesson 15–Lesson 16; Unit 13, Lesson 1–Lesson 4; Lesson 9–Lesson 10
• analyze and evaluate the mathematical thinking and strategies of others;	Unit 1, Lesson 3–Lesson 4; Lesson 6; Lesson 12–Lesson 15; Unit 3, Lesson 1–Lesson 5; Unit 5, Lesson 4–Lesson 5; Lesson 8–Lesson 12; Lesson 14; Lesson 16; Unit 7, Lesson 11; Lesson 13; Lesson 16; Unit 9, Lesson 10; Unit 11, Lesson 16; Unit 13, Lesson 1–Lesson 4; Lesson 9–Lesson 10
• use the language of mathematics to express mathematical ideas precisely.	Unit 1, Lesson 3–Lesson 4; Lesson 6; Lesson 12–Lesson 15; Unit 2, Lesson 5; Unit 3, Lesson 1–Lesson 5; Unit 5, Lesson 3–Lesson 6; Lesson 8–Lesson 12; Lesson 16; Unit 7, Lesson 11; Lesson 16; Unit 9, Lesson 10; Unit 11, Lesson 15–Lesson 16; Unit 13, Lesson 1–Lesson 4; Lesson 9–Lesson 10

Connections Standard	
• recognize and use connections among mathematical ideas;	Unit 4, Lesson 1; Lesson 3; Lesson 4; Unit 5, Lesson 4; Lesson 10; Lesson 12; Lesson 14; Unit 7, Lesson 12–Lesson 13; Unit 8, Lesson 1–Lesson 3; Unit 9, Lesson 10; Lesson 14; Unit 10, Lesson 1–Lesson 3; Unit 12, Lesson 1–Lesson 5; Unit 14, Lesson 2
• understand how mathematical ideas interconnect and build on one another to produce a coherent whole;	Unit 5, Lesson 4; Lesson 10; Lesson 12; Lesson 14; Unit 7, Lesson 12–Lesson 13; Unit 9, Lesson 10; Lesson 14
• recognize and apply mathematics in contexts outside of mathematics.	Unit 1, Lesson 2–Lesson 3; Lesson 6–Lesson 15; Unit 3, Lesson 2–Lesson 8; Unit 5, Lesson 2–Lesson 11; Lesson 13–Lesson 16; Unit 7, Lesson 2; Lesson 4; Lesson 6; Lesson 8–Lesson 13; Lesson 15–Lesson 16; Unit 9, Lesson 2–Lesson 13; Unit 10, Lesson 1–Lesson 3; Unit 11, Lesson 2–Lesson 7; Lesson 9–Lesson 21; Unit 12, Lesson 2; Unit 13, Lesson 1–Lesson 10; Unit 14, Lesson 2

Representation Standard	
• create and use representations to organize, record, and communicate mathematical ideas;	Unit 1, Lesson 1–Lesson 4; Unit 2, Lesson 2; Lesson 4; Unit 3, Lesson 6–Lesson 8; Unit 4, Lesson 2; Unit 5, Lesson 4; Lesson 7; Lesson 10–Lesson 11; Lesson 14; Lesson 16; Unit 6, Lesson 1; Unit 7, Lesson 1–Lesson 5; Lesson 7–Lesson 8; Lesson 16; Unit 9, Lesson 1–Lesson 3; Lesson 5–Lesson 8; Lesson 11; Lesson 13; Unit 10, Lesson 2; Unit 11, Lesson 1–Lesson 7; Lesson 9–Lesson 17; Unit 12, Lesson 2–Lesson 4; Unit 13, Lesson 1–Lesson 4; Lesson 10; Unit 14, Lesson 1–Lesson 3
• select, apply, and translate among mathematical representations to solve problems;	Unit 1, Lesson 3–Lesson 5; Unit 3, Lesson 6–Lesson 8; Unit 5, Lesson 4; Lesson 7; Lesson 10–Lesson 11; Lesson 16; Unit 7, Lesson 1–Lesson 5; Lesson 7–Lesson 8; Lesson 16; Unit 9, Lesson 1; Lesson 3; Lesson 5–Lesson 8; Lesson 11; Unit 10, Lesson 2; Unit 11, Lesson 1–Lesson 7; Lesson 9–Lesson 17
• use representations to model and interpret physical, social, and mathematical phenomena.	Unit 3, Lesson 6–Lesson 8; Unit 5, Lesson 4; Lesson 7; Lesson 10–Lesson 11; Lesson 14; Unit 7, Lesson 1–Lesson 5; Lesson 7–Lesson 8; Lesson 16; Unit 9, Lesson 1–Lesson 3; Lesson 5–Lesson 8; Lesson 11; Unit 11, Lesson 1–Lesson 7; Lesson 9–Lesson 17; Unit 13, Lesson 1–Lesson 4; Lesson 10

Area and Perimeter

IN UNIT 8, students continue to explore perimeter and area. In Unit 7, students found the perimeters of triangles and quadrilaterals by measuring the sides and adding the lengths. In Unit 4, students learned that the area of a rectangle is the number of square units that fit inside it, and then used the area to model multiplication. In this unit, students find perimeters and areas of figures drawn on a dot array, determine when a real-world problem involves perimeter or area, and develop algebraic formulas for perimeter and area of rectangles and squares.

Skills Trace

Grade 2	Grade 3	Grade 4
• Find the area of figures by counting square units. • Estimate the area of unusual figures. • Find the perimeter of squares, rectangles, and triangles.	• Find perimeter and area of figures drawn on a dot array by counting units. • Estimate the area of irregular shapes. • Determine whether a real-life problem requires finding perimeter or area, and then solve the problem. • Recognize that rectangles with the same perimeter may have different areas and rectangles with the same area may have different perimeters. • Use formulas for the area and perimeter of squares and rectangles.	• Find and estimate perimeter and area of irregular and complex shapes. • Recognize that rectangles with the same perimeter may have different areas and rectangles with the same area may have different perimeters. • Use formulas for the area and perimeter of squares, rectangles, and parallelograms.

Unit 8 Contents

Big Idea Area and Perimeter

Planning Unit 8

NCTM Curriculum Focal Points and Connections Key: **1.** Number and Operations and Algebra **2.** Number and Operations **3.** Geometry **4.** Algebra **5.** Measurement **6.** Data Analysis **7.** Number and Operations

Lesson NCTM Focal Points NCTM Standards	Resources	Materials for Lesson Activities	Materials for Going Further
8-1 **Explore Perimeter and Area** NCTM Focal Points: 5.2, 5.3, 5.4 NCTM Standards: 3, 4, 9	TE pp. 609–618 SAB pp. 285–290 H&R pp. 205–206 AC 8-1 MCC 29	String ✓ MathBoard materials ✓ Centimeter Ruler Centimeter Grid Paper (TRB M31) Inch Grid Paper (TRB M42) Overhead projector (optional) Blank transparency (optional) Index cards CD cases	Centimeter Grid Paper (TRB M31) Colored pencils ✓ MathBoard materials or Centimeter Dot Paper (TRB M28) Inch Grid Paper (TRB M42) Math Journals
8-2 **Relate Perimeter and Area** NCTM Focal Points: 5.2, 5.3, 5.4 NCTM Standards: 3, 4, 9	TE pp. 619–624 SAB pp. 291–292 H&R pp. 207–208 AC 8-2 MCC 30	✓ MathBoard materials ✓ Centimeter Ruler *Spaghetti and Meatballs for All!* by Marilyn Burns	Square inch tiles ✓ MathBoard materials or Centimeter Dot Paper (TRB M28) ✓ Centimeter Rulers Math Journals
8-3 **Formulas for Perimeter and Area** NCTM Focal Points: 5.2, 5.3, 5.4 NCTM Standards: 3, 4, 9	TE pp. 625–632 SAB pp. 293–296 H&R pp. 209–210 AC 8-3 MCC 31, 32 AG Quick Quiz	None	Geoboards Rubber bands ✓ Rulers Index cards ✓ MathBoard materials Math Journals
✓ Unit Review and Test	TE pp. 633–636 SAB pp. 297–300 AG Unit 8 Tests		

Resources/Materials Key: TE: Teacher Edition SAB: Student Activity Book H&R: Homework and Remembering AC: Activity Cards MCC: Math Center Challenge AG: Assessment Guide ✓: Grade 3 kits TRB: Teacher's Resource Book

NCTM Standards and Expectations Key: 1. Number and Operations 2. Algebra 3. Geometry 4. Measurement 5. Data Analysis and Probability 6. Problem Solving 7. Reasoning and Proof 8. Communication 9. Connections 10. Representation

Hardcover Student Book

- Together, the Hardcover Student Book and its companion Activity Workbook contain all of the pages in the consumable Student Activity Book.

Manipulatives and Materials

- Essential materials for teaching *Math Expressions* are available in the Grade 3 kits. These materials are indicated by a ✓ in these lists. At the front of this Teacher Edition is more information about kit contents, alternatives for the materials, and use of the materials.

Independent Learning Activities

Ready-Made Math Challenge Centers

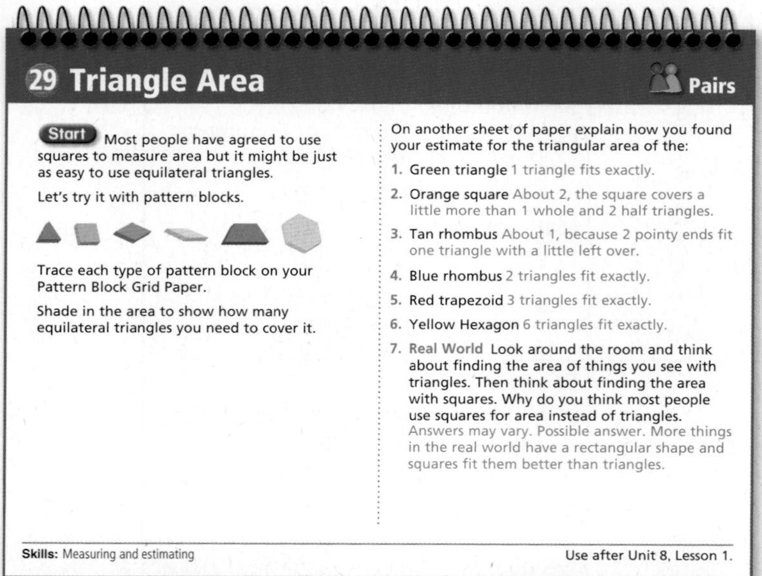

29 Triangle Area Pairs

Start Most people have agreed to use squares to measure area but it might be just as easy to use equilateral triangles.

Let's try it with pattern blocks.

Trace each type of pattern block on your Pattern Block Grid Paper.

Shade in the area to show how many equilateral triangles you need to cover it.

On another sheet of paper explain how you found your estimate for the triangular area of the:

1. Green triangle 1 triangle fits exactly.
2. Orange square About 2, the square covers a little more than 1 whole and 2 half triangles.
3. Tan rhombus About 1, because 2 pointy ends fit one triangle with a little left over.
4. Blue rhombus 2 triangles fit exactly.
5. Red trapezoid 3 triangles fit exactly.
6. Yellow Hexagon 6 triangles fit exactly.
7. Real World Look around the room and think about finding the area of things you see with triangles. Then think about finding the area with squares. Why do you think most people use squares for area instead of triangles. Answers may vary. Possible answer. More things in the real world have a rectangular shape and squares fit them better than triangles.

Skills: Measuring and estimating — Use after Unit 8, Lesson 1.

Grouping Pairs

Materials Pattern blocks, Pattern Block Grid Paper (TRB M47)

Objective Students apply the concept of area with triangular units

Connections Measurement and Estimation

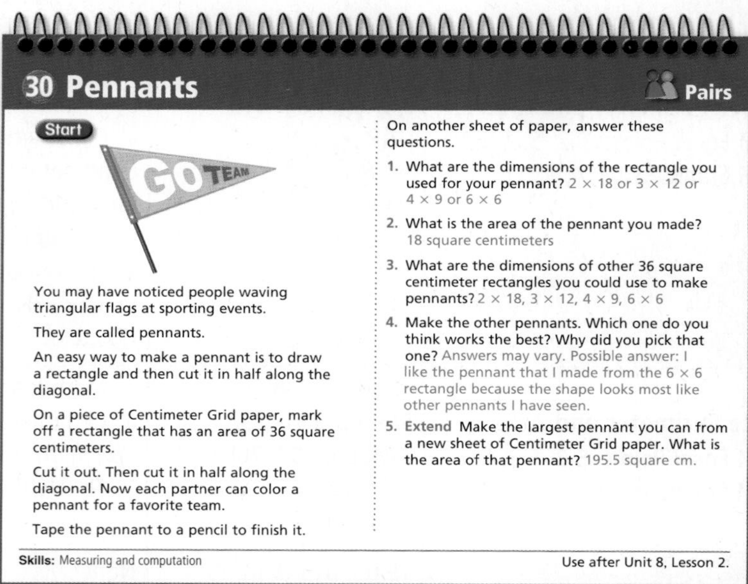

30 Pennants Pairs

Start

You may have noticed people waving triangular flags at sporting events.

They are called pennants.

An easy way to make a pennant is to draw a rectangle and then cut it in half along the diagonal.

On a piece of Centimeter Grid paper, mark off a rectangle that has an area of 36 square centimeters.

Cut it out. Then cut it in half along the diagonal. Now each partner can color a pennant for a favorite team.

Tape the pennant to a pencil to finish it.

On another sheet of paper, answer these questions.

1. What are the dimensions of the rectangle you used for your pennant? 2×18 or 3×12 or 4×9 or 6×6
2. What is the area of the pennant you made? 18 square centimeters
3. What are the dimensions of other 36 square centimeter rectangles you could use to make pennants? 2×18, 3×12, 4×9, 6×6
4. Make the other pennants. Which one do you think works the best? Why did you pick that one? Answers may vary. Possible answer: I like the pennant that I made from the 6×6 rectangle because the shape looks most like other pennants I have seen.
5. Extend Make the largest pennant you can from a new sheet of Centimeter Grid paper. What is the area of that pennant? 195.5 square cm.

Skills: Measuring and computation — Use after Unit 8, Lesson 2.

Grouping Pairs

Materials Markers, Centimeter Grid Paper (TRB M31)

Objective Students apply the concept of area to triangles.

Connections Measurement and Real World

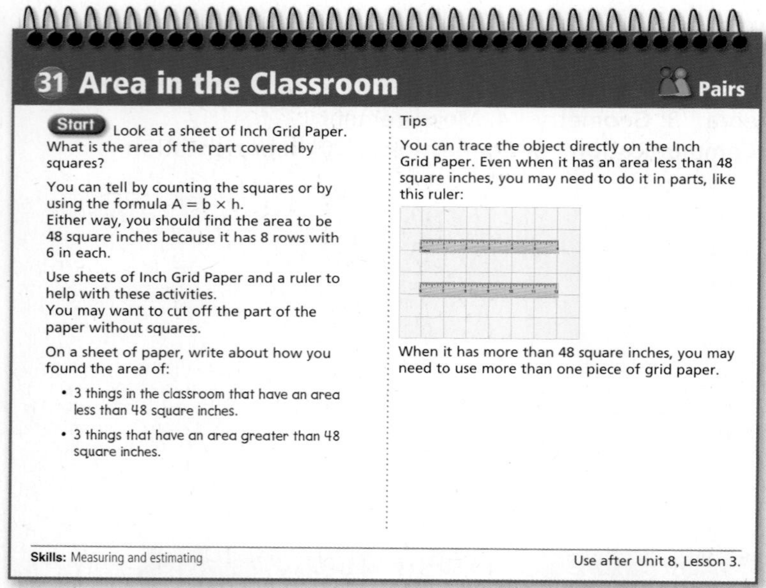

31 Area in the Classroom Pairs

Start Look at a sheet of Inch Grid Paper. What is the area of the part covered by squares?

You can tell by counting the squares or by using the formula $A = b \times h$.
Either way, you should find the area to be 48 square inches because it has 8 rows with 6 in each.

Use sheets of Inch Grid Paper and a ruler to help with these activities.
You may want to cut off the part of the paper without squares.

On a sheet of paper, write about how you found the area of:

- 3 things in the classroom that have an area less than 48 square inches.
- 3 things that have an area greater than 48 square inches.

Tips

You can trace the object directly on the Inch Grid Paper. Even when it has an area less than 48 square inches, you may need to do it in parts, like this ruler:

When it has more than 48 square inches, you may need to use more than one piece of grid paper.

Skills: Measuring and estimating — Use after Unit 8, Lesson 3.

Grouping Pairs

Materials Scissors, ruler, calculator, Inch Grid Paper (TRB M42)

Objective Students find the area of real-world objects.

Connections Measurement and Real World

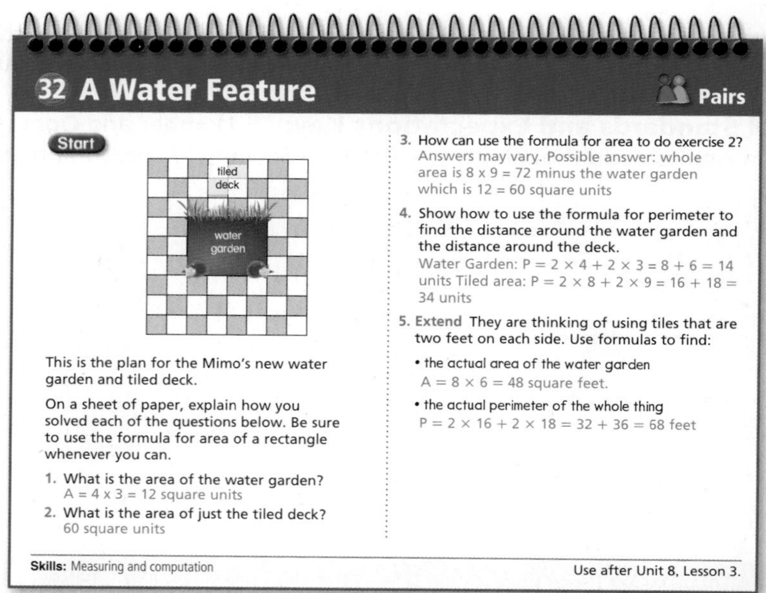

32 A Water Feature Pairs

Start

This is the plan for the Mimo's new water garden and tiled deck.

On a sheet of paper, explain how you solved each of the questions below. Be sure to use the formula for area of a rectangle whenever you can.

1. What is the area of the water garden? $A = 4 \times 3 = 12$ square units
2. What is the area of just the tiled deck? 60 square units
3. How can use the formula for area to do exercise 2? Answers may vary. Possible answer: whole area is $8 \times 9 = 72$ minus the water garden which is $12 = 60$ square units
4. Show how to use the formula for perimeter to find the distance around the water garden and the distance around the deck. Water Garden: $P = 2 \times 4 + 2 \times 3 = 8 + 6 = 14$ units Tiled area: $P = 2 \times 8 + 2 \times 9 = 16 + 18 = 34$ units
5. Extend They are thinking of using tiles that are two feet on each side. Use formulas to find:
   - the actual area of the water garden $A = 8 \times 6 = 48$ square feet.
   - the actual perimeter of the whole thing $P = 2 \times 16 + 2 \times 18 = 32 + 36 = 68$ feet

Skills: Measuring and computation — Use after Unit 8, Lesson 3.

Grouping Pairs

Materials None

Objective Students use formulas to solve real-world area and perimeter problems.

Connections Computation and Measurement

Ready-Made Math Resources

Technology — Tutorials, Practice, and Intervention

Use online, individualized intervention and support to bring students to proficiency.

Help students practice skills and apply concepts through exciting math adventures.

Extend and enrich students' understanding of skills and concepts through engaging, interactive lessons and activities.

Visit **Education Place**®
www.eduplace.com

Visit www.eduplace.com/mx2t/ and find family, teacher, and student materials, activities, games, and more.

Literature Links

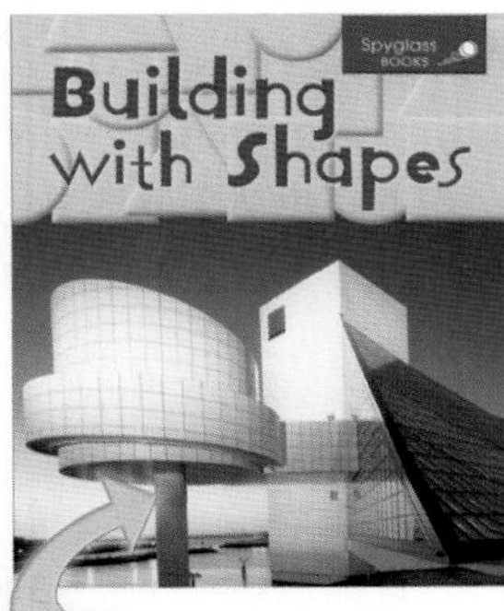

Building with Shapes

Building with Shapes
In this read through of Rebecca Weber's book, students will find out how geometric shapes and forms are used in creating structures in our world. The photographs are very instructive, as is the glossary at the end of the book.

Literature Connection

Spaghetti and Meatballs for All!: A Mathematical Story, by Marilyn Burns, illustrated by Gordon Silveria (Scholastic Press, 1997)

Unit 8 Assessment

✓ Unit Objectives Tested	Unit Test Items	Lessons
8.1 Find perimeters and areas of figures drawn on a dot array by counting units; estimate area and perimeter.	1–4	1
8.2 Determine whether a real-life problem requires finding perimeter or area, and then solve the problem.	9–10	1
8.3 Recognize that rectangles with the same perimeter may have different areas and rectangles with the same area may have different perimeters.	5–6	2
8.4 Use formulas for the area and perimeter of squares and rectangles.	7–8	3

Assessment and Review Resources

Formal Assessment

Student Activity Book

- Unit Review and Test (pp. 297–300)

Assessment Guide

- Quick Quizzes (p. A73)
- Test A–Open Response (pp. A74–A77)
- Test B–Multiple Choice (pp. A78–A80)
- Performance Assessment (pp. A81–A83)

Test Generator CD-ROM

- Open Response Test
- Multiple Choice Test
- Test Bank Items

Informal Assessment

Teacher Edition

- Ongoing Assessment (in every lesson)
- Quick Practice (in every lesson)
- Portfolio Suggestions (p. 635)

Math Talk

- Math Talk in Action (p. 626)
- Solve and Discuss (pp. 615, 616)
- Student Pairs (p. 613)
  Helping Partners (p. 613)
- Small Groups (pp. 615, 616)
- In Activities (pp. 610, 611, 622)

Review Opportunities

Homework and Remembering

- Review of recently taught topics
- Spiral Review

Teacher Edition

- Unit Review and Test (pp. 633–636)

Test Generator CD-ROM

- Custom Review Sheets

Unit 8 Teaching Resources

Differentiated Instruction

Individualizing Instruction		
	Level	Frequency
Activities	• Intervention • On Level • Challenge	All 3 in every lesson
	Level	Frequency
Math Writing Prompts	• Intervention • On Level • Challenge	All 3 in every lesson
Math Center Challenges	For advanced students	
	4 in every unit	

Reaching All Learners		
English Language Learners	Lessons	Pages
	1, 2, 3	609, 619, 625
Extra Help	Lesson	Page
	1	612

Strategies for English Language Learners

Present this problem to all students. Offer the different levels of support to meet students' levels of language proficiency.

Objective To review properties of squares and rectangles.

Problem Give students a mixture of squares and rectangles and have them sort the shapes. Help students describe the groups.

Newcomer

- Guide students to sort the shapes into a group of squares and a group of rectangles that are not squares.

Beginning

- Say: **There are 2 groups. A group of squares and a group of rectangles that are not squares.** Have students repeat.
- Model the shapes. Say: **Squares have 4 equal sides. The other rectangles have only 2 pairs of equal sides.** Have children repeat.

Intermediate

- Ask: **How many groups did you make?** 2 **What shapes can we use to name the groups?** squares and rectangles
- **How many sides do squares have?** 4 **Rectangles?** 4 **Are all 4 sides of each square equal?** yes **Are all 4 sides of each of the other rectangles equal?** no

Advanced

- Have students name the groups. Invite them to use simple sentences to tell how squares and other rectangles are alike and different.

Connections

Literature Connection
Lesson 2, page 624

Art Connection
Lesson 3, page 632

Putting Research into Practice for Unit 8

From Current Research: Measurement and Formulas

Prior to grade 3, students should have begun to develop an understanding of what it means to measure an object, that is, identifying an attribute to be measured, choosing an appropriate unit, and comparing that unit to the object being measured. They should have had many experiences with measuring length and should also have explored ways to measure liquid volume, weight, and time. In grades 3–5, students should deepen and expand their understanding and use of measurement. For example, they should measure other attributes such as area and angle. They need to begin paying closer attention to the degree of accuracy when measuring and use a wider variety of measurement tools. They should also begin to develop and use formulas for the measurement of certain attributes, such as area.

National Council of Teachers of Mathematics. *Principles and Standards for School Mathematics.* Reston: NCTM, 2000. 171.

Relating Area and Perimeter

Students in grades 3–5 should explore how measurements are affected when one attribute to be measured is held constant and the other is changed. For example, consider the area of four tiles joined along adjacent sides (see fig. 5.18). The area of each tile is a square unit. When joined, the area of the resulting polygon is always four square units, but the perimeter varies from eight to ten units, depending on how the tiles are arranged. Or suppose students are given twenty toothpicks with which to build a rectangle. How many different rectangles are possible if all twenty toothpicks are used? This activity provides an opportunity to discuss the relationship of area to perimeter. It also highlights the importance of organizing solutions systematically.

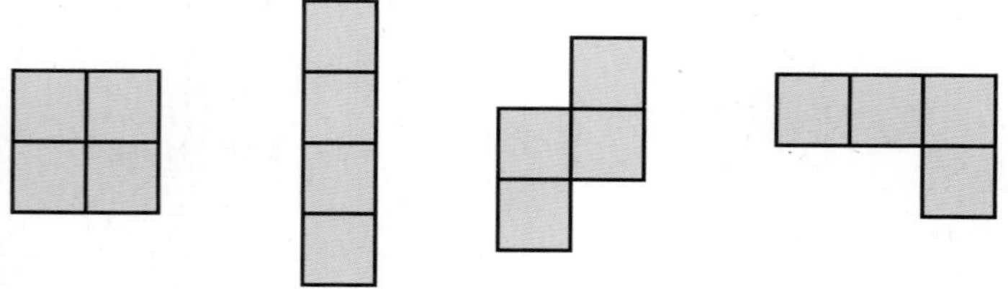

Fig. **5.18.** Polygons with the same area and different perimeters

National Counci! of Teachers of Mathematics. *Principles and Standards for School Mathematics.* Reston: NCTM, 2000. 172.

Other Useful References: Measurement

Nitabach, E, & R. Lehrer. "Developing Spatial Sense through Area Measurement." *Teaching Children Mathematics* (Apr. 1996): 473–476.

Wilson, P.S. and R.E. Rowland. "Teaching Measurement." *Research Ideas for the Classroom: Early Childhood Mathematics.* Ed. R.J. Jensen. Old Tappan, NJ: Macmillan, 1993. 171–194.

Other Useful References: Perimeter and Area

Chappell, Michaele F. and Denisse R. Thompson. "Perimeter or Area? Which Measure Is It?" *Mathematics Teaching in the Middle School* 5.1 (Sept. 1999): 20.

Ferrer, Bellasanta B., Bobbie Hunter, Kathryn C. Irwin, Maureen J. Sheldon, Charles S. Thompson, Catherine P. Vistro-Yu. "By the Unit or Square Unit?" *Mathematics Teaching in the Middle School* 7.3 (Nov. 2001): 132.

Malloy, Carol E. "Perimeter and Area through the van Hiele Model." *Mathematics Teaching in the Middle School* 5.2 (Oct. 1999): 87.

Whitin, Phyllis. "Promoting Problem-Posing Explorations." *Teaching Children Mathematics* 11.4 (Nov. 2004): 180.

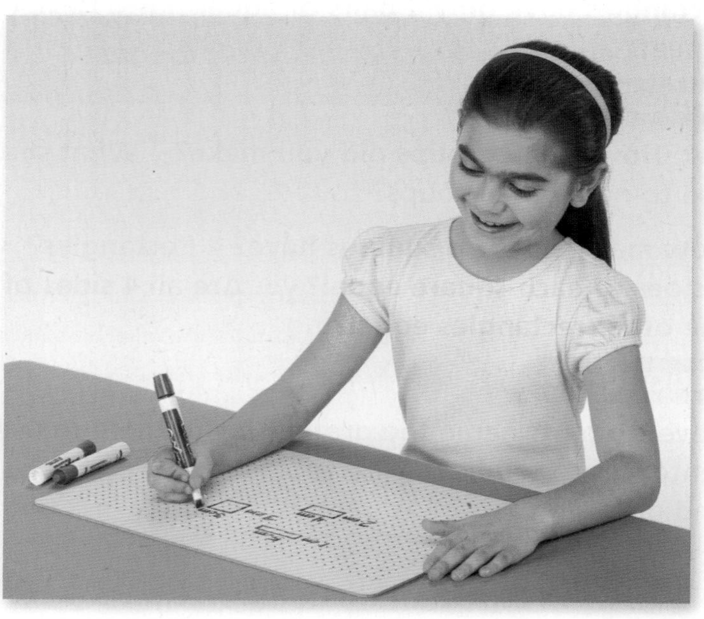

Getting Ready to Teach Unit 8

In this unit, students continue to explore area and perimeter. At the end of the unit they generalize to write formulas for area and perimeter.

Area and Perimeter

Lesson 1

In the previous units, students found the perimeter of rectangles by measuring and adding lengths of sides, and the area of rectangles by counting squares. They also used area models for multiplication. In this unit, students find the perimeter and area of figures drawn on centimeter dot arrays.

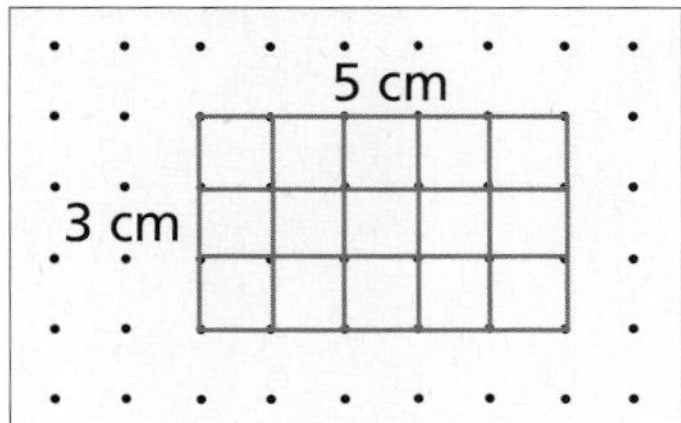

Perimeter = 5 + 5 + 3 + 3 = 16 16 cm
Area = 3 × 5 = 15 15 sq cm

Students also estimate perimeter and area.

Relating Perimeter and Area

Lesson 2

In this unit's activities, students draw on a dot array all the possible rectangles with a given perimeter with whole unit side lengths. Then they find the area of the rectangles. They observe for a given perimeter, the longest, skinniest rectangle has the least area and the most "square-like" rectangle has the greatest area.

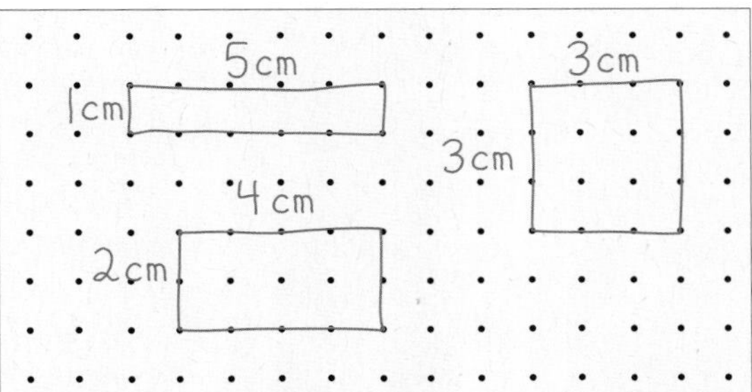

Students also draw all the possible rectangles with a given area with whole unit side lengths. and find the perimeters. They observe that for a given area, the longest, skinniest rectangle has the greatest perimeter and the most "square-like" rectangle has the least perimeter.

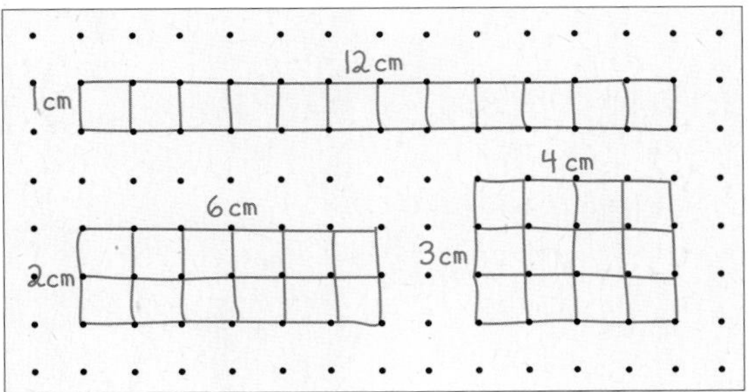

Algebraic Formulas

Lesson 3

As students progress through this unit, most of them will develop shortcuts that allow them to find the perimeter and area of rectangles without counting unit segments or unit squares. In the last lesson, students generalize these shortcuts as rules, first in words and then with algebraic symbols. Then they have opportunities to use these rules, or formulas, to find perimeter and area of rectangles.

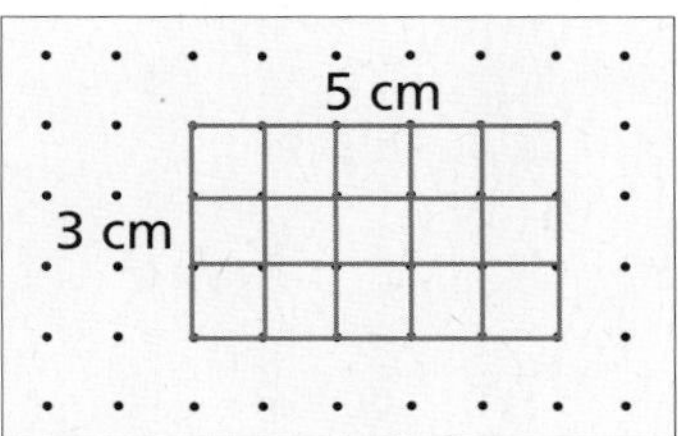

Perimeter = (2 × 5) + (2 × 3) = 10 + 6 = 16 = 16 cm
Area = 5 × 3 = 15 = 15 sq cm

Problem Solving

In *Math Expressions* a research-based, algebraic problem-solving approach that focuses on problem types is used: understand the situation, represent the situation with a math drawing or an equation, solve the problem, and see that the answer makes sense.

In this unit students consider some real-life problems and determine whether the solution requires them to find perimeter and/or area.

Use Mathematical Processes

Lessons 1, 2, and 3

The mathematical process skills of problem solving, reasoning and proof, communication, connections, and representation are emphasized throughout this unit as students explore area and perimeter, represent area and perimeter in drawings, make generalizations, and derive formulas.

Explore Perimeter and Area

Lesson Objectives

- Recognize the difference between a centimeter and a square centimeter.
- Find perimeter and area by counting linear units (perimeter) or square units (area).
- Determine whether a real-world situation involves finding area or perimeter.
- Estimate perimeter and area.

Vocabulary

perimeter
area
square unit
square centimeter
square inch
square mile

The Day at a Glance

Today's Goals	Materials	
1 Teaching the Lesson **A1:** Find the perimeters and areas of figures on a dot array. **A2:** Find the areas of figures by counting whole- and half-squares. **A3:** Solve real-world problems involving area and perimeter. **A4:** Estimate perimeter and area.	**Lesson Activities** Student Activity Book pp. 285–290 or Student Hardcover Book pp. 285–290 and Activity Workbook pp. 133–134 (includes Family Letter) Homework and Remembering pp. 205–206 ✓ MathBoard materials Centimeter Dot Paper (TRB M28) ✓ Centimeter rulers (TRB M26) Overhead projector Transparency of Student Activity Book pages (optional) Index cards	CD Cases Centimeter rulers String Centimeter Grid paper (TRB M31) **Going Further** Activity Cards 8-1 Centimeter Grid paper (TRB M31) Colored pencils MathBoard materials or Centimeter Dot paper (TRB M28) Inch Grid paper (TRB M42) Math Journals
2 Going Further ▸ Differentiated Instruction		
3 Homework and Spiral Review		

Keeping Skills Sharp

Daily Routines

Logic Problem Use *all, some*, or *no* to complete each sentence.

1. If all rhombi have 4 equal sides, then _____ rhombi are squares. some
2. If all rectangles are parallelograms with 4 right angles, than _____ squares are rectangles. all

English Language Learners

Draw a rectangle on the board. Write *perimeter* and *area*. Trace around the rectangle. Say: ***Perimeter* is the distance around.**

- **Beginning** Shade the inside of the rectangle. Say: ***Area* is the space inside.** Have children repeat.
- **Intermediate** Ask: **Is *area* the distance around?** no **The space inside?** yes Say: ***Perimeter* is the distance ___.** around
- **Advanced** Have children tell how *perimeter* and *area* differ.

1 Teaching the Lesson

Activity 1

Find Perimeter and Area on a Dot Array

 15 MINUTES

Goal: Find the perimeters and areas of figures on a dot array.

Materials: MathBoard materials or Centimeter-Dot Paper (TRB M28), Centimeter Ruler (TRB M26) (1 per student), Student Activity Book or Hardcover Book p. 285, overhead projector and transparency of Student Book p. 285 (optional)

 **NCTM Standards:**
Measurement
Geometry
Connections

▶ Explore and Discuss Perimeter

WHOLE CLASS

Math Talk 

For this activity, have students use the dot arrays on their MathBoards or Centimeter-Dot Paper (TRB M28). Explain that since the dots are 1 cm apart, both vertically and horizontally, students can use the array to draw horizontal and vertical line segments with whole-centimeter lengths.

Ask students to draw a vertical line segment 3 cm long. Circulate as students are working. If you see students connect three dots instead of four, remind them that the length of a line segment is the number of units—in this case, centimeters—it contains, not the number of dots.

- How many dots did you connect to make a 3-cm line segment? 4 dots

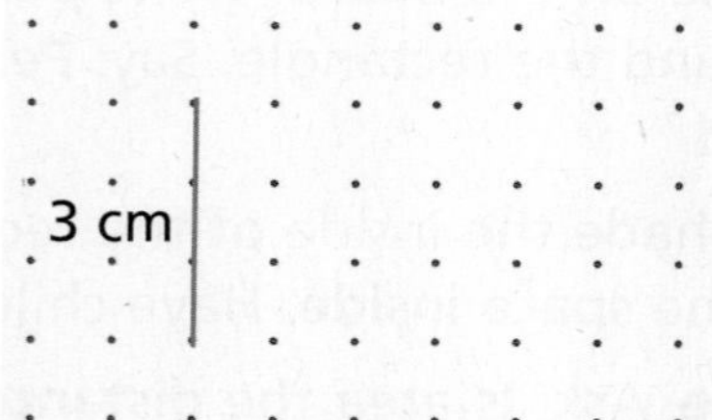

Ask for Ideas Elicit from students what they know about perimeter.

Next, ask students to draw a horizontal line segment 5 cm long starting from one end of the 3-cm line segment.

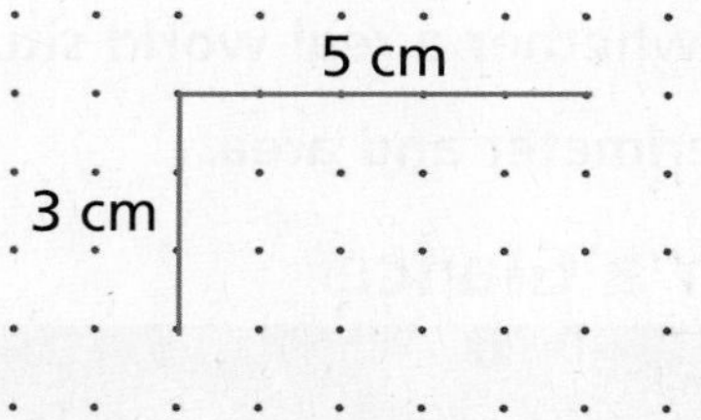

- How many dots did you connect to make a 5-cm line segment? 6 dots

Then ask students to draw two more line segments to form a rectangle. Have students predict the lengths of the line segments they would need to draw to form a rectangle. They should recall that the opposite sides of a rectangle are the same length, so the new sides will have lengths of 3 cm and 5 cm.

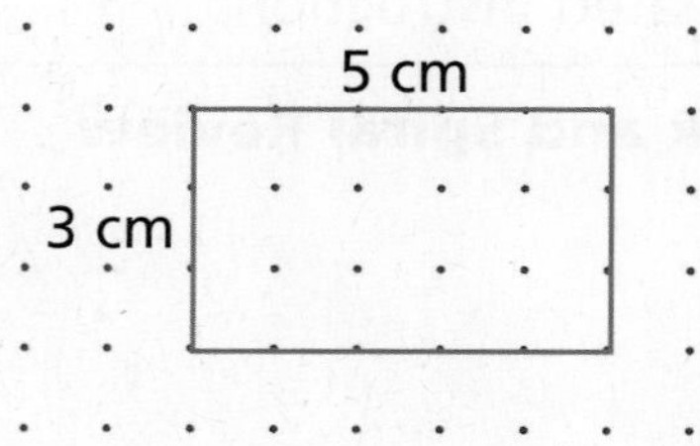

- What does the perimeter of a figure mean? Perimeter is the distance around the figure.
- What is the perimeter of your rectangle? 16 cm
- How did you find the perimeter? Possible answers: I added the lengths of the sides, 5 cm + 5 cm + 3 cm + 3 cm = 16 cm; I added 5 and 3 and then multiplied by 2; I multiplied 5 by 2, then 3 by 2, and added the sums.

▶ Explore and Discuss Area

WHOLE CLASS

Math Talk 

Ask students to leave the rectangle on their dot arrays and draw a square with each side 1 cm long.

Explain to students that they can use this small square as a square unit to measure the area of a rectangle.

- What is the area of a rectangle? the number of square units inside the figure
- How can you use square units to find the area of a rectangle? You can count the number of square units that fit inside the rectangle.

Explain to students that because each side of this square is 1 cm long, it is called *1 square centimeter.* Tell students that they can use the abbreviation *sq cm* for square centimeter.

- If a square unit has sides measuring 1 inch, what would you call the unit? 1 square inch
- If a square unit has sides measuring 1 mile, what would you call the unit? 1 square mile

Ask students to find the area of the 3 cm by 5 cm rectangle they drew. 15 sq cm

After several minutes, encourage volunteers to explain how they found the area of their rectangle. Many students will draw and count 15 individual square centimeters inside their rectangle.

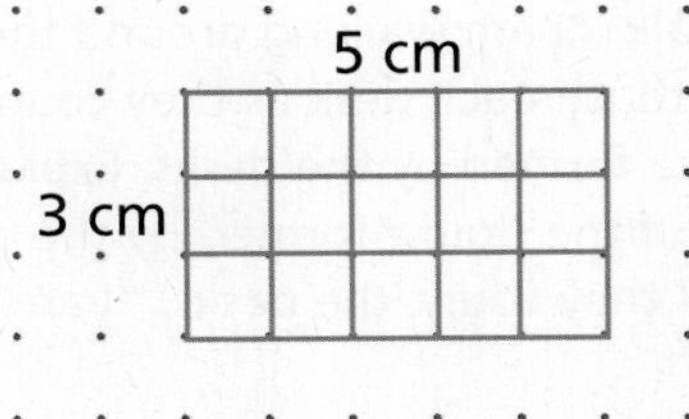

Other students might use different strategies. For example, they might draw one row or column of squares and then multiply by 3 or 5 to find the product.

1 row is 5 sq cm.
3 rows are 3 × 5, or 15 sq cm.

1 column is 3 sq cm.
5 columns are 5 × 3, or 15 sq cm.

Some students might realize that they can simply multiply the lengths of the adjacent sides to find the area. Encourage students to present their different strategies and methods, but it is not necessary to spend too much time discussing them. Students will revisit these strategies in more detail in Lesson 3.

Before moving on, review with the class the difference between centimeters and square centimeters as units of measure.

- Is length measured in centimeters or square centimeters? centimeters
- Is perimeter measured in centimeters or square centimeters? centimeters
- Is area measured in centimeters or square centimeters? square centimeters

Activity continued ▶

▶ Visualize Perimeter and Area

WHOLE CLASS

Tell students that it is possible to find the perimeter and area of any closed figure. Draw this figure on the class MathBoard and ask students to copy it onto their own dot arrays.

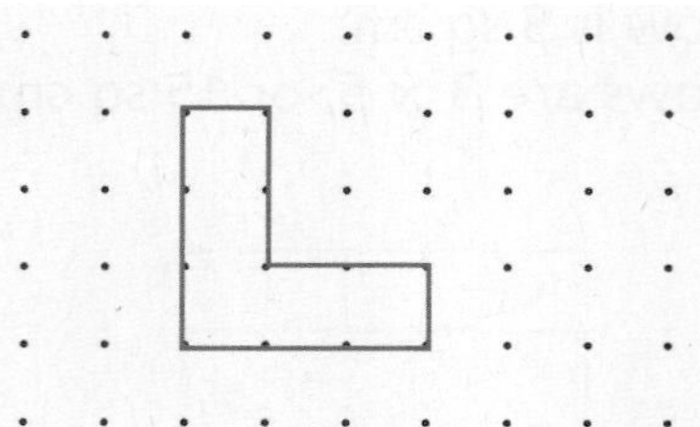

Ask students to find the perimeter and area of the figure and have volunteers share their work. See below for an example of students' work.

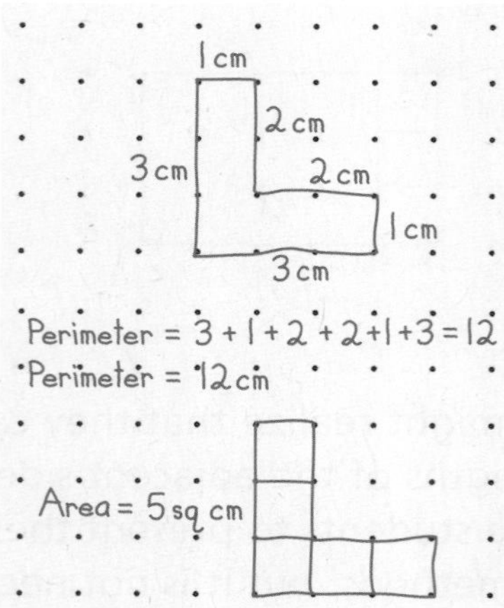

For this example, make sure that students express perimeter in centimeters and area in square centimeters.

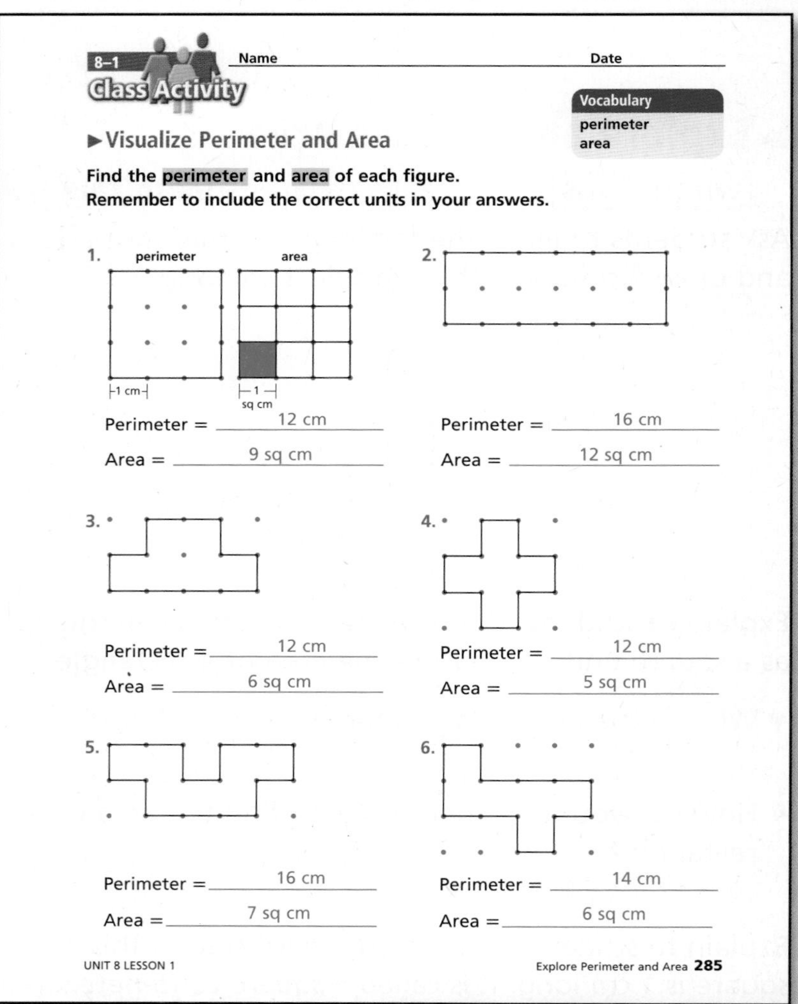

8–1 Class Activity Name Date

Vocabulary
perimeter
area

▶ Visualize Perimeter and Area

Find the perimeter and area of each figure.
Remember to include the correct units in your answers.

1. perimeter area
1 cm 1 sq cm
Perimeter = 12 cm
Area = 9 sq cm

2. Perimeter = 16 cm
Area = 12 sq cm

3. Perimeter = 12 cm
Area = 6 sq cm

4. Perimeter = 12 cm
Area = 5 sq cm

5. Perimeter = 16 cm
Area = 7 sq cm

6. Perimeter = 14 cm
Area = 6 sq cm

UNIT 8 LESSON 1 Explore Perimeter and Area **285**

Student Activity Book page 285

Refer students to Student Book page 285 and ask them to complete exercises 1–6 independently. Remind students that the dots are 1 cm apart. When they are finished, you might display an overhead transparency of the page and ask volunteers to present their solutions.

Differentiated Instruction

Extra Help Push 6 desks together in 2 × 3 array. Have students walk around them. Explain that they are moving around the perimeter of the figure formed by the desks. Have them repeat as they walk, "I am walking around the perimeter." Then have them touch each desk as they count the number of desks in the figure formed by the desks. Explain that they are finding the area of the figure formed by the desks. Have each student repeat as they count the desks, "I am finding the area."

Activity 2

Find Area by Counting Whole- and Half-Squares

 **10 MINUTES**

Goal: Find the areas of figures by counting whole- and half-squares.

Materials: Student Activity Book pages 285–286, overhead projector and overhead transparency of Student Book page 286 (optional)

 **NCTM Standards:**
Measurement
Geometry
Connections

▶ Count Whole- and Half-Square Units to Find Area PAIRS

Point out to **Student Pairs** that the figures in exercises 1–6 on Student Book page 285 are made of whole- square centimeters. Also point out that figures may sometimes contain half-square centimeters or other partial units.

Refer students to Student Book page 286 and have **Student Pairs** complete exercise 7.

When students are finished, you may wish to display an overhead transparency of Student Book page 286 or draw an enlarged version of the figure in exercise 7 on the board.

Ask a volunteer to explain how to find the area of the figure. Possible explanation: We divided the figure into whole-centimeters and then used arrows to show which half-squares we would combine to form whole-squares. Then we counted all of the whole-squares to find the area.

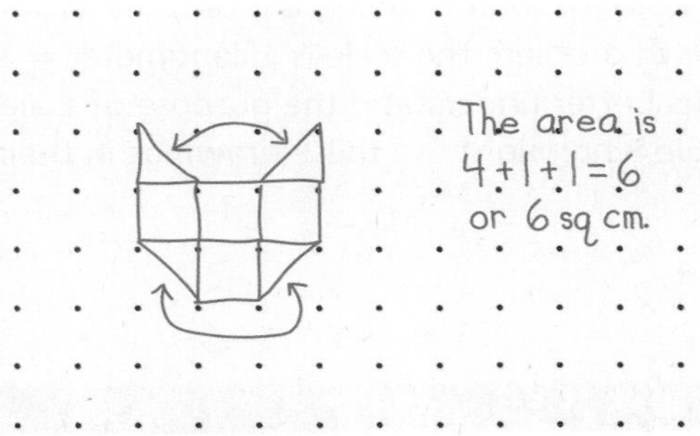

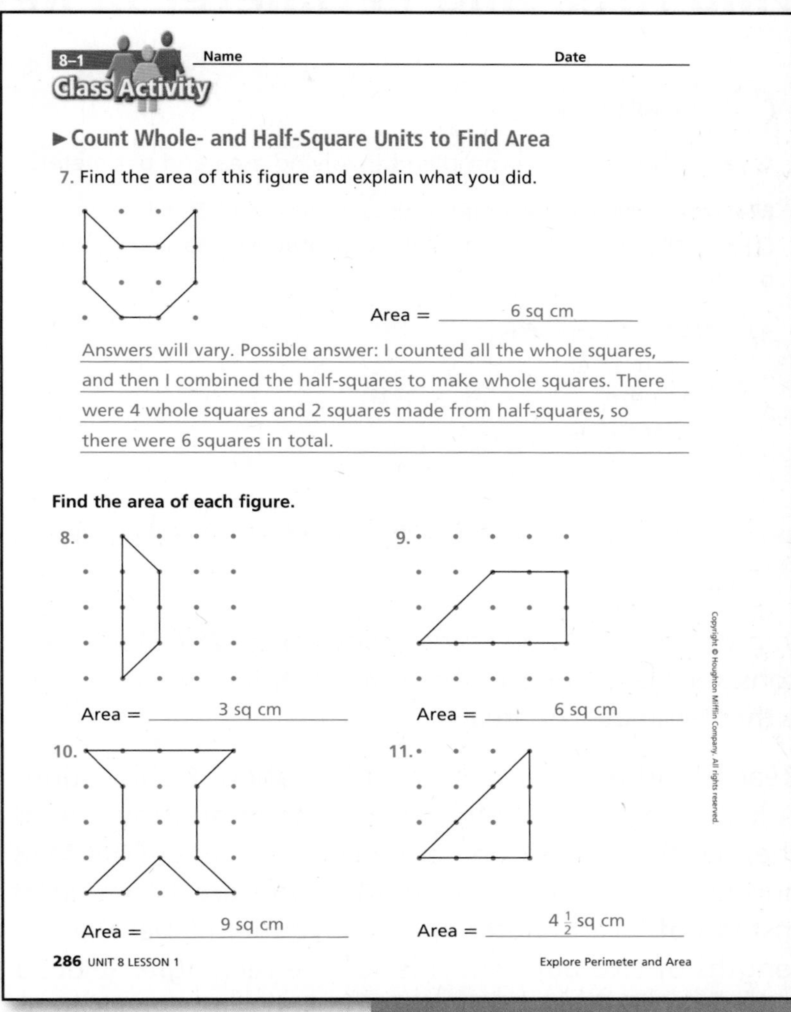

8–1 Class Activity Name Date

▶ Count Whole- and Half-Square Units to Find Area

7. Find the area of this figure and explain what you did.

Area = 6 sq cm

Answers will vary. Possible answer: I counted all the whole squares, and then I combined the half-squares to make whole squares. There were 4 whole squares and 2 squares made from half-squares, so there were 6 squares in total.

Find the area of each figure.

8. Area = 3 sq cm

9. Area = 6 sq cm

10. Area = 9 sq cm

11. Area = $4\frac{1}{2}$ sq cm

286 UNIT 8 LESSON 1 Explore Perimeter and Area

Student Activity Book page 286

Ask **Student Pairs** to complete exercises 8–11. When they are finished, discuss their answers. Keep in mind that some students may have difficulty with exercise 11 because it has an odd number of half-squares. You may wish to have students check their answers with a **Helping Partner**.

 **Class Management**

Looking Ahead Students will need a sheet of Centimeter-Dot Paper (TRB M28) to complete the Homework page for this lesson.

Activity 3

Find Area and Perimeter in Real-World Situations

 15 MINUTES

Goal: Solve real-world problems involving area and perimeter.

Materials: MathBoard materials or Centimeter-Dot Paper (TRB M28), Student Activity Book or Hardcover Book pp. 287–288

 **NCTM Standards:**
Measurement
Geometry
Connections

▶ Solve Area and Perimeter Problems

WHOLE CLASS

In problems 12–15 on Student Book page 287, students consider real-world situations in which they must find either perimeter or area.

Read aloud the first word problem about Debra's floor. Ask students to draw the floor on the dot array side of their MathBoards or on Centimeter-Dot Paper (TRB M28) and tell them to pretend that the dots are 1 foot apart instead of 1 centimeter apart. Have them label the lengths of two adjacent sides of the rectangle. Select a volunteer to share his or her drawing with the class.

Read aloud problem 12 and have students solve it on their own. When they are finished, choose two or three students to share their explanations.

Next, read aloud problem 13 and give students several minutes before inviting them to share their solutions.

Read aloud the word problem about Deshawn's fence. Ask students to draw the rectangular space in Deshawn's backyard on the dot array side of their MathBoards, and tell them to pretend that the dots are 1 yard apart instead of 1 centimeter apart.

Students can complete problems 14 and 15 as a class or on their own, depending on their understanding of perimeter and area. In problem 14, they should reason that the fencing required is the distance around the rectangle; therefore, they need to find the perimeter.

When students are finished, encourage them to brainstorm other real-world situations that ask for perimeter or area. Then have them solve problem 16.

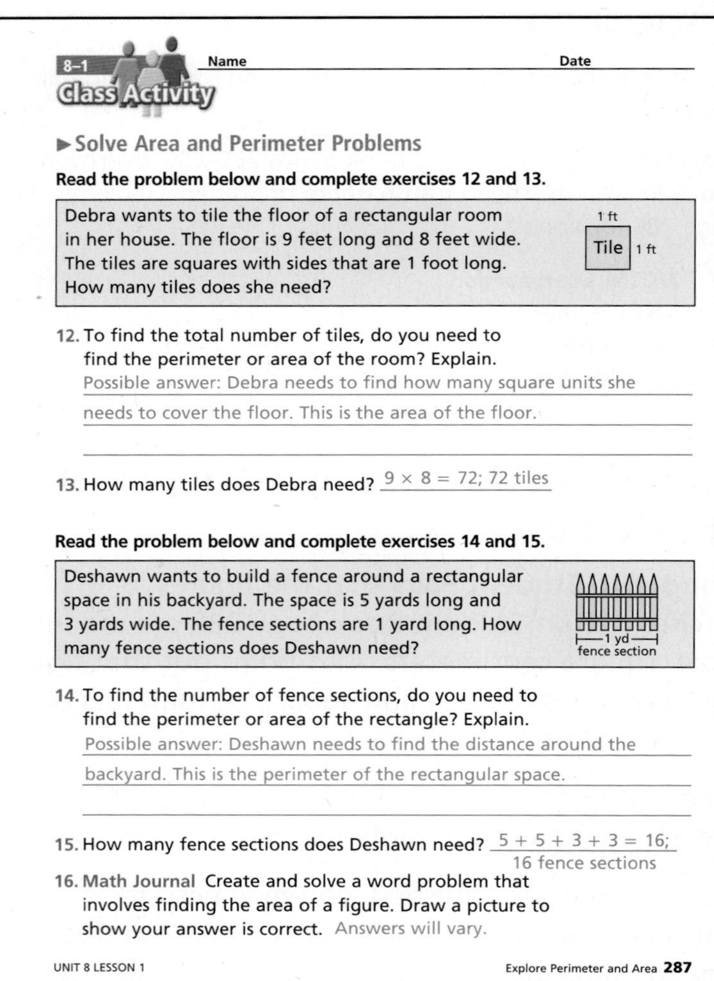
8–1 Class Activity Name Date

▶ Solve Area and Perimeter Problems

Read the problem below and complete exercises 12 and 13.

Debra wants to tile the floor of a rectangular room in her house. The floor is 9 feet long and 8 feet wide. The tiles are squares with sides that are 1 foot long. How many tiles does she need?

12. To find the total number of tiles, do you need to find the perimeter or area of the room? Explain.
Possible answer: Debra needs to find how many square units she needs to cover the floor. This is the area of the floor.

13. How many tiles does Debra need? $9 \times 8 = 72$; 72 tiles

Read the problem below and complete exercises 14 and 15.

Deshawn wants to build a fence around a rectangular space in his backyard. The space is 5 yards long and 3 yards wide. The fence sections are 1 yard long. How many fence sections does Deshawn need?

14. To find the number of fence sections, do you need to find the perimeter or area of the rectangle? Explain.
Possible answer: Deshawn needs to find the distance around the backyard. This is the perimeter of the rectangular space.

15. How many fence sections does Deshawn need? $5 + 5 + 3 + 3 = 16$; 16 fence sections

16. Math Journal Create and solve a word problem that involves finding the area of a figure. Draw a picture to show your answer is correct. Answers will vary.

UNIT 8 LESSON 1 Explore Perimeter and Area 287

Student Activity Book page 287

Teaching Note

Math Background You might explain to students that their drawings are what we call *scale drawings.* A scale drawing is the same shape as a real object but it is usually smaller. In their scale drawings of Debra's floor, for example, 1 centimeter represents 1 foot. The scale for their drawing is 1 centimeter = 1 foot. In the fence word problem the scale is 1 centimeter = 1 yard. To help students better understand the purpose of scale drawings, discuss people who might use these drawings in their everyday work.

Ongoing Assessment

Ask students to create and solve a real-world problem that involves area and perimeter.

Activity 4

Estimate Perimeter and Area in the Real World

 **20 MINUTES**

Goal: Estimate the perimeter and area of squares, rectangles and irregular figures.

Materials: Student Activity Book or Hardcover Book p. 288, Index cards (1 per small group), CD cases (1 per small group), centimeter rulers, MathBoard materials, Centimeter Grid Paper (TRB M31), string

 **NCTM Standards:**
Measurement
Geometry
Connections

8–1 Class Activity

Name ________ Date ________

▶ Estimate Perimeter and Area

17. Estimate the perimeter of an index card and CD case in centimeters. Record your estimates in the table. Then find the actual perimeters.

18. Estimate the area of an index card and CD case in centimeters. Record your estimates in the table. Then find the actual areas using a calculator. Estimates may vary.

	Perimeter		Area	
Object	Estimate (cm)	Actual (cm)	Estimate (cm^2)	Actual (cm^2)
Index card	about 40 cm	60 cm	about 100 cm^2	94.75 cm^2
CD case	about 52 cm	53 cm	about 140 cm^2	168 cm^2

▶ Estimate the Perimeter and Area of Irregular Figures

19. Use centimeter grid paper (TRB M31). Trace your hand with fingers together and thumb out on the grid. Estimate the perimeter and area.

Perimeter: About ________ cm Area: About ________ cm^2

Answers will vary. Check that students' estimates are reasonable.

288 UNIT 8 LESSON 1 Explore Perimeter and Area

Student Activity Book page 288

▶ Estimate Perimeter and Area

SMALL GROUPS

Have **Small Groups** of students draw a line segment that is 1 centimeter long on their MathBoards.

Then have them generate a list of benchmarks that can help estimate lengths in centimeters. A sample list is below:

1 centimeter

width of 1 finger
width of a staple
width of a paper clip

Now have **Small Groups** of students estimate the perimeter of the index card and CD case using a benchmark or visual image of a centimeter. Students should record their estimates in the table on Student Activity Book page 288.

Using the **Solve and Discuss** structure, have **Small Groups** share their estimates and strategies with the class.

Next have **Small Groups** use a centimeter ruler to calculate the actual perimeters. Review how to round measurements to the nearest centimeter, if necessary.

Students should record their actual perimeters in the table and compare how close their estimates were to the actual results.

Next show students a centimeter square cut from centimeter grid paper.

Have students shade one square centimeter on their centimeter grid paper.

Then have students generate a list of benchmarks that can help estimate area in square centimeters. A sample list is below:

1 square centimeter

area of thumbnail
button on telephone
piece of cereal

1 Teaching the Lesson (continued)

Next have **Small Groups** of students estimate the area of the index card and CD case using their benchmark or visualize an image of a square centimeter and record their estimates in the table.

Using the **Solve and Discuss** structure, have **Small Groups** share their estimates and strategies for finding the area with the class.

Next have **Small Groups** trace the index card and CD case on centimeter grid paper and count the whole and half squares to find the actual area.

Students should record their actual perimeters in the table and compare how close their estimates were to the actual results.

▶ Estimate the Perimeter and Area of Irregular Figures SMALL GROUPS

Give each student a sheet of centimeter grid paper (TRB M31). Have **Small Groups** trace around one of their hands with fingers together and thumb out. Have one student place their hand on the grid, while another student traces around the hand.

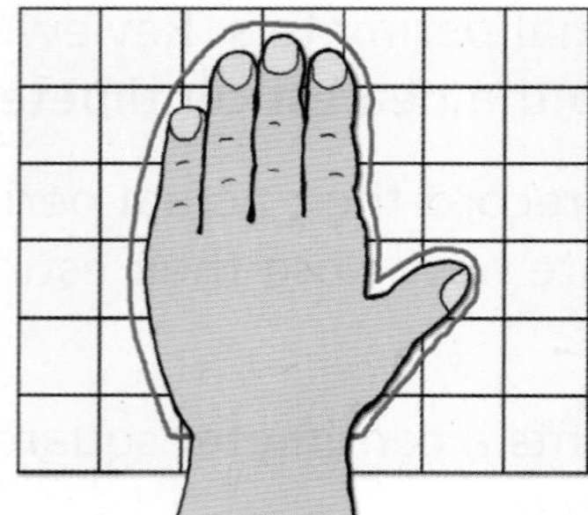

Have **Small Groups** think of ways they can estimate the perimeter and area of an irregular figure and share their strategies with the class. Some possible strategies:

Perimeter:

- Count the squares whose lengths are covered or almost covered.
- Trace the outline of the hand with string. Then measure the string with a centimeter ruler.

Area:

- Count squares that are covered or almost covered.
- Count whole squares and half squares.

Have each **Small Group** try a different strategy and compare their results.

Suggest that **Small Groups** who are counting squares and half squares use colored pencils to shade the partial squares that form about one whole square the same color.

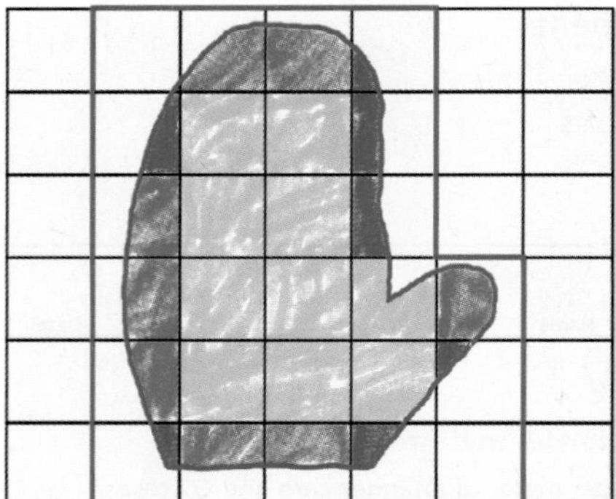

Some students may suggest drawing an L-shape on the grid paper, and then count the squares in the L-shape. This will give students an overestimate. Counting whole and partial squares will result in an estimate closer to the actual area.

2 Going Further

Differentiated Instruction

Intervention

Activity Card 8-I

Count Square Units

Activity Card 8-1

Work: In pairs

Use:

- TRB M31 (Centimeter-Grid Paper)
- Colored pencils

1. **On Your Own** Outline a figure on grid paper. Use both whole and half squares, as shown below. Trade papers with your partner to find the area.
2. **Think** How many whole squares are in the figure? How many half squares? How many squares in all?
3. Write the area under the figure.
4. **Analyze** What strategy did you use to keep track of the squares as you counted them?

Unit 8, Lesson 1

Activity Note There are several ways for students to keep track of the squares they count. For example, they can check off counted squares or shade squares in different colors.

Math Writing Prompt

Explain a Method Victor wants to find the area of a figure drawn on a centimeter grid made from whole-squares and half-squares. Explain to Victor how he can find the area of the figure.

Software Support

Warm Up 45.25

On Level

Activity Card 8-I

Solve a Word Problem

Activity Card 8-1

Work: In pairs

Use:

- MathBoard materials or TRB M28 (Centimeter-Dot Paper)

1. Read the word problem below. Work together to make a drawing to help you solve the problem.

   Shina's family wants to build a patio from square, cement tiles, 1 ft × 1 ft. The finished patio should be 7 ft × 3 ft. How many tiles do they need? How many feet of wood do they need to add a wood border around the patio?

2. What shape is the patio? How long is the patio? How wide is it? A rectangle; 7 ft long; 3 ft wide
3. **Think** What measurement gives you the number of tiles needed for the patio? What measurement gives you the number of feet of wood needed for the border? Area; perimeter

Unit 8, Lesson 1

Activity Note Review the formulas for area and perimeter before assigning this activity. Tell students that each square on the grid represents one square foot. Students can use counting to check answers.

Math Writing Prompt

Explain the Difference What is the difference between finding the area and finding the perimeter of the same figure.

Software Support

Shapes Ahoy: Ship Shapes, Level X

Challenge

Activity Card 8-I

Estimate Area

Activity Card 8-1

Work: In pairs

Use:

- TRB M42 (Inch-Grid Paper)
- Colored pencils

Decide:

Who will be Student 1 and who will be Student 2.

1. **Student 1:** Stand with one foot on the grid.
2. **Student 2:** Trace the outline of your partner's shoe.

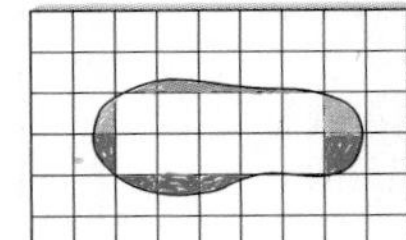

3. Estimate the area.
4. **Analyze** How can you use the partial squares in the drawing to find the total number of squares?

Unit 8, Lesson 1

Activity Note To keep track of the partial squares, suggest that students use the same color to shade the partial squares that equal about one whole square.

Math Writing Prompt

Make a Drawing Draw a small rectangle inside a larger rectangle on a dot array. Shade the small rectangle. How can you find the area of the unshaded part without counting squares?

DESTINATION Math

Software Support

Course II: Module 3: Unit 1: Area

3 Homework and Spiral Review

8–1 Homework **Goal:** Additional Practice

This Homework page gives students an opportunity to practice finding perimeter and area.

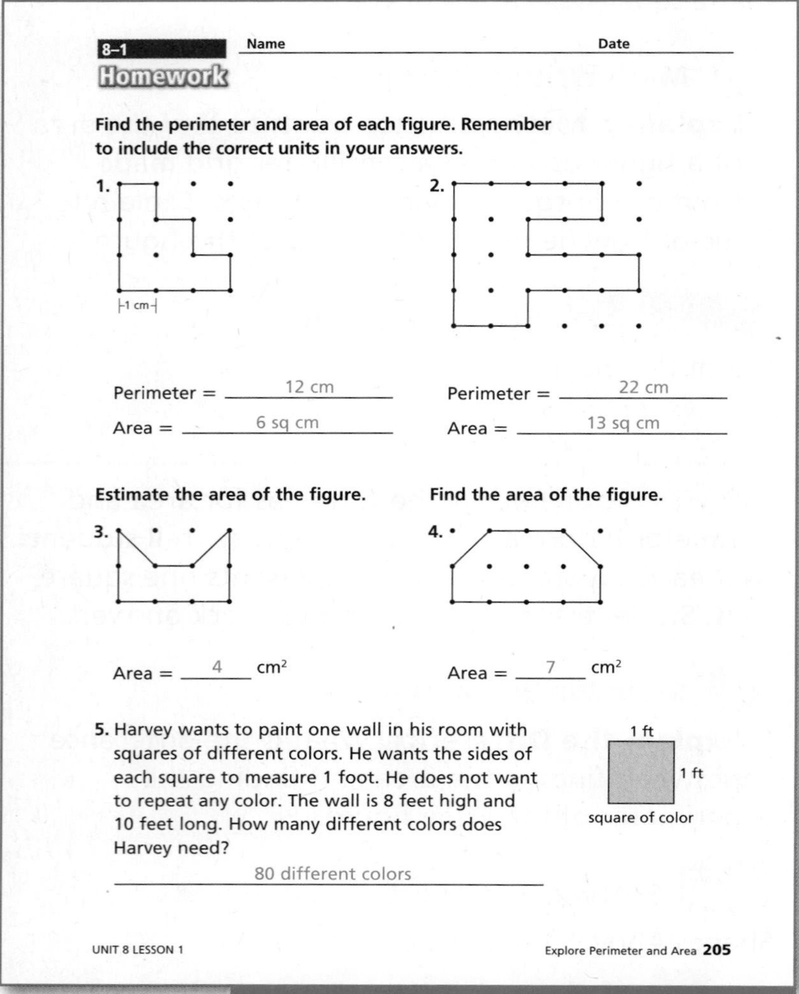

8–1 Homework — Name ________ Date ________

Find the perimeter and area of each figure. Remember to include the correct units in your answers.

1. ├1 cm┤
Perimeter = 12 cm
Area = 6 sq cm

2. Perimeter = 22 cm
Area = 13 sq cm

Estimate the area of the figure.

3. Area = 4 cm^2

Find the area of the figure.

4. Area = 7 cm^2

5. Harvey wants to paint one wall in his room with squares of different colors. He wants the sides of each square to measure 1 foot. He does not want to repeat any color. The wall is 8 feet high and 10 feet long. How many different colors does Harvey need?

1 ft, 1 ft, square of color

80 different colors

UNIT 8 LESSON 1 — Explore Perimeter and Area 205

Homework and Remembering page 205

8–1 Remembering **Goal:** Spiral Review

This Remembering page would be appropriate anytime after today's lesson.

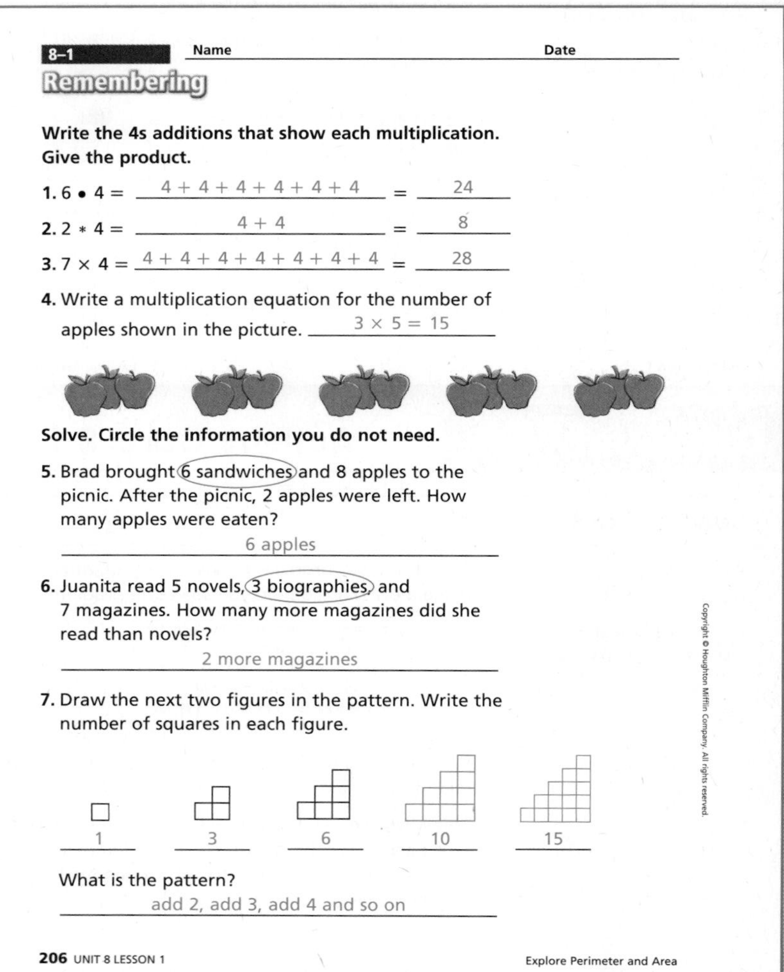

8–1 Remembering — Name ________ Date ________

Write the 4s additions that show each multiplication. Give the product.

1. $6 \bullet 4 = 4 + 4 + 4 + 4 + 4 + 4 = 24$
2. $2 * 4 = 4 + 4 = 8$
3. $7 \times 4 = 4 + 4 + 4 + 4 + 4 + 4 + 4 = 28$
4. Write a multiplication equation for the number of apples shown in the picture. $3 \times 5 = 15$

Solve. Circle the information you do not need.

5. Brad brought (6 sandwiches) and 8 apples to the picnic. After the picnic, 2 apples were left. How many apples were eaten?
6 apples

6. Juanita read 5 novels, (3 biographies,) and 7 magazines. How many more magazines did she read than novels?
2 more magazines

7. Draw the next two figures in the pattern. Write the number of squares in each figure.
1 3 6 10 15
What is the pattern? add 2, add 3, add 4 and so on

Copyright © Houghton Mifflin Company. All rights reserved.

206 UNIT 8 LESSON 1 — Explore Perimeter and Area

Homework and Remembering page 206

Home and School Connection

Family Letter Have students take home the Family Letter on Student Activity Book page 289 or Activity Workbook page 133. This letter explains how the concepts of perimeter and area are developed in *Math Expressions.* It gives parents and guardians a better understanding of the learning that goes on in math class and creates a bridge between school and home. A Spanish translation of this letter is on the following page.

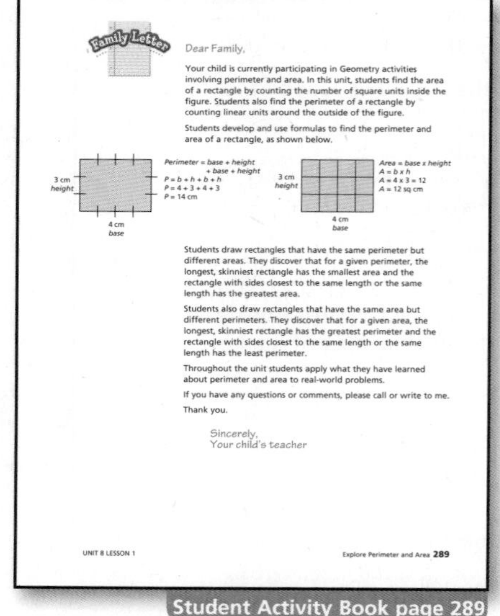

Family Letter

Dear Family,

Your child is currently participating in Geometry activities involving perimeter and area. In this unit, students find the area of a rectangle by counting the number of square units inside the figure. Students also find the perimeter of a rectangle by counting linear units around the outside of the figure.

Students develop and use formulas to find the perimeter and area of a rectangle, as shown below.

3 cm height, 4 cm base
Perimeter = base + height + base + height
$P = b + h + b + h$
$P = 4 + 3 + 4 + 3$
$P = 14$ cm

3 cm height, 4 cm base
Area = base x height
$A = b \times h$
$A = 4 \times 3 = 12$
$A = 12$ sq cm

Students draw rectangles that have the same perimeter but different areas. They discover that for a given perimeter, the longest, skinniest rectangle has the smallest area and the rectangle with sides closest to the same length or the same length has the greatest area.

Students also draw rectangles that have the same area but different perimeters. They discover that for a given area, the longest, skinniest rectangle has the greatest perimeter and the rectangle with sides closest to the same length or the same length has the least perimeter.

Throughout the unit students apply what they have learned about perimeter and area to real-world problems.

If you have any questions or comments, please call or write to me.

Thank you.

Sincerely,
Your child's teacher

UNIT 8 LESSON 1 — Explore Perimeter and Area 289

Student Activity Book page 289

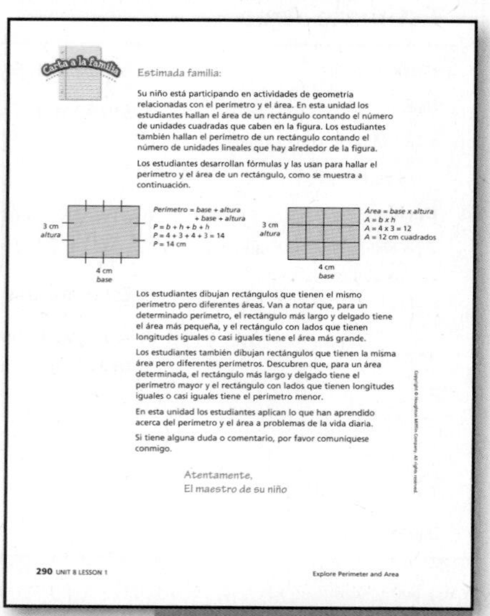

Carta a la familia

Estimada familia:

Su niño está participando en actividades de geometría relacionadas con el perímetro y el área. En esta unidad los estudiantes hallan el área de un rectángulo contando el número de unidades cuadradas que caben en la figura. Los estudiantes también hallan el perímetro de un rectángulo contando el número de unidades lineales que hay alrededor de la figura.

Los estudiantes desarrollan fórmulas y las usan para hallar el perímetro y el área de un rectángulo, como se muestra a continuación.

3 cm altura, 4 cm base
Perímetro = base + altura + base + altura
$P = b + h + b + h$
$P = 4 + 3 + 4 + 3 = 14$
$P = 14$ cm

3 cm altura, 4 cm base
Área = base x altura
$A = b \times h$
$A = 4 \times 3 = 12$
$A = 12$ cm cuadrados

Los estudiantes dibujan rectángulos que tienen el mismo perímetro pero diferentes áreas. Van a notar que, para un determinado perímetro, el rectángulo más largo y delgado tiene el área más pequeña, y el rectángulo con lados que tienen longitudes iguales o casi iguales tiene el área más grande.

Los estudiantes también dibujan rectángulos que tienen la misma área pero diferentes perímetros. Descubren que, para un área determinada, el rectángulo más largo y delgado tiene el perímetro mayor y el rectángulo con lados que tienen longitudes iguales o casi iguales tiene el perímetro menor.

En esta unidad los estudiantes aplican lo que han aprendido acerca del perímetro y el área a problemas de la vida diaria.

Si tiene alguna duda o comentario, por favor comuníquese conmigo.

Atentamente,
El maestro de su niño

Copyright © Houghton Mifflin Company. All rights reserved.

290 UNIT 8 LESSON 1 — Explore Perimeter and Area

Student Activity Book page 290

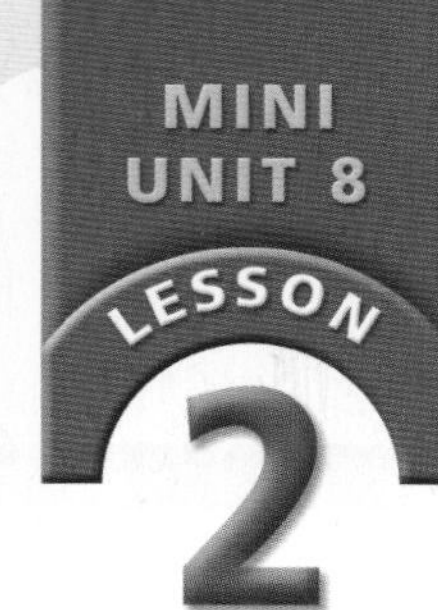

Relate Area and Perimeter

Lesson Objectives

- Discover that rectangles with the same perimeter can have different areas.
- Discover that rectangles with the same area can have different perimeters.

Vocabulary
perimeter
area

The Day at a Glance

Today's Goals	Materials	
1 Teaching the Lesson **A1:** Draw all of the possible rectangles with a given perimeter and sides whose lengths are whole numbers, and find and compare their areas. **A2:** Draw all of the possible rectangles with a given area and sides whose lengths are whole numbers, and find and compare their perimeters.	**Lesson Activities** Student Activity Book pp. 291–292 or Student Hardcover Book pp. 291–292 and Activity Workbook pp. 135–136 (includes tables) Homework and Remembering pp. 207–208 MathBoard materials or Centimeter Dot Paper (TRB M28) Centimeter ruler or Centimeter Ruler (TRB M26) *Spaghetti and Meatballs for All* by Marilyn Burns (Scholastic Press, 1997)	**Going Further** Activity Cards 8-2 Square-inch tiles or paper cut into square inches Centimeter Dot Paper (TRB M28) Centimeter ruler or Centimeter Ruler (TRB M26) Math Journals
2 Going Further ▸ Differentiated Instruction		
3 Homework and Spiral Review		

Use Math Talk today!

Keeping Skills Sharp

Daily Routines

Homework Review Ask students to place their homework at the corner of their desks. As you circulate during Quick Practice, check that students completed the assignment, and see whether any problem(s) caused difficulty for many students.

Create a Pattern Create a growing pattern using geometric figures. If necessary, use pattern blocks and counters to visually create the pattern. Then, trace the figures onto paper. Share with the class.

English Language Learners

Draw a 2 row × 4 unit rectangle and a 1 row × 5 unit rectangle. Guide students to find the *perimeter* and *area* of each rectangle.

- **Beginning** Say: **The *perimeter* of the rectangles is the same. The *area* of the rectangles is different.** Have children repeat.
- **Intermediate** Ask: **Is the *perimeter* of the rectangles the same?** yes **Is the *area* of the rectangles the same?** no
- **Advanced** Have children tell about the *areas* and *perimeters* of the rectangles.

1 Teaching the Lesson

Activity 1

Same Perimeter with a Different Area

 **30 MINUTES**

Goal: Draw all of the possible rectangles with a given perimeter and sides whose lengths are whole numbers, and find and compare their areas.

Materials: Student Activity Book or Hardcover Book p. 291 and Activity Workbook p. 135, MathBoard materials or Centimeter-Dot Paper (TRB M28), centimeter ruler or Centimeter Ruler (TRB M26) (1 per student)

 **NCTM Standards:**
Geometry
Measurement
Connections

▶ Explore Rectangles with the Same Perimeter WHOLE CLASS

Refer students to Student Book page 291. Read aloud the directions in exercise 1 and make sure students know what to do. Ask students to complete the exercise either on the dot array side of their MathBoards or on Centimeter-Dot Paper (TRB M28). Remind students that in Unit 2, they drew all of the possible rectangles with a given perimeter. If students are having difficulty with the exercise, ask these questions:

- If you add the lengths of all four sides, you get 12 cm. What do you get if you add the lengths of the two adjacent sides? 6 cm
- How can you use this information to help you draw a rectangle? I can find two numbers that add to 6 and use them as lengths of sides.

Ask volunteers to share their rectangles with the rest of the class. There are three possible rectangles.

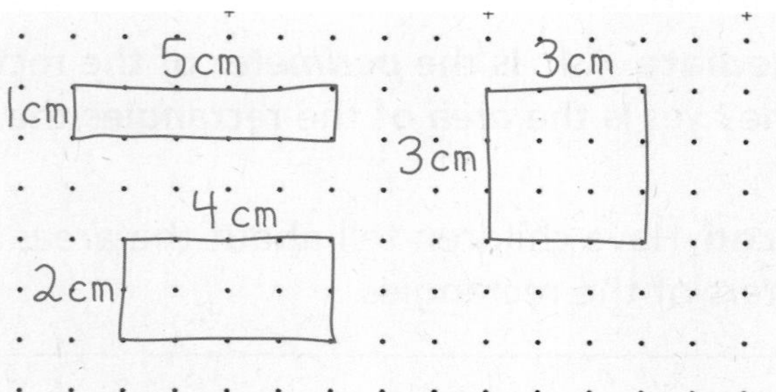

Name Date

▶ Explore Rectangles with the Same Perimeter

Complete.

1. On a centimeter dot array, draw all possible rectangles with a **perimeter** of 12 cm and sides whose lengths are whole centimeters. Label the lengths of two adjacent sides of each rectangle.
2. Find and label the **area** of each rectangle. In the table, record the lengths of the sides and the area of each rectangle.
3. Compare the shapes of the rectangles with the least and greatest areas.
Possible answer: The rectangle with the least area is long and skinny; the rectangle with the greatest area is a square.

Rectangles with Perimeter 12 cm

Lengths of Two Adjacent Sides	Area
1 cm, 5 cm	5 sq cm
2 cm, 4 cm	8 sq cm
3 cm, 3 cm	9 sq cm

4. On a centimeter dot array, draw all possible rectangles with a perimeter of 22 cm and sides whose lengths are whole centimeters. Label the lengths of two adjacent sides of each rectangle.
5. Find and label the area of each rectangle. In the table, record the lengths of the sides and the area of each rectangle.

Rectangles with Perimeter 22 cm

Lengths of Two Adjacent Sides	Area
1 cm, 10 cm	10 sq cm
2 cm, 9 cm	18 sq cm
3 cm, 8 cm	24 sq cm
4 cm, 7 cm	28 sq cm
5 cm, 6 cm	30 sq cm

6. Compare the shapes of the rectangles with the least and greatest areas.
Possible answer: The rectangle with the least area is long and skinny; the rectangle with the greatest area has side lengths close to the same length.

UNIT 8 LESSON 2 Relate Area and Perimeter 291

Student Activity Book page 291

Teaching Note

Watch For! Some students might draw each of the non-square rectangles twice, with different orientations. In other words, they might draw a rectangle with a 1-cm width and a 5-cm length, and a rectangle with a 5-cm width and a 1-cm length. If this happens, explain that because these rectangles are the same size and shape—that is, because they are congruent—they are considered to be the same rectangle.

Ask students whether they used any strategies to check that they drew all of the possible rectangles. If necessary, remind students that in Unit 2 they discovered that the lengths of two adjacent sides add to half of the perimeter. So to find all of the possible lengths of sides for rectangles with a perimeter of

12 cm, they can find all the different pairs of whole numbers that add to 6: 1 and 5, 2 and 4, and 3 and 3. Connect this to the partners of 6. Students can make rectangles with adjacent sides of all of the partners of half of the perimeter.

- What is the perimeter of each rectangle that you drew? 12 cm
- Are they all the same shape? no
- Do you think they all have the same area? no

Have students complete exercises 2 and 3. Then discuss their answers. They should notice that the rectangle with the least area is long and skinny and that the rectangle with the greatest area is a square.

Ask students to examine all of the rectangles and their completed table. They should see that as the lengths of the adjacent sides become closer to the same length the area increases.

Next, have students complete exercise 4.

Ask several volunteers to share their rectangles with the rest of the class. There are five possible rectangles.

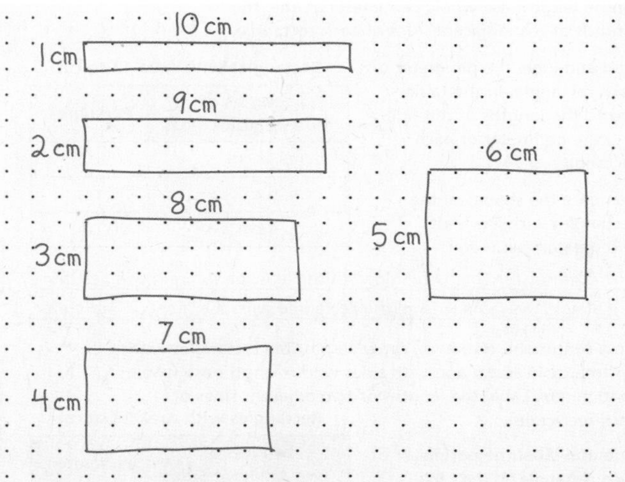

Ask students to complete exercises 5 and 6. Then discuss their answers. They should recognize that the rectangle with the least area is long and skinny. The rectangle with the greatest area looks the most like a square.

Activity 2

Same Area with a Different Perimeter

 **30 MINUTES**

Goal: Draw all of the possible rectangles with a given area and sides whose lengths are whole numbers, and find and compare their perimeters.

Materials: Student Activity Book or Hardcover Book p. 292 and Activity Workbook p. 136, MathBoard materials or Centimeter Dot Paper (TRB M28), centimeter ruler or Centimeter Ruler (TRB M26) (1 per student)

 **NCTM Standards:**
Geometry
Measurement
Connections

▶ Explore Rectangles with the Same Area WHOLE CLASS

Read aloud the directions in exercise 7 on Student Book page 292. Ask students to complete the exercise either on the dot array side of their MathBoards or on Centimeter Dot Paper (TRB M28).

When students are finished, ask several volunteers to share their rectangles. There are three possibilities.

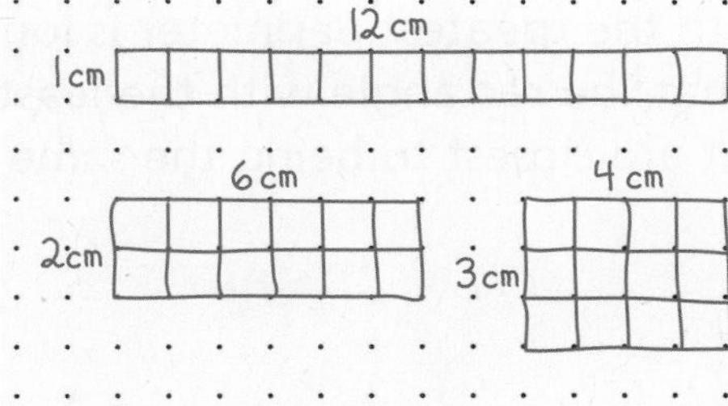

Activity continued ▶

Teaching the Lesson (continued)

8–2 Class Activity Name Date

► Explore Rectangles with the Same Area

Complete.

7. On a centimeter dot array, draw all possible rectangles with an area of 12 sq cm and sides whose lengths are whole centimeters. Label the lengths of two adjacent sides of each rectangle.
8. Find and label the perimeter of each rectangle. In the table, record the lengths of the sides and the perimeter of each rectangle.
9. Compare the shapes of the rectangles with the least and greatest perimeter.

Rectangles with Area 12 sq cm

Lengths of Two Adjacent Sides	Perimeter
1 cm, 12 cm	26 cm
2 cm, 6 cm	16 cm
3 cm, 4 cm	14 cm

Possible answer: The rectangle with the least perimeter has sides that are almost the same length; the rectangle with the greatest perimeter is long and skinny.

10. On a centimeter dot array, draw all possible rectangles with an area of 18 sq cm and with sides whose lengths are whole centimeters. Label the lengths of two adjacent sides of each rectangle.
11. Find and label the perimeter of each rectangle. In the table, record the lengths of the sides and the perimeter of each rectangle.
12. Compare the shapes of the rectangles with the least and greatest perimeter.

Rectangles with Area 18 sq cm

Lengths of Two Adjacent Sides	Perimeter
1 cm, 18 cm	38 cm
2 cm, 9 cm	22 cm
3 cm, 6 cm	18 cm

Possible answer: The rectangle with the least perimeter is twice as long as it is wide. The rectangle with the greatest perimeter is long and skinny.

292 UNIT 8 LESSON 2 Relate Area and Perimeter

Student Activity Book page 292

Ask students whether they used any strategies to check that they drew all of the possible rectangles. If necessary, remind them that to find all of the possible rectangles with an area of 12 sq cm, they can find all the different pairs of whole numbers with a product of 12: 1 and 12, 2 and 6, and 3 and 4.

Point out that although their rectangles look different, they all have an area of 12 sq cm.

Ask students to complete exercises 8 and 9 and then discuss their answers. They should notice that the rectangle with the greatest perimeter is long and skinny and that the rectangle with the least perimeter has sides that are closest to being the same length.

Next, have students work through exercises 10 and 11. There are three possible rectangles.

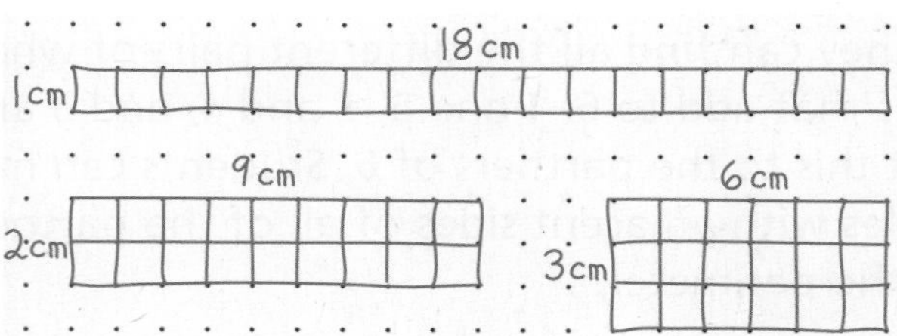

Math Talk You might summarize the discussion by asking the following questions:

- When you drew all the rectangles with the same perimeter, what did the rectangle with the least area look like? The rectangle was long and skinny.
- What did the rectangle with the greatest area look like? The rectangle had sides that were closest to being the same length or were the same length.
- When you drew all the rectangles with the same area, what did the rectangle with the greatest perimeter look like? It was long and skinny.
- What did the rectangle with the least perimeter look like? The rectangle had sides that were closest to being the same length.

Class Management

Looking Ahead Students will need a sheet of Centimeter-Dot Paper (TRB M28) to complete their homework.

Ongoing Assessment

Ask students the following questions:

► Donya has 24 square tiles. She wants to make a rectangular patio with the greatest possible area. Describe the shape of the rectangle she should use for her patio.

► Alejandro wants to make a rectangular garden that is 25 sq m. He plans to put up a deer fence around the garden. He wants to use the least possible amount of fencing. Describe the shape of the rectangle he should use.

2 Going Further

Differentiated Instruction

Intervention — Activity Card 8-2

Tile Mirror — Activity Card 8-2

Work: In pairs

Use:
- 20 square-inch tiles

1. **Work Together** Model and solve the word problem below.

   Mr. Uralov is making a rectangular mirror with 20 square mirror tiles that are 1 foot x 1 foot. What are the possible lengths of adjacent sides he can use for his rectangular mirror?

2. Use the tiles to create as many rectangles as you can. Make a list of all the possible lengths and widths that you find. 20 ft × 1 ft; 10 ft × 2 ft; 5 ft × 4 ft
3. **Analyze** How did you find your answer?

Unit 8, Lesson 2

Activity Note Stress the connection between the total number of tiles and the area of the mirror. Then have students make an organized list of all the pairs of factors whose product is 20.

Math Writing Prompt

Make a Drawing Ester is making a rectangular wall hanging using 16 squares of fabric. Draw the different rectangles she can use. Explain how you know that you have drawn all possibilities.

Software Support

Warm Up 44.26

On Level — Activity Card 8-2

Rabbit Run — Activity Card 8-2 

Work: In pairs

Use:
- TRB M28 (Centimeter-Dot Paper)
- TRB M26 (Centimeter Ruler)

1. **Work Together** Model and solve the word problem below.

   Philippe has 16 feet of fencing to make a rectangular run for his rabbit. He wants the run to have the greatest possible area. What dimensions should he use for his rabbit run?

2. **Think** How does the 16 feet of fencing relate to the measure of each rectangle? It is the measure of the perimeter.
3. Use the dot paper to model all the rectangular runs that use 16 feet of fencing. How many rectangles did you find? Which one has the greatest possible area? 4; a 4 ft × 4 ft square

Unit 8, Lesson 2

Activity Note The perimeter of the run is 16 ft. So length plus width equals 8 ft. Students can make an organized list of all pairs of addends whose sum is 8, and then find the pair with the greatest product.

Math Writing Prompt

Explain a Method Lelia has 14 inches of ribbon to use as a border for a rectangular picture frame. How can Lelia find all of the possible rectangles with a perimeter of 14 inches?

Software Support

Shapes Ahoy: Ship Shapes, Level W

Challenge — Activity Card 8-2

Find Lengths of Sides — Activity Card 8-2

Work: In pairs

Use:
- TRB M28 (Centimeter-Dot Paper)
- TRB M26 (Centimeter Ruler)

1. **Work Together** Model and solve the word problem below.

   Melissa drew a rectangle with an area of 20 sq cm and a perimeter of 24 cm. What are the length and width of the rectangle?

2. How many rectangles could Melissa draw with an area of 20 sq cm? What are the length and width of the rectangle with a perimeter of 24 cm? 3; 2 cm × 10 cm rectangle
3. **Analyze** Could you have solved this problem another way? Explain.

Unit 8, Lesson 2

Activity Note Some students may find all possible rectangles with a perimeter of 24 cm, and then identify the one with an area of 20 sq cm.

Math Writing Prompt

Explain Your Thinking Can you use addition to find all of the possible rectangles for a given perimeter, and multiplication to find all of the possible rectangles for a given area? Explain.

Software Support

Course II: Module 3: Unit 1: Area

3 Homework and Spiral Review

Goal: Additional Practice

This Homework page gives students practice comparing rectangles with a given area or perimeter.

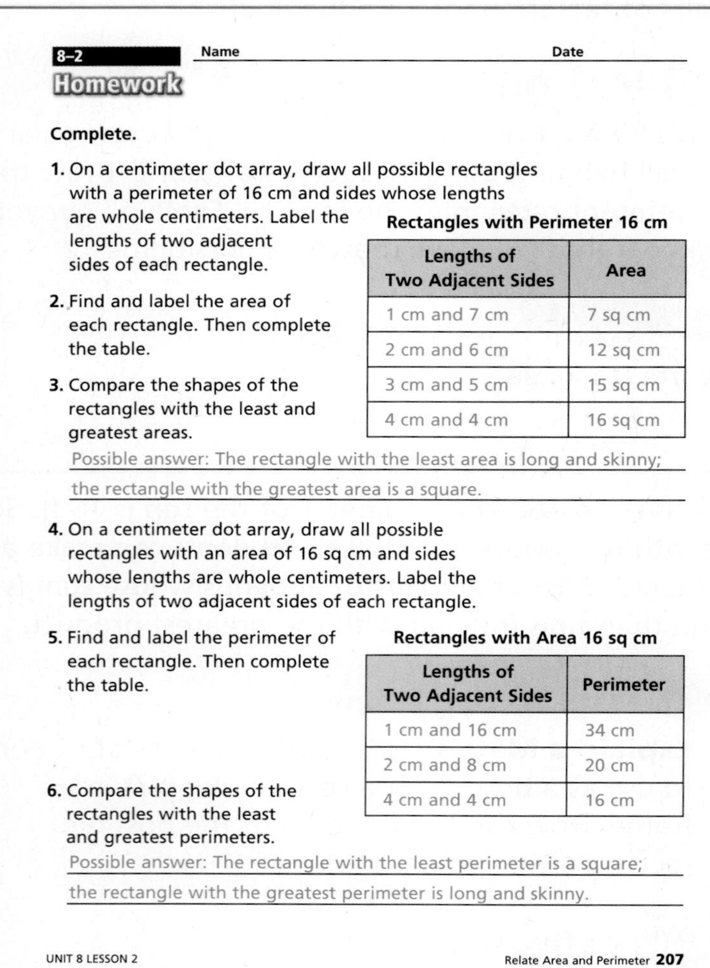

8–2 Homework Name ______ Date ______

Complete.

1. On a centimeter dot array, draw all possible rectangles with a perimeter of 16 cm and sides whose lengths are whole centimeters. Label the lengths of two adjacent sides of each rectangle.
2. Find and label the area of each rectangle. Then complete the table.
3. Compare the shapes of the rectangles with the least and greatest areas.
   Possible answer: The rectangle with the least area is long and skinny; the rectangle with the greatest area is a square.

Rectangles with Perimeter 16 cm

Lengths of Two Adjacent Sides	Area
1 cm and 7 cm	7 sq cm
2 cm and 6 cm	12 sq cm
3 cm and 5 cm	15 sq cm
4 cm and 4 cm	16 sq cm

4. On a centimeter dot array, draw all possible rectangles with an area of 16 sq cm and sides whose lengths are whole centimeters. Label the lengths of two adjacent sides of each rectangle.
5. Find and label the perimeter of each rectangle. Then complete the table.
6. Compare the shapes of the rectangles with the least and greatest perimeters.
   Possible answer: The rectangle with the least perimeter is a square; the rectangle with the greatest perimeter is long and skinny.

Rectangles with Area 16 sq cm

Lengths of Two Adjacent Sides	Perimeter
1 cm and 16 cm	34 cm
2 cm and 8 cm	20 cm
4 cm and 4 cm	16 cm

UNIT 8 LESSON 2 Relate Area and Perimeter 207

Homework and Remembering page 207

Goal: Spiral Review

This Remembering page would be appropriate anytime after today's lesson.

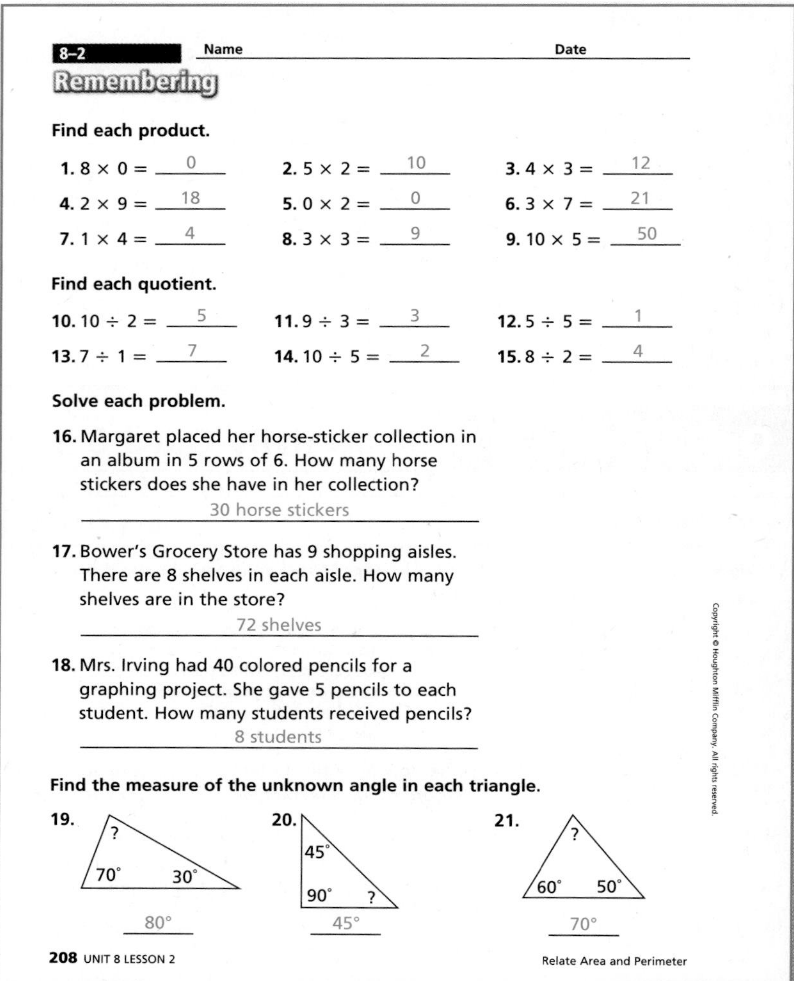

8–2 Remembering Name ______ Date ______

Find each product.

1. $8 \times 0 =$ 0
2. $5 \times 2 =$ 10
3. $4 \times 3 =$ 12
4. $2 \times 9 =$ 18
5. $0 \times 2 =$ 0
6. $3 \times 7 =$ 21
7. $1 \times 4 =$ 4
8. $3 \times 3 =$ 9
9. $10 \times 5 =$ 50

Find each quotient.

10. $10 \div 2 =$ 5
11. $9 \div 3 =$ 3
12. $5 \div 5 =$ 1
13. $7 \div 1 =$ 7
14. $10 \div 5 =$ 2
15. $8 \div 2 =$ 4

Solve each problem.

16. Margaret placed her horse-sticker collection in an album in 5 rows of 6. How many horse stickers does she have in her collection?
    30 horse stickers
17. Bower's Grocery Store has 9 shopping aisles. There are 8 shelves in each aisle. How many shelves are in the store?
    72 shelves
18. Mrs. Irving had 40 colored pencils for a graphing project. She gave 5 pencils to each student. How many students received pencils?
    8 students

Find the measure of the unknown angle in each triangle.

19. ?, 70°, 30° — 80°
20. 45°, 90°, ? — 45°
21. ?, 60°, 50° — 70°

208 UNIT 8 LESSON 2 Relate Area and Perimeter

Homework and Remembering page 208

Home or School Connection

Literature Connection

Spaghetti and Meatballs for All! Have students read *Spaghetti and Meatballs for All!* by Marilyn Burns (Scholastic Press, 1997). After reading the story, present students with this related word problem to solve:

Your family is having a picnic. You plan to put together 12 smaller square tables to make one large rectangular table so everyone can sit as a group. How would you arrange the 12 tables so that you could have the greatest number of seated guests? How would you arrange the 12 tables so that you could have the greatest tabletop area?

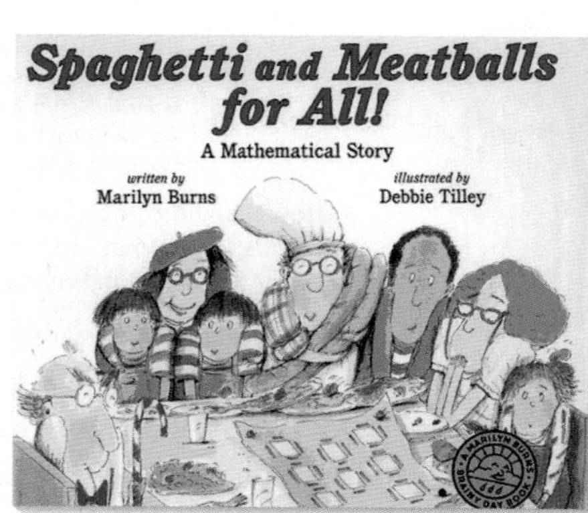

Formulas for Area and Perimeter

Lesson Objectives

- Develop methods for finding the area and perimeter of a rectangle without counting individual squares or unit lengths.
- Use symbols to write rules (formulas) for finding the area and perimeter of a rectangle.

Vocabulary
base
height
formula

The Day at a Glance

Today's Goals	Materials	
1 Teaching the Lesson **A1:** Develop a formula for the area of a rectangle. **A2:** Develop a formula for the perimeter of a rectangle. **A3:** Develop formulas for the area and perimeter of a square.	**Lesson Activities** Student Activity Book pp. 293–296 or Student Hardcover Book pp. 293–296 Homework and Remembering pp. 209–210 Quick Quiz (Assessment Guide)	**Going Further** Activity Cards 8-3 Geoboards Rubber Bands Inch Rulers Index cards Mathboard Materials Math Journals
2 Going Further ► Differentiated Instruction		
3 Homework and Spiral Review		

Use Math Talk today!

Keeping Skills Sharp

Daily Routines

Homework Review Let students work together to check their work. Initially, pair less able students with more able students. Remind students to use what they know about helping others.

Congruent Figures Draw two figures that are congruent. Explain how you can test that they are congruent.

Possible answer:

When you flip, slide, or turn one figure and it fits exactly on top of the other, the figures are congruent. After turning and sliding Triangle B,it fits exactly on top of Triangle A. The triangles are congruent.

English Language Learners

Draw a 3 row × 4 unit rectangle. Point and say: **This is the *base*. This is the *height*.** Have students repeat. Label the lengths of each.

- **Beginning** Point to the base. Say: **The *base* is 4 units.** Point to the height. Say: **The *height* is 3 units.** Have students repeat.
- **Intermediate** Say: **The *base* is 4 units.** Ask: **Is the *height* 4 units?** no **Is the *height* 3?** yes
- **Advanced** Have students tell the difference between the *base* and *height* of a rectangle.

1 Teaching the Lesson

Activity 1

Area Formula for a Rectangle

 **20 MINUTES**

Goal: Develop a formula for the area of a rectangle.

Materials: Student Activity Book or Hardcover Book pp. 293–294

 **NCTM Standards:**
Geometry
Measurement
Connections

▶ Find the Area of a Rectangle

INDIVIDUALS

Refer students to Student Book page 293 and ask them to complete exercises 1–3 independently.

At this point, many students will count individual square centimeters to find the area. To encourage other methods of calculating area, the rectangle in exercise 3 is not drawn on a grid. Nevertheless, some students might choose to draw square centimeters to help them find the area of this rectangle.

Discuss students' answers and then ask:

- If you know the lengths of two adjacent sides of any rectangle, how can you find its area? You can find the area by multiplying the lengths of the two adjacent sides.

Draw a rectangle and label the sides as shown below.

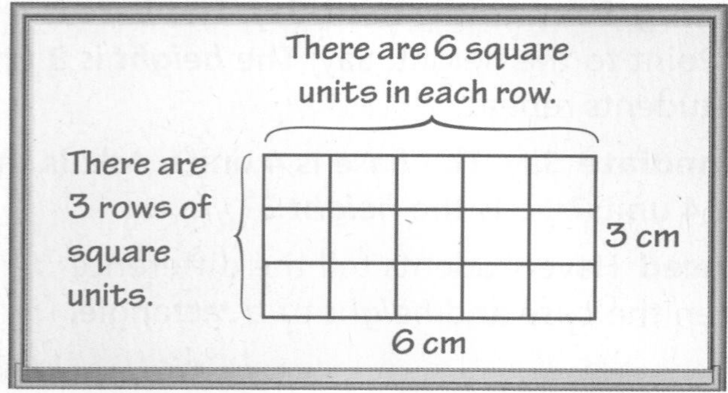

Have students work in pairs to find its area.

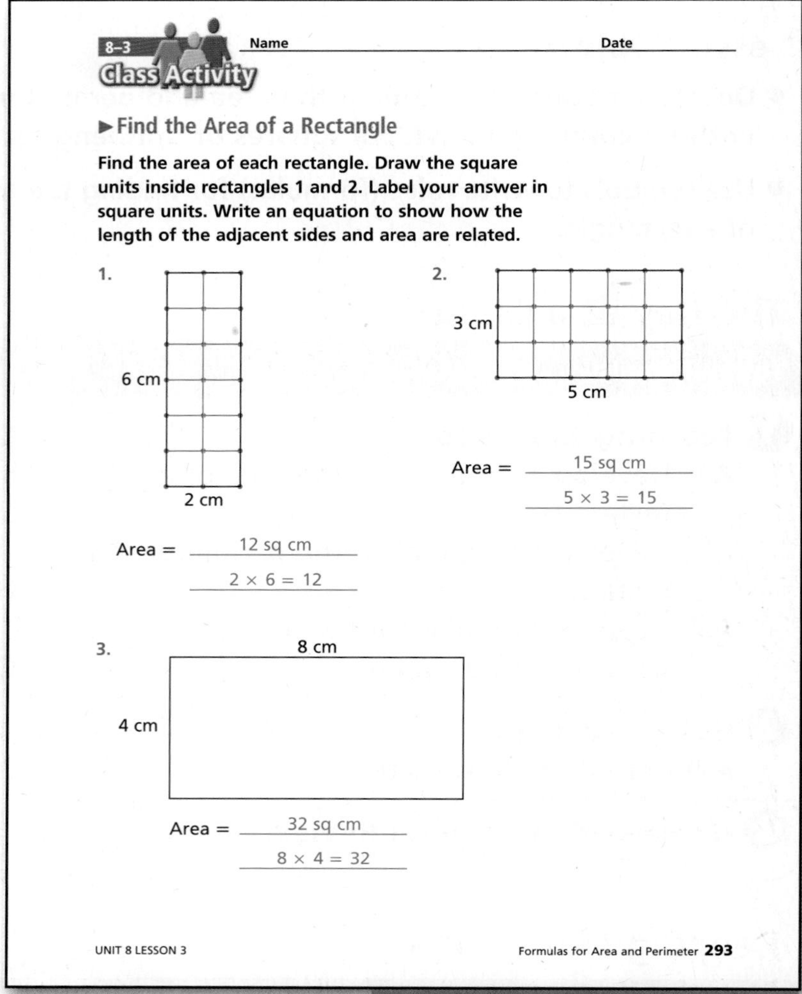
8–3 Class Activity
Name
Date

▶ Find the Area of a Rectangle

Find the area of each rectangle. Draw the square units inside rectangles 1 and 2. Label your answer in square units. Write an equation to show how the length of the adjacent sides and area are related.

1. 6 cm, 2 cm

Area = 12 sq cm
2 × 6 = 12

2. 3 cm, 5 cm

Area = 15 sq cm
5 × 3 = 15

3. 8 cm, 4 cm

Area = 32 sq cm
8 × 4 = 32

UNIT 8 LESSON 3 Formulas for Area and Perimeter 293

Student Activity Book page 293

Math Talk in Action

Adita: What can I do to find the area of the rectangle?

Lian: Multiply 6 and 3. The area is 18 square centimeters.

Adita: I see. There are 3 rows with 6 square units in each. This is represented by the equation 6 × 3 = 18.

If necessary, help students see why this method works. Students can think of the length of one side as the number of rows of square units in an array and the other side as the number of square units in each row. The total number of square units, or the area, is the product of these two numbers.

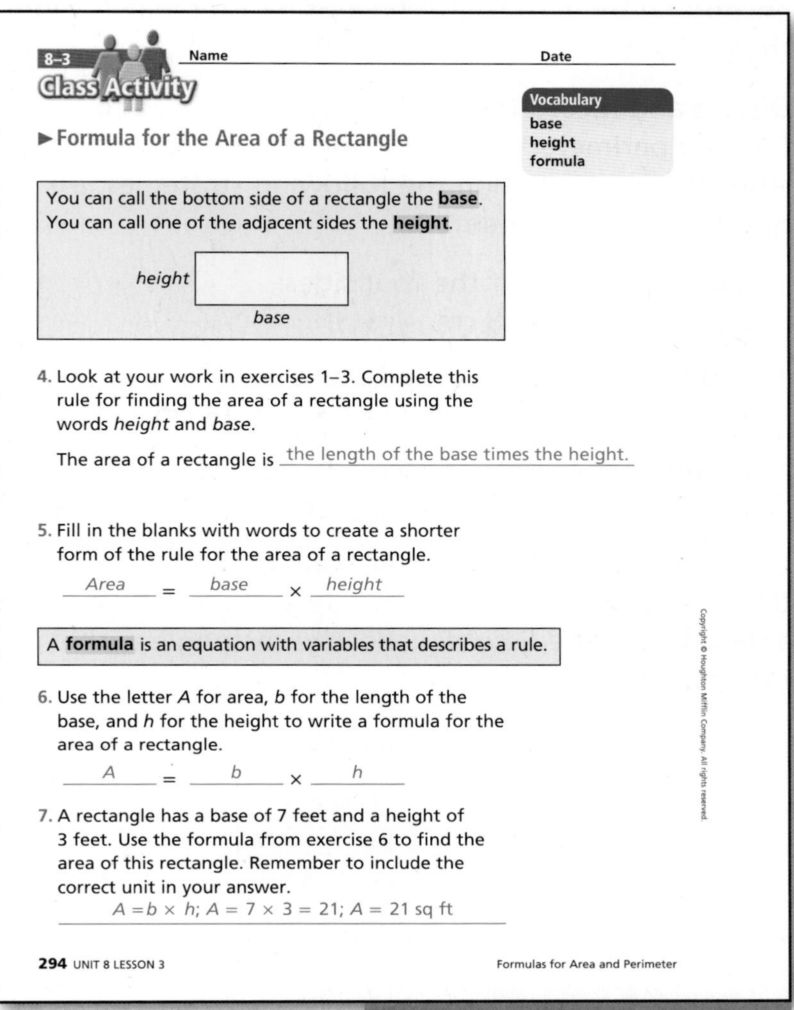
8–3 Class Activity

Name ______ Date ______

Vocabulary
base
height
formula

► Formula for the Area of a Rectangle

You can call the bottom side of a rectangle the **base**.
You can call one of the adjacent sides the **height**.

height

base

4. Look at your work in exercises 1–3. Complete this rule for finding the area of a rectangle using the words *height* and *base*.

   The area of a rectangle is the length of the base times the height.

5. Fill in the blanks with words to create a shorter form of the rule for the area of a rectangle.

   Area = base × height

A **formula** is an equation with variables that describes a rule.

6. Use the letter *A* for area, *b* for the length of the base, and *h* for the height to write a formula for the area of a rectangle.

   A = *b* × *h*

7. A rectangle has a base of 7 feet and a height of 3 feet. Use the formula from exercise 6 to find the area of this rectangle. Remember to include the correct unit in your answer.

   A = *b* × *h*; *A* = 7 × 3 = 21; *A* = 21 sq ft

294 UNIT 8 LESSON 3 Formulas for Area and Perimeter

Student Activity Book page 294

► Formula for the Area of a Rectangle

WHOLE CLASS

Tell students that they will now write a rule for finding the area of a rectangle. This kind of rule is called a *formula.* Ask them to look at the rectangle on Student Book page 294. Explain that they can call the bottom side the base. An adjacent side can be called the height.

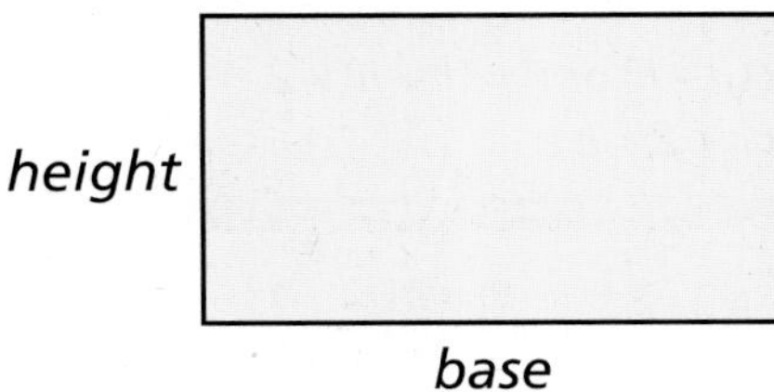

Work through exercises 4 and 5 together. Ask students to suggest a rule, in words, for calculating the area of a rectangle with known measurements for the base and height. If they need help, point out that exercise 4 gives the beginning of the rule. Write the rule on the board.

> The area of a rectangle is the length of the base times the height.

Next, establish a shorter form of the rule for area.

> Area = base x height

Together, test the rule using the rectangle in exercise 1. Explain that in order to calculate the area, you replace the words *base* and *height* with the given values.

> Area = base x height
> Area = 2 x 6 = 12
> Area = 12 sq cm

Explain to students that a formula is a rule that uses letters instead of words. Read aloud exercise 6. Then work with students to establish this formula: A = b x h

Explain that this equation is called a formula for the area of a rectangle.

Together, solve exercise 7, using the formula and substituting 7 for *b* and 3 for *h.*

> A = b x h
> A = 7 x 3 = 21
> A = 21 sq ft

- What unit do we use for the area of this rectangle? square feet

Activity 2

Perimeter Formula for a Rectangle

20 MINUTES

Goal: Develop a formula for the perimeter of a rectangle.

Materials: Student Activity Book or Hardcover Book page 295

NCTM Standards:
Geometry
Measurement
Connections

▶ Formula for the Perimeter of a Rectangle WHOLE CLASS

Refer students to Student Book page 295. Have them work independently to find the perimeter of the rectangles in exercises 8–12.

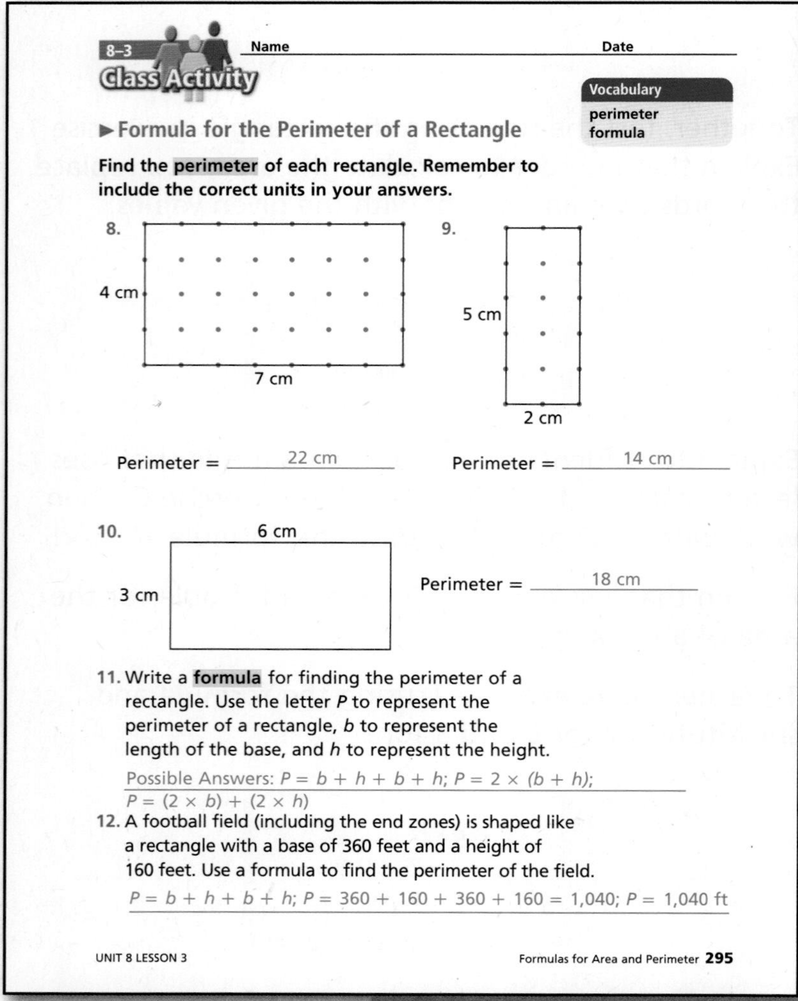

8-3 Class Activity

Name Date

Vocabulary
perimeter
formula

▶ Formula for the Perimeter of a Rectangle

Find the perimeter of each rectangle. Remember to include the correct units in your answers.

8. 4 cm, 7 cm

Perimeter = 22 cm

9. 5 cm, 2 cm

Perimeter = 14 cm

10. 6 cm, 3 cm

Perimeter = 18 cm

11. Write a formula for finding the perimeter of a rectangle. Use the letter P to represent the perimeter of a rectangle, b to represent the length of the base, and h to represent the height.

Possible Answers: $P = b + h + b + h$; $P = 2 \times (b + h)$; $P = (2 \times b) + (2 \times h)$

12. A football field (including the end zones) is shaped like a rectangle with a base of 360 feet and a height of 160 feet. Use a formula to find the perimeter of the field.

$P = b + h + b + h$; $P = 360 + 160 + 360 + 160 = 1{,}040$; $P = 1{,}040$ ft

UNIT 8 LESSON 3 Formulas for Area and Perimeter 295

Student Activity Book page 295

If you notice students counting individual centimeters, encourage them to try to think of a faster way to find the perimeter.

Discuss and record the methods students used to find the perimeter of the rectangle in exercise 10. If students don't mention the following strategies, ask questions to elicit them.

- Add the lengths of the four sides: $3 + 6 + 3 + 6 = 18$ cm
- Add the lengths of two adjacent sides, and multiply the sum by 2: $(3 + 6) \times 2 = 9 \times 2 = 18$ cm
- Multiply the length of each adjacent side by 2, and add the products: $(3 \times 2) + (6 \times 2) = 6 + 12 = 18$ cm

Draw a rectangle on the board and remind students that they can call the bottom side the *base* and an adjacent side the *height.* Label the rectangle with b for base and h for height.

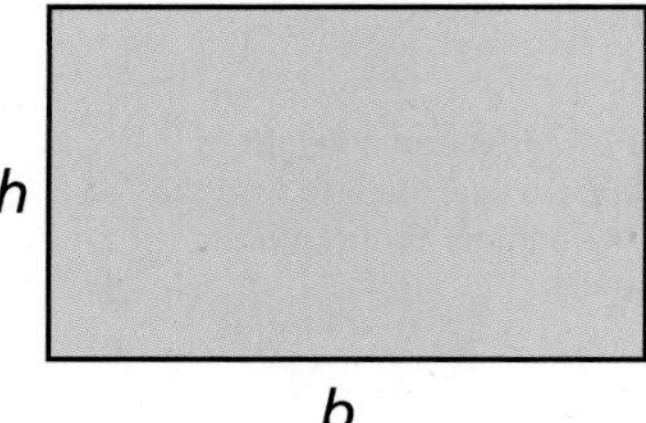

Ask students to try to complete exercise 11 independently before you invite volunteers to share their formulas for the perimeter of a rectangle. There are several correct formulas. Record each on the board.

$P = b + h + b + h$
(or any other formula that shows the sum of the lengths of the four sides, such as $P = h + b + h + b$ or $P = h + h + b + b$)

$P = 2 \times (b + h)$ or $P = (b + h) \times 2$
$P = 2 \times b + 2 \times h$

If a student suggests $P = 2 \times b + h$ or $P = b + h \times 2$, explain that when an equation includes both multiplication and addition, you multiply first. To specify that you want to add first, you can use parentheses: $P = 2 \times (b + h)$ or $P = (b + h) \times 2$. Students will learn about parentheses and order of operations in more depth in Unit 5.

Don't worry if students have difficulty coming up with a formula for perimeter on their own. They will continue to explore formulas for area and perimeter in later grades.

Have students solve problem 12 using a formula of their choice. Remind them to include the correct unit in their answer.

Activity 3

Perimeter and Area Formulas for a Square

 **20 MINUTES**

Goal: Develop formulas for the area and perimeter of a square.

Materials: Student Activity Book or Hardcover Book p. 296

 **NCTM Standards:**
Geometry
Measurement
Connections

▶ Formulas for the Perimeter and Area of a Square WHOLE CLASS

Tell students that since a square is a special kind of rectangle, they can use the same formulas that they used for a rectangle to find the area and perimeter of a square.

- What is special about the values of b and h for a square? They are the same.

Refer students to Student Book page 296 and have them find the perimeter and area of each square in exercises 13–15. Discuss their answers.

Point out that while the formulas for a rectangle work for a square, there are also special formulas for a square.

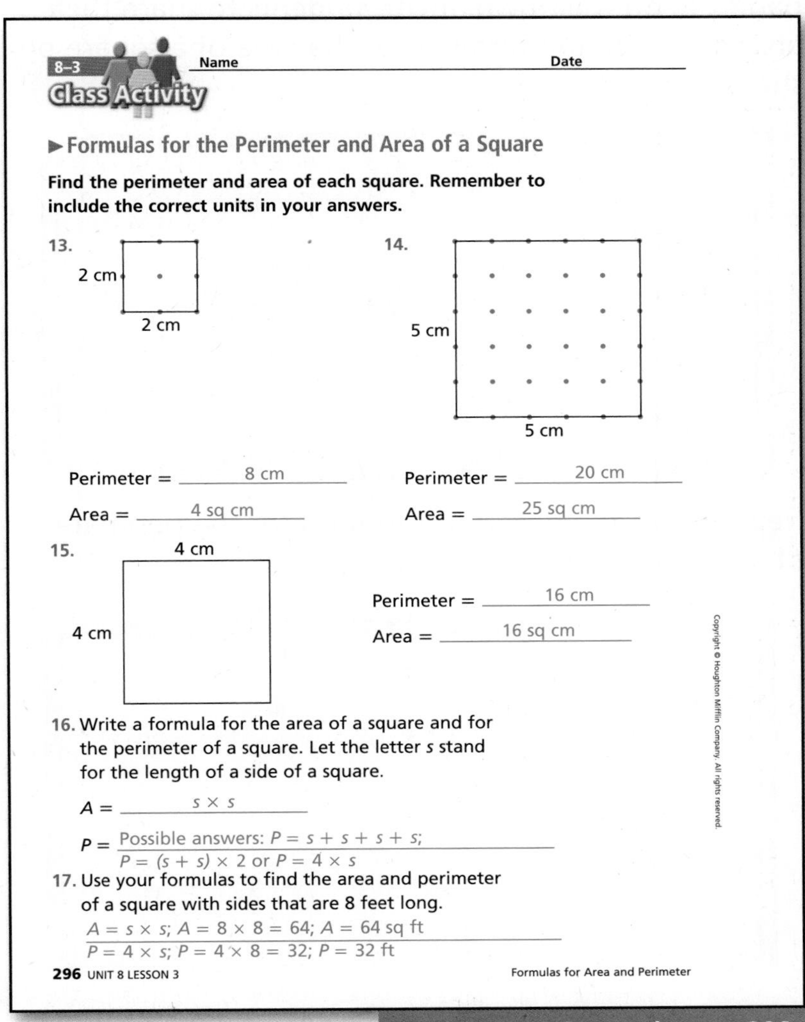

8–3 Class Activity Name Date

▶ Formulas for the Perimeter and Area of a Square

Find the perimeter and area of each square. Remember to include the correct units in your answers.

13. 2 cm, 2 cm

Perimeter = 8 cm

Area = 4 sq cm

14. 5 cm, 5 cm

Perimeter = 20 cm

Area = 25 sq cm

15. 4 cm, 4 cm

Perimeter = 16 cm

Area = 16 sq cm

16. Write a formula for the area of a square and for the perimeter of a square. Let the letter s stand for the length of a side of a square.

$A =$ $s \times s$

$P =$ Possible answers: $P = s + s + s + s$; $P = (s + s) \times 2$ or $P = 4 \times s$

17. Use your formulas to find the area and perimeter of a square with sides that are 8 feet long.

$A = s \times s$; $A = 8 \times 8 = 64$; $A = 64$ sq ft

$P = 4 \times s$; $P = 4 \times 8 = 32$; $P = 32$ ft

Student Activity Book page 296

Activity continued ▶

Draw a square on the board and label each side *s*. Remind students that all sides of a square are the same length.

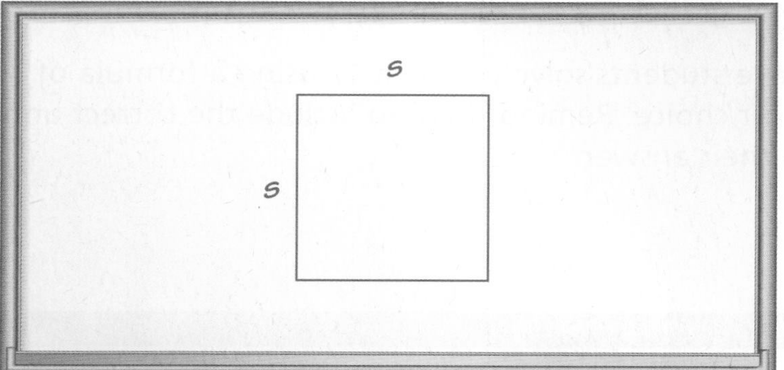

Ask students to complete exercise 16 on Student Book page 296 on their own. Invite students to share their answers; write the formula for the area of a square on the board.

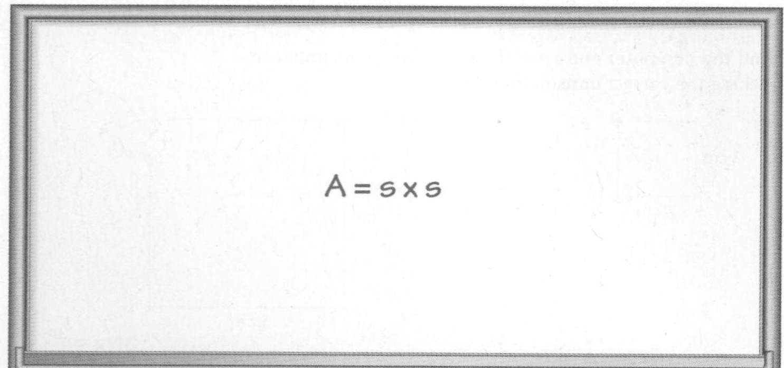

Next, record the different formulas for the perimeter of a square on the board.

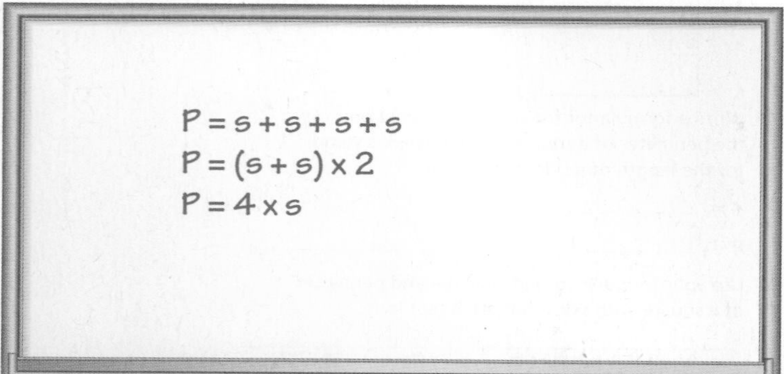

Ask students to use one of the formulas for the perimeter and area of a square to complete exercise 17 on Student Book page 296. When they are finished, discuss their answers and write the solution on the board.

$P = 4 \times s$	$A = s \times s$
$P = 4 \times 8 = 32$	$A = 8 \times 8 = 64$
$P = 32$ feet	$A = 64$ square feet

- In what unit are the sides of the square measured? feet
- What unit should we use for the perimeter? feet
- What unit should we use for the area? square feet

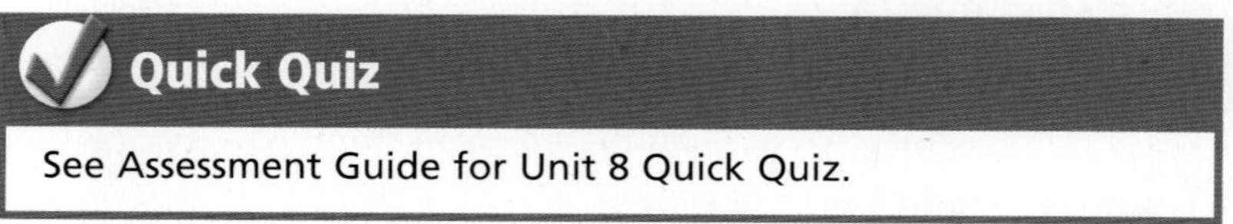

Quick Quiz

See Assessment Guide for Unit 8 Quick Quiz.

Ongoing Assessment

Ask students to solve these problems using formulas:

- A rectangular planter box has sides that are 8 feet long and 4 feet wide. What is the area of the planter box?
- Whitney has a rectangular painting with sides that are 3 feet long and 2 feet wide. What is the perimeter of Whitney's painting?
- One side of a square cake is 9 inches long. What is the area of the cake? What is the perimeter?

2 Going Further

Differentiated Instruction

Intervention

Activity Card 8-3

Geoboard Rectangles — Activity Card 8-3 ●

Work: In pairs

Use:

- Geoboard
- Rubber band

Decide:

Who will be Student 1 and who will be Student 2 for the first round.

1. **Student 1:** Create a rectangle on the geoboard.
2. **Student 2:** Use formulas to calculate the area and perimeter. Remember! Area is measured in square units.
3. Check your answers by counting. Then change roles and create another rectangle.

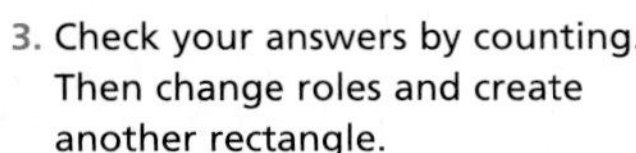

4. **Analyze** What do you count to check perimeter? What do you count to check area? Explain.
Lengths of sides; squares inside the shape

Unit 8, Lesson 3

Activity Note Review the formulas for area and perimeter before assigning this activity. Point out the different units used for each measurement.

Math Writing Prompt

Explain a Method Thomas wants to know the area of a room. He starts covering the room with squares of paper with sides that are 1 foot long. Explain an easier way to find the area.

Software Support

Warm Up 45.25

On Level

Activity Card 8-3

Estimate Classroom Areas — Activity Card 8-3 ▲

Work: In pairs

Use:

- Inch rulers
- Index cards

1. Find a flat surface shaped like a rectangle. Work together to estimate the perimeter and area.
2. Measure to check your estimates. Round to the nearest whole inch. Then use formulas to calculate perimeter and area.

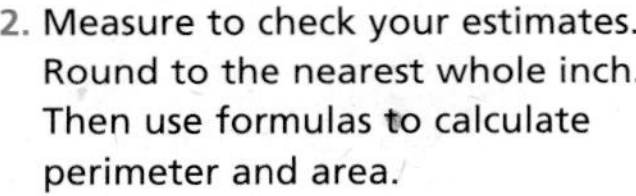

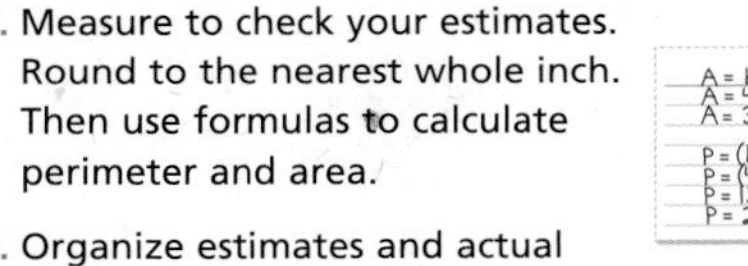

3. Organize estimates and actual measurements in a table to compare results.
4. **Analyze** How did you estimate each measure? Which was greater, the estimates or the actual measures?

Unit 8, Lesson 3

Activity Note Have students discuss strategies that they used to estimate area and perimeter. Some students may use nonstandard units such as the length of a calculator to estimate lengths.

Math Writing Prompt

You Decide Emilio says he can use multiplication to find the area of a rectangle. Do you agree or disagree? Draw a picture to explain your thinking.

Software Support

Shapes Ahoy: Ship Shapes, Level X

Challenge

Activity Card 8-3

Dimensions of Squares — Activity Card 8-3 ■

Work: In pairs

Use:

- MathBoard materials

1. **Work Together** Read the word problem below.

   Ana has a square photograph that has an area of 25 square inches. She wants to find the perimeter of the photo to make a picture frame. Use the area and perimeter formulas for a square to help you find the perimeter of the frame.

2. Write the formulas for area and perimeter of a square. **Think** What do you know about the sides of a square with an area of 25 square inches? Each side measures 5 in.
3. Use the formula for perimeter of a square to solve the problem. P = (L + W) × 2; P = (5 + 5) × 2; P = 20)
4. Have your partner check your work.

Unit 8, Lesson 3

Activity Note If time allows, have students do the same activity for square photographs with areas of 36 sq in. and 64 sq in.

Math Writing Prompt

Predict and Verify Is the perimeter of a rectangle with whole-centimeter lengths of sides even or odd? Test your prediction. Explain your findings.

Software Support

Course II: Module 3: Unit 1: Area

3 Homework and Spiral Review

Goal: Additional Practice

✓ Include students' completed Homework page as part of their portfolios.

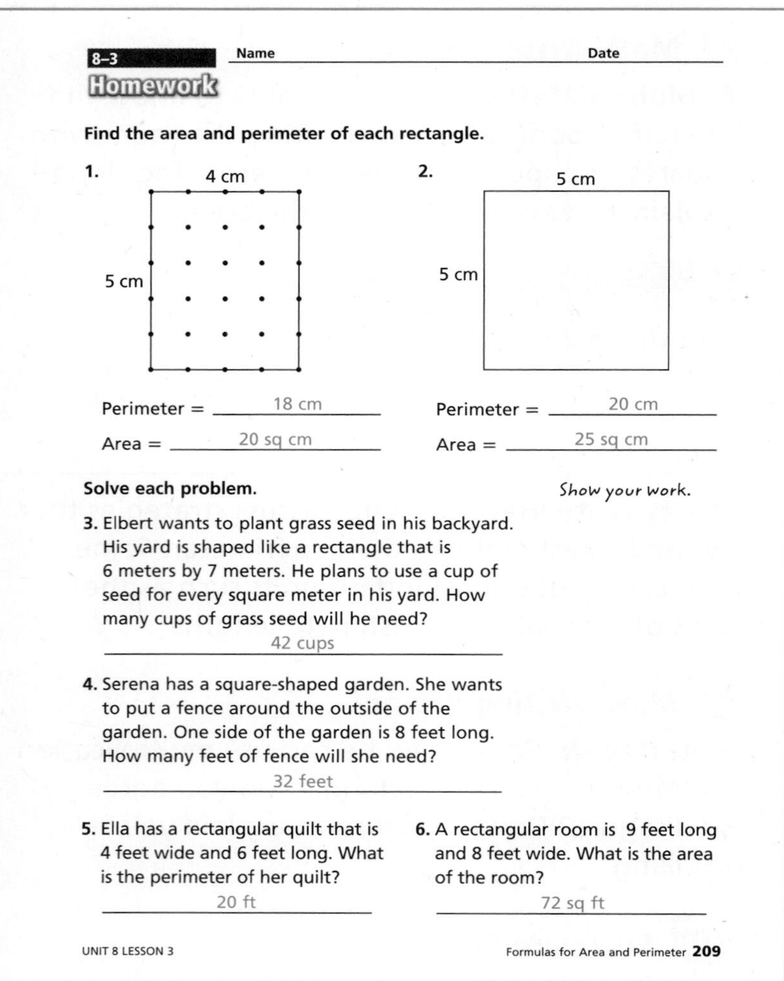

8–3 Homework   Name ______ Date ______

Find the area and perimeter of each rectangle.

1. 4 cm by 5 cm

Perimeter = 18 cm

Area = 20 sq cm

2. 5 cm by 5 cm

Perimeter = 20 cm

Area = 25 sq cm

Solve each problem. *Show your work.*

3. Elbert wants to plant grass seed in his backyard. His yard is shaped like a rectangle that is 6 meters by 7 meters. He plans to use a cup of seed for every square meter in his yard. How many cups of grass seed will he need?
42 cups

4. Serena has a square-shaped garden. She wants to put a fence around the outside of the garden. One side of the garden is 8 feet long. How many feet of fence will she need?
32 feet

5. Ella has a rectangular quilt that is 4 feet wide and 6 feet long. What is the perimeter of her quilt?
20 ft

6. A rectangular room is 9 feet long and 8 feet wide. What is the area of the room?
72 sq ft

UNIT 8 LESSON 3   Formulas for Area and Perimeter **209**

Homework and Remembering page 209

8–3 Remembering **Goal:** Spiral Review

This Remembering page would be appropriate anytime after today's lesson.

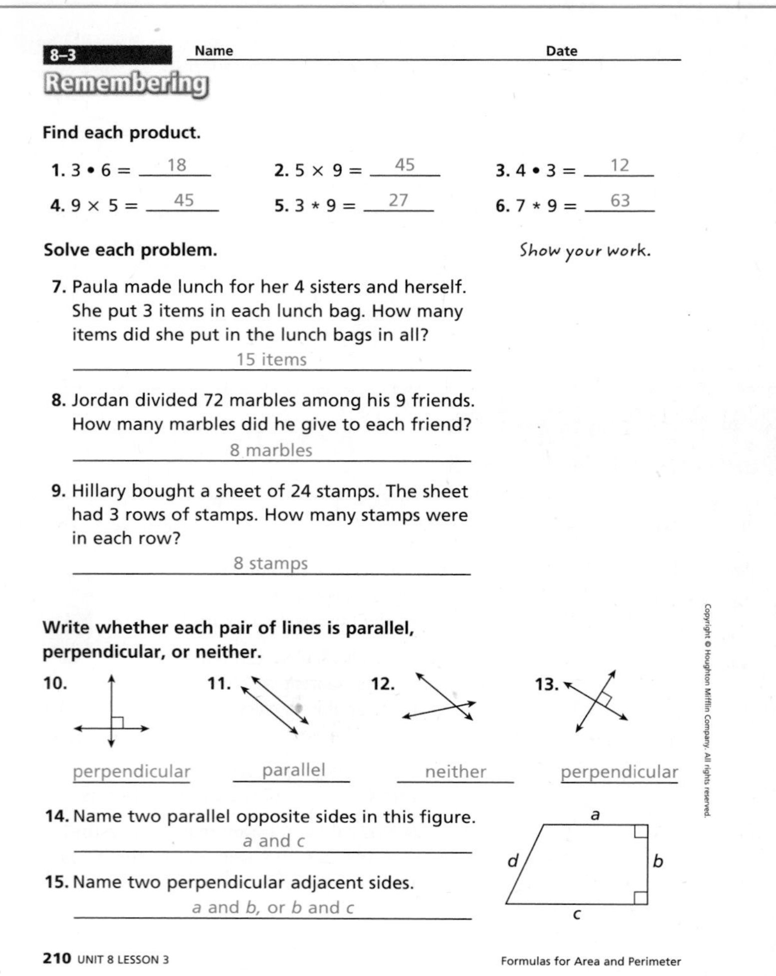

8–3 Remembering   Name ______ Date ______

Find each product.

1. 3 • 6 = 18
2. 5 × 9 = 45
3. 4 • 3 = 12
4. 9 × 5 = 45
5. 3 * 9 = 27
6. 7 * 9 = 63

Solve each problem. *Show your work.*

7. Paula made lunch for her 4 sisters and herself. She put 3 items in each lunch bag. How many items did she put in the lunch bags in all?
15 items

8. Jordan divided 72 marbles among his 9 friends. How many marbles did he give to each friend?
8 marbles

9. Hillary bought a sheet of 24 stamps. The sheet had 3 rows of stamps. How many stamps were in each row?
8 stamps

Write whether each pair of lines is parallel, perpendicular, or neither.

10. perpendicular
11. parallel
12. neither
13. perpendicular

14. Name two parallel opposite sides in this figure.
a and *c*

15. Name two perpendicular adjacent sides.
a and *b*, or *b* and *c*

210 UNIT 8 LESSON 3   Formulas for Area and Perimeter

Homework and Remembering page 210

Home or School Activity

Art Connection

Picture Frames Have students make a picture frame by gluing together craft sticks. Have them decorate their frames with small objects like beads, shells, buttons, rocks, sequins, or dried flowers.

Ask students to measure the length and width of their frame and use formulas to calculate its perimeter and area (the area of the picture that the frame can hold).

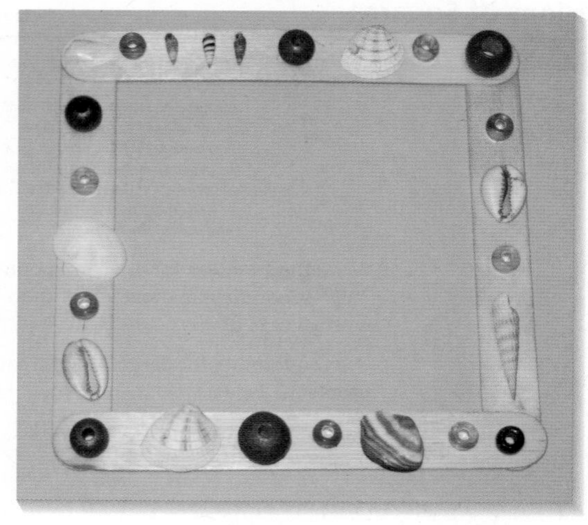

Unit Review and Test

Lesson Objective

- **Assess student progress on unit objectives.**

The Day at a Glance

Today's Goals	Materials
1 Assessing the Unit ▶ Assess student progress on unit objectives. ▶ Use activities from unit lessons to reteach content.	Unit 8 Test, Student Activity Book pp. 297–300 or Hardcover Book pp. 297–300 and Activity Workbook pp. 137–140 Unit 8 Test, Form A or B, Assessment Guide (optional) Unit 8 Performance Assessment, Assessment Guide (optional)
2 Extending the Assessment ▶ Use remediation for common errors.	
There is no homework assignment on a test day.	

Keeping Skills Sharp

Daily Routines 5 MINUTES	
If you are doing a unit review day, go over the homework. If this is a test day, omit the homework review.	**Review and Test Day** You may want to choose a quiet game or other activity (reading a book or working on homework for another subject) for students who finish early.

1 Assessing the Unit

Assess Unit Objectives

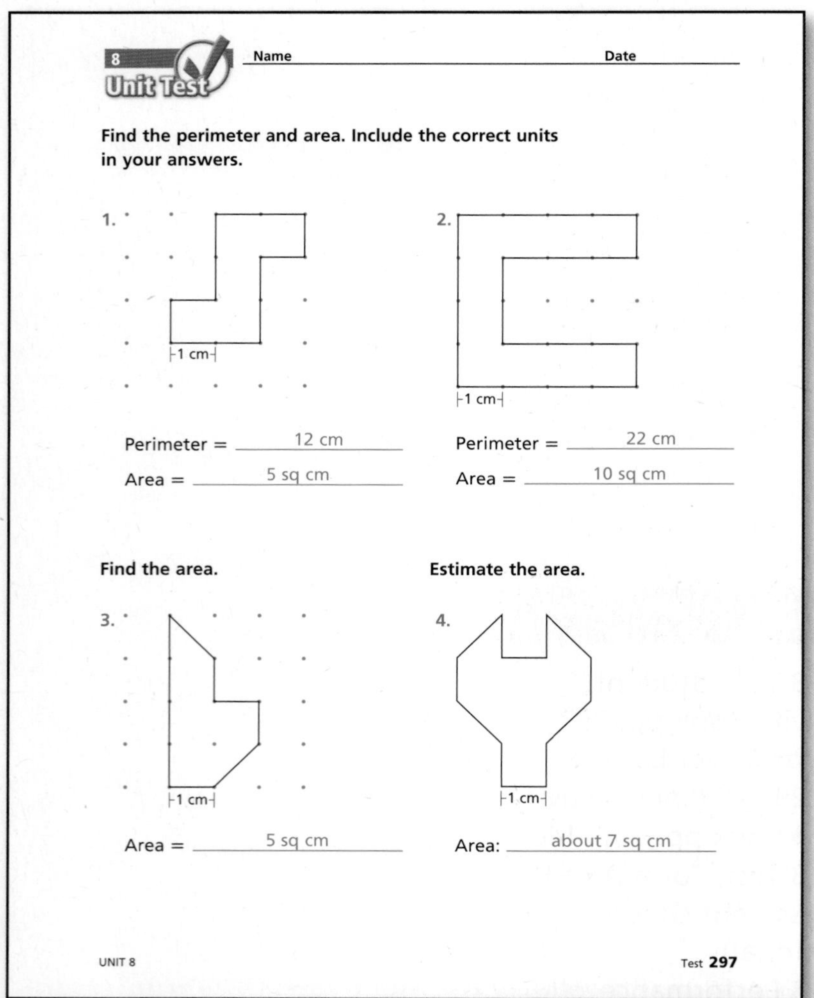

8 Unit Test Name ____ Date ____

Find the perimeter and area. Include the correct units in your answers.

1\.

Perimeter = 12 cm

Area = 5 sq cm

2\.

Perimeter = 22 cm

Area = 10 sq cm

Find the area.

3\.

Area = 5 sq cm

Estimate the area.

4\.

Area: about 7 sq cm

UNIT 8 Test 297

Student Activity Book page 297

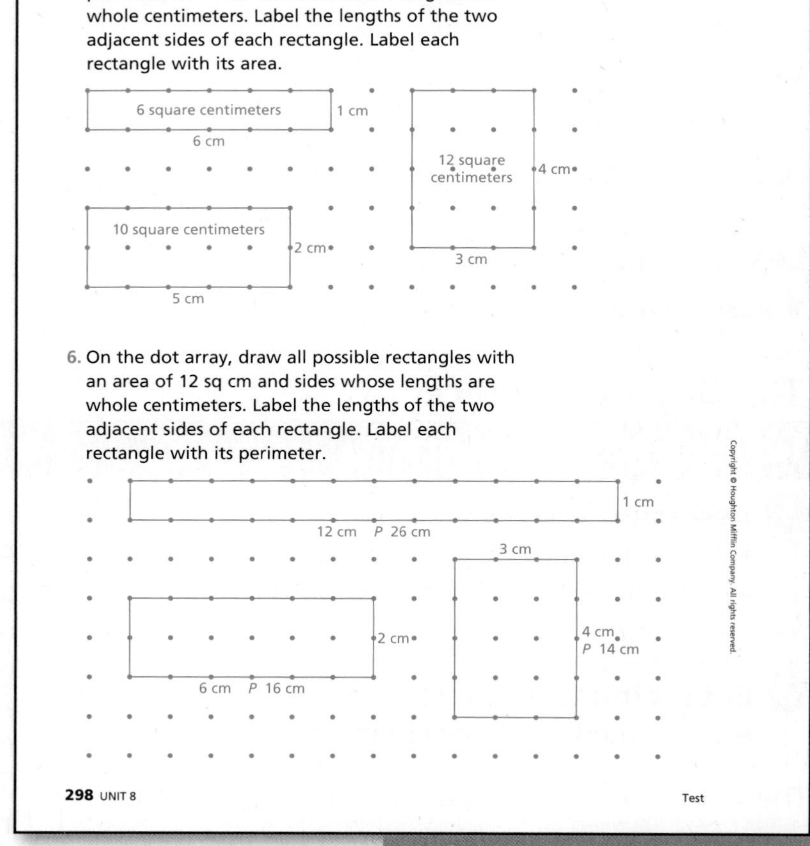

8 Unit Test Name ____ Date ____

5\. On the dot array, draw all possible rectangles with a perimeter of 14 cm and sides whose lengths are whole centimeters. Label the lengths of the two adjacent sides of each rectangle. Label each rectangle with its area.

6\. On the dot array, draw all possible rectangles with an area of 12 sq cm and sides whose lengths are whole centimeters. Label the lengths of the two adjacent sides of each rectangle. Label each rectangle with its perimeter.

298 UNIT 8 Test

Student Activity Book page 298

45 MINUTES (more if schedule permits)

Goal: Assess student progress on unit objectives.

Materials: Student Activity Book or Hardcover Book pp. 297–300 and Activity Workbook pp. 137–140; Assessment Guide (optional)

▶ Review and Assessment

If your students are ready for assessment on the unit objectives, use either the test on the Student Activity Book pages or one of the forms of the Unit 8 Test in the Assessment Guide to assess student progress. To assign a numerical score for all of these test forms, use 10 points for each questions.

The chart to the right lists the test items, the unit objectives they cover, and the lesson activities in which the objective is covered in this unit.

Unit Test Items	Unit Objectives Tested	Activities to Use for Reteaching
1–4	**8.1** Find perimeters and areas of figures drawn on a dot array by counting units; estimate area and perimeter.	Lesson 1, Activities 1 and 2
9, 10	**8.2** Determine whether a real-life problem requires finding perimeter or area, and then solve the problem.	Lesson 1, Activity 3

Name Date

7. Use the letter *A* to represent the area of the rectangle, *b* to represent the length of the base, and *h* to represent the height.

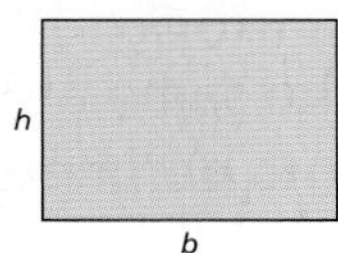

Write a formula for the area of the rectangle.

$A = b \times h$

Use your formula to find the area of a rectangle with a height of 3 feet and a base of 5 feet.

A = 5 × 3 = 15; 15 sq ft

8. Use the letter *P* to represent the perimeter of the rectangle, *b* to represent the length of the base, and *h* to represent the height.

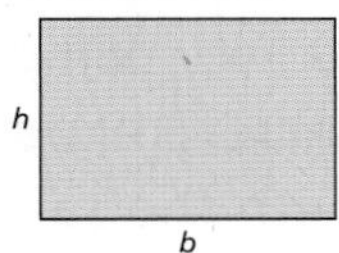

Write a formula for the perimeter of the rectangle.

$P = 2\ (b + h)$ or (2 × b) + (2 × h)

Use your formula to find the perimeter of a rectangle with a width of 3 feet and a length of 5 feet.

P = 2 × (5 + 3) = 16; 16 ft

UNIT 8 Test 299

Student Activity Book page 299

8 Unit Test

Name Date

9. Liana wants to put a rope around a rectangular space in her yard where she plans to plant a vegetable garden. The garden will be 8 meters long and 6 meters wide. How much rope does Liana need?

28 m

10. **Extended Response** David is sewing together a quilt from quilt squares his grandmother made. He wants the quilt to be a rectangle, with sides of length 5 feet and 7 feet. The quilt squares have sides of length 1 foot.

1 foot
1 foot
Quilt square

To find the number of quilt squares he needs, do you need to find the perimeter of the quilt or the area? Explain your reasoning.

area; You want to find the number of square units inside the quilt, so you need to find the area.

How many quilt squares does David need? Explain how you found your answer.

35 quilt squares; Multiply 5 feet by 7 feet to give an area of 35 square feet. Since each quilt square is 1 ft by 1 ft, you need 35 quilt squares.

Draw a picture of the quilt to show your answer is correct. Drawings may vary.

7 ft
5 ft

300 UNIT 8 Test

Student Activity Book page 300

Unit Test Items	Unit Objectives Tested	Activities to Use for Reteaching
5, 6	**8.3** Recognize that rectangles with the same perimeter may have different areas and rectangles with the same area may have different perimeters.	Lesson 2, Activities 1 and 2
7, 8	**8.4** Use formulas for the area and perimeter of squares and rectangles.	Lesson 3, Activities 1–3

▸ Assessment Resources

Form A Free Response Test (Assessment Guide)

Form B Multiple-Choice Test (Assessment Guide)

Performance Assessment (Assessment Guide)

▸ Portfolio Assessment

Teacher-selected Items for Student Portfolios:

- Homework, Lesson 3
- Class Activity work, Lessons 1, 2

Student-selected Items for Student Portfolios:

- Favorite Home or School Activity
- Best Writing Prompt

2 Extending the Assessment

Common Errors

Activities for Remediation

Unit Objective 8.1

Find perimeters and areas of figures drawn on a dot array by counting units; estimate area and perimeter.

Common Error: Adds the Incorrect Number of Sides When Finding Perimeter

Some students may not add the correct number of sides of a figure when finding the perimeter.

Remediation Tell students that the perimeter of a figure is the distance around the outside of the figure, so they need to count the length of each side of the figure once. Suggest that they work out a system to be sure that they add the lengths of all sides once. For instance, they may want to check off or highlight each side after they have counted it. Or, if they are writing number sentences, they can compare the number of addends to the number of sides of the figure.

Common Error: Counts Partial Units as Whole Units

Some students may count partial units as whole units when finding area of figures on dot arrays.

Remediation Demonstrate how estimating area on a dot array requires looking at partial units and visualizing how to combine them to estimate whole units. Suggest they color the partial units that combine to make about one whole unit of the same color.

Unit Objective 8.2

Determine whether a real-life problem requires finding perimeter or area, and then solve the problem.

Common Error: Doesn't Correctly Identify If a Problem Involves Area or Perimeter

Some students may have difficulty identifying if a problem requires them to find the area or the perimeter of a figure.

Remediation Suggest that students draw a diagram. Once they have drawn the diagram, ask them to identify what information they are asked to find. If the question is about the distance around a figure, they need to find its perimeter. If the question is about the amount of surface inside the figure, they need to find its area.

Unit Objective 8.3

Recognize that rectangles with the same perimeter may have different areas and rectangles with the same area may have different perimeters.

Common Error: Doesn't Recognize that Rectangles with the Same Perimeter May Have Different Areas

Students may think that if two rectangles have the same perimeter they must have the same area.

Remediation Provide students with string and geoboards. Have them use one length of string to create a rectangle on the geoboard. Have them experiment to make other rectangles with the same length of string. This activity will provide students with concrete experience that different rectangles can have the same perimeter.

Common Error: Doesn't Recognize that Rectangles with the Same Area May Have Different Perimeters

Students may think that if two rectangles have the same area they must have the same perimeter.

Remediation Provide students with 12 square tiles and have them model different rectangles with the 12 square tiles. Have them trace each rectangle on inch-grid paper and find the perimeter of each one. Ask them to record the perimeter and area on each rectangle. This activity will provide students with concrete experience that rectangles with the same area can have different perimeters.

Unit Objective 8.4

Use formulas for the area and perimeter of squares and rectangles.

Common Error: Uses the Perimeter Formula to Find Area

Some students may confuse the area and perimeter formulas.

Remediation Remind students of the area model for multiplication. This may help them remember that area involves multiplication.

Common Error: Uses the Area Formula to Find Perimeter

Some students may confuse the area and perimeter formulas.

Remediation Remind students that the perimeter is the distance around the outside of the figure. To find perimeter, they add all the side lengths together, so the perimeter formula for rectangles involves addition.

Multiplication and Division with 6, 7, and 8 and Problem Solving

IN UNIT 9, students learn multiplications and divisions for the factors 6, 7, and 8, while continuing to practice with the factors covered in Unit 4. This unit also focuses on word problems. Students are introduced to multiplication comparison word problems, write their own word problems of various types, and solve word problems involving several steps.

Skills Trace		
Grade 2	**Grade 3**	**Grade 4**
• Recall basic multiplications and divisions with 2 through 5. • Explore equal groups and array models. • Write related addition and multiplication equations. • Solve a variety of word problems involving multiplication.	• Recall basic multiplications and divisions with 0 through 10. • Write multiplication equations to represent repeated groups, arrays, and area models. • Write related addition and multiplication and multiplication and division equations. • Solve a variety of word problems involving multiplication and division, including comparison and multi-step word problems.	• Review basic multiplications and divisions with 0 through 12, and practice multi-digit multiplication. • Explore factors, multiples, and prime numbers. • Write situation and solution equations for multiplication and division. • Solve a variety of word problems involving multiplication and division, including combination problems.

Unit 9 Contents

Unit 9 Assessment

✓ Unit Objectives Tested	Unit Test Items	Lessons
9.1 Recall basic multiplications and divisions with 0 through 10.	1–12	1, 3, 5, 8–9
9.2 Solve a variety of word problems involving multiplication and division including comparison and multi-step word problems.	13–20	4, 6–7, 10–13

Assessment and Review Resources

Formal Assessment

Student Activity Book

- Unit Review and Test (pp. 375–376)

Assessment Guide

- Quick Quizzes (pp. A84, A85, A86)
- Test A–Open Response (pp. A87–A88)
- Test B–Multiple Choice (pp. A89–A91)
- Performance Assessment (pp. A92–A94)

Test Generator CD-ROM

- Open Response Test
- Multiple Choice Test
- Test Bank Items

Informal Assessment

Teacher Edition

- Ongoing Assessment (in every lesson)
- Quick Practice (in every lesson)
- Portfolio Suggestions (p. 753)

Math Talk

- ▸ The Learning Classroom (p. 720)
- ▸ Math Talk in Action (pp. 640, 658, 675, 680, 687, 705, 728)
- ▸ Solve and Discuss (pp. 651, 667, 670, 680, 688, 696, 698, 719, 735, 741)
- ▸ Student Pairs (pp. 648, 656, 666, 674, 684, 694, 702, 710, 711, 716, 726, 734, 740, 742) Helping Partners (pp. 729, 736)
- ▸ Small Groups (p. 644, 652)
- ▸ Scenarios (p. 720)
- ▸ In Activities (pp. 652, 661, 678, 698, 712, 717, 719, 722, 746, 747)

Review Opportunities

Homework and Remembering

- Review of recently taught topics
- Spiral Review

Teacher Edition

- Unit Review and Test (pp. 751–754)

Test Generator CD-ROM

- Custom Review Sheets

Planning Unit 9

NCTM Curriculum Focal Points and Connections Key: **1.** Number and Operations and Algebra **2.** Number and Operations **3.** Geometry **4.** Algebra **5.** Measurement **6.** Data Analysis **7.** Number and Operations

Lesson NCTM Focal Points NCTM Standards	Resources	Materials for Lesson Activities	Materials for Going Further
9-1 **Multiply and Divide with 6** NCTM Focal Points: 1.3, 1.10, 4.1, 4.2, 4.3, 4.4 NCTM Standards: 1, 2, 10	TE pp. 637–646 SAB pp. 301–304 H&R pp. 211–214 AC 9-1	✓ Class Multiplication Table Poster ✓ Pointer ✓ MathBoard materials	Calculators 6s Match (TRB M100) Math Journals
9-2 **Solve Area Word Problems** NCTM Focal Point: 1.9 NCTM Standards: 1, 2, 4, 6, 10	TE pp. 647–654 SAB pp. 305–308 H&R pp. 215–218 AC 9-2	Check Up materials ✓ Strategy Cards Transparency of Student Book p. 307 (optional) Overhead projector (optional)	✓ Connecting Cubes ✓ Number Cubes Centimeter Grid Paper (TRB M31) Math Journals
9-3 **Multiply and Divide with 8** NCTM Focal Points: 1.1, 1.2, 1.3, 1.8, 1.10, 4.1, 4.2, 4.3, 4.4 NCTM Standards: 1, 2, 10	TE pp. 655–664 SAB pp. 309–312 H&R pp. 219–222 AC 9-3 MCC 33	Check Up materials ✓ Strategy Cards ✓ Class Multiplication Table Poster ✓ Pointer ✓ MathBoard materials	✓ Two-color counters ✓ Index cards ✓ MathBoard materials Math Journals
9-4 **Write Word Problems and Equations** NCTM Focal Points: 1.1, 1.2, 1.3 NCTM Standard: 1, 4, 6	TE pp. 665–672 SAB pp. 313–316 H&R pp. 223–224 AC 9-4	Blank Sprint Answer Sheet (TRB M57) Signature Sheet Check up materials ✓ Strategy Cards	Fill in the Blanks (TRB M103) Math Journals
9-5 **Multiply and Divide with 7** NCTM Focal Points: 1.1, 1.2, 1.8, 4.1, 4.2, 4.3, 4.4 NCTM Standard: 1, 2, 6, 10	TE pp. 673–682 SAB pp. 317–318 H&R pp. 225–228 AC 9-5 AG Quick Quiz 1	Check Up materials ✓ Strategy Cards ✓ Class Multiplication Table Poster ✓ Pointer ✓ MathBoard materials	Index cards Game Cards (TRB M25) Math Journals
9-6 **Comparison Word Problems** NCTM Focal Points: 1.9, 4.5 NCTM Standards: 1, 2, 6, 8, 9, 10	TE pp. 683–692 SAB pp. 319–326 H&R pp. 229–230 AC 9-6 MCC 34	Check Up materials ✓ Strategy Cards Transparency of Student Book p. 323 (optional) Overhead projector (optional)	✓ MathBoard materials ✓ Two-color counters Index cards Game Cards (TRB M25) Comparison Logic Problems (TRB M106) Math Journals
9-7 **More Comparison Word Problems** NCTM Focal Points: 1.9, 4.5, 6.2 NCTM Standards: 1, 2, 5, 6, 10	TE pp. 693–700 SAB pp. 327–330 H&R pp. 231–232 AC 9-7	Check Up materials ✓ Strategy Cards ✓ MathBoard materials	✓ Connecting Cubes Centimeter Grid Paper (TRB M31) Scissors Crayons Math Journals
9-8 **Square Numbers** NCTM Focal Points: 1.3, 4.3 NCTM Standards: 1, 2, 4, 10	TE pp. 701–708 SAB pp. 331–334 H&R pp. 233–238 AC 9-8	Blank Sprint Answer Sheet (TRB M57) Signature Sheet Check Up materials ✓ Strategy Cards *Sea Squares* by Joy N. Hulme	Centimeter Grid Paper (TRB M31) Scissors ✓ Number Cubes Multiplication Riddles (TRB M108) Math Journals

Resources/Materials Key: TE: Teacher Edition SAB: Student Activity Book H&R: Homework and Remembering AC: Activity Cards MCC: Math Center Challenge AG: Assessment Guide ✓: Grade 3 kits TRB: Teacher's Resource Book

NCTM Standards and Expectations Key: **1.** Number and Operations **2.** Algebra **3.** Geometry **4.** Measurement **5.** Data Analysis and Probability **6.** Problem Solving **7.** Reasoning and Proof **8.** Communication **9.** Connections **10.** Representation

Lesson NCTM Focal Points NCTM Standards	Resources	Materials for Lesson Activities	Materials for Going Further
9-9 **Practice with 6s, 7s, and 8s** NCTM Focal Points: 1.8, 4.3 NCTM Standards: 1, 2	TE pp. 709–714 SAB pp. 335–344 H&R pp. 239–240 AC 9-9 MCC 35 AG Quick Quiz 2	Folders Check Up materials ✓ Strategy Cards Transparency of Student Book page 343 (optional) Overhead projector (optional)	Game Cards (TRB M25) Codebuster (TRB M114) Symbol Cards (TRB M115) Math Journals
9-10 **Solve Mixed Word Problems** NCTM Focal Point: 1.9 NCTM Standards: 1, 6, 7, 8, 9	TE pp. 715–724 SAB pp. 345–350 H&R pp. 241–242 AC 9-10	Signature Sheet Check Up materials ✓ Strategy Cards	Drawing paper Symbol Cards (TRB M115) Math Journals
9-11 **Solve Multi-Step Word Problems** NCTM Focal Points: 1.2, 1.3, 1.9 NCTM Standards: 1, 2, 6, 10	TE pp. 725–732 SAB pp. 351–354 H&R pp. 243–244 AC 9-11	Check Up materials ✓ Strategy Cards	Highlighters Game Cards (TRB M25) Symbol Cards (TRB M115) Index cards Secret Code Cards ✓ MathBoard materials Math Journals
9-12 **Solve Complex Multi-Step Word Problems** NCTM Focal Point: 1.9 NCTM Standards: 1, 2, 6	TE pp. 733–738 SAB pp. 355–360 H&R pp. 245–246 AC 9-12 MCC 36	Folders Check Up materials ✓ Strategy Cards	✓ MathBoard materials Math Journals
9-13 **Play Multiplication and Division Games** NCTM Focal Point: 1.9 NCTM Standards: 1, 2, 6, 10	TE pp. 739–744 SAB pp. 361–368 H&R pp. 247–248 AC 9-13 AG Quick Quiz 3	Check Up materials ✓ Strategy Cards Game Cards (TRB M25) Game Boards and Game Rules from U7 L13, 15; U9, L9	Game Cards (TRB M25) Calculator (optional) Math Journals
9-14 **Use Mathematical Processes** NCTM Focal Points: 1.2, 5.2, 6.2 NCTM Standards: 6, 7, 8, 9, 10	TE pp. 745–750 SAB pp. 369–370; H&R pp. 249–250 AC 9-14	None	Game Cards (TRB M25) Grid paper Math Journals
✓ Unit Review and Test	TE pp. 751–754 SAB pp. 371–396 AG Unit 9 Tests		

Hardcover Student Book

- Together, the Hardcover Student Book and its companion Activity Workbook contain all of the pages in the consumable Student Activity Book.

Manipulatives and Materials

- Essential materials for teaching *Math Expressions* are available in the Grade 3 kits. These materials are indicated by a ✓ in these lists. At the front of this Teacher Edition is more information about kit contents, alternatives for the materials, and use of the materials.

Independent Learning Activities

Ready-Made Math Challenge Centers

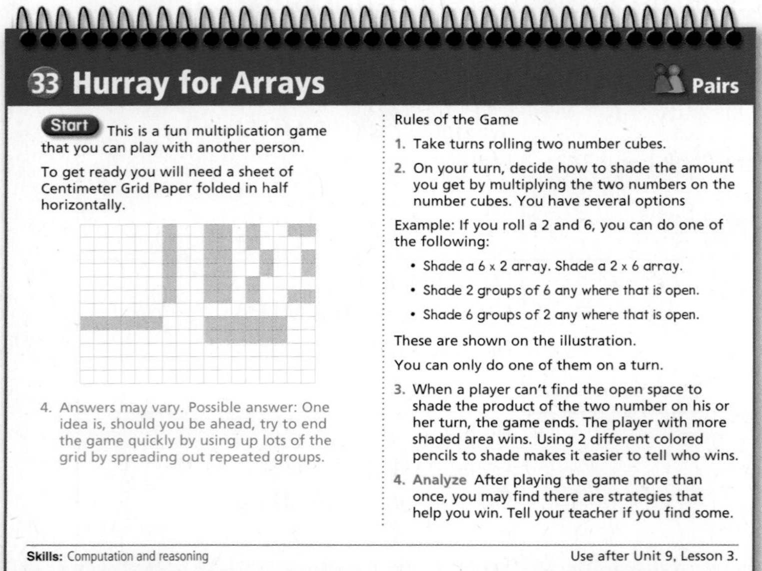

33 Hurray for Arrays — Pairs

Start This is a fun multiplication game that you can play with another person.

To get ready you will need a sheet of Centimeter Grid Paper folded in half horizontally.

Rules of the Game

1. Take turns rolling two number cubes.
2. On your turn, decide how to shade the amount you get by multiplying the two numbers on the number cubes. You have several options

Example: If you roll a 2 and 6, you can do one of the following:

- Shade a 6 x 2 array. Shade a 2 x 6 array.
- Shade 2 groups of 6 any where that is open.
- Shade 6 groups of 2 any where that is open.

These are shown on the illustration.

You can only do one of them on a turn.

3. When a player can't find the open space to shade the product of the two number on his or her turn, the game ends. The player with more shaded area wins. Using 2 different colored pencils to shade makes it easier to tell who wins.
4. **Analyze** After playing the game more than once, you may find there are strategies that help you win. Tell your teacher if you find some.

4. Answers may vary. Possible answer: One idea is, should you be ahead, try to end the game quickly by using up lots of the grid by spreading out repeated groups.

Skills: Computation and reasoning — Use after Unit 9, Lesson 3.

Grouping Pairs

Materials Two different-colored pencils, two number cubes, Centimeter Grid Paper (TRB M31)

Objective Students represent multiplication facts with drawings.

Connections Representation and Reasoning

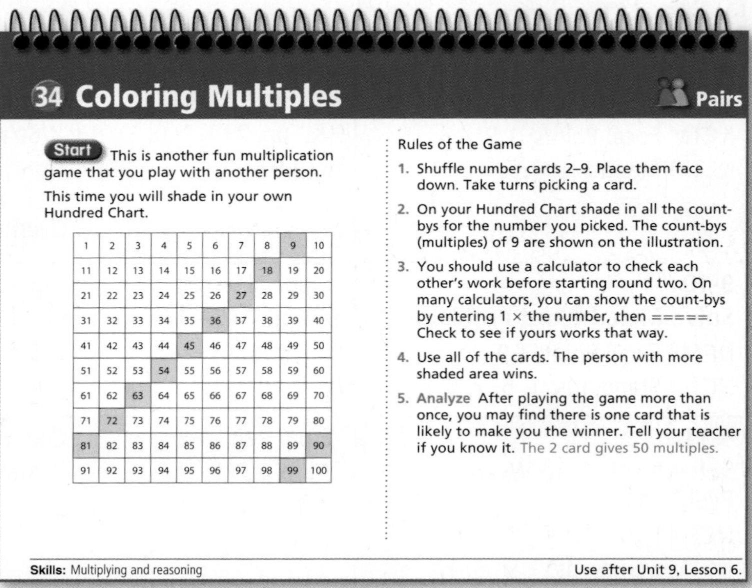

34 Coloring Multiples — Pairs

Start This is another fun multiplication game that you play with another person.

This time you will shade in your own Hundred Chart.

1	2	3	4	5	6	7	8	9	10
11	12	13	14	15	16	17	18	19	20
21	22	23	24	25	26	27	28	29	30
31	32	33	34	35	36	37	38	39	40
41	42	43	44	45	46	47	48	49	50
51	52	53	54	55	56	57	58	59	60
61	62	63	64	65	66	67	68	69	70
71	72	73	74	75	76	77	78	79	80
81	82	83	84	85	86	87	88	89	90
91	92	93	94	95	96	97	98	99	100

Rules of the Game

1. Shuffle number cards 2–9. Place them face down. Take turns picking a card.
2. On your Hundred Chart shade in all the count-bys for the number you picked. The count-bys (multiples) of 9 are shown on the illustration.
3. You should use a calculator to check each other's work before starting round two. On many calculators, you can show the count-bys by entering 1 × the number, then =====. Check to see if yours works that way.
4. Use all of the cards. The person with more shaded area wins.
5. **Analyze** After playing the game more than once, you may find there is one card that is likely to make you the winner. Tell your teacher if you know it. The 2 card gives 50 multiples.

Skills: Multiplying and reasoning — Use after Unit 9, Lesson 6.

Grouping Pairs

Materials Calculator, Hundred Chart (TRB M34), playing cards

Objective Students count by multiples of a number.

Connections Computation and Reasoning

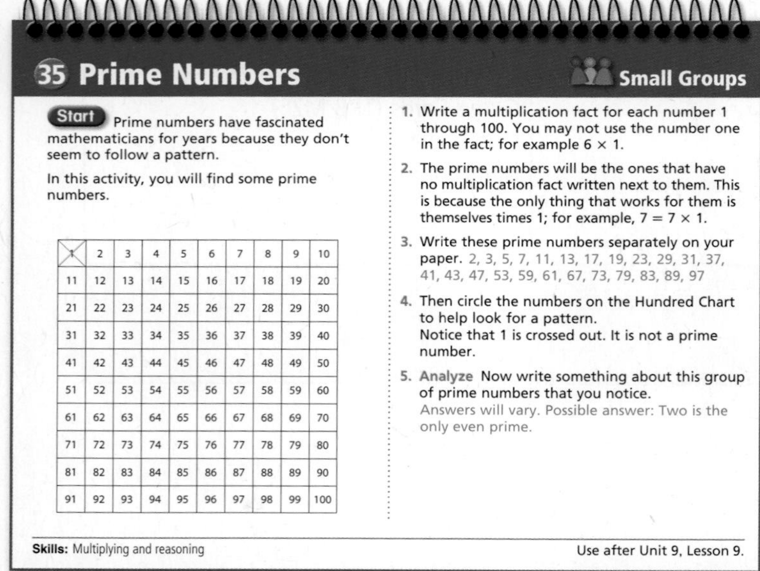

35 Prime Numbers — Small Groups

Start Prime numbers have fascinated mathematicians for years because they don't seem to follow a pattern.

In this activity, you will find some prime numbers.

1	2	3	4	5	6	7	8	9	10
11	12	13	14	15	16	17	18	19	20
21	22	23	24	25	26	27	28	29	30
31	32	33	34	35	36	37	38	39	40
41	42	43	44	45	46	47	48	49	50
51	52	53	54	55	56	57	58	59	60
61	62	63	64	65	66	67	68	69	70
71	72	73	74	75	76	77	78	79	80
81	82	83	84	85	86	87	88	89	90
91	92	93	94	95	96	97	98	99	100

1. Write a multiplication fact for each number 1 through 100. You may not use the number one in the fact; for example 6 × 1.
2. The prime numbers will be the ones that have no multiplication fact written next to them. This is because the only thing that works for them is themselves times 1; for example, 7 = 7 × 1.
3. Write these prime numbers separately on your paper. 2, 3, 5, 7, 11, 13, 17, 19, 23, 29, 31, 37, 41, 43, 47, 53, 59, 61, 67, 73, 79, 83, 89, 97
4. Then circle the numbers on the Hundred Chart to help look for a pattern. Notice that 1 is crossed out. It is not a prime number.
5. **Analyze** Now write something about this group of prime numbers that you notice. Answers will vary. Possible answer: Two is the only even prime.

Skills: Multiplying and reasoning — Use after Unit 9, Lesson 9.

Grouping Small Groups

Materials Calculator, Hundred Chart (TRB M34)

Objective Students use multiplication facts to identify prime numbers.

Connections Computation and Algebra

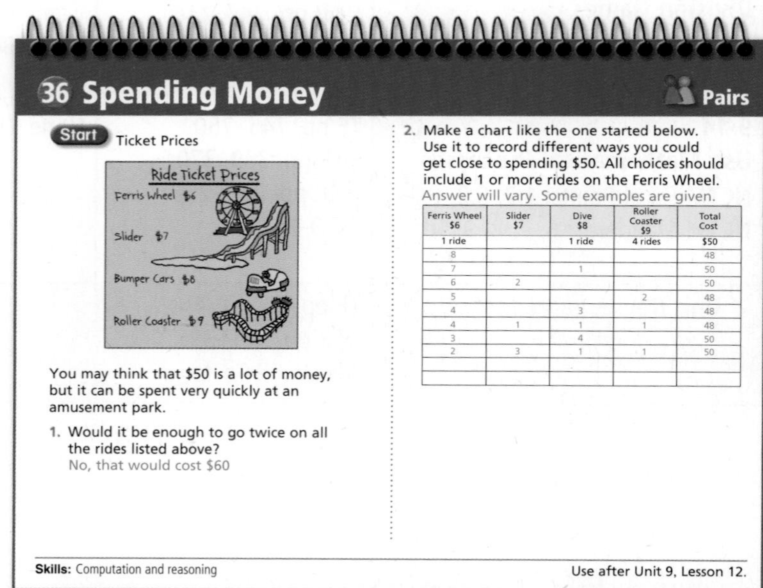

36 Spending Money — Pairs

Start Ticket Prices

You may think that $50 is a lot of money, but it can be spent very quickly at an amusement park.

1. Would it be enough to go twice on all the rides listed above? No, that would cost $60
2. Make a chart like the one started below. Use it to record different ways you could get close to spending $50. All choices should include 1 or more rides on the Ferris Wheel. Answer will vary. Some examples are given.

Ferris Wheel $6	Slider $7	Dive $8	Roller Coaster $9	Total Cost
1 ride		1 ride	4 rides	$50
8				48
7		1		50
6	2			50
5			2	48
4		3		48
4	1	1	1	48
3		4		50
2	3	1	1	50

Skills: Computation and reasoning — Use after Unit 9, Lesson 12.

Grouping Pairs

Materials Calculator

Objective Students use multiple operations to show different ways to spend money.

Connections Data and Real World

Ready-Made Math Resources

Technology — Tutorials, Practice, and Intervention

Use online, individualized intervention and support to bring students to proficiency.

Help students practice skills and apply concepts through exciting math adventures.

Extend and enrich students' understanding of skills and concepts through engaging, interactive lessons and activities.

Visit **Education Place**®
www.eduplace.com

Visit www.eduplace.com/mx2t/ and find family, teacher, and student materials, activities, games, and more.

Literature Links

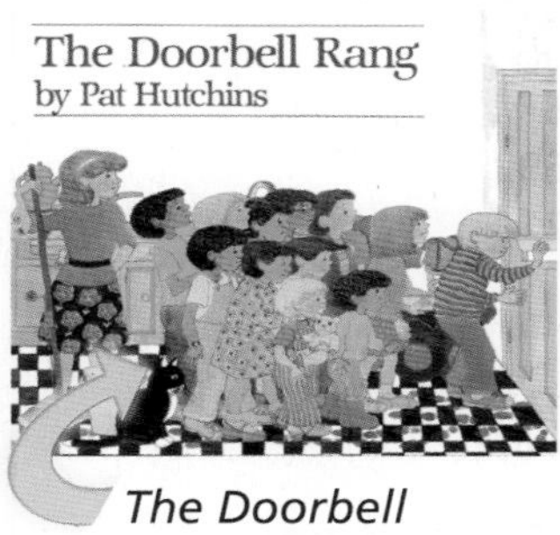

The Doorbell Rang

The Doorbell Rang

What do you do when lots of unexpected guests come to the house and you have just a certain number of cookies to share? Pat Hutchins presents an enjoyable solution in her book about both division and sharing.

Literature Connection

- *Sea Squares,* by Joy N. Hulme, illustrated by Carol Schwartz (Hyperion Books, 1993)

Unit 9 Teaching Resources

Differentiated Instruction

Individualizing Instruction		
	Level	Frequency
Activities	• Intervention • On Level • Challenge	All 3 in every lesson
	Level	Frequency
Math Writing Prompts	• Intervention • On Level • Challenge	All 3 in every lesson
Math Center Challenges	For advanced students	
	4 in every unit	

Reaching All Learners		
	Lessons	Pages
English Language Learners	1, 2, 3, 4, 5, 6, 7, 8, 9, 10, 11, 12, 13, 14	643, 651, 662, 668, 677, 686, 695, 704, 711, 719, 727, 736, 741, 747
	Lessons	Pages
Extra Help	1, 2, 3, 4, 5, 6, 7, 11, 13	642, 650, 659, 667, 678, 686, 697, 727, 741
	Lessons	Pages
Advanced Learners	5, 8	680, 703
	Lesson	Page
Alternate Approach	10	718

Strategies for English Language Learners

Present this problem to all students. Offer the different levels of support to meet students' levels of language proficiency.

Objective To provide support with multiplication vocabulary.

Problem Draw a 6 × 4 dot array on the board. Help students identify the factors and product.

Newcomer

- Say: **This is a 6 × 4 array.** Have students repeat. Write 6 × 4 = __.
- Point as you say: **We *multiply* 6 *by* 4. We get 24. 6 *times* 4 is 24.** Have students repeat.

Beginning

- Ask: **Is this an array?** yes **How many rows are there?** 6 **How many columns are there?** 4 **Can we *multiply* 6 *by* 4 to find the total number of dots?** yes
- Say: **6 and 4 are factors. 6 *times* 4 is 24. 24 is the *product*.** Have students repeat.

Intermediate

- Say: **I want to find the total number of dots. I *multiply* 6 by __.** 4 Write 6 × 4 = __ and say: **6 *times* 4 is __.** 24
- Ask: **Is 6 a *factor* or the *product*?** factor **Is 4 a factor or the product?** factor Say: **The product is __.** 24

Advanced

- Have students identify the array, the factors, and the product.
- Write 6 × 4 = 24. Point to the ×. Say: **This means *multiply by* or __.** times

Connections

Art Connection
Lesson 7, page 700

Language Arts Connection
Lesson 12, page 738

Math to Math Connection
Lesson 5, page 682

Real-World Connections
Lesson 2, page 654
Lesson 4, page 672
Lesson 6, page 692
Lesson 9, page 714

Science Connections
Lesson 10, page 724
Lesson 11, page 732

Social Studies Connection
Lesson 3, page 664

Literature Connection
Lesson 8, page 708

Multicultural Connection
Lesson 13, page 744

Putting Research into Practice for Unit 9

From our Curriculum Research Project: Multiplication and Division Consolidation

In this unit, students will use various strategies to learn multiplications and divisions for 6s, 7s, and 8s, while continuing to practice with the factors covered earlier in Unit 7. Research has found that many students find the 6s, 7s, and 8s multiplications to be the most difficult multiplications. Some strategies we will have students use include: starting with a known count-by and then adding on, using a known multiplication and doubling, and combining two known multiplications.

Also in this unit, students are introduced to comparison problems involving multiplication and division. Such comparisons involve one quantity that is a number of times as many as or as much as another. To solve these types of problems, students learn that they can use multiplication and division and they begin to use unit fraction language ("one fifth as many as"). Student activity pages may summarize student strategies to stimulate discussion and reflection.

–Karen Fuson, Author
Math Expressions

You can use 6s multiplications that you know to find 6s multiplications that you don't know. Here are the strategies for 6 × 6.

- **Strategy 1:** Start with 5 × 6, and count by 6 from there.
  5 × 6 = 30, plus 6 more is 36. So, 6 × 6 = 36.
- **Strategy 2:** Double a 3s multiplication.
  6 × 6 is twice 6 × 3, which is 18. So, 6 × 6 = 18 + 18 = 36.
- **Strategy 3:** Combine two multiplications you know.

4 × 6 = 24	4 sixes are 24.
2 × 6 = 12	2 sixes are 12.
6 × 6 = 36	6 sixes are 36.

Here are two ways to show Strategy 3 with drawings.

From Current Research: Multiplication

The remaining 15 multiplication combinations (and their commutative counterparts) may be computed by skip counting or by building on known combinations. For example, 3 × 6 must be 6 more than 2 × 6, which is 12. So 3 × 6 is 18. Similarly, 4 × 7 must be twice 2 × 7, which is 14. So 4 × 7 is 28 . . . To compute multiples of 6, one can build on the multiples of 5. So, for example, 6 × 8 must be 8 more than 5 × 8, which is 40. So 6 × 8 is 48. If students are comfortable with such strategies for multiplication by 3, 4, and 6, only three multiplication combinations remain: 7 × 7, 7 × 8, and 8 × 8. These can be derived from known combinations in many creative ways.

National Research Council. "Developing Proficiency with Whole Numbers." *Adding It Up: Helping Students Learn Mathematics.* Washington, D.C.: National Academy Press, 2001: page 192.

Other Useful References: Multiplication

Baroody, A.J. *Children's Mathematical Thinking: A Developmental Framework for Preschool, Primary, and Special Education Teachers.* New York: Teachers College Press, 1987.

Baroody, A.J. "The roles of estimation and the commutativity principle in the development of third-graders' mental multiplication." *Journal of Experimental Child Psychology,* 74 [Special issue on mathematical cognition] (1999): 157–193.

Steffe, L. "Children's multiplying schemes." *The Development of Multiplicative Reasoning in the Learning of Mathematics.* Eds. G. Harel & J. Confrey, Albany: State University of New York Press, 1994: 3–39.

Thornton, C.A. "Emphasizing thinking strategies in basic fact instruction." *Journal for Research in Mathematics Education,* 9 (1978): 214–227.

Getting Ready to Teach Unit 9

In this unit, students continue practicing with the factors covered in Unit 7, learn multiplications and divisions for 6, 7, and 8, and extend their skills with an introduction to double-digit multiplication.

Math Expressions Vocabulary

As you teach this unit, check understanding of these terms:

- array problem
- repeated-groups problem
- area problem

See Glossary on pages T1–T17.

Multiplication Strategies and for 6s, 7s, and 8s

Starting with a Known Count-by and Then Adding On

Lessons 1, 3, 5, 9, and 13

Given a multiplication example that students don't know, we encourage them to try to figure out the answer using the count-bys they already know.

$6 \times 6 = \square$

Start with a 5s count-by you know: $5 \times 6 = 30$

Then count by 6 from there: 30 plus 6 more is 36.
So $6 \times 6 = 36$.

Using a Known Multiplication and Doubling

Lessons 1, 3, 5, 9, and 13

Another strategy we encourage students to use when they see a new multiplication they do not know is to see if using doubles can help. For example, for a 6s multiplication they don't know doubling a 3s multiplication can give the correct answer.

$6 \times 6 = \square$

6×6 is twice 6×3.

$6 \times 3 = 18$. Then $18 + 18 = 36$. So, $6 \times 6 = 36$.

Combining Two Known Multiplications

Lessons 1, 3, 5, 9, and 13

A strategy to find the answer to a new multiplication or a multiplication they don't recall is for students to think about two multiplications they do know. The products can be added to find the product of the example they don't know or recall.

$6 \times 6 = \square$

$4 \times 6 = 24$	4 sixes are 24
$2 \times 6 = 12$	2 sixes are 12
$6 \times 6 = 36$	6 sixes are 36

Using a Drawing to Combine Two Known Multiplications

Lessons 1, 3, 5, 9, and 13

Here are two ways to show combining two known multiplications to find the product of a multiplication they do not know.

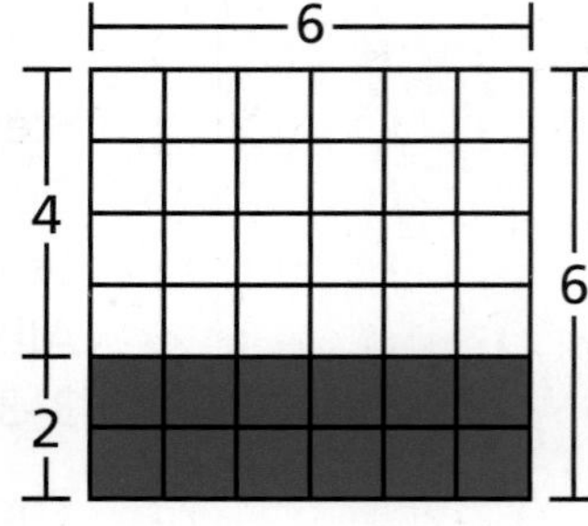

unshaded area: $4 \times 6 = 24$
shaded area: $2 \times 6 = 12$
total area: $6 \times 6 = 36$

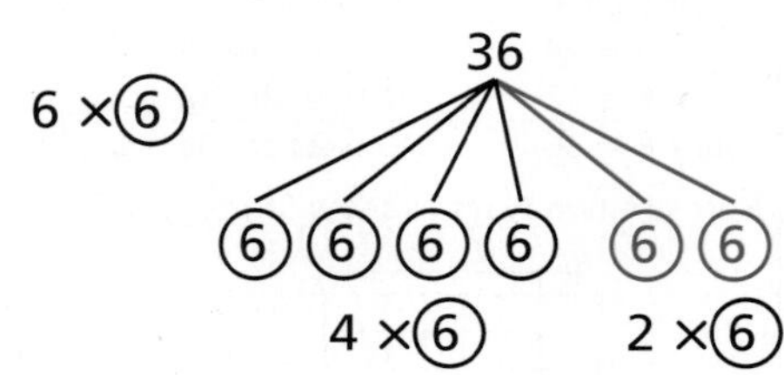

Explanation:
6 groups of 6 is 4 groups of 6 plus 2 groups of 6.

Patterns

Using Patterns to Help Multiply and Divide

Lessons 1, 3, 5, 8, and 13

Our goal is to encourage students to use patterns, such as count-bys, doubling, and patterns in the multiplications and divisions they already know to make proficiency with these facts easier. Using patterns can be a helpful strategy that they may use whenever they encounter examples or concepts that are new or difficult.

Problem Solving

In *Math Expressions* a research-based, algebraic problem-solving approach that focuses on problem types is used: understand the situation, represent the situation with a math drawing or an equation, solve the problem, and see that the answer makes sense.

Representing Word Problems

Lessons 2, 4, 6, 7, 10, 11, 12, and 13

Students using *Math Expressions* are taught a variety of ways to represent word problems. Some are conceptual in nature (making math drawings), while others are symbolic (writing equations). Students move from using math drawings to solving problems symbolically with equations. The following are the math drawings students use to represent multiplication and division word problems in this unit.

"As Many As" Comparisons

Lessons 6, 7, 10, 11, 12, and 13

Students encounter problems involving one quantity that is a number of times *as many as* another quantity. These problems involve comparing equal groups. We work with students to find that they can solve these types of problems by using multiplication. They learn how to make comparison drawings to help.

Bobby has 3 hockey pucks. Wayne has 15 hockey pucks.

Wayne has ____________ times as many hockey pucks as Bobby.

Students draw the number of hockey pucks each friend has. They circle groups of the smaller amount of hockey pucks: 3. Then they tell how many groups of hockey pucks each friend has: 1 group and 5 groups. We discuss how to tell how many times as many hockey pucks the friend with the greater amount has than the other friend: 5 times as many.

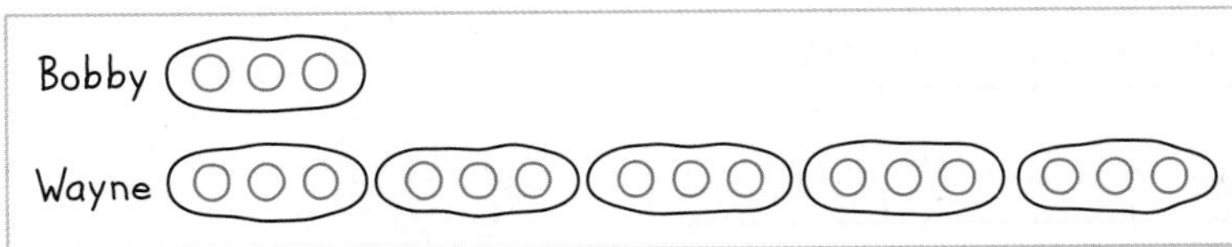

$W = 5 \times B$ **$B = \frac{1}{5} \times W$**

Later, students advance to drawing comparison bars, such as the following:

Bobby | 3 |

Wayne | 3 | 3 | 3 | 3 | 3 |

$W = 5 \times B$ **$B = \frac{1}{5} \times W$**

Each comparison can be said in two ways:

Bobby has $\frac{1}{5}$ as many as Wayne has.

Wayne has 5 times as many as Bobby has.

Students hear and practice the unit fraction language, but we do not expect mastery in this unit.

Fraction Comparisons
Lessons 6, 7, 10, 11, 12, and 13

To solve a comparison problem that involves a unit fraction, students learn to use division.

Eduardo has 12 posters in his room.

Manuela has $\frac{1}{3}$ as many posters as Eduardo.

How many posters does Manuela have?

$\frac{1}{3}$ as many means to divide into 3 equal groups and take 1.

Students divide 12 into 3 equal groups. Students may make drawings or comparison bars or use their multiplication and division knowledge. 12 posters put into 3 equal groups gives 4 posters in each group. So Manuela has 4 posters.

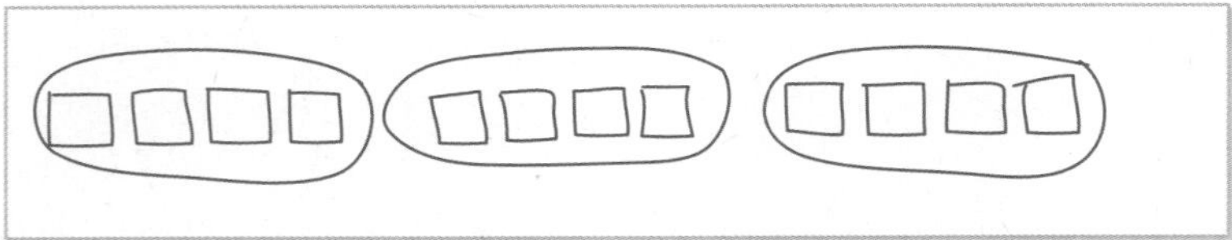

Use Mathematical Processes
Lesson 14

The NCTM process skills of problem solving, reasoning and proof, communication, connections, and representation are interwoven through all lessons throughout the year. The last lesson of this unit allows students to extend their use of mathematical processes to other situations.

NCTM Process Skill	Activity and Goal
Representation	1: Create a bar graph to represent data. 3: Make a drawing to support conclusions. 4: Draw an array to represent a situation.
Communication	1: Write a story problem. 2: Share and discuss answers. 3: Discuss results. 4: Share arrays and explain how they represent the problem. 5: Discuss information that is missing.
Connections	1: Math and Social Studies: Number Sense and Graphing
Reasoning and Proof	1: Analyze information in a bar graph to answer questions. 2: Prove or disprove conclusions. 3: Make generalizations about adding even and odd numbers.
Problem Solving	1: Solve problems using a bar graph. 2: Solve problems involving perimeter.

Multiply and Divide with 6

Lesson Objectives

- Explore patterns in 6s count-bys, multiplications, and divisions.
- Use a variety of strategies to solve multiplication problems.

Vocabulary
function table

The Day at a Glance

Today's Goals	Materials	
1 Teaching the Lesson **A1:** Explore patterns in 6s count-bys, multiplications, and divisions. **A2:** Use function tables. **A3:** Discuss strategies for finding 6 × 6, 6 × 7, and 6 × 8.	**Lesson Activities** Student Activity Book pp. 301–304 or Student Hardcover Book pp. 301–304 and Activity Workbook pp. 141–142 (includes Family Letter) Homework and Remembering pp. 211–214 Class Multiplication Table Poster or Poster (TRB M50) Pointer MathBoard materials	**Going Further** Class multiplication Table Activity Cards 9–1 Student Book p. 301 Calculators 6s Match (TRB M100) Math Journals
2 Going Further ► Differentiated Instruction		
3 Homework and Spiral Review		

Use Math Talk today!

Keeping Skills Sharp

Quick Practice — 5 MINUTES

Goal: Practice 3s count-bys, multiplications, and divisions.

Materials: Class Multiplication Table Poster, pointer
Display the Class Multiplication Table Poster. Use the number "3" for these activities.

Repeated Quick Practice
Use these Quick Practice activities from previous lessons.

3s Multiplications in Order (See Unit 7 Lesson 4.)

Mixed 3s Multiplications (See Unit 7 Lesson 2.)

Mixed 3s Divisions (See Unit 7 Lesson 5.)

Daily Routines

Nonroutine Problem Two pens cost 30¢ in all. One pen costs two times as much as the other pen. How much does each pen cost? Explain how you found your answer.

30¢ in all — first pen; 2 times the cost of the first pen

There are 3 equal amounts. So, 30 ÷ 3 = 10; 30¢ – 10¢ = 20¢; The pens cost 10¢ and 20¢.

1 Teaching the Lesson

Activity 1

6s Multiplications and Divisions

 **20 MINUTES**

Goal: Explore patterns in 6s count-bys, multiplications, and divisions.

Materials: Class Multiplication Table Poster or Class Multiplication Table Poster (TRB M50), pointer, MathBoard materials, Student Activity Book or Hardcover Book p. 301

 **NCTM Standards:**
Number and Operations
Representation

The Learning Classroom

Building Concepts The first part of Activity 1 outlines a way to involve the entire class in summarizing what they have already learned about multiplication. To support building coherence, remember to have students summarize on a regular basis. For instance, you might have students take turns summarizing the previous day's lesson at the beginning of math class. They can just say one or two sentences. Students do this in Japanese elementary school classes. An alternative may be to have a student summarize at the end of the lesson. Either way, if you do this regularly, students will get used to making mental summaries of the math concepts discussed and making conceptual connections.

▶ Identify Multiplications Not Yet Studied

WHOLE CLASS

Begin by reviewing the multiplications students have learned so far. Have students look at the Class Multiplication Table Poster. If you don't have the poster, give each child a copy of Class Multiplication Table Poster (TRB M50.)

- You've already learned lots of multiplications. Let's go through the table and circle those you still have left to learn.

For each column, ask students which multiplications they have not yet studied. They should recognize that they have studied all the multiplications in the 1s, 2s, 3s, 4s, 5s, and 9s columns and most of those in the 6s, 7s, and 8s columns. When you are finished, the nine multiplications below should be circled.

Class Multiplication Table

X	1	2	3	4	5	6	7	8	9
1	1 · 1 = 1	1 · 2 = 2	1 · 3 = 3	1 · 4 = 4	1 · 5 = 5	1 · 6 = 6	1 · 7 = 7	1 · 8 = 8	1 · 9 = 9
2	2 × 1 = 2	2 × 2 = 4	2 × 3 = 6	2 × 4 = 8	2 × 5 = 10	2 × 6 = 12	2 × 7 = 14	2 × 8 = 16	2 × 9 = 18
3	3 * 1 = 3	3 * 2 = 6	3 * 3 = 9	3 * 4 = 12	3 * 5 = 15	3 * 6 = 18	3 * 7 = 21	3 * 8 = 24	3 * 9 = 27
4	4 · 1 = 4	4 · 2 = 8	4 · 3 = 12	4 · 4 = 16	4 · 5 = 20	4 · 6 = 24	4 · 7 = 28	4 · 8 = 32	4 · 9 = 36
5	5 × 1 = 5	5 × 2 = 10	5 × 3 = 15	5 × 4 = 20	5 × 5 = 25	5 × 6 = 30	5 × 7 = 35	5 × 8 = 40	5 × 9 = 45
6	6 * 1 = 6	6 * 2 = 12	6 * 3 = 18	6 * 4 = 24	6 * 5 = 30	6 * 6 = 36	6 * 7 = 42	6 * 8 = 48	6 * 9 = 54
7	7 · 1 = 7	7 · 2 = 14	7 · 3 = 21	7 · 4 = 28	7 · 5 = 35	7 · 6 = 42	7 · 7 = 49	7 · 8 = 56	7 · 9 = 63
8	8 × 1 = 8	8 × 2 = 16	8 × 3 = 24	8 × 4 = 32	8 × 5 = 40	8 × 6 = 48	8 × 7 = 56	8 × 8 = 64	8 × 9 = 72
9	9 * 1 = 9	9 * 2 = 18	9 * 3 = 27	9 * 4 = 36	9 * 5 = 45	9 * 6 = 54	9 * 7 = 63	9 * 8 = 72	9 * 9 = 81
10	10 · 1 = 10	10 · 2 = 20	10 · 3 = 30	10 · 4 = 40	10 · 5 = 50	10 · 6 = 60	10 · 7 = 70	10 · 8 = 80	10 · 9 = 90

- There are 90 multiplications in this table, and you have only 9 more to learn. That means you know 81 of these multiplications!
- Today we will focus on the 6s column. We will look at all the multiplications in the column, but keep in mind that only three are new to you.

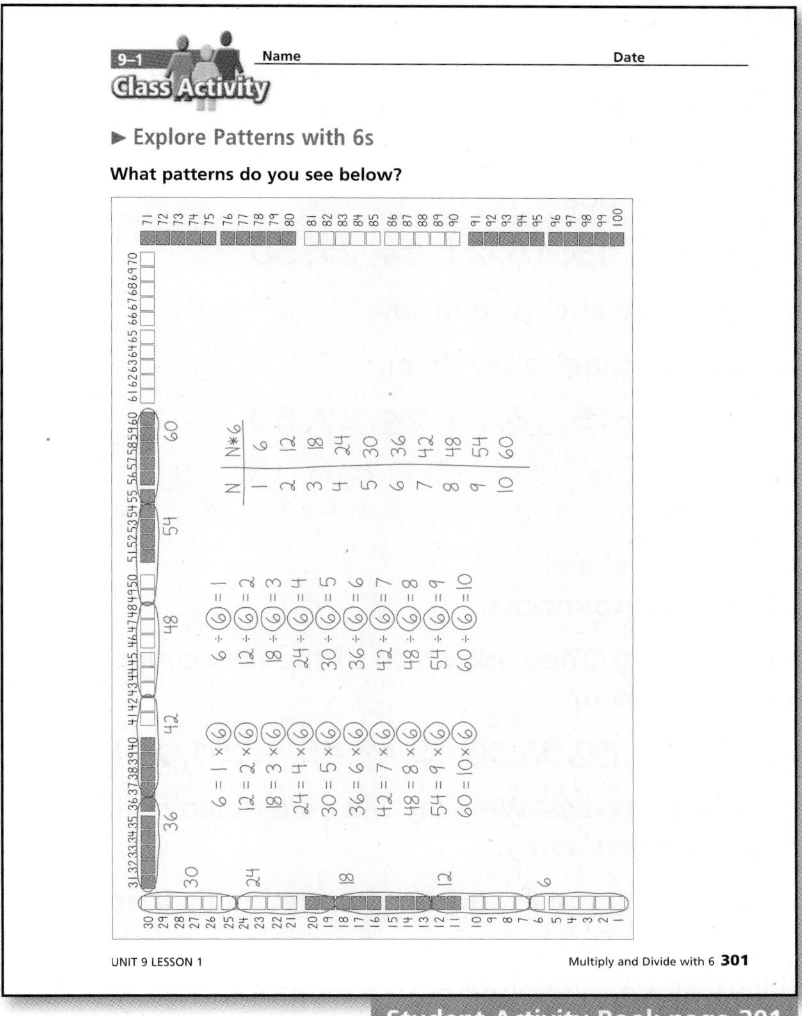

Student Activity Book page 301

► Explore Patterns with 6s WHOLE CLASS

Tell students that today they will be thinking of things that come in groups of 6. Ask students what everyday things come in groups of 6. cans of juice or soda, legs on an insect, eggs in a half dozen, and so on

Model the steps of this activity on the Class MathBoard as students follow along on their MathBoards. The completed board is shown above on Student Activity Book page 301. You can use it to facilitate a summary discussion of the patterns in 6s.

Have students circle sequential groups of 6, up to 60, on the Number Path and write the totals so far next to each group. After they circle the first group, have them say in unison, "1 group of 6 is 6"; after they circle the second group, have them say, "2 groups of 6 are 12"; and so on.

Activity continued ►

Teaching Note

Math Background When one number is a count-by of a second number, the first number is *divisible* by the second number. That is, the 2s count-bys (2, 4, 6, 8, 10, 12, . . .) are all divisible by 2, the 3s count-bys (3, 6, 9, 12, 15, 18, . . .) are all divisible by 3, the 4s count-bys (4, 8, 12, 16, 20, 24) are all divisible by 4, and so on.

As students proceed in their study of mathematics, it will become increasingly important for them to become skilled at recognizing whether one number is divisible by another. The work with count-bys in Units 4 and 5 helps build the foundation for that skill. In later grades they will learn the following basic divisibility rules.

A whole number is divisible by:

- 2 if its ones digit is even
- 3 if the sum of its digits is divisible by 3
- 4 if the number formed by the tens digit and the ones digit is divisible by 4
- 5 if its ones digit is 0 or 5
- 8 if the number formed by its hundreds, tens, and ones digits is divisible by 8
- 9 if the sum of its digits is divisible by 9
- 10 if its ones digit is 0

As students explore patterns with 6s in Activity 1, they will discover that every 6s count-by is an even number and is also a 3s count-by. So they are intuitively developing an additional divisibility rule.

- A whole number is divisible by 6 if it is divisible by 2 and by 3.

Math Talk in Action

Tamar: I think that the 6s count-bys are also all 2s count-bys. They're even numbers.

Jameel: And they're all 3s count-bys, too.

Rosita: Oh, look! Line up the 6s count-bys with the 3s count-bys under them, like this.

6	12	18	24	30	36	42	48	54	60
3	6	9	12	15	18	21	24	27	30

Compare them. I think the 6s count-bys are all twice as big as the 3s count-bys under them.

Benjamin: Look at every third 6s count-by: 18, 36, 54. Those are all 9s count-bys, too.

Shelly: Add the digits in the 6s count-bys that have two digits. $1 + 2 = 3$, $1 + 8 = 9$, $2 + 4 = 6$, $3 + 0 = 3$, $3 + 6 = 9$, $4 + 2 = 6$, $4 + 8 = 12$, $5 + 4 = 9$, $6 + 0 = 6$. The totals are all 3s count-bys.

Kwan: That works for 6, too. Just think about a 0 in the tens place. $0 + 6 = 6$. That's a 3s count-by.

Annette: Is there a pattern for the totals? You've got 6, 3, 9, 6, 3, 9, 6, 12, 9. Oh! The 12 isn't right.

Duri: Yes, it is! Add $1 + 2 = 3$ and put that in instead of 12. Then you get 6, 3, 9, 6, 3, 9, 6, 3, 9.

After students have circled all ten groups, point to each group in order as students say, "1 group of 6 is 6," "2 groups of 6 are 12," "3 groups of 6 are 18," and so on.

Next, ask students to say just the 6s count-bys. Point to the totals as students say them aloud: 6, 12, 18, 24, 30, 36, 42, 48, 54, 60

- When you said the 6s count-bys, did you hear any 3s count-bys? yes I'm going to write the 3s count-bys on the board. Who can tell me what to write?

Write the 3s count-bys on the board.

3, 6, 9, 12, 15, 18, 21, 24, 27, 30

- Which of these numbers are also 6s count-bys? 6, 12, 18, 24, 30

Underline these numbers as students say them.

3, <u>6</u>, 9, <u>12</u>, 15, <u>18</u>, 21, <u>24</u>, 27, <u>30</u>

- What pattern do you see? Every other 3s count-by is a 6s count-by. Why does this make sense? Because there are two 3s in 6; if you put two groups of 3 together, you get a group of 6.
- Let's continue our list of 3s count-bys.

Elicit the 3s count-bys up to 60. Then ask which of the new count-bys are 6s count-bys, and underline them.

3, <u>6</u>, 9, <u>12</u>, 15, <u>18</u>, 21, <u>24</u>, 27, <u>30</u>, 33, <u>36</u>, 39, <u>42</u>, 45, <u>48</u>, 51, <u>54</u>, 57, <u>60</u>

- Let's read this list of 3s count-bys. We'll say the underlined numbers loudly and the other numbers softly.

Read the list as a group, saying the 6s count-bys more loudly than the other numbers.

Next, as students follow along, write and read a multiplication equation for each count-by.

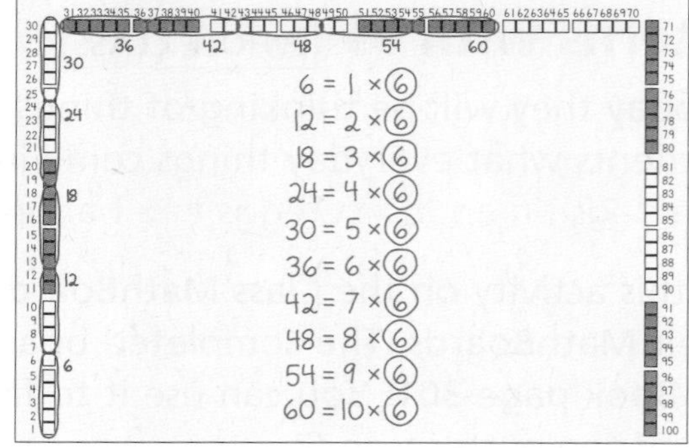

Point to one of the multiplications. Write an = sign after the multiplication, and ask students to help you write a repeated addition expression. Do this for one or two more multiplications.

Ask students to describe the patterns they see in the count-bys and equations. See the **Math Talk in Action** in the side column.

▶ Use the Class Multiplication Table Poster WHOLE CLASS

In the Class Multiplication Table Poster, point to the equations in the 6s column in order and have the class read them aloud, using fingers to show the multiplier.

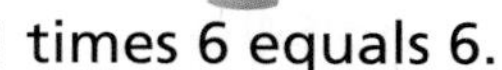
1 times 6 equals 6.

2 times 6 equals 12.

3 times 6 equals 18.

Point to each equation in the 6s column again, this time having students say only the count-bys. Again, have them use their fingers to indicate the multipliers.

6

12

18

▶ Use Fingers to Multiply WHOLE CLASS

Present 6s multiplications and have students count up on their fingers to find the answers. For example, to find 4×6, they should count by 6s, raising a finger for each count-by, until 4 fingers are raised.

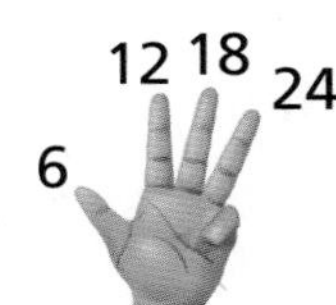

4 times 6 equals 24.

Ask students how they could use the "5s shortcut" to find 8×6 quickly. Start with all 5 fingers up on one hand, say 30, and count up from there.

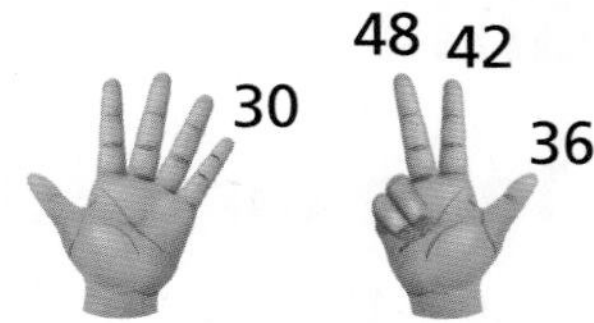

8 times 6 equals 48.

Have students use the shortcut to find 7×6 and 9×6.

▶ Divide with 6s WHOLE CLASS

Erase the repeated addition expressions from the Class MathBoard. Work with students to write the first two or three related division equations, and then have them work independently to write the rest. See side column.

Activity continued ▶

Teaching Note

Watch For! Students have learned that multiplication is commutative. Since they are learning to relate multiplication and division, they might mistakenly assume that division, too, is commutative. As a result, in Activity 1 they might write equations like $6 \div 24 = 4$.

Discuss the differences between multiplication and division. Review the terms associated with each operation. For multiplication, point out that each of the numbers being multiplied has the same name – factor. Display an example like the following.

$$4 \times 6 = 24$$

factors (4, 6) product (24)

Compare this to division, in which each part has a different name.

$$24 \div 6 = 4$$

dividend (24) divisor (6) quotient (4)

Stress that, when a division is written in this form, the dividend must always be written first.

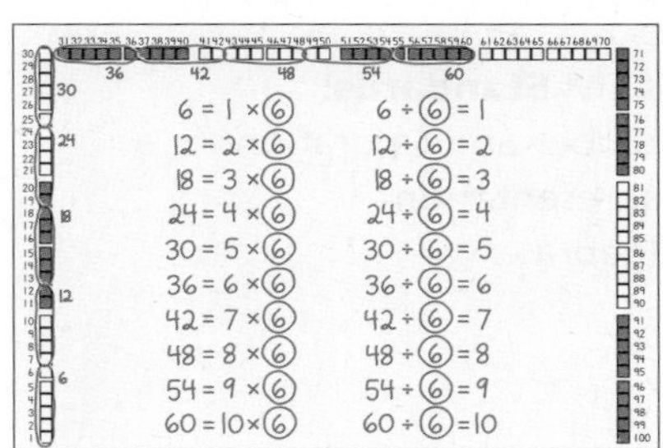

Differentiated Instruction

Extra Help Egg cartons that are split into half-dozen sections can provide tactile learners with a visual model for 6s multiplications and divisions. Remove the lids from several half-dozen cartons. Then, for example, give students the cartons and 24 counters. Have them find how many of the cartons they can fill with the counters, placing one counter in each indentation.

After they fill 4 half-dozen cartons, lead them to see that 4 is the unknown number in both $24 \div 6 = \square$ and $\square \times 6 = 24$. Repeat this activity for other 6s multiplications and divisions.

Have students turn over their MathBoards. Hide the division equations on the Class MathBoard. Write the following division and related unknown multiplication problem on the board.

$$24 \div 6 = \square \qquad \square \times 6 = 24$$

Ask students to try to find the unknown number without using count-bys. They should think "What number times 6 is 24?" and consider the multiplications they know. (They may use count-bys if they can't figure out the answer this way.) Repeat for $18 \div 6$, $30 \div 6$, and $54 \div 6$.

Then write the following division and related unknown multiplication problem on the board.

$$42 \div 6 = \square \qquad \square \times 6 = 42$$

For the divisions $36 \div 6$, $42 \div 6$, and $48 \div 6$, most students will need to use count-bys. Have students count up on their fingers to find the answers. Seven fingers will be raised, indicating that there are 7 groups of 6 in 42. So, $42 \div 6 = 7$.

Ask students how they could have used the "5s shortcut" to find the unknown number. Start with all 5 fingers up on one hand, say "30," and count by 6s from there until you reach 42.

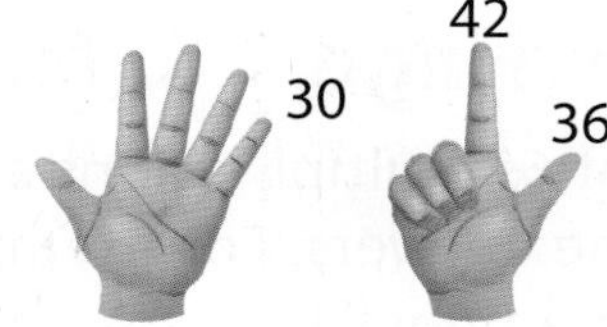

7 times 6 equals 42.

Have students use count-bys to find $36 \div 6$ and $48 \div 6$.

Activity 2

Introduce Function Tables with a Variable

 **15 MINUTES**

Goal: Use function tables.

Materials: MathBoard materials

 **NCTM Standards:**
Number and Operations
Representation
Algebra

▶ Make a Function Table for 6s Count-bys WHOLE CLASS

On the Class MathBoard, make a two-column table with column heads N and $N * 6$. Tell students that you are making a special kind of table called a *function table*. Remind students that a function table shows what happens when a rule is applied to certain numbers. Point to the first column and explain that N means "any number"; we can write any number we want in this column. Then explain that $N * 6$ is the rule that tells us what do with the numbers in the N column. This rule tells us to multiply each number by 6.

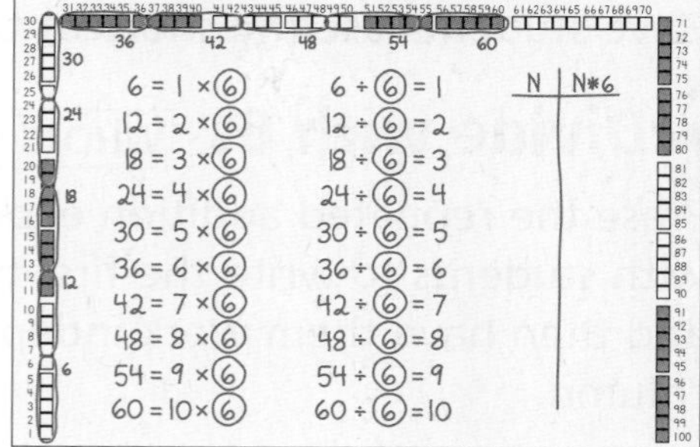

Write 1 as the first entry in the N column.

- Use 1 for the first value of N. What does the rule say to do with 1? Multiply it by 6.
- What is the answer when the rule is used? 6

Write 6 in the $N * 6$ column, next to the number 1.

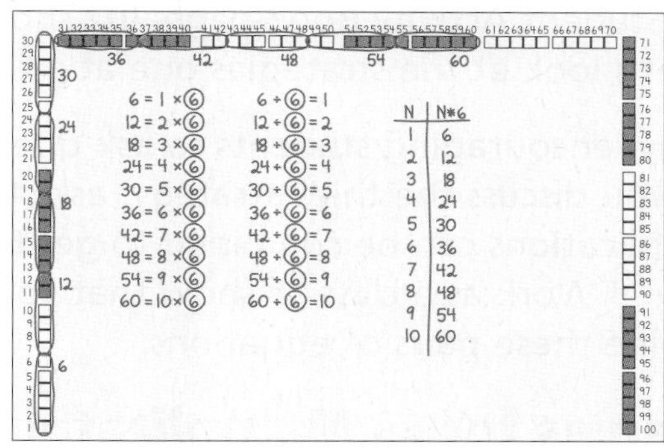

Now write 2 as the second entry in the N column.

- Use 2 for the value of N. What happens to the 2? Multiply it by 6.
- What is the answer? 12
- Write 12 in the $N * 6$ column, next to the number 2.

Continue this process for N values 3, 4, and 5. Then ask students to complete the table for consecutive N values through 10.

When students are finished, point out that the numbers in the $N * 6$ column are the 6s count-bys. Point to the row with the numbers 4 and 24.

- This row shows that the fourth 6s count-by is 24. In other words, 4×6 is 24.
- You can see from the table that you can find any count-by by counting up or counting back from a count-by you know.
- It is usually easiest to start with a "close count-by," one that is near the one you want to find. For example, to find 7×6, start at 5×6, or 30, and count up by two more 6s: 30 plus 6 is 36, plus 6 more is 42. (Point to 30, 36, and 42 as you say these numbers.)
- Suppose you want to find 8×6 and you know that 9×6 is 54. You can count back by one 6: 54 minus 6 is 48. (Point to 54 and 48 as you say these numbers.)

Ask a volunteer to explain how to count up or count back to find 6×6.

If your school district has expressions as a topic to be covered, use this opportunity to introduce 6n for $N * 6$

Teaching Note

Make a Tens-Number Strategy

To help students count up or back by 6s, you may want to discuss the Make a Tens-Number strategy. This is an extension of the Make a Ten strategy discussed in Unit 1. To use this strategy to count up, first add part of the 6 to make a tens-number, and then add the part that is left over. The following are two examples.

- To find $36 + 6$, start with 36. Add 4 to get 40, and then add 2 more to get 42. In symbols, $36 + 6 = 36 + 4 + 2 = 40 + 2 = 42$.
- To find $48 + 6$, start with 48. Add 2 to get 50, and then add 4 more to get 54. In symbols, $48 + 6 = 48 + 2 + 4 = 50 + 4 = 54$.

To use the Make a Tens-Number strategy to count back, subtract part of the 6 to get to a tens number, and then subtract the rest of the 6. The following are two examples.

- To find $42 - 6$, start with 42. Subtract 2 to get 40, and then subtract 4 more to get 36. In symbols, $42 - 6 = 42 - 2 - 4 = 40 - 4 = 36$.
- To find $54 - 6$, start with 54. Subtract 4 to get 50, and then subtract 2 more to get 48. In symbols, $54 - 6 = 54 - 4 - 2 = 50 - 2 = 48$.

In upcoming lessons, students will adapt this strategy to count up and back by 8s and 7s.

English Language Learners

Draw and identify a *function table* on the board.

- **Beginning** Ask: **Does the table show 6 count-bys?** yes
- **Intermediate and Advanced** Ask: **Does the table show all the equations?** no Say: **It shows 6 ___.** count-bys

Activity 3

Strategies for 6s Multiplications

 **15 MINUTES**

Goal: Discuss strategies for finding 6 × 6, 6 × 7, and 6 × 8.

Materials: MathBoard materials, Student Activity Book or Hardcover Book p. 302, Homework and Remembering p. 213

 **NCTM Standards:**
Number and Operations
Representation

 **Ongoing Assessment**

Ask questions such as the following:

- ▶ What unknown multiplication problem can you use to find 54 ÷ 6? What is the unknown number?
- ▶ Suppose you know that 8 × 3 = 24. How can you use that multiplication to find 8 × 6?
- ▶ How can you make a function table for the 4s count-bys?

 **Class Management**

Looking Ahead Remind students to take home the 6s chart on Homework and Remembering page 211. At this time, you may want to have students fill in the Study Plan box on Homework and Remembering page 213. Students should practice their 6s tonight.

▶ Strategies for Multiplying with 6 WHOLE CLASS

Start this activity by saying something like the following.

- You have learned several strategies for figuring out multiplications you don't know. Student Activity Book page 302 shows three ways you can find 6 × 6. Let's look at the strategies one at a time.

Discuss each strategy, encouraging students to ask questions if they don't understand. When you discuss the third strategy, ask students what other pairs of multiplications can be combined to get 6 × 6. 5 × 6 and 1 × 6; 3 × 6 and 3 × 6 Work as a class to show that you get the correct answer if you combine these pairs of equations.

▶ Apply Strategies for 6s Multiplications PAIRS

Have **Student Pairs** solve and present their answers to problem 1. If possible, make sure all three strategies are presented. Do the same for problem 2.

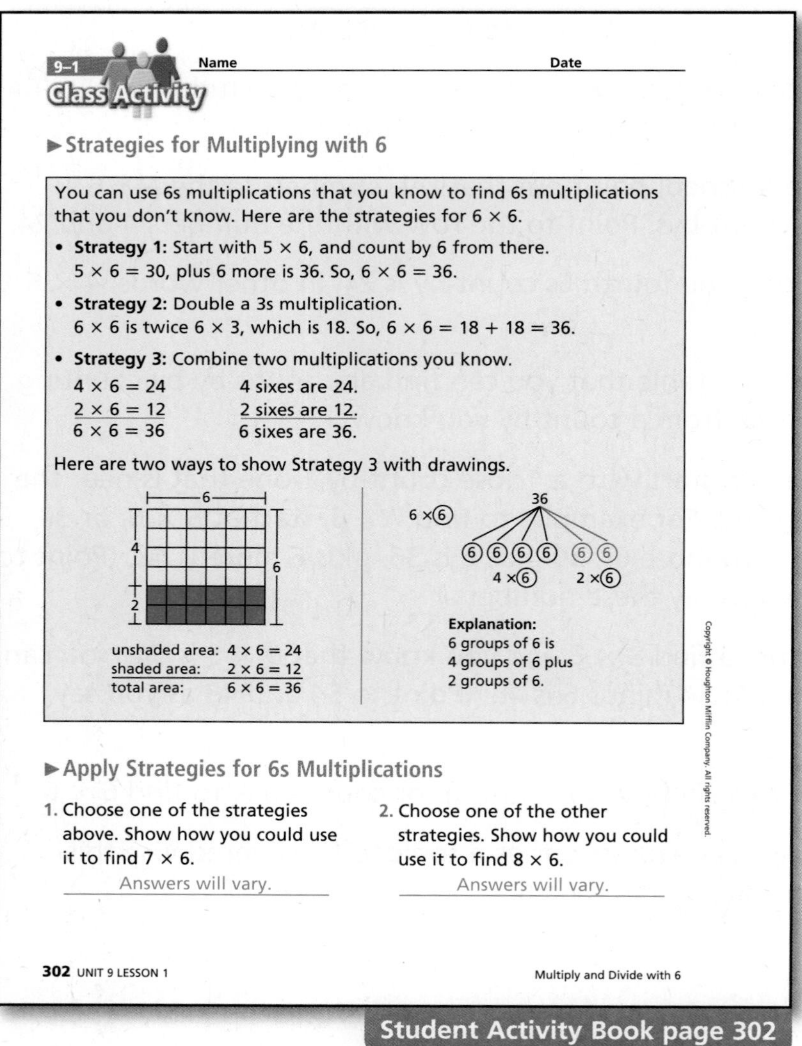
9–1 Class Activity Name ________ Date ________

▶ Strategies for Multiplying with 6

You can use 6s multiplications that you know to find 6s multiplications that you don't know. Here are the strategies for 6 × 6.

- **Strategy 1:** Start with 5 × 6, and count by 6 from there. 5 × 6 = 30, plus 6 more is 36. So, 6 × 6 = 36.
- **Strategy 2:** Double a 3s multiplication. 6 × 6 is twice 6 × 3, which is 18. So, 6 × 6 = 18 + 18 = 36.
- **Strategy 3:** Combine two multiplications you know.

4 × 6 = 24	4 sixes are 24.
2 × 6 = 12	2 sixes are 12.
6 × 6 = 36	6 sixes are 36.

Here are two ways to show Strategy 3 with drawings.

▶ Apply Strategies for 6s Multiplications

1. Choose one of the strategies above. Show how you could use it to find 7 × 6.
Answers will vary.

2. Choose one of the other strategies. Show how you could use it to find 8 × 6.
Answers will vary.

302 UNIT 9 LESSON 1 Multiply and Divide with 6

Student Activity Book page 302

2 Going Further

Differentiated Instruction

Intervention — Activity Card 9-I

6s Calculator Patterns

Activity Card 9-1

Work: On your own

Use:

- Calculator
- Student Activity Book page 301

1. Use your calculator to make patterns using 6s. Press the number 6 key on your calculator and then press the + key.

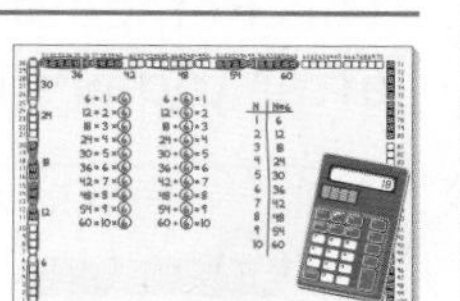

2. Each time you press the + key, say the multiplication equation whose product the display shows. So the first equation is $6 \times 1 = 6$.
3. Continue the key pattern until the display shows 60. What is the second product on the display? What is the next multiplication equation you will say? 12; $6 \times 2 = 12$
4. **Analyze** Suppose you forgot which equation to say after the display shows 42. What number could you use to divide 42 to help you remember the multiplication equation? 6

Unit 9, Lesson 1

Activity Note Use the Number Path on Student Activity Book page 301 to stress that multiplication is repeated addition. Students will see that by first pressing the keys 6 + and then = ten times generates 6, 12, ... 60.

Math Writing Prompt

Number Sense How do you know that the quotient $42 \div 6$ must be greater than the quotient $36 \div 6$?

Software Support

Warm Up 12.15

On Level — Activity Card 9-I

6s Strategy Match

Activity Card 9-1

Work: In pairs

Use:

- TRB M100 (6s Match)

1. **Work Together** Match each 6s multiplication with the strategy you can use to find the product.

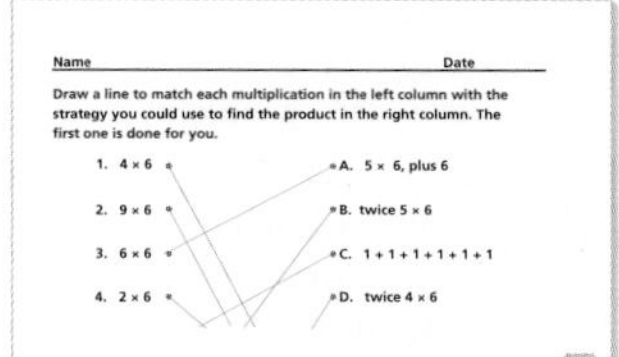

2. **Think** How does doubling help you to find 4×6? The product of 2×6 is 12, and 4 is twice 2, so 4×6 is double 12, or 24.
3. When you have completed the activity, discuss other strategies that you could use to find the products in the left column.

Unit 9, Lesson 1

Activity Note Challenge students to find as many strategies as possible to calculate each product, once they have completed the activity.

Math Writing Prompt

Explain Your Thinking Explain why an odd number cannot be a 6s count-by.

Software Support

Country Countdown: Counting Critters, Level F

Challenge — Activity Card 9-I

Find the Missing Rule

Activity Card 9-1

Work: In pairs

1. **On Your Own** Create three function tables with missing multiplication or division rules.
2. Exchange tables with your partner and find each missing rule.
3. Exchange tables again and check the results.
4. Discuss the strategies you used to find the missing rules.

N	?
7	28
2	8
5	20
9	36
1	4
3	12
6	24
10	40
4	16
8	32

Rule N × 4

N	?
40	5
8	1
24	3
64	8
16	2
48	6
72	9
32	4
80	10
56	7

Rule N ÷ 8

Unit 9, Lesson 1

Activity Note A multiplication rule has a table whose values increase from the first column to the second. A division rule exists for a table whose values decrease from the first column to the second.

Math Writing Prompt

Investigate Math How can you use the fact that 9×6 is equal to 54 to find the product 9×12?

DESTINATION Math®

Software Support

Course II: Module 2: Unit 2: Finding Products less than 100

Homework and Spiral Review

9–1 Homework **Goal:** Additional Practice

This Homework page provides practice multiplying and dividing 6s and using function tables.

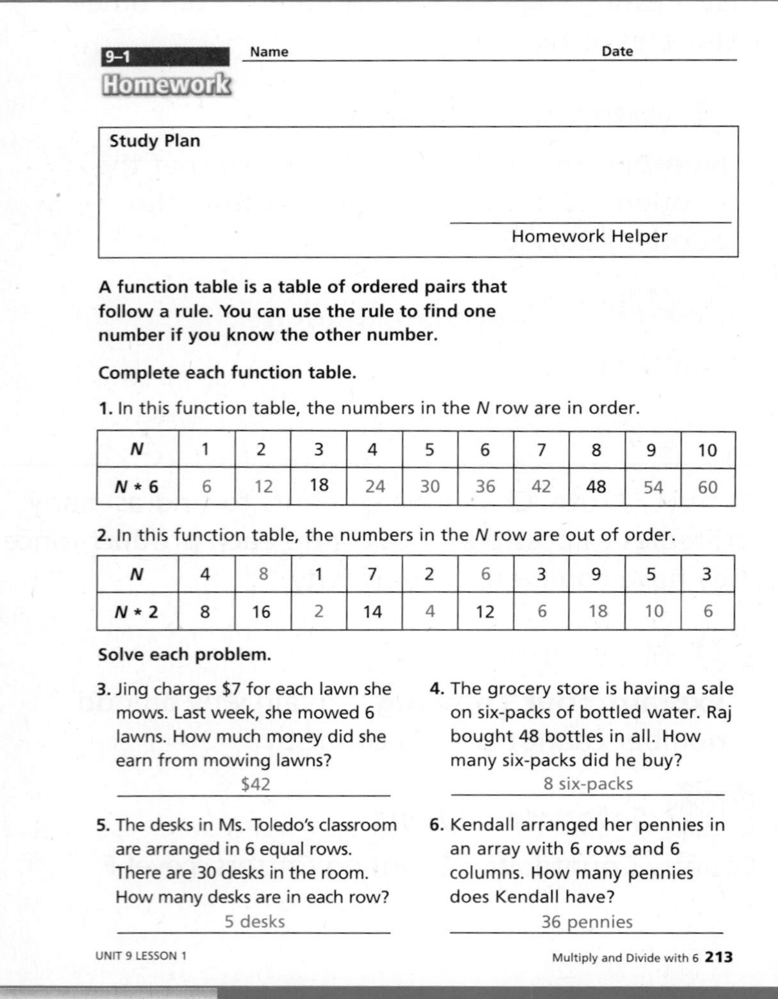

9–1 Homework Name Date

Study Plan

Homework Helper

A function table is a table of ordered pairs that follow a rule. You can use the rule to find one number if you know the other number.

Complete each function table.

1. In this function table, the numbers in the *N* row are in order.

N	1	2	3	4	5	6	7	8	9	10
N * 6	6	12	18	24	30	36	42	48	54	60

2. In this function table, the numbers in the *N* row are out of order.

N	4	8	1	7	2	6	3	9	5	3
N * 2	8	16	2	14	4	12	6	18	10	6

Solve each problem.

3. Jing charges $7 for each lawn she mows. Last week, she mowed 6 lawns. How much money did she earn from mowing lawns? $42

4. The grocery store is having a sale on six-packs of bottled water. Raj bought 48 bottles in all. How many six-packs did he buy? 8 six-packs

5. The desks in Ms. Toledo's classroom are arranged in 6 equal rows. There are 30 desks in the room. How many desks are in each row? 5 desks

6. Kendall arranged her pennies in an array with 6 rows and 6 columns. How many pennies does Kendall have? 36 pennies

UNIT 9 LESSON 1 Multiply and Divide with 6 **213**

Homework and Remembering page 213

9–1 Remembering **Goal:** Spiral Review

This Remembering page would be appropriate anytime after today's lesson.

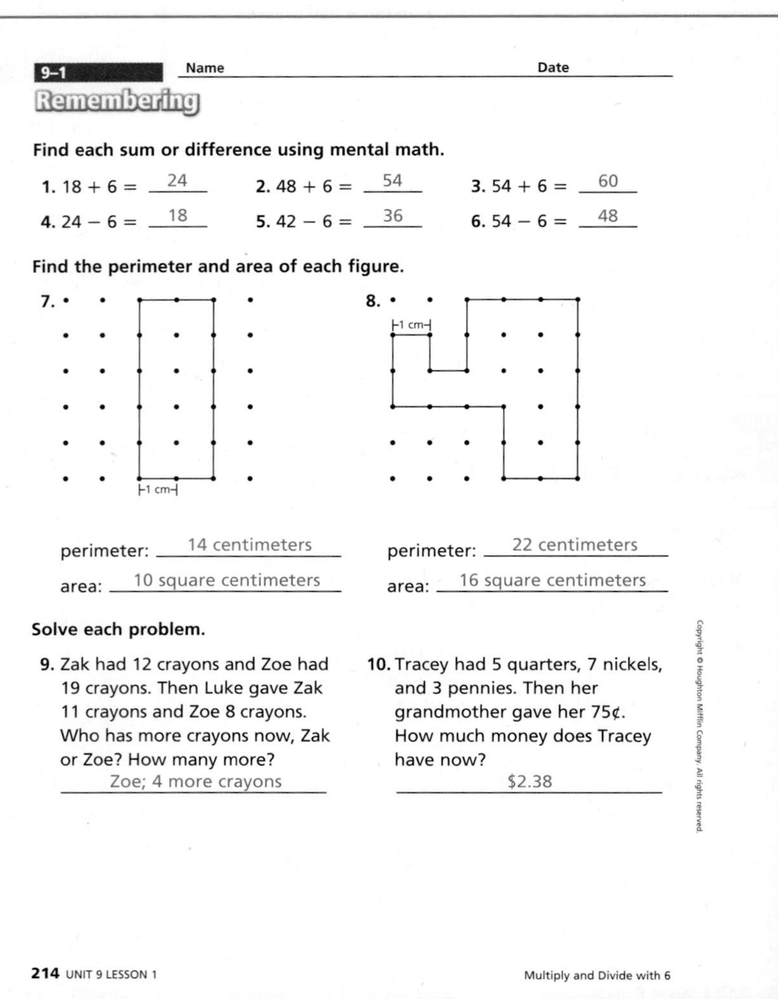

9–1 Remembering Name Date

Find each sum or difference using mental math.

1. 18 + 6 = 24
2. 48 + 6 = 54
3. 54 + 6 = 60
4. 24 − 6 = 18
5. 42 − 6 = 36
6. 54 − 6 = 48

Find the perimeter and area of each figure.

7. 1 cm

perimeter: 14 centimeters

area: 10 square centimeters

8. 1 cm

perimeter: 22 centimeters

area: 16 square centimeters

Solve each problem.

9. Zak had 12 crayons and Zoe had 19 crayons. Then Luke gave Zak 11 crayons and Zoe 8 crayons. Who has more crayons now, Zak or Zoe? How many more? Zoe; 4 more crayons

10. Tracey had 5 quarters, 7 nickels, and 3 pennies. Then her grandmother gave her 75¢. How much money does Tracey have now? $2.38

214 UNIT 9 LESSON 1 Multiply and Divide with 6

Homework and Remembering page 214

Home and School Connection

Family Letter Have children take home the Family Letter on Student Activity Book page 303 or Activity Workbook p. 141. A Spanish translation of this letter is on the following page. This letter explains how the concepts of multiplication comparisons and multi-step word problems are developed in *Math Expressions.* It gives parents and guardians a better understanding of the learning that goes on in math class and creates a bridge between school and home.

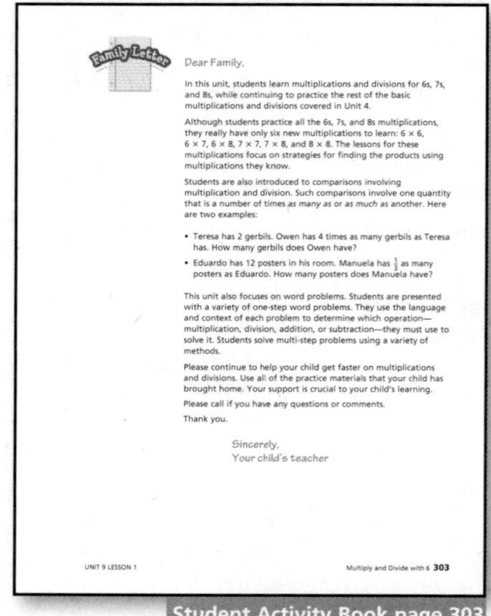

Family Letter

Dear Family,

In this unit, students learn multiplications and divisions for 6s, 7s, and 8s, while continuing to practice the rest of the basic multiplications and divisions covered in Unit 4.

Although students practice all the 6s, 7s, and 8s multiplications, they really have only six new multiplications to learn: 6 × 6, 6 × 7, 6 × 8, 7 × 7, 7 × 8, and 8 × 8. The lessons for these multiplications focus on strategies for finding the products using multiplications they know.

Students are also introduced to comparisons involving multiplication and division. Such comparisons involve one quantity that is a number of times *as many as* or *as much as* another. Here are two examples:

- Teresa has 2 gerbils. Owen has 4 times as many gerbils as Teresa has. How many gerbils does Owen have?
- Eduardo has 12 posters in his room. Manuela has $\frac{1}{3}$ as many posters as Eduardo. How many posters does Manuela have?

This unit also focuses on word problems. Students are presented with a variety of one-step word problems. They use the language and context of each problem to determine which operation—multiplication, division, addition, or subtraction—they must use to solve it. Students solve multi-step problems using a variety of methods.

Please continue to help your child get faster on multiplications and divisions. Use all of the practice materials that your child has brought home. Your support is crucial to your child's learning.

Please call if you have any questions or comments.

Thank you.

Sincerely,
Your child's teacher

UNIT 9 LESSON 1 Multiply and Divide with 6 **303**

Student Activity Book page 303

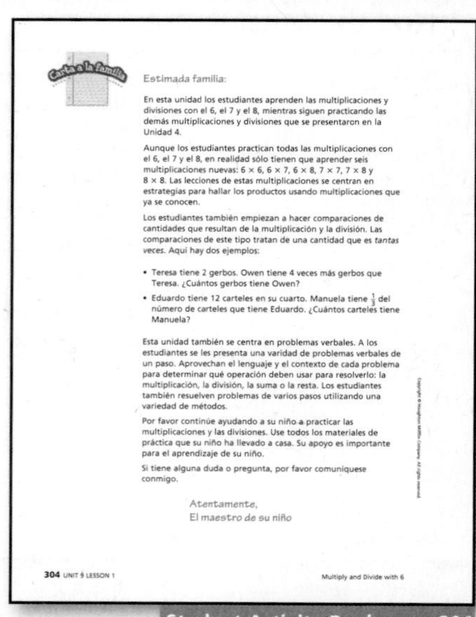

Carta a la familia

Estimada familia:

En esta unidad los estudiantes aprenden las multiplicaciones y divisiones con el 6, el 7 y el 8, mientras siguen practicando las demás multiplicaciones y divisiones que se presentaron en la Unidad 4.

Aunque los estudiantes practican todas las multiplicaciones con el 6, el 7 y el 8, en realidad sólo tienen que aprender seis multiplicaciones nuevas: 6 × 6, 6 × 7, 6 × 8, 7 × 7, 7 × 8 y 8 × 8. Las lecciones de estas multiplicaciones se centran en estrategias para hallar los productos usando multiplicaciones que ya se conocen.

Los estudiantes también empiezan a hacer comparaciones de cantidades que resultan de la multiplicación y la división. Las comparaciones de este tipo tratan de una cantidad que es *tantas veces*. Aquí hay dos ejemplos:

- Teresa tiene 2 gerbos. Owen tiene 4 veces más gerbos que Teresa. ¿Cuántos gerbos tiene Owen?
- Eduardo tiene 12 carteles en su cuarto. Manuela tiene $\frac{1}{3}$ del número de carteles que tiene Eduardo. ¿Cuántos carteles tiene Manuela?

Esta unidad también se centra en problemas verbales. A los estudiantes se les presenta una varidad de problemas verbales de un paso. Aprovechan el lenguaje y el contexto de cada problema para determinar qué operación deben usar para resolverlo: la multiplicación, la división, la suma o la resta. Los estudiantes también resuelven problemas de varios pasos utilizando una variedad de métodos.

Por favor continúe ayudando a su niño a practicar las multiplicaciones y las divisiones. Use todos los materiales de práctica que su niño ha llevado a casa. Su apoyo es importante para el aprendizaje de su niño.

Si tiene alguna duda o pregunta, por favor comuníquese conmigo.

Atentamente,
El maestro de su niño

304 UNIT 9 LESSON 1 Multiply and Divide with 6

Student Activity Book page 304

Solve Area Word Problems

Vocabulary
length
width
area
perimeter
Fast-Area Drawing

Lesson Objective

- Develop strategies for solving real-world area problems.

The Day at a Glance

Today's Goals	Materials	
1 Teaching the Lesson **A1:** Practice count-bys, multiplications, and divisions. **A2:** Solve Missing Number puzzles. **A3:** Solve word problems involving area.	**Lesson Activities** Student Activity Book pp. 305–310 or Student Hardcover Book pp. 305–310 and Activity Workbook pp. 143–145 (includes Study Sheet, Number Puzzle, and Check Sheet Homework and Remembering pp. 215–218 Check Up materials Signature Sheet Study Sheets A-C Check Sheets 1–7 Dry-erase markers Sheet protectors Study sheet answer strips Quick Check Answer Strips	Cardstock Strategy Cards Transparency of Student Activity Book page 307 (optional) Overhead projector (optional) **Going Further** Activity Cards 9–2 Connecting Cubes Number Cubes Centimeter Grid paper (TRB M31) Math Journals
2 Going Further ► Problem Solving Strategy: Draw a Picture ► Differentiated Instruction		
3 Homework and Spiral Review		

Use Math Talk today!

Keeping Skills Sharp

Quick Practice — 5 MINUTES	Daily Routines
Goal: Practice 6s count-bys, multiplications, and divisions. **Materials:** Class Multiplication Table Poster, pointer Use the Class Poster and the number "6" for these activities. **Repeated Quick Practice** Use these Quick Practice activities from previous lessons. **6s Multiplications in Order** (See Unit 7 Lesson 4.) **Mixed 6s Multiplications** (See Unit 7 Lesson 2.) **Mixed 6s Divisions** (See Unit 7 Lesson 5.)	**Homework Review** Have students discuss their incorrect answers. **Mental Math** Use a mental math strategy to add 47 + 38. Explain how you found your answer. 85; I added on 3 of the 38 to 47 to make 50. I added 30 from the 35 to 50 and got 80. I added 5 to 80 and got 85.

Teaching the Lesson

Activity 1

Check Up and Independent Study

5 MINUTES

Goal: Practice count-bys, multiplications, and divisions.

Materials: Check Up materials: Signature Sheet (Student Activity Book pp. 205–206 or Activity Workbook p. 77); Study Sheets A–C (Student Activity Book pp. 207–208; 243–244; 305–306 or Activity Workbook pp. 78, 89, 143), Check Sheets 1–7 (Student Activity Book pp. 223–224; 229–230; 234; 251–252; 267–268; 273–274 or Activity Workbook pp. 83, 85, 87, 118, 123–124, 129), dry-erase markers (1 per student), sheet protectors (1 per student), Study Sheet Answer Strips (TRB M54), Check Sheet Answer Strips (TRB M55), cardstock; Strategy Cards, Homework and Remembering page 217

NCTM Standard:
Number and Operations

▶ Check Up with 6s PAIRS

Give a sheet protector to each student. Have students write their names on Study Sheet C (from Student Book page 305 or Activity Workbook page 143), and slip it into a sheet protector. Explain that this sheet includes count-bys, multiplications, and divisions for the rest of the factors students will study. Give **Student Pairs** a few minutes to test one another using Study Sheets A–C and collect signatures. For students who have already collected signatures on Study Sheets, have them use Check Sheets 1–7. Then give students a minute or two to study independently using their Study Sheet, Check Sheets, or Strategy Cards. You may want to have Study Sheets and Check Sheet Answer Strips (TRB M54–M55) available.

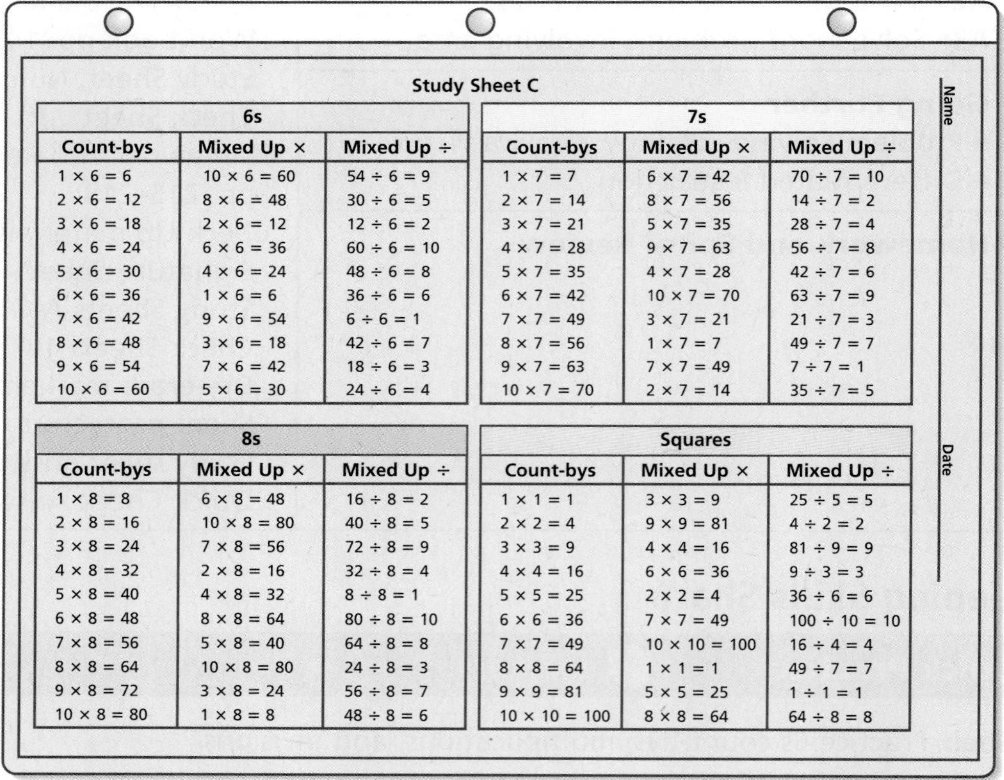

Study Sheet C

Name

Date

6s		
Count-bys	Mixed Up ×	Mixed Up ÷
1 × 6 = 6	10 × 6 = 60	54 ÷ 6 = 9
2 × 6 = 12	8 × 6 = 48	30 ÷ 6 = 5
3 × 6 = 18	2 × 6 = 12	12 ÷ 6 = 2
4 × 6 = 24	6 × 6 = 36	60 ÷ 6 = 10
5 × 6 = 30	4 × 6 = 24	48 ÷ 6 = 8
6 × 6 = 36	1 × 6 = 6	36 ÷ 6 = 6
7 × 6 = 42	9 × 6 = 54	6 ÷ 6 = 1
8 × 6 = 48	3 × 6 = 18	42 ÷ 6 = 7
9 × 6 = 54	7 × 6 = 42	18 ÷ 6 = 3
10 × 6 = 60	5 × 6 = 30	24 ÷ 6 = 4

7s		
Count-bys	Mixed Up ×	Mixed Up ÷
1 × 7 = 7	6 × 7 = 42	70 ÷ 7 = 10
2 × 7 = 14	8 × 7 = 56	14 ÷ 7 = 2
3 × 7 = 21	5 × 7 = 35	28 ÷ 7 = 4
4 × 7 = 28	9 × 7 = 63	56 ÷ 7 = 8
5 × 7 = 35	4 × 7 = 28	42 ÷ 7 = 6
6 × 7 = 42	10 × 7 = 70	63 ÷ 7 = 9
7 × 7 = 49	3 × 7 = 21	21 ÷ 7 = 3
8 × 7 = 56	1 × 7 = 7	49 ÷ 7 = 7
9 × 7 = 63	7 × 7 = 49	7 ÷ 7 = 1
10 × 7 = 70	2 × 7 = 14	35 ÷ 7 = 5

8s		
Count-bys	Mixed Up ×	Mixed Up ÷
1 × 8 = 8	6 × 8 = 48	16 ÷ 8 = 2
2 × 8 = 16	10 × 8 = 80	40 ÷ 8 = 5
3 × 8 = 24	7 × 8 = 56	72 ÷ 8 = 9
4 × 8 = 32	2 × 8 = 16	32 ÷ 8 = 4
5 × 8 = 40	4 × 8 = 32	8 ÷ 8 = 1
6 × 8 = 48	8 × 8 = 64	80 ÷ 8 = 10
7 × 8 = 56	5 × 8 = 40	64 ÷ 8 = 8
8 × 8 = 64	10 × 8 = 80	24 ÷ 8 = 3
9 × 8 = 72	3 × 8 = 24	56 ÷ 8 = 7
10 × 8 = 80	1 × 8 = 8	48 ÷ 8 = 6

Squares		
Count-bys	Mixed Up ×	Mixed Up ÷
1 × 1 = 1	3 × 3 = 9	25 ÷ 5 = 5
2 × 2 = 4	9 × 9 = 81	4 ÷ 2 = 2
3 × 3 = 9	4 × 4 = 16	81 ÷ 9 = 9
4 × 4 = 16	6 × 6 = 36	9 ÷ 3 = 3
5 × 5 = 25	2 × 2 = 4	36 ÷ 6 = 6
6 × 6 = 36	7 × 7 = 49	100 ÷ 10 = 10
7 × 7 = 49	10 × 10 = 100	16 ÷ 4 = 4
8 × 8 = 64	1 × 1 = 1	49 ÷ 7 = 7
9 × 9 = 81	5 × 5 = 25	1 ÷ 1 = 1
10 × 10 = 100	8 × 8 = 64	64 ÷ 8 = 8

Have students complete the Study Plan box on Homework and Remembering page 217. They should include any multiplications or divisions they missed in the Check Up. Remind students to bring home the Home Study Sheet C on Homework and Remembering page 215 to use for studying and testing with their Homework Helper.

Activity 2

Solve Missing Number Puzzles

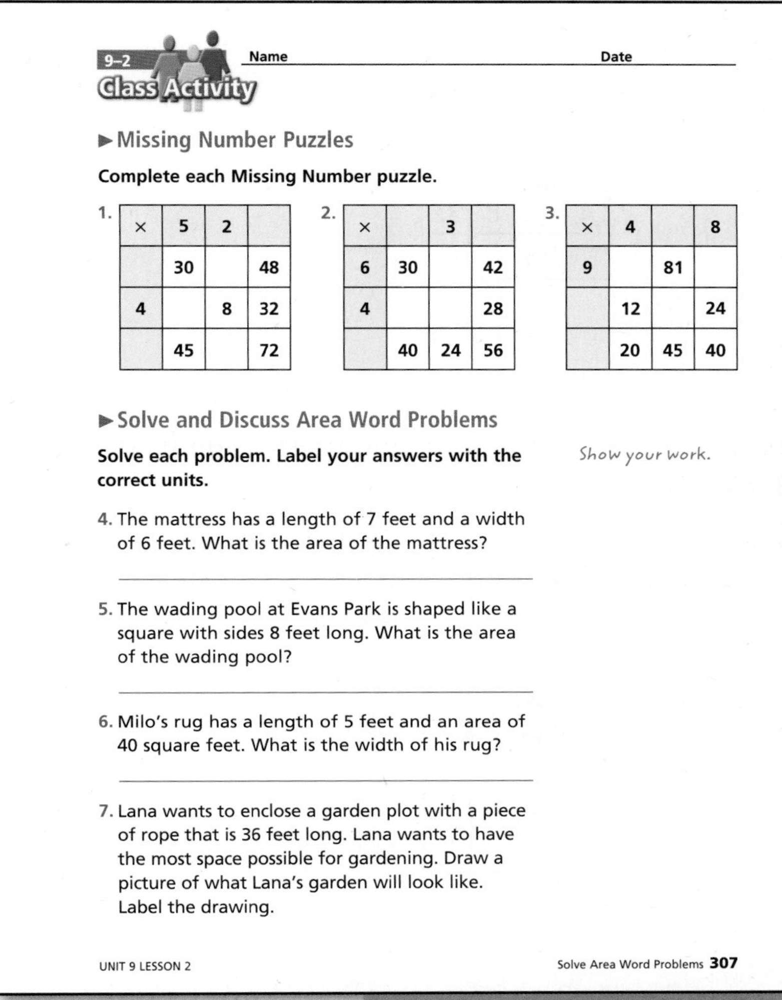

9–2 Class Activity

Name ______________________ Date __________

▶ Missing Number Puzzles

Complete each Missing Number puzzle.

1.

×	5	2	
	30		48
4		8	32
	45		72

2.

×		3	
6	30		42
4			28
	40	24	56

3.

×	4		8
9		81	
	12		24
	20	45	40

▶ Solve and Discuss Area Word Problems

Solve each problem. Label your answers with the correct units.

Show your work.

4. The mattress has a length of 7 feet and a width of 6 feet. What is the area of the mattress?

5. The wading pool at Evans Park is shaped like a square with sides 8 feet long. What is the area of the wading pool?

6. Milo's rug has a length of 5 feet and an area of 40 square feet. What is the width of his rug?

7. Lana wants to enclose a garden plot with a piece of rope that is 36 feet long. Lana wants to have the most space possible for gardening. Draw a picture of what Lana's garden will look like. Label the drawing.

UNIT 9 LESSON 2 Solve Area Word Problems 307

Student Activity Book page 307

20 MINUTES

Goal: Solve Missing Number puzzles.

Materials: Student Activity Book or Hardcover Book p. 307 and Activity Workbook p. 144, transparency of Student Book p. 307 (optional), Overhead projector (optional)

NCTM Standards:
Number and Operations
Algebra

▶ Missing Number Puzzles WHOLE CLASS

Ask students to look at the first Missing Number puzzle. Display a transparency of Student Book page 307, or re-create the puzzle on the board. Tell students that the numbers in the shaded part of the puzzle are factors and that those in the unshaded part are products.

Point to the 8 in the puzzle, and ask if anyone can explain how this product is related to the factors in the shaded squares. Help students see that 8 is the product of 4, the factor in the shaded square to its left, and 2, the factor in the shaded square above it.

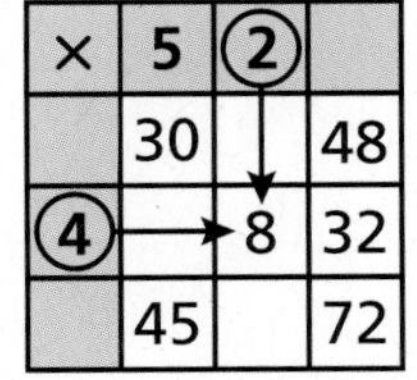

Multiply the number in the shaded square to the left by the number in the shaded square above.

$4 \times 2 = 8$

Activity continued ▶

Teaching Note

Math Background In this lesson, students will work with algebraic concepts as they find missing factors in multiplication. Finding missing factors will also expand students understanding of relationships between multiplication and division.

Teaching Note

What to Expect from Students
When seeing the puzzles for the first time, students may confuse them with the multiplication table, and how the factors in a multiplication table are ordered from least to greatest. Let students know that in these puzzles, the factors that are listed in a row or column are not ordered in a particular way, but they should note that the relationship of the factors and how they meet to form a product is still the same.

1 Teaching the Lesson (continued)

Differentiated Instruction

Extra Help Some students may have difficulty with the examples in the puzzles that involve finding the missing factor or divisor. Provide students with counters. Have them model the larger number (the product or the dividend). Then have students model the smaller number. Tell them that the smaller number represents one equal group. Ask, how many of these equal groups of 4 do we need to make the larger number?

larger number ●●●●●●●●●●●●●●●●●●●●●●●●●●●●●●●● 32

smaller number ○○○○ 4

Students should make more equal groups until they reach the larger number. Ask, how many smaller groups make up the larger group?

Teaching Note

Language and Vocabulary To reinforce algebraic concepts and to help **English learners**, have students practice reading equations aloud:

$\square \times 5 = 30$

Ask, *What number times 5 is equal to 30?*

$4 \times \square = 32$

Ask, *4 times what number is equal to 32?*

- Look at the empty square to the left of the 8. What number belongs in this square? 20 How do you know? I multiplied the factor in the shaded square to the left of the empty square, 4, by the factor in the shaded square above it, 5.

×	(5)	2	
	30		48
(4)		8	32
	45		72

$4 \times 5 = \square$

Write 20 in the square on the transparency, and have students do the same on Student Book page 307.

- Now look at the empty shaded square above the 4. What number belongs here? 6 How did you figure this out? The factor in the empty square times 5 must equal 30. So the factor must be 6.

×	(5)	2	
◯	30		48
4	20	8	32
	45		72

$\square \times 5 = 30$

If necessary, work with the class to fill in more of the squares. Then have students work independently to complete the second and third puzzles, providing help as needed. You might need to mention that sometimes it will be impossible to fill in a particular square until other parts of the puzzle have been completed. Select two students who finish early to fill in the puzzles on the transparency or to draw them on the board. When most students have finished, discuss the solutions.

Activity 3

Solve Area Word Problems

▶ Solve and Discuss Area Word Problems

WHOLE CLASS

Math Talk 

Using the **Solve and Discuss** structure, have students solve problem 4 on Student Activity Book page 307. You may need to explain that the words *length* and *width* refer to the lengths of adjacent sides of a rectangle. It doesn't matter which side is called the length and which is called the width. Some students may need to sketch the rectangle, but at this point very few should need to draw and count individual unit squares. If you see students doing this, remind them of the work they did with area in Unit D, and ask if they can think of a faster way to find the area.

Introduce the idea of using a Fast-Area Drawing to help solve problem 4. Explain that a Fast-Area Drawing is a quick sketch of a rectangle labeled with the given information, including the units. The rectangle's area goes in the center of the rectangle. Emphasize that students don't need to worry about making the sides appropriate lengths or drawing them perfectly straight.

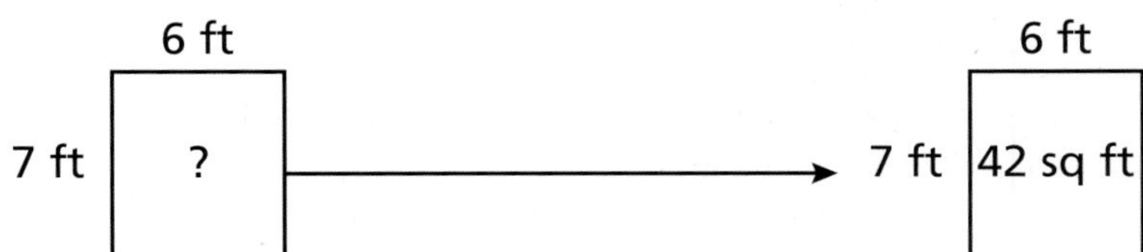

Label the lengths of the sides. The area is the unknown number.

Multiply the lengths of the sides to find the area.

Using **Solve and Discuss**, have students solve problems 5–7. Encourage them to try using Fast-Area Drawings.

Problem 6 gives the area of a rectangle and the length of one of its sides, and students must find the length of the other side.

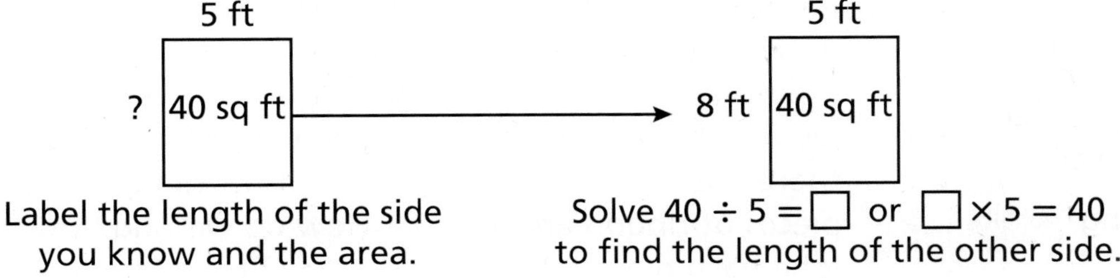

Label the length of the side you know and the area.

Solve $40 \div 5 = \square$ or $\square \times 5 = 40$ to find the length of the other side.

Problem 7 will be challenging for many students. Lead students to understand that while there are many different rectangles with a perimeter of 36 feet, the length and width of the rectangles always total 18. You may want to have students create an organized list of the lengths and widths that total 18 and the area of each rectangle.

 **25 MNUTES**

Goal: Solve word problems involving area.

Materials: Student Activity Book or Hardcover Book p. 307

 **NCTM Standards:**

Number and Operations
Measurement
Problem Solving
Representation

English Language Learners

Draw a rectangle and a square. Have children identify the length and width.

- **Beginning** Say: **Is *area* the *length* × *width*?** yes
- **Intermediate and Advanced** Ask: **What do I find when I multiply *length* × *width*?** area

Class Management

Looking Ahead Remind students to take home the Home Study Sheet C on Homework and Remembering page 215.

Ongoing Assessment

Ask questions such as the following:

- ▶ Find the area of a rectangle that has a length of 7 feet and a width of 5 feet.
- ▶ If you know the length of a side and the area of a rectangle, how can you find the width?

2 Going Further

Problem-Solving Strategy: Draw a Picture

Goal: Use the strategy of drawing a picture to solve problems.

Materials: Student Activity Book or Hardcover Book p. 308

 **NCTM Standards:**

Number and Operations
Measurement
Problem Solving
Representation

▶ Discuss the Draw a Picture Strategy

WHOLE CLASS

Math Talk

Ask students to describe how they have used the strategy of drawing pictures to help them solve problems. Possible responses: Equal-Shares Drawings, Comparison Bars, Area Drawings, Arrays, Repeated Groups

Have students discuss uses in daily life of the Draw a Picture Strategy to solve problems. Possible response: Arrange furniture in a room.

Explain to students that they will be working on word problems today. Also explain that when they read a word problem that involves thinking about what something looks like, drawing a picture is a good strategy to help them understand the situation.

▶ Problem-Solving Strategy: Draw a Picture

WHOLE CLASS

Have a volunteer read aloud problem 1 on Student Book page 308. Discuss students' ideas for how drawing a picture can help solve the word problem. Students may suggest that a picture would be easier than words to see the information in the problem.

- How can we show the ribbon with a drawing? Make a long rectangle.
- How do we show the pieces Ana cut in the drawing? We divide the long strip into three equal pieces. How do we find the length of each of the 3 pieces? Divide. $18 \div 3 = 6$
- How do we show the small pieces that Ana cut in the drawing? Draw lines to divide each of the three pieces in half.

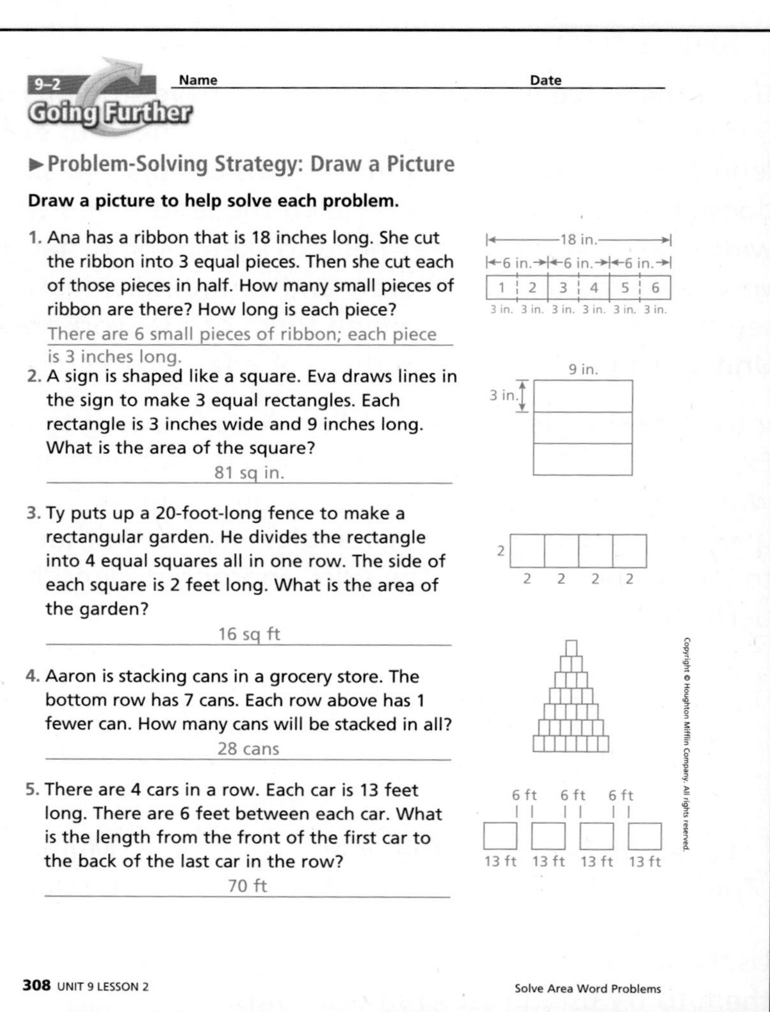

9–2 Going Further   Name   Date

▶ Problem-Solving Strategy: Draw a Picture

Draw a picture to help solve each problem.

1. Ana has a ribbon that is 18 inches long. She cut the ribbon into 3 equal pieces. Then she cut each of those pieces in half. How many small pieces of ribbon are there? How long is each piece?
   There are 6 small pieces of ribbon; each piece is 3 inches long.
2. A sign is shaped like a square. Eva draws lines in the sign to make 3 equal rectangles. Each rectangle is 3 inches wide and 9 inches long. What is the area of the square?
   81 sq in.
3. Ty puts up a 20-foot-long fence to make a rectangular garden. He divides the rectangle into 4 equal squares all in one row. The side of each square is 2 feet long. What is the area of the garden?
   16 sq ft
4. Aaron is stacking cans in a grocery store. The bottom row has 7 cans. Each row above has 1 fewer can. How many cans will be stacked in all?
   28 cans
5. There are 4 cars in a row. Each car is 13 feet long. There are 6 feet between each car. What is the length from the front of the first car to the back of the last car in the row?
   70 ft

308 UNIT 9 LESSON 2   Solve Area Word Problems

Student Activity Book page 308

- Re-read the problem to find what it asks for. What do we need to find? How many small pieces of ribbon are there? How long is each piece? How can we use the drawing to find how many small pieces there are? Count the small pieces. How many small pieces of ribbon are there? 6 How do we find how long each piece is? Divide. $6 \div 2 = 3$ How long is each piece? 3 inches

Have students complete problems 2–5 independently. To help students get started, encourage them to think about how they might draw a picture to show the situation or object described.

When students have completed their work, have students use **Solve and Discuss** to share their pictures and methods for solving the problems.

Intervention — Activity Card 9-2

Models for Area Problems
Activity Card 9-2 ●

Work: In pairs

Use:
- Connecting cubes
- Homework page 217

1. **Work Together** Use connecting cubes to model and solve area problems on Homework page 217.
2. Read exercise 4. Then look at the model below. How does the model represent the tabletop? The table top measures 3 ft by 6 ft; the model has 3 rows of 6 cubes each.

3. Count by 6s to find the area. Record the area in square units. 18 sq ft
4. Repeat the activity to solve problems 5–7.

Unit 9, Lesson 2

Activity Note Remind students that area is a measure of square units covering a surface. Students can check their work by counting the number of cubes.

Math Writing Prompt

Make a Drawing Which of these rectangles has a greater area? Rectangle A: length of 5 in., width of 4 in.; Rectangle B: length of 8 in., width of 2 in. Make a drawing to help explain how you know.

Software Support

Warm Up 45.24

On Level — Activity Card 9-2

Roll a Rectangle
Activity Card 9-2 ▲

Work: In pairs

Use:
- 2 Number cubes (labeled 1–6)
- TRB M31 (Centimeter Grid Paper)

Decide:

Who will be Student 1 and who will be Student 2 for the first round.

1. **Student 1:** Roll a number cube to choose the length of a rectangle.
2. **Student 2:** Roll the other number cube to choose the width.
3. Together draw a rectangle on grid paper, using the length and width you rolled.

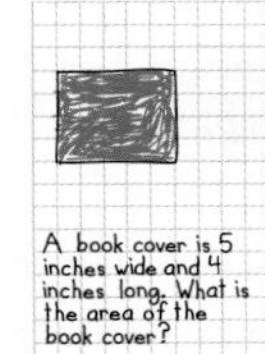

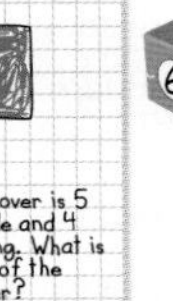

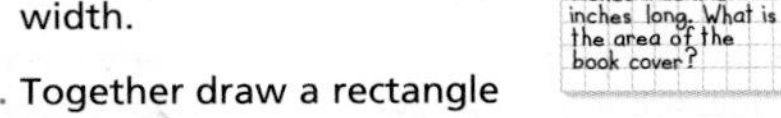

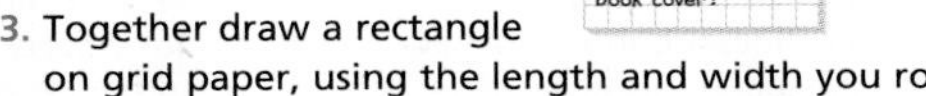

4. **Student 1:** Write a word problem for the drawing.
5. **Student 2:** Solve the problem.
6. Switch roles and repeat the activity.

Unit 9, Lesson 2

Activity Note Encourage students to include word problems giving the area and one dimension, with the second dimension as the answer.

Math Writing Prompt

Summarize Explain how you would find the area of the classroom floor.

Software Support

Shapes Ahoy: Ship Shapes, Level X

Challenge — Activity Card 9-2

Find the Greatest
Activity Card 9-2 ■

Work: In pairs

Use:
- TRB M31 (Centimeter-Grid Paper)

1. **Work Together** Solve these two problems.
   - Find the length and width of the rectangle with the greatest area if its perimeter is 24 inches. $6 \times 6 = 36$ square inches
   - Find the length and width of the rectangle with the greatest perimeter if its area is 18 square inches. $1 + 18 + 1 + 18 = 38$ inches
2. Draw all the possible rectangles on grid paper. Include the lengths and widths.
3. **Analyze** How does a rectangular shape need to change to increase the area or the perimeter? The area increases as the figure becomes more like a square; the perimeter increases as the figure becomes longer and narrower.

Unit 9, Lesson 2

Activity Note The rectangle with the greatest area is 6×6. The rectangle with the greatest perimeter is 1×18. The difference between length and width decreases as area increases. The difference increases as the perimeter increases.

Math Writing Prompt

Explain Your Thinking Explain how to estimate the area of your footprint.

Software Support

Course II: Module 3: Unit 1: Area

3 Homework and Spiral Review

9–2 **Homework** **Goal:** Additional Practice

✓ Include students' completed Homework page as part of their portfolios.

9–2 **Remembering** **Goal:** Spiral Review

This Remembering page would be appropriate anytime after today's lesson.

9–2 Homework Name ______ Date ______

Study Plan

______ Homework Helper

Complete each Missing Number puzzle.

1.

×	4	3	**6**
9	**36**	27	54
2	8	6	12
3	**12**	**9**	18

2.

×	**7**	5	**6**
4	**28**	20	**24**
6	42	**30**	36
8	**56**	40	**48**

3.

×	8	6	**4**
5	40	**30**	20
7	**56**	**42**	28
3	24	18	**12**

Solve each problem. Label your answers with the correct units.

4. Raul built a rectangular tabletop with a length of 3 feet and a width of 6 feet. What is the area of the tabletop?
18 sq ft

5. Li Fong covered the rectangular floor of his tree house with 48 square feet of carpeting. If one side of the floor has a length of 6 feet, what is the length of the adjacent side?
8 ft

6. Frances wants to paint a rectangular wall that has a width of 8 feet and a height of 9 feet. She has a quart of paint that will cover 85 square feet. What is the area of the wall? Does Frances have enough paint?
72 sq ft; yes

7. Willis cut out a paper rectangle with an area of 42 square centimeters. If one side has a length of 6 centimeters, what is the length of the adjacent side?
7 cm

UNIT 9 LESSON 2 Solve Area Word Problems 217

Homework and Remembering page 217

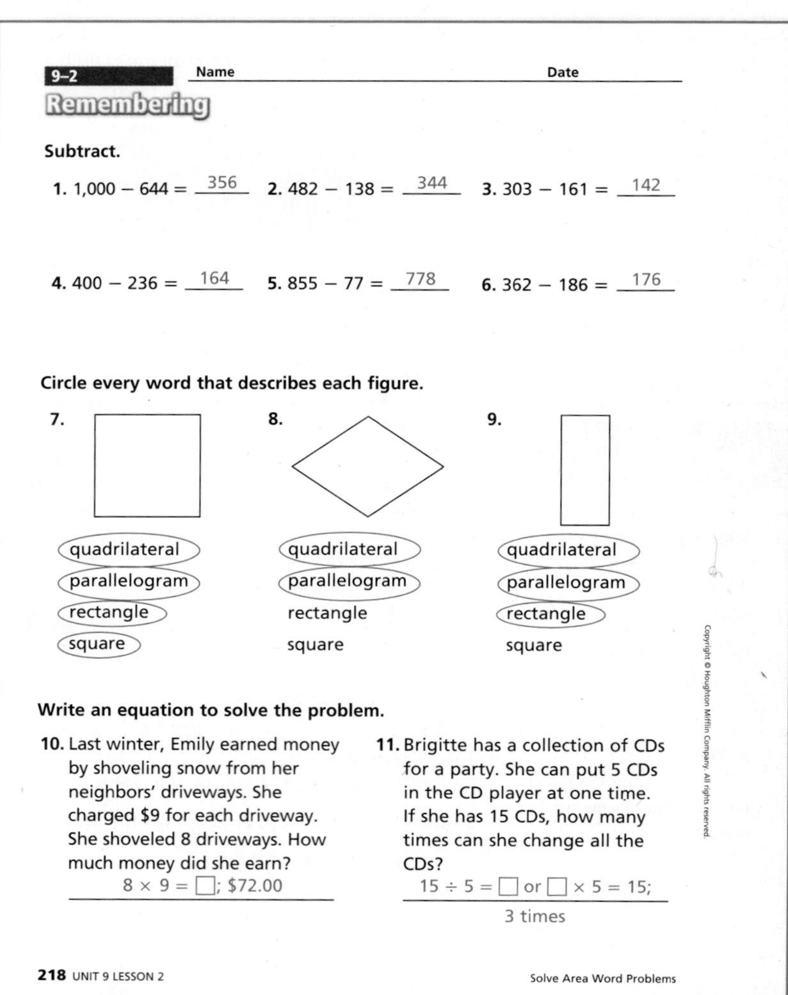
9–2 Remembering Name ______ Date ______

Subtract.

1. 1,000 − 644 = 356
2. 482 − 138 = 344
3. 303 − 161 = 142
4. 400 − 236 = 164
5. 855 − 77 = 778
6. 362 − 186 = 176

Circle every word that describes each figure.

7. (quadrilateral) (parallelogram) (rectangle) (square)

8. (quadrilateral) (parallelogram) rectangle square

9. (quadrilateral) (parallelogram) (rectangle) square

Write an equation to solve the problem.

10. Last winter, Emily earned money by shoveling snow from her neighbors' driveways. She charged $9 for each driveway. She shoveled 8 driveways. How much money did she earn?
8 × 9 = □; $72.00

11. Brigitte has a collection of CDs for a party. She can put 5 CDs in the CD player at one time. If she has 15 CDs, how many times can she change all the CDs?
15 ÷ 5 = □ or □ × 5 = 15; 3 times

218 UNIT 9 LESSON 2 Solve Area Word Problems

Homework and Remembering page 218

Home or School Activity

Real-World Connection

How Much Paint? A gallon of paint covers about 350 square feet. If a room is 9 feet wide by 10 feet long and each wall is 8 feet high, is a gallon of paint enough to cover the walls? Encourage students to draw and label a picture before finding the area of the walls.

Multiply and Divide with 8

Lesson Objectives

- Explore patterns in 8s count-bys, multiplications, and divisions.
- Use a variety of strategies to solve multiplication problems.

Vocabulary
Fast-Array drawing

The Day at a Glance

Today's Goals	Materials	
1 Teaching the Lesson A1: Practice count-bys, multiplications, and divisions. A2: Explore patterns in 8s count-bys, multiplications, and divisions. A3: Discuss strategies for finding 7 × 8 and 8 × 8. A4: Find the missing numbers in Fast-Array drawings.	**Lesson Activities** Student Activity Book pp. 309–312 or Student Hardcover Book pp. 309–312 Homework and Remembering pp. 219–222 Check Up materials Signature Sheets Study Sheets A-C Check Sheets 1–8 Dry-erase markers Sheet protectors Study Sheet Answer Strips Check Sheet Answer Strips Cardstock Strategy Cards Class Multiplication Table Poster Pointer	**Going Further** Activity Cards 9–3 Two-color counters Index cards MathBoard materials Math Journals Use Math Talk today!
2 Going Further ▸ Differentiated Instruction		
3 Homework and Spiral Review		

Keeping Skills Sharp

Quick Practice (5 MINUTES)

Goal: Practice 6s count-bys, multiplications, and divisions.

Materials: Class Multiplication Table Poster, pointer
Use the Class Poster and the number "6" for these activities.

Repeated Quick Practice
Use these Quick Practice activities from previous lessons.

6s Multiplications in Order (See Unit 7 Lesson 4.)

Mixed 6s Multiplications (See Unit 7 Lesson 2.)

Mixed 6s Divisions (See Unit 7 Lesson 5.)

Daily Routines

Homework Review Plan to set aside some time to work with students who had difficulty with parts of the homework.

Place Value Find the number that is 1,000 less than two thousand seventy-nine. 2,079; 1,079

1 Teaching the Lesson

Activity 1

Check Up and Independent Study

10 MINUTES

Goal: Practice count-bys, multiplications, and divisions.

Materials: Check Up materials: Signature Sheet; Study Sheets A–C, Check Sheets 1–8, dry-erase markers (1 per student), sheet protectors (1 per student), Study Sheet Answer Strips (TRB M54), Check Sheet Answer Strips (TRB M55), cardstock; Strategy Cards, Homework and Remembering p. 221

NCTM Standard:
Number and Operations

▶ Check Up with 6s PAIRS

Give **Student Pairs** a few minutes to test one another using Study Sheets A–C and collect signatures. For students who have already collected signatures on Study Sheets, have them use Check Sheets 1–8. You may want to have Study Sheet and Check Sheet Answer Strips (TRB M54–M55) available.

After **Student Pairs** have tested one another, give students two or three minutes to study independently using their Study Sheets, Check Sheets, or Strategy Cards. Then have students complete their Study Plan box at the top of Homework and Remembering page 221. Student should include 8s practice along with any multiplications or divisions they missed in the Check Up.

Activity 2

8s Multiplications and Divisions

25 MINUTES

Goal: Explore patterns in 8s count-bys, multiplications, and divisions.

Materials: Class Multiplication Table Poster, pointer, MathBoard materials, Student Activity Book or Hardcover Book p. 311

NCTM Standards:
Number and Operations
Algebra
Representation

▶ Explore Patterns with 8s WHOLE CLASS

Refer students to the 8s column of the Class Multiplication Table Poster. Ask which multiplications in the column they haven't studied yet. There are only two: 7×8 and 8×8.

Tell students that today they will be thinking about groups of 8. Ask what things in the real world come in groups of 8. legs on a spider, arms on an octopus, sides on a stop sign, pints in a gallon, and so on

Model the steps of this activity on the Class MathBoard as students follow along on their MathBoards. The completed board is reproduced on Student Book page 311. You can use it to facilitate a summary discussion of 8s patterns.

Have students circle sequential groups of 8, up to 80, on the Number Path and write the totals so far next to each group. After they circle the first group, have them say in unison, "1 group of 8 is 8"; after they circle the second group, have them say, "2 groups of 8 are 16"; and so on.

After students have circled all the groups, point to each group in order as students say in unison, "1 group of 8 is 8," "2 groups of 8 are 16," "3 groups of 8 are 24," and so on.

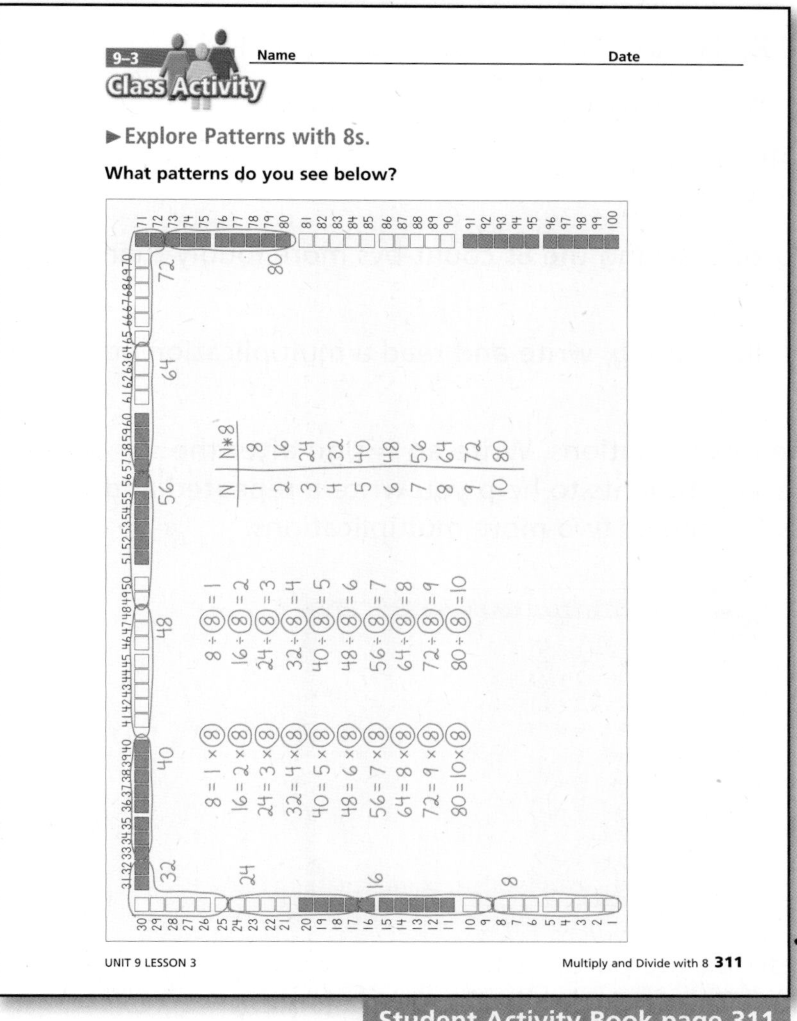
9-3 Class Activity

Name Date

► Explore Patterns with 8s.

What patterns do you see below?

N	N*8
1	8
2	16
3	24
4	32
5	40
6	48
7	56
8	64
9	72
10	80

8 = 1 × 8
16 = 2 × 8
24 = 3 × 8
32 = 4 × 8
40 = 5 × 8
48 = 6 × 8
56 = 7 × 8
64 = 8 × 8
72 = 9 × 8
80 = 10 × 8

8 ÷ 8 = 1
16 ÷ 8 = 2
24 ÷ 8 = 3
32 ÷ 8 = 4
40 ÷ 8 = 5
48 ÷ 8 = 6
56 ÷ 8 = 7
64 ÷ 8 = 8
72 ÷ 8 = 9
80 ÷ 8 = 10

UNIT 9 LESSON 3 Multiply and Divide with 8 **311**

Student Activity Book page 311

Teaching Note

Math Background The following pattern relates the 8s to the 10s.

1 × 8 = 1 ten	−	2 ones
2 × 8 = 2 tens	−	4 ones
3 × 8 = 3 tens	−	6 ones
4 × 8 = 4 tens	−	8 ones
5 × 8 = 5 tens	−	10 ones

In general, for any whole number N:

$N \times 8 = N$ tens − $(2 \times N)$ ones

Your students might discover this pattern on their own as they become more familiar with 8s multiplications. If you think students will find this pattern interesting or helpful, you may want to present it, even if no one mentions it. You might start by asking them to recall the pattern that relates the 9s to the 10s ($N \times 9 = N$ tens − N ones). Then ask whether they can find a similar pattern involving 8s.

Next, point to the totals on the class MathBoard as students say just the 8s count-bys aloud: 8, 16, 24, 32, 40, 48, 56, 64, 72, 80

- When we said the 8s count-bys, did you hear any 4s count-bys? yes I'm going to write the 4s count-bys on the board. Who can tell me what to write?

Write the 4s count-bys on the board.

4, 8, 12, 16, 20, 24, 28, 32, 36, 40

- Which of these numbers are also 8s count-bys? 8, 16, 24, 32, 40

Underline these numbers as students say them.

4, <u>8</u>, 12, <u>16</u>, 20, <u>24</u>, 28, <u>32</u>, 36, <u>40</u>

- What pattern do you see? Every other 4s count-by is also an 8s count-by. Why does this make sense? Because there are two 4s in 8; if you put two groups of 4 together, you get a group of 8.

Continue the list of 4s count-bys up to 80.

Activity continued ►

Teaching the Lesson (continued)

Math Talk in Action

Andrei: The 8s count-bys are like the 6s count-bys and the 4s count-bys and the 10s count-bys – They're all 2s count-bys.

Taylor: So the 8s count-bys are all even numbers!

Dennis: You can do the same thing we did with the 6s count-bys and 3s count-bys. Line up the 8s count-bys with the 4s count-bys under them.

8	16	24	32	40	48	56	64	72	80
4	8	12	16	20	24	28	32	36	40

The 8s count-bys are all two times the 4s count-bys under them.

JaNette: I see a pattern in the ones digits. It goes 8, 6, 4, 2, 0. Then it starts over again: 8, 6, 4, 2, 0.

Esteban: Remember how we matched up the 6s count-bys? I think you can do the same thing with the 8s count-bys. Just don't look at 80. Start at the outside and go to the center. The ones digits all add to 10. $8 + 2 = 10$, $6 + 4 = 10$, $4 + 6 = 10$, $2 + 8 = 10$.

Mai Lin: Also, try adding the numbers – not just the ones. $8 + 72 = 80$, $16 + 64 = 80$, $24 + 56 = 80$, $32 + 48 = 80$. You get 80 each time!

Yusef: Remember how we added the digits in the 6s count-bys? Can we do something like that here?

Celia: I think so. You think about 8 like 08 and add $0 + 8 = 8$. Then you add $1 + 6 = 7$, $2 + 4 = 6$, $3 + 2 = 5$, $4 + 0 = 4$, $4 + 8 = 12$, $5 + 6 = 11$, $6 + 4 = 10$, $7 + 2 = 9$, $8 + 0 = 8$. So you get 8, 7, 6, 5, 4, 12, 11, 10, 9, 8.

Jacob: Oh! You can do more with the 12, 11, and 10. Keep adding: $1 + 2 = 3$, $1 + 1 = 2$, $1 + 0 = 1$. Now you have 8, 7, 6, 5, 4, 3, 2, 1, 9, 8.

Then ask which of the new count-bys are 8s count-bys. Underline these numbers.

4, 8, 12, 16, 20, 24, 28, 32, 36, 40, 44, 48,
52, 56, 60, 64, 68, 72, 76, 80

- Read the list of 4s count-bys. Say the underlined numbers loudly and the other numbers softly.

Read the list as a group, saying the 8s count-bys more loudly than the other numbers.

Next, as students follow along, write and read a multiplication equation for each count-by.

Point to one of the multiplications. Write an = sign after the multiplication, and ask students to help you write a repeated addition expression. Do this for one or two more multiplications.

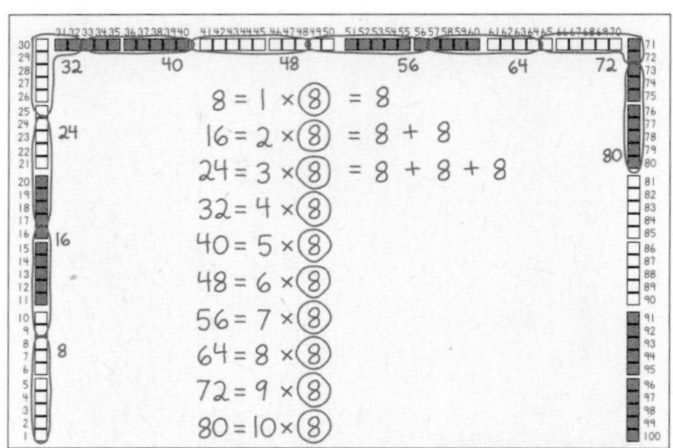

Ask students to describe the patterns they see in the count-bys and equations. (See **Math Talk in Action** in the side column.)

▶ Use the Class Multiplication Table Poster

WHOLE CLASS

On the Class Multiplication Table Poster, point to the equations in the 8s column in order and have the class read them aloud, using fingers to show the multiplier.

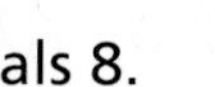
1 times 8 equals 8.

2 times 8 equals 16.

3 times 8 equals 24.

Point to each equation in the 8s column again, this time having students say only the count-bys. Again, have them use their fingers to indicate the multipliers.

8

16

24

▶ Use Fingers to Multiply WHOLE CLASS

Present 8s multiplications and have students count up on their fingers to find the answers. For example, to find 4 × 8, they should count by 8s, raising a finger for each count-by, until 4 fingers are raised.

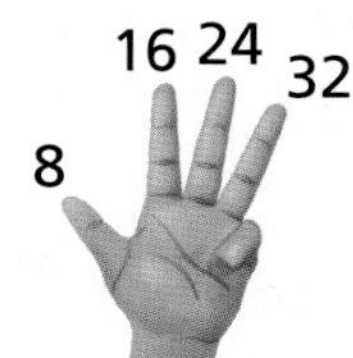

4 times 8 equals 32.

Ask how students could use the "5s shortcut" to find 7 × 8 quickly. Start with all 5 fingers up on one hand, say 40, and count up from there.

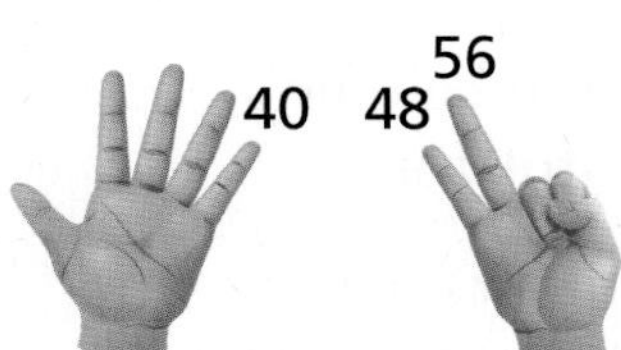

7 times 8 equals 56.

Have students use the shortcut to find 6 × 8 and 9 × 8.

▶ Divide with 8s WHOLE CLASS

Erase the repeated addition expressions from the Class MathBoard. Work with students to write the first two or three related division equations, and then have them work independently to write the rest.

8 = 1 × ⑧ 8 ÷ ⑧ = 1
16 = 2 × ⑧ 16 ÷ ⑧ = 2
24 = 3 × ⑧ 24 ÷ ⑧ = 3
32 = 4 × ⑧ 32 ÷ ⑧ = 4
40 = 5 × ⑧ 40 ÷ ⑧ = 5
48 = 6 × ⑧ 48 ÷ ⑧ = 6
56 = 7 × ⑧ 56 ÷ ⑧ = 7
64 = 8 × ⑧ 64 ÷ ⑧ = 8
72 = 9 × ⑧ 72 ÷ ⑧ = 9
80 = 10 × ⑧ 80 ÷ ⑧ = 10

Have students turn over their MathBoards. Hide the division equations on the Class MathBoard. Write the following division and related unknown multiplication equation on the board.

$24 \div 8 = \square \qquad \square \times 8 = 24$

Ask students to try to find the unknown number without using count-bys. They should think "What number times 8 is 24?" and consider the multiplications they know. (They may use count-bys if they can't figure out the answer this way.) Repeat for 16 ÷ 8, 32 ÷ 8, and 72 ÷ 8.

Activity continued ▶

Differentiated Instruction

Extra Help Some students might still be having difficulty finding the missing number in a multiplication equation. Encourage them to draw a picture of the situation, using whichever image they find most helpful.

Repeated Groups

For instance, they can think of $\square \times 8 = 24$ as a repeated groups situation: *How many groups of 8 have a total of 24?* Then they can draw groups of 8 dots until they have drawn 24 dots in all.

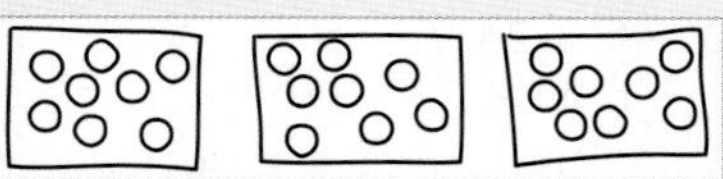

3 groups of 8 dots equal 24 dots in all.
3 × 8 = 24

Area Model

Some students might prefer to think of an area model: *How many rows of 8 squares have a total of 24 in all?* Give them grid paper and have them color rows of 8 squares until they have colored 24 squares in all.

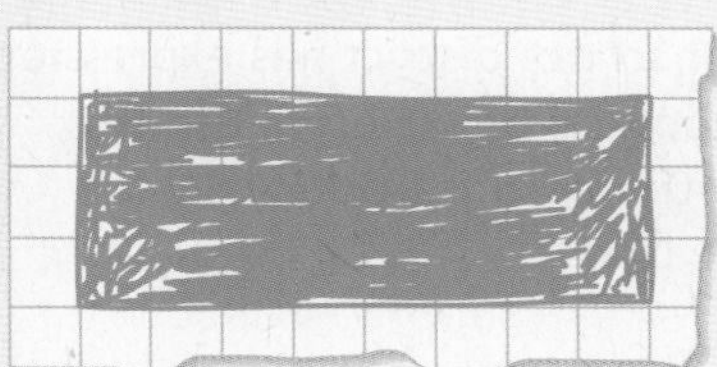

A 3-by-8 rectangle equals 24 squares.
3 × 8 = 24

Fast-Area Drawing

Other students might use a Fast-Area Drawing to represent $\square \times 8 = 24$.

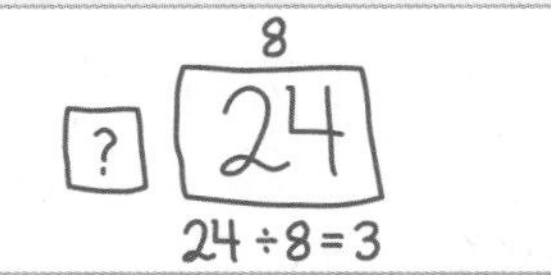

Teaching Note

Math Background To help students count up or back by 8s, you might want to discuss the Make a Ten strategy. The following are two examples.

- To find 56 + 8, start with 56. Add 4 to get 60, and then add 4 more to get 64. In symbols, $56 + 8 = 56 + 4 + 4 = 60 + 4 = 64$.
- To find 32 − 8, start with 32. Subtract 2 to get 30, and then subtract 6 more to get 24. In symbols, $32 - 8 = 32 - 2 - 6 = 30 - 6 = 24$.

Teaching Note

An **algebraic expression** consists of one or more variables. It usually contains some constants and one or more operations.

$$N * 8 + 2$$

variable (N) constants (8, 2)

If your school district has expressions as a topic to be covered, use this opportunity to introduce 8*N* for *N* * 8.

For the divisions 48 ÷ 8, 56 ÷ 8, and 64 ÷ 8, most students will need to use count-bys. Write the following division and related unknown multiplication equation on the board.

$$56 \div 8 = \square \qquad \square \times 8 = 56$$

Have students count up on their fingers to find the answers. Seven fingers will be raised, indicating that there are 7 groups of 8 in 56. So, 56 ÷ 8 = 7.

Ask how students could have used the "5s shortcut" to find the unknown number. Start with all 5 fingers up on one hand, say "40," and count by 8s from there until you reach 56.

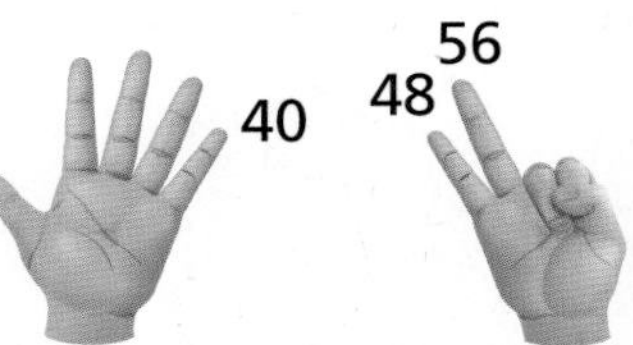

56 divided by 8 equals 7.

▶ Make a Function Table for 8s Count-bys WHOLE CLASS

Make a two-column table with column heads *N* and *N* * 8 on the Class MathBoard.

- Make a function table. The first column of this table is labeled *N*. What does *N* stand for? any number You can put any number in this column.
- The second column is labeled *N* * 8. This is the rule for the function table. What does this rule say to do? Multiply each number in the *N* column by 8.

Write 1 as the first entry in the *N* column.

- Use 1 for our first value of *N*. What does the rule say to do with 1? Multiply it by 8. What is the answer when the rule is used? 8

Enter 8 in the second column. Then write 2 as the second entry in the first column.

- Now use 2 for the value of *N*. What happens to 2? Multiply it by 8. What is the answer when that's done? 16 Write 16 in the *N* * 8 column, next to the 2.

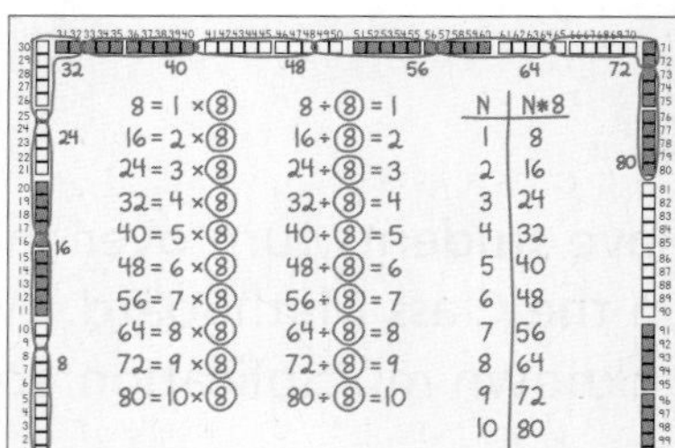

Repeat this process for *N* values 3 and 4. Then ask students to complete the table for *N* values through 10.

Point out that the numbers in the *N* * 8 column are the 8s count-bys.

- You can see from the table that you can find any count-by by counting up or counting back from a count-by you know. Remember, it is easiest to start with a count-by that is close to the one you want to find.

Ask a volunteer to explain how to find 7 × 8 by counting up from 5 × 8. Ask another to explain how to find 8 × 8 by counting back from 9 × 8.

Activity 3

Strategies for 8s Multiplications

▶ Discuss Strategies for 7 × 8 and 8 × 8

WHOLE CLASS

Math Talk 

Write the following two multiplication equations on the board.

$7 \times 8 = \square \qquad 8 \times 8 = \square$

Ask for a volunteer to describe a strategy for finding the product in the first multiplication. Allow the student to come to the board to explain if necessary. Encourage other students to ask questions if they don't understand. Then ask if anyone can think of a different strategy. Allow as many different methods as possible to be presented. If no one mentions the following methods, you might suggest them yourself.

- Start with 5 × 8, and count by 8 from there.
  5 × 8 = 40, plus 8 more is 48, plus 8 more is 56. So, 7 × 8 = 56.
- Combine two multiplications you know.

4 × 8 = 32	4 eights are 32.
3 × 8 = 24	3 eights are 24.
7 × 8 = 56	7 eights are 56.

- Double a 4s multiplication.
  7 × 8 is twice as much as 7 × 4, which is 28. So, 7 × 8 = 28 + 28 = 56.

Repeat this process for 8 × 8. For this product, students might suggest starting at 9 × 8, or 72, and subtracting 8 to get 64.

 **10 MINUTES**

Goal: Discuss strategies for finding 7 × 8 and 8 × 8.

 **NCTM Standard:**
Number and Operations

Teaching Note

Watch For! When using the doubling strategy for multiplication, some students might erroneously double both factors. For instance, they might consider the multiplication 6 × 8 to be double 3 × 4. Then, recalling that 3 × 4 = 12, they might find 6 × 8 by adding 12 + 12 = 24.

Always encourage students to consider the reasonableness of their answers. In this case, if a student recalls that 6 × 5 = 30, point out that the product 6 × 8 must be greater than 30, and so 24 is not a reasonable answer.

Activity 4

Complete Fast-Array Drawings

▶ Review Fast-Array Drawings

WHOLE CLASS

Draw the Fast-Array drawing at right on the board.

Remind students that they learned about Fast-Array drawings in Unit 7 and that one appears on each Strategy Card. Review the key features of a Fast-Array drawing, eliciting as much information as possible from students. Make sure the points at the top of the following page are made.

```
   4
 OOOO
 O
 O
 O
8O  32
 O
 O
 O
 O
```

Activity continued ▶

 **10 MINUTES**

Goal: Find the missing numbers in Fast-Array drawings.

Materials: Student Activity Book or Hardcover Book p. 312

 **NCTM Standards:**
Number and Operations
Representation

Teaching the Lesson (continued)

Ongoing Assessment

Give students the following multiplication equation.

6 × 8 = ☐

Ask questions such as the following:

- ▶ How can you find the unknown number using 5 × 8 = 40?
- ▶ How can you find the unknown number using 3 × 8 = 24?
- ▶ How can you find the unknown number using 2 × 8 = 16 and 4 × 8 = 32?

After students have determined that the unknown number is 48, give them the following division equation.

48 ÷ 8 = ☐

Ask:

- ▶ What is the unknown number in this equation? How do you know?

Class Management

Looking Ahead Remind students to take home the 8s chart and the Home Check Sheet 8 on Homework and Remembering pages 219–220.

English Language Learners

Draw an 8×4 array and an 8×4 *fast array*. Have students point to the *fast array*.

- **Beginning** Ask: **Is the *product* the number in the center or on the side?** center **Are 8 and 4 the *factors*?** yes
- **Intermediate** Say: **The center number is the ___.** product **8 and 4 are ___.** factors
- **Advanced** Have children tell how the arrays are alike and different. Make sure they use *factor* and *product* correctly.

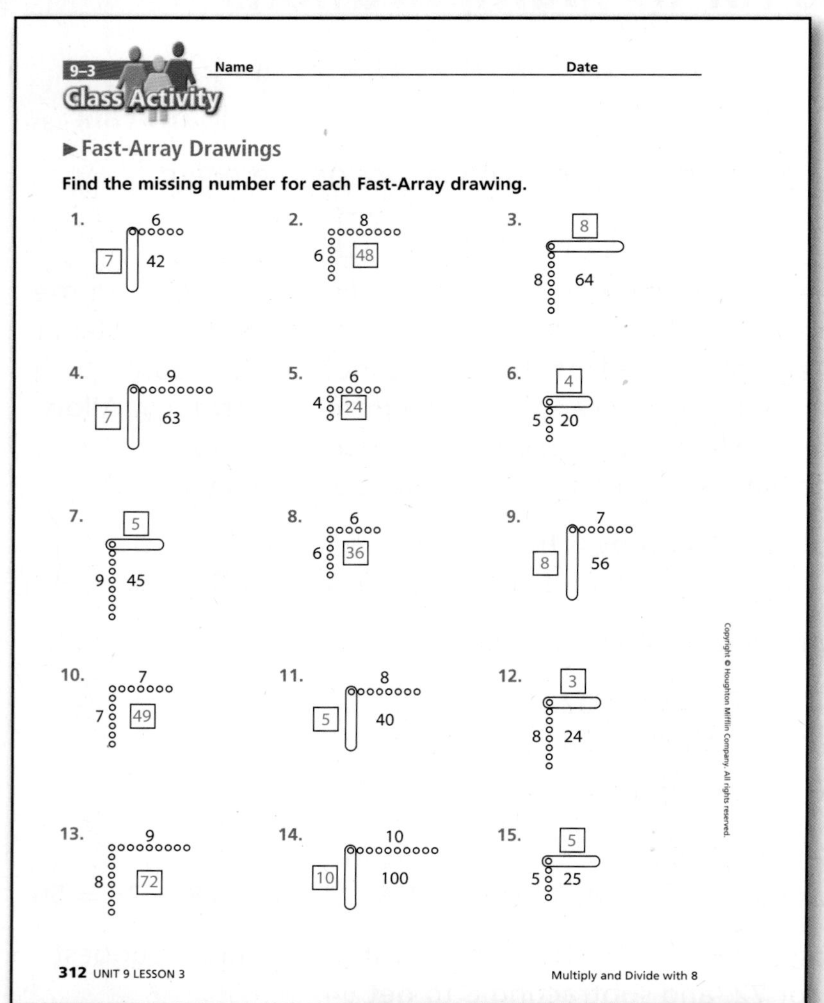

9–3 Class Activity Name Date

▶ Fast-Array Drawings

Find the missing number for each Fast-Array drawing.

1. 6; [7]; 42
2. 8; 6; [48]
3. [8]; 8; 64
4. 9; [7]; 63
5. 6; 4; [24]
6. [4]; 5; 20
7. [5]; 9; 45
8. 6; 6; [36]
9. 7; [8]; 56
10. 7; 7; [49]
11. 8; [5]; 40
12. [3]; 8; 24
13. 9; 8; [72]
14. 10; [10]; 100
15. [5]; 5; 25

312 UNIT 9 LESSON 3 Multiply and Divide with 8

Student Activity Book page 312

- The two numbers on the sides are factors. The number in the center is the product.
- You can multiply the two side numbers (the factors) to get the center number (the product).
- You can divide the center number by either of the side numbers to get the other side number.
- You can write eight equations for each Fast-Array drawing. Elicit the eight equations for this Fast-Array drawing:

8 × 4 = 32	4 × 8 = 32	32 ÷ 8 = 4	32 ÷ 4 = 8
32 = 8 × 4	32 = 4 × 8	4 = 32 ÷ 8	8 = 32 ÷ 4

▶ Fast-Array Drawings INDIVIDUALS

Give students a few minutes to find the unknown number in each of the Fast-Array drawings on Student Book page 312, and then discuss the answers.

2 Going Further

Differentiated Instruction

Intervention

Activity Card 9-3

Models for 8s Strategies

Activity Card 9-3 ●

Work: On your own

Use:

- 56 two-color counters
- MathBoard materials

1. Use counters on your MathBoard to break down a multiplication expression into two expressions that are easier to multiply.
2. Arrange counters into rows using a single color to represent 7 × 8. Then turn over two rows of counters to show the expressions 5 × 8 plus 2 × 8.

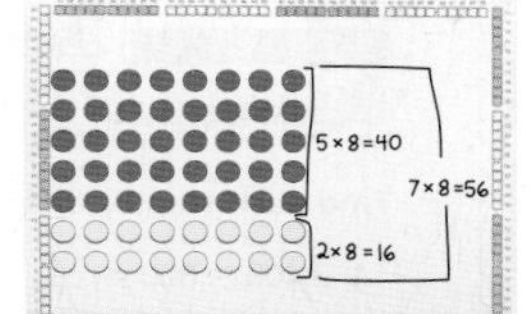

3. Repeat the activity two more times. Break down 6 × 8 into 3 × 8 plus 3 × 8. Break down 4 × 8 into 5 × 8 minus 1 × 8.

Unit 9, Lesson 3

Activity Note Some students may have difficulty modeling 4 × 8 as the difference between two multiplications. Show this breakdown as 5 rows of 8, with 1 row turned over. Four rows are the product.

Math Writing Prompt

Explain Your Thinking A student wrote 48 ÷ 8 = 8. Is the quotient correct? Explain how you can check by multiplying.

Software Support

Warm Up 12.20

On Level

Activity Card 9-3

8s Equation Game

Activity Card 9-3 ▲

Work: In pairs

Use:

- 20 Index cards

1. Make a set of 20 game cards as shown at the right.

8	18	30	48	60
12	20	32	50	64
14	24	40	54	72
16	28	42	56	80

2. Shuffle the cards and place them facedown in a stack. Take turns picking a card and deciding if the number you pick is an 8s count-by. If it is not, your partner takes a turn.
3. If the card you draw is an 8s count-by, use the number to write a correct 8s multiplication equation and a correct 8s division equation.
4. Score 1 point for each correct equation. When all cards have been drawn, the higher score wins.

Unit 9, Lesson 3

Activity Note Players should check each other's equations. If a player writes an incorrect equation, the turn is forfeited to the other player, who also gets a point for correcting the equation.

Math Writing Prompt

Choose a Strategy Which 8s multiplication is hardest for you to remember? What strategy do you use to help you remember it?

Software Support

Numberopolis: Cross Town Number Line, Level R

Challenge

Activity Card 9-3

Break the Code

Activity Card 9-3 ■

Work: In pairs

1. Each symbol in the equations represents a one-digit number. Use the equations to find the code for each symbol. Begin with the multiplication equations.

♥ − 3 = ✻ ● × ▲ = 24
● × ♥ = 48 ■ + ✻ = ★
20 ÷ ✻ = ▲ ◆ − ★ = ■
■ + 3 = ✻ ✿ + ● = ★

○ = 6, ♡ = 8, △ = 4, ✳ = 5, □ = 2, ☆ = 7, ◊ = 9, ✿ = 1

2. Think Which one-digit numbers are factors of both 24 and 48? Which of these factors could work in both equations? 1, 2, 3, 4, 6, and 8; 6 × 8 and 6 × 4
3. Now use substitution to find the values of the symbols in the remaining equations. Make a list of all the symbols and their values.

Unit 9, Lesson 3

Activity Note If time permits, have each student create a different code and use it to write an original set of equations. Partners should exchange equations and try to break the codes.

Math Writing Prompt

Investigate Math How can you use the fact that 56 ÷ 8 is equal to 7 to find the quotient 112 ÷ 8?

DESTINATION Math® **Software Support**

Course II: Module 2: Unit 3: Dividing by a 1-digit Number

Homework and Spiral Review

9–3 **Homework** **Goal:** Additional Practice

This Homework page provides practice in multiplying and dividing 8s.

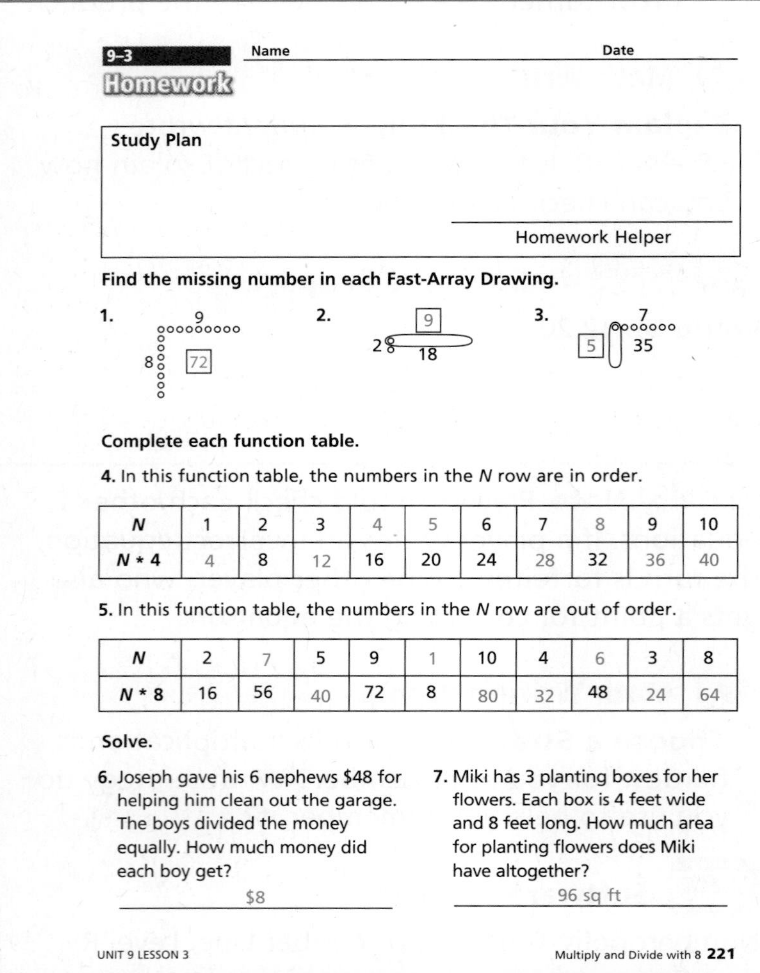

9–3 Homework Name Date

Study Plan

Homework Helper

Find the missing number in each Fast-Array Drawing.

1. 9, 8, 72
2. 9, 2, 18
3. 7, 5, 35

Complete each function table.

4. In this function table, the numbers in the *N* row are in order.

N	1	2	3	4	5	6	7	8	9	10
N * 4	4	8	12	16	20	24	28	32	36	40

5. In this function table, the numbers in the *N* row are out of order.

N	2	7	5	9	1	10	4	6	3	8
N * 8	16	56	40	72	8	80	32	48	24	64

Solve.

6. Joseph gave his 6 nephews $48 for helping him clean out the garage. The boys divided the money equally. How much money did each boy get?
$8

7. Miki has 3 planting boxes for her flowers. Each box is 4 feet wide and 8 feet long. How much area for planting flowers does Miki have altogether?
96 sq ft

UNIT 9 LESSON 3 Multiply and Divide with 8 **221**

Homework and Remembering page 221

9–3 **Remembering** **Goal:** Spiral Review

This Remembering page would be appropriate anytime after today's lesson.

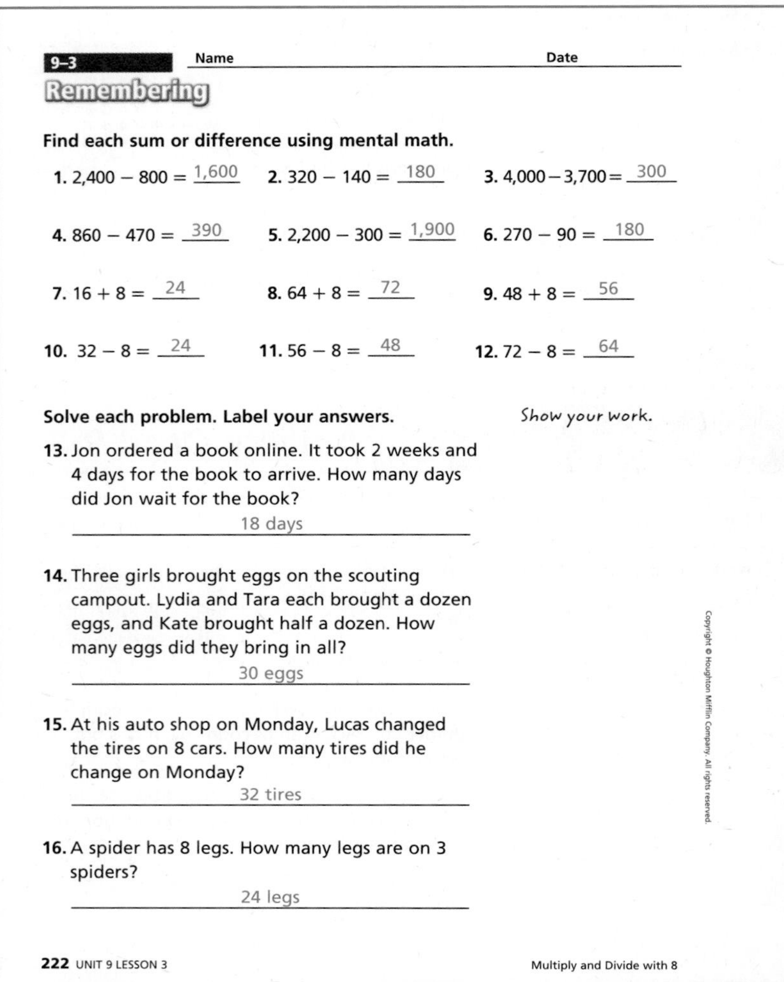

9–3 Remembering Name Date

Find each sum or difference using mental math.

1. 2,400 − 800 = 1,600
2. 320 − 140 = 180
3. 4,000 − 3,700 = 300
4. 860 − 470 = 390
5. 2,200 − 300 = 1,900
6. 270 − 90 = 180
7. 16 + 8 = 24
8. 64 + 8 = 72
9. 48 + 8 = 56
10. 32 − 8 = 24
11. 56 − 8 = 48
12. 72 − 8 = 64

Solve each problem. Label your answers. *Show your work.*

13. Jon ordered a book online. It took 2 weeks and 4 days for the book to arrive. How many days did Jon wait for the book?
18 days

14. Three girls brought eggs on the scouting campout. Lydia and Tara each brought a dozen eggs, and Kate brought half a dozen. How many eggs did they bring in all?
30 eggs

15. At his auto shop on Monday, Lucas changed the tires on 8 cars. How many tires did he change on Monday?
32 tires

16. A spider has 8 legs. How many legs are on 3 spiders?
24 legs

222 UNIT 9 LESSON 3 Multiply and Divide with 8

Homework and Remembering page 222

Home or School Activity

Social Studies Connection

Chess The game of chess is played on a board with 8 rows (called ranks) of 8 squares. There are 8 columns, called files. Each player has 16 game pieces. There are 8 pawns, 2 rooks (they look like towers), 2 knights (horses), 2 bishops, a queen, and a king. Show students what the board and game pieces look like. Have students find the area of the chess board. Then have students look up the correct placement of the game pieces and the moves permitted by each piece. Encourage students to learn how to play!

Write Word Problems and Equations

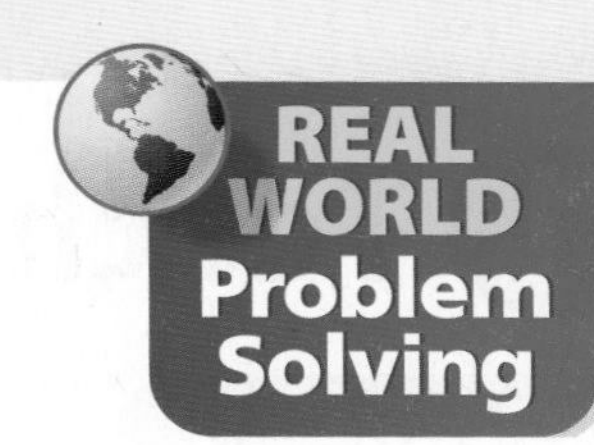

Vocabulary
array problem
repeated-groups problem
area problem
equation
variable

Lesson Objective

- **Write multiplication and division word problems of various types.**

The Day at a Glance

Today's Goals	Materials	
1 Teaching the Lesson **A1:** Take Sprints for 6s multiplications and divisions. **A2:** Practice count-bys, multiplications, and divisions. **A3:** Solve word problems, identify types of word problems, and write word problems. **A4:** Write equations with variables (Extension).	**Lesson Activities** Student Activity Book pp. 313–316 or Student Hardcover Book pp. 313–316 and Activity Workbook pp. 146–148 (includes Check Sheet and Special Format) Homework and Remembering pp. 223–224 Blank Sprint Answer Sheet (TRB M57) Check Up materials Signature sheet Study Sheets A-C Check Sheets 1–8 Dry-erase markers Sheet protectors	Study Sheet Answer Strips (TRB M54) Check Sheet Answer Strips (TRB M55) Cardstock Strategy cards
2 Going Further ▸ Differentiated Instruction		**Going Further** Activity Cards 9–4 Fill in the Blanks (TRB M103) Math Journals
3 Homework and Spiral Review		

Use Math Talk today!

Keeping Skills Sharp

Quick Practice (5 MINUTES)

Goal: Practice 8s count-bys, multiplications, and divisions.

Materials: Class Multiplication Table Poster, pointer
Display the Class Multiplication Table Poster. Use the number "8" for these activities.

Repeated Quick Practice
Use these Quick Practice activities from previous lessons.

8s Multiplications in Order (See Unit 7 Lesson 4.)

Mixed 8s Multiplications (See Unit 7 Lesson 2.)

Mixed 8s Divisions (See Unit 7 Lesson 5.)

Daily Routines

Homework Review Let students work together to check their work and correct errors.

Strategy Problem An extra-large popcorn costs 89¢, a large popcorn costs 81¢, and a medium popcorn costs 73¢. If the pattern continues, how much will the small popcorn cost? Explain.
65¢; Small is after medium.

89¢ → -8¢ → 81¢ → -8¢ → 73¢ → -8¢ → 65¢

1 Teaching the Lesson

Activity 1

Assess 6s

 5 MINUTES

Goal: Take Sprints for 6s multiplications and divisions.

Materials: Student Activity Book p. 313 or Activity Workbook p. 146, Blank Sprint Answer Sheet (TRB M57), Signature Sheet (Student Activity Book pp. 205–206 or Activity Workbook p. 77)

 **NCTM Standard:**
Number and Operations

 **Class Management**

If students are struggling with count-bys, you might give a count-by Sprint.

▶ Sprints for 6s PAIRS

Direct students to Student Book page 313 or Activity Workbook p. 146 and read the two Sprints below.

$\times 6$	$\div 6$
a. 4×6 24	**a.** $12 \div 6$ 2
b. 9×6 54	**b.** $30 \div 6$ 5
c. 1×6 6	**c.** $6 \div 6$ 1
d. 5×6 30	**d.** $54 \div 6$ 9
e. 7×6 42	**e.** $24 \div 6$ 4
f. 2×6 12	**f.** $48 \div 6$ 8
g. 8×6 48	**g.** $18 \div 6$ 3
h. 3×6 18	**h.** $36 \div 6$ 6
i. 6×6 36	**i.** $60 \div 6$ 10
j. 10×6 60	**j.** $42 \div 6$ 7

Have **Student Pairs** check each other's work as you read the answers, marking any incorrect answers, and getting any signatures.

Activity 2

Check Up and Independent Study

 5 MINUTES

Goal: Practice count-bys, multiplications, and divisions.

Materials: Check Up materials: Signature Sheet; Study Sheets A–C, Check Sheets 1–8, dry-erase markers (1 per student), sheet protectors (1 per student), Study Sheet Answer Strips (TRB M54), Check Sheet Answer Strips (TRB M55), cardstock; Strategy Cards, Homework and Remembering page 223

 **NCTM Standard:**
Number and Operations

▶ Check Up with 6s and 8s PAIRS

Give **Student Pairs** a few minutes to test one another using Study Sheets A–C and collect signatures. For students who have already collected signatures on Study Sheets, have them use Check Sheets 1–8. You may want to have Study Sheet and Check Sheet Answer Strips (TRB M54–M55) available.

After **Student Pairs** have tested one another, give students two or three minutes to study independently using their Study Sheets, Check Sheets, or Strategy Cards. Then have students complete their Study Plan box on Homework and Remembering page 223, including any multiplications or divisions they missed during the Check Up or Sprint.

Activity 3

Write Word Problems

9–4 Class Activity

Name ______ Date ______

► Identify the Type and Choose the Operation

Solve. Then circle what type it is and what operation you use.

1. Students in Mr. Till's class hung their paintings on the wall. They made 6 rows, with 5 paintings in each row. How many paintings did the students hang?
   30 paintings

   Circle one: (array) repeated groups area
   Circle one: (multiplication) division

2. Write your own problem that is the same type as problem 1. Answers will vary.

3. There are 8 goldfish in each tank at the pet store. If there are 56 goldfish in all, how many tanks are there?
   7 tanks

   Circle one: array (repeated groups) area
   Circle one: multiplication (division)

4. Write your own problem that is the same type as problem 3. Answers will vary.

5. Pierre built a rectangular pen for his rabbits. The pen is 4 feet wide and 6 feet long. What is the area of the pen? 24 square feet

   Circle one: array repeated groups (area)
   Circle one: (multiplication) division

314 UNIT 9 LESSON 4 Write Word Problems and Equations

Student Activity Book page 314

40 MINUTES

Goal: Solve word problems, identify types of word problems, and write word problems.

Materials: Student Activity Book or Hardcover Book pp. 314–316 and Activity Workbook pp. 147–148

NCTM Standards:
Number and Operations
Measurement
Problem Solving

► Identify the Type and Choose the Operation

WHOLE CLASS

Math Talk Tell students that today they will use **Solve and Discuss** to solve word problems and then write and share similar problems of their own.

Have students look at problem 1 on Student Book page 314. Read the word problem aloud. Give students a minute or two to solve it, and then have a volunteer present the solution. As a class, establish that this is an array multiplication problem, and have students ring the appropriate choices to identify it as such.

For problem 2, make sure students understand that they should write an array problem involving multiplication. Give them a few minutes to work individually or in pairs on their problems.

Activity continued ►

Differentiated Instruction

Extra Help If some students have difficulty writing their own word problems, you might try one of the following ideas.

- ► Have them cross out the nouns and numbers and replace them with other nouns and numbers. Make sure they consider whether the numbers they are replacing are factors or products.
- ► Have them sketch the array, rectangle, or groups for the given problem and then add or erase one column, row, or group. Then help them think of a situation for the revised drawing. ("What could this be? Six rows of what? Groups of 8 what?")

Ongoing Assessment

As students work on problems 3–10, observe their written responses. Ask questions such as the following:

- How did you decide that this is an array problem (or a repeated groups problem or an area problem)?
- How did you decide that you should multiply (or divide) to solve this problem?
- How do you know that the problem you wrote is the same type as the problem that was given to you?

English Language Learners

Give students as much support as possible as they write their own word problems.

- **Beginning** Model how to change the nouns and numbers in a word problem to make a new one.
- **Intermediate and Advanced** Have students work in pairs. First they tell the new word problem, then write it.

Class Management

Looking Ahead The student problems you collect at the end of this lesson will be used for Activity 5 (Communication) in Lesson 14 (Use Mathematical Processes). You might want to photocopy the problems, make transparencies of them, or write them on large pieces of chart paper for this purpose.

9–4 Class Activity Name ______ Date ______

6. Write your own problem that is the same type as problem 5. Answers will vary.

Solve the word problem. Then circle what type it is and circle the operation you would use.

7. Paulo arranged 72 baseball cards in 9 rows and a certain number of columns. How many columns did he arrange the cards into? 8 columns

Circle one: (array) repeated groups area
Circle one: multiplication (division)

8. Write your own problem that is the same type as Problem 7. Answers will vary.

9. The store sells bottles of juice in six-packs. Mr. Lee bought 9 six-packs for a picnic. How many bottles did he buy? 54 bottles of juice

Circle one: array (repeated groups) area
Circle one: (multiplication) division

10. Write your own problem that is the same type as Problem 9. Answers will vary.

11. Math Journal Write an area multiplication problem. Draw a Fast Array to solve it.

UNIT 9 LESSON 4 Write Word Problems and Equations **315**

Student Activity Book page 315

Choose two or three students to read their problems aloud. Have the class discuss whether each problem is of the correct type. Some students will write a problem similar to the given problem, using the same situation but changing the numbers. Others may come up with their own array situations.

Repeat this process for problems 3–10. Encourage students to be creative and invent their own problem situations. As time allows, have students share their word problems for problem 11.

End the lesson by asking students to copy their best problem onto a blank sheet of paper. Collect the problems. Tell students that, in a few days, you will present some of their problems to the class to solve.

Activity 4

Write Equations with Variables

▶ Introduce Variables WHOLE CLASS

 **20 MINUTES**

Goal: Write equations with variables for word problems.

Materials: Student Activity Book or Hardcover Book pp. 314–316

 **NCTM Standards:**
Algebra
Number and Operations

Have students look back at problem 9 on Student Book page 315. Read aloud the problem. Then write this equation on the board.

$$9 \times 6 = \square$$

Discuss with students what each part of the equation represents.

- What does the 9 represent? The 9 represents the number of six-packs Mr. Lee bought.
- What does the 6 represent? The 6 represents the number of juice bottles in each six-pack.
- What does the box represents? The box represents the total number of bottles that Mr. Lee bought.

Explain to students that the box represents the unknown number. Point out that you can also use any letter to represent an unknown number. That letter is called a *variable*.

- What letter shall we use to represent the variable instead of a box? Possible answer: Use the letter b. It may help to remember that the b represents the total number of bottles.

Write $6 \times 9 = b$ on the board.

- What does the variable b represent? The total number of bottles.

Next have students look back at problem 3 on Student Book page 314. Read the problem aloud. Then write these equations on the board.

$56 = \square \times 8$ $\quad 56 \div 8 = \square$

- What does the 56 represent? The total number of fish.
- What does the 8 represent? The number of fish in each tank.
- What does the box represent? The unknown number of tanks.
- What letter could we use to represent the the number of tanks? Any letter.
- Let's use the letter t.

Write $56 = t \times 8$ and $56 \div 8 = t$ on the board.

- What does the variable t represent? The number of tanks.

❶ Teaching the Lesson (continued)

Teaching Note

Watch For! When writing multiplication equations, if students begin to use the letter *x* for the variable, encourage them to use the other symbols for multiplication (such as * •) instead of the times sign. In this example, $3 \times x = 12$ can be very confusing. Or tell them to use a letter other than *x* to avoid the confusion.

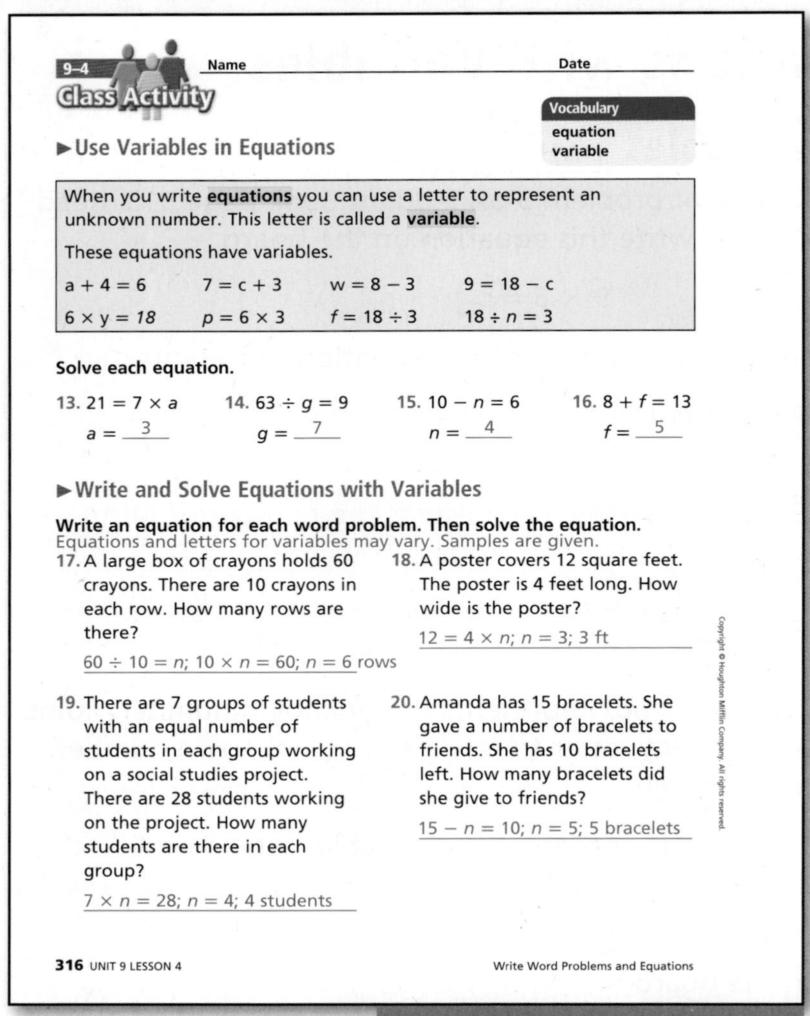

9–4 Class Activity

Name ______ Date ______

Vocabulary
equation
variable

► Use Variables in Equations

When you write **equations** you can use a letter to represent an unknown number. This letter is called a **variable**.

These equations have variables.

$a + 4 = 6$	$7 = c + 3$	$w = 8 - 3$	$9 = 18 - c$
$6 \times y = 18$	$p = 6 \times 3$	$f = 18 \div 3$	$18 \div n = 3$

Solve each equation.

13. $21 = 7 \times a$ $a =$ 3
14. $63 \div g = 9$ $g =$ 7
15. $10 - n = 6$ $n =$ 4
16. $8 + f = 13$ $f =$ 5

► Write and Solve Equations with Variables

Write an equation for each word problem. Then solve the equation.
Equations and letters for variables may vary. Samples are given.

17. A large box of crayons holds 60 crayons. There are 10 crayons in each row. How many rows are there?
$60 \div 10 = n$; $10 \times n = 60$; $n = 6$ rows

18. A poster covers 12 square feet. The poster is 4 feet long. How wide is the poster?
$12 = 4 \times n$; $n = 3$; 3 ft

19. There are 7 groups of students with an equal number of students in each group working on a social studies project. There are 28 students working on the project. How many students are there in each group?
$7 \times n = 28$; $n = 4$; 4 students

20. Amanda has 15 bracelets. She gave a number of bracelets to friends. She has 10 bracelets left. How many bracelets did she give to friends?
$15 - n = 10$; $n = 5$; 5 bracelets

316 UNIT 9 LESSON 4   Write Word Problems and Equations

Student Activity Book page 316

► Use Variables in Equations WHOLE CLASS

Direct students' attention to the top of Student Activity Book page 316 and have a volunteer read aloud the definition of *variable*.

Have students complete exercises 13–16 and then discuss their answers as a class. Make sure students understand that any letter could have been used for the variable.

► Write and Solve Equations with Variables

INDIVIDUALS

Have students solve problems 17–20 independently. Then use the **Solve and Discuss** structure to share their solution methods and strategies. Have volunteers who used different equations, present their work. For example, in problems 17, 18, and 19, students can use either multiplication or division equations to represent the problem.

2 Going Further

Differentiated Instruction

Intervention — Activity Card 9-4

Fill in the Blanks

Activity Card 9-4

Work: In pairs

Use:

- TRB M103 (Fill in the Blanks)

1. **Work Together** Write two word problems on the page by filling in the blanks.
2. Use information from the picture to complete each problem. You can write problems about all the stickers together, or you can write about just the smile or flower stickers.

Naomi has 4 pages of stickers.
There are 5 smile stickers on each page.
How many smile stickers are there in all?
Answer: 20 smile stickers

Naomi has 4 pages of stickers.
There are 36 stickers in all.
How many stickers are on each page?
Answer: 9 stickers

3. After you have completed your problems, check your answers. Then discuss each problem with your partner.
   - What type of problem is it — array, repeated-groups, or area?
   - What operation did you use to find the answer?

Unit 9, Lesson 4

Activity Note Review the different types of problems with students before they begin the activity. Point out clue words such as *in all* to help them identify the operation needed.

Math Writing Prompt

Explain Your Thinking How is an array problem different from a repeated-group problem?

Software Support

Warm Up 45.24

On Level — Activity Card 9-4

Choose a Topic

Activity Card 9-4

Work: In pairs

Decide:

Who will be Student 1 and who will be Student 2 for the first activity.

1. **Work Together** Make a list of your favorite topics for word problems. Some topics that you could choose are shown below.

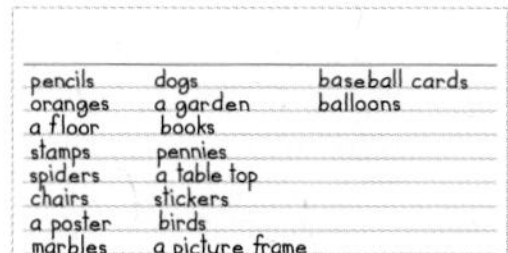

2. **Student 1:** Choose a topic from your list. Write a multiplication problem about the topic.
3. **Student 2:** Write a division problem about the same topic. Then exchange papers and solve the problem.
4. Repeat the activity with a different topic.

Unit 9, Lesson 4

Activity Note Suggest that students illustrate their problems to reinforce identification of the type of problem they are solving.

Math Writing Prompt

Same Numbers, Different Operations How can you rewrite a multiplication word problem as a division word problem? Give an example.

Software Support

Numberopolis: Carnival Stories, Level S

Challenge — Activity Card 9-4

Problems, Problems, Problems

Activity Card 9-4

Work: On your own

1. Write three different multiplication or division word problems. Be sure that each problem is a different type — array, repeated-group, or area.
2. Illustrate your problems and identify each problem by type and operation. Then solve each problem.

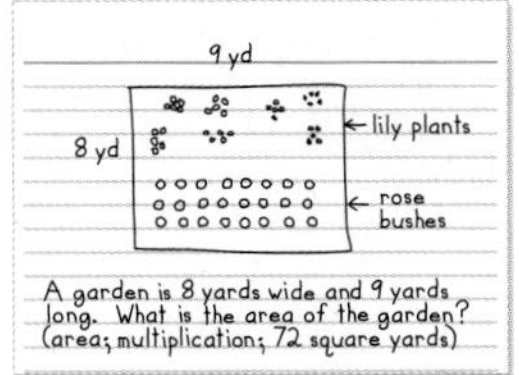

Unit 9, Lesson 4

Activity Note To make the activity more challenging, have students choose a topic and then write three different types of multiplication or division word problems within that topic.

Math Writing Prompt

Summarize Explain how you know if a word problem is an array, repeated-groups, or area problem.

Software Support

Course II: Module 2: Unit 2: Repeated Addition and Arrays

3 Homework and Spiral Review

9–4 Homework **Goal:** Additional Practice

This Homework page provides practice in identifying types of word problems.

9–4 Homework

Name ______________________ Date ____________

Study Plan
______________ Homework Helper

Solve. Then circle what type it is and what operation you used.

1. The area of a photograph is 15 square inches. If the width of the photograph is 3 inches, what is its length?

   5 inches

   array   repeated groups   (area)

   multiplication   (division)

2. Mrs. Divita divided 64 beetles equally among the 8 students in the science club. How many beetles did each student receive?

   8 beetles

   array   (repeated groups)   area

   multiplication   (division)

3. Write your own problem that is the same type as problem 1.

   Answers will vary.

4. Write your own problem that is the same type as problem 2.

   Answers will vary.

Find the missing number in each Fast-Array Drawing.

5. 9, [6], 54

6. 4, 7, [28]

7. [6], 6, 36

UNIT 9 LESSON 4   Write Word Problems and Equations **223**

Homework and Remembering page 223

9–4 Remembering **Goal:** Spiral Review

This Remembering page would be appropriate anytime after today's lesson.

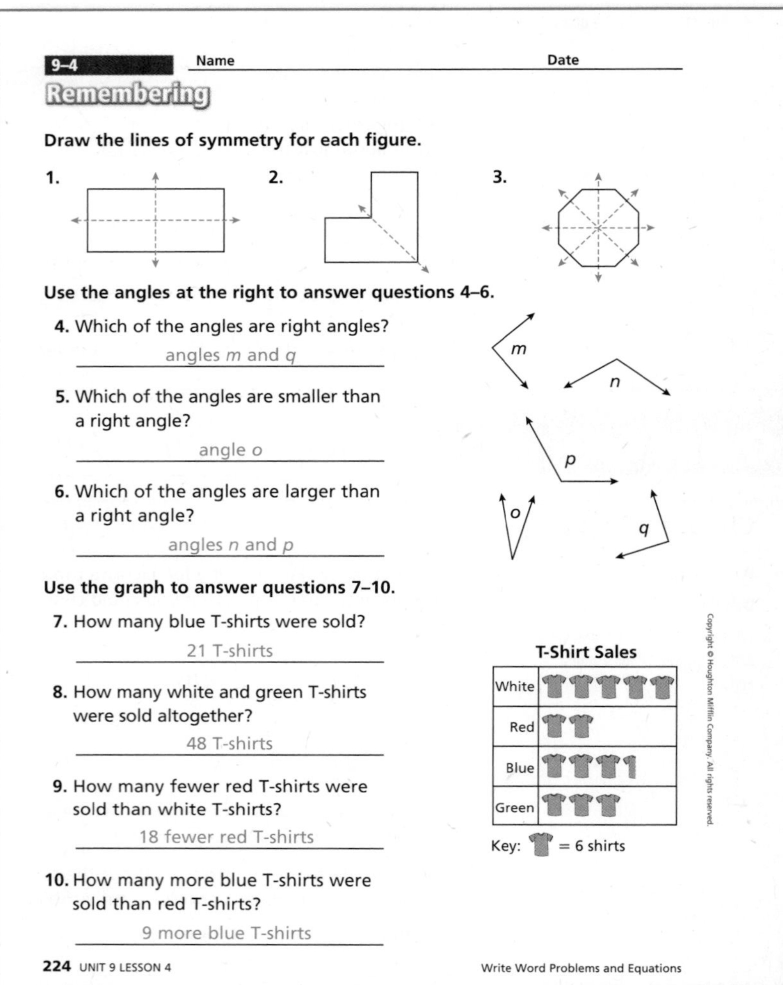

9–4 Remembering

Name ______________________ Date ____________

Draw the lines of symmetry for each figure.

1. 2. 3.

Use the angles at the right to answer questions 4–6.

4. Which of the angles are right angles?

   angles *m* and *q*

5. Which of the angles are smaller than a right angle?

   angle *o*

6. Which of the angles are larger than a right angle?

   angles *n* and *p*

Use the graph to answer questions 7–10.

7. How many blue T-shirts were sold?

   21 T-shirts

8. How many white and green T-shirts were sold altogether?

   48 T-shirts

9. How many fewer red T-shirts were sold than white T-shirts?

   18 fewer red T-shirts

10. How many more blue T-shirts were sold than red T-shirts?

    9 more blue T-shirts

T-Shirt Sales

White	5 shirts
Red	2 shirts
Blue	3½ shirts
Green	3 shirts

Key: 1 shirt = 6 shirts

224 UNIT 9 LESSON 4   Write Word Problems and Equations

Homework and Remembering page 224

Home or School Activity

Real-World Connection

Chores at Home and School Ask students what chores they do at school or home. Have them make a list and then ask them to think of some tasks that might lead to multiplication and division problems. Have students write word problems about their chores.

I clean the whiteboard in class every day. It takes 5 minutes. How many minutes does it take each week?

Multiply and Divide with 7

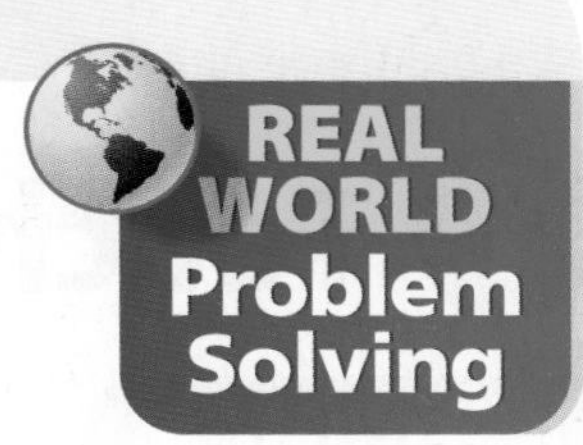

Lesson Objectives

- Explore patterns in 7s count-bys, multiplications, and divisions.
- Use a variety of strategies to solve multiplication problems.

The Day at a Glance

Today's Goals	Materials	
1 Teaching the Lesson **A1:** Practice count-bys, multiplications, and divisions. **A2:** Explore patterns in 7s count-bys, multiplications, and divisions. **A3:** Discuss strategies for finding 7 × 7. **A4:** Find the missing numbers in Fast-Array Drawings.	**Lesson Activities** Student Activity Book pp. 317–318 or Student Hardcover Book pp. 317–318 Homework and Remembering pp. 225–228 Check Up materials Signature Sheet Blank Sprint Answer Sheets Study sheets A-C Check Sheets 1–8 Dry-erase markers Sheet protectors Study Sheet Answer Strips Check Sheet Answer Strips Cardstock Strategy cards	Class Multiplication Table Poster, Pointer MathBoard materials Quick Quiz 1 (Assessment Guide)
2 Going Further ► Problem-Solving Strategy: More Guess and Check ► Differentiated Instruction		**Going Further** Activity Cards 9–5 Game Cards (TRB M25) Index Cards Math Journals
3 Homework and Spiral Review		Use Math Talk today!

Keeping Skills Sharp

Quick Practice — 5 MINUTES

Goal: Practice 8s count-bys, multiplications, and divisions.

Materials: Class Multiplication Table Poster, pointer
Display the Class Multiplication Table Poster. Use the number "8" for these activities.

Repeated Quick Practice
Use these Quick Practice activities from previous lessons.

8s Multiplications in Order (See Unit 7 Lesson 4.)

Mixed 8s Multiplications (See Unit 7 Lesson 2.)

Mixed 8s Divisions (See Unit 7 Lesson 5.)

Daily Routines

Homework Review Have students share the word problems they wrote.

Logical Reasoning Alex, Josh, and Julie either have a bike, skateboard, or roller blades. Josh does not have the skateboard. Alex does not have the roller blades or the skateboard. Which does each person have? Alex: Bike; Josh: Roller Blades; Julie: Skateboard

	Bike	Skateboard	Rollerblades
Alex	yes	no	no
Josh	no	no	yes
Julie	no	yes	no

1 Teaching the Lesson

Activity 1

Check Up and Independent Study

 **5 MINUTES**

Goal: Practice count-bys, multiplications, and divisions.

Materials: Check Up materials: Signature Sheet (Student Activity Book pp. 205–206 or Activity Workbook p. 77); Blank Sprint Answer Sheets (TRB M57); Study Sheets A–C (Student Activity Book pp. 207–208; 243–244; 305–306, or Activity Workbook pp. 78, 89, 143), Check Sheets 1–8 (Student Activity Book pp. 223–224; 229–230; 234; 251–252; 267–268; 273–274; 309–310 or Activity Workbook pp. 83, 85, 87, 118, 123–124, 129, 145), dry-erase markers (1 per student), sheet protectors (1 per student), Study Sheet Answer Strips (TRB M54), Check Sheet Answer Strips (TRB M55), cardstock; Strategy Cards, Homework and Remembering p. 227

✓ **NCTM Standard:**
Number and Operations

▶ Check Up with 6s and 8s PAIRS

Give **Student Pairs** a few minutes to test one another using Study Sheets A–C and collect signatures or use Check Sheets 1–8. You may want to have Study Sheet and Check Sheet Answer Strips (TRB M54–M55) available.

Students who made mistakes on the 6s Sprints from Lesson 4 (or who were absent) may take repeat or make up Sprints. Students can record their answers on a Blank Sprint Answer Sheet (TRB M57).

After **Student Pairs** have tested one another, give students two or three minutes to study independently using their Study Sheets, Check Sheets, or Strategy Cards. Then have students complete their Study Plan box on Homework and Remembering page 227. They should include 7s practice along with any multiplications or divisions they may have missed in the Check Up.

Activity 2

7s Multiplications and Divisions

 **25 MINUTES**

Goal: Explore patterns in 7s count-bys, multiplications, and divisions.

Materials: Class Multiplication Table Poster, pointer, MathBoard materials, Student Activity Book or Hardcover Book p. 317

 **NCTM Standards:**
Number and Operations
Algebra
Representation

▶ Explore Patterns with 7s WHOLE CLASS

Refer students to the 7s column of the Class Multiplication Table Poster. Ask which multiplications in the column they haven't learned yet. There is only one: 7×7.

Tell students that today they will be thinking about groups of 7. Ask what things in the real world come in groups of 7. days in a week, score for a touchdown with the extra point, and so on

Model the steps of this activity on the Class MathBoard as students follow along on their MathBoards. The completed board is reproduced on Student Activity Book page 317. You can use it to facilitate a summary discussion of 7s patterns.

Have students circle sequential groups of 7, up to 70, on the Number Path and write the totals so far next to each group. After they circle the first group, have them say in unison, "1 group of 7 is 7"; after they circle the second group, have them say, "2 groups of 7 are 14"; and so on.

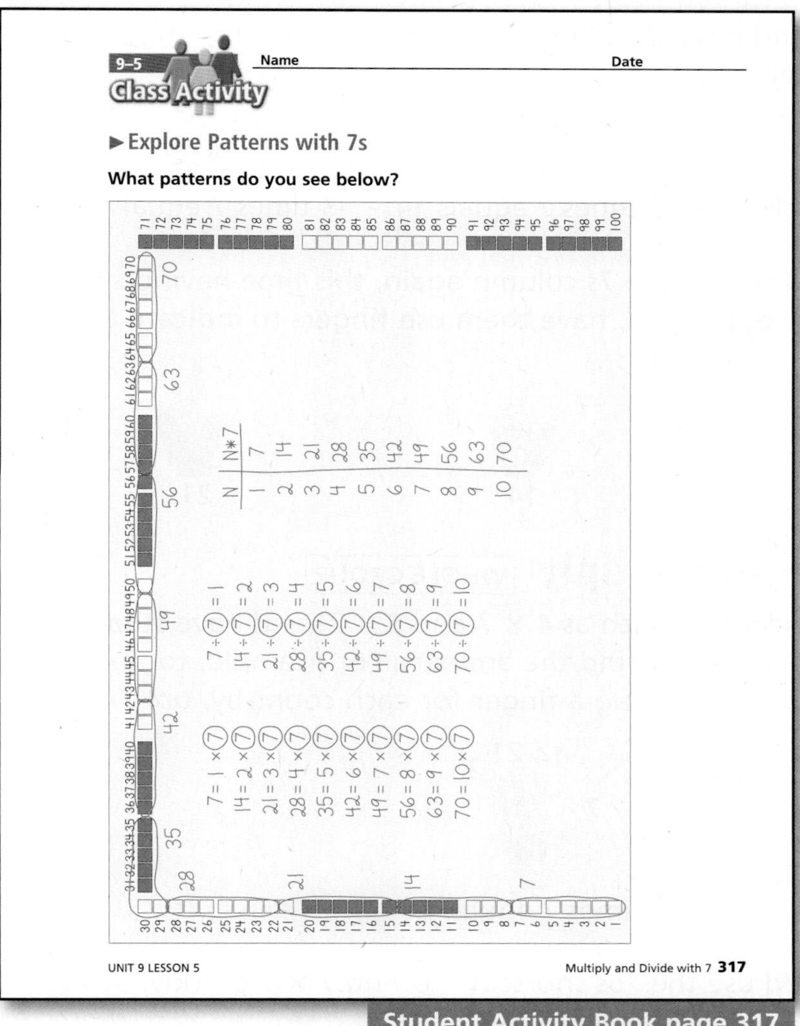

9–5 **Class Activity** Name Date

► **Explore Patterns with 7s**

What patterns do you see below?

N	N*7
1	7
2	14
3	21
4	28
5	35
6	42
7	49
8	56
9	63
10	70

7 = 1 × 7 7 ÷ 7 = 1
14 = 2 × 7 14 ÷ 7 = 2
21 = 3 × 7 21 ÷ 7 = 3
28 = 4 × 7 28 ÷ 7 = 4
35 = 5 × 7 35 ÷ 7 = 5
42 = 6 × 7 42 ÷ 7 = 6
49 = 7 × 7 49 ÷ 7 = 7
56 = 8 × 7 56 ÷ 7 = 8
63 = 9 × 7 63 ÷ 7 = 9
70 = 10 × 7 70 ÷ 7 = 10

UNIT 9 LESSON 5   Multiply and Divide with 7 **317**

Student Activity Book page 317

Point to the groups in order as students say, "1 group of 7 is 7," "2 groups of 7 are 14," "3 groups of 7 are 21," and so on.

Next, point to the totals on the class MathBoard as students say just the 7s count-bys. 7, 14, 21, 28, 35, 42, 49, 56, 63, 70

Then, as students follow along, write and read a multiplication equation for each count-by.

Point to one of the multiplications. Write an = sign following it, and ask students to help you write a repeated addition expression. Repeat for one or two more multiplications. See side column.

Ask students what patterns they see in the count-bys and equations. See **Math Talk in Action** in the side column.

Activity continued ▶

Math Talk in Action

What patterns do you see in the 7s count-bys?

Sari: Well, the 7s count-bys are not all even numbers and they're not all odd numbers.

Malcolm: No, but *every other one* is an even number. And every other one is an odd number!

Aneka: So they're like the 3s count-bys!

James: Let's try that match-up with the 7s count-bys. We can't use 70, though.

7, 14, 21, 28, 35, 42, 49, 56, 63

Start with 7 and 63 and go to the center. The same thing happens. The ones digits add to 10. Look: 7 + 3 = 10, 4 + 6 = 10, 1 + 9 = 10, 8 + 2 = 10.

Natalie: And the pairs of numbers add to 70! 7 + 63 = 70, 14 + 56 = 70, 21 + 49 = 70, 28 + 42 = 70.

Billy: So you can match up the 6s count-bys so they add to 60, the 7s count-bys so they add to 70, and the 8s count-bys so they add to 80.

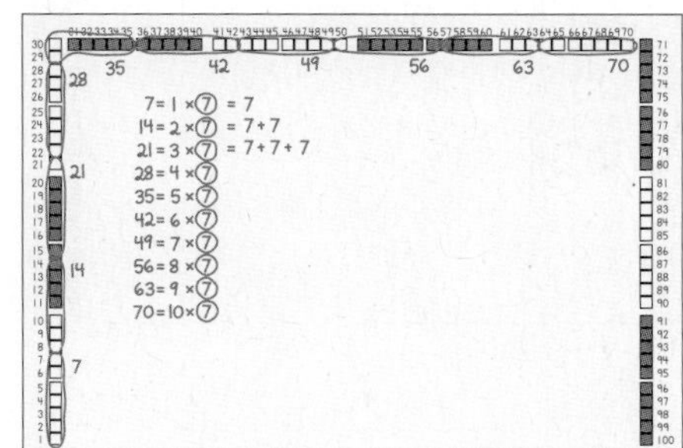

① Teaching the Lesson (continued)

Teaching Note

Watch For! Students who attempt to use the "5s shortcut" for the 7s multiplications — or any other multiplications — might arrive at an incorrect answer because they have not yet mastered the 5s count-bys. You might want to have these students work with a partner to do additional Check Ups with 5s. Encourage them also to ask their Homework Helper to review the 5s chart with them.

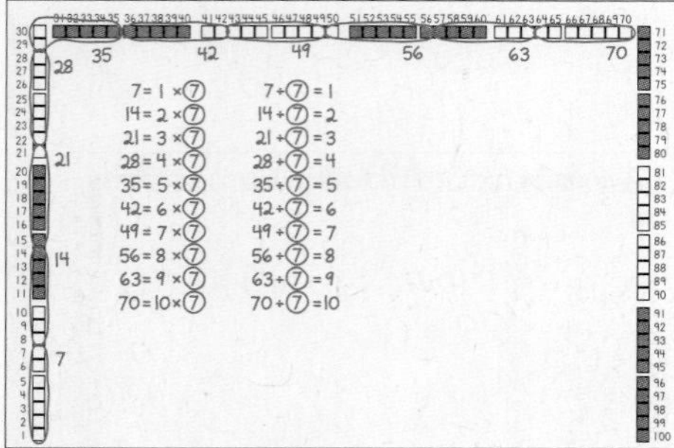

▶ Use the Class Multiplication Table Poster WHOLE CLASS

In the Class Multiplication Table Poster, point to the equations in the 7s column in order and have the class read them aloud, using fingers to show the multiplier.

1 times 7 equals 7. 2 times 7 equals 14. 3 times 7 equals 21.

Point to each equation in the 7s column again, this time having students say only the count-bys. Again, have them use fingers to indicate the multipliers.

7 14 21

▶ Use Fingers to Multiply WHOLE GROUP

Present 7s multiplications (such as 4 × 7 and 8 × 7) and have students count up on their fingers to find the answers. For example, to find 4 × 7, they should count by 7s, raising a finger for each count-by, until 4 fingers are raised.

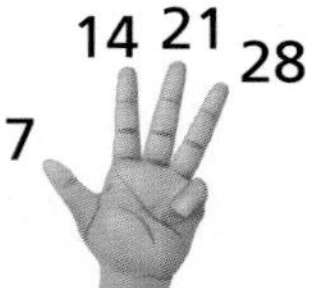

4 times 7 equals 28.

Ask how they could use the "5s shortcut" to find 7 × 7 quickly. Start with all 5 fingers up on one hand, say "35," and count up from there.

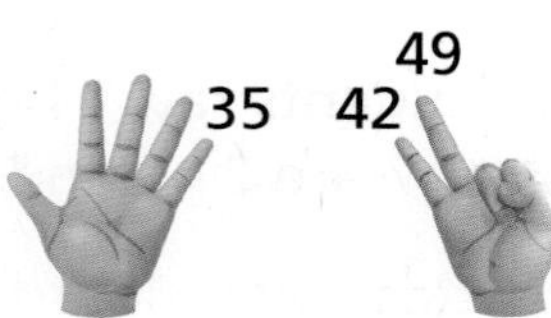

7 times 7 equals 49.

Have students use the shortcut to find 6 × 7 and 8 × 7.

▶ Divide with 7s WHOLE GROUP

Erase the addition expressions from the Class MathBoard. Work with students to write the first two or three division equations, and then have them work independently to write the rest.

Have students turn over their MathBoards. Hide the division equations on the Class MathBoard. Write the following division and related unknown multiplication equation on the board.

$$28 \div 7 = \square \qquad \square \times 7 = 28$$

Ask students to try to find the unknown number without using count-bys. They should think "What number times 7 is 28?" and consider the multiplications they know. (They may use count-bys if they can't figure out the answer this way.) Repeat for 14 ÷ 7, 35 ÷ 7, and 63 ÷ 7.

For the divisions 42 ÷ 7, 49 ÷ 7, and 56 ÷ 7, most students will need to use count-bys. Write the following division and related multiplication equation on the board.

$$56 \div 7 = \square \qquad \square \times 7 = 56$$

Have students count up on their fingers to find the answer. Eight fingers will be raised, indicating that there are 8 groups of 7 in 56. So, 56 ÷ 7 = 8.

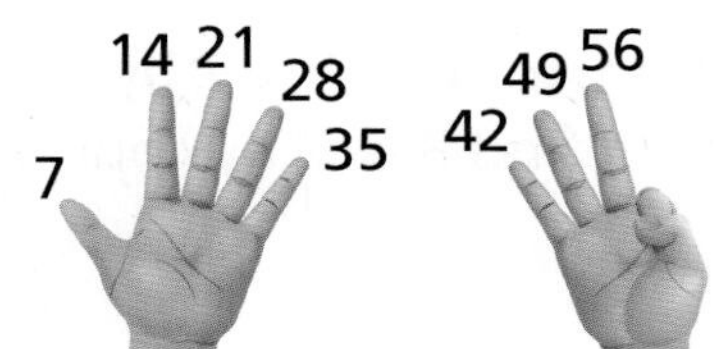

56 divided by 7 equals 8.

Ask students how they could have used the "5s shortcut" to find the unknown number. Start with all 5 fingers up on one hand, say "35," and count by 7s from there until you reach 56.

▶ Make a Function Table for 7s Count-bys WHOLE CLASS

On the Class MathBoard, make a two-column table with column heads *N* and *N* * 7.

- The first column of this function table is labeled *N*. What does *N* mean? any number
- The second column is labeled *N* * 7. This is the rule for our function table. What does this rule tell us to do? Multiply each number in the *N* column by 7.

Activity continued ▶

Teaching Note

Math Background A function is a relationship between two sets of numbers in which each member of one set is paired with exactly one member of the other set. The function table in this lesson, for example, shows each of the first ten counting numbers paired with the first ten 7s count-bys. The relationship that determines the pairing is "Multiply by 7."

As students progress in their study of mathematics, they will study increasingly complex functions. However, no matter how complex the function, the basic concept remains the same. To make the concept more accessible to young children, some people like to illustrate a "function machine" like this with models.

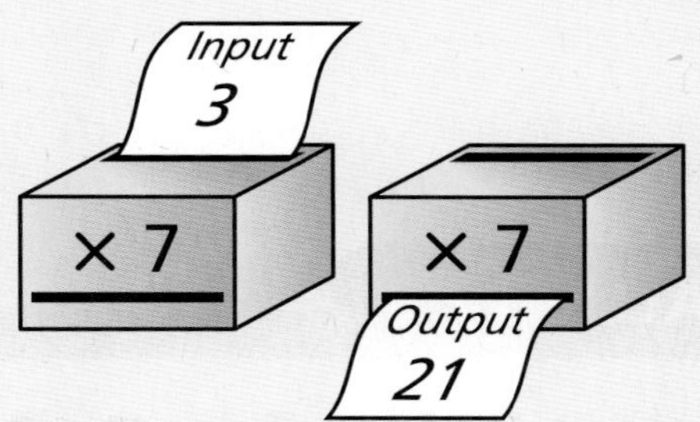

In this depiction of a function, the numbers of one set are *input* into the machine, the machine operates on the number, and exactly one member of the second set is *output.* For this reason, in some teaching resources you may see the terms *Input* and *Output* at the top of a function table.

English Language Learners

Write a 7 count-bys *function table* on the board. Say: **The *function* is the action.**

- **Beginning** Point to N×7. Say: **This means multiply all the numbers by __.** 7 Ask: **Is this the *function*?** yes
- **Intermediate and Advanced** Ask: **What tells us the action?** N×7 Say: **N×7 is the __.** function

Teaching Note

Math Background To help students count up or back by 7s, you might want to discuss the Make-a-Ten strategy. The following are two examples.

- To find 56 + 7, start with 56. Add 4 to get 60, and then add 3 more to get 63. In symbols, 56 + 7 = 56 + 4 + 3 = 60 + 3 = 63.
- To find 35 − 7, start with 35. Subtract 5 to get 30, and then subtract 2 more to get 28. In symbols, 35 − 7 = 35 − 5 − 2 = 30 − 2 = 28.

Have a volunteer work at the Class MathBoard as other students work on their MathBoards. Ask students to write the whole numbers from 1 to 10 in the *N* column, and then use the rule to fill in the *N* ∗ 7 column.

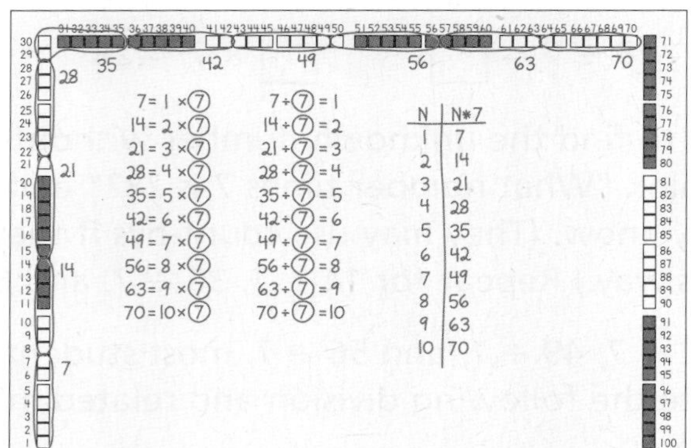

Point out that the numbers in the *N* ∗ 7 column are the 7s count-bys.

- We can see from the table that we can find any count-by by counting up or counting back from a count-by we know. Remember, it is easiest to start with a count-by that is close to the one we want to find.

Ask a volunteer to explain how to find 7 × 7 by counting up from 5 × 7. Ask another to explain how to find 8 × 7 by counting back from 9 × 7.

Activity 3

Strategies for 7s Multiplications

 **10 MINUTES**

Goal: Discuss strategies for finding 7 × 7.

 **NCTM Standard:** Number and Operations

Differentiated Instruction

Extra Help 7 × 8 is one of the hardest multiplications for students to learn. Set up the equation like 56 = 7 × 8, and show them the digits 5, 6, 7, 8 are in sequential order.

▶ Discuss Strategies for 7 × 7  

Write the following multiplication equation on the board.

$$7 \times 7 = \square$$

Ask for a volunteer to describe a strategy for finding the product. Allow the student to come to the board to explain if necessary. Encourage other students to ask questions if they don't understand. Then ask if anyone can think of a different strategy. Allow as many different methods as possible to be presented. If no one mentions the following methods, you might suggest them yourself.

- Start with 5 × 7, and count by 7 from there.

  5 × 7 = 35, plus 7 more is 42, plus 7 more is 49. So, 7 × 7 = 49.

- Combine two multiplications you know.

4 × 7 = 28	4 sevens are 28.
3 × 7 = 21	3 sevens are 21.
7 × 7 = 49	7 sevens are 49.

Activity 4

Complete Fast-Array Drawings

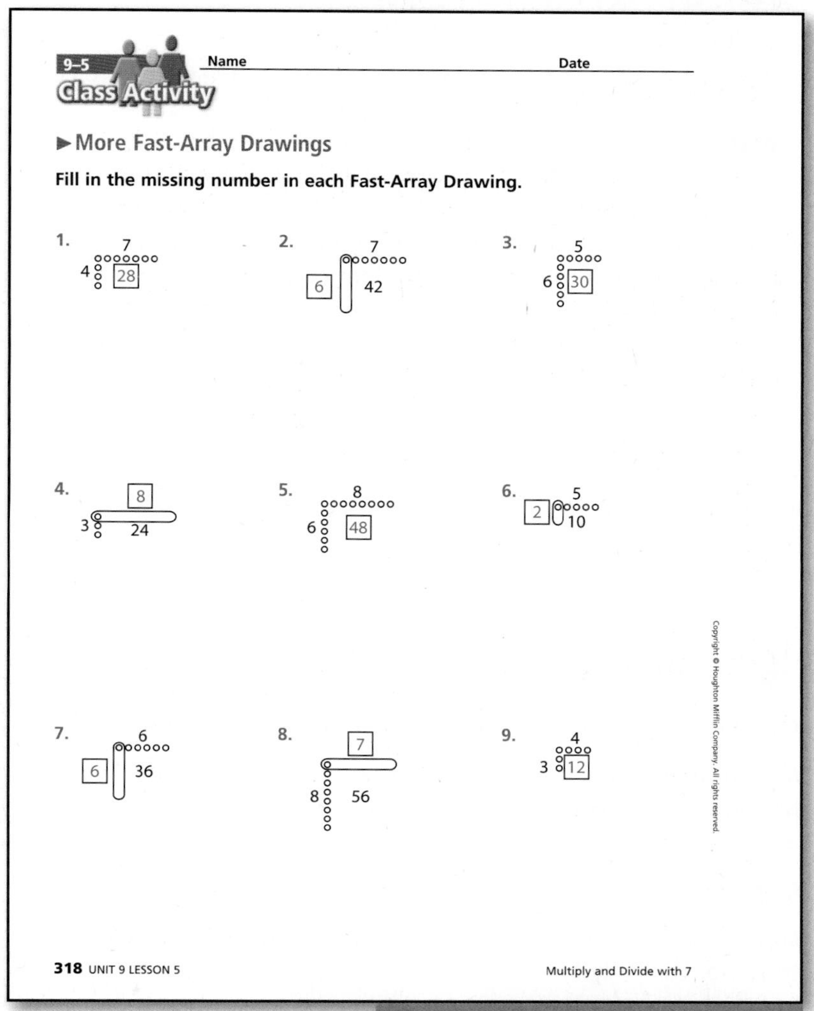

9–5 Class Activity Name Date

▶ More Fast-Array Drawings

Fill in the missing number in each Fast-Array Drawing.

1. 7, 4, [28]
2. 7, [6], 42
3. 5, 6, [30]
4. [8], 3, 24
5. 8, 6, [48]
6. 5, [2], 10
7. 6, [6], 36
8. [7], 8, 56
9. 4, 3, [12]

318 UNIT 9 LESSON 5 Multiply and Divide with 7

Student Activity Book page 318

▶ More Fast-Array Drawings WHOLE CLASS

On the board, make this Fast-Array Drawing.

9

5 45

Remind students that a Fast-Array Drawing shows the number of items in each row, the number of items in each column, and the total. Your drawing represents an array with 5 rows and 9 columns. The total, 45, is written in the center.

Have students complete the Fast-Array Drawings on Student Book page 318. Explain that they must find the missing number in each drawing. Give them a few minutes to do the exercises, and then discuss the answers.

10 MINUTES

Goal: Find the missing numbers in Fast-Array Drawings.

Materials: Student Activity Book or Hardcover Book p. 318

NCTM Standards:
Number and Operations
Representation

Ongoing Assessment

Ask questions such as the following:

- ▶ If you know that 7 + 7 = 14, what 7s multiplication can you do?
- ▶ If you know that 2 × 7 = 14, and 7 more is 21, what 7s multiplication do you know?
- ▶ If you know that 2 × 7 = 14 and 3 × 7 = 21, how can you combine them to do another 7s multiplication?
- ▶ If you know that 5 × 7 = 35, what 7s division can you do?

Class Management

Looking Ahead Remind students to take home the 7s chart on Homework and Remembering page 227.

Quick Quiz

See Assessment Guide for Unit 9 Quick Quiz 1.

2 Going Further

Problem Solving Strategy: More Guess and Check

Goal: Use the Guess and Check strategy to solve problems.

Materials: MathBoard materials

✓ **NCTM Standard:**
Problem Solving

▶ Review the Guess and Check Strategy WHOLE CLASS

Tell students you are thinking of two numbers whose sum is 10. Ask them to guess what the numbers might be. Make a list of their answers on the board.

Now tell them that you will give them more information: One number is 4 times the other. Ask if any of their guesses fits this new information. Yes, 2 and 8, because 8 is equal to 4 times 2.

- Sometimes you start working on a problem by taking a guess based on part of the given information. Then you check your guess using all the information. If the guess doesn't work, you use what you have learned to revise your guess and try again.

▶ Use the Guess and Check Strategy WHOLE CLASS

Write these word problems and have students solve them using **Solve and Discuss**. Encourage them to share their thinking about how they made their guesses and how they checked if a guess was correct. See **Math Talk in Action** for a sample classroom discussion.

1. Dori's father is 4 times as old as Dori. The sum of their ages is 40 years. How old is Dori? 8 How old is her father? 32
2. A sweater and a hat together cost $32. The sweater costs 3 times as much as the hat. What is the cost of the hat? $8 What is the cost of the sweater? $24
3. A 36-inch rope is cut into two pieces. One piece is 8 times as long as the other. How long is the shorter piece? 4 inches How long is the longer piece? 32 inches
4. A 40-inch ribbon is cut into two pieces. One piece is 4 inches longer than the other. How long is the shorter piece? 18 inches How long is the longer piece? 22 inches

Teaching Note

Watch For! In problems 1–3, students need to break a quantity into two parts that are related by multiplication. As a result, they might read problem 4 too quickly, assume it is similar, and think that one piece is 4 times as long as the other. Encourage them to read the problem carefully and note that one piece is *4 inches longer* than the other. Lead them to see that the lengths of the two pieces are related by an addition (or subtraction) of 4 inches.

Math Talk in Action

Cammie: I think Dori is 10 years old. 4 times 10 equals 40.

Karl: It doesn't say that 4 times her age is 40. It says that 4 times her age is her father's age. So we have to figure out how old he is.

Cammie: Well, what if she's 10? Does that mean her father is 40?

Lupita: Yes, and that's too much. 10 plus 40 is 50. Their ages together can only be 40.

Karl: So her age has to be less than 10. I say we should try 6.

Cammie: O.K. If Dori is 6, her father is 4 times 6. That's 24.

Lupita: But now it's not enough. 6 plus 24 is only 30.

Karl: So let's try something in between. How about 8? That's right in the middle between 6 and 10.

Lupita: If Dori is 8, her father is 4 times 8.

Cammie: Look! 4 times 8 is 32, and 8 plus 32 is 40. That's it!

Differentiated Instruction

Advanced Learners Give students the following problem to solve using the Guess and Check strategy.

There are 15 animals in the barnyard. Some are chickens and some are cows. There are 48 legs in all. How many of the animals are chickens? How many are cows? 6; 9

Intervention — Activity Card 9-5

Picture This!

Activity Card 9-5

Work: In pairs

Use:

- 10 Index cards

1. **Work Together** Write the 7s multiplications from 1 × 7 through 10 × 7 on index cards, one per card.
2. Shuffle the cards and place them in a stack facedown. Each person takes a card and draws a picture to show the multiplication.
3. Exchange papers with your partner. Write a multiplication and a division equation that the picture could represent.

6 × 7

6 × 7 = 42
42 ÷ 7 = 6

4. Repeat the activity until all the cards are taken.

Unit 9, Lesson 5

Activity Note Drawings to represent a multiplication can show an array or repeated grouping. They can also show an area. Remind students of these different types of situations, all of which can illustrate a multiplication.

Math Writing Prompt

Describe a Strategy Explain how to use a multiplication you know to find 6 × 7.

Software Support

Warm Up 12.27

On Level — Activity Card 9-5

Take the Tens

Activity Card 9-5

Work: In pairs

Use:

- TRB M25 (Game Cards)

1. Shuffle the cards and place them in a stack facedown to play the game *Take the Tens.*
2. Take turns. Take a card and multiply the number on the card by 7. If the product is correct, your score increases by the number of points equal to the tens digit of the product. If the product is 0 or 7, you score no points.
3. Continue playing until all the cards have been taken. The player with the higher score wins.

4   4 × 7 = 28

Unit 9, Lesson 5

Activity Note Students should check each other's multiplications. If a product is incorrect, you may suggest that the player forfeit the turn and return the card to the bottom of the stack.

Math Writing Prompt

Choose a Strategy What strategies can you use to help you find multiplications you don't remember?

Software Support

Country Countdown: Counting Critters, Level V

Challenge — Activity Card 9-5

Ns and More *Ns*!

Activity Card 9-5

Work: In pairs

1. Copy and complete each function table shown. Write the whole numbers from 1 through 9, in order, in the *N* column.
2. Describe any patterns that you see in the right-hand column of each table.
3. **Analyze** Look at each table carefully. Is there more than one pattern to describe? Discuss your results with your partner.

1. N | N + N   2. N | N − N   3. N | N × N   4. N | N ÷ N

N	N + N
1	2
2	4
3	6
4	8
5	10
6	12
7	14
8	16
9	18

Each number is 2 more than the one before.

Unit 9, Lesson 5

Activity Note Patterns may vary. For example, patterns in the addition function may be described as increasing each number in the second column by 2 or counting by 2s, or multiplying by 2.

Math Writing Prompt

Different Ways Suppose that the "7" key on your calculator is broken. Describe two different ways you could use your calculator to find 7 × 6.

Software Support

Course II: Module 2: Unit 2: Repeated Addition and Arrays

Homework and Spiral Review

9–5 **Homework** **Goal:** Additional Practice

This Homework page provides practice in multiplying and dividing with 7.

9–5 **Remembering** **Goal:** Spiral Review

This Remembering page would be appropriate anytime after today's lesson.

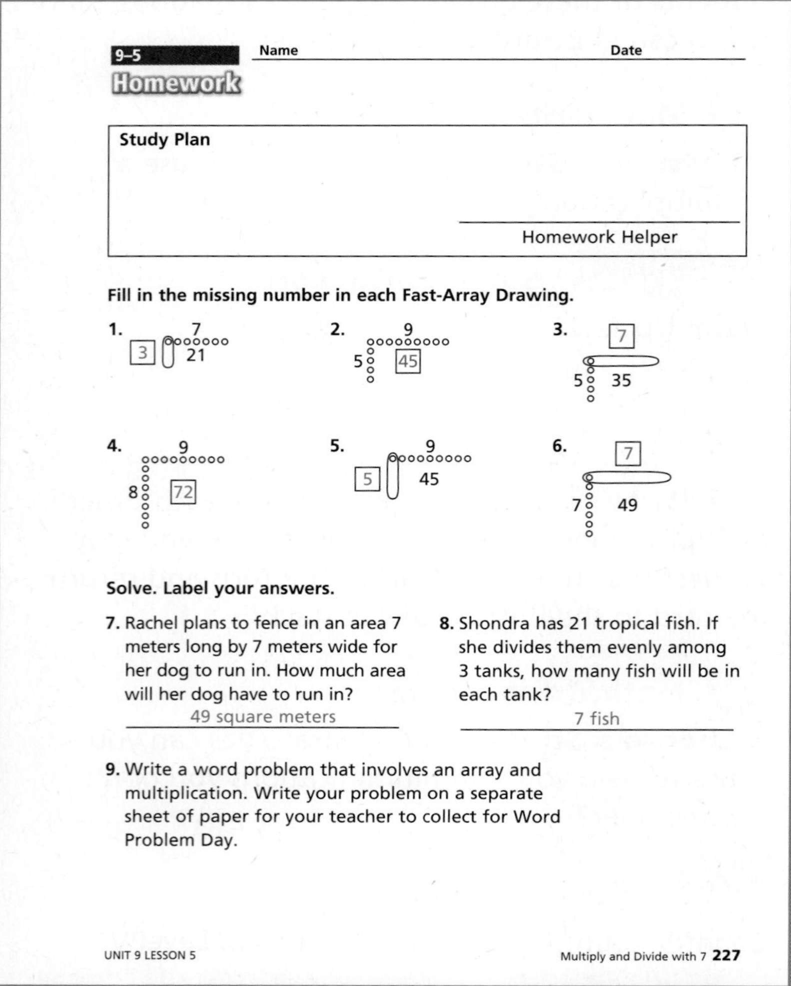

9–5 Homework Name Date

Study Plan

Homework Helper

Fill in the missing number in each Fast-Array Drawing.

1. 7; 3; 21
2. 9; 5; 45
3. 7; 5; 35
4. 9; 8; 72
5. 9; 5; 45
6. 7; 7; 49

Solve. Label your answers.

7. Rachel plans to fence in an area 7 meters long by 7 meters wide for her dog to run in. How much area will her dog have to run in? 49 square meters
8. Shondra has 21 tropical fish. If she divides them evenly among 3 tanks, how many fish will be in each tank? 7 fish
9. Write a word problem that involves an array and multiplication. Write your problem on a separate sheet of paper for your teacher to collect for Word Problem Day.

UNIT 9 LESSON 5 Multiply and Divide with 7 227

Homework and Remembering page 227

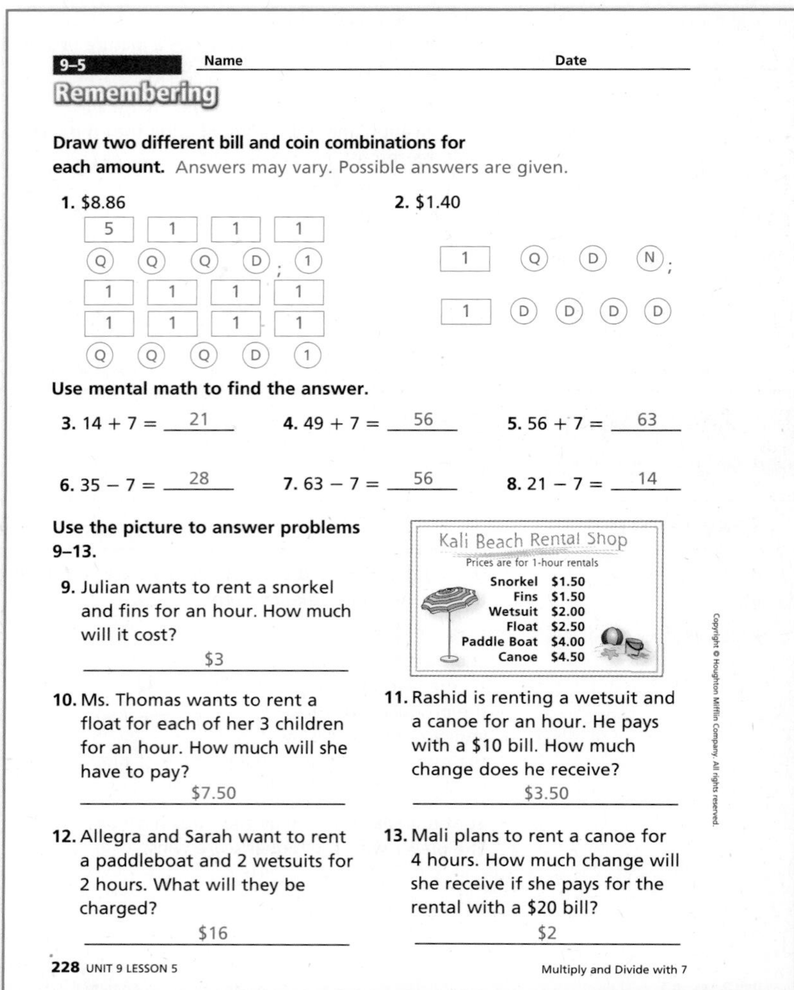

9–5 Remembering Name Date

Draw two different bill and coin combinations for each amount. Answers may vary. Possible answers are given.

1. $8.86
   5 1 1 1 Q Q Q D 1;
   1 1 1 1 1 1 1 1 Q Q Q D 1
2. $1.40
   1 Q D N;
   1 D D D D

Use mental math to find the answer.

3. 14 + 7 = 21
4. 49 + 7 = 56
5. 56 + 7 = 63
6. 35 − 7 = 28
7. 63 − 7 = 56
8. 21 − 7 = 14

Use the picture to answer problems 9–13.

Kali Beach Rental Shop
Prices are for 1-hour rentals

Snorkel	$1.50
Fins	$1.50
Wetsuit	$2.00
Float	$2.50
Paddle Boat	$4.00
Canoe	$4.50

9. Julian wants to rent a snorkel and fins for an hour. How much will it cost? $3
10. Ms. Thomas wants to rent a float for each of her 3 children for an hour. How much will she have to pay? $7.50
11. Rashid is renting a wetsuit and a canoe for an hour. He pays with a $10 bill. How much change does he receive? $3.50
12. Allegra and Sarah want to rent a paddleboat and 2 wetsuits for 2 hours. What will they be charged? $16
13. Mali plans to rent a canoe for 4 hours. How much change will she receive if she pays for the rental with a $20 bill? $2

228 UNIT 9 LESSON 5 Multiply and Divide with 7

Homework and Remembering page 228

Home or School Activity

Math-to-Math Connection

Calendar 7s Have students look at calendars to help them count by 7s. Have students find the 7 and move down the column to practice 7s multiplications to 4 × 7. Then have them continue: 35, 42, 49, 56, 63, 70. Challenge students to find any other number patterns on the calendar.

April

Sun	Mon	Tues	Wed	Thurs	Fri	Sat
1	2	3	4	5	6	7
8	9	10	11	12	13	14
15	16	17	18	19	20	21
22	23	24	25	26	27	28
29	30					

Comparison Word Problems

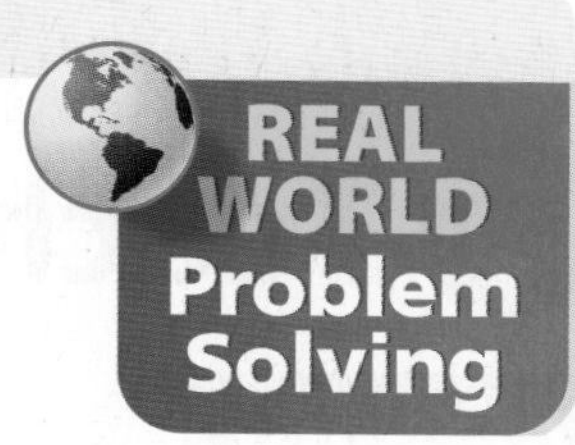

Vocabulary
times
fraction

Lesson Objective

- Solve comparison word problems involving multiplication and division.

The Day at a Glance

Today's Goals	Materials	
1 Teaching the Lesson **A1:** Practice count-bys, multiplications, and divisions. **A2:** Review basic multiplications and divisions. **A3:** Solve comparison word problems. **2 Going Further** ▸ Extension: Common Multiples ▸ Differentiated Instruction **3 Homework and Spiral Review**	**Lesson Activities** Student Activity Book pp. 319–326 or Student Hardcover Book pp. 319–326 and Activity Workbook pp. 149–150 (includes Dashes 5-8 and Special Format) Homework and Remembering pp. 229–230 Folders Check Up materials Signature sheet Study Sheets A-C Check Sheets 1–8 Dry-erase markers Sheet protectors Study Sheet Answer Strips Check Sheet Answer Strips Cardstock, Strategy Cards	Overhead projector (optional) Transparency of Student Book page 323 (optional) **Going Further** Activity Cards 9–6 MathBoard materials Index Cards Two-counters Game Cards (TRB M25) Comparison Logic Problems (TRB M106) Math Journals 123 Use Math Talk today!

Keeping Skills Sharp

Quick Practice 5 MINUTES	Daily Routines
Goal: Practice 7s count-bys, multiplications, and divisions. **Materials:** Class Multiplication Table Poster, pointer Use the Class Poster and the number "7" for these activities. **Repeated Quick Practice** Use these Quick Practice activities from previous lessons. **7s Multiplications in Order** (See Unit 7 Lesson 4.) **Mixed 7s Multiplications** (See Unit 7 Lesson 2.) **Mixed 7s Divisions** (See Unit 7 Lesson 5.)	**Homework Review** Check if students completed the assignment and if any problem caused difficulty. **Nonroutine Problem** Yom has 8 coins worth $1.06. What are the coins? Explain. 3 quarters, 2 dimes, 2 nickels, 1 penny; Add different values to find 8 coins worth $1.06.

1 Teaching the Lesson

Activity 1

Check Up and Independent Study

 5 MINUTES

Goal: Practice count-bys, multiplications, and divisions.

Materials: Folders, Check Up materials: Signature Sheet; Study Sheets A–C, Check Sheets 1–8, dry-erase markers (1 per student), sheet protectors (1 per student), Study Sheet Answer Strips (TRB M54), Check Sheet Answer Strips (TRB M55), cardstock; Strategy Cards, Homework and Remembering p. 229

 **NCTM Standards:**
Number and Operations
Communication

▶ Check Up PAIRS

Give **Student Pairs** a few minutes to test each other using Study Sheets A–C and Check Sheets 1–8 and collect signatures. You may want to have Study Sheet and Check Sheet Answer Strips (TRB M54–M55) available. After **Student Pairs** have tested each other, give students a few minutes to study independently using their Study Sheets, Check Sheets, or Strategy Cards. Then have students complete their Study Plan box on Homework and Remembering page 229. Students should include any multiplications and divisions they missed in the Check Up.

Activity 2

Mixed Practice

 10 MINUTES

Goal: Review basic multiplications and divisions.

Materials: Student Activity Book pp. 319–322 or Activity Workbook p. 149

 **NCTM Standard:**
Number and Operations

▶ Dashes 5–8 INDIVIDUALS

Have students complete the Dashes on Student Book page 319 or Activity Workbook p. 149. You can have them complete one Dash at a time, with breaks in between, or do all four at once. Time the Dashes, or let students complete them at their own pace. Students can check their answers on Student Book page 321. A second Dash is included on the back for retesting if needed.

Activity 3

Comparison Word Problems

9-6 Class Activity Name Date

▶ Comparison Statements

Use the sentences and pictures below to complete the comparison statements.

Martina has 6 tennis balls. Chris has 2 tennis balls.

Martina

Chris

1. Martina has 4 more tennis balls than Chris.
2. Chris has 4 fewer tennis balls than Martina.
3. Martina has 3 times as many tennis balls as Chris.
4. Chris has $\frac{1}{3}$ as many tennis balls as Martina.

Use the sentences and pictures below to complete the comparison statements.

Bobby has 3 hockey pucks. Wayne has 15 hockey pucks.

Bobby

Wayne

5. Write a comparison statement about the hockey pucks using the word *more*. Wayne has 12 more hockey pucks than Bobby.
6. Write a comparison statement about the hockey pucks using the word *fewer*. Bobby has 12 fewer hockey pucks than Wayne.
7. Wayne has 5 times as many hockey pucks as Bobby.
8. Bobby has $\frac{1}{5}$ as many hockey pucks as Wayne.

UNIT 9 LESSON 6 Comparison Word Problems 323

Student Activity Book page 323

▶ Comparison Statements WHOLE CLASS

Remind students that, in earlier lessons, they solved problems that involved comparing two amounts. Those comparison problems used the word *more* or *fewer* and often asked about the *difference* between two amounts.

Direct students to Student Book page 323. Have them look at the first sentence and picture to help them answer the first four statements. Select students to read the completed statements and explain how they found the answers.

Activity continued ▶

35 MINUTES

Goal: Solve comparison word problems.

Materials: Student Activity Book or Hardcover Book pp. 323–325, overhead projector (optional), transparency of Student Book page 323 (optional)

NCTM Standards:
Number and Operations
Algebra
Problem Solving
Representation

Class Management

You might prepare a transparency of Student Activity Book page 323 to help facilitate the lesson.

Teaching Note

Math Background In this lesson, the multiplication-related phrase, *"times as many as"* and a fractional-related phrase such as, *"one third as many"* are used to compare two groups. The concept of equal groups is key to comparing from a multiplication or fractional point of view. Students have compared groups by identifying each item as one. Now, they will see two or more items as one group when comparing.

❶ Teaching the Lesson (continued)

Differentiated Instruction

Extra Help Some students may have difficulty separating the larger group into equal smaller groups of the correct number. Show students how to use an index card to measure and mark off the size of the smaller group. They can then use the marked part of the index card to measure smaller groups in the larger group.

Teaching Note

Fractions The discussion of fractions in this lesson is informal. Students aren't expected to master these ideas at this time. Fraction concepts will be the focus of Unit 6.

English Language Learners

Say: **A *fraction* is a part of the whole.** Draw a pizza cut into 8 slices on the board.

- **Beginning** Say: **I eat 1 of 8 equal slices.** Write $\frac{1}{8}$. Say: **This is a *fraction*.** Have students repeat.
- **Intermediate** Ask: Is **1 slice 1 of 8 equal parts?** yes Write $\frac{1}{8}$. Ask: **Is $\frac{1}{8}$ a *fraction*?** yes
- **Advanced** Ask: **1 slice is 1 of how many equal parts?** 8 Write $\frac{1}{8}$. Say: $\frac{1}{8}$ **is a __.** fraction

Point out that statements 1 and 2 can be completed either by subtracting or by solving an addition problem. Tell students that there is another type of comparison that requires using multiplication. Introduce the idea that when we compare two amounts using multiplication, we consider the smaller amount to be the group. Ask,

- What is the smaller amount in this situation? 2 tennis balls Circle groups of 2 tennis balls in the picture.

Circle the groups on the transparency as students do so on their page.

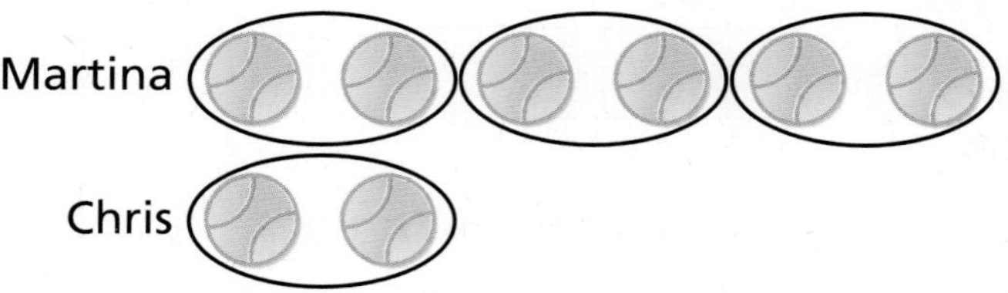

- Chris has 1 group of 2 tennis balls, and Martina has 3 groups of 2 tennis balls. Martina has *3 times as many* tennis balls as Chris.

Have students complete problem 3. Point out that the completed statement describes the larger amount—the number of balls Martina has—in terms of the smaller amount—the number of balls Chris has. It is also possible to make the opposite comparison, to describe the smaller amount in terms of the larger amount.

- In this situation, we say that Chris has one third as many tennis balls as Martina.

Write "one third" on the board, and explain that one third is a *fraction.*

- Does anyone know what a fraction is?

Some students may know that a fraction is a number that shows a part of a whole or a part of a group.

- Who knows how to write one third using numbers?

Have a student write one third in fraction notation on the board, or write it yourself.

One third $\frac{1}{3}$

- What does $\frac{1}{3}$ mean? 1 of 3 equal parts or groups

Show students this drawing to help them visually see $\frac{1}{3}$ of a set.

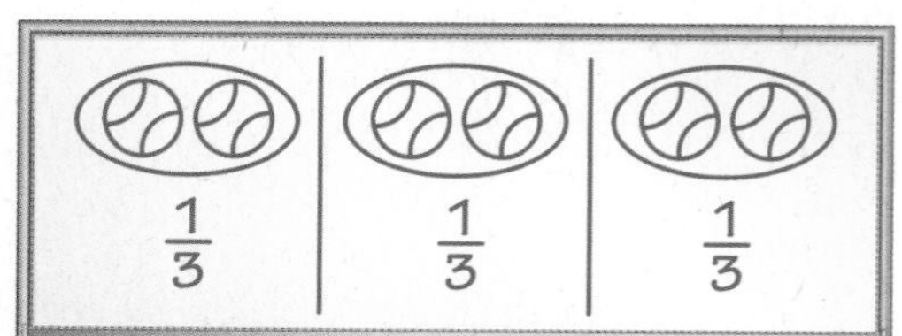

Have students write $\frac{1}{3}$ in the blank in problem 4. Read the completed statement aloud, and ask if anyone can explain what it means. See **Math Talk in Action** in the side column.

Have students work independently to solve problems 5–8, and then discuss the answers. To solve problems 7 and 8, students should consider the smaller amount, 3 hockey pucks, to be the group.

Solve and Discuss Have students complete problems 9–16. You might explain that, from problem 9 on, the comparison statements no longer include the word "times"; students will have to write this in as part of the answer.

Ask students to look for a pattern in the number they wrote for the last two problems in each group of problems. In each problem, one blank has a whole number and the other has a fraction that is 1 over the whole number.

9–6 Name ________________ Date ________

Class Activity

Make a math drawing to show the situation. Then use the sentences to write and complete the comparison statements.

Abby has 8 comic books. Pascal has 2 comic books.

Abby
Pascal

9. Write a comparison statement about the comic books using the word *more*.
Abby has 6 more comic books than Pascal.

10. Write a comparison statement about the comic books using the word *fewer*.
Pascal has 6 fewer comic books than Abby.

11. Abby has 4 times as many comic books as Pascal.

12. Pascal has $\frac{1}{4}$ as many comic books as Abby.

Kai has 3 paintbrushes. Neeta has 18 paintbrushes.

Kai
Neeta

13. Write a comparison statement about the paintbrushes using the word *more*.
Neeta has 15 more paintbrushes than Kai.

14. Write a comparison statement about the paintbrushes using the word *fewer*.
Kai has 15 fewer paintbrushes than Neeta.

15. Kai has $\frac{1}{6}$ as many paint brushes as Neeta.

16. Neeta has 6 times as many paint brushes as Kai.

324 UNIT 9 LESSON 6 Comparison Word Problems

Student Activity Book page 324

Activity continued ▶

Math Talk in Action

Who can explain what the statement "Chris has $\frac{1}{3}$ as many tennis balls as Martina" means?

Jada: The top number in the fraction, 1, is the number of equal groups in the smaller amount. The smaller amount is 1 group of 2 tennis balls.

Nick: The bottom number, 3, is the number of equal groups in the larger amount. The larger amount has 3 groups of 2 tennis balls.

Adam: I think the statement says that Chris has 1 group and Martina has 3 groups.

You are all correct!

Teaching Note

Language and Vocabulary Write the fractions below on the board. Ask a volunteer to read them aloud, and then read them aloud yourself.

$\frac{1}{2}, \frac{1}{3}, \frac{1}{4}, \frac{1}{5}, \frac{1}{6}, \frac{1}{7}, \frac{1}{8}, \frac{1}{9}, \frac{1}{10}$

Ask students what pattern they hear in the fraction names. They should notice that, except for $\frac{1}{2}$, the names are all "one" followed by the words used to describe the order of things arranged in a line—third, fourth, fifth, sixth, and so on. The exception is $\frac{1}{2}$, which is read "one half."

The Learning Classroom

Helping Community Students can work in pairs to role-play the problem situations on Student Book pages 323–325. Each student can reinforce how many items and groups he or she has, as the pairs try to find the appropriate multiplication and fraction language to compare.

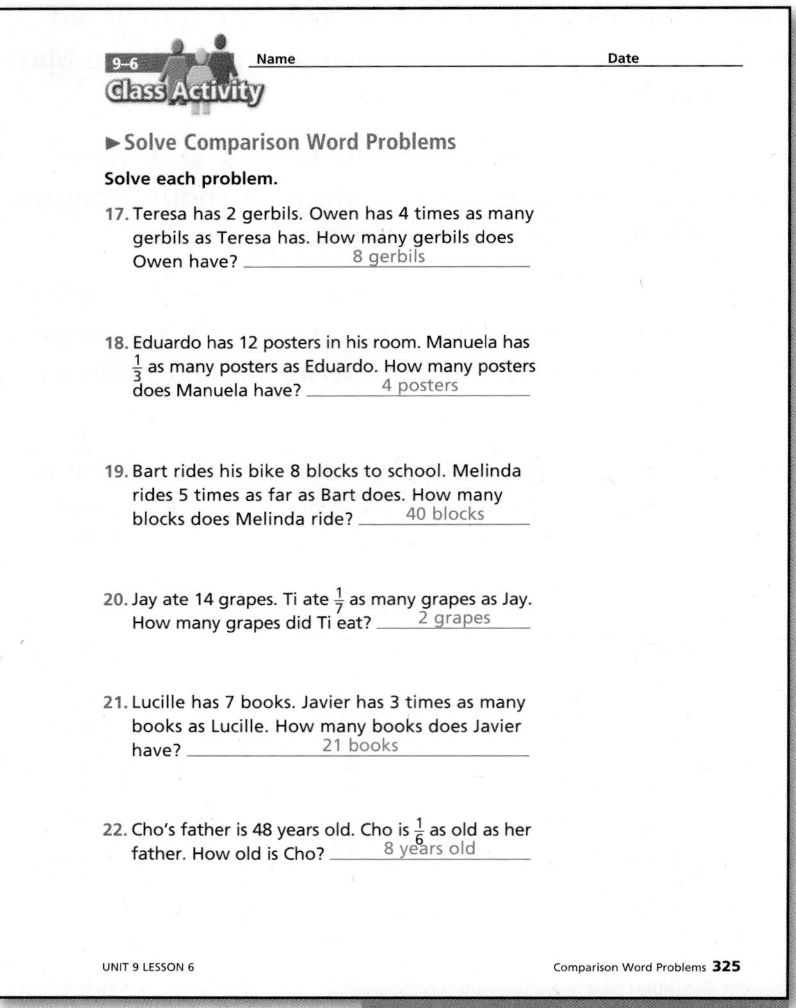

9–6 Class Activity Name Date

▶ Solve Comparison Word Problems

Solve each problem.

17. Teresa has 2 gerbils. Owen has 4 times as many gerbils as Teresa has. How many gerbils does Owen have? 8 gerbils

18. Eduardo has 12 posters in his room. Manuela has $\frac{1}{3}$ as many posters as Eduardo. How many posters does Manuela have? 4 posters

19. Bart rides his bike 8 blocks to school. Melinda rides 5 times as far as Bart does. How many blocks does Melinda ride? 40 blocks

20. Jay ate 14 grapes. Ti ate $\frac{1}{7}$ as many grapes as Jay. How many grapes did Ti eat? 2 grapes

21. Lucille has 7 books. Javier has 3 times as many books as Lucille. How many books does Javier have? 21 books

22. Cho's father is 48 years old. Cho is $\frac{1}{6}$ as old as her father. How old is Cho? 8 years old

UNIT 9 LESSON 6 Comparison Word Problems 325

Student Activity Book page 325

▶ Solve Comparison Word Problems WHOLE CLASS

Using **Solve and Discuss,** have students solve problems 17–22 on Student Book page 325. In these comparison problems, students are given one amount and a comparison statement, and they must find the other amount. Encourage them to make simple drawings to represent the situations. Have student volunteers share their drawings with the class.

Here are some possible methods for solving problems 17 and 18.

Problem 17 The 2 gerbils Teresa has is the smaller amount, so consider 2 gerbils to be the group.

Owen has 4 times as many, so he has 4 groups of 2 gerbils, or 8 gerbils.

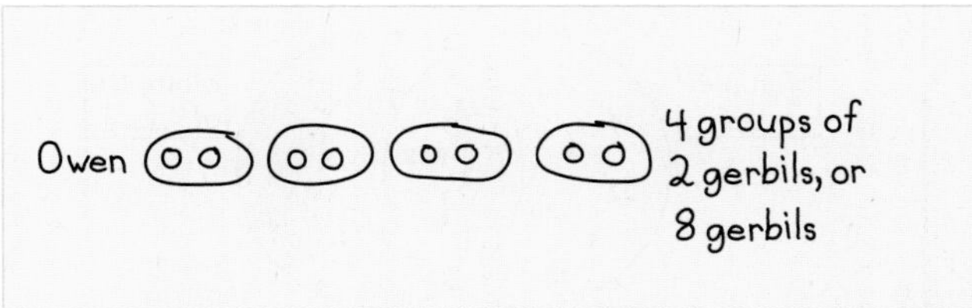

Problem 18 The 12 posters Eduardo has is the larger amount. Manuela has $\frac{1}{3}$ as many. To find the number she has, divide 12 posters into 3 equal groups.

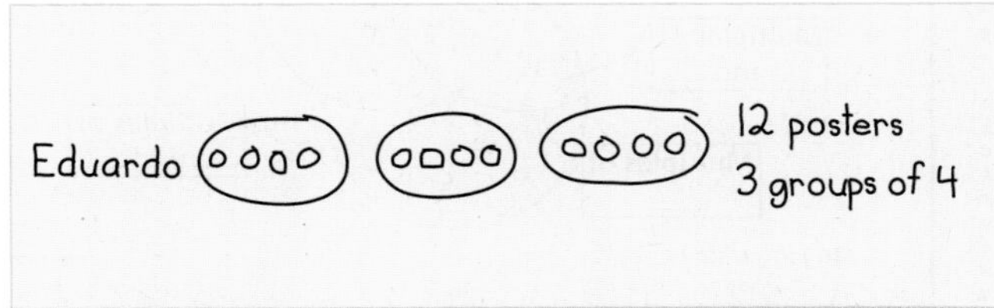

Manuela has 1 group of posters, or 4 posters.

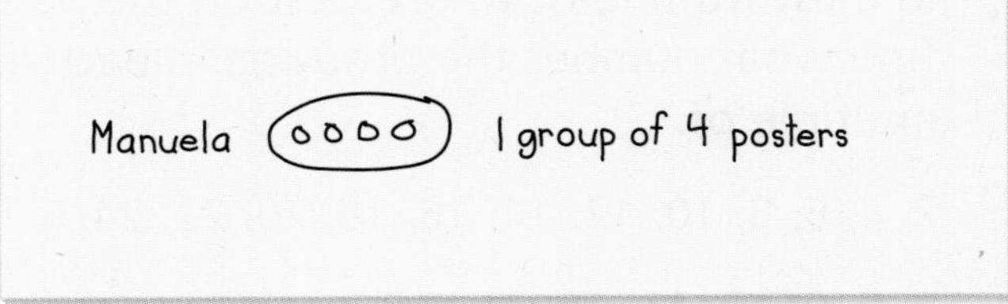

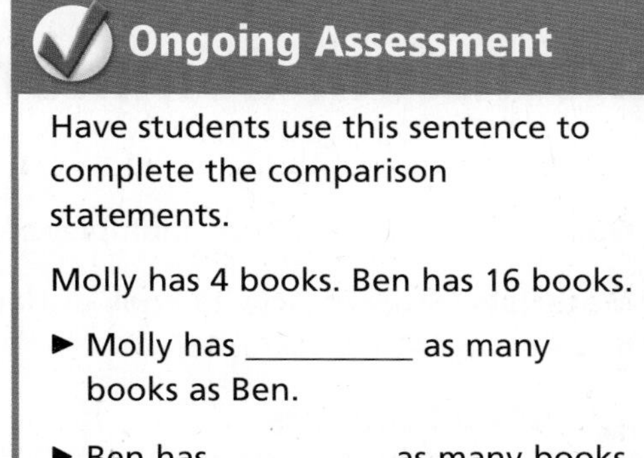

Ongoing Assessment

Have students use this sentence to complete the comparison statements.

Molly has 4 books. Ben has 16 books.

- Molly has __________ as many books as Ben.
- Ben has __________ as many books as Molly.

2 Going Further

Extension: Common Multiples

Goal: Explore the common multiples of two numbers.

Materials: Student Activity Book or Hardcover Book p. 326 and Activity Workbook p. 150.

NCTM Standards:
Number and Operations
Algebra
Representation

▶ Introduce Venn Diagrams WHOLE CLASS

A Venn diagram is a picture that is used to show the relationships of sets or groups. Draw the following on the board.

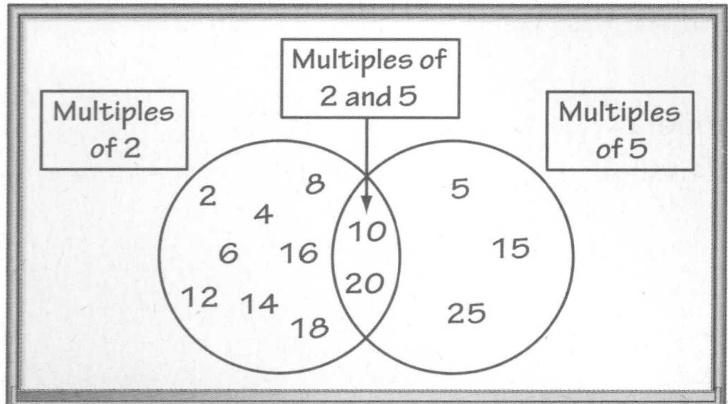

Explain to students that the numbers that are in the left circle are multiples of 2 and the numbers that are in the right circle are multiples of 5. Explain that a *multiple* is the product of a number and any other number. For example, 0, 6, 12, 18, and 24 are multiples of 6 because each is the product of 6 and another number. $0 \times 6 = 0$, $1 \times 6 = 6$, $2 \times 6 = 12$, $3 \times 6 = 18$, and $4 \times 6 = 24$.

Emphasize that the numbers in the intersection (where the circles overlap) are multiples of both 2 and 5.

▶ Use a Venn Diagram to Show Relationships WHOLE CLASS

Tell students that the rule they are going to sort with involves multiples. Direct students to Student Activity Book page 326.

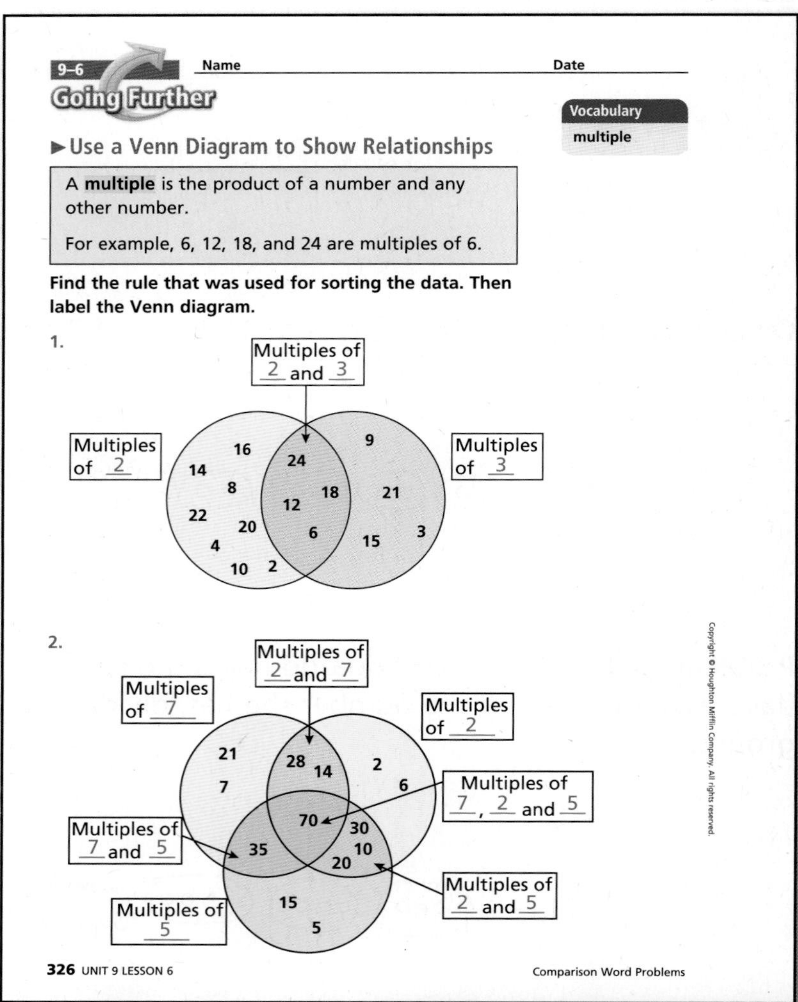

Student Activity Book page 326

Write the products given in the circles in exercise 1 in a list from least to greatest on the board. Then find what number the products in each list are a multiple of.

2, 4, 6, 8, 10, 12, 14, 16, 18, 20, 22, 24 – Multiples of 2

3, 6, 9, 12, 15, 18, 21, 24 – Multiples of 3

Circle the numbers that are in both lists. Tell students that these numbers are called common multiples of 2 and 3. Point out these numbers in the overlapping parts of the circle.

Have students use this method to help them find the sorting rules for exercise 2.

Intervention — Activity Card 9-6

Compare with Counters
Activity Card 9-6 ●

Work: In pairs

Use:
- MathBoard materials
- 30 Counters
- Homework page 229

1. **Work Together** Model the comparisons on Homework page 229. First, use counters to represent the greater amount. Then separate the counters into groups of the same number as the lesser amount.
2. Look at the model for Sam's and Brenna's marbles. Why is Sam's marble collection divided into groups of 3? 18 marbles is the greater. So Sam's marbles are divided into groups of 3 which is the lesser amount.

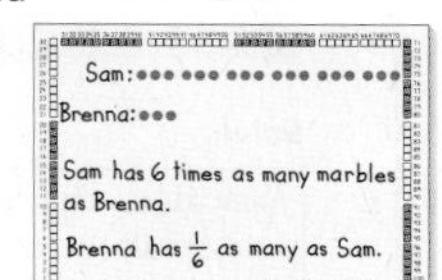

3. **Think** How does the fraction $\frac{1}{6}$ relate to the model for Problem 1? Sam has 6 groups of 3 marbles and Brenna has one group of 3. So Brenna has $\frac{1}{6}$ as many as Sam.
4. Continue modeling the other Homework problems.

Unit 9, Lesson 6

Activity Note Be sure that students can distinguish between the comparisons using "as many as" and "more than." Point out that "as many as" implies multiplication, and "more than" implies subtraction.

Math Writing Prompt
Make a Drawing Make a drawing to show 3 items that are alike and another drawing to show 4 times as many of these items. Explain how you knew how many items to draw for "4 times as many."

Soar to Success Math **Software Support**

Warm Up 9.07

On Level — Activity Card 9-6

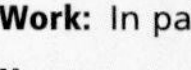

Multiplication Comparison Problems
Activity Card 9-6 ▲

Work: In pairs

Use:
- 5 index cards
- TRB M25 (Game Cards)

Decide:

Who will be Student 1 and who will be Student 2 for the first round.

1. Write an item name on each index card. Shuffle the cards and place them face down in a pile. Place the shuffled Game Cards face down in a pile.

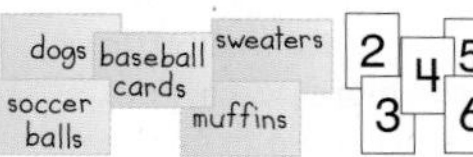

2. **Student 1:** Pick an item card. Then pick a Game Card to represent the lesser number of items in a comparison situation. Next, choose a multiple of that number as the greater number of items to be compared.
3. **Student 2:** Write two comparison statements, using the item and numbers your partner chose. Be sure to include a fraction and the words "times as many as" in the statements you write.

Unit 9, Lesson 6

Activity Note Students should recognize the word and number patterns in these types of comparisons. For any given item and number, the following two comparisons are valid: Sue has 7 times as many items as Beth. So Beth has $\frac{1}{7}$ as many items as Sue.

Math Writing Prompt
Summarize Explain how the statements "Michael has 8 times as many books as Angie" and "Angie has $\frac{1}{8}$ as many books as Michael" are related.

Harcourt Mega Math Grades K-6 **Software Support**

Country Countdown: Harrison's Comparisons, Level I

Challenge — Activity Card 9-6

Comparison Logic Problems
Activity Card 9-6 ■

Work: In pairs

Use:
- TRB M106 (Comparison Logic Problems)

1. **Work Together** Solve the comparison logic problems on TRB M106.

Tony is having a party. Use these clues to help answer the questions at the end:
- The number of friends at the party was less than 20.
- Tony had to open more than 2 bags of favors to give out one favor to each friend at the party.
- Each bag of favors had 7 favors in it.
- Some of the friends are sitting at a small table. The rest of the friends are sitting at a large table.
- The small table has $\frac{1}{3}$ as many friends as the large table.

2. Read each problem. Decide which clues to use first. In the problem above, what do the clues about favors tell you about the number of friends at the party? At least 15 friends were at the party.

Unit 9, Lesson 6

Activity Note If time allows, have pairs of students write their own logic problem and challenge other pairs to solve it.

Math Writing Prompt
Investigate Math Suppose you find 4 times a number and then you find $\frac{1}{4}$ of the answer. What number do you get? Explain.

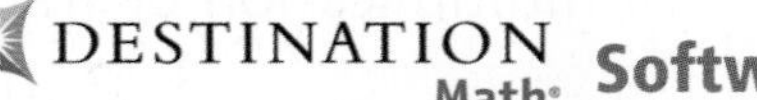

Software Support

Course II: Module 2: Unit 3: Dividing by a 1-digit Number

3 Homework and Spiral Review

9–6 Homework **Goal:** Additional Practice

This Homework page provides practice in solving comparison problems involving multiplication and division.

9–6 Homework Name ______ Date ______

Study Plan

______ Homework Helper

Complete the comparison statements.

Sam has 18 marbles. Brenna has 3 marbles.

1. Write a comparison statement about the marbles using the word *more*.
   Sam has 15 more marbles than Brenna.
2. Write a comparison statement about the marbles using the word *fewer*.
   Brenna has 15 fewer marbles than Sam.
3. Brenna has $\frac{1}{6}$ as many marbles as Sam.
4. Sam has 6 times as many marbles as Brenna.

Tara swam 5 laps at the pool. Canyon swam 15 laps.

5. Canyon swam 3 times as many laps as Tara.
6. Tara swam $\frac{1}{3}$ as many laps as Canyon.

Solve.

7. Mia sold 9 calendars. Ellen sold 3 times as many calendars. How many calendars did Ellen sell?
   27 calendars
8. Alfredo walked 24 miles in the walk-a-thon. His friend Terence walked $\frac{1}{3}$ as many miles. How many miles did Terence walk?
   8 miles

UNIT 9 LESSON 6 Comparison Word Problems 229

Homework and Remembering page 229

9–6 Remembering **Goal:** Spiral Review

This Remembering page would be appropriate anytime after today's lesson.

9–6 Remembering Name ______ Date ______

Solve.

Isaac drew this large rectangle, which is made up of two small rectangles.

1. Find the area of the large rectangle by finding the areas of the two small rectangles and adding them.
   $5 \times 6 = 30$ square units; $3 \times 6 = 18$ square units; total = 48 square units
2. Find the area of the large rectangle by multiplying the number of rows by the number of square units in each row.
   $8 \times 6 = 48$ square units

6
5
3
8

Use the bar graph to solve problems 3–6.

Trees in Caspian's Orchard

Tree: Plum, Peach, Pear, Apple

0 5 10 15 20 25 30 35 40 45 50 55 60

Number of Trees

3. How many more peach trees than pear trees are in Caspian's orchard?
   15 more peach trees
4. How many pear and apple trees are in Caspian's orchard altogether?
   80 trees
5. How many plum, peach, and pear trees are in Caspian's orchard?
   110 trees
6. Write a problem using the information from the bar graph. Solve your problem.
   Answers will vary

230 UNIT 9 LESSON 6 Comparison Word Problems

Homework and Remembering page 230

Home or School Activity

Real-World Connection

Survey Count and Comparisons Have students choose two items to count in the real world, such as number of cars and bicycles that go by in 10 minutes. Have them keep a tally of the data as they carry out the survey. Then students make any comparisons they can, using *more* or *less* or multiplication or fraction language.

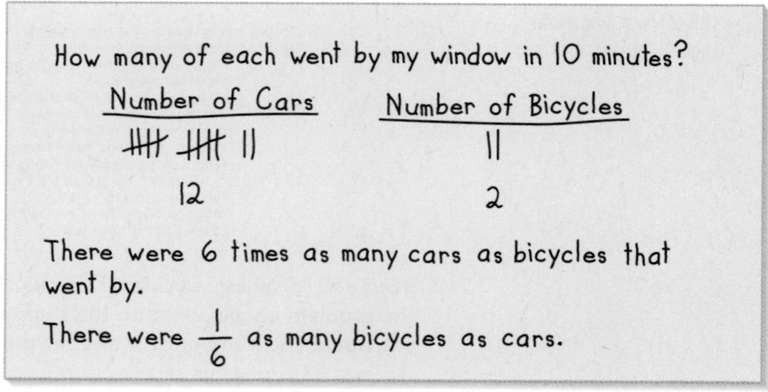

More Comparison Word Problems

Lesson Objectives

- Develop strategies for solving comparison word problems.
- Complete comparison statments based on information in a bar graph.

Vocabulary
fraction

The Day at a Glance

Today's Goals	Materials	
1 Teaching the Lesson A1: Practice count-bys, multiplications, and divisions. A2: Use simple drawings to solve comparison problems involving larger numbers. A3: Complete comparison statments based on information in a bar graph. A4: Solve addition, subtraction, multiplication, and division comparison problems.	**Lesson Activities** Student Activity Book pp. 327–330 or Student Hardcover Book pp. 327–330 Homework and Remembering pp. 231–232 Check Up materials Folders Signature Sheet Blank Sprint Answer Sheet Study Sheets A-C Check Sheets 1–8 Dry-erase markers Sheet protectors Study Sheet Answer Strips Check Sheet Answer Strips Cardstock Strategy cards Mathboard materials	**Going Further** Activity Cards 9–7 Scissors Crayons Connecting Cubes Centimeter Grid Paper Math Journals
2 Going Further ▸ Differentiated Instruction		
3 Homework and Spiral Review		

Use Math Talk today!

Keeping Skills Sharp

Quick Practice — 5 MINUTES

Goal: Practice 7s count-bys, multiplications, and divisions.

Materials: Class Multiplication Table Poster, pointer
Use the Class Poster and the number "7" for these activities.

Repeated Quick Practice
Use these Quick Practice activities from previous lessons.

7s Multiplications in Order (See Unit 7 Lesson 4.)

Mixed 7s Multiplications (See Unit 7 Lesson 2.)

Mixed 7s Divisions (See Unit 7 Lesson 5.)

Daily Routines

Homework Review If students give incorrect answers, have them explain how they found the answers.

Area Lionel plans to fence in an area 6 feet long by 10 feet wide for his garden. How much area will his garden have? 60 square feet

1 Teaching the Lesson

Activity 1

Check Up and Independent Study

5 MINUTES

Goal: Practice count-bys, multiplications, and divisions.

Materials: Folders, Check Up materials: Signature Sheet; Blank Sprint Answer Sheet (TRB M57); Study Sheets A–C, Check Sheets 1–8, dry-erase markers (1 per student), sheet protectors (1 per student), Study Sheet Answer Strips (TRB M54), Check Sheet Answer Strips (TRB M55), cardstock; Strategy Cards, Homework and Remembering p. 231

NCTM Standard:
Number and Operations

▶ Check Up with 6s, 7s, and 8s PAIRS

Give **Student Pairs** a few minutes to test each other using Study Sheets A–C and collect signatures. For students who have collected signatures on Study Sheets A–C, have them study with Check Sheets 1–8. You may want to have Study Sheet and Check Sheet Answer Strips (TRB M54–M55) available.

Then give them 2 or 3 minutes to study independently using their Study Sheets, Check Sheets, or Strategy Cards. Also have them complete their Study Plan box on Homework and Remembering page 231. Students should include any multiplications and divisions they missed in the Check Up. Remind students to place all Check Up Materials in their folders.

Activity 2

Draw Comparison Bars

20 MINUTES

Goal: Use simple drawings to solve comparison problems involving larger numbers.

Materials: MathBoard materials, Student Activity Book or Hardcover Book pp. 327–328

NCTM Standard:
Number and Operations
Algebra
Problem Solving
Representation

▶ Use Comparison Bars WHOLE CLASS

Read the introduction to problems 1 and 2 on Student Book page 327 aloud. Remind students that they have solved problems like this by drawing individual objects. In this situation, that would mean drawing 42 objects for the blue ribbons alone! Tell students that they should try to come up with a simpler drawing to represent the situation. Give them a few minutes to work, and then ask a few students to share their solutions and drawings.

If students don't share this strategy, remind students they can use Comparison Bars to solve comparison problems involving multiplication and division. Demonstrate how to do this for problems 1 and 2.

9–7 Class Activity

Name ______ Date ______

► Use Comparison Bars

Draw comparison bars to help you solve each problem.

Jadzia's dog Roscoe competes in dog shows. He has won 42 blue ribbons and 6 red ribbons.

1. Roscoe has won 7 times as many blue ribbons as red ribbons.
2. Roscoe has won $\frac{1}{7}$ as many red ribbons as blue ribbons.

red ribbons | 6 |

blue ribbons | 6 | 6 | 6 | 6 | 6 | 6 | 6 |

Daphne is 7 years old. Her grandfather is 56 years old.

3. Daphne is $\frac{1}{8}$ as old as her grandfather.
4. Daphne's grandfather is 8 times as old as Daphne.

Daphne's age | 7 |

Grandfather's age | 7 | 7 | 7 | 7 | 7 | 7 | 7 | 7 |

Beatrice has 48 dolls. Cathy has 8 dolls.

5. Beatrice has 6 times as many dolls as Cathy.
6. Cathy has $\frac{1}{6}$ as many dolls as Beatrice.

Beatrice's dolls | 8 | 8 | 8 | 8 | 8 | 8 |

Cathy's dolls | 8 |

UNIT 9 LESSON 7 More Comparison Word Problems 327

Student Activity Book page 327

- The smaller amount, 6 ribbons, is the group. Use a labeled bar to represent this group.

red ribbons | 6 |

- To show the number of blue ribbons, put copies of the 6-bar together, counting up by 6 as you draw each bar, until you reach 42.

red ribbons | 6 |

blue ribbons | 6 | 6 | 6 | 6 | 6 | 6 | 6 |

Count: 6 12 18 24 30 36 42

- There is 1 group of 6 for red ribbons and 7 groups of 6 for blue ribbons, so Roscoe has won 7 times as many blue ribbons as red ribbons. Equivalently, he has won $\frac{1}{7}$ as many red ribbons as blue ribbons.

Give students a few minutes to work on problems 3–6 independently. Then discuss their answers and strategy for solving.

Activity continued ►

Teaching Note

Math Background Students have explored using the multiplication-related phrase, *"times as many as"* and a fractional-related phrase such as, *"one third as many"* to compare two groups. In this lesson, the students will continue to use the language to solve comparison problems involving larger factors: 6s, 7s, and 8s.

English Language Learners

Draw comparison bars on the board for the problems on Student Activity Book p. 327. Have students count the bars for the ribbons.

- **Beginning** Point and make comparisons. Have students repeat. Continue with other problems.
- **Intermediate** Say: **There are 6 ___.** red ribbons **There are 7 *times as many* ___.** blue ribbons Continue with other problems.
- **Advanced** Have students work in pairs to make comparisons. Invite volunteers to share their sentences.

Teaching Note

Watch For! Watch for students who find that the larger group is 1 time less than the correct comparison. They may get this idea from the concept of *"how many more."* Have students say the pattern of multiplications: 1 × 6, 2 × 6, 3 × 6, 4 × 6, 5 × 6, 6 × 6, 7 × 6 as they point to each group, and then compare the last multiplication to the smaller group. 7 × 6 is 7 times as many as 1 × 6 (not 6 times as many). It is helpful to have such students write the count-bys below the longer bar.

Note here contrasting additive comparison bars

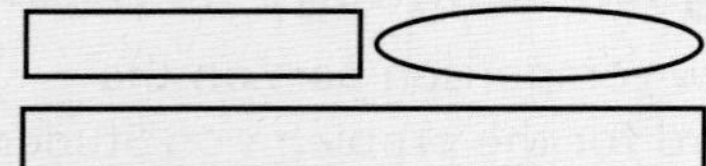

and multiplicative comparison bars with repeated equal groups such as we are using here for these multiplicative comparison problems. Discuss the difference between the two kinds of comparison bars on Student Book page 328.

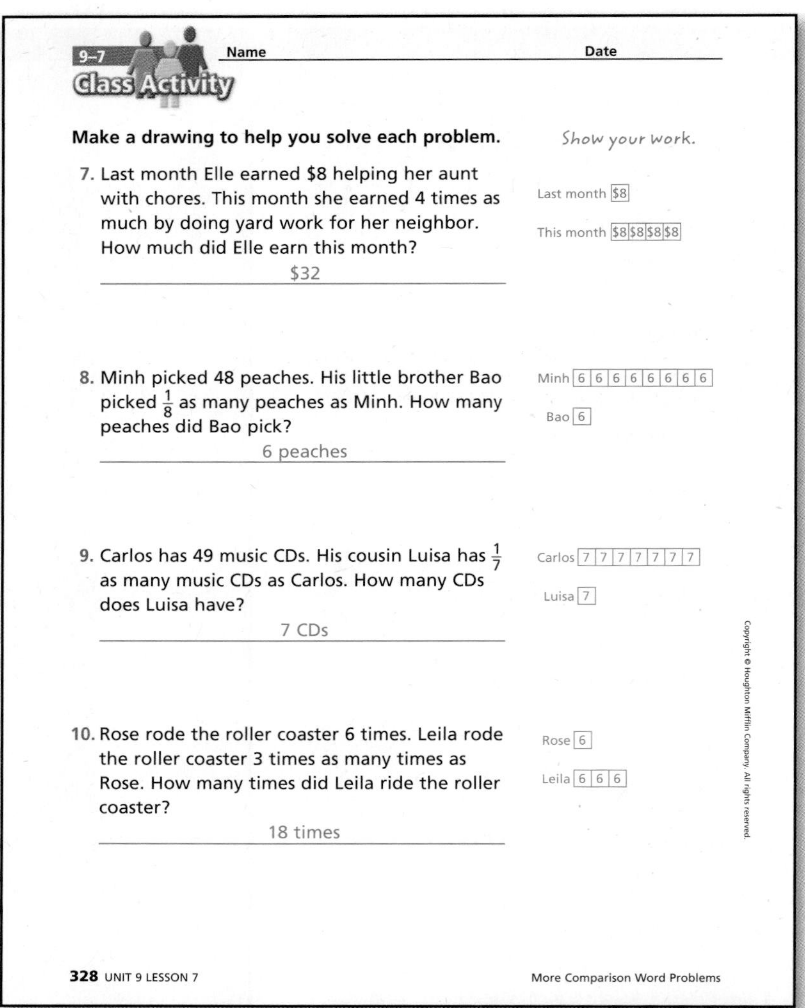

9–7 Class Activity — Name ________ Date ________

Make a drawing to help you solve each problem. *Show your work.*

7. Last month Elle earned $8 helping her aunt with chores. This month she earned 4 times as much by doing yard work for her neighbor. How much did Elle earn this month? $32

8. Minh picked 48 peaches. His little brother Bao picked $\frac{1}{8}$ as many peaches as Minh. How many peaches did Bao pick? 6 peaches

9. Carlos has 49 music CDs. His cousin Luisa has $\frac{1}{7}$ as many music CDs as Carlos. How many CDs does Luisa have? 7 CDs

10. Rose rode the roller coaster 6 times. Leila rode the roller coaster 3 times as many times as Rose. How many times did Leila ride the roller coaster? 18 times

328 UNIT 9 LESSON 7 — More Comparison Word Problems

Student Activity Book page 328

Using the **Solve and Discuss** structure, have students solve problems 7–10.

- A comparison situation involves a larger amount and a smaller amount. Which of these problems tell you the smaller amount? Problems 7 and 10
- What's the smaller amount in Problem 7? $8 What other information are you given? Elle earned 4 times as much this month as last month.

Write the following on the board:

Smaller Amount	Comparison
$8	4 times as much

- The problem asks you to find the larger amount. What amount did you find? $32

Add this information to the board, in a different color if possible.

Smaller Amount	Comparison	Larger Amount
$8	4 times as much	$32

- If a problem gives you the smaller amount and the comparison, how can you find the larger amount? Multiply the smaller amount by the number in the comparison. What equation can we write for this problem? $8 \times 4 = 32$

Repeat this procedure for problem 10.

- Which of the problems tell you the larger amount? Problems 8 and 9
- What is the larger amount in problem 8? 48 peaches What other information are you given? Bao picked $\frac{1}{8}$ as many peaches.
- What is the smaller amount? 6 peaches

Add this information to the board.

Larger Amount	Comparison	Smaller Amount
48 peaches	$\frac{1}{8}$ as much	6 peaches

- If a problem gives you the larger amount and the comparison, how can you find the smaller amount? Divide the larger amount by the bottom number in the comparison fraction. $48 \div 8 = 6$

Repeat this procedure for problem 9.

Activity 3

Interpret a Bar Graph

▶ Use a Bar Graph to Compare WHOLE CLASS

Have students solve problems 11–14 on Student Activity Book page 329.

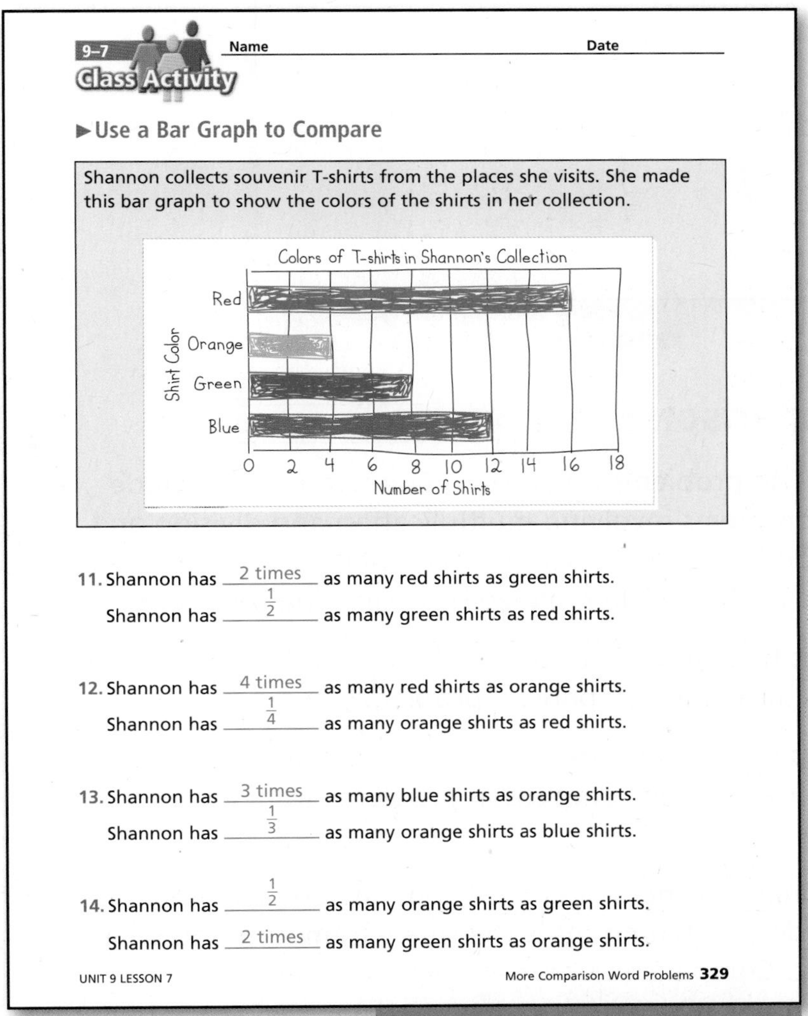

9–7 Class Activity Name Date

▶ Use a Bar Graph to Compare

Shannon collects souvenir T-shirts from the places she visits. She made this bar graph to show the colors of the shirts in her collection.

11. Shannon has 2 times as many red shirts as green shirts.
Shannon has $\frac{1}{2}$ as many green shirts as red shirts.

12. Shannon has 4 times as many red shirts as orange shirts.
Shannon has $\frac{1}{4}$ as many orange shirts as red shirts.

13. Shannon has 3 times as many blue shirts as orange shirts.
Shannon has $\frac{1}{3}$ as many orange shirts as blue shirts.

14. Shannon has $\frac{1}{2}$ as many orange shirts as green shirts.
Shannon has 2 times as many green shirts as orange shirts.

UNIT 9 LESSON 7 More Comparison Word Problems 329

Student Activity Book page 329

15 MINUTES

Goal: Complete comparison statements based on information in a bar graph.

Materials: Student Activity Book or Hardcover Book p. 329

NCTM Standards:
Number and Operations
Algebra
Data Analysis
Problem Solving
Representation

Teaching Note

Math Background Students will now use multiplication and fraction language to compare bars in bar graphs. Using bars is an introduction to length models and comparing wholes, rather than groups.

Differentiated Instruction

Extra Help Some students may have difficulty with the increments of 2 as they find the number that each bar represents. Have the students write in the numbers which complete the horizontal axis to show increments of 1.

Activity 4

Solve Mixed Comparison Problems

 15 MINUTES

Goal: Solve addition, subtraction, multiplication, and division comparison problems.

Materials: Student Activity Book or Hardcover Book p. 330

 **NCTM Standards:**
Number and Operations
Problem Solving
Algebra

Teaching Note

What to Expect from Students
Some students may automatically try to use the new drawing technique of drawing comparison bars to solve the mixed-set of problems. Remind students that they may find problems that can be solved another way. Also remind students that if they choose to draw pictures to help solve the problems, they do not need to draw each individual item. The comparison bars for additive *more/less* comparisons have an oval difference and the multiplicative comparison bars show repeated groups and use numbers. Stress with students that the comparison bars for additive more/less comparisons have oval differences and the multiplicative comparison bars share repeated groups.

Ongoing Assessment

Ask questions such as the following:

- ▶ What number is $\frac{1}{8}$ as many as 48?
- ▶ What number is 6 times as many as 6?

9–7 Class Activity

Name ________ Date ________

▶ Solve Comparison Problems

Solve.

15. Maddie took 21 photographs on her vacation. Jack took $\frac{1}{3}$ as many photos as Maddie. How many photos did Jack take?
7 photos

16. Franco has 18 toy cars. Roberto has 6 more toy cars than Franco. How many toy cars does Roberto have?
24 toy cars

17. Arvin delivered 42 newspapers. Kelly delivered 7 fewer papers than Arvin. How many papers did Kelly deliver?
35 papers

18. Jasmine's dog weighs 8 pounds. Shaunda's dog weighs 5 times as much as Jasmine's dog. How much does Shaunda's dog weigh?
40 pounds

19. Charles is $\frac{1}{4}$ as old as his father. His father is 36 years old. How old is Charles?
9 years old

330 UNIT 9 LESSON 7 More Comparison Word Problems

Student Activity Book page 330

▶ Solve Comparison Problems WHOLE CLASS

Math Talk The problems on Student Book page 330 include two comparison problems involving multiplication and division and two involving addition and subtraction. Using **Solve and Discuss**, have students solve the problems. Summarize by asking the following:

- What key words help you figure out whether a word problem is an addition or a subtraction comparison problem? more, fewer
- What key words help you figure out whether a word problem is a multiplication or a division comparison problem? as many as, as much as

Emphasize that when solving any kind of comparison problem, it is important to decide which amount is the smaller amount and which is the larger amount. Comparison bars can help with this.

Intervention — Activity Card 9-7

Cube Train Graphs

Activity Card 9-7 ●

Work: In pairs

Use:

- Connecting Cubes

1. Use cubes to show the following cube trains.
   - Train A has 4 cubes.
   - Train B has 2 times as many cubes as Train A.
   - Train C has 3 times as many cubes as Train A.
   - Train D has 4 times as many cubes as Train A.
2. Begin by building Train A as shown below. Then use Train A to help you build the other trains.

3. Use the cube trains to copy and complete the comparisons below using fractions.
   - Train B is ? as many cubes as Train D. $\frac{1}{2}$
   - Train A has ? as many cubes as Train C. $\frac{1}{3}$
   - Train A has ? as many cubes as Train D. $\frac{1}{4}$

Unit 9, Lesson 7

Activity Note If students have difficulty completing the comparisons, suggest that they count how many times the smaller train can fit on the larger train. Then use that number to write the fraction.

Math Writing Prompt

Explain Your Thinking Explain how to compare 16 cubes and 4 cubes using "times as many" and a fraction.

Software Support

Warm Up 9.08

On Level — Activity Card 9-7

Build a Bar Graph

Activity Card 9-7 ▲

Work: In pairs

Use:

- TRB M31 (Centimeter-Grid Paper)
- Scissors
- Crayons

1. Copy the bar graph on grid paper.

Number of Hours of TV Watched in a Week
Person: Raj, Lucy
Number of Hours: 0 2 4 6 8 10 12 14 16

2. Shade and cut out strips of paper in the following unit lengths: 16, 8, 4, and 2 units.

Number of Hours of TV Watched in a Week
Person: Raj, Lucy
Number of Hours: 0 2 4 6 8 10 12 14 16

3. Take turns. Choose two strips of paper to represent the hours spent watching TV. Then compare the two amounts, using multiplication or fraction language.
4. Place the strips on the graph to check the comparisons you make.

Unit 9, Lesson 7

Activity Note Students can use the bar graph to compare strips by comparing number of hours each strip represents or by visually comparing how many times the smaller strip fits along the larger strip.

Math Writing Prompt

Make a Drawing Explain how to make a drawing to show that one Comparison Bar is $\frac{1}{4}$ as long as another bar.

Software Support

Country Countdown: White Water Graphing, Level F

Challenge — Activity Card 9-7

Surveys for Bar Graphs

Activity Card 9-7 ■

Work: In pairs

1. Read the information below about tickets sold at four different movies.

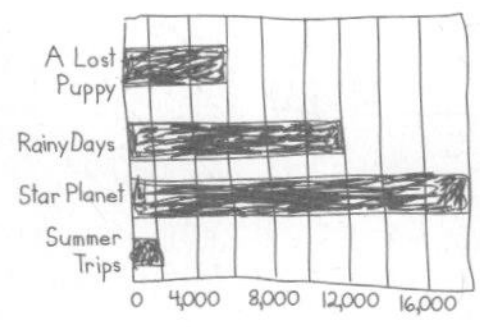

This past weekend, 6 thousand people bought tickets to see the film *A Lost Puppy*. *Rainy Days* sold 2 times as many tickets as *A Lost Puppy*. *Star Planet* sold 3 times as many tickets as *A Lost Puppy*. *Summer Trips* sold $\frac{1}{3}$ as many tickets as *A Lost Puppy*.

2. **Work Together** Draw a horizontal bar graph showing how many people bought tickets to see each movie.

Unit 9, Lesson 7

Activity Note Have students discuss how they determined the number of tickets sold. Then have students exchange graphs to check.

Math Writing Prompt

Summarize Explain how to solve this problem: Erin read 3 times as many books as Kevin read. Kevin read $\frac{1}{2}$ as many books as Juan. Juan read 12 books. Who read the most books?

Software Support

Course II: Module 2: Unit 3: Meaning of Division

3 Homework and Spiral Review

9–7 Homework Goal: Additional Practice

This Homework page provides practice in solving multiplication and division comparison problems.

9–7 **Homework** Name ______ Date ______

Study Plan
Homework Helper

Complete the sentence.

Kristi is training for a marathon. This month she ran 36 miles. Last month she ran only 6 miles.

Show your work.

1. Kristi ran 6 times as many miles this month as last month.
   This month 6 6 6 6 6 6
   Last month 6
2. Kristi ran $\frac{1}{6}$ as many miles last month as this month.

Make a drawing to help you solve each problem.

3. Darnell swam 8 miles last month. He plans to swim 3 times as many miles this month. How many miles does he plan to swim this month? 24 miles
   Last month 8
   This month 8 8 8
4. Geoff rode 64 miles on his bike last month. He rode $\frac{1}{8}$ as many miles this month as last month. How many miles did he ride this month? 8 miles
   Last month 8 8 8 8 8 8 8 8
   This month 8
5. Molly ran in 4 races at the track meet. Her sister Sophie ran in 8 races. How many times more races did Sophie run in than Molly? 2 times
   Molly 2 2
   Sophie 2 2 2 2
6. Tamara made 8 baskets in the championship game. Lucia made $\frac{1}{4}$ as many baskets as Tamara. How many baskets did Lucia make? 2 baskets
   Tamara 2 2 2 2
   Lucia 2

UNIT 9 LESSON 7 More Comparison Word Problems 231

Homework and Remembering page 231

9–7 Remembering Goal: Spiral Review

This Remembering page would be appropriate anytime after today's lesson.

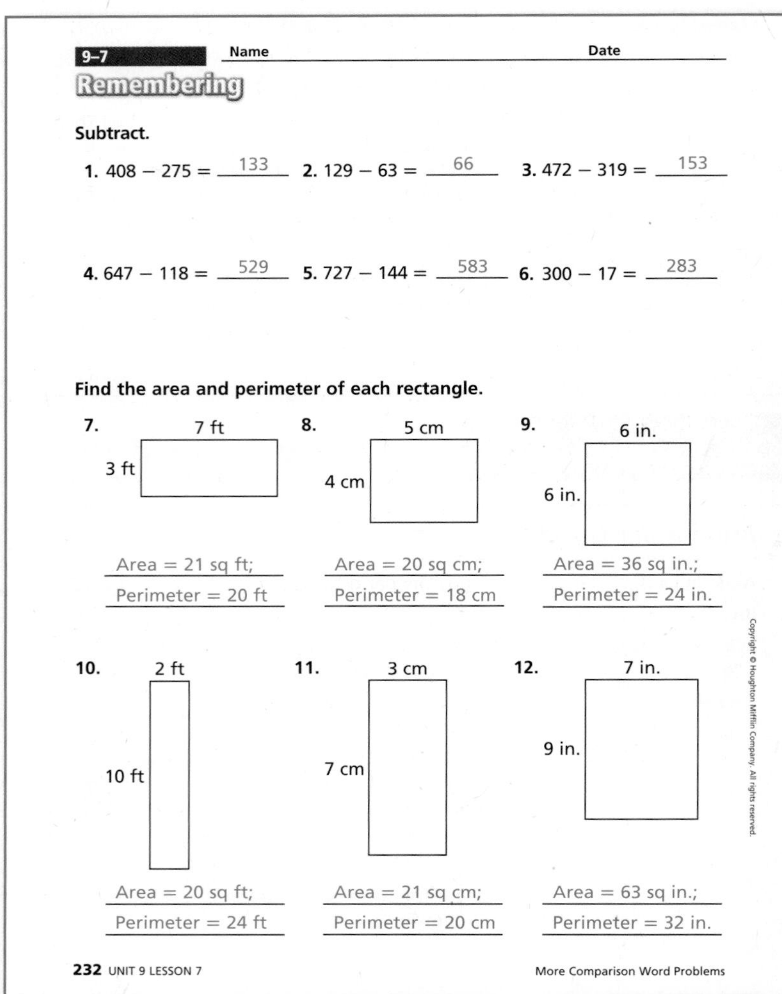

9–7 **Remembering** Name ______ Date ______

Subtract.

1. 408 − 275 = 133
2. 129 − 63 = 66
3. 472 − 319 = 153
4. 647 − 118 = 529
5. 727 − 144 = 583
6. 300 − 17 = 283

Find the area and perimeter of each rectangle.

7. 7 ft by 3 ft — Area = 21 sq ft; Perimeter = 20 ft
8. 5 cm by 4 cm — Area = 20 sq cm; Perimeter = 18 cm
9. 6 in. by 6 in. — Area = 36 sq in.; Perimeter = 24 in.
10. 2 ft by 10 ft — Area = 20 sq ft; Perimeter = 24 ft
11. 3 cm by 7 cm — Area = 21 sq cm; Perimeter = 20 cm
12. 7 in. by 9 in. — Area = 63 sq in.; Perimeter = 32 in.

232 UNIT 9 LESSON 7 More Comparison Word Problems

Homework and Remembering page 232

Home or School Activity

Art Connection

More or Fewer in a Picture Have students either draw a picture or find a picture in a book, magazine, or newspaper. The picture should have many items in it. Have them describe the picture using comparison words such as *more, fewer, times, as many as,* and so on.

Square Numbers

Lesson Objectives

- Understand what a square number is.
- Describe patterns in the square numbers in the multiplication table.

Vocabulary
square unit
area
square number

The Day at a Glance

Today's Goals	Materials	
1 Teaching the Lesson **A1:** Take Sprints for 8s multiplications and divisions. **A2:** Practice count-bys, multiplications, and divisions. **A3:** Discuss square numbers.	**Lesson Activities** Student Activity Book pp. 331–334 or Student Hardcover Book pp. 331–334 and Activity Workbook pp. 151–153 (includes Check Sheets and Special Formats) Homework and Remembering pp. 233–238 Blank Sprint Answer Sheet (TRB M57) Signature Sheet Check Up materials Blank Sprint Answer Sheet Study Sheets A-C Check Sheets 1–9 Dry-erase markers Sheet protectors Study Sheet Answer Strips Check Sheet Answer Strips	Cardstock Strategy Cards *Sea Squares* by Joy N. Hulme (Hyperion Books, 1993) **Going Further** Student Activity Book p. 334 Activity Cards 9–8 Scissors Centimeter Grid Paper (TRB M31) Number Cubes Multiplication Riddles (TRB M108) Math Journals
2 Going Further ▶ Differentiated Instruction		
3 Homework and Spiral Review		

Use Math Talk today!

Keeping Skills Sharp

Quick Practice — 5 MINUTES

Goal: Use the 5s Shortcut.

Materials: Class Multiplication Table Poster, pointer

5s Shortcut Display the Multiplication Table Poster. The **Student Leader** points to any equation with a multiplier of 6 or more and reads it aloud. Then, starting with the "5 ×" equation in the same column, the leader points to one equation at a time as students say the count-bys. When students reach the original equation, the leader says "Equation," and the class says the equation. You may wish to lead the activity first and then have a leader take over.

Daily Routines

Homework Review Have students show and explain their drawings. As a class, review for any errors.

Estimation 167 students bought lunch. Of these students, 84 bought pizza and the rest bought spaghetti. Round each number to the nearest ten to find about how many students bought spaghetti. about 90 students

1 Teaching the Lesson

Activity 1

Assess 8s

 5 MINUTES

Goal: Take Sprints for 8s multiplications and divisions.

Materials: Student Activity Book p. 331 or Activity Workbook p. 151, Blank Sprint Answer Sheet (TRB M57), Signature Sheet

 **NCTM Standard:** Number and Operations

 Class Management

If students are struggling with count-bys, you might give a count-by Sprint.

▶ Sprints for 8s INDIVIDUALS

Direct students to Student Activity Book page 331 or Activity Workbook p. 151 and read aloud the two Sprints below.

× 8	÷ 8
a. 3 × 8 = 24	a. 16 ÷ 8 = 2
b. 1 × 8 = 8	b. 32 ÷ 8 = 4
c. 7 × 8 = 56	c. 40 ÷ 8 = 5
d. 10 × 8 = 80	d. 48 ÷ 8 = 6
e. 2 × 8 = 16	e. 8 ÷ 8 = 1
f. 5 × 8 = 40	f. 64 ÷ 8 = 8
g. 6 × 8 = 48	g. 80 ÷ 8 = 10
h. 4 × 8 = 32	h. 72 ÷ 8 = 9
i. 8 × 8 = 64	i. 56 ÷ 8 = 7
j. 9 × 8 = 72	j. 24 ÷ 8 = 3

Have **Student Pairs** check one another's work as you read the answers, marking any incorrect answers and getting signatures.

Activity 2

Check Up and Independent Study

 5 MINUTES

Goal: Practice count-bys, multiplications, and divisions

Materials: Check Up materials: Signature Sheet, Blank Sprint Answer Sheet (TRB M57), Study Sheets A–C, Check Sheets 1–9, dry-erase markers (1 per student), sheet protectors (1 per student), Study Sheet Answer Strips (TRB M54), Check Sheet Answer Strips (TRB M55), cardstock; Strategy Cards, Homework and Remembering p. 235

 **NCTM Standard:** Number and Operations

▶ Check Up with 6s, 7s, and 8s PAIRS

Give **Student Pairs** a few minutes to test each other using Study Sheets A–C and collect signatures. For students who have already collected signatures on Study Sheets A–C, have them study with Check Sheets 1–9. You may want to have Study Sheet and Check Sheet Answer Strips (TRB M54–M55) available.

Then give them 2 or 3 minutes to study independently using their Study Sheets, Check Sheets, or Strategy Cards. Also have students complete their Study Plan box on Homework and Remembering page 235. Students should include any multiplications and divisions they missed in the Check Up. Remind students to place all their Check Up materials in their folders.

Activity 3

Square Numbers

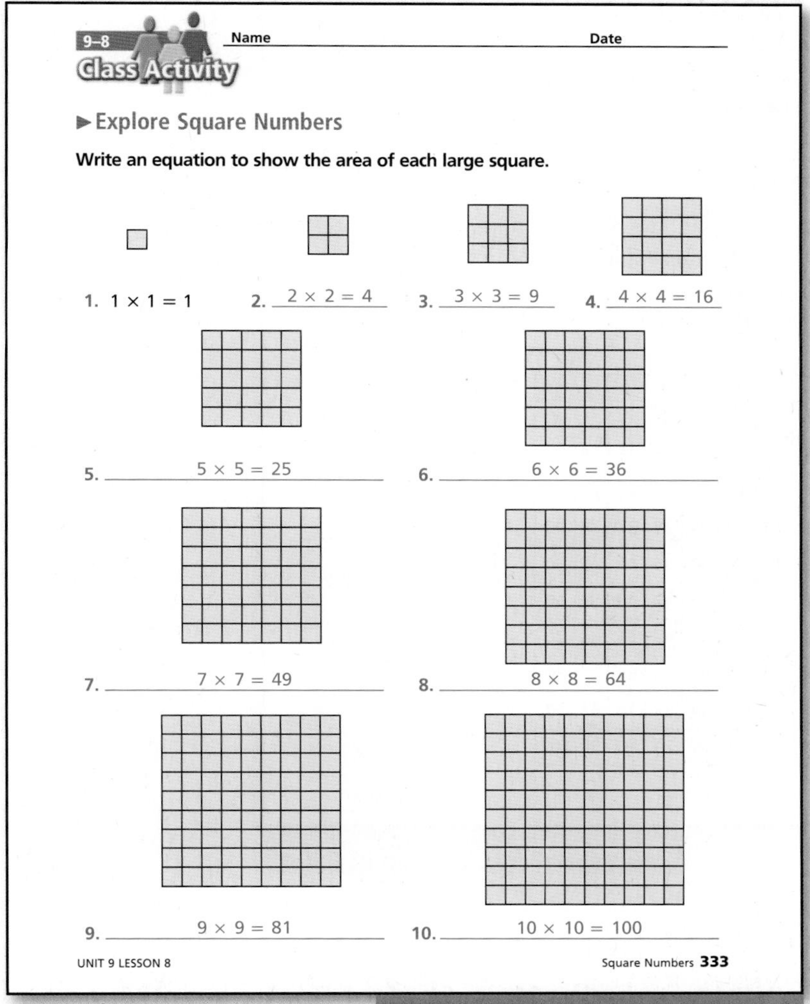
9–8 Class Activity

Name Date

▶ Explore Square Numbers

Write an equation to show the area of each large square.

1. 1 × 1 = 1
2. 2 × 2 = 4
3. 3 × 3 = 9
4. 4 × 4 = 16
5. 5 × 5 = 25
6. 6 × 6 = 36
7. 7 × 7 = 49
8. 8 × 8 = 64
9. 9 × 9 = 81
10. 10 × 10 = 100

UNIT 9 LESSON 8 Square Numbers 333

Student Activity Book page 333

35 MINUTES

Goal: Discuss square numbers.

Materials: Student Activity Book or Hardcover Book pp. 333–334 and Activity Workbook p. 153

NCTM Standards:
Number and Operations
Algebra
Measurement
Representation

▶ Explore Square Numbers WHOLE CLASS

Have students look at exercises 1–10 on Student Book page 333. Explain that the little squares in the drawings are square units. Ask how all the drawings are alike. They all show squares made up of square units. Ask how they are different. The large squares are different sizes.

Ask students to write an equation to show the area of each square. Exercise 1 is done for them. Tell them they don't have to label the units.

Activity continued ▶

Differentiated Instruction

Advanced Learners You might ask more advanced students to try to find a pattern in the number of unit squares added from one square to the next.

The number of squares added with each step follows the pattern 3, 5, 7, 9, 11, ... The illustration below shows the pattern visually.

1

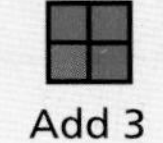
Add 3

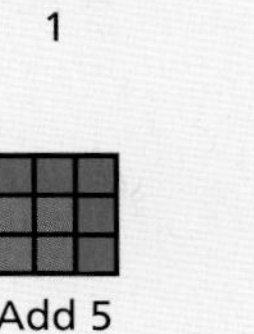
Add 5

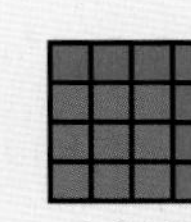
Add 7

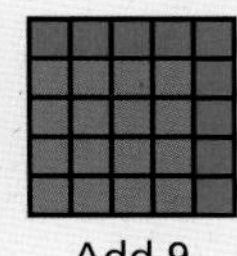
Add 9

Add 11

Extra Help Some students may be distracted by all of the area models on Student Book page 333, as they are working on one exercise. Provide students with a few sheets of black construction paper to use to cover the other exercises, as they work on each one of the models.

Teaching the Lesson (continued)

Class Management

You may want to create a transparency of the multiplication table on Student Book page 334, and have students come to the overhead to circle the products. If an overhead projector is not available, draw the table on a sheet of chart paper and post it on a wall.

English Language Learners

Make sure students understand *square number.* Draw arrays for 2×2, 3×3, and 4×4. Have students find the products.

- **Beginning** Ask: **What shape are these arrays?** square Say: **The products are *square numbers.*** Have students repeat.
- **Intermediate** Say: **When we multiply a number by itself the array is ___.** square Ask: **Are the products *square numbers*?** yes
- **Advanced** Have students describe the arrays and tell what happens when a number is multiplied by itself.

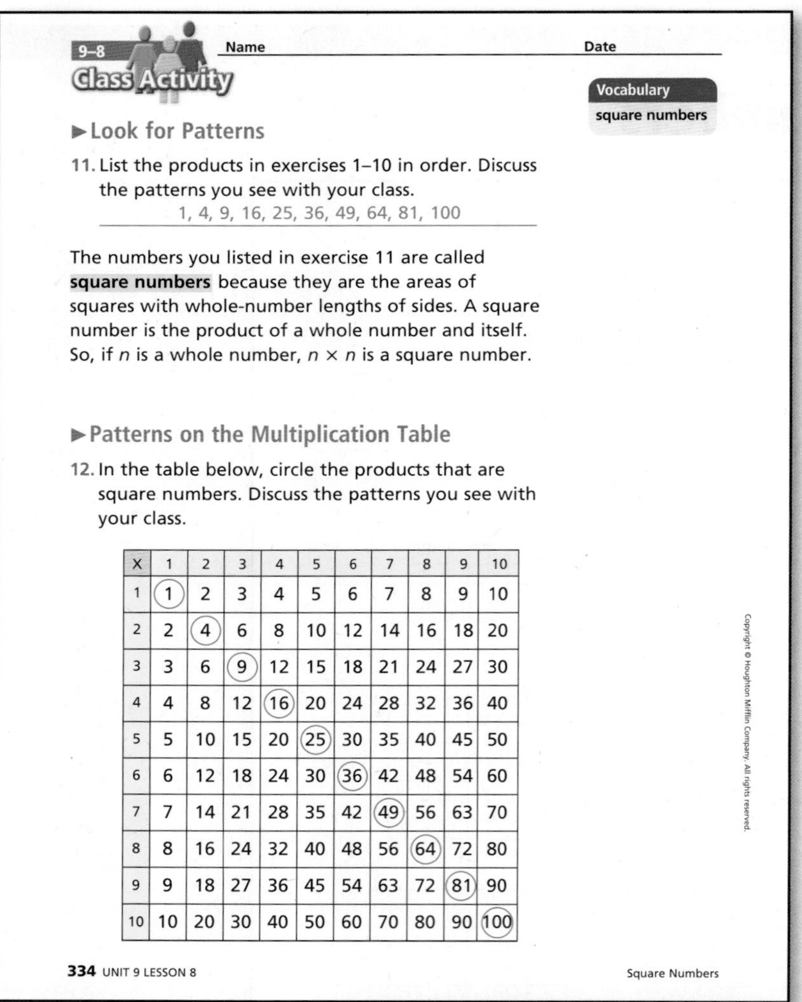

9–8 **Class Activity** Name ______ Date ______

Vocabulary
square numbers

▶ **Look for Patterns**

11. List the products in exercises 1–10 in order. Discuss the patterns you see with your class.
1, 4, 9, 16, 25, 36, 49, 64, 81, 100

The numbers you listed in exercise 11 are called **square numbers** because they are the areas of squares with whole-number lengths of sides. A square number is the product of a whole number and itself. So, if n is a whole number, $n \times n$ is a square number.

▶ **Patterns on the Multiplication Table**

12. In the table below, circle the products that are square numbers. Discuss the patterns you see with your class.

×	1	2	3	4	5	6	7	8	9	10
1	(1)	2	3	4	5	6	7	8	9	10
2	2	(4)	6	8	10	12	14	16	18	20
3	3	6	(9)	12	15	18	21	24	27	30
4	4	8	12	(16)	20	24	28	32	36	40
5	5	10	15	20	(25)	30	35	40	45	50
6	6	12	18	24	30	(36)	42	48	54	60
7	7	14	21	28	35	42	(49)	56	63	70
8	8	16	24	32	40	48	56	(64)	72	80
9	9	18	27	36	45	54	63	72	(81)	90
10	10	20	30	40	50	60	70	80	90	(100)

334 UNIT 9 LESSON 8 Square Numbers

Student Activity Book page 334

▶ Look for Patterns WHOLE CLASS

Now have students turn to exercise 11 on Student Book page 334, and list the products from exercises 1–10 in order, as you list them on the board. 1, 4, 9, 16, 25, 36, 49, 64, 81, 100

Explain that these numbers are called *square numbers.* Have a student read the definition of square numbers below exercise 11.

▶ Patterns on the Multiplication Table WHOLE CLASS

Explain that the chart in exercise 12 is a multiplication table. The numbers in the shaded squares are the factors, and the numbers in the unshaded squares are the products. Each product is found by multiplying the number in the shaded square to its left by the number in the shaded square above it.

Have a student explain how to find 4×4, by tracing across the 4-row and down the 4-column. Ask the student to circle the product, 16, on the transparency, while students circle it on their pages. Then have students work independently to find and circle all the square numbers.

- What pattern do you see in the square numbers you circled? They form a diagonal from the upper left to the lower right.
- The diagonal of square numbers divides the table in half. Look at the numbers below the diagonal and the numbers above it. Do you notice anything interesting?

X	1	2	3	4	5	6	7	8	9	10
1	1	2	3	4	5	6	7	8	9	10
2	2	4	6	8	10	12	14	16	18	20
3	3	6	9	12	15	18	21	24	27	30
4	4	8	12	16	20	24	28	32	36	40
5	5	10	15	20	25	30	35	40	45	50
6	6	12	18	24	30	36	42	48	54	60
7	7	14	21	28	35	42	49	56	63	70
8	8	16	24	32	40	48	56	64	72	80
9	9	18	27	36	45	54	63	72	81	90
10	10	20	30	40	50	60	70	80	90	100

Students should notice that for each number on one side of the diagonal, there is a matching number on the other side of the diagonal. For a sample of classroom dialogue, see **Math Talk in Action** in the side column.

- The diagonal is like a line of symmetry for the table. If the table is folded along this diagonal, each number on one half would match with the same number on the other half.

Ask students to put an X through the number 21 in the bottom half of the table, as you do the same.

- What multiplication equation goes with this 21? $7 \times 3 = 21$

Write $7 \times 3 = 21$ on the board. Then ask students to find and put an X through the matching 21 on the top half of the table.

- What multiplication equation goes with this 21? $3 \times 7 = 21$

Write $3 \times 7 = 21$ on the board, next to $7 \times 3 = 21$.

$$3 \times 7 = 21 \qquad 7 \times 3 = 21$$

Repeat this for two or three more pairs of numbers. Ask students what they notice about each pair of equations. The factors in one equation are the same as those in the other, but in a different order. Remind students that multiplication is commutative, meaning that the order of the factors can be switched without changing the product.

X	1	2	3	4	5	6	7	8	9	10
1	1	2	3	4	5	6	7	8	9	10
2	2	4	6	8	10	12	14	16	18	20
3	3	6	9	12	15	18	21	24	27	30
4	4	8	12	16	20	24	28	32	36	40
5	5	10	15	20	25	30	35	40	45	50
6	6	12	18	24	30	36	42	48	54	60
7	7	14	21	28	35	42	49	56	63	70
8	8	16	24	32	40	48	56	64	72	80
9	9	18	27	36	45	54	63	72	81	90
10	10	20	30	40	50	60	70	80	90	100

Activity continued ►

Math Talk in Action

Abdul: I see a diagonal line when you look at all the square numbers. Then on each side of the diagonal line, you can see numbers that are the same.

Why do you think those numbers are the same?

Abdul: The numbers are multiplied in the other order, but the answer is the same.

Can you give an example?

Abdul: $4 \times 3 = 12$ and $3 \times 4 = 12$.

Why is there no matching product for a square number?

Abdul: Each number is multiplied by itself.

Ongoing Assessment

Ask questions such as the following:

- ► What is the shape of a model that represents a whole number multiplied by itself?
- ► How do you know that a product is a square number?

The Learning Classroom

Building Concepts Students have had several experiences completing related divisions for multiplications. Now, you may wish to have students write the related divisions before them. Ask students why they think there are fewer related divisions for square numbers than for other products. Since the two factors in the multiplication are the same, there's only one related division for each square number.

Class Management

Looking Ahead In the next lesson, students will use the 12 remaining Strategy Cards (6s, 7s, and 8s) from Unit 4. Students will practice with them and combine them with the rest of the cards to complete the deck. Students will work to separate the multiplication and division cards and play a game with them.

Also remind students to take home the Home Check Sheet 9 on Homework and Remembering page 233. Students will use this Check Sheet to study with their Homework Helper.

▶ Practice Multiplication and Division of Square Numbers WHOLE CLASS

Now practice solving square number multiplication equations. Begin by presenting the problems in order.

Say . . .	Then write . . .
1 times 1 is . . .? 1	$1 \times 1 = 1$
2 times 2 is . . .? 4	$2 \times 2 = 4$
3 times 3 is . . .? 9	$3 \times 3 = 9$
4 times 4 is . . .? 16	$4 \times 4 = 16$
5 times 5 is . . .? 25	$5 \times 5 = 25$
6 times 6 is . . .? 36	$6 \times 6 = 36$
7 times 7 is . . .? 49	$7 \times 7 = 49$
8 times 8 is . . .? 64	$8 \times 8 = 64$
9 times 9 is . . .? 81	$9 \times 9 = 81$
10 times 10 is . . .? 100	$10 \times 10 = 100$

Next, have students read the products aloud as you point to them: 1, 4, 9, 16, 25, 36, 49, 64, 81, 100

Erase the multiplication equations, or stand in front of them. Say the square number multiplication problems in mixed order. Give students a few seconds to determine the answer to each problem, and then have them say the answer aloud at your signal.

Next, give students the square number division problems in order, and have them say the answers aloud. After each answer, write the equation on the board.

Say . . .	Then write . . .
1 divided by 1 is . . .? 1	$1 \div 1 = 1$
4 divided by 2 is . . .? 2	$4 \div 2 = 2$
9 divided by 3 is . . .? 3	$9 \div 3 = 3$
16 divided by 4 is . . .? 4	$16 \div 4 = 4$
25 divided by 5 is . . .? 5	$25 \div 5 = 5$
36 divided by 6 is . . .? 6	$36 \div 6 = 6$
49 divided by 7 is . . .? 7	$49 \div 7 = 7$
64 divided by 8 is . . .? 8	$64 \div 8 = 8$
81 divided by 9 is . . .? 9	$81 \div 9 = 9$
100 divided by 10 is . . .? 10	$100 \div 10 = 10$

Erase or hide the division equations. Say some square-number division problems in mixed order, and have students give the answers aloud at your signal.

2 Going Further

Differentiated Instruction

Intervention — Activity Card 9-8

Count-Bys for Square Numbers — Activity Card 9-8 ●

Work: In pairs

Use:

- Student Activity Book page 334
- Scissors
- TRB M31 (Centimeter-Grid Paper)

1. Use centimeter-grid paper to cut out squares with unit sides from 1 to 10.
2. Now place the squares one at a time on the multiplication table on Student Activity Book page 334. Align each square with the top left corner of the table as shown below. Then write the multiplication that each square represents.

×	1	2	3	4	5	6	7	8	9	10
1						6	7	8	9	10
2						12	14	16	18	20
3		5 × 5 = 25				18	21	24	27	30
4						24	28	32	36	40
5						30	35	40	45	50
6	6	12	18	24	30	(36)	42	48	54	60

3. **Analyze** Why are the numbers 1, 4, 9, 16, 25, 36, 49, 64, 81, and 100 called square numbers? They can each be represented by square figures.

Unit 9, Lesson 8

Activity Note Students should notice that the number under the lower right corner of each square placed on the table equals the product of the multiplication equation represented by the square.

Math Writing Prompt

Summarize Explain why numbers like 1, 4, 9, and 16 are called square numbers.

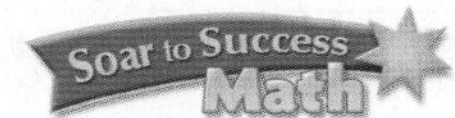

Software Support

Warm Up 12.27

On Level — Activity Card 9-8

Square Number Cube Toss — Activity Card 9-8 ▲

Work: In pairs

Use:

- 2 Number cubes labeled 3–8

1. Take turns tossing the two number cubes to score points in a game.

2. After your toss, say the multiplication equation that uses the two numbers as factors. Score one point for saying the correct product. Score two points if the correct product is a square number.
3. Record each equation and the score for each player. The first player to score 10 points wins the game.

Unit 9, Lesson 8

Activity Note When both number cubes show the same number, the product is always a square number. A variation on the rules of the game could require forfeiting points for an incorrect product.

Math Writing Prompt

Explain Your Thinking Explain a strategy that will help you remember the multiplications for square numbers.

Software Support

Ice Station Exploration: Arctic Algebra, Level P

Challenge — Activity Card 9-8

Multiplication Puzzles — Activity Card 9-8 ■

Work: In pairs

Use:

- TRB M108 (Multiplication Riddles)

1. **Work Together** Find the answers to the multiplication riddles. Use the multiplication table on the page to help.

   1. Deon is thinking of three square numbers. All three numbers are less than 100. The first square number is $\frac{1}{4}$ as many as the second one. The third one is 9 times as many as the first one. Which square numbers are Deon thinking of? 9, 36, 81

   2. Elena is thinking of a number. One of its multiples is 24. The number is a multiple of 6 numbers in the multiplication table. What number is Elena thinking of? 12

2. **Think** How can you identify the square numbers on the multiplication table? Lightly shade each square number. The square numbers are on the diagonal from the top left corner to the bottom right corner.
3. **Analyze** How do you know when a number is a multiple of another number? Any product in the table is a multiple of every counting number from 1 to 10 that appears in the same column or row.

Unit 9, Lesson 8

Activity Note Have pairs make up their own multiplication riddles for other pairs to solve if time permits.

Math Writing Prompt

Critical Thinking Is the product of 9 and a number the same as twice the product of 3 and that number? Explain why or why not.

DESTINATION Math® **Software Support**

Course II: Module 2: Unit 2: Finding Products less than 100

3 Homework and Spiral Review

Goal: Additional Practice

This Homework page provides practice in using square numbers.

9–8 Homework

Name Date

Study Plan

Homework Helper

Write a multiplication equation for each square array.

1. $3 \times 3 = 9$
2. $5 \times 5 = 25$
3. $6 \times 6 = 36$

Solve.

4. Julia used 1 foot square stone tiles to make a patio. She laid the tiles in a square, 7 tiles wide by 7 tiles long. What is the area of Julia's new patio? 49 sq ft

5. Sal brought 2 dozen apples to a science club meeting. He divided the apples equally among the 8 people there. How many apples did he give each person? 3 apples

6. Lehie has 21 crystals in her collection. Her brother Tomer has 7 crystals. How many more crystals does Lehie have than Tomer? 14 more crystals

7. Emmanuel collected 49 leaves last week. He collected the same number of leaves each day. How many leaves did he collect on Monday? 7 leaves

Complete.

8.

×	6	4	8
4	24	16	32

9.

×	5	4	9
9	45	36	81

10.

×	8	7	3
8	64	56	24

UNIT 9 LESSON 8 Square Numbers 235

Homework and Remembering page 235

9–8 Remembering **Goal:** Spiral Review

This Remembering page would be appropriate anytime after today's lesson.

9–8 Remembering

Name Date

Solve.

1. Isabel had \$37. She bought 2 CDs for \$11 each. Then she earned some money babysitting. Now she has \$53. How much did she earn babysitting? \$38

2. Arnon planted 4 apple trees and 7 peach trees. Jenn planted 5 more apple trees than Arnon and 4 fewer peach trees. How many trees did Jenn plant in all? 12 trees

3. Brigitte scored 234 points in a pinball game. Lee scored 394. In a second game, Lee scored 164 points, and Brigitte scored 307 points. Altogether, who scored the most points? How many more? Lee; 17 more

4. Julian caught 8 fish, Tana caught 6, Stewart caught 11, and Ana caught 4. They threw the 9 smallest fish back into the water. Then they each caught 2 more fish. How many fish do they have now? 28 fish

Draw 2 rectangles that each have a perimeter of 12 centimeters. Write the area inside each figure. Drawings will vary.

5.

236 UNIT 9 LESSON 8 Square Numbers

Homework and Remembering page 236

Home or School Activity

Literature Connection

Sea Squares Have students read the book *Sea Squares* by Joy N. Hulme. Have them make a list of the square numbers described in the book and the related multiplications. For example, 8 "octos" have 64 legs, $8 \times 8 = 64$. Then students can think of their own example of animals and a square number and draw it. They should write the related multiplication.

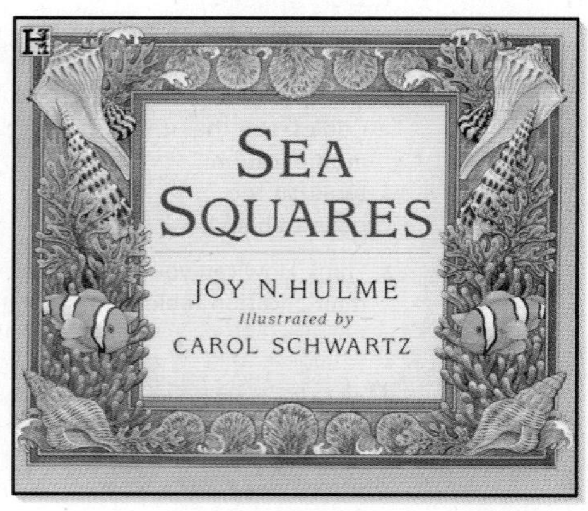

Practice with 6s, 7s, and 8s

Vocabulary

square number
Distributive Property of Multiplication

Lesson Objective

- **Practice 6s, 7s, and 8s multiplications and divisions.**

The Day at a Glance

Today's Goals	Materials
1 Teaching the Lesson **A1:** Practice count-bys, multiplications, and divisions. **A2:** Complete multiplication and division Dashes. **A3:** Use remaining Strategy Cards and play a game.	**Lesson Activities** Student Activity Book pp. 335–344 or Student Hardcover Book pp. 335–344 and Activity Workbook pp. 154–158 (includes Check Sheets, Dashes 9-12, Game Rules, and Special Format) Transparency of Student Book page 343 (optional) Overhead projector (optional) Homework and Remembering pp. 239–240 Quick Quiz 2 (Assessment Guide) Folders Check Up materials Signature Sheet Blank Sprint Answer Sheet Study Sheets A-C Check Sheets 1–11 Dry-erase markers Sheet protectors Study Sheet Answer Strips Check Sheet Answer Strips Cardstock Strategy cards Multiplication and Division Strategy Cards
2 Going Further ► Extension: Multiply and Divide with 11 and 12 ► Differentiated Instruction	**Going Further** Activity Cards 9–9 Codebuster (TRB M114) Symbol Cards (TRB M115) Game Cards (TRB M25) Math Journals
3 Homework and Spiral Review	

Use Math Talk today!

Keeping Skills Sharp

Quick Practice — 5 MINUTES

Goal: Use the 5s Shortcut.

Materials: Class Multiplication Table Poster, pointer

5s Shortcut The **Student Leader** points to and reads aloud an equation on the table with a multiplier of 6 or more. Then, starting with the "5 ×" equation in the same column, the leader points to one equation at a time as students say the count-bys. When students reach the original equation, the leader says "Equation," and the class says the equation. (See Unit 9 Lesson 8.)

Daily Routines

Homework Review Have students work together to discuss and correct difficulties with the homework.

Function Machine A function machine divides each input by 8. What is the output when the input is 16? 80? 8? 64? 2; 10; 1; 8

1 Teaching the Lesson

Activity 1

Check Up and Independent Study

 10 MINUTES

Goal: Practice count-bys, multiplications, and divisions.

Materials: Folders, Check Up materials: Signature Sheet, Blank Sprint Answer Sheet (TRB M57), Study Sheets A–C, Check Sheets 1–11, dry-erase markers (1 per student), sheet protectors (1 per student), Study Sheet Answer Strips (TRB M54), Check Sheet Answer Strips (TRB M55), cardstock; Strategy Cards, Homework and Remembering p. 239

 **NCTM Standard:**
Number and Operations

 **Class Management**

Looking Ahead Remind students to take home the Home Check Sheets 10 and 11 on Homework and Remembering pages 237–238.

▶ Check Up with 6s, 7s, and 8s PAIRS

Give **Student Pairs** a few minutes to test each other using Study Sheets A–C and collect signatures. For students who have already collected signatures on Study Sheets, have them use Check Sheets 1–11. You may want to have Study Sheet and Check Sheet Answer Strips (TRB M54–M55) available.

Students who made mistakes on the 8s Sprints from Lesson 8 (or who were absent) may take repeat or make-up Sprints at this time. Students can record their answers on Blank Sprint Answer Sheet (TRB M57).

Give students several minutes to study independently, using their Study Sheets, Check Sheets, and Strategy Cards. Have them complete their Study Plan box on Homework and Remembering page 239. They should include any multiplications or divisions they missed in the Check Up. Remind students to place all their Check Up materials in their folders.

Activity 2

Mixed Practice

 10 MINUTES

Goal: Complete multiplication and division Dashes.

Materials: Student Activity Book or Hardcover Book pages 337–340 and Activity Workbook p. 156

 **NCTM Standard:**
Number and Operations

▶ Dashes 9–12 INDIVIDUALS

Have students complete Dashes 9–12 on Student Activity Book page 337 or Activity Workbook p. 156. You can have them complete one Dash at a time, with breaks in between, or do all four at once. Time the Dashes, or let students complete them at their own pace. Students can check their answers against those on Student Book page 339. A second Dash is included on the back for retesting if needed.

Activity 3

Use the Strategy Cards

▶ Play *High Card Wins* PAIRS

Distribute the 12 remaining Strategy Cards. Give **Student Pairs** a minute or two to practice with them, and then have them combine them with the rest of the Strategy Cards. Tell students the deck is now complete.

Have students separate the multiplication and division cards. Tell them they can use either set to play the *High Card Wins* game. Read the rules of the game aloud (see below), and make sure students know what to do. You might demonstrate by playing a few rounds with a volunteer.

Give **Student Pairs** several minutes to play the game with a partner. Tell them to try to play the game at least once with the multiplication cards and once with the division cards.

Name Date

▶ Play *High Card Wins*

Read the rules for playing *High Card Wins*. Then play the game with your partner.

Rules for *High Card Wins*

Number of players: 2
What you will need: 1 set of multiplication Strategy Cards *or* 1 set of division Strategy Cards

1. Shuffle the cards. Then deal all the cards evenly between the two players.
2. Players put their stacks in front of them, problem side up.
3. Each player takes the top card from his or her stack and puts it problem side up in the center of the table.
4. Each player says the answer (product or quotient) and then turns the card over to check. Then do one of the following:
   - If one player says the wrong answer, the other player takes both cards and puts them at the bottom of his or her pile.
   - If both players say the wrong answer, both players take back their cards and put them at the bottom of their piles.
   - If both players say the correct answer, the player with the higher product takes both cards and puts them at the bottom of his or her pile. If the answers are the same, the players set the cards aside and play another round. The winner of the next round takes all the cards.
5. When time is up, the player with the most cards wins.

UNIT 9 LESSON 9 Play *High Card Wins* **341**

Student Activity Book page 341

20 MINUTES

Goal: Use remaining Strategy Cards and play a game.

Materials: Student Activity Book or Hardcover Book p. 341 and Activity Workbook p. 157, Multiplication and Division Strategy Cards

NCTM Standard:
Number and Operations

Basic Multiplication and Divisions Assessment

To check students' fluency with basic multiplications and divisions, use Student Book pages 371–374.

Answers to these tests can be found on TRB pages M121–M124 in the Teacher's Resource Book.

English Language Learners

Model several rounds of Higher Card Wins with a volunteer.

Ongoing Assessment

Ask questions such as the following:

- ▶ How do you find the answer to a basic multiplication you do not recall?
- ▶ How do you find the quotient for a basic division?

See Assessment Guide for Unit 9 Quick Quiz 2.

2 Going Further

Extension: Multiply and Divide with 11 and 12

Goal: Study the 11s and 12s multiplications and divisions.

Materials: Student Activity Book or Hardcover Book p. 343 and Activity Workbook p. 158, transparency of Student Book page 343 and overhead projector (optional)

NCTM Standards:
Number and Operations
Algebra

Class Management

You may want to create a transparency of the multiplication table and have students come to the overhead to complete the products. If an overhead projector is not available, draw the table on a sheet of chart paper and post it on a wall.

▶ Multiply and Divide with 11 and 12

WHOLE CLASS

Explain that the charts show the 11s and 12s multiplications and divisions. Encourage students to look for patterns.

Math Talk To summarize ask the following:

- What patterns do you see in the 11s multiplications and divisions? The digits in each product are the same up to 9 × 11.
- What patterns do you see in the 12s multiplications and divisions? Each next product is 12 more. The products are all even numbers.

▶ Multiplication Table 11s and 12s

WHOLE CLASS

Tell students they will fill in the multiplication table to show products for the 11s and 12s multiplications. Help students understand that they can use the strategy of using multiplications they know to complete the table.

Explain that they already know 7s and 5s and 10s and 2s multiplications, so they can use them to find 8 times 12.

Have students share their methods and direct them to Student Activity Book page 343 to check their solutions.

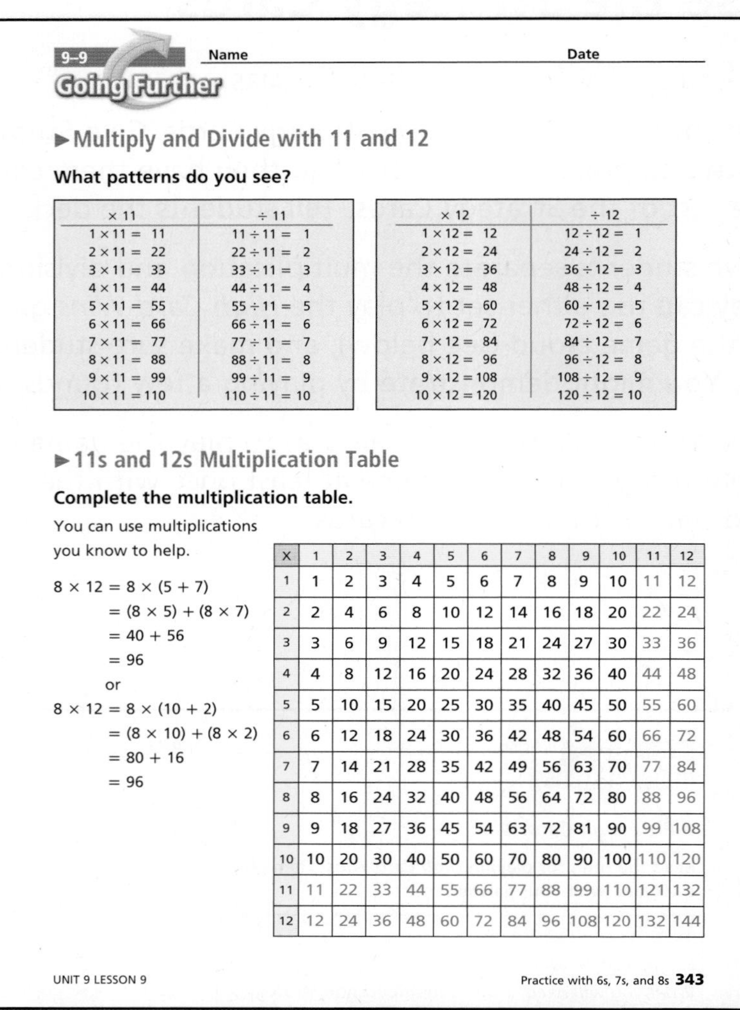

9–9 Going Further   Name ______ Date ______

▶ Multiply and Divide with 11 and 12

What patterns do you see?

× 11	÷ 11
1 × 11 = 11	11 ÷ 11 = 1
2 × 11 = 22	22 ÷ 11 = 2
3 × 11 = 33	33 ÷ 11 = 3
4 × 11 = 44	44 ÷ 11 = 4
5 × 11 = 55	55 ÷ 11 = 5
6 × 11 = 66	66 ÷ 11 = 6
7 × 11 = 77	77 ÷ 11 = 7
8 × 11 = 88	88 ÷ 11 = 8
9 × 11 = 99	99 ÷ 11 = 9
10 × 11 = 110	110 ÷ 11 = 10

× 12	÷ 12
1 × 12 = 12	12 ÷ 12 = 1
2 × 12 = 24	24 ÷ 12 = 2
3 × 12 = 36	36 ÷ 12 = 3
4 × 12 = 48	48 ÷ 12 = 4
5 × 12 = 60	60 ÷ 12 = 5
6 × 12 = 72	72 ÷ 12 = 6
7 × 12 = 84	84 ÷ 12 = 7
8 × 12 = 96	96 ÷ 12 = 8
9 × 12 = 108	108 ÷ 12 = 9
10 × 12 = 120	120 ÷ 12 = 10

▶ 11s and 12s Multiplication Table

Complete the multiplication table.

You can use multiplications you know to help.

$$8 \times 12 = 8 \times (5 + 7)$$
$$= (8 \times 5) + (8 \times 7)$$
$$= 40 + 56$$
$$= 96$$
or
$$8 \times 12 = 8 \times (10 + 2)$$
$$= (8 \times 10) + (8 \times 2)$$
$$= 80 + 16$$
$$= 96$$

X	1	2	3	4	5	6	7	8	9	10	11	12
1	1	2	3	4	5	6	7	8	9	10	11	12
2	2	4	6	8	10	12	14	16	18	20	22	24
3	3	6	9	12	15	18	21	24	27	30	33	36
4	4	8	12	16	20	24	28	32	36	40	44	48
5	5	10	15	20	25	30	35	40	45	50	55	60
6	6	12	18	24	30	36	42	48	54	60	66	72
7	7	14	21	28	35	42	49	56	63	70	77	84
8	8	16	24	32	40	48	56	64	72	80	88	96
9	9	18	27	36	45	54	63	72	81	90	99	108
10	10	20	30	40	50	60	70	80	90	100	110	120
11	11	22	33	44	55	66	77	88	99	110	121	132
12	12	24	36	48	60	72	84	96	108	120	132	144

UNIT 9 LESSON 9   Practice with 6s, 7s, and 8s **343**

Student Activity Book page 343

Ask a volunteer to show how to find 5 × 12 using 3s and 9s.

$$\begin{aligned} 5 \times 12 &= 5 \times (3 + 9) \\ &= (5 \times 3) + (5 \times 9) \\ &= 15 + 45 \\ &= 60 \end{aligned}$$

Students can work independently to complete the 11s and 12s multiplications in the multiplication table using any strategy they know.

- What patterns did you notice when you were trying to find the products for the 11s and 12s multiplications in the multiplication chart? You can still use count-bys to find the next product after the 10s multiplications; 11 × 12 has the same product as 12 × 11.

Intervention — Activity Card 9-9

High Product Wins

Activity Card 9-9 ●

Work: In pairs

Use:

- 2 sets of TRB M25 (Game Cards)

1. Shuffle the Game Cards and place them face down in a pile. Each student chooses two cards and multiplies the numbers. The student with the greater product wins the round and earns points equal to the product.

6 7  9 3

$6 \times 7 = 42$ $9 \times 3 = 27$

Hilda's score	Isaac's score
42	0

2. Each student discards the original cards and picks two new cards for the next round. Continue until all the cards have been used. The student with the higher score wins the game.

Unit 9, Lesson 9

Activity Note Students should keep score on a separate piece of paper. Encourage students to check each other's products before awarding points.

Math Writing Prompt

Understanding Multiplication Explain a strategy you can use to find the product of 8×7.

Software Support

Warm Up 12.27

On Level — Activity Card 9-9

Codebuster

Activity Card 9-9 ▲

Work: In pairs

Use:

- TRB M114 (Codebuster)

1. Find the missing numbers for the equations on the page.
2. Break the code by matching the numbers you found for each letter in the equations with the letters in the Secret Answer.

W	O	U	L	D		Y	O	U		L	I	K	E		T	O		G	O
6	35	48	42	9		49	35	48		42	2	63	32		3	35		1	35

T	O		T	H	E		S	Q	U	A	R	E		D	A	N	C	E	?
3	35		3	4	32		7	30	48	18	8	32		9	18	24	5	32	

3. **Analyze** How did you break the code?
4. Make up your own codebuster problem and secret message for other student pairs to solve.

Unit 9, Lesson 9

Activity Note If time permits, have students share their strategies for breaking the code. This will reinforce their number sense and enhance skills with operations.

Math Writing Prompt

Explain Your Thinking Suppose you do not know the product of 6×8. Explain two different strategies that could help you find the product.

Software Support

The Number Games: Up, Up, and Array, Level B

Challenge — Activity Card 9-9

Multiplication and Division Scramble

Activity Card 9-9 ■

Work: In small groups

Use:

- 3 sets of TRB M25 (Game Cards)
- 15 sets of TRB M115 (Symbol Cards)

1. Shuffle and deal out an equal number of Game Cards to each student.
2. The first student makes a multiplication or division equation, using the cards.
3. The next student builds another equation on the first equation.
4. Continue taking turns building onto the equations until all the Game Cards have been used or until no one can make another equation.
5. The student with the fewest Game Cards left wins the game.

$6 \times 8 = 48$ (across); $63 \div 7 = 9$ (across); $8 \times 7 = 56$ (down)

Unit 9, Lesson 9

Activity Note Be sure that students position the operation symbols correctly when operating with two-digit numbers vertically to avoid misuse of the symbols.

Math Writing Prompt

Investigate Math Naomi wrote $11 \times (7 + 5)$ to help find the product of 11×12. Explain how Naomi could use the other number sentences to find the product.

DESTINATION Math® **Software Support**

Course II: Module 2: Unit 3: Meaning of Division

3 Homework and Spiral Review

9–9 Homework Goal: Additional Practice

This Homework page provides practice with 6s, 7s, and 8s multiplications and divisions.

9–9 Homework

Name ________ Date ________

Study Plan
Homework Helper

Solve.

1. Sarah's chickens laid 3 dozen eggs over the weekend. She divided them equally into cartons to give away to her 6 closest neighbors. How many eggs did she put in each carton?
   6 eggs
2. Latisha needs 60 square feet of cloth. She has a rectangular piece of cloth that measures 3 ft by 9 ft, and a square piece that measures 5 ft on a side. Does she have enough cloth? If not, how much more does she need?
   no; 8 sq ft more

Complete each function table.

3.

N	2	6	3	7	10	8	9	1	5	4
6 * *N*	12	36	18	42	60	48	54	6	30	24

4.

N	4	10	6	3	8	2	7	5	9	1
***N* * 7**	28	70	42	21	56	14	49	35	63	7

Fill in the missing number in each Fast-Array.

5. 7; 6; 42
6. 6; 9; 54
7. 8; 7; 56

UNIT 9 LESSON 9 Practice with 6s, 7s, and 8s **239**

Homework and Remembering page 239

9–9 Remembering Goal: Spiral Review

This Remembering page would be appropriate anytime after today's lesson.

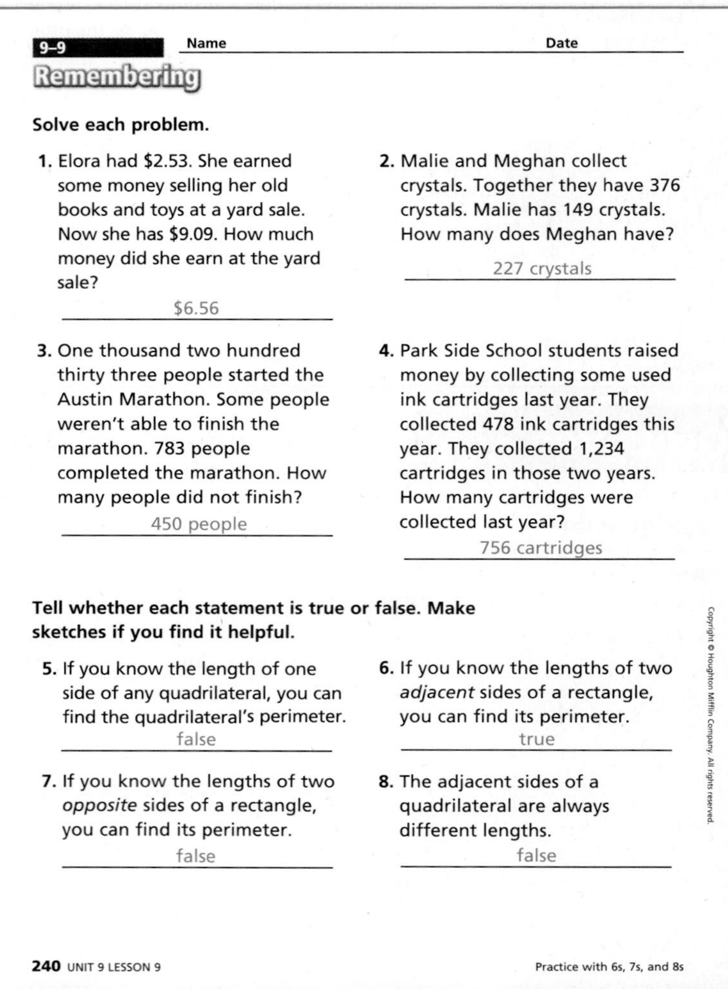

9–9 Remembering

Name ________ Date ________

Solve each problem.

1. Elora had $2.53. She earned some money selling her old books and toys at a yard sale. Now she has $9.09. How much money did she earn at the yard sale?
   $6.56
2. Malie and Meghan collect crystals. Together they have 376 crystals. Malie has 149 crystals. How many does Meghan have?
   227 crystals
3. One thousand two hundred thirty three people started the Austin Marathon. Some people weren't able to finish the marathon. 783 people completed the marathon. How many people did not finish?
   450 people
4. Park Side School students raised money by collecting some used ink cartridges last year. They collected 478 ink cartridges this year. They collected 1,234 cartridges in those two years. How many cartridges were collected last year?
   756 cartridges

Tell whether each statement is true or false. Make sketches if you find it helpful.

5. If you know the length of one side of any quadrilateral, you can find the quadrilateral's perimeter.
   false
6. If you know the lengths of two *adjacent* sides of a rectangle, you can find its perimeter.
   true
7. If you know the lengths of two *opposite* sides of a rectangle, you can find its perimeter.
   false
8. The adjacent sides of a quadrilateral are always different lengths.
   false

240 UNIT 9 LESSON 9 Practice with 6s, 7s, and 8s

Homework and Remembering page 240

Home or School Activity

Real-World Connection

Careers and Hourly Wages Have students do research to find examples of hourly wages for different careers or occupations. They can make a table to show the amount of pay per hour (rounded to the nearest dollar), and the earnings for 8 hours of work in one day. If students find that some hourly wages are greater than $10, have them use a calculator to find the daily earnings.

Career or Occupation	Pay per Hour	Daily Earnings (for 8 hours)
Animal Shelter Worker	$8	$64
Baker	$7	$56
Cook	$7	$56
Crossing Guard	$8	$64
Dog Walker	$6	$48
Forest Firefighter	$10	$80
Jewelry Salesperson	$9	$72
Video Game Tester	$8	$64

Solve Mixed Word Problems

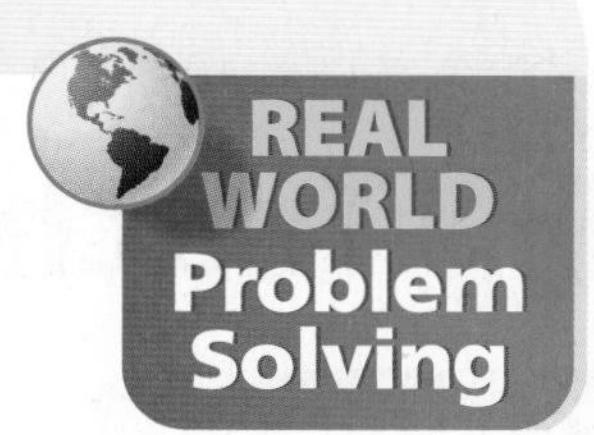

Vocabulary

square number
Distributive Property of Multiplication

Lesson Objectives

- Choose the operation to solve a word problem.
- Write word problems for given equations.

The Day at a Glance

Today's Goals	Materials	
1 Teaching the Lesson **A1:** Take Sprints for 7s multiplications and divisions. **A2:** Practice count-bys, multiplications, and divisions. **A3:** Discuss how to determine which operation to use to solve a word problem. **A4:** Use the "information part" of a word problem to write an appropriate "question part." **A5:** Write word problems for given equations. **2 Going Further** ▸ Problem Solving Strategy: Open-Ended Problems ▸ Differentiated Instruction **3 Homework and Spiral Review**	**Lesson Activities** Student Activity Book pp. 345–350 or Student Hardcover Book pp. 345–350 and Activity Workbook pp. 159–160 (includes Check Sheet) Homework and Remembering pp. 241–242 Signature Sheet Check Up materials Study Sheets A-C Check Sheets 1–11 Dry-erase markers Sheet protectors Study Sheet Answer Strips Check Sheet Answer Strips Cardstock Strategy Cards	**Going Further** Activity Cards 9–10 Homework and Remembering p. 241 Drawing Paper Symbol Cards (TRB M115) Math Journals Use Math Talk today!

Keeping Skills Sharp

Quick Practice — 5 MINUTES

Goal: Use the 5s Shortcut.

Materials: Class Multiplication Table Poster, pointer

5s Shortcut The **Student Leader** points to any equation on the Class Multiplication Table Poster with a multiplier of 6 or more and reads it aloud. Then, starting with the "5 ×" equation in the same column, the leader points to one equation at a time as students say the count-bys. When students reach the original equation, the leader says "Equation," and the class says the equation in unison. (See Unit 9 Lesson 8.)

Daily Routines

Homework Review Have students explain how they found their errors.

Strategy Problem There are 2 books on the first shelf, 6 books on the second shelf, 12 books on the third shelf, and 20 books on the fourth shelf. How many books are on the tenth shelf? 110 books; Solved a simpler problem; applied the pattern in given rows: add the first 10 even numbers.

1 Teaching the Lesson

Activity 1

Assess 7s

 5 MINUTES

Goal: Take Sprints for 7s multiplications and divisions.

Materials: Student Activity Book p. 345 or Activity Workbook p. 159, (TRB M57), Signature Sheet

 **NCTM Standard:**
Number and Operations

 **Class Management**

If students are struggling with count-bys, you might give a count-by Sprint.

▶ Sprints for 7s WHOLE CLASS

Direct students to Student Activity Book page 345 or Activity Workbook p. 159 and give the two Sprints below.

× 7	÷ 7
a. 7 × 7 49	**a.** 63 ÷ 7 9
b. 2 × 7 14	**b.** 42 ÷ 7 6
c. 9 × 7 63	**c.** 7 ÷ 7 1
d. 1 × 7 7	**d.** 56 ÷ 7 8
e. 4 × 7 28	**e.** 28 ÷ 7 4
f. 10 × 7 70	**f.** 14 ÷ 7 2
g. 3 × 7 21	**g.** 21 ÷ 7 3
h. 5 × 7 35	**h.** 49 ÷ 7 7
i. 6 × 7 42	**i.** 70 ÷ 7 10
j. 8 × 7 56	**j.** 35 ÷ 7 5

Have **Student Pairs** check each other's work as you read the answers, marking any incorrect answers, and getting signatures.

Activity 2

Check Up and Independent Study

 5 MINUTES

Goal: Practice count-bys, multiplications, and divisions.

Materials: Check Up materials: Signature Sheet, Study Sheets A–C, Check Sheets 1–11, dry-erase markers (1 per student), sheet protectors (1 per student), Study Sheet Answer Strips (TRB M54), Check Sheet Answer Strips (TRB M55), cardstock; Strategy Cards, Homework and Remembering p. 241

 **NCTM Standard:**
Number and Operations

▶ Check Up with 6s, 7s, and 8s PAIRS

Give **Student Pairs** a few minutes to test each other, using Study Sheets A–C and collect signatures. For students who have collected signatures for Study Sheets, have them use Check Sheets 1–11. You may want to have Study Sheet and Check Sheet Answer Strips (TRB M54–M55) available.

Then give them 2 or 3 minutes to study independently using their Study Sheets, Check Sheets, or Strategy Cards. Also have students complete their Study Plan box on Homework and Remembering page 241. Students should include any multiplications or divisions they missed in the Sprint or Check Up. Remind students to put all Check Up materials in their folders.

Activity 3

Determine Which Operation to Use

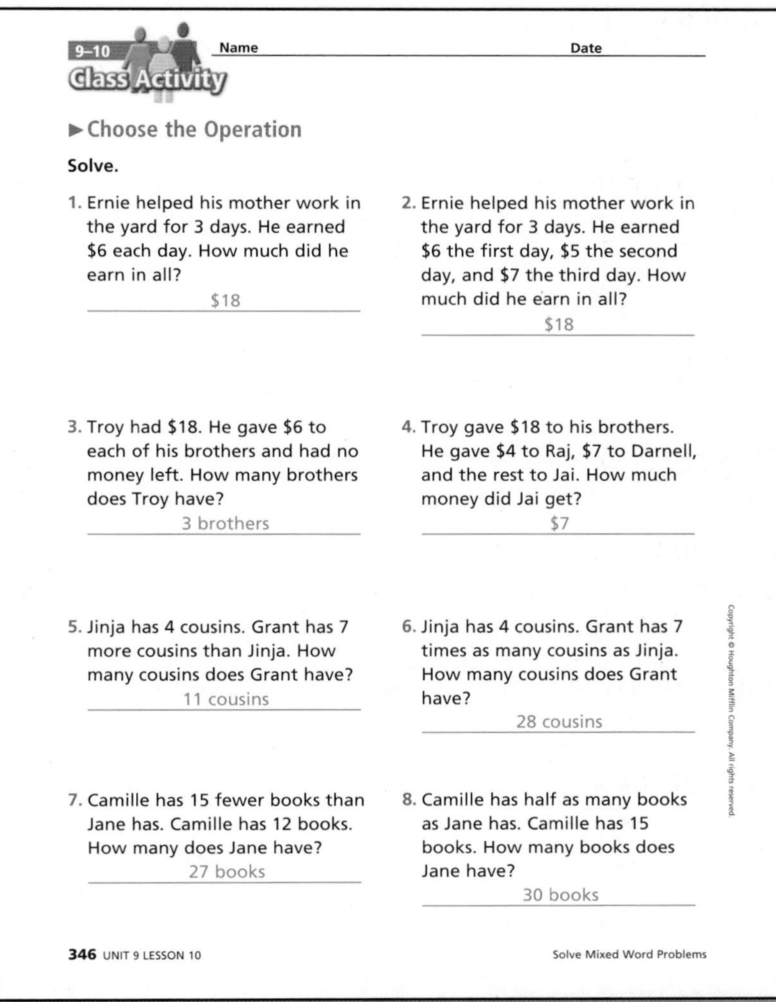

9–10 Class Activity

Name ______ Date ______

► Choose the Operation

Solve.

1. Ernie helped his mother work in the yard for 3 days. He earned $6 each day. How much did he earn in all? $18

2. Ernie helped his mother work in the yard for 3 days. He earned $6 the first day, $5 the second day, and $7 the third day. How much did he earn in all? $18

3. Troy had $18. He gave $6 to each of his brothers and had no money left. How many brothers does Troy have? 3 brothers

4. Troy gave $18 to his brothers. He gave $4 to Raj, $7 to Darnell, and the rest to Jai. How much money did Jai get? $7

5. Jinja has 4 cousins. Grant has 7 more cousins than Jinja. How many cousins does Grant have? 11 cousins

6. Jinja has 4 cousins. Grant has 7 times as many cousins as Jinja. How many cousins does Grant have? 28 cousins

7. Camille has 15 fewer books than Jane has. Camille has 12 books. How many does Jane have? 27 books

8. Camille has half as many books as Jane has. Camille has 15 books. How many books does Jane have? 30 books

346 UNIT 9 LESSON 10 Solve Mixed Word Problems

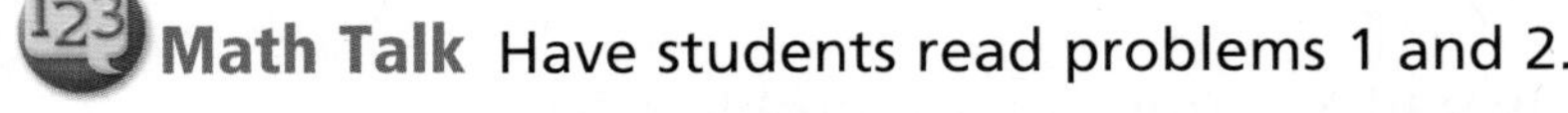

Student Activity Book page 346

► Choose the Operation WHOLE CLASS

Math Talk Have students read problems 1 and 2.

- **What is the same about these problems?** Both problems ask for the total Ernie earned.
- **What is different about these problems?** In problem 1, Ernie earns the same amount each day. In problem 2, he earns a different amount each day.
- **Which operation would you use to solve problem 1?** multiplication **How do you know?** Because I need to find the total in 3 groups of the same size.
- **Could you solve problem 1 by adding?** yes **How?** Find 6 + 6 + 6.

Activity continued ►

20 MINUTES

Goal: Discuss how to determine which operation to use to solve a word problem.

Materials: Student Activity Book or Hardcover Book pp. 346–347

NCTM Standards:
Number and Operations
Problem Solving
Reasoning and Proof
Communication

Class Management

Looking Ahead The next few lessons focus on word problems. In this lesson, each problem involves one operation. Students must reason about the situation and the language to determine which operation to use. The problems in Lessons 11 and 12 involve two or more operations; those in Lesson 12 are more complex. If your students struggle with word problems, you may want to spend two days on this lesson and two days on Lesson 11, and assign Lesson 12 only to more advanced students.

Alternate Approach

Counters for Problems Students can use counters to model comparing one-to-one, and comparing equal groups.

Have students use counters to model problem 5 on Student Book page 346. They should show two groups — one for Jinja's cousins and one for Grant's cousins, and use a different color for each group. Have students match the counters between the groups one-to-one, until they see that Grant has 7 more cousins than Jinja.

Jinja ●●●●
Grant ○○○○○○○○○○○

Continue similarly for problem 6. Highlight the difference between comparing equal groups of 4 counters, rather than one-counter-to-one counter.

Jinja ●●●●
Grant ○○○○ ○○○○ ○○○○ ○○○○ ○○○○ ○○○○ ○○○○

Class Management

Looking Ahead In Lesson 14, students will solve some of the problems they have written for homework. Before that lesson, select problems of a variety of types from those you have collected. Try to choose an equal number of multiplication and division problems. To save time, you may want to create a transparency or a handout of the problems, or write them on the board before you begin the lesson.

- Which operation would you use to solve problem 2? addition Could you solve the problem by multiplying? no Why? Because the groups are different sizes.

Solve problems 1 and 2 quickly, eliciting information from students. Then have students read problems 3 and 4.

- What is the same about these problems? In both problems, Troy gives $18 to his brothers.
- What is different about them? In problem 3, Troy gives the same amount to each brother. In problem 4, he gives a different amount to each brother. The questions are also different.
- Which operation would you use to solve problem 3? division How do you know? Because I need to find how many groups of $6 are in $18; I am dividing $18 into equal groups of $6.
- Could you solve problem 3 by subtracting? yes How? Start with 18, and subtract 6 until you reach 0. Count the number of 6s you subtracted.
- Which operation would you use to solve problem 4? subtraction Can you solve the problem by dividing? no Why? Because Troy is not dividing the money equally; the groups are different sizes.

Solve problems 3 and 4 quickly, and then have students read problems 5 and 6.

- What is the same about these problems? In both problems, Jinja has 4 cousins and Grant has more cousins than Jinja. Both ask how many cousins Grant has.
- What is different about these problems? Problem 5 tells how many more cousins Grant has than Jinja. Problem 6 tells how many times as many cousins Grant has than Jinja.
- Which operation would you use to solve problem 5? addition How do you know? Because it asks how many "more" cousins Grant has. It gives the smaller amount and the difference, so you need to add to find the larger amount.
- Which operation would you use to solve problem 6? multiplication How do you know? The problem asks "how many times as many." You need to multiply the smaller amount by 7 to find the larger amount.

You may want to draw Comparison Bars for problems 5 and 6.

Problem 5

Jinja [4](7)
Grant [?]

Problem 6

Jinja [4]
Grant [4|4|4|4|4|4|4] Total = ?

Have students solve problems 7 and 8 on their own. Discuss their solutions.

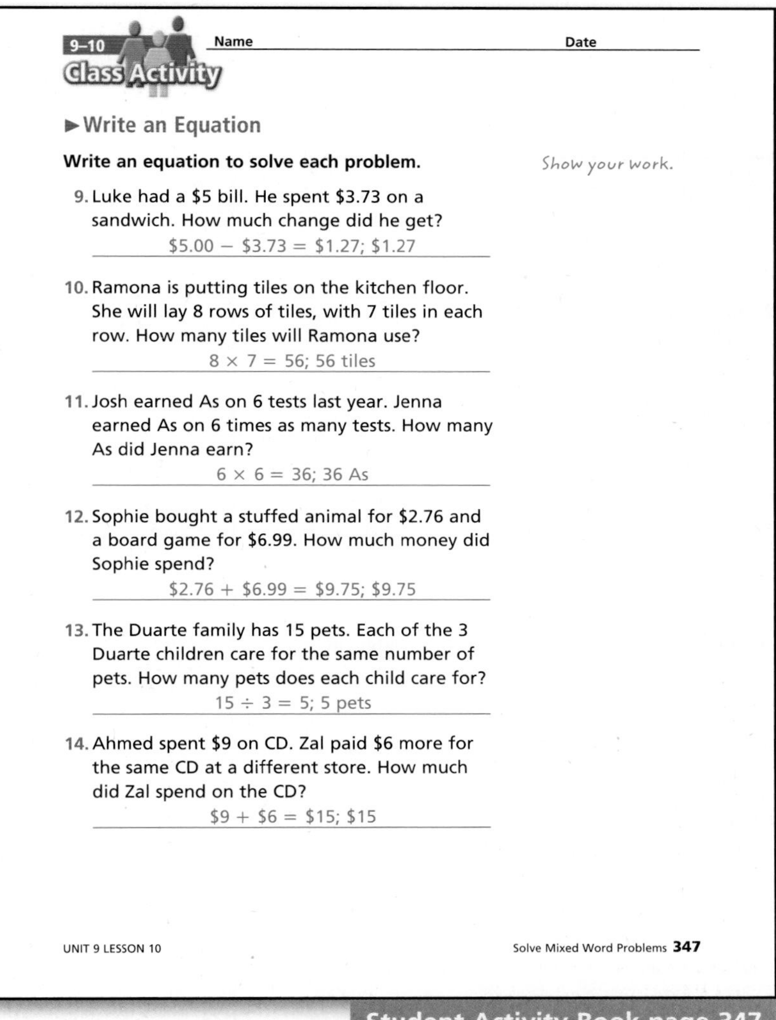
9–10 Class Activity

Name ____ Date ____

▶ Write an Equation

Write an equation to solve each problem. *Show your work.*

9. Luke had a $5 bill. He spent $3.73 on a sandwich. How much change did he get?
$5.00 − $3.73 = $1.27; $1.27

10. Ramona is putting tiles on the kitchen floor. She will lay 8 rows of tiles, with 7 tiles in each row. How many tiles will Ramona use?
8 × 7 = 56; 56 tiles

11. Josh earned As on 6 tests last year. Jenna earned As on 6 times as many tests. How many As did Jenna earn?
6 × 6 = 36; 36 As

12. Sophie bought a stuffed animal for $2.76 and a board game for $6.99. How much money did Sophie spend?
$2.76 + $6.99 = $9.75; $9.75

13. The Duarte family has 15 pets. Each of the 3 Duarte children care for the same number of pets. How many pets does each child care for?
15 ÷ 3 = 5; 5 pets

14. Ahmed spent $9 on CD. Zal paid $6 more for the same CD at a different store. How much did Zal spend on the CD?
$9 + $6 = $15; $15

UNIT 9 LESSON 10 Solve Mixed Word Problems **347**

Student Activity Book page 347

▶ Write an Equation WHOLE CLASS

Using the **Solve and Discuss** structure, have students solve problems 9–14 on Student Activity Book page 347. Presenters should explain how they figured out which operations to use.

Math Talk As students explain their strategies and tell which operation they used for each word problem, have them describe the key words that helped them choose the operation. Operations and possible key words are given below:

Problem 9: subtraction; how much change

Problem 10: multiplication; in each row

Problem 11: multiplication; times as many

Problem 12: addition; how much

Problem 13: division; each

Problem 14: addition; how much

Teaching Note

Watch For! Make sure students understand that using key words can help them solve word problems, but they need to read the complete context of the word problem to see what operation to use, as some key words can mean different operations. Remind students about the distinction between *situation equations* and *solution equations.* They can write either one. In later lessons, there will be problems where they may want to write *situation equations.*

English Language Learners

Draw pictures on the board to provide support with vocabulary for the word problems.

- **Beginning** Draw a $5 bill, a tiled floor, a test paper with an A grade, and a stuffed animal. Identify each one and have students repeat.
- **Intermediate** Point to each picture. Have students work in pairs to find the vocabulary in the word problems.
- **Advanced** Ask students questions to help them make sentences with the vocabulary.

Activity 4

Write Questions

 15 MINUTES

Goal: Use the "information part" of a word problem to write an appropriate "question part."

Materials: Student Activity Book or Hardcover Book p. 348

 **NCTM Standards:**
Number and Operations
Problem Solving
Communication
Connections

The Learning Classroon

Scenarios You may wish to have Student Pairs act out the situations in the "information part" of the word problems on Student Book page 348. They can act out the situations as they work to write an appropriate question. This strategy can be especially helpful for students in understanding the action in the situations, and then the operation required.

Teaching Note

Watch For! Watch for students who consistently write a "question part" that asks for the total number of items. Ask them to try to solve their own problems to see if the question makes sense for the situation.

9–10 Class Activity Name ______ Date ______

▶ Write the Question

Write a question for the given information and solve.
Sample questions and solutions given. Check students' work.

15. Anna read 383 pages this month. Chris read 416 pages.
Question: Possible answer: How many pages did they read altogether?
Solution: 383 + 416 = 799 pages

16. Marisol had 128 beads in her jewelry box. She gave away 56 of them.
Question: Possible answer: How many beads does she have left?
Solution: 128 − 56 = 72 beads

17. Louis put 72 marbles in 8 bags. He put the same number of marbles in each bag.
Question: Possible answer: How many marbles did he put in each bag?
Solution: 72 ÷ 8 = 9 marbles

18. Geoff planted 4 pots of seeds. He planted 6 seeds in each pot.
Question: Possible answer: How many seeds did Geoff plant?
Solution: 4 × 6 = 24 seeds

19. Last week, Marly read for 2 hours. Jamal read for 7 times as many hours as Marly did.
Question: Possible answer: How many hours did Jamal read?
Solution: 2 × 7 = 14 hours

348 UNIT 9 LESSON 10 Solve Mixed Word Problems

Student Activity Book page 348

▶ Write the Question INDIVIDUALS

Have students look back at problems 1–14 on Student Book pages 346–347. Point out that all of the problems give some information and then ask a question. Explain that in problems 15–19 on Student Book page 348, students will be given only the information part of the problems; they must write the questions themselves. Tell them there may be more than one reasonable question for each situation.

Give students time to complete problems 15–19, and then have volunteers share their questions and solutions.

Activity 5

Write Word Problems to Match Equations

9–10 Class Activity

Name ______ Date ______

▶ Write the Problem

Write a problem that can be solved using the given equation. Then solve.
Sample problems and solutions given. Check students' work.

20. $9 \times 6 = \square$ **Solution:** $9 \times 6 = 54$ eggs

Jordan has 9 cartons of eggs. Each carton holds a half dozen eggs. How many eggs does he have?

21. $324 - 176 = \square$ **Solution:** $324 - 176 = \$148$

Lehla had $324 to spend on supplies for the astronomy club's camping trip. She spent $176 on food. How much money does she have left?

22. $56 \div 7 = \square$ **Solution:** $56 \div 7 = 8$ toy cars

Cameron divided 56 toys cars evenly among the 7 guests at his birthday party. How many toy cars did each guest receive?

23. $459 + 635 = \square$ **Solution:** $459 + 635 = 1{,}094$ cans

Julian's team collected 459 aluminum cans to raise money for the soccer league. Tamara's team collected 635 cans. How many cans did they collect in all?

24. **Math Journal** Choose an operation. Write a word problem that involves that operation. Write an equation to solve your word problem.

UNIT 9 LESSON 10 Solve Mixed Word Problems **349**

Student Activity Book page 349

▶ Write the Problem WHOLE CLASS

Explain that in problems 20–23, on Student Book page 349, students must write a word problem for a given equation and then give the solution to the problem. You might do the first problem as a class so students know what to do. Give students several minutes to work on their problems, and then select students to share their problems and solutions.

Have students answer question 24, and then have them share their problems with the class.

15 MINUTES

Goal: Write word problems for given equations.

Materials: Student Activity Book or Hardcover Book p. 349

NCTM Standards:
Number and Operations
Problem Solving
Communication
Connections

Ongoing Assessment

Ask questions such as the following:

- ▶ What key words in a problem tell you to multiply?
- ▶ What can you say about the groups in a word problem that uses division?

2 Going Further

Problem Solving Strategy: Open-Ended Problems

Goal: Solve open-ended word problems with 3s multiplications and divisions.

Materials: Student Activity Book or Hardcover Book p. 351

NCTM Standards:
Number and Operations
Problem Solving

▶ Solve Open-Ended Problems

WHOLE CLASS

Explain to students that some of the problems they encounter in their math books sometimes have just one correct answer and only one way to solve it. However, in real-life situations, some problems may be solved in many different ways and have many different correct answers.

Read aloud problem 1 on Student Book page 350.

- What steps do you need to solve the problem? Possible answer: First find out the total cost of all the things she needs, and then find out how much money Hilda will have left after she buys them. Then see if she has enough money to buy the markers or the calculator.

Point out to students that although the pencils are 4 for $1.00, they can be purchased individually. Ask students how much one pencil costs. 25¢

Have students work in pairs to solve problem 1. Have volunteers come to the board and explain their solutions.

Math Talk Ask the following questions:

- Did anyone think of this problem in a different way?
- Does anyone have the same answer, but found it in a different way?
- Does anyone have a different answer? How did you get that answer?

In problem 2, students will need to pay attention to the fact that the items are being sold in a package that contains more than one item. You might suggest that students create a table to help organize their choices. The table to the right shows one possible solution to the problem.

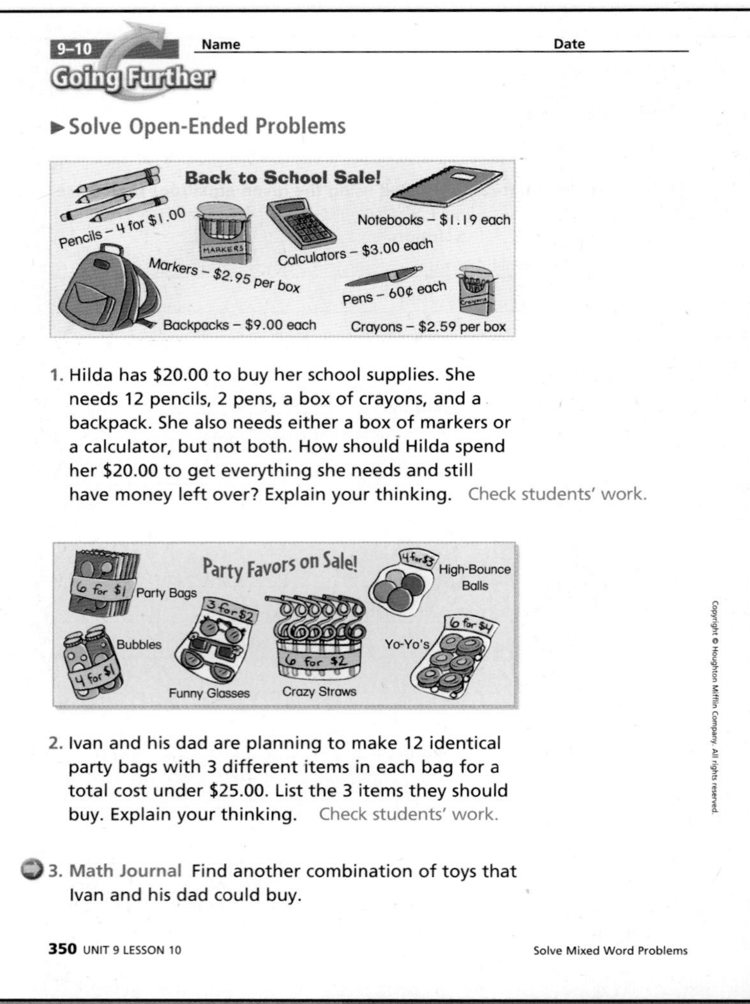
9–10 Going Further Name Date

▶ Solve Open-Ended Problems

1. Hilda has $20.00 to buy her school supplies. She needs 12 pencils, 2 pens, a box of crayons, and a backpack. She also needs either a box of markers or a calculator, but not both. How should Hilda spend her $20.00 to get everything she needs and still have money left over? Explain your thinking. Check students' work.

2. Ivan and his dad are planning to make 12 identical party bags with 3 different items in each bag for a total cost under $25.00. List the 3 items they should buy. Explain your thinking. Check students' work.

3. Math Journal Find another combination of toys that Ivan and his dad could buy.

350 UNIT 9 LESSON 10 Solve Mixed Word Problems

Student Activity Book page 350

Have students work individually or in pairs to solve the problem. Then have volunteers come to the board to explain their solutions.

Item	Number of Items in a Package	Number of Packages Needed to get 12 Items	Cost of Each Package	Total Cost of 12 Items
Party bags	6	2	$1	$2
High-bounce balls	4	3	$3	$9
Bubbles	4	3	$1	$3
Funny glasses	3	4	$2	$8
Total Cost				$22

Intervention Activity Card 9-10

Picture It

Activity Card 9-10

Work: In pairs

Use:

- Homework and Remembering, page 241
- Drawing paper

1. Read Problem 1 on Homework page 241. Discuss how you could create a drawing, cartoon, or diagram to make the problem easier to understand.

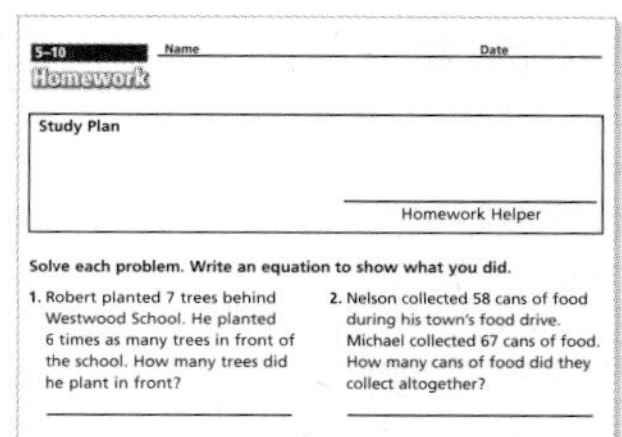

2. **Work Together** Create your drawing and then solve the problem. Continue the activity by making pictures for the remaining problems on the page.

Unit 9, Lesson 10

Activity Note For problems with large numbers, suggest that students create symbols to represent groups of 10 items in their drawings.

Math Writing Prompt

Choose the Operation Write a list of words that tell you to multiply in a word problem. Then write a list of words that tell you to divide.

Software Support

Warm Up 12.29

On Level Activity Card 9-10

Four Problems Rotate

Activity Card 9-10

Work: In small groups

Use:

- TRB M115 (Symbol Cards)

1. Work in a group of 4. Shuffle and deal out the symbol cards, one to each student in the group.
2. Write a word problem that can be solved using the operation on your symbol card.

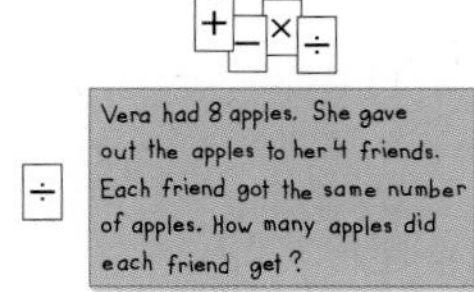

3. Pass your word problem to the student on your right and then solve the problem you receive.
4. For each correct answer, score 1 point. The first student to score 5 points wins.

Unit 9, Lesson 10

Activity Note Before beginning the activity, ask students to describe each of the four operations in terms of combining, grouping, comparing, or increasing groups of items.

Math Writing Prompt

Explain Your Thinking Thelma uses beads to make earrings. She uses the same number of beads to make each earring. Which operation would Thelma use to find how many earrings she could make? Explain.

Software Support

Numberopolis: Carnival Stories, Level T

Challenge Activity Card 9-10

What Are Our Ages?

Activity Card 9-10

Work: In pairs

1. Read the logical reasoning problem below. Work together to solve the problem.

   Katy is trying to figure out the ages of her three cousins. Her cousins Alec, Sara, and Tommy give her these clues. Alec is $\frac{1}{3}$ as many years old as Tommy. Tommy is not the oldest. All of the cousins are older than 2 years old. The oldest cousin is 11 years old and is 8 years older than Alec. How old is each cousin?

   Alec: 3; Tommy: 9; Sara: 11

2. **Analyze** Which operation did you use to solve the problem? How did you choose it?
3. Write your own logical reasoning problem and exchange with another pair to solve.

Unit 9, Lesson 10

Activity Note If students have difficulty, suggest they use the clues to organize the three cousins in order of their ages along a number line.

Math Writing Prompt

You Decide Can every word problem that can be solved by adding also be solved by multiplying? Give an example.

DESTINATION Math®

Software Support

Course II: Module 2: Unit 3: Fractional Parts

3 Homework and Spiral Review

9–10 Homework **Goal:** Additional Practice

Include students' completed Homework page as part of their portfolios.

9–10 Homework Name Date

Study Plan

Homework Helper

Solve each problem. Write an equation to show what you did.

1. Robert planted 7 trees behind Westwood School. He planted 6 times as many trees in front of the school. How many trees did he plant in front?
   42 trees; $7 \times 6 = 42$

2. Nelson collected 58 cans of food during his town's food drive. Michael collected 67 cans of food. How many cans of food did they collect altogether?
   125 cans of food; $58 + 67 = 125$

3. On a snorkeling trip, Betina spotted 27 different kinds of fish. Her younger sister Lucia spotted one third as many. How many different kinds of fish did Lucia spot?
   9 kinds; $27 \div 3 = 9$

4. Arnon earned $27 delivering newspapers last week. He spent $9 on a book about snakes. How much money does he have left?
   $18; $27 – 9 = $18

Write a question to finish each word problem. Then solve the problem.

5. Sonya has 272 coins in her collection. Her brother Erez has 298 coins.
   Question: Possible answer: How many coins do they have altogether?
   Solution: 570 coins

6. Richard folded 32 shirts and stacked them in 4 equal piles.
   Question: Possible answer: How many shirts were in each stack?
   Solution: 8 shirts

UNIT 9 LESSON 10 Solve Mixed Word Problems **241**

Homework and Remembering page 241

9–10 Remembering **Goal:** Spiral Review

This Remembering page would be appropriate anytime after today's lesson.

9–10 Remembering Name Date

Round each number to the nearest ten.

1. 94 90
2. 309 310
3. 82 80
4. 888 890

Round each number to the nearest hundred.

5. 192 200
6. 538 500
7. 389 400
8. 856 900

Solve each problem.

9. Pedro's class cut out 314 paper snowflakes to decorate their classroom. Natalie's class cut out 229 snowflakes. How many fewer snowflakes did Natalie's class make?
   85 fewer snowflakes

10. Kai and Marcia spent Saturday doing jigsaw puzzles. They put together puzzles with 500 pieces, 1,200 pieces, and 150 pieces. How many puzzle pieces did they put together in all?
   1,850 puzzle pieces

Fill in the missing number in each Fast Array drawing.

11. 6, 6, 36
12. 6, 8, 48
13. 9, 6, 54
14. 7, 5, 35
15. 7, 9, 63
16. 8, 8, 64

242 UNIT 9 LESSON 10 Solve Mixed Word Problems

Homework and Remembering page 242

Home or School Activity

Science Connection

Lightning and Thunder Explain to students that they can find the distance they are from a storm. When they spot lightning, they can count the seconds between the lightning and the sound of the thunder, and divide the number of seconds by 5 to find the number of miles away the storm is. Have students complete the table. If time allows read Patricia Pollaco's book, *Thunder Cake.*

Time Between Lightning and Thunder (in seconds)	Distance You Are From Storm (in miles)
15	3
25	5
20	4
30	6
35	7

Solve Multi-Step Word Problems

Vocabulary
expression
evaluate

Lesson Objective

- Develop strategies for solving multi-step word problems.

The Day at a Glance

Today's Goals	Materials	
1 Teaching the Lesson **A1:** Practice count-bys, multiplications, and divisions. **A2:** Use the order of operations to write and evaluate expressions. **A3:** Solve multi-step word problems.	**Lesson Activities** Student Activity Book pp. 351–354 or Student Hardcover Book pp. 351–354 Homework and Remembering pp. 243–244 Check Up materials Signature Sheet Blank Sprint Answer Sheets Study Sheets A-C Check Sheets 1–11 Dry-erase markers Sheet protectors Study Sheet Answer Strips Check Sheet Answer Strips Cardstock Strategy Cards Cardstock Strategy cards	**Going Further** Activity Cards 9–11 Highlighters Homework p. 243 Game Cards (TRB M25) Symbol Cards (TRB M115) Index cards Secret Code Cards MathBoard materials Math Journals
2 Going Further ► Extension: Multiply 2- and 3-Digit Numbers by 1-Digit Numbers ► Differentiated Instruction		
3 Homework and Spiral Review		

Use Math Talk today!

Keeping Skills Sharp

Quick Practice — 5 MINUTES	Daily Routines
Goal: Practice mixed multiplications and divisions. **Materials:** Class Multiplication Table Poster, pointer **Mixed Multiplications** The Student Leader says "Close your eyes" and points to any equation in the table. The leader reads the multiplication aloud and pauses. The leader then says "Answer," and students say the answer in unison. Then students open their eyes and say the complete equation. Repeat for about 10 equations. **Mixed Divisions** Use the same procedure as above with the leader reading the related division aloud.	**Homework Review** Have students share the questions they wrote for homework and have the class solve. **Skip Count** Skip count backward by 10s from 1,000 to 870 and then from 345 to 215.

1 Teaching the Lesson

Activity 1

Check Up and Independent Study

 5 MINUTES

Goal: Practice count-bys, multiplications, and divisions.

Materials: Check Up materials: Signature Sheet, Blank Sprint Answer Sheet (TRB M57), Study Sheets A–C, Check Sheets 1–11, dry-erase markers (1 per student), sheet protectors (1 per student), Study Sheet Answer Strips (TRB M54), Check Sheet Answer Strips (TRB M55), cardstock; Strategy Cards, Homework and Remembering p. 243

 **NCTM Standard:**
Number and Operations

▶ Check Up with 6s, 7s, and 8s PAIRS

Give **Student Pairs** a few minutes to test each other using Study Sheets A–C and collect signatures. For students who have already collected signatures on the Study Sheets, have them use Check Sheets 1–11. You may want to have Study Sheet and Check Sheet Answer Strips (TRB M54–M55) available.

Students who made mistakes on the 7s Sprints from Lesson 10 (or who were absent) may take repeat or make-up sprints at this time. Students can record their answers on Blank Sprint Answer Sheet (TRB M57).

Then give them 2 or 3 minutes to study independently using their Study Sheets, Check Sheets, or Strategy Cards. Also have students complete their Study Plan box on Homework and Remembering page 243. Students should include any multiplications and divisions they missed in the Check Up.

Activity 2

Order of Operations

 15 MINUTES

Goal: Use the order of operations to write and evaluate expressions.

Materials: Student Activity Book page 351

 **NCTM Standards:**
Number and Operations
Problem Solving
Algebra
Representation

▶ Introduce Order of Operations WHOLE CLASS

In the next activity and in the next two lessons, students will solve word problems involving two or more operations. Writing such expressions correctly requires an understanding of order of operations. Specifically;

- If a mathematical expression does not contain parentheses, multiplication and division are done before addition and subtraction.
- To indicate that addition or subtraction should be done before multiplication and division, parentheses must be used. Parentheses mean "Do this first."

9–11 Class Activity

Name ______ Date ______

▶ Use Order of Operations

This exercise involves subtraction and multiplication:

$10 - 3 \times 2$

1. What do you get if you subtract first and then multiply? 14

2. What do you get if you multiply first and then subtract? 4

To make sure everyone has the same answer to problems like this one, people have decided that multiplication and division will be done *before* addition and subtraction. The answer you found in question 2 is correct.

If you want to tell people to add or subtract first, you must use parentheses. Parentheses mean "Do this first." For example, if you want people to subtract first in the exercise above, write it like this:

$(10 - 3) \times 2$

Find the answer.

3. $5 + 4 \times 2 =$ 13
4. $(9 - 3) \times 6 =$ 36
5. $8 \div 2 + 2 =$ 6
6. $6 \times (8 - 1) =$ 42

Rewrite each statement, using symbols and numbers instead of words.

7. Add 4 and 3, and multiply the total by 8. $(4 + 3) \times 8$

8. Multiply 3 by 8, and add 4 to the total. $3 \times 8 + 4$

UNIT 9 LESSON 11 Solve Multi-Step Word Problems **351**

Student Activity Book page 351

▶ Use Order of Operations SMALL GROUPS

On Student Book page 351, exercises 1–8 introduce and provide practice with order of operations. Have Small Groups work on them independently and then discuss the answers as a class. For exercise 8, explain that although it is not necessary to put parentheses around 3×8, it is not wrong to include them.

The Learning Classroom

Building Concepts Students will not be tested specifically on the order of operations. Some students will solve the problems by doing the steps one at a time. Others will write a single expression to represent an entire problem and then evaluate that expression. Many students may write and evaluate expressions incorrectly, but in a way that gives the correct answer. When students present solutions to word problems, encourage them to use parentheses and apply the order of operations correctly. In time they will internalize these ideas.

Differentiated Instruction

Extra Help Some students may have difficulty focusing on the individual operations when they see an expression with more than one symbol. Have students rewrite the expressions in exercises 3–6 on Student Book page 351 as two separate number sentences. For example, for $5 + 4 \times 2$, begin by rewriting the expression as:

$4 \times 2 = \square$ and

$\square + 5 = \bigcirc$

English Language Learners

Write *My Dear Aunt Sally* on the board. Say: **When I can't remember the order of operations, I think of *My Dear Aunt Sally.*** Underline the first letter of each word and say: **My – M – Multiplication. Dear – D – Division. Aunt – A – Addition. Sally – S – Subtraction.** Have students repeat.

Activity 3

Solve Multi-Step Word Problems

 15 MINUTES

Goal: Solve multi-step word problems.

Materials: Student Activity Book or Hardcover Book p. 352

 **NCTM Standards:**
Number and Operations
Problem Solving
Algebra

Math Talk in Action

How can you find how many people were on the roller coaster in problem 9?

Amir: First I'm going to find the total number of seats on the roller coaster. I can do that by multiplying 7 × 4. That's 28 seats.

Then what do you do?

Amir: Next, I'm going to subtract the number of empty seats. 28 − 3 = 25. There were 25 people on the roller coaster.

Very good. This is one strategy. It uses separate steps. Can anyone write one *expression* that shows all the operations at once?

There is a pause while Nicole writes this expression:

$7 \times 4 - 3$

Are parentheses needed?

Nicole: No, because you need to do multiplication before subtraction, anyway.

What are the steps we use to *evaluate* this expression?

There is a pause while Nicole writes the following:

$7 \times 4 - 3 = 28 - 3 = 25$

Nicole: First you multiply and then you subtract.

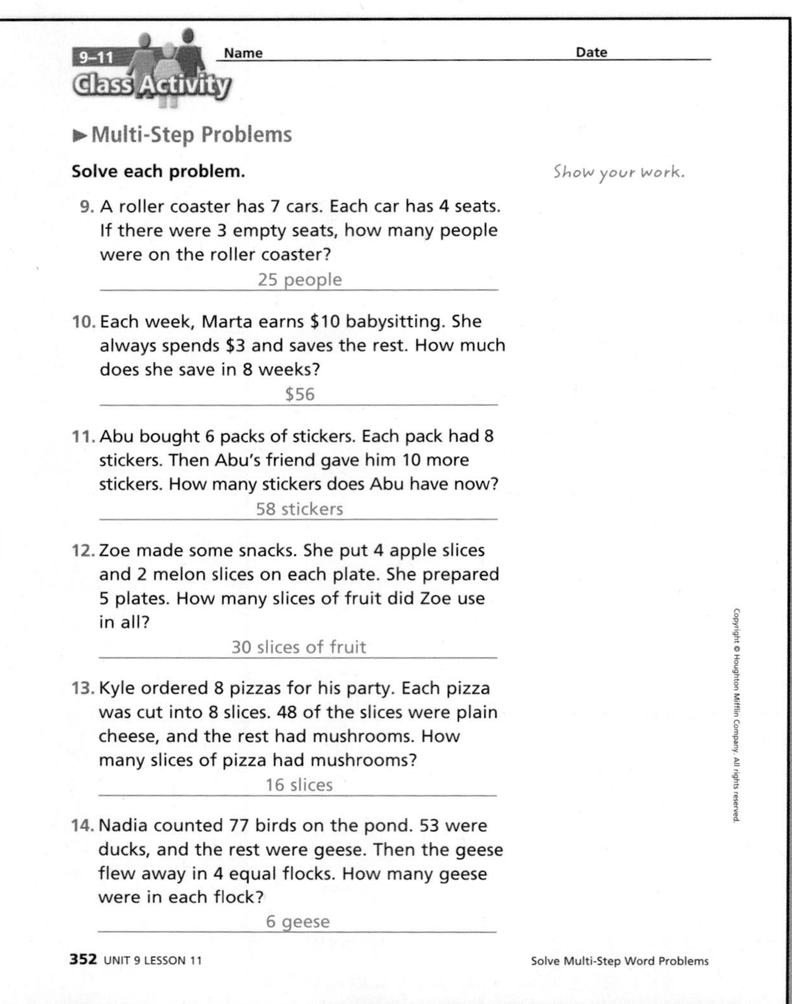

9–11 Class Activity Name ______ Date ______

▶ Multi-Step Problems

Solve each problem. *Show your work.*

9. A roller coaster has 7 cars. Each car has 4 seats. If there were 3 empty seats, how many people were on the roller coaster?
25 people

10. Each week, Marta earns $10 babysitting. She always spends $3 and saves the rest. How much does she save in 8 weeks?
$56

11. Abu bought 6 packs of stickers. Each pack had 8 stickers. Then Abu's friend gave him 10 more stickers. How many stickers does Abu have now?
58 stickers

12. Zoe made some snacks. She put 4 apple slices and 2 melon slices on each plate. She prepared 5 plates. How many slices of fruit did Zoe use in all?
30 slices of fruit

13. Kyle ordered 8 pizzas for his party. Each pizza was cut into 8 slices. 48 of the slices were plain cheese, and the rest had mushrooms. How many slices of pizza had mushrooms?
16 slices

14. Nadia counted 77 birds on the pond. 53 were ducks, and the rest were geese. Then the geese flew away in 4 equal flocks. How many geese were in each flock?
6 geese

352 UNIT 9 LESSON 11 Solve Multi-Step Word Problems

Student Activity Book page 352

▶ Multi-Step Problems WHOLE CLASS

Tell students that today they will work on word problems that take two or more steps to solve. Read problem 9 aloud. Using the **Solve and Discuss** structure, have students solve it. If students don't suggest the methods suggested in the **Math Talk in Action** in the side column, bring them up yourself.

Then have students solve problems 10–14. See an example of how students may solve problem 10 on the next page.

Problem 10 Some students will figure out how much Marta saves each week and then multiply by 8:

$$(10 - 3) \times 8 = 7 \times 8$$
$$= 56 \text{ dollars}$$

Others will subtract the total she spends in 8 weeks from the total she earns.

$$8 \times 10 - 8 \times 3 = 80 - 24$$
$$= 56 \text{ dollars}$$

▶ More Multi-Step Problems INDIVIDUALS

9–11 Class Activity Name ____ Date ____

▶ More Multi-Step Problems

Solve each problem. Draw a picture if you need to. *Show your work.*

15. Lakesha has filled two pages of her stamp book. Both pages have 5 rows of stamps. On one page, there are 5 stamps in each row. On the opposite page, there are 3 stamps in each row. How many stamps are on the two pages?
40 stamps

16. Kagami baked 86 blueberry muffins. Her sisters ate 5 of them. Kagami divided the remaining muffins equally among 9 plates. How many muffins did she put on each plate?
9 muffins

17. Lucia had 42 plums. Jorge had 12 more plums than Lucia. Jorge divided his plums equally among 6 people. How many plums did each person get?
9 plums

18. Dana arranged her books on 5 shelves, with 8 books on each shelf. Hassan arranged his books on 4 shelves, with 9 books on each shelf. Who has more books? How many more?
Dana; 4 more books

19. Juana has 21 shirts. Leslie had one third as many shirts as Juana, but then she bought 4 more. How many shirts does Leslie have now?
11 shirts

UNIT 9 LESSON 11 Solve Multi-Step Word Problems **353**

Student Activity Book page 353

Have students solve problems 15–19. Discuss students' answers and strategies with the class. Have students who have difficulty check their answers with a **Helping Partner**.

Teaching Note

What to Expect From Students To solve problem 15, some students will find the number of stamps on each page and then add.

$$5 \times 5 + 5 \times 3 = 25 + 15$$
$$= 40 \text{ stamps}$$

Others will add the number in each row for the two pages and then multiply the total by 5.

$$(5 + 3) \times 5 = 8 \times 5$$
$$= 40 \text{ stamps}$$

Students probably will not be able to solve problem 18 by writing a single expression. They must first figure out how many books each person has and then subtract that smaller amount from the larger amount.

Multi-Step Mastery These multi-step problems and those later in this unit and in Unit 5 are challenging for third graders. They are not for mastery by all. After today, you may wish to separate your class into two groups and have the less-advanced students work on more difficult single-step problems (or problems at their present learning level) while the rest work on multi-step problems. This is especially true if you have mainstreamed special needs students.

Ongoing Assessment

- Give an example of when you need to use more than one operation to solve a problem.
- What is the correct order of operations in an expression?

2 Going Further

Extension: Multiply 2- and 3-Digit Numbers by 1-Digit Numbers

Goal: Multiply 2- and 3-digit numbers by 1-digit numbers with regrouping.

Materials: Student Activity Book or Hardcover Book p. 354

✓ **NCTM Standards:**
Number and Operations
Problem Solving

▶ Multiply 2- and 3-Digit Numbers by 1-Digit Numbers WHOLE CLASS

Have a volunteer read aloud the word problem at the top of Student Book page 354.

- What information does the problem give? there are 26 cars in the water ride; 7 people fit in each car
- What does the problem ask for? how many people can fit in all the cars of the water ride
- What operation can we use to solve the problem? Multiplication, because each car can fit the same number of people. We need to find 26 × 7.

Write 26 × 7 = ☐ on the board:

Have students share ideas about how they can multiply 26 × 7. They might suggest drawing a picture, using count-bys, using repeated addition, as well as other strategies. Tell students that today, they see methods for multiplying that involve breaking-apart the larger number and then using multiplications they know.

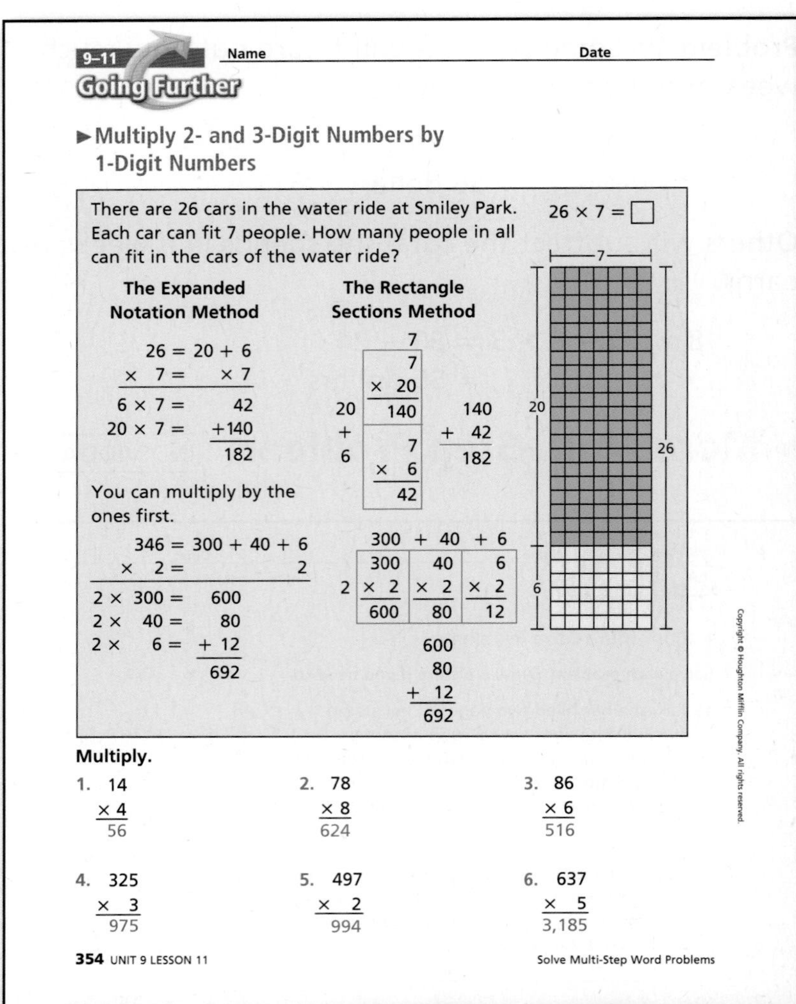
9–11 Going Further Name Date

▶ Multiply 2- and 3-Digit Numbers by 1-Digit Numbers

There are 26 cars in the water ride at Smiley Park. Each car can fit 7 people. How many people in all can fit in the cars of the water ride?

26 × 7 = ☐

The Expanded Notation Method

26 = 20 + 6
× 7 = × 7
6 × 7 = 42
20 × 7 = +140
182

You can multiply by the ones first.

346 = 300 + 40 + 6
× 2 = 2
2 × 300 = 600
2 × 40 = 80
2 × 6 = + 12
692

The Rectangle Sections Method

7; 20 + 6: 7 × 20 = 140; 7 × 6 = 42; 140 + 42 = 182

300 + 40 + 6; 2: 300 × 2 = 600; 40 × 2 = 80; 6 × 2 = 12; 600 + 80 + 12 = 692

Multiply.

1. 14 × 4 = 56
2. 78 × 8 = 624
3. 86 × 6 = 516
4. 325 × 3 = 975
5. 497 × 2 = 994
6. 637 × 5 = 3,185

354 UNIT 9 LESSON 11 — Solve Multi-Step Word Problems

Student Activity Book page 354

Work through the **Expanded Notation, Rectangle Sections**, and **Array** methods shown on Student Activity Book page 354 with the class.

Students can work independently or in Helping Pairs to solve the problems at the bottom of Student Activity Book page 354. Have them use a separate sheet of paper to show their work.

When students have completed the problems, use **Solve and Discuss** for sharing students' methods.

Intervention Activity Card 9-11

Highlight the Operation
Activity Card 9-11

Work: In pairs

Use:
- One yellow and one pink highlighter
- Homework and Remembering, page 243

Decide:

Who will be Student 1 and who will be Student 2 for the first problem.

1. Read the first problem on Homework page 243
2. **Student 1:** Use the yellow highlighter to mark the part of the problem that you need to solve first.
3. **Student 2:** Use the pink highlighter to mark the part of the problem that you must solve next.

> 1. The tour boats at the Laguna can carry 8 passengers. Jacob watched 6 boats float by. Three of the boats had 2 empty seats. The others were full. How many passengers were on the 6 boats?

4. **Work Together** Write an equation and solve the problem. Then continue highlighting and solving the remaining problems on the page.

Unit 9, Lesson 11

Activity Note If students have difficulty identifying the separate parts of a problem, have them answer the following questions: What do I need to know? What do I know now?

Math Writing Prompt

Explain Your Thinking Explain the steps you would take to solve $5 \times (7 - 3) = \square$. Use words like *first, next,* and *then*.

Software Support

Warm Up 12.39

On Level Activity Card 9-11

Mixed Up Expressions
Activity Card 9-11

Work: In pairs

Use:
- TRB M25 (Game Cards)
- TRB M115 (Symbol Cards)
- Index cards

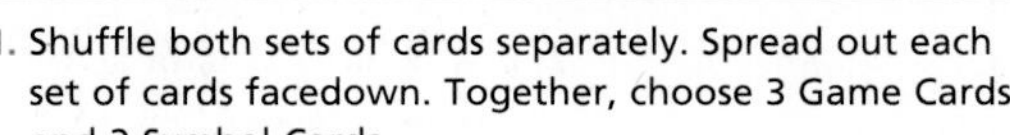

1. Shuffle both sets of cards separately. Spread out each set of cards facedown. Together, choose 3 Game Cards and 2 Symbol Cards.
2. Try to make all the possible expressions with the 3 digits and 2 operations that you chose. Use the index cards to write parentheses to use in your expressions.

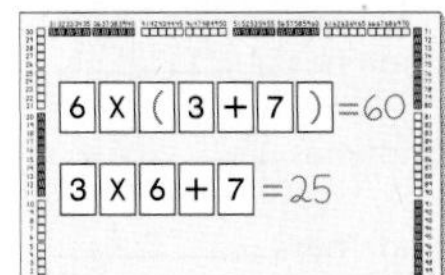

3. **Analyze** How can you show an expression with the greatest possible value and one with the least possible value using your cards?

Unit 9, Lesson 11

Activity Note Review the order of operations and the use of parentheses before students begin this activity.

Math Writing Prompt

You Decide The Puzzled Penguin solved $2 + 6 \times 7 = 56$. Is he correct? Explain why or why not.

Software Support

Ice Station Exploration: Arctic Algebra, Level H

Challenge Activity Card 9-11

Guess and Check
Activity Card 9-11

Work: In pairs

Use:
- Secret Code Cards
- MathBoard materials

1. Shuffle the Secret Code cards and put them into two piles face down—tens and ones.
2. You and your partner each pick a card from one of the piles. Now form a two-digit number.
3. **Work Together** Write at least 5 different equations to equal the number you made. Be sure to use at least 2 operations in each equation. Use parentheses too if you like.

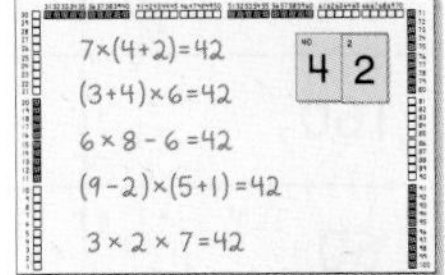

Unit 9, Lesson 11

Activity Note Students may use the strategy of Guess and Check or they may use number sense and order of operations to write the 5 equations.

Math Writing Prompt

Compare How is finding the product of 26×7 the same as finding the product of 6×7? How is it different?

Software Support

Course II: Module 2: Unit 2: Finding Products less than 100

3 Homework and Spiral Review

9–11 **Homework** **Goal:** Additional Practice

This Homework page provides practice in solving multi-step word problems.

9–11 **Homework** Name ____ Date ____

Study Plan
____ Homework Helper

Solve each problem.

1. The tour boats at the Laguna can carry 8 passengers. Jacob watched 6 boats float by. Three of the boats had 2 empty seats. The others were full. How many passengers were on the 6 boats?
   42 passengers
2. Jerome bought 8 packs of baseball cards at a garage sale. Each pack had 10 cards. He gave his younger sister 3 cards from each pack. How many cards does Jerome have left?
   56 cards
3. Zoe cut a pan of brownies into 5 rows and 6 columns. She gave 6 brownies to her family, and divided the rest evenly among the 8 people at her scout meeting. How many brownies did each person at her scout meeting get?
   3 brownies
4. Four girls helped Mr. Day plant a garden. For their help, he gave the girls $24 to share equally. Later, Mrs. Day gave each girl $2 for helping to clean up. How much money did each girl get?
   $8
5. Grace made 7 bouquets for the bridesmaids in a wedding. She put 3 roses, 4 tulips, and 2 lilies in each bouquet. How many flowers did she use in all?
   63 flowers
6. Takala put 9 marbles in the box, Jackie put in 7, and Laird put in 11. Then they divided the marbles evenly among themselves. How many did each person get?
   9 marbles

UNIT 9 LESSON 11 Solve Multi-Step Word Problems **243**

Homework and Remembering page 243

9–11 **Remembering** **Goal:** Spiral Review

This Remembering page would be appropriate anytime after today's lesson.

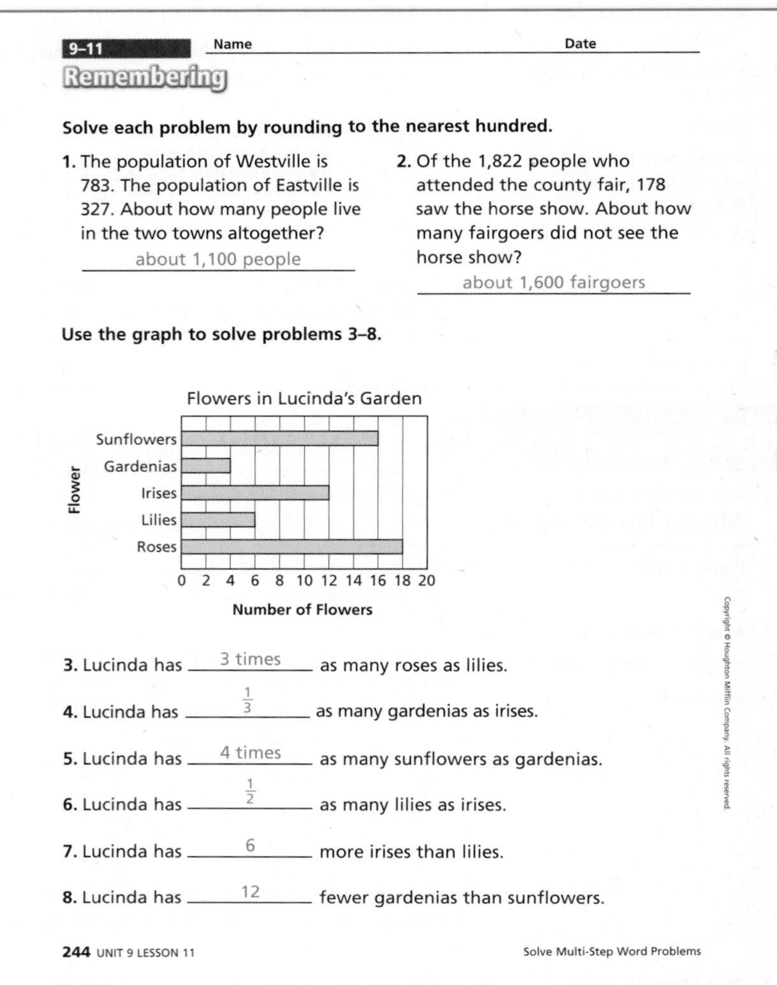

9–11 **Remembering** Name ____ Date ____

Solve each problem by rounding to the nearest hundred.

1. The population of Westville is 783. The population of Eastville is 327. About how many people live in the two towns altogether?
   about 1,100 people
2. Of the 1,822 people who attended the county fair, 178 saw the horse show. About how many fairgoers did not see the horse show?
   about 1,600 fairgoers

Use the graph to solve problems 3–8.

3. Lucinda has 3 times as many roses as lilies.
4. Lucinda has $\frac{1}{3}$ as many gardenias as irises.
5. Lucinda has 4 times as many sunflowers as gardenias.
6. Lucinda has $\frac{1}{2}$ as many lilies as irises.
7. Lucinda has 6 more irises than lilies.
8. Lucinda has 12 fewer gardenias than sunflowers.

244 UNIT 9 LESSON 11 Solve Multi-Step Word Problems

Homework and Remembering page 244

Home or School Activity

Science Connection

How Crickets Tell Temperature Explain to students that the snowy tree cricket chirps at rates that change with the air temperature and that they can compute the temperature (in degrees Fahrenheit) by counting the number of chirps each minute and using the following formula:

$$\frac{(\text{Number of chirps in one minute} - 40)}{4} + 50$$

Have students complete the table at the right. Students may check their answers with a calculator.

Number of Chirps per Minute N	$N-40$	$\frac{N-40}{4}$	Temperature $\frac{N-40}{4} + 50$
140	100	25	75°
80	40	10	60°
160	120	30	80°
60	20	5	55°
120	80	20	70°

Solve Complex Multi-Step Word Problems

Vocabulary
twice
half

Lesson Objective

- Develop strategies for solving multi-step word problems.

The Day at a Glance

Today's Goals	Materials
1 Teaching the Lesson **A1:** Practice count-bys, multiplications, and divisions. **A2:** Complete multiplication and division Dashes for whole number factors from 2 through 9. **A3:** Discuss and solve complex multi-step word problems.	**Lesson Activities** Student Activity Book pp. 355–360 or Student Hardcover Book pp. 355–360 and Activity Workbook pp. 161–162 (includes Dashes 13–16, 17–20) Homework and Remembering pp. 245–246 Folders Check Up materials Signature Sheet Study Sheets A-C Check Sheets 1–11 Dry-erase markers Sheet protectors Study Sheet Answer Strips Check Sheet Answer Strips Cardstock Strategy Cards
2 Going Further ▸ Differentiated Instruction	**Going Further** Activity Cards 9–12 MathBoard materials Homework p. 245 Math Journals
3 Homework and Spiral Review	

Use Math Talk today!

Keeping Skills Sharp

Quick Practice — 5 MINUTES

Goal: Practice mixed multiplications and divisions.

Materials: Class Multiplication Table Poster, pointer

Mixed Multiplications The leader says "Close your eyes" and points to any equation in the table. The leader reads aloud the multiplication equation and pauses for a few seconds. The leader then says "Answer," and students say the answer in unison. Then students open their eyes and say the complete equation. Repeat for about 10 equations. (See Unit 9 Lesson 11.)

Mixed Divisions Use the same procedure as above with the leader reading the related division aloud. (See Unit 9 Lesson 11.)

Daily Routines

Homework Review Encourage students to write situation equations to solve word problems.

Analyze Data The students voted for their favorite subject. 4 students voted for science. 7 students voted for math. 5 students voted for reading. Create a line plot and write a conclusion using the data.

Possible answer: Fewer students liked reading than math.

Science	Math	Reading
xxxx	xxxxxxx	xxxxx

Favorite Subject in School

1 Teaching the Lesson

Activity 1

Check Up and Independent Study

10 MINUTES

Goal: Practice count-bys, multiplications, and divisions.

Materials: Folders, Check Up materials: Signature Sheet, Study Sheets A–C, Check Sheets 1–11, dry-erase markers (1 per student), sheet protectors (1 per student), Study Sheet Answer Strips (TRB M54), Check Sheet Answer Strips (TRB M55), cardstock; Strategy Cards, Homework and Remembering p. 245

NCTM Standard:
Number and Operations

▶ Check Up with 0s–10s PAIRS

Give **Student Pairs** a few minutes to test one another using Study Sheets A–C and collect signatures. For students who have collected signatures, have them use Check Sheets 1–11. You may want to have Study Sheet and Check Sheet Answer Strips (TRB M54–M55) available.

Give students 2 or 3 minutes to study independently, using their Study Sheets, Check Sheets, and Strategy Cards. Also have them complete their Study Plan box on Homework and Remembering page 245. Students should include any multiplications and divisions they missed in the Check Up.

Class Management

Remind students to put all their Check Up materials in their folders.

Activity 2

Mixed Practice

15 MINUTES

Goal: Complete multiplication and division Dashes for whole number factors from 2 through 9.

Materials: Student Activity Book pages 355–358 or Activity Workbook p.161

NCTM Standard:
Number and Operations

▶ Dashes 13–16 INDIVIDUALS

Have students complete Dashes 13–16 on Student Activity Book page 355 or Activity Workbook p. 161. You can have them complete one Dash at a time, with breaks in between, or do all four at once. Time the Dashes, or let students complete them at their own pace. Students can check their answers against those on page 357. A second Dash is included on the back for retesting if needed.

Activity 3

Solve Complex Word Problems

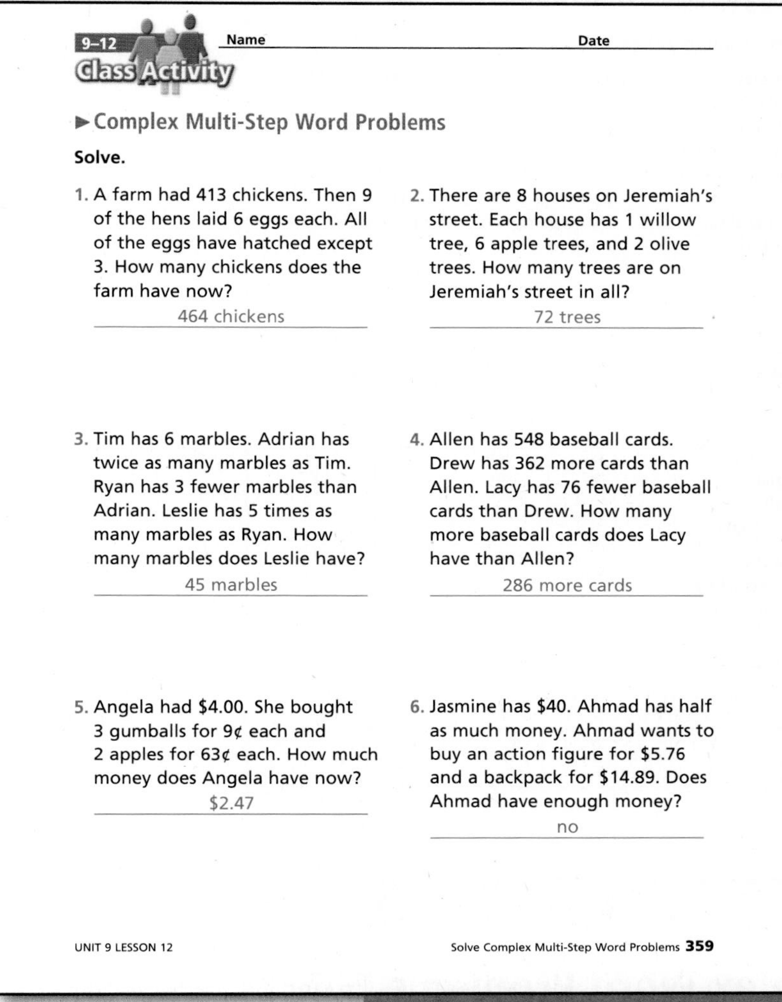

9–12 Class Activity

Name Date

► Complex Multi-Step Word Problems

Solve.

1. A farm had 413 chickens. Then 9 of the hens laid 6 eggs each. All of the eggs have hatched except 3. How many chickens does the farm have now?
   464 chickens

2. There are 8 houses on Jeremiah's street. Each house has 1 willow tree, 6 apple trees, and 2 olive trees. How many trees are on Jeremiah's street in all?
   72 trees

3. Tim has 6 marbles. Adrian has twice as many marbles as Tim. Ryan has 3 fewer marbles than Adrian. Leslie has 5 times as many marbles as Ryan. How many marbles does Leslie have?
   45 marbles

4. Allen has 548 baseball cards. Drew has 362 more cards than Allen. Lacy has 76 fewer baseball cards than Drew. How many more baseball cards does Lacy have than Allen?
   286 more cards

5. Angela had $4.00. She bought 3 gumballs for 9¢ each and 2 apples for 63¢ each. How much money does Angela have now?
   $2.47

6. Jasmine has $40. Ahmad has half as much money. Ahmad wants to buy an action figure for $5.76 and a backpack for $14.89. Does Ahmad have enough money?
   no

UNIT 9 LESSON 12 Solve Complex Multi-Step Word Problems **359**

Student Activity Book page 359

► Complex Multi-Step Word Problems WHOLE CLASS

The problems in this activity build on the problems students solved in Lesson 11. They are slightly more difficult, but the essential strategies are the same. Most of the problems can be solved either by doing the steps separately or by writing and evaluating an expression. Using the **Solve and Discuss** structure, have students solve problems 1–6. Below and in the side column are comments on a few of the trickier problems.

Problem 6: Students who try to write and evaluate a single expression may have trouble because the final result will be less than 0. It is probably easiest to solve this problem in steps.

- Find the amount Ahmad has: $40 ÷ 2 = $20
- Find the total cost of the items: $5.76 + $14.89 =$20.65
- Compare the total cost to the amount Ahmad has: The cost is more than $20, so Ahmad does not have enough.

Activity continued ►

 **20 MINUTES**

Goal: Discuss and solve complex multi-step word problems.

Materials: Student Activity Book or Hardcover Book pp. 359–360

 **NCTM Standards:**
Number and Operations
Algebra
Problem Solving

Teaching Note

What to Expect from Students
Most students will find it easiest to keep track of the information in problem 3 if they solve it step by step, considering one person at a time.

Tim: 6 marbles

Adrian: twice as many as Tim
$2 \times 6 = 12$ marbles

Ryan: 3 fewer than Adrian
$12 - 3 = 9$ marbles

Leslie: 5 times as many as Ryan
$5 \times 9 = 45$ marbles

Some students will be able to write and evaluate a single expression:

$$\begin{aligned} 5 \times (2 \times 6 - 3) &= 5 \times (12 - 3) \\ &= 5 \times 9 \\ &= 45 \text{ marbles} \end{aligned}$$

These problems are not for mastery by all at this grade level.

Teaching the Lesson (continued)

English Language Learners

Draw pictures to help students identify new vocabulary in these word problems.

- **Beginning** Point to and identify each picture. Have students repeat. Point again and have children identify the picture.
- **Intermediate** Point to each picture. Have students work in pairs to find the vocabulary in the word problems.
- **Advanced** Ask students questions to help them make sentences with the vocabulary.

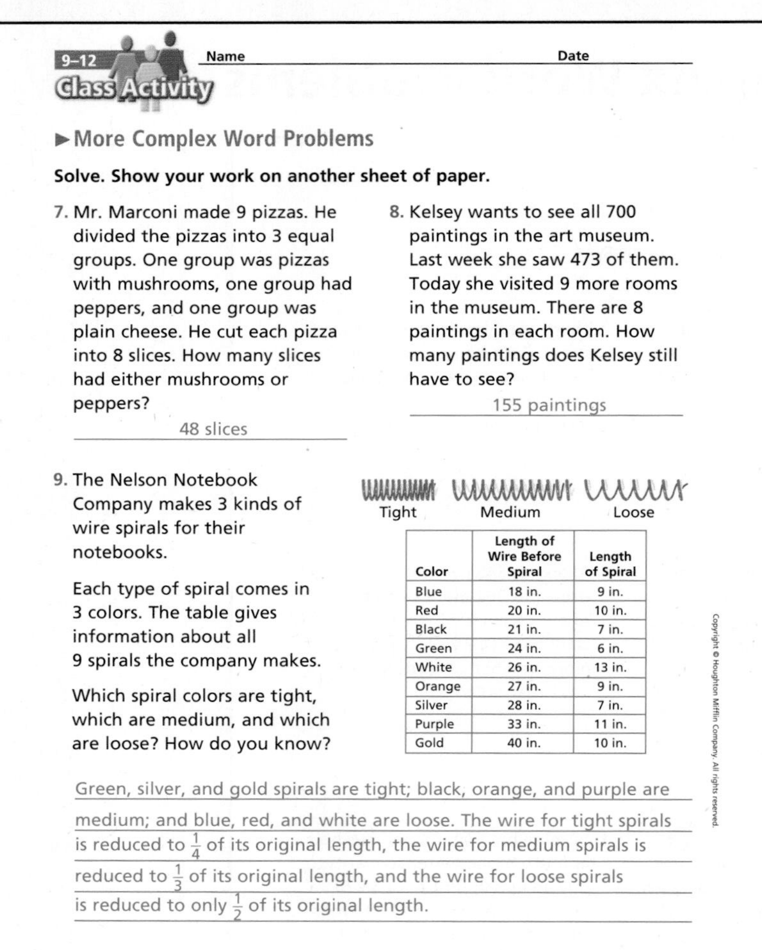

9–12 Class Activity Name ______ Date ______

▶ More Complex Word Problems

Solve. Show your work on another sheet of paper.

7. Mr. Marconi made 9 pizzas. He divided the pizzas into 3 equal groups. One group was pizzas with mushrooms, one group had peppers, and one group was plain cheese. He cut each pizza into 8 slices. How many slices had either mushrooms or peppers?
   48 slices

8. Kelsey wants to see all 700 paintings in the art museum. Last week she saw 473 of them. Today she visited 9 more rooms in the museum. There are 8 paintings in each room. How many paintings does Kelsey still have to see?
   155 paintings

9. The Nelson Notebook Company makes 3 kinds of wire spirals for their notebooks.

   Each type of spiral comes in 3 colors. The table gives information about all 9 spirals the company makes.

   Which spiral colors are tight, which are medium, and which are loose? How do you know?

Color	Length of Wire Before Spiral	Length of Spiral
Blue	18 in.	9 in.
Red	20 in.	10 in.
Black	21 in.	7 in.
Green	24 in.	6 in.
White	26 in.	13 in.
Orange	27 in.	9 in.
Silver	28 in.	7 in.
Purple	33 in.	11 in.
Gold	40 in.	10 in.

Green, silver, and gold spirals are tight; black, orange, and purple are medium; and blue, red, and white are loose. The wire for tight spirals is reduced to $\frac{1}{4}$ of its original length, the wire for medium spirals is reduced to $\frac{1}{3}$ of its original length, and the wire for loose spirals is reduced to only $\frac{1}{2}$ of its original length.

Student Activity Book page 360

▶ More Complex Word Problems PAIRS

Have students who experienced difficulty with the word problems on page 359 work with a **Helping Partner** to solve the problems on Student Book page 360. Problems 9 is a challenge, so you may want to have students work through it as a class. Students should discover the following:

- The blue, red, and white spirals are $\frac{1}{2}$ as long as the original wire. These are the loose spirals.
- The black, orange, and purple spirals are $\frac{1}{3}$ as long as the original wire. These are the medium spirals.
- The green, silver, and gold spirals are $\frac{1}{4}$ as long as the original wires. These are the tight spirals.

Some students may have trouble understanding the relationship between the length of the spiral relative to the original wire length and the tightness of the spiral. You might ask them to imagine pressing on the ends of a spring. As they press, the spring gets shorter and its coils get tighter (closer together). A spring pressed to $\frac{1}{3}$ its original length is tighter than a spring pressed to only $\frac{1}{2}$ its original length.

Ongoing Assessment

As students are solving the problems, ask questions such as the following:

- ▶ How did you know to use that operation?
- ▶ How can you find the number you need to continue solving the problem?

2 Going Further

Differentiated Instruction

Intervention

Activity Card 9-12

Act It Out! Activity Card 9-12

Work: In pairs

Use:

- MathBoard materials
- Homework page 245

1. Read problem 1 on Homework page 245.
2. **Work Together** Organize the information. Then choose a strategy to help you solve the problem. You can draw a picture, act it out, or use counters.
3. Write an equation to solve the problem. Discuss your work with others and compare strategies.

17 roses + 6 groups of 3 roses =
17 + 18 = 35 roses

4. Repeat the activity with the remaining problems.

Unit 9, Lesson 12

Activity Note For problems with larger numbers, such as in problems 3 and 5, suggest that students use base-ten blocks to model the situation.

Math Writing Prompt

Explain Your Thinking What kinds of word problems might a carpenter have to solve? Give 2 examples.

Software Support

Warm Up 12.39

On Level

Activity Card 9-12

Three to a Word Problem Activity Card 9-12

Work: In small groups

Decide:

Who will be Student 1, who will be Student 2, and who will be Student 3.

1. Work in groups of 3 to create a problem.
2. **Student 1:** Think of an action that relates to an operation. Describe the action to begin the problem. Record the problem as you work.
3. **Student 2:** Continue the problem, using another action related to a different operation.
4. **Student 3:** Finish the problem, using a third action that relates to yet another operation.
5. Exchange with another group to solve.

One day, I made three cakes. Then I decided to make three more cakes. I cut each cake into 8 slices. Then I gave $\frac{1}{4}$ of each cake to Sammy. Then I gave one more slice of each cake to my neighbor. How many slices did I have left?

Unit 9, Lesson 12

Activity Note Remind students that at each stage of the problem, the numbers must make sense. Students should mentally check their numbers and operations as they add each part to the final problem.

Math Writing Prompt

Summarize Write about two or three different strategies you can use to solve a complex word problem.

Software Support

Fraction Action: Fraction Flare Up, Level C

Challenge

Activity Card 9-12

Logic Problems Activity Card 9-12

Work: In pairs

1. Solve the problem below.

- Mario made 4 pizzas for customers. Mario put a different topping on each of three pies: broccoli, red peppers, sausage. He made one plain.
- Each customer ordered a different pie.
- Customer A does not like vegetables.
- Customer B ordered a green topping.
- Customer C does not like toppings.
- Customer D only eats pizzas with peppers.

What kind of pizza did each customer order?

Tips for Writing Problems
- Include at least one clue with the words does not.
- Include one clue with the word only.

Customer A – sausage
Customer B – broccoli
Customer C – plain
Customer D – red peppers

2. Then work together to write a similar problem. Exchange your problem with another pair.
3. **Discuss** Check each other's solution.

Unit 9, Lesson 12

Activity Note Students should try to include at least one clue with the words *does not,* and one clue with the word *only*. Their problem should take several steps to solve.

Math Writing Prompt

Justify Explain why the order of steps is important in solving a multi-step problem.

DESTINATION Math® **Software Support**

Course II: Module 2: Unit 2: Finding Products less than 100

3 Homework and Spiral Review

Goal: Additional Practice

✓ Include students' completed Homework page as part of their portfolios.

9–12 **Homework**

Name ______ Date ______

Study Plan

______
Homework Helper

Solve each problem.

1. Shamariah collects silk roses. She had 17 silk roses in a vase. Six friends each gave her 3 more roses. How many roses does Shamariah have now?
   35 roses

2. Robin has 42 quarters. Jay has 1/7 as many quarters as Robin has. Tori has 4 times as many quarters as Jay. How many quarters does Tori have?
   24 quarters

3. A pet store had 9 corn snakes. 7 of the snakes laid 8 eggs each. All but 5 of the eggs hatched. How many corn snakes does the pet store have now?
   60 corn snakes

4. In a paper airplane contest, Amanda's plane flew 19 ft farther than Darren's plane. Darren's plane flew twice as far as Rachel's plane. Rachel's plane flew 23 ft. How far did Amanda's plane fly?
   65 ft

5. Jenna divided 120 daisies into 2 equal groups. Then she divided one group equally into 10 small bunches, and she divided the other group equally into 6 large bunches. She gave her grandmother one large bunch and one small bunch. How many daisies did Jenna give her grandmother?
   16 daisies

UNIT 9 LESSON 12 Solve Complex Multi-Step Word Problems **245**

Homework and Remembering page 245

9–12 **Remembering** **Goal:** Spiral Review

This Remembering page would be appropriate anytime after today's lesson.

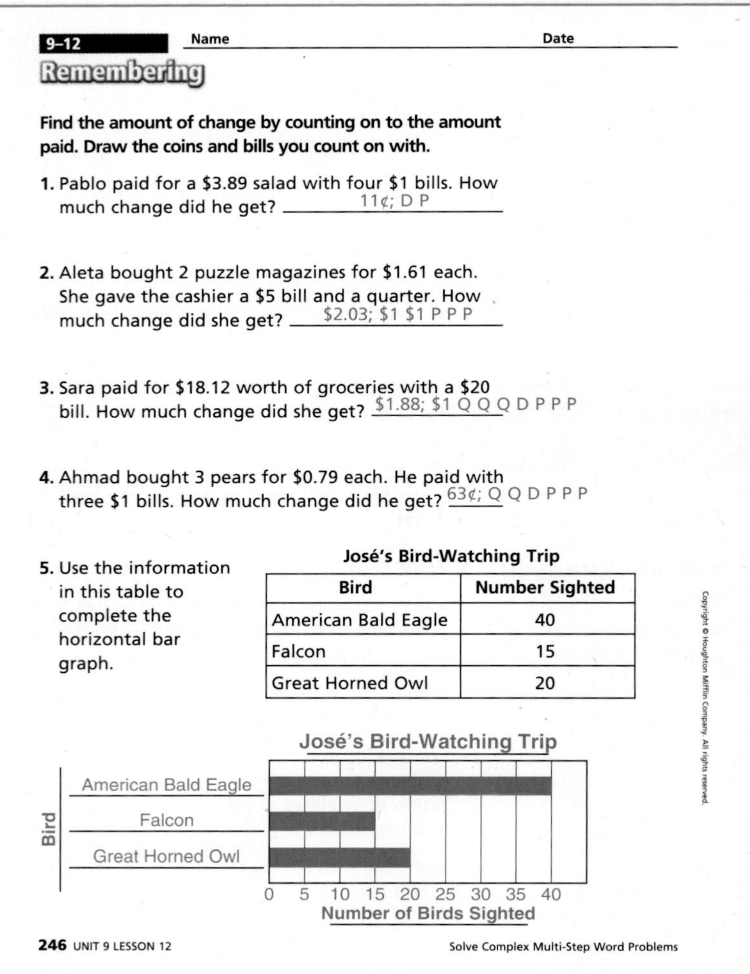
9–12 Remembering

Name ______ Date ______

Find the amount of change by counting on to the amount paid. Draw the coins and bills you count on with.

1. Pablo paid for a $3.89 salad with four $1 bills. How much change did he get? 11¢; D P

2. Aleta bought 2 puzzle magazines for $1.61 each. She gave the cashier a $5 bill and a quarter. How much change did she get? $2.03; $1 $1 P P P

3. Sara paid for $18.12 worth of groceries with a $20 bill. How much change did she get? $1.88; $1 Q Q Q D P P P

4. Ahmad bought 3 pears for $0.79 each. He paid with three $1 bills. How much change did he get? 63¢; Q Q D P P P

5. Use the information in this table to complete the horizontal bar graph.

José's Bird-Watching Trip

Bird	Number Sighted
American Bald Eagle	40
Falcon	15
Great Horned Owl	20

246 UNIT 9 LESSON 12 Solve Complex Multi-Step Word Problems

Homework and Remembering page 246

Home or School Activity

Language Arts Connection

Write a Poem Have students write a word problem as a poem. Have them try to include more than one operation that is needed to solve the problem. You may wish to provide some suggestions to help students get started.

Mom cut a pie, so we could share.
We all asked please, please make it fair.
All pieces the same, there were eight.
But we were four and had to wait.
'Til someone found out what to do.
Is it equal to each have two?

Each person needs to have a seat.
We don't know how, it is a feat.
Ten guests came, then forty-three more.
Six tables found, and none in store.
"All groups the same!" said Nate and Kate.
Five guests leave! The answer is eight!

Play Multiplication and Division Games

Vocabulary
input
output
rule

Lesson Objective

- **Develop strategies for solving multi-step word problems.**
- **Practice multiplications and divisions.**

The Day at a Glance

Today's Goals	Materials	
1 Teaching the Lesson **A1:** Practice count-bys, multiplications, and divisions. **A2:** Take Dashes for all factors. **A3:** Solve a variety of word problems. **A4:** Play Strategy Card games.	**Lesson Activities** Student Activity Book pp. 361–368 or Student Hardcover Book pp. 361–368 and Activity Workbook pp. 163–164 (Special Format and Game Rules) Homework and Remembering pp. 247–248 Quick Quiz 3 (Assessment Guide) Check Up materials Signature Sheet Study Sheets A-C Check Sheets 1–11 Dry-erase markers Sheet protectors Study Sheet Answer Strips Check Sheet Answer Strips	Cardstock Strategy cards Game Cards (TRB M25) Game Boards and game rules from U7 L13, 15; U9 L9 **Going Further** Activity Cards 9–13 Game Cards Calculator (optional) Math Journals
2 Going Further ▸ Differentiated Instruction		
3 Homework and Spiral Review		

Use Math Talk today!

Keeping Skills Sharp

Quick Practice — 5 MINUTES

Goal: Practice multiplication and division.

Materials: Class Multiplication Table Poster, pointer

Mixed Multiplications The **Student Leader** says "Close your eyes", points to any equation, reads the multiplication aloud, and pauses. The leader then says "Answer," and students say the answer in unison. Then students open their eyes and say the complete equation. Repeat for about 10 equations. (See Unit 9 Lesson 11.)

Mixed Divisions Use the same procedure as above with the leader reading the related division aloud. (See Unit 9 Lesson 11.)

Daily Routines

Homework Review Let students work together to check their work. Remind students to use what they know about helping others.

Skip Count Have students skip count by 100s beginning at 100 and ending at 1,000.

1 Teaching the Lesson

Activity 1

Check Up and Independent Study

10 MINUTES

Goal: Practice count-bys, multiplications, and divisions.

Materials: Check Up materials: Signature Sheet, Study Sheets A–C, Check Sheets 1–11, dry-erase markers, sheet protectors, Study Sheet Answer Strips (TRB M54), Check Sheet Answer Strips (TRB M55), cardstock; Strategy Cards, Homework and Remembering p. 247

NCTM Standard:
Number and Operations

Class Management

At the end of this unit, you may still have students that have not collected all their signatures. Encourage students to continue studying in order to gain fluency with basic multiplications and divisions.

▶ Check Up with 0s and 10s PAIRS

Give **Student Pairs** a few minutes to test each other using Study Sheets A–C and collect signatures. For students who have collected signatures on Study Sheets, have them study with Check Sheets 1–11. You may want to have Study Sheet and Check Sheet Answer Strip (TRB M54–M55) available.

Give students 2 or 3 minutes to study independently, using their Study Sheets, Check Sheets, and Strategy Cards. Also have them complete their Study Plan box on Homework and Remembering page 247. Students should include any multiplications and divisions they missed in the Check Up. Remind students to put all their Check Up materials in their folders.

Activity 2

Mixed Practice

15 MINUTES

Goal: Take Dashes for all factors.

Materials: Student Activity Book pp. 361–364 or Activity Workbook p. 162

NCTM Standard:
Number and Operations

▶ Dashes 17–20 INDIVIDUALS

Have students complete Dashes 17–20 on Student Activity Book page 361 or Activity Workbook p. 162. You can have them complete one Dash at a time, with breaks in between, or do all four at once. Time the Dashes, or let students complete them at their own pace. Students can check their answers against those on page 363. A second Dash is included for retesting if needed.

Activity 3

Solve Word Problems

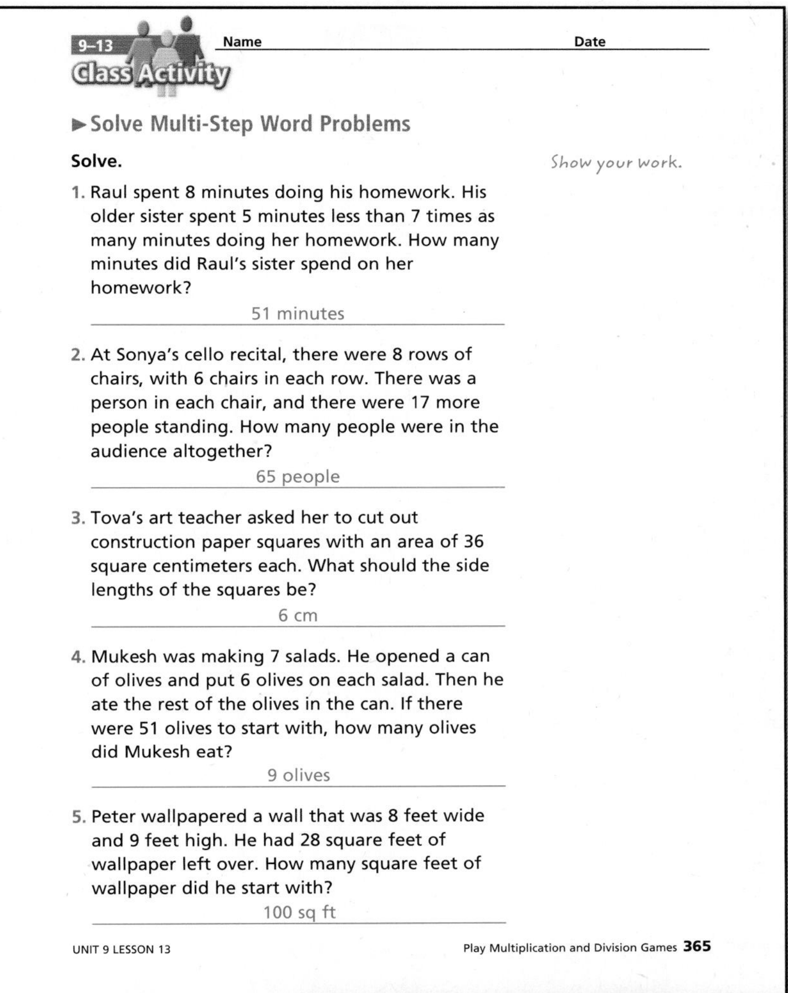
9–13 Class Activity

Name Date

▶ Solve Multi-Step Word Problems

Solve.

Show your work.

1. Raul spent 8 minutes doing his homework. His older sister spent 5 minutes less than 7 times as many minutes doing her homework. How many minutes did Raul's sister spend on her homework?
   51 minutes
2. At Sonya's cello recital, there were 8 rows of chairs, with 6 chairs in each row. There was a person in each chair, and there were 17 more people standing. How many people were in the audience altogether?
   65 people
3. Tova's art teacher asked her to cut out construction paper squares with an area of 36 square centimeters each. What should the side lengths of the squares be?
   6 cm
4. Mukesh was making 7 salads. He opened a can of olives and put 6 olives on each salad. Then he ate the rest of the olives in the can. If there were 51 olives to start with, how many olives did Mukesh eat?
   9 olives
5. Peter wallpapered a wall that was 8 feet wide and 9 feet high. He had 28 square feet of wallpaper left over. How many square feet of wallpaper did he start with?
   100 sq ft

UNIT 9 LESSON 13 Play Multiplication and Division Games **365**

Student Activity Book page 365

▶ Solve Multi-Step Word Problems WHOLE GROUP

Math Talk Using the **Solve and Discuss** structure, have students complete problems 1–5. If they make drawings, encourage them to use Equal-Shares Drawings, Fast-Array Drawings, or Fast-Area drawings, to show each individual item. As students work, ask questions, such as:

Problem 1: Is *7 times as many as* the same as *7 more than*? Explain.

Problem 2: When there are 8 rows with 6 chairs in each row, what does it look like?

Problem 3: How is finding the area of a square different from finding the area of a rectangle?

Problem 4: What operation do you need to use first?

Problem 5: How will you find the amount of wallpaper Peter used?

 **15 MINUTES**

Goal: Solve a variety of word problems.

Materials: Student Activity Book or Hardcover Book p. 365

 **NCTM Standards:**
Number and Operations
Problem Solving

English Language Learners

Draw examples of an *Equal-Shares*, a *Fast-Array*, and a *Fast-Area Drawing.* Provide examples of word problems for each.

- **Beginning** Point to each type of drawing. Identify it and have students repeat. Tell students the word problem related to the problem.
- **Intermediate** As you say each word problem guide students to tell which drawing represents it.
- **Advanced** Write the problems on the board. Have students match the drawings and problems.

Differentiated Instruction

Extra Help For problems 3 and 5, students may need a review of area and how to find area. Help students recall that the area of a figure is the number of square units needed to cover it without overlapping. Show them how to multiply the length by the width of a rectangle to find area. Tell students they should write the result in square units.

Activity 4

Play Games

 **15 MINUTES**

Goal: Play Strategy Card games.

Materials: Student Activity Book or Hardcover Book pp. 366–367 and Activity Workbook p. 163–164, Game Cards (TRB M25) (1–9, 1 set per pair); Strategy Cards, Game boards and game rules from Unit 7 Lessons 13, 15; Unit 9 Lesson 9

 **NCTM Standards:**
Number and Operations
Algebra
Representation

Basic Multiplication and Divisions Assessment

To check students' fluency with basic multiplications and divisions, use Student Activity Book pages 369–372.

Answers to these tests can be found on TRB pages M121–M124 in the Teacher's Resource Book.

Ongoing Assessment

Ask questions such as the following:

- Does the rule you found work for each and every set of input and output numbers in the table?
- When you are solving a multi-step problem, what can you use?

Quick Quiz

See Assessment Guide for Unit 9 Quick Quiz 3.

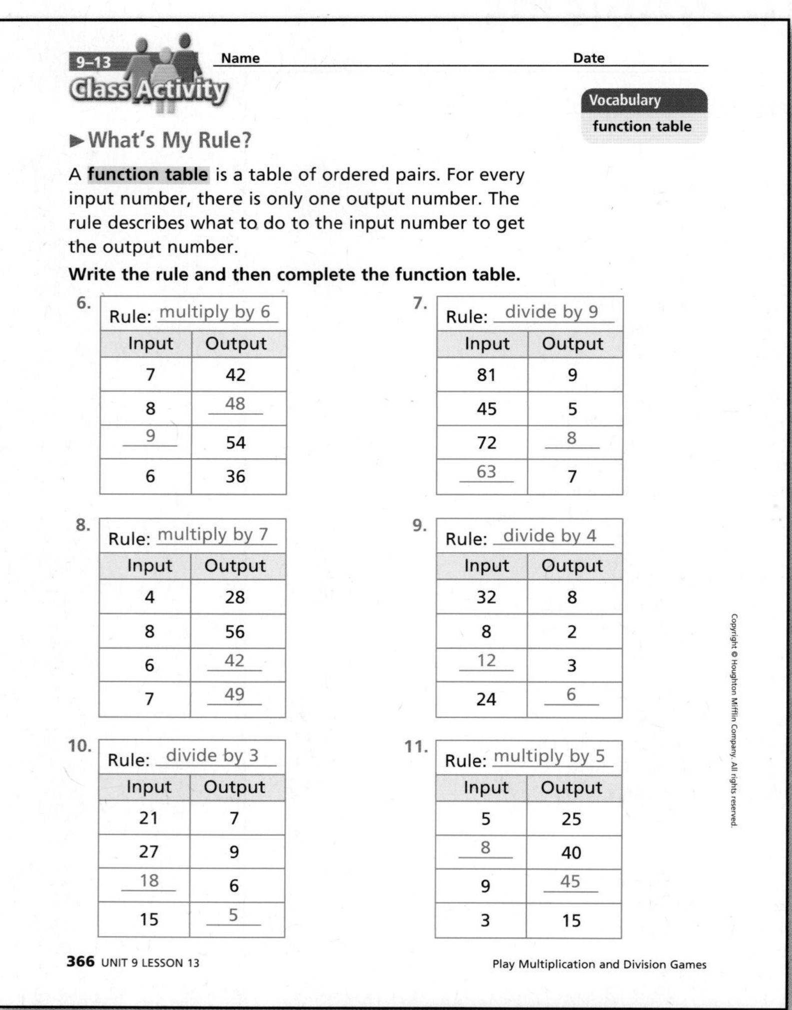

9–13 Class Activity Name ______ Date ______

Vocabulary: function table

▶ What's My Rule?

A **function table** is a table of ordered pairs. For every input number, there is only one output number. The rule describes what to do to the input number to get the output number.

Write the rule and then complete the function table.

6. Rule: multiply by 6

Input	Output
7	42
8	48
9	54
6	36

7. Rule: divide by 9

Input	Output
81	9
45	5
72	8
63	7

8. Rule: multiply by 7

Input	Output
4	28
8	56
6	42
7	49

9. Rule: divide by 4

Input	Output
32	8
8	2
12	3
24	6

10. Rule: divide by 3

Input	Output
21	7
27	9
18	6
15	5

11. Rule: multiply by 5

Input	Output
5	25
8	40
9	45
3	15

366 UNIT 9 LESSON 13 Play Multiplication and Division Games

Student Activity Book page 366

▶ What's My Rule? PAIRS

Use the *What's My Rule* tables on Student Book page 366 to discuss how to find the rule for a function table. Then have **Students Pairs** complete the six tables. As time allows, challenge students to add another row to each table.

▶ Play Games WHOLE CLASS

Read aloud the directions to *Division Three-in-a-Row* on Student Book page 367. Students will need their *Three-in-a-Row* game grids from Unit 7 Lesson 15 to play the game. As time allows, have students use the remaining time to play *Solve the Stacks, Multiplication Three-in-a-Row, Division Race,* or *High Card Wins*. Students should have saved their game boards and rules, but if you need replacements, you can find them in the Teacher's Resource Book.

2 Going Further

Intervention

Activity Card 9-13

One-Card Predictor — Activity Card 9-13 ●

Work: In pairs

Use:

- TRB M25 (Game Cards)

Decide:

Who will be Student 1 and who will be Student 2 for the first round.

1. **Student 1:** Choose a Game Card without showing it to your partner. Then follow these steps mentally and say the final product:
   - Multiply your number by 5.
   - Multiply that answer by 2.
2. **Student 2:** Guess the number on your partner's card. Try dividing the product by 10 or saying the digit in the tens place.

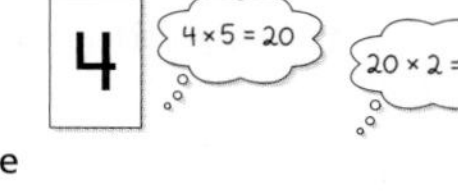

3. Change roles and play for three more rounds.

Unit 9, Lesson 13

Activity Note Ask students why both dividing by 10 and saying the digit in the tens place give the number on the card. Students should make the connection to base 10 and to the product $5 \times 2 = 10$.

Math Writing Prompt

Explain Your Thinking Think of a game you play. Write about how addition, subtraction, multiplication, and division are used to play the game.

Software Support

Warm Up 12.31

On Level

Activity Card 9-13

Guess My Number — Activity Card 9-13 ▲

Work: In pairs

Use:

- TRB M25 (Game Cards)

Decide:

Who will be Student 1 and who will be Student 2 for the first round.

1. **Student 1:** Choose a Game Card without showing it to your partner. Then follow these steps mentally and say the final result:
   - Multiply your number by 5.
   - Multiply that answer by 2.
   - Add 7.
   - Add 5.
   - Subtract 12.
2. **Student 2:** Guess the number on your partner's card. Try dividing the product by 10.

3. Change roles and play for three more rounds.

Unit 9, Lesson 13

Activity Note Students should play several rounds, switching roles, and try to find a pattern to discover why the trick works. Suggest that they think about the effect of using opposite operations.

Math Writing Prompt

Summarize Write a strategy you know for finding the answer to any multiplication or division.

Software Support

The Number Games: Up, Up, and Array, Level A

Challenge

Activity Card 9-13

Two-Digit Predictor — Activity Card 9-13 ■

Work: In pairs

Use:

- 2 TRB M25 (Game Cards)
- Calculator (optional)

Decide:

Who will be Student 1 and who will be Student 2 for the first round.

1. **Student 1:** Choose a Game Card. Place it face down without showing it to your partner. Follow these steps:
   - Multiply your number by 2.
   - Add 2 to the answer.
   - Multiply that answer by 5. (Call this result A, but don't tell your partner.)
2. **Student 2:** Choose a Game Card. Place it face down to the right of your partner's card. Subtract your number from 10 and share this result B.
3. **Student 1:** Subtract result B from result A. Turn over both cards. What do you notice? They show the difference A – B.

   Subtract 8 from 70 and then turn over the cards! They show the answer!

   6 2
4. Repeat the activity with different Game Cards.

Unit 9, Lesson 13

Activity Note Suggest that students record their work to keep track of results as they complete each step of the activity.

Math Writing Prompt

Investigate Math Explain why you can guess the number chosen by a friend if the friend multiplies the number by 5 and then multiplies that result by 2.

Software Support

Course II: Module 2: Unit 2: Finding Products less than 100

3 Homework and Spiral Review

9–13 Homework **Goal:** Additional Practice

✓ Include students' completed Homework page as part of their portfolios.

9–13 Homework

Name ______________________ Date ______________

Study Plan

____
Homework Helper

Solve each problem.

1. Julia used square tiles to make a design. She laid the tiles in a square, 8 tiles wide by 8 tiles long. Each tile has an area of 1 square inch. What is the area of Julia's tile design?
   64 sq in.

2. Bart lives 6 blocks from his grandparents. Melinda lives 8 times as far from her grandparents as Bart does. How many blocks does Melinda live from her grandparents?
   48 blocks

3. Rose rode the roller coaster 9 times. Leila rode the roller coaster $\frac{1}{3}$ as many times as Rose. Joseph rode the roller coaster 8 times as many times as Leila. How many more times did Joseph ride the roller coaster than Rose?
   15 more times

4. Shondra has 72 roses and 48 lilies. She wants to make 8 bouquets with them, with the same number of each type of flower in each bouquet. How many flowers will be in each bouquet?
   15 flowers

5. Willis wants to paint two walls in a room. The ceiling is 8 feet high. One wall is 8 feet wide, and the other 9 feet wide. He has 2 quarts of paint that will each cover 75 square feet. What is the area of the walls he wants to paint? Does he have enough paint?
   136 sq ft; yes

6. Randall bought 7 computer games at a yard sale. He paid \$4 each for 4 of the games, and \$5 each for the rest. How much money did he spend?
   \$31

UNIT 9 LESSON 13 — Play Multiplication and Division Games **247**

Homework and Remembering page 247

9–13 Remembering **Goal:** Spiral Review

This Remembering page would be appropriate anytime after today's lesson.

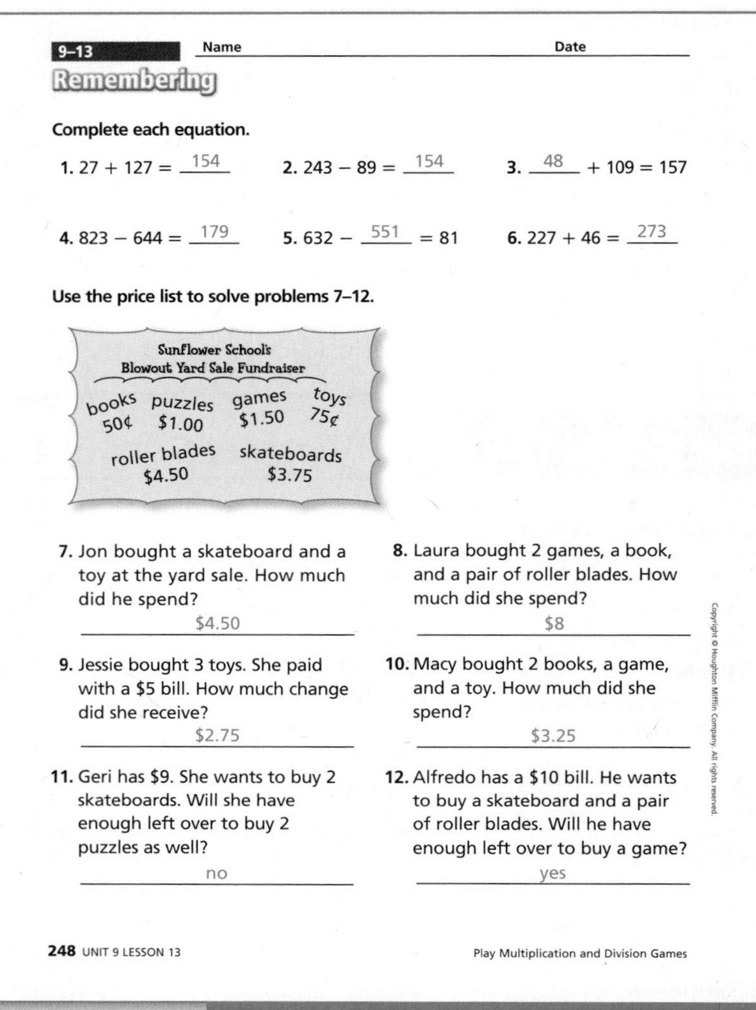

9–13 Remembering

Name ______________________ Date ______________

Complete each equation.

1. 27 + 127 = 154
2. 243 − 89 = 154
3. 48 + 109 = 157
4. 823 − 644 = 179
5. 632 − 551 = 81
6. 227 + 46 = 273

Use the price list to solve problems 7–12.

7. Jon bought a skateboard and a toy at the yard sale. How much did he spend?
   \$4.50

8. Laura bought 2 games, a book, and a pair of roller blades. How much did she spend?
   \$8

9. Jessie bought 3 toys. She paid with a \$5 bill. How much change did she receive?
   \$2.75

10. Macy bought 2 books, a game, and a toy. How much did she spend?
    \$3.25

11. Geri has \$9. She wants to buy 2 skateboards. Will she have enough left over to buy 2 puzzles as well?
    no

12. Alfredo has a \$10 bill. He wants to buy a skateboard and a pair of roller blades. Will he have enough left over to buy a game?
    yes

248 UNIT 9 LESSON 13 — Play Multiplication and Division Games

Homework and Remembering page 248

Home or School Activity

Multicultural Connection

Chinese Multiplication Table The Chinese developed a unique multiplication table that only used one digit numbers for products.

For example: 9 × 3 = 27 → 2 + 7 = 9
6 × 8 = 48 → 4 + 8 = 12 → 1 + 2 = 3

Have students create a Chinese multiplication table. First, they create a traditional multiplication table on 10 × 10 Grid Paper (TRB M43). Then they can place a sheet of tracing paper over their grid to fill in the one digit product. Discuss the patterns you see.

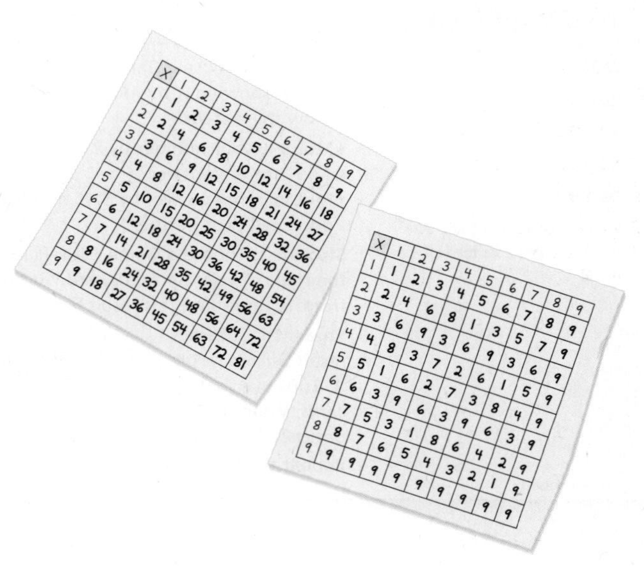

Use Mathematical Processes

Lesson Objectives

- **Apply mathematical concepts and skills in meaningful contexts.**
- **Reinforce the NCTM process skills embedded in this unit, and in previous units, with a variety of problem-solving situations.**

The Day at a Glance

Today's Goals	Materials	
1 Teaching the Lesson **A1: Math Connection** Make a bar graph to display data; answer questions about the data in a bar graph; write a story problem about the data in a bar graph. **A2: Problem Solving** Given the perimeter, find the rectangle with the greatest area or the smallest area; given the dimensions of 2 rectangles, find the rectangle with the greatest area or the greatest perimeter. **A3: Reasoning and Proof** Make generalizations about the results of adding even and odd numbers. **A4: Representation** Draw an array for a situation and explain why the array represents the situation **A5: Communication** Identify if a word problem has too much information, not enough information, or hidden information.	**Lesson Activities** Student Activity Book pp. 369–370 or Student Hardcover Book pp. 369–370 Homework and Remembering (pp. 249–250)	**Going Further** TRB M25 (Game Cards) Grid paper Math Journals
2 Going Further ▸ Differentiated Instruction		
3 Homework and Spiral Review		

Use Math Talk today!

Keeping Skills Sharp

Quick Practice/ Daily Routines	
If you wish to include Quick Practice or a Daily Routine, choose content based on the needs of your class.	**Class Management** Select activities from this lesson that support important goals and objectives, or that help students prepare for state or district tests.

1 Teaching the Lesson

Activity 1

Connections

Math and Social Studies

 20 MINUTES

Goals: Make a bar graph to display data; answer questions about the data in a bar graph; write a story problem about the data in a bar graph.

Materials: Student Activity Book or Hardcover Book p. 369.

 **NCTM Standards:**

Problem Solving | Connections | Communication
Representation | Reasoning and Proof

9–14 Class Activity

Name ______ Date ______

▶ Math and Social Studies

Every state has a state bird.

- The meadowlark is the state bird of 6 states.
- The robin is the state bird of half of the number of states that have the meadowlark as a state bird.
- The wren is the state bird of 1 fewer states than the states with the robin as state bird.
- The bluebird is the state bird of twice the number of states with the wren as state bird.

1. On a piece of grid paper, make a graph that shows the data about state birds above. Check student's work. Their graphs should show 6 states with a meadowlark, 3 states with a robin, 2 states with a wren, and 4 states with a bluebird.
2. Put the birds in order from most often used as a state bird to least often used as a state bird.
meadowlark, bluebird, robin, wren
3. The number of states with a cardinal as state bird is one more than the number of states with the meadowlark as the state bird. How many states have the cardinal as state bird?
7 states
4. Write a word problem about the data in the graph and give the answer. Trade problems with a partner and solve.
Answers will vary. Sample: How many times the number of wrens as state birds is the number of meadowlarks as state birds? 3 times

UNIT 9 LESSON 14 Use Mathematical Processes 369

Student Activity Book page 369

▶ Discuss State Birds

Task 1 Introduce the activity to the class.

Tell students that every state in the United States has a state bird.

▶ Do you know what the state bird is of our state? Answers will vary depending on the state.

▶ Make and Read a Graph Math Talk 

Task 2 Have students complete exercise 1 on Student Book page 369. When students have completed the activity, discuss the following:

▶ How did you find the number of states that have a robin for state bird? Find half of 6.

▶ How did you find the number of states that have a wren for state bird? Subtract 1 from 3.

▶ How did you find the number of states that have a bluebird for state bird? Multiply 2×2.

Have students share their graphs with the class.

Go over exercises 2 and 3. Have students share the word problems they wrote for exercise 4 with the class.

Teaching Note

State Flowers Have students research state flowers in books or on the Internet. Have them make a graph to show the results of their research.

Activity 2

Problem Solving

Street Chalk Art Fair

 20 MINUTES

Goals: Given the perimeter, find the rectangle with the greatest area or the smallest area; given the dimensions of 2 rectangles, find the rectangle with the greatest area or the greatest perimeter.

Materials: Student Activity Book or Hardcover Book p. 370

 **NCTM Standards:**
Problem Solving
Reasoning and Proof
Connections
Communication

9–14 Name Date

▶ Street Chalk Art Fair

Around the country cities block off streets and hold Chalk Art Fairs. Each person or group is given a rectangle outlined on the street for their chalk painting.

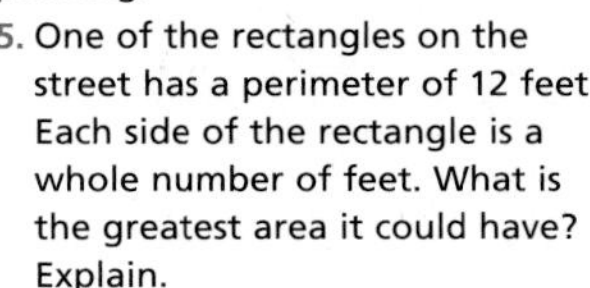

5. One of the rectangles on the street has a perimeter of 12 feet. Each side of the rectangle is a whole number of feet. What is the greatest area it could have? Explain.
9 square feet. The 3 possible rectangles are 1 ft by 5 ft with an area of 5 sq feet, 2 ft by 4 ft with an area of 8 sq feet, and 3 ft by 3 ft with an area of 9 sq feet. The greatest area is 9 sq feet.

6. One of the rectangles has a perimeter of 16 feet. Each side of the rectangle is a whole number of feet. What is the smallest area it could have? Explain.
7 square feet. The 4 possible rectangles are 1 ft by 7 ft with an area of 7 sq feet, 2 ft by 6 ft with an area of 12 sq feet, 3 ft by 5 ft with an area of 15 sq feet, and 4 ft by 4 ft with an area of 16 sq feet. The smallest area is 7 sq feet.

7. Lupe and her friends have their choice of a rectangle that is 9 feet by 2 feet or a rectangle that is 4 feet by 5 feet. They want to choose the rectangle with the greatest area. Which rectangle should they choose? Explain.
The 9 ft by 2 ft rectangle has an area of 18 sq ft. The 4 ft by 5 ft rectangle has an area of 20 sq ft. They should choose the 4 ft by 5 ft rectangle.

8. Which of the rectangles described in Problem 7 should Lupe and her friends choose if they want the rectangle with the greatest perimeter? Explain.
The 9 ft by 2 ft rectangle has a perimeter of 22 sq feet. The 4 ft by 5 ft rectangle a perimeter of 18 ft. They should choose the 9 ft by 2 ft rectangle.

370 UNIT 9 LESSON 14 Use Mathematical Processes

Student Activity Book page 370

▶ Discuss Rectangular Chalk Art Drawings

Task 1 Begin with a whole class discussion.

- ▶ Have you ever been to a fair where people make drawings with chalk in rectangles that are marked on the street? Allow students to share their experiences.

Tell students that they are going to solve some problems about a Chalk Art Fair.

▶ Find Perimeter and Area of Drawings

Math Talk

Task 2 When students have completed the exercises on Student Book page 370, discuss the answers to exercises 5 through 8.

- ▶ If rectangle A has a greater area than rectangle B, is it always true that rectangle A has a greater perimeter too? No.
- ▶ Which exercises on Student Book page 370 give an example where the rectangle with the greatest area is not the rectangle with the greatest perimeter? exercises 7–8.

English Language Learners

Draw a 2 × 3 rectangle on the board. Write *perimeter* and *area*.

- **Beginning** Ask: **Do I add all 4 sides to find *area* or *perimeter*?** perimeter **Do I multiply the length and width to find area?** yes
- **Intermediate and Advanced** Say: **I add all 4 sides to find the ___.** perimeter **I multiply length times width to find ___.** area

Activity 3

Adding Even and Odd Numbers

 10 MINUTES

Goal: Make generalizations about the results of adding even and odd numbers.

 **NCTM Standards:**
Problem Solving Reasoning and Proof
Communication Representation

Make a statement about the result of adding 2 odd numbers, adding 2 even numbers, and adding an even number and an odd number. Give an example to support each statement. See right column for answer.

Reasoning and Proof

Hold a whole-class discussion of the problem.

- What pictures could you draw to support your statements? Answers will vary. Sample pictures are given.

× × ○ ○ ○ ○	× ○ ○ ○ ○ ○	× ○ ○ ○ ○
2 + 4 = 6	1 + 5 = 6	1 + 4 = 5

When you add 2 odd numbers, the answer is even. (5 + 7 = 12) When you add 2 even numbers, the answer is even. (6 + 4 = 10) When you add an even number and an odd number, the answer is odd. (7 + 4 = 11)

Activity 4

Draw an Array

 10 MINUTES

Goal: Draw an array for a situation and explain why the array represents the situation.

✓ **NCTM Standards:**
Problem Solving Representation
Connections Communication

Chung has a sheet of stamps with 5 rows and 4 stamps in each row. Draw an array to show the sheet of stamps. See right column for array.

Representation

Discuss the problem with the class.

- Show your array and explain why it represents the situation. Have students show their arrays.
- Are there other arrays that would have a total of 20? 10 by 2 array, 20 by 1 array

Activity 5

What Kind of Problem?

 10 MINUTES

Goal: Identify if a word problem has too much information, not enough information, or hidden information.

Materials: Student-Written Word problems from Lesson 4

 **NCTM Standards:**
Problem Solving Communication Connections

Select some of the student-written word problems from Lesson 4 in this unit and solve them as a class. Ask students what kind of problem each problem is — too much information, not enough information, or hidden information? See right column for answer.

Communication

Hold a whole-class discussion of the problems.

- If the problem has too much information, ask the students what information is not necessary to solve the problem.
- If the problem does not have enough information, ask the students what information they would need to solve the problem.
- If the problem has hidden information, ask the students to identify the hidden information.

Sample problem: Carol has 4 times as many apples as oranges. How many oranges does she have? Not enough information

2 Going Further

Intervention — Activity Card 9-14

Pictures of Squared Numbers — Activity Card 9-14

Work: On your own

Use:

- TRB M25 (Game Cards)
- TRB M31 (Centimeter-Grid Paper)

1. Choose a Game Card.
2. Find the square number for the number on the card.
3. Draw a picture to show the square number on grid paper.

Unit 9, Lesson 14

Activity Note This activity is an opportunity for students to practice the process skill of communication. They also apply what they learned about multiplication and square numbers in this unit.

Math Writing Prompt

The Square of 1 Find the square number for 1. Take the answer and find the square of that number. If you keep doing that will you ever get an answer greater than 1? Explain.

Software Support

Warm Up 12.27

On Level — Activity Card 9-14

Get Close to the Square — Activity Card 9-14

Work: In pairs

Use:

- TRB M25 (Game Cards)

1. **Work Together** Choose a game card. Find the square number for the number on the card.
2. Each player chooses another game card without looking and uses that number to write a multiplication problem with 2 different factors. Try to get a product that is as close to the square number as possible.
3. Each player writes the difference between the square number and their product.
4. At the end of 5 rounds, each player adds up all of the differences.
5. The player with the lowest score wins.
6. **Discuss** Why doesn't the player with the highest score win?

Unit 9, Lesson 14

Activity Note This activity is an opportunity for students to practice the process skill of representation. They also apply what they learned about multiplication and square numbers in this unit.

Math Writing Prompt

Using Square Numbers Write about a time when you might want to find the square of a number.

Software Support

Ice Station Exploration: Arctic Algebra, Level P

Challenge — Activity Card 9-14

What Number Am I Thinking Of — Activity Card 9-14

Work In pairs

Use:

- TRB M25 (Game Cards)

Decide:

Who will be Student 1 and who will be Student 2 for the first round.

1. **Student 1:** Choose a Game Card without showing it to your partner. Find the square number for the number on the card. Give your partner clues for the square number.

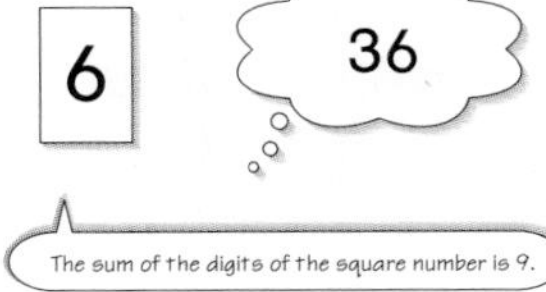

2. **Student 2:** Listen to the clues. Try to figure out the number in as few clues as you can.
3. Switch roles and continue.

Unit 9, Lesson 14

Activity Note Students practice the process skill of reasoning and apply what they learned about multiplication and square numbers in this unit.

Math Writing Prompt

Number Pattern Make a list of square numbers starting with the square of 1 and ending with the square of 9. Describe the pattern in differences between one square number and the next.

DESTINATION Math **Software Support**

Course II: Module 2: Unit 2: Finding Products less than 100

Homework and Spiral Review

9–14 Homework **Goal:** Additional Practice

Include student's completed Homework page as part of their portfolios.

9–14 Remembering **Goal:** Spiral Review

This Remembering page would be appropriate anytime after today's lesson.

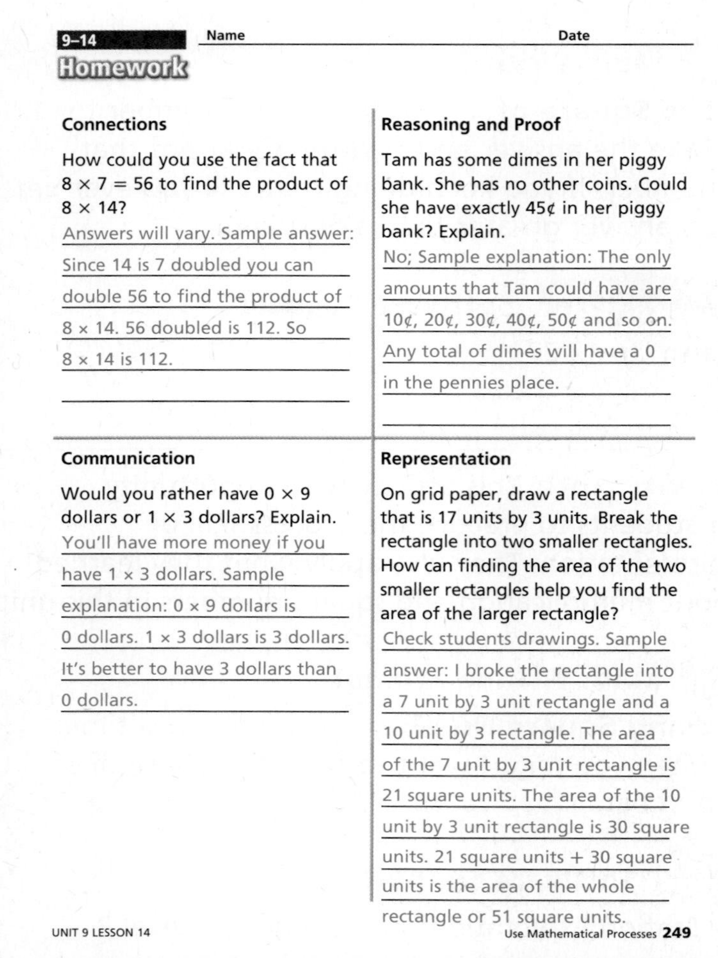

9–14 Homework Name ______ Date ______

Connections

How could you use the fact that 8 × 7 = 56 to find the product of 8 × 14?

Answers will vary. Sample answer: Since 14 is 7 doubled you can double 56 to find the product of 8 × 14. 56 doubled is 112. So 8 × 14 is 112.

Reasoning and Proof

Tam has some dimes in her piggy bank. She has no other coins. Could she have exactly 45¢ in her piggy bank? Explain.

No; Sample explanation: The only amounts that Tam could have are 10¢, 20¢, 30¢, 40¢, 50¢ and so on. Any total of dimes will have a 0 in the pennies place.

Communication

Would you rather have 0 × 9 dollars or 1 × 3 dollars? Explain.

You'll have more money if you have 1 × 3 dollars. Sample explanation: 0 × 9 dollars is 0 dollars. 1 × 3 dollars is 3 dollars. It's better to have 3 dollars than 0 dollars.

Representation

On grid paper, draw a rectangle that is 17 units by 3 units. Break the rectangle into two smaller rectangles. How can finding the area of the two smaller rectangles help you find the area of the larger rectangle?

Check students drawings. Sample answer: I broke the rectangle into a 7 unit by 3 unit rectangle and a 10 unit by 3 rectangle. The area of the 7 unit by 3 unit rectangle is 21 square units. The area of the 10 unit by 3 unit rectangle is 30 square units. 21 square units + 30 square units is the area of the whole rectangle or 51 square units.

UNIT 9 LESSON 14 Use Mathematical Processes 249

Homework and Remembering page 249

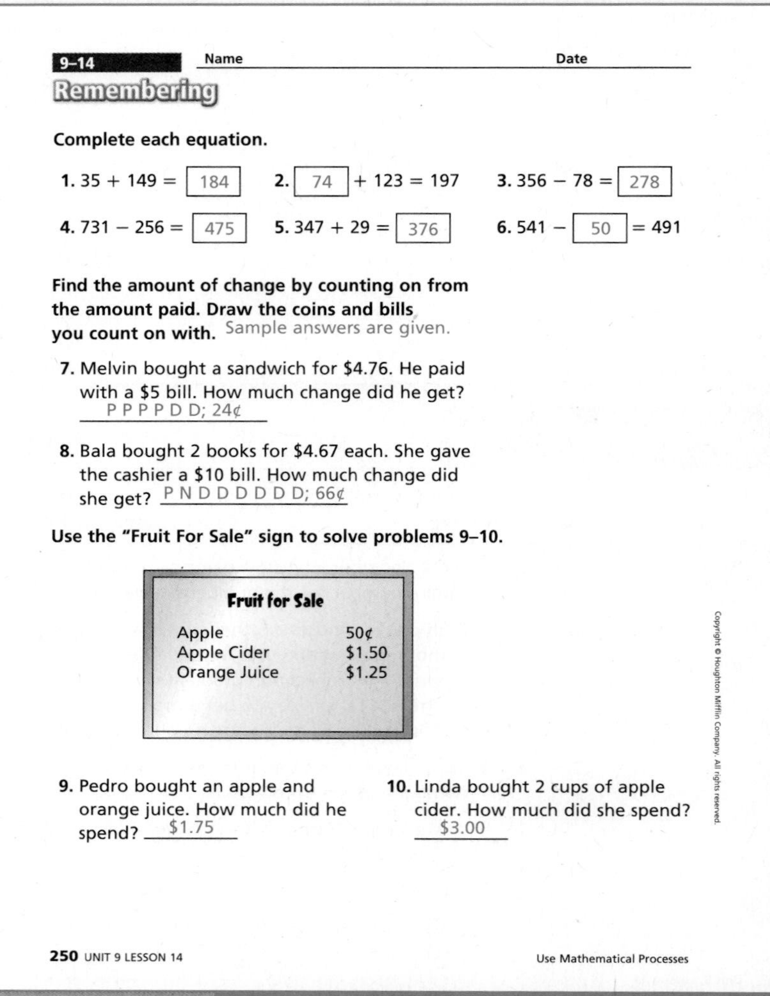

9–14 Remembering Name ______ Date ______

Complete each equation.

1. 35 + 149 = 184
2. 74 + 123 = 197
3. 356 − 78 = 278
4. 731 − 256 = 475
5. 347 + 29 = 376
6. 541 − 50 = 491

Find the amount of change by counting on from the amount paid. Draw the coins and bills you count on with. Sample answers are given.

7. Melvin bought a sandwich for $4.76. He paid with a $5 bill. How much change did he get? P P P P D D; 24¢
8. Bala bought 2 books for $4.67 each. She gave the cashier a $10 bill. How much change did she get? P N D D D D D D; 66¢

Use the "Fruit For Sale" sign to solve problems 9–10.

Fruit for Sale	
Apple	50¢
Apple Cider	$1.50
Orange Juice	$1.25

9. Pedro bought an apple and orange juice. How much did he spend? $1.75
10. Linda bought 2 cups of apple cider. How much did she spend? $3.00

250 UNIT 9 LESSON 14 Use Mathematical Processes

Homework and Remembering page 250

Home or School Activity

Language Arts Connection

Letter Patterns Give each student a different letter of the alphabet. Have students make a pattern with slides, flips, and turns of the letter. Have each student give their pattern to a partner. Have the partner look at the pattern and tell which movement was done to the letter and find the pattern.

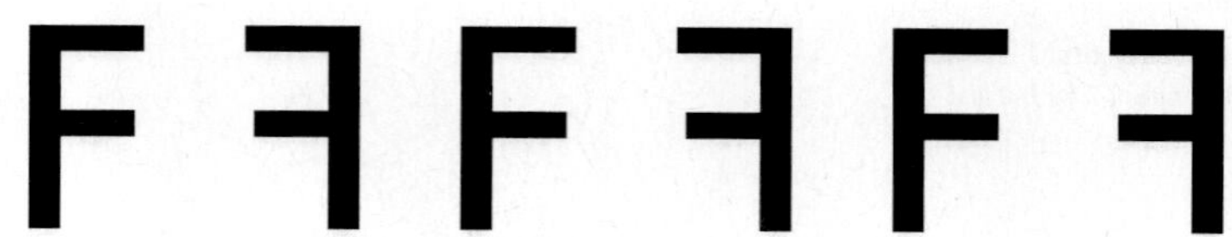

Unit Review and Test

Lesson Objective

- **Assess student progress on unit objectives.**

The Day at a Glance

Today's Goals	Materials
1 Assessing the Unit **A1:** Assess student progress on unit objectives. **A2:** Use activities from unit lessons to reteach content. **2 Extending the Assessment** ► Use remediation for common errors. There is no homework assignment on a test day.	Unit 9 Test, Student Activity Book or Harcover Book pp. 375–376 Unit 9 Test, Form A or B, Assessment Guide (optional) Unit 9 Performance Assessment, Assessment Guide (optional) Basic Multiplications Test, Student Activity Book pp. 371–372 or Hardcover Book pp. 371–372 and Activity Workbook pp. 165–166 Basic Divisions Test, Student Activity Book pp. 373–374 or Hardcover Book pp. 371–372 and Activity Workbook pp. 167–168

Keeping Skills Sharp

Quick Practice 5 MINUTES	
Goal: Review any skills you choose to meet the needs of your class. If you are doing a unit review day, use any of the Quick Practice activities that provide support for your class. If this is a test day, omit Quick Practice.	**Review and Test Day** You may want to choose a quiet game or other activity (reading a book or working on homework for another subject) for students who finish early.

1 Assessing the Unit

Assess Unit Objectives

 **45 MINUTES** (more if schedule permits)

Goal: Assess student progress on unit objectives.

Materials: Student Activity Book or Hardcover Book pp. 375–376; Assessment Guide Unit 9 Test Form A or B (optional); Assessment Guide Unit 9 Performance Assessment (optional); Basic Multiplications Test, Student Activity Book pp. 371–372 or Hardcover Book pp. 371–372 and Activity Workbook pp. 165–166; Basic Divisions Test, Student Activity Book pp. 373–374 or Hardcover Book pp. 371–372 and Activity Workbook pp. 167–168

▶ Review and Assessment

If your students are ready for assessment on the unit objectives, you may use either the test on the Student Book pages or one of the forms of the Unit 9 Test in the Assessment Guide to assess student progress.

If you feel that students need some review first, you may use the test on the Student Book pages as a review of unit content, and then use one of the forms of the Unit 9 Test in the Assessment Guide to assess student progress.

To assign a numerical score for all of these test forms, use 5 points for each question.

You may also choose to use the Unit 9 Performance Assessment. Scoring for that assessment can be found in its rubric in the Assessment Guide.

▶ Reteaching Resources

The chart at the right lists the test items, the unit objectives they cover, and the lesson activities in which the objective is covered in this unit. You may revisit these activities with students who do not show mastery of the objectives.

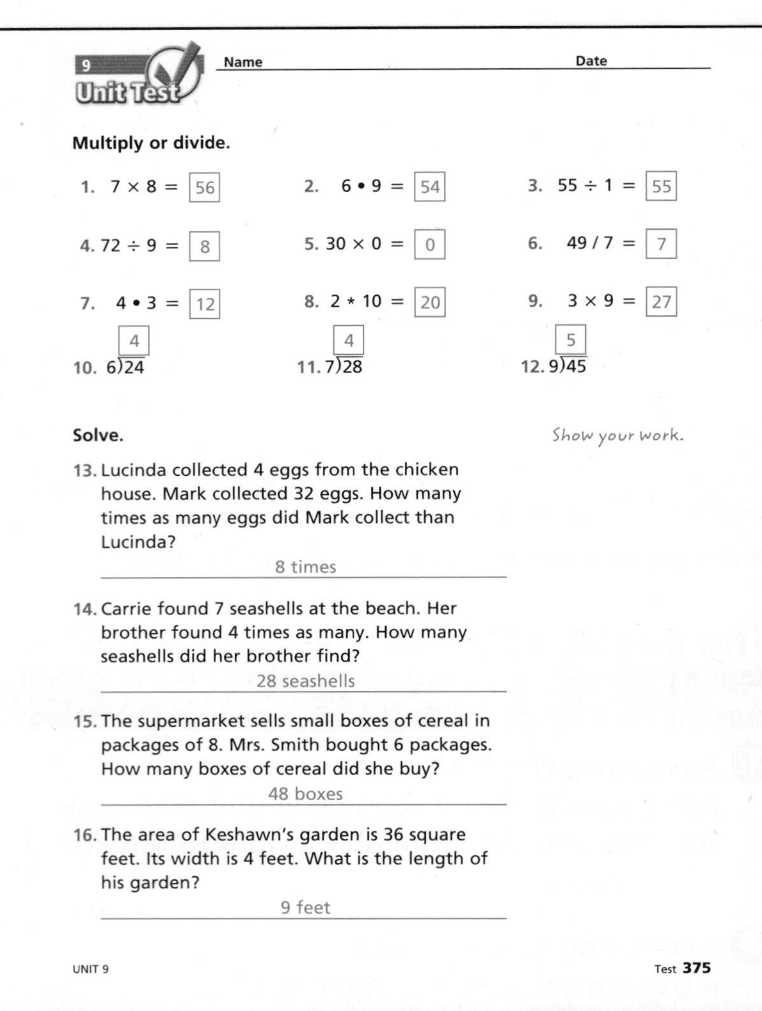
9 Unit Test Name Date

Multiply or divide.

1. 7 × 8 = 56
2. 6 • 9 = 54
3. 55 ÷ 1 = 55
4. 72 ÷ 9 = 8
5. 30 × 0 = 0
6. 49 / 7 = 7
7. 4 • 3 = 12
8. 2 * 10 = 20
9. 3 × 9 = 27
10. 6)24 — 4
11. 7)28 — 4
12. 9)45 — 5

Solve. *Show your work.*

13. Lucinda collected 4 eggs from the chicken house. Mark collected 32 eggs. How many times as many eggs did Mark collect than Lucinda? 8 times

14. Carrie found 7 seashells at the beach. Her brother found 4 times as many. How many seashells did her brother find? 28 seashells

15. The supermarket sells small boxes of cereal in packages of 8. Mrs. Smith bought 6 packages. How many boxes of cereal did she buy? 48 boxes

16. The area of Keshawn's garden is 36 square feet. Its width is 4 feet. What is the length of his garden? 9 feet

UNIT 9 Test 375

Student Activity Book page 375

Unit Test Items	Unit Objectives Tested	Activities to Use for Reteaching
1–12	**9.1** Recall basic multiplications and divisions with 0 through 10.	Lesson 1, Activity 1 Lesson 3, Activity 2 Lesson 5, Activity 2 Lesson 8, Activity 2 Lesson 9, Activities 1–3
13–20	**9.2** Solve a variety of word problems involving multiplication and division including comparison and multi-step word problems.	Lesson 4, Activity 3 Lesson 6, Activity 3 Lesson 7, Activity 4 Lesson 10, Activity 3 Lesson 11, Activity 3 Lesson 12, Activity 3 Lesson 13, Activity 3

Name _______________ Date _______

Write an equation to solve the problem.

17. A class has 35 goldfish and 5 fish bowls. How many fish will be in each bowl if the same number of fish are in each bowl?

$35 \div 5 = 7$; 7 goldfish

Solve.

18. Mr. Howell arranged 56 books on 8 shelves with the same number on each shelf. How many books were on each shelf?

7 books

19. Mr. Alberto has 48 students to divide into teams of 8. Mr. Yates has 81 students to divide into teams of 9. How many more teams does Mr. Yates have than Mr. Alberto?

3 more teams.

*20. **Extended Response** Marcie has 7 bean bag dolls. Lucy has 3 times as many dolls as Marcie. Janice has twice as many dolls as Marcie and Lucy combined. How many more dolls does Janice have than Marcie? Explain the steps you used to solve the problem.

49 more dolls; Possible answer: Lucy has 3 times as many dolls as Marcie or $3 \times 7 = 21$. Janice has twice as many dolls as Marcie and Lucy combined or $7 + 21 = 28$. $28 + 28 = 56$. So Janice has 56 dolls. Subtract $56 - 7 = 49$.

*Item 20 also assesses the process skills of Reasoning and Proof, Communication, and Math Connection.

376 UNIT 9 Test

Student Activity Book page 376

▶ Assessment Resources

Free Response Tests

Unit 9 Test, Student Book pages 375–376

Unit 9 Test, Form A, Assessment Guide

Basic Multiplications Test, Student Book pp. 371–372, and Basic Divisions Test, Student Book pp. 373–374, or Activity Workbook pp. 165–168

*Answers to the Basic Multiplications and Divisions Tests can be found in the Teacher's Resource Book (M121–M124).

Extended Response Item

The last item in the Student Book test and in the Form A test will require an extended response as an answer.

Multiple Choice Test

Unit 9 Test, Form B, Assessment Guide

Performance Assessment

Unit 9 Performance Assessment, Assessment Guide

Unit 9 Performance Assessment Rubric, Assessment Guide

▶ Portfolio Assessment

Teacher-selected Items for Student Portfolios:

- Homework, Lessons 2, 10, 12, 13, and 14
- Class Activity work, Lessons 4, 7, 11, 13, and 14.

Student-selected Items for Student Portfolios:

- Favorite Home or School Activity
- Best Writing Prompt

2 Extending the Assessment

Common Errors

Activities for Remediation

Unit Objective 9.1

Recall basic multiplications and divisions with 0 through 10.

Common Error: Computation Errors

Students may have difficulty remembering basic multiplications and divisions.

Remediation Have students use the Strategy Cards to practice the multiplications and divisions they do not recall. Students can also make an audio tape or CD of the basic multiplications they need to learn with a pause before saying the answer. They can then use the tape to practice those basic multiplications and divisions.

Common Error: Doesn't Distinguish × From +

Students may add instead of multiply.

Remediation Have students circle the operation symbol and name the operation they will use.

Common Error: Doesn't Recognize the Commutative Property

Students recall one arrangement of two factors but not the other.

Remediation Remind students that switching the order of the factors does not change the product. Demonstrate that the Commutative Property can be used, for example, to find 6×4 if they know 4×6.

Unit Objective 9.2

Solve a variety of word problems involving multiplication and division including comparison and multi-step word problems.

Common Error: Difficulty Deciding Whether to Multiply or Divide

Students may have difficulty determining if a word problem involves multiplication or division.

Remediation Have students work in pairs to analyze a variety of multiplication and division problems. Have them list the similarities and differences between problems. For example:

- Both problems involve equal groups.
- When you need to find the total, you use multiplication.
- When you are separating the total, you use division.

Common Error: Chooses an Incorrect Operation

Students may have difficulty determining whether a word problem involves multiplication or addition.

Remediation Remind students that while both addition and multiplication are used to find a total, addition is used for both equal and unequal groups. Multiplication can only be used for equal groups. Have students create word problems to represent each meaning.

Common Error: Difficulty with Multi-Step Problems

Students may have difficulty determining the steps required to solve a multi-step problem.

Remediation Have students act out the problem using lists, drawings, or manipulatives. This will allow them to concretely see which steps must be performed and the order of the steps.

Common Error: Difficulty Sequencing

Students may struggle to try to determine the steps, and the number of steps, that are needed to solve a problem.

Remediation Provide students with a wide variety of multi-step problems. For each problem, work with the students to make a list of the information they need to solve the problem. Then use the list to organize the steps that are needed to solve the problem.

Unit 10 Overview

Time

UNIT 10 EXTENDS the skills in telling time that students developed in the previous grade level. This unit begins with students telling time to the hour, half-hour, quarter-hour, five minutes, and one minute. The features of calendars are reviewed, and students find elapsed time in days, weeks, and months. They also find elapsed time on clocks in hours and minutes and solve real-world problems involving elapsed time. The final lesson in this unit provides students with practice multiplying and dividing by 6, by relating a minute to a 6° rotation of the minute hand.

Skills Trace

Grade 2	Grade 3	Grade 4
• Read and write time to the hour and to the minute. • Read and write time as *after the hour* and *before the hour.* • Solve real-world problems involving elapsed time, including hours and half-hours. • Read a calendar and a function table.	• Read and write time to the hour, half-hour, quarter-hour, 5 minutes, and 1 minute. • Solve real-world problems involving elapsed time. • Relate clock angles to elapsed time.	• Convert units of time with calendar units. • Solve problems involving the passing of time and elapsed time with calendar units. • Add and subtract units of time.

Unit 10 Contents

Big Idea Time

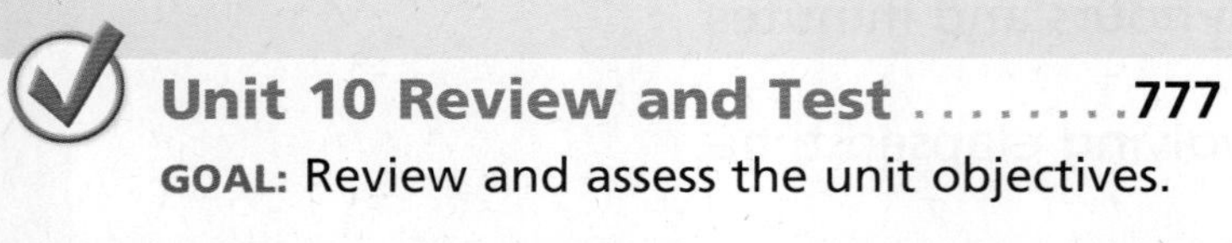

Planning Unit 10

NCTM Curriculum Focal Points and Connections Key: **1.** Number and Operations and Algebra **2.** Number and Operations **3.** Geometry **4.** Algebra **5.** Measurement **6.** Data Analysis **7.** Number and Operations

Lesson NCTM Focal Points NCTM Standards	Resources	Materials for Lesson Activities	Materials for Going Further
10-1 **Tell Time** NCTM Standards: 4, 9	TE pp. 755–762 SAB pp. 376A–376B; 377–382 H&R pp. 251–252 AC 10-1 MCC 37	Scissors Prong fasteners Analog clock Digital clock ✓ Time Poster Paper Clock (TRB M125)	Paper Clock (TRB M125) Math Journals
10-2 **Elapsed Time** NCTM Standards: 4, 9, 10	TE pp. 763–770 SAB pp. 383–388 H&R pp. 253–254 AC 10-2 MCC 38, 39	Paper Clock (TRB M125)	Paper Clock (TRB M125) Index Cards Sheet protectors Dry-erase markers Math Journals
10-3 **Clock Angles** NCTM Standards: 4, 9	TE pp. 771–776 SAB pp. 389–390 H&R pp. 255–256 AC 10-3 MCC 40 AG Quick Quiz	None	Index cards Math Journals
✓ **Unit Review and Test**	TE pp. 777–780 SAB pp. 391–392 AG Unit 10 Tests		

Resources/Materials Key: TE: Teacher Edition SAB: Student Activity Book H&R: Homework and Remembering AC: Activity Cards MCC: Math Center Challenge AG: Assessment Guide ✓: Grade 3 kits TRB: Teacher's Resource Book

Hardcover Student Book

- Together, the Hardcover Student Book and its companion Activity Workbook contain all of the pages in the consumable Student Activity Book.

Manipulatives and Materials

- Essential materials for teaching *Math Expressions* are available in the Grade 3 kits. These materials are indicated by a ✓ in these lists. At the front of this Teacher Edition is more information about kit contents, alternatives for the materials, and use of the materials.

Independent Learning Activities

Ready-Made Math Challenge Centers

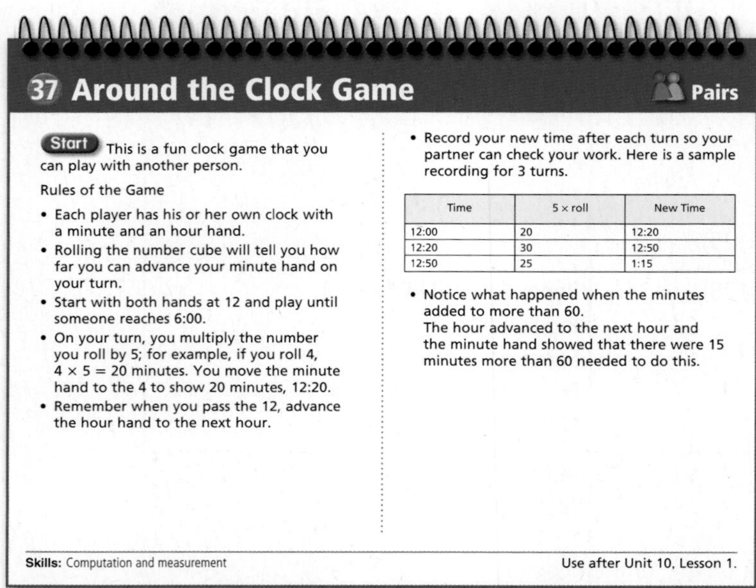

37 Around the Clock Game — Pairs

Start This is a fun clock game that you can play with another person.

Rules of the Game

- Each player has his or her own clock with a minute and an hour hand.
- Rolling the number cube will tell you how far you can advance your minute hand on your turn.
- Start with both hands at 12 and play until someone reaches 6:00.
- On your turn, you multiply the number you roll by 5; for example, if you roll 4, $4 \times 5 = 20$ minutes. You move the minute hand to the 4 to show 20 minutes, 12:20.
- Remember when you pass the 12, advance the hour hand to the next hour.

- Record your new time after each turn so your partner can check your work. Here is a sample recording for 3 turns.

Time	5 × roll	New Time
12:00	20	12:20
12:20	30	12:50
12:50	25	1:15

- Notice what happened when the minutes added to more than 60.
  The hour advanced to the next hour and the minute hand showed that there were 15 minutes more than 60 needed to do this.

Skills: Computation and measurement — Use after Unit 10, Lesson 1.

Pairs

Number cube, Paper Clock (TRB M125)

Students read, write and add analog time.

Measurement and Computation

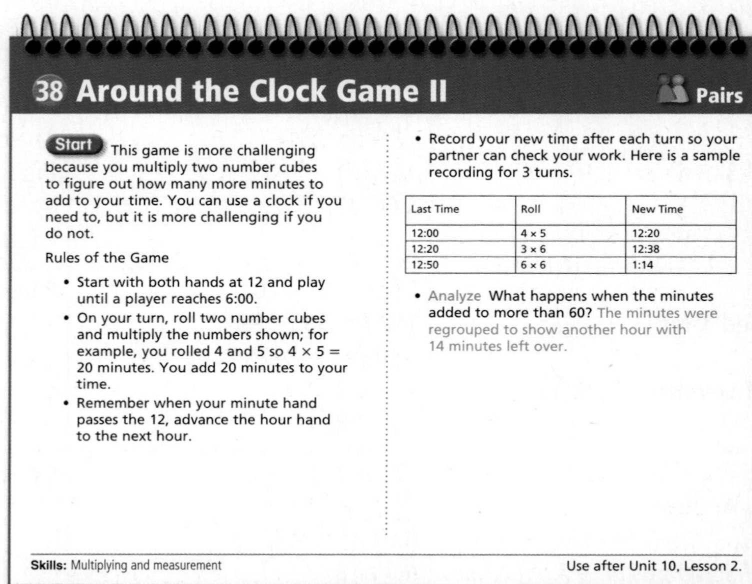

38 Around the Clock Game II — Pairs

Start This game is more challenging because you multiply two number cubes to figure out how many more minutes to add to your time. You can use a clock if you need to, but it is more challenging if you do not.

Rules of the Game

- Start with both hands at 12 and play until a player reaches 6:00.
- On your turn, roll two number cubes and multiply the numbers shown; for example, you rolled 4 and 5 so $4 \times 5 =$ 20 minutes. You add 20 minutes to your time.
- Remember when your minute hand passes the 12, advance the hour hand to the next hour.

- Record your new time after each turn so your partner can check your work. Here is a sample recording for 3 turns.

Last Time	Roll	New Time
12:00	4 × 5	12:20
12:20	3 × 6	12:38
12:50	6 × 6	1:14

- Analyze What happens when the minutes added to more than 60? The minutes were regrouped to show another hour with 14 minutes left over.

Skills: Multiplying and measurement — Use after Unit 10, Lesson 2.

Pairs

Two number cubes, Paper Clock (TRB M125)

Students read, write, and add analog time.

Measurement and Computation

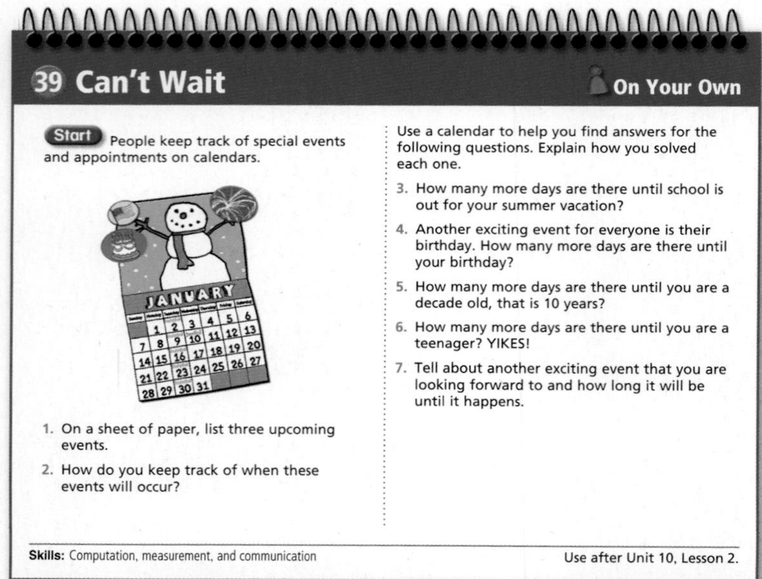

39 Can't Wait — On Your Own

Start People keep track of special events and appointments on calendars.

1. On a sheet of paper, list three upcoming events.
2. How do you keep track of when these events will occur?

Use a calendar to help you find answers for the following questions. Explain how you solved each one.

3. How many more days are there until school is out for your summer vacation?
4. Another exciting event for everyone is their birthday. How many more days are there until your birthday?
5. How many more days are there until you are a decade old, that is 10 years?
6. How many more days are there until you are a teenager? YIKES!
7. Tell about another exciting event that you are looking forward to and how long it will be until it happens.

Skills: Computation, measurement, and communication — Use after Unit 10, Lesson 2.

Individuals

Calculator, calendar

Students use a calendar to calculate time duration.

Computation and Communication

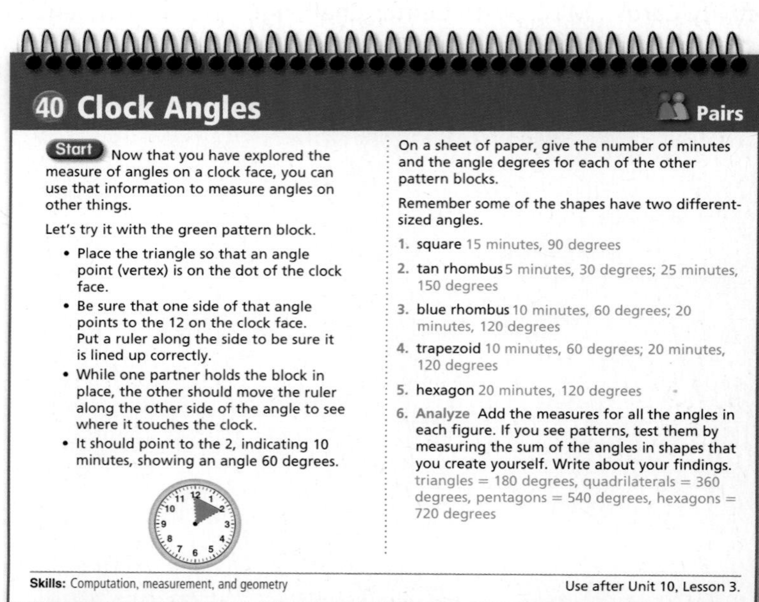

40 Clock Angles — Pairs

Start Now that you have explored the measure of angles on a clock face, you can use that information to measure angles on other things.

Let's try it with the green pattern block.

- Place the triangle so that an angle point (vertex) is on the dot of the clock face.
- Be sure that one side of that angle points to the 12 on the clock face. Put a ruler along the side to be sure it is lined up correctly.
- While one partner holds the block in place, the other should move the ruler along the other side of the angle to see where it touches the clock.
- It should point to the 2, indicating 10 minutes, showing an angle 60 degrees.

On a sheet of paper, give the number of minutes and the angle degrees for each of the other pattern blocks.

Remember some of the shapes have two different-sized angles.

1. square 15 minutes, 90 degrees
2. tan rhombus 5 minutes, 30 degrees; 25 minutes, 150 degrees
3. blue rhombus 10 minutes, 60 degrees; 20 minutes, 120 degrees
4. trapezoid 10 minutes, 60 degrees; 20 minutes, 120 degrees
5. hexagon 20 minutes, 120 degrees
6. Analyze Add the measures for all the angles in each figure. If you see patterns, test them by measuring the sum of the angles in shapes that you create yourself. Write about your findings. triangles = 180 degrees, quadrilaterals = 360 degrees, pentagons = 540 degrees, hexagons = 720 degrees

Skills: Computation, measurement, and geometry — Use after Unit 10, Lesson 3.

Pairs

Pattern blocks, Paper Clock (TRB M125)

Students use a clock face to determine angle measure.

Measurement and Computation

Ready-Made Math Resources

Technology — Tutorials, Practice, and Intervention

Use online, individualized intervention and support to bring students to proficiency.

Help students practice skills and apply concepts through exciting math adventures.

Extend and enrich students' understanding of skills and concepts through engaging, interactive lessons and activities.

Visit **Education Place**®
www.eduplace.com

Visit www.eduplace.com/mx2t/ and find family, teacher, and student materials, activities, games, and more.

Literature Links

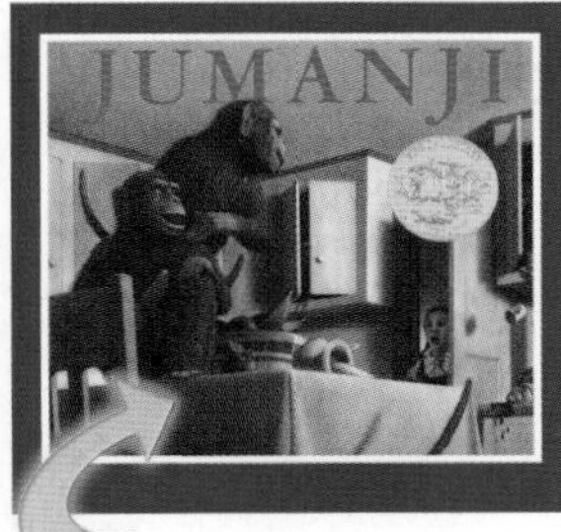

Jumanji

Jumanji
The surreal illustrations in Chris Van Allsburg's book complement the strange and mysterious tale of a boy and girl who find a game board in a park. They begin to play it only to find out they must complete the game in a certain time frame or ELSE! Have students chart a minute-by-minute timeline for the game while you read.

Literature Connection

Secret Treasures and Magical Measures: Adventures in Measurement: Temperature, Time, Length, Weight, Volume, Angles, Shapes, and Money, by Chris Kensler (Simon & Schuster, 2003)

Unit 10 Assessment

Unit Objectives Tested	Unit Test Items	Lessons
10.1 Read and write time to the hour, half-hour, quarter-hour, 5 minutes, and 1 minute.	1–6	1
10.2 Solve real-world problems involving elapsed time.	7–8, 10	2
10.3 Relate clock angles to elapsed time.	9	3

Assessment and Review Resources

Formal Assessment

Student Activity Book
- Unit Review and Test (pp. 391–392)

Assessment Guide
- Quick Quiz (p. A95)
- Test A–Open Response (pp. A96–A97)
- Test B–Multiple Choice (pp. A98–A99)
- Performance Assessment (pp. A100–A102)

Test Generator CD-ROM
- Open Response Test
- Multiple Choice Test
- Test Bank Items

Informal Assessment

Teacher Edition
- Ongoing Assessment (in every lesson)
- Math Talk (in every lesson)
- Portfolio Suggestions (p. 778)

Math Talk
- Math Talk in Action (pp. 765, 768, 773)
- Student Pairs (pp. 760, 767)
  Helping Partners (pp. 757, 760, 768)
- Small Groups (p. 773)
- In Activities (pp. 766, 767)
- Scenarios (p. 767)

Review Opportunities

Homework and Remembering
- Review of recently taught topics
- Spiral Review

Teacher Edition
- Unit Review and Test (pp. 777–780)

Test Generator CD-ROM
- Custom Review Sheets

Unit 10 Teaching Resources

Differentiated Instruction

Individualizing Instruction		
	Level	Frequency
Activities	• Intervention • On Level • Challenge	All 3 in every lesson
	Level	Frequency
Math Writing Prompts	• Intervention • On Level • Challenge	All 3 in every lesson
Math Center Challenges	For advanced students	
	4 in every unit	

Reaching All Learners		
English Language Learners	Lessons	Pages
	1, 2, 3	755, 763, 771
Extra Help	Lesson	Page
	1	758

Strategies for English Language Learners

Present this problem to all students. Offer the different levels of support to meet students' levels of language proficiency.

Objective To make sure students can identify the parts of a clock.

Problem Draw a large clock on the board. Point to the hands, the numbers, and the tick marks. Have students identify each part.

Newcomer

- Point to the numbers then the tick marks. Say: **These are the *hours*. These are the *minutes*.** Have students repeat.
- Point to each hand. Say: **The small hand is the *hour hand*. The large hand is the *minute hand hand*.** Have students repeat.

Beginning

- Ask: **Are the numbers the *hours* or the *minutes*?** hours Point to the tick marks. Say: **These are the ___.** minutes hand.
- Point to the hour hand. Ask: **Is this the *minute hand*?** no **Is this the *hour hand*?** yes

Intermediate

- Point and say: **The numbers tell us the ___.** hour **The tick marks tell us the ___.** minutes
- Ask: **Is the large hand the *hour hand* or *minute hand*?** minute hand

Advanced

- Say: **The small hand points to the numbers to tell us the ___.** hour **The large hand point to the tick marks to tell us the ___.** minutes

Connections

Art Connection
Lesson 2, page 770

Literature Connection
Lesson 3, page 776

Putting Research into Practice for Unit 10

From Current Research: Reading Time

For years, teachers have observed students' frustration as they grappled with learning to read an analog clock (see, e.g., Kelly and Burke [1998]). We ourselves have felt frustrated, not fully understanding why learning to tell time is difficult for students or how to help. Unfortunately, much of our past instruction has been based on an incomplete understanding of the idea that "two aspects of time have to be distinguished in teaching: firstly, one must try to develop a concept of time in a child; and secondly, one must teach the child to 'tell the time' (teaching clock time)" (Grauberg 1998, p. 50). Moreover, the tools commonly used for time instruction, including manipulative clock faces and paper-and-pencil activities, may not be sufficient for developing children's understanding. These tools usually focus on telling time, not on developing concepts of time.

Teachers of young children generally concur that their students learn mathematical concepts best when they construct their understanding through concrete experiences. When we remember that time can be neither seen nor touched but experienced and measured only indirectly with such tools as clocks, we begin to understand why time-related concepts are difficult for our students to learn. From the body of research available, as well as from our own firsthand teaching experiences, we know that "everything to do with understanding and using time concepts develops rather late" (Dickson, Brown, and Gibson 1984 [cited in Grauberg 1998, p. 50]).

Monroe, Eula Ewing, Michelle P. Orme, and Lynnette B. Erickson. "Working Cotton: Toward an Understanding of Time." *Teaching Children Mathematics* 8.8 (April 2002): 475.

History of Time

Harris, Art. "Historical Roots of Our Calendar." *Mathematics Teaching in the Middle School* 8.4 (Dec. 2002): 196.

http://physics.nist.gov/GenInt/Time/time.html, A NIST Physics Laboratory Presentation, A Walk Through Time, The Evolution of Time Measurement through the Ages

http://www.britannica.com/clockworks/main.html, Britannica.com Presents Clockworks, From Sundials to the Atomic Second

http://webexhibits.org/calendars/index.html, WebExhibits, Calendars through the Ages

Calendar Patterns

Owens, Iva. "Calendar Patterns" *Student Math Notes.* (May 2004).

Angles of Rotation

Pagni, David L. "Angles, Time, and Proportion." *Mathematics Teaching in the Middle School* 10.9 (May 2005): 436.

Getting Ready to Teach Unit 10

In this unit, students build upon their time-telling skills from previous grades. Students review telling time to the hour and minute and extend their knowledge of elapsed time to include calendar and time units.

Summary of Time Concepts and Connections

Telling Time

Lesson 1

In the previous grade, students were introduced to telling time to the hour and to five minutes on analog clocks. In Unit 10, students begin by reviewing the features and functions of clocks and telling time to the hour. Then they read time to 15 minutes, 5 minutes, and 1 minute, learning that a single time can be said in several different ways.

Elapsed Time on a Calendar

Lesson 2

In the previous grade, students used a calendar to explore how a year is divided into months, weeks, and days and they used ordinal numbers to say dates and to refer to days, weeks, or months in position. In Unit 10, students review the features and functions of calendars and find elapsed time in days, weeks, and months including solving real-world problems.

Elapsed Time on Clocks

Lesson 2

In the previous grade, students found elapsed time in hours and half-hours from a start time and an end time. In this unit, students find elapsed time in hours and minutes including solving real-world problems. The principle that clocks are comprised of iterated units, like all measuring tools, is reinforced as students count the sectors that the clock hands have traveled through to find elapsed time.

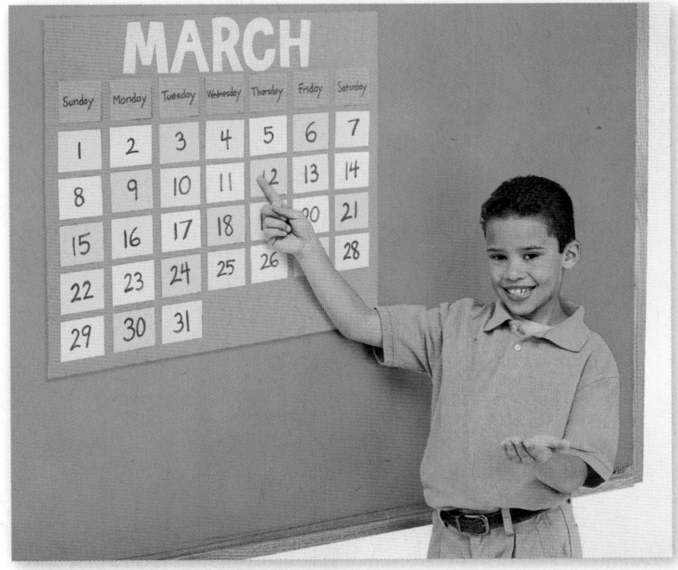

Clock Angles

Lesson 3

In Unit 10, students relate elapsed time on a clock to angles of rotation. They begin by identifying the angle of rotation when the minute hand has traveled 15 minutes, 30 minutes, 45 minutes, and 60 minutes. They then establish that the minute hand has a 6° rotation each minute it travels. By dividing and multiplying by 6, students complete exercises about finding the angle of rotation of different elapsed times and finding end times from start times and angles of rotation of the minute hand.

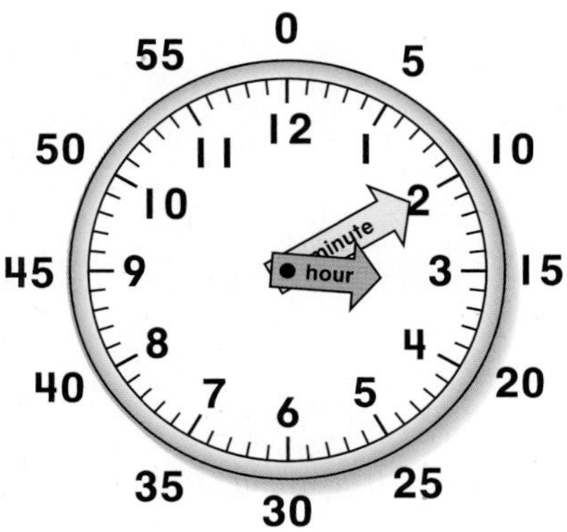

Students use their 5 count-bys to read minutes and their 6 multiples to find angles of rotation.

Problem Solving

In *Math Expressions* a research-based, algebraic problem-solving approach that focuses on problem types is used: understand the situation, represent the situation with a math drawing or an equation, solve the problem, and see that the answer makes sense. In this unit students solve some real-life problems involving elapsed time.

Use Mathematical Processes

Lessons 1, 2, and 3

The mathematical process skills of problem solving, reasoning and proof, communication, connections, and representation are emphasized through out this unit as students tell time in different ways, find elapsed time on a clock or calendar, and connect rotations of clock hands to angles.

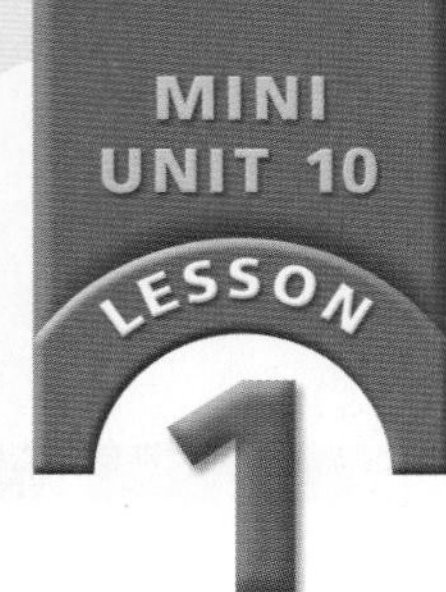

Tell Time

Lesson Objectives

- Tell time to the hour, half-hour, and quarter-hour.
- Tell time to 5 minutes and to 1 minute.
- State times using the words *before* and *after* with the appropriate hour.

Vocabulary
quarter-hour
half-hour
A.M.
P.M.

The Day at a Glance

Today's Goals	Materials	
1 Teaching the Lesson **A1:** Read and write time to the hour, half-hour, quarter-hour and describe it in different ways **A2:** Read and write time to 5 minutes and to 1 minute. **A3:** State times using the words *before* and *after* with the appropriate hour.	**Lesson Activities** Student Activity Book pp. 376A–382 or Student Hardcover Book pp. 377–382 and Activity Workbook pp. 169–174 (includes Family Letter and Special Formats) Homework and Remembering pp. 251–252 Scissors Prong fasteners Analog clock, digital clock, or Time Poster Paper Clock (TRB M125)	**Going Further** Activity Cards 10-1 Paper Clocks Math Journals
2 Going Further ▸ Differentiated Instruction		
3 Homework and Spiral Review		

Use Math Talk today!

Keeping Skills Sharp

Daily Routines	English Language Learners
Perimeter Dan wants to put fencing around his garden. The garden is a rectangle with a length of 3 feet and a width of 5 feet. How many feet of fencing does Dan need? 16 feet	Draw a clock divided into quarters on the board. Shade in a quarter. Have students count the parts. Say: **1 part of 4 is a *quarter***. Model a *quarter-hour* on a paper clock. Continue with *half-hour*. • **Beginning** Hold up the paper clock, and point to the 3. Say: **When the minute hand is here it is a *quarter-hour***. Have students repeat. • **Intermediate** Hold up the paper clock. Ask: **Is the minute hand showing a *quarter-hour*?** yes • **Advanced** Hold up the paper clock. Ask: **Where do I put the minute hand to show a *quarter-hour*?** on the 3

1 Teaching the Lesson

Activity 1

Hour, Half-Hour, Quarter-Hour

 **30 MINUTES**

Goal: Read and write time to the hour, half-hour, and quarter-hour and describe it in different ways.

Materials: Student Activity Book pp. 376A–378 or Hardcover Book pp. 377–378 and Activity Workbook pp. 169–171, scissors, prong fasteners (1 per student), analog clock, digital clock, or Time Poster, Paper Clock (TRB M125)

 **NCTM Standards:**
Measurement
Connections

▶ Make an Analog Clock INDIVIDUALS

Have students make their own analog clock from Student Activity Book page 376A or Activity Workbook p. 169. Instruct them to cut out the hands of the clock and attach them to the Paper Clock using prong fasteners.

Display 1:30 on an analog clock, on the Time Poster, or on a quick sketch. If you have access to the *Math Expressions* Materials Kit, the Time Poster is included. Ask students to place the hands on their paper clocks to show the same time. Draw the 5s count-bys around the hour numbers as shown.

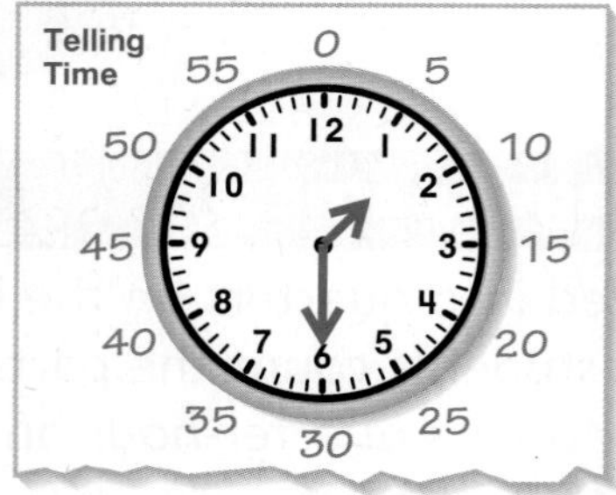

Analog Clock on Time Poster

Ask for Ideas Review what students know about reading time on an analog clock. Elicit as much as possible from students throughout the lesson.

Discuss how the 5s count-bys are used to read the minutes on an analog clock (the 1 is 5 minutes, the 2 is $2 \times 5 = 10$ minutes, etc.) Review the other aspects of time including *minute hand, hour hand, clockwise, 60 minutes = 1 hour, 12 hours = 1 clock go-around, a.m.* and *p.m.* as describing each *12-hour go-around.*

Brainstorm ways to remember all of these aspects of time. For example, some students remember that the minute hand is longer than the hour hand because the word minute is longer than the word hour and because minutes can get bigger than hours (they go up to 59 and hours only go up to 12).

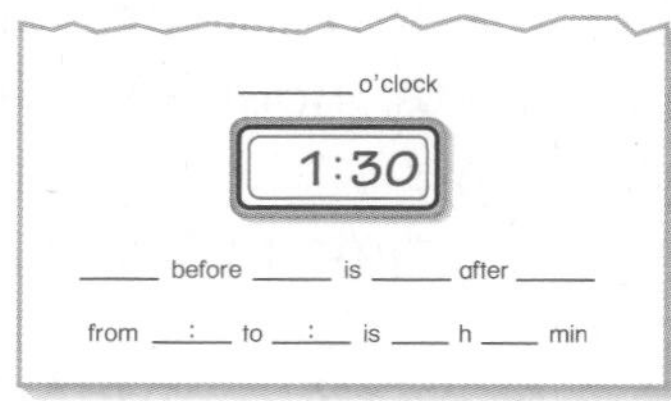

Relate the left-right digital way of writing time to the way we say time: "hour then minutes."

▶ Review Units of Time WHOLE CLASS

Write the following chart on the board and have student volunteers help you fill it in.

Units of Time

1 hour = __ 60 _______ minutes

1 minute = __ 60 ______ seconds

24 hours = __ 1 ______ day

Once the chart is complete, you may want to keep it posted in the room for the next few days so students can use it as a reference when solving problems that include measuring in mixed units of time.

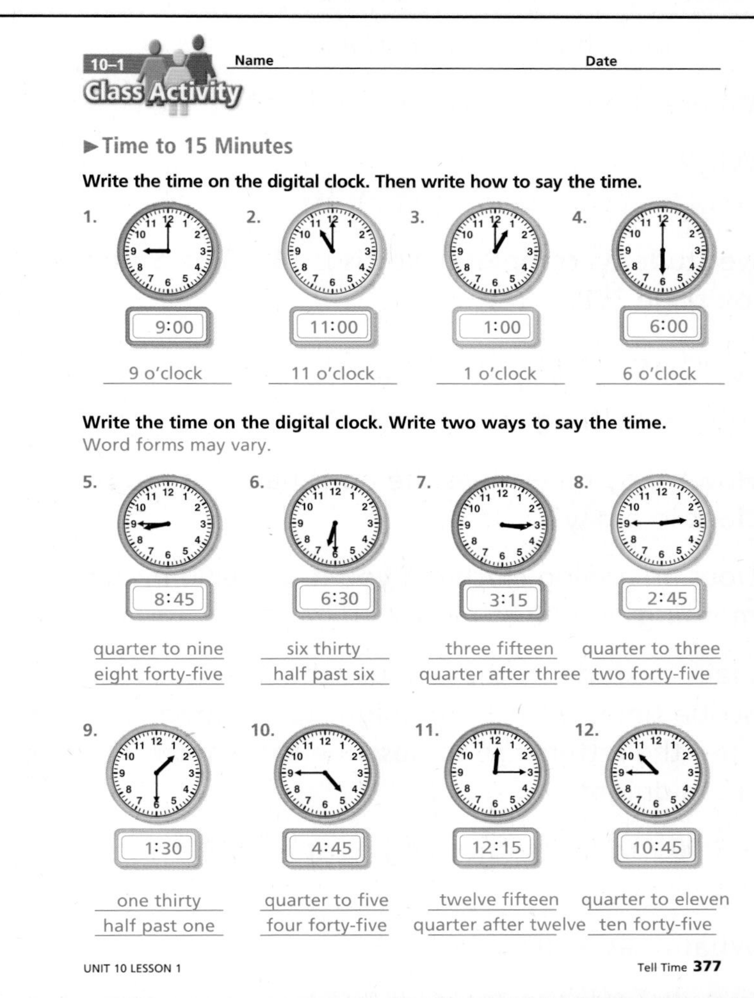

10-1 Class Activity

Name ____________ Date ____________

► Time to 15 Minutes

Write the time on the digital clock. Then write how to say the time.

	Digital clock	How to say it
1.	9:00	9 o'clock
2.	11:00	11 o'clock
3.	1:00	1 o'clock
4.	6:00	6 o'clock

Write the time on the digital clock. Write two ways to say the time.
Word forms may vary.

	Digital clock	Two ways to say it
5.	8:45	quarter to nine eight forty-five
6.	6:30	six thirty half past six
7.	3:15	three fifteen quarter after three
8.	2:45	quarter to three two forty-five
9.	1:30	one thirty half past one
10.	4:45	quarter to five four forty-five
11.	12:15	twelve fifteen quarter after twelve
12.	10:45	quarter to eleven ten forty-five

UNIT 10 LESSON 1 Tell Time **377**

Student Activity Book page 377

► Time to 15 Minutes WHOLE CLASS

Time to the Hour Display 3:00 on an analog clock or the Time Poster. Ask students to move the hands on their paper clocks to show the same time.

- What time does this clock show? 3 o'clock
- How do you know? The hour hand is at 3 and the minute hand is at 12.

Ask students to complete exercises 1–4 on Student Activity Book page 377.

Fifteen Minutes After the Hour Display the time 3:15. Ask students to show the same time on their clocks.

- How many minutes after the hour does this clock show? 15 minutes
- How do you know? I counted by 5s from 12 to 3 and I got 15.
- Where is the hour hand? Just a little past the 3.

Ask students how they can say the time shown on the clock. Write their answers on the board.

fifteen minutes after three
three-fifteen
quarter after three

Explain to students that when the minute hand is pointing to the 3, it has gone one quarter of the way around the face of the clock so it shows one quarter of an hour past the hour.

Half Past the Hour Change the time on your clock to 3:30. Ask students to do the same on their paper clocks. Repeat the questions you asked for Fifteen Minutes After the Hour.

Ask students how they can say the time shown on the clock. Write their answers on the board.

three-thirty
thirty minutes after three
half past three

- How does the minute hand show that it is half past the hour? When the minute hand is at the 6 it has gone halfway around the clock.

Forty-Five Minutes After the Hour Repeat with 3:45. Be sure that students note that the hour hand is three-quarters of the way between the 3 and the 4. Some students may read the time as quarter to four. Later activities in the unit focus on reading time before and after the hour.

Have students complete Student Activity Book page 377. Discuss their answers as a class.

Throughout this unit, pair **English learners** having difficulty with a **Helping Partner** to practice showing and reading times in different ways.

Activity continued ►

❶ Teaching the Lesson (continued)

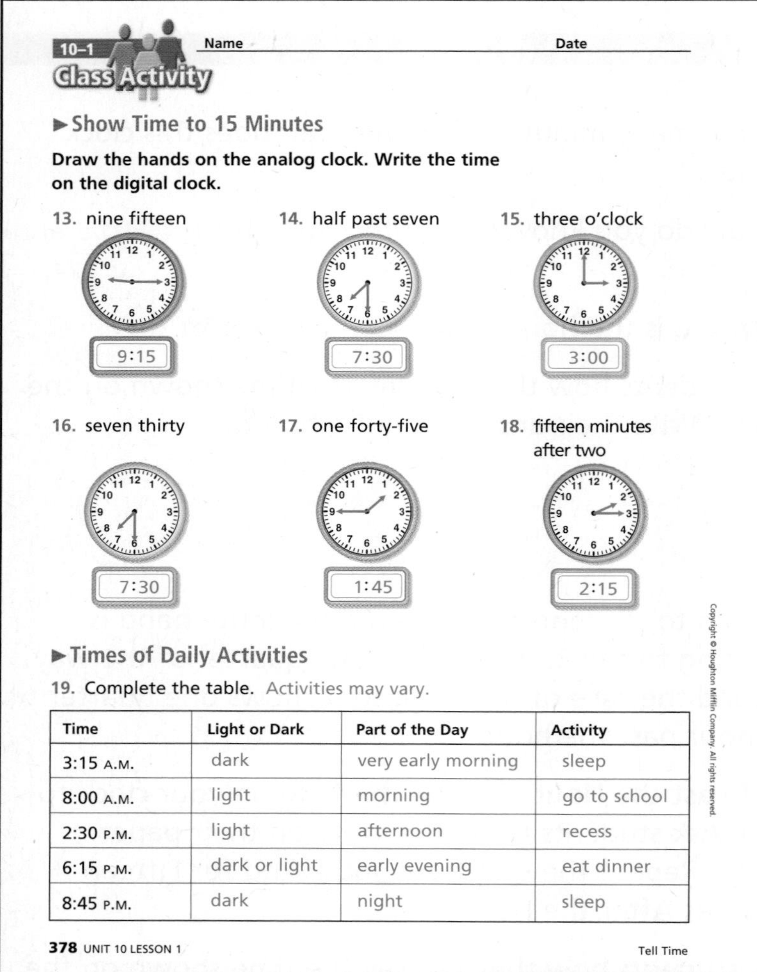

10–1 Class Activity

Name ________ Date ________

► Show Time to 15 Minutes

Draw the hands on the analog clock. Write the time on the digital clock.

13. nine fifteen — 9:15
14. half past seven — 7:30
15. three o'clock — 3:00
16. seven thirty — 7:30
17. one forty-five — 1:45
18. fifteen minutes after two — 2:15

► Times of Daily Activities

19. Complete the table. Activities may vary.

Time	Light or Dark	Part of the Day	Activity
3:15 A.M.	dark	very early morning	sleep
8:00 A.M.	light	morning	go to school
2:30 P.M.	light	afternoon	recess
6:15 P.M.	dark or light	early evening	eat dinner
8:45 P.M.	dark	night	sleep

378 UNIT 10 LESSON 1 — Tell Time

Student Activity Book page 378

► Show Time to 15 Minutes WHOLE CLASS

Write these times in words on the board:

four-fifteen	one o'clock	three-forty-five
six-thirty	half past nine	quarter after two

Ask volunteers to show each time on their paper clocks to the class and to write the times in numbers on the board.

Work through exercise 13 with the class.

- Where should the hour hand go? a little after the 9
- Is the hour hand long or short? short
- Where should the minute hand go? at the 3
- Why? The time is 15 minutes after the hour. I skip counted by 5s to 15 and got to 3.

Have students complete exercises 14–18 on Student Book page 378.

► Times of Daily Activities INDIVIDUALS

Display an analog clock.

- How many times does the hour hand go around a clock in a day? 2 times
- Does an analog clock tell you if it is 8:00 in the morning or 8:00 at night? no

Explain to students that we use the letters A.M. to describe times from 12 midnight to 12 noon, and that we use the letters P.M. to describe times from 12 noon to 12 midnight.

- Is 9:00 A.M. in the morning or at night? in the morning
- What does 9:00 P.M. mean? 9:00 at night

Discuss the first row of the table in exercise 19 and then ask students to complete the table individually.

Differentiated Instruction

Extra Help Provide students with Paper Clock (TRB M125.) Ask them to fold it in half at the 9 and the 3. Ask them why we read a time as "half-past the hour" when the minute hand is at the 6. Have them fold the clock in half again from the 12 to the 6. Ask them why we read a time as "quarter after the hour" when the minute hand is at the 3.

Ongoing Assessment

Ask students to show 4:15 and 8:30 on their paper clocks. Ask them to tell an activity they often do at 4:15 P.M. and an activity they often do at 8:30 A.M.

Activity 2

Tell Time to 5 Minutes and 1 Minute

 **15 MINUTES**

Goal: Read and write time to 5 minutes and to 1 minute.

Materials: Paper clocks from Activity 1, Student Activity Book or Hardcover Book p. 379, analog clock or Time Poster

 **NCTM Standards:**
Measurement
Connections

▶ Time to 5 Minutes WHOLE CLASS

Display 8:25 on an analog clock or the Time Poster. Ask students to show the same time on their clocks.

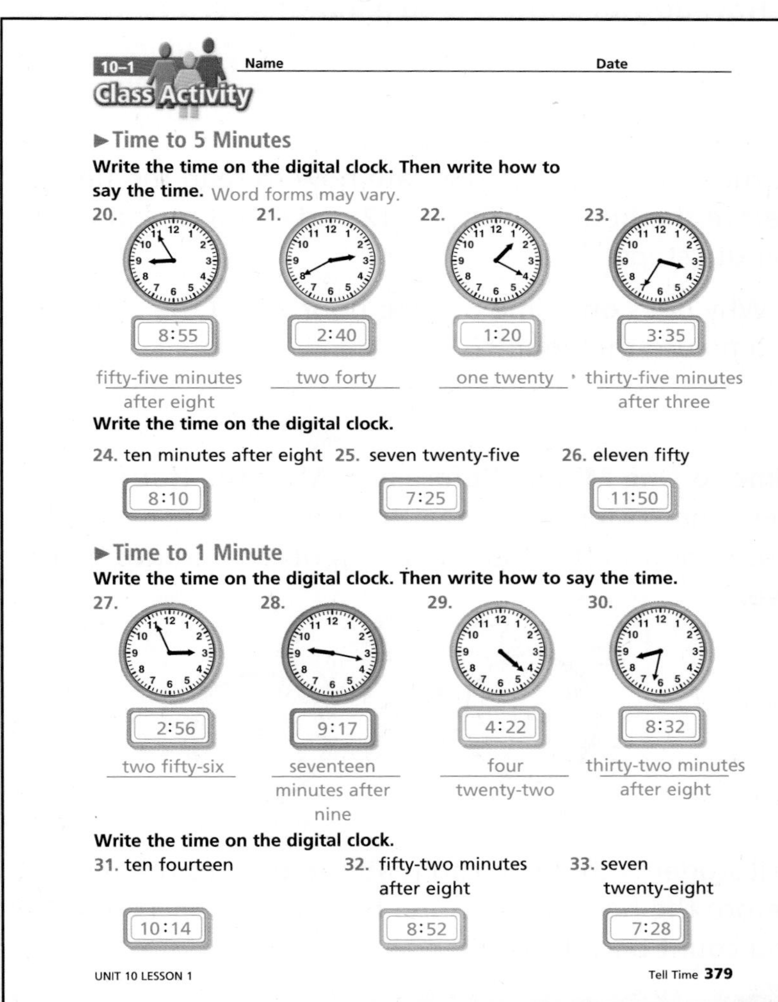

10–1 Class Activity Name Date

▶ Time to 5 Minutes

Write the time on the digital clock. Then write how to say the time. Word forms may vary.

20. 8:55 fifty-five minutes after eight
21. 2:40 two forty
22. 1:20 one twenty
23. 3:35 thirty-five minutes after three

Write the time on the digital clock.

24. ten minutes after eight 8:10
25. seven twenty-five 7:25
26. eleven fifty 11:50

▶ Time to 1 Minute

Write the time on the digital clock. Then write how to say the time.

27. 2:56 two fifty-six
28. 9:17 seventeen minutes after nine
29. 4:22 four twenty-two
30. 8:32 thirty-two minutes after eight

Write the time on the digital clock.

31. ten fourteen 10:14
32. fifty-two minutes after eight 8:52
33. seven twenty-eight 7:28

UNIT 10 LESSON 1 Tell Time 379

Student Activity Book page 379

Work through this and several other examples of telling time to 5 minutes using skip counting by 5s.

Ask students to work individually to complete exercises 20–23 on Student Book page 379.

Write these times in words on the board:

three forty-five	*ten minutes after five*
ten-twenty	*thirty-five minutes after two*

Invite volunteers to show each time on their paper clocks to the class and to write the times in numbers on the board.

Ask students to work individually to complete exercises 24–26 on Student Book page 379.

▶ Time to 1 Minute WHOLE CLASS

Ask students to look at the numbers and tick marks on their paper clocks.

Display 1:37 on an analog clock or the Time Poster. Ask students to show the same time on their clocks.

Ask students to count together by 5s until they reach the 7. 5, 10, 15, 20, 25, 30, 35

Then ask them to count on by 1s until they reach the minute hand. 36, 37

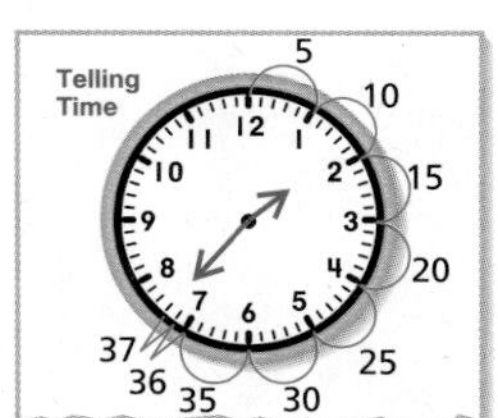

- What time does the clock show? thirty-seven minutes after one

Ask students to complete exercises 27–30.

Write these times in words on the board:

three forty-two	*seven minutes after five*
ten thirty-nine	*twelve minutes after two*

Invite volunteers to show each time on their paper clocks to the class and to write the times in numbers on the board.

Ask students to complete exercises 31–33.

1 Teaching the Lesson (continued)

Activity 3

Before and After the Hour

 15 MINUTES

Goal: State times using the words *before* and *after* with the appropriate hour.

Materials: analog clock or Time poster, paper clocks from Activity 1, Student Activity Book or Hardcover Book p. 380

 **NCTM Standards:**
Measurement
Connections

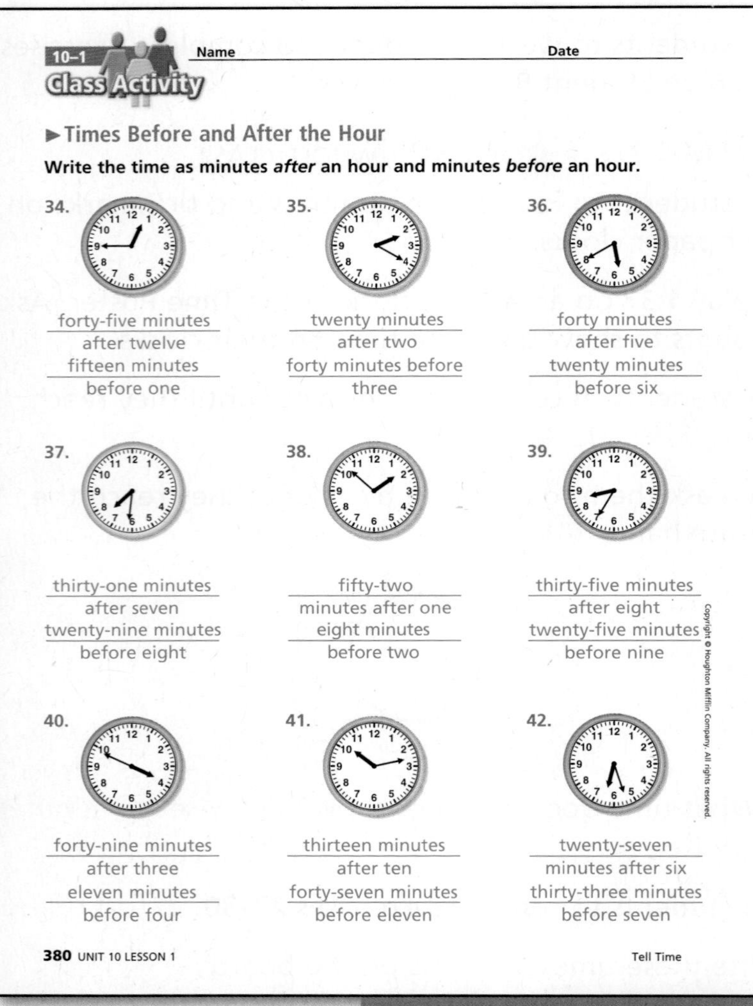
10–1 Class Activity

Name ______ Date ______

► Times Before and After the Hour

Write the time as minutes *after* an hour and minutes *before* an hour.

34. forty-five minutes after twelve / fifteen minutes before one

35. twenty minutes after two / forty minutes before three

36. forty minutes after five / twenty minutes before six

37. thirty-one minutes after seven / twenty-nine minutes before eight

38. fifty-two minutes after one / eight minutes before two

39. thirty-five minutes after eight / twenty-five minutes before nine

40. forty-nine minutes after three / eleven minutes before four

41. thirteen minutes after ten / forty-seven minutes before eleven

42. twenty-seven minutes after six / thirty-three minutes before seven

380 UNIT 10 LESSON 1 Tell Time

Student Activity Book page 380

► Times Before and After the Hour

WHOLE CLASS

Display 2:50 on an analog clock or on the Time Poster. Ask students to place the hands on their clocks to show the same time.

Tell students that they can read this time as before the hour or after the hour. Using the Time Poster, draw an arrow from the 12 to the 10 to outline the minutes after the hour. Draw a second arrow in a different color in the opposite direction from 12 back to 10 to outline the minutes before the next hour.

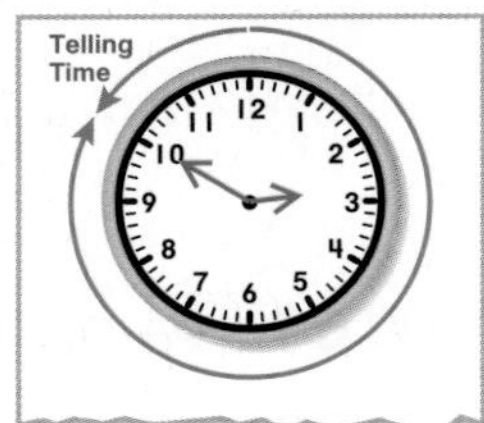

- What is the time after the hour? 50 minutes after 2
- How do you know it is 50 minutes after 2? The minute hand is at the 10 so I skip counted by 5s from the 12 to the 10 and got 50. The hour hand is between the 2 and the 3 so the time is after 2.

In the same way, demonstrate how to read the time as before the hour, starting at 12 and counting back by 5-minute steps.

- Why does one time use the hour 2 and the other time use the hour 3? The first time is the minutes after the last hour, which is 2. The second time is the minutes before the next hour, which is 3.

Time to One Minute Before and After the Hour Use the Time Poster and repeat the procedure for "forty-two minutes after four" and "eighteen minutes before five."

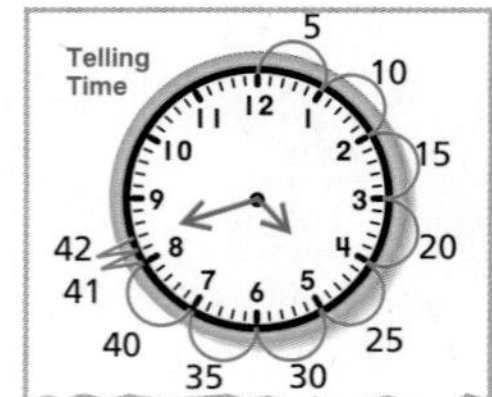

Tell students that you can read the time to the minute before the hour by counting by 5s and then 1s but that you count back from 12.

Math Talk Ask students to work in pairs then have **Student Pairs** complete exercises 34–42. Discuss their answers as a class. Have **Student Pairs** who have difficulty check their work with **Helping Partners.**

2 Going Further

Differentiated Instruction

Intervention — Activity Card 10-1

Guess My Time — Activity Card 10-1 ●

Work: In pairs

Use:

- 2 Paper clock

Decide:

Who will be Student 1 and who will be Student 2 for the first round.

1. **Student 1:** Secretly display a time on the clock. Give your partner clues about the position of the clock hands.
2. **Student 2:** Use the clues to guess the time.

Clue: The hour hand is between 4 and 5 and the minute hand is pointing to the 3. What time is it?

Answer: 4:15

3. Change roles and repeat the activity.

Unit 10, Lesson 1

Activity Note Students can use the paper clocks from the lesson. The student who is guessing the time should use or draw a clock to represent the clues about the positions of the clock hands.

Math Writing Prompt

Explain a Method To read the time 2:37, Pepita counted by 1s to 37. Explain a faster way to find the number of minutes after the hour.

Software Support

Warm Up 48.13

On Level — Activity Card 10-1

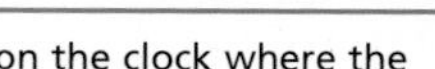

Time Before and After — Activity Card 10-1 ▲

Work: In pairs

Use:

- Paper clock

Decide:

Who will be Student 1 and who will be Student 2 for the first round.

1. **Student 1:** Display a time on the clock where the minute hand is between the 6 and the 12.
2. **Student 2:** Read the time in two ways. Use the words *before* and *after*.

The time after the hour is 52 minutes after 9.

The time before the hour is 8 minutes before 10.

3. Switch roles and repeat the activity.

Unit 10, Lesson 1

Activity Note Students can use the paper clocks from the lesson. Remind them that *before the hour* means counting minutes from the minute hand forward to 12. *After the hour* means counting minutes from 12 forward to the minute hand.

Math Writing Prompt

Explain Your Thinking Why is 37 minutes after 7 the same time as 23 minutes before 8? Explain your thinking.

Software Support

Country Countdown: Clock-a-Doodle-Doo, Level J

Challenge — Activity Card 10-1

Round Times — Activity Card 10-1 ■

Work: In pairs

Use:

- Paper clock

Decide:

Who will be Student 1 and who will be Student 2 for the first round.

1. **Student 1:** Show a time on the paper clock.
2. **Student 2:** Round the time to the nearest five minutes. Read the time using the word *about*.

The time is about 9:20.

3. Switch roles and repeat the activity.

Unit 10, Lesson 1

Activity Note Students can use the paper clocks from the lesson. Have students discuss when it makes sense to round the time and when it is necessary to be exact in naming the time.

Math Writing Prompt

Support an Opinion Fred says it is easier to tell the time before the hour on an analog clock than on a digital clock. Do you agree or disagree? Explain your thinking with examples.

Software Support

Course II: Module 3: Unit 2: Time

3 Homework and Spiral Review

10–1 Homework **Goal:** Additional Practice

This Homework page provides practice with reading and writing times in numbers and words.

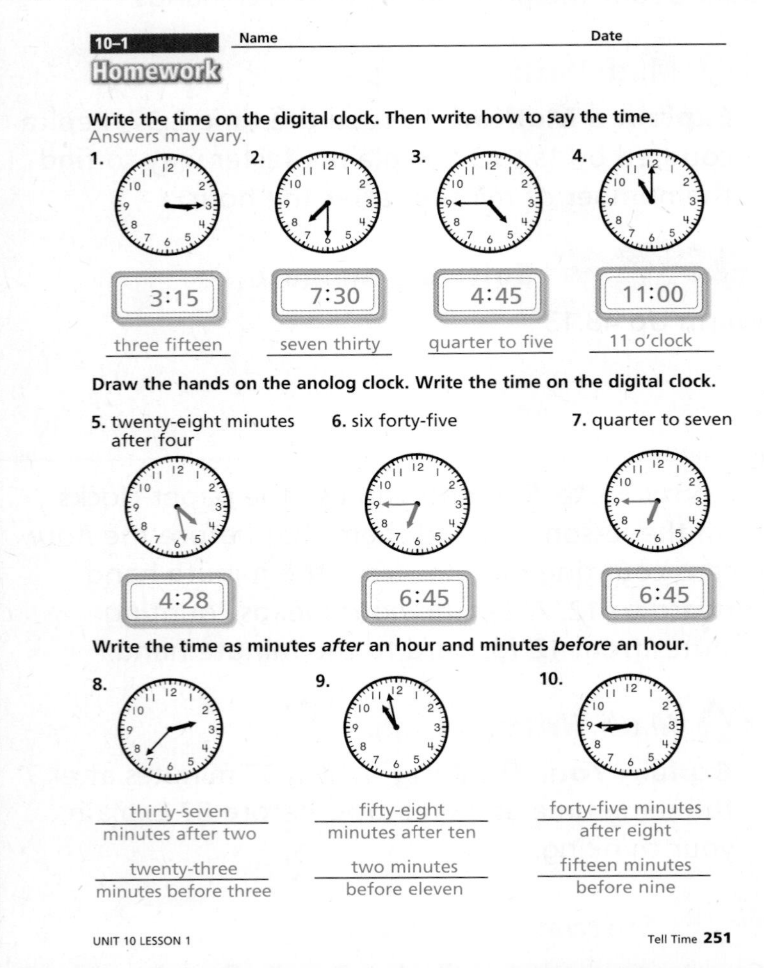

10–1 Homework Name ______ Date ______

Write the time on the digital clock. Then write how to say the time.
Answers may vary.

1. 3:15 — three fifteen
2. 7:30 — seven thirty
3. 4:45 — quarter to five
4. 11:00 — 11 o'clock

Draw the hands on the anolog clock. Write the time on the digital clock.

5. twenty-eight minutes after four — 4:28
6. six forty-five — 6:45
7. quarter to seven — 6:45

Write the time as minutes *after* an hour and minutes *before* an hour.

8. thirty-seven minutes after two; twenty-three minutes before three
9. fifty-eight minutes after ten; two minutes before eleven
10. forty-five minutes after eight; fifteen minutes before nine

UNIT 10 LESSON 1 Tell Time **251**

Homework and Remembering page 251

10–1 Remembering **Goal:** Spiral Review

This Remembering page would be appropriate anytime after today's lesson.

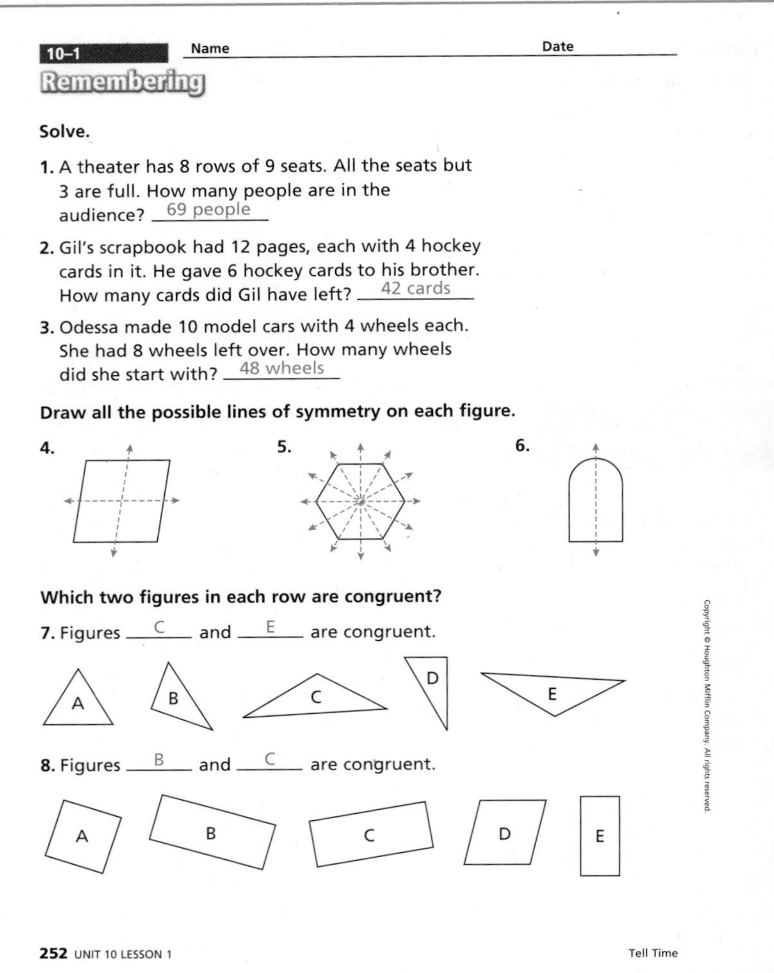

10–1 Remembering Name ______ Date ______

Solve.

1. A theater has 8 rows of 9 seats. All the seats but 3 are full. How many people are in the audience? 69 people
2. Gil's scrapbook had 12 pages, each with 4 hockey cards in it. He gave 6 hockey cards to his brother. How many cards did Gil have left? 42 cards
3. Odessa made 10 model cars with 4 wheels each. She had 8 wheels left over. How many wheels did she start with? 48 wheels

Draw all the possible lines of symmetry on each figure.

4. 5. 6.

Which two figures in each row are congruent?

7. Figures C and E are congruent.

8. Figures B and C are congruent.

252 UNIT 10 LESSON 1 Tell Time

Homework and Remembering page 252

Home and School Connection

Family Letter Have students take home the Family Letter on Student Activity Book page 381 or Activity Workbook page 173. A Spanish translation of this letter is on the following page. This letter explains how the concept of time is developed in *Math Expressions.* It gives parents and guardians a better understanding of the learning that goes on in math class and creates a bridge between school and home.

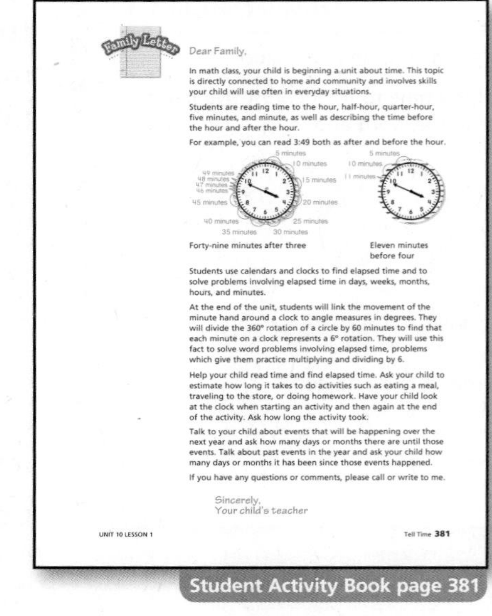

Family Letter

Dear Family,

In math class, your child is beginning a unit about time. This topic is directly connected to home and community and involves skills your child will use often in everyday situations.

Students are reading time to the hour, half-hour, quarter-hour, five minutes, and minute, as well as describing the time before the hour and after the hour.

For example, you can read 3:49 both as after and before the hour.

Forty-nine minutes after three — Eleven minutes before four

Students use calendars and clocks to find elapsed time and to solve problems involving elapsed time in days, weeks, months, hours, and minutes.

At the end of the unit, students will link the movement of the minute hand around a clock to angle measures in degrees. They will divide the 360° rotation of a circle by 60 minutes to find that each minute on a clock represents a 6° rotation. They will use this fact to solve word problems involving elapsed time, problems which give them practice multiplying and dividing by 6.

Help your child read time and find elapsed time. Ask your child to estimate how long it takes to do activities such as eating a meal, traveling to the store, or doing homework. Have your child look at the clock when starting an activity and then again at the end of the activity. Ask how long the activity took.

Talk to your child about events that will be happening over the next year and ask how many days or months there are until those events. Talk about past events in the year and ask your child how many days or months it has been since those events happened.

If you have any questions or comments, please call or write to me.

Sincerely,
Your child's teacher

UNIT 10 LESSON 1 Tell Time **381**

Student Activity Book page 381

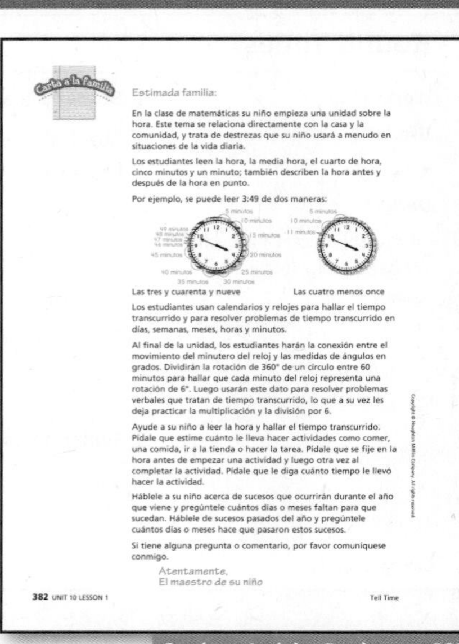

Carta a la familia

Estimada familia:

En la clase de matemáticas su niño empieza una unidad sobre la hora. Este tema se relaciona directamente con la casa y la comunidad, y trata de destrezas que su niño usará a menudo en situaciones de la vida diaria.

Los estudiantes leen la hora, la media hora, el cuarto de hora, cinco minutos y un minuto; también describen la hora antes y después de la hora en punto.

Por ejemplo, se puede leer 3:49 de dos maneras:

Las tres y cuarenta y nueve — Las cuatro menos once

Los estudiantes usan calendarios y relojes para hallar el tiempo transcurrido y para resolver problemas de tiempo transcurrido en días, semanas, meses, horas y minutos.

Al final de la unidad, los estudiantes harán la conexión entre el movimiento del minutero del reloj y las medidas de ángulos en grados. Dividirán la rotación de 360° de un círculo entre 60 minutos para hallar que cada minuto del reloj representa una rotación de 6°. Luego usarán este dato para resolver problemas verbales que tratan de tiempo transcurrido, lo que a su vez les deja practicar la multiplicación y la división por 6.

Ayude a su niño a leer la hora y hallar el tiempo transcurrido. Pídale que estime cuánto le lleva hacer actividades como comer, una comida, ir a la tienda o hacer la tarea. Pídale que se fije en la hora antes de empezar una actividad y luego otra vez al completar la actividad. Pídale que le diga cuánto tiempo le llevó hacer la actividad.

Háblele a su niño acerca de sucesos que ocurrirán durante el año que viene y pregúntele cuántos días o meses faltan para que sucedan. Háblele de sucesos pasados del año y pregúntele cuántos días o meses hace que pasaron estos sucesos.

Si tiene alguna pregunta o comentario, por favor comuníquese conmigo.

Atentamente,
El maestro de su niño

382 UNIT 10 LESSON 1 Tell Time

Student Activity Book page 382

Elapsed Time

Lesson Objectives

- Use ordinal numbers.
- Determine elapsed time in days, weeks, months, hours, and minutes.
- Use elapsed time to find start and end dates and times.

Vocabulary

calendar
month
year
day
week
ordinal number
elapsed time

The Day at a Glance

Today's Goals

1 Teaching the Lesson

A1: Determine how much time has passed in days, weeks, and months, and use elapsed time to find start and end dates.

A2: Determine how much time has passed in hours and minutes, and use elapsed time to find start and end times.

2 Going Further

▸ Differentiated Instruction

3 Homework and Spiral Review

Materials

Lesson Activities

Student Activity Book pp. 383–388 or Student Hardcover Book pp. 383–388
Homework and Remembering pp. 253–254
Paper clocks from Lesson 1 or Paper Clock (TRB M125)

Going Further

Student Activity Book pp. 383–384
Activity Cards 10-2
Index cards
Sheet Protectors
Dry-erase markers
Paper clocks
Math Journals

Keeping Skills Sharp

Daily Routines

Homework Review Ask students if they had difficulty with any part of the homework. Plan to set aside some time to work with students needing extra help.

Strategy Problem Di's sister is 3 times as old as Di. The sum of their ages is 24 years. How old is Di? How old is her sister? Explain how you found your answer.
6; 18; I drew a picture.

24 years altogether
Di's age
her sister's age

I guessed numbers for Di's age.

Di's Age	*Sister's Age*	*Sum*
4	12	16 < 24
5	15	20 < 24
6	18	24

English Language Learners

Have students point to a calendar in the classroom. Use a flip calendar to review the months of the year and ordinal numbers.

- **Beginning** Open the calendar to January. Say: **January is the 1st month**. Have students repeat. Continue with other months.
- **Intermediate** Ask: **What is the 1st month of the year?** January Open the calendar to show students they are correct. Continue with other months.
- **Advanced** Have students tell the order of the months. For each one, ask if anyone has a birthday that month. Help students use ordinal numbers to tell what day. For example, January 17th.

1 Teaching the Lesson

Activity 1

Elapsed Time on a Calendar

 30 MINUTES

Goal: Determine how much time has passed in days, weeks, and months, and use elapsed time to find start and end dates.

Materials: Student Activity Book or Hardcover Book pp. 383–386.

 **NCTM Standards:**
Measurement
Representation

10–2 Class Activity

Name ______________________ Date ____________

▶ Features of Calendars

January

Sun	Mon	Tues	Wed	Thurs	Fri	Sat
	1	2	3	4	5	6
7	8	9	10	11	12	13
14	15	16	17	18	19	20
21	22	23	24	25	26	27
28	29	30	31			

February

Sun	Mon	Tues	Wed	Thurs	Fri	Sat
				1	2	3
4	5	6	7	8	9	10
11	12	13	14	15	16	17
18	19	20	21	22	23	24
25	26	27	28			

March

Sun	Mon	Tues	Wed	Thurs	Fri	Sat
				1	2	3
4	5	6	7	8	9	10
11	12	13	14	15	16	17
18	19	20	21	22	23	24
25	26	27	28	29	30	31

April

Sun	Mon	Tues	Wed	Thurs	Fri	Sat
1	2	3	4	5	6	7
8	9	10	11	12	13	14
15	16	17	18	19	20	21
22	23	24	25	26	27	28
29	30					

May

Sun	Mon	Tues	Wed	Thurs	Fri	Sat
		1	2	3	4	5
6	7	8	9	10	11	12
13	14	15	16	17	18	19
20	21	22	23	24	25	26
27	28	29	30	31		

June

Sun	Mon	Tues	Wed	Thurs	Fri	Sat
					1	2
3	4	5	6	7	8	9
10	11	12	13	14	15	16
17	18	19	20	21	22	23
24	25	26	27	28	29	30

UNIT 10 LESSON 2 Elapsed Time 383

Student Activity Book page 383

10–2 Class Activity

Name ______________________ Date ____________

July

Sun	Mon	Tues	Wed	Thurs	Fri	Sat
1	2	3	4	5	6	7
8	9	10	11	12	13	14
15	16	17	18	19	20	21
22	23	24	25	26	27	28
29	30	31				

August

Sun	Mon	Tues	Wed	Thurs	Fri	Sat
			1	2	3	4
5	6	7	8	9	10	11
12	13	14	15	16	17	18
19	20	21	22	23	24	25
26	27	28	29	30	31	

September

Sun	Mon	Tues	Wed	Thurs	Fri	Sat
						1
2	3	4	5	6	7	8
9	10	11	12	13	14	15
16	17	18	19	20	21	22
23	24	25	26	27	28	29
30						

October

Sun	Mon	Tues	Wed	Thurs	Fri	Sat
	1	2	3	4	5	6
7	8	9	10	11	12	13
14	15	16	17	18	19	20
21	22	23	24	25	26	27
28	29	30	31			

November

Sun	Mon	Tues	Wed	Thurs	Fri	Sat
				1	2	3
4	5	6	7	8	9	10
11	12	13	14	15	16	17
18	19	20	21	22	23	24
25	26	27	28	29	30	

December

Sun	Mon	Tues	Wed	Thurs	Fri	Sat
						1
2	3	4	5	6	7	8
9	10	11	12	13	14	15
16	17	18	19	20	21	22
23	24	25	26	27	28	29
30	31					

384 UNIT 10 LESSON 2 Elapsed Time

Student Activity Book page 384

▶ Features of Calendars WHOLE CLASS

Have students look at the calendars on Student Book pages 383–384 to answer the following questions. Make sure students are reading across the page to see how the months are ordered.

- How many months are in one year? 12
- How many days are in one year? 365
- About how many weeks are in one month? 4
- How many days are in one week? 7

You may want to add these units of time to the chart you made the other day.

- How many Wednesdays are there in June? 4
- On what day of the week does this January begin? Monday
- Which months have 30 days? September, April, June, and November
- Which month has 28 days and each leap year 29 days? February

- Which months have 31 days? January, March, May, July, August, October, and December

▶ Use a Calendar WHOLE CLASS

10-2 Class Activity

Name Date

Vocabulary
month day
week elapsed time

▶ Use a Calendar

Use the calendars on pages 383–384 to complete exercises 1–3.

1. What is the fourth **month** of the year? April
2. What is the date of the twenty-second **day** of the third month? March 22
3. What day of the **week** is the third day of the seventh month? Tuesday

▶ Elapsed Time on a Calendar

Write the elapsed time.

4. August 1 to November 1 is 3 months.
5. 7:00 A.M. May 2 to 7:00 A.M. May 19 is 17 days.

Write the month.

6. Eight months after March November
7. Six months before December June

Write the date.

8. Seven days after the third of July July 10
9. Two weeks after November 2 November 16
10. Four days before June 10 June 6
11. One week before August 23 August 16

UNIT 10 LESSON 2 Elapsed Time 385

Student Activity Book page 385

Explain to students that ordinal numbers are numbers that show the position of items that are arranged in a sequence. Tell students that ordinal numbers are used to describe dates: for example, we say "the second of June" or "April ninth."

Ask questions such as the following.

- What is the first month of the year? January second month? February sixth month? June
- What month of the year is July? seventh
- For this month, what day of the week is the fifth? seventh? tenth? twentieth?

Have students complete exercises 1–3 on Student Activity Book 385 and then discuss their answers.

▶ Elapsed Time on a Calendar

WHOLE CLASS

- How many years, months, and days old are you? Answer will vary.
  Have a volunteer explain how they found the answer.

Write "8:00 A.M. June 2nd to 8:00 A.M. June 11th" on the board. Engage students in discussion (see **Math Talk in Action**) about how to find the number of days that passed.

Ask students to work individually to complete exercises 4–11. Discuss their answers.

Math Talk in Action

How did you find the number of days that have elapsed?

Anna: I counted on my fingers. I counted from June 2nd to June 3rd as 1 day. Then I continued on: June 4th – 2 days, June 5th – 3, June 6th – 4, June 7th – 5, June 8th – 6, June 9th – 7, June 10th – 8, June 11th – 9. There are 9 days from June 2nd to June 11th.

Roscoe: I subtracted 2 from 11 and got 9 so there are 9 days from June 2nd to June 11th.

Alexi: I used a number line. There are 9 spaces between the 2nd and the 11th so there are 9 days from June 2nd to June 11th.

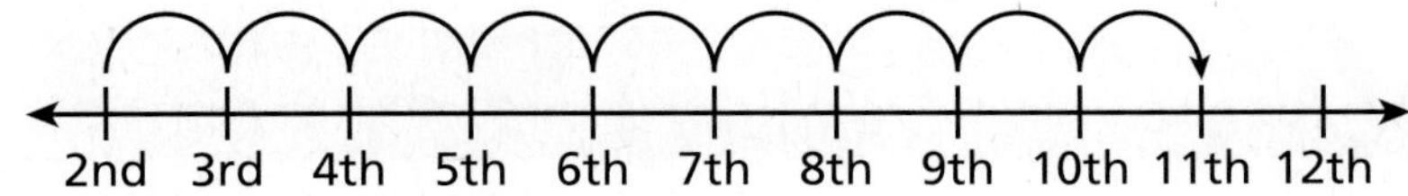

Meda: I used a calendar. I counted each space from June 3rd to June 11th. There were 9 spaces so there are 9 days from June 2nd to June 11th.

Activity continued ▶

10-2 Class Activity Name ______ Date ______

▶ Solve Problems About Elapsed Time on a Calendar

Solve. *Show your work.*

12. Garnetta worked on her project from October 4 to October 11. She then had 4 more days to complete it. How many days did she work on her project?
11 days

13. David's family left for their vacation on June 3. After 2 weeks, they returned home. What date did they arrive home?
June 17

14. Randi planted flower seeds in the house on January 15. On May 15, she planted the small plants outside. Three months later, they bloomed. How long did it take the seeds to grow into blooming plants?
7 months

15. Irene went to the aquarium on July 16. Bruce went to the aquarium 1 week later. Chantal went to the aquarium 4 days after Bruce. On what date did Chantal go to the aquarium?
July 27

16. Marilyn went to the History Museum on August 5. Alison went 1 week later. If Charlie went to the History Museum 3 days before Alison, what date did he go?
August 9

386 UNIT 10 LESSON 2 Elapsed Time

Student Activity Book page 386

▶ Solve Problems About Elapsed Time on a Calendar INDIVIDUALS

Have students complete Student Book page 386. Discuss their answers.

Teaching Note

Watch For! Some students may incorrectly include the start date in their count to find an end date. Explain to students that a day is an interval of time. Suggest they use a number line to help them visualize a day as a unit of elapsed time.

Ongoing Assessment

- ▶ How many days are there from January 1st to January 15th?
- ▶ How many weeks are there from February 4th to February 25th?
- ▶ What is the month four months after July?
- ▶ What is the elapsed time from 12:30 P.M. to 4:45 P.M.?

Activity 2

Elapsed Time on a Clock

 30 MINUTES

Goal: Determine how much time has passed in hours and minutes, and use elapsed time to find start and end times.

Materials: Student Activity Book or Hardcover Book pp. 387–388, paper clocks from Lesson 1 or Paper Clock (TRB M125)

 **NCTM Standards:**
Measurement
Connections

▶ Discuss Minutes and Hours

 WHOLE CLASS

Math Talk 

Lead a discussion to review minutes and hours as measures of time.

- What units do we usually use to measure time on a clock? minutes and hours
- What are some things you can do in about one minute? Possible answers: walk from the school entrance to the classroom, write a note, tie your shoelaces
- What are some things you can do in about one hour? Possible answers: have a lunch break, do my homework, watch a television program

Next, focus on elapsed time periods in students' daily lives.

- How much time do you spend traveling to school each day? Possible answers: 5 minutes, 15 minutes, 20 minutes
- How much time do you spend sleeping each night? Possible answers: 9 hours, 10 hours
- How much time do you spend eating breakfast each day? Possible answers: 10 minutes, 15 minutes
- Suppose you wake up at 7:00 and leave for school at 8:15. How many hours and minutes is it from the time you woke up until you left for school? 1 hour and 15 minutes

Discuss Strategies Write "1:30 P.M. to 4:47 P.M." on the board. Ask students to share different methods for finding how much time has passed from the start time to the end time.

Some students may count on their fingers. For example, they could count each finger as an hour and then add the leftover minutes "2:30, 3:30, 4:30. That's three hours and seventeen minutes."

Other students may use a time line to help them find elapsed time.

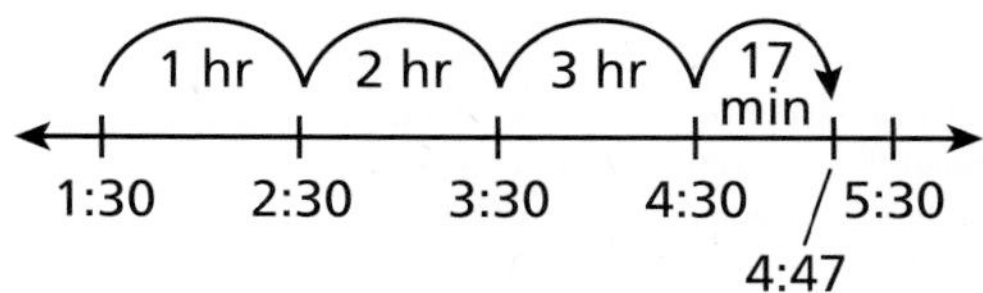

▶ Find Elapsed Time by Acting It Out

WHOLE CLASS

Math Talk

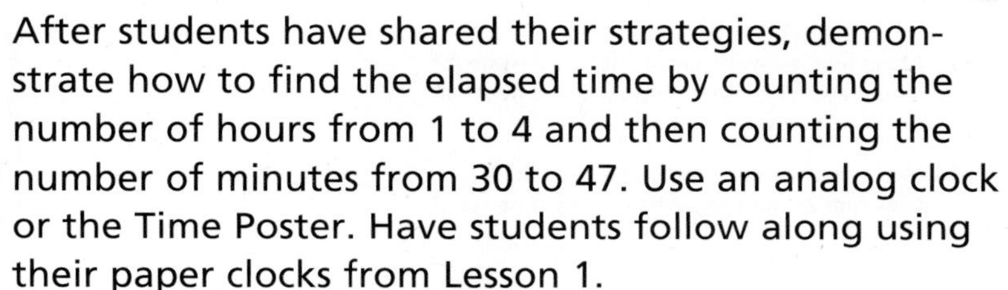

After students have shared their strategies, demonstrate how to find the elapsed time by counting the number of hours from 1 to 4 and then counting the number of minutes from 30 to 47. Use an analog clock or the Time Poster. Have students follow along using their paper clocks from Lesson 1.

3 hours

17 minutes

Some students find it helpful to visualize the clock going around for each hour rather than counting the hour hand changes on the clock face. Model this strategy if no student mentions it. The minute changes can be shown by moving the finger along to show how the tip of the minute hand moves.

What is the elapsed time from 1:30 P.M. to 4:47 P.M.?
3 hours and 17 minutes

Review the use of A.M. for times from 12:00 midnight to 12:00 noon and P.M. from 12:00 noon to 12:00 midnight.

▶ Minutes and Seconds Extension

PAIRS

Challenge **Students Pairs** to time each other with a stop watch using minutes and seconds in an activity that takes less than 2 minutes such as writing twenty multiplication or division facts with answers. Or have one student start the stop watch and stop it after a few minutes and seconds and have the other student estimate how many minutes and seconds have passed. Ask each student to complete exercise 17. Students can use the paper clocks from Lesson 1 if necessary. Discuss their answers as a class.

▶ Elapsed Time in Minutes and Hours

INDIVIDUALS

10–2 Class Activity Name ______ Date ______

▶ Elapsed Time in Minutes and Hours

17. Find the elapsed time.

Start Time	End Time	Elapsed Time
4:00 P.M.	7:00 P.M.	3 hours
7:45 A.M.	8:15 A.M.	30 minutes
2:17 P.M.	7:17 P.M.	5 hours
11:00 A.M.	2:00 P.M.	3 hours
11:55 A.M.	4:25 P.M.	4 hours and 30 minutes

18. Find the end time.

Start Time	Elapsed Time	End Time
1:00 P.M.	2 hours	3:00 P.M.
4:15 A.M.	4 hours	8:15 A.M.
4:55 P.M.	18 minutes	5:13 P.M.
2:15 A.M.	1 hour and 15 minutes	3:30 A.M.
11:55 A.M.	2 hours and 5 minutes	2:00 P.M.

19. Find the start time.

Start Time	Elapsed Time	End Time
1:15 P.M.	3 hours	4:15 P.M.
2:30 P.M.	15 minutes	2:45 P.M.
9:20 A.M.	2 hours and 35 minutes	11:55 A.M.
2:22 A.M.	1 hour and 20 minutes	3:42 A.M.

UNIT 10 LESSON 2 Elapsed Time 387

Student Activity Book page 387

The Learning Classroom

Scenarios This scenario can foster a sense of involvement in a real-life application that provides a meaningful context for counting minutes and hours on an analog clock to find the elapsed time between the start and end times. The main purpose of this Act-It-Out scenario is to demonstrate how elapsed time is useful when finding how long an activity takes or when that activity actually started or ended.

Activity continued ▶

Demonstrate how to find the end time for a show that starts at 2:30 P.M. and ends 2 hours and 12 minutes later. Use an analog clock or the Time poster. Have students follow along using their paper clocks from Lesson 1.

What time will the show end? 4:42 P.M.

Ask students to work individually to complete exercise 18. Discuss their answers as a class.

Ask students how they could find the start time if they know the end time and the elapsed time. See **Math Talk in Action** for a sample classroom discussion.

Math Talk in Action

Look at the table in exercise 19. How can you find the start time if you only know the end time and elapsed time?

Brie: First, I would use my paper clock to show the end time. Then, I would move back the clock hands the amount of time that elapsed to show the start time.

That's a good strategy. Does anyone have a different method?

Deacon: I would use subtraction. 4 hours and 15 minutes minus 3 hours is 1 hour and 15 minutes or 1:15.

Maddie: I would use backward hops on a number line to find the start time.

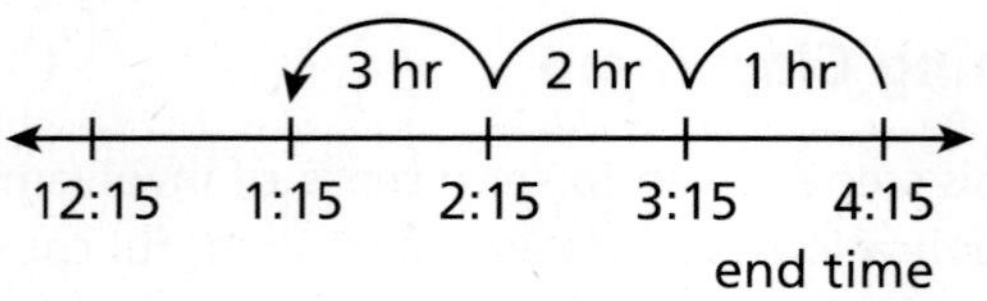

Have students complete exercise 19. Discuss their answers as a class.

▶ Solve Problems About Elapsed Time on a Clock INDIVIDUALS

10–2 Class Activity

Name ______________ Date ______________

▶ Solve Problems About Elapsed Time on a Clock

Solve. Use your clock if you need to. *Show your work.*

20. Loretta left her friend's house at 3:45. She had been there for 2 hours and 20 minutes. What time did she get there?
1:25

21. Berto spent from 3:45 P.M. to 4:15 P.M. doing math homework and from 4:30 P.M. to 5:10 P.M. doing social studies homework. How much time did he spend on his math and social studies homework?
1 hour and 10 minutes

22. Ed arrived at a biking trail at 9:00 A.M. He biked for 1 hour and 45 minutes. He spent 20 minutes riding home. What time did he get home?
11:05 A.M.

23. Mario finished swimming at 10:45. He swam for 1 hour and 15 minutes. What time did he start?
9:30

24. Vasco finished cleaning his room at 4:30. It took him 25 minutes. What time did he start?
4:05

25. Eric has basketball practice from 3:30 P.M. to 4:15 P.M. He has violin practice at 5:30. Today basketball practice ended 30 minutes late and it takes Eric 15 minutes to walk to violin practice. Will he be on time? Explain.
Yes; Basketball will end at 4:45 P.M. and he will get to violin practice at 5:00 P.M.

388 UNIT 10 LESSON 2 Elapsed Time

Student Activity Book page 388

Have students complete word problems 20–25 on Student Book page 388. Have students who experience difficulty, discuss their answers with a **Helping Partner**. Then check the answers as a class.

Teaching Note

Language and Vocabulary The abbreviation A.M. stands for *ante meridiem* and the abbreviation P.M. stands for *post meridiem*. These are Latin words: *ante* means "before," *post* means "after," and *meridiem* means "noon." Note that we do not use either A.M. or P.M. to refer to 12 midnight or 12 noon.

2 Going Further

Differentiated Instruction

Intervention — Activity Card 10-2

Daily Schedule

Activity Card 10-2 ●

Work On your own

Use:

- Paper clock

1. Create a schedule of your morning activities from the time you wake up until the end of lunch.
2. Write a start time, an end time, and an elapsed time for each activity as shown below.

Activity	Start Time	End Time	Elapsed Time
Shower	6:30 A.M.	6:37 A.M.	7 minutes
Brush Teeth	6:40 A.M.	6:43 A.M.	3 minutes
Dress	6:45 A.M.	7:00 A.M.	15 minutes
Breakfast	7:00 A.M.	7:20 A.M.	20 minutes

3. Think How can you use the minute hand on the clock to help you find the elapsed time for each activity? Begin with the start time and count minutes as you move the hand to the end time.

Unit 10, Lesson 2

Activity Note Students can use the paper clocks from Lesson 1. Have them compare the total number of elapsed minutes on the chart with the number of minutes calculated by using the minute hand of the clock to mark off the elapsed time.

Math Writing Prompt

Explain a Method Meda started playing badminton at 4:15 P.M. She finished at 5:30 P.M. Explain how to find out how long she played.

Software Support

Warm Up 48.15

On Level — Activity Card 10-2

Match Up Game

Activity Card 10-2 ▲

Work: In pairs

Use:

- 8 Index cards
- Paper clocks

1. On Your Own Create four pairs of cards. On one of each pair, show an end time and an elapsed time. On the other, show the start time.

   end time: 3:50
   elapsed time:
   2 hours and
   10 minutes

   start time:
   1:40

2. Put all the cards together upside down on the table. Take turns flipping them over to find the matching sets.
3. Use your paper clocks to show start and end times.

   Analyze What strategies did you use to match the pairs?

Unit 10, Lesson 2

Activity Note Students can use the paper clocks from Lesson 1. Suggest that they use strategies such as counting on from the start time, first with hours and then with minutes. They could also count back from the end time, using a clock as a visual aid.

Math Writing Prompt

Make a Drawing A radio show ended at 4:55 P.M. It was 30 minutes long. Explain how to find the start time of the show using a clock or a number line. Include a drawing in your explanation.

Software Support

Country Countdown: Clock-a-Doodle-Doo, Level K

Challenge — Activity Card 10-2

Look for Patterns

Activity Card 10-2 ■

Work: In pairs

Use:

- Student Activity Book pages 383-384
- Sheet protectors
- Dry-erase markers

1. Work Together Look for patterns on the calendar. Examine groups of numbers in rows, columns, and along diagonals.
2. What pattern is shown by the circled numbers in the example below? The numbers increase by 7.

March

Sun	Mon	Tues	Wed	Thurs	Fri	Sat
				1	2	3
4	5	6	7	8	9	10
11	12	13	14	15	16	17
18	19	20	21	22	23	24
25	26	27	28	29	30	31

3. Look for examples of at least three different patterns. Circle each group of numbers that form a pattern. Then describe each pattern.

Unit 10, Lesson 2

Activity Note Patterns include numbers that are multiples of 7 in one column, numbers that increase or decrease by 6 along some diagonals, and numbers that increase or decrease by 8 along other diagonals.

Math Writing Prompt

Investigate Mathematics Describe an activity you might do in about 2 hours. Create an elapsed time problem about the activity and include a solution.

Software Support

Course II: Module 3: Unit 2: Time

Homework and Spiral Review

Goal: Additional Practice

Include students' completed Homework page as part of their portfolios.

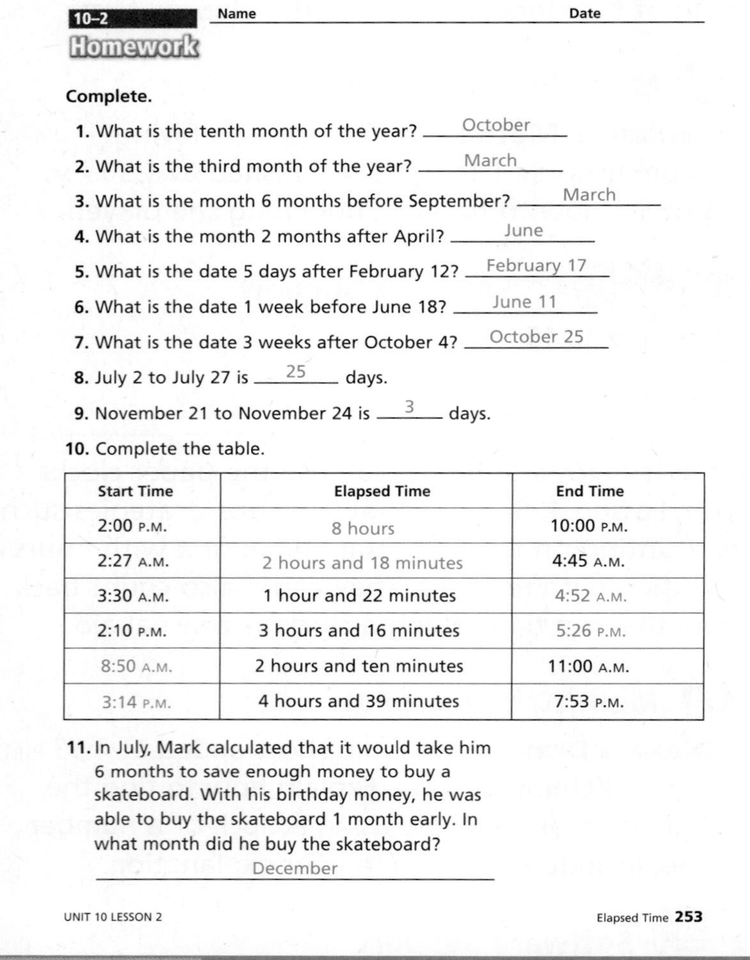

10–2 Homework

Name Date

Complete.

1. What is the tenth month of the year? October
2. What is the third month of the year? March
3. What is the month 6 months before September? March
4. What is the month 2 months after April? June
5. What is the date 5 days after February 12? February 17
6. What is the date 1 week before June 18? June 11
7. What is the date 3 weeks after October 4? October 25
8. July 2 to July 27 is 25 days.
9. November 21 to November 24 is 3 days.
10. Complete the table.

Start Time	Elapsed Time	End Time
2:00 P.M.	8 hours	10:00 P.M.
2:27 A.M.	2 hours and 18 minutes	4:45 A.M.
3:30 A.M.	1 hour and 22 minutes	4:52 A.M.
2:10 P.M.	3 hours and 16 minutes	5:26 P.M.
8:50 A.M.	2 hours and ten minutes	11:00 A.M.
3:14 P.M.	4 hours and 39 minutes	7:53 P.M.

11. In July, Mark calculated that it would take him 6 months to save enough money to buy a skateboard. With his birthday money, he was able to buy the skateboard 1 month early. In what month did he buy the skateboard? December

UNIT 10 LESSON 2 Elapsed Time 253

Homework and Remembering page 253

Goal: Spiral Review

This Remembering page would be appropriate anytime after today's lesson.

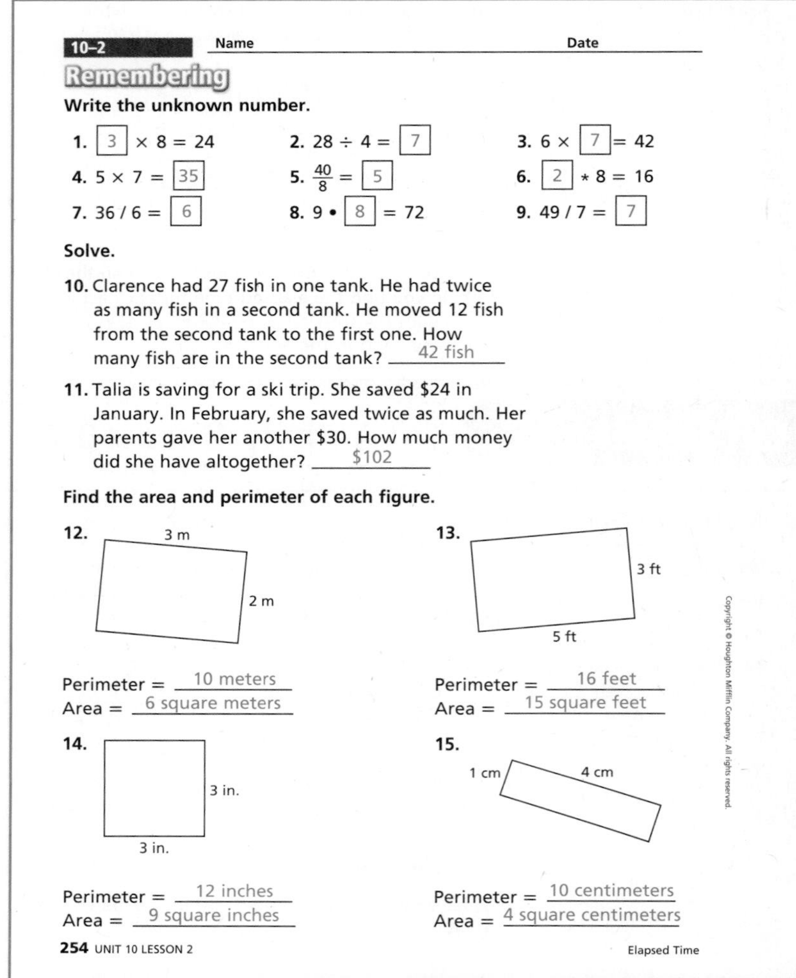

10–2 Remembering

Name Date

Write the unknown number.

1. 3 × 8 = 24
2. 28 ÷ 4 = 7
3. 6 × 7 = 42
4. 5 × 7 = 35
5. $\frac{40}{8}$ = 5
6. 2 * 8 = 16
7. 36 / 6 = 6
8. 9 • 8 = 72
9. 49 / 7 = 7

Solve.

10. Clarence had 27 fish in one tank. He had twice as many fish in a second tank. He moved 12 fish from the second tank to the first one. How many fish are in the second tank? 42 fish
11. Talia is saving for a ski trip. She saved $24 in January. In February, she saved twice as much. Her parents gave her another $30. How much money did she have altogether? $102

Find the area and perimeter of each figure.

12. (3 m, 2 m) Perimeter = 10 meters; Area = 6 square meters
13. (5 ft, 3 ft) Perimeter = 16 feet; Area = 15 square feet
14. (3 in., 3 in.) Perimeter = 12 inches; Area = 9 square inches
15. (1 cm, 4 cm) Perimeter = 10 centimeters; Area = 4 square centimeters

254 UNIT 10 LESSON 2 Elapsed Time

Homework and Remembering page 254

Home and School Activity

Art Connection

Make a Calendar Have students make and decorate calendar pages for one or two months. Copy one or two blank calendar pages from Calendar (TRB M126) for each student. Have them add month titles, week titles, and dates to each page. Encourage them to decorate their calendars with such visuals as animals, landscapes, activities, holidays, or weather related to the months they have chosen.

Clock Angles

Lesson Objectives

- **Relate elapsed time on a clock to angles of rotation.**
- **Apply multiples of 6.**

Vocabulary
degrees

The Day at a Glance

Today's Goals	Materials	
1 Teaching the Lesson **A1:** Relate the number of degrees in a quarter, half, and full rotation of the minute hand on a clock to the number of minutes elapsed. **A2:** Find the number of degrees the minute hand on a clock rotates in one minute and multiply and divide by 6 to solve problems.	**Lesson Activities** Student Activity Book pp. 389–390 or Student Hardcover Book pp. 389–390 Homework and Remembering pp. 255–256 Quick Quiz (Assessment Guide) *Secret Treasures and Magical Measures: Adventures in Measuring: Time, Temperature, Length, Weight, Volume, Angles, Shapes and Money* by Chris Kensler (Simon & Schuster, 2003)	**Going Further** Activity Cards 10-3 Index cards Math Journals
2 Going Further ▶ Differentiated Instruction		
3 Homework and Spiral Review		

Use Math Talk today!

Keeping Skills Sharp

Daily Routines

Homework Review Let students work together to check their work. Initially, pair less able students with more able students. Remind students to use what they know about helping others.

Area Ishwar plans to carpet a square section of his room. The length and width of this section are 5 feet. How much carpet does Ishwar need for this section of his room? 25 square feet

English Language Learners

Model how *degrees* measure a turn in a rotation. Draw a clock, shade in a quarter, and mark the right angle. Say: **The minute hand turns around the clock.**

- **Beginning** Point to the right angle. Ask: **Does this mean 90°?** yes Say: **A quarter-hour is a 90° turn**. Have students repeat.
- **Intermediate** Ask: **Did I draw a 90° angle?** yes Say: **The minute hand is on a quarter-hour.** Ask: **How many *degrees* did it turn?** 90°
- **Advanced** Point and ask: **How many degrees is this?** 90° **Does a quarter-hour equal a 90° turn?** yes

1 Teaching the Lesson

Activity 1

Quarter, Half, Three-Quarter, and Full Turns

25 MINUTES

Goal: Relate the number of degrees in a quarter, half, and full rotation of the minute hand on a clock to the number of minutes elapsed.

Materials: Student Activity Book or Hardcover Book p. 389

NCTM Standards:
Measurement
Connections

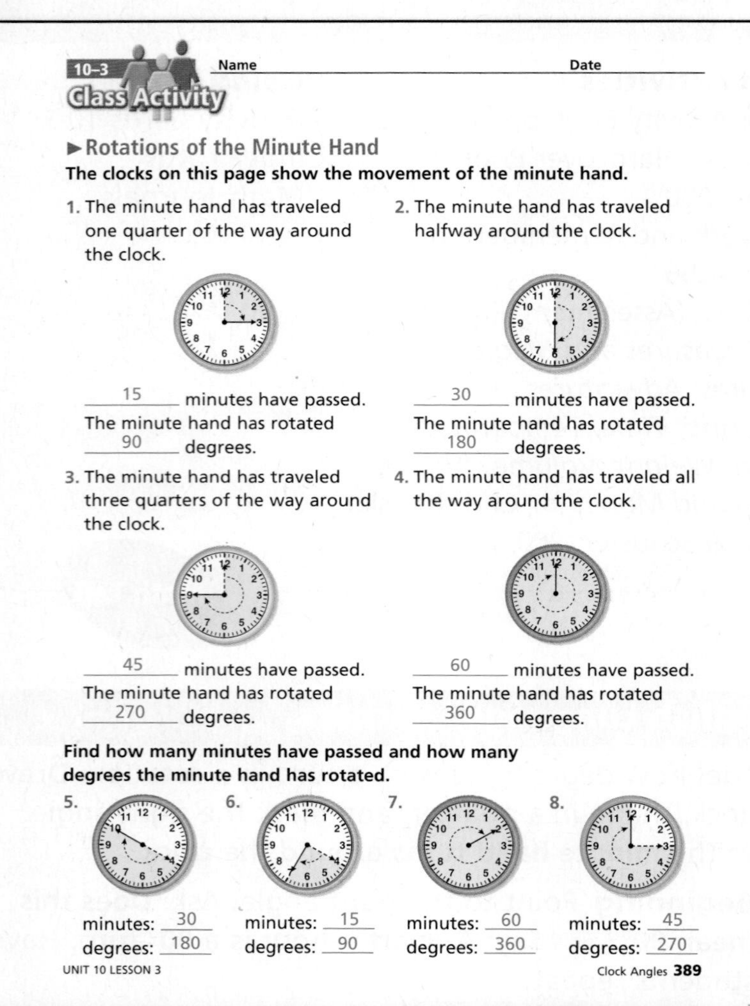

10-3 Class Activity Name ________ Date ________

► Rotations of the Minute Hand

The clocks on this page show the movement of the minute hand.

1. The minute hand has traveled one quarter of the way around the clock.

   15 minutes have passed.
   The minute hand has rotated 90 degrees.

2. The minute hand has traveled halfway around the clock.

   30 minutes have passed.
   The minute hand has rotated 180 degrees.

3. The minute hand has traveled three quarters of the way around the clock.

   45 minutes have passed.
   The minute hand has rotated 270 degrees.

4. The minute hand has traveled all the way around the clock.

   60 minutes have passed.
   The minute hand has rotated 360 degrees.

Find how many minutes have passed and how many degrees the minute hand has rotated.

5. minutes: 30 degrees: 180
6. minutes: 15 degrees: 90
7. minutes: 60 degrees: 360
8. minutes: 45 degrees: 270

UNIT 10 LESSON 3 Clock Angles **389**

Student Activity Book page 389

► Rotations of the Minute Hand

WHOLE CLASS

Refer students to Student Book page 389.

Explain that each clock shows the movement of the minute hand. These clocks do not show the hour hand. The dotted arrows show where the minute hand started and how far it has traveled.

Explain that in exercise 1, the minute hand started at 12, as shown by the dashed arrow. The minute hand then rotated one quarter of the way around the clock, ending at the 3.

- How many minutes does it take the minute hand to rotate one quarter of the way around a clock? 15 minutes
- How many degrees does the minute hand rotate in a quarter turn? 90°

Have students complete exercises 2–4 and then discuss their answers.

Then ask students to look at the clocks in exercises 5–8. Explain that the dashed arrow shows where the minute hand started and the solid arrow shows where it stopped.

- How are the placements of the minute hands different from those in exercises 1–4? In exercises 1–4, the minute hand always started at 12. In these exercises, it starts in different places.

Have students compare the clocks in exercises 2 and 5.

- How are the clocks in exercises 2 and 5 similar? The minute hand has traveled halfway around each clock.
- How are they different? In exercise 2, the minute hand starts at 12. In exercise 5, it starts at 4.
- How much time has passed in exercise 2? 30 minutes in exercise 5? 30 minutes

Students should realize that it takes 30 minutes for the minute hand to make a half turn, no matter where it starts. Work through other examples like 15 minutes before and 15 minutes after the hour if necessary.

Give students a few minutes to complete exercises 5–8 and then discuss their answers. Offer other examples using the same number of minutes that have passed as in exercises 6–8 if necessary.

Activity 2

Multiply and Divide by 6 to Solve Time Problems

 **35 MINUTES**

Goal: Find the number of degrees the minute hand on a clock rotates in one minute and multiply and divide by 6 to solve problems.

Materials: Student Activity Book or Hardcover Book p. 390

 **NCTM Standards:**
Measurement
Connections

▶ Introduce Degrees of Rotation in One Minute SMALL GROUPS

Have student volunteers explain how many degrees the minute hand rotates in 30 minutes. 180° Have students work in **Small Groups** to use their answer to determine how many degrees the minute hand rotates in one minute. Make sure the following points are made.

- You can use a division equation.

  18 tens ÷ 3 tens = [6]

- You can use a multiplication equation.

  [6] × 3 tens = [18 tens]

Both of these examples show the minute hand rotates 6° in one minute.

Then have students figure out how many degrees the minute hand rotates in 60 minutes? 360°

Have students work in **Small Groups** and use their answer to verify how many degrees the minute hand rotates in one minute.

After a few minutes, have groups share their ideas with the class. See **Math Talk in Action** for a sample classroom dialogue.

Math Talk in Action

How did you start finding the number of degrees the minute hand rotates in one minute?

Han Suk: I wanted to find the number of degrees if I divided 360° into 60 equal groups. I wrote this division problem:

36 tens ÷ 6 tens = □

Joseph: I wrote a missing factor multiplication instead:

□ × 6 tens = 36 tens

How can you solve Han Suk's division problem?

Priscilla: To solve 360 ÷ 60, I can think of 60 as the group size, so I can ask myself "How many groups of 60 are in 360?"

I can add 60 repeatedly until I reach 360. Then count the number of 60s I added:

60 + 60 = 120	(two 60s so far)
120 + 60 = 180	(three 60s)
180 + 60 = 240	(four 60s)
240 + 60 = 300	(five 60s)
300 + 60 = 360	(six 60s altogether)

There are six 60s in 360, so 360 ÷ 60 = 6. This means the minute hand rotates 6° in one minute.

Activity continued ▶

10-3 Class Activity

Name ______________________ Date ______________

Vocabulary
degrees

► Degrees of Rotation in 1 Minute

The minute hand rotates 6 degrees (°) in 1 minute.
Complete the sentence.

9. Between 12:00 and 12:08, the minute hand rotates __48__ degrees.
10. Between 12:00 and 12:07, the minute hand rotates __42__ degrees.
11. Between 12:00 and 12:10, the minute hand rotates __60__ degrees.

► Elapsed Time

Complete the sentence.

12. From 4:16 to 4:25, __9__ minutes pass. The minute hand rotates __54__ degrees.
13. From 2:43 to 2:48, __5__ minutes pass. The minute hand rotates __30__ degrees.
14. From 8:55 to 9:01, __6__ minutes pass. The minute hand rotates __36__ degrees.
15. From 12:59 to 1:01, __2__ minutes pass. The minute hand rotates __12__ degrees.

► Find End Times Using Clock Angles

Solve.

16. A clock starts at 4:15. What time is it after the minute hand rotates 18 degrees? __4:18__
17. A clock starts at 7:57. What time is it after the minute hand rotates 24 degrees? __8:01__
18. A clock starts at 10:59. What time is it after the minute hand rotates 42 degrees? __11:06__

390 UNIT 10 LESSON 3 Clock Angles

Student Activity Book page 390

► Degrees of Rotation in 1 Minute

WHOLE CLASS

Have students look at Student Book page 390 and work through exercise 9 as a class.

- At 12:00, where does the minute hand point? at the 12
- How many minutes pass between 12:00 and 12:08? 8 minutes
- How many degrees does the minute hand rotate in this time? 48°
- How do you know? The hand rotates 6° in 1 minute, so in 8 minutes it rotates 8 times as much, or 48°.

Have students complete exercises 10–11 and then discuss their answers.

► Elapsed Time

INDIVIDUALS

Have students look at exercise 12. Make sure they understand that they need to first determine how many minutes have passed and then how many degrees the minute hand rotates in that amount of time. Have students complete exercises 12–15. They may have trouble with exercises 14 and 15 because the time crosses over the hour.

► Find End Times Using Clock Angles

INDIVIDUALS

Exercises 16–18 involve dividing by 6. Read exercise 16 aloud. Give students a minute or two to solve it, and then have a volunteer present his or her solution. Students should reason that, if 1 minute passes for every 6°, then in 18°, 18 ÷ 6, or 3, minutes pass. The new time is 4:18. Then have students complete exercises 17 and 18.

Quick Quiz

See Assessment Guide for Unit 10 Quick Quiz.

Ongoing Assessment

Ask students these questions:

- ► How many degrees does the minute hand rotate between 3:00 and 3:09?
- ► A clock starts at 2:18. What time is it after the minute hand has rotated 48°?

2 Going Further

Differentiated Instruction

Intervention — Activity Card 10-3

Matching Game — Activity Card 10-3

Work: In pairs

Use:

- 16 Index cards

1. On Your Own Make four pairs of matching cards. Write 90°, 180°, 270°, and 360° on four of the cards, one measure on each card.
2. The other four cards each show start and end time positions for the minute hand to represent one of the four degree measures.

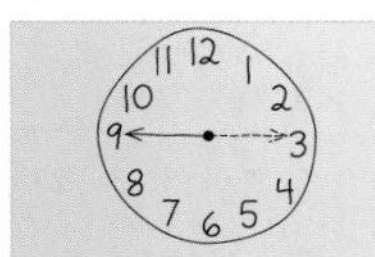

3. Shuffle all 8 pairs of cards. Put them face down.
4. Take turns turning over one pair of cards. Try to find as many matching pairs as you can each time.

Unit 10, Lesson 3

Activity Note Be sure that students use the dashed line to indicate the end time position of the minute hand. Otherwise, they will not be able to distinguish between 90° and 270°. A single hand indicates 360°.

Math Writing Prompt

Explain Your Thinking How many degrees of rotation is one minute? Explain how you know.

Software Support

Warm Up 35.23

On Level — Activity Card 10-3

Angle of Rotation Snap — Activity Card 10-3

Work: In pairs

Use:

- 20 index cards

1. Each student makes five pairs of matching cards. One card in each pair shows an end time and an angle of rotation that is a multiple of 6. The other card shows the start time.

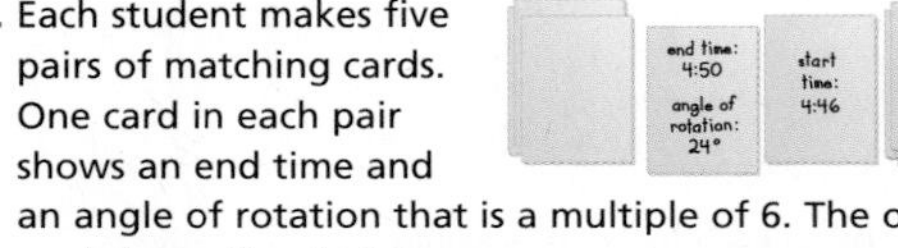

2. Shuffle all the cards and make two equal piles facedown. Using one pile, each student flips over a card. If the cards match, the first student to call the match wins the cards.
3. When all the cards in a draw pile are faceup, leave the top card faceup and turn over the cards from the other pile to make a new draw pile.
4. The game ends when one player has all the cards.

Unit 10, Lesson 3

Activity Note Angles of rotation must be multiples of 6 for this game. Students can divide the angle by 6 and then count back by that number of minutes from the end time to find the matching start time.

Math Writing Prompt

Use Reasoning A clock showed 1:25. The minute hand then rotated 42°. Explain how to find the time at the end of the rotation.

Software Support

Country Countdown: Clock-a-Doodle-Doo, Level K

Challenge — Activity Card 10-3

Create Your Own Problem — Activity Card 10-3

Work: In pairs

1. On Your Own Create a problem about elapsed time. Include a starting time and an angle of rotation.

I left home at 2:15. While I walked to my friend's house, the minute hand on my watch rotated 36°. What time did I get to my friend's house?

2. Exchange your problem with your partner and solve. Then exchange problems again to check the results.

Unit 10, Lesson 3

Activity Note Angles of rotation must be multiples of 6 for this activity to be manageable. As an additional challenge, tell students to create problems that have a missing angle measure, given both times.

Math Writing Prompt

Explain a Method How can you use a clock face to help you estimate the angle of a partly opened door?

Software Support

Course II: Module 3: Unit 2: Time

3 Homework and Spiral Review

Goal: Additional Practice

This Homework page provides practice calculating elapsed minutes and rotation in degrees of the minute hand.

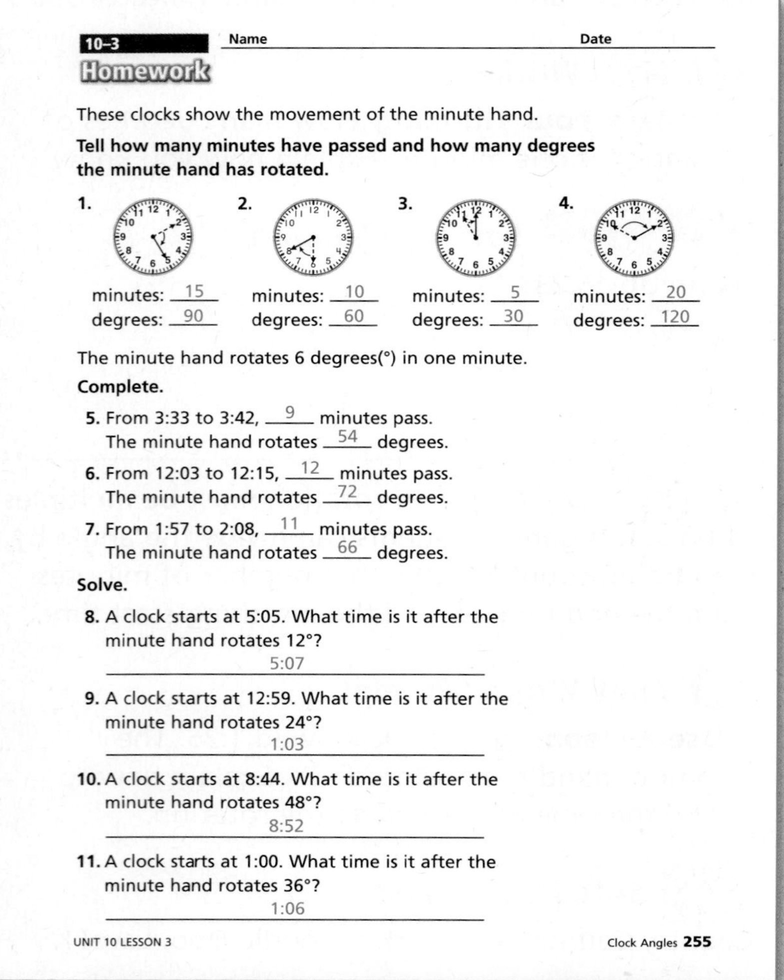

10–3 Homework Name Date

These clocks show the movement of the minute hand.

Tell how many minutes have passed and how many degrees the minute hand has rotated.

1. minutes: 15 degrees: 90
2. minutes: 10 degrees: 60
3. minutes: 5 degrees: 30
4. minutes: 20 degrees: 120

The minute hand rotates 6 degrees(°) in one minute.

Complete.

5. From 3:33 to 3:42, 9 minutes pass. The minute hand rotates 54 degrees.
6. From 12:03 to 12:15, 12 minutes pass. The minute hand rotates 72 degrees.
7. From 1:57 to 2:08, 11 minutes pass. The minute hand rotates 66 degrees.

Solve.

8. A clock starts at 5:05. What time is it after the minute hand rotates 12°? 5:07
9. A clock starts at 12:59. What time is it after the minute hand rotates 24°? 1:03
10. A clock starts at 8:44. What time is it after the minute hand rotates 48°? 8:52
11. A clock starts at 1:00. What time is it after the minute hand rotates 36°? 1:06

UNIT 10 LESSON 3 Clock Angles 255

Homework and Remembering page 255

Goal: Spiral Review

This Remembering page would be appropriate anytime after today's lesson.

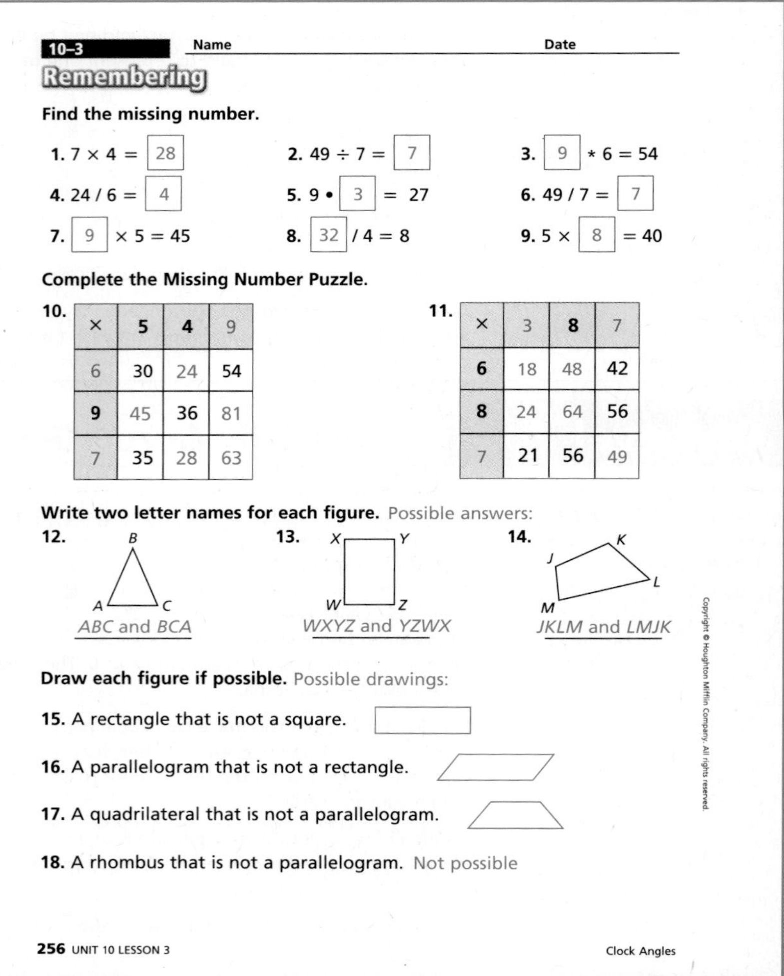

10–3 Remembering Name Date

Find the missing number.

1. 7 × 4 = 28
2. 49 ÷ 7 = 7
3. 9 * 6 = 54
4. 24 / 6 = 4
5. 9 • 3 = 27
6. 49 / 7 = 7
7. 9 × 5 = 45
8. 32 / 4 = 8
9. 5 × 8 = 40

Complete the Missing Number Puzzle.

10.

×	5	4	9
6	30	24	54
9	45	36	81
7	35	28	63

11.

×	3	8	7
6	18	48	42
8	24	64	56
7	21	56	49

Write two letter names for each figure. Possible answers:

12. ABC and BCA
13. WXYZ and YZWX
14. JKLM and LMJK

Draw each figure if possible. Possible drawings:

15. A rectangle that is not a square.
16. A parallelogram that is not a rectangle.
17. A quadrilateral that is not a parallelogram.
18. A rhombus that is not a parallelogram. Not possible

256 UNIT 10 LESSON 3 Clock Angles

Homework and Remembering page 256

Home or School Activity

Literature Connection

Secret Treasures and Magical Measures: Adventures in Measurement: Temperature, Time, Length, Weight, Volume, Angles, Shapes, and Money Read aloud Chris Kensler's book (Simon & Schuster, 2003) to extend students' understanding. You may want to share parts of this book at different times throughout the unit. Students can try some of the suggested activities.

Unit Review and Test

Lesson Objective

- **Assess student progress on unit objectives.**

The Day at a Glance

Today's Goals	Materials
1 Assessing the Unit ► Assess student progress on unit objectives. ► Use activities from unit lessons to reteach content. **2 Extending the Assessment** ► Use remediation for common errors. There is no homework assignment on a test day.	Unit 10 Test, Student Activity Book pp. 391–392 or Hardcover Book pp. 391–392 and Activity Workbook pp. 175–176 Unit 10 Test, Form A or B, Assessment Guide (optional) Unit 10 Performance Assessment, Assessment Guide (optional)

Keeping Skills Sharp

Daily Routines — 5 MINUTES	
If you are doing a unit review day, go over the homework. If this is a test day, omit the homework review.	**Review and Test Day** You may want to choose a quiet game or other activity (reading a book or working on homework for another subject) for students who finish early.

1 Assessing the Unit

Assess Unit Objectives

45 MINUTES (more if schedule permits)

Goal: Assess student progress on unit objectives.

Materials: Student Activity Book pp. 391–392 or Hardcover Book pp. 391–392 and Activity Workbook pp. 175–176; Assessment Guide Unit 10 Test Form A or B (optional); Assessment Guide Unit 10 Performance Assessment (optional)

▶ Review and Assessment

If your students are ready for assessment on the unit objectives, you may use either the test on the Student Activity Book pages or one of the forms of the Unit 10 Test in the Assessment Guide to assess student progress.

If you feel that students need some review first, you may use the test on the Student Activity Book pages as a review of unit content, and then use one of the forms of the Unit 10 Test in the Assessment Guide to assess student progress.

To assign a numerical score for all of these test forms, use 10 points for each question.

You may also choose to use the Unit 10 Performance Assessment. Scoring for that assessment can be found in its rubric in the Assessment Guide.

▶ Reteaching Resources

The chart lists the test items, the unit objectives they cover, and the lesson activities in which the objective is covered in this unit. You may revisit these activities with students who do not show mastery of the objectives.

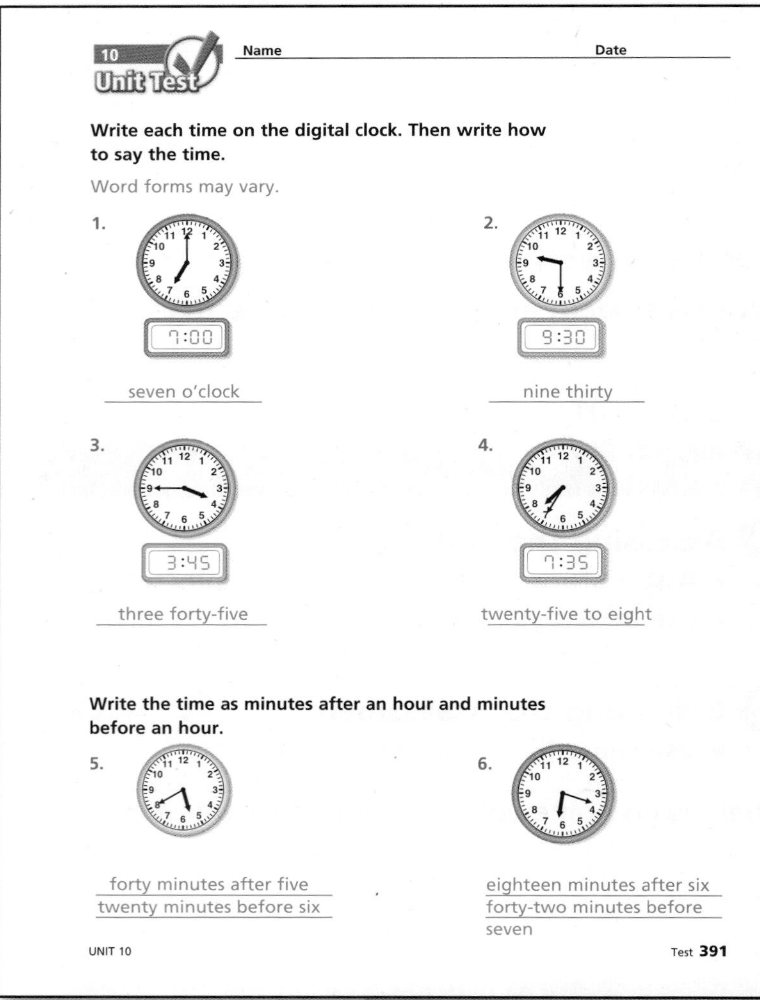

10 Unit Test Name Date

Write each time on the digital clock. Then write how to say the time.

Word forms may vary.

1. 7:00 seven o'clock

2. 9:30 nine thirty

3. 3:45 three forty-five

4. 7:35 twenty-five to eight

Write the time as minutes after an hour and minutes before an hour.

5. forty minutes after five / twenty minutes before six

6. eighteen minutes after six / forty-two minutes before seven

UNIT 10 Test 391

Student Activity Book page 391

Unit Test Items	Unit Objectives Tested	Activities to Use for Reteaching
1–6	**10.1** Read and write time to the hour, half-hour, quarter-hour, 5 minutes, and 1 minute.	Lesson 1, Activity 1 Lesson 1, Activity 2
7, 8, 10	**10.2** Solve real-world problems involving elapsed time.	Lesson 2, Activity 1 Lesson 2, Activity 2
9	**10.3** Relate clock angles to elapsed time.	Lesson 3, Activity 2

10 Unit Test

Name ______ Date ______

Solve.

Show your work.

7. Diego went to his grandparents' house on August 3. He stayed there until August 21. How many days did he stay at his grandparents' house?
18 days

8. At 8:45 Tamara went to basketball practice. Her practice lasted 1 hour and 15 minutes. What time did she finish her practice?
10:00

9. A clock shows 7:00. What time is it after the minute hand rotates 90°? Use the clock in exercise 1 if you need to.
7:15

10. **Extended Response** Carla finished her homework at 8:30. She had spent 30 minutes on math and 45 minutes on a science report. Show what time she started her homework on the clock below.

Explain how you found your answer.
Check students' work.

392 UNIT 10 Test

Student Activity Book page 392

▶ Assessment Resources

Free Response Tests
Unit 10 Test, Student Book pages 391–392
Unit 10 Test, Form A, Assessment Guide

Extended Response Item
The last item in the Student Book test and in the Form A test will require an extended response as an answer.

Multiple Choice Test
Unit 10 Test, Form B, Assessment Guide

Performance Assessment
Unit 10 Performance Assessment, Assessment Guide
Unit 10 Performance Assessment Rubric, Assessment Guide

▶ Portfolio Assessment

Teacher-selected Items for Student Portfolios:

- Homework, Lesson 2
- Class Activity work, Lessons 1, 3

Student-selected Items for Student Portfolios:

- Favorite Home or School Activity
- Best Writing Prompt

2 Extending the Assessment

Common Errors

Activities for Remediation

Unit Objective 10.1

Read and write time to the hour, half-hour, quarter-hour, 5 minutes, and 1 minute.

Common Error: Confuses the Hour and Minute Hands

In reading time on an analog clock, students may confuse the hour and the minute hands.

Remediation Explain to students that the minute hand has to be longer because it points to the tick marks between the numbers. If the minute hand were not long, we would not be able to easily read the number of minutes past the hour. Point out that we don't need to know which tick mark the hour hand points to, so the hour hand is shorter.

Common Error: Identifies the Previous Hour When Telling the Time Before the Hour

In telling time before the hour, students may use the number that the hour hand has just passed.

Remediation Tell students that when they are reading the time as before or after the hour, they must study the position of the hour hand. Remind them that when they are reading a time after an hour, they need to look at the previous hour. When they are reading a time before the hour, they must look at the next hour.

Unit Objective 10.2

Solve real-world problems involving elapsed time.

Common Error: Includes Start Time in Count of Elapsed Time on a Clock

In finding elapsed time, students may count the beginning time as the first hour and include it in the elapsed time.

Remediation Reinforce that an hour is a unit of time. Demonstrate on a clock, that one hour is the time it takes for the hour hand to move from one number to the next. Explain that when they are finding elapsed time, they are counting the number of hour units that have passed.

Common Error: Omits Minutes in Elapsed Time

Students may not include minutes in elapsed times involving hours and minutes.

Remediation Have students draw the start time and the end time on one clock face. Ask them to use one color to highlight the elapsed hours and another color to highlight the elapsed minutes on the clock face.

Common Error: Miscounts Days in Elapsed Time

In finding elapsed time in days, students may count the first date as one elapsed day.

Remediation Reinforce that a day is a 24-hour period. Demonstrate how to find elapsed time in days using a calendar and emphasize that a day is the unit of time from one date to the next. Have students use their own calendars to find elapsed time in days. Have them draw an arrow from the first date to the next date and count this arrow as one day. Then tell students to continue making arrows between dates until they reach the end date. The number of arrows is the elapsed time in days.

Unit Objective 10.3

Relate clock angles to elapsed time.

Common Error: Doesn't Know Benchmarks for Angle Measures on a Circle

Some students may not know the benchmarks of 90°, 180°, 270°, and 360° on a circle.

Remediation Have students draw a horizontal line segment on a clock face between the 3 and the 9 and a vertical line segment between the 12 and the 6. Remind students that the angle between the 12 and the 3 is a right angle and measures 90°. Ask students to note that the angle between the 12 and the 6 is twice the size as between the 12 and the 3 and ask them what the angle measure is. Continue for a rotation from the 12 to the 9 and from the 12 all the way around the clock face back to 12. Then ask students to stand and face the front of the class. Ask them to turn 90°, 180°, 270°, and 360°.

Exploring Fractions, Decimals, Probability, and Division with Remainders

UNIT 11 INTRODUCES the meaning of a fraction and basic computation involving fractions. Hands-on activities help students visualize what it means to add, subtract, and compare fractions with the same denominator or different denominators. Students apply their understanding of fractions to write the probability of simple events. To connect fractions with division, the final section of this unit introduces students to division with remainders, improper fractions, and mixed numbers.

Skills Trace

Grade 2	Grade 3	Grade 4
• Explore the terms *half* and *equal shares.* • Identify and represent unit and non-unit fractions. • Compare fractions using fraction strips. • Write money amounts as fractions. • Describe events as *impossible, possible,* or *certain*, decide whether events are *likely* or *unlikely* to happen, and discuss *fair* and *unfair* games.	• Write a fraction to represent a part of a whole and a part of a set. • Find a fraction of a number or set. • Write equivalent fractions and improper fractions as mixed numbers. • Add, subtract, and compare fractions. • Describe events as *impossible, possible,* or *certain* and decide whether events are *likely* or *unlikely* to happen. • Introduce 2-digit division, and interpret remainders.	• Write a fraction to represent a part of a whole and a part of a set. • Find a fraction of a number or set. • Find equivalent fractions and simplify fractions. • Add, subtract, and compare fractions and mixed numbers. • Relate probability to fractions and determine the probability of an event, find all the possible outcomes, and record probability in a line plot. • Practice multi-digit division (including division with money), and interpret remainders.

Unit 11 Contents

Big Idea Fraction Concepts

REAL WORLD Problem Solving

Big Idea Use Fraction Concepts

REAL WORLD Problem Solving

Big Idea Equivalent Fractions

Unit 11 Contents

Planning Unit 11

NCTM Curriculum Focal Points and Connections Key: **1.** Number and Operations and Algebra **2.** Number and Operations **3.** Geometry **4.** Algebra **5.** Measurement **6.** Data Analysis **7.** Number and Operations

Lesson NCTM Focal Points NCTM Standards	Resources	Materials for Lesson Activities	Materials for Going Further
11-1 **Fractions as Parts of a Whole** NCTM Focal Points: 2.1, 2.4, 2.5 NCTM Standards: 1, 10	TE pp. 781–790 SAB pp. 393–398 H&R pp. 257–258 AC 11-1	Blank transparency (optional) Overhead projector (optional) ✓ MathBoard materials	Crayons or colored pencils ✓ Pattern blocks Paper clips Spinner F (TRB M141) Centimeter Grid Paper (TRB M31) Scissors Math Journals
11-2 **Fractions as Part of a Set** NCTM Focal Points: 2.2, 2.4, 2.5 NCTM Standards: 1, 10	TE pp. 791–796 SAB pp. 399–400 H&R pp. 259–260 AC 11-2 MCC 41	✓ Connecting cubes	✓ Two-color counters Fraction Stickers (TRB M127) Fraction Venn Diagram (TRB M128) Math Journals
11-3 **Unit Fractions of Sets and Numbers** NCTM Focal Points: 2.2, 2.5 NCTM Standards: 1, 6, 10	TE pp. 797–802 SAB pp. 401–402 H&R pp. 261–262 AC 11-3	✓ MathBoard materials *The Big Orange Splot* by Daniel Pinkwater	Paper cups ✓ Two-color counters ✓ Play money Math Journals
11-4 **Compare with Fractions** NCTM Focal Point: 2.5 NCTM Standards: 1, 5, 6, 10	TE pp. 803–808 SAB pp. 403–404 H&R pp. 263–264 AC 11-4	None	✓ MathBoard materials ✓ Connecting cubes ✓ Two-color counters Index cards Plastic bowl Math Journals
11-5 **Practice Fractional Comparisons** NCTM Focal Point: 2.5 NCTM Standards: 1, 5, 6, 10	TE pp. 809–814 SAB pp. 405–406 H&R pp. 265–266 AC 11-5 AG Quick Quiz 1	✓ MathBoard materials *Jump, Kangaroo, Jump* by Stuart J. Murphy	✓ Connecting cubes Sticky notes Fraction of a Day (TRB M129) Crayons or colored markers Math Journals
11-6 **Find a Fraction of a Set or a Number** NCTM Focal Point: 2.2 NCTM Standards: 1, 6, 10	TE pp. 815–822 SAB pp. 407–410 H&R pp. 267–268 AC 11-6	None	Paper plates ✓ Two-color counters Index cards Math Journals
11-7 **Fractions on Circle Graphs** NCTM Focal Points: 2.1, 2.5 NCTM Standards: 1, 2, 5, 10	TE pp. 823–828 SAB pp. 411–412 H&R pp. 269–270 AC 11-7	None	Fraction Circle Model (TRB M130) Crayons or markers Math Journals

Resources/Materials Key: TE: Teacher Edition SAB: Student Activity Book H&R: Homework and Remembering AC: Activity Cards MCC: Math Center Challenge AG: Assessment Guide ✓: Grade 3 kits TRB: Teacher's Resource Book

Lesson NCTM Focal Points NCTM Standards	Resources	Materials for Lesson Activities	Materials for Going Further
11-8 **Explore Probability** NCTM Focal Point: 2.2 NCTM Standards: 1, 5, 8	TE pp. 829–840 SAB pp. 413–418; 416A–416B H&R pp. 271–272 AC 11-8 AG Quick Quiz 2	Marbles (white and black) Clear container Coins Paper Bags (TRB M131) Cubes (red and blue) or paper squares Paper clips Spin a Word (TRB M161)	Spinner C (TRB M61) ✓ MathBoard materials or blank paper Paper bag ✓ Play money Math Journals
11-9 **Introduce Equivalence** NCTM Focal Points: 2.5, 2.9 NCTM Standards: 1, 10	TE pp. 841–848 SAB pp. 418A–418B; 419–420 H&R pp. 273–274 AC 11-9 MCC 42	Envelopes Fraction tiles Fraction Strips (TRB M134)	Fraction Strips (TRB M134) Crayons or colored pencils Equivalent Fractions Match Up (TRB M135) Index Cards Math Journals
11-10 **Explore Equivalence** NCTM Focal Points: 2.1, 2.5, 2.9 NCTM Standards: 1, 10	TE pp. 849–854 SAB pp. 421–424; 424A–424B H&R pp. 275–276 AC 11-10	Transparency of Student Activity Book p. 423 (optional) Overhead projector (optional) ✓ Rulers Paper clips	Equivalent Fraction Strips (TRB M142) Spinner F (TRB M141) Paper clips Inch-Grid Paper (TRB M42) ✓ Two-color counters ✓ MathBoard materials Math Journals
11-11 **Equivalence Patterns** NCTM Focal Points: 2.5, 2.9 NCTM Standards: 1, 6, 10	TE pp. 855–862 SAB pp. 424C–424D; 425–426 H&R pp. 277–278 AC 11-11	Envelopes Scissors ✓ MathBoard materials Game Board for Halves (TRB M137) Game Board for Thirds (TRB M138)	Index Cards ✓ MathBoard materials Math Journals
11-12 **Find Equivalent Fractions by Multiplying** NCTM Focal Points: 2.5, 2.9 NCTM Standards: 1, 6, 10	TE pp. 863–868 SAB pp. 427–428 H&R pp. 279–280 AC 11-12	Multiplication Table Rows (from Lesson 11) Equivalent Fractions Box (from Lesson 11) Equivalence Chains (TRB M140) Math Journals *Mega-Fun Fractions* by Martin Lee and Marcia Miller	Spinner E (TRB M132) Paper clip ✓ Number Cube Multiplication Table Rows and Equivalent Fraction Box Game Cards (TRB M25) Math Journals

Hardcover Student Book

- Together, the Hardcover Student Book and its companion Activity Workbook contain all of the pages in the consumable Student Activity Book.

Manipulatives and Materials

- Essential materials for teaching *Math Expressions* are available in the Grade 3 kit. These materials are indicated by a ✓ in these lists. At the front of this Teacher Edition is more information about kit contents, alternatives for the materials, and use of the materials.

NCTM Curriculum Focal Points and Connections Key: 1. Number and Operations and Algebra 2. Number and Operations 3. Geometry 4. Algebra 5. Measurement 6. Data Analysis 7. Number and Operations

Lesson NCTM Focal Points NCTM Standards	Resources	Materials for Lesson Activities	Materials for Going Further
11-13 **Find Equivalent Fractions by Dividing** NCTM Focal Points: 2.5, 2.9 NCTM Standards: 1, 6, 10	TE pp. 869–874 SAB pp. 429–430 H&R pp. 281–282 AC 11-13 AG Quick Quiz 3	✓ MathBoard materials *The Fraction Family Heads West* by Marti Dryk	Spinner F (TRB M141) Paper clips Sticky notes Index Cards Math Journals
11-14 **Add Any Fractions** NCTM Focal Point: 2.5 NCTM Standards: 1, 6, 10	TE pp. 875–884 SAB pp. 430A–430B; 431–434 H&R pp. 283–284 AC 11-14	Sheet protectors Dry erase markers Transparency of Student Activity Book p. 430A (optional) Overhead projector (optional)	Equivalent Fraction Strips Spinner F (TRB M141) Paper clips ✓ MathBoard materials Math Journals
11-15 **Compare and Subtract Fractions** NCTM Focal Points: 2.5, 2.6, 2.7, 2.8 NCTM Standards: 1, 6, 8, 10	TE pp. 885–892 SAB pp. 435–438 H&R pp. 285–286 AC 11-15 MCC 43	Equivalent Fraction Strips (TRB M140)	Fraction Circle Model (TRB M130) Colored pencils Sentence strips ✓ MathBoard materials Math Journals
11-16 **Whole Numbers and Fractions on a Number Line** NCTM Focal Points: 2.3, 2.5, 2.6, 2.7 NCTM Standards: 1, 8 ,10	TE pp. 893–900 SAB pp. 439–442 H&R pp. 287–288 AC 11-16	Transparency of Student Activity Book pp. 441–442 (optional) Overhead projector (optional) *Piece = Part = Portion: Fractions = Decimals = Percents* by Scott Gifford	Blank paper Equivalent Fraction Strips (from Student Activity Book p. 430A, Lesson 11–14) Math Journals
11-17 **Fractions and Decimals** NCTM Focal Point: 2.4 NCTM Standard: 1	TE pp. 901–912 SAB pp. 443–446 H&R pp. 289–290 AC 11-17 AG Quick Quiz 4	Tenths and Hundredths Grids (TRB M162)	✓ Play money 10 × 10 Grid (TRB M43) Crayons or markers Math Journals
11-18 **Improper Fractions and Mixed Numbers** NCTM Focal Points: 2.3, 2.5 NCTM Standards: 1, 6, 10	TE pp. 913–920 SAB pp. 447–448 H&R pp. 291–292 AC 11-18	✓ MathBoard materials	✓ Number cubes ✓ MathBoard materials Index Cards Spinner E (TRB M132) Paper clip Math Journals

Resources/Materials Key: TE: Teacher Edition SAB: Student Activity Book H&R: Homework and Remembering AC: Activity Cards MCC: Math Center Challenge AG: Assessment Guide ✓: Grade 3 kits TRB: Teacher's Resource Book

NCTM Standards and Expectations Key: **1.** Number and Operations **2.** Algebra **3.** Geometry **4.** Measurement **5.** Data Analysis and Probability **6.** Problem Solving **7.** Reasoning and Proof **8.** Communication **9.** Connections **10.** Representation

Lesson NCTM Focal Points NCTM Standards	Resources	Materials for Lesson Activities	Materials for Going Further
11-19 **Introduce Division with Remainders** NCTM Focal Point: 1.9 NCTM Standards: 1, 6	TE pp. 921–926 SAB pp. 449–450 H&R pp. 293–294 AC 11-19	*A Remainder of One* by Elinor J. Pinczes	Multiplication Table (TRB M50) Index cards ✓ Number cubes ✓ MathBoard materials Spinner G (TRB M143) Paper clips Counters Math Journals
11-20 **Understand Remainders** NCTM Focal Point: 1.6 NCTM Standards: 1, 6	TE pp. 927–934 SAB pp. 451–452 H&R pp. 295–296 AC 11-20 MCC 44	Sentence strips ✓ Two-color counters Sticky notes	Math Journals
11-21 **Practice Division with Remainders** NCTM Focal Point: 1.10 NCTM Standards: 1, 6	TE pp. 935–940 SAB pp. 453–454 H&R pp. 297–298 AC 11-21 AG Quick Quiz 5	*The Great Divide* by Dayle Ann Dodds	Inch Grid Paper (TRB M42) ✓ MathBoard materials Math Journals
11-22 **Use Mathematical Processes** NCTM Focal Points: 2.1, 2.2, 3.4, 3.6 NCTM Standards: 6, 8, 9, 10	TE pp. 941–946 SAB pp. 455–456 H&R pp. 299–300 AC 11-22	Map of Northeastern United States (TRB M163) Crayons	✓ Two-color counters Spinner C (TRB M61) Paper clip Pencil Spinner E (TRB M132) Connecting Cubes Paper bags Math Journals
✓ Unit Review and Test	TE pp. 947–950 SAB pp. 457–460 AG Unit 11 Tests		

Hardcover Student Book

- Together, the Hardcover Student Book and its companion Activity Workbook contain all of the pages in the consumable Student Activity Book.

Manipulatives and Materials

- Essential materials for teaching *Math Expressions* are available in the Grade 3 kit. These materials are indicated by a ✓ in these lists. At the front of this Teacher Edition is more information about kit contents, alternatives for the materials, and use of the materials.

Independent Learning Activities

Ready-Made Math Challenge Centers

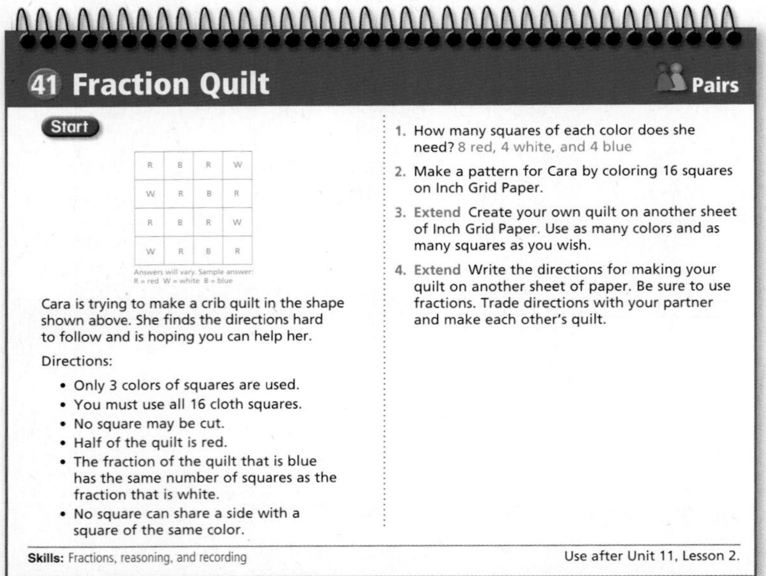

41 Fraction Quilt — Pairs

Start

R	B	R	W
W	R	B	R
R	B	R	W
W	R	B	R

Answers will vary. Sample answer: R = red W = white B = blue

Cara is trying to make a crib quilt in the shape shown above. She finds the directions hard to follow and is hoping you can help her.

Directions:

- Only 3 colors of squares are used.
- You must use all 16 cloth squares.
- No square may be cut.
- Half of the quilt is red.
- The fraction of the quilt that is blue has the same number of squares as the fraction that is white.
- No square can share a side with a square of the same color.

1. How many squares of each color does she need? 8 red, 4 white, and 4 blue
2. Make a pattern for Cara by coloring 16 squares on Inch Grid Paper.
3. Extend Create your own quilt on another sheet of Inch Grid Paper. Use as many colors and as many squares as you wish.
4. Extend Write the directions for making your quilt on another sheet of paper. Be sure to use fractions. Trade directions with your partner and make each other's quilt.

Skills: Fractions, reasoning, and recording — Use after Unit 11, Lesson 2.

Grouping Pairs

Materials Crayons or markers, Inch Grid Paper (TRB M42)

Objective Students represent fractional parts of a whole.

Connections Fractions and Representation

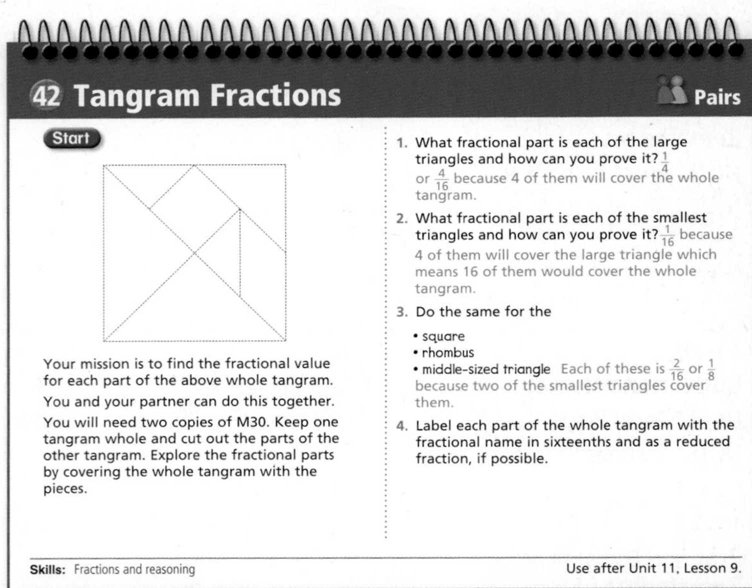

42 Tangram Fractions — Pairs

Start

Your mission is to find the fractional value for each part of the above whole tangram.

You and your partner can do this together.

You will need two copies of M30. Keep one tangram whole and cut out the parts of the other tangram. Explore the fractional parts by covering the whole tangram with the pieces.

1. What fractional part is each of the large triangles and how can you prove it? $\frac{1}{4}$ or $\frac{4}{16}$ because 4 of them will cover the whole tangram.
2. What fractional part is each of the smallest triangles and how can you prove it? $\frac{1}{16}$ because 4 of them will cover the large triangle which means 16 of them would cover the whole tangram.
3. Do the same for the
   - square
   - rhombus
   - middle-sized triangle Each of these is $\frac{2}{16}$ or $\frac{1}{8}$ because two of the smallest triangles cover them.
4. Label each part of the whole tangram with the fractional name in sixteenths and as a reduced fraction, if possible.

Skills: Fractions and reasoning — Use after Unit 11, Lesson 9.

Grouping Pairs

Materials Scissors, Tangrams (TRB M30)

Objective Students find fractional parts of a whole.

Connections Fractions and Reasoning

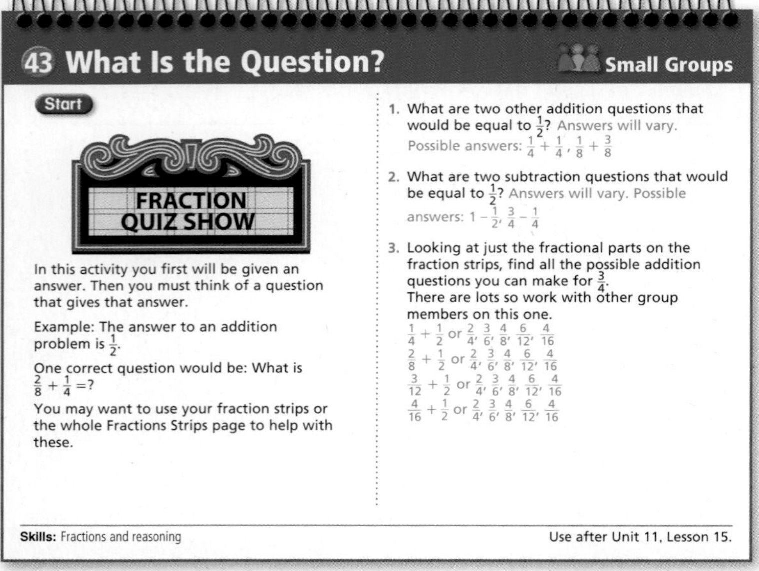

43 What Is the Question? — Small Groups

Start

In this activity you first will be given an answer. Then you must think of a question that gives that answer.

Example: The answer to an addition problem is $\frac{1}{2}$.

One correct question would be: What is $\frac{2}{8} + \frac{1}{4} = ?$

You may want to use your fraction strips or the whole Fractions Strips page to help with these.

1. What are two other addition questions that would be equal to $\frac{1}{2}$? Answers will vary. Possible answers: $\frac{1}{4} + \frac{1}{4}$, $\frac{1}{8} + \frac{3}{8}$
2. What are two subtraction questions that would be equal to $\frac{1}{2}$? Answers will vary. Possible answers: $1 - \frac{1}{2}$, $\frac{3}{4} - \frac{1}{4}$
3. Looking at just the fractional parts on the fraction strips, find all the possible addition questions you can make for $\frac{3}{4}$. There are lots so work with other group members on this one.
   $\frac{1}{4} + \frac{1}{2}$ or $\frac{2}{4}, \frac{3}{6}, \frac{4}{8}, \frac{6}{12}, \frac{4}{16}$
   $\frac{2}{8} + \frac{1}{2}$ or $\frac{2}{4}, \frac{3}{6}, \frac{4}{8}, \frac{6}{12}, \frac{4}{16}$
   $\frac{3}{12} + \frac{1}{2}$ or $\frac{2}{4}, \frac{3}{6}, \frac{4}{8}, \frac{6}{12}, \frac{4}{16}$
   $\frac{4}{16} + \frac{1}{2}$ or $\frac{2}{4}, \frac{3}{6}, \frac{4}{8}, \frac{6}{12}, \frac{4}{16}$

Skills: Fractions and reasoning — Use after Unit 11, Lesson 15.

Grouping Small Groups

Materials Fraction Strips (TRB M134)

Objective Students write addition and subtraction equations with fractions.

Connections Fractions and Communication

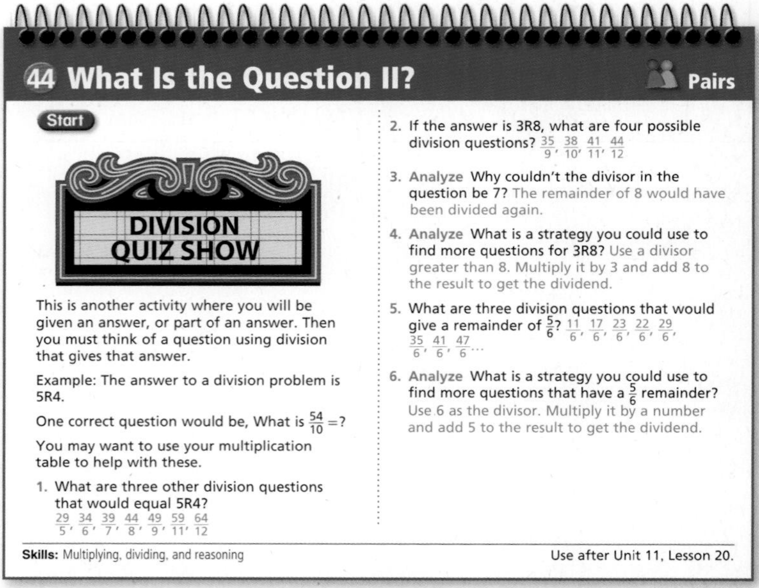

44 What Is the Question II? — Pairs

Start

This is another activity where you will be given an answer, or part of an answer. Then you must think of a question using division that gives that answer.

Example: The answer to a division problem is 5R4.

One correct question would be, What is $\frac{54}{10} = ?$

You may want to use your multiplication table to help with these.

1. What are three other division questions that would equal 5R4? $\frac{29}{5}, \frac{34}{6}, \frac{39}{7}, \frac{44}{8}, \frac{49}{9}, \frac{59}{11}, \frac{64}{12}$
2. If the answer is 3R8, what are four possible division questions? $\frac{35}{9}, \frac{38}{10}, \frac{41}{11}, \frac{44}{12}$
3. Analyze Why couldn't the divisor in the question be 7? The remainder of 8 would have been divided again.
4. Analyze What is a strategy you could use to find more questions for 3R8? Use a divisor greater than 8. Multiply it by 3 and add 8 to the result to get the dividend.
5. What are three division questions that would give a remainder of $\frac{5}{6}$? $\frac{11}{6}, \frac{17}{6}, \frac{23}{6}, \frac{22}{6}, \frac{29}{6}, \frac{35}{6}, \frac{41}{6}, \frac{47}{6}\ldots$
6. Analyze What is a strategy you could use to find more questions that have a $\frac{5}{6}$ remainder? Use 6 as the divisor. Multiply it by a number and add 5 to the result to get the dividend.

Skills: Multiplying, dividing, and reasoning — Use after Unit 11, Lesson 20.

Grouping Pairs

Materials Class Multiplication Table (TRB M50)

Objective Students use division to solve problems.

Connections Computation and Reasoning

Ready-Made Math Resources

Technology — Tutorials, Practice, and Intervention

Use online, individualized intervention and support to bring students to proficiency.

Help students practice skills and apply concepts through exciting math adventures.

Extend and enrich students' understanding of skills and concepts through engaging, interactive lessons and activities.

Visit **Education Place®**
www.eduplace.com

Visit www.eduplace.com/mx2t/ and find family, teacher, and student materials, activities, games, and more.

Literature Links

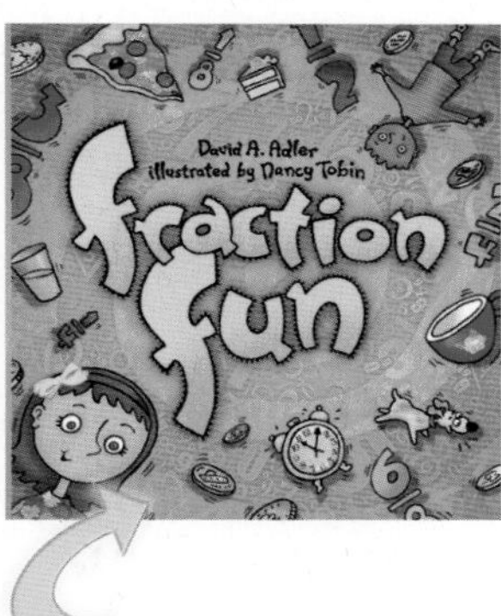

Fraction Fun

Fraction Fun
Using everyday objects David Adler and Nancy Tobin's book explores basic fraction concepts in an engaging way. There is plenty here to fill a few days of enrichment extension discussion and activity!

Literature Connections

- *The Big Orange Splot,* by Daniel Manus Pinkwater (Redbound by Sagebrush, 1999)
- *Jump, Kangaroo, Jump,* by Stuart J. Murphy, illustrated by Kevin O'Malley (HarperTrophy, 1999)
- *Mega-Fun Fractions,* by Martin Lee and Marcia Miller (Teaching Resources, 2002)
- *The Fraction Family Heads West,* by Marti Dryk, Ph.D., illustrated by Trevor Romain, D.M. (Bookaloppy Press, 1997)
- *Piece = Part = Portion: Fractions = Decimals = Percents,* by Scott Gifford, photographs by Shmuel Thaler (Tricycle Press, 2003)
- *A Remainder of One: A Mathematical Folktale,* by Elinor J. Pinczes, illustrated by Bonnie Mackain (Houghton Mifflin, 1995)
- *The Great Divide,* by Dayle Ann Dodds, illustrated by Tracy Mitchell (Candlewick Press, 2005)

Unit 11 Assessment

✓ Unit Objectives Tested	Unit Test Items	Lessons
11.1 Write a fraction to represent a part of a whole and a part of a set.	1–2	1–2
11.2 Find a fraction of a number.	3–4	3, 6
11.3 Express the probability of an event and use it to make predictions.	10–11	8
11.4 Write equivalent fractions and decimals.	5–8, 12–13	9, 11–13, 17
11.5 Compare fractions and decimals.	9, 14	15–17
11.6 Add and subtract fractions made from the same unit fractions and fractions made from different unit fractions.	18–21	14–15
11.7 Write an improper fraction as a mixed number and vice versa.	16–17	18
11.8 Divide 2-digit numbers to 90 by 1-digit numbers and interpret remainders.	15, 23	19–21
11.9 Use fractions to solve problems, compare data on a bar graph, and to interpret circle graphs.	22, 24–25	4–5, 7

Assessment and Review Resources

Formal Assessment

Student Activity Book

- Unit Review and Test (pp. 457–460)

Assessment Guide

- Quick Quizzes (pp. A103–A107)
- Test A–Open Response (pp. A108–A111)
- Test B–Multiple Choice (pp. A112–A116)
- Performance Assessment (pp. A117–A118)

Test Generator CD-ROM

- Open Response Test
- Multiple Choice Test
- Test Bank Items

Informal Assessment

Teacher Edition

- Ongoing Assessment (in every lesson)
- Quick Practice (in every lesson)
- Portfolio Suggestions (p. 949)

Math Talk

- The Learning Classroom (p. 858)
- Math Talk in Action (pp. 783, 788, 805, 810, 817, 879, 904, 917, 932, 942, 943)
- Solve and Discuss (pp. 799, 806, 812, 817, 818, 826, 890, 922, 923, 928, 931)
- Student Pairs (pp. 820, 834, 835, 836, 838, 908, 931)
  Helping Partners (pp. 819, 910)
- Small Groups (p. 932)
- In Activities (pp. 784, 794, 830, 832, 842, 864, 872, 922)
- Scenarios (p. 820)

Review Opportunities

Homework and Remembering

- Review of recently taught topics
- Spiral Review

Teacher Edition

- Unit Review and Test (pp. 947–950)

Test Generator CD-ROM

- Custom Review Sheets

Unit 11 Teaching Resources

Differentiated Instruction

Individualizing Instruction		
Activities	Level	Frequency
	• Intervention • On Level • Challenge	All 3 in every lesson
Math Writing Prompts	Level	Frequency
	• Intervention • On Level • Challenge	All 3 in every lesson
Math Center Challenges	For advanced students	
	4 in every unit	

Reaching All Learners		
English Language Learners	Lessons	Pages
	1, 2, 3, 4, 5, 6, 7, 9, 10, 11, 12, 13, 14, 15, 16, 18, 19, 20, 21, 22	785, 793, 798, 804, 811, 816, 826, 843, 852, 860, 865, 870, 876, 889, 897, 914, 922, 929, 936, 943
Extra Help	Lessons	Pages
	1, 2, 4, 6, 7, 11, 12, 13, 15, 16, 18, 20, 21	784, 792, 805, 819, 825, 857, 864, 870, 871, 872, 887, 896, 914, 917, 932, 938
Special Needs	Lesson	Page
	9	842
Alternate Approach	Lessons	Pages
	3, 5, 9, 11, 15, 19, 20	799, 811, 842, 889, 922, 930

Strategies for English Language Learners

Present this problem to all students. Offer the different levels of support to meet students' levels of language proficiency.

Objective To familiarize students with the concept that fractions are equal parts of a whole.

Problem Write *fraction* on the board. Have students fold and cut a piece of paper into 4 equal parts, then shade 1 part.

Newcomer

- Say: **I have 4 equal parts. Together they make 1 whole.** Have students repeat. Hold up 1 part. Say: **This is 1 out of 4 equal parts.** Have students repeat.

Beginning

- Ask: **How many equal parts do you have?** 4 **Together, do they make 1 whole?** yes **How many parts did you shade?** 1 Write $\frac{1}{4}$. Say: **I shaded $\frac{1}{4}$.** Have students repeat.

Intermediate

- Hold up 1 piece. Ask: **Is this 1 out of 4 equal parts?** yes Write $\frac{1}{4}$. Ask: **Is this a whole number or a *fraction*?** fraction Say: **$\frac{1}{4}$ means 1 out of 4 __.** equal parts

Advanced

- Ask: **How many equal parts do you have?** 4 Write $\frac{1}{4}$. Ask: **The *fraction* $\frac{1}{4}$ means 1 out of 4 __.** equal parts

Connections

Social Studies Connection
Lesson 4, p. 808

Art Connections
Lesson 2, p. 796; Lesson 8, p. 840; Lesson 9, p. 848; Lesson 11, p. 862

Language Arts Connections
Lesson 7, p. 828; Lesson 18, p. 920

Math-to-Math Connection
Lesson 17, p. 912

Real-World Connection
Lesson 22, p. 946

Music Connection
Lesson 14, p. 884

Technology Connection
Lesson 20, p. 934

Science Connections
Lesson 6, p. 822; Lesson 10, p. 854

Literature Connections
Lesson 3, p. 802; Lesson 5, p. 814; Lesson 12, p. 868; Lesson 13, p. 874; Lesson 16, p. 900; Lesson 19, p. 926; Lesson 21, p. 940

Multicultural Connection
Lesson 15, p. 892

Putting Research into Practice for Unit 11

From Our Curriculum Research Project: Fractions

In this unit, students will learn about the meaning of fractions. They will see fractions as equal parts of a whole or a set. Students explore fractions in a variety of ways. They fold paper strips to make fractions and they shade fractions of a figure and a set. We have students start with the idea of a unit fraction and then continue with the idea that other fractions can be built from unit fractions.

Also in this unit, students are introduced to addition, subtraction, and comparisons of fractions. Students will rename fractions with different denominators so that they can be compared, added, and subtracted. Students will also write improper fractions as mixed numbers, using division with remainders to help them. Thinking of fractions as made up of unit fractions is key to conceptual understanding of all these.

–Karen Fuson, Author
Math Expressions

From Current Research: Fractions

Many researchers who have studied what students know about operations with fractions... recommend that instruction emphasize conceptual understanding from the beginning. More specifically, say these researchers, instruction should build on students' intuitive understanding of fractions and use objects or contexts that help students make sense of the operations. The rationale for that approach is that students need to understand the key ideas in order to have something to connect with procedural rules. For example, students need to understand why the sum of two fractions can be expressed as a single number only when the parts are of the same size. That understanding can lead them to see the need for constructing common denominators.

National Research Council. "Developing Proficiency with Whole Numbers." *Adding It Up: Helping Children Learn Mathematics.* Washington, D.C.: National Academy Press, 2001. 192.

Other Useful References: Fractions

Bezuk, N.D., and M. Bieck. "Current research on rational numbers and common fractions: Summary and implications for teachers." *Research Ideas for the Classroom: Middle Grades Mathematics.* Ed. D.T. Owens. New York: Macmillan, 1993. 118–136.

Mack, N.K. "Learning fractions with understanding: Building on informal knowledge." *Journal for Research in Mathematics Education,* 21, (1990): 16–32.

Peck, D.M., and S.M. Jencks. "Conceptual issues in the teaching and learning of fractions." *Journal for Research in Mathematics Education,* 12, 1981. 339–348.

Streefland, L. "Fractions: A realistic approach." *Rational numbers: An Integration of Research* Eds. T.P. Carpenter, E. Fennema, & T.A. Romberg. Hillsdale, NJ: Erlbaum, 1993. 289–325.

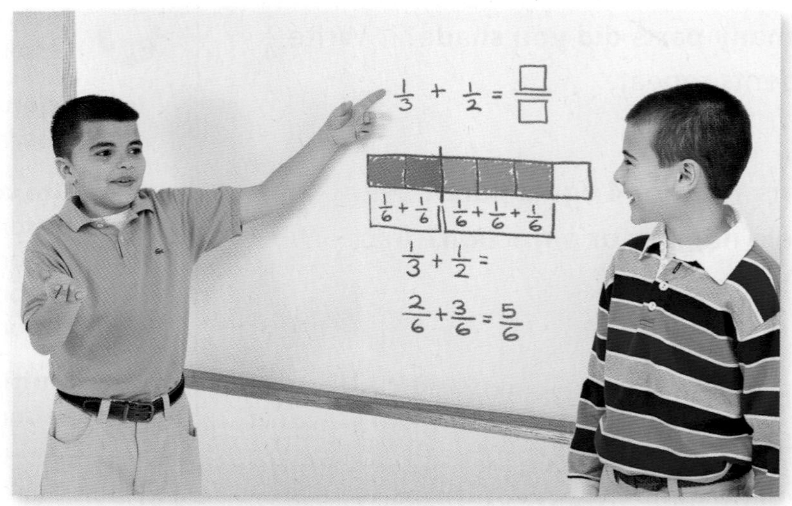

Math Expressions Vocabulary

As you teach this unit, check understanding of this term:

- fracture

See Glossary on pages T1–T17.

Getting Ready to Teach Unit 11

In this unit students continue to develop fraction concepts and relate them to probability concepts and decimals.

Meaning of Fractions

Fractions as Parts of a Whole

Lessons 1 and 7

Students will explore the meaning of a fraction as equal parts of a whole. The whole is divided into a number of equal parts. The number under the fraction bar tells how many equal parts the whole is divided into and is called the *denominator*. The number above the fraction bar tells how many parts we are talking about and is called the *numerator*. From the beginning, we show that unit fractions can be combined to form other fractions of a whole.

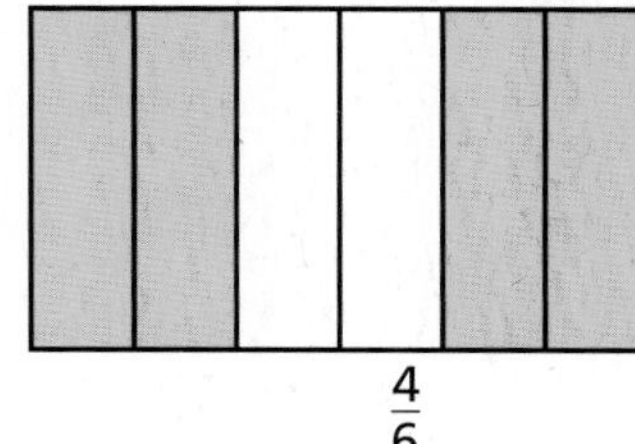

$\frac{4}{6}$

$$\frac{1}{6}+\frac{1}{6}+\frac{1}{6}+\frac{1}{6}=\frac{4}{6}$$

$$4 \times \frac{1}{6}=\frac{4}{6}$$

$\frac{1}{6}$ = one of 6 equal parts

It is also important that students understand that the size of a fractional part is relative to the size of the whole.

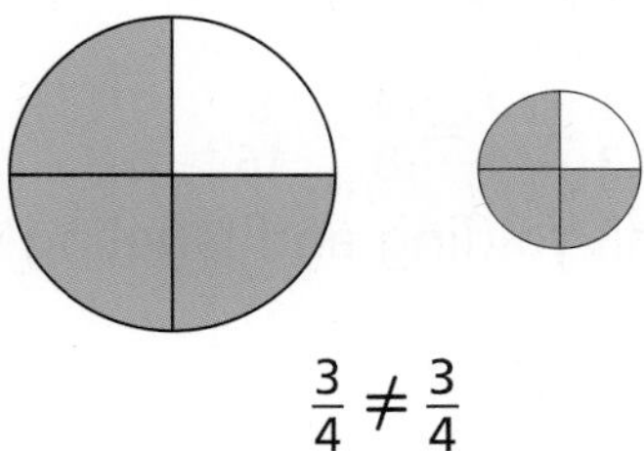

$$\frac{3}{4} \neq \frac{3}{4}$$

Fractions as Parts of a Set

Lesson 2

Students will also explore the meaning of fractions as parts of a set. To represent the fraction of the set of coins that are pennies in the example below, we can write two equivalent fractions.

What fraction of the coins are pennies?

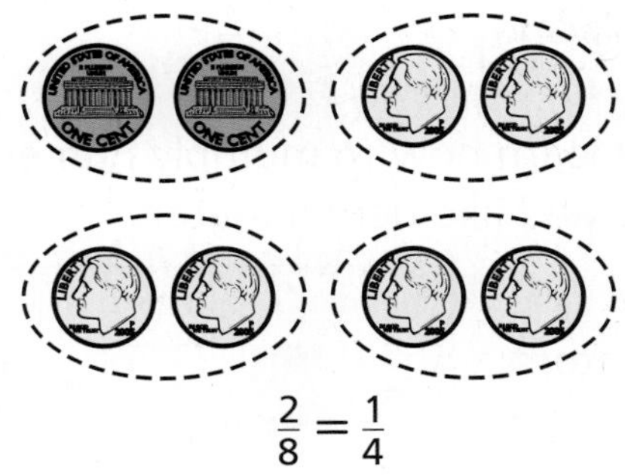

$$\frac{2}{8}=\frac{1}{4}$$

Fraction of a Set or Number

Lessons 3 and 6

Students will first find a unit fraction of a set or number and then find a non-unit fraction of a set or number. For example, in the problem below students first find $\frac{1}{6}$ of 12 by grouping the 12 objects into 6 groups of 2. Then they find that 2 groups of $\frac{1}{6}$ is 4 or $\frac{2}{6}$ of 12 = 4.

$\frac{1}{6}$ of 12 = 2 so $\frac{2}{6}$ of 12 = 4

Representation of Fractions Builds Understanding for Adding and Subtracting

Lessons 1, 2, and 3

We help students model a unit fraction, such as $\frac{1}{3}$ and $\frac{1}{4}$, using drawings, pictures, and strips of paper. They see fractions as equal parts of figures or sets. When we discuss fractions other than unit fractions, such as $\frac{2}{3}$ and $\frac{3}{4}$, we show the idea that these are the sum of unit fractions. For example, $\frac{3}{4} = \frac{1}{4} + \frac{1}{4} + \frac{1}{4}$ or $3 \times \frac{1}{4} = \frac{3}{4}$. Visualizing a non-unit fraction as a combination of unit fractions helps students when adding or subtracting to see that the parts we are talking about are combined or separated, but the number of equal parts stays the same.

Research has shown that many students have difficulty computing with fractions because they do not understand the underlying meaning of fractions. If students learn only algorithms for adding and subtracting fractions, studies show they may not be able to recall these algorithms later. Our visual, conceptual approach enables students to understand and explain fraction computation.

Working with Fractions

Finding Equivalent Fractions

Lessons 9, 10, 11, 12, and 13

Students explore equivalent fractions by making models of the same-sized whole strip. They start with folding equal strips into halves, fourths, eighths, and sixteenths. They write a chain of equivalent fractions:

$$\frac{1}{2} = \frac{2}{4} = \frac{4}{8} = \frac{8}{16}$$

For thirds, sixths, and twelfths, they follow this folding and labeling sequence and write the equivalent fraction chains.

$\frac{1}{3}$	$\frac{1}{3}$	$\frac{1}{3}$

$\frac{1}{6}$	$\frac{1}{6}$	$\frac{1}{6}$	$\frac{1}{6}$	$\frac{1}{6}$	$\frac{1}{6}$

$\frac{1}{12}$	$\frac{1}{12}$	$\frac{1}{12}$	$\frac{1}{12}$	$\frac{1}{12}$	$\frac{1}{12}$	$\frac{1}{12}$	$\frac{1}{12}$	$\frac{1}{12}$	$\frac{1}{12}$	$\frac{1}{12}$	$\frac{1}{12}$

They write the following equivalent fraction chains:

$$\frac{1}{3} = \frac{2}{6} = \frac{4}{12}$$

$$\frac{2}{3} = \frac{4}{6} = \frac{8}{12}$$

Comparing, Adding, and Subtracting Fractions

Lessons 4, 5, 14, 15, and 16

To compare, add, or subtract fractions, students learn how to multiply numerators and denominators to rename fractions. They find equivalent fractions and like denominators.

Students can now compare, add, or subtract the fractions, $\frac{1}{3}$ and $\frac{1}{4}$, using their common denominators to write equivalent fractions: $\frac{4}{12}$ and $\frac{3}{12}$.

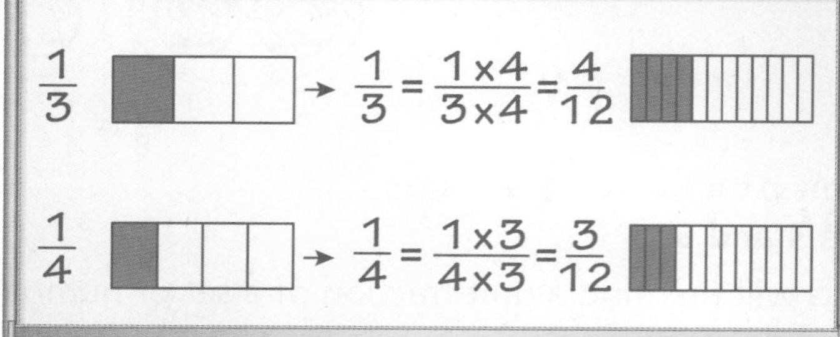

Students cut out and put together rows of the multiplication table to see many equivalent fractions for a given fraction. The column number tells them the common multiple to find each equivalent multiple.

$$\frac{2}{7} \overset{\times 2}{=} \frac{4}{14} \overset{\times 3}{=} \frac{6}{21} \overset{\times 4}{=} \frac{8}{28} \overset{\times 5}{=} \frac{10}{35} \overset{\times 6}{=} \frac{12}{42} \overset{\times 7}{=} \frac{14}{49} \overset{\times 8}{=} \frac{16}{56} \overset{\times 9}{=} \frac{18}{63} \overset{\times 10}{=} \frac{20}{70}$$

Students also add, subtract, and compare fractions on number lines.

Relate Fractions to Probability and Decimals

Probability

Lesson 8

In this unit students apply what they know about fractions to explore probability concepts.

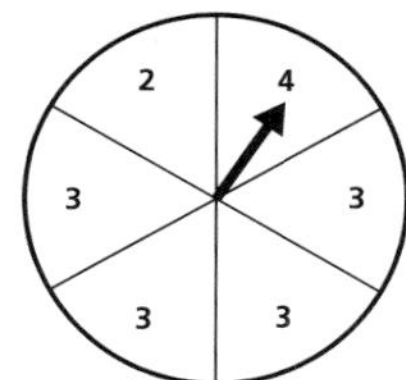

The probability of spinning a 3 is likely. There are 4 out of 6 or $\frac{4}{6}$ chances.

Decimals

Lesson 17

Students also discover the relationship between fractions and decimals using money.

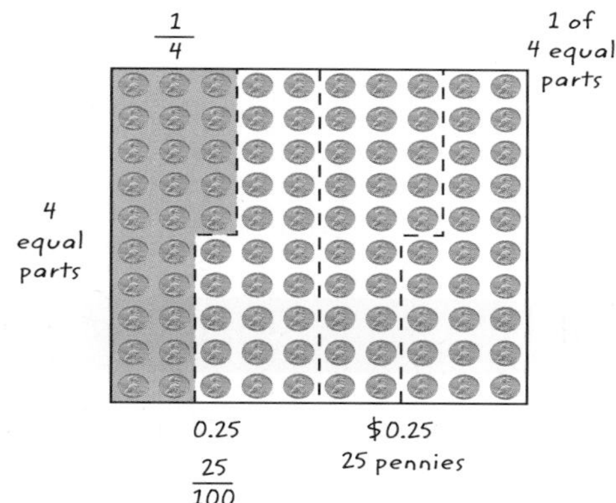

Problem Solving

In *Math Expressions* a research-based, algebraic problem-solving approach that focuses on problem types is used: understand the situation, represent the situation with a math drawing or an equation, solve the problem, and see that the answer makes sense. In this unit students solve problems involving fractions, probability, decimals, and division with remainders.

Representing Word Problems

Students using *Math Expressions* are taught a variety of ways to represent word problems. Some are conceptual in nature (making math drawings), while others are symbolic (writing equations). Students move from using math drawings to solving problems symbolically with equations. In this unit students use a variety of drawings to solve word problems.

Use Mathematical Processes

Lesson 22

The NCTM process skills of problem solving, reasoning and proof, communication, connections, and representation are interwoven through all lessons throughout the year. The last lesson of this unit allows students to extend their use of mathematical processes to other situations.

NCTM Process Skill	Activity and Goal
Representation	1: Make geometric designs. 2: Design a spinner. 4: Make a list to represent outcomes.
Communication	1: Share designs. 2: Discuss how to determine fairness of spinners. 3: Discuss number of colors needed to color a map. 5: Discuss the process of elimination.
Connections	1: Math and Art: Geometric Figures in Designs
Reasoning and Proof	2: Analyze spinners to determine fairness or probability. 3: Find the fewest number of colors needed to color a map. 4: Analyze to be sure all ways are represented. 5: Use process of elimination to find the correct answer.
Problem Solving	2: Design a spinner to meet given probability requirements. 3: Solve spatial color problems. 4: Solve a problem by making a list. 5: Solve a problem through process of elimination.

1 Teaching the Lesson

Activity 1

Understand Unit Fractions

 15 MINUTES

Goal: Use fraction strips to explore unit fractions.

Materials: Student Activity Book or Hardcover Book p. 393 and Activity Workbook p. 177 (includes special format), blank transparency and overhead projector (optional)

 **NCTM Standards:**
Number and Operations
Representation

 **Class Management**

You may wish to use an overhead transparency instead of drawing the diagrams on the board.

Teaching Note

Language and Vocabulary Students often have trouble remembering which name goes with each part of the fraction. You might suggest they think of the first letter of *denominator:* the **d**enominator is the number that is **d**own, or the number of pieces that the whole is **d**ivided into. To help students remember that the numerator is the top number, look at the u in numerator. The number that is **up** is the n**u**merator. Be sure that **English learners** participate in this important verbal-visual activity.

▶ The Meaning of Fractions WHOLE CLASS

Write the following situation on the board.

Shaundra had a long ribbon. She divided the ribbon into three equal pieces to make bracelets for her friends.

Tell students you are going to make a drawing to show how Shaundra divided her ribbon. Draw the following on the board.

1 whole

Use your drawing to introduce the idea of a *fraction.*

- I drew a long bar to represent the ribbon. I labeled it "1 whole" because it represents one whole ribbon. I divided the whole into three equal parts for the three bracelets.
- We can use fractions to name parts of wholes. Does anyone know what fraction of the whole each part of the ribbon is? $\frac{1}{3}$

Label each part $\frac{1}{3}$, and read the fraction aloud as *one third.* Tell students that Shaundra used one third of the whole ribbon to make each bracelet. Shade one of the parts, and tell students that you have shaded one third.

1 whole

$\frac{1}{3}$	$\frac{1}{3}$	$\frac{1}{3}$

Leave this drawing on the board for the next activity. Discuss the following points:

- The bottom number of the fraction, 3, tells how many equal parts the whole is divided into.
- The top number, 1, tells how many of the equal parts we are talking about.

Explain that the top number of a fraction is called the *numerator* and the bottom number is called the *denominator*. Use these terms to label the fraction.

1 ⟵ numerator
3 ⟵ denominator

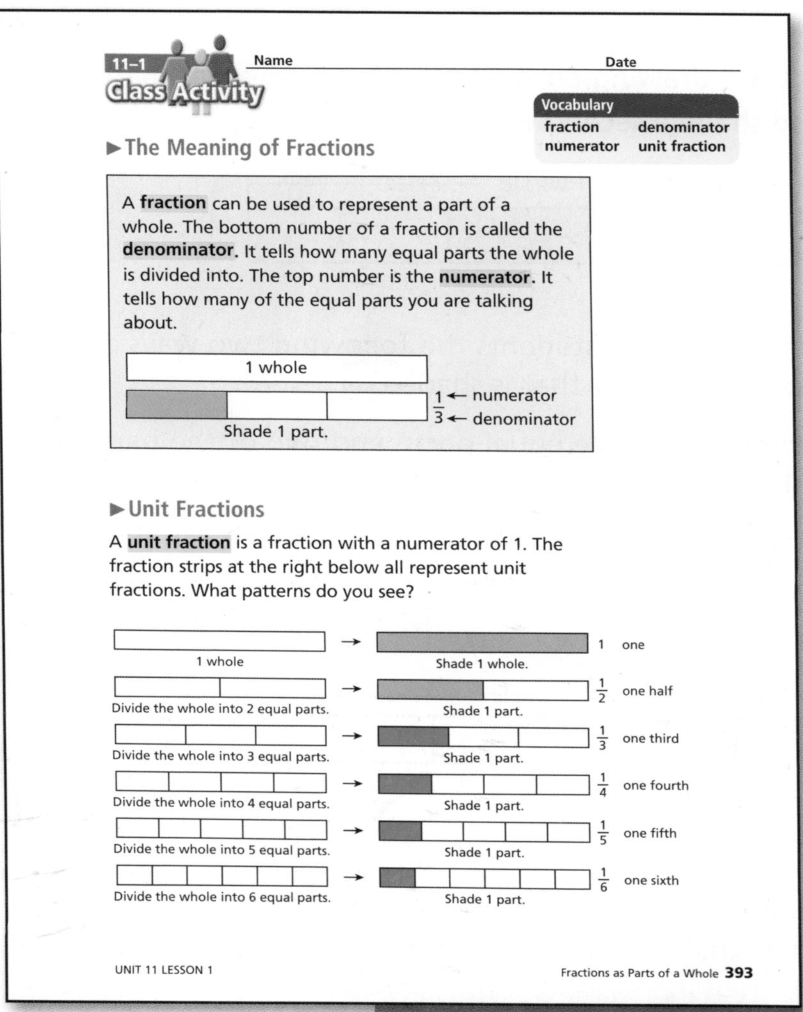

11–1 Class Activity

Name Date

Vocabulary
fraction denominator
numerator unit fraction

► The Meaning of Fractions

A **fraction** can be used to represent a part of a whole. The bottom number of a fraction is called the **denominator.** It tells how many equal parts the whole is divided into. The top number is the **numerator.** It tells how many of the equal parts you are talking about.

1 whole

Shade 1 part. 1 ← numerator, 3 ← denominator

► Unit Fractions

A **unit fraction** is a fraction with a numerator of 1. The fraction strips at the right below all represent unit fractions. What patterns do you see?

1 whole	→	Shade 1 whole.	1	one
Divide the whole into 2 equal parts.	→	Shade 1 part.	$\frac{1}{2}$	one half
Divide the whole into 3 equal parts.	→	Shade 1 part.	$\frac{1}{3}$	one third
Divide the whole into 4 equal parts.	→	Shade 1 part.	$\frac{1}{4}$	one fourth
Divide the whole into 5 equal parts.	→	Shade 1 part.	$\frac{1}{5}$	one fifth
Divide the whole into 6 equal parts.	→	Shade 1 part.	$\frac{1}{6}$	one sixth

UNIT 11 LESSON 1 Fractions as Parts of a Whole **393**

Student Activity Book page 393

► Unit Fractions WHOLE CLASS

Explain that a fraction with 1 as the numerator, such as $\frac{1}{3}$, is called a *unit fraction.* Ask students for other examples of unit fraction $\frac{1}{2}$, $\frac{1}{4}$, and so on

Have students look at the fraction strips showing unit fractions on Student Book page 393. Explain that the strip in the top row shows the whole. Point out that the number 1 is used to represent 1 whole. In each of the following rows, students need to divide the strip into equal parts, and then shade one part. The unit fraction representing the shaded part is given in both numbers and words.

Have students explain the patterns they see in the fraction strips. See **Math Talk in Action** in the side column for a sample classroom discussion.

Teaching Note

Math Background When working with fraction bars, strips, and other region models for fractions as parts of wholes, some students may have difficulty seeing the whole. For instance, some students think, "I see 1 shaded part and 2 parts that are not shaded, so the fraction is $\frac{1}{2}$."

In this fraction lesson, we always show the divided whole first without shading, and then show it again with a fractional part shaded. This helps students see that the fractional part is "embedded" in the whole.

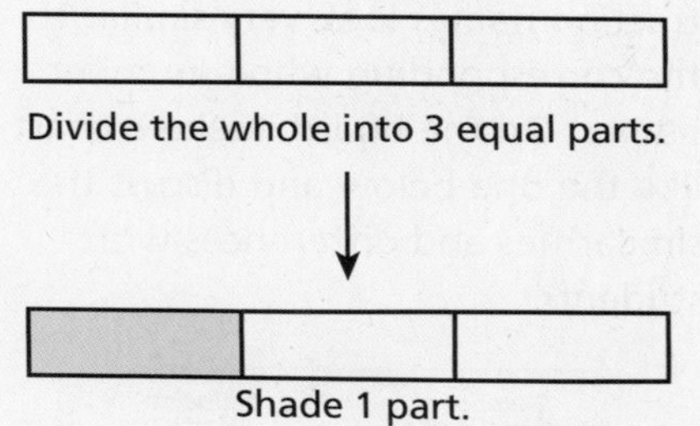

Math Talk in Action

What patterns do you see in the fraction strips?

Eli: All the fractions have a numerator of 1.

Yes, all the fractions are unit fractions.

Ben: The denominators increase by 1 with each row.

Correct, this is because the number of parts increases by 1 with each row.

Trina: The smaller the part is, the large[r] the denominator of the unit fraction is.

Yes, the larger the denominator is, th[e] smaller the part is. This is because th[e] more parts you divide the whole int[o] the smaller each part must be.

Activity 2

Build Fractions from Unit Fractions

15 MINUTES

Goal: Use fraction bars to relate unit fractions to non-unit fractions.

Materials: Student Activity Book or Hardcover Book p. 394 and Activity Workbook p. 177 (includes special format), MathBoard materials, blank transparency and overhead projector (optional)

NCTM Standards:
Number and Operations
Representation

Differentiated Instruction

Extra Help Some students might have difficulty reading and writing fraction names, especially since some fraction names look very similar to the corresponding whole-number names. On the board, make a chart like the one below and discuss the similarities and differences with students.

Number of Equal Parts	Name of Parts
two	halves
three	thirds
four	fourths
five	fifths
six	sixths
seven	sevenths
eight	eighths
nine	ninths
ten	tenths

int out that the words *fourths*, hs, *sevenths*, and *tenths* are ed just by attaching the suffix the corresponding whole- r name. Ask students to how the other listed fraction e different from these. Pay ention to the word *halves*, it appears somewhat the singular form of *half*.

e
e
o,

▸ Discuss and Introduce Building Fractions from Unit Fractions

WHOLE CLASS

Math Talk

Refer students to the $\frac{1}{3}$ drawing on the board (or on the transparency) from Activity 1 and shade a second equal part.

1 whole

$\frac{1}{3}$	$\frac{1}{3}$	$\frac{1}{3}$

By asking questions, elicit from students the following two ways of representing the part of the bar that is shaded.

- The whole is divided into three equal parts, and two of the parts are shaded, so the shaded part can be represented by the fraction $\frac{2}{3}$.
- The shaded part is two of the $\frac{1}{3}$ parts put together, so it can be expressed as $\frac{1}{3} + \frac{1}{3}$.

Label the drawing as shown below.

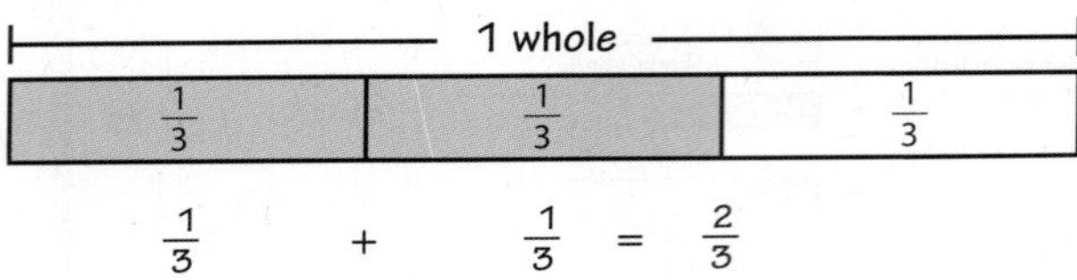

Now, shade all three parts of the fraction bar. Again, elicit two ways of representing the part that is shaded—as a single fraction and as a sum of unit fractions.

- For the fraction $\frac{3}{3}$, the whole bar is shaded. This gives us another way to represent the shaded part. What number can we write to represent 1 whole? 1

1 whole

$\frac{1}{3}$	$\frac{1}{3}$	$\frac{1}{3}$

$\frac{1}{3} + \frac{1}{3} + \frac{1}{3} = \frac{3}{3}$

Point out that the fractions $\frac{2}{3}$ and $\frac{3}{3}$ were built by adding unit fractions.

Explain that we can also show the shaded part of each strip using multiplication.

- For all the fraction strips, we showed the shaded part by adding $\frac{1}{3}$ repeatedly. For the second bar, how many one thirds did we add? 2 What multiplication equation can we write to show this? $2 \times \frac{1}{3} = \frac{2}{3}$

Ask a volunteer to write the part shaded on each strip as a product of a

Work through another example with students. Write on the board (or overhead transparency) as students work along with you on their MathBoards. Draw a bar and divide it into four equal parts. To make dividing the bar easier, you might suggest that students first divide the bar in half and then divide each half in half.

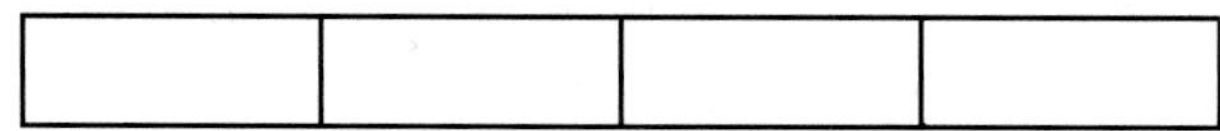

- How many equal parts is the bar divided into? 4 What part of the whole does each part represent? $\frac{1}{4}$

Have students write $\frac{1}{4}$ in each of the four equal parts. Shade one of the parts. Ask students how much is shaded, and then write $\frac{1}{4}$ on the board.

$\frac{1}{4}$	$\frac{1}{4}$	$\frac{1}{4}$	$\frac{1}{4}$

$\frac{1}{4}$

Shade a second part. Ask students what addition equation shows how much is shaded. Write the equation on the board. Then ask what multiplication equation shows how much is shaded and write it on the board.

$\frac{1}{4}$	$\frac{1}{4}$	$\frac{1}{4}$	$\frac{1}{4}$

$\frac{1}{4} + \frac{1}{4} = \frac{2}{4}$

$2 \times \frac{1}{4} = \frac{2}{4}$

Shade a third part, and elicit and record both an addition and multiplication equation.

$\frac{1}{4}$	$\frac{1}{4}$	$\frac{1}{4}$	$\frac{1}{4}$

$\frac{1}{4} + \frac{1}{4} + \frac{1}{4} = \frac{3}{4}$

$3 \times \frac{1}{4} = \frac{3}{4}$

Shade the last part, and elicit and record both an addition and multiplication equation.

$\frac{1}{4}$	$\frac{1}{4}$	$\frac{1}{4}$	$\frac{1}{4}$

$\frac{1}{4} + \frac{1}{4} + \frac{1}{4} + \frac{1}{4} = \frac{4}{4}$ or 1

$4 \times \frac{1}{4} = \frac{4}{4}$ or 1

- For the fraction $\frac{4}{4}$, the whole bar is shaded. This gives us another way to represent the shaded part. What number can we write to represent 1 whole? 1

Activity continued ▶

Teaching Note

Critical Thinking Students will begin to study equivalent fractions in Lesson 9, but you can introduce the concept by giving them a critical thinking exercise like the following.

Draw the two pictures below on the board, one above the other.

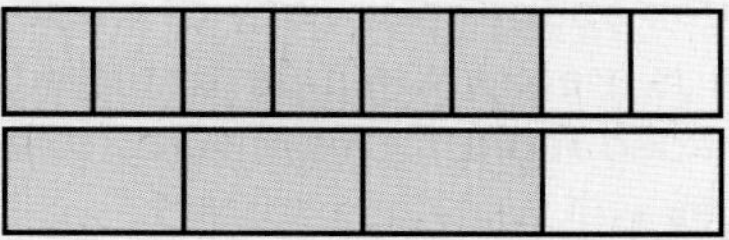

Ask students to describe how the pictures are alike and how they are different. Possible answer: Alike – The rectangles are both the same size, and the same amount of each one is shaded. Different – The top rectangle is divided into eight equal parts, six of the parts are shaded, so six eighths of the top rectangle is shaded. The bottom rectangle is divided into four equal parts, three of the parts are shaded, so three fourths of the bottom rectangle is shaded. Lead students to conclude that the fractions $\frac{6}{8}$ and $\frac{3}{4}$ name the same amount.

English Language Learners

Write *equal parts* on the board. Draw these 2 rectangles:

A  B 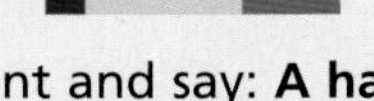

- **Beginning** Point and say: **A has 3 *equal parts*.** Ask: **Does B have *equal parts*?** no
- **Intermediate** Ask: **Which rectangle has *equal parts*?** A
- **Advanced** Have students describe the parts of each shape.

Teaching Note

Watch For! *Math Expressions* emphasizes the concept that any fraction is the sum of unit fractions as a means of helping students avoid two common errors related to fractions.

- When looking at a drawing with a fractional part shaded, students who understand this concept will first think of the unit fraction that represents each part, and then think about how many of these parts are put together to form the shaded region. This ensures that they will write the correct denominator and avoid the common error of writing

$$\frac{\text{number of shaded parts}}{\text{number of parts not shaded}}.$$

- Students who understand this concept have a much easier time understanding why we add only the numerators when we add like fractions. For example, they will see $\frac{1}{4} + \frac{1}{4}$ as two $\frac{1}{4}$ parts put together, which is $\frac{2}{4}$. This helps avoid the common error of adding the numerators and also adding the denominators to obtain $\frac{2}{8}$.

Help students make generalizations about fractions that are equal to 1.

- Why is any fraction with the same numerator and denominator equal to 1? Possible explanation: If you make a fraction bar for the fraction, then all the parts will be shaded. This means the whole bar is shaded.

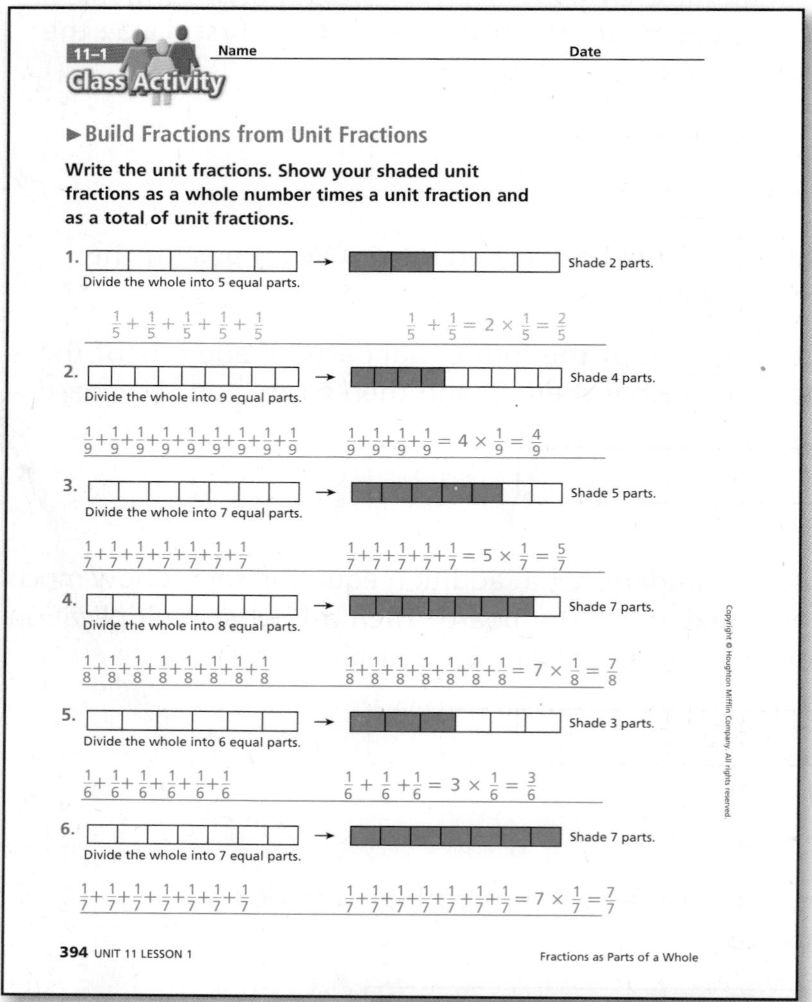

11–1 Class Activity Name Date

▶ Build Fractions from Unit Fractions

Write the unit fractions. Show your shaded unit fractions as a whole number times a unit fraction and as a total of unit fractions.

1. Divide the whole into 5 equal parts. → Shade 2 parts.
$\frac{1}{5}+\frac{1}{5}+\frac{1}{5}+\frac{1}{5}+\frac{1}{5}$ $\frac{1}{5}+\frac{1}{5}=2\times\frac{1}{5}=\frac{2}{5}$

2. Divide the whole into 9 equal parts. → Shade 4 parts.
$\frac{1}{9}+\frac{1}{9}+\frac{1}{9}+\frac{1}{9}+\frac{1}{9}+\frac{1}{9}+\frac{1}{9}+\frac{1}{9}+\frac{1}{9}$ $\frac{1}{9}+\frac{1}{9}+\frac{1}{9}+\frac{1}{9}=4\times\frac{1}{9}=\frac{4}{9}$

3. Divide the whole into 7 equal parts. → Shade 5 parts.
$\frac{1}{7}+\frac{1}{7}+\frac{1}{7}+\frac{1}{7}+\frac{1}{7}+\frac{1}{7}+\frac{1}{7}$ $\frac{1}{7}+\frac{1}{7}+\frac{1}{7}+\frac{1}{7}+\frac{1}{7}=5\times\frac{1}{7}=\frac{5}{7}$

4. Divide the whole into 8 equal parts. → Shade 7 parts.
$\frac{1}{8}+\frac{1}{8}+\frac{1}{8}+\frac{1}{8}+\frac{1}{8}+\frac{1}{8}+\frac{1}{8}+\frac{1}{8}$ $\frac{1}{8}+\frac{1}{8}+\frac{1}{8}+\frac{1}{8}+\frac{1}{8}+\frac{1}{8}+\frac{1}{8}=7\times\frac{1}{8}=\frac{7}{8}$

5. Divide the whole into 6 equal parts. → Shade 3 parts.
$\frac{1}{6}+\frac{1}{6}+\frac{1}{6}+\frac{1}{6}+\frac{1}{6}+\frac{1}{6}$ $\frac{1}{6}+\frac{1}{6}+\frac{1}{6}=3\times\frac{1}{6}=\frac{3}{6}$

6. Divide the whole into 7 equal parts. → Shade 7 parts.
$\frac{1}{7}+\frac{1}{7}+\frac{1}{7}+\frac{1}{7}+\frac{1}{7}+\frac{1}{7}+\frac{1}{7}$ $\frac{1}{7}+\frac{1}{7}+\frac{1}{7}+\frac{1}{7}+\frac{1}{7}+\frac{1}{7}+\frac{1}{7}=7\times\frac{1}{7}=\frac{7}{7}$

394 UNIT 11 LESSON 1 Fractions as Parts of a Whole

Student Activity Book page 394

▶ Build Fractions from Unit Fractions INDIVIDUALS

Have students complete exercises 1–6 on Student Book page 394, and then discuss the answers. Some students may find it useful to label each part of the divided bar with the appropriate unit fraction. Then have students look back at all the answers.

- Look at the numerator of each fraction and the number of unit fractions you added together or the whole number you multiplied by. How are they related? The numerator is the number of unit fractions added together and the same as the whole number you multiplied by.

Fractions of Wholes

▶ Fractions as Part of a Whole WHOLE CLASS

Have students look at exercise 7 on Student Book page 395.

- What is the whole in this problem? a rectangle How many equal parts is the whole divided into? 8 What fraction shows 1 whole divided into 8 equal parts? $\frac{8}{8}$ Have students then shade 3 parts in the second drawing. In the second picture, how many parts are shaded? 3 So what fraction of the rectangular region is shaded? $\frac{3}{8}$
- How can we show the shaded part by adding unit fractions or multiplying a whole number by a unit fraction? Each small rectangle is $\frac{1}{8}$. Because three rectangles are shaded, the shaded part is $\frac{1}{8} + \frac{1}{8} + \frac{1}{8}$, which is $3 \times \frac{1}{8} = \frac{3}{8}$.

Have students complete exercises 7–12, and then discuss the answers.

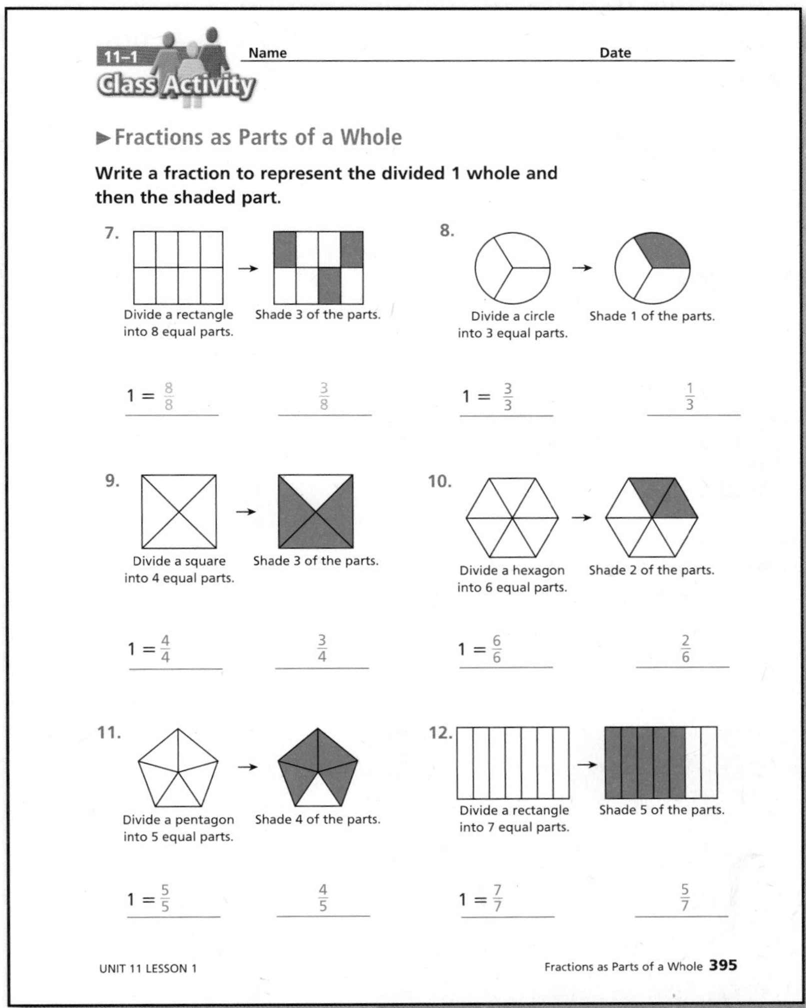

11–1 Class Activity Name Date

▶ Fractions as Parts of a Whole

Write a fraction to represent the divided 1 whole and then the shaded part.

7. Divide a rectangle into 8 equal parts. → Shade 3 of the parts.
$1 = \frac{8}{8}$ $\frac{3}{8}$

8. Divide a circle into 3 equal parts. → Shade 1 of the parts.
$1 = \frac{3}{3}$ $\frac{1}{3}$

9. Divide a square into 4 equal parts. → Shade 3 of the parts.
$1 = \frac{4}{4}$ $\frac{3}{4}$

10. Divide a hexagon into 6 equal parts. → Shade 2 of the parts.
$1 = \frac{6}{6}$ $\frac{2}{6}$

11. Divide a pentagon into 5 equal parts. → Shade 4 of the parts.
$1 = \frac{5}{5}$ $\frac{4}{5}$

12. Divide a rectangle into 7 equal parts. → Shade 5 of the parts.
$1 = \frac{7}{7}$ $\frac{5}{7}$

UNIT 11 LESSON 1 Fractions as Parts of a Whole 395

Student Activity Book page 395

 15 MINUTES

Goal: Use fractions to describe parts of a whole.

Materials: Student Activity Book or Hardcover Book pp. 395–396, and Activity Workbook pp. 179–180 (includes special format)

 **NCTM Standards:**
Number and Operations
Representation

Differentiated Instruction

Advanced Learners Give students a set of pattern blocks. Have them arrange the blocks to show as many fractional relationships as they can among the blocks.

For instance, two red trapezoids together completely cover the yellow hexagon. So if the yellow hexagon is called one whole, then the red trapezoid is one half. Similarly the blue parallelogram is one third of the hexagon, and the green triangle is one sixth.

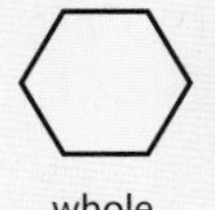
whole

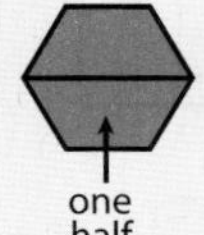
one half

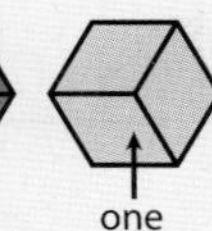
one third

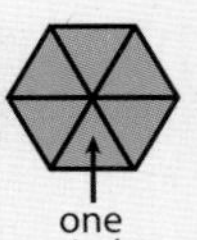
one sixth

Activity continued ▶

1 Teaching the Lesson (continued)

Math Talk in Action

Sunil: I think that the Penguin's drawing is right. There are three parts and he shaded one of them. Isn't that one third?

Heather: It's only one third if the parts are equal, isn't it?

Martin: That's right. And those parts don't look equal, do they?

Yun Mi: No, they're not equal. Look at the part that the Penguin shaded. The line on one side goes from corner to corner on the square. That makes half the square.

Andre: Right! And those other two parts are half of a half. That makes them smaller than the part that the Penguin shaded.

Taneeka: So how do you fix it to make one third?

Roberto: I think you have to draw the parts a different way.

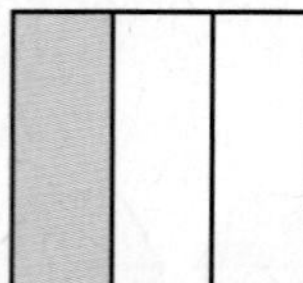

Ongoing Assessment

Ask questions such as the following:

- What is a fraction?
- What is the meaning of the top number in a fraction? the bottom number?
- How would you make a picture to show one ninth of a circle?
- How can you name the shaded part of this whole?

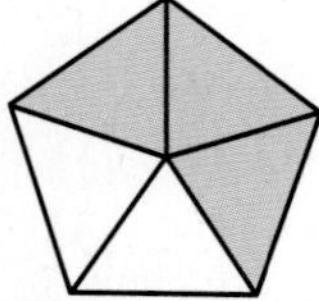

After discussing exercise 9, you might ask students if they can think of another way of dividing and shading a square to show $\frac{3}{4}$.

Next, have students complete exercises 13–16, and choose students to present their answers. For exercises 13–15, select students who divided the shapes in different ways. Make sure students are dividing the regions into parts that are approximately equal.

For exercise 16, be sure students understand that the size of the fractional part is relative to the size of the whole. In this exercise, $\frac{1}{4}$ of the large square is not equal to $\frac{1}{4}$ of the small square because the wholes are not of equal size. To reinforce this concept, draw two circles of different sizes, have volunteers shade $\frac{1}{2}$ of each, and compare the sizes of the parts shaded. Then do the same with two rectangles of different sizes by having volunteers shade $\frac{2}{3}$ of each.

Finally, read and discuss the letter from the Puzzled Penguin. Encourage students not only to explain why the drawing is incorrect, but also to suggest a way to correct it. See the **Math Talk in Action** in the side column page for a sample classroom discussion.

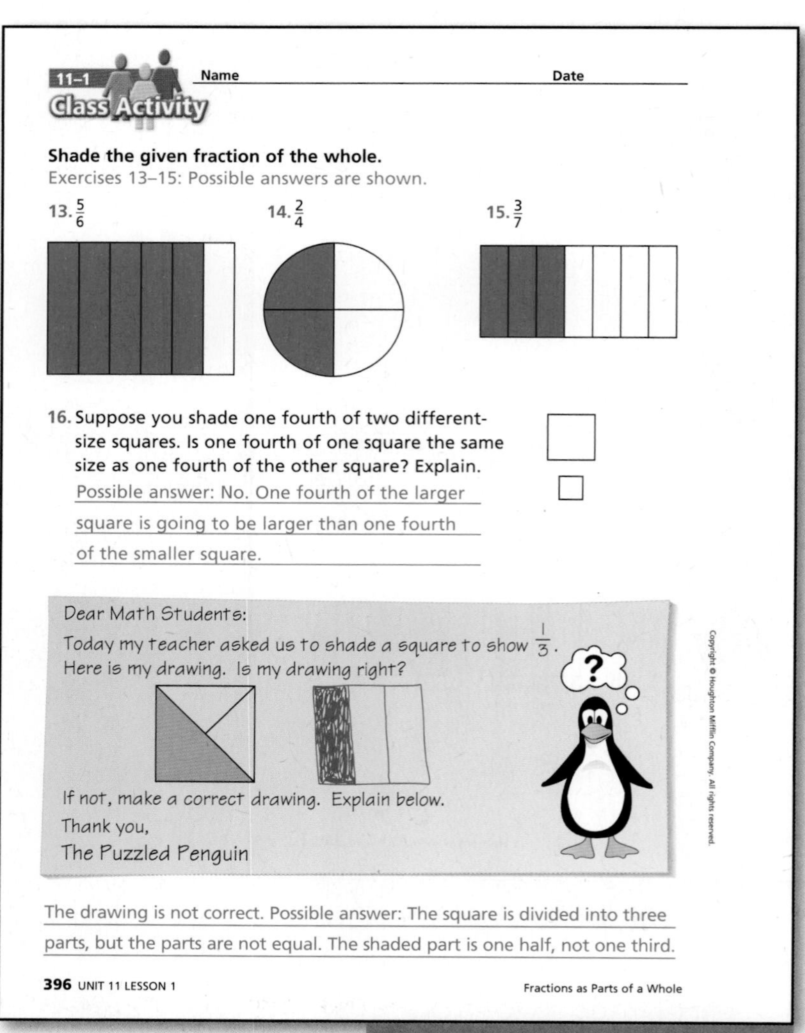

11-1 Class Activity Name ______ Date ______

Shade the given fraction of the whole.

Exercises 13–15: Possible answers are shown.

13. $\frac{5}{6}$ 14. $\frac{2}{4}$ 15. $\frac{3}{7}$

16. Suppose you shade one fourth of two different-size squares. Is one fourth of one square the same size as one fourth of the other square? Explain.

Possible answer: No. One fourth of the larger square is going to be larger than one fourth of the smaller square.

Dear Math Students:

Today my teacher asked us to shade a square to show $\frac{1}{3}$. Here is my drawing. Is my drawing right?

If not, make a correct drawing. Explain below.

Thank you,

The Puzzled Penguin

The drawing is not correct. Possible answer: The square is divided into three parts, but the parts are not equal. The shaded part is one half, not one third.

Student Activity Book page 396

2 Going Further

Differentiated Instruction

Intervention — Activity Card 11-1

Folding Fractions — Activity Card 11-1

Work: In small groups

Use:

- Crayons or colored pencils

1. **Work Together** Fold and color a paper model for each fraction listed below.

   $\frac{1}{4}$ $\frac{3}{4}$ $\frac{2}{4}$ $\frac{2}{3}$ $\frac{1}{6}$ $\frac{5}{6}$ $\frac{1}{8}$ $\frac{4}{8}$

2. The model below shows the fraction $\frac{1}{3}$.
   Think How can you use the model to show $\frac{2}{6}$?
   Fold the paper in half so that each column has two sections.

3. Compare your results with other groups.

Unit 11, Lesson 1

Activity Note Adjusting a model to represent related fractions will help students understand fractions. For example, fourths divided in half can show eighths.

Math Writing Prompt

Explain Your Thinking Which is bigger: $\frac{1}{5}$ of a square, or $\frac{1}{6}$ of the same square? How do you know?

Software Support

Warm Up 5.04

On Level — Activity Card 11-1

Fill All Four — Activity Card 11-1

Work: In pairs

Use:

- Two sets of pattern blocks (2 hexagons, 48 triangles, 16 trapezoids, 24 parallelograms)
- TRB M141 (Spinner F)
- Paper clips

1. **On Your Own** Trace four hexagons on a sheet of paper. Then work with your partner to set up your spinner like the one shown at the right.

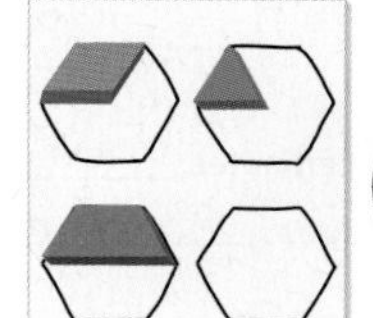

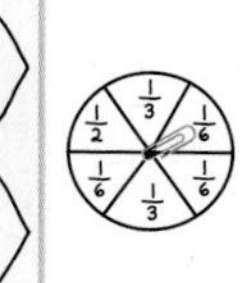

2. Take turns spinning the spinner. For each spin, place a pattern block on one of your hexagons according to the rules listed below.

   $\frac{1}{6}$ = triangle $\frac{1}{3}$ = parallelogram $\frac{1}{2}$ = trapezoid

3. Be careful where you place each block. Once a block is placed, it cannot be removed. The first player to fill all four hexagons wins!

Unit 11, Lesson 1

Activity Note Extend the activity by having students write the sum of the fractions represented by the hexagon they complete.

Math Writing Prompt

Look for a Pattern If $\frac{1}{8}$ of a figure is shaded, what part is not shaded? What if $\frac{2}{8}$ are shaded? $\frac{3}{8}$? What is the pattern? Explain how you found the pattern rule.

Software Support

Fraction Action: Fraction Flare Up, Level B

Challenge — Activity Card 11-1

Grid Paper Fractions — Activity Card 11-1

Work: In small groups

Use:

- TRB M31 (Centimeter-Grid Paper)
- Scissors

1. Cut out several 4-unit by 4-unit squares from the grid paper.
2. **Work Together** Cut one square into two identical halves. Three possible answers are shown below. Find as many ways as possible to make two identical halves.

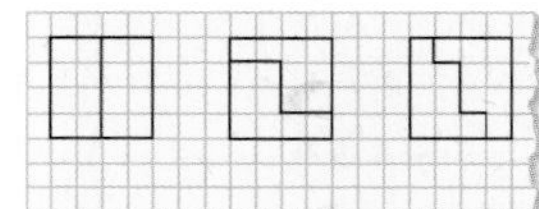

3. Now repeat the activity. This time, divide the squares into identical fourths.
4. **Analyze** How can you be sure the fractional parts are identical? Each part has the same shape and an equal number of squares.

Unit 11, Lesson 1

Activity Note Be sure that students understand that they may only cut the squares along the grid lines.

Math Writing Prompt

Investigate Math What do you think the fraction $\frac{5}{4}$ means? Draw a picture to explain your thinking.

Software Support

Course II: Module 2: Unit 3: Fractional Parts

3 Homework and Spiral Review

11-1 Homework **Goal:** Additional Practice

This Homework page provides practice in representing fractions.

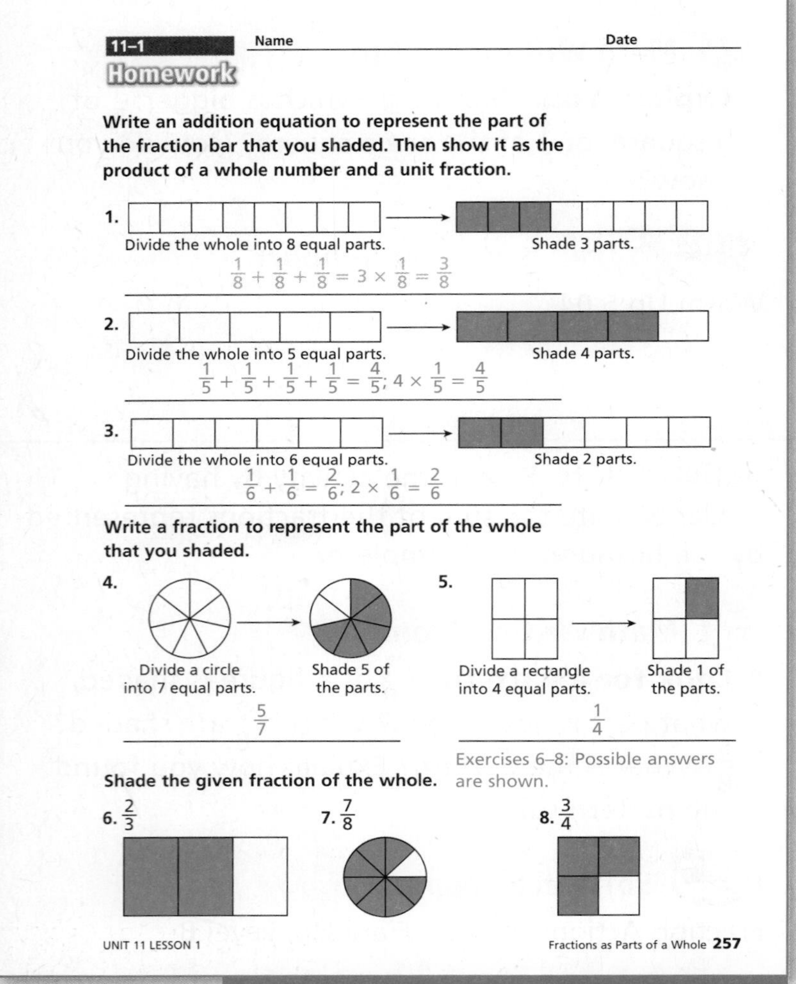

11–1 Homework Name Date

Write an addition equation to represent the part of the fraction bar that you shaded. Then show it as the product of a whole number and a unit fraction.

1. Divide the whole into 8 equal parts. → Shade 3 parts.
$\frac{1}{8} + \frac{1}{8} + \frac{1}{8} = 3 \times \frac{1}{8} = \frac{3}{8}$

2. Divide the whole into 5 equal parts. → Shade 4 parts.
$\frac{1}{5} + \frac{1}{5} + \frac{1}{5} + \frac{1}{5} = \frac{4}{5}; 4 \times \frac{1}{5} = \frac{4}{5}$

3. Divide the whole into 6 equal parts. → Shade 2 parts.
$\frac{1}{6} + \frac{1}{6} = \frac{2}{6}; 2 \times \frac{1}{6} = \frac{2}{6}$

Write a fraction to represent the part of the whole that you shaded.

4. Divide a circle into 7 equal parts. → Shade 5 of the parts.
$\frac{5}{7}$

5. Divide a rectangle into 4 equal parts. → Shade 1 of the parts.
$\frac{1}{4}$

Shade the given fraction of the whole. Exercises 6–8: Possible answers are shown.

6. $\frac{2}{3}$

7. $\frac{7}{8}$

8. $\frac{3}{4}$

UNIT 11 LESSON 1 Fractions as Parts of a Whole **257**

Homework and Remembering page 257

11-1 Remembering **Goal:** Spiral Review

This Remembering page would be appropriate anytime after today's lesson.

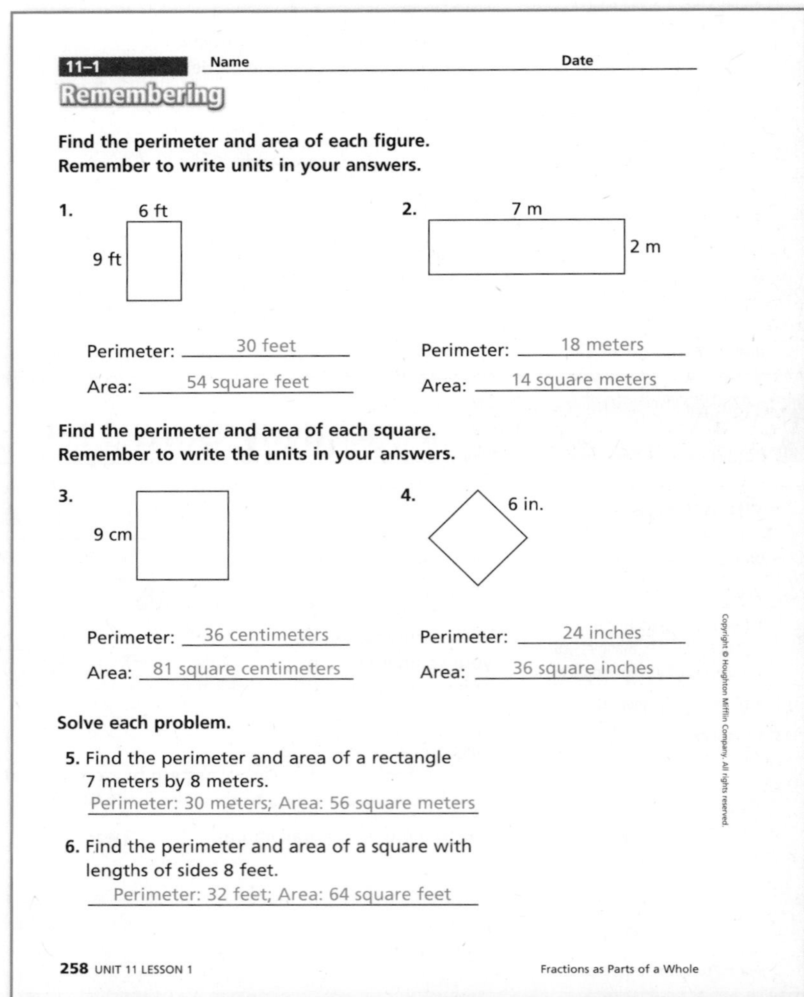

11–1 Remembering Name Date

Find the perimeter and area of each figure. Remember to write units in your answers.

1. 6 ft by 9 ft
Perimeter: 30 feet
Area: 54 square feet

2. 7 m by 2 m
Perimeter: 18 meters
Area: 14 square meters

Find the perimeter and area of each square. Remember to write the units in your answers.

3. 9 cm
Perimeter: 36 centimeters
Area: 81 square centimeters

4. 6 in.
Perimeter: 24 inches
Area: 36 square inches

Solve each problem.

5. Find the perimeter and area of a rectangle 7 meters by 8 meters.
Perimeter: 30 meters; Area: 56 square meters

6. Find the perimeter and area of a square with lengths of sides 8 feet.
Perimeter: 32 feet; Area: 64 square feet

258 UNIT 11 LESSON 1 Fractions as Parts of a Whole

Homework and Remembering page 258

Home and School Connection

Family Letter Have children take home the Family Letter on Student Book page 397. A Spanish translation of this letter is on the following page. This letter explains how the concept of fractions is developed in *Math Expressions.* It gives parents and guardians a better understanding of the learning that goes on in math class and creates a bridge between school and home.

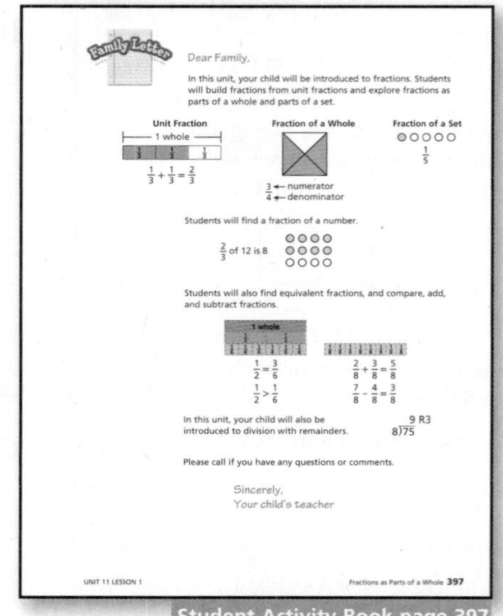

Family Letter

Dear Family,

In this unit, your child will be introduced to fractions. Students will build fractions from unit fractions and explore fractions as parts of a whole and parts of a set.

Unit Fraction — Fraction of a Whole — Fraction of a Set

$\frac{1}{3} + \frac{1}{3} = \frac{2}{3}$ — 3 ← numerator, 4 ← denominator — $\frac{1}{5}$

Students will find a fraction of a number.

$\frac{2}{3}$ of 12 is 8

Students will also find equivalent fractions, and compare, add, and subtract fractions.

$\frac{1}{2} = \frac{3}{6}$ $\frac{1}{2} > \frac{1}{6}$ $\frac{2}{8} + \frac{3}{8} = \frac{5}{8}$ $\frac{7}{8} - \frac{4}{8} = \frac{3}{8}$

In this unit, your child will also be introduced to division with remainders. 9 R3 8)75

Please call if you have any questions or comments.

Sincerely,
Your child's teacher

UNIT 11 LESSON 1 Fractions as Parts of a Whole 397

Student Activity Book page 397

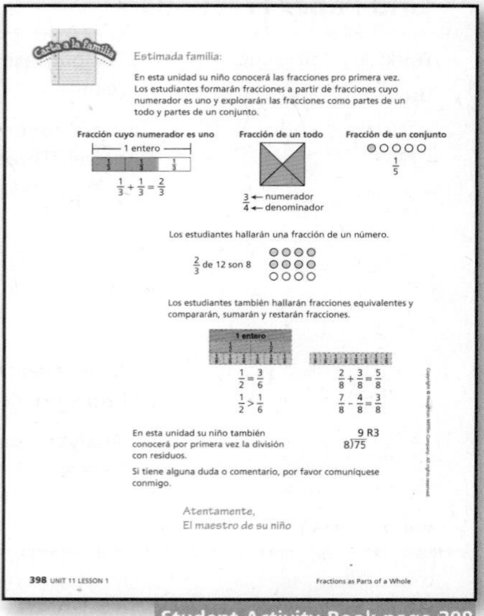

Carta a la familia

Estimada familia:

En esta unidad su niño conocerá las fracciones por primera vez. Los estudiantes formarán fracciones a partir de fracciones cuyo numerador es uno y explorarán las fracciones como partes de un todo y partes de un conjunto.

Fracción cuyo numerador es uno — Fracción de un todo — Fracción de un conjunto

$\frac{1}{3} + \frac{1}{3} = \frac{2}{3}$ — 3 ← numerador, 4 ← denominador — $\frac{1}{5}$

Los estudiantes hallarán una fracción de un número.

$\frac{2}{3}$ de 12 son 8

Los estudiantes también hallarán fracciones equivalentes y compararán, sumarán y restarán fracciones.

$\frac{1}{2} = \frac{3}{6}$ $\frac{1}{2} > \frac{1}{6}$ $\frac{2}{8} + \frac{3}{8} = \frac{5}{8}$ $\frac{7}{8} - \frac{4}{8} = \frac{3}{8}$

En esta unidad su niño también conocerá por primera vez la división con residuos. 9 R3 8)75

Si tiene alguna duda o comentario, por favor comuníquese conmigo.

Atentamente,
El maestro de su niño

398 UNIT 11 LESSON 1 Fractions as Parts of a Whole

Student Activity Book page 398

Fractions as Parts of a Set

Lesson Objectives

- Represent fractions in a variety of ways.
- Use fractions to prepresent parts of sets.

Vocabulary
set

The Day at a Glance

Today's Goals	Materials	
1 Teaching the Lesson **A1:** Review using fractions to represent parts of wholes. **A1:** Use fractions to represent parts of sets.	**Lesson Activities** Student Activity Book pp. 399–400 or Student Hardcover Book pp. 399–400 and Activity Workbook pp. 183–184 (includes Special Format) Homework and Remembering pp. 259–260 Connecting Cubes	**Going Further** Activity Cards 11-2 Two Color Counters Fraction Stickers (TRB M127) Fraction Venn Diagram (TRB M128) Math Journals
2 Going Further ► Differentiated Instruction		
3 Homework and Spiral Review		

Use Math Talk today!

Keeping Skills Sharp

Quick Practice — 5 MINUTES

Goal: Use a fraction to represent part of a group.

Fractions in Action The **Student Leader** selects a group of 6 to 10 students to come to the front of the room. The leader tells some of the students in the group to raise his or her hand. The leader then asks the class what fraction of the group has his or her hand raised. On the leader's signal, the class answers in unison.

The leader changes the size of the group by having some students sit down or having new students come up to the front. Then the leader chooses which students should raise their hands and repeats the process.

Prior to the **Student Leader,** you may wish to lead this activity for the first time so students understand what to do.

Daily Routines

Homework Review Ask students to place their homework at the corner of their desks. As you circulate during Quick Practice, check that students completed the assignment, and see whether any problem caused difficulty for many students.

Skip Count Skip count backward by 100s starting from 1,000 and ending with 200.

Teaching the Lesson

Activity 1

Review Fractions as Parts of Wholes

20 MINUTES

Goal: Review using fractions to represent parts of wholes.

Materials: Student Activity Book or Hardcover Book p. 399 and Activity Workbook p. 183, connecting cubes

NCTM Standards:
Number and Operations
Representation

Differentiated Instruction

Extra Help For Activity 1, tactile learners can use connecting cubes to model the fractions in exercise 7. If white cubes are available, have students use those to represent the part of the whole that is not shaded. They can use any other color to represent the shaded part. For instance, they can model $\frac{4}{5}$ by making a cube train of four red cubes and one white cube.

Students can also use the cubes in Activity 2 to model fractions as parts of sets, but the cubes should remain disconnected. In exercise 12, for instance, they can use seven red cubes and four white cubes to model $\frac{7}{11}$.

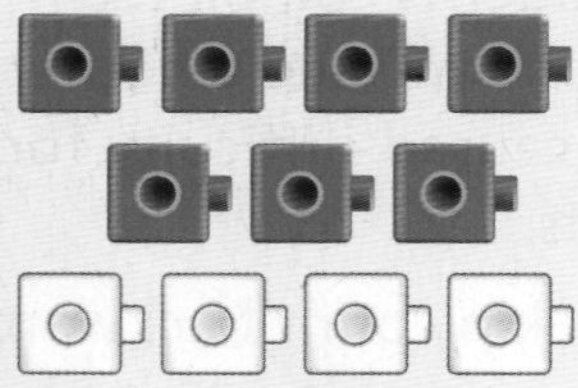

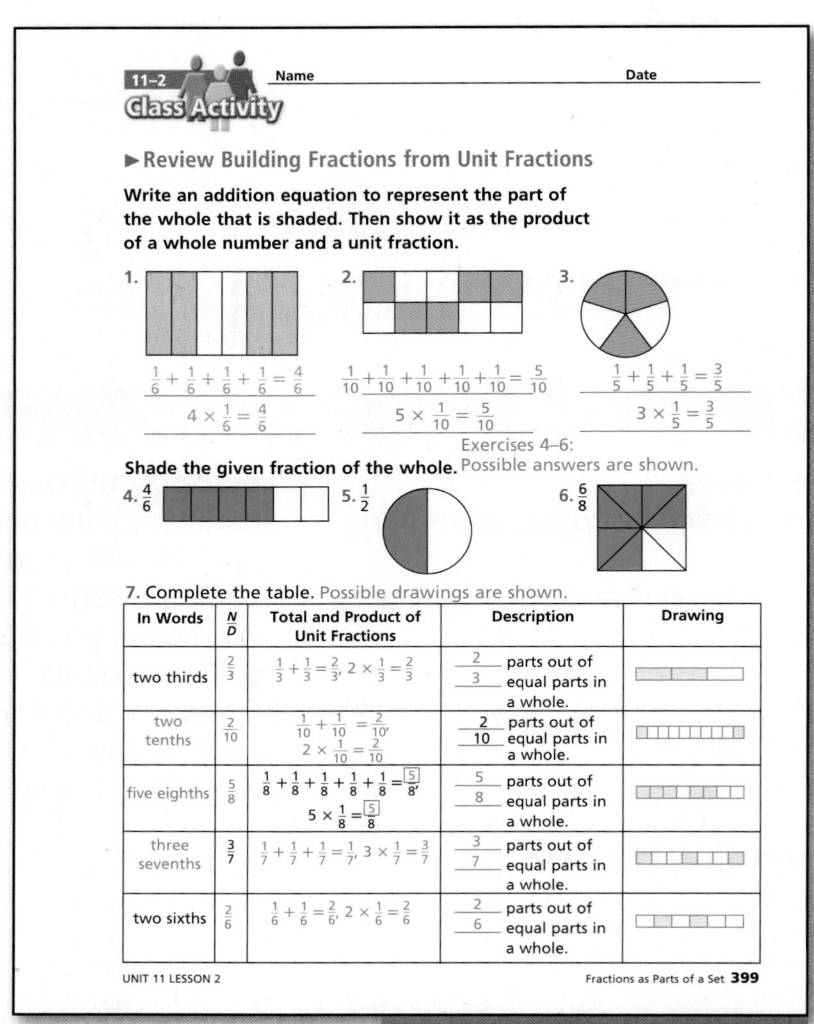

11–2 Class Activity

Name ____________ Date ____________

► Review Building Fractions from Unit Fractions

Write an addition equation to represent the part of the whole that is shaded. Then show it as the product of a whole number and a unit fraction.

1. $\frac{1}{6}+\frac{1}{6}+\frac{1}{6}+\frac{1}{6}=\frac{4}{6}$
   $4 \times \frac{1}{6}=\frac{4}{6}$

2. $\frac{1}{10}+\frac{1}{10}+\frac{1}{10}+\frac{1}{10}+\frac{1}{10}=\frac{5}{10}$
   $5 \times \frac{1}{10}=\frac{5}{10}$

3. $\frac{1}{5}+\frac{1}{5}+\frac{1}{5}=\frac{3}{5}$
   $3 \times \frac{1}{5}=\frac{3}{5}$

Shade the given fraction of the whole. Exercises 4–6: Possible answers are shown.

4. $\frac{4}{6}$
5. $\frac{1}{2}$
6. $\frac{6}{8}$

7. Complete the table. Possible drawings are shown.

In Words	$\frac{N}{D}$	Total and Product of Unit Fractions	Description	Drawing
two thirds	$\frac{2}{3}$	$\frac{1}{3}+\frac{1}{3}=\frac{2}{3}$, $2 \times \frac{1}{3}=\frac{2}{3}$	2 parts out of 3 equal parts in a whole.	
two tenths	$\frac{2}{10}$	$\frac{1}{10}+\frac{1}{10}=\frac{2}{10}$, $2 \times \frac{1}{10}=\frac{2}{10}$	2 parts out of 10 equal parts in a whole.	
five eighths	$\frac{5}{8}$	$\frac{1}{8}+\frac{1}{8}+\frac{1}{8}+\frac{1}{8}+\frac{1}{8}=\frac{5}{8}$, $5 \times \frac{1}{8}=\frac{5}{8}$	5 parts out of 8 equal parts in a whole.	
three sevenths	$\frac{3}{7}$	$\frac{1}{7}+\frac{1}{7}+\frac{1}{7}=\frac{1}{7}$, $3 \times \frac{1}{7}=\frac{3}{7}$	3 parts out of 7 equal parts in a whole.	
two sixths	$\frac{2}{6}$	$\frac{1}{6}+\frac{1}{6}=\frac{2}{6}$, $2 \times \frac{1}{6}=\frac{2}{6}$	2 parts out of 6 equal parts in a whole.	

UNIT 11 LESSON 2 Fractions as Parts of a Set **399**

Student Activity Book page 399

► Review Building Fractions from Unit Fractions

WHOLE CLASS

Have students turn to Student Book page 399. Exercises 1–3 give students practice in writing fractions to describe parts of a whole. Point out that these exercises do not first show the whole without shading. Students need to keep in mind that the whole is the entire shape, including the parts that are shaded as well as the parts that are not shaded. Give students a few minutes to complete these exercises, and then have them share their answers.

Exercises 4–6 review dividing and shading wholes to represent given fractions. Give students time to do the exercises and then select students to share their answers.

Have students look at the table in exercise 7. Discuss the different ways the fraction $\frac{2}{3}$ is shown. Allow students to complete the table independently, and then select students to share their answers.

Activity 2

Fractions of Sets

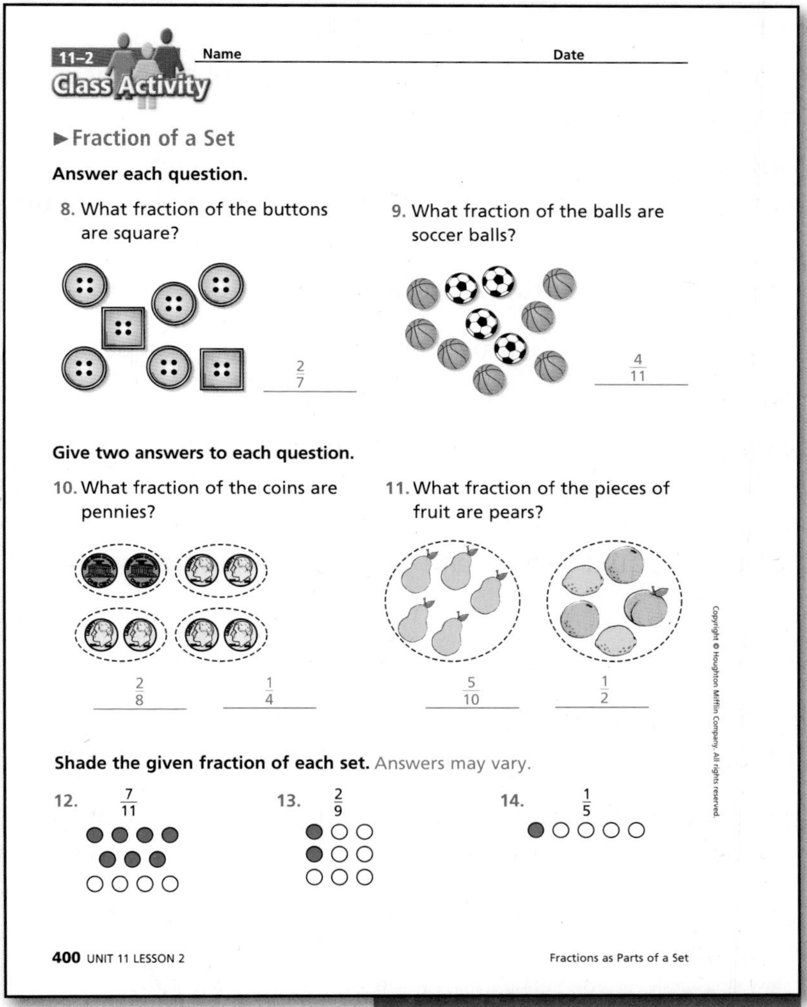

11–2 Class Activity Name Date

► Fraction of a Set

Answer each question.

8. What fraction of the buttons are square? $\frac{2}{7}$

9. What fraction of the balls are soccer balls? $\frac{4}{11}$

Give two answers to each question.

10. What fraction of the coins are pennies? $\frac{2}{8}$ $\frac{1}{4}$

11. What fraction of the pieces of fruit are pears? $\frac{5}{10}$ $\frac{1}{2}$

Shade the given fraction of each set. Answers may vary.

12. $\frac{7}{11}$

13. $\frac{2}{9}$

14. $\frac{1}{5}$

400 UNIT 11 LESSON 2 Fractions as Parts of a Set

Student Activity Book page 400

► Fraction of a Set WHOLE CLASS

Explain to students that parts of collections, or *sets,* can be represented with fractions. Tell students to look at the set of buttons in exercise 8.

- In earlier exercises, you found what fraction of a *whole* bar or shape was shaded. In this exercise, you need to find what fraction of a *whole* set of buttons are square buttons.
- How many buttons are in the whole set? 7 How many of the buttons are square? 2 So what fraction of all the buttons are square? $\frac{2}{7}$

Activity continued ►

 30 MINUTES

Goal: Use fractions to represent parts of sets.

Materials: Student Activity Book or Hardcover Book p. 400 and Activity Workbook p. 184 (includes special format)

 **NCTM Standards:**
Number and Operations
Representation

Teaching Note

Watch For! When working with set models for fractions, some students may have difficulty seeing the whole. For example, in exercise 8, students might think, "I see 2 square buttons and 5 round buttons, so the fraction is $\frac{2}{5}$." Emphasize that the whole is the *whole set,* which is *all* the buttons. You might want to suggest that students draw a circle around the set to remind them what the whole is.

English Language Learners

Write *set* on the board. Hold up a box of crayons. Say: **This is a *set* of crayons.**

- **Beginning** Ask: **Are they all the same color?** no **Are they all crayons?** yes
- **Intermediate** Ask: **What is different about these crayons?** colors **Are things in a *set* always exactly the same?** no
- **Advanced** Have students find other *sets* of things in the classroom. pictures, cards, books

1 Teaching the Lesson (continued)

Teaching Note

Math Background Exercises 10 and 11 are an informal introduction to the concept of equivalent fractions. For now, you might want to mention that sometimes two fractions name the same part of a whole. Students will study equivalent fractions in depth in lessons 9–13.

Ongoing Assessment

Ask questions such as the following:

- What fraction names the shaded part?

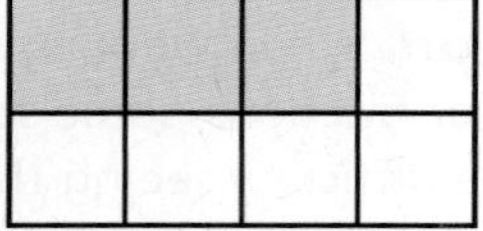

- What fraction names the shaded part?

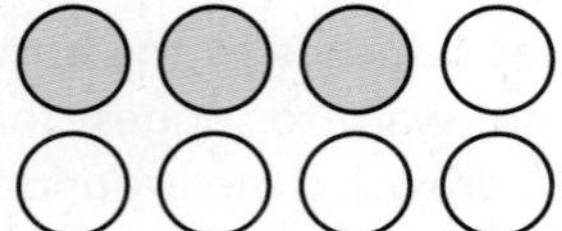

- How are these two pictures of three eighths alike? How are they different?

Remind students that they represented fractions of wholes as sums of unit fractions. Discuss the fact that fractions of sets can also be represented in this way.

- What fraction of the whole set does each button represent? $\frac{1}{7}$
- So how can we show the part of the set that is square buttons as a sum of unit fractions? $\frac{1}{7} + \frac{1}{7}$

Have students complete exercise 9, and then review the answer. Ask students to identify the whole and to express the specified part as a sum of unit fractions.

Next, tell students to look at the set of coins in exercise 10.

- How many coins are in this set? 8 How many of the coins are pennies? 2 So what fraction of the coins are pennies? $\frac{2}{8}$
- There is another way to think about this exercise. Notice that the set is divided into equal parts, or groups, with two coins in each group. How many equal groups are there? 4 How many of the groups are made of pennies? 1 So 1 of the 4 equal groups are pennies. What fraction is this? $\frac{1}{4}$

Point out that exercise 10 appears to have two correct answers.

- If you think of the individual coins as the equal parts, then 2 out of 8 equal parts, or $\frac{2}{8}$, of the set is pennies.
- If you think of the groups of 2 coins as the equal parts, then 1 out of 4 equal parts, or $\frac{1}{4}$, of the set is pennies.

Have students complete exercise 11. After all students have completed their work, discuss the answer.

Next, have students complete exercises 12–14, which require them to shade a given fraction of a set.

Math Talk Have students think of places they see fractions, such as the supermarket. As a class, discuss each use and decide if the fraction is a fraction of a whole or fraction of set. To review, ask the following questions:

- If I bought 2/3 pound of red apples, would this represent a fraction of a whole or a fraction of a set? Explain. Fraction of a whole; 1 whole pound of the same type of fruit was split into 3 equal pieces.
- If 2/3 of the fruit on the table was red apples and the rest was pears, would 2/3 represent a fraction of a whole or a fraction of a set? Explain. Fraction of a set; The whole set of the fruit had different types of fruit.

2 Going Further

Differentiated Instruction

Intervention — Activity Card 11-2

Model Fractions — Activity Card 11-2 ●

Work: In pairs

Use:

- Two-color counters

1. Display 12 red counters. Flip one counter over to yellow.
2. What fraction of the counters are yellow? Red? $\frac{1}{12}$, $\frac{11}{12}$
3. Now arrange the counters in 3 rows of 4, all showing red. Flip the top row to yellow. What fraction of the counters are yellow? $\frac{4}{12}$ or $\frac{1}{3}$
4. Flip another row over to yellow. What fraction is yellow now? $\frac{8}{12}$ or $\frac{2}{3}$
5. Repeat the activity, beginning with the same array of 12 red counters. Turn over one column at a time. Name the fraction of yellow counters each time. $\frac{3}{12}$ or $\frac{1}{4}$, $\frac{6}{12}$ or $\frac{1}{2}$, $\frac{9}{12}$ or $\frac{3}{4}$

Unit 11, Lesson 2

Activity Note Challenge students to name each fractional part in more than one way if possible. Focus attention on the number of rows or columns.

Math Writing Prompt

Explain Your Thinking Sylvie made a bracelet with 1 red bead, 3 blue beads, and 4 white beads. Use fractions to describe what part of the beads is red, what part is blue, and what part is white.

Software Support

Warm Up 5.08

On Level — Activity Card 11-2

Sticky Fraction Problems — Activity Card 11-2 ▲

Work: In pairs

Use:

- TRB M127 (Fraction Stickers)

One page in Judy's scrapbook has the 15 stickers shown below. Use the stickers to solve each problem. Give more than one answer to each problem if possible.

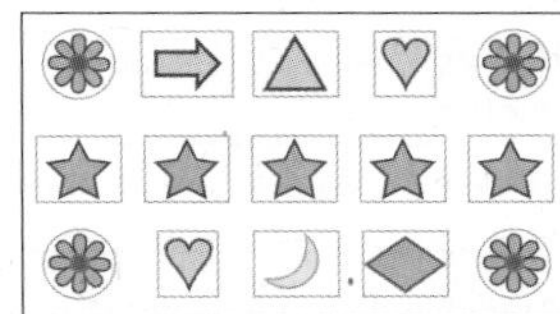

- What fraction of the sticker shapes on the page have no straight edges? $\frac{7}{15}$
- Judy gave 5 stickers to her friend Erin. What fraction of the stickers did Judy keep? $\frac{10}{15}$, or $\frac{2}{3}$

Unit 11, Lesson 2

Activity Note Have students make up their own fraction problems about the stickers and exchange with another pair to solve.

Math Writing Prompt

Critical Thinking Exactly $\frac{1}{4}$ of the crayons in a box are blue. Does this mean that there are exactly four crayons in the box? Explain.

Software Support

Fraction Action: Fraction Flare Up, Level C

Challenge — Activity Card 11-2

Fractions and Venn Diagrams — Activity Card 11-2 ■

Work: In small groups

Use:

- TRB M128 (Fraction Venn Diagram)

1. Use the Fraction Venn Diagram to show what you know about geometric shapes and fractions. Work together to answer each question.
2. Now create your own Venn Diagram. Write several fraction questions to share with another group.

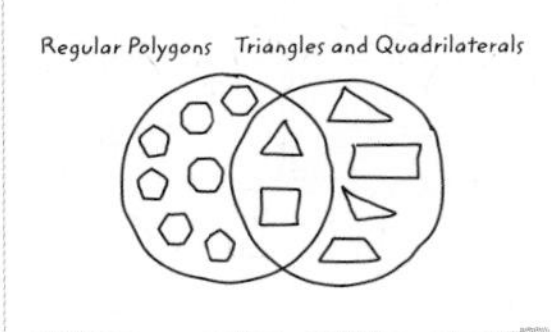

Unit 11, Lesson 2

Activity Note Before the activity review that a square is both a rectangle and a rhombus.

Math Writing Prompt

Estimate Fractions There are 5 green marbles in a bag of 24 marbles. Greg says the number of green marbles is close to one fourth of all the marbles. Do you agree or disagree? Explain.

Software Support

Course II: Module 2: Unit 3: Fractional Parts

3 Homework and Spiral Review

Goal: Additional Practice

This Homework page provides practice in using fractions to represent parts of sets.

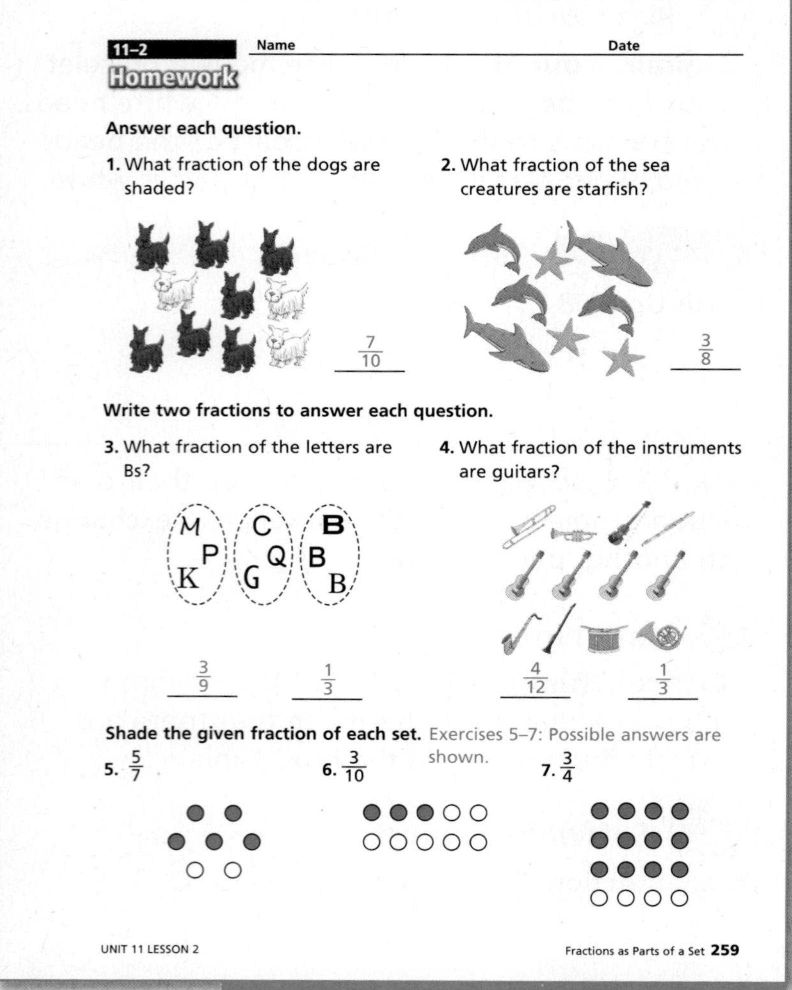

11–2 Homework — Name ______ Date ______

Answer each question.

1. What fraction of the dogs are shaded? $\frac{7}{10}$
2. What fraction of the sea creatures are starfish? $\frac{3}{8}$

Write two fractions to answer each question.

3. What fraction of the letters are Bs?

M P K | C Q G | B B B

$\frac{3}{9}$ $\frac{1}{3}$

4. What fraction of the instruments are guitars? $\frac{4}{12}$ $\frac{1}{3}$

Shade the given fraction of each set. Exercises 5–7: Possible answers are shown.

5. $\frac{5}{7}$
6. $\frac{3}{10}$
7. $\frac{3}{4}$

UNIT 11 LESSON 2 Fractions as Parts of a Set 259

Homework and Remembering page 259

Goal: Spiral Review

This Remembering page would be appropriate anytime after today's lesson.

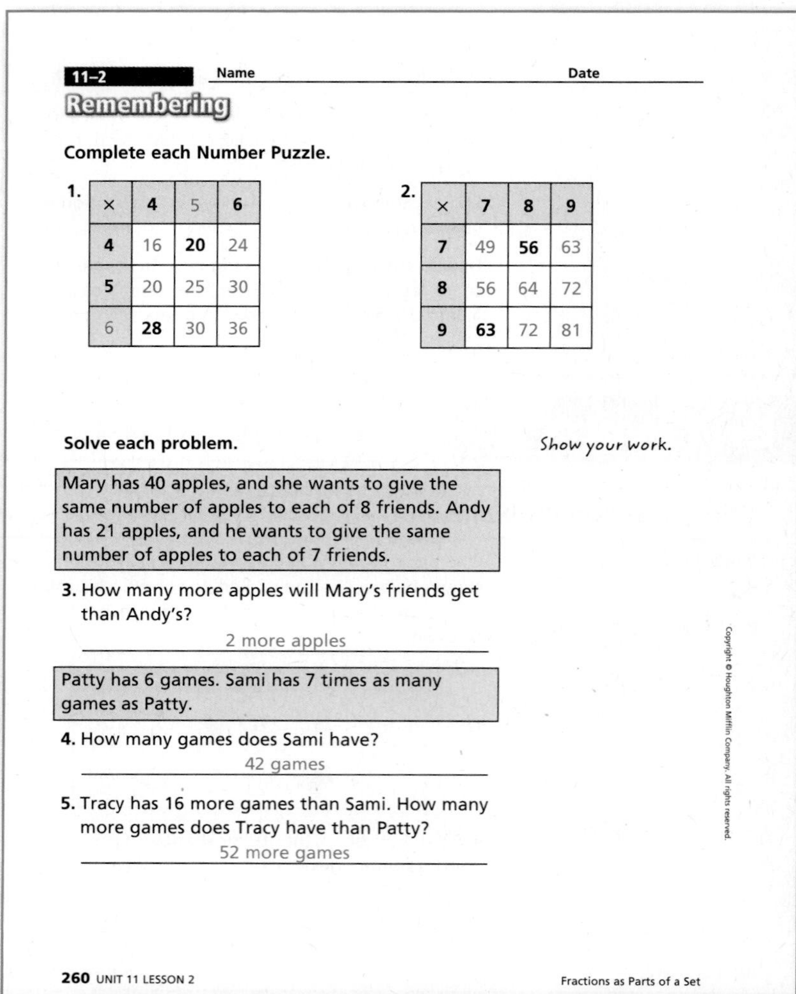

11–2 Remembering — Name ______ Date ______

Complete each Number Puzzle.

1.

×	4	5	6
4	16	20	24
5	20	25	30
6	28	30	36

2.

×	7	8	9
7	49	56	63
8	56	64	72
9	63	72	81

Solve each problem. *Show your work.*

Mary has 40 apples, and she wants to give the same number of apples to each of 8 friends. Andy has 21 apples, and he wants to give the same number of apples to each of 7 friends.

3. How many more apples will Mary's friends get than Andy's? 2 more apples

Patty has 6 games. Sami has 7 times as many games as Patty.

4. How many games does Sami have? 42 games
5. Tracy has 16 more games than Sami. How many more games does Tracy have than Patty? 52 more games

260 UNIT 11 LESSON 2 Fractions as Parts of a Set

Homework and Remembering page 260

Home or School Activity

Art Connection

Fraction Designs Have students trace a 1 inch-by-3 inch rectangle a number of times on paper or poster board to make a design that forms a square or rectangle. Then have them color the small rectangles using 3 or 4 different colors. Have students use a fraction to describe what part of the rectangle or square is each color. Display the completed designs around the room.

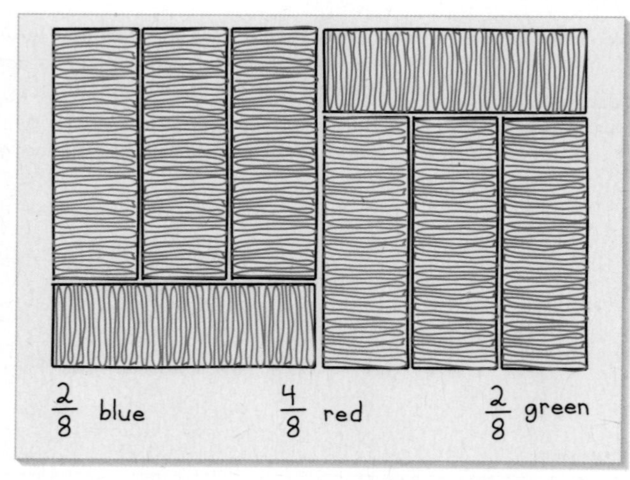

Unit Fractions of Sets and Numbers

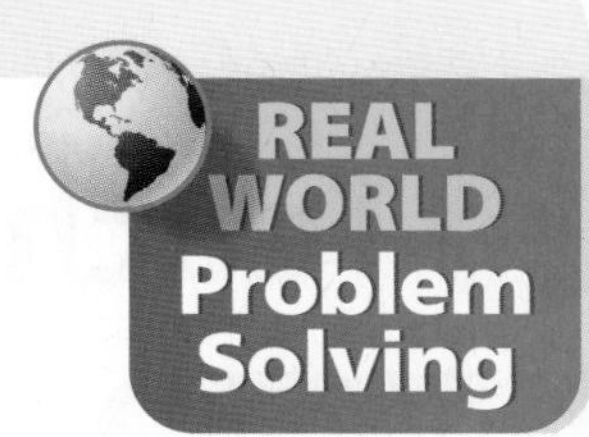

Lesson Objective

- Find a unit fraction of an amount.

The Day at a Glance

Today's Goals	Materials	
1 Teaching the Lesson A1: Write three equations to represent dividing a set into equal parts. A2: Solve word problems involving finding a unit fraction of a set. A3: Consolidate ideas about unit fractions of sets.	**Lesson Activities** Student Activity Book pp. 401–402 or Student Hardcover Book pp. 401–402 Homework and Remembering pp. 261–262 MathBoard Materials *The Big Orange Splot* by Daniel Pinkwater (Scholastic Inc., 1977)	**Going Further** Activity Cards 11-3 Paper Cups (6) Two-color counters (36) Play Money Math Journals
2 Going Further ► Differentiated Instruction		
3 Homework and Spiral Review		

Use Math Talk today!

Keeping Skills Sharp

Quick Practice — 5 MINUTES

Goal: Use a fraction to represent part of a group.

Fractions in Action The **Student Leader** selects a group of 6 to 10 students to come to the front of the room and tells some of these students to raise his or her hand. The leader then asks the class what fraction of the group has his or her hand raised. On the leader's signal, the class answers in unison.

The leader changes the size of the group by having some students sit down or having new students come to the front. Then the leader chooses new students to raise their hands and repeats the process. (See Unit 11 Lesson 2.)

Daily Routines

Homework Review Ask students if they had difficulty with any part of the homework. Plan to set aside some time to work with students needing extra help.

What's Wrong? Akiko added 77 and 68 and got a sum of 135. What did Akiko do wrong? What is the correct sum? Forgot to carry the ten, or forgot to add the carried ten; 145

1 Teaching the Lesson

Activity 1

Find Unit Fractions of Sets

15 MINUTES

Goal: Write three equations to represent dividing a set into equal parts.

Materials: MathBoard materials

NCTM Standards:
Number and Operations
Representation

Teaching Note

What to Expect from Students
As students write the three equations in Activity 1, you might find that the multiplication equation is not as intuitive to them as the other equations. Students might have difficulty conceptualizing what it means to multiply by a fraction. You can help them understand by relating multiplication by a fraction to multiplication by a whole number.

- Remind students that the product 4×3 means "4 times as many as 3."
- Tell them that, in the same way, $\frac{1}{4} \times 12$ means "$\frac{1}{4}$ times as many as 12." This is usually stated as "$\frac{1}{4}$ as many as 12."
- Remind students that, when solving comparison problems in Unit 5, they found "$\frac{1}{4}$ as many" by dividing by 4.

English Language Learners

Draw a bouquet of flowers, a sharp crayon, a dull crayon, and a seal on the board to provide vocabulary support for Activity 2.

► Explore Unit Fractions of Sets WHOLE CLASS

Work on the board as students follow along on their MathBoards. Have students draw a set of 12 circles. Then ask them to divide the set of 12 circles into four equal parts.

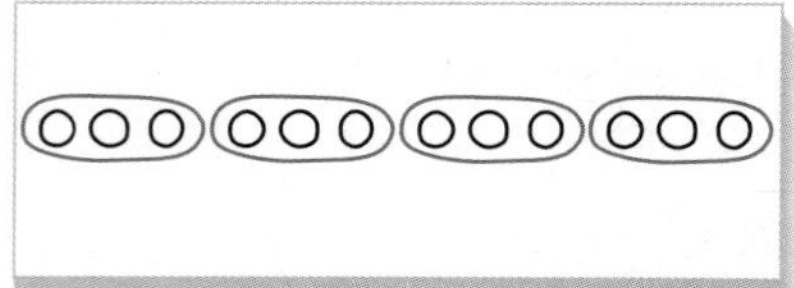

- You divided the set of 12 circles into four equal parts. What fraction of the set is each part? $\frac{1}{4}$ How many circles are in each part? 3
- The drawing shows that $\frac{1}{4}$ of 12 equals 3. Let's write that as an equation next to the drawing.
- Can anyone think of another equation to show what we did?

If necessary, help students see that, because they divided the 12 circles into 4 equal groups, they can also write the equation $12 \div 4 = 3$. Have students write this equation under the first equation.

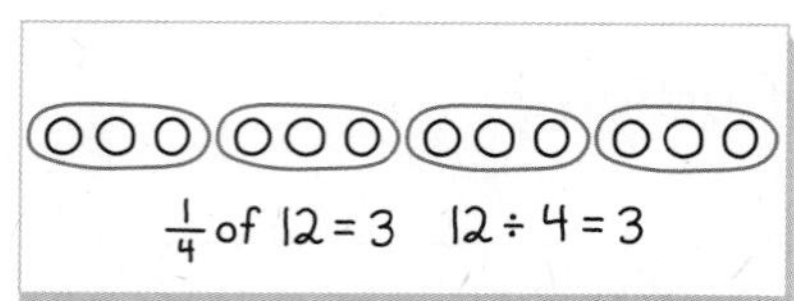

Tell students that there is one more equation they can write to show their work. Write the equation $\frac{1}{4} \times 12 = 3$ under the other equations.

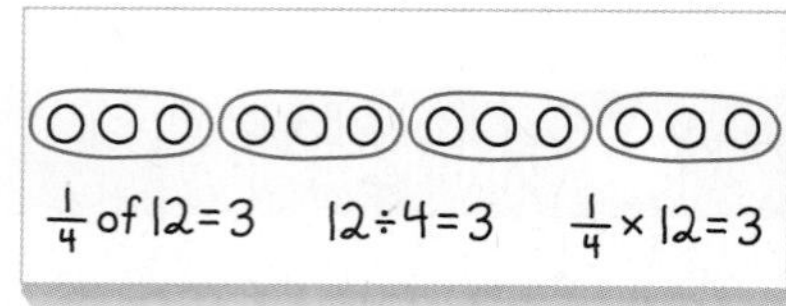

Review all three equations, repeating that "$\frac{1}{4}$ of 12," "$\frac{1}{4}$ times 12," and "12 divided by 4" all mean the same thing.

Tell students not to erase the drawing or the equations. At a different place on the board, have them draw three rows of 6 circles. Ask them to divide the set of circles into three equal parts. Ask students to write three different equations to show what they did. Select students to share their drawings and equations.

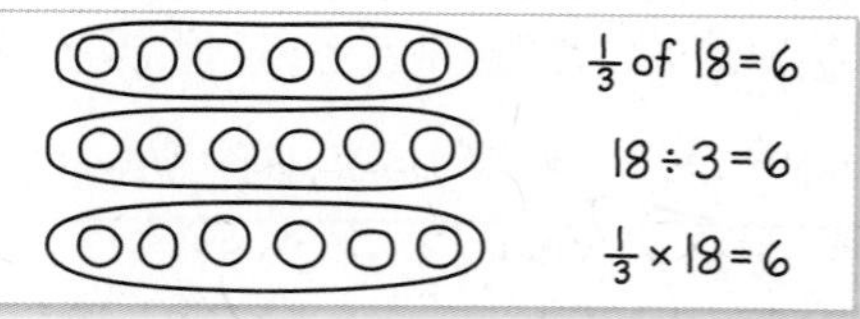

Activity 2

Solve Word Problems Involving Unit Fractions of Sets

11-3 Class Activity   Name ____________ Date ____________

▶ Solve Word Problems Involving Unit Fractions of Sets

Solve each problem.

Show your work.

1. One sixth of Kiera's cousins have red hair. Kiera has 12 cousins. How many cousins have red hair?
   2 cousins
2. One third of the students on the bus are in the third grade. There are 15 students on the bus. How many students are in the third grade?
   5 students
3. One half of Angel's crayons are sharp. Angel has 14 crayons. How many crayons are sharp?
   7 crayons
4. One fourth of the roses in a bouquet are pink. There are 24 roses in the bouquet. How many roses are pink?
   6 roses
5. One tenth of the trees in the forest are oak trees. There are 90 trees in the forest. How many trees are oak trees?
   9 trees
6. There are 56 seals at the seashore. One eighth of the seals are swimming. How many seals are swimming?
   7 seals

UNIT 11 LESSON 3   Unit Fractions of Sets and Numbers 401

Student Activity Book page 401

20 MINUTES

Goal: Solve word problems involving finding a unit fraction of a set.

Materials: Student Activity Book or Hardcover Book p. 401

NCTM Standards:
Problem Solving
Representation

▶ Solve Word Problems Involving Unit Fractions of Sets WHOLE CLASS

Math Talk Using **Solve and Discuss,** have students solve problem 1 on Student Book page 401. Discuss some possible solution methods.

- Find $\frac{1}{6}$ of 12. This is the same as dividing 12 by 6. Because $12 \div 6 = 2$, Kiera has 2 cousins with red hair.
- Draw 12 circles to show the 12 cousins. Divide the circles into 6 groups. There are 2 circles in each group. One group represents the red-haired cousins, so Kiera has 2 cousins with red hair.

Have students solve problems 2–6. Point out that drawings are not practical for large numbers such as in problem 5, and encourage them to try a numerical solution method. Discuss the new method.

Alternate Approach

Area Models Here are two other ways to visualize multiplication by a unit fraction. Each shows the multiplication $\frac{1}{4} \times 8$. You might want to present one or both of these to your students.

- Think of $\frac{1}{4} \times 8$ as 8 copies of $\frac{1}{4}$. If the area of a circle is a whole, then the area of a quarter circle is $\frac{1}{4}$. The figure below shows that 8 copies of $\frac{1}{4}$ make 2 wholes, so $\frac{1}{4} \times 8 = 2$.

   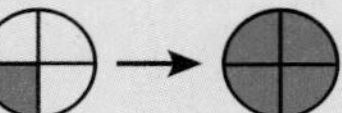

 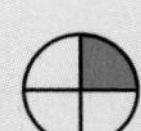  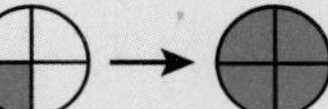

- Think of $\frac{1}{4} \times 8$ as the area of a rectangle that is $\frac{1}{4}$ unit wide and 8 units long. The figure below shows how to rearrange the pieces to form whole square units. The area is 2 square units, so $\frac{1}{4} \times 8 = 2$.

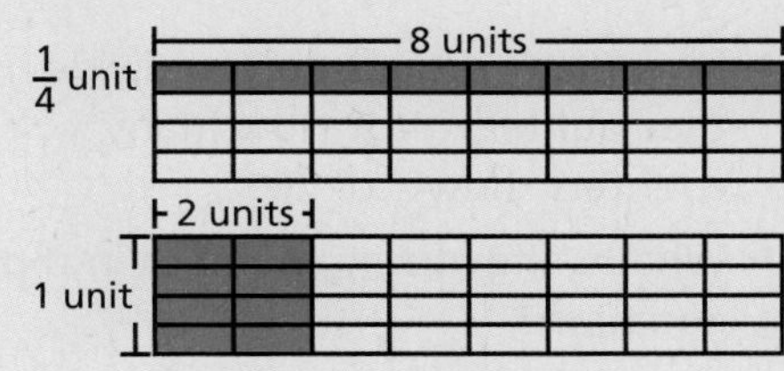

Activity 3

Consolidate Ideas

 15 MINUTES

Goal: Consolidate ideas about unit fractions of sets.

Materials: Student Activity Book or Hardcover Book p. 402

 **NCTM Standards:**
Number and Operations
Representation

Differentiated Instruction

Language and Vocabulary Explain to students that the word *equivalent* means having an equal value. In mathematics, it means representing the same number. *Equivalent equations* are equations that have the same solution. Have students work in pairs to write and read several equations and their equivalents. Have them take turns and correct each other's work.

Ongoing Assessment

Provide students with a set of counters and the equation below.

$\frac{1}{4}$ of 20 = $\square$

Ask questions such as the following:

- How many groups do you divide the counters into? How many counters show $\frac{1}{4}$ of 20?
- What is the missing number in the equation?
- What multiplication equation has the same meaning as this equation? What division equation is equivalent to the equation?

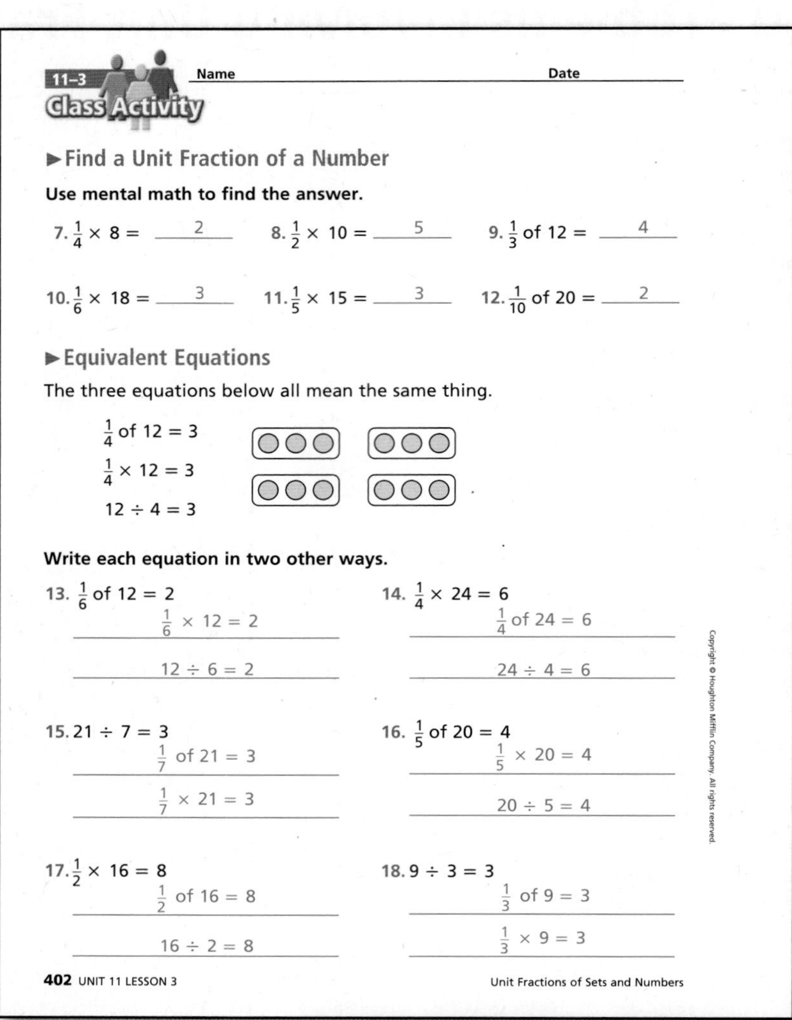

11–3 Class Activity Name ______ Date ______

▶ Find a Unit Fraction of a Number

Use mental math to find the answer.

7. $\frac{1}{4} \times 8 =$ 2
8. $\frac{1}{2} \times 10 =$ 5
9. $\frac{1}{3}$ of 12 = 4
10. $\frac{1}{6} \times 18 =$ 3
11. $\frac{1}{5} \times 15 =$ 3
12. $\frac{1}{10}$ of 20 = 2

▶ Equivalent Equations

The three equations below all mean the same thing.

$\frac{1}{4}$ of 12 = 3
$\frac{1}{4} \times 12 = 3$
$12 \div 4 = 3$

Write each equation in two other ways.

13. $\frac{1}{6}$ of 12 = 2
$\frac{1}{6} \times 12 = 2$
$12 \div 6 = 2$

14. $\frac{1}{4} \times 24 = 6$
$\frac{1}{4}$ of 24 = 6
$24 \div 4 = 6$

15. $21 \div 7 = 3$
$\frac{1}{7}$ of 21 = 3
$\frac{1}{7} \times 21 = 3$

16. $\frac{1}{5}$ of 20 = 4
$\frac{1}{5} \times 20 = 4$
$20 \div 5 = 4$

17. $\frac{1}{2} \times 16 = 8$
$\frac{1}{2}$ of 16 = 8
$16 \div 2 = 8$

18. $9 \div 3 = 3$
$\frac{1}{3}$ of 9 = 3
$\frac{1}{3} \times 9 = 3$

402 UNIT 11 LESSON 3 Unit Fractions of Sets and Numbers

Student Activity Book page 402

▶ Find a Unit Fraction of a Number WHOLE CLASS

Have students look at exercises 7–12 on Student Book page 402. Read aloud each multiplication. Remind students that "of" means multiplication.

▶ Equivalent Equations WHOLE CLASS

Now have students look at the three equivalent equations given on Student Activity Book page 426.

$$\frac{1}{4} \text{ of } 12 = 3 \qquad \frac{1}{4} \times 12 = 3 \qquad 12 \div 4 = 3$$

Tell students that exercises 13–18 give them one form of an equation, and they must write the other two equivalent forms. Give students a few minutes to complete the exercises, and then discuss the answers.

For the remainder of the lesson, have students suggest word problems that involve finding a unit fraction of a number. Discuss and solve each problem as a class, and then have students write three different equations to represent the problem.

2 Going Further

Differentiated Instruction

Intervention — Activity Card 11-3

Paper Cup Fractions — Activity Card 11-3

Work: In pairs

Use:
- 6 paper cups
- 36 counters

1. Use paper cups and counters to model $\frac{1}{4}$ of 24. Divide 24 counters equally among 4 cups.
2. **Think** How many are in each cup? 6
   What division equation does this show? $24 \div 4 = 6$
3. Now write a multiplication equation that the model represents, using the fraction $\frac{1}{4}$. $\frac{1}{4} \times 24 = 6$
4. Repeat the activity three more times. Use paper cups and counters to model each fractional part below. Then write a multiplication equation for each model.
   $\frac{1}{4}$ of 20 $\quad$ $\frac{1}{4}$ of 36 $\quad$ $\frac{1}{3}$ of 24
5. **Analyze** How did you decide how many cups to use for each model? The denominator of the fraction tells how many cups.

Unit 11, Lesson 3

Activity Note Remind students that the expression $\frac{1}{4}$ of 24 is the same as the multiplication expression $\frac{1}{4} \times 24$. Discuss how each fraction relates to the number of cups needed to model the expression.

Math Writing Prompt

Make a Drawing A pillow has 11 fabric squares on it. Jumari said, "Half of the squares are red." Can this be true? Explain your thinking with a picture.

Software Support

Warm Up 5.05

On Level — Activity Card 11-3

Mental Math Challenge — Activity Card 11-3

Work: In pairs

1. Copy the list of multiplication exercises below onto a sheet of paper.

$\frac{1}{3} \times 18$	$\frac{1}{7} \times 35$	$\frac{1}{5} \times 25$
$\frac{1}{5} \times 30$	$\frac{1}{3} \times 27$	$\frac{1}{9} \times 45$
$\frac{1}{4} \times 16$	$\frac{1}{8} \times 40$	$\frac{1}{4} \times 28$
$\frac{1}{6} \times 42$	$\frac{1}{2} \times 14$	$\frac{1}{7} \times 56$

2. Take turns. Choose a multiplication and use mental math to name the product.
3. If the product is correct, the player scores one point and crosses off the chosen multiplication.
4. When the entire list has been crossed off, the player with the greater number of points wins.

Unit 11, Lesson 3

Activity Note Tell students that both partners should agree on each product named before crossing out the exercise and awarding a point for the answer.

Math Writing Prompt

You Decide Chelsea had 12 marbles. She said that $\frac{1}{3}$ were red, $\frac{1}{3}$ were green, $\frac{1}{3}$ were orange, and $\frac{1}{3}$ were purple. Can the marbles be grouped like this? Explain.

Software Support

Fraction Action: Number Line Mine, Level L

Challenge — Activity Card 11-3

Unit Fractions of Money Amounts — Activity Card 11-3

Work: In pairs

Use:
- Play money

1. Each equation below represents the amount of money that one member of a group should receive. Each fraction tells how many members are in each group.

$\frac{1}{2}$ of \$9 = ☐	\$4.50
$\frac{1}{4}$ of \$11 = ☐	\$2.75
$\frac{1}{5}$ of \$7 = ☐	\$1.40
$\frac{1}{8}$ of \$14 = ☐	\$1.75

2. Solve the first equation. Use play money to represent \$9. Trade bills and coins until you have a set of coins and a set of bills that can be divided into 2 equal groups.
3. How many bills are in each group? How many coins? How much does each person receive? Four \$1 bills; 2 quarters; \$4.50
4. Solve the remaining equations in the same way.

Unit 11, Lesson 3

Activity Note Using smaller bills and coins will increase the likelihood of having an assortment of bills and coins that can be divided equally into different-size groups.

Math Writing Prompt

Work Backward What is the missing number in the equation below? Explain how you found the answer.

$\square \times \frac{1}{4} = 8$

DESTINATION Math®

Software Support

Course II: Module 3: Unit 2: Money

3 Homework and Spiral Review

Goal: Additional Practice

This Homework page provides practice in finding a fraction of a set.

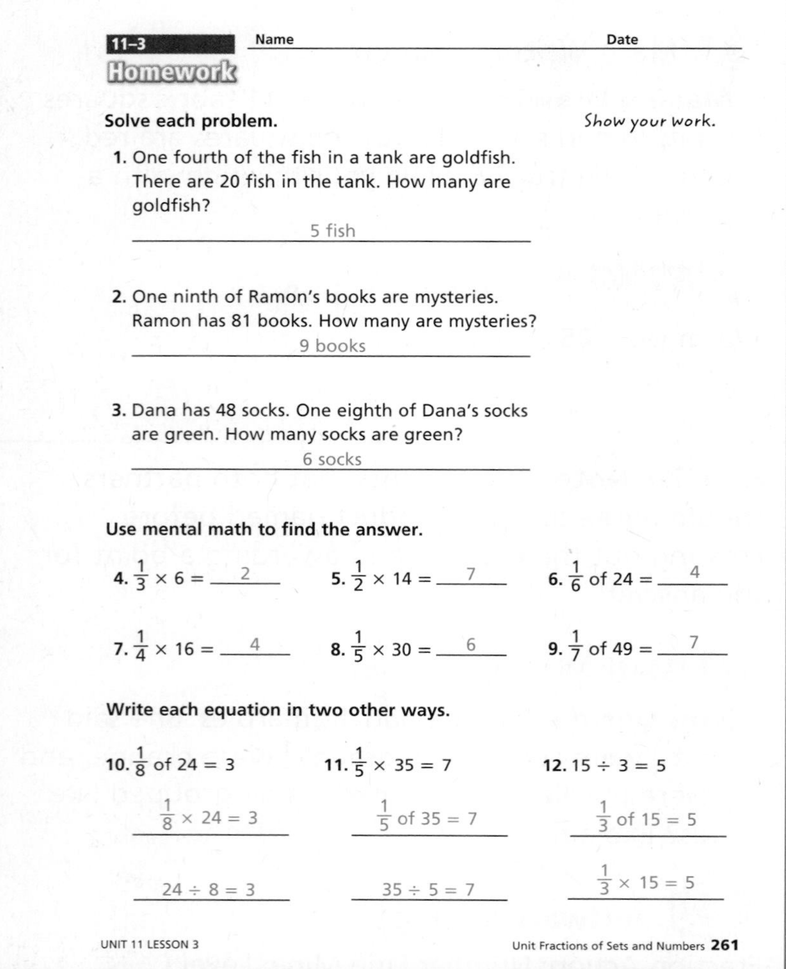

11–3 Homework   Name ______ Date ______

Solve each problem.   *Show your work.*

1. One fourth of the fish in a tank are goldfish. There are 20 fish in the tank. How many are goldfish? 5 fish
2. One ninth of Ramon's books are mysteries. Ramon has 81 books. How many are mysteries? 9 books
3. Dana has 48 socks. One eighth of Dana's socks are green. How many socks are green? 6 socks

Use mental math to find the answer.

4. $\frac{1}{3} \times 6 =$ 2
5. $\frac{1}{2} \times 14 =$ 7
6. $\frac{1}{6}$ of $24 =$ 4
7. $\frac{1}{4} \times 16 =$ 4
8. $\frac{1}{5} \times 30 =$ 6
9. $\frac{1}{7}$ of $49 =$ 7

Write each equation in two other ways.

10. $\frac{1}{8}$ of $24 = 3$ — $\frac{1}{8} \times 24 = 3$; $24 \div 8 = 3$
11. $\frac{1}{5} \times 35 = 7$ — $\frac{1}{5}$ of $35 = 7$; $35 \div 5 = 7$
12. $15 \div 3 = 5$ — $\frac{1}{3}$ of $15 = 5$; $\frac{1}{3} \times 15 = 5$

UNIT 11 LESSON 3   Unit Fractions of Sets and Numbers 261

Homework and Remembering page 261

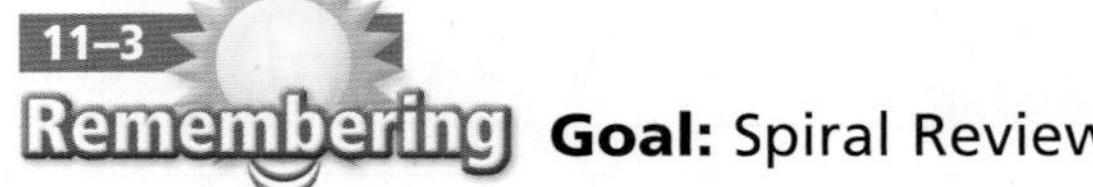

Goal: Spiral Review

This Remembering page would be appropriate anytime after today's lesson.

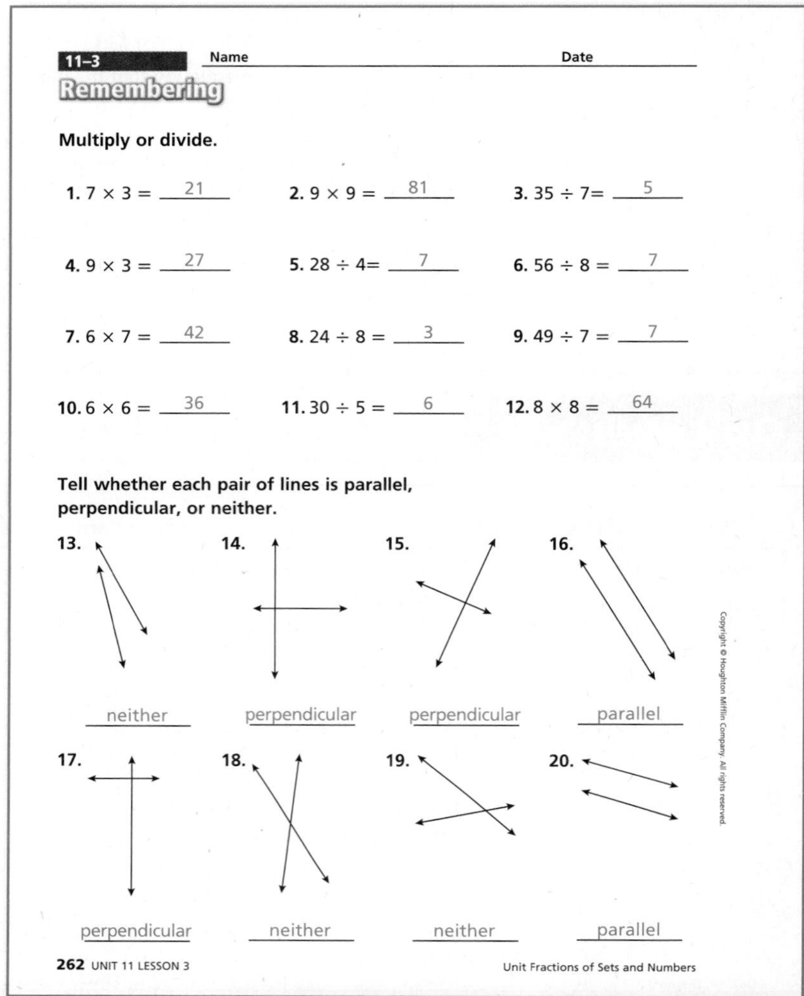

11–3 Remembering   Name ______ Date ______

Multiply or divide.

1. $7 \times 3 =$ 21
2. $9 \times 9 =$ 81
3. $35 \div 7 =$ 5
4. $9 \times 3 =$ 27
5. $28 \div 4 =$ 7
6. $56 \div 8 =$ 7
7. $6 \times 7 =$ 42
8. $24 \div 8 =$ 3
9. $49 \div 7 =$ 7
10. $6 \times 6 =$ 36
11. $30 \div 5 =$ 6
12. $8 \times 8 =$ 64

Tell whether each pair of lines is parallel, perpendicular, or neither.

13. neither
14. perpendicular
15. perpendicular
16. parallel
17. perpendicular
18. neither
19. neither
20. parallel

Copyright © Houghton Mifflin Company. All rights reserved.

262 UNIT 11 LESSON 3   Unit Fractions of Sets and Numbers

Homework and Remembering page 262

Home or School Activity

Literature Connection

The Big Orange Splot Read aloud Daniel Pinkwater's book or have students read the book on their own. Have students explain each page of the book and describe as many fraction examples they can find. Challenge students to design their own Fraction House and have classmates describe the houses in fractional parts.

Compare with Fractions

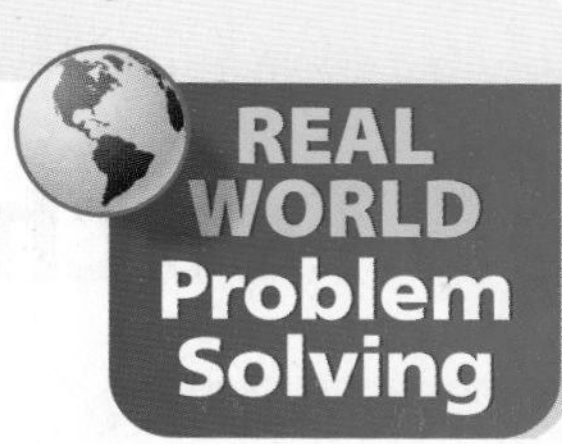

Lesson Objectives

- Make "as many as" comparison statements, and represent them with multiplication equations.
- Make comparison statements about information in a bar graph.
- Solve word problems involving comparisons and multiplication.

Vocabulary
comparison

The Day at a Glance

Today's Goals	Materials	
1 Teaching the Lesson **A1:** Make "as many as" comparison statements. **A2:** Solve word problems involving comparisons and multiplication.	**Lesson Activities** Student Activity Book pp. 403–404 or Student Hardcover Book pp. 403–404 Homework and Remembering pp. 263–264	**Going Further** Activity Cards 11-4 Mathboard materials Connecting cubes (12 Red, 6 Blue, 4 White, 3 Yellow, 2 Green for each student) Two-color counters (100) Plastic Bowl Index Cards (12) Math Journals
2 Going Further ▸ Differentiated Instruction		
3 Homework and Spiral Review		

Use **Math Talk** *today!*

Keeping Skills Sharp

Quick Practice — 5 MINUTES

Goal: Use a fraction to represent part of a group.

Fractions in Action The **Student Leader** selects a group of 6 to 10 students to come to the front of the room and tells some of these students to raise his or her hand. The leader then asks the class what fraction of the group has his or her hand raised. On the leader's signal, the class answers in unison.

The leader changes the size of the group, chooses new students to raise their hands, and repeats the process. (See Unit 11 Lesson 2.)

Daily Routines

Homework Review If students give incorrect answers, have them explain how they found the answers. This will determine where the error was made.

Strategy Problem The temperature was 69°F at 12 P.M., 72°F at 1 P.M., and 75°F at 2 P.M. If the pattern continues, what will be the temperature at 3 P.M.? Explain. 78°F; Used a pattern, +3°F.

69°F → +3°F → 72°F → +3°F → 75°F → +3°F → 78°F

1 Teaching the Lesson

Activity 1

Comparisons Involving Fractions

 **25 MINUTES**

Goal: Make "as many as" comparison statements.

Materials: Student Activity Book or Hardcover Book p. 403

 **NCTM Standards:**
Number and Operations
Data Analysis and Probability
Representation

Teaching Note

Math Background Throughout Units 7 and 9, students explored the relationships between multiplication and division. In this unit, students should try to achieve mastery of the following concepts.

- Division undoes multiplication, and vice versa.

  $3 \times 5 = 15 \Leftrightarrow 15 \div 5 = 3$

- Dividing by a number is the same as multiplying by the unit fraction with that number as the denominator.

  $10 \div 5 = 2 \Leftrightarrow \frac{1}{5} \times 10 = 2$

English Language Learners

Make sure students can use the comparison language needed. Draw these chocolate bars on the board.

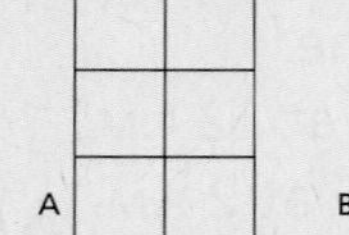

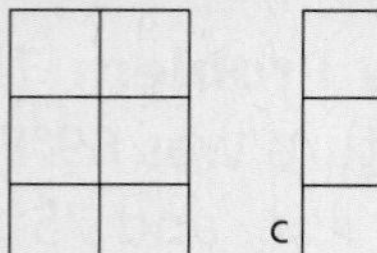

A B C

Ask: **Are chocolate bars A and B equal?** yes **Is A *as* big *as* B?** yes **Does B have *as many* pieces *as* A?** yes **Does A have 2 *times as many* pieces as C?** yes Say: **C has __ as many pieces as A.** half

▸ Review Comparison Statements WHOLE CLASS

Write the following statements on the board or overhead.

Jie has 5 markers. Yasir has 15 markers.

Ask students to make some comparison statements about the numbers of markers that Jie and Yasir have. Write the statements on the board. Make sure all four of the following comparisons are mentioned.

- Yasir has 10 more markers than Jie.
- Jie has 10 fewer markers than Yasir.
- Yasir has 3 times as many markers as Jie.
- Jie has $\frac{1}{3}$ as many markers as Yasir.

Remind students that the first statement can be represented with an addition equation. Write the addition equation on the board, and add labels to show which quantity is the number of markers Jie has (J) and which is the number of markers Yasir has (Y).

$$\underset{Y}{15} = 5 + \underset{J}{10}$$

Give students time to write and label equations for the other statements, and have volunteers present their answers.

- Jie has 10 fewer markers than Yasir.

$$\underset{J}{5} = \underset{Y}{15} - 10$$

- Yasir has 3 times as many markers as Jie.

$$\underset{Y}{15} = 3 \times \underset{J}{5}$$

- Jie has $\frac{1}{3}$ as many markers as Yasir.

$$\underset{J}{5} = \underset{Y}{15} \div 3 \quad \text{or} \quad \underset{J}{5} = \frac{1}{3} \text{ of } \underset{Y}{15} \quad \text{or} \quad \underset{J}{5} = \frac{1}{3} \times \underset{Y}{15}$$

Make sure all three possibilities are mentioned for the "$\frac{1}{3}$ as many" statement. Remind students that, in Unit 5, they learned "$\frac{1}{3}$ as many as 15" is $15 \div 3$. Now they know two more ways to think about this situation: $\frac{1}{3}$ of 15 and $\frac{1}{3} \times 15$.

11–4 Class Activity

Name ______________________ Date __________

▶ Use a Bar Graph to Compare

Use the bar graph below to complete exercises 1–4.

Markers in Students' Desks

Student: Jie, Yasir, Derek, Keisha, Amanda

0 5 10 15 20 25 30

Number of Markers

Fill in the blanks.

1. Jie has $\frac{1}{3}$ as many markers as Yasir has.
   Yasir has 3 times as many markers as Jie has.
2. Derek has 4 times as many markers as Jie has.
   Jie has $\frac{1}{4}$ as many markers as Derek has.
3. Derek has 2 times as many markers as Keisha has.
   Keisha has $\frac{1}{2}$ as many markers as Derek has.
4. Amanda has 2 times as many markers as Yasir has.
   Yasir has $\frac{1}{2}$ as many markers as Amanda has.

UNIT 11 LESSON 4 Compare with Fractions **403**

Student Activity Book page 403

▶ Use a Bar Graph to Compare WHOLE CLASS

Have students look at the bar graph on Student Book page 403. Make sure they understand what the graph shows and how to read it. Point out that the scale is marked in intervals of 5. If you feel your students have a good understanding of multiplication comparisons, have them solve problems 1–4 independently, and then discuss the solutions. Otherwise, work through the problems as a class.

Divide the class into two random groups to do the "comparison chant." See **Math Talk in Action** in the side column for a sample classroom discussion.

Differentiated Instruction

Extra Help Have students use two-color counters to represent the numbers of markers that Jie and Yasir have.

To show that Yasir has ten more markers than Jie, and that Jie has ten fewer markers than Yasir, have students line up 15 counters showing red and 5 counters showing yellow, as below.

To show that Yasir has 3 times as many markers as Jie, and that Jie has one third as many markers as Yasir, have students divide 15 counters showing red into 3 groups of 5. Then they can place a row of 5 counters showing yellow next to them.

Math Talk in Action

Jie and Yasir

Students: 5 and 15

Boys, compare Jie to Yasir.

Boys: 5 is $\frac{1}{3}$ as many as 15.

Girls, compare Yasir to Jie.

Girls: 15 is 3 times as many as 5.

Repeat for Derek and Keisha, and Amanda and Yasir.

Activity 2

Comparison Word Problems

 25 MINUTES

Goal: Solve word problems involving comparisons and multiplication.

Materials: Student Activity Book or Hardcover Book p. 404

 **NCTM Standards:**

Number and Operations
Problem Solving
Representation

Ongoing Assessment

Ask questions such as the following:

- Seth has four times as many pencils as Darnell. What is another "as many as" statement you can make about the numbers of pencils?
- Ina has one fifth as many crayons as Nomi. What is another "as many as" statement you can make about the numbers of crayons?
- Charlie has 8 pens and Aliana has 16 pens. What are two "as many as" statements you can make about the numbers of pens?

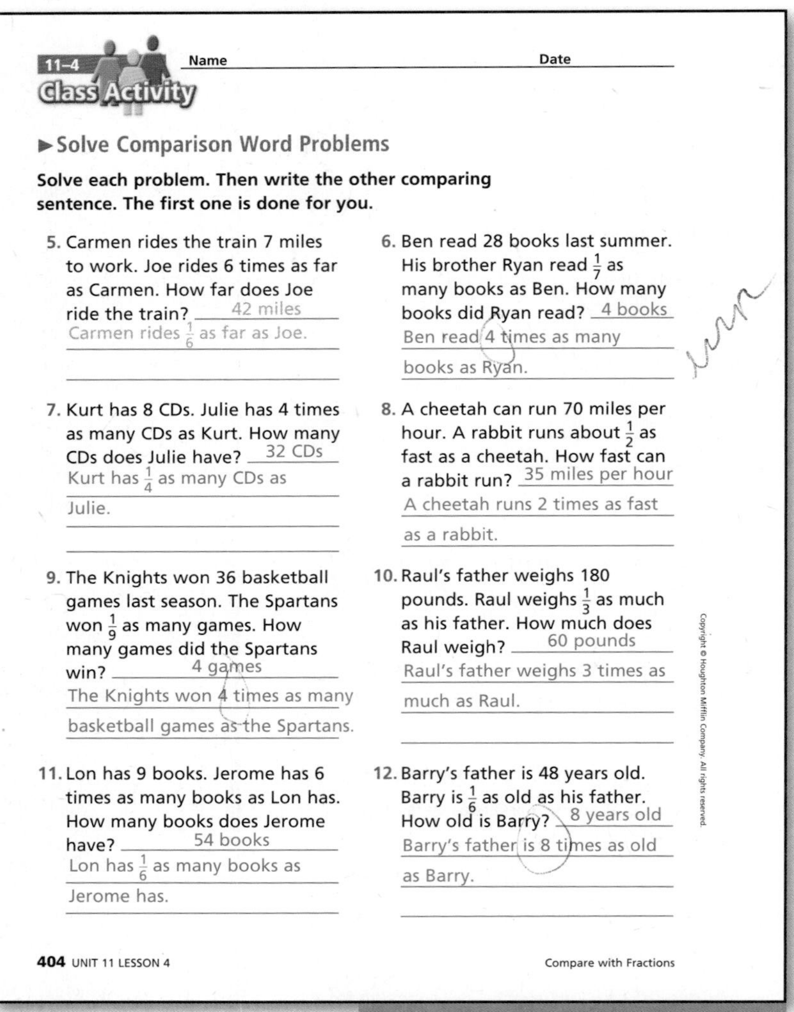

11–4 Class Activity Name ________ Date ________

▶ Solve Comparison Word Problems

Solve each problem. Then write the other comparing sentence. The first one is done for you.

5. Carmen rides the train 7 miles to work. Joe rides 6 times as far as Carmen. How far does Joe ride the train? 42 miles
Carmen rides $\frac{1}{6}$ as far as Joe.

6. Ben read 28 books last summer. His brother Ryan read $\frac{1}{7}$ as many books as Ben. How many books did Ryan read? 4 books
Ben read 4 times as many books as Ryan.

7. Kurt has 8 CDs. Julie has 4 times as many CDs as Kurt. How many CDs does Julie have? 32 CDs
Kurt has $\frac{1}{4}$ as many CDs as Julie.

8. A cheetah can run 70 miles per hour. A rabbit runs about $\frac{1}{2}$ as fast as a cheetah. How fast can a rabbit run? 35 miles per hour
A cheetah runs 2 times as fast as a rabbit.

9. The Knights won 36 basketball games last season. The Spartans won $\frac{1}{9}$ as many games. How many games did the Spartans win? 4 games
The Knights won 4 times as many basketball games as the Spartans.

10. Raul's father weighs 180 pounds. Raul weighs $\frac{1}{3}$ as much as his father. How much does Raul weigh? 60 pounds
Raul's father weighs 3 times as much as Raul.

11. Lon has 9 books. Jerome has 6 times as many books as Lon has. How many books does Jerome have? 54 books
Lon has $\frac{1}{6}$ as many books as Jerome has.

12. Barry's father is 48 years old. Barry is $\frac{1}{6}$ as old as his father. How old is Barry? 8 years old
Barry's father is 8 times as old as Barry.

Student Activity Book page 404

▶ Solve Comparison Word Problems WHOLE CLASS

Using **Solve and Discuss,** have students solve problems 6–12. The first one is done for them.

Students may have some difficulty solving problems 8 and 10, which requires finding $\frac{1}{2}$ of 70 and $\frac{1}{3}$ of 180. The following are two possible ways students might reason about these problems.

- Think about repeated addition. For problem 8, think of a number which, when added to itself, gives 70. For problem 10, think of a number which, when added together three times, gives 180.
- Think of 10-sticks. 70 is seven 10-sticks, so half of 70 is three and a half 10-sticks, which is 35. 180 is eighteen 10-sticks, so one third of 180 is 18 tens ÷ 3, or 6 tens, which is 60.

After the solutions have been presented, go back to problems 6, 8, 9, and 10. Work with students to write three different equations for each problem. For example, for problem 9, write the following.

$$4 = \frac{1}{9} \text{ of } 36 \qquad 4 = \frac{1}{9} \times 36 \qquad 4 = 36 \div 9$$

2 Going Further

Differentiated Instruction

Intervention

Activity Card 11-4

Fraction Towers Activity Card 11-4 ●

Work: In pairs

Use:

- MathBoard materials
- Connecting cubes (12 red, 6 blue, 4 white, 3 yellow, 2 green for each student)

1. On Your Own Make five separate cube towers, using connecting cubes of the same color.
2. Compare your towers with the towers that your partner made. Work together to write as many statements as you can about the number of cubes in the towers. Each statement should use the words "as many as."

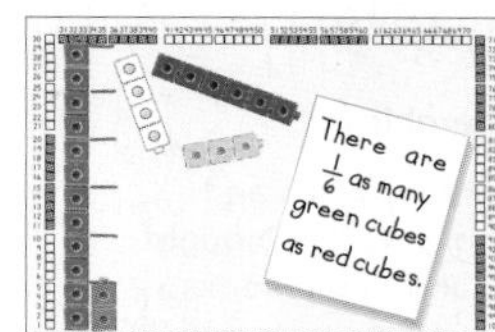

Unit 11, Lesson 4

Activity Note Show students how to place two towers next to each other and then move the shorter tower up along the taller one, marking off lengths.

Math Writing Prompt

Reasoning Jason has 10 stickers. Is it possible for Sari to have exactly one fourth as many stickers? Explain your answer.

Software Support

Warm Up 5.07

On Level

Activity Card 11-4

Empty the Bowl Activity Card 11-4 ▲

Work: In pairs

Use:

- 100 Counters
- Plastic bowl
- 12 Index cards

1. Work Together Place 100 counters in the bowl. Then write the expressions below on 12 index cards. Shuffle the cards and place them face down.

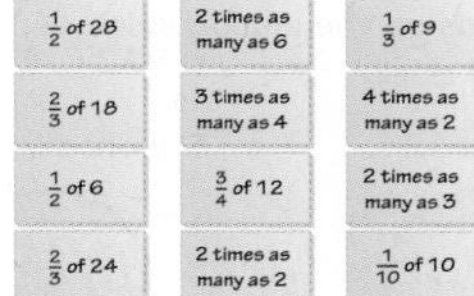

2. Take turns. Choose the top card and decide how many counters the expression represents. Then take that number of counters out of the bowl.
3. When the bowl is empty, the player with the greater number of counters wins.

Unit 11, Lesson 4

Activity Note Make sure that each player checks each other's work to make sure that the correct number of counters is being removed.

Math Writing Prompt

Explain Your Thinking Which is more: one fifth as many as a number of marbles, or one fourth as many as the same number of marbles? Explain your thinking.

Software Support

Fraction Action: Number Line Mine, Level L

Challenge

Activity Card 11-4

Break the Code Activity Card 11-4 ■

Work: In pairs

1. Use the statements below to break the code and find what number each symbol represents.

✿ is four times as many as ●.
★ is one fifth as many as ✿.
♦ is one tenth as many as seventy.
♥ is half as many as ▲.
● plus twice as many as ♦ is nineteen.
▲ is three times as many as ★.

♦ = 7,
● = 5,
✿ = 20,
★ = 4,
▲ = 12,
♥ = 6

2. Think How can you decide which statement you should use to begin to break the code? Look for a statement with only one symbol.
3. Analyze Is there a better strategy than guess and check to help you break the code? Use each symbol you decode to find the value of another symbol related to it.

Unit 11, Lesson 4

Activity Note If time permits, have each student create a different code and use it to write a new set of "as many as" statements for a partner to decode.

Math Writing Prompt

Investigate Math Fill in the blanks. Explain.

● is two times as many as ■.
■ is one fourth as many as ▲.
● is ______ as many as ▲.

DESTINATION Math®

Software Support

Course II: Module 2: Unit 3: Fractional Parts

3 Homework and Spiral Review

11–4 Homework **Goal:** Additional Practice

This Homework page provides practice in making comparison statements and representing them with multiplication equations.

11–4 Remembering **Goal:** Spiral Review

This Remembering page would be appropriate anytime after today's lesson.

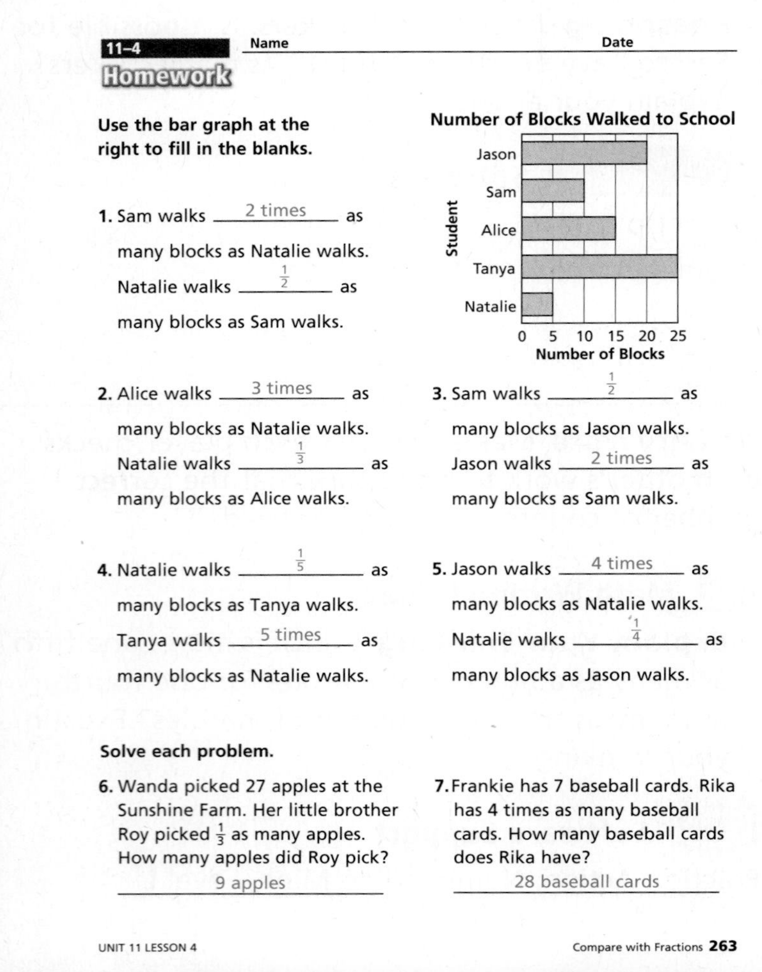

11–4 Homework Name ______ Date ______

Use the bar graph at the right to fill in the blanks.

Number of Blocks Walked to School

1. Sam walks 2 times as many blocks as Natalie walks. Natalie walks $\frac{1}{2}$ as many blocks as Sam walks.

2. Alice walks 3 times as many blocks as Natalie walks. Natalie walks $\frac{1}{3}$ as many blocks as Alice walks.

3. Sam walks $\frac{1}{2}$ as many blocks as Jason walks. Jason walks 2 times as many blocks as Sam walks.

4. Natalie walks $\frac{1}{5}$ as many blocks as Tanya walks. Tanya walks 5 times as many blocks as Natalie walks.

5. Jason walks 4 times as many blocks as Natalie walks. Natalie walks $\frac{1}{4}$ as many blocks as Jason walks.

Solve each problem.

6. Wanda picked 27 apples at the Sunshine Farm. Her little brother Roy picked $\frac{1}{3}$ as many apples. How many apples did Roy pick?
9 apples

7. Frankie has 7 baseball cards. Rika has 4 times as many baseball cards. How many baseball cards does Rika have?
28 baseball cards

UNIT 11 LESSON 4 Compare with Fractions **263**

Homework and Remembering page 263

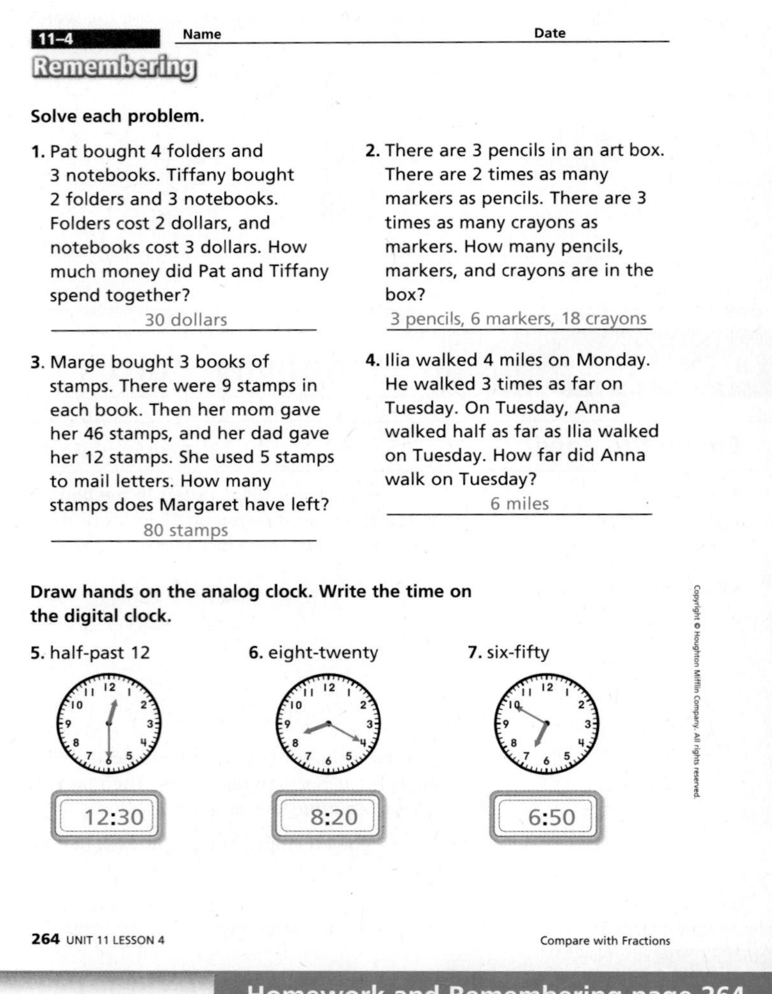

11–4 Remembering Name ______ Date ______

Solve each problem.

1. Pat bought 4 folders and 3 notebooks. Tiffany bought 2 folders and 3 notebooks. Folders cost 2 dollars, and notebooks cost 3 dollars. How much money did Pat and Tiffany spend together?
30 dollars

2. There are 3 pencils in an art box. There are 2 times as many markers as pencils. There are 3 times as many crayons as markers. How many pencils, markers, and crayons are in the box?
3 pencils, 6 markers, 18 crayons

3. Marge bought 3 books of stamps. There were 9 stamps in each book. Then her mom gave her 46 stamps, and her dad gave her 12 stamps. She used 5 stamps to mail letters. How many stamps does Margaret have left?
80 stamps

4. Ilia walked 4 miles on Monday. He walked 3 times as far on Tuesday. On Tuesday, Anna walked half as far as Ilia walked on Tuesday. How far did Anna walk on Tuesday?
6 miles

Draw hands on the analog clock. Write the time on the digital clock.

5. half-past 12 — 12:30

6. eight-twenty — 8:20

7. six-fifty — 6:50

264 UNIT 11 LESSON 4 Compare with Fractions

Homework and Remembering page 264

Home or School Activity

Social Studies Connection

State Capitals Have students research and list all the state capitals. Then have them answer questions such as:

- What fraction of the names of the capitals begin with a vowel?
- What fraction of the names of the capitals have more than 5 letters?

State	Capital
Alabama	Montgomery
Alaska	Juneau
Arizona	Phoenix
Arkansas	Little Rock
California	Sacramento
Colorado	Denver

Practice Fractional Comparisons

Lesson Objectives

- Make "as many as" comparison statements.
- Solve word problems involving multiplication.

Vocabulary
comparison

The Day at a Glance

Today's Goals	Materials	
1 Teaching the Lesson **A1:** Complete comparison statements based on information in a bar graph. **A2:** Solve word problems involving multiplication comparisons.	**Lesson Activities** Student Activity Book pp. 405–406 or Student Hardcover Book pp. 405–406 Homework and Remembering pp. 265–266 Quick Quiz 1 (Assessment Guide) MathBoard materials *Jump, Kangaroo, Jump!* by Stuart J. Murphy (HarperTrophy, 1999)	**Going Further** Activity Cards 11-5 Connecting cubes Sticky notes Fraction of the Day (TRB M129) Crayons or colored markers Math Journals
2 Going Further ▸ Differentiated Instruction		
3 Homework and Spiral Review		

Use Math Talk today!

Keeping Skills Sharp

Quick Practice — 5 MINUTES

Goal: Use a fraction to represent part of a group.

Fractions in Action The **Student Leader** selects a group of 6 to 10 students to come to the front of the room and tells some of these students to raise his or her hand. The leader then asks the class what fraction of the group has his or her hand raised. On the leader's signal, the class answers in unison.

The leader changes the size of the group by having some students sit down or having new students come to the front. The leader chooses new students to raise their hands and repeats the procedure. (See Unit 11 Lesson 2.)

Daily Routines

Homework Review For students who did not read the bar graph correctly, have them follow each bar to the right and write the total at the end. Review as a class.

Place Value Decide if the second number is *1,000 more* or *1,000 less* than the first number.

1. 3,108 → 2,108 1,000 less
2. 5,914 → 6,914 1,000 more
3. 2,076 → 3,076 1,000 more

1 Teaching the Lesson

Activity 1

Practice Comparisons Involving Fractions

 **25 MINUTES**

Goal: Complete comparison statements based on information in a bar graph.

Materials: Student Activity Book or Hardcover Book p. 405

 **NCTM Standards:**
Number and Operations
Data Analysis and Probability
Representation

Math Talk in Action

Daffodils and Daisies
Students: 8 and 2

Compare Daffodils to Daisies.
Students: 8 is 4 times as many as 2.

Compare Daisies to Daffodils in a different way.
Students: 2 is $\frac{1}{4}$ as many as 8.

Repeat for several other sets of flowers.

Ongoing Assessment

Observe as students do the exercises on Student Book page 405. Ask questions such as the following:

- How do you know that 4 times as many people like daffodils as like daisies?
- In exercise 2, how did you decide where to write *2 times* and where to write $\frac{1}{2}$?
- How will you decide the comparison between the number of people who like lilies and the number of people who like roses?

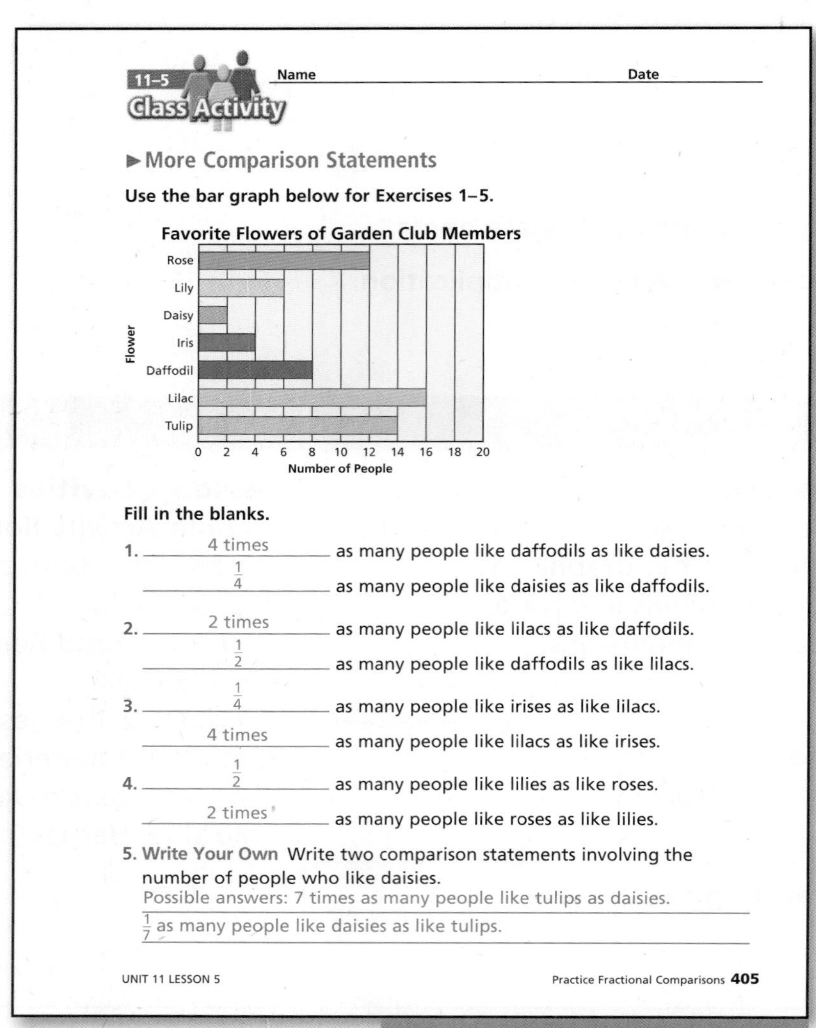

11-5 Class Activity   Name ______ Date ______

► More Comparison Statements

Use the bar graph below for Exercises 1–5.

Fill in the blanks.

1. 4 times as many people like daffodils as like daisies.
   $\frac{1}{4}$ as many people like daisies as like daffodils.
2. 2 times as many people like lilacs as like daffodils.
   $\frac{1}{2}$ as many people like daffodils as like lilacs.
3. $\frac{1}{4}$ as many people like irises as like lilacs.
   4 times as many people like lilacs as like irises.
4. $\frac{1}{2}$ as many people like lilies as like roses.
   2 times as many people like roses as like lilies.
5. **Write Your Own** Write two comparison statements involving the number of people who like daisies.
   Possible answers: 7 times as many people like tulips as daisies.
   $\frac{1}{7}$ as many people like daisies as like tulips.

UNIT 11 LESSON 5   Practice Fractional Comparisons **405**

Student Activity Book page 405

► More Comparison Statements WHOLE CLASS

Have students look at the bar graph on Student Book page 405. Make sure students understand what the graph shows and how to read it. Point out that the scale is marked in intervals of 2. Work through exercise 1 as a class, and then have students complete exercises 2–5 independently.

Have students do the "comparison chant." See **Math Talk in Action** for a sample classroom discussion.

Activity 2

Comparison Word Problems

▶ Make a Drawing to Solve Comparison Word Problems WHOLE CLASS

Write the following problem on the board.

Donato has 6 CDs.
Melodie has 4 times as many CDs as Donato has.
How many CDs does Melodie have?

Ask a volunteer to read the problem. Then ask questions such as the following:

- Do we know exactly how many CDs Donato or Melodie has? Yes. Donato has 6 CDs. How can we show that with a drawing? Draw a comparison bar for Donato.

D | 6 |

- How many CDs does Melodie have? She has 4 times as many as Donato. How can we show 4 times as many as 6? Make a comparison bar of 4 groups of 6. What multiplication does the drawing show? $4 \times 6 = 24$ So how many CDs does Melodie have? 24 CDs

M | 6 | 6 | 6 | 6 |

Next, write the following problem on the board.

Polly has 21 action figures.
Elian has $\frac{1}{3}$ as many action figures as Polly.
How many action figures does Elian have?

Ask a volunteer to read aloud the problem. Use **Solve and Discuss** for the problem.

P | 21 |

E | |

$\frac{1}{3} \times 21 = 7$

25 MINUTES

Goal: Solve word problems involving multiplication comparisons.

Materials: MathBoard materials, Student Activity Book or Hardcover Book p. 406

NCTM Standards:
Number and Operations
Problem Solving
Representation

Alternate Approach

Equal-Shares Drawings Some students may prefer to picture fractional comparisons by making Equal-Shares Drawings. For example, they can picture "$\frac{1}{3}$ as many as 21" as shown below.

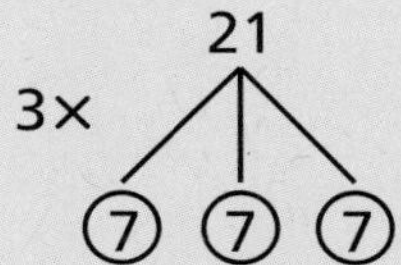

Students might also find Equal-Shares Drawings to be particularly helpful when a problem involves greater numbers.

English Language Learners

On the board, write: *Naomi ate 4 cookies. Wendy ate $\frac{1}{2}$ as many cookies as Naomi. Jude ate 2 times as many cookies as Naomi.* Draw groups of 2, 4, and 8 cookies. Help students identify who ate each group.

- **Beginning** Say: ***$\frac{1}{2}$ as many* means *less*.** Ask: **Who ate less than Naomi?** Wendy Continue with *2 times as many.*
- **Intermediate** Ask: **Which means *less*, *$\frac{1}{2}$ as many* or *2 times as many*?** $\frac{1}{2}$ **Who ate 2 cookies?** Wendy
- **Advanced** Have students tell which comparison means more and which means less, then identify the groups.

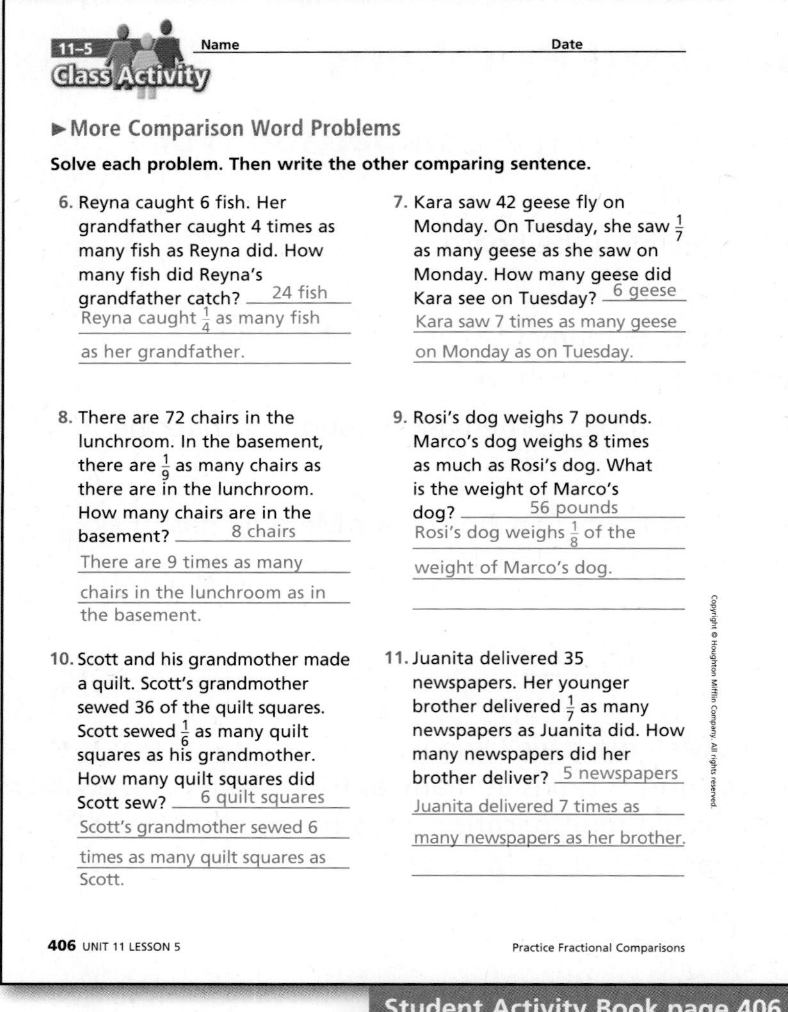

11–5 Class Activity Name Date

▶ More Comparison Word Problems

Solve each problem. Then write the other comparing sentence.

6. Reyna caught 6 fish. Her grandfather caught 4 times as many fish as Reyna did. How many fish did Reyna's grandfather catch? 24 fish
Reyna caught $\frac{1}{4}$ as many fish as her grandfather.

7. Kara saw 42 geese fly on Monday. On Tuesday, she saw $\frac{1}{7}$ as many geese as she saw on Monday. How many geese did Kara see on Tuesday? 6 geese
Kara saw 7 times as many geese on Monday as on Tuesday.

8. There are 72 chairs in the lunchroom. In the basement, there are $\frac{1}{9}$ as many chairs as there are in the lunchroom. How many chairs are in the basement? 8 chairs
There are 9 times as many chairs in the lunchroom as in the basement.

9. Rosi's dog weighs 7 pounds. Marco's dog weighs 8 times as much as Rosi's dog. What is the weight of Marco's dog? 56 pounds
Rosi's dog weighs $\frac{1}{8}$ of the weight of Marco's dog.

10. Scott and his grandmother made a quilt. Scott's grandmother sewed 36 of the quilt squares. Scott sewed $\frac{1}{6}$ as many quilt squares as his grandmother. How many quilt squares did Scott sew? 6 quilt squares
Scott's grandmother sewed 6 times as many quilt squares as Scott.

11. Juanita delivered 35 newspapers. Her younger brother delivered $\frac{1}{7}$ as many newspapers as Juanita did. How many newspapers did her brother deliver? 5 newspapers
Juanita delivered 7 times as many newspapers as her brother.

406 UNIT 11 LESSON 5 Practice Fractional Comparisons

Student Activity Book page 406

▶ More Comparison Word Problems WHOLE CLASS

Using **Solve and Discuss,** have students solve problems 6–11 on Student Book page 406. Have students use numeric solution methods whenever possible. However, if they are not sure how to proceed with a given problem, suggest that they draw comparison bars.

After the solutions have been presented, go back to problems 7, 8, 10, and 11. Work with students to write three different equations for each problem. For example, the following are the three equations for problem 7.

$$6 = \frac{1}{7} \text{ of } 42 \qquad 6 = \frac{1}{7} \times 42 \qquad 6 = 42 \div 7$$

Quick Quiz

See Assessment Guide for Unit 11 Quick Quiz 1.

2 Going Further

Differentiated Instruction

Intervention — Activity Card 11-5

Display Data in Different Ways — Activity Card 11-5

Work: In pairs

Use:

- Connecting cubes
- Sticky notes

1. Look at the data below. Use connecting cubes to represent the number of votes for each type of muffin. Use a different color for each flavor.

Favorite Types of Muffins

Types of Muffins	Number of Votes
Blueberry	8
Cranberry	16
Bran	2
Apple	12
Corn	4

2. Use a sticky note to label each tower of cubes.

3. Write several "as many as" comparisons about the data that your towers show.

Unit 11, Lesson 5

Activity Note Each pair of flavors can be compared in two ways. For example, there are $\frac{1}{2}$ as many bran muffins as corn, and twice as many corn as bran.

Math Writing Prompt

Make a Drawing Make a drawing to show the difference between "3 times as many as 6" and "$\frac{1}{3}$ as many as 6."

Software Support

Warm Up 5.07

On Level — Activity Card 11-5

"As Many As" Riddles — Activity Card 11-5

Work: In pairs

1. **Work Together** Solve each of the four riddles below. Find the mystery number in each riddle.

    1. Six times as many as this number is 48. What is the number? 8
    2. One seventh as many as this number is 9. What is the number? 63
    3. One more than three times as many as this number is 10. What is the number? 3
    4. Two less than one eighth as many as this number is 5. What is the number? 56

2. **Analyze** What strategies did you use to solve the riddles?
3. **On Your Own** Write four "as many as" riddles and exchange with your partner to solve.

Unit 11, Lesson 5

Activity Note Students may use guess-and-test as a strategy for some of the riddles. Others such as Riddle 1 can be solved by using opposite operations.

Math Writing Prompt

Explain Your Thinking Explain how finding $\frac{1}{3}$ as many as a number is related to division.

Software Support

Fraction Action: Number Line Mine, Level L

Challenge — Activity Card 11-5

Fractions of a Day — Activity Card 11-5

Work: In pairs

Use:

- TRB M129 (Fraction of a Day)
- Crayons or colored markers

1. **Work Together** Make a list of things you do during a school day. Then estimate how much time you spend doing those activities.
2. Organize the information in a table. Then use the table to complete the circle graph on TRB M129. Each part of the circle represents 1 hour.

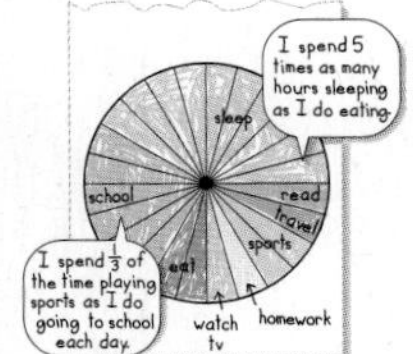

3. Write as many "as many as" comparison statements as possible, using the data.

Unit 11, Lesson 5

Activity Note Have students round their estimates to whole hours before transferring the data to the circle graph.

Math Writing Prompt

Investigate Math What is equal to *10 times as many as* $\frac{1}{2}$? Explain your answer.

Software Support

Course II: Module 2: Unit 3: Fractional Parts

3 Homework and Spiral Review

Goal: Additional Practice

✓ Include students' completed Homework page as part of their portfolios.

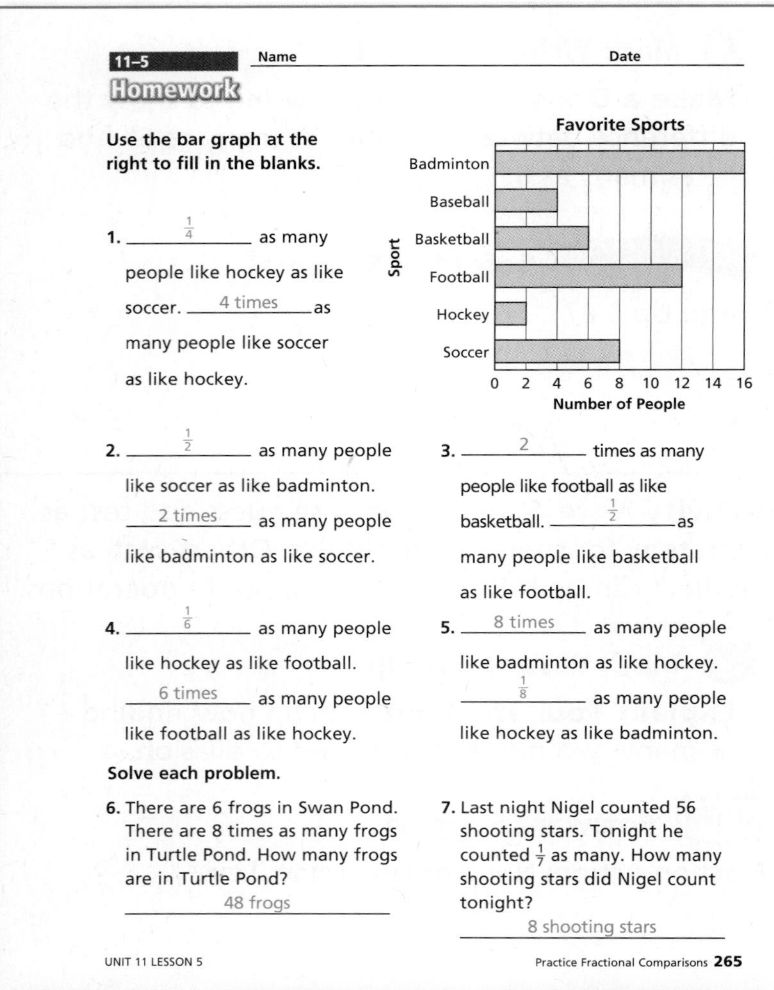

11–5 Name ______ Date ______

Homework

Use the bar graph at the right to fill in the blanks.

Favorite Sports

Sport: Badminton, Baseball, Basketball, Football, Hockey, Soccer

Number of People: 0 2 4 6 8 10 12 14 16

1. $\frac{1}{4}$ as many people like hockey as like soccer. 4 times as many people like soccer as like hockey.

2. $\frac{1}{2}$ as many people like soccer as like badminton. 2 times as many people like badminton as like soccer.

3. 2 times as many people like football as like basketball. $\frac{1}{2}$ as many people like basketball as like football.

4. $\frac{1}{6}$ as many people like hockey as like football. 6 times as many people like football as like hockey.

5. 8 times as many people like badminton as like hockey. $\frac{1}{8}$ as many people like hockey as like badminton.

Solve each problem.

6. There are 6 frogs in Swan Pond. There are 8 times as many frogs in Turtle Pond. How many frogs are in Turtle Pond? 48 frogs

7. Last night Nigel counted 56 shooting stars. Tonight he counted $\frac{1}{7}$ as many. How many shooting stars did Nigel count tonight? 8 shooting stars

UNIT 11 LESSON 5 Practice Fractional Comparisons **265**

Homework and Remembering page 265

11–5 Remembering **Goal:** Spiral Review

This Remembering page would be appropriate anytime after today's lesson.

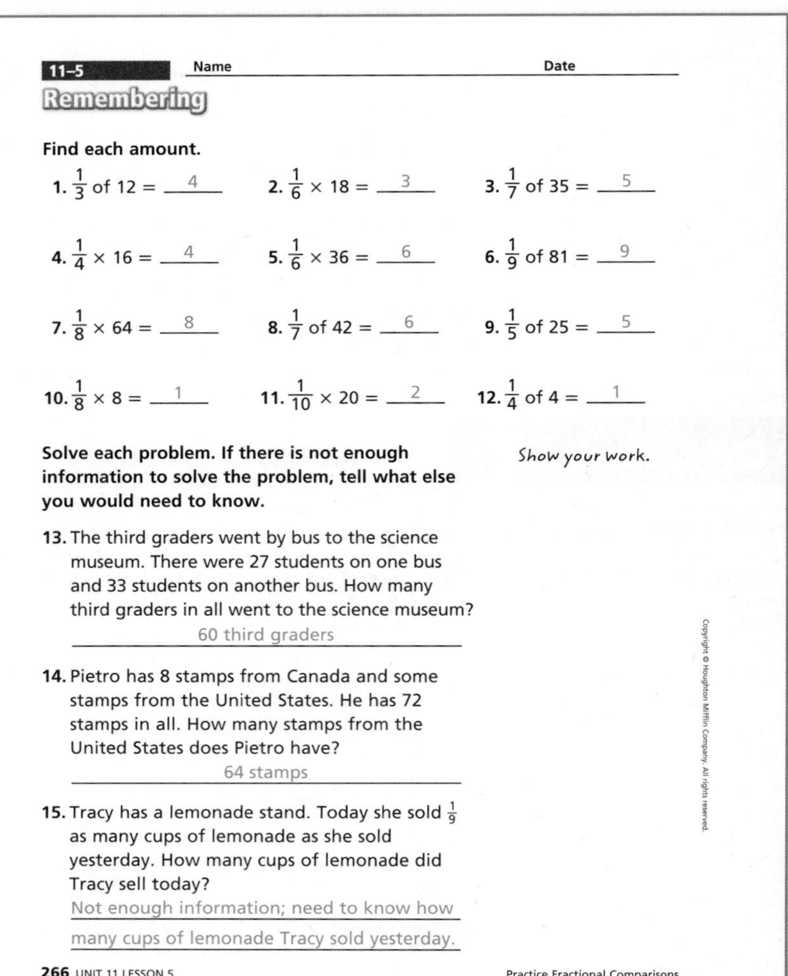

11–5 Name ______ Date ______

Remembering

Find each amount.

1. $\frac{1}{3}$ of 12 = 4
2. $\frac{1}{6} \times 18$ = 3
3. $\frac{1}{7}$ of 35 = 5
4. $\frac{1}{4} \times 16$ = 4
5. $\frac{1}{6} \times 36$ = 6
6. $\frac{1}{9}$ of 81 = 9
7. $\frac{1}{8} \times 64$ = 8
8. $\frac{1}{7}$ of 42 = 6
9. $\frac{1}{5}$ of 25 = 5
10. $\frac{1}{8} \times 8$ = 1
11. $\frac{1}{10} \times 20$ = 2
12. $\frac{1}{4}$ of 4 = 1

Solve each problem. If there is not enough information to solve the problem, tell what else you would need to know. *Show your work.*

13. The third graders went by bus to the science museum. There were 27 students on one bus and 33 students on another bus. How many third graders in all went to the science museum? 60 third graders

14. Pietro has 8 stamps from Canada and some stamps from the United States. He has 72 stamps in all. How many stamps from the United States does Pietro have? 64 stamps

15. Tracy has a lemonade stand. Today she sold $\frac{1}{9}$ as many cups of lemonade as she sold yesterday. How many cups of lemonade did Tracy sell today? Not enough information; need to know how many cups of lemonade Tracy sold yesterday.

Copyright © Houghton Mifflin Company. All rights reserved.

266 UNIT 11 LESSON 5 Practice Fractional Comparisons

Homework and Remembering page 266

Home or School Activity

Literature Connection

Jump, Kangaroo, Jump! Read aloud *Jump, Kangaroo, Jump!* by Stuart J. Murphy, illustrated by Kevin O' Malley (HarperTrophy, 1999). Have students act out the 12 kangaroos in the story playing tug-of-war and having races. Then have students divide a group of 24 into the same fractional parts. You may want to adapt some of the activities in the book for class activities.

Find a Fraction of a Set or a Number

Lesson Objective

- Discover a method for multiplying a whole number by any fraction.

Vocabulary

whole number	set
product	multiple

The Day at a Glance

Today's Goals	Materials	
1 Teaching the Lesson **A1:** Find a fractional part of a set. **A2:** Solve problems involving finding a fraction of a number. **A3:** Write a rule for multiplying a whole number by a fraction.	**Lesson Activities** Student Activity Book pp. 407–410 or Student Hardcover Book pp. 407–410 and Activity Workbook p. 185 (includes table) Homework and Remembering pp. 267–268	**Going Further** Activity Cards 11-6 Paper Plates Two-color counters Index cards (12) Math Journals
2 Going Further ► Differentiated Instruction		
3 Homework and Spiral Review		

123 Use Math Talk today!

Keeping Skills Sharp

Quick Practice — 5 MINUTES

Goal: Practice "as many as" comparisons.

Comparison Chant Divide the class into two groups. The **Student Leader** writes a factor and one of its count-bys on the board. The leader asks one group to compare the first number to the second, and then asks the second group to compare the second number to the first. Repeat with several more pairs of numbers.

Student Leader: Group 1, compare 5 to 20. Group 2, compare 20 to 5.

Group 1: 5 is $\frac{1}{4}$ as many as 40.

Group 2: 20 is 4 times as many as 5.

Daily Routines

Homework Review Let students work together to check their work. Remind students to use what they know about helping others.

Create a Pattern Create a shrinking pattern using geometric figures. If necessary, use pattern blocks and counters to visually create the pattern. Then, trace the figures onto paper. Have the class find the next figure in your pattern.

1 Teaching the Lesson

Activity 1

Fractional Parts of Sets

15 MINUTES

Goal: Find a fractional part of a set.

Materials: Student Activity Book or Hardcover Book p. 407 and Activity Workbook p. 185

 **NCTM Standards:**
Number and Operations
Problem Solving
Representation

English Language Learners

Guide students to tell about the table. Write *set* and *fractional part* on the board.

- **Beginning** Point to the table. Ask: **Are there 4 sets of t-shirts?** yes **Are the colors *fractional parts*?** yes
- **Intermediate** Ask: **Is each size a *set* or a *fractional part*?** set Say: **Each color is a *fractional part* of a __.** set
- **Advanced** Have students tell about the *sets* and *fractional parts* on the table.

11–6 Class Activity  Name Date

▶ Explore Fractional Parts of a Set

1. The Promo Company prints T-shirts for the rock band MathGrlzz. Complete the table to show how many shirts of each size and color they printed on Monday.

MathGrlzz Shirts Printed on Monday

	$\frac{1}{6}$ Yellow	$\frac{2}{6}$ Red	$\frac{3}{6}$ Blue
18 small shirts	3	6	9
36 medium shirts	6	12	18
54 large shirts	9	18	27
48 extra large shirts	8	16	24

2. The Promo Company also prints caps and hats for MathGrlzz. Complete the table to show how many caps or hats of each type and color they printed on Monday.

MathGrlzz Caps and Hats Printed on Monday

	$\frac{1}{7}$ Yellow	$\frac{4}{7}$ Red	$\frac{2}{7}$ Blue
49 baseball caps	7	28	14
21 knit caps	3	12	6
35 floppy hats	5	20	10
14 straw hats	2	8	4

UNIT 11 LESSON 6 Find a Fraction of a Set or a Number **407**

Student Activity Book page 407

▶ Explore Fractional Parts of a Set WHOLE CLASS

Have students read problem 1 on Student Book page 407 and have them look at the table. Make sure they understand what the completed table should show.

- Let's start with the first row. The company printed 18 small shirts. What fraction of the shirts were yellow? $\frac{1}{6}$ So $\frac{1}{6}$ of the 18 small shirts were yellow. How many shirts is this? 3 shirts How did you figure this out? $\frac{1}{6}$ of 18 is 18 divided by 6, which is 3.

Ask students what three equations can be written to show this

$$\frac{1}{6} \text{ of } 18 = 3 \qquad \frac{1}{6} \times 18 = 3 \qquad 18 \div 6 = 3$$

Point out that "of" and "x" mean the same thing.

- The table also tells us that $\frac{2}{6}$ of the 18 small shirts were red. How can we find $\frac{2}{6}$ of 18?

Give students a few minutes to try to figure this out independently.

After a few minutes, ask students to share their answers and explain how they found them. See the **Math Talk in Action** in the side column for two common solution methods.

Be sure the numerical method is discussed. Write the following on the board.

$\frac{2}{6}$ of $18 = 6$ $\qquad$ $\frac{2}{6} \times 18 = 6$ $\qquad$ $(18 \div 6) \times 2 = 6$

Next, point out that $\frac{3}{6}$ of the 18 small shirts are blue. Ask students to figure out how many this is, and then select students to share their solutions. Make sure the method of multiplying $\frac{1}{6}$ of 18, or 3, multiplied by 3 to get 9 is mentioned. (Some students may see that, because the total number of small shirts is 18, you can find the number of blue shirts by figuring that the number of red and yellow shirts combined is 9, then subtracting 9 from 18.)

Using the **Solve and Discuss** structure, have students complete the remaining three rows of the table. Encourage them to try to find the answers numerically. They can make drawings to check their answers if they need to. Ask questions about the completed table.

- How do the numbers in the *Red* column compare to the numbers in the *Yellow* column? They are twice as much. Why? because $\frac{2}{6}$ of a number is twice as much as $\frac{1}{6}$ of the number.
- How do the numbers in the *Blue* column compare to the numbers in the *Yellow* column? They are 3 times as much. Why? because $\frac{3}{6}$ of a number is 3 times as much as $\frac{1}{6}$ of the number

Have students complete the three rows of the table in problem 2. Discuss the answers and ask questions about the completed table, as you did for the table in problem 1.

Teaching Note

Math Background The numerical method of calculating $\frac{2}{6} \times 18$ can be shown in symbols as follows.

$$\begin{aligned} &\tfrac{2}{6} \times 18 \\ &= (2 \times \tfrac{1}{6}) \times 18 \\ &= 2 \times (\tfrac{1}{6} \times 18) \\ &= 2 \times 3 \\ &= 6 \end{aligned}$$

Math Talk in Action

Duane: We learned that $\frac{2}{6}$ is $2 \times \frac{1}{6}$ .I think that $\frac{2}{6}$ of 18 must be twice as much as $\frac{1}{6}$ of 18.

Keleigh: Well, $\frac{1}{6}$ of 18 is 3.

Javier: So $\frac{2}{6}$ of 18 is 2 times 3. That's 6!

Amaya: Can we make a drawing instead?

Luca: Sure. Divide 18 things into 6 equal groups, like this.

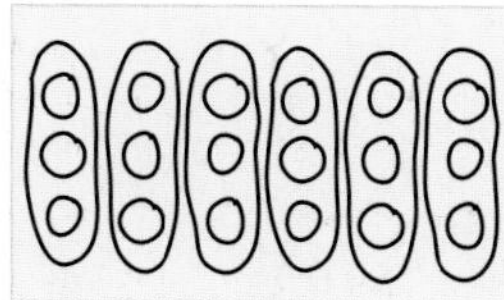

Nevaeh: There are 3 things in each group. So it shows that $\frac{1}{6}$ of 18 is 3.

Osvaldo: Right! Now color the things in 2 of the groups, like this.

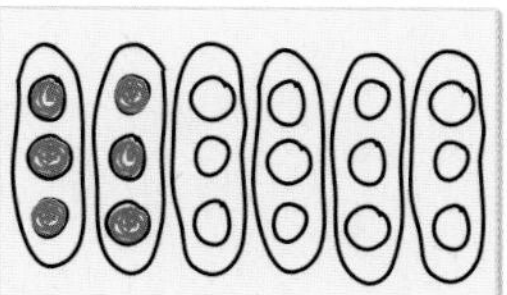

Caroline: You colored 6 things. So $\frac{2}{6}$ of 18 is 6!

Activity 2

Solve Word Problems

 10 MINUTES

Goal: Solve problems involving finding a fraction of a number.

Materials: Student Activity Book or Hardcover Book p. 408

 **NCTM Standards:**
Number and Operations
Problem Solving
Representation

Differentiated Instruction

Advanced Learners Give students the following problem.

Lizbeth baked 24 muffins. She gave $\frac{1}{3}$ of them to her mother and $\frac{5}{8}$ of them to her cousin. She kept the rest of the muffins. How many muffins did Lizbeth keep? 1

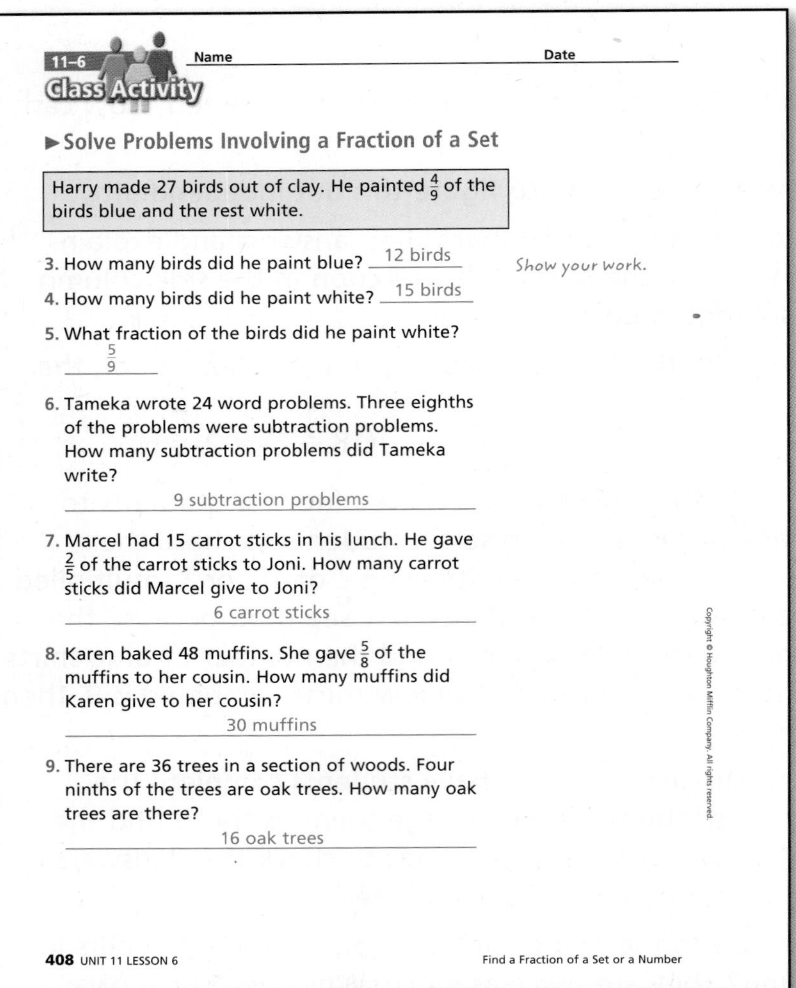
11–6 Class Activity Name ______ Date ______

▶ Solve Problems Involving a Fraction of a Set

Harry made 27 birds out of clay. He painted $\frac{4}{9}$ of the birds blue and the rest white.

3. How many birds did he paint blue? 12 birds

Show your work.

4. How many birds did he paint white? 15 birds

5. What fraction of the birds did he paint white? $\frac{5}{9}$

6. Tameka wrote 24 word problems. Three eighths of the problems were subtraction problems. How many subtraction problems did Tameka write? 9 subtraction problems

7. Marcel had 15 carrot sticks in his lunch. He gave $\frac{2}{5}$ of the carrot sticks to Joni. How many carrot sticks did Marcel give to Joni? 6 carrot sticks

8. Karen baked 48 muffins. She gave $\frac{5}{8}$ of the muffins to her cousin. How many muffins did Karen give to her cousin? 30 muffins

9. There are 36 trees in a section of woods. Four ninths of the trees are oak trees. How many oak trees are there? 16 oak trees

Copyright © Houghton Mifflin Company. All rights reserved.

408 UNIT 11 LESSON 6 Find a Fraction of a Set or a Number

Student Activity Book page 408

▶ Solve Problems Involving a Fraction of a Set

WHOLE CLASS

Using **Solve and Discuss,** have students solve problems 3–9 on Student Book page 408. Encourage them to use numeric methods.

In problems 3–5, you might ask students to add the fraction of blue birds to the fraction of white birds. Although students have not formally learned to add fractions, they can do this by thinking of each fraction as a sum of unit fractions, or by drawing a fraction bar divided into ninths and then shading $\frac{4}{9}$ and $\frac{5}{9}$. Ask them why the answer, $\frac{9}{9}$, or 1, makes sense. because $\frac{9}{9}$ is 1 whole, which is all the birds, and the blue and white birds together make up all the birds.

Activity 3

Write and Use a Rule

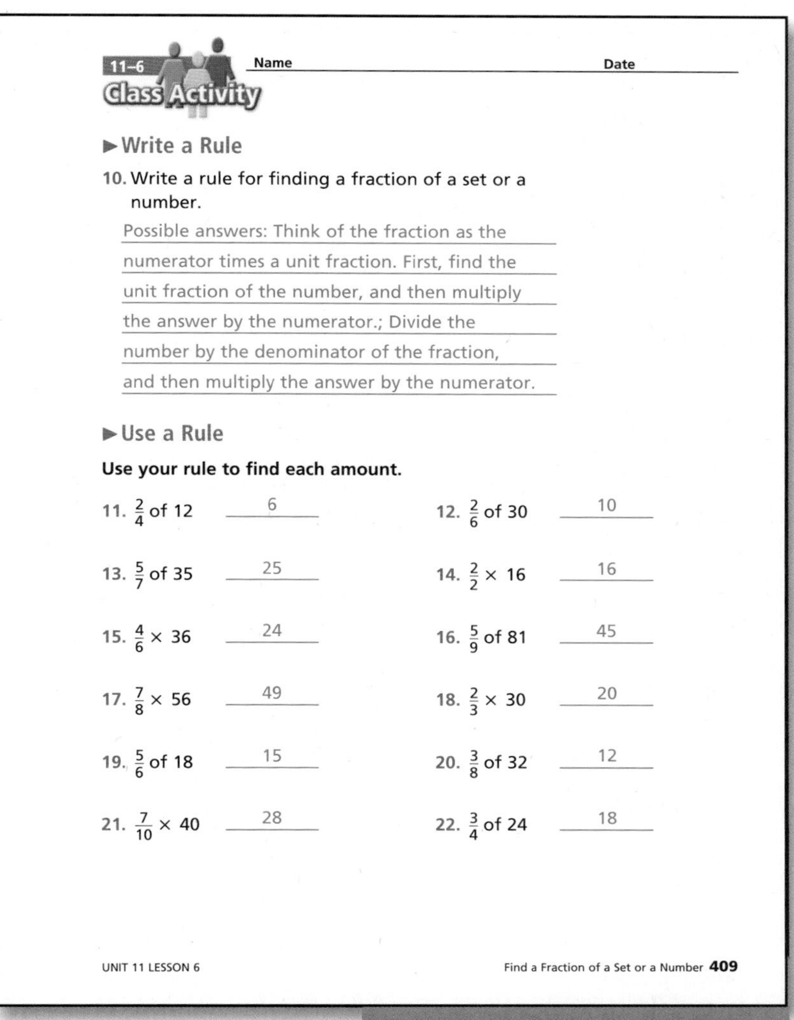

11–6 Class Activity

Name ______ Date ______

► Write a Rule

10. Write a rule for finding a fraction of a set or a number.

Possible answers: Think of the fraction as the numerator times a unit fraction. First, find the unit fraction of the number, and then multiply the answer by the numerator.; Divide the number by the denominator of the fraction, and then multiply the answer by the numerator.

► Use a Rule

Use your rule to find each amount.

11. $\frac{2}{4}$ of 12 ___6___
12. $\frac{2}{6}$ of 30 ___10___
13. $\frac{5}{7}$ of 35 ___25___
14. $\frac{2}{2} \times 16$ ___16___
15. $\frac{4}{6} \times 36$ ___24___
16. $\frac{5}{9}$ of 81 ___45___
17. $\frac{7}{8} \times 56$ ___49___
18. $\frac{2}{3} \times 30$ ___20___
19. $\frac{5}{6}$ of 18 ___15___
20. $\frac{3}{8}$ of 32 ___12___
21. $\frac{7}{10} \times 40$ ___28___
22. $\frac{3}{4}$ of 24 ___18___

UNIT 11 LESSON 6 Find a Fraction of a Set or a Number **409**

Student Activity Book page 409

► Write a Rule WHOLE CLASS

Ask if anyone can think of a rule that can be used to find a fraction of a number. Write the rules on the board and test that they work. The following are two possibilities.

- First find the unit fraction of the number, and then multiply the answer by the numerator.
- Divide the number by the denominator of the fraction, and then multiply the answer by the numerator.

Have students complete exercise 10 on Student Book page 409.

► Use a Rule INDIVIDUALS

Have students complete exercises 11–22 on Student Book page 409 independently. Assign **Helping Partners** to work with students who are having difficulty.

 **10 MINUTES**

Goal: Write a rule for multiplying a whole number by a fraction.

Materials: Student Activity Book or Hardcover Book p. 409

 **NCTM Standard:**
Number and Operations

Differentiated Instruction

Extra Help Explain to students that when they write a rule, they write steps that tell in general how to do something. Tell students that it might be helpful when writing a rule if they first write the steps for a particular example, and then write the steps using math vocabulary that will explain how to do it for all examples.

Ongoing Assessment

- ► If you know that $\frac{1}{9}$ of a number is 4, how can you find $\frac{8}{9}$ of that number?
- ► How can you use this drawing to find $\frac{5}{7}$ of 21?

2 Going Further

Problem Solving: Act it Out

Goal: Solve a problem by using models to act it out.

Materials: counters, Student Activity Book or Hardcover Book p. 410

✓ **NCTM Standard:**
Problem Solving

Teaching Note

Math Background The *Act It Out* problem solving strategy focuses on recreating the actions described in a problem. It does not require the use of the specific objects involved. For instance, students do not have to use T-shirts to act out a problem about T-shirts. Rather, they can use counters, cubes, or other objects to represent the T-shirts.

Students can use the *Act It Out* strategy as a method for solving a problem, or they can use it to check their solution.

▶ Solve a Problem by Acting It Out

PAIRS

Have **Student Pairs** read problem 1 on Student Book page 410. In each pair, one student should play the part of Olivia, while another student should play Olivia's aunt. Lead students in the solution of the problem.

- How many daisies did Olivia pick? 28 We don't have daisies here in the classroom, so pretend that the counters are the daisies. Everyone who is playing Olivia, count out 28 counters.
- What fraction of the daisies did Olivia give to her aunt? $\frac{5}{7}$ How do we divide the counters into sevenths? make 7 equal groups Work together to divide the 28 counters into 7 groups.
- How many counters are in each group? 4 counters How many groups of 4 did Olivia give to her aunt? 5 groups Everyone who is playing Olivia, give 5 groups of 4 counters to the student playing Olivia's aunt. How many counters do you have left? 8 counters So how many daisies did Olivia keep? 8 daisies

Have students work in pairs to solve problems 2–6.

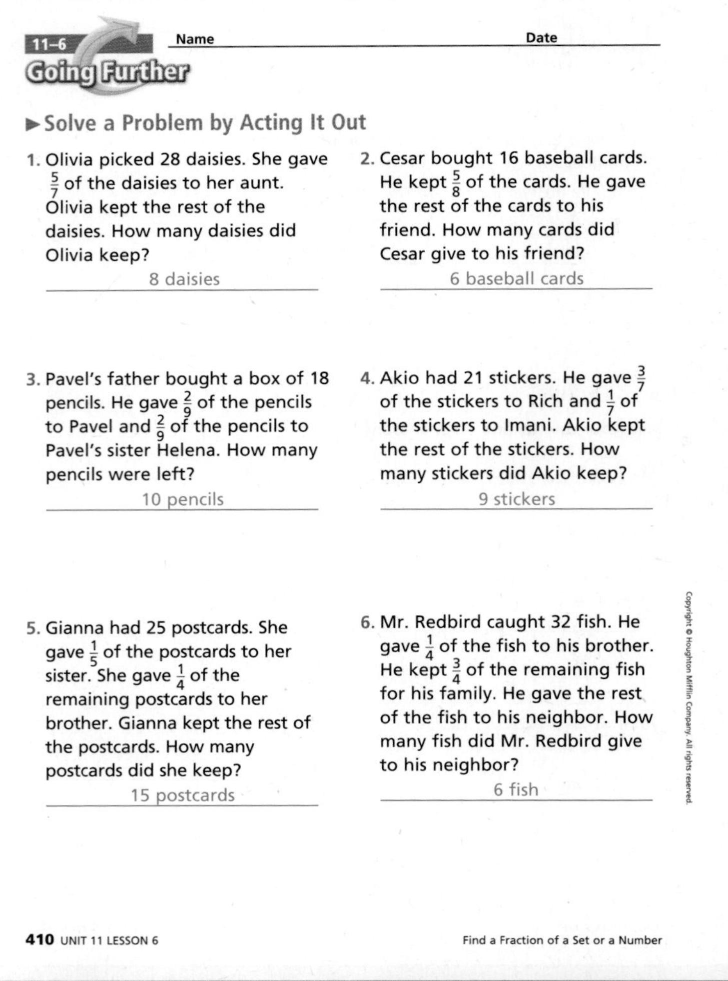
11–6 Going Further

Name ______ Date ______

▶ Solve a Problem by Acting It Out

1. Olivia picked 28 daisies. She gave $\frac{5}{7}$ of the daisies to her aunt. Olivia kept the rest of the daisies. How many daisies did Olivia keep?
8 daisies

2. Cesar bought 16 baseball cards. He kept $\frac{5}{8}$ of the cards. He gave the rest of the cards to his friend. How many cards did Cesar give to his friend?
6 baseball cards

3. Pavel's father bought a box of 18 pencils. He gave $\frac{2}{9}$ of the pencils to Pavel and $\frac{2}{9}$ of the pencils to Pavel's sister Helena. How many pencils were left?
10 pencils

4. Akio had 21 stickers. He gave $\frac{3}{7}$ of the stickers to Rich and $\frac{1}{7}$ of the stickers to Imani. Akio kept the rest of the stickers. How many stickers did Akio keep?
9 stickers

5. Gianna had 25 postcards. She gave $\frac{1}{5}$ of the postcards to her sister. She gave $\frac{1}{4}$ of the remaining postcards to her brother. Gianna kept the rest of the postcards. How many postcards did she keep?
15 postcards

6. Mr. Redbird caught 32 fish. He gave $\frac{1}{4}$ of the fish to his brother. He kept $\frac{3}{4}$ of the remaining fish for his family. He gave the rest of the fish to his neighbor. How many fish did Mr. Redbird give to his neighbor?
6 fish

410 UNIT 11 LESSON 6 Find a Fraction of a Set or a Number

Student Activity Book page 410

Teaching Note

Watch For! In problem 5, students must give away $\frac{1}{5}$ of 25 counters. Then they must give away $\frac{1}{4}$ of the *remaining* counters. If students do not read the problem carefully, they might attempt to give away $\frac{1}{4}$ of the original 25 counters.

In problem 6, students might quickly read the fractions $\frac{1}{4}$ and $\frac{3}{4}$ and assume that, since $\frac{1}{4}$ and $\frac{3}{4}$ together make 1 whole, there were no fish left to give to the neighbor.

The Learning Classroom

Scenarios The main purpose of this Act-It-Out scenario is to demonstrate when finding a fraction of a set is used everyday. Each scenario can also foster a sense of involvement in a real-life application that provides a meaningful context for multiplying fractions and whole numbers to find fractions of a set and then deciding how this amount is used in each scenario.

Intervention — Activity Card 11-6

Model Fractions of a Set
Activity Card 11-6

Work: In pairs

Use:

- Paper plates
- Counters

1. Use paper plates and 15 counters to model $\frac{2}{3}$ of 15. Use the denominator of $\frac{2}{3}$ to decide how many equal groups you need to make.
2. Put an equal number of counters on each plate. How did you decide how many counters to put on each plate? 15 can be divided into 3 groups of 5.

3. Use the numerator of $\frac{2}{3}$ to decide how many groups to count. What is $\frac{2}{3}$ of 15? 10
4. Repeat the activity to find $\frac{2}{3}$ of 21. 14

Unit 11, Lesson 6

Activity Note If students have difficulty deciding on the number in each group, suggest that they distribute the counters among the 3 plates until all the counters have been used.

Math Writing Prompt

Explain Your Thinking Explain how to find $\frac{3}{7}$ of 21.

Software Support

Warm Up 5.09

On Level — Activity Card 11-6

Fractional Parts Game
Activity Card 11-6

Work: In pairs

Use:

- 12 Index cards

1. Make the set of 12 index cards shown below.

$\frac{3}{5}$ of 45	$\frac{3}{7}$ of 21	14
$\frac{4}{5}$ of 40	20	21
$\frac{7}{8}$ of 24	27	$\frac{7}{9}$ of 18
32	$\frac{5}{6}$ of 24	9

2. Shuffle the cards and place them face down in a 3 × 4 array. Take turns choosing two cards and checking to see if they match.
3. Keep each matched pair and return the others.
4. When all the pairs are matched, the player with more matched pairs wins.

Unit 11, Lesson 6

Activity Note As students make sets of matching cards, be sure that students check each other's work.

Math Writing Prompt

Connected Math If you spend $\frac{1}{4}$ of a 24-hour day working on your boat, how many hours did you work? Explain how you found your answer.

Software Support

Fraction Action: Number Line Mine, Level L

Challenge — Activity Card 11-6

Fractions of Time
Activity Card 11-6

Work: In small groups

1. **Work Together** Solve each equation below. For equation 4, use the relationship 1 month = 30 days.

1. $\frac{3}{4}$ of a year = __?__ months
2. $\frac{6}{7}$ of a week = __?__ days
3. $\frac{5}{6}$ of a day = __?__ hours
4. $\frac{2}{5}$ of a month = __?__ days
5. $\frac{5}{6}$ of an hour = __?__ minutes
6. $\frac{7}{10}$ of a minute = __?__ seconds

1.9 2.6 3.20 4.12 5.50 6.42

2. Next, write an original set of equations about fractions of time and exchange with another group to solve.

Unit 11, Lesson 6

Activity Note Suggest that students make a table of measures of time before beginning this activity.

Math Writing Prompt

Work Backward Solve the following equation. Explain how you found the solution.

$$\frac{5}{8} \times \square = 40$$

DESTINATION Math

Software Support

Course II: Module 2: Unit 3: Fractional Parts

Homework and Spiral Review

11–6 **Homework** **Goal:** Additional Practice

This Homework page provides practice in finding a fraction of a number.

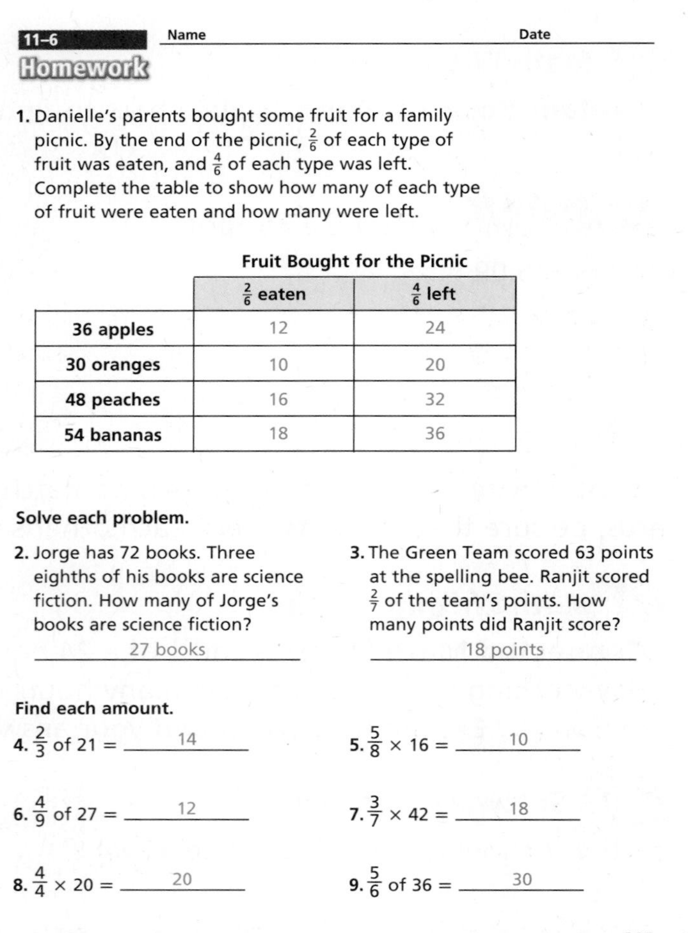

11–6 Homework Name Date

1. Danielle's parents bought some fruit for a family picnic. By the end of the picnic, $\frac{2}{6}$ of each type of fruit was eaten, and $\frac{4}{6}$ of each type was left. Complete the table to show how many of each type of fruit were eaten and how many were left.

Fruit Bought for the Picnic

	$\frac{2}{6}$ eaten	$\frac{4}{6}$ left
36 apples	12	24
30 oranges	10	20
48 peaches	16	32
54 bananas	18	36

Solve each problem.

2. Jorge has 72 books. Three eighths of his books are science fiction. How many of Jorge's books are science fiction? 27 books

3. The Green Team scored 63 points at the spelling bee. Ranjit scored $\frac{2}{7}$ of the team's points. How many points did Ranjit score? 18 points

Find each amount.

4. $\frac{2}{3}$ of 21 = 14
5. $\frac{5}{8} \times 16$ = 10
6. $\frac{4}{9}$ of 27 = 12
7. $\frac{3}{7} \times 42$ = 18
8. $\frac{4}{4} \times 20$ = 20
9. $\frac{5}{6}$ of 36 = 30

UNIT 11 LESSON 6 Find a Fraction of a Set or a Number 267

Homework and Remembering page 267

11–6 **Remembering** **Goal:** Spiral Review

This Remembering page would be appropriate anytime after today's lesson.

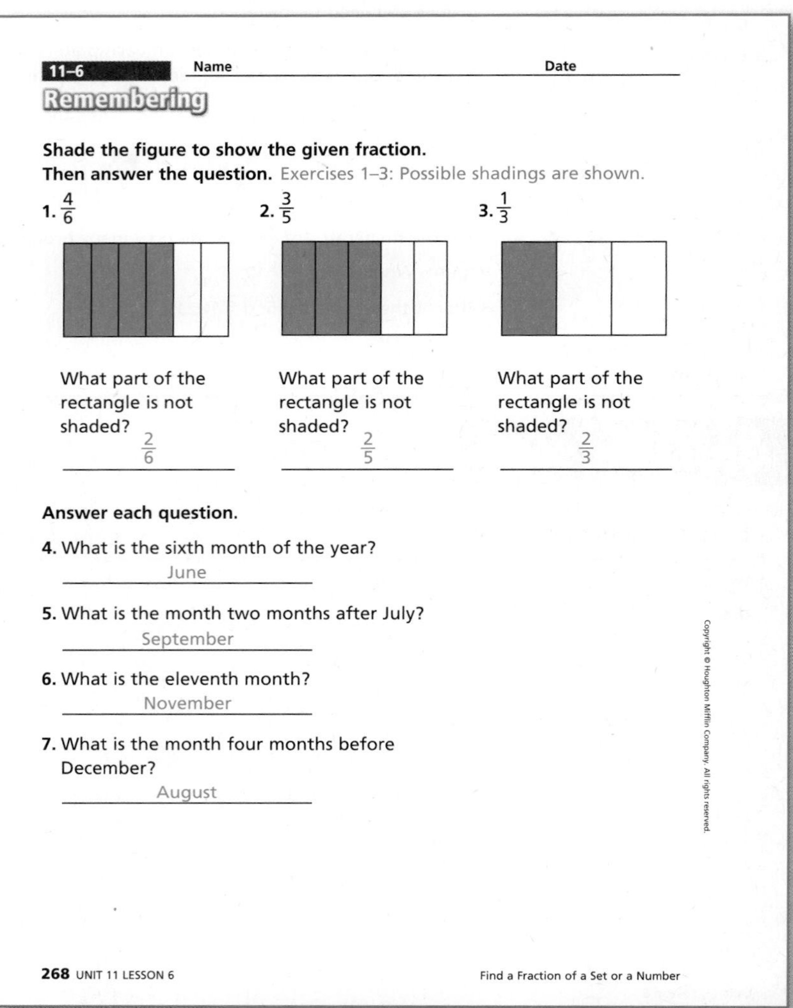

11–6 Remembering Name Date

Shade the figure to show the given fraction. Then answer the question. Exercises 1–3: Possible shadings are shown.

1. $\frac{4}{6}$ What part of the rectangle is not shaded? $\frac{2}{6}$
2. $\frac{3}{5}$ What part of the rectangle is not shaded? $\frac{2}{5}$
3. $\frac{1}{3}$ What part of the rectangle is not shaded? $\frac{2}{3}$

Answer each question.

4. What is the sixth month of the year? June
5. What is the month two months after July? September
6. What is the eleventh month? November
7. What is the month four months before December? August

268 UNIT 11 LESSON 6 Find a Fraction of a Set or a Number

Homework and Remembering page 268

Home or School Activity

Science Connection

Weight on the Planets An object has weight because of the pull of gravity. On Mars, gravity is about $\frac{4}{10}$ the strength of gravity on Earth. On Venus, gravity is about $\frac{9}{10}$ of Earth's. Have students make a poster showing about how much a 20 pound dog, a 10 pound cat, a 50 pound foal, a 100 pound person, and a 200 pound pig would weigh on Earth, Venus, and Mars.

Weights on Different Planets

	Dog	Cat	Foal	Person	Pig
Earth	20 pounds	10 pounds	50 pounds	100 pounds	200 pounds
Mars	8 pounds	4 pounds	20 pounds	40 pounds	80 pounds
Venus	18 pounds	9 pounds	45 pounds	90 pounds	180 pounds

Fractions on Circle Graphs

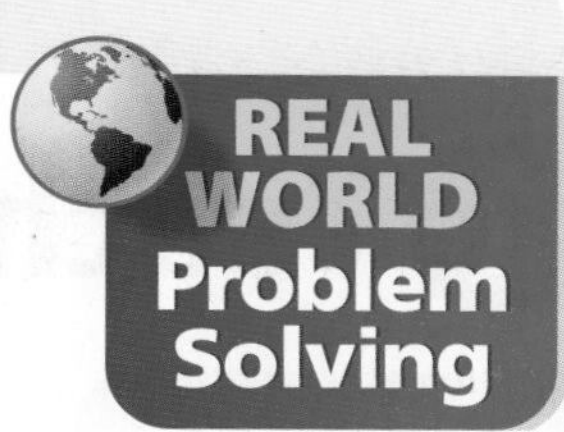

Lesson Objectives

- Interpret circle graphs.
- Identify fractions on a circle graph.

Vocabulary
circle graph

The Day at a Glance

Today's Goals	Materials	
1 Teaching the Lesson **A1:** Read a circle graph and find fractions of numbers to solve problems. **A2:** Identify fractions on a circle graph and solve problems about the circle graph.	**Lesson Activities** Student Activity Book pp. 411–412 or Student Hardcover Book pp. 411–412 and Activity Workbook pp. 186–188 (includes Special Formats) Homework and Remembering pp. 269–270	**Going Further** Activity Cards 11-7 Fraction Circle Model (TRB M130) Crayons or markers Math Journals
2 Going Further ► Differentiated Instruction		
3 Homework and Spiral Review		

Use Math Talk today!

Keeping Skills Sharp

Quick Practice	Daily Routines	
Goal: Practice "as many as" comparisons. **Comparison Chant** Divide the class into two groups. The **Student Leader** writes a factor and one of its count-bys on the board. The leader asks one group to compare the first number to the second. Then, the leader asks the second group to compare the second number to the first. Repeat with several more pairs of numbers. (See Unit 11 Lesson 6.)	**Homework Review** Ask students if they had difficulty with any part of the homework. Plan to set aside some time to work with students needing extra help.	**Nonroutine Problem** Mrs. Yoshira wants to buy pens and pencils for her 24 students. Pencils are sold in packs of 4 pencils for \$1 or packs of 6 pencils for \$1.50. Pens are sold in packs of 2 pens for \$0.50 or packs of 8 pens for \$2.00. How many packs of pens and pencils should she buy? How much will it cost? \$12; Possible answer: 6 packs of 4 pencils each and 3 packs of 8 pens each

1 Teaching the Lesson

Activity 1

Read Circle Graphs

 25 MINUTES

Goal: Read a circle graph and find fractions of numbers to solve problems.

Materials: Student Activity Book or Hardcover Book p. 411 and Activity Workbook p. 186 (includes table)

 **NCTM Standards:**
Number and Operations
Algebra
Data Analysis and Probability
Representation

Teaching Note

Math Background Circle graphs are useful for comparing items with respect to the whole. For example, the circle graph in this activity allows us to understand the fractional value of each type of beanbag animal with respect to the entire collection. A bar graph is an appropriate choice when it is important to compare numbers of items, but not important to understand their relationship to the whole. If a bar graph had been used to represent the beanbag collection, we could easily compare numbers of types of beanbags, but we would not have a clear picture of the fraction of the beanbags that were bears, for example.

Teaching Note

Language and Vocabulary Sometimes circle graphs are called pie charts. You may want to introduce this term with a visual representation.

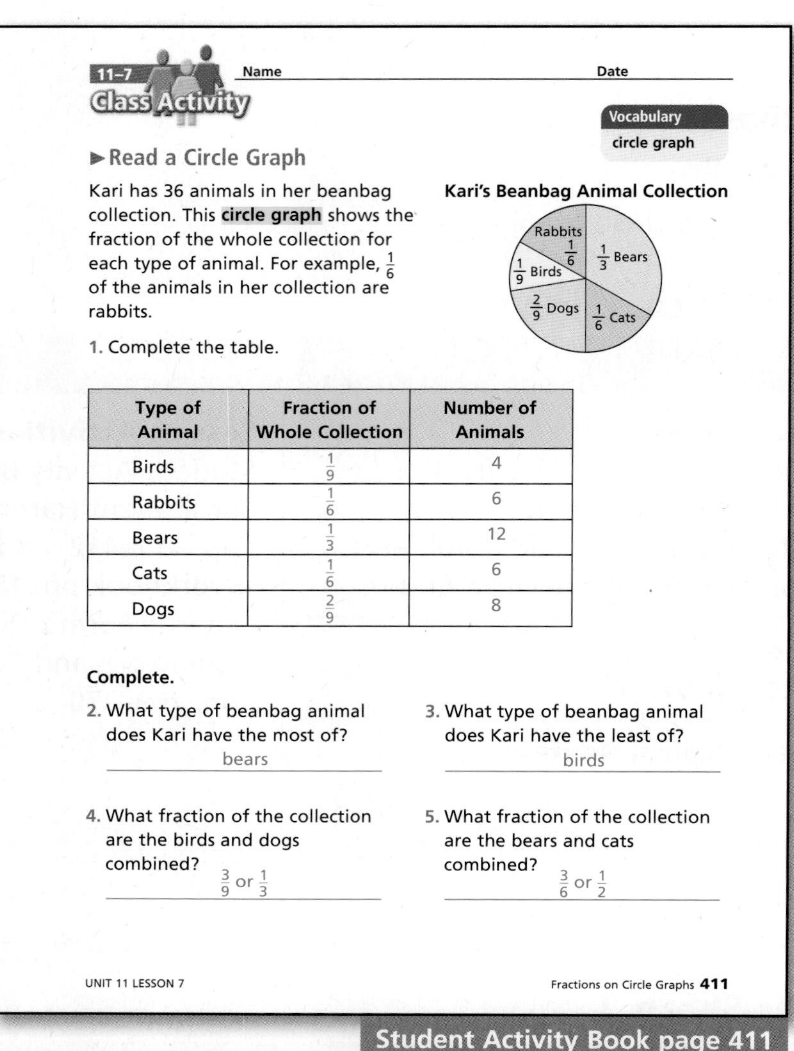

11–7 Class Activity Name ____ Date ____

Vocabulary
circle graph

► Read a Circle Graph

Kari has 36 animals in her beanbag collection. This **circle graph** shows the fraction of the whole collection for each type of animal. For example, $\frac{1}{6}$ of the animals in her collection are rabbits.

Kari's Beanbag Animal Collection

1. Complete the table.

Type of Animal	Fraction of Whole Collection	Number of Animals
Birds	$\frac{1}{9}$	4
Rabbits	$\frac{1}{6}$	6
Bears	$\frac{1}{3}$	12
Cats	$\frac{1}{6}$	6
Dogs	$\frac{2}{9}$	8

Complete.

2. What type of beanbag animal does Kari have the most of? bears

3. What type of beanbag animal does Kari have the least of? birds

4. What fraction of the collection are the birds and dogs combined? $\frac{3}{9}$ or $\frac{1}{3}$

5. What fraction of the collection are the bears and cats combined? $\frac{3}{6}$ or $\frac{1}{2}$

UNIT 11 LESSON 7 Fractions on Circle Graphs 411

Student Activity Book page 411

► Read a Circle Graph WHOLE CLASS

Math Talk

Have students look at the circle graph on Student Book page 411. Explain that a circle graph shows how a whole is divided into fractional parts. Discuss some features of the graph:

- The whole circle represents Kari's whole beanbag animal collection.
- The sections represent the different types of animals in the collection.
- The larger a section is, the more animals it represents. For example, because the bears section is larger than the cats section, we know Kari has more bears in her collection than cats.
- Each section represents the fraction of the whole collection. For example, because the bear section is $\frac{1}{3}$ of the whole circle, we know that $\frac{1}{3}$ of Kari's whole collection is bears.

Work with students to complete the first two rows of the table. Note that finding the number of bears requires calculating 36 ÷ 3. Although this is not a division students have learned, they should be able to figure it out. For example, they can reason that 36 is 3 × 10, or 30, plus two more 3s. Therefore, 36 = 3 × 12, or 36 ÷ 3 × 12.

Have students solve problems 2–5 using **Solve and Discuss**. For problems 2 and 3, be sure to discuss the fact that students can find the answer by comparing the numbers of animals *or* by comparing the sizes of the sections of the graph.

There are at least three ways students might solve problem 4:

- $\frac{2}{9}$ of the animals are dogs and $\frac{1}{9}$ are birds. So $\frac{2}{9} + \frac{1}{9} = \frac{1}{9} + \frac{1}{9} + \frac{1}{9} = \frac{3}{9}$ are dogs and birds combined.
- There are 4 + 8, or 12, birds and dogs altogether. 12 animals out of 36 is $\frac{12}{36}$ of the collection.
- The birds section and the dogs section combined are the same size as the bears section, so the birds and dogs combined must make up $\frac{1}{3}$ of the collection.

Notice that these three approaches give three different, but equivalent, answers. Explain to students that, in an upcoming lesson, they will see that $\frac{12}{36}$, $\frac{3}{9}$, and $\frac{1}{3}$ fractions are equivalent.

For problem 5, students may reason these ways:

- The bears and cats sections combined make up $\frac{1}{2}$ of the circle, so bears and cats make up half the collection.
- 12 bears and 6 cats make 18 bears and cats. 18 animals out of 36 is $\frac{18}{36}$ of the collection.

Again, these methods give two different, but equivalent fractions.

Differentiated Instruction

Extra Help To reinforce students' understanding of finding a fraction of a number, you might demonstrate how $\frac{1}{9}$ of 18 is the same as 18 ÷ 9 = 2. For example, use counters to show the example below:

$\frac{1}{9}$ **of 18** = 2	**18 ÷ 9** = 2
There are 18 counters. They are in 9 equal groups, and one group is circled. So, one ninth of the counters are circled.	There are 18 counters, divided into 9 equal groups. Each group has 2 counters. So, 18 divided by 9 is 2.

Activity 2

Identify Fractions on a Circle Graph

► Label and Use a Circle Graph WHOLE CLASS

In this activity students must label each section of the graph with fractions. Students should be able to identify the $\frac{1}{2}$ section easily. For the green section, you might suggest that students decide how many of these sections fit in the whole. This should help them identify the green section as $\frac{1}{4}$ of the circle. Then you might have students figure out how many of the blue sections fit in one half of the circle (4) and consequently, how many sections fit in the whole circle (8).

Activity continued ►

25 MINUTES

Goal: Identify fractions on a circle graph and solve problems about the circle graph.

Materials: Student Activity Book or Hardcover Book p. 412 and Activity Workbook p. 187 (includes table)

NCTM Standards:
Number and Operations
Algebra, Representation
Data Analysis and Probability

Teaching the Lesson (continued)

Ongoing Assessment

Have students look at Kari's Beanbag Animal Collection circle graph on Student Book page 411. Ask students the following questions:

- What two types of animals besides bears and cats make up one half of the collection?
- Explain how a circle graph can help you see which beanbag animals make up half of the collection.

English Language Learners

Write *equivalent* on the board. Draw the circle graph from Student Activity Book page 412.

- **Beginning** Ask: **Are the blue and yellow sections as big as the green section?** yes Say: **$\frac{2}{8}$ and $\frac{1}{4}$ are *equivalent*.** Have students repeat.
- **Intermediate** Ask: **What two sections are the same size as the green section?** blue and yellow **Are $\frac{2}{8}$ and $\frac{1}{4}$ *equivalent*?** yes
- **Advanced** Ask: **Which 2 sections are *equivalent* to the green section?** blue and yellow

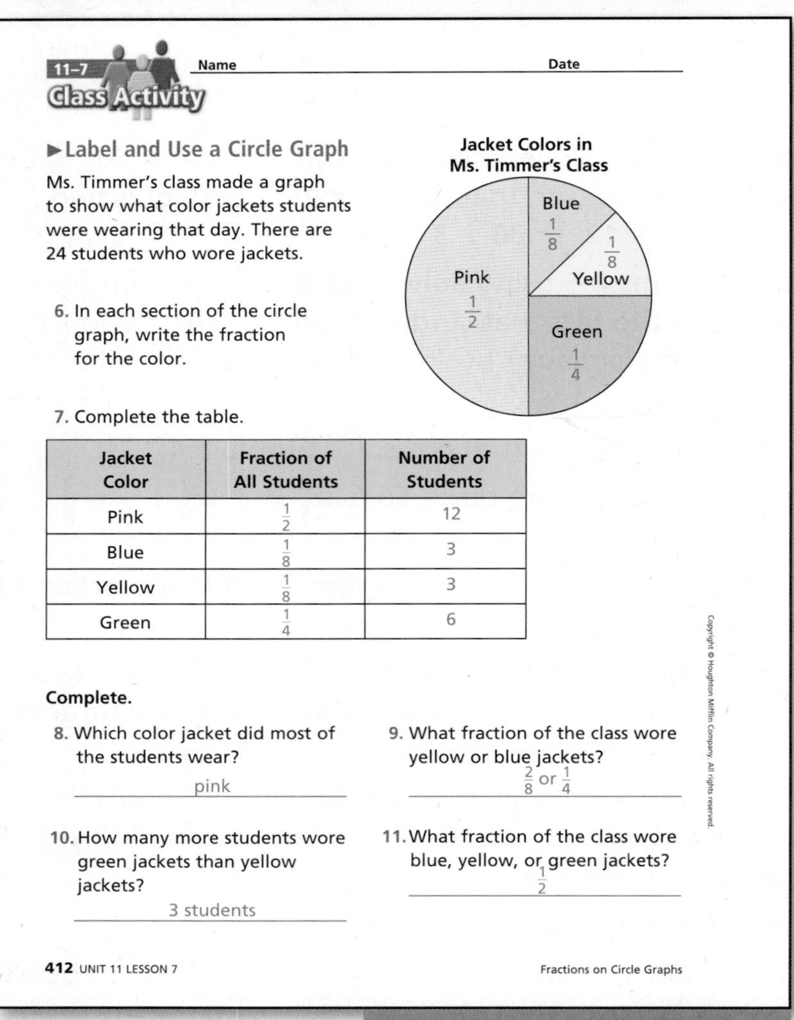
11–7 Class Activity Name Date

▶ Label and Use a Circle Graph

Ms. Timmer's class made a graph to show what color jackets students were wearing that day. There are 24 students who wore jackets.

6. In each section of the circle graph, write the fraction for the color.

7. Complete the table.

Jacket Color	Fraction of All Students	Number of Students
Pink	$\frac{1}{2}$	12
Blue	$\frac{1}{8}$	3
Yellow	$\frac{1}{8}$	3
Green	$\frac{1}{4}$	6

Complete.

8. Which color jacket did most of the students wear? pink

9. What fraction of the class wore yellow or blue jackets? $\frac{2}{8}$ or $\frac{1}{4}$

10. How many more students wore green jackets than yellow jackets? 3 students

11. What fraction of the class wore blue, yellow, or green jackets? $\frac{1}{2}$

412 UNIT 11 LESSON 7 Fractions on Circle Graphs

Student Activity Book page 412

Have students complete exercise 6 on Student Book page 412. Discuss the answers. Be sure students have correct answers before completing the table in exercise 7. Have students solve problems 8–11 using **Solve and Discuss.**

Problem 8 can be solved by comparing the size of each section of the graph.

For problems 9 through 11, students must find a fraction of a number.

For problem 9, $\frac{1}{8}$ of the class wore yellow jackets and $\frac{1}{8}$ of the class wore blue jackets. Add the fractions. $\frac{1}{8} + \frac{1}{8} = \frac{2}{8}$.

Problem 10 may be solved in several ways. You might see students first write down the number of green jackets, then the number of yellow jackets, then subtract. Or they may notice that 2 yellow sections fit in one green section. So, if you take away one yellow section from the green section, you are left with half a green section, or $\frac{1}{2}$ of 6 = 3.

2 Going Further

Differentiated Instruction

Intervention — Activity Card 11-7

Make a Fraction Circle — Activity Card 11-7 ●

Work: In pairs

Use:
- TRB M130 (Fraction Circle Model)
- Crayons or markers

1. Use the fraction circle to trace two circles on paper.
2. Divide one circle into 4 sections and the other circle into 3 sections as shown below.

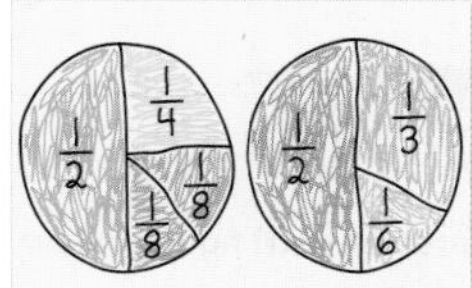

3. Color both circles, using different colors for sections that represent different fractions.
4. **Analyze** How many different ways can you make half a circle, using the fractions $\frac{1}{4}$, $\frac{1}{3}$, $\frac{1}{6}$, or $\frac{1}{8}$? $\frac{1}{4}$, $\frac{1}{4}$. $\frac{1}{8}$, $\frac{1}{8}$, $\frac{1}{8}$, $\frac{1}{8}$. $\frac{1}{6}$, $\frac{1}{6}$, $\frac{1}{6}$. $\frac{1}{3}$, $\frac{1}{6}$. $\frac{1}{4}$, $\frac{1}{8}$, $\frac{1}{8}$

Unit 11, Lesson 7

Activity Note Students should divide the first circle into eighths and the second into sixths to reinforce their understanding of unit fraction relationships.

Math Writing Prompt

Explain Your Thinking Janie's circle graph has 6 equal parts. She wants to shade $\frac{1}{2}$ of the graph blue. Explain how she can figure out how to shade the correct number of parts on her graph.

Software Support

Warm Up 5.11

On Level — Activity Card 11-7

Make a Circle Graph — Activity Card 11-7 ▲

Work: On your own

Use:
- TRB M130 (Fraction Circle Model)
- Red, blue, and green crayons or markers

1. Divide the circle into 8 parts, using 4 lines. First divide the circle in half. Then divide each half in half again. Next, divide each of the four sections in half.
2. Use the information below to make a circle graph about Leeza's marble collection. Use shading to show how many of each color marble Leeza has in her collection.

> Leeza has 8 marbles in her collection.
> $\frac{1}{4}$ of the marbles are blue.
> Three of the marbles are green.
> The rest of the marbles are red.

Unit 11, Lesson 7

Activity Note The graph should show three red sections, two blue sections, and three green sections. Discuss how the graph makes it easy to compare different types of marbles in the collection.

Math Writing Prompt

Explain Your Thinking When would you use a circle graph to display information instead of a bar graph? Give an example.

Software Support

Shapes Ahoy: Ship Shapes, Level T

Challenge — Activity Card 11-7

Graph Data — Activity Card 11-7 ■

Work: In pairs

Use:
- Crayons or markers
- TRB M130 (Fraction Circle Model)

1. **Work Together** Conduct a survey and record your results. Ask 12 of your classmates this question: "Which subject do you like the best – Math, Reading, or Spelling?"
2. Make a circle graph to display the results of your survey.
3. **Discuss** How many sections should your graph display? 12 How many different colors should you use on the graph? 3
4. **Analyze** Does the graph make it easier to make comparisons? Why or why not? Write several comparison statements about the data shown in the graph.

Unit 11, Lesson 7

Activity Note Students may be able to divide their circle into fewer than 12 sections, depending on their survey results. However, using the 12 sections may make it easier to display their results accurately.

Math Writing Prompt

Justify Sahara said that $\frac{3}{8}$ of the pie has been eaten. Explain how a picture can show that there is about $\frac{1}{2}$ of the pie left.

Software Support

Course II: Module 2: Unit 3: Fractional Parts

3 Homework and Spiral Review

11–7 Homework **Goal:** Additional Practice

✓ Include students' completed Homework page as part of their portfolios.

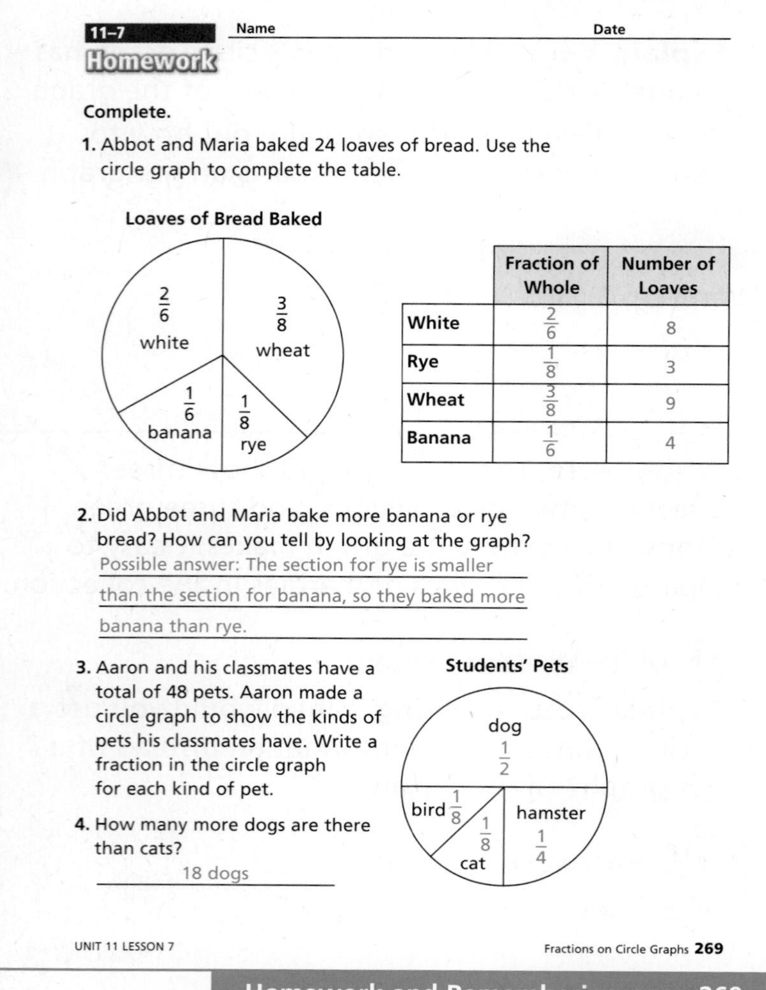

11–7 Homework Name ______ Date ______

Complete.

1. Abbot and Maria baked 24 loaves of bread. Use the circle graph to complete the table.

Loaves of Bread Baked

	Fraction of Whole	Number of Loaves
White	$\frac{2}{6}$	8
Rye	$\frac{1}{8}$	3
Wheat	$\frac{3}{8}$	9
Banana	$\frac{1}{6}$	4

2. Did Abbot and Maria bake more banana or rye bread? How can you tell by looking at the graph?
Possible answer: The section for rye is smaller than the section for banana, so they baked more banana than rye.

3. Aaron and his classmates have a total of 48 pets. Aaron made a circle graph to show the kinds of pets his classmates have. Write a fraction in the circle graph for each kind of pet.

Students' Pets

4. How many more dogs are there than cats?
18 dogs

UNIT 11 LESSON 7 Fractions on Circle Graphs **269**

Homework and Remembering page 269

11–7 Remembering **Goal:** Spiral Review

This Remembering page would be appropriate anytime after today's lesson.

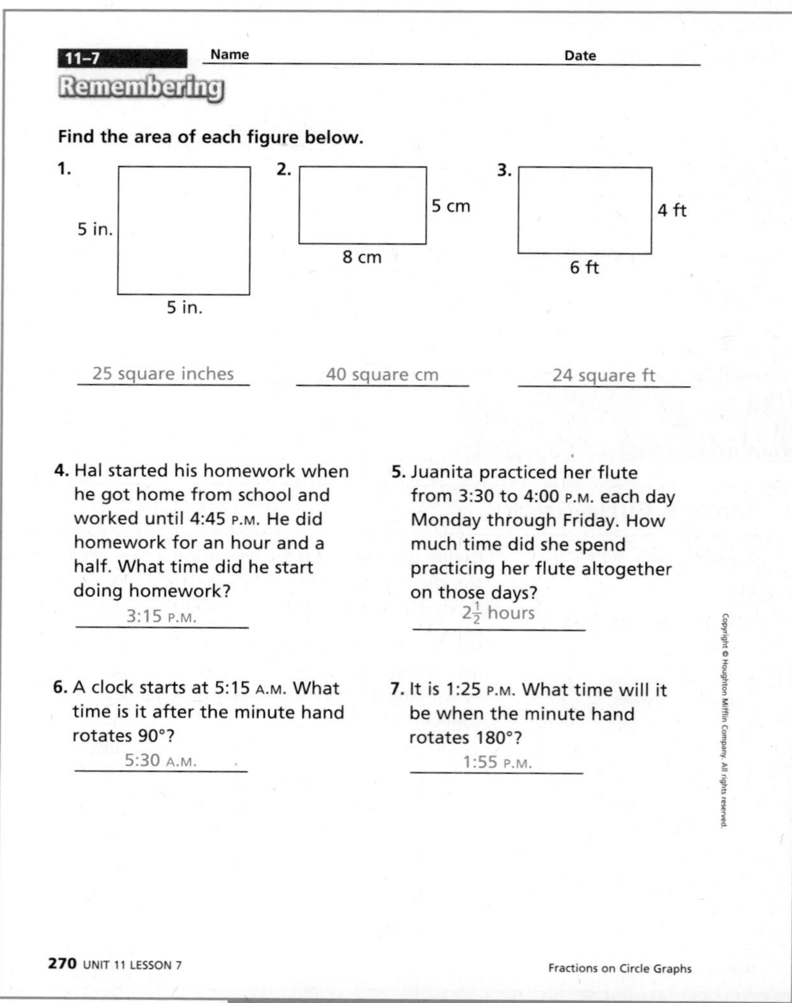

11–7 Remembering Name ______ Date ______

Find the area of each figure below.

1. 5 in. by 5 in.
25 square inches

2. 8 cm by 5 cm
40 square cm

3. 6 ft by 4 ft
24 square ft

4. Hal started his homework when he got home from school and worked until 4:45 P.M. He did homework for an hour and a half. What time did he start doing homework?
3:15 P.M.

5. Juanita practiced her flute from 3:30 to 4:00 P.M. each day Monday through Friday. How much time did she spend practicing her flute altogether on those days?
$2\frac{1}{2}$ hours

6. A clock starts at 5:15 A.M. What time is it after the minute hand rotates 90°?
5:30 A.M.

7. It is 1:25 P.M. What time will it be when the minute hand rotates 180°?
1:55 P.M.

270 UNIT 11 LESSON 7 Fractions on Circle Graphs

Homework and Remembering page 270

Home or School Activity

Language Arts Connection

Circle Graphs in the News Have students look in newspapers and bring in any circle graphs they find. Display the graphs. Ask questions such as:

What does the whole circle graph represent? Which had the most ______? What fraction could you write for the section that represents ______? How does the section that represents ______ compare with the section that represents _____?

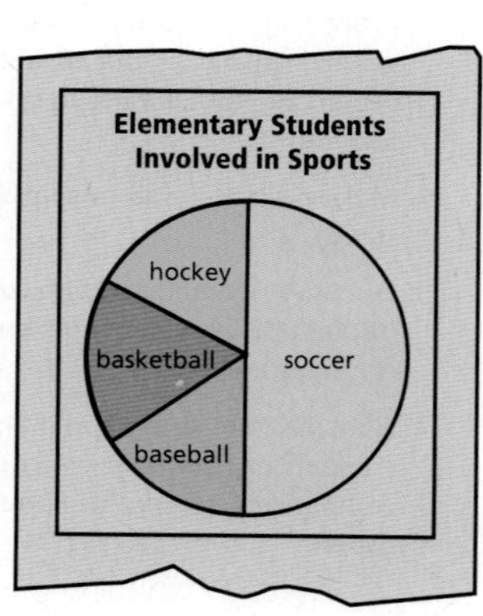

Explore Probability

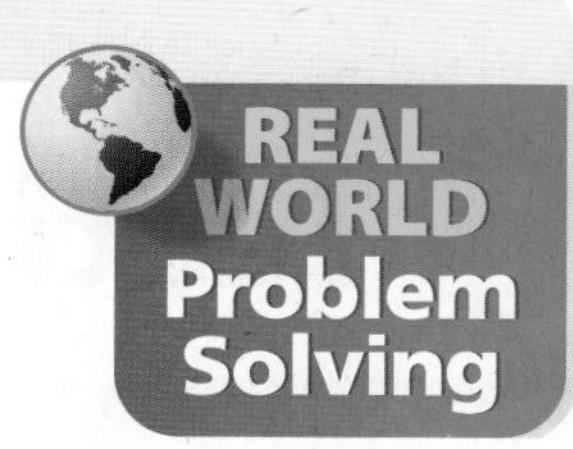

Lesson Objectives

- Understand the meaning of probability, how to determine the probability of an event, and predict future events.
- Understand how probability relates to fractions.

Vocabulary

likely	experiment
certain	outcome
equally likely	unlikely
probability	impossible
event	combination

The Day at a Glance

Today's Goals	Materials	
1 Teaching the Lesson **A1:** Understand the meaning of probability. **A2:** Record the probability of an event in two ways. **A3:** Conduct experiments to predict future events. **A4:** Find all possible outcomes of an experiment.	**Lesson Activities** Student Activity Book pp. 413–418 or Student Hardcover Book pp. 413–418 and Activity Workbook pp. 189–190 (includes Cut-Outs) Homework and Remembering pp. 271–272 Quick Quiz 2 (Assessment Guide) Marbles (3 white and 4 black) Clear container Coins (dimes and pennies) Paper bags (TRB M131) Cubes (6 red and 6 blue) or paper squares Paper clips Spin-a-Word (TRB M161)	**Going Further** Activity Cards 11-8 Spinner C (TRB M61) Mathboard materials or blank paper Paper bag Play money Math Journals
2 Going Further		
3 Homework and Spiral Review		

123 Use Math Talk today!

Keeping Skills Sharp

Quick Practice — 5 MINUTES

Goal: Practice "as many as" comparisons.

Comparison Chant Divide the class into two groups. The **Student Leader** writes a factor and one of its count-bys on the board. The leader asks Group 1 to compare the first number to the second. Then, the leader asks Group 2 to compare the second number to the first. Repeat with several more pairs of numbers. (See Unit 11 Lesson 6.)

Daily Routines

Homework Review If students give incorrect answers, have them explain how they found these answers. This can help determine if the error is conceptual or procedural.

Estimation Use rounding to the nearest ten to decide if the answer is reasonable. Then find the answer to see if you were right.

1. 218 + 74 is about 180
   not reasonable; 292
2. 463 − 55 is about 400
   reasonable; 408

1 Teaching the Lesson

Activity 1

Introduce Probability

 25 MINUTES

Goal: Describe events as impossible, unlikely, equally likely, likely, or certain.

Materials: 3 white marbles and 4 black marbles, clear container, coin, Paper bags (TRB M131), 6 red cubes or paper squares, 6 blue cubes or paper squares, Student Activity Book or Hardcover Book page 413

 **NCTM Standards:**
Number and Operations
Communication
Data Analysis and Probability

Teaching Note

Language and Vocabulary
If the phrase "equally likely" is confusing for students, you may want to use the common phrase "a fifty-fifty chance."

English Language Learners

Write the words *more likely* and *unlikely* on the board. Display a container filled with six blue cubes and one red cube.

- **Beginning** Say: **There are six blue cubes and one red cube. What color cube is *more likely* to be picked?** a blue cube
- **Intermediate** Ask: **Is it *unlikely* you will pick a red cube? Why?** yes; there are more blue cubes than red cubes
- **Advanced** Have children name other examples that are more *likely* or *unlikely*.

▶ Discuss the Meaning of Probability

WHOLE CLASS

Math Talk 

Ask students to name some things that are *certain* or will *always* happen. For example, it is certain that the sun will set tomorrow. Explain that many things in life, however, are not certain, but we can think of how *likely* things are to happen. Write the following on the board:

impossible unlikely equally likely likely certain

Suggest some events and ask students which term best describes the chances that the events will happen. Here are some examples:

- Students will have math homework tonight.
- It will rain tomorrow.
- Today's lunch will include a vegetable.
- Jen will be chosen to be a Student Leader.

Ask students to offer other suggestions.

Then, put 3 white marbles and 1 black marble in a clear container and display where the class can see the marbles.

- If I reach in and take out a marble without looking, am I more likely to get a white marble or a black marble? Why? A white one; there are more white ones in the container
- Which color am I less likely to choose? Why? Black; there is only 1 black marble and 3 white ones.
- Suppose I had 50 white marbles and 1 black marble in the container? What is likely to happen when I draw a marble from the container? What is unlikely to happen? Drawing a white marble; drawing a black marble

Then put 2 black marbles and 2 white marbles in the clear container.

- If I reach in and take out a marble without looking, am I more likely to draw a white one or a black one? Neither is more likely.

How could you describe the likelihood of drawing white? black? equally likely; equally likely

Put 4 black marbles in the clear container.

- What is certain when I draw a marble? drawing a black one
- What is impossible when I draw a marble? drawing a white one

▶ Express Probability Using Words

Distribute Paper Bags (TRB M133) to students to reinforce using words to express probability. Each student places a number of cubes or paper squares in the first bag so the label is correct. Students draw squares of the correct color to record the results. Repeat the step for the other bags.

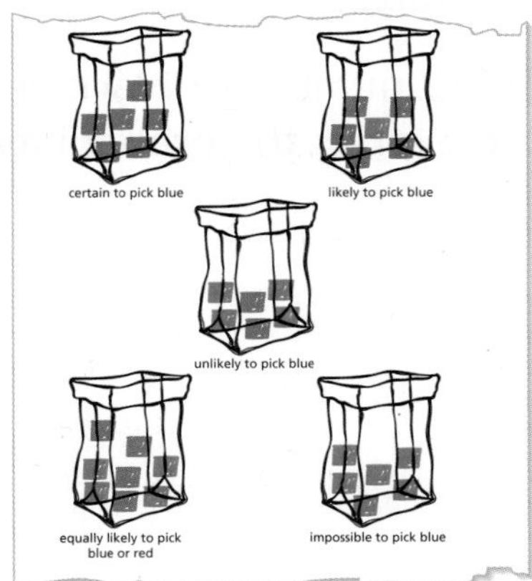

Then discuss if there's another way to place the squares in each bag to have it correctly labeled.

Activity continued ▶

Quick Quiz

See Assessment Guide for Unit 11 Quick Quiz 2.

▶ Discuss Probability as a Fraction

Math Talk 

Tell students that probability is a mathematical way of stating the likelihood that an event will happen. An event that is *impossible* has a probability of 0, and an event that is *certain* has a probability of 1. Other predictions of what will happen can be expressed as a fraction between 0 and 1.

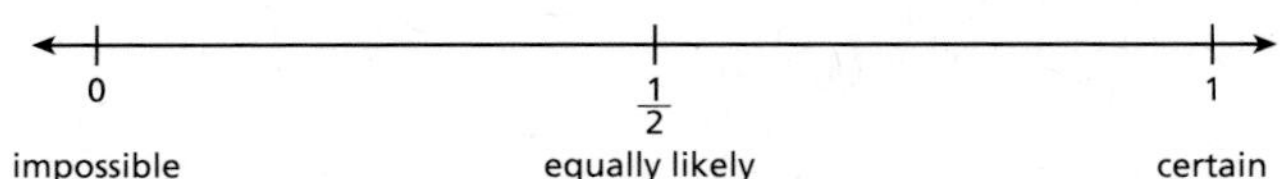

Show the clear container with 2 black marbles and 2 white marbles.

There are 4 marbles altogether and two of them are white. The probability that I will draw a white marble is 2 out of 4. This can be expressed as a fraction $\frac{2}{4}$.

- What is the probability of drawing a black marble? 2 out of 4 or $\frac{2}{4}$ or $\frac{1}{2}$

Show the container with 3 white marbles and 1 black marble.

- What is the probability of drawing a white marble? 3 out of 4 or $\frac{3}{4}$
- What is the probability of drawing a black marble? 1 out of 4 or $\frac{1}{4}$

Show the container with 4 white marbles.

- What is the probability of drawing a black marble? 0 out of 1 or $\frac{0}{1}$ or 0
- What is the probability of drawing a white marble? 1 out of 1 or $\frac{1}{1}$ or 1

Have volunteers put a different number of black and white marbles in the container for the class to express the probability as a fraction.

11–8 Class Activity

Name Date

Vocabulary
probability
likely
unlikely
certain
impossible
equally likely
event

▶ Use the Language of Probability

Probability describes how likely it is that something will happen. You can use words or a number from 0 to 1 to describe it.

Use the spinner at the right. Write the words *likely, unlikely, equally likely, impossible,* or *certain* to describe the likelihood of the event.

1. Spinning a 2 unlikely
2. Spinning a 3 likely
3. Spinning either a 2 or a 4 equally likely
4. Spinning a 5 impossible
5. Spinning a number less than 5 certain

▶ Record Probability in Two Ways

Use the spinner above to write the probability of the event.

6. What is the probability of spinning a 3?
4 out of 6 or $\frac{4}{6}$
7. What is the probability of spinning a 2?
1 out of 6 or $\frac{1}{6}$
8. What is the probability of spinning a 4?
1 out of 6 or $\frac{1}{6}$
9. What is the probability of spinning a 1?
0
10. What is the probability of spinning a number less than 5?
1

UNIT 11 LESSON 8 Explore Probability 413

Student Activity Book page 413

▶ Use the Language of Probability INDIVIDUALS

Have students look at the spinner on Student Activity Book page 413 and complete exercises 1–5, using words to express probability.

▶ Record Probability in Two Ways WHOLE CLASS

Work together as a class to write the probability of spinning each number in exercises 6–10. For example:

- How many total sections are in the spinner? 6
- How many sections are labeled 3? 4
- What is the probability of spinning a 3? 4 out of 6
- How can you write that as a fraction? $\frac{4}{6}$

Teaching Note

Math Background Some students may see that 4 out of 6 or $\frac{4}{6}$ is the same as 2 out of 3 or $\frac{2}{3}$. Equivalent fractions will be formally taught in the next few lessons.

Activity 2

Record the Probability of an Event

 15 MINUTES

Goal: Record the results of a probability experiment.

Materials: coins, Student Activity Book page 414

 **NCTM Standards:**
Number and Operations
Communication
Data Analysis and Probability

Teaching Note

Math Background The probability of $\frac{1}{2}$ for tossing a head is *theoretical probability*. It is found by analyzing the possible outcomes. Students can use the results of their coin tosses to find an experimental probability for tossing heads. For example, a pair of students gets heads on 9 out of 20 tosses, their experimental probability of tossing heads is $\frac{9}{20}$ which is close to $\frac{10}{20}$ or $\frac{1}{2}$. The more times the coin is tossed, the closer the theoretical and experimental probabilities will be.

Note the fractions for the combined results. They should be very close to $\frac{1}{2}$.

11–8 Class Activity Name ____ Date ____

▶ Conduct a Coin Toss Experiment

When you toss a coin, heads or tails are equally likely to land up. This means they have the same chance of occurring. Heads has a 1 out of 2 chance of happening. You can expect to get heads about half the time, or about 1 out of every 2 tosses.

11. What is the probability written as a fraction of heads landing up when you toss a coin? $\frac{1}{2}$

12. Toss a coin 20 times and keep a tally. Results will vary.

Heads	Tails

13. How many tosses did you make? ____ Answers will vary.

14. I tossed heads ____ out of ____ tosses. Answers will vary.

15. I tossed tails ____ out of ____ tosses. Answers will vary.

16. Did you get heads for about $\frac{1}{2}$ of your tosses? Answers will vary.

17. **Explain** If the probability of getting heads is $\frac{1}{2}$, why do you think you and your partner may not have tossed heads half of the time? Possible explanation: Probability tells us what we can expect to happen. It does not tell us exactly what will happen.

18. Work with your teacher to combine the results for your class.
Class results: Heads: ____ Tails: ____
Did your class get heads closer to one half than you did in exercise 14? In most cases the answer will be "Yes".

414 UNIT 11 LESSON 8 Explore Probability

Student Activity Book page 414

▶ Conduct a Coin Toss Experiment PAIRS

Give each **Student Pair** a coin and have them work on exercises 11–17 on Student Book page 414. When students have finished, discuss the results as a class.

Then work together with students to complete exercise 18 by combining the results for all the **Student Pairs** in the class.

Discuss with the class that doing at least 50 trials in an experiment will give a better idea of the outcome for a larger group than a small number of trials.

Ask students what they would expect the number of heads and the number of tails tossed to be out of 200 tosses. 100 heads, 100 tails

Activity 3

Predict Future Events

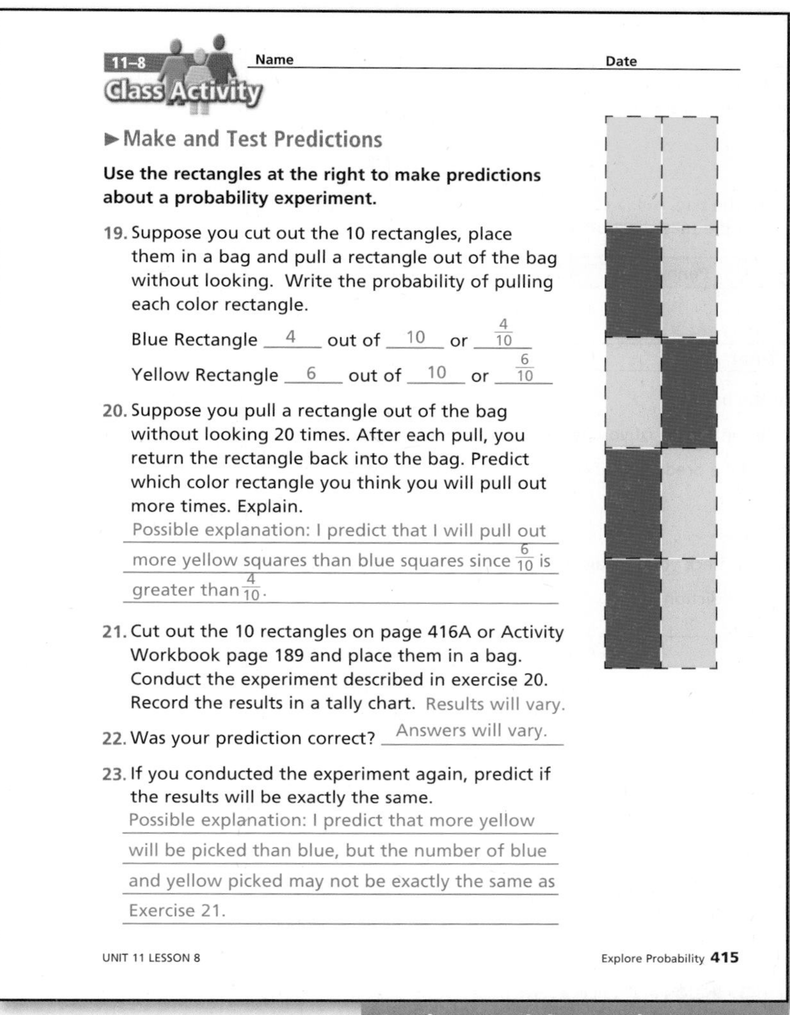

11-8 Class Activity

Name ____ Date ____

► Make and Test Predictions

Use the rectangles at the right to make predictions about a probability experiment.

19. Suppose you cut out the 10 rectangles, place them in a bag and pull a rectangle out of the bag without looking. Write the probability of pulling each color rectangle.

Blue Rectangle 4 out of 10 or $\frac{4}{10}$

Yellow Rectangle 6 out of 10 or $\frac{6}{10}$

20. Suppose you pull a rectangle out of the bag without looking 20 times. After each pull, you return the rectangle back into the bag. Predict which color rectangle you think you will pull out more times. Explain.
Possible explanation: I predict that I will pull out more yellow squares than blue squares since $\frac{6}{10}$ is greater than $\frac{4}{10}$.

21. Cut out the 10 rectangles on page 416A or Activity Workbook page 189 and place them in a bag. Conduct the experiment described in exercise 20. Record the results in a tally chart. Results will vary.

22. Was your prediction correct? Answers will vary.

23. If you conducted the experiment again, predict if the results will be exactly the same.
Possible explanation: I predict that more yellow will be picked than blue, but the number of blue and yellow picked may not be exactly the same as Exercise 21.

UNIT 11 LESSON 8 Explore Probability 415

Student Activity Book page 415

15 MINUTES

Goal: Predict future events.

Materials: Student Activity Book pp. 415–416A or Hardcover Book pp. 415–416, and Activity Workbook p. 189, 10 coins (dimes and pennies) per student pair

NCTM Standards:
Number and Operations
Communication
Data Analysis and Probability

► Make and Test Predictions PAIRS

Have students look at the rectangles on Student Book page 415 to write the probability of picking a blue or yellow piece of paper to make a prediction of which color they will choose most often. Then have **Student Pairs** complete exercises 19 and 20.

For exercise 21, students cut out the 10 rectangular pieces on Student Activity Book page 416A or Activity Workbook p. 189, conduct the experiment, and record the results. Students will analyze the results in exercises 22–23.

When students have finished, have volunteers share their results and predictions about the results if the experiment is repeated.

Activity continued ►

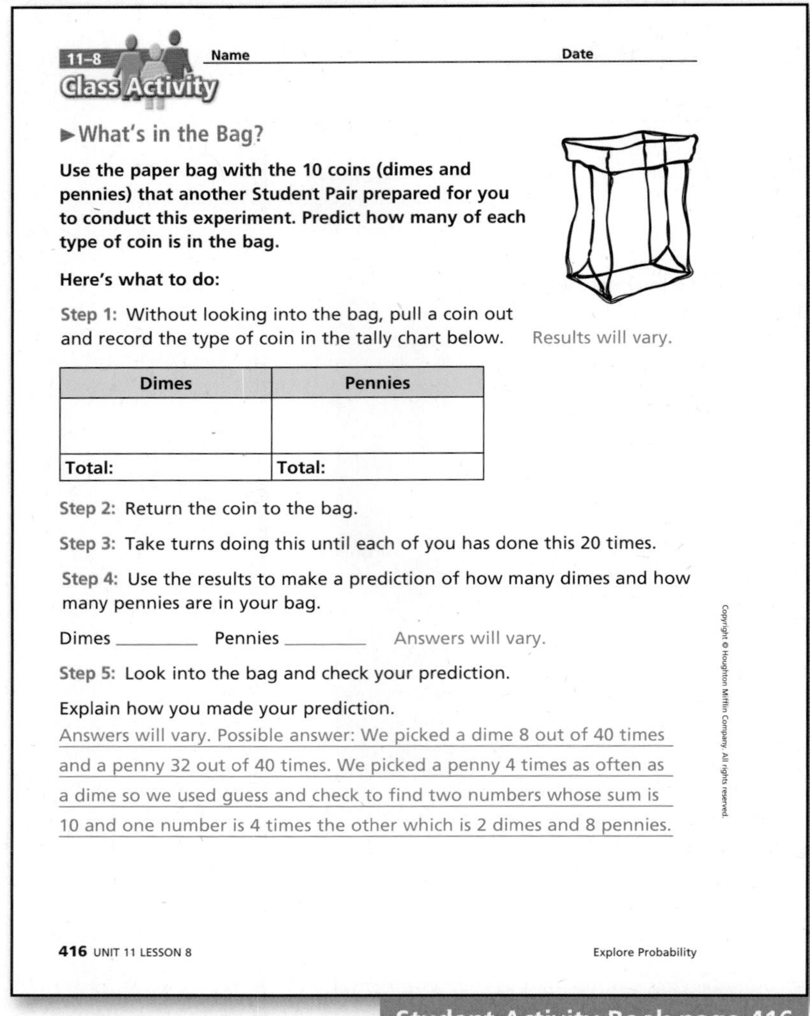
11-8 Class Activity

Name Date

▶ What's in the Bag?

Use the paper bag with the 10 coins (dimes and pennies) that another Student Pair prepared for you to conduct this experiment. Predict how many of each type of coin is in the bag.

Here's what to do:

Step 1: Without looking into the bag, pull a coin out and record the type of coin in the tally chart below. Results will vary.

Dimes	Pennies
Total:	Total:

Step 2: Return the coin to the bag.

Step 3: Take turns doing this until each of you has done this 20 times.

Step 4: Use the results to make a prediction of how many dimes and how many pennies are in your bag.

Dimes ________ Pennies ________ Answers will vary.

Step 5: Look into the bag and check your prediction.

Explain how you made your prediction.

Answers will vary. Possible answer: We picked a dime 8 out of 40 times and a penny 32 out of 40 times. We picked a penny 4 times as often as a dime so we used guess and check to find two numbers whose sum is 10 and one number is 4 times the other which is 2 dimes and 8 pennies.

416 UNIT 11 LESSON 8 Explore Probability

Student Activity Book page 416

▶ What's in the Bag? PAIRS

Have each **Student Pair** prepare a bag with 10 coins (dimes and pennies), fold the top of the bag down, and give it to another **Student Pair**.

Tell students that they will be using probability to predict what coins are in the bag. Be sure they understand that they are not to look in the bag when they are choosing and that they should return the coin each time after they record the type of coin.

After students have completed Student Book page 416, invite students to share how they made their predictions and if their methods worked.

Activity 4

All Possible Outcomes

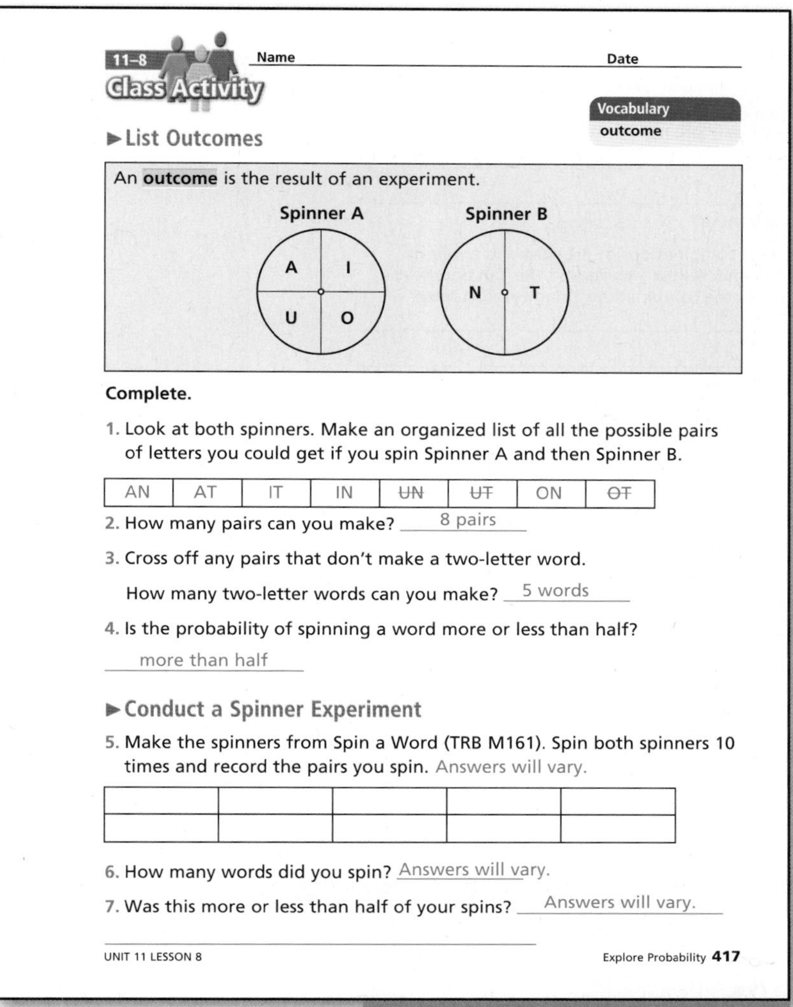

11-8 Class Activity

Name ______ Date ______

Vocabulary
outcome

► List Outcomes

An **outcome** is the result of an experiment.

Spinner A: A, I, U, O

Spinner B: N, T

Complete.

1. Look at both spinners. Make an organized list of all the possible pairs of letters you could get if you spin Spinner A and then Spinner B.

AN	AT	IT	IN	~~UN~~	~~UT~~	ON	~~OT~~

2. How many pairs can you make? 8 pairs
3. Cross off any pairs that don't make a two-letter word.
   How many two-letter words can you make? 5 words
4. Is the probability of spinning a word more or less than half?
   more than half

► Conduct a Spinner Experiment

5. Make the spinners from Spin a Word (TRB M161). Spin both spinners 10 times and record the pairs you spin. Answers will vary.

6. How many words did you spin? Answers will vary.
7. Was this more or less than half of your spins? Answers will vary.

UNIT 11 LESSON 8 Explore Probability 417

Student Activity Book page 417

► List Outcomes WHOLE CLASS

Introduce the term *outcome* as the result of a probability experiment on the top of Student Book page 417. Explain that if you toss a coin, the possible outcomes are heads or tails. Explain how to make an organized list of all the possible outcomes from spinning the spinners by starting with one letter on the left spinner and pairing it with both letters on the second spinner and so on. Then have students complete exercises 1–4.

► Conduct a Spinner Experiment INDIVIDUALS

Have students use Spin-a-Word (TRB M161) to make the spinners and do the experiment.

After students have recorded the results from 10 spins and complete exercises 5–7, discuss the results as a class.

- How did your actual results compare with probability in exercise 4? Answers may vary.

Activity continued ►

20 MINUTES

Goal: Identify all possible outcomes for a probability experiment.

Materials: paper clips, pencils, Student Activity Book or Hardcover Book pp. 417–418, Spin-a-Word (TRB M161), cut outs from Student Activity Book p. 416A or Activity Workbook p. 189

NCTM Standards:
Number and Operations
Communication
Data Analysis and Probability

11–8 Glass Activity

Name ______ Date ______

▶ Combinations

Use the T-shirts and shorts cutouts to complete this activity.
Here's what to do:

Step 1: Make all the different combinations of a T-shirt and a pair of shorts using the Red T-shirt and the Tan and Navy pairs of shorts. Record the combinations using the first letter of the color of the item.

RT RN

How many combinations are there? 2

Step 2: Make all the different combinations of a T-shirt and a pair of shorts using the Red and Yellow T-shirts and the Tan and Navy pairs of shorts. Record the combinations using the first letter of the color of the item.

RT RN YT YN

How many combinations are there? 4

Step 3: Make all the different combinations of a T-shirt and a pair of shorts using the three T-shirts and the Tan and Navy pairs of shorts. Record the combinations using the first letter of the color of the item.

RT RN YT YN BN BT

How many combinations are there? 6

Step 4: Make all the different combinations of a T-Shirt and a pair of shorts using the three T-shirts and all three pairs of shorts. Record the combinations using the first letter of the color of the item.

RT RN RB YT YN YB BN BT BB

How many combinations are there? 9

What pattern do you see?
If you multiply the number of T- shirts by the number of shorts you get the number of combinations.

418 UNIT 11 LESSON 8 Explore Probability

Student Activity Book page 418

▶ Combinations PAIRS

Have students cut out the T-shirts and shorts on Student Activity Book page 416A or Activity Workbook page 189 and complete Student Book page 418.

If **Student Pairs** have difficulty discovering the pattern, write out the number of T- Shirts and pairs of shorts used in each step:

1 T-shirt 2 pairs of shorts

2 T-shirts 2 pairs of shorts

3 T-shirts 3 pairs of shorts

Quick Quiz

See Assessment Guide for Unit 11 Quick Quiz 2.

2 Going Further

Differentiated Instruction

Intervention — Activity Card 11-8

Describe a Spinner — Activity Card 11-8 ●

Work: In pairs

Use:
- 4 copies of Spinner C (TRB M61)
- Crayons

1. Choose a color.
2. Create 4 spinners to show the following:
   - likely to spin that color
   - unlikely to spin that color
   - certain to spin that color
   - impossible to spin that color
3. Describe each spinner.
4. Trade with another pair and discuss.
5. **Analyze** How would you color a spinner so it is equally likely you will spin blue and yellow? Color equal (2) sections blue and yellow.

Certain to land on blue.
Impossible to land on red.

Unit 11, Lesson 8

Activity Note If pairs have difficulty with the vocabulary, explain that *impossible* and *certain* are direct opposites *(can't happen* versus *will happen).* Likewise, the terms *unlikely* and *likely* are also direct opposites.

Math Writing Prompt

Write About It Suppose there are 15 red marbles, 5 green marbles, and 3 yellow marbles. Is choosing a blue marble *likely, certain,* or *impossible?*

Software Support

Warm Up 52.05

On Level — Activity Card 11-8

Heads or Tails? — Activity Card 11-8 ▲

Work: On your own

Use:
- MathBoard materials or blank paper
- 2 coins

1. List all the possible outcomes when tossing two coins. (For this chart, heads and tails and tails and heads are the same.)

2. Flip both coins at the same time and record the results in a tally chart 20 times.
3. Then write the probability as a fraction.

Unit 11, Lesson 8

Activity Note Encourage students to physically manipulate the two pennies in order to find all of the possible outcomes when tossing both coins.

Math Writing Prompt

Explain Suppose you choose a cube (without looking) from a bag with 5 green cubes and 2 red cubes. Which cube are you most likely to choose? Explain.

Software Support

Numberopolis: Wash 'n Spin, Level F

Challenge — Activity Card 11-8

What's in the Bag? — Activity Card 11-8 ■

Work: In pairs

Use:
- MathBoard materials or blank paper
- Paper bag
- Play Money (12 dimes and 12 pennies)

Decide:

Who will be Student 1 and who will be Student 2 for the first round.

1. **Student 1:** Put 12 coins in a paper bag (for example 8 dimes and 4 pennies).
2. **Student 2:** Choose one coin at a time, record the type of coin in a tally chart, and then return the coin to the bag. Continue this 20 times and then predict the number of each type of coin in the bag.
3. **Student 1:** Reveal the coins and compare them to the prediction.
4. Switch roles and repeat the steps.

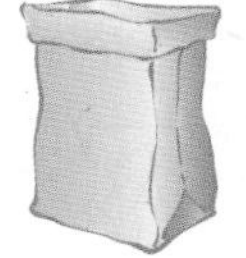
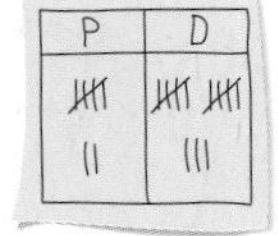

Unit 11, Lesson 8

Activity Note Encourage students to write the probability for each coin to help them make their predictions on how many coins are in the bag.

Math Writing Prompt

Predict Suppose you roll two number cubes (labeled 1–6) and add to find the sum. Which total do you predict is the most likely outcome for a roll? Explain. 7 is the sum most likely to be rolled.

DESTINATION Math®

Software Support

Course II: Module 3: Unit 2: Money

 Homework and Spiral Review

11-8 Homework **Goal:** Additional Practice

This Homework page provides practice with probability.

11-8 Homework Name ______ Date ______

Look at the bag of marbles and use the words *impossible, certain, equally likely, likely,* or *unlikely* to describe the event of picking a marble out of the bag.

1. Pick a black marble equally likely
2. Pick a white marble impossible
3. Pick a striped marble less likely
4. Pick a marble certain

Use the bag of marbles above to complete. Write the probability in two ways.

5. What is the probability of picking a black marble? $\frac{3}{6}$ or $\frac{1}{2}$; 3 out of 6 chance
6. What is the probability of picking a white marble? 0; 0 out of 0 chance
7. What is the probability of picking a marble with dots? $\frac{2}{6}$ or $\frac{1}{3}$; 2 out of 6 chance
8. What is the probability of picking a marble with stripes? $\frac{1}{6}$ 1 out of 6 chance

Look at the spinner, list the outcomes, and predict what you are more likely to spin.

9. red, green, blue; red

Red	Red
Green	Blue

10. 1, 3, 4; 4

Spinner sections: 4, 4, 4, 4, 4, 3, 1, 1

UNIT 11 LESSON 8 Discover Probability 271

Homework and Remembering page 271

11-8 Remembering **Goal:** Spiral Review

This Remembering page would be appropriate anytime after today's lesson.

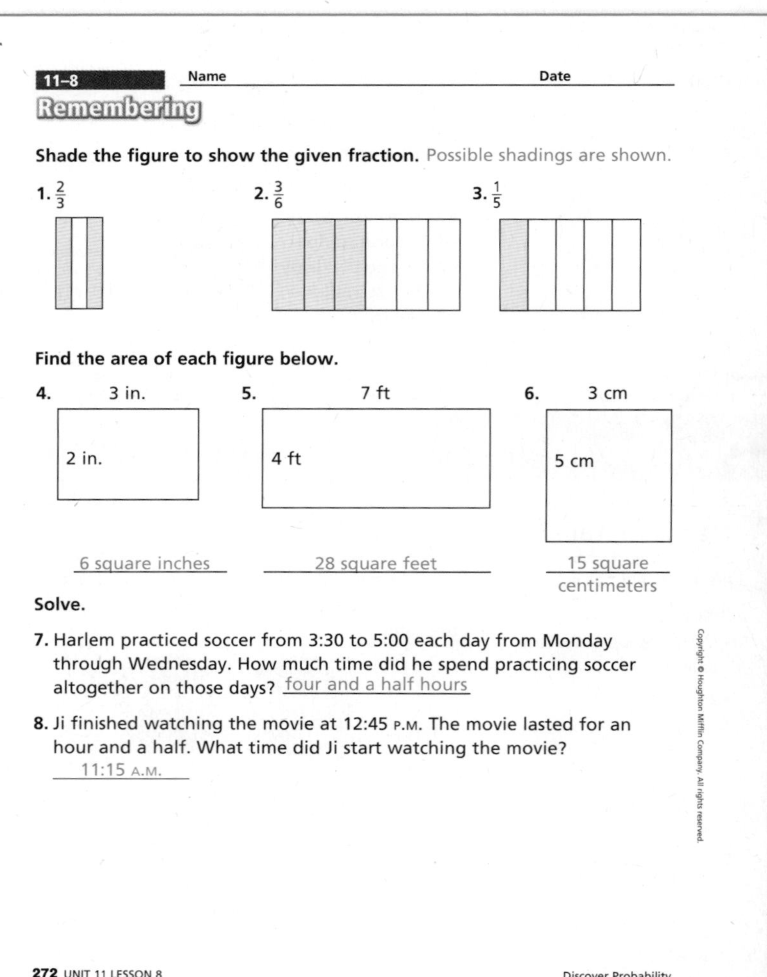
11-8 Remembering Name ______ Date ______

Shade the figure to show the given fraction. Possible shadings are shown.

1. $\frac{2}{3}$ 2. $\frac{3}{6}$ 3. $\frac{1}{5}$

Find the area of each figure below.

4. 3 in. by 2 in. — 6 square inches
5. 7 ft by 4 ft — 28 square feet
6. 3 cm by 5 cm — 15 square centimeters

Solve.

7. Harlem practiced soccer from 3:30 to 5:00 each day from Monday through Wednesday. How much time did he spend practicing soccer altogether on those days? four and a half hours
8. Ji finished watching the movie at 12:45 P.M. The movie lasted for an hour and a half. What time did Ji start watching the movie? 11:15 A.M.

Copyright © Houghton Mifflin Company. All rights reserved.

272 UNIT 11 LESSON 8 Discover Probability

Homework and Remembering page 272

Home or School Activity

 Art Connection

Game Design Have students design their own probability game. They may want to design a fair game in which the likelihood of winning is the same for all players or design one that would allow one player to win most of the time. Then play the game and test their predictions.

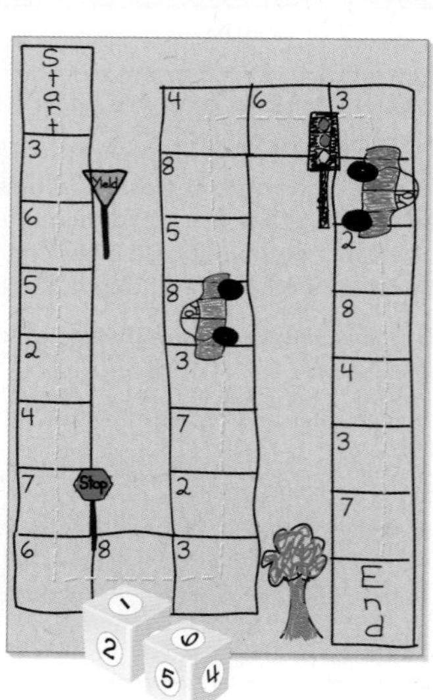

Introduce Equivalence

Vocabulary

equivalent fractions
equivalence chain
denominator
numerator

Lesson Objective

- **Informally explore equivalent fractions.**

The Day at a Glance

Today's Goals	Materials	
1 Teaching the Lesson **A1:** Use fraction strips to find equivalent fractions. **2 Going Further** ▸ Differentiated Instruction **3 Homework and Spiral Review**	**Lesson Activities** Student Activity Book pp. 418A–420 or Student Hardcover Book pp. 418A–420 and Activity Workbook pp. 191–192 (includes Cut-Outs) Homework and Remembering pp. 273—274 Envelopes Fraction Tiles Fraction Strips (TRB M134)	**Going Further** Activity Cards 11-9 Fraction Strips (TRB M134) Crayons or colored pencils Equivalent Fraction Match Up (TRB M135) Index Cards (16) Math Journals

Use Math Talk today!

Keeping Skills Sharp

Quick Practice

Goal: Practice "as many as" comparisons.

Comparison Chant The class is divided into two groups. The **Student Leader** writes a factor and one of its count-bys on the board. The leader asks one group to compare the first number to the second, and then asks the second group to compare the second number to the first. The leader repeats the process with several more pairs of numbers. (See Unit 11 Lesson 6.)

Daily Routines

Homework Review Ask students to place their homework at the corner of their desks. As you circulate during Quick Practice, check that students completed the assignment, and see whether any problem caused difficulty for many students.

Analyze Data The students voted for their favorite color. 3 students voted for blue. 5 students voted for red. 2 students voted for green. 6 students voted for orange. Create a line plot using the data. Then, write a conclusion about the data.

Possible answer: Green was liked the least of all the colors.

1 Teaching the Lesson

Activity

Fold Fraction Strips

 45 MINUTES

Goal: Use fraction strips to find equivalent fractions.

Materials: Student Activity Book pp. 418A–420 or Hardcover Book pp. 419–420 and Activity Workbook p. 191 (includes cut outs), envelopes (1 per student), fraction tiles, Fraction Strips (TRB M134)

 **NCTM Standards:**
Number and Operations
Representation

 Alternate Approach

Fraction Tiles Students with limited dexterity might find it difficult to create fraction strips by the folding process described in the Activity. You might prefer to provide these students with a set of commercially produced fraction bars. These sets generally include models for halves, fourths, eighths, thirds, sixths, and twelfths, as well as fifths and tenths.

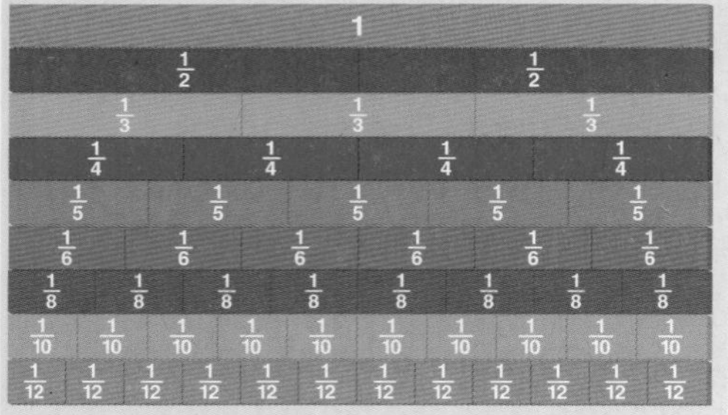

Differentiated Instruction

Special Needs If some students have difficulty cutting and manipulating the paper fraction strips, laminate the page before you cut out the strips for them. Laminated strips will be easier to pick up and move around as the students use them.

▶ Make Fraction Strips for $\frac{1}{2}$s, $\frac{1}{4}$s, $\frac{1}{8}$s, and $\frac{1}{16}$s

WHOLE CLASS

Have students cut out the 8 paper strips on Student Activity Book page 418A or Activity Workbook p. 189. Point out that all the strips are the same length. Explain to students that they will be folding the strips to show different fractions.

Have students take one strip and label it 1 whole.

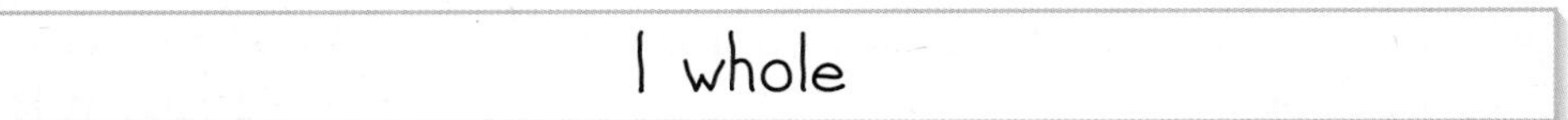

Next, have students take a second strip and fold it in half. Suggest that students trace the fold with a pencil, to make the division easier to see.

- How many equal parts is your strip of paper divided into? 2 What fraction of a whole does each part represent? $\frac{1}{2}$

Have students write $\frac{1}{2}$ in each section.

Now, have students use a third strip and fold it into fourths.

- Does anyone have any ideas about how you might do this? Remember the four parts must be equal.

The following are two ways that students can do this.

- Fold the strip in half and then, without unfolding it, fold it in half again.
- Fold the strip in half. Unfold it, and then fold each half in half by folding each end to the center.

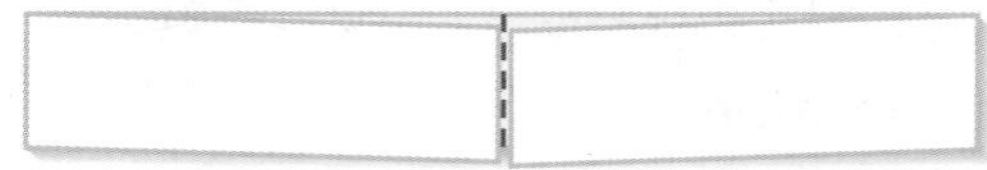

Again, suggest students draw a line on each fold to make the divisions easier to see.

- How many equal parts did we divide the strip into? 4 What fraction should we write in each part? $\frac{1}{4}$

Have students label their strips.

Tell students to use a new strip and ask them to suggest methods for folding the strip into eighths. Have them fold the strip, trace the folds, and label the parts.

Next, ask students how they can fold another strip into sixteenths. Have them fold and label the strip.

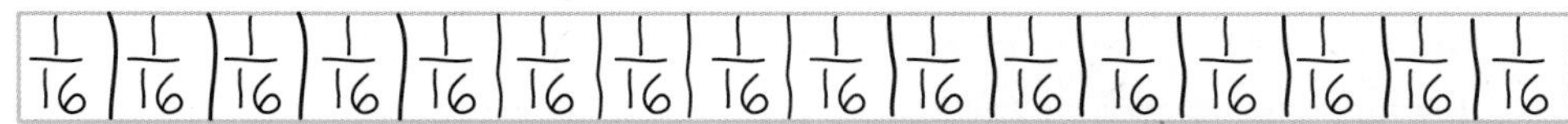

Have students place the halves strip above the fourths strip, aligning the ends as shown.

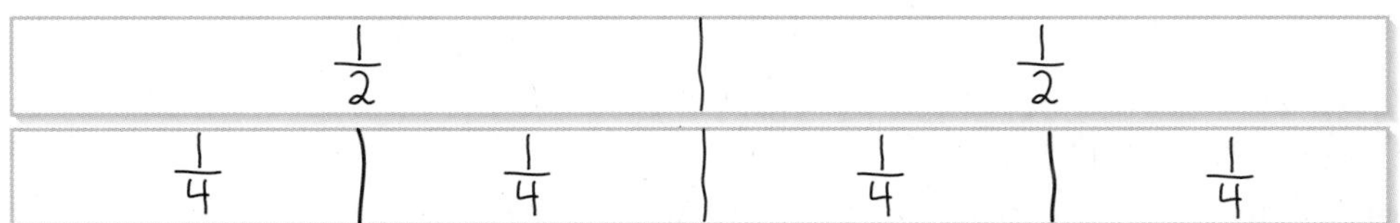

- Look at how the parts of your strips match up. How many fourths make a half? 2

Write the following on the board:

2 fourths = 1 half $\quad \frac{2}{4} = \frac{1}{2}$

Tell students we say that $\frac{2}{4}$ and $\frac{1}{2}$ are *equivalent fractions*. Equivalent fractions are fractions that name the same amount. Explain that the fraction strips that they just made can be used to find other pairs of equivalent fractions.

Activity continued ▶

Differentiated Instruction

Extra Help Point out that the word equivalent has equal in it. Cross out the "i" "v," and "ent" in equivalent to see the word *equal*. We show that fractions are equivalent using an equal sign.

English Language Learners

Write *equivalent* on the board. Provide students with inch and centimeter rulers. Ask: **Are inches and centimeters equal?** no Guide students to draw a 2-in. line and a 5-cm line, then measure each in both units.

- **Beginning** Ask: **Are the lines the same length?** yes **Is 2 inches *equivalent* to 5 centimeters?** yes
- **Intermediate** Say: **2 inches and 5 centimeters are __.** equivalent
- **Advanced** Have students tell about the lines. Invite them to find how many centimeters are equivalent to 1 inch.

Differentiated Instruction

Advanced Learners Have students complete this equivalence chain. Present the chain as shown below. Tell them to use any patterns they see to fill in the blanks.

$$\frac{1}{2} = \frac{2}{4} = \frac{\square}{6} = \frac{4}{8} = \frac{\square}{\square} = \frac{\square}{12} = \frac{\square}{\square}$$

$$\frac{1}{2} = \frac{2}{4} = \frac{3}{6} = \frac{4}{8} = \frac{5}{10} = \frac{6}{12} = \frac{7}{14}$$

Then ask them to identify what fraction in this chain would have 30 as the denominator, and what fraction would have 30 as the numerator. $\frac{15}{30}, \frac{30}{60}$

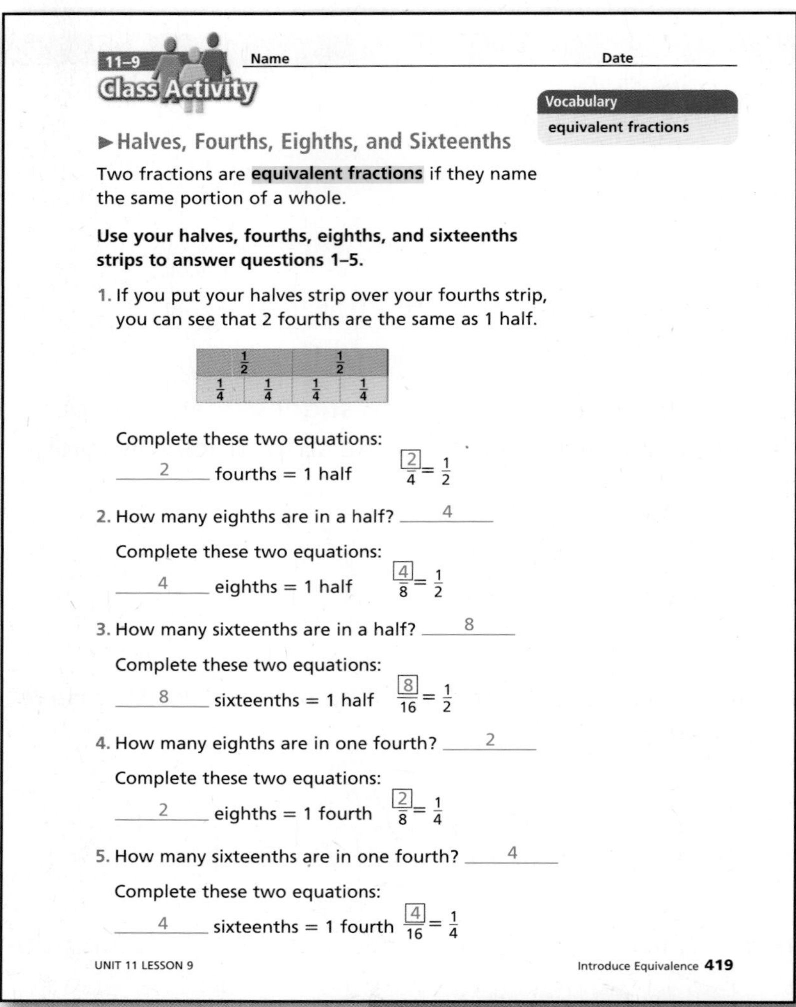
11–9 Class Activity

Name ______ Date ______

Vocabulary
equivalent fractions

▶ Halves, Fourths, Eighths, and Sixteenths

Two fractions are **equivalent fractions** if they name the same portion of a whole.

Use your halves, fourths, eighths, and sixteenths strips to answer questions 1–5.

1. If you put your halves strip over your fourths strip, you can see that 2 fourths are the same as 1 half.

$\frac{1}{2}$		$\frac{1}{2}$	
$\frac{1}{4}$	$\frac{1}{4}$	$\frac{1}{4}$	$\frac{1}{4}$

Complete these two equations:

2 fourths = 1 half $\qquad \frac{2}{4} = \frac{1}{2}$

2. How many eighths are in a half? 4

Complete these two equations:

4 eighths = 1 half $\qquad \frac{4}{8} = \frac{1}{2}$

3. How many sixteenths are in a half? 8

Complete these two equations:

8 sixteenths = 1 half $\qquad \frac{8}{16} = \frac{1}{2}$

4. How many eighths are in one fourth? 2

Complete these two equations:

2 eighths = 1 fourth $\qquad \frac{2}{8} = \frac{1}{4}$

5. How many sixteenths are in one fourth? 4

Complete these two equations:

4 sixteenths = 1 fourth $\qquad \frac{4}{16} = \frac{1}{4}$

UNIT 11 LESSON 9 Introduce Equivalence 419

Student Activity Book page 419

▶ Halves, Fourths, Eighths, and Sixteenths WHOLE CLASS

Refer students to Student Book page 419. Work together to complete exercise 1. Then have them use their fraction strips to complete exercises 2–5. Discuss the answers as a class.

Explain to students they just used fraction strips to find three fractions that are equivalent to $\frac{1}{2}$. Write the following equivalent fractions on the board.

$$\frac{2}{4} = \frac{1}{2} \qquad \frac{4}{8} = \frac{1}{2} \qquad \frac{8}{16} = \frac{1}{2}$$

- We can write an *equivalence chain* to show that all the fractions are equivalent.

Write the following equivalence chain on the board.

$$\frac{1}{2} = \frac{2}{4} = \frac{4}{8} = \frac{8}{16}$$

- How are these fractions all alike?

Students should notice that the numerator is half the denominator, or, equivalently, that the denominator is twice the numerator.

► Make Fraction Strips for Thirds, Sixths, and Twelfths WHOLE CLASS

Have students start with a new, unfolded fraction strip. Tell them to try to figure out how to fold the strip to make thirds. This is not easy to do. You might suggest that they make an S shape and then "squish" it together, keeping the three sections the same length.

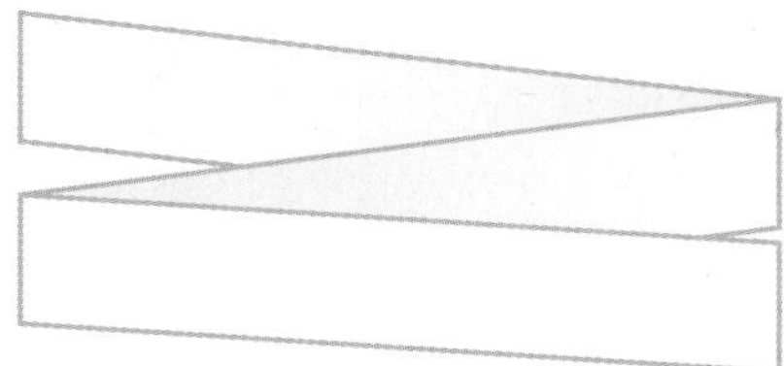

Have students trace the folds and label the equal parts.

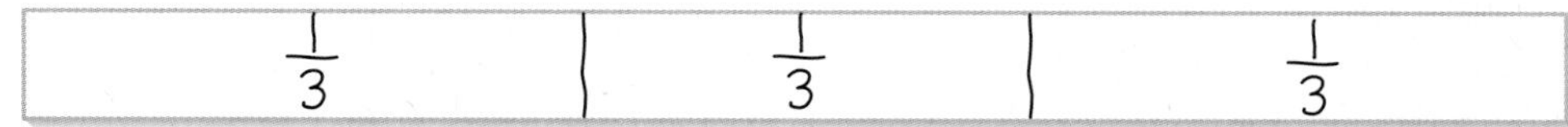

Tell students to start with another strip. Ask them to suggest methods for folding the strip into sixths. This can be done by dividing a strip into thirds and then folding each third in half. Have them fold the strip, trace the folds, and label the parts.

Next, ask students how they can fold another strip into twelfths. This can be done by folding the strip into sixths and then dividing each sixth in half. Have them fold and label the strip.

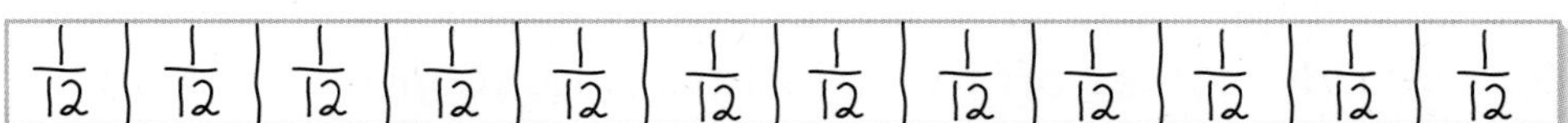

Have students place the thirds strip above the sixths strip, aligning the ends as shown.

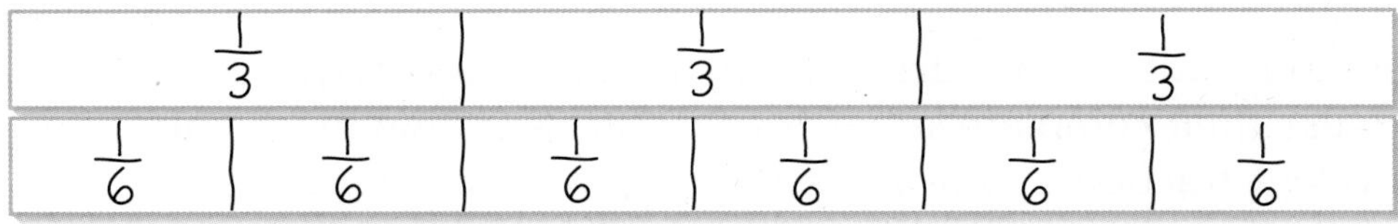

- Look at how the parts of your strips match up. How many sixths make a third? 2

Activity continued ►

Teaching Note

What to Expect from Students
When folding a strip to make thirds, some students might be tempted to fold three equal sections with some extra left over, and then just tear off the extra. Point out that tearing off part of the strip changes the whole. In order to use the strips to find equivalent fractions, the whole must be the same for all the strips.

Ongoing Assessment

Ask questions such as the following:

- ► What does it mean for two fractions to be equivalent?
- ► How can you use your fraction strips to tell if two fractions are equivalent?
- ► Are $\frac{3}{6}$ and $\frac{1}{2}$ equivalent fractions?

Class Management

At the end of today's activity, have students put their fraction strips in an envelope and take them home to use for homework.

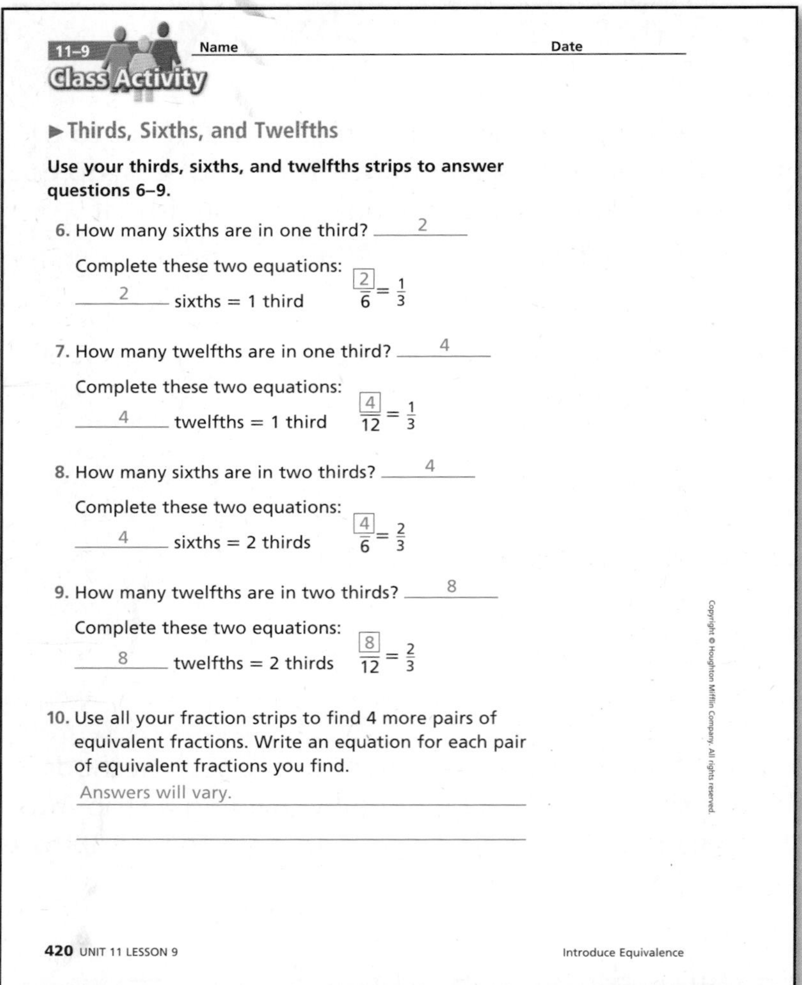

11–9 Class Activity Name Date

► Thirds, Sixths, and Twelfths

Use your thirds, sixths, and twelfths strips to answer questions 6–9.

6. How many sixths are in one third? 2

Complete these two equations:

2 sixths = 1 third $\frac{2}{6} = \frac{1}{3}$

7. How many twelfths are in one third? 4

Complete these two equations:

4 twelfths = 1 third $\frac{4}{12} = \frac{1}{3}$

8. How many sixths are in two thirds? 4

Complete these two equations:

4 sixths = 2 thirds $\frac{4}{6} = \frac{2}{3}$

9. How many twelfths are in two thirds? 8

Complete these two equations:

8 twelfths = 2 thirds $\frac{8}{12} = \frac{2}{3}$

10. Use all your fraction strips to find 4 more pairs of equivalent fractions. Write an equation for each pair of equivalent fractions you find.

Answers will vary.

420 UNIT 11 LESSON 9 Introduce Equivalence

Student Activity Book page 420

► Thirds, Sixths, and Twelfths WHOLE CLASS

Refer students to Student Book page 420. Have them use their fraction strips to complete exercises 6–9. Note that students may have difficulty if they did not fold their strips accurately. If so, give them a strip with sections already marked off from Fraction Strips (Copymaster M134), or allow them to work with another student.

When students are done, have them help you write the following two equivalence chains.

$$\frac{1}{3} = \frac{2}{6} = \frac{4}{12} \qquad \frac{2}{3} = \frac{4}{6} = \frac{8}{12}$$

Direct the students to exercise 10 on Student Book page 420 and have them use their complete set of fraction strips to find more pairs of equivalent fractions. Have students share what other equivalent fractions they discovered. Have students look for and discuss the similarities between original fraction and the simplified equivalent fraction. Possible response: Both numerators and denominators are even numbers, divisible by at least 2.

2 Going Further

Differentiated Instruction

Intervention

Activity Card 11-9

Visualize Equivalent Fractions — Activity Card 11-9 ●

Work: On your own

Use:
- TRB M134 (Fraction Strips)
- Crayons or colored pencils

1. Cut out fraction strips that you can use to model equivalent fractions.
2. Choose the fraction strip that shows $\frac{2}{3}$. Then color additional strips to show the same amount.

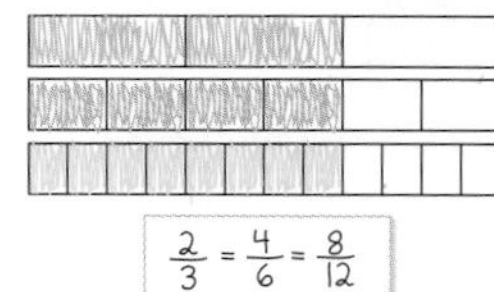

3. Write the equivalence chain that the models show. Repeat the activity for $\frac{1}{2}$, $\frac{3}{4}$, and $\frac{3}{12}$.
4. **Analyze** What patterns do you see in the equivalence chains that you write?

Unit 11, Lesson 9

Activity Note Remind students to align fraction strips on the left before identifying equivalent fractions. Each set of strips can identify a second equivalence with the sections that are not colored.

Math Writing Prompt

Make a Drawing Make a drawing to show why $\frac{3}{4}$ and $\frac{6}{8}$ are equivalent fractions. Explain your thinking.

Software Support

Warm Up 6.08

On Level

Activity Card 11-9

Equivalent Fractions Match Up — Activity Card 11-9 ▲

Work: In pairs

Use:
- TRB M135 (Equivalent Fractions Match Up)

1. Cut out the cards on Equivalent Fractions Match Up. Then shuffle the cards and place them face down in a 4 × 4 array.
2. Take turns choosing two cards. If the cards are not equivalent, return the cards face down.
3. If the cards are equivalent, keep the cards.
4. When all the cards have been matched, the player with the greater number of matches wins the game.

Unit 11, Lesson 9

Activity Note Students should check each other's matches and record the equivalent fractions that each match represents.

Math Writing Prompt

Explain Your Thinking Artie cut a large pizza into 4 equal pieces and ate 2 pieces. Rafael cut a small pizza into 8 equal pieces and ate 4 pieces. Did they both eat the same amount of pizza? If not, who ate more? Explain your answer.

Software Support

Fraction Action: Fraction Flare Up, Level D

Challenge

Activity Card 11-9

Greater Than, Less Than, Equal — Activity Card 11-9 ■

Work: In pairs

Use:
- TRB M142 (Fractions Strips)
- 16 Index cards

1. Write the fractions below on 16 index cards.

   $\frac{1}{2}$, $\frac{1}{1}$, $\frac{3}{4}$, $\frac{5}{6}$, $\frac{2}{8}$, $\frac{2}{12}$, $\frac{3}{6}$, $\frac{4}{16}$

   $\frac{1}{4}$, $\frac{2}{3}$, $\frac{1}{8}$, $\frac{4}{12}$, $\frac{8}{8}$, $\frac{6}{8}$, $\frac{2}{16}$, $\frac{2}{4}$

2. Play a fraction equivalence game. Shuffle and give 8 cards to each player. Players stack their cards face down. Both players turn over the top card and compare fractions. Use fraction strips to help you compare.
3. The player with the greater fraction takes both cards. If fractions are equivalent, players take only their own card.
4. Continue until all of the cards are taken. The player with more cards wins.

Unit 11, Lesson 9

Activity Note Some students may use other strategies to compare fractions, such as comparing numerators and denominators to identify fractions greater or less than $\frac{1}{2}$.

Math Writing Prompt

Investigate Math How many twentieths are equivalent to a half? a fourth? a fifth? a tenth? Explain how you found your answer.

Course II: Module 2: Unit 3: Fractional Parts

3 Homework and Spiral Review

11–9 Homework **Goal:** Additional Practice

This Homework page provides practice in finding equivalent fractions.

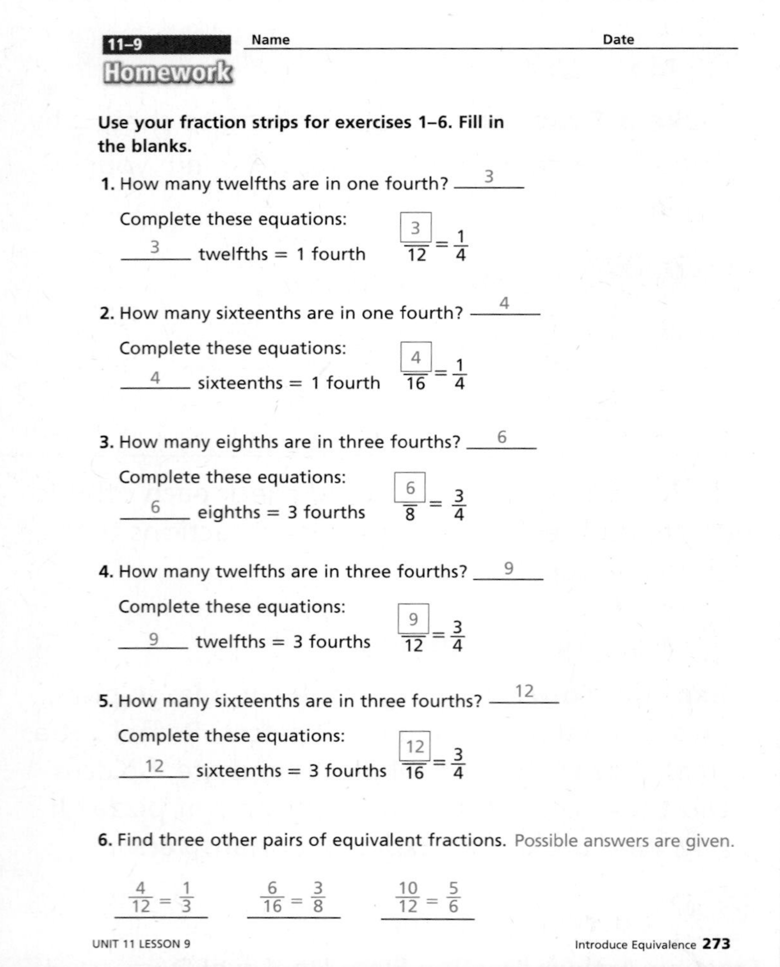

11–9 Homework Name ______ Date ______

Use your fraction strips for exercises 1–6. Fill in the blanks.

1. How many twelfths are in one fourth? 3

   Complete these equations:

   3 twelfths = 1 fourth $\quad \frac{3}{12} = \frac{1}{4}$

2. How many sixteenths are in one fourth? 4

   Complete these equations:

   4 sixteenths = 1 fourth $\quad \frac{4}{16} = \frac{1}{4}$

3. How many eighths are in three fourths? 6

   Complete these equations:

   6 eighths = 3 fourths $\quad \frac{6}{8} = \frac{3}{4}$

4. How many twelfths are in three fourths? 9

   Complete these equations:

   9 twelfths = 3 fourths $\quad \frac{9}{12} = \frac{3}{4}$

5. How many sixteenths are in three fourths? 12

   Complete these equations:

   12 sixteenths = 3 fourths $\quad \frac{12}{16} = \frac{3}{4}$

6. Find three other pairs of equivalent fractions. Possible answers are given.

   $\frac{4}{12} = \frac{1}{3}$ $\quad \frac{6}{16} = \frac{3}{8}$ $\quad \frac{10}{12} = \frac{5}{6}$

UNIT 11 LESSON 9 Introduce Equivalence **273**

Homework and Remembering page 273

11–9 Remembering **Goal:** Spiral Review

This Remembering page would be appropriate anytime after today's lesson.

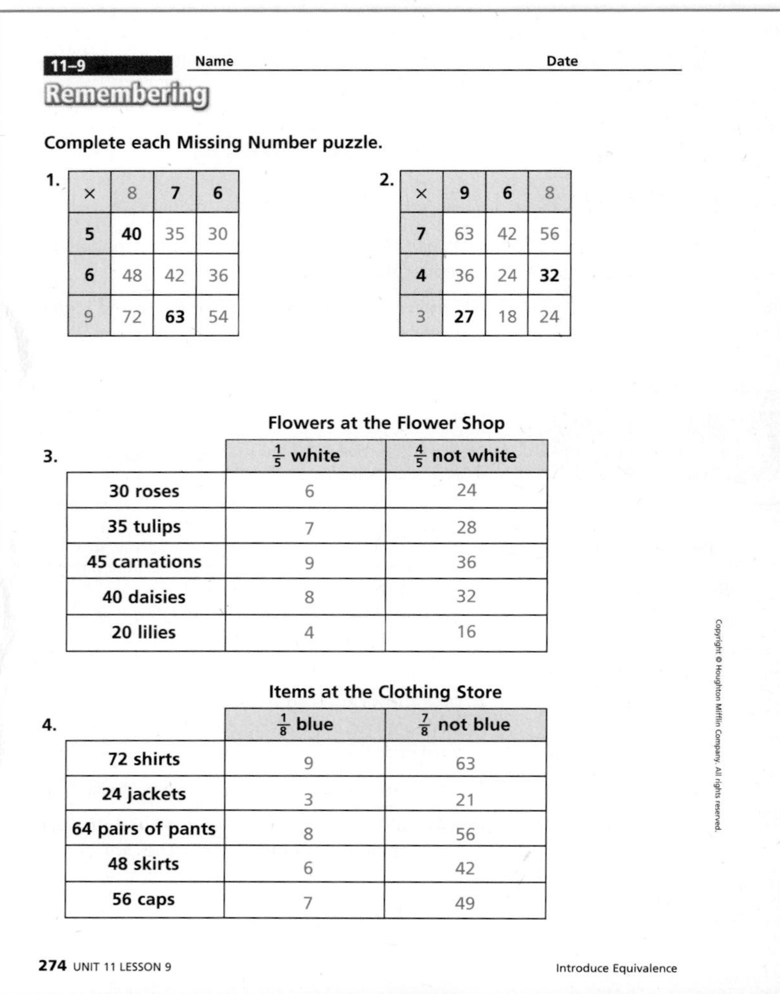

11–9 Remembering Name ______ Date ______

Complete each Missing Number puzzle.

1.

×	8	7	6
5	40	35	30
6	48	42	36
9	72	63	54

2.

×	9	6	8
7	63	42	56
4	36	24	32
3	27	18	24

3. **Flowers at the Flower Shop**

	$\frac{1}{5}$ white	$\frac{4}{5}$ not white
30 roses	6	24
35 tulips	7	28
45 carnations	9	36
40 daisies	8	32
20 lilies	4	16

4. **Items at the Clothing Store**

	$\frac{1}{8}$ blue	$\frac{7}{8}$ not blue
72 shirts	9	63
24 jackets	3	21
64 pairs of pants	8	56
48 skirts	6	42
56 caps	7	49

274 UNIT 11 LESSON 9 Introduce Equivalence

Homework and Remembering page 274

Home or School Activity

Art Connection

Make a Paper Quilt Have students fold a large sheet of paper into halves, fourths, eighths, and so on until they cannot fold it any more. Then have them unfold the paper and color each of the sections with crayons or markers to make a paper quilt. Ask them to use fractions to describe the quilt.

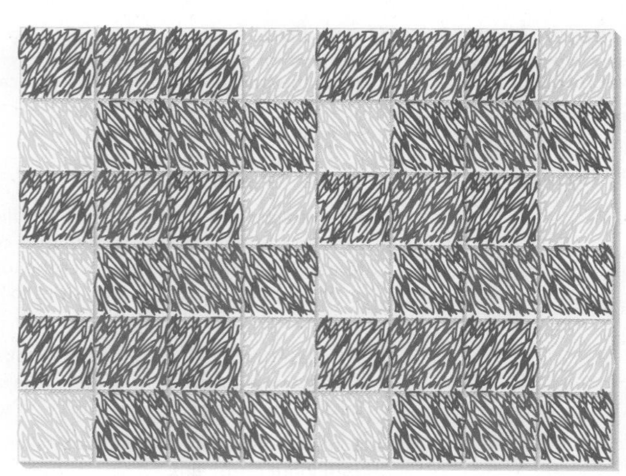

Explore Equivalence

Lesson Objective

- **Make discoveries about equivalent fractions while playing a game.**

Vocabulary
whole
equivalent fractions

The Day at a Glance

Today's Goals	Materials	
1 Teaching the Lesson **A:** Play a game involving equivalent fractions, and record and discuss observations. **2 Going Further** ▶ Differentiated Instruction **3 Homework and Spiral Review**	**Lesson Activities** Student Activity Book pp. 421–424B or Student Hardcover Book pp. 421–424 and Activity Workbook pp. 193–198 (includes Game Rules and Game Boards) Homework and Remembering pp. 275–276 Transparency of Student Activity Book page 443 and overhead projector (optional) Rulers Paper clips	**Going Further** Activity Cards 11-10 Equivalent Fraction Strips (TRB M142) Spinner F (TRB M141) Paper clips Inch-Grid Paper (TRB M42) Two-color counters MathBoard materials Math Journals

Use Math Talk today!

Keeping Skills Sharp

Quick Practice	Daily Routines	
Goal: Practice "as many as" comparisons. **Comparison Chant** The **Student Leader** writes a factor and one of its count-bys on the board. The leader has one group compare the first number to the second and a second group compare the second number to the first. Repeat. (See Unit 11 Lesson 6.)	**Homework Review** Let students work together to check their work. Remind students to use what they know about helping others.	**Strategy Problem** In June, Tia drove 497 miles. She drove a total of 783 miles in June and July. How many miles did Tia drive in July? How can smaller numbers help? 286 miles; Smaller numbers help focus on the operations. Subtract 6 miles in June from 10 miles in June and July to find she drove 4 miles in July. So, I subtract 497 from 783.

1 Teaching the Lesson

Activity

Fraction Game

 45 MINUTES

Goal: Play a game involving equivalent fractions, and record and discuss observations.

Materials: Transparency of Student Book p. 423 and overhead projector (optional), rulers, paper clips, Student Activity Book pp. 421–424A or Hardcover Book pp. 421–424 and Activity Workbook pp. 193–197 (includes game boards, rules, and cut outs)

 **NCTM Standards:**
Number and Operations
Representation

Teaching Note

What to Expect from Students Some students might be confused because the fraction labels on the sections of the spinners on Student Book page 424A are generally not related to the relative sizes of the sections. For example, on the first spinner for the Halves Game board, the section labeled *take one sixteenth* makes up one half of the spinner, not one sixteenth.

Before students play the game, you might want to discuss this issue. For each spinner, you might ask students what fraction of the spinner each section makes up, and which section the pointer is most likely or least likely to land on.

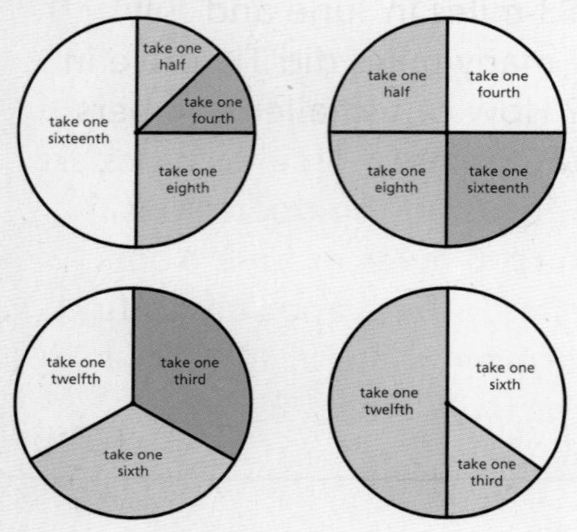

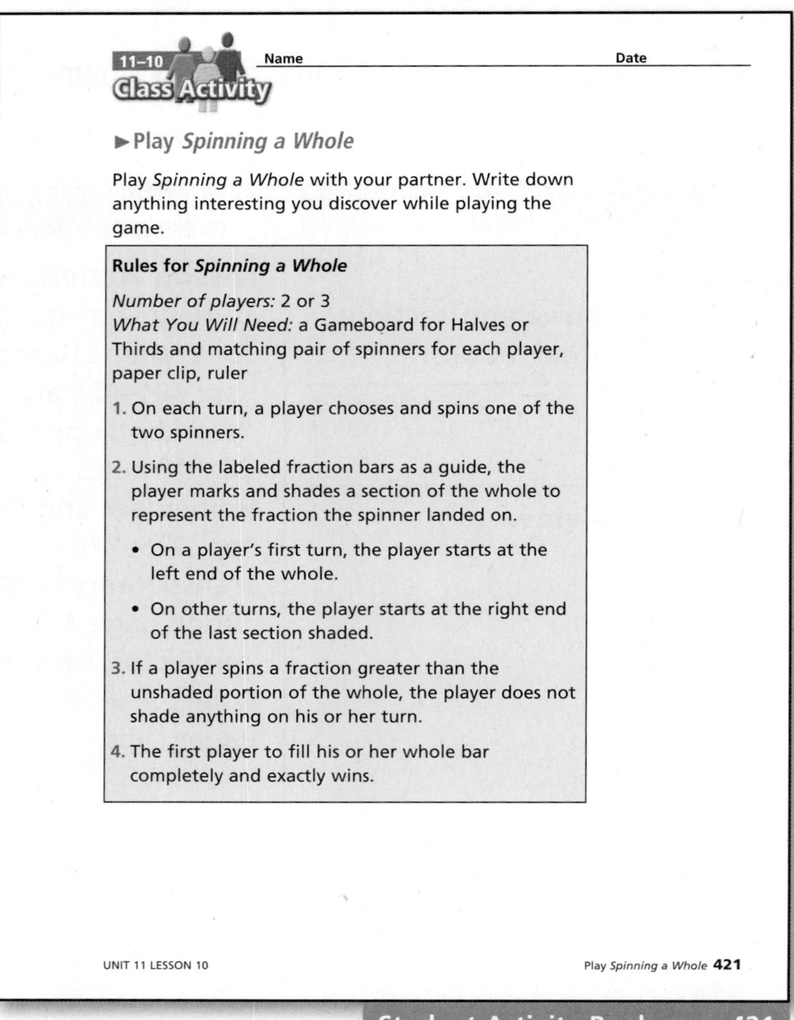
11–10 Class Activity

Name Date

► Play *Spinning a Whole*

Play *Spinning a Whole* with your partner. Write down anything interesting you discover while playing the game.

Rules for *Spinning a Whole*

Number of players: 2 or 3

What You Will Need: a Gameboard for Halves or Thirds and matching pair of spinners for each player, paper clip, ruler

1. On each turn, a player chooses and spins one of the two spinners.
2. Using the labeled fraction bars as a guide, the player marks and shades a section of the whole to represent the fraction the spinner landed on.
   - On a player's first turn, the player starts at the left end of the whole.
   - On other turns, the player starts at the right end of the last section shaded.
3. If a player spins a fraction greater than the unshaded portion of the whole, the player does not shade anything on his or her turn.
4. The first player to fill his or her whole bar completely and exactly wins.

UNIT 11 LESSON 10 Play *Spinning a Whole* **421**

Student Activity Book page 421

► Play *Spinning a Whole* WHOLE CLASS

Refer students to Student Activity Book pages 423–424A or Activity Workbook pp. 193–197, which include the Game Board for Halves, the Game Board for Thirds, and the game spinners for halves and thirds.

To help explain the game, you may want to display an overhead transparency of the Game Board for Halves, and have students look at their copy of this game board and the corresponding spinners. Point out that the top of the game board shows fraction strips, and the bottom shows undivided wholes. Tell students that they will use one of the wholes for each game.

Read aloud the rules for the game on Student page 421. Ask students to imagine that on your first turn, you spin $\frac{1}{8}$. Show students how to use the fraction strips, a ruler, and a pencil to mark off a $\frac{1}{8}$ section on the first whole. Shade and label the section.

Game Board for Halves

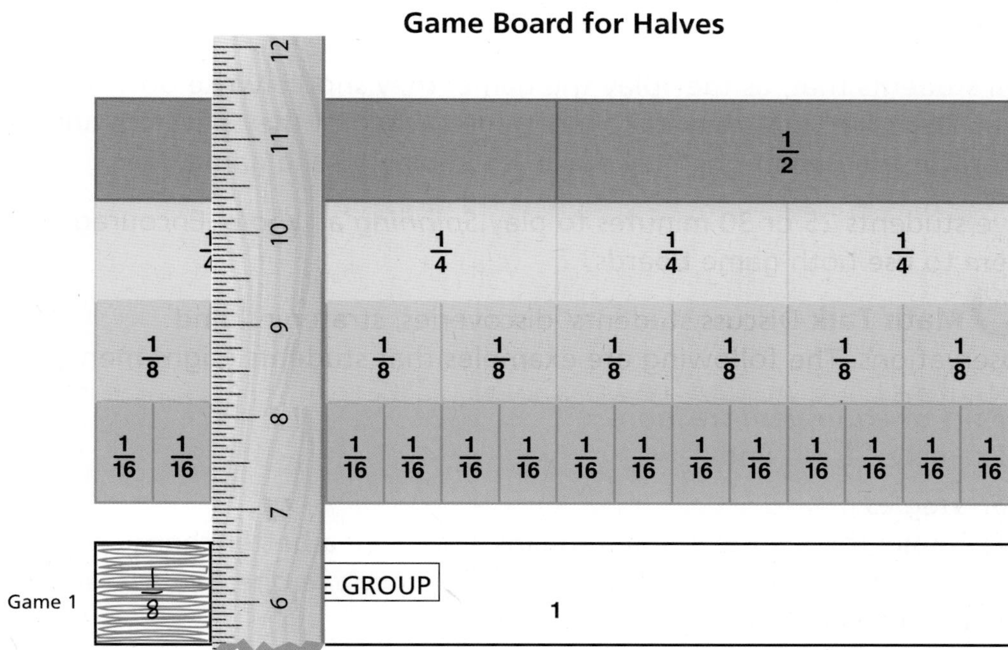

Ask students to imagine that, on your second turn, you spin $\frac{1}{4}$. Explain that you need to start at the end of the $\frac{1}{8}$ section you just shaded and mark off a $\frac{1}{4}$ section. However, none of the sections on the fourths bar begin at the end of the $\frac{1}{8}$ section. Ask students if they have any suggestions for how you could mark off $\frac{1}{4}$. If necessary, help students see that you could combine two $\frac{1}{8}$ sections or four $\frac{1}{16}$ sections to get a section equivalent to $\frac{1}{4}$. Demonstrate this on the overhead.

Game Board for Halves

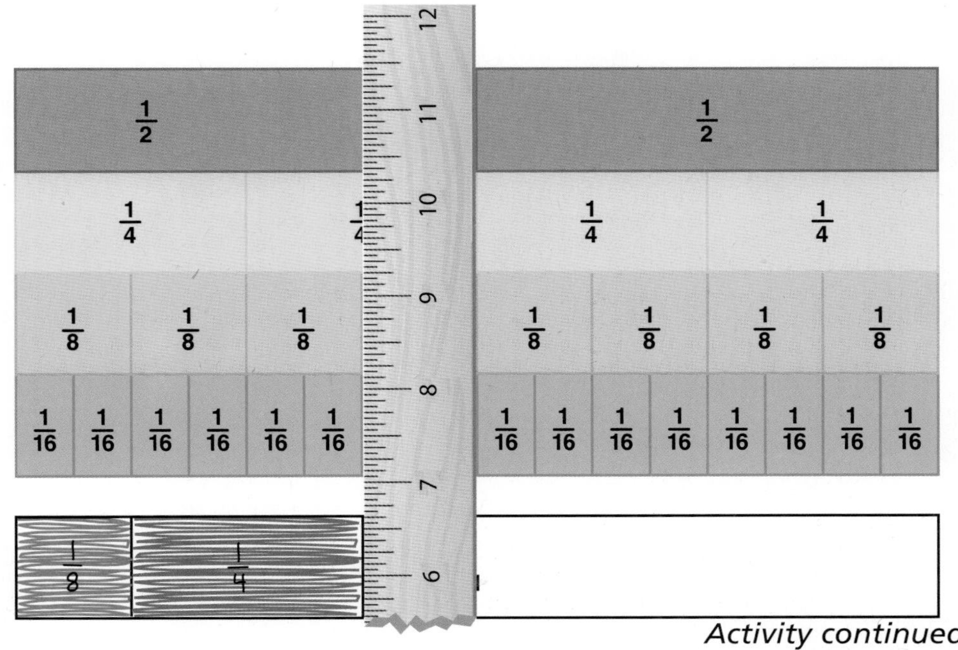

Activity continued ▶

Teaching Note

Watch For! After the first turn spinning, make sure students are adding on fractions from where they last shaded on the whole strip.

1 Teaching the Lesson (continued)

Class Management

Remind students to take home the Game Board for Halves, Game Board for Thirds, and spinners so that they can play *Spinning a Whole* for homework. These gameboards are available on Copymasters M137–M138.

Ongoing Assessment

Observe as students play *Spinning a Whole*. Ask questions such as:

- ► You marked off $\frac{1}{12}$ of the whole. What if your next spin is $\frac{1}{3}$? How would you mark that off?
- ► You marked off most of the whole. What fraction do you think you must spin to complete it? Why?

English Language Learners

As students play, walk around and provide support with telling about observations and strategies.

- **Beginning** Point to a board and ask: **Is $\frac{1}{16} + \frac{1}{16}$ equivalent to $\frac{2}{8}$?** yes **Are there more pieces on the bottom or top?** bottom
- **Intermediate** Say: **From the top to the bottom the pieces get __.** smaller Ask: **What is $\frac{1}{8} + \frac{1}{8}$ equivalent to?** $\frac{1}{4}$
- **Advanced** Ask: **How many 16ths pieces are equivalent to $\frac{1}{2}$?** 8 **What is 16 ÷ 8?** 2

Explain that players continue to take turns spinning and marking off sections until one player has filled one whole (*completely* and *exactly*). If a player spins a fraction greater than the part of the whole that remains, the player may not shade anything on that turn. For example, if $\frac{1}{6}$ of the whole remains, and a player spins $\frac{1}{4}$, that player may *not* shade a section.

Tell students that, as they play the game, they should write down equivalent fractions they discover, game strategies they develop, and interesting observations they make while playing the game.

Give students 25 or 30 minutes to play *Spinning a Whole*. Encourage them to use both game boards.

Math Talk Discuss students' discoveries, strategies, and observations. The following are examples that students might mention.

- *Pairs of equivalent fractions*
  Example: $\frac{4}{12} = \frac{1}{3}$ and $\frac{6}{16} = \frac{3}{8}$
- *Strategies*
  Example: If $\frac{1}{12}$ of the whole remains, you have a better chance of winning if you spin the spinner in which the *take one twelfth* section makes up the larger part of the circle.
- *Fraction Sums*
  Example: $\frac{1}{4} + \frac{1}{8} = \frac{6}{16}$ and $\frac{1}{3} + \frac{1}{6} = \frac{3}{6}$
- *Visual and Numeric Patterns*
  Example: As you move from the top fraction strip to the bottom, the number of pieces and the size of the denominator double with each bar, but the size of the pieces is halved with each bar.

This activity is excellent for **English learners** because it involves explaining discoveries and observations and summarizing strategies.

2 Going Further

Intervention — Activity Card 11-10

Spin and Compare

Activity Card 11-10

Work: In pairs

Use:

- TRB M142 (Equivalent Fraction Strips)
- TRB M141 (Spinner F)
- Paper clips

1. Work Together Cut the fraction strips and make a 6-part spinner to play a fraction game.
2. Take turns. Each player spins the spinner and then models the fraction, using the fraction strips. Compare fractions. If the fractions are equivalent, each player gets 1 point. Otherwise, the player with the greater fraction gets 1 point.

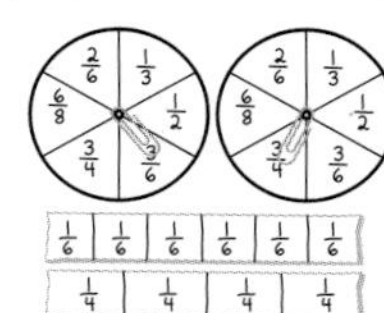

3. Continue playing until one player gets 5 points to win.

Unit 11, Lesson 10

Activity Note There are three pairs of equivalent fractions on the spinner: $\frac{1}{2} = \frac{3}{6}, \frac{2}{6} = \frac{1}{3}, \frac{6}{8} = \frac{3}{4}$. Modeling fractions will reinforce this understanding.

Math Writing Prompt

Model Fractions Draw a picture to explain if $\frac{3}{5}$ is equivalent to $\frac{4}{10}$.

Software Support

Warm Up 6.08

On Level — Activity Card 11-10

Four in a Row

Activity Card 11-10

Work: In pairs

Use:

- TRB M42 (Inch-Grid Paper)
- Two-color counters
- TRB M141 (Spinner F)
- Paper clips

1. Outline a 7 × 7 rectangle on one piece of grid paper. Create a game board and spinner like the ones below.

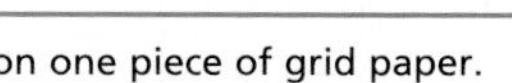

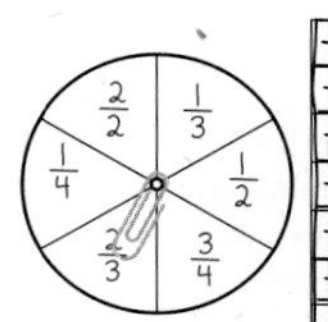

2. Take turns spinning the spinner and finding an equivalent fraction on the board. Mark the fraction with a counter in your color.
3. The first player to mark four in a row (across, up and down, or diagonally) wins the game.

Unit 11, Lesson 10

Activity Note Unit fractions such as $\frac{6}{6}$ do not appear on the spinner. However, students only need to mark 4 fractions in a row to win the game.

Math Writing Prompt

Make a Drawing Brie divided a circle into 8 equal pieces. She colored $\frac{1}{2}$ of the pieces green and $\frac{1}{2}$ of the pieces orange. How many eighths are orange? Make a drawing to explain your answer.

Software Support

Fraction Action: Fraction Flare Up, Level D

Challenge — Activity Card 11-10

Design a Spinner

Activity Card 11-10

Work: On your own

Use:

- MathBoard materials

1. Use the instructions below to design a spinner on your MathBoard.

Design a Spinner that:

- Has an equal probability of landing or not landing on a fraction equivalent to $\frac{1}{2}$.
- Is more likely to land on a fraction equivalent to $\frac{3}{4}$ than not.
- Has an equal probability of landing on fractions equivalent to $\frac{1}{6}$ or $\frac{1}{3}$.

2. Be sure to use a different fraction on each section of your spinner.
3. Exchange spinners with a classmate. Check to see if the spinner follows all the rules above.

Unit 11, Lesson 10

Activity Note Review the meaning of probability in this context before students begin this activity.

Math Writing Prompt

You Decide Miguel said that he ate $\frac{1}{4}$ of the large pizza. He ate an even number of pieces. How do you think the pizza was sliced? Make drawings to explain your thinking.

Software Support

Course II: Module 2: Unit 3: Fractional Parts

Homework and Spiral Review

11–10 Homework **Goal:** Additional Practice

This Homework page provides practice in finding equivalent fractions.

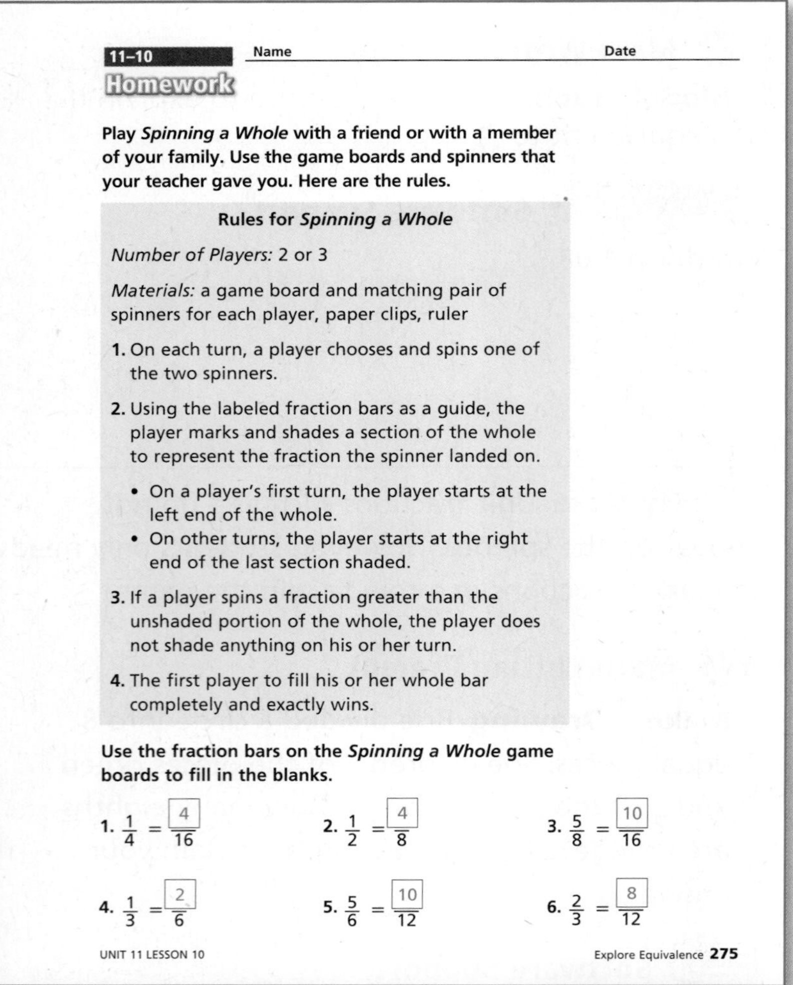

11–10 **Homework** Name ____________ Date ____________

Play *Spinning a Whole* with a friend or with a member of your family. Use the game boards and spinners that your teacher gave you. Here are the rules.

Rules for *Spinning a Whole*

Number of Players: 2 or 3

Materials: a game board and matching pair of spinners for each player, paper clips, ruler

1. On each turn, a player chooses and spins one of the two spinners.
2. Using the labeled fraction bars as a guide, the player marks and shades a section of the whole to represent the fraction the spinner landed on.
   - On a player's first turn, the player starts at the left end of the whole.
   - On other turns, the player starts at the right end of the last section shaded.
3. If a player spins a fraction greater than the unshaded portion of the whole, the player does not shade anything on his or her turn.
4. The first player to fill his or her whole bar completely and exactly wins.

Use the fraction bars on the *Spinning a Whole* game boards to fill in the blanks.

1. $\frac{1}{4} = \frac{4}{16}$
2. $\frac{1}{2} = \frac{4}{8}$
3. $\frac{5}{8} = \frac{10}{16}$
4. $\frac{1}{3} = \frac{2}{6}$
5. $\frac{5}{6} = \frac{10}{12}$
6. $\frac{2}{3} = \frac{8}{12}$

UNIT 11 LESSON 10 Explore Equivalence **275**

Homework and Remembering page 275

11–10 Remembering **Goal:** Spiral Review

This Remembering page would be appropriate anytime after today's lesson.

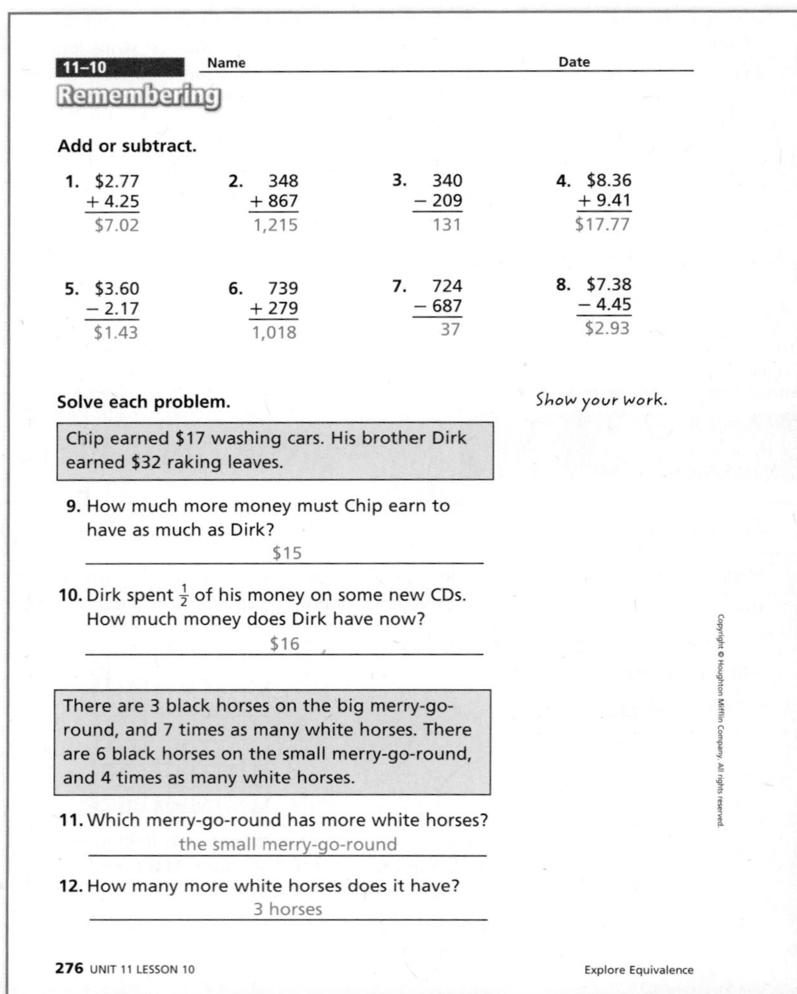

11–10 **Remembering** Name ____________ Date ____________

Add or subtract.

1. $2.77 + 4.25 = \$7.02$
2. $348 + 867 = 1{,}215$
3. $340 - 209 = 131$
4. $8.36 + 9.41 = \$17.77$
5. $3.60 - 2.17 = \$1.43$
6. $739 + 279 = 1{,}018$
7. $724 - 687 = 37$
8. $7.38 - 4.45 = \$2.93$

Solve each problem. *Show your work.*

Chip earned $17 washing cars. His brother Dirk earned $32 raking leaves.

9. How much more money must Chip earn to have as much as Dirk? $15
10. Dirk spent $\frac{1}{2}$ of his money on some new CDs. How much money does Dirk have now? $16

There are 3 black horses on the big merry-go-round, and 7 times as many white horses. There are 6 black horses on the small merry-go-round, and 4 times as many white horses.

11. Which merry-go-round has more white horses? the small merry-go-round
12. How many more white horses does it have? 3 horses

276 UNIT 11 LESSON 10 Explore Equivalence

Homework and Remembering page 276

Home or School Activity

Science Connection

Fractions in the Sky Around the world, scientists and meterologists watch the sky at weather stations. They use fractions to describe what they see in the sky. When there aren't any clouds, they write $\frac{0}{8}$. If clouds cover half the sky they write $\frac{4}{8}$ which is equivalent to $\frac{1}{2}$. If clouds cover all the sky, they write $\frac{8}{8}$. Have students track weather data for one week and write the fractions in the sky.

Equivalence Patterns

Vocabulary
fraction
equivalent fraction
equivalence chain
fracture
simpler fraction

Lesson Objective

- Find equvalent fractions.

The Day at a Glance

Today's Goals	Materials	
1 Teaching the Lesson **A1:** Write equivalence chains. **A2:** Discover patterns in equivalence chains. **2 Going Further** ▸ Differentiated Instruction **3 Homework and Spiral Review**	**Lesson Activities** Student Activity Book pp. 424C–426 or Student Hardcover Book pp. 425–426 and Activity Workbook pp. 199–200 (includes Cut-Outs) Homework and Remembering pp. 277–278 Scissors Envelopes MathBoard materials Game board for Halves (TRB M137) Game board for Thirds (TRB M138)	**Going Further** Activity Cards 11-11 Index Cards MathBoard materials Math Journals

Use **Math Talk** *today!*

Keeping Skills Sharp

Quick Practice — 5 MINUTES

Goal: Identify equivalent fractions.

Unit Fraction Equivalents Have a **Student Leader** write $\frac{1}{2}$ on the board. Then the leader says "one-half" and "fourths" and the class responds with the "fourths" equivalent for $\frac{1}{2}$.

Leader: One half. Fourths.

Class: Two fourths.

The leader then says "eighths" and "sixteenths" and asks the class to respond with the equivalent fraction.

Daily Routines

Homework Review Ask students if they had difficulty with any part of the homework. Review these parts.

Mental Math Find each difference using mental math.

1. 4,000 – 1,500 2,500
2. 6,500 – 3,000 3,500
3. 5,500 – 2,300 3,200

1 Teaching the Lesson

Activity 1

Make Equivalence Chains

 **40 MINUTES**

Goal: Write equivalence chains.

Materials: Student Activity Book pp. 424c–425 or Hardcover Book P. 425 and Activity Workbook p. 199 (includes cut outs), envelopes, scissors, MathBoard materials

 **NCTM Standards:**
Number and Operations
Problem Solving
Representation

 **Class Management**

Looking Ahead For the first part of this activity, students will need only the rows they cut from the Multiplication Table Rows. Have them set aside the Equivalent Fraction Box in a safe place. At the end of the lesson, have students place both the Equivalent Fraction Box and Multiplication Table Rows in an envelope.

Teaching Note

Watch For! After students cut apart the rows of numbers, they may think that they can slide the rows side to side and line up the numbers in different ways. This assumption is incorrect. Emphasize that the only correct way to use the rows is to align the ends.

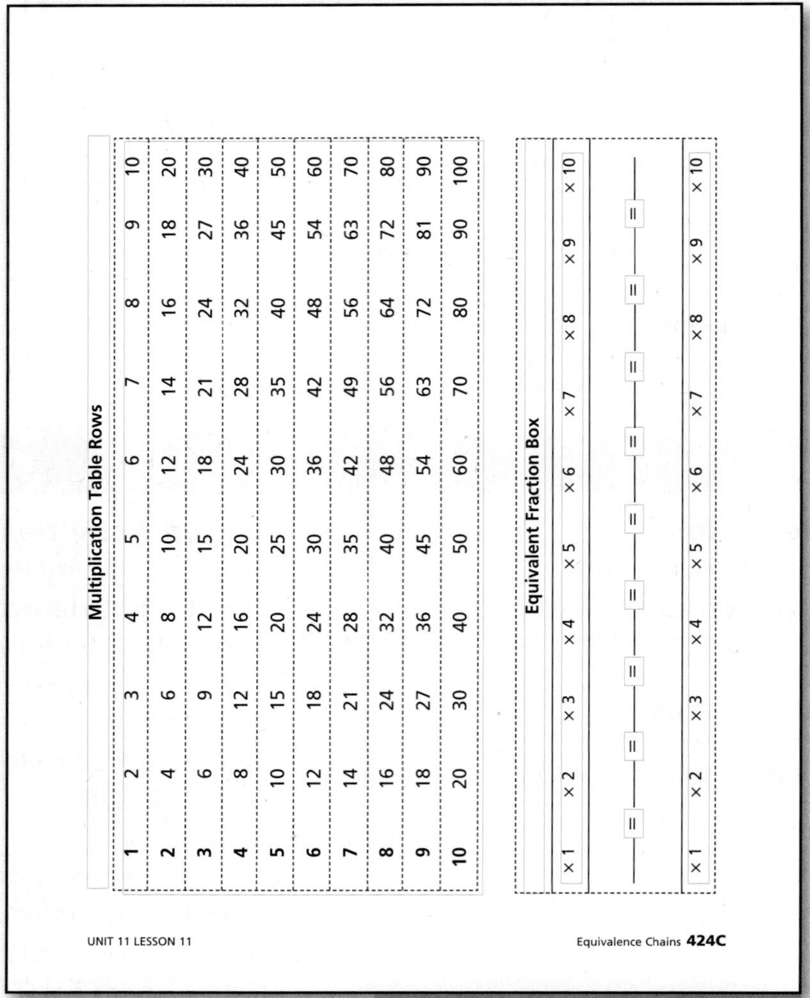

Multiplication Table Rows

1	2	3	4	5	6	7	8	9	10
2	4	6	8	10	12	14	16	18	20
3	6	9	12	15	18	21	24	27	30
4	8	12	16	20	24	28	32	36	40
5	10	15	20	25	30	35	40	45	50
6	12	18	24	30	36	42	48	54	60
7	14	21	28	35	42	49	56	63	70
8	16	24	32	40	48	56	64	72	80
9	18	27	36	45	54	63	72	81	90
10	20	30	40	50	60	70	80	90	100

Equivalent Fraction Box

× 1	× 2	× 3	× 4	× 5	× 6	× 7	× 8	× 9	× 10
=	=	=	=	=	=	=	=	=	
× 1	× 2	× 3	× 4	× 5	× 6	× 7	× 8	× 9	× 10

UNIT 11 LESSON 11 Equivalence Chains **424C**

Student Activity Book page 424c

▶ Multiplication Table Rows WHOLE CLASS

Refer students to the Multiplication Table Rows on Student Book page 424c.

- Look at the table called Multiplication Table Rows. Where have you seen numbers organized like this before? multiplication tables

Have students cut along the dashed lines to separate the 10 rows and the Equivalent Fraction Box. Give them time to experiment with the Multiplication Rows by stacking them two at a time with the ends aligned.

- What do the stacked rows form? a row of fractions
  (Note that students may make improper fractions, which will be addressed later in the unit.)
- How are the fractions related? They are equivalent.

Have students align the 2 row above the 7 row. Ask them to name some fractions they see. Possible answers: $\frac{2}{7}, \frac{4}{14}, \frac{10}{35}, \frac{20}{70}$

2	4	6	8	10	12	14	16	18	20
7	14	21	28	35	42	49	56	63	70

- How is $\frac{2}{7}$ related to $\frac{6}{21}$? 6 is 3 times as many as 2, and 21 is 3 times as many as 7.
- What number do you multiply by 2 and 7 in $\frac{2}{7}$ to relate it to $\frac{10}{35}$? The 2 and the 7 are multiplied by 5.
- What patterns do you see? Each number in the top row is 2 multiplied by 2, 3, 4, up to 10 and each number in the bottom row is 7 multiplied by 2, 3, 4, up to 10.

Point out that a row of fractions such as $\frac{2}{7}, \frac{4}{14}, \frac{6}{21}$ and so on is an example of an *equivalence chain*. It is a chain of equivalent fractions.

▶ Model Equivalence Chains WHOLE CLASS

To show that an equivalence chain is a chain of equivalent fractions, refer students to exercise 1 on Student book page 425. Have several students each copy two models of $\frac{2}{7}$ onto the board as the rest of the class works at their seats.

Have the students at the board 3-fracture each part of one of the models.

$\frac{2}{7}$

$\frac{6}{21}$

$$\frac{2}{7} \overset{\times 3}{=} \frac{6}{21} \quad (\times 3)$$

- Look at the model that has been 3-fractured. How many shaded parts are there? 6 How many parts in all? 21 What fraction is shaded in the fractured model? $\frac{6}{21}$
- How is it possible that something with more unit fractions is the same amount as something with fewer unit fractions? $\frac{6}{21}$ has more unit fractions, but those unit fractions are smaller.
- How is each equivalent fraction formed in an equivalence chain? You multiply the numerator and denominator in each fraction by the same number.
- Why does fracturing make equivalent fractions? The amount stays the same, but the number of unit fractions is different.

Activity continued ▶

Teaching Note

Watch For! Some students may think 3-fracture means to draw 3 lines in each part of the model rather than to divide the part into 3 pieces. Refer to the fractured model of $\frac{2}{7}$ and point out that it takes only 2 lines to 3-fracture. You can use other models to show that it takes one line to 2-fracture. Summarize that in each case one less line than the fracture number is needed.

Differentiated Instruction

Extra Help Some students may need extra practice fracturing fractions. They can fold paper strips in half to practice 2-fracturing and in thirds to practice 3-fracturing. Encourage students to draw dashed lines on the folds to show the fractures.

The Learning Classroom

Math Talk To encourage students to relate equivalent fractions and simpler fractions, ask questions such as:

- What number do you multiply both 2 and 7 by, to make the equivalent fraction $\frac{12}{42}$? 6
- What number could you divide both 12 and 42 by, to make the simpler fraction $\frac{2}{7}$? Explain. Possible answer: 6; I multiplied $\frac{2}{7}$ by 6 to make $\frac{12}{42}$ so I divide $\frac{12}{42}$ by 6 to make $\frac{2}{7}$
- Are there other fractions equivalent to $\frac{12}{42}$? yes Which of those fractions are simpler than $\frac{12}{42}$? $\frac{6}{21}$, $\frac{4}{14}$

$\frac{3}{5} = \frac{6}{10} = \frac{9}{15} = \frac{12}{20} = \frac{15}{25} = \frac{18}{30} = \frac{21}{35} = \frac{24}{40} = \frac{27}{45} = \frac{30}{50}$

► Equivalent Fraction Box WHOLE CLASS

For this activity, students will need the rows from the Multiplication Table Rows and the Equivalent Fraction Box. Have students put the 2 and 7 rows in the Equivalent Fraction Box in the spaces between the multipliers.

×1	×2	×3	×4	×5	×6	×7	×8	×9	×10
$\frac{2}{7}$ =	$\frac{4}{14}$ =	$\frac{6}{21}$ =	$\frac{8}{28}$ =	$\frac{10}{35}$ =	$\frac{12}{42}$ =	$\frac{14}{49}$ =	$\frac{16}{56}$ =	$\frac{18}{63}$ =	$\frac{20}{70}$
×1	×2	×3	×4	×5	×6	×7	×8	×9	×10

- Find the fraction $\frac{6}{21}$. What does the "×3" above the 6 mean? Why is "×3" below the 21? 2 has been multiplied by 3 to get 6; both the numerator and denominator of $\frac{2}{7}$ need to be multiplied by the same number to form an equivalent fraction.
- What number do you multiply the numerator and denominator in $\frac{2}{7}$ by to make the equivalent fraction $\frac{8}{28}$? 4
- What fraction do you get if you multiply both the 2 and 7 in $\frac{2}{7}$ by 8? $\frac{16}{56}$
- How do you know that $\frac{4}{14}$ and $\frac{6}{21}$ are equivalent to each other? Because they are both equivalent to $\frac{2}{7}$
- If you multiply the numerator and denominator of $\frac{4}{14}$ by 2, what equivalent fraction will you get? $\frac{8}{28}$
- What pattern do you notice in the rows for finding equivalent fractions by multiplying the numerator and denominator of the fraction $\frac{4}{14}$ by 2, 3, 4, and so on. Every other fraction from $\frac{4}{14}$ shows an equivalent fraction to $\frac{4}{14}$ by multiplying the numerator and denominator by 2, 3, 4, and so on.
- What fractions with smaller numbers called simpler fractions do you see in the row that results from dividing the numerator and denominator of $\frac{20}{70}$ by the same number?

  $\frac{20 \div 2}{70 \div 2} = \frac{10}{35}$; $\frac{20 \div 5}{70 \div 5} = \frac{4}{14}$; $\frac{20 \div 10}{70 \div 10}$
- Summarize what the Equivalent Fraction Box shows. You can make equivalent fractions by multiplying or dividing both the top and bottom numbers by the same number. That number is the column number in the multiplication table for those multiples of the fraction.

Have students practice making equivalence chains using the Equivalent Fraction Box with different number rows and write the chains on their MathBoards. See side column for an example of student work.

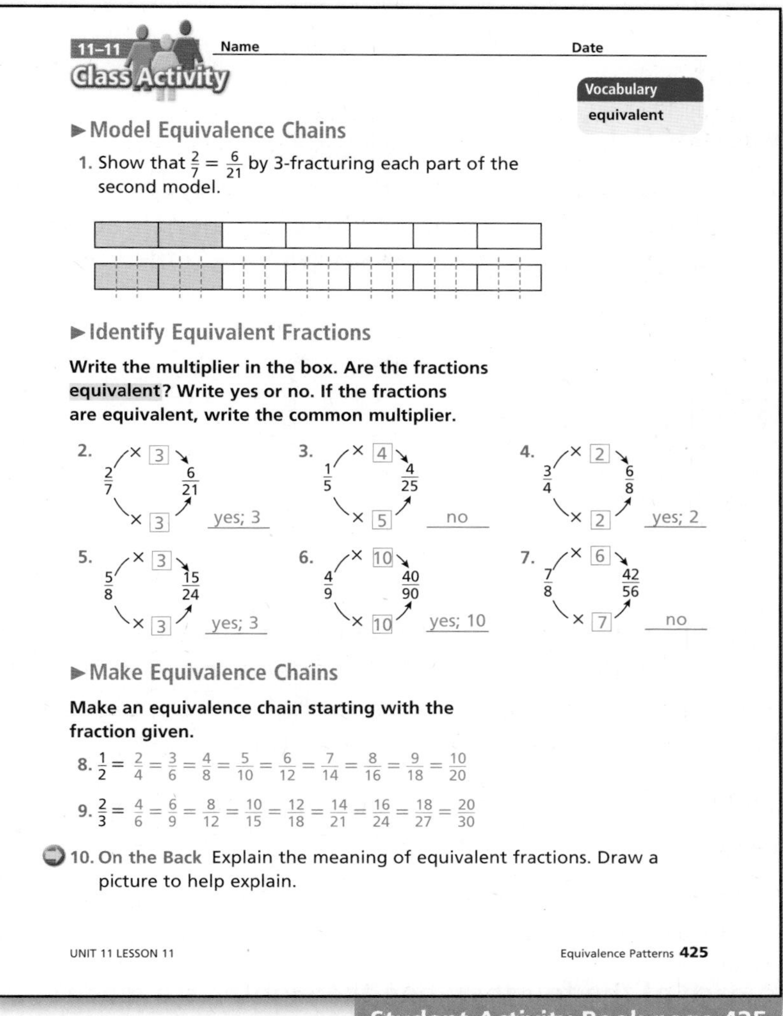

11–11 Class Activity

Name Date

Vocabulary
equivalent

► Model Equivalence Chains

1. Show that $\frac{2}{7} = \frac{6}{21}$ by 3-fracturing each part of the second model.

► Identify Equivalent Fractions

Write the multiplier in the box. Are the fractions equivalent? Write yes or no. If the fractions are equivalent, write the common multiplier.

2. $\frac{2}{7}$ ×3 $\frac{6}{21}$ ×3 yes; 3
3. $\frac{1}{5}$ ×4 $\frac{4}{25}$ ×5 no
4. $\frac{3}{4}$ ×2 $\frac{6}{8}$ ×2 yes; 2
5. $\frac{5}{8}$ ×3 $\frac{15}{24}$ ×3 yes; 3
6. $\frac{4}{9}$ ×10 $\frac{40}{90}$ ×10 yes; 10
7. $\frac{7}{8}$ ×6 $\frac{42}{56}$ ×7 no

► Make Equivalence Chains

Make an equivalence chain starting with the fraction given.

8. $\frac{1}{2} = \frac{2}{4} = \frac{3}{6} = \frac{4}{8} = \frac{5}{10} = \frac{6}{12} = \frac{7}{14} = \frac{8}{16} = \frac{9}{18} = \frac{10}{20}$

9. $\frac{2}{3} = \frac{4}{6} = \frac{6}{9} = \frac{8}{12} = \frac{10}{15} = \frac{12}{18} = \frac{14}{21} = \frac{16}{24} = \frac{18}{27} = \frac{20}{30}$

10. On the Back Explain the meaning of equivalent fractions. Draw a picture to help explain.

UNIT 11 LESSON 11 Equivalence Patterns 425

Student Activity Book page 425

► Identify Equivalent Fractions WHOLE CLASS

Read aloud the directions to exercises 2–7 on Student Book page 425. Be sure students understand that they should first write the correct multiplier in the box. Point out that they may not be the same for both the numerator and denominator.

- How will you decide if the fractions are equivalent? The equivalent fractions will have a common multiplier.

Have students complete exercises 2–7. Have student volunteers explain their answers.

Teaching Note

Watch For! Some students may not realize that the multipliers must be the same in exercises 2–7 for the fractions to be equivalent. Have students use two number rows to show the first fraction and see the pattern of common multipliers of the first fraction. Also point out that multipliers that are the same are called common multipliers.

Activity 2

Understand Equivalent Fractions

 15 MINUTES

Goal: Discover patterns in equivalence chains.

Materials: Game Board for Halves (Copymaster M137), Game Board for Thirds (Copymaster M138), MathBoard materials, Student Activity Book or Hardcover Book pp. 425–426

 **NCTM Standards:**
Number and Operations
Problem Solving
Representation

Class Management

If students need to replace their Game Boards for Halves and Thirds, use Copymasters M137–M138 in the Teacher's Resource Book.

English Language Learners

Write *fracture* on the board. Draw a $\frac{1}{2}$ model on the board. Ask: **Does this model show $\frac{1}{2}$?** yes Draw 1 fracture in each part.

- **Beginning** Point and say: **The dotted lines are *fractures*.** Have students repeat.
- **Intermediate** Ask: **Do the dotted lines break each part into smaller parts?** yes **Are they *fractures*?** yes
- **Advanced** Have students tell how the *fractures* changed the model.

 Ongoing Assessment

Have students write an equivalence chain with five fractions for $\frac{1}{4}$. They can use number strips, the Equivalent Fraction Box, or other models to help.

▶ Make Equivalence Chains WHOLE CLASS

Have students find $\frac{1}{2}$ on the Game Board for Halves. As they look down the Game Board for Halves, ask them to name the equivalent fractions they see. Ask them to write an equivalence chain starting with $\frac{1}{2}$ on their MathBoards.

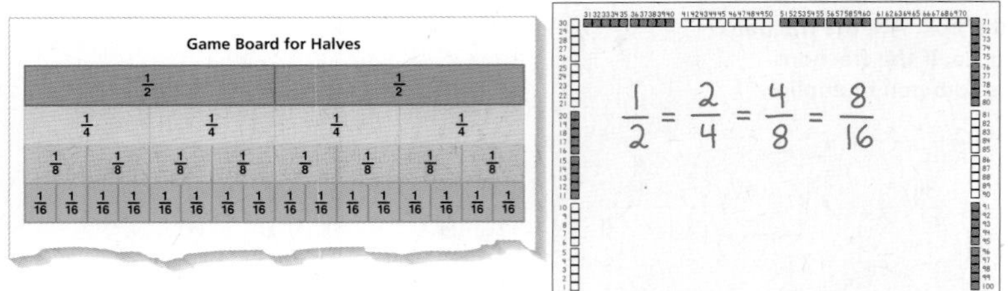

Discuss the fracturing represented on the game board. Help the class see that each fraction in a row must be halved to make the next row of smaller fractions. For example, the whole must be halved to make the 2 halves, the 2 halves must each be halved to make the 4 fourths.

- What happens to the whole when the 2 halves are made? It is split into 2 parts. It is 2-fractured.
- What happens to each of the halves when the fourths are made? They are each 2-fractured.
- What happens to each of the fourths when the eighths are made? They are each 2-fractured.

Discuss the fact that when each part is 2-fractured, the number of new parts is *2 times as many.* Help students see that the equivalence chain shows this doubling pattern and that the game board shows that there are more pieces, but they get smaller.

- When the 1 whole is 2-fractured, how many fractional parts do we end up with? 2 When the 2 halves are 2-fractured, how many fractional parts do we get? 4
- Do you see a pattern? The equivalence chain may help you. Each time something is 2-fractured, the number of new parts is 2 times as many.

Then have students examine the Game Board for Thirds. Ask them to write an equivalence chain for $\frac{2}{3}$ on their MathBoards: $\frac{2}{3}, \frac{4}{6}, \frac{8}{12}$

Discuss the results.

- What was done to each third to make sixths? Each was divided into 2 parts. It was 2-fractured.
- What happens to each sixth when twelfths are made? Each sixth is 2-fractured. There are 2 times as many, so we get 8 twelfths.

Have students complete exercises 8–10 on Student Activity Book page 449.

2 Going Further

Differentiated Instruction

Intervention — Activity Card 11-11

Draw Equivalent Fractions — Activity Card 11-11 ●

Work: In pairs

Use:
- 6 Index cards
- MathBoard materials

Decide:

Who will be Student 1 and who will be Student 2 for the first round.

1. **Work Together** Make a set of index cards, one for each of the following fractions: $\frac{1}{3}, \frac{3}{4}, \frac{3}{5}, \frac{5}{7}, \frac{3}{8}, \frac{4}{9}$.
2. Shuffle the cards and place them face down. **Student 1:** Choose a card and model the fraction.
3. **Student 2:** Fracture the diagram and write the equivalent fractions that the model shows.

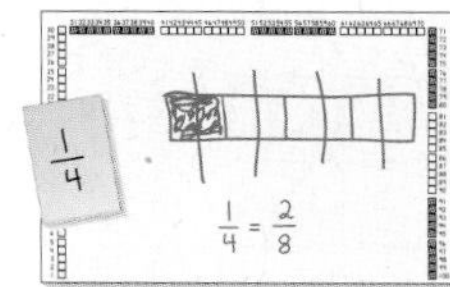

4. Change roles and repeat the activity for each fraction listed above. $\frac{1}{3} = \frac{2}{6}, \frac{3}{4} = \frac{3}{8}, \frac{3}{5} = \frac{6}{10}, \frac{5}{7} = \frac{10}{14}, \frac{3}{8} = \frac{6}{16}, \frac{4}{9} = \frac{8}{18}$

Unit 11, Lesson 11

Activity Note Be sure that students understand that a single vertical line drawn in each section of the fraction diagram will 2-fracture the diagram.

Math Writing Prompt

Explain Your Thinking Explain how you can find an equivalent fraction for $\frac{4}{8}$. Include a drawing in your answer.

Software Support

Warm Up 5.11

On Level — Activity Card 11-11

Match Equivalent Fractions — Activity Card 11-11 ▲

Work: In pairs

Use:
- 12 index cards

1. Write the following fractions on index cards, one on each card:

   $\frac{1}{4}, \frac{2}{8}, \frac{6}{15}, \frac{2}{5}, \frac{8}{10}, \frac{4}{5}$

   $\frac{3}{6}, \frac{1}{2}, \frac{2}{3}, \frac{8}{12}, \frac{5}{15}, \frac{1}{3}$
2. Shuffle the cards. Place them face down in a 4×3 array.
3. Take turns. Turn over two cards and decide if you have a match. If the cards do not match, turn the cards back over.
4. If the cards do match, take the cards and score 1 point. When all the cards have been matched, the player with the higher score wins.

Unit 11, Lesson 11

Activity Note After students have played the game, have them share the strategies that they used to decide if two fractions were equivalent.

Math Writing Prompt

Summarize Explain how you can tell if two fractions are equivalent.

Software Support

Fraction Action: Fraction Flare Up, Level D

Challenge — Activity Card 11-11

Guess My Equivalent — Activity Card 11-11 ■

Work: In pairs

1. Take turns with your partner to play a game about equivalent fractions.

2. Use what you know about equivalent fractions. Give clues or guess the fraction that matches the clues.

Unit 11, Lesson 11

Activity Note Students should give two clues for each round of the game. One clue should give the equivalent value. The other clue should give information about the numerator or denominator.

Math Writing Prompt

Critical Thinking Can a fraction with a 3 in the denominator be equivalent to $\frac{1}{2}$? Explain why or why not.

DESTINATION Math® **Software Support**

Course II: Module 2: Unit 3: Fractional Parts

Homework and Spiral Review

11–11 Homework Goal: Additional Practice

Include student's completed Homework page as part of their portfolios.

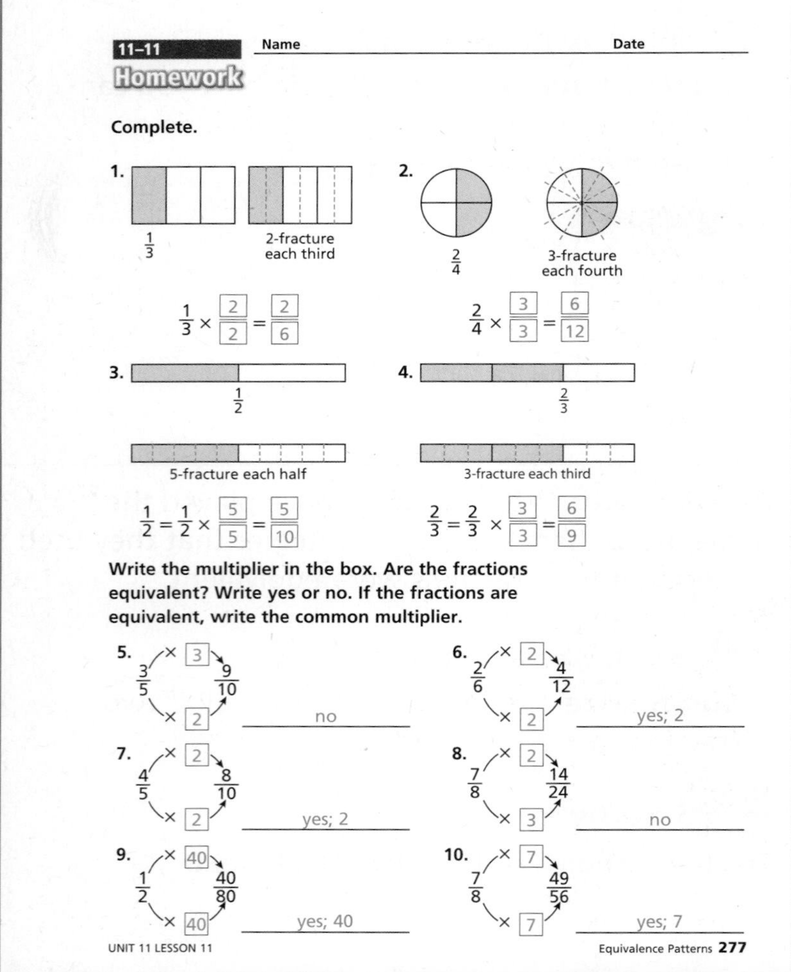

11–11 Homework Name ______ Date ______

Complete.

1. $\frac{1}{3}$ — 2-fracture each third

$\frac{1}{3} \times \frac{2}{2} = \frac{2}{6}$

2. $\frac{2}{4}$ — 3-fracture each fourth

$\frac{2}{4} \times \frac{3}{3} = \frac{6}{12}$

3. $\frac{1}{2}$ — 5-fracture each half

$\frac{1}{2} = \frac{1}{2} \times \frac{5}{5} = \frac{5}{10}$

4. $\frac{2}{3}$ — 3-fracture each third

$\frac{2}{3} = \frac{2}{3} \times \frac{3}{3} = \frac{6}{9}$

Write the multiplier in the box. Are the fractions equivalent? Write yes or no. If the fractions are equivalent, write the common multiplier.

5. $\frac{3}{5}$ (× 3, × 2) $\frac{9}{10}$ — no
6. $\frac{2}{6}$ (× 2, × 2) $\frac{4}{12}$ — yes; 2
7. $\frac{4}{5}$ (× 2, × 2) $\frac{8}{10}$ — yes; 2
8. $\frac{7}{8}$ (× 2, × 3) $\frac{14}{24}$ — no
9. $\frac{1}{2}$ (× 40, × 40) $\frac{40}{80}$ — yes; 40
10. $\frac{7}{8}$ (× 7, × 7) $\frac{49}{56}$ — yes; 7

UNIT 11 LESSON 11 Equivalence Patterns 277

Homework and Remembering page 277

11–11 Remembering Goal: Spiral Review

This Remembering page would be appropriate anytime after today's lesson.

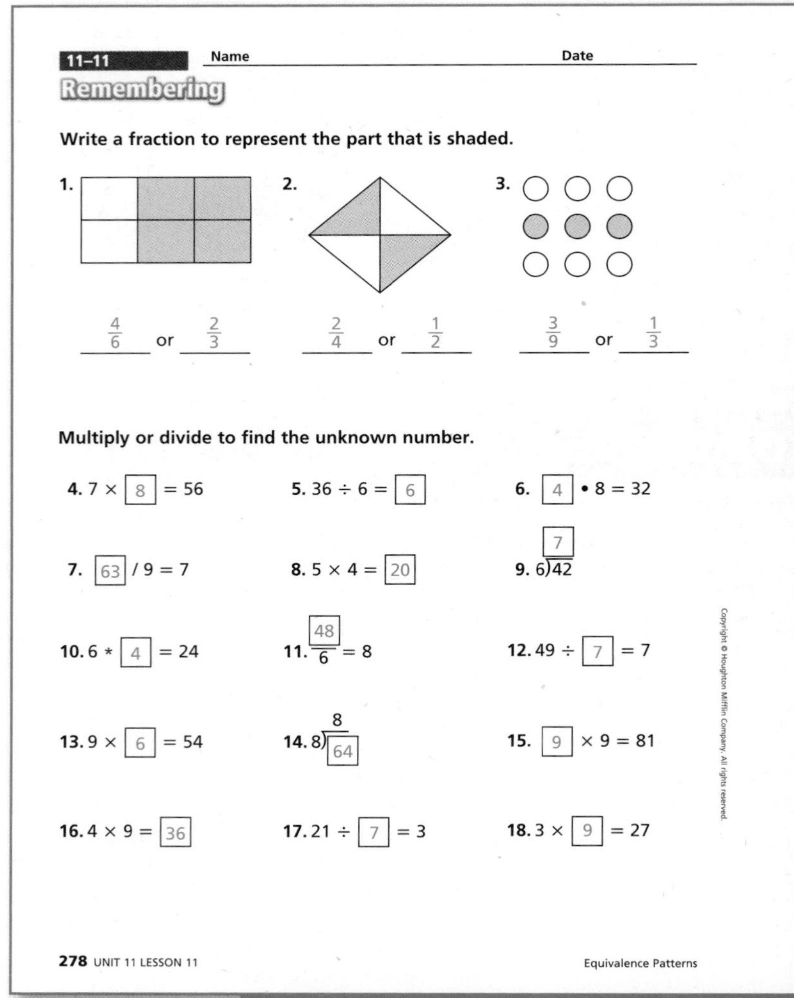

11–11 Remembering Name ______ Date ______

Write a fraction to represent the part that is shaded.

1. $\frac{4}{6}$ or $\frac{2}{3}$
2. $\frac{2}{4}$ or $\frac{1}{2}$
3. $\frac{3}{9}$ or $\frac{1}{3}$

Multiply or divide to find the unknown number.

4. 7 × [8] = 56
5. 36 ÷ 6 = [6]
6. [4] • 8 = 32
7. [63] / 9 = 7
8. 5 × 4 = [20]
9. 6)42 = [7]
10. 6 * [4] = 24
11. $\frac{[48]}{6}$ = 8
12. 49 ÷ [7] = 7
13. 9 × [6] = 54
14. 8)[64] = 8
15. [9] × 9 = 81
16. 4 × 9 = [36]
17. 21 ÷ [7] = 3
18. 3 × [9] = 27

278 UNIT 11 LESSON 11 Equivalence Patterns

Homework and Remembering page 278

Home or School Activity

Art Connection

Paper Folding Provide students with directions for some simple paper folding models. Have students use colored paper to create one of the models. Ask students to identify the fractions created by the folds.

Find Equivalent Fractions by Multiplying

UNIT 11 LESSON 12

Vocabulary

equivalent fraction
equivalence chain
fraction
fracture
unit fraction
common multiplier

Lesson Objective

- Find equivalent fractions by multiplying.

The Day at a Glance

Today's Goals	Materials	
1 Teaching the Lesson **A1:** Multiply to find equivalent fractions. **A2:** Relate fracturing to multiplying to find equivalent fractions. **2 Going Further** ▶ Differentiated Instruction **3 Homework and Spiral Review**	**Lesson Activities** Student Activity Book pp. 427–428 or Student Hardcover Book pp. 427–428 and Activity Workbook p. 201 (includes Special Formats) Homework and Remembering pp. 279–280 Equivalent Chains (TRB M140) Multiplication Table Rows (from Lesson 11) Equivalent Fraction Box (from Lesson 11) Math Journals *Mega-Fun Fractions* by Martin Lee and Marcia Miller (Teaching Resources, 2002)	**Going Further** Activity Cards 11-12 Spinner E (TRB M132) Paper clip Number Cube labeled 1–6 Multiplication Table Rows and Equivalent Fraction Box Game Cards (TRB M25) Index Cards Math Journals

Keeping Skills Sharp

Quick Practice

Goal: Find equivalent fractions.

Unit Fraction Equivalents Have a **Student Leader** write $\frac{1}{3}$ on the board. Then the leader says "one third" and "sixths." The class responds with the "sixths" equivalent for $\frac{1}{3}$, two sixths. The leader then says "ninths" and "twelfths" and asks the class to respond with the equivalent fraction.

Daily Routines

Homework Review If students give incorrect answers, have them explain how they found the answers. This can help you determine whether the error is conceptual or procedural.

Logical Reasoning Kai, Todd, and Jun chose blue, red, or green, but not the same color. Jun does not like blue. Kai does not like green or blue. Which color did each choose? Kai: red; Todd: blue; Jun: green

	Blue	Red	Green
Kai	no	yes	no
Todd	yes	no	no
Jun	no	no	yes

1 Teaching the Lesson

Activity 1

Equivalent Fractions

 **30 MINUTES**

Goal: Multiply to find equivalent fractions.

Materials: Multiplication Table Rows and Equivalent Fraction Box (from Lesson 11) or Equivalence Chains (TRB M140), Student Activity Book or Hardcover Book p. 427, Math Journals

 **NCTM Standards:**
Number and Operations
Problem Solving
Representation

Teaching Note

Watch For! Be alert to students who use the Equivalent Fraction Box incorrectly and multiply only the top or the bottom number of a fraction rather than both numbers by the common multiplier. This misunderstanding of how to model and write equivalent fractions will lead to errors when students write equivalent fractions using multiplications.

Differentiated Instruction

Extra Help Some students might benefit from fracturing models and writing multiplications for additional examples besides $\frac{3}{4}$ and $\frac{15}{20}$. Guide them through the 2-fracturing of $\frac{3}{4}$ to write the equivalent fraction $\frac{6}{8}$ using the two multiplier notations. Repeat for $\frac{3}{4}$ and $\frac{18}{24}$ (6-fracture).

▶ Relate Equivalent Fractions by Multiplying

WHOLE CLASS

Have students use the Multiplication Table Rows and Equivalent Fraction Boxes they cut out yesterday to show equivalent fractions to $\frac{3}{4}$.

×1	×2	×3	×4	×5	×6	×7	×8	×9	×10
3	6	9	12	15	18	21	24	27	30
=	=	=	=	=	=	=	=	=	=
4	8	12	16	20	24	28	32	36	40
×1	×2	×3	×4	×5	×6	×7	×8	×9	×10

 **Math Talk** To begin the discussion ask the following questions:

- How is $\frac{21}{28}$ related to $\frac{3}{4}$? 21 is 7 times as many as 3 and 28 is 7 times as many as 4.
- If you wanted to write the equivalent fraction $\frac{27}{36}$, what number would you multiply the numerator and denominator of $\frac{3}{4}$ by? 9
- How do you make the fraction $\frac{15}{20}$ from $\frac{3}{4}$? Multiply the numerator and the denominator in $\frac{3}{4}$ by 5.

The Equivalent Fraction Box shows that to get to $\frac{15}{20}$ from $\frac{3}{4}$, both the numerator and denominator must be multiplied by 5.

These models can be represented numerically in two ways.

$$\frac{3}{4} \overset{\times 5}{\underset{\times 5}{=}} \frac{15}{20} \quad \text{or} \quad \frac{3}{4} = \frac{3 \times 5}{4 \times 5} = \frac{15}{20}$$

These notations also represent 5-fracturing. When the denominator is multiplied by 5, that means that there are 5 times as many pieces. Multiplying the numerator by 5 means that 5 times as many pieces are selected.

- What do the 5s mean? They show the common multiplier. They tell how many times the simpler fraction was fractured.
- Why don't the 5s change the value of the fraction $\frac{3}{4}$? Both the numerator and denominator in the fraction are fractured in the same way. The same amount is divided into different unit fractions.

To review, have students share other fractions equivalent to $\frac{3}{4}$.

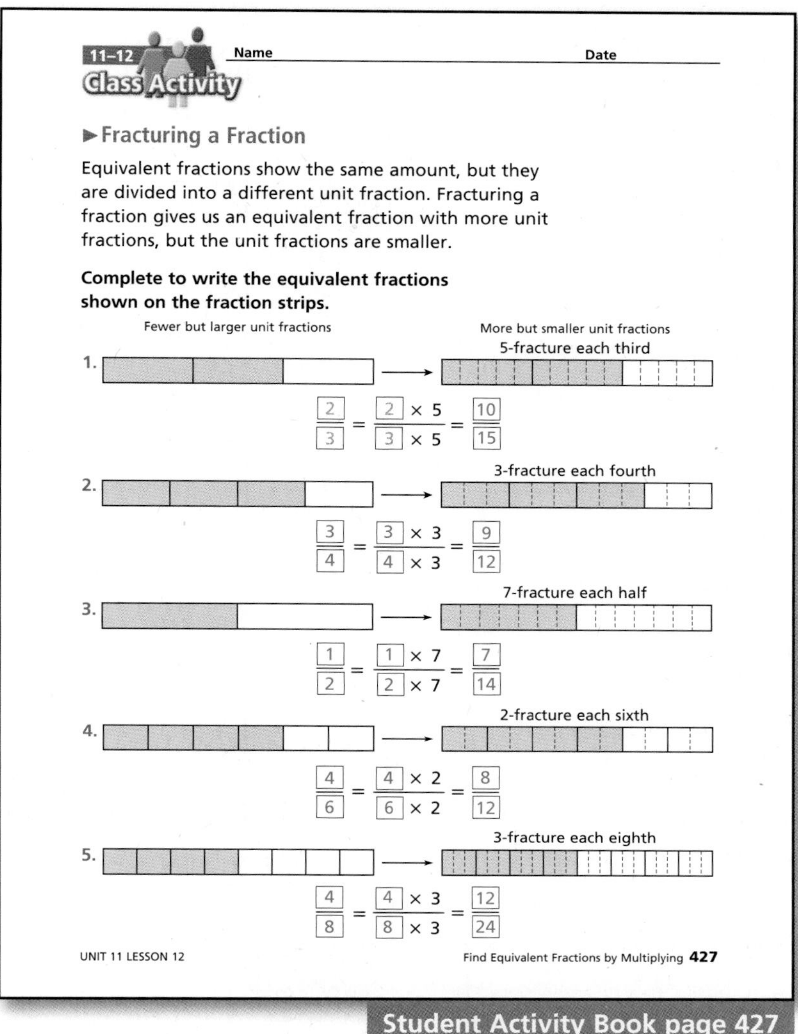

11–12 Class Activity Name Date

▶ Fracturing a Fraction

Equivalent fractions show the same amount, but they are divided into a different unit fraction. Fracturing a fraction gives us an equivalent fraction with more unit fractions, but the unit fractions are smaller.

Complete to write the equivalent fractions shown on the fraction strips.

Fewer but larger unit fractions — More but smaller unit fractions

1. 5-fracture each third

$\frac{2}{3} = \frac{2 \times 5}{3 \times 5} = \frac{10}{15}$

2. 3-fracture each fourth

$\frac{3}{4} = \frac{3 \times 3}{4 \times 3} = \frac{9}{12}$

3. 7-fracture each half

$\frac{1}{2} = \frac{1 \times 7}{2 \times 7} = \frac{7}{14}$

4. 2-fracture each sixth

$\frac{4}{6} = \frac{4 \times 2}{6 \times 2} = \frac{8}{12}$

5. 3-fracture each eighth

$\frac{4}{8} = \frac{4 \times 3}{8 \times 3} = \frac{12}{24}$

UNIT 11 LESSON 12 Find Equivalent Fractions by Multiplying **427**

Student Activity Book page 427

▶ Fracturing a Fraction INDIVIDUALS

Direct students to exercise 1 on Student Book page 427. Ask them to identify the two equivalent fractions shown in the drawings. $\frac{2}{3}$ and $\frac{10}{15}$

- Compare the number and size of the unit fractions in each model. $\frac{2}{3}$ has fewer pieces but the unit fractions are larger.
- Why does the fraction with smaller numbers ($\frac{2}{3}$) have larger pieces? The whole is divided into fewer parts, so each part is larger.
- Why does the number 5 appear in the top and bottom of the multiplication equation? The model for $\frac{10}{15}$ shows $\frac{2}{3}$ after it has been 5-fractured. The 5s show how the simpler fraction was fractured.

After students complete exercise 1, have them work individually or in Helping Pairs to complete exercises 2–5.

Teaching Note

Watch For! When students write equivalent fractions with a multiplication equation, be sure that they write the numerator as one unit (3 × 5) completely above the fraction bar and the denominator as one unit (4 × 5) completely below. It is incorrect to write $\frac{3}{4} \times 5 = \frac{15}{20}$. Although it is correct to write $\frac{3}{4} \times \frac{5}{5} = \frac{15}{20}$, this shows multiplication by a fraction which is not taught at this level.

English Language Learners

Write *common multiplier* on the board. Write $\frac{2}{5}$.

- **Beginning** Say: **Let's multiply 2 × 2 and 5 × 2.** Write $\frac{4}{10}$. Say: **We get $\frac{4}{10}$. 2 is the *common multiplier*.**
- **Intermediate** Write $\frac{4}{10}$. Ask: **What times 2 is 4?** 2 **What times 5 is 10?** 2 **Is 2 the *common multiplier*?** yes
- **Advanced** Write $\frac{4}{10}$. Ask: **What can we multiply 2 and 5 by to get $\frac{4}{10}$?** 2 Say: **2 is the __.** common multiplier

1 Teaching the Lesson (continued)

Activity 2

Show Equivalent Fractions with Fractions Strips

 20 MINUTES

Goal: Relate fracturing to multiplying to find equivalent fractions.

Materials: Student Activity Book or Hardcover Book p. 428 or Activity Workbook p. 201 (includes special format)

 **NCTM Standards:**
Number and Operations
Problem Solving
Representation

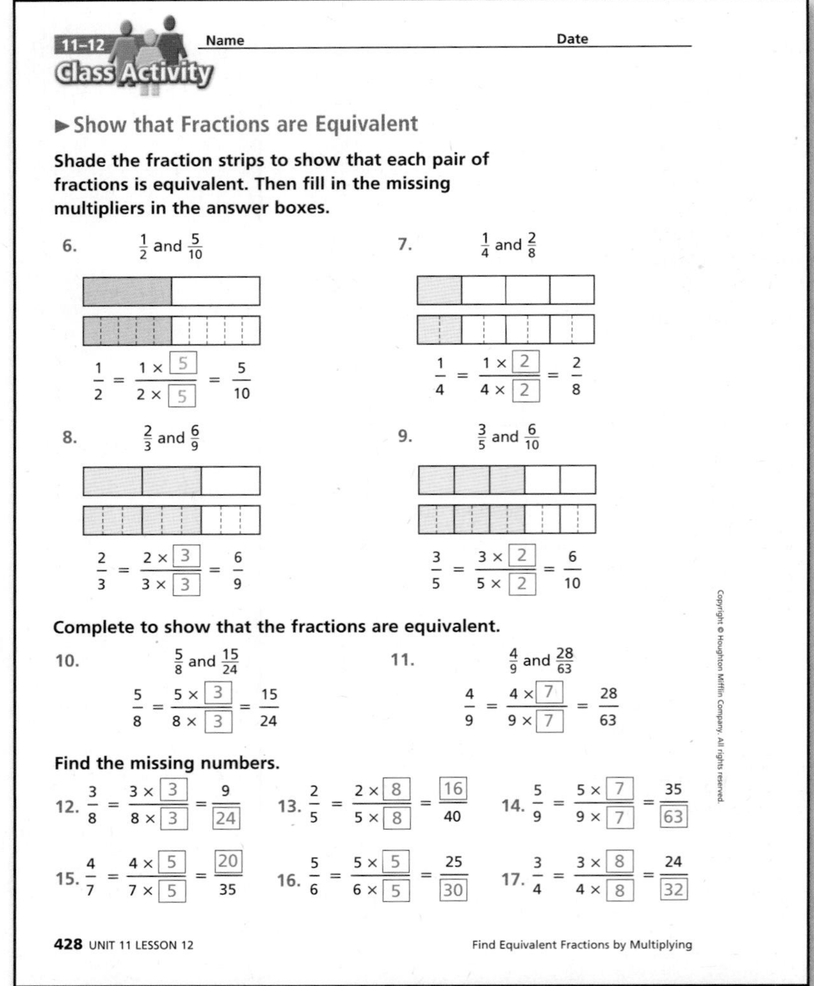

11–12 Class Activity

Name Date

▶ Show that Fractions are Equivalent

Shade the fraction strips to show that each pair of fractions is equivalent. Then fill in the missing multipliers in the answer boxes.

6. $\frac{1}{2}$ and $\frac{5}{10}$

$\frac{1}{2} = \frac{1 \times 5}{2 \times 5} = \frac{5}{10}$

7. $\frac{1}{4}$ and $\frac{2}{8}$

$\frac{1}{4} = \frac{1 \times 2}{4 \times 2} = \frac{2}{8}$

8. $\frac{2}{3}$ and $\frac{6}{9}$

$\frac{2}{3} = \frac{2 \times 3}{3 \times 3} = \frac{6}{9}$

9. $\frac{3}{5}$ and $\frac{6}{10}$

$\frac{3}{5} = \frac{3 \times 2}{5 \times 2} = \frac{6}{10}$

Complete to show that the fractions are equivalent.

10. $\frac{5}{8}$ and $\frac{15}{24}$

$\frac{5}{8} = \frac{5 \times 3}{8 \times 3} = \frac{15}{24}$

11. $\frac{4}{9}$ and $\frac{28}{63}$

$\frac{4}{9} = \frac{4 \times 7}{9 \times 7} = \frac{28}{63}$

Find the missing numbers.

12. $\frac{3}{8} = \frac{3 \times 3}{8 \times 3} = \frac{9}{24}$

13. $\frac{2}{5} = \frac{2 \times 8}{5 \times 8} = \frac{16}{40}$

14. $\frac{5}{9} = \frac{5 \times 7}{9 \times 7} = \frac{35}{63}$

15. $\frac{4}{7} = \frac{4 \times 5}{7 \times 5} = \frac{20}{35}$

16. $\frac{5}{6} = \frac{5 \times 5}{6 \times 5} = \frac{25}{30}$

17. $\frac{3}{4} = \frac{3 \times 8}{4 \times 8} = \frac{24}{32}$

428 UNIT 11 LESSON 12 Find Equivalent Fractions by Multiplying

Student Activity Book page 428

▶ Show that Fractions are Equivalent INDIVIDUALS

Direct students to exercise 6 on Student Book page 428. Have them use the fraction strips to show that $\frac{1}{2}$ and $\frac{5}{10}$ are equivalent.

- How many times did you fracture $\frac{1}{2}$ to show the equivalent fraction $\frac{5}{10}$? The fraction is fractured 5 times.
- What common multiplier belongs in the top and bottom answer boxes to get an equivalent fraction? 5 Why? Because the fraction was 5-fractured

Then have students complete exercises 7–17 individually or in helping pairs.

Ongoing Assessment

Have students identify the common multiplier for the equivalent fractions $\frac{2}{5}$ and $\frac{8}{20}$, then write the multiplication to show these fractions are equivalent.

Intervention Activity Card 11-12

Find Equivalent Fractions Numerically — Activity Card 11-12

Work: In pairs

Use:
- TRB M132 (Spinner E)
- Paper clip
- Number cube labeled 1–6
- TRB M140 (Multiplication Table Rows and Equivalent Fraction Box)

1. Make a spinner like the one shown below.
2. Spin the spinner and toss the number cube. To find an equivalent fraction use the number on the cube to multiply the numerator and the denominator of the fraction on the spinner. Record your work.

$\frac{2}{3} = \frac{2 \times 4}{3 \times 4} = \frac{8}{12}$

3. Check the equivalent fractions you find by using the Multiplication Table Rows and Equivalent Fraction Box.
4. Repeat the activity 4 times.

Unit 11, Lesson 12

Activity Note Have students list the equivalent fractions that they find. Students can also check their equivalent fractions by using fraction strips.

Math Writing Prompt

Justify the Answer Anna says that $\frac{5}{6}$ of the students are going on a class field trip. Bill says that $\frac{20}{24}$ are going on the field trip. Explain why they are both correct.

Software Support

Warm Up 20.17

On Level Activity Card 11-12

Multipliers to 10 — Activity Card 11-12

Work: In small groups

Use:
- TRB M132 (Spinner E)
- Paper clip
- TRB M25 (Game Cards 2–9)

1. Make a spinner like the one shown. Shuffle the Game Cards and place them face down.
2. One student spins the spinner. Each student draws a Game Card.
3. To find an equivalent fraction use the Game Card number as the multiplier for the numerator and denominator for the fraction on the spinner. Record all questions.

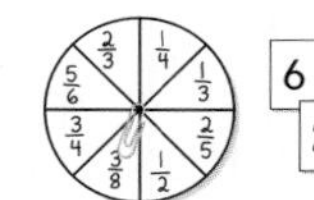
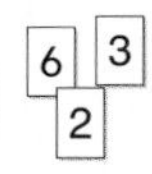

$\frac{3}{8} = \frac{3 \times 6}{8 \times 6} = \frac{18}{48}$ $\frac{3}{8} = \frac{3 \times 3}{8 \times 3} = \frac{9}{24}$ $\frac{3}{8} = \frac{3 \times 2}{8 \times 2} = \frac{6}{16}$

4. Select different cards and write equations until you record eight equivalent fractions.
5. Repeat the activity by spinning the fraction spinner again.

Unit 11, Lesson 12

Activity Note Students should repeat the activity as time allows by spinning the spinner again and reshuffling the Game Cards to use again.

Math Writing Prompt

Investigate Math Explain how to find the missing numbers in this equation. $\frac{4}{7} = \frac{(4 \times \square)}{(7 \times \square)} = \frac{\square}{49}$

Software Support

Fraction Action: Number Line Mine, Level E

Challenge Activity Card 11-12

Highest Multiplier — Activity Card 11-12

Work: In pairs

Use:
- 18 index cards

1. Label 18 index cards with the fractions shown below. Place the cards face down in an array.

$\frac{24}{32}$	$\frac{16}{28}$	$\frac{45}{54}$	$\frac{7}{21}$	$\frac{18}{48}$	$\frac{2}{3}$
$\frac{6}{24}$	$\frac{3}{8}$	$\frac{10}{25}$	$\frac{4}{7}$	$\frac{3}{4}$	$\frac{8}{12}$
$\frac{5}{6}$	$\frac{1}{4}$	$\frac{18}{36}$	$\frac{1}{3}$	$\frac{2}{5}$	$\frac{1}{2}$

2. Players take turns turning over two cards. If the cards show a fraction and its simplest form, the player keeps the cards after identifying the multiplier.
3. If the fractions are not equivalent or the player cannot identify the multiplier, the cards are returned face down.
4. Play continues until all cards are used.
5. The player with more cards wins.

Unit 11, Lesson 12

Activity Note Suggest that students first decide if one or both fractions are in simplest form. If only one fraction is in simplest form, they can then identify the multiplier by looking at the numerators.

Math Writing Prompt

Reasoning Explain why a simplified fraction is an equivalent fraction.

Software Support

Course II: Module 2: Unit 3: Fractional Parts

3 Homework and Spiral Review

11–12 Homework **Goal:** Additional Practice

This Homework page provides practice in finding equivalent fractions using multiplication.

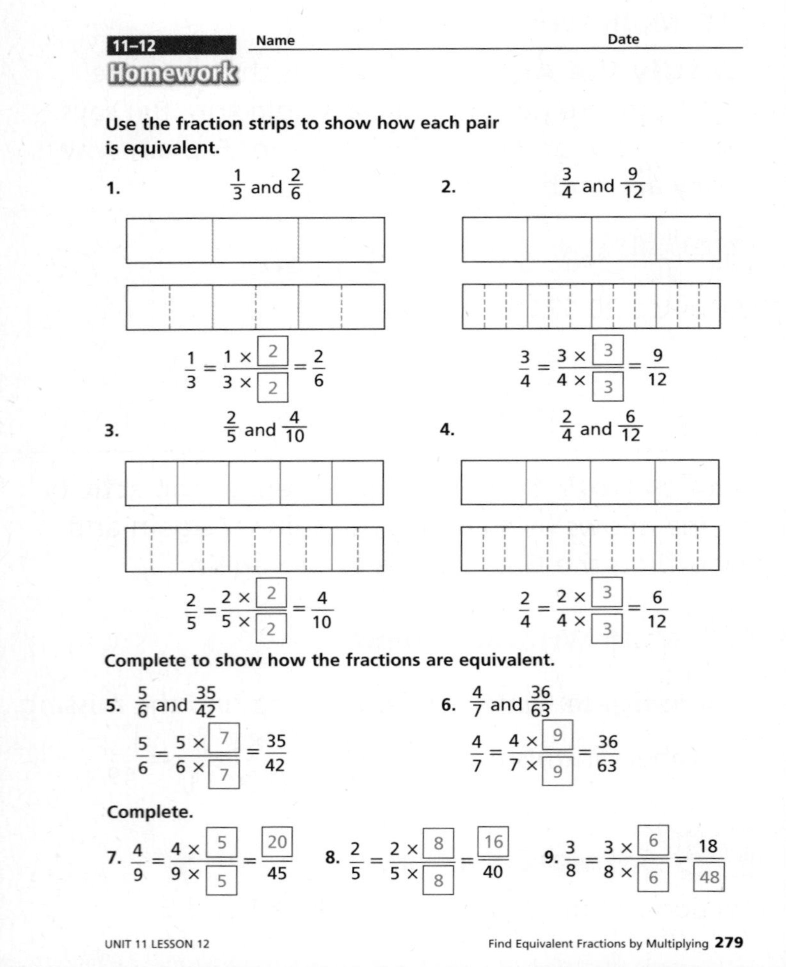

11–12 Homework

Name Date

Use the fraction strips to show how each pair is equivalent.

1. $\frac{1}{3}$ and $\frac{2}{6}$

$\frac{1}{3} = \frac{1 \times 2}{3 \times 2} = \frac{2}{6}$

2. $\frac{3}{4}$ and $\frac{9}{12}$

$\frac{3}{4} = \frac{3 \times 3}{4 \times 3} = \frac{9}{12}$

3. $\frac{2}{5}$ and $\frac{4}{10}$

$\frac{2}{5} = \frac{2 \times 2}{5 \times 2} = \frac{4}{10}$

4. $\frac{2}{4}$ and $\frac{6}{12}$

$\frac{2}{4} = \frac{2 \times 3}{4 \times 3} = \frac{6}{12}$

Complete to show how the fractions are equivalent.

5. $\frac{5}{6}$ and $\frac{35}{42}$

$\frac{5}{6} = \frac{5 \times 7}{6 \times 7} = \frac{35}{42}$

6. $\frac{4}{7}$ and $\frac{36}{63}$

$\frac{4}{7} = \frac{4 \times 9}{7 \times 9} = \frac{36}{63}$

Complete.

7. $\frac{4}{9} = \frac{4 \times 5}{9 \times 5} = \frac{20}{45}$

8. $\frac{2}{5} = \frac{2 \times 8}{5 \times 8} = \frac{16}{40}$

9. $\frac{3}{8} = \frac{3 \times 6}{8 \times 6} = \frac{18}{48}$

UNIT 11 LESSON 12 Find Equivalent Fractions by Multiplying 279

Homework and Remembering page 279

11–12 Remembering **Goal:** Spiral Review

This Remembering page would be appropriate anytime after today's lesson.

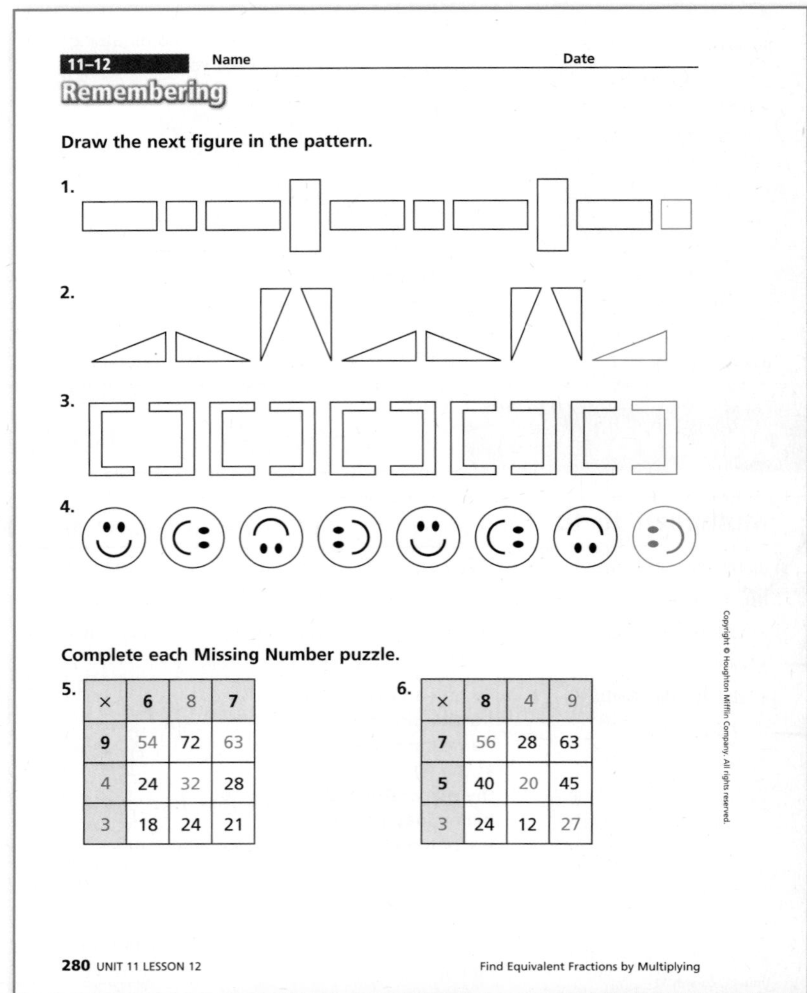

11–12 Remembering

Name Date

Draw the next figure in the pattern.

1.

2.

3.

4.

Complete each Missing Number puzzle.

5.

×	6	8	7
9	54	72	63
4	24	32	28
3	18	24	21

6.

×	8	4	9
7	56	28	63
5	40	20	45
3	24	12	27

280 UNIT 11 LESSON 12 Find Equivalent Fractions by Multiplying

Homework and Remembering page 280

Home or School Activity

Literature Connection

Fraction Poems The book *Mega-Fun Fractions* by Martin Lee and Marcia Miller (Teaching Resources, 2002) has many fraction activities for students. Read aloud the poem "Half" on page 40 of the book. Have students discuss what the poem means and then have them write their own poems about fractions.

At home it seems like chores
take up half the day.

I'd rather spend two-fourths
of the day in play!

Find Equivalent Fractions by Dividing

Vocabulary

fraction
equivalence chain
fracture
simplify
simpler fraction

Lesson Objective

- Find equivalent fractions by dividing.

The Day at a Glance

Today's Goals	Materials	
1 Teaching the Lesson **A1:** Visualize a simpler fraction. **A2:** Simplify fractions. **2 Going Further** ► Differentiated Instruction **3 Homework and Spiral Review**	**Lesson Activities** Student Activity Book pp. 429–430 or Student Hardcover Book pp. 429–430 and Activity Workbook p. 202 (includes special formats) Homework and Remembering pp. 281–282 MathBoard materials Quick Quiz 3 (Assessment Guide) *The Fraction Family Heads West* by Marti Dryk (Bookaloopy Press, 1997)	**Going Further** Activity Cards 11-13 Spinner F (TRB M141) Paper clips Sticky notes Index cards Math Journals

Use Math Talk today!

Keeping Skills Sharp

Quick Practice — X MINUTES

Goal: Write equivalence chains.

Equivalence Chains Have a **Student Leader** write a fraction on the board (for example $\frac{2}{3}$). As volunteers take turns identifying the equivalent fractions for the fraction in order $\left(\text{up to } \frac{10\times \text{ numerator}}{10\times \text{ denominator}}\right)$, the **Student Leader** writes the fractions on the board as an equivalence chain.

$\frac{2}{3} = \frac{4}{6} = \frac{6}{9} = \frac{8}{12} = \frac{10}{15} = \frac{12}{18} = \frac{14}{21} = \frac{16}{24} = \frac{18}{27} = \frac{20}{30}$

Daily Routines

Homework Review Have students discuss the difficulties from the homework. Allow students to help.

Calendar How much time has elapsed between 9 A.M. November 11 to 9 A.M. November 26? Explain. 15 days; Possible explanation: I subtracted 11 from 26.

1 Teaching the Lesson

Activity 1

Visualize a Simpler Fraction

 25 MINUTES

Goal: Visualize a simpler fraction.

Materials: MathBoard materials, Student Activity Book or Hardcover Book p. 429

 **NCTM Standards:**
Number and Operations
Problem Solving
Representation

Math Backgrounnd

Language and Vocabulary Point out to students that fracturing and grouping are opposites. Fracturing splits a unit fraction into smaller pieces. Grouping puts smaller unit fractions together into a larger one.

Differentiated Instruction

Extra Help Some students might benefit from using the Multiplication Table Rows and Equivalent Fraction Boxes to show equivalent fractions in simpler form. They can use inverse operations to simplify any fraction to the first one in the row.

English Language Learners

Write *simplify* on the board. Draw design A and B.

A  B 

- **Beginning** Say: **A is simple. B is not.** Erase the extra lines in B. Say: **I *simplified* B.**
- **Intermediate** Ask: **Which design is simple?** A Erase the extra lines in B. Ask: **Did I *simplify* B?** yes
- **Advanced** Have students tell how to *simplify* B.

▶ Group to Find an Equivalent Fraction WHOLE CLASS

Have students draw fractions strips on their MathBoards to show that $\frac{6}{8}$ is equivalent to $\frac{3}{4}$. Draw the strips on the board. Have students follow the same steps on their Mathboards.

Point out that they can change the fraction $\frac{6}{8}$ to the fraction $\frac{3}{4}$ by grouping the smaller unit fractions in twos.

Draw rings on the model to show the groupings, and then write the two ways the model can be represented numerically.

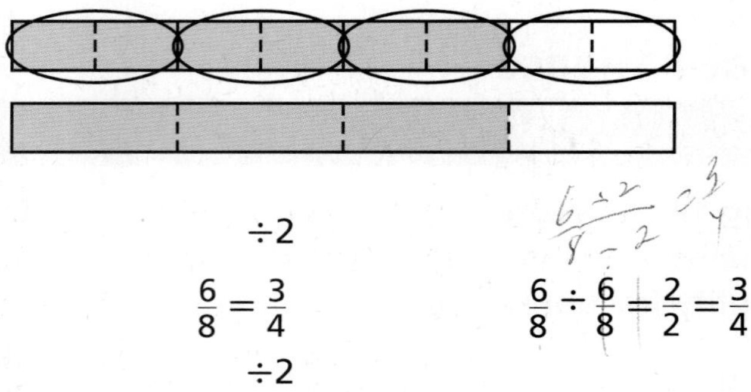

$$\frac{6}{8} \overset{\div 2}{\underset{\div 2}{=}} \frac{3}{4} \qquad \frac{6}{8} \div \frac{6}{8} = \frac{2}{2} = \frac{3}{4}$$

- What fraction did you start with? $\frac{6}{8}$ What simpler fraction did you show by grouping the $\frac{1}{8}$s? $\frac{3}{4}$
- How did you group $\frac{6}{8}$ to show $\frac{3}{4}$? group the eighths into groups of 2
- How did you show this change numerically? show "÷ 2" in the first notation; divide the numerator and denominator of $\frac{6}{8}$ by 2 in the second notation

Have students draw two fraction strips on their MathBoards to show that $\frac{2}{3}$ and $\frac{10}{15}$ are equivalent as a volunteer does the same at the board.

- How could you group $\frac{10}{15}$ into $\frac{2}{3}$? Possible answers: Group the fifteenths together in groups of 5; Divide the numerator and denominator by 5

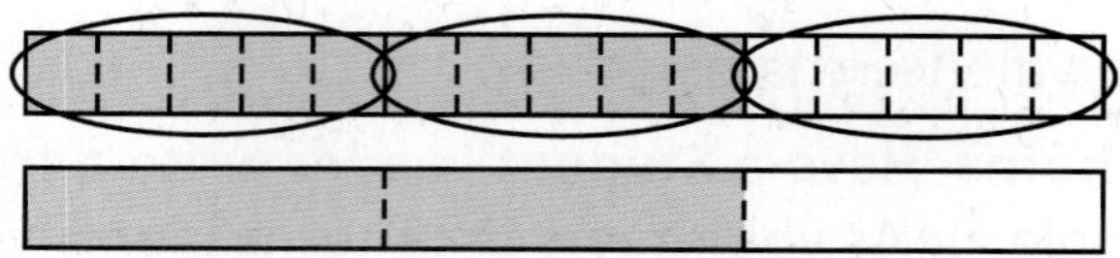

Ask students to write the two ways to show the grouping numerically. Explain that when you divide the numerator and denominator of a fraction by the same number, you *simplify* the fraction.

$$\frac{10}{15} \overset{\div 5}{\underset{\div 5}{=}} \frac{2}{3} \qquad \frac{10}{15} = \frac{10 \div 5}{15 \div 5} = \frac{2}{3}$$

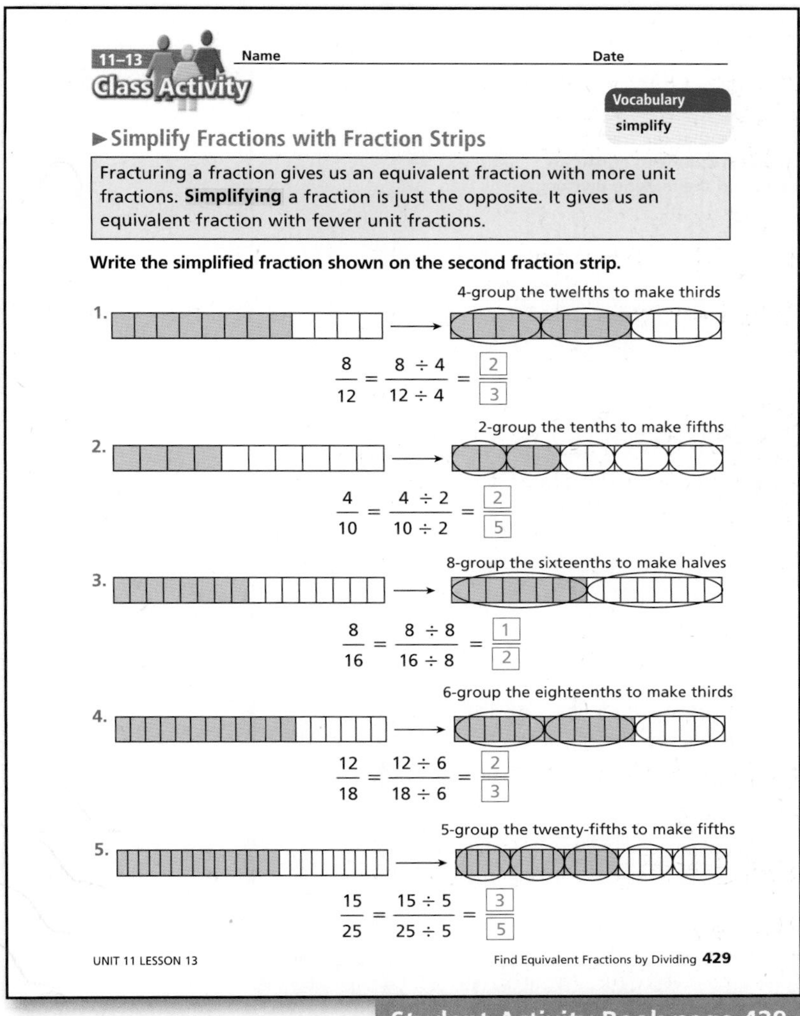

11–13 Class Activity

Name ______________________ Date ____________

Vocabulary
simplify

► Simplify Fractions with Fraction Strips

Fracturing a fraction gives us an equivalent fraction with more unit fractions. **Simplifying** a fraction is just the opposite. It gives us an equivalent fraction with fewer unit fractions.

Write the simplified fraction shown on the second fraction strip.

1. 4-group the twelfths to make thirds

$\frac{8}{12} = \frac{8 \div 4}{12 \div 4} = \frac{2}{3}$

2. 2-group the tenths to make fifths

$\frac{4}{10} = \frac{4 \div 2}{10 \div 2} = \frac{2}{5}$

3. 8-group the sixteenths to make halves

$\frac{8}{16} = \frac{8 \div 8}{16 \div 8} = \frac{1}{2}$

4. 6-group the eighteenths to make thirds

$\frac{12}{18} = \frac{12 \div 6}{18 \div 6} = \frac{2}{3}$

5. 5-group the twenty-fifths to make fifths

$\frac{15}{25} = \frac{15 \div 5}{25 \div 5} = \frac{3}{5}$

UNIT 11 LESSON 13 | Find Equivalent Fractions by Dividing **429**

Student Activity Book page 429

► Simplify Fractions with Fraction Strips INDIVIDUALS

Refer students to Student Book page 429. Guide them through exercise 1.

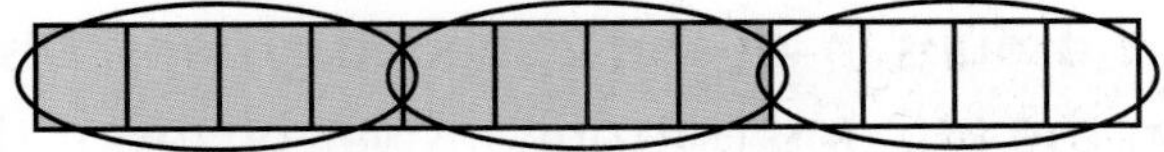

- How is the fraction $\frac{8}{12}$ grouped? The fraction is 4-grouped
  How do you know? There are 4 parts in each circled group
- How many groups are there in all? 3
- How many groups are shaded? 2
- What is the simplified fraction? $\frac{2}{3}$

Have students work as individuals or in Helping Pairs to complete the page.

Teaching Note

Watch For! Students may think that the number of groups, rather than the number of parts in a group, tells how a fraction has been grouped. In exercise 1, for example, they might think that $\frac{8}{12}$ has been 3-grouped because there are 3 groups. Point out that the number of parts in each circled section (4) tells how the fraction has been grouped (4-grouped). Emphasize this point by reviewing the other models on the page.

Teaching Note

Language and Vocabulary A *simpler* fraction is any equivalent fraction with a smaller numerator and denominator. The *simplest* fraction is an equivalent fraction with the smallest possible numerator and denominator. You can simplify a fraction to any simpler fraction.

Differentiated Instruction

Extra Help The concept of *simplifying* a fraction to make larger unit fractions, (by dividing the numerator and denominator by the same number) and *fracturing* to make smaller unit fractions (by multiplying the numerator and denominator by the same number) may be difficult for some students. Have students work in pairs to practice simplifying fractions.

Activity 2

Simplify Fractions by Dividing

 **30 MINUTES**

Goal: Simplify fractions.

Materials: Student Activity Book or Hardcover Book p. 430 and Activity Workbook p. 202 (includes special format)

✔ **NCTM Standards:**
Number and Operations
Representation

Differentiated Instruction

Extra Help When students simplify fractions without models for the first time, they may find it easier to look at the relationship between just the numerators first and then the denominators. Have students use a yellow marker or highlighter to identify the numerators in each fraction pair and discuss the relationship between the numbers. First ask how many times more is the greater number than the smaller one? Then repeat for the denominator pair. Next ask if the same multiplier relates these two numbers.

Ongoing Assessment

Have students find a simpler fraction for $\frac{4}{6}$, $\frac{7}{14}$, and $\frac{8}{20}$.

Quick Quiz

See Assessment Guide for Unit 11 Quick Quiz 3.

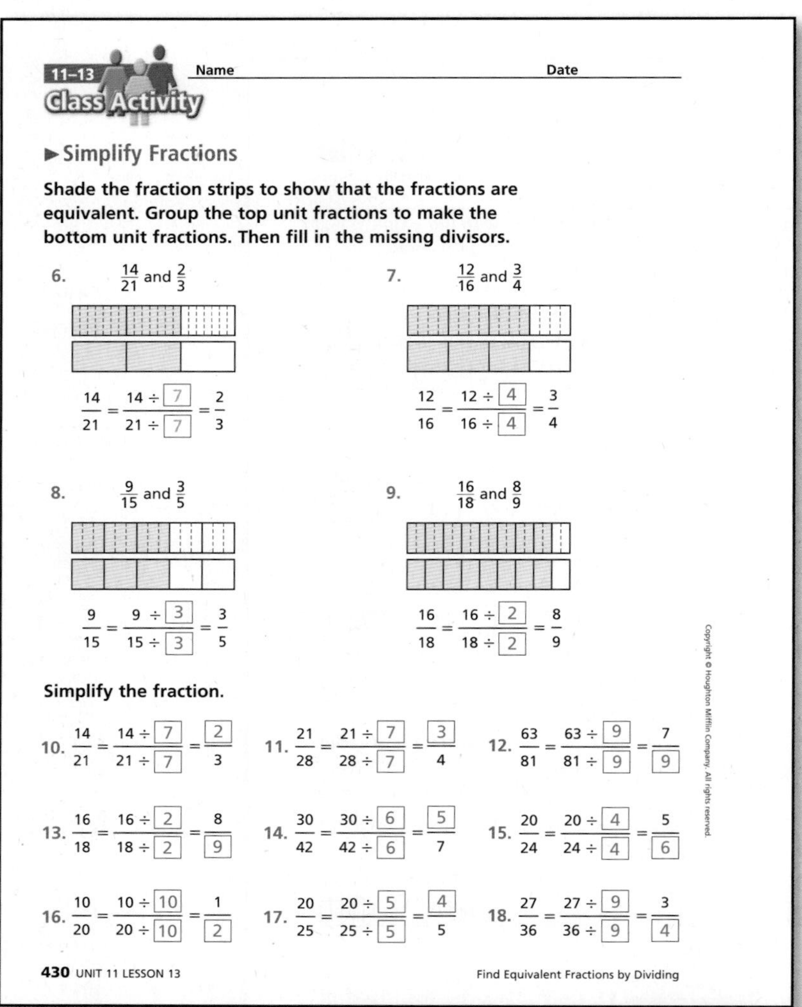

11–13 Class Activity Name ______ Date ______

▶ Simplify Fractions

Shade the fraction strips to show that the fractions are equivalent. Group the top unit fractions to make the bottom unit fractions. Then fill in the missing divisors.

6. $\frac{14}{21}$ and $\frac{2}{3}$

$\frac{14}{21} = \frac{14 \div \boxed{7}}{21 \div \boxed{7}} = \frac{2}{3}$

7. $\frac{12}{16}$ and $\frac{3}{4}$

$\frac{12}{16} = \frac{12 \div \boxed{4}}{16 \div \boxed{4}} = \frac{3}{4}$

8. $\frac{9}{15}$ and $\frac{3}{5}$

$\frac{9}{15} = \frac{9 \div \boxed{3}}{15 \div \boxed{3}} = \frac{3}{5}$

9. $\frac{16}{18}$ and $\frac{8}{9}$

$\frac{16}{18} = \frac{16 \div \boxed{2}}{18 \div \boxed{2}} = \frac{8}{9}$

Simplify the fraction.

10. $\frac{14}{21} = \frac{14 \div \boxed{7}}{21 \div \boxed{7}} = \frac{\boxed{2}}{3}$

11. $\frac{21}{28} = \frac{21 \div \boxed{7}}{28 \div \boxed{7}} = \frac{\boxed{3}}{4}$

12. $\frac{63}{81} = \frac{63 \div \boxed{9}}{81 \div \boxed{9}} = \frac{7}{\boxed{9}}$

13. $\frac{16}{18} = \frac{16 \div \boxed{2}}{18 \div \boxed{2}} = \frac{8}{\boxed{9}}$

14. $\frac{30}{42} = \frac{30 \div \boxed{6}}{42 \div \boxed{6}} = \frac{\boxed{5}}{7}$

15. $\frac{20}{24} = \frac{20 \div \boxed{4}}{24 \div \boxed{4}} = \frac{5}{\boxed{6}}$

16. $\frac{10}{20} = \frac{10 \div \boxed{10}}{20 \div \boxed{10}} = \frac{1}{\boxed{2}}$

17. $\frac{20}{25} = \frac{20 \div \boxed{5}}{25 \div \boxed{5}} = \frac{\boxed{4}}{5}$

18. $\frac{27}{36} = \frac{27 \div \boxed{9}}{36 \div \boxed{9}} = \frac{3}{\boxed{4}}$

430 UNIT 11 LESSON 13 Find Equivalent Fractions by Dividing

Student Activity Book page 430

▶ Simplify Fractions WHOLE CLASS

Direct students' attention to exercise 6 on Student Book page 430.

Math Talk Discuss how students can use the blank models to show the equivalent fractions $\frac{14}{21}$ and $\frac{2}{3}$. Guide students as they 7-group the fraction $\frac{14}{21}$ to make 3 groups in all and 2 shaded groups. Discuss why the number 7 belongs in the top and bottom answer boxes of the numerical representation of this problem. Then have students work as individuals or in helping pairs to complete exercises 7–9.

Encourage students to complete the equations in exercises 10–18 without using models. Review and discuss the answers when everyone has finished, having a few students share their methods at the board.

2 Going Further

Differentiated Instruction

Intervention — Activity Card 11-13

Simplify Fractions

Activity Card 11-13 ●

Work: In small groups

Use:
- TRB M141 (Spinner F)
- Paper clips

1. Make a spinner like the one below. Take turns spinning the spinner.

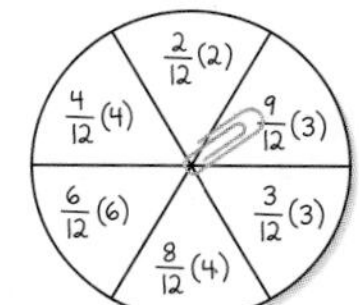

2. On Your Own Divide the numerator and denominator of the fraction by the number in parentheses next to it. Write a division equation to show your results.
3. Continue until all the fractions on the spinner have been used.
4. Analyze Compare your results with other members in your group.

Unit 11, Lesson 13

Activity Note After students have completed the activity, have them identify which fractions are in simplest form after dividing and then discuss how to simplify the ones that are not in simplest form.

Math Writing Prompt

Explain Your Thinking Explain how you know that the fraction $\frac{8}{12}$ can be simplified to $\frac{2}{3}$.

Software Support

Warm Up 20.11

On Level — Activity Card 11-13

Find the Hidden Number

Activity Card 11-13 ▲

Work: In pairs

Use:
- Sticky notes

Decide:

Who will be Student 1 and who will be Student 2 for the first round.

1. Student 1: Secretly write a pair of equivalent fractions on a sheet of paper. Then cover one of the four numbers with a sticky note.
2. Student 2: Find the hidden numerator or denominator and write the number on top of the sticky note. Then work with your partner to check that both fractions are equivalent.

$$\frac{4}{5} = \frac{12}{15}$$

3. Discuss How can you decide if two fractions are equivalent? Is there more than one way?

Unit 11, Lesson 13

Activity Note Suggest that students use multiplication to write equivalent fractions. Students can check their answers and the equivalence by using either multiplication or division.

Math Writing Prompt

Summarize Summarize the steps you would use to find a missing denominator in a pair of equivalent fractions. Use $\frac{5}{\square} = \frac{20}{24}$ as an example.

Software Support

Fraction Action: Number Line Mine, Level E

Challenge — Activity Card 11-13

Make a Match

Activity Card 11-13 ■

Work: In pairs

Use:
- 24 Index cards

1. Label 24 index cards as shown. Then arrange them into an array face down.

$\frac{21}{28}$	$\frac{24}{40}$	$\frac{32}{56}$	$\frac{24}{32}$	$\frac{9}{18}$	$\frac{14}{35}$
$\frac{18}{36}$	$\frac{30}{40}$	$\frac{8}{48}$	$\frac{16}{32}$	$\frac{16}{24}$	$\frac{18}{45}$
$\frac{45}{72}$	$\frac{32}{40}$	$\frac{27}{36}$	$\frac{27}{90}$	$\frac{27}{49}$	$\frac{10}{40}$
$\frac{40}{48}$	$\frac{32}{36}$	$\frac{10}{20}$	$\frac{35}{40}$	$\frac{35}{42}$	$\frac{24}{56}$

2. Both players turn over one card and calculate the equivalent fraction in simplest form.
3. Each player names the divisor used to simplify the fraction. The player with the greater divisor earns 1 point. Equal divisors earn 1 point for both players.
4. After all the cards are used, the higher score wins.

Unit 11, Lesson 13

Activity Note Before awarding points, players should check each other's calculations by dividing both the numerator and denominator, using the named divisor.

Math Writing Prompt

Reasoning Explain why a simplified fraction is an equivalent fraction.

Software Support

Course II: Module 2: Unit 3: Fractional Parts

3 Homework and Spiral Review

Goal: Additional Practice

This Homework page provides practice in finding equivalent fractions using division.

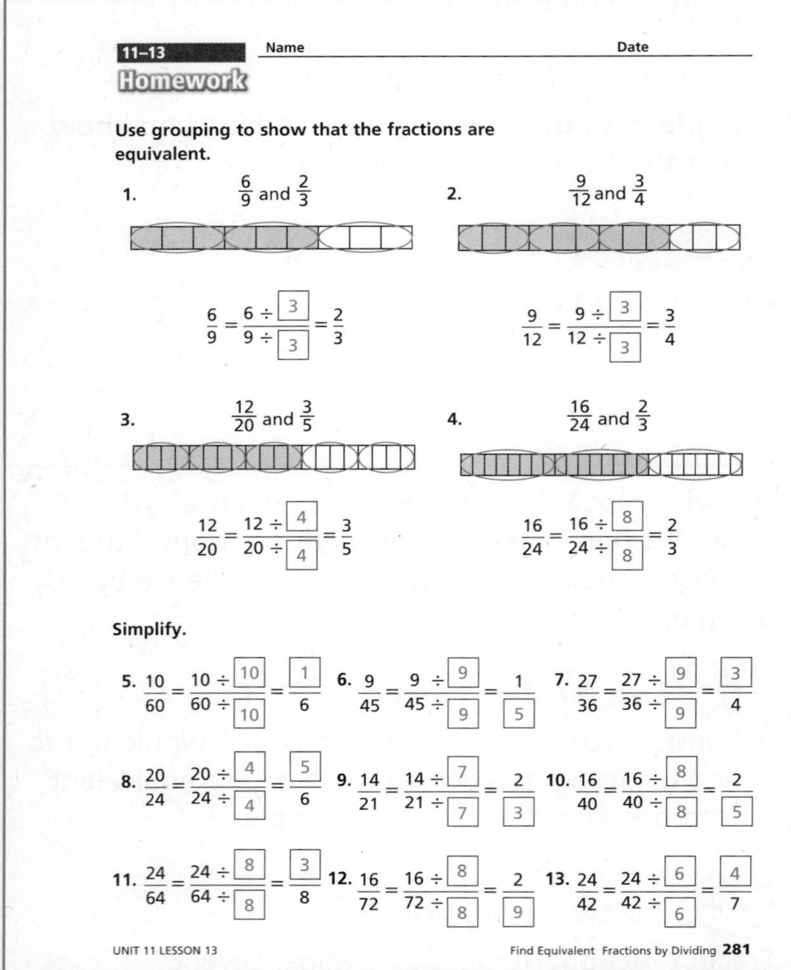

11–13 Homework Name ____ Date ____

Use grouping to show that the fractions are equivalent.

1. $\frac{6}{9}$ and $\frac{2}{3}$ $\qquad \frac{6}{9} = \frac{6 \div \boxed{3}}{9 \div \boxed{3}} = \frac{2}{3}$

2. $\frac{9}{12}$ and $\frac{3}{4}$ $\qquad \frac{9}{12} = \frac{9 \div \boxed{3}}{12 \div \boxed{3}} = \frac{3}{4}$

3. $\frac{12}{20}$ and $\frac{3}{5}$ $\qquad \frac{12}{20} = \frac{12 \div \boxed{4}}{20 \div \boxed{4}} = \frac{3}{5}$

4. $\frac{16}{24}$ and $\frac{2}{3}$ $\qquad \frac{16}{24} = \frac{16 \div \boxed{8}}{24 \div \boxed{8}} = \frac{2}{3}$

Simplify.

5. $\frac{10}{60} = \frac{10 \div \boxed{10}}{60 \div \boxed{10}} = \frac{\boxed{1}}{6}$

6. $\frac{9}{45} = \frac{9 \div \boxed{9}}{45 \div \boxed{9}} = \frac{1}{\boxed{5}}$

7. $\frac{27}{36} = \frac{27 \div \boxed{9}}{36 \div \boxed{9}} = \frac{\boxed{3}}{4}$

8. $\frac{20}{24} = \frac{20 \div \boxed{4}}{24 \div \boxed{4}} = \frac{\boxed{5}}{6}$

9. $\frac{14}{21} = \frac{14 \div \boxed{7}}{21 \div \boxed{7}} = \frac{2}{\boxed{3}}$

10. $\frac{16}{40} = \frac{16 \div \boxed{8}}{40 \div \boxed{8}} = \frac{2}{\boxed{5}}$

11. $\frac{24}{64} = \frac{24 \div \boxed{8}}{64 \div \boxed{8}} = \frac{\boxed{3}}{8}$

12. $\frac{16}{72} = \frac{16 \div \boxed{8}}{72 \div \boxed{8}} = \frac{2}{\boxed{9}}$

13. $\frac{24}{42} = \frac{24 \div \boxed{6}}{42 \div \boxed{6}} = \frac{\boxed{4}}{7}$

UNIT 11 LESSON 13 Find Equivalent Fractions by Dividing 281

Homework and Remembering page 281

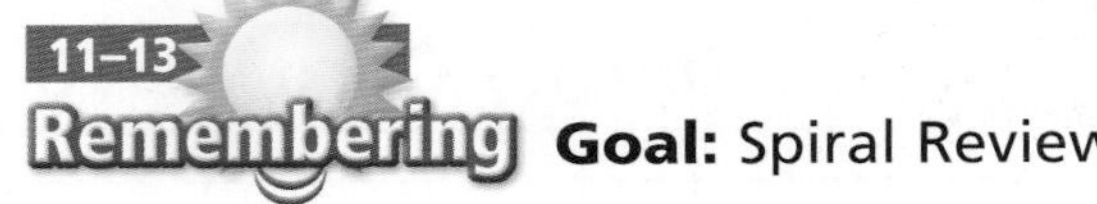

Goal: Spiral Review

This Remembering page would be appropriate anytime after today's lesson.

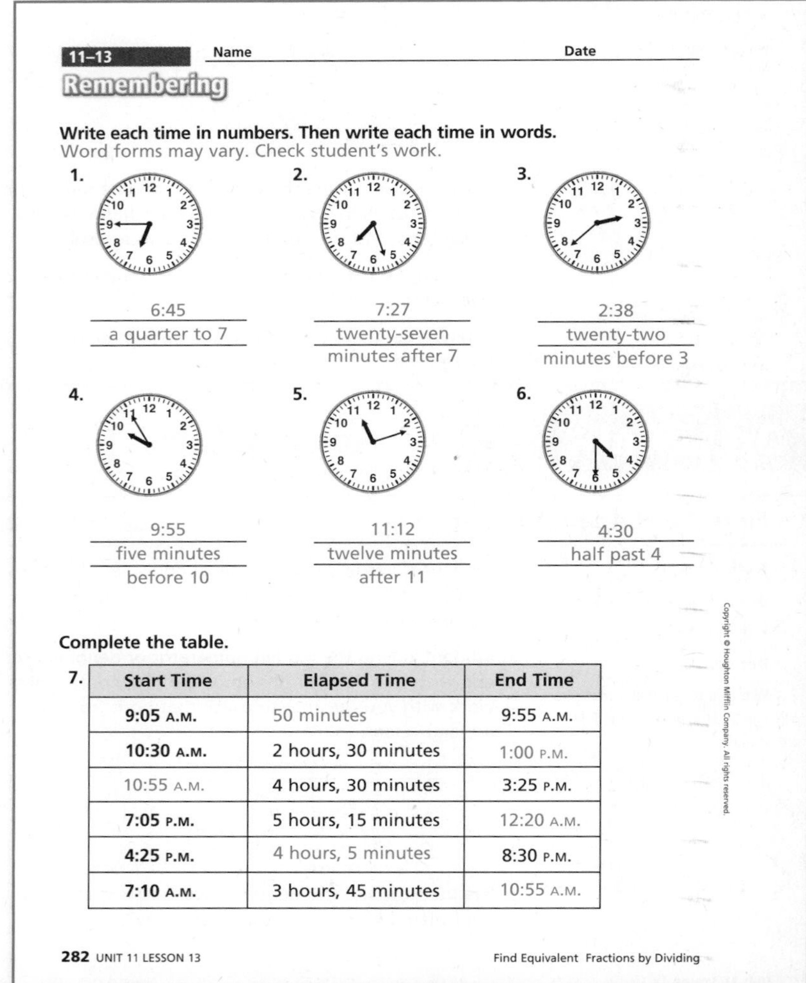

11–13 Remembering Name ____ Date ____

Write each time in numbers. Then write each time in words.
Word forms may vary. Check student's work.

1. 6:45 — a quarter to 7
2. 7:27 — twenty-seven minutes after 7
3. 2:38 — twenty-two minutes before 3
4. 9:55 — five minutes before 10
5. 11:12 — twelve minutes after 11
6. 4:30 — half past 4

Complete the table.

7.

Start Time	Elapsed Time	End Time
9:05 A.M.	50 minutes	9:55 A.M.
10:30 A.M.	2 hours, 30 minutes	1:00 P.M.
10:55 A.M.	4 hours, 30 minutes	3:25 P.M.
7:05 P.M.	5 hours, 15 minutes	12:20 A.M.
4:25 P.M.	4 hours, 5 minutes	8:30 P.M.
7:10 A.M.	3 hours, 45 minutes	10:55 A.M.

282 UNIT 11 LESSON 13 Find Equivalent Fractions by Dividing

Homework and Remembering page 282

Home or School Activity

Literature Connection

The Fraction Family Heads West Read aloud Marti Dryk's picture book about the Fraction Family heading to California during the 1849 Gold Rush. As you read along in the book, have students simplify each family members' fractional name like $\frac{14}{21}$, $\frac{8}{32}$, and so on. To extend the activity, give each student a fractional name and have them simplify that fraction.

Add Any Fractions

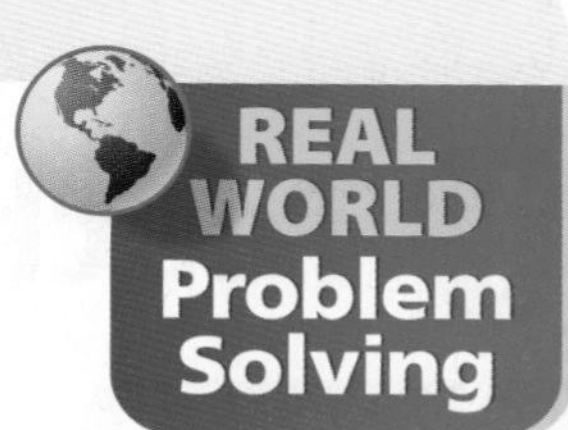

Lesson Objectives

- Add fractions with unlike and like denominators.
- Understand the term *rename* as it relates to fractions.
- Recognize common errors in adding fractions.

Vocabulary

fraction
equivalent fraction
equivalence chain
unlike fraction
denominator
common denominator
unit fraction

The Day at a Glance

Today's Goals	Materials	
1 Teaching the Lesson **A1:** Add fractions with like and unlike denominators. **A2:** Devise strategies for avoiding common errors in fraction addition. **2 Going Further** ▸ Differentiated Instruction **3 Homework and Spiral Review**	**Lesson Activities** Student Activity Book pp. 430A–434 or Student Hardcover Book pp. 431–434 and Activity Workbook pp. 203–206 (includes Special Formats and Cut-Outs) Homework and Remembering pp. 283–284 Sheet protectors and dry erase markers Transparency of Student Activity Book p. 430A and overhead projector (optional)	**Going Further** Activity Cards 11-14 Equivalent Fraction Strips Spinner F (TRB M141) Paper clips MathBoard materials Math Journals

Use **Math Talk** today!

Keeping Skills Sharp

Quick Practice — 5 MINUTES

Goal: Write equivalence chains.

Equivalence Chains Have a **Student Leader** write a fraction on the board, such as $\frac{3}{4}$. As volunteers take turns identifying the equivalent fractions for the fraction in order $\left(\text{up to} \frac{10\times \text{ numerator}}{10\times \text{ denominator}}\right)$, the **Student Leader** writes the fractions on the board as an equivalence chain. (See Unit 11 Lesson 13.)

$$\frac{3}{4} = \frac{6}{8} = \frac{9}{12} = \frac{15}{20} = \frac{18}{24} = \frac{18}{24} = \frac{21}{28} = \frac{24}{32} = \frac{27}{36} = \frac{30}{40}$$

Daily Routines

Homework Review Let students work together to check their work.

Nonroutine Problem Joe has 8 coins that total $1.25. Which coins does Joe have? 3 quarters, 5 dimes

1 Teaching the Lesson

Activity 1

Add Like and Unlike Fractions

 35 MINUTES

Goal: Add fractions with unlike and like denominators.

Materials: Student Activity Book p. 430A–432, or Hardcover Book pp. 431–432 and Acivity Workbook pp. 203–205 (includes special format), sheet protectors and dry erase markers, transparency of Student Activity Book p. 430A and overhead projector (optional)

 **NCTM Standards:**
Number and Operations
Problem Solving
Representation

 **Class Management**

Looking Ahead You may want to make a transparency of Student Book page 430A to use for this lesson.

English Language Learners

Write *like*, *unlike*, $\frac{1}{4}$, and $\frac{3}{4}$ on the board.

- **Beginning** Point and ask: **Are the *denominators* the same?** yes Say: **The fractions have *like denominators*.** Have students repeat. Continue with *numerator* and *unlike*.
- **Intermediate** Ask: **What is the same in the fractions?** denominator **Do they have *like denominators*?** yes
- **Advanced** Have students tell what is *like* and *unlike* about the fractions.

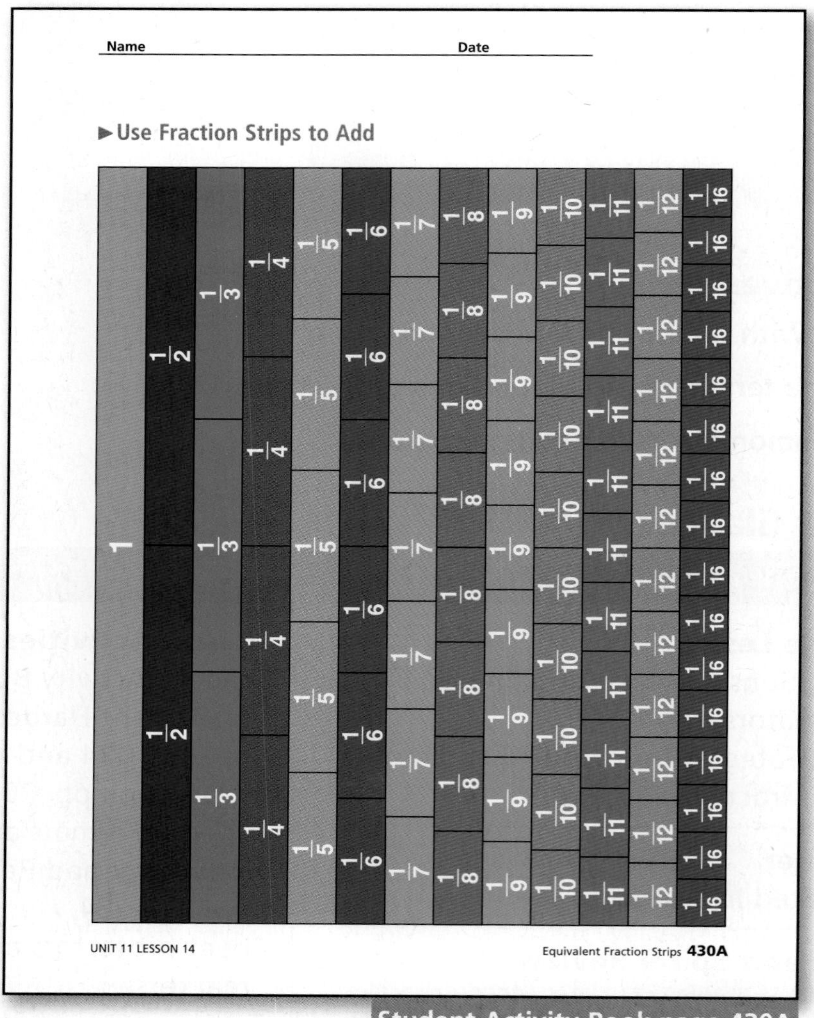
Name Date

▶ Use Fraction Strips to Add

UNIT 11 LESSON 14 Equivalent Fraction Strips 430A

Student Activity Book page 430A

▶ Use Fraction Strips to Add WHOLE CLASS

Direct students' attention to the fraction strips on Student Book page 430A and have them place this page into a sheet protector. Ask students to describe any patterns they see in the fraction strips and have them identify equivalent fractions.

Now, ask students how they can use the fraction strips to add $\frac{3}{6}$ and $\frac{2}{6}$. Have students share their strategies. Explain to students that fractions made from the same unit fraction have the same denominator and are called *like fractions*. These fractions can be added as they are. Students can use the fractions strips to see that they are just adding that many (numerators) of those unit fractions.

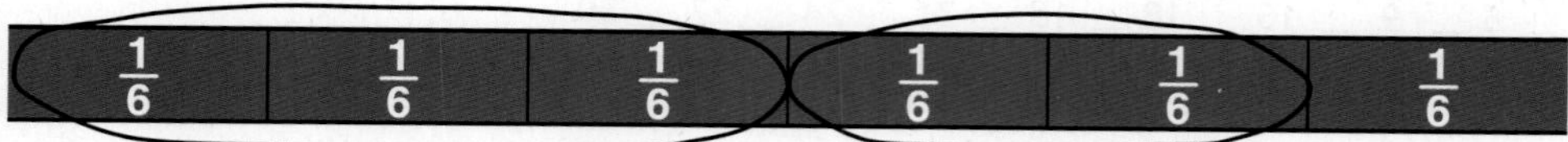

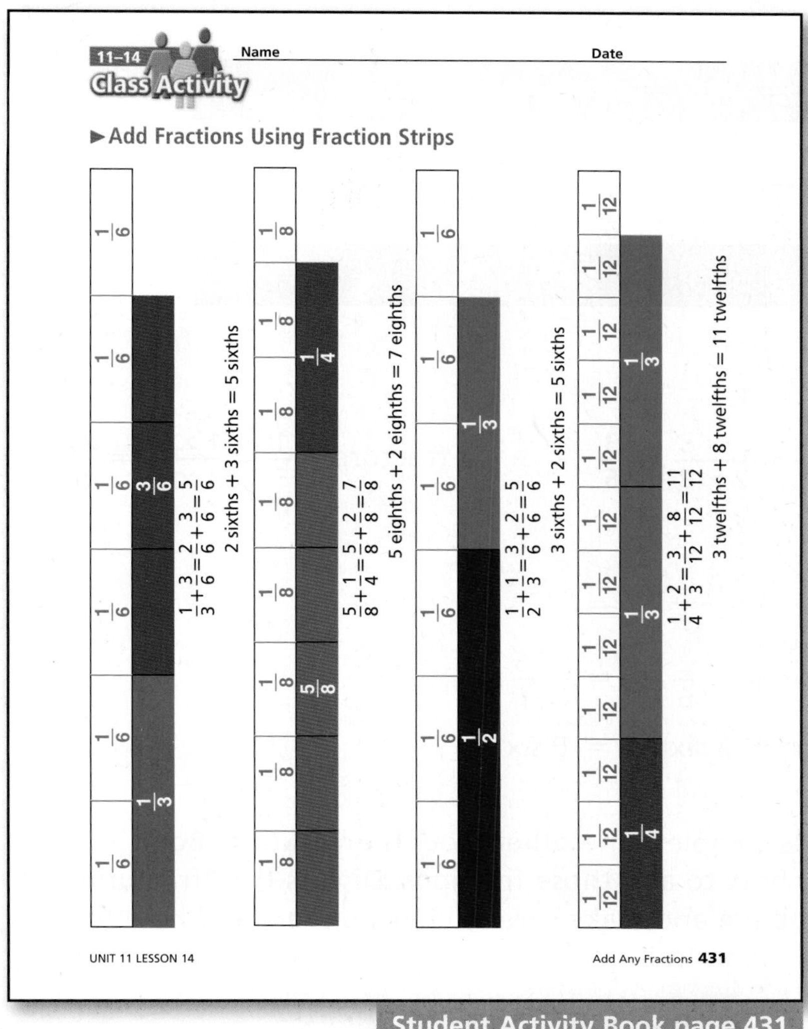

11–14 Class Activity

Name ________________________ Date ____________

► Add Fractions Using Fraction Strips

$\frac{1}{3} + \frac{3}{6} = \frac{2}{6} + \frac{3}{6} = \frac{5}{6}$

2 sixths + 3 sixths = 5 sixths

$\frac{5}{8} + \frac{1}{4} = \frac{5}{8} + \frac{2}{8} = \frac{7}{8}$

5 eighths + 2 eighths = 7 eighths

$\frac{1}{2} + \frac{1}{3} = \frac{3}{6} + \frac{2}{6} = \frac{5}{6}$

3 sixths + 2 sixths = 5 sixths

$\frac{1}{4} + \frac{2}{3} = \frac{3}{12} + \frac{8}{12} = \frac{11}{12}$

3 twelfths + 8 twelfths = 11 twelfths

UNIT 11 LESSON 14 — Add Any Fractions 431

Student Activity Book page 431

► Add Fractions Using Fraction Strips WHOLE CLASS

Write the following addition exercise on the board.

$$\frac{1}{2} + \frac{1}{3} = ?$$

- What do you notice about the denominators? They are not the same.

Explain to students that if two fractions are not made from the same unit fraction, one or both of them needs to be changed or renamed.

- How can we rename $\frac{1}{2}$ and $\frac{1}{3}$ so we can add them? Find equivalent fractions that are made from the same unit fraction. Then the fractions would have the same denominator.

Tell students to use the third model on Student Book page 431.

Activity continued ►

Math Background

Language and Vocabulary You may want to introduce the term rename. Explain that some people think of writing equivalent fractions as "renaming." Ask why the term makes sense. The value of the fraction is the same; the fraction has a new name.

The Learning Classroom

Building Concepts Challenge students who quickly find the unit fraction *sixths* for $\frac{1}{2} + \frac{1}{3}$ to find another possible unit fraction (twelfths). They can then compare these two options for solving the addition exercise and decide which is easier.

① Teaching the Lesson (continued)

Have students draw the fractures on the third model on Student Book page 431 to show equivalent fractions using sixths. Have them label the strips using multiplication notation, and then complete the addition.

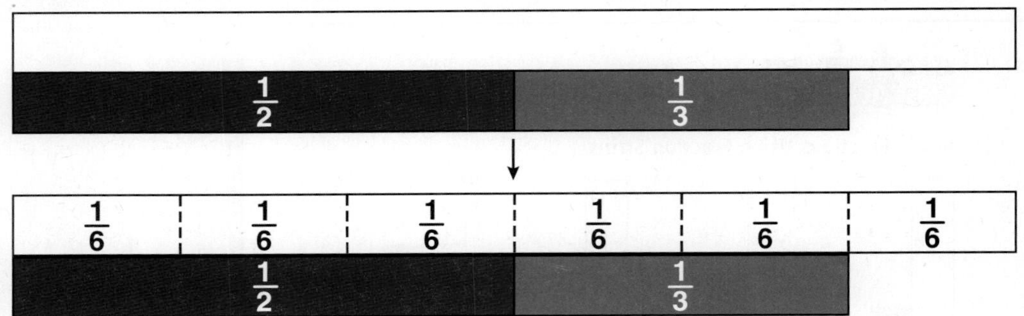

3-fracture $\frac{1}{2} = \frac{1 \times 3}{2 \times 3} = \frac{3}{6}$ 2-fracture $\frac{1}{3} = \frac{1 \times 2}{3 \times 2} = \frac{2}{6}$

$$\frac{1}{2} + \frac{1}{3} =$$

$$\frac{3}{6} + \frac{2}{6} = \frac{5}{6}$$

3 sixths + 2 sixths = 5 sixths

Now have students complete the other models on Student Book page 431 to show how to add those fractions. Discuss the "fracturing" aspect of each problem and make sure students understand how to write the answers numerically.

Teaching Note

Math Background When students write their addition solutions, encourage them to label the fractions with word name denominators, such as sixths or eighths. These labels will remind students that denominators are like units, such as inches or pounds, to be carried over to the answer rather than added together.

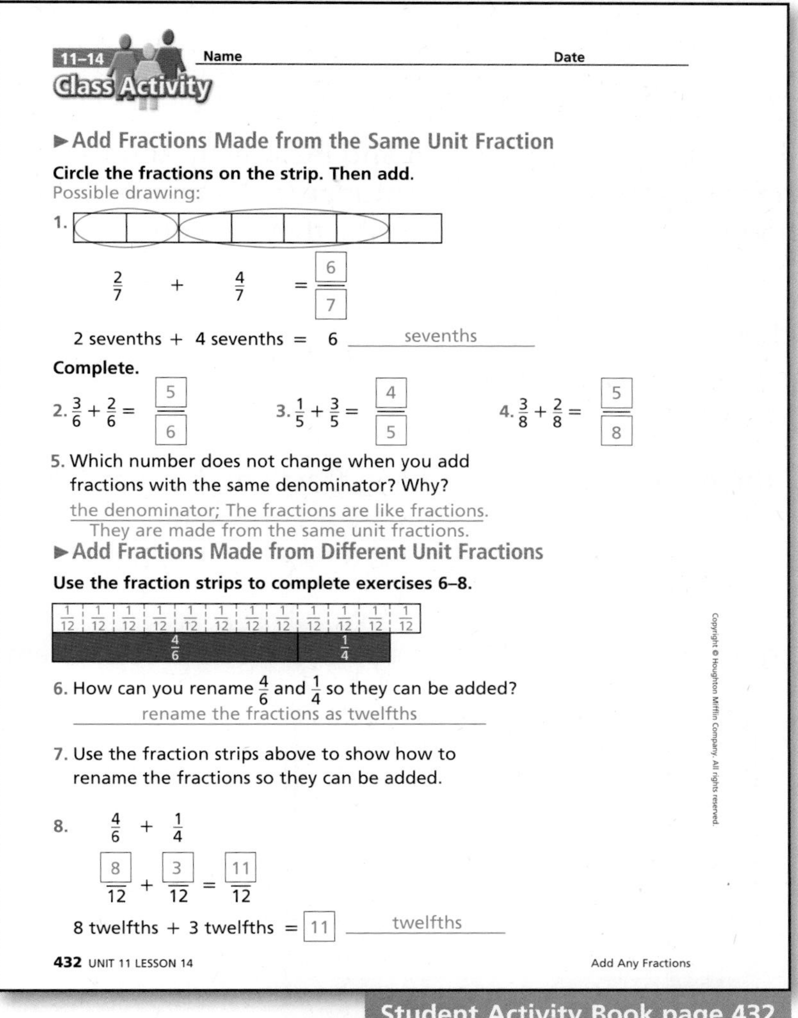

11–14 Name Date

Class Activity

► Add Fractions Made from the Same Unit Fraction

Circle the fractions on the strip. Then add.

Possible drawing:

1.

$\frac{2}{7} + \frac{4}{7} = \frac{6}{7}$

2 sevenths + 4 sevenths = 6 sevenths

Complete.

2. $\frac{3}{6} + \frac{2}{6} = \frac{5}{6}$

3. $\frac{1}{5} + \frac{3}{5} = \frac{4}{5}$

4. $\frac{3}{8} + \frac{2}{8} = \frac{5}{8}$

5. Which number does not change when you add fractions with the same denominator? Why?

the denominator; The fractions are like fractions. They are made from the same unit fractions.

► Add Fractions Made from Different Unit Fractions

Use the fraction strips to complete exercises 6–8.

$\frac{1}{12}$ $\frac{1}{12}$ $\frac{1}{12}$ $\frac{1}{12}$ $\frac{1}{12}$ $\frac{1}{12}$ $\frac{1}{12}$ $\frac{1}{12}$ $\frac{1}{12}$ $\frac{1}{12}$ $\frac{1}{12}$ $\frac{1}{12}$

$\frac{4}{6}$ $\frac{1}{4}$

6. How can you rename $\frac{4}{6}$ and $\frac{1}{4}$ so they can be added?

rename the fractions as twelfths

7. Use the fraction strips above to show how to rename the fractions so they can be added.

8. $\frac{4}{6} + \frac{1}{4}$

$\frac{8}{12} + \frac{3}{12} = \frac{11}{12}$

8 twelfths + 3 twelfths = 11 twelfths

432 UNIT 11 LESSON 14 Add Any Fractions

Student Activity Book page 432

► Add Fractions Made from the Same Unit Fraction WHOLE CLASS

Have students look at the denominators in exercise 1 on Student Book page 432. Remind them that if two unit fractions are made from the same unit fraction, they can be added as they are. Then have them compare the fraction strip model with the numeric form. Have students use their fraction strips to complete exercises 2–4 and summarize what they did to complete exercise 5. Help students understand that "sevenths" is like a unit name, such as inches or pounds, so it doesn't change.

► Add Fractions Made from Different Unit Fractions WHOLE CLASS

Refer students to the bottom of Student Book page 432 and have them look at the denominators. Remind them that if fractions are not made from the same unit, one or both of them will need to be renamed. Encourage students to use their fraction strips to help them rename the fractions to complete exercises 6–8. Have student volunteers explain how they added $\frac{4}{6}$ and $\frac{1}{4}$. See the **Math Talk in Action** for a sample discussion.

Teaching Note

Watch For! Some students may think that fractions with the same numerator, such as $\frac{3}{4}$ and $\frac{3}{5}$, have been made with the same unit fraction. You might need to use fraction strips to review the meaning of unit fractions with these students.

Math Talk in Action

To add $\frac{4}{6}$ and $\frac{1}{4}$, do we need to rename one or both fractions?

Cora: Both fractions.

That's correct. Can anyone tell me an equivalent fraction for each fraction?

Sadie: You could use twelths. $\frac{4}{6} = \frac{8}{12}$ and $\frac{1}{4} = \frac{3}{12}$.

How do we add those fractions?

Martin: $\frac{8}{12}$ and $\frac{3}{12}$ is $\frac{11}{12}$.

Activity 2

Avoid Common Errors

 **20 MINUTES**

Goal: Devise strategies for avoiding common errors in fraction addition.

Materials: Student Activity Book or Hardcover Book p. 433 and Activity Workbook p. 206 (includes special format)

 **NCTM Standards:**
Number and Operations
Problem Solving
Representation

▶ Common Errors When Adding Fractions WHOLE CLASS

Some students see the numbers in a fraction and incorrectly add the numerators and then the denominators. Ask students to summarize in their own words how they add fractions and why they add only the numerators.

- How do you add two fractions, such as $\frac{1}{4}$ and $\frac{2}{3}$? First find equivalent fractions with the same denominator. Then add the numerators and write the sum over the denominator.
- Why do we add the numerators when adding fractions, but not the denominators? The numerators tell how many pieces we have. The denominators just tell what kind of unit fractions we are adding together.

Write the following (incorrect) equations on the board and discuss them.

$$\frac{1}{4} + \frac{1}{4} = \frac{2}{8}$$

$$\frac{1}{2} + \frac{1}{2} = \frac{2}{4}$$

- Look at the first equation. Is the answer correct? No
- Why is it wrong? You get an answer that is equivalent to one of the fractions you added. A total has to be larger than the numbers added.

If students give answers such as "You shouldn't add the bottom numbers," ask for a concept-based response such as you are adding fourths so you should end up with fourths.

- Look at the second equation. Is the answer correct? No
- Why is it wrong? Again you get an answer that is equivalent to one of the fractions you added. A total has to be larger than the numbers added.

Then have students correct the equations and discuss how they corrected them.

Write this example and the drawings given below on the board.

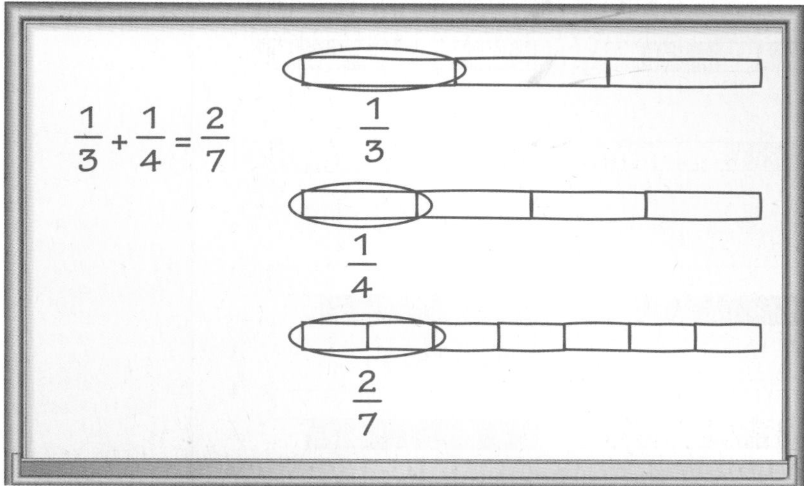

Have students examine the drawings. Discuss why $\frac{2}{7}$ is not a logical answer to the equation.

- What do the drawings show us? The answer is smaller than one of the addends.
- Does $\frac{2}{7}$ look like a reasonable answer to the equation? No, because $\frac{2}{7}$ isn't even as long as $\frac{1}{3}$. So $\frac{2}{7}$ couldn't be the sum of $\frac{1}{3}$ and $\frac{1}{4}$.

Ask students to think of ways that might help them avoid this error. If your students are having trouble with this, discuss the following strategies.

- Think of the denominator or the unit fraction as a "last name", like a unit. You must add inches to inches or hours to hours. You can't add inches to feet or hours to seconds.
- Write the fraction names to remember not to add the denominators together. Instead of $\frac{2}{6}$, write $\frac{2}{\text{6ths}}$ or $\frac{2}{\text{sixths}}$

Have a volunteer come to the board and add $\frac{1}{3}$ and $\frac{1}{4}$ correctly drawing fraction bars to show the answer is correct.

Activity continued ►

Teaching Note

Watch For! A common error made by students in adding fractions is adding the numerators and then adding the denominators. Students need to understand that the sum of two numbers must be greater than either of the two addends. Before students can use this concept with fractions, they must understand it with whole numbers. They can practice it with whole numbers using classroom objects or base-ten blocks to model simple whole number addition problems before moving on to fraction bars.

Teaching the Lesson (continued)

Ongoing Assessment

Ask students to add $\frac{2}{8} + \frac{5}{8}$, $\frac{1}{2} + \frac{1}{4}$ and $\frac{2}{3} + \frac{1}{4}$. As they add, have them explain their thinking aloud.

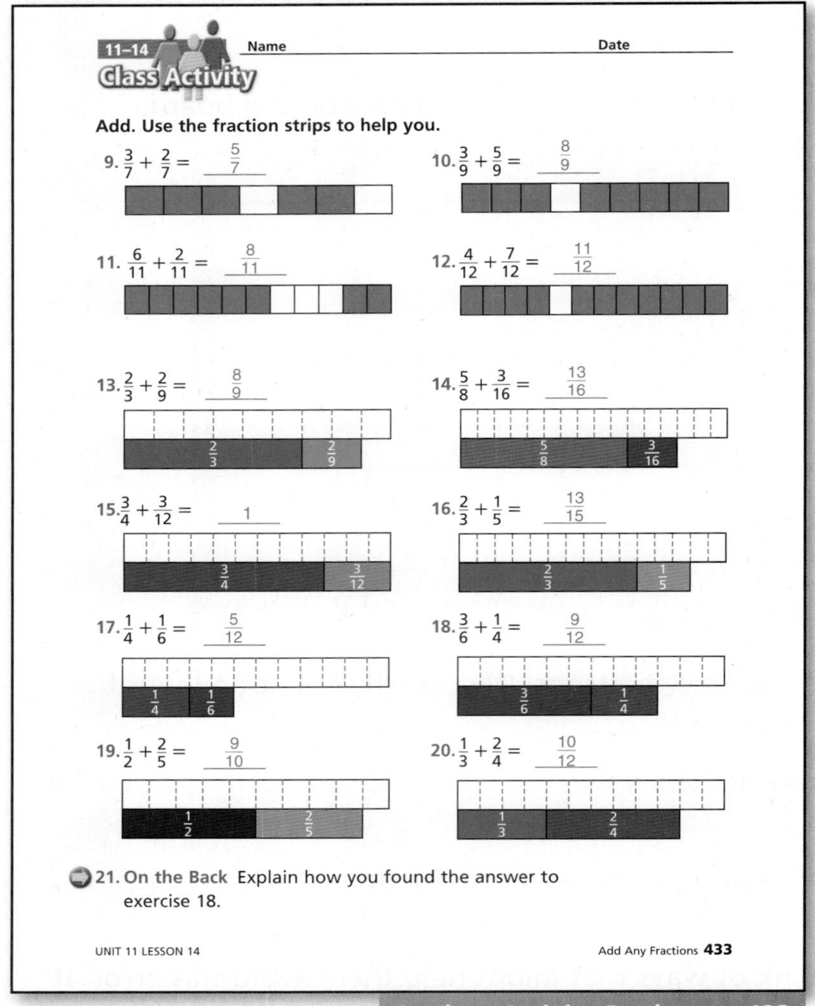

11–14 Class Activity

Name Date

Add. Use the fraction strips to help you.

9. $\frac{3}{7} + \frac{2}{7} =$ $\frac{5}{7}$

10. $\frac{3}{9} + \frac{5}{9} =$ $\frac{8}{9}$

11. $\frac{6}{11} + \frac{2}{11} =$ $\frac{8}{11}$

12. $\frac{4}{12} + \frac{7}{12} =$ $\frac{11}{12}$

13. $\frac{2}{3} + \frac{2}{9} =$ $\frac{8}{9}$

14. $\frac{5}{8} + \frac{3}{16} =$ $\frac{13}{16}$

15. $\frac{3}{4} + \frac{3}{12} =$ 1

16. $\frac{2}{3} + \frac{1}{5} =$ $\frac{13}{15}$

17. $\frac{1}{4} + \frac{1}{6} =$ $\frac{5}{12}$

18. $\frac{3}{6} + \frac{1}{4} =$ $\frac{9}{12}$

19. $\frac{1}{2} + \frac{2}{5} =$ $\frac{9}{10}$

20. $\frac{1}{3} + \frac{2}{4} =$ $\frac{10}{12}$

21. On the Back Explain how you found the answer to exercise 18.

UNIT 11 LESSON 14 Add Any Fractions 433

Student Activity Book page 433

▶ Practice Fraction Addition INDIVIDUALS

Have students work on their own to complete the exercises on Student Book page 433. After students complete the page, have them work in pairs to check their answers.

Be sure students understand that two fractions made from the same unit fraction can be added as they are. Fractions not made from the same unit fraction cannot be added. One or both of them need to be changed or renamed so both are made from the same unit fraction, that is, they have the same denominator.

2 Going Further

Differentiated Instruction

Intervention

Activity Card 11-14

Possible Answers Activity Card 11-14 ●

Work: In pairs

Use:

- Equivalent Fraction Strips (Student Activity Book page 430 A)

1. Cut out the fraction strips from page 430 A.
2. Work Together Choose two unit fraction strips to add together. Then choose another fraction strip that might show the sum of the two unit fractions.
3. Compare Does the third fraction strip show the sum? If not, can you find another fraction strip with a part that matches the sum exactly?
4. When you find the sum, write an equation telling what the fraction strips show. Then repeat the activity two more times.

$\frac{1}{2} + \frac{1}{3} =$ ____

$\frac{3}{6} + \frac{2}{6} = \frac{5}{6}$

Unit 11, Lesson 14

Activity Note Students can use the fraction strips from the lesson. After students find the sum, discuss any patterns that students observe between the denominators of the unit fractions and the denominator of the sum.

Math Writing Prompt

Use a Model Explain how you could use fraction strips to show that $\frac{2}{3} + \frac{1}{4}$ does not equal $\frac{1}{2}$.

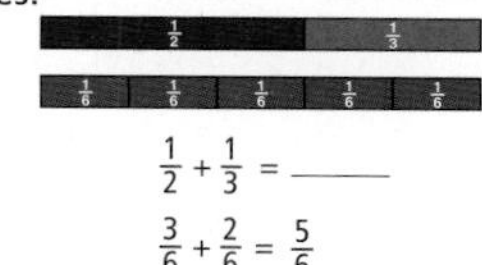

Software Support

Warm Up 20.14

On Level

Activity Card 11-14

Add Fractions Activity Card 11-14 ▲

Work: In pairs

Use:

- Equivalent Fraction Strips (Student Activity Book page 430 A)
- TRB M141 (Spinner F)
- 2 Paper clips

1. Work Together Make two spinners as shown below.
2. Spin both spinners and then add the two fractions. How can you use fraction strips to help you find and write the sum?

$\frac{1}{6} + \frac{1}{4} = \square$

$\frac{2}{12} + \frac{3}{12} = \frac{5}{12}$

3. Analyze If a fraction expressed as a sum has a numerator greater than the denominator, how does that fraction compare to 1?
4. Spin the spinners again and repeat the activity.

Unit 11, Lesson 14

Activity Note Have students write each sum as shown in the model, using the common denominator for each addend. Save SAB 430A for Activity Card 11-16 ▲.

Math Writing Prompt

Summarize Summarize the steps you take to add any two unlike fractions.

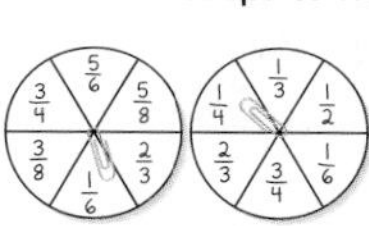

Software Support

Fraction Action: Fraction Flare Up, Level I

Challenge

Activity Card 11-14

Follow the Rules Activity Card 11-14 ■

Work: On your own

Use:

- MathBoard materials
- Equivalent Fraction Strips (from Student Activity Book 430 A)

1. Copy the grid below. Then use the rules to find the missing fractions.

A $\frac{1}{2}$	B $\frac{1}{8}$	C $\frac{5}{8}$
D $\frac{1}{4}$	E O	F $\frac{1}{4}$
G $\frac{3}{4}$	H $\frac{1}{8}$	I $\frac{7}{8}$

Add A and B to get C.
Add A and D to get G.
Add D and E to get F.
Add C and F to get I.

2. Think How many eighths are equivalent to $\frac{1}{2}$? How many fourths? 4; 2
3. Exchange papers with a classmate to check your answers.

Unit 11, Lesson 14

Activity Note If time allows, challenge students to create their own puzzle that follows the same rules. Display the puzzles for others to solve on their own.

Math Writing Prompt

Analyze Can the sum of two unit fractions equal $\frac{7}{12}$? If so, identify the fractions. If not, explain why not.

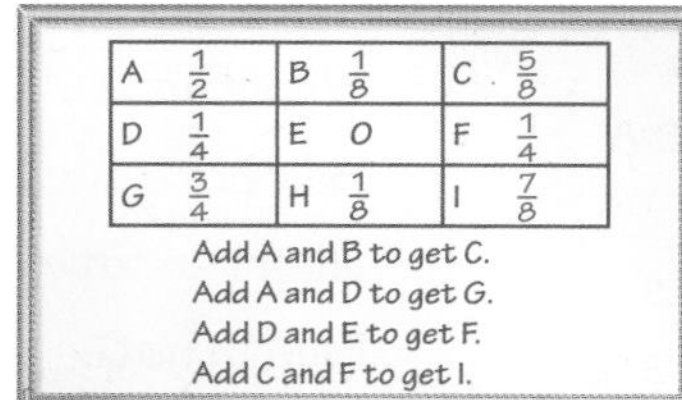

DESTINATION Math® **Software Support**

Course II: Module 2: Unit 3: Fractional Parts

3 Homework and Spiral Review

Goal: Additional Practice

This Homework page provides practice in using equivalent fractions.

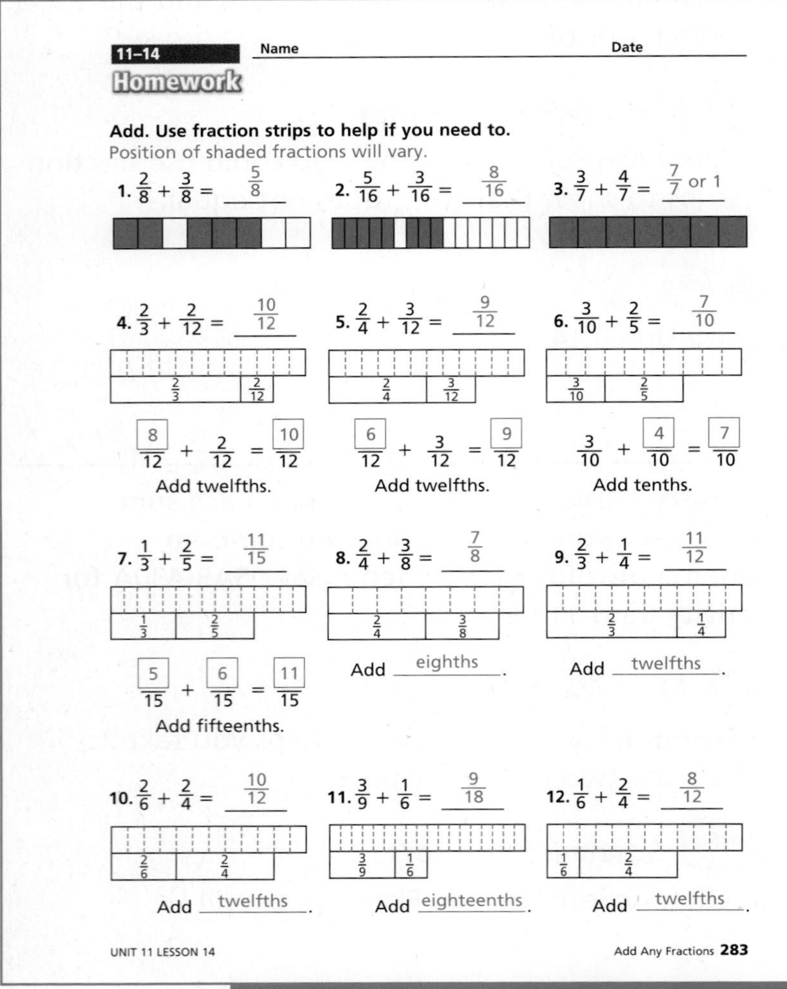

11–14 Homework Name ____ Date ____

Add. Use fraction strips to help if you need to.

Position of shaded fractions will vary.

1. $\frac{2}{8} + \frac{3}{8} = \frac{5}{8}$
2. $\frac{5}{16} + \frac{3}{16} = \frac{8}{16}$
3. $\frac{3}{7} + \frac{4}{7} = \frac{7}{7}$ or 1
4. $\frac{2}{3} + \frac{2}{12} = \frac{10}{12}$ $\quad \frac{8}{12} + \frac{2}{12} = \frac{10}{12}$ Add twelfths.
5. $\frac{2}{4} + \frac{3}{12} = \frac{9}{12}$ $\quad \frac{6}{12} + \frac{3}{12} = \frac{9}{12}$ Add twelfths.
6. $\frac{3}{10} + \frac{2}{5} = \frac{7}{10}$ $\quad \frac{3}{10} + \frac{4}{10} = \frac{7}{10}$ Add tenths.
7. $\frac{1}{3} + \frac{2}{5} = \frac{11}{15}$ $\quad \frac{5}{15} + \frac{6}{15} = \frac{11}{15}$ Add fifteenths.
8. $\frac{2}{4} + \frac{3}{8} = \frac{7}{8}$ Add eighths.
9. $\frac{2}{3} + \frac{1}{4} = \frac{11}{12}$ Add twelfths.
10. $\frac{2}{6} + \frac{2}{4} = \frac{10}{12}$ Add twelfths.
11. $\frac{3}{9} + \frac{1}{6} = \frac{9}{18}$ Add eighteenths.
12. $\frac{1}{6} + \frac{2}{4} = \frac{8}{12}$ Add twelfths.

UNIT 11 LESSON 14 Add Any Fractions 283

Homework and Remembering page 283

Goal: Spiral Review

This Remembering page would be appropriate anytime after today's lesson.

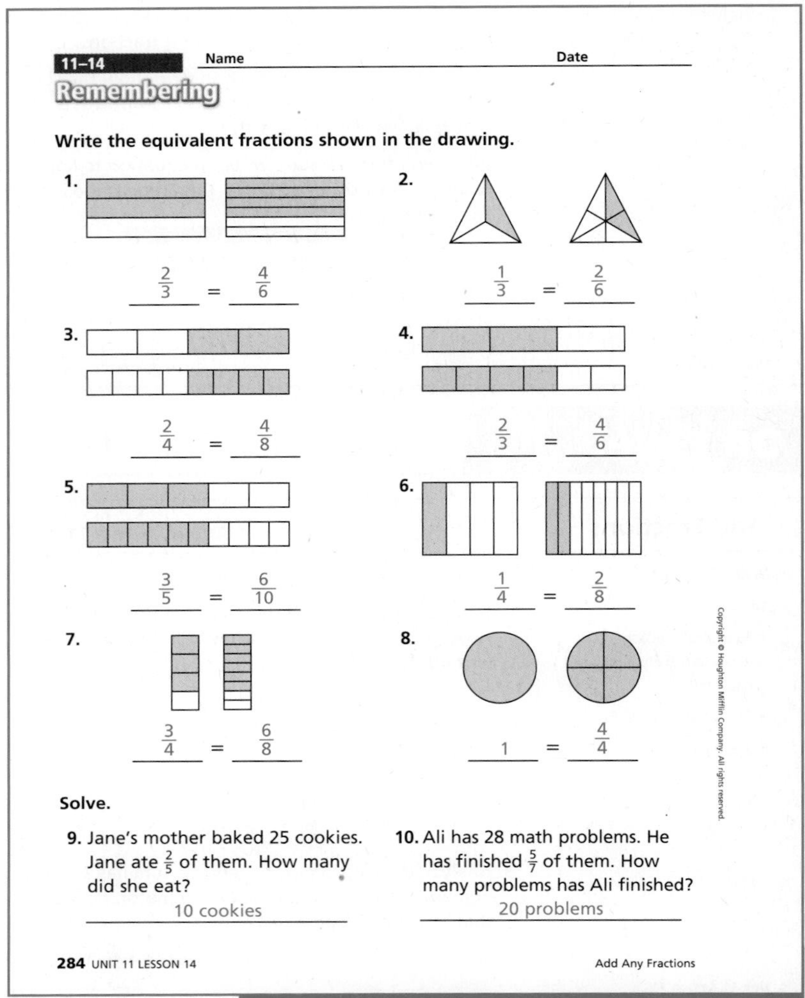

11–14 Remembering Name ____ Date ____

Write the equivalent fractions shown in the drawing.

1. $\frac{2}{3} = \frac{4}{6}$
2. $\frac{1}{3} = \frac{2}{6}$
3. $\frac{2}{4} = \frac{4}{8}$
4. $\frac{2}{3} = \frac{4}{6}$
5. $\frac{3}{5} = \frac{6}{10}$
6. $\frac{1}{4} = \frac{2}{8}$
7. $\frac{3}{4} = \frac{6}{8}$
8. $1 = \frac{4}{4}$

Solve.

9. Jane's mother baked 25 cookies. Jane ate $\frac{2}{5}$ of them. How many did she eat? 10 cookies
10. Ali has 28 math problems. He has finished $\frac{5}{7}$ of them. How many problems has Ali finished? 20 problems

284 UNIT 11 LESSON 14 Add Any Fractions

Homework and Remembering page 284

Home or School Activity

Music Connection

Musical Notes Display the table on the right for students to see how musical notes are written. You may want to display examples of sheet music and if musical instruments are available, show students how to play whole, half, quarter, and eighth notes. If instruments are not available, clap the notes. If time allows, challenge students to use the musical notation to write addition exercises for others to solve.

Name	Note	Value
Whole note	𝅝	1
Half note	𝅗𝅥	$\frac{1}{2}$
Quarter note	♩	$\frac{1}{4}$
Eighth note	♪	$\frac{1}{8}$
Sixteenth note	𝅘𝅥𝅯	$\frac{1}{16}$

Compare and Subtract Fractions

Lesson Objectives

- Compare and subtract like fractions.
- Compare and subtract unlike fractions by finding equivalent fractions with a common denominator.
- Solve word problems that involve comparing, adding, and subtracting fractions.

Vocabulary

comparison problem
equivalent fraction
numerator
denominator

The Day at a Glance

Today's Goals	Materials	
1 Teaching the Lesson **A1:** Subtract like and unlike unit fractions. **A2:** Add, compare, and subtract fractons and solve fraction word problems. **2 Going Further** ► Differentiated Instruction **3 Homework and Spiral Review**	**Lesson Activities** Student Activity Book pp. 435–438 or Student Hardcover Book pp. 435–438 and Activity Workbook p. 207 (includes Special Formats) Homework and Remembering pp. 285–286 Equivalent fraction strips (from Lesson 14)	**Going Further** Activity Cards 11-15 2 copies of Fractions Circle Model (TRB M130) Colored pencils Sentence strips MathBoard materials Math Journals

Use Math Talk today!

Keeping Skills Sharp

Quick Practice — 5 MINUTES

Goal: Write equivalence chains.

Equivalence Chains Have a **Student Leader** write a fraction on the board. As volunteers take turns identifying the equivalent fractions for the fraction in order $\left(\text{up to} \frac{10\times \text{ numerator}}{10\times \text{ denominator}}\right)$, the **Student Leader** writes the fractions on the board as an equivalence chain.

$$\frac{2}{6} = \frac{4}{12} = \frac{6}{18} = \frac{8}{24} = \frac{10}{30} = \frac{12}{36} = \frac{14}{42} = \frac{16}{48} = \frac{18}{54} = \frac{20}{60}$$

Daily Routines

Homework Review Have students show the work they used to get any incorrect answers. Review as a class.

Nonroutine Problem In a row of the audience, $\frac{7}{10}$ are students, $\frac{1}{5}$ are teachers, and 4 are alumni. How many people are sitting in the row? 40 people

1 Teaching the Lesson

Activity 1

Relate Fraction Addition and Subtraction

 25 MINUTES

Goal: Subtract like and unlike unit fractions.

Materials: Student Activity Book or Hardcover Book p. 435 and Activity Workbook p. 207 (includes special format)

 **NCTM Standards:**
Number and Operations
Problem Solving
Communication
Representation

Teaching Note

Watch For! Students might be confused by the comparison subtraction situation in this problem. You might remind students briefly of the three types of subtraction situations: take apart, unknown partner, and **comparison**. To solve this problem, we must **compare** the amount Amrita decorated to the amount Sam decorated and then find the fraction that represents the difference. The same outcome can be achieved by subtracting the fraction Sam decorated from the fraction Amrita decorated.

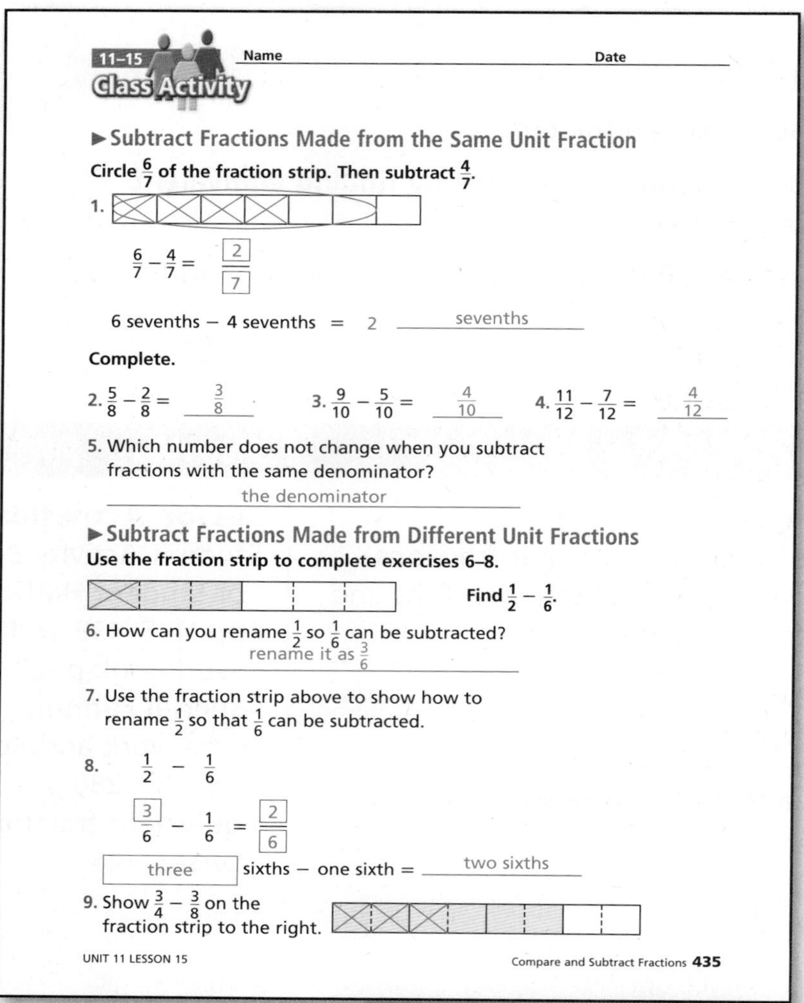

11–15 Class Activity Name Date

► Subtract Fractions Made from the Same Unit Fraction

Circle $\frac{6}{7}$ of the fraction strip. Then subtract $\frac{4}{7}$.

1. $\frac{6}{7} - \frac{4}{7} = \frac{2}{7}$

6 sevenths − 4 sevenths = 2 sevenths

Complete.

2. $\frac{5}{8} - \frac{2}{8} =$ $\frac{3}{8}$
3. $\frac{9}{10} - \frac{5}{10} =$ $\frac{4}{10}$
4. $\frac{11}{12} - \frac{7}{12} =$ $\frac{4}{12}$
5. Which number does not change when you subtract fractions with the same denominator? the denominator

► Subtract Fractions Made from Different Unit Fractions

Use the fraction strip to complete exercises 6–8.

Find $\frac{1}{2} - \frac{1}{6}$.

6. How can you rename $\frac{1}{2}$ so $\frac{1}{6}$ can be subtracted? rename it as $\frac{3}{6}$
7. Use the fraction strip above to show how to rename $\frac{1}{2}$ so that $\frac{1}{6}$ can be subtracted.
8. $\frac{1}{2} - \frac{1}{6}$

$\frac{3}{6} - \frac{1}{6} = \frac{2}{6}$

three sixths − one sixth = two sixths

9. Show $\frac{3}{4} - \frac{3}{8}$ on the fraction strip to the right.

UNIT 11 LESSON 15 Compare and Subtract Fractions 435

Student Activity Book page 435

► Subtract Fractions Made from the Same Unit Fraction WHOLE CLASS

Write the following problem on the board and read it aloud to the class.

Sam and Amrita are decorating a cake. Sam decorated $\frac{1}{6}$ of the cake and Amrita decorated $\frac{2}{6}$ of the cake. How much more of the cake did Amrita decorate than Sam?

Remind students that if two fractions are from the same unit fraction, they have the same denominator and can be subtracted as they are. Ask students how to solve this problem. Subtract Sam's fraction of the cake. $\frac{2}{6} - \frac{1}{6} = \frac{1}{6}$

Have students complete exercises 1–5 on Student Book page 435.

▶ Subtract Fractions Made from Different Unit Fractions WHOLE CLASS

Write the following problem on the board and read it aloud to the class.

Neil and Keo are decorating a cake. Neil decorated $\frac{1}{4}$ of the cake and Keo decorated $\frac{1}{3}$ of the cake. How much of the cake have they decorated together?

Remind students that if two fractions are not made from the same unit fraction, one or both of them will need to be renamed. Students will have to find an equivalent fraction for one or both, so both fractions are the same unit fraction. Some students may need to use their Fraction strips from lesson 14 to help them find common denominators.

Let students work on this problem for a minute before leading a discussion about renaming methods.

- Can we add $\frac{1}{3}$ and $\frac{1}{4}$ as they are? No, we have to rename both of them.
- What equivalent fractions can we use? $\frac{4}{12}$ and $\frac{3}{12}$

Elicit the equations showing $\frac{n}{n}$ to remind the class how renaming works. Then have students find the total. $\frac{7}{12}$

Keo

$\frac{1}{3} \rightarrow \frac{1}{3} = \frac{1 \times 4}{3 \times 4} = \frac{4}{12}$

Neil

$\frac{1}{4} \rightarrow \frac{1}{4} = \frac{1 \times 3}{4 \times 3} = \frac{3}{12}$

$\frac{4}{12} + \frac{3}{12} = \frac{7}{12}$

Finally, present a subtraction problem, using the same fractions:

How much more of the cake did Keo decorate than Neil?

- What should we do to solve this problem? Subtract Neil's fraction of the cake from Keo's.

Help students discover that, because they have already renamed $\frac{1}{4}$ and $\frac{1}{3}$ in the previous problem, they can use that information again to help solve this problem.

$\frac{1}{3} - \frac{1}{4} =$

$\frac{4}{12} - \frac{3}{12} = \frac{1}{12}$

Have students complete exercises 6–9 on the bottom of Student Book page 435 and discuss the answers as a class.

Differentiated Instruction

Extra Help To help children understand how much more of the cake Keo decorated than Neil, you may want to use the same graphic on the board that was used for adding how much Keo and Neil decorated in all. Have a student compare Keo's fraction to Neil's fraction, and find the fraction that represents the difference.

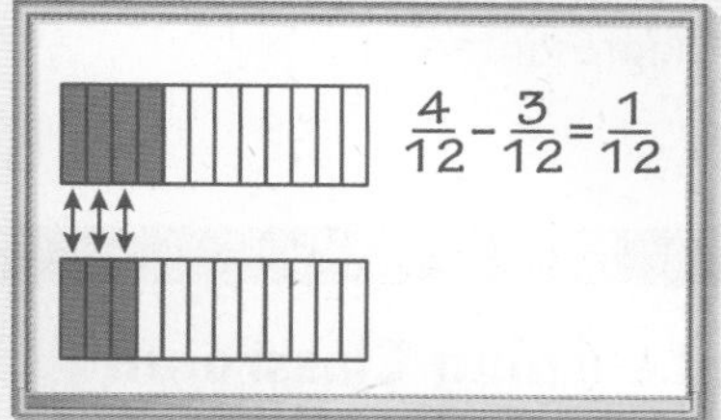

Teaching Note

Math Background It may be helpful as students get deeper into adding and subtracting fractions to reinforce the notion of renaming by multiplying the numerator and denominator by $\frac{n}{n}$. Any fraction with the same numerator and denominator is a whole, or 1. In this way, multiplying the numerator and denominator by $\frac{n}{n}$ is the same as multiplying by 1, and the fraction that is being renamed retains its original value.

Activity 2

Compare and Compute with Fractions

 25 MINUTES

Goal: Add, compare, and subtract fractions and solve fraction word problems.

Materials: Equivalent Fraction Strips (from Lesson 14) or (TRB M142), Student Activity Book or Hardcover Book pp. 436–438

 **NCTM Standards:**
Number and Operations
Problem Solving
Communication
Representation

The Learning Classroom

Building Concepts Students may discover "tricks" that allow them to compare fractions with different denominators without renaming. For example, when the numerators are the same, and the denominators are different, the fraction with the greater denominator represents a smaller amount.

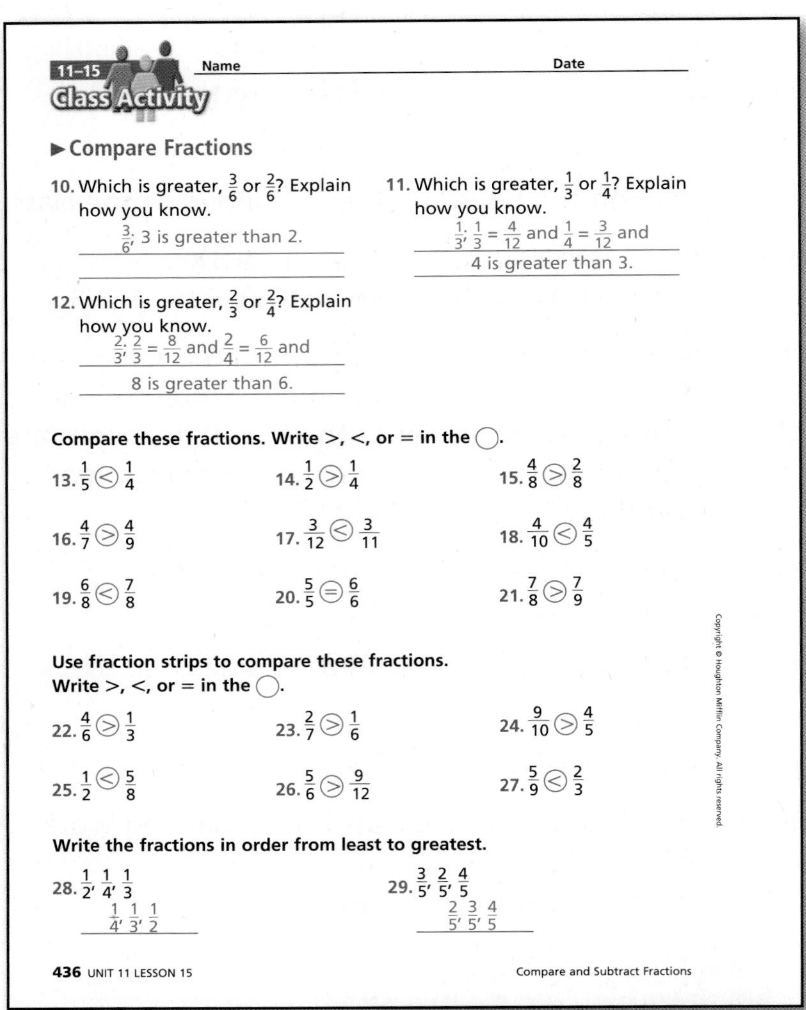

11–15 Class Activity Name Date

▶ Compare Fractions

10. Which is greater, $\frac{3}{6}$ or $\frac{2}{6}$? Explain how you know.
$\frac{3}{6}$; 3 is greater than 2.

11. Which is greater, $\frac{1}{3}$ or $\frac{1}{4}$? Explain how you know.
$\frac{1}{3}$; $\frac{1}{3} = \frac{4}{12}$ and $\frac{1}{4} = \frac{3}{12}$ and 4 is greater than 3.

12. Which is greater, $\frac{2}{3}$ or $\frac{2}{4}$? Explain how you know.
$\frac{2}{3}$; $\frac{2}{3} = \frac{8}{12}$ and $\frac{2}{4} = \frac{6}{12}$ and 8 is greater than 6.

Compare these fractions. Write >, <, or = in the ◯.

13. $\frac{1}{5} < \frac{1}{4}$
14. $\frac{1}{2} > \frac{1}{4}$
15. $\frac{4}{8} > \frac{2}{8}$
16. $\frac{4}{7} > \frac{4}{9}$
17. $\frac{3}{12} < \frac{3}{11}$
18. $\frac{4}{10} < \frac{4}{5}$
19. $\frac{6}{8} < \frac{7}{8}$
20. $\frac{5}{5} = \frac{6}{6}$
21. $\frac{7}{8} > \frac{7}{9}$

Use fraction strips to compare these fractions. Write >, <, or = in the ◯.

22. $\frac{4}{6} > \frac{1}{3}$
23. $\frac{2}{7} > \frac{1}{6}$
24. $\frac{9}{10} > \frac{4}{5}$
25. $\frac{1}{2} < \frac{5}{8}$
26. $\frac{5}{6} > \frac{9}{12}$
27. $\frac{5}{9} < \frac{2}{3}$

Write the fractions in order from least to greatest.

28. $\frac{1}{2}, \frac{1}{4}, \frac{1}{3}$
$\frac{1}{4}, \frac{1}{3}, \frac{1}{2}$

29. $\frac{3}{5}, \frac{2}{5}, \frac{4}{5}$
$\frac{2}{5}, \frac{3}{5}, \frac{4}{5}$

436 UNIT 11 LESSON 15 Compare and Subtract Fractions

Student Activity Book page 436

▶ Compare Fractions WHOLE CLASS

Discuss exercise 10 on Student Activity Book page 462. Then present this comparison word problem, using fractions with unlike denominators to help students visualize exercise 11.

Justine decorated $\frac{5}{6}$ of a cake and Ben decorated $\frac{2}{3}$ of the cake. Who decorated more of the cake?

- What do we need to know to solve this problem? Which is larger, $\frac{5}{6}$ or $\frac{2}{3}$?
- How can we tell which is larger? By renaming the fractions so that they have the same denominator. See side column for an example.

Have students solve the problem. $\frac{5}{6} > \frac{4}{6}$ so $\frac{5}{6} > \frac{2}{3}$; Justine decorated more of the cake.

Before students complete exercises 12–29 on Student Book page 436, remind them to make sure they have fractions with the same denominator before comparing them.

Justine	Ben
$\frac{5}{6}$	$\frac{2 \times 2}{3 \times 2} = \frac{4}{6}$

$\frac{5}{6} > \frac{4}{6}$ so $\frac{5}{6} > \frac{2}{3}$

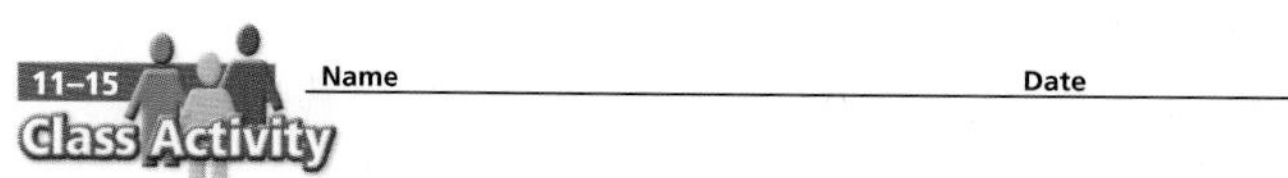

11–15 Class Activity

Name ______________________ Date ____________

▶ Add, Compare, and Subtract Fractions

Add, compare, and subtract each pair of fractions.

Add	Compare	Subtract
30. $\frac{3}{8} + \frac{5}{8} = \frac{8}{8}$	$\frac{3}{8} < \frac{5}{8}$	$\frac{5}{8} - \frac{3}{8} = \frac{2}{8}$
31. $\frac{1}{4} + \frac{1}{3} = \frac{7}{12}$ $\frac{3}{12} + \frac{4}{12} = \frac{7}{12}$	$\frac{1}{4} < \frac{1}{3}$	$\frac{1}{3} - \frac{1}{4} =$ $\frac{4}{12} - \frac{3}{12} = \frac{1}{12}$
32. $\frac{1}{3} + \frac{1}{2} = \frac{5}{6}$ $\frac{2}{6} + \frac{3}{6} = \frac{5}{6}$	$\frac{1}{3} < \frac{1}{2}$	$\frac{1}{2} - \frac{1}{3} =$ $\frac{3}{6} - \frac{2}{6} = \frac{1}{6}$
33. $\frac{5}{6} + \frac{1}{3}$ $\frac{7}{6}$ $\frac{5}{6} + \frac{2}{6} = \frac{7}{6}$	$\frac{5}{6} < \frac{1}{3}$	$\frac{5}{6} - \frac{1}{3} =$ $\frac{5}{6} - \frac{2}{6} = \frac{3}{6}$
34. $\frac{1}{2} + \frac{2}{4} = 1$ $\frac{2}{4} + \frac{2}{4} = \frac{4}{4}$ or 1	$\frac{1}{2} = \frac{2}{4}$	$\frac{1}{2} - \frac{2}{4} =$ $\frac{2}{4} - \frac{2}{4} = 0$

UNIT 11 LESSON 15 — Compare and Subtract Fractions **437**

Student Activity Book page 437

▶ Add, Compare, and Subtract Fractions WHOLE CLASS

Have students complete exercises 30–34 on Student Book page 437. Complete the first exercise together and then give students time to finish the table. Discuss the results. Remind students that once they rename fractions in the first column of the table, they do not need to do it again for the next two columns.

- Can you subtract before you compare? No Why or why not? Possible answer: You must make sure you know which fraction is greater, so you know which fraction to subtract from.

Activity continued ▶

Alternate Approach

Equivalent Fraction Strips Students may want to use Equivalent Fraction Strips (from Lesson 14) to help complete exercises 30–34. For example, to complete exercise 33, students might use these fraction strips:

$$\frac{5}{6} + \frac{1}{3} = \underline{\qquad}$$

$\frac{1}{6}$	$\frac{1}{6}$	$\frac{1}{6}$	$\frac{1}{6}$	$\frac{1}{6}$
$\frac{1}{3}$				

Here students can visually translate $\frac{1}{3}$ into $\frac{2}{6}$ in order to add. Students can also visualize the comparison. They will see that $\frac{5}{6}$ is greater than $\frac{1}{3}$. If you feel your students need this reinforcement, you will probably want to spend an extra day on this lesson.

English Language Learners

Write $\frac{3}{4} > \frac{1}{4}$ and $\frac{1}{4} < \frac{3}{4}$ on the board. Make sure students can read the expressions. Point to $\frac{3}{4} > \frac{1}{4}$.

- **Beginning** Say: **$\frac{3}{4}$ is *greater than* $\frac{1}{4}$.** Have students repeat. Point and say: **Does the symbol point to the smaller fraction?** yes Continue with *less than*.
- **Intermediate** Ask: **Is $\frac{3}{4}$ *greater* or *less than* $\frac{1}{4}$?** greater than Continue with *less than*.
- **Advanced** Have students read the expressions aloud and tell about where the symbols point.

Ongoing Assessment

Ask students the following questions:

- ► Can you subtract $\frac{1}{3} - \frac{1}{5}$ without renaming? No
- ► How would you rename $\frac{1}{3}$ and $\frac{1}{5}$? Multiply $\frac{1}{3}$ by $\frac{5}{5}$ and $\frac{1}{5}$ by $\frac{3}{3}$ to get $\frac{5}{15}$ and $\frac{3}{15}$
- ► Do you change the value of a fraction when you rename it? No

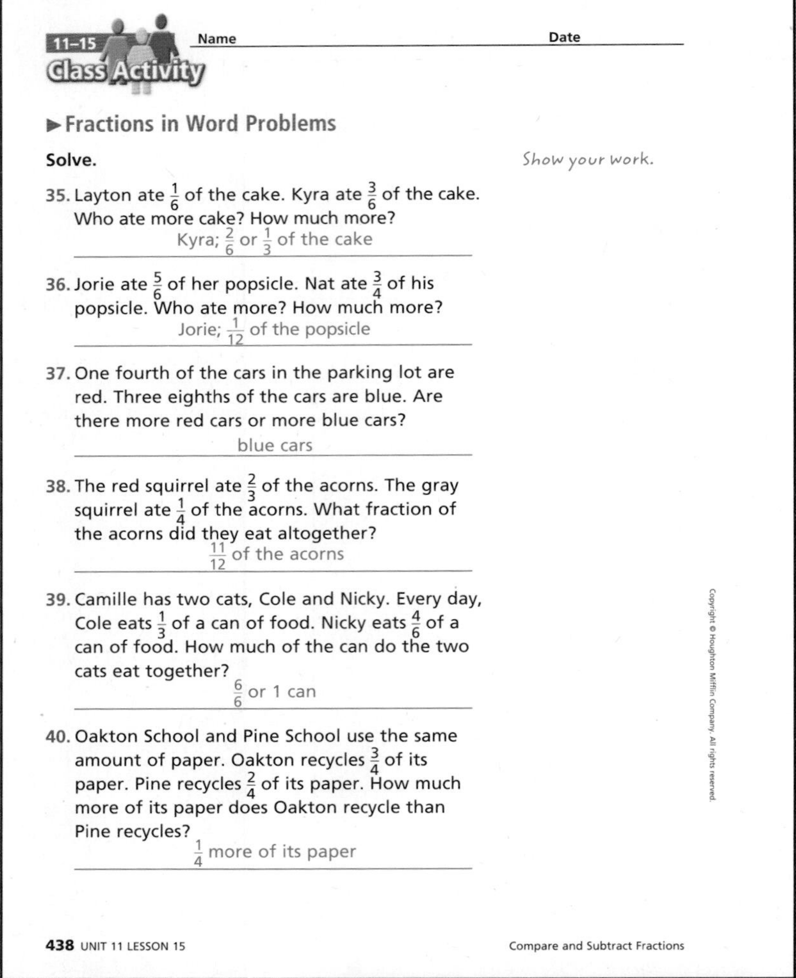

11–15 Class Activity Name Date

► Fractions in Word Problems

Solve. *Show your work.*

35. Layton ate $\frac{1}{6}$ of the cake. Kyra ate $\frac{3}{6}$ of the cake. Who ate more cake? How much more? Kyra; $\frac{2}{6}$ or $\frac{1}{3}$ of the cake

36. Jorie ate $\frac{5}{6}$ of her popsicle. Nat ate $\frac{3}{4}$ of his popsicle. Who ate more? How much more? Jorie; $\frac{1}{12}$ of the popsicle

37. One fourth of the cars in the parking lot are red. Three eighths of the cars are blue. Are there more red cars or more blue cars? blue cars

38. The red squirrel ate $\frac{2}{3}$ of the acorns. The gray squirrel ate $\frac{1}{4}$ of the acorns. What fraction of the acorns did they eat altogether? $\frac{11}{12}$ of the acorns

39. Camille has two cats, Cole and Nicky. Every day, Cole eats $\frac{1}{3}$ of a can of food. Nicky eats $\frac{4}{6}$ of a can of food. How much of the can do the two cats eat together? $\frac{6}{6}$ or 1 can

40. Oakton School and Pine School use the same amount of paper. Oakton recycles $\frac{3}{4}$ of its paper. Pine recycles $\frac{2}{4}$ of its paper. How much more of its paper does Oakton recycle than Pine recycles? $\frac{1}{4}$ more of its paper

438 UNIT 11 LESSON 15 Compare and Subtract Fractions

Student Activity Book page 438

► Fractions in Word Problems WHOLE CLASS

Math Talk Use the **Solve and Discuss** structure to work through Student Book page 438. Ask students to explain how they found the equivalent fractions in each problem. You may find that students draw a picture to help write equivalent fractions or continue to use Fraction Strips. Some discussion questions you might ask include:

- For which problems do you have to rename only one fraction? 37, 39
- For which problems do you not have to rename fractions? 35, 40
- In problem 38, by what number did you multiply the numerator and denominator of $\frac{2}{3}$? Possible answer: I multiplied both by 4, to rename $\frac{2}{3}$ as twelfths. Why? I did that because $\frac{1}{4}$ can also be renamed as twelfths.

Teaching Note

Watch For! Some students may continue to add and subtract numerators and denominators. If this is the case, review Student Activity Book page 461, exercises 1 and 2. Make sure students are clear that the denominator is the bottom number, and that it does not change when adding and subtracting.

2 Going Further

Differentiated Instruction

Intervention

Activity Card 11-15

Build a Whole Activity Card 11-15 ●

Work: In pairs

Use:

- 2 copies of TRB M130 (Fraction Circle Model)
- Math Journal
- Colored pencils

1. **Work Together** Choose one fraction circle piece to begin making a fraction circle. Then find one or more different fraction pieces to complete the circle. Copy the circle into your Math Journal, shading each piece to show different units.

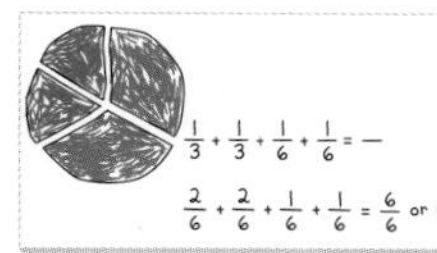

2. Write an addition sentence to describe the circle. Rename the fractions in the addition sentence so the denominators are the same.
3. **Discuss** What strategy can you use to choose a denominator for the addition sentence you write?

Unit 11, Lesson 15

Activity Note Be sure that students understand that the activity requires using at least two different unit fractions to complete the circle.

Math Writing Prompt

Explain Your Thinking Explain how you would subtract $\frac{1}{4}$ from $\frac{1}{2}$.

Software Support

Warm Up 20.14

On Level

Activity Card 11-15

Mixed Up Word Problems Activity Card 11-15 ▲

Work: In pairs

Use:

- Sentence strips

1. **Work Together** Use each sentence strip below to make a word problem that you can solve.

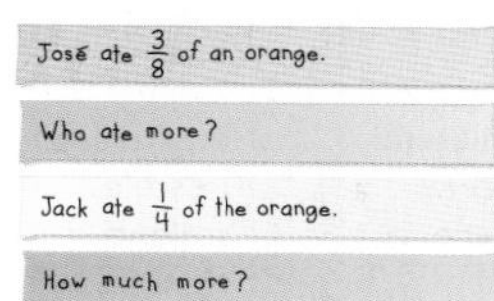

2. Reorganize the strips and solve the problem. Write an equation to show your work.
3. **On Your Own** Write a fraction word problem. Make sentence strips to exchange with your partner. Solve the problem. Exchange again to check your partner's results.

Unit 11, Lesson 15

Activity Note Students should use fractions with different denominators in their word problems and ask questions that require comparison, as in the given model.

Math Writing Prompt

Compare How is adding fractions similar to subtracting fractions? How is it different?

Software Support

Fraction Action: Fraction Flare Up, Level J

Challenge

Activity Card 11-15

Addition and Subtraction Paths Activity Card 11-15 ■

Work: In pairs

Use:

- MathBoard materials

1. Copy the path below on a sheet of paper. Work together to find the missing operation signs to make the path correct. Use the symbols for addition or subtraction.

$\frac{1}{2}$ + ☐ = $\frac{5}{8}$; $\frac{1}{4}$ − $\frac{1}{8}$

$\frac{3}{4}$ − ☐ = $\frac{9}{8}$; $\frac{1}{8}$ + $\frac{1}{2}$

2. **On Your Own** Make another fraction path and exchange with your partner to solve. Exchange again to check your partner's work.
3. **Discuss** What strategies did you use to choose the missing operations?

Unit 11, Lesson 15

Activity Note Students should realize that rewriting the fractions to have a common denominator will make it easier to choose the correct operations.

Math Writing Prompt

Explain Your Thinking Kyle thinks that $\frac{1}{2}$ is less than $\frac{1}{4}$ because 2 is less than 4. Is this correct? Explain.

Software Support

Course II: Module 2: Unit 3: Fractional Parts

Homework and Spiral Review

11–15 Homework Goal: Additional Practice

✓ Include students' completed Homework page as part of their portfolios.

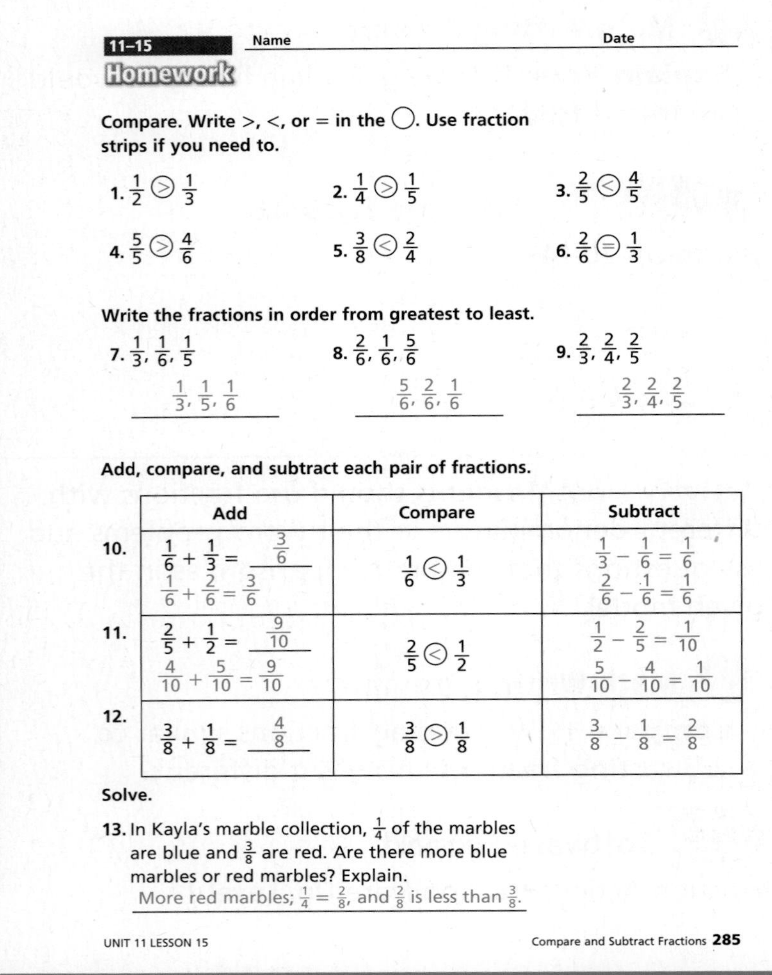

11–15 Homework Name ____ Date ____

Compare. Write >, <, or = in the ◯. Use fraction strips if you need to.

1. $\frac{1}{2} > \frac{1}{3}$
2. $\frac{1}{4} > \frac{1}{5}$
3. $\frac{2}{5} < \frac{4}{5}$
4. $\frac{5}{5} > \frac{4}{6}$
5. $\frac{3}{8} < \frac{2}{4}$
6. $\frac{2}{6} = \frac{1}{3}$

Write the fractions in order from greatest to least.

7. $\frac{1}{3}, \frac{1}{6}, \frac{1}{5}$ — $\frac{1}{3}, \frac{1}{5}, \frac{1}{6}$
8. $\frac{2}{6}, \frac{1}{6}, \frac{5}{6}$ — $\frac{5}{6}, \frac{2}{6}, \frac{1}{6}$
9. $\frac{2}{3}, \frac{2}{4}, \frac{2}{5}$ — $\frac{2}{3}, \frac{2}{4}, \frac{2}{5}$

Add, compare, and subtract each pair of fractions.

	Add	Compare	Subtract
10.	$\frac{1}{6} + \frac{1}{3} = \frac{3}{6}$; $\frac{1}{6} + \frac{2}{6} = \frac{3}{6}$	$\frac{1}{6} < \frac{1}{3}$	$\frac{1}{3} - \frac{1}{6} = \frac{1}{6}$; $\frac{2}{6} - \frac{1}{6} = \frac{1}{6}$
11.	$\frac{2}{5} + \frac{1}{2} = \frac{9}{10}$; $\frac{4}{10} + \frac{5}{10} = \frac{9}{10}$	$\frac{2}{5} < \frac{1}{2}$	$\frac{1}{2} - \frac{2}{5} = \frac{1}{10}$; $\frac{5}{10} - \frac{4}{10} = \frac{1}{10}$
12.	$\frac{3}{8} + \frac{1}{8} = \frac{4}{8}$	$\frac{3}{8} > \frac{1}{8}$	$\frac{3}{8} - \frac{1}{8} = \frac{2}{8}$

Solve.

13. In Kayla's marble collection, $\frac{1}{4}$ of the marbles are blue and $\frac{3}{8}$ are red. Are there more blue marbles or red marbles? Explain.
More red marbles; $\frac{1}{4} = \frac{2}{8}$, and $\frac{2}{8}$ is less than $\frac{3}{8}$.

UNIT 11 LESSON 15 Compare and Subtract Fractions 285

Homework and Remembering page 285

11–15 Remembering Goal: Spiral Review

This Remembering page would be appropriate anytime after today's lesson.

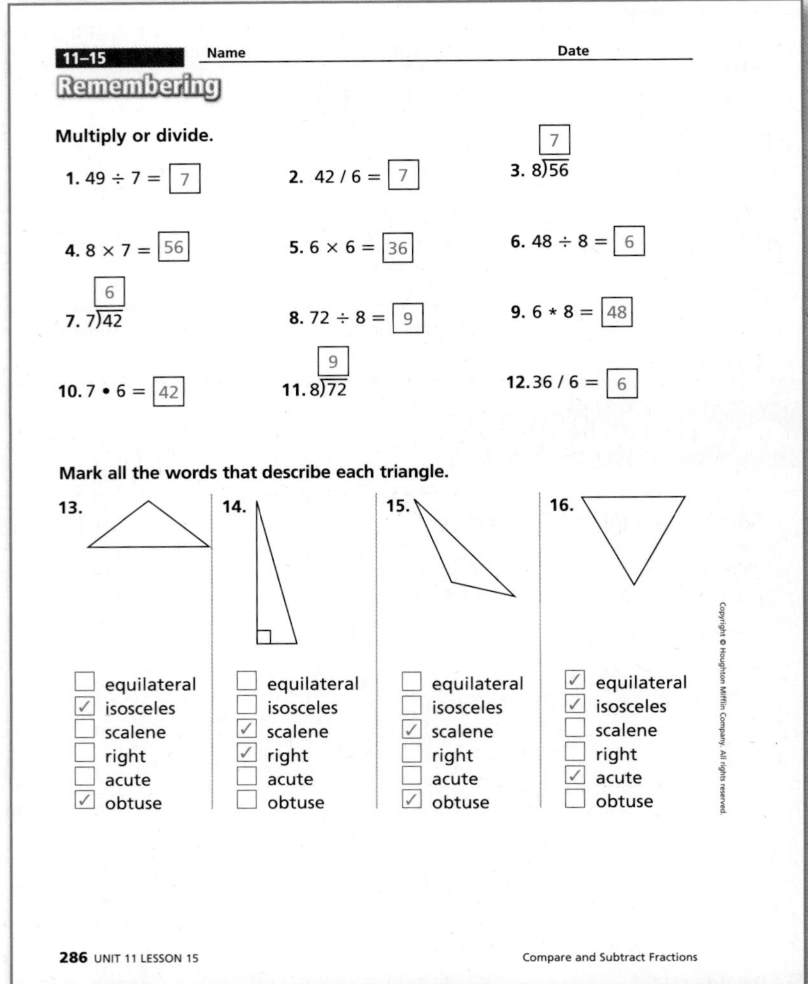

11–15 Remembering Name ____ Date ____

Multiply or divide.

1. 49 ÷ 7 = 7
2. 42 / 6 = 7
3. 8)56 → 7
4. 8 × 7 = 56
5. 6 × 6 = 36
6. 48 ÷ 8 = 6
7. 7)42 → 6
8. 72 ÷ 8 = 9
9. 6 * 8 = 48
10. 7 • 6 = 42
11. 8)72 → 9
12. 36 / 6 = 6

Mark all the words that describe each triangle.

13. ☐ equilateral ☑ isosceles ☐ scalene ☐ right ☐ acute ☑ obtuse

14. ☐ equilateral ☐ isosceles ☑ scalene ☑ right ☐ acute ☐ obtuse

15. ☐ equilateral ☐ isosceles ☑ scalene ☐ right ☐ acute ☑ obtuse

16. ☑ equilateral ☑ isosceles ☐ scalene ☐ right ☑ acute ☐ obtuse

286 UNIT 11 LESSON 15 Compare and Subtract Fractions

Homework and Remembering page 286

Home or School Activity

Multicultural Connection

Egyptian Fractions Explain to students that Early Egyptians developed and used a system for fractions. Display the chart on the right and have students practice writing the fractions. Have students use the symbols to write addition or subtraction exercises for others to solve. If time allows, challenge students to create their own fractional symbols.

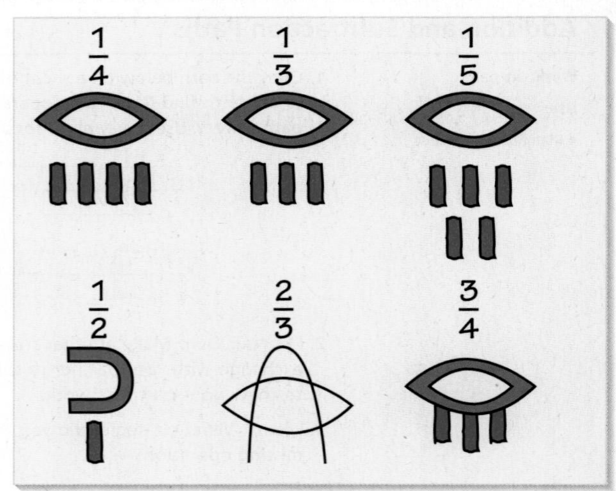

Whole Numbers and Fractions on a Number Line

Lesson Objectives

- **Locate points on a number line.**
- **Add and subtract fractions on a number line.**
- **Compare fractions on a number line.**

Vocabulary

improper fraction
decimal

The Day at a Glance

Today's Goals	Materials	
1 Teaching the Lesson **A1:** Locate numbers on a number line. **A2:** Compare fractions on a number line. **A3:** Add and subtract fractions on a number line. **2 Going Further** ▶ Differentiated Instruction **3 Homework and Spiral Review**	**Lesson Activities** Student Activity Book pp. 439–442 or Student Hardcover Book pp. 439–442 and Activity Workbook pp. 208–210 (includes Special Formats) Homework and Remembering pp. 287–288 Transparency of Student Activity Book pp. 441–442 and overhead projector (optional) *Piece = Part = Portion: Fractions = Decimals = Percents by Scott Gifford* (Tricycle Press, 2003)	**Going Further** Activity Cards 11-16 Blank paper Equivalent Fraction Strips (from Student Activity Book p. 430A, Lesson 11-14) Math Journals

Use **Math Talk** *today!*

Keeping Skills Sharp

Quick Practice — 5 MINUTES

Goal: Write equivalence chains.

Equivalence Chains Have a **Student Leader** write a fraction on the board and have volunteers identify the equivalent fractions. (See Unit 11 Lesson 13.)

Daily Routines

Homework Review Set aside time to work with students needing help.

Elapsed Time Linh's lesson starts at 4:00 P.M. It takes 35 minutes to get there. Linh has to stop at the post office, which will take 15 minutes. What is the latest time Linh should leave her house? 3:10 P.M.

Teaching the Lesson

Activity 1

Whole Numbers and Fractions on a Number Line

15 MINUTES

Goal: Identify and locate whole numbers and fractions on a number line.

Materials: Student Activity Book pp. 439–440 or Hardcover Book pp. 439–440 and Activity Workbook p. 208

NCTM Standards:
Number and Operations

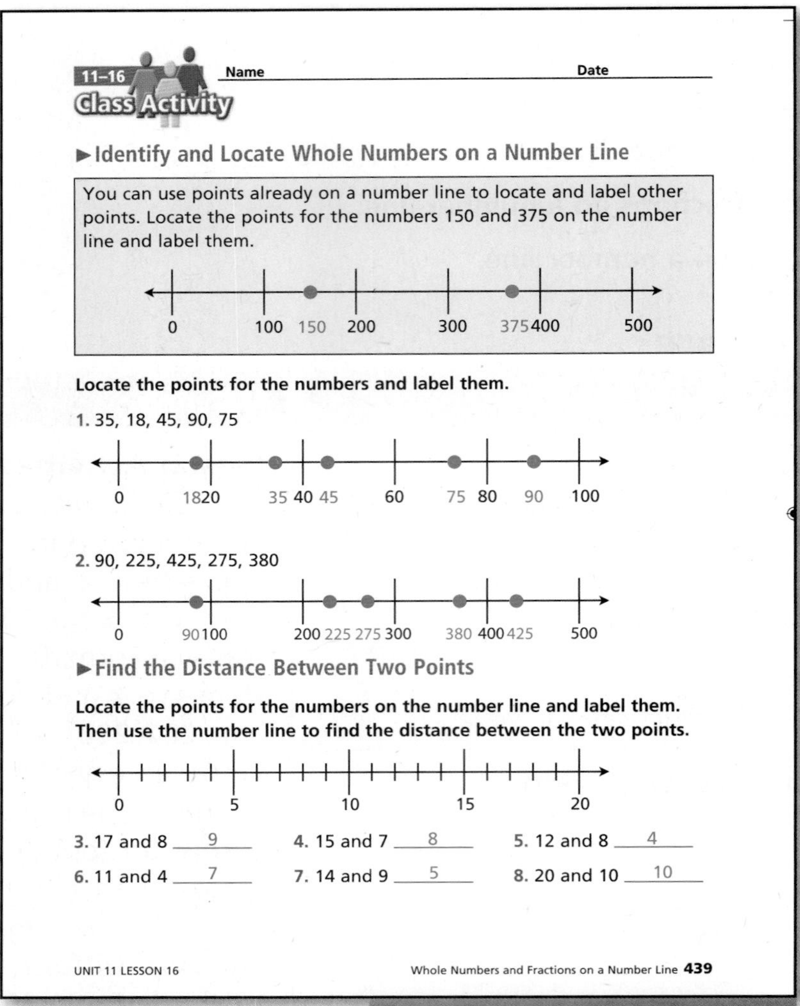

11–16 Class Activity

Name Date

▶ Identify and Locate Whole Numbers on a Number Line

You can use points already on a number line to locate and label other points. Locate the points for the numbers 150 and 375 on the number line and label them.

0 100 150 200 300 375 400 500

Locate the points for the numbers and label them.

1. 35, 18, 45, 90, 75

0 18 20 35 40 45 60 75 80 90 100

2. 90, 225, 425, 275, 380

0 90 100 200 225 275 300 380 400 425 500

▶ Find the Distance Between Two Points

Locate the points for the numbers on the number line and label them. Then use the number line to find the distance between the two points.

0 5 10 15 20

3. 17 and 8 9
4. 15 and 7 8
5. 12 and 8 4
6. 11 and 4 7
7. 14 and 9 5
8. 20 and 10 10

UNIT 11 LESSON 16 Whole Numbers and Fractions on a Number Line 439

Student Activity Book page 439

▶ Identify and Locate Whole Numbers on a Number Line WHOLE CLASS

Draw the number line on the board and review with students how to identify and locate these numbers on it: 2 ,4, 7, and 9.

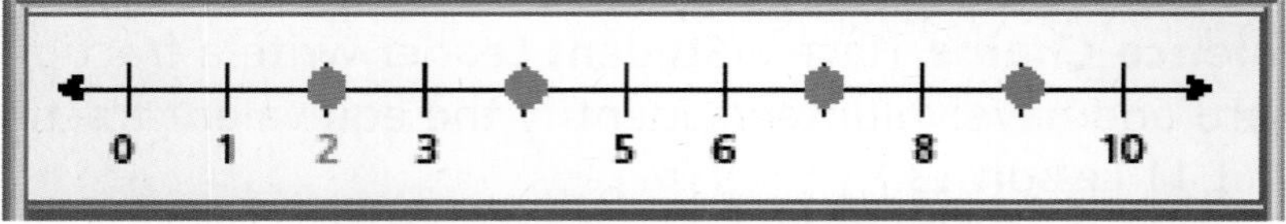

Then have them complete exercises 1–2 on Student Book page 439.

▶ Find the Distance Between Two Points WHOLE CLASS

Review with students how to find the difference between two points on a number line. (By counting the spaces between the points or by subtracting the numbers.)

Then have students complete exercises 3–6 on Student Book page 439.

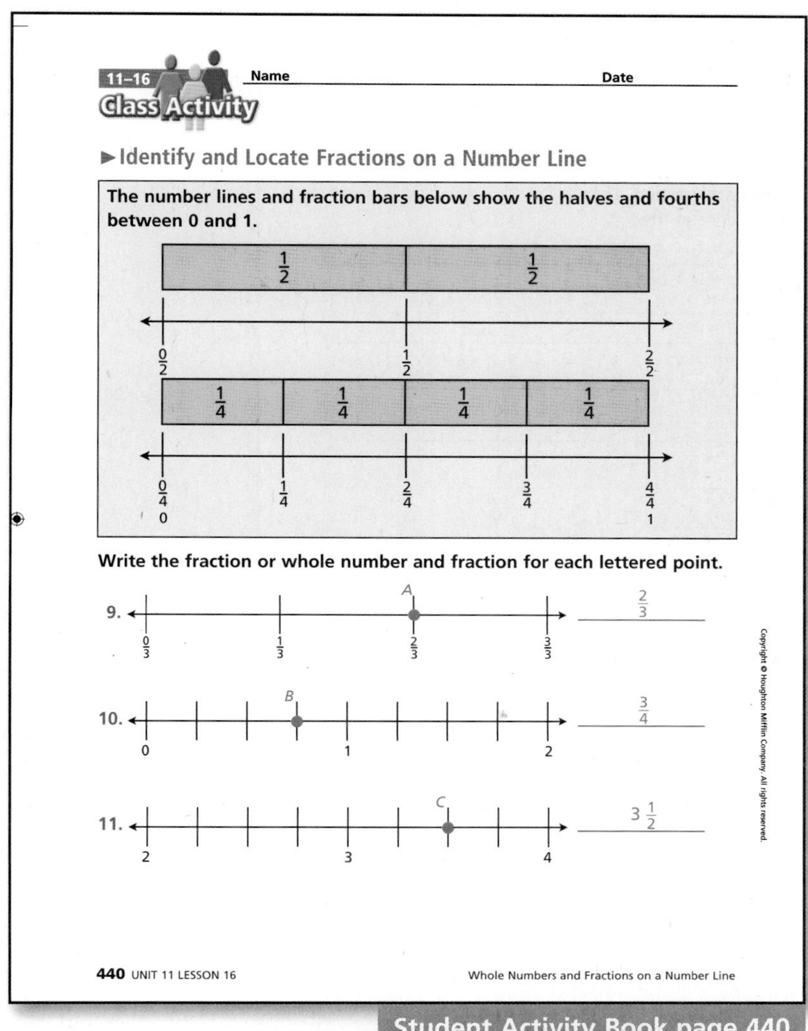

Student Activity Book page 440

▶ Identify and Locate Fractions on a Number Line

WHOLE CLASS

Have students look at the number line and fraction bars on the top of Student Book page 440. Discuss the similarities and differences between the number line and fraction bars.

Then have students work together as a class to identify each point on the number lines. Point out in exercises 10 and 11 that the fractional relationships that occur between 1 and 2, 2 and 3, and 3 and 4 are the same as the relationships that occur between 0 and 1. To help students identify the points, help them identify the unit fractions for each tick mark on the number line.

Teaching Note

Math Background Exercises 7 and 8 go beyond one whole, so the concept of mixed numbers is introduced. Formal lessons and instruction on mixed numbers occur in subsequent lessons.

1 Teaching the Lesson

Activity 2

Use a Number Line to Compare Fractions

15 MINUTES

Goal: Compare fractions on a number line.

Materials: Student Activity Book or Hardcover Book p. 441 and Activity Workbook p. 209, transparency of Student Book page 441 and overhead projector (optional)

NCTM Standards:
Number and Operations
Communication
Representation

Differentiated Instruction

Extra Help You may need to review the symbols for greater than and less than. Remind students that the sign always points to the lesser number.

$\frac{1}{3} < \frac{1}{2}$ is less than

$\frac{1}{2} > \frac{1}{3}$ is greater than

Teaching Note

Benchmarks and Comparing Fractions You may wish to introduce the benchmarks 0, $\frac{1}{2}$, and 1. Draw this number line on the board.

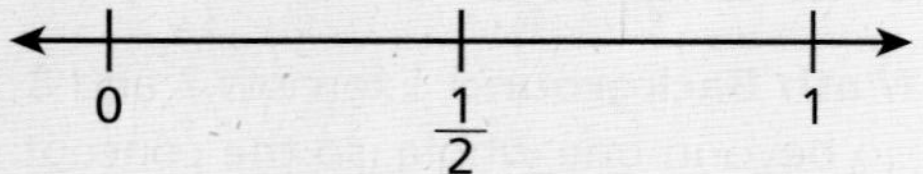

Ask if $\frac{3}{8}$ is closer to 0, 1, or $\frac{1}{2}$. Show that $\frac{4}{8}$ is equal to $\frac{1}{2}$ and $\frac{3}{8}$ is less than $\frac{1}{2}$. Then ask students about $\frac{6}{10}$. Lead them to see that $\frac{5}{10} = \frac{1}{2}$, so $\frac{6}{10}$ is greater than $\frac{1}{2}$. Given that, students can conclude that $\frac{4}{8} < \frac{6}{10}$. Repeat this activity using other pairs of fractions to compare.

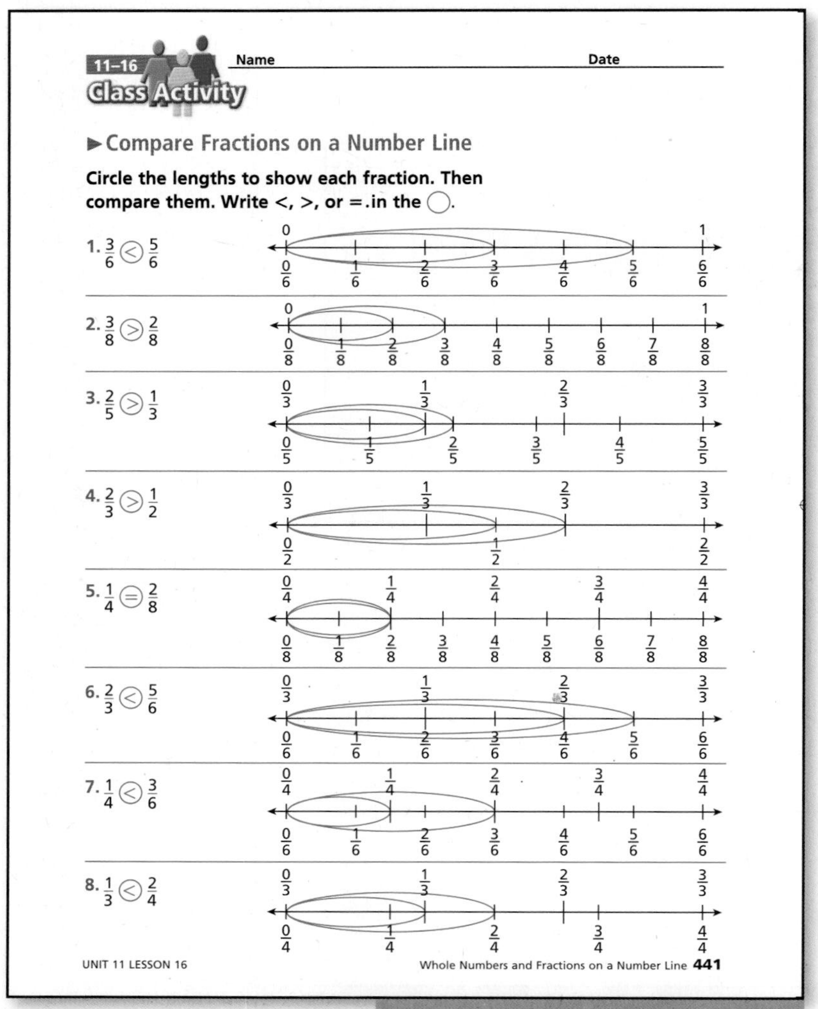

11–16 Class Activity

Name Date

► Compare Fractions on a Number Line

Circle the lengths to show each fraction. Then compare them. Write <, >, or = in the ◯.

1. $\frac{3}{6} < \frac{5}{6}$
2. $\frac{3}{8} > \frac{2}{8}$
3. $\frac{2}{5} > \frac{1}{3}$
4. $\frac{2}{3} > \frac{1}{2}$
5. $\frac{1}{4} = \frac{2}{8}$
6. $\frac{2}{3} < \frac{5}{6}$
7. $\frac{1}{4} < \frac{3}{6}$
8. $\frac{1}{3} < \frac{2}{4}$

UNIT 11 LESSON 16 Whole Numbers and Fractions on a Number Line 441

Student Activity Book page 441

► Compare Fractions on a Number Line WHOLE CLASS

Refer students to exercise 1 on Student Book page 441. You may wish to make an overhead transparency of the page to demonstrate how to locate the fractions on the number line. Tell students that today they will use a number line to compare fractions. Ask students to mark the lengths for $\frac{3}{6}$ and $\frac{5}{6}$ on the number line to represent the fractions they want to compare.

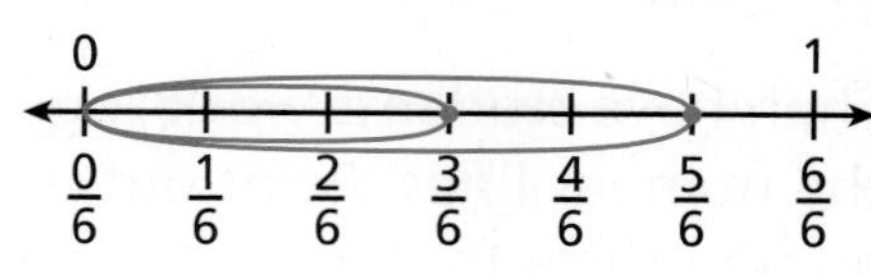

- Which fraction is longer? $\frac{5}{6}$; it has 5 of the $\frac{1}{6}$ lengths.
- Which comparison sign will you write in the circle? less than (<)

Have students use the same steps to complete exercises 2–8.

Activity 3

Use a Number Line to Add and Subtract Fractions

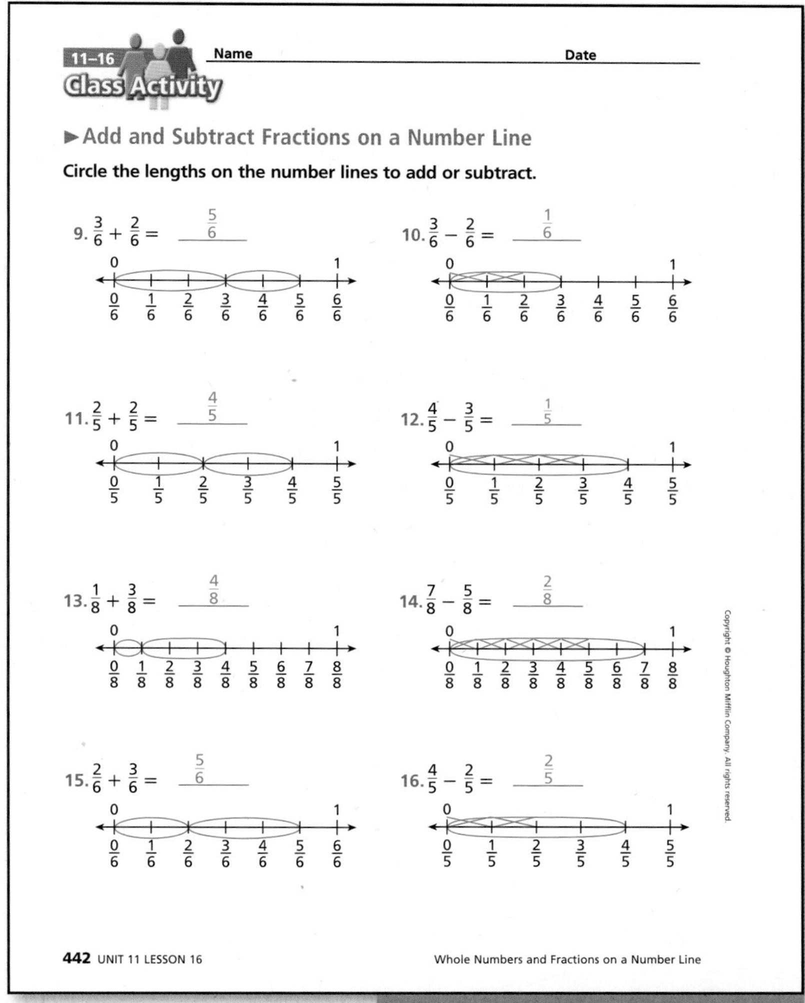

11–16 Class Activity Name ______ Date ______

▶ Add and Subtract Fractions on a Number Line

Circle the lengths on the number lines to add or subtract.

9. $\frac{3}{6} + \frac{2}{6} =$ $\frac{5}{6}$

10. $\frac{3}{6} - \frac{2}{6} =$ $\frac{1}{6}$

11. $\frac{2}{5} + \frac{2}{5} =$ $\frac{4}{5}$

12. $\frac{4}{5} - \frac{3}{5} =$ $\frac{1}{5}$

13. $\frac{1}{8} + \frac{3}{8} =$ $\frac{4}{8}$

14. $\frac{7}{8} - \frac{5}{8} =$ $\frac{2}{8}$

15. $\frac{2}{6} + \frac{3}{6} =$ $\frac{5}{6}$

16. $\frac{4}{5} - \frac{2}{5} =$ $\frac{2}{5}$

442 UNIT 11 LESSON 16 Whole Numbers and Fractions on a Number Line

Student Activity Book page 442

▶ Add and Subtract Fractions on a Number Line WHOLE CLASS

Have students look at the first number line on Student Book page 442. Elicit solution methods from students. These will involve viewing the fractions as made of unit fractions and adding or subtracting these fraction lengths.

 **15 MINUTES**

Goal: Add and subtract fractions on a number line.

Materials: Student Activity Book or Hardcover Book p. 442 and Activity Workbook p. 210 (includes special format), transparency of Student Book p. 442 and overhead projector (optional)

 **NCTM Standards:**
Number and Operations
Communication
Representation

Class Management

You may wish to make an overhead transparency of the page to demonstrate how to add and subtract fractions on a number line.

English Language Learners

Write *length* on the board. Draw a number line with lengths of $\frac{1}{6}$. Ask: **Is this a *number line*?** yes Point to 1 length.

- **Beginning** Say: **This is 1 *length*. It equals $\frac{1}{6}$.** Have students repeat. Ask: **How many *lengths* are there?** 6 **Are they all equal?** yes
- **Intermediate** Ask: **Is this 1 *length*?** yes **Does it equal $\frac{1}{6}$?** yes Gesture and say: **Each *length* equals __.** $\frac{1}{6}$
- **Advanced** Have students identify the lengths and tell about the number line.

Then have students write the unit fraction involved in the addition or subtraction.

$$\frac{3}{6} + \frac{2}{6} = \square$$

$$\frac{1}{6} + \frac{1}{6} + \frac{1}{6} + \frac{1}{6} + \frac{1}{6} = \frac{5}{6}$$

$$\frac{3}{6} - \frac{2}{6} = \square$$

$$\cancel{\frac{1}{6}} + \cancel{\frac{1}{6}} + \frac{1}{6} = \frac{1}{6}$$

Now direct students to exercises 11 and 12 on Student Book page 442 and elicit methods from students. Encourage them to write the unit fractions involved in the addition and subtraction as well. The following are examples of what students may do.

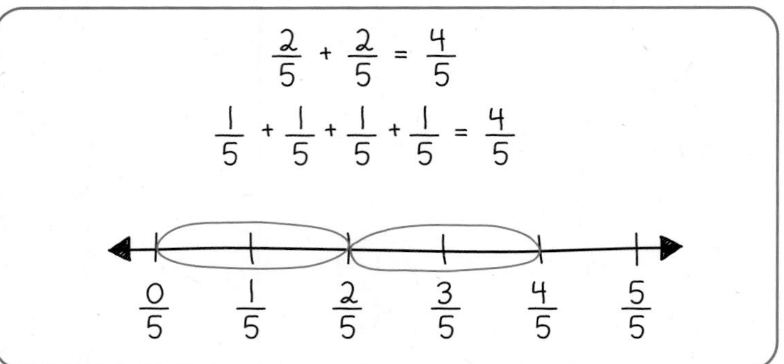

$$\frac{4}{5} - \frac{3}{5} = \frac{1}{5}$$

$$\cancel{\frac{1}{5}} + \cancel{\frac{1}{5}} + \cancel{\frac{1}{5}} + \frac{1}{5} = \frac{1}{5}$$

0/5 1/5 2/5 3/5 4/5 5/5

Differentiated Instruction

Intervention — Activity Card 11-16

Fold a Number Line

Activity Card 11-16

Work: On your own

Use:

- Blank paper

1. Fold a piece of paper in half.
2. Open the paper and draw a number line. Mark 0 and 1. Use the folded line to mark $\frac{1}{2}$ on the number line.
3. Repeat the process for thirds and fourths. Mark $\frac{1}{3}$, $\frac{2}{3}$, and $\frac{1}{4}$, $\frac{2}{4}$, and $\frac{3}{4}$.

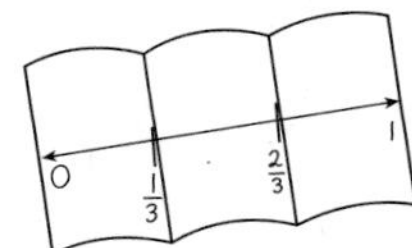

4. **Analyze** Is $\frac{2}{3}$ greater than or less than $\frac{2}{4}$? How do you know? $\frac{2}{3}$ is closer to 1 on the number line.

Unit 11, Lesson 16

Activity Note When students fold fourths, encourage them to fold the paper in half first and then fold each half in half.

Math Writing Prompt

Compare and Contrast How is a number line for fourths different than a number line for thirds? How is it the same?

Software Support

Warm Up 9.09

On Level — Activity Card 11-16

Model Number Lines

Activity Card 11-16

Work: On your own

Use:

- Equivalent Fraction Strips (from Student Activity Book 430 A, Lesson 11–14)

1. Place four $\frac{1}{4}$ fraction bars side-by-side.
2. Draw and label a number line with fourths above or below it.
3. Repeat for other fractions.

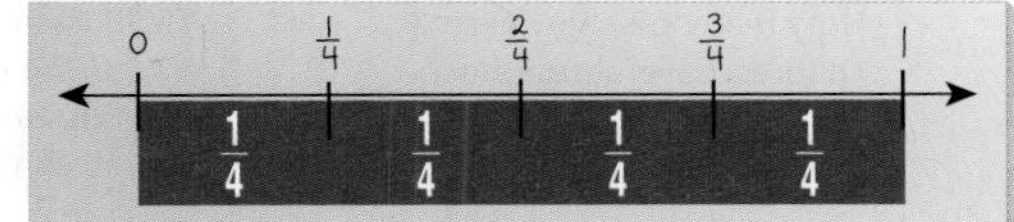

Unit 11, Lesson 16

Activity Note Make sure students line up the fraction bars right next to each other in order to create their number line.

Math Writing Prompt

Math Connection How can you use a number line to show that $\frac{2}{4}$ and $\frac{1}{4}$ are equivalent? Explain your thinking.

Software Support

Fraction Action: Number Line Mine, Level E

Challenge — Activity Card 11-16

Sums of 1

Activity Card 11-16

Work: In pairs

Use:

- Blank paper

Decide:

Who will be Student 1 and Student 2 for the first round.

1. **Student 1:** Write an addition equation with missing addends, such as $\frac{3}{4}$ + _____ = 1.
2. **Student 2:** Try and solve your partner's equation.

$\frac{3}{4}$ + _______ = 1

3. Switch roles and repeat the steps.

Unit 11, Lesson 16

Activity Note Encourage students to use number lines to check that their equations are correct.

Math Writing Prompt

Extend How do you think you can use a number line to compare two fractions?

DESTINATION Math® **Software Support**

Course II: Module 2: Unit 3: Fractional Parts

3 Homework and Spiral Review

Goal: Additional Practice

✓ Include students' completed Homework page as part of their portfolios.

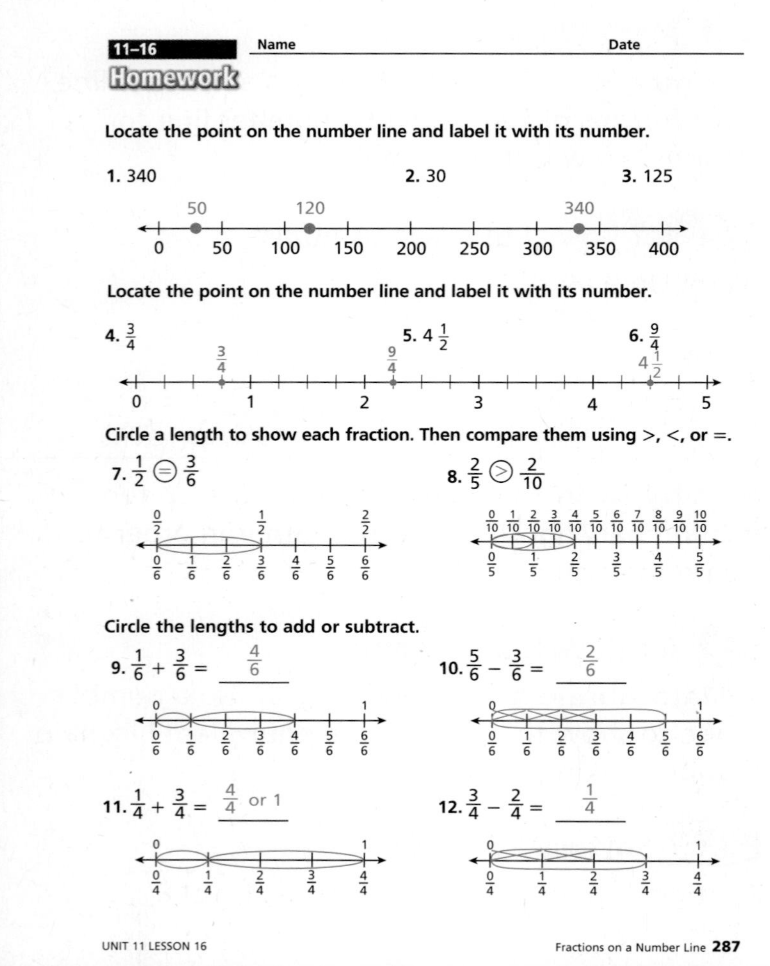

11–16 Homework Name Date

Locate the point on the number line and label it with its number.

1. 340 2. 30 3. 125

(Number line 0 to 400 in steps of 50, with points labeled 50, 120, 340)

Locate the point on the number line and label it with its number.

4. $\frac{3}{4}$ 5. $4\frac{1}{2}$ 6. $\frac{9}{4}$

(Number line 0 to 5, with points labeled $\frac{3}{4}$, $\frac{9}{4}$, $4\frac{1}{2}$)

Circle a length to show each fraction. Then compare them using >, <, or =.

7. $\frac{1}{2}$ = $\frac{3}{6}$ 8. $\frac{2}{5}$ > $\frac{2}{10}$

Circle the lengths to add or subtract.

9. $\frac{1}{6} + \frac{3}{6} = \frac{4}{6}$ 10. $\frac{5}{6} - \frac{3}{6} = \frac{2}{6}$

11. $\frac{1}{4} + \frac{3}{4} = \frac{4}{4}$ or 1 12. $\frac{3}{4} - \frac{2}{4} = \frac{1}{4}$

UNIT 11 LESSON 16 Fractions on a Number Line 287

Homework and Remembering page 287

Goal: Spiral Review

This Remembering page would be appropriate anytime after today's lesson.

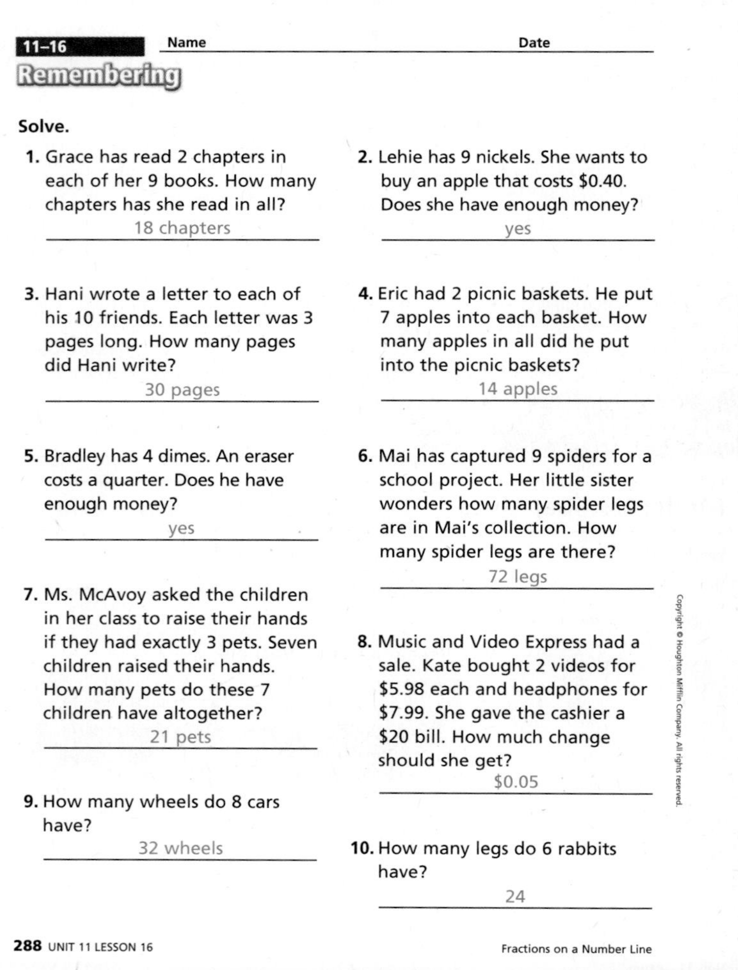

11–16 Remembering Name Date

Solve.

1. Grace has read 2 chapters in each of her 9 books. How many chapters has she read in all? 18 chapters
2. Lehie has 9 nickels. She wants to buy an apple that costs $0.40. Does she have enough money? yes
3. Hani wrote a letter to each of his 10 friends. Each letter was 3 pages long. How many pages did Hani write? 30 pages
4. Eric had 2 picnic baskets. He put 7 apples into each basket. How many apples in all did he put into the picnic baskets? 14 apples
5. Bradley has 4 dimes. An eraser costs a quarter. Does he have enough money? yes
6. Mai has captured 9 spiders for a school project. Her little sister wonders how many spider legs are in Mai's collection. How many spider legs are there? 72 legs
7. Ms. McAvoy asked the children in her class to raise their hands if they had exactly 3 pets. Seven children raised their hands. How many pets do these 7 children have altogether? 21 pets
8. Music and Video Express had a sale. Kate bought 2 videos for $5.98 each and headphones for $7.99. She gave the cashier a $20 bill. How much change should she get? $0.05
9. How many wheels do 8 cars have? 32 wheels
10. How many legs do 6 rabbits have? 24

288 UNIT 11 LESSON 16 Fractions on a Number Line

Homework and Remembering page 288

Home or School Activity

Literature Connection

Piece = Part = Portion: Fractions = Decimals = Percents Read aloud Scott Gifford's book about fractions (Tricycle Press, 2003). Then have students list wholes that can be fractured as shown in the book.

Fractions and Decimals

Vocabulary
decimals
tenths
hundredths
decimal point

Lesson Objective

- **Explore related fractions and decimals**

The Day at a Glance

Today's Goals	Materials	
1 Teaching the Lesson **A1:** Observe patterns of related fractions and decimals. **A2:** Write equivalent fractions and decimals. **A3** Write decimals greater than1 and equivalent decimals. **A4** Compare decimals and fractions	**Lesson Activities** Student Activity Book pp. 443–446 or Student Hardcover Book pp. 443–446 and Activity Workbook pp. 211–212 (includes Special Format) Homework and Remembering pp. 289–290 Quick Quiz 4 (Assessment Guide) Tenths and Hundredths Grids (TRB M162)	**Going Further** Activity Cards 11-17 Play money (Pennies 100) 10 × 10 Grid (TRB M43) Crayons or markers Math Journals
2 Going Further ▸ Differentiated Instruction		
3 Homework and Spiral Review		

Keeping Skills Sharp

Quick Practice	Daily Routines	
Goal: Write equivalence chains. **Equivalence Chains** Have a **Student Leader** write a fraction on the board and have volunteers identify the equivalent fractions. (See Unit 11 Lesson 13.)	**Homework Review** Have students discuss the difficulties and errors from their homework. Encourage students to help each other correct these errors.	**Nonroutine Problem** Two tickets cost 40¢ in all. One ticket costs three times as much as the other ticket. How much does each ticket cost? Explain how you found your answer. 40¢ in all: first ticket; 3 times the cost of the first ticket There are 4 equal amounts. So, 40 ÷ 4 = 10; 40¢ − 10¢ = 30¢; The tickets cost 10¢ and 30¢.

1 Teaching the Lesson

Activity 1

Relate Fractions, Decimals, and Money

 **20 MINUTES**

Goal: Observe patterns of related fractions and decimals

Materials: Student Book p. 443

 **NCTM Standards:**
Numbers and Operations
Communication
Representation

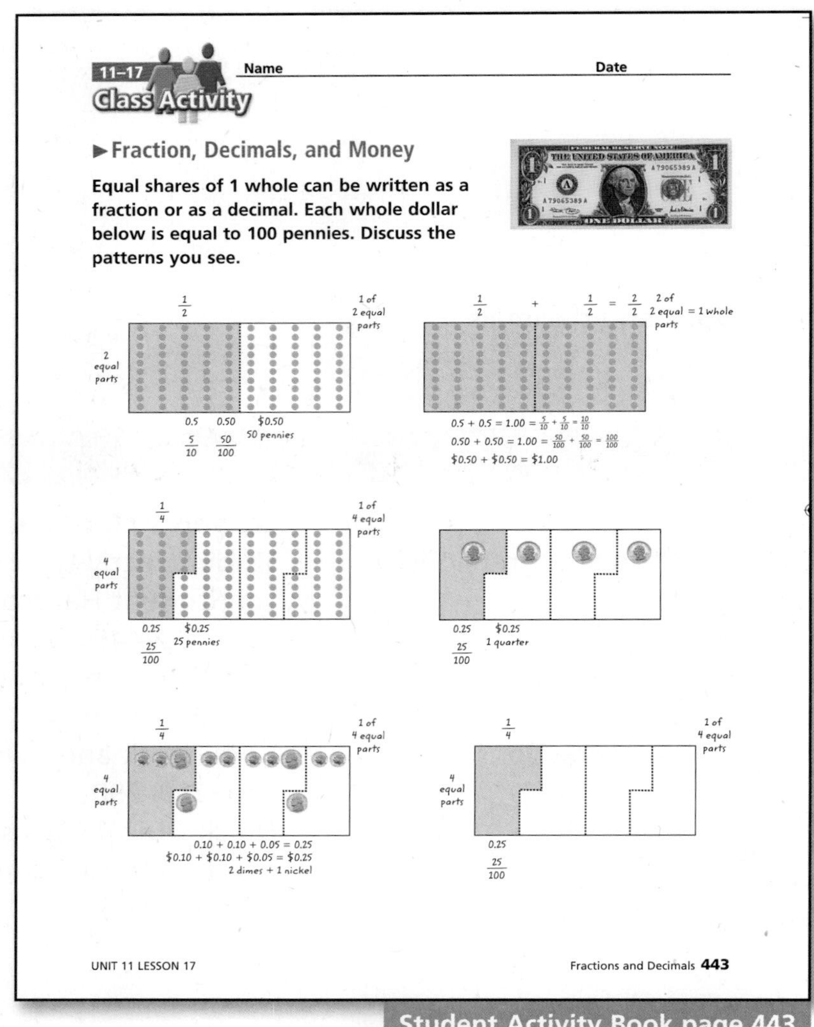

11–17 Class Activity

Name ______ Date ______

▶ Fraction, Decimals, and Money

Equal shares of 1 whole can be written as a fraction or as a decimal. Each whole dollar below is equal to 100 pennies. Discuss the patterns you see.

UNIT 11 LESSON 17 Fractions and Decimals **443**

Student Activity Book page 443

▶ Fractions, Decimals, and Money WHOLE CLASS

Ask For Ideas Give students an opportunity to share what they know about fractions, decimals, and money, and describe how they can relate to each other.

In today's activities, students will use money to discover patterns that relate fractions and decimal numbers.

Invite a volunteer to read aloud the paragraph at the top of Student Activity Book page 443. Then have students focus their attention on the two dollars that are shown as collections of 100 pennies at the top of the page, and discuss any patterns they see. (The goal of the discussion is for students to think of hundredths—whether written as a fraction or as a decimal—as pennies in a dollar and think of tenths as dimes in a dollar, when a dollar is used to represent 1 whole.)

Math Talk Make sure the following points are included in the discussion.

- The whole is one dollar and is made of 100 pennies.
- The whole has been divided into two equal parts because each equal part has 50 pennies.
- The fraction $\frac{1}{2}$ means 1 of 2 equal parts. The bottom number (the denominator) tells how many equal parts have been made, and the top number (the numerator) tells how many of those parts we have taken.
- If we think of the 100 pennies as the whole, we can see that half of the whole is 50 pennies, which is the fraction $\frac{50}{100}$.
- If we think of each column as a dime, the whole is 10 dimes, and half of the whole is 5 dimes, which is the fraction $\frac{5}{10}$.
- We have 1 whole whenever we have a fraction of the form $\frac{n}{n}$ (such as $\frac{2}{2}$, $\frac{10}{10}$, or $\frac{100}{100}$ for example) because we have taken as many unit fractions as we divided the 1 whole into, so we get the 1 whole back again.

Use the example $\frac{1}{2} + \frac{1}{2} = \frac{2}{2}$ to explain what fraction addition really is:

- The bottom number just tells the kind of unit fraction we have (the number of equal parts we made), and the top number tells how many of such unit fractions (equal parts) we put together to make the fraction.

Teaching Note

Common Error Understanding that $0.5 = 0.50$ will be difficult for those students who ignore the decimal numbers and instead view the relationship as one of whole numbers ($5 \neq 50$). Thinking of 0.5 as 5 dimes can help these students see and remember that $0.5 = 0.50$.

Math Talk Now have students look at the next 4 dollars—those that are divided into 4 equal parts—and discuss patterns they see. Be sure the discussion includes these points.

- The whole is one dollar and is made of 100 pennies.
- The whole has been divided into four equal parts because each equal part has 25 pennies.
- The fraction $\frac{1}{4}$ means 1 of 4 equal parts. The bottom number (the denominator) tells how many equal parts have been made, and the top number (the numerator) tells how many of those parts we have taken.
- If we think of the 100 pennies as the whole, we can see that one-fourth of the whole is 25 pennies or 1 quarter, which is the fraction $\frac{25}{100}$.
- Be sure that students discuss both common terms for $\frac{1}{4}$: *one fourth* and *one quarter*. Also point out a way to remember the term *one quarter* is to think that the value of a quarter coin is 25 pennies, or $\frac{25}{100}$.
- If we think of as $\frac{1}{4}$ of a dollar as 25¢ or 2 dimes and 1 nickel, we can see that 20 pennies is replaced by 2 dimes and 5 pennies is replaced by a nickel.
- In the fourth dollar the $\frac{1}{4}$s are blank. What other ways with coins could we represent twenty five hundredths?

Math Talk in Action

Yuri: We could use 1 dime, 2 nickels and 5 pennies. That equals 25¢.

Bethany: How about 1 dime and 3 nickels. That's $\frac{1}{4}$ of a dollar.

Abdi: We could use 5 nickels. That equals 25 pennies.

These are all good ways to help us remember that $\frac{1}{4} = \frac{25}{100} = 0.25 =$ \$0.25 = 25¢.

Ongoing Assessment

- Name a fraction and a decimal to represent 1 penny if the whole is 100 pennies. Explain how you know.
- Name a fraction and a decimal to represent 1 dime if the whole is 10 dimes. Explain how you know.

Activity 2

Practice the Relationships

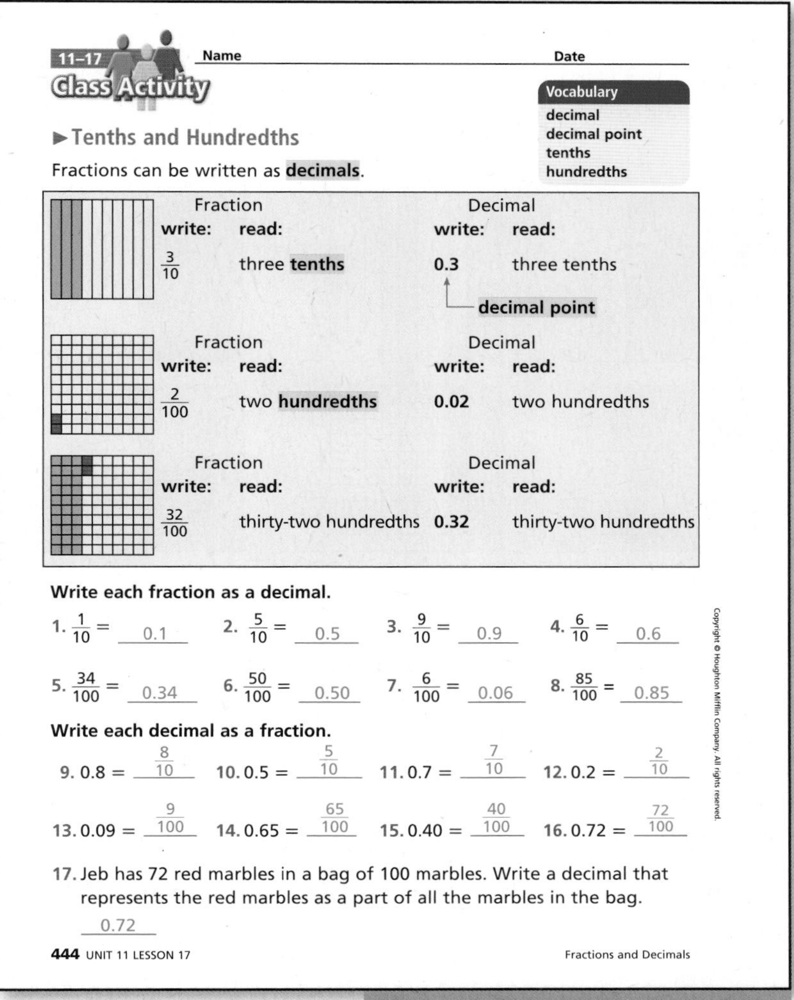

11–17 Class Activity

Name Date

Vocabulary
decimal
decimal point
tenths
hundredths

► Tenths and Hundredths

Fractions can be written as **decimals**.

Fraction write:	read:	Decimal write:	read:
$\frac{3}{10}$	three **tenths**	0.3 (decimal point)	three tenths
$\frac{2}{100}$	two **hundredths**	0.02	two hundredths
$\frac{32}{100}$	thirty-two hundredths	0.32	thirty-two hundredths

Write each fraction as a decimal.

1. $\frac{1}{10}$ = 0.1
2. $\frac{5}{10}$ = 0.5
3. $\frac{9}{10}$ = 0.9
4. $\frac{6}{10}$ = 0.6
5. $\frac{34}{100}$ = 0.34
6. $\frac{50}{100}$ = 0.50
7. $\frac{6}{100}$ = 0.06
8. $\frac{85}{100}$ = 0.85

Write each decimal as a fraction.

9. 0.8 = $\frac{8}{10}$
10. 0.5 = $\frac{5}{10}$
11. 0.7 = $\frac{7}{10}$
12. 0.2 = $\frac{2}{10}$
13. 0.09 = $\frac{9}{100}$
14. 0.65 = $\frac{65}{100}$
15. 0.40 = $\frac{40}{100}$
16. 0.72 = $\frac{72}{100}$
17. Jeb has 72 red marbles in a bag of 100 marbles. Write a decimal that represents the red marbles as a part of all the marbles in the bag. 0.72

444 UNIT 11 LESSON 17 Fractions and Decimals

Student Activity Book page 444

► Tenths and Hundredths WHOLE CLASS

Have students look at the top of Student Book page 444.

- What coins could you use in the place of the columns? dimes
- What coins could you use in place of the small squares? pennies
- What number is shown in the top grid? $\frac{3}{10}$ or 0.3
- Have a volunteer read the fraction and decimal that the top grid represents. Repeat for the models showing hundredths.
- What do you notice about the 3 tenths and 30 hundredths? They are represented by the same amount on the grid. They are equal.

20 MINUTES

Goal: Write equivalent fractions and decimals.

Materials: Student Book p. 444, Tenths and Hundredths Grids (TRB M162)

NCTM Standards:
Number and Operations
Communication
Representation

English Language Learners

Write 0.33 on the board.

- **Beginning** Point to the decimal number. Say: **This is a decimal.** Point to the *decimal point* and say: **This is a decimal point.** Have children repeat.
Intermediate Ask: **Does a decimal always have a decimal point?** yes
Point to the decimal point. Ask: **What is the name of this dot?** decimal point
- **Intermediate and Advanced** Point to the decimal. Ask: **How do you say this decimal?** thirty-three hundredths
Point to the decimal point. Ask: **What is the name of this dot?** decimal point

Teaching Note

Common Error Understanding that 0.1 = 0.10 and 0.2 = 0.20 will be difficult for those students who ignore the decimal numbers and instead view the relationships as whole numbers (1 ≠ 10 and 2 ≠ 20). Thinking of 0.1 as 1 dime can help these students see and remember that 0.1 = 0.10, and thinking of 0.2 as 2 dimes can help them see and remember that 0.2 = 0.20.

Class Management

Students will need the Tenths and Hundredths Grids (TRB M162) they used in this activity for the next activity.

Distribute Tenths and Hundredths Grids (TRB M162) to **Student Pairs.**

In the first set of tenths and hundredths grids, give students decimals such as 0.5 and 0.55 to show the relationships between tenths and hundredths. Have them write the fraction and decimal shown next to their grid.

Example:

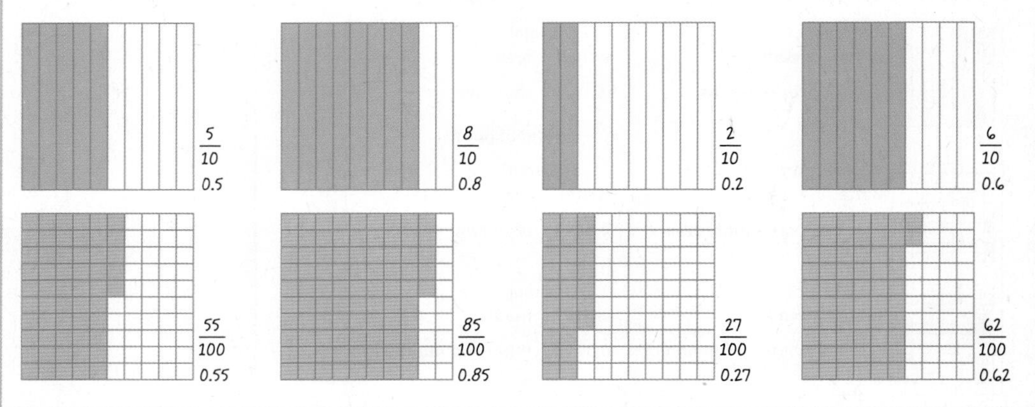

- What relationships do you see between tenths and hundredths? $\frac{5}{10}$ is 50 hundredths, 8 tenths is 80 hundredths and so on.

In the second set of tenths and hundredths grids, have **Student Pairs** take turns shading grids for their partner to write the fractions and decimals represented by the shading.

Tell students they will now practice the relationships without models. Allow students to use grids if needed.

Then have students complete exercises 1–17 on Student Book page 444. Tell students if they have difficulty with problem 17 to think about how they would represent the marbles on a hundredths grid.

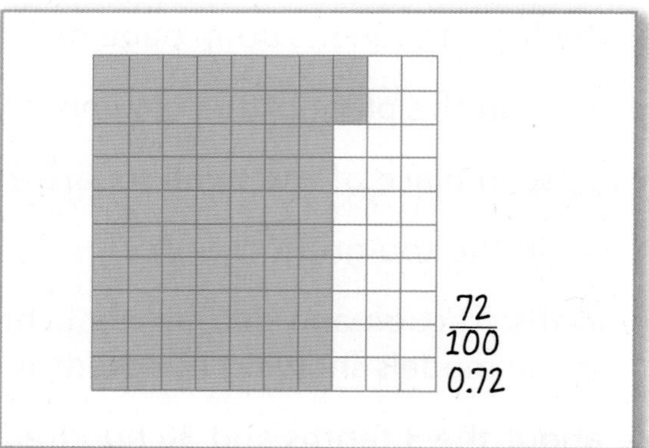

Activity 3

Equivalent Decimals

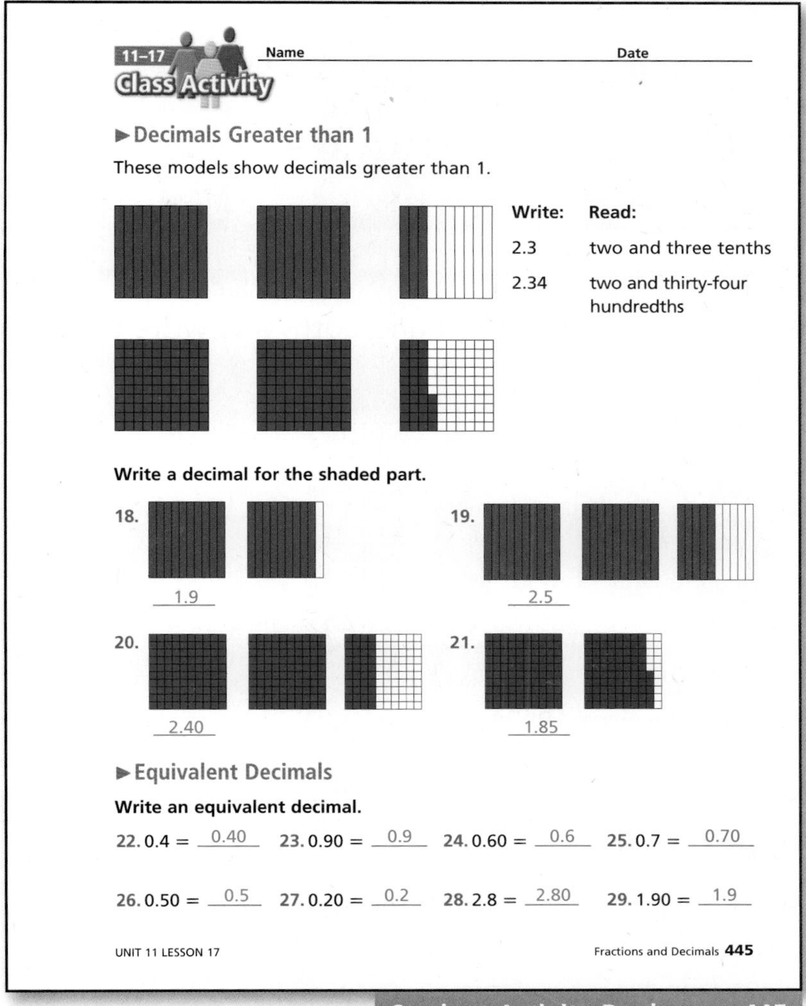

11–17 Class Activity Name ____ Date ____

► Decimals Greater than 1

These models show decimals greater than 1.

Write:	Read:
2.3	two and three tenths
2.34	two and thirty-four hundredths

Write a decimal for the shaded part.

18. 1.9
19. 2.5
20. 2.40
21. 1.85

► Equivalent Decimals

Write an equivalent decimal.

22. 0.4 = 0.40 23. 0.90 = 0.9 24. 0.60 = 0.6 25. 0.7 = 0.70

26. 0.50 = 0.5 27. 0.20 = 0.2 28. 2.8 = 2.80 29. 1.90 = 1.9

UNIT 11 LESSON 17 Fractions and Decimals 445

Student Activity Book page 445

Goal: Write equivalent decimals including decimals greater than 1.

Materials: Student Book p. 445, Tenths and Hundredths Grids (TRB M162) from Activity 2

NCTM Standards:
Number and Operations
Communication
Representation

► Decimals Greater than 1 WHOLE CLASS

Ask for Ideas How could you represent a decimal greater than 1 such as one and five tenths on a grid? Shade 1 whole grid and shade 5 tenths of the next whole grid.

Direct students to the grids on the top of Student Book page 445.

- What decimals do the grids show? Two and three tenths and two and thirty-four hundredths.
- Which decimal is greater, 2.3 or 2.34? 2.34
- How do you know? Because two and thirty-four hundredths is four hundredth more than two and three tenths.

Activity continued ►

On the third set of grids on the Tenths and Hundredths Grids (TRB M162) from the last activity, have **Student Pairs** shade 3 whole squares of tenths and 4 tenths and write the decimal it represents.

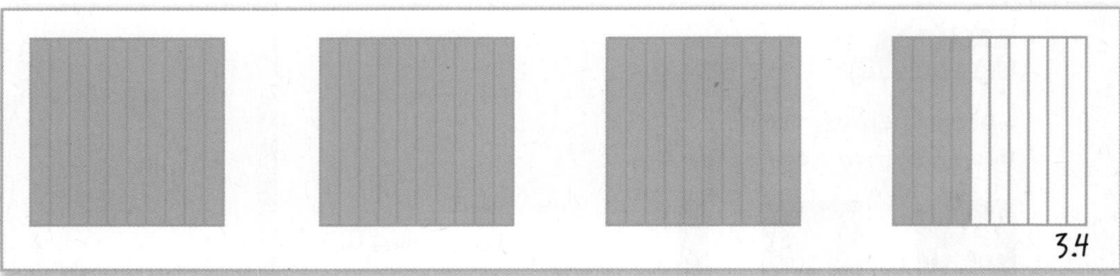

In the next row have them show 2 and 35 hundredths and write the decimal.

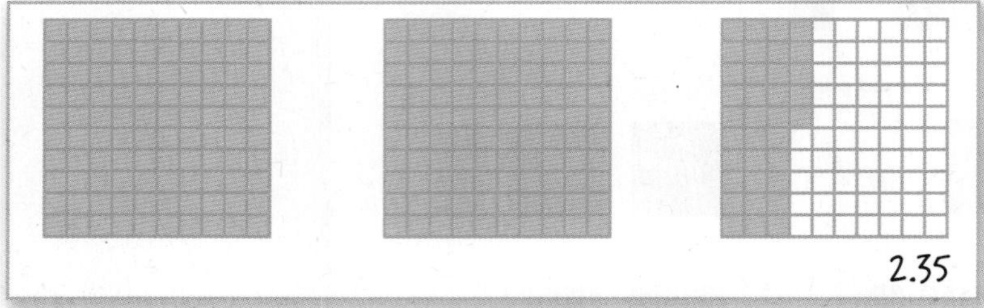

Have students complete exercises 18–21.

▶ Equivalent Decimals

On the last set of grids have students represent equivalent tenths and hundredths.

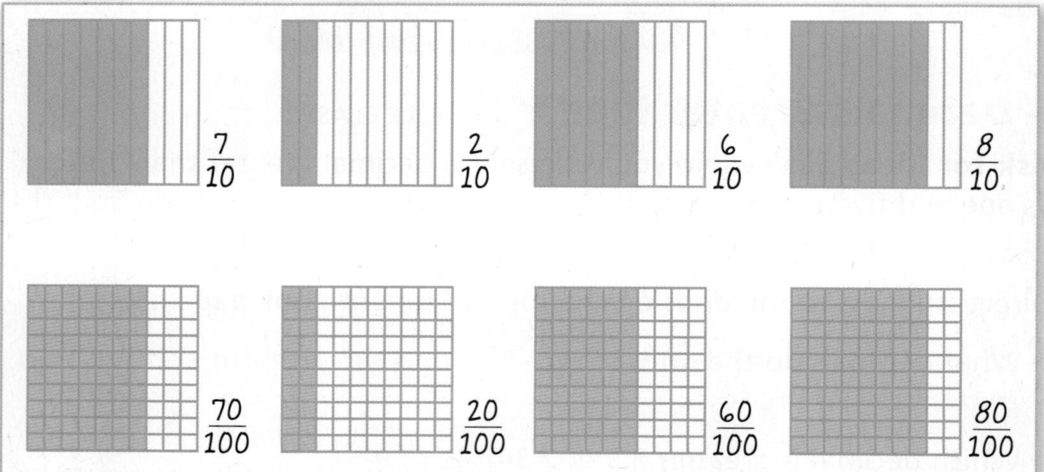

Then have students complete exercises 22–29.

Activity 4

Compare Fractions and Decimals

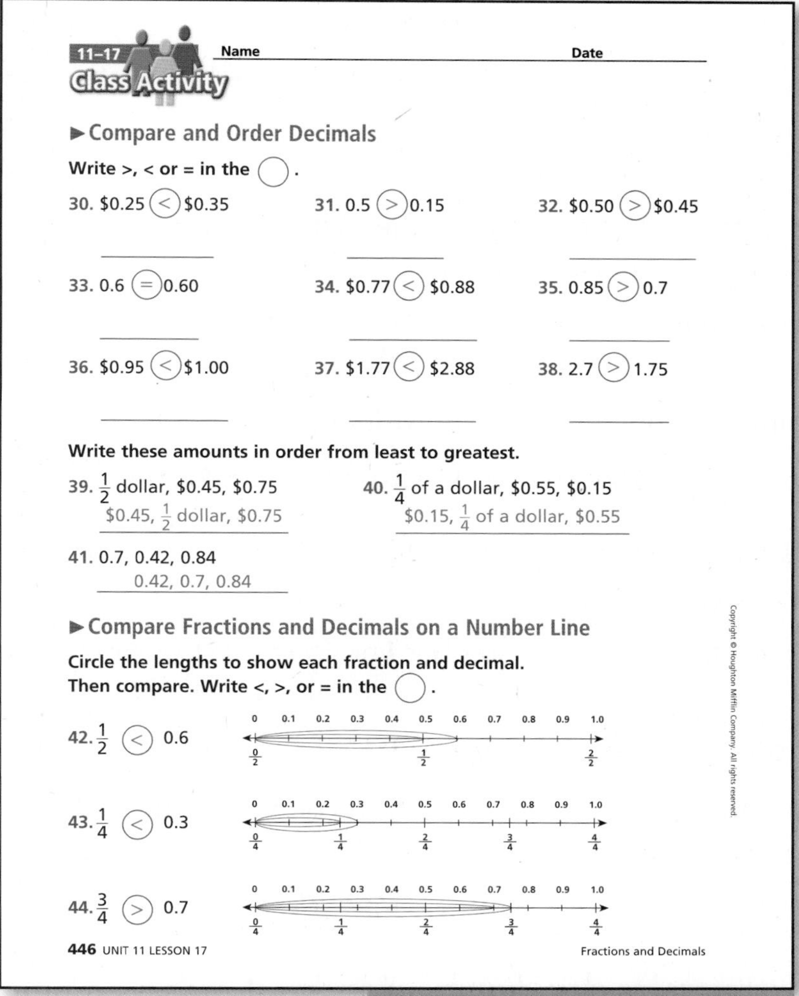

11–17 Class Activity   Name   Date

► Compare and Order Decimals

Write >, < or = in the ◯.

30. \$0.25 (<) \$0.35   31. 0.5 (>) 0.15   32. \$0.50 (>) \$0.45

33. 0.6 (=) 0.60   34. \$0.77 (<) \$0.88   35. 0.85 (>) 0.7

36. \$0.95 (<) \$1.00   37. \$1.77 (<) \$2.88   38. 2.7 (>) 1.75

Write these amounts in order from least to greatest.

39. $\frac{1}{2}$ dollar, \$0.45, \$0.75
\$0.45, $\frac{1}{2}$ dollar, \$0.75

40. $\frac{1}{4}$ of a dollar, \$0.55, \$0.15
\$0.15, $\frac{1}{4}$ of a dollar, \$0.55

41. 0.7, 0.42, 0.84
0.42, 0.7, 0.84

► Compare Fractions and Decimals on a Number Line

Circle the lengths to show each fraction and decimal. Then compare. Write <, >, or = in the ◯.

42. $\frac{1}{2}$ (<) 0.6

43. $\frac{1}{4}$ (<) 0.3

44. $\frac{3}{4}$ (>) 0.7

446 UNIT 11 LESSON 17   Fractions and Decimals

Student Activity Book page 446

► Compare and Order Decimals

Write the following on the board:

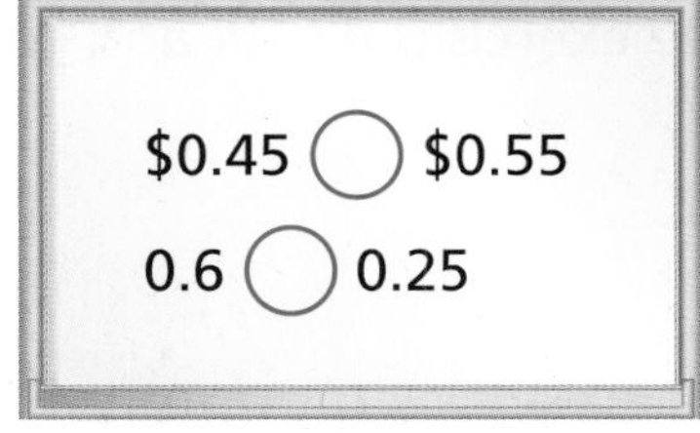

- How can you compare the decimals in the first row? Think: 45 cents is greater than 55 cents
- How can you compare the decimals in the second row? Think: 6 tenths or 60 hundredths is greater than 25 hundredths.
- How might the Puzzled Penguin compare these two decimals? Possible response: The Puzzled Penguin might ignore the decimal points and compare 6 and 25.

Activity continued ▶

Goal: Compare and order decimals and fractions.

Materials: Student Activity Book or Hardcover Book p. 446 and Activity Workbook p. 211

 **NCTM Standards:**
Number and Operations
Communication
Representation

❶ Teaching the Lesson (continued)

Write the following on the board:

2.3 ◯ 1.35

1.75 ◯ 1.7

- How would you compare the decimals in the first row? Compare the whole numbers, 2.3 is greater.
- How would you compare the decimals in the second row? Think: 75 hundredths is 5 hundredths greater than 7 tenths.

Have students complete exercises 30–41 individually.

Have struggling students check their work with a **Helping Partner.**

▶ Compare Fractions and Decimals on a Number Line WHOLE CLASS

How did you compare fractions on a number line in the last lesson? I circled length to show the fractions. Then compared the lengths.

Tell students they can compare decimals and fractions the same way.

Draw the following number line on the board to compare $\frac{3}{5}$ and 0.7. Have a volunteer draw lengths to compare the fraction and decimal.

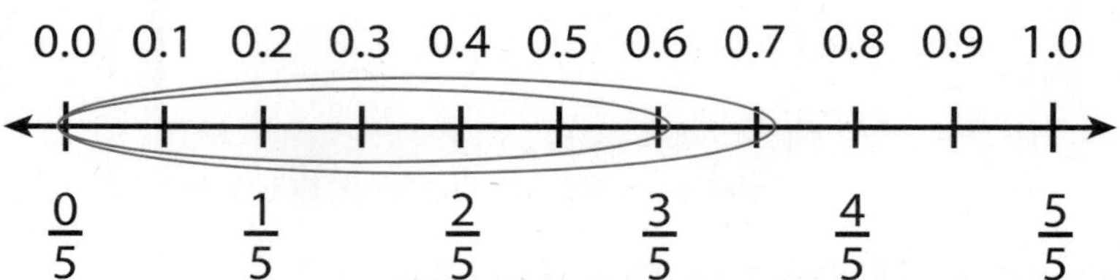

- Which length is longer? The length for 0.7

Then have students complete exercises 42–44 and compare their answers with another student.

Write $\frac{3}{5}$ ◯ 00.7 on the board.

- What symbol would you write in the circle? <

Quick Quiz

See Assessment Guide for Unit 11 Quick Quiz 4.

2 Going Further

Differentiated Instruction

Intervention

Activity Card 11-17

Model Hundredths

Activity Card 11-17 ●

Work: In pairs

Use:

- Play money (100 pennies)
- 4 TRB M43 (10 × 10 grid)
- Crayons or markers

Decide:

Who will be Student 1 and who will be Student 2 for the first round.

1. **Student 1:** Choose a fraction from the list below. Then model it on the grid by coloring the correct number of squares.

   $\frac{45}{100}$ $\frac{25}{100}$ $\frac{10}{100}$ $\frac{75}{100}$

2. **Student 2:** Model the same fraction using pennies. Then write the fraction as a decimal number.

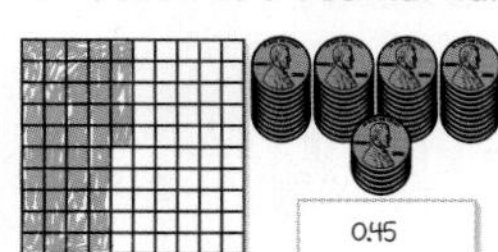

3. Change roles and model another fraction.

Unit 11, Lesson 17

Activity Note Tell students that the grid represents one dollar, and each square represents one penny. Ask students what part of the grid would represent a dime, quarter, and nickel. (10, 25, and 5 squares)

Math Writing Prompt

Compare Explain how fractions are like decimals.

Software Support

Warm Up 24.27

On Level

Activity Card 11-17

Fractions and Decimals

Activity Card 11-17 ▲

Work: In pairs

Use:

- 4 copies of TRB M43 (10 × 10 Grid)
- Crayons or markers

1. **Work Together** Model and write fractions in decimal form.
2. **Think** If the number 1 represents one whole, how can you write 1 as a fraction with the denominator 100? $\frac{100}{100}$
3. Model the number 1 on a grid. Then think of the number 1 as 1 dollar and write the equivalent decimal. 1.00
4. Model each of the following fractions on a grid: $\frac{1}{2}, \frac{1}{4}, \frac{1}{5}$
5. Write the fraction and decimal equivalent for each.

$\frac{1}{2} + \frac{50}{100} = 0.50$

Unit 11, Lesson 17

Activity Note For step 5 encourage students to write fraction and decimal equivalents using hundredths.

Math Writing Prompt

Connected Math How can you decide which is greater, $\frac{1}{2}$ or $\frac{3}{4}$ cup of juice? Explain your thinking.

Software Support

Fraction Action: Fraction Flare Up, Level N

Challenge

Activity Card 11-17

Fractions of a Dollar

Activity Card 11-17 ■

Work: On your own

Use:

- TRB M43 (10 × 10 grid)
- 4 different colored markers or crayons

1. Choose a different color for each coin type and make a key to show the colors you choose.

   Key: Penny, Nickel, Dime, Quarter

2. Suppose you have 100 coins in a collection. Use the four colors to fill the 10 × 10 grid.
3. Write the fraction and decimal equivalents of the part of the collection that each coin represents.

Penny: $\frac{10}{100} = 0.10$
Nickel: $\frac{10}{100} = 0.10$
Dime: $\frac{30}{100} = 0.30$
Quarter: $\frac{50}{100} = 0.50$
$\frac{100}{100} = 1.00$

Unit 11, Lesson 17

Activity Note Be sure that students understand that the sum of the fractions and decimals represents the entire collection of coins, but not their total value. Challenge students to calculate the value separately.

Math Writing Prompt

Number Sense Is $\frac{5}{8} + \frac{1}{2}$ greater or less than one whole? Explain how you know without adding.

Software Support

Course II: Module 2: Unit 3: Fractional Parts

Homework and Spiral Review

11–17 Homework **Goal:** Additional Practice

Include students' completed Homework page as part of their portfolios.

11–17 Remembering **Goal:** Spiral Review

This Remembering page would be appropriate anytime after today's lesson.

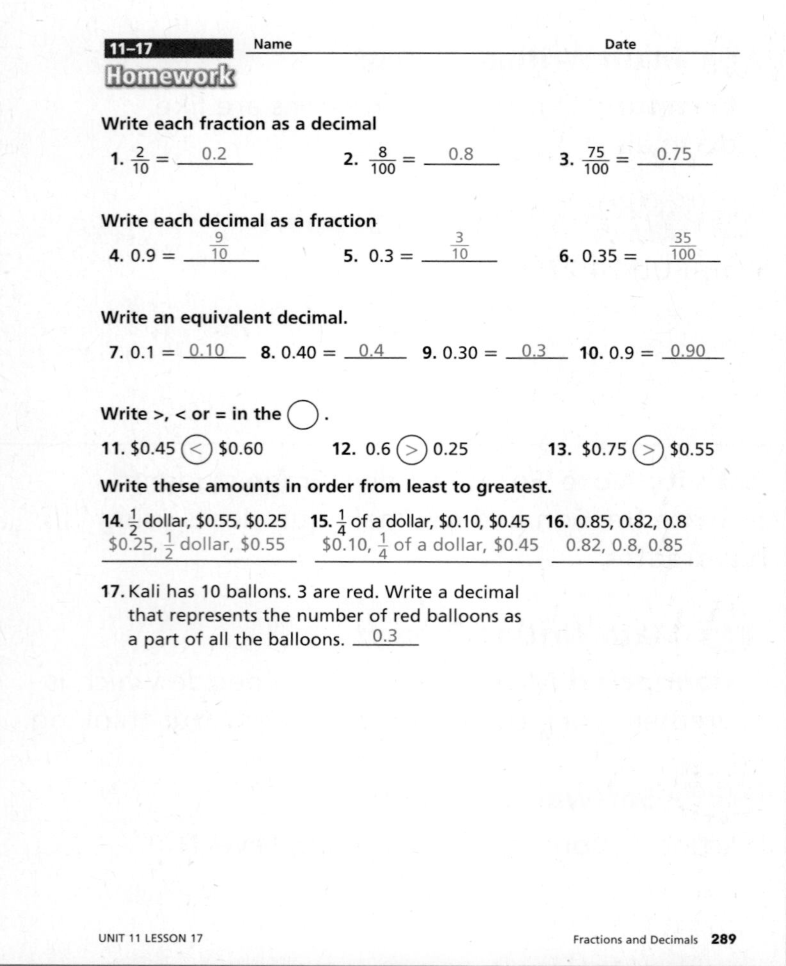

11–17 Homework Name ______ Date ______

Write each fraction as a decimal

1. $\frac{2}{10}$ = 0.2
2. $\frac{8}{100}$ = 0.8
3. $\frac{75}{100}$ = 0.75

Write each decimal as a fraction

4. 0.9 = $\frac{9}{10}$
5. 0.3 = $\frac{3}{10}$
6. 0.35 = $\frac{35}{100}$

Write an equivalent decimal.

7. 0.1 = 0.10
8. 0.40 = 0.4
9. 0.30 = 0.3
10. 0.9 = 0.90

Write >, < or = in the ◯.

11. \$0.45 (<) \$0.60
12. 0.6 (>) 0.25
13. \$0.75 (>) \$0.55

Write these amounts in order from least to greatest.

14. $\frac{1}{2}$ dollar, \$0.55, \$0.25 — \$0.25, $\frac{1}{2}$ dollar, \$0.55
15. $\frac{1}{4}$ of a dollar, \$0.10, \$0.45 — \$0.10, $\frac{1}{4}$ of a dollar, \$0.45
16. 0.85, 0.82, 0.8 — 0.82, 0.8, 0.85

17. Kali has 10 ballons. 3 are red. Write a decimal that represents the number of red balloons as a part of all the balloons. 0.3

UNIT 11 LESSON 17 Fractions and Decimals 289

Homework and Remembering page 289

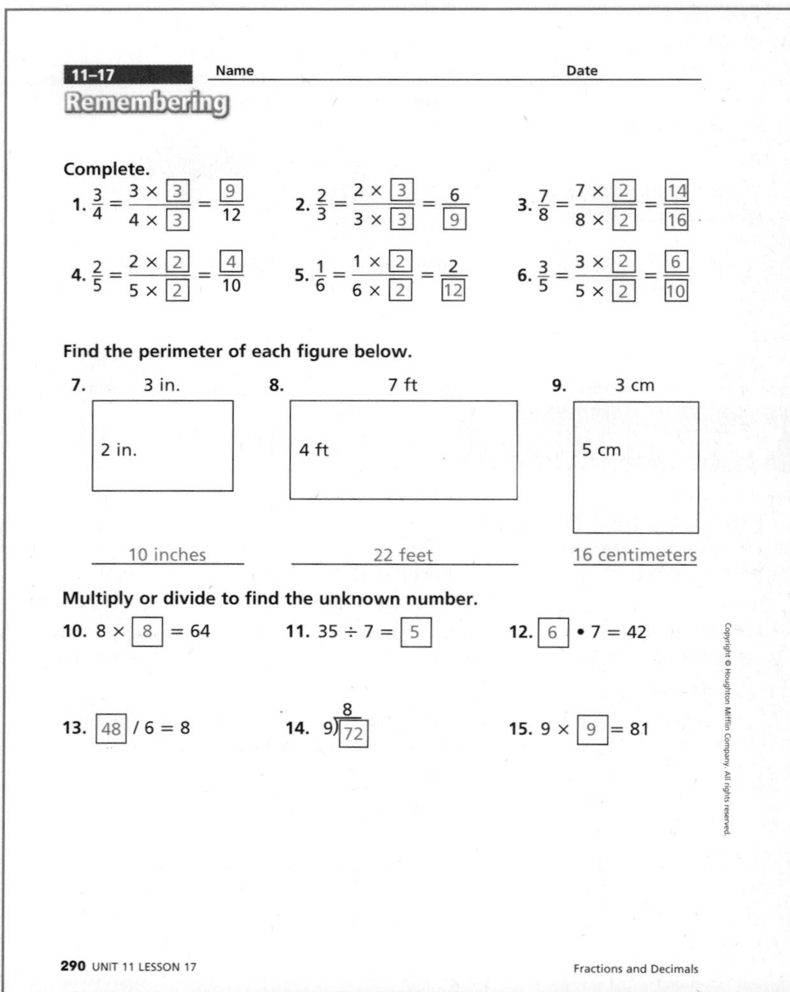

11–17 Remembering Name ______ Date ______

Complete.

1. $\frac{3}{4} = \frac{3 \times \boxed{3}}{4 \times \boxed{3}} = \frac{\boxed{9}}{12}$
2. $\frac{2}{3} = \frac{2 \times \boxed{3}}{3 \times \boxed{3}} = \frac{6}{\boxed{9}}$
3. $\frac{7}{8} = \frac{7 \times \boxed{2}}{8 \times \boxed{2}} = \frac{\boxed{14}}{\boxed{16}}$
4. $\frac{2}{5} = \frac{2 \times \boxed{2}}{5 \times \boxed{2}} = \frac{\boxed{4}}{10}$
5. $\frac{1}{6} = \frac{1 \times \boxed{2}}{6 \times \boxed{2}} = \frac{2}{\boxed{12}}$
6. $\frac{3}{5} = \frac{3 \times \boxed{2}}{5 \times \boxed{2}} = \frac{\boxed{6}}{\boxed{10}}$

Find the perimeter of each figure below.

7. 3 in. by 2 in. — 10 inches
8. 7 ft by 4 ft — 22 feet
9. 3 cm by 5 cm — 16 centimeters

Multiply or divide to find the unknown number.

10. 8 × [8] = 64
11. 35 ÷ 7 = [5]
12. [6] • 7 = 42
13. [48] / 6 = 8
14. 9)[72] = 8
15. 9 × [9] = 81

290 UNIT 11 LESSON 17 Fractions and Decimals

Homework and Remembering page 290

Home or School Activity

Math-to-Math Connection

Decimal Numbers in the Metric System of Measurement Describe how metric units of measurement are based on a system of 10s. For example, one meter can be divided into 100 equal units. Each of these 100 equal units is called a centimeter, and is the same length as 0.01 m. Have students create a table to show the decimal equivalent in meters for units of linear measure.

Metric Unit of Length	How Many Meters in Fractions?	How Many Meters in Decimals?
Decimeter	$\frac{1}{10}$	0.1
Centimeter	$\frac{1}{100}$	0.01
Millimeter	$\frac{1}{1,000}$	0.001

Improper Fractions and Mixed Numbers

Lesson Objectives

- **Understand improper fractions and mixed numbers.**
- **Apply the terms *improper fraction* and *mixed number*.**
- **Rename improper fractions as mixed numbers and mixed numbers as improper fractions.**

Vocabulary
fraction
numerator
denominator
improper fraction
mixed number

The Day at a Glance

Today's Goals	Materials	
1 Teaching the Lesson **A1:** Understand improper fractions and mixed numbers. **A2:** Use drawings to write mixed numbers as improper fractions and vice versa. **A3:** Write mixed numbers as improper fractions and vice versa.	**Lesson Activities** Student Activity Book pp. 447–448 or Student Hardcover Book pp. 447–448 Homework and Remembering pp. 291–292 MathBoard materials	**Going Further** Activity Cards 11-18 Number Cubes labeled (2, 3, 5, 7, 8 and 9) MathBoard materials Index cards Spinner E (TRB M132) Paper clips Math Journals
2 Going Further ► Differentiated Instruction		
3 Homework and Spiral Review		

Use Math Talk today!

Keeping Skills Sharp

Quick Practice

Goal: Identify fractions greater than a given fraction.

Greater Fraction Game Have a **Student Leader** write $\frac{1}{3}$ on the board and challenge groups to find a greater fraction. Each group that names an appropriate fraction within 30 seconds earns one point. The game continues with other fractions, such as $\frac{3}{8}$, $\frac{1}{2}$, $\frac{2}{5}$, and $\frac{1}{4}$, until a group earns three points.

Daily Routines

Homework Review Ask students to place their homework at the corner of their desks. As you circulate during Quick Practice, check that students complete the assignment, and see whether any problem caused difficulty for many students.

Analyze Data Helga counted the vehicles that drove past in ten minutes. 6 were trucks. 4 were cars. 3 were motorcycles. 5 were bicycles. Create a tally chart and write a conclusion about the data.

Vehicles Counted

Vehicle	*Amount*
Trucks	𝍸 |
Cars	||||
Motorcycles	|||
Bicycles	𝍸

Possible answer: More trucks drove by than any other vehicle.

1 Teaching the Lesson

Activity 1

Introduce Improper Fractions and Mixed Numbers

 25 MINUTES

Goal: Understand improper fractions and mixed numbers.

Materials: MathBoard materials

 **NCTM Standards:**
Number and Operations
Problem Solving
Representation

Differentiated Instruction

Extra Help To help students visualize the whole and then the piece(s) of a whole you may want to use this drawing for $\frac{5}{4}$.

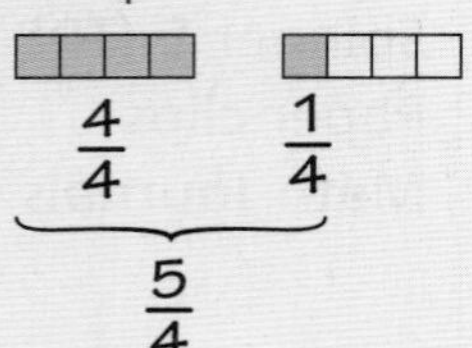

English Language Learners

Write *proper fraction, improper fraction,* $\frac{1}{2}$, $\frac{2}{2}$, and $\frac{3}{2}$ on the board.

- **Beginning** Point and say: **$\frac{1}{2}$ is less than 1. It is a *proper fraction*.** Have students repeat. Continue with other fractions.
- **Intermediate** Ask: **Is $\frac{1}{2}$ less than, equal to, or greater than 1?** less than **Is it a *proper fraction*?** yes Continue with other fractions.
- **Advanced** Ask: **Which fraction is less than 1?** $\frac{1}{2}$ **What kind of fraction is it?** proper Continue with other fractions.

▶ Introduce Improper Fractions WHOLE CLASS

Write the following addition exercise on the board. Have students find the answer on their MathBoards. Ask a volunteer to work at the board and explain how to find equivalent fractions to find the answer.

$$\frac{1}{2} + \frac{3}{4}$$

$$\frac{2}{4} + \frac{3}{4} = \frac{5}{4}$$

Have the volunteer point to the fraction that is the sum.

- How is this fraction different from other fractions you have worked with? The numerator is greater than the denominator.

Tell students that a fraction that has a numerator that is greater or equal to the denominator is called an *improper fraction*. Fractions that you worked with earlier that had the numerator smaller than the denominator are called *proper fractions*.

Present these three drawings on the board to show ways to model the improper fraction $\frac{5}{4}$.

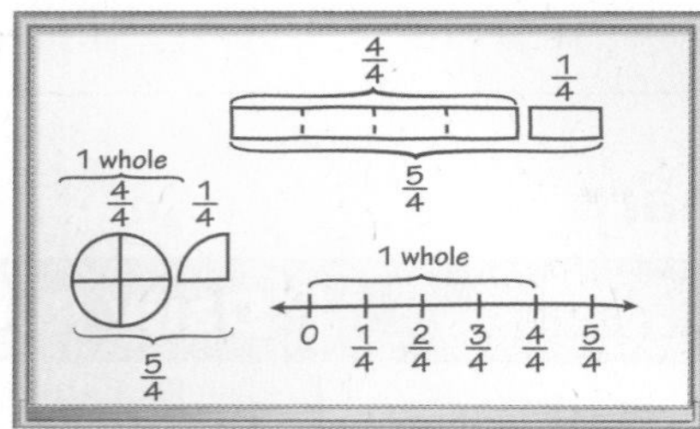

 **Math Talk**

Discuss how the drawings represent $\frac{5}{4}$.

- Describe what you see in the fraction strip drawing. There is one whole divided into fourths plus one fourth more.
- How many fourths are shown in all? 5
- How do we write that as a fraction? $\frac{5}{4}$

Continue using this type of questioning for the circle graph model and the number line.

Emphasize that an improper fraction is equal to or greater than 1. Point out that $\frac{4}{4}$ is also an improper fraction.

▶ Introduce Mixed Numbers WHOLE CLASS

Point out that each drawing on the board also shows that 1 whole is hidden inside the improper fraction and the fraction $\frac{1}{4}$ is added on.

- How many wholes, or $\frac{4}{4}$, are hidden in $\frac{5}{4}$? 1 What fraction is there besides $\frac{4}{4}$ or the whole? $\frac{1}{4}$

Explain that $\frac{5}{4}$ can also be written as $1\frac{1}{4}$ because there is 1 whole plus $\frac{1}{4}$. Explain that numbers like $1\frac{1}{4}$ are called *mixed numbers*.

- Why do you think we call $1\frac{1}{4}$ a *mixed number*? A mixed number is a whole number "mixed" with a fraction.

Write $1\frac{1}{4}$ under each drawing on the board

Then ask several volunteers to make drawings of $\frac{8}{5}$ on the board. Ask them to label the "hidden whole" and the "extra fifths" in $\frac{8}{5}$. Students in their seats should make the drawings on their MathBoards. Students may draw either fraction strips, circle graphs or number line models. One possible drawing is shown below.

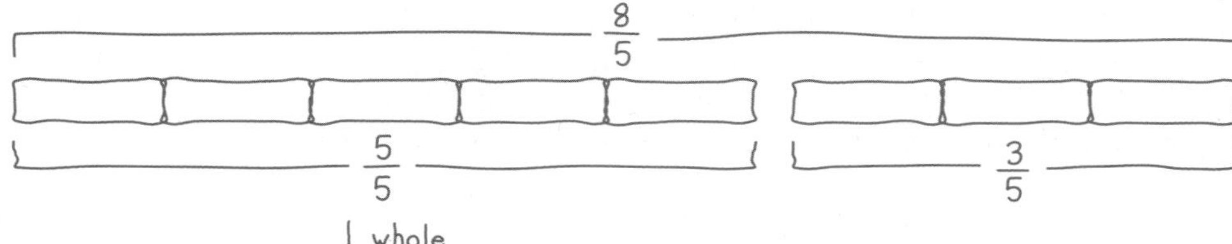

Now ask students to use their drawings to rename $\frac{8}{5}$ as a mixed number.

- How many hidden wholes and extra fifths do you see in your drawing? One hidden whole, $\frac{5}{5}$, and then 3 extra fifths.
- What mixed number could we write for $\frac{8}{5}$? $1\frac{3}{5}$ How do you know? There is 1 whole hidden in $\frac{8}{5}$. The extra part is $\frac{3}{5}$. So $\frac{8}{5}$ equals 1 whole plus $\frac{3}{5}$, or $1\frac{3}{5}$

Then ask volunteers to model $\frac{8}{3}$ and write it as a mixed number on the board as the other students model it on their MathBoards. Use the same type of questions as above to help students rename $\frac{8}{3}$ as a mixed number.

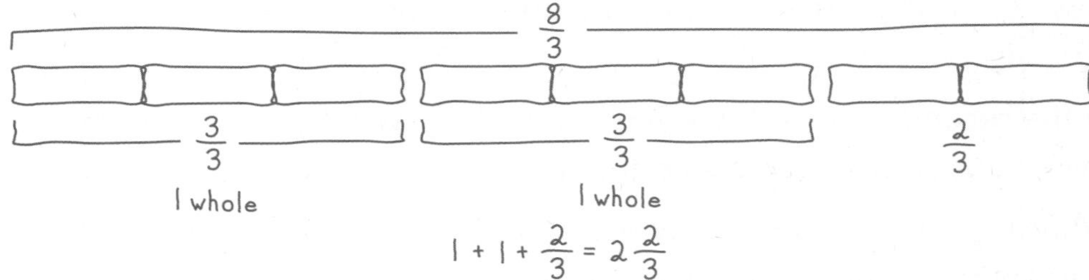

If students need additional practice, repeat the activity for $\frac{5}{2}$, $\frac{7}{3}$, and $\frac{9}{4}$.

Teaching Note

Language and Vocabulary A mixed number "mixes" a whole number and a fraction. You might want to remind students that *whole numbers* are the counting numbers (1, 2, 3, 4...) and zero.

Activity 2

Identify Improper Fractions and Mixed Numbers

10 MINUTES

Goal: Use drawings to write mixed numbers as improper fractions and vice versa.

Materials: Student Activity Book or Hardcover Book p. 447

NCTM Standards:
Number and Operations
Problem Solving
Representation

The Learning Classroom

Building Concepts Have students draw fraction strips to represent $\frac{4}{3}$ and $\frac{7}{3}$. Ask them to compare and contrast the two models, naming at least one similarity and one difference.

► Use Models to Visualize Mixed Numbers and Improper Fractions WHOLE CLASS

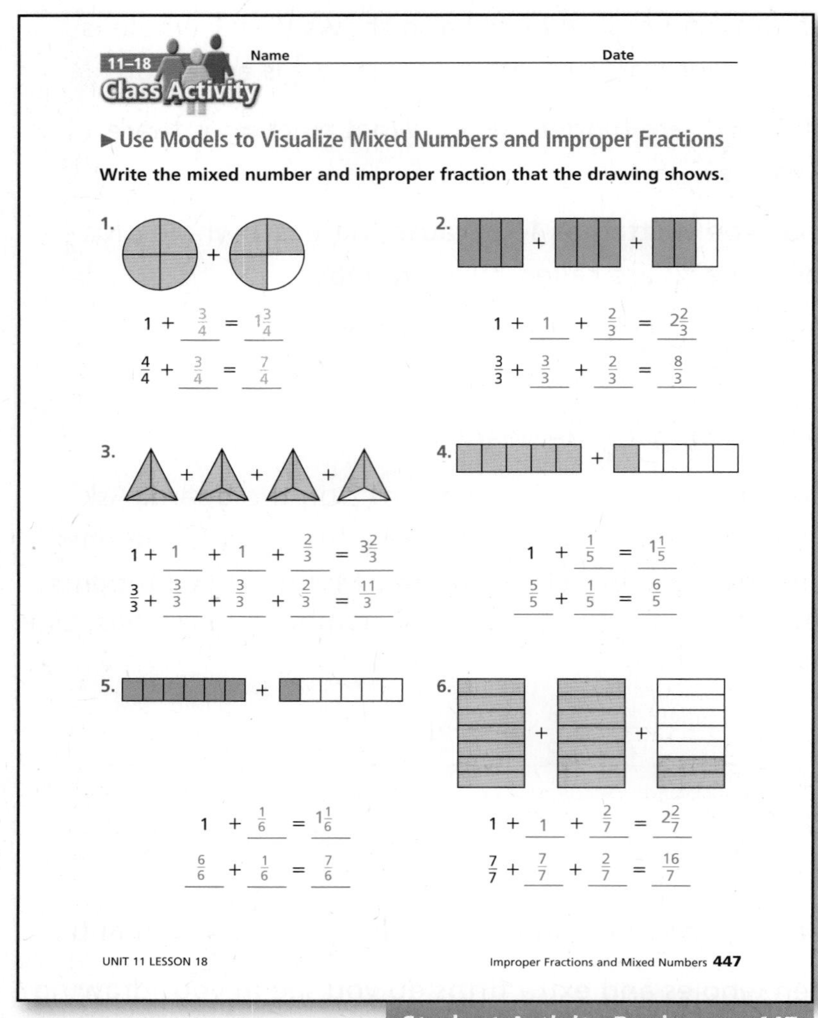

11–18 Class Activity Name Date

► Use Models to Visualize Mixed Numbers and Improper Fractions

Write the mixed number and improper fraction that the drawing shows.

1. $1 + \frac{3}{4} = 1\frac{3}{4}$

$\frac{4}{4} + \frac{3}{4} = \frac{7}{4}$

2. $1 + 1 + \frac{2}{3} = 2\frac{2}{3}$

$\frac{3}{3} + \frac{3}{3} + \frac{2}{3} = \frac{8}{3}$

3. $1 + 1 + 1 + \frac{2}{3} = 3\frac{2}{3}$

$\frac{3}{3} + \frac{3}{3} + \frac{3}{3} + \frac{2}{3} = \frac{11}{3}$

4. $1 + \frac{1}{5} = 1\frac{1}{5}$

$\frac{5}{5} + \frac{1}{5} = \frac{6}{5}$

5. $1 + \frac{1}{6} = 1\frac{1}{6}$

$\frac{6}{6} + \frac{1}{6} = \frac{7}{6}$

6. $1 + 1 + \frac{2}{7} = 2\frac{2}{7}$

$\frac{7}{7} + \frac{7}{7} + \frac{2}{7} = \frac{16}{7}$

UNIT 11 LESSON 18 Improper Fractions and Mixed Numbers 447

Student Activity Book page 447

Have students look at Student Book page 447. Explain that they will write the improper fraction and the mixed number represented by each drawing. Complete the first exercise as a class.

- What kind of fraction does the first drawing show? fourths How do you know? The whole is divided into four parts.
- How many fourths are we adding to the 1 whole? $\frac{3}{4}$ What is 1 whole plus $\frac{3}{4}$? $1\frac{3}{4}$ Is the answer a mixed number or improper fraction? mixed number
- In the second equation, we see the 1 whole written as $\frac{4}{4}$. Once again, how many fourths are we adding to the $\frac{4}{4}$? $\frac{3}{4}$
- What is $\frac{4}{4}$ plus $\frac{3}{4}$? $\frac{7}{4}$ Is the answer a mixed number or an improper fraction? improper fraction

Have students complete the page. Check the answers as a class.

1 Teaching the Lesson (continued)

Activity 3

Convert Between Mixed Numbers and Improper Fractions

▶ Convert Without Making Drawings WHOLE CLASS

Have students look at the two equations they completed in exercise 6 on Student Book page 447.

How can we figure out that $2\frac{2}{7}$ equals $\frac{16}{7}$ without using a drawing? First we could rename each of the 2 wholes as $\frac{7}{7}$. Then we could add each $\frac{7}{7}$ to $\frac{2}{7}$. We would have $\frac{7}{7} + \frac{7}{7} + \frac{2}{7} = \frac{17}{7}$ That's the second equation we completed in exercise 6.

$$1 + 1 + \frac{2}{7} = 2\frac{2}{7}$$

$$\frac{7}{7} + \frac{7}{7} + \frac{2}{7} = \frac{16}{7}$$

Some students may propose multiplying 7 times 2, and then adding the 2 from $\frac{2}{7}$, to find out how many sevenths there are. That method is fine as long as they understand the concept behind the algorithm.

Then ask students how to convert the other way—how to figure out that $\frac{16}{7}$ equals $2\frac{2}{7}$ without using a drawing. Offer hints if necessary. See **Math Talk in Action** for a sample classroom discussion.

Math Talk in Action

How can we figure out that $\frac{16}{7}$ equals $2\frac{2}{7}$?

Annika: First, we have to find out how many wholes are hidden in $\frac{16}{7}$.

Larry: Right. Then we have to find how many sevenths are left over.

Keiko: 1 whole is $\frac{7}{7}$. If we take 1 whole away, we have $\frac{9}{7}$ left. If we take another whole away, we have $\frac{2}{7}$ left.

Annika: Once we have $\frac{2}{7}$, we can't subtract any more wholes.

Keiko: We subtracted 2 wholes and had $\frac{2}{7}$ left over. So, $\frac{16}{7}$ equals $2\frac{2}{7}$.

Activity continued ▶

15 MINUTES

Goal: Write mixed numbers as improper fractions and vice versa.

Materials: Student Activity Book or Hardcover Book p. 448

NCTM Standards:
Number and Operations
Problem Solving
Representation

Differentiated Instruction

Extra Help One way to show students how to identify the improper fraction shown by a drawing is to first count the number of sections in the whole. This number tells the type of fraction, such as halves, fourths, or fifths, that is shown. The next step is to count the total number of sections shown in the whole or wholes and the extra parts and write that number over the number of sections shown in the whole. If students have difficulty identifying the improper fraction, show them this two-step process as an alternate method.

Teaching the Lesson (continued)

Ongoing Assessment

Have students write $\frac{5}{3}$ as a mixed number and $1\frac{3}{5}$ as an improper fraction. Encourage them to draw a picture and explain their thinking as part of the answer.

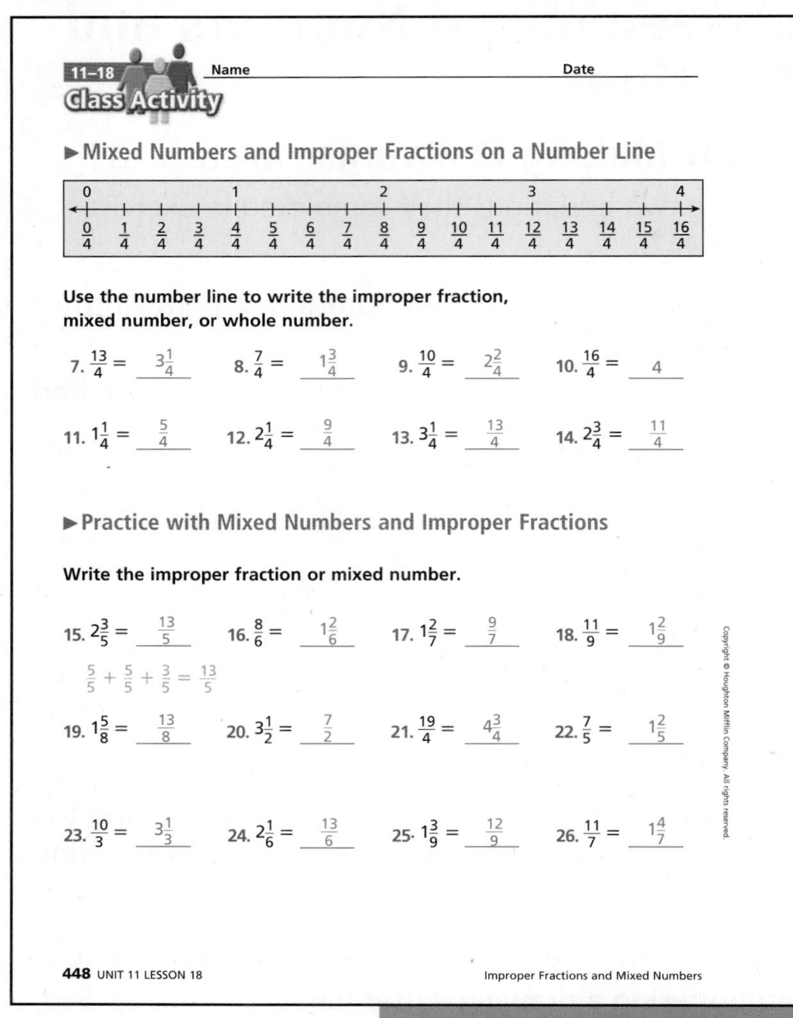

11–18 Class Activity Name ______ Date ______

► Mixed Numbers and Improper Fractions on a Number Line

0 1 2 3 4

$\frac{0}{4}$ $\frac{1}{4}$ $\frac{2}{4}$ $\frac{3}{4}$ $\frac{4}{4}$ $\frac{5}{4}$ $\frac{6}{4}$ $\frac{7}{4}$ $\frac{8}{4}$ $\frac{9}{4}$ $\frac{10}{4}$ $\frac{11}{4}$ $\frac{12}{4}$ $\frac{13}{4}$ $\frac{14}{4}$ $\frac{15}{4}$ $\frac{16}{4}$

Use the number line to write the improper fraction, mixed number, or whole number.

7. $\frac{13}{4} = 3\frac{1}{4}$ 8. $\frac{7}{4} = 1\frac{3}{4}$ 9. $\frac{10}{4} = 2\frac{2}{4}$ 10. $\frac{16}{4} = 4$

11. $1\frac{1}{4} = \frac{5}{4}$ 12. $2\frac{1}{4} = \frac{9}{4}$ 13. $3\frac{1}{4} = \frac{13}{4}$ 14. $2\frac{3}{4} = \frac{11}{4}$

► Practice with Mixed Numbers and Improper Fractions

Write the improper fraction or mixed number.

15. $2\frac{3}{5} = \frac{13}{5}$ 16. $\frac{8}{6} = 1\frac{2}{6}$ 17. $1\frac{2}{7} = \frac{9}{7}$ 18. $\frac{11}{9} = 1\frac{2}{9}$

$\frac{5}{5} + \frac{5}{5} + \frac{3}{5} = \frac{13}{5}$

19. $1\frac{5}{8} = \frac{13}{8}$ 20. $3\frac{1}{2} = \frac{7}{2}$ 21. $\frac{19}{4} = 4\frac{3}{4}$ 22. $\frac{7}{5} = 1\frac{2}{5}$

23. $\frac{10}{3} = 3\frac{1}{3}$ 24. $2\frac{1}{6} = \frac{13}{6}$ 25. $1\frac{3}{9} = \frac{12}{9}$ 26. $\frac{11}{7} = 1\frac{4}{7}$

448 UNIT 11 LESSON 18 Improper Fractions and Mixed Numbers

Student Activity Book page 448

► Mixed Numbers and Improper Fractions on a Number Line WHOLE CLASS

Refer students to Student Book page 448. Ask them to find $\frac{15}{4}$ on the number line.

- How many wholes are hidden in $\frac{15}{4}$? 3 How do you know? $\frac{15}{4}$ is more than 3 and less than 4
- How many fourths more than 3 is $\frac{15}{4}$? $\frac{3}{4}$ more
- How would you write $\frac{15}{4}$ as a mixed number? $3\frac{3}{4}$

Have students complete exercises 7–14.

► Practice with Mixed Numbers and Improper Fractions WHOLE CLASS

Complete exercises 15 and 16 together as a class. Have students complete the page. Encourage them to draw pictures to help them if necessary.

Intervention — Activity Card 11-18

Improper Fraction to Mixed Number
Activity Card 11-18

Work: In pairs

Use:
- 2 Number cubes (labeled 2, 3, 5, 7, 8, and 9)
- MathBoard materials

1. Work Together Change improper fractions to mixed numbers. Toss the two number cubes. If both numbers are the same, toss the cubes again.
2. Use the numbers to make an improper fraction. Then make a drawing to model the improper fraction.

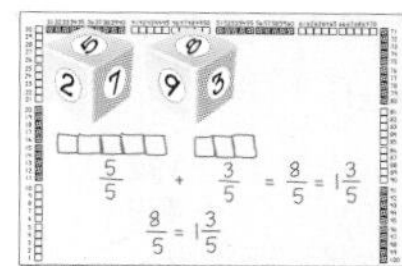

3. Think Suppose you toss an 8 and a 5. How does a drawing help you to rename the improper fraction $\frac{8}{5}$ as a mixed number?
4. Toss the number cubes again to repeat the activity.

Unit 11, Lesson 18

Activity Note Guide students to use the denominator of the improper fraction to model the fraction as a sum that is easy to write as a mixed number.

Math Writing Prompt

You Decide Why is $\frac{8}{5}$ an improper fraction but $\frac{5}{8}$ is not? Explain how you know.

Software Support

Warm Up 5.13

On Level — Activity Card 11-18

Find the Match
Activity Card 11-18

Work: In pairs

Use:
- Index cards

1. Copy the numbers below onto the cards. Shuffle the cards and place them face down in an array.

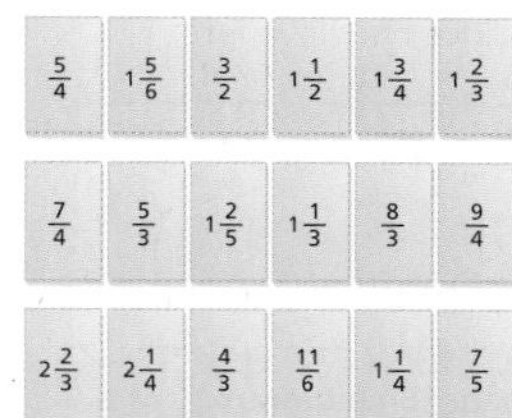

$\frac{5}{4}$	$1\frac{5}{6}$	$\frac{3}{2}$	$1\frac{1}{2}$	$1\frac{3}{4}$	$1\frac{2}{3}$
$\frac{7}{4}$	$\frac{5}{3}$	$1\frac{2}{5}$	$1\frac{1}{3}$	$\frac{8}{3}$	$\frac{9}{4}$
$2\frac{2}{3}$	$2\frac{1}{4}$	$\frac{4}{3}$	$\frac{11}{6}$	$1\frac{1}{4}$	$\frac{7}{5}$

2. Take turns turning over two cards. Keep the cards if they show two equal numbers. If not, return the cards to the array face down.
3. Continue until all the cards have been matched.

Unit 11, Lesson 18

Activity Note Before students begin the activity, tell them that each matching pair shows an improper fraction and its corresponding mixed number.

Math Writing Prompt

Real-World Application Describe places where you have seen or used mixed numbers or improper fractions.

Software Support

Fraction Action: Number Line Mine, Level F

Challenge — Activity Card 11-18

Improper Fraction Totals
Activity Card 11-18

Work: In pairs

Use:
- TRB M132 (Spinner E)
- Paper clip

Decide:

Who will be Student 1 and who will be Student 2 for the first round.

1. Work Together Make a spinner like the one below. Then spin the spinner twice. Write the two fractions.

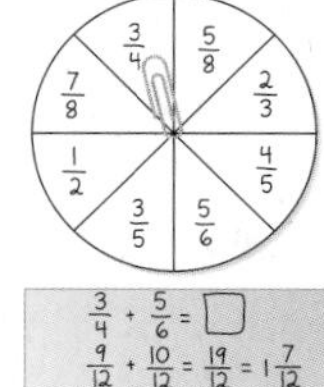

$\frac{3}{4} + \frac{5}{6} = \square$

$\frac{9}{12} + \frac{10}{12} = \frac{19}{12} = 1\frac{7}{12}$

2. Student 1: Add the fractions and show the answer as an improper fraction.
3. Student 2: Rename the sum as a mixed number.
4. Change roles and repeat the activity.

Unit 11, Lesson 18

Activity Note Before beginning the activity, have students review strategies for renaming fractions with common denominators.

Math Writing Prompt

Explain Your Thinking Would you ever have to write an improper fraction as a mixed number when you add two mixed numbers? Explain.

Software Support

Course II: Module 2: Unit 3: Fractional Parts

 Homework and Spiral Review

11–18 Homework **Goal:** Additional Practice

This Homework page provides practice in writing mixed numbers as improper fractions and vice-versa.

11–18 Remembering **Goal:** Spiral Review

This Remembering page would be appropriate anytime after today's lesson.

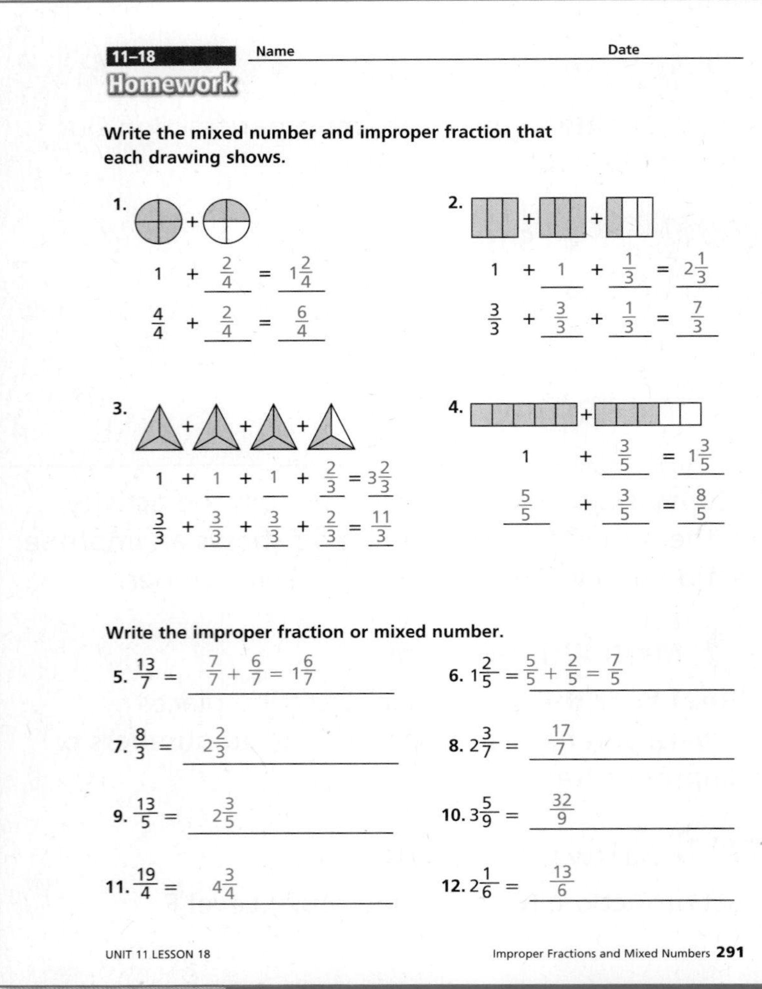

11–18 Homework Name ______ Date ______

Write the mixed number and improper fraction that each drawing shows.

1. $1 + \frac{2}{4} = 1\frac{2}{4}$

   $\frac{4}{4} + \frac{2}{4} = \frac{6}{4}$

2. $1 + 1 + \frac{1}{3} = 2\frac{1}{3}$

   $\frac{3}{3} + \frac{3}{3} + \frac{1}{3} = \frac{7}{3}$

3. $1 + 1 + 1 + \frac{2}{3} = 3\frac{2}{3}$

   $\frac{3}{3} + \frac{3}{3} + \frac{3}{3} + \frac{2}{3} = \frac{11}{3}$

4. $1 + \frac{3}{5} = 1\frac{3}{5}$

   $\frac{5}{5} + \frac{3}{5} = \frac{8}{5}$

Write the improper fraction or mixed number.

5. $\frac{13}{7} = \frac{7}{7} + \frac{6}{7} = 1\frac{6}{7}$
6. $1\frac{2}{5} = \frac{5}{5} + \frac{2}{5} = \frac{7}{5}$
7. $\frac{8}{3} = 2\frac{2}{3}$
8. $2\frac{3}{7} = \frac{17}{7}$
9. $\frac{13}{5} = 2\frac{3}{5}$
10. $3\frac{5}{9} = \frac{32}{9}$
11. $\frac{19}{4} = 4\frac{3}{4}$
12. $2\frac{1}{6} = \frac{13}{6}$

UNIT 11 LESSON 18 Improper Fractions and Mixed Numbers **291**

Homework and Remembering page 291

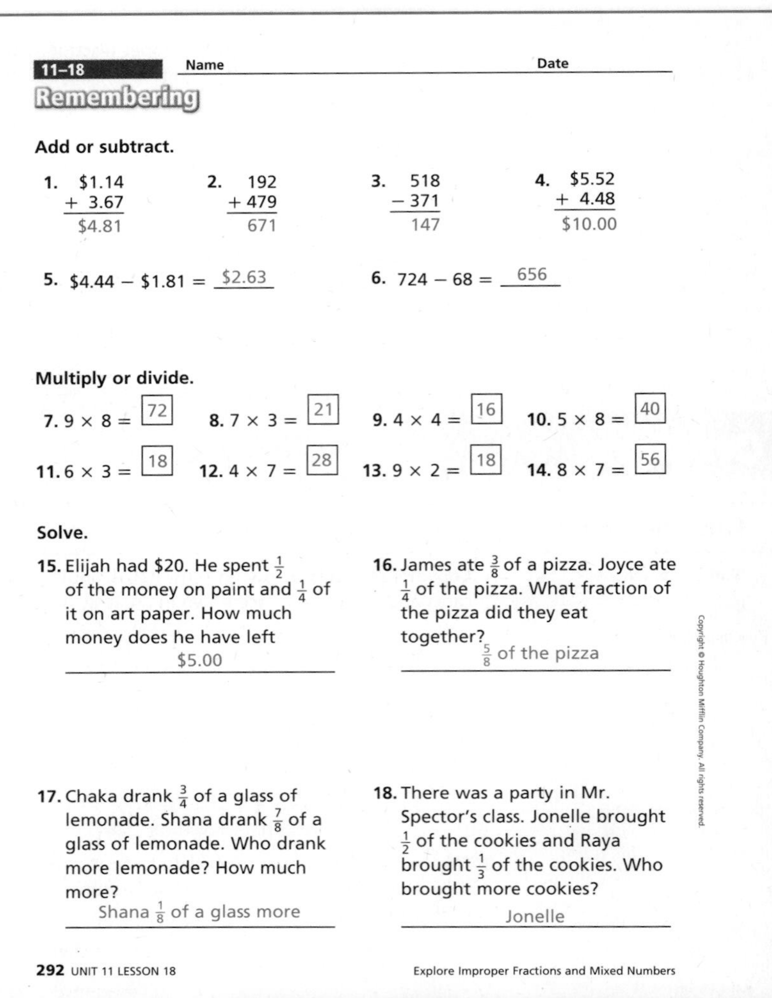

11–18 Remembering Name ______ Date ______

Add or subtract.

1. $1.14 + 3.67 = $4.81
2. 192 + 479 = 671
3. 518 − 371 = 147
4. $5.52 + 4.48 = $10.00
5. $4.44 − $1.81 = $2.63
6. 724 − 68 = 656

Multiply or divide.

7. 9 × 8 = 72
8. 7 × 3 = 21
9. 4 × 4 = 16
10. 5 × 8 = 40
11. 6 × 3 = 18
12. 4 × 7 = 28
13. 9 × 2 = 18
14. 8 × 7 = 56

Solve.

15. Elijah had $20. He spent $\frac{1}{2}$ of the money on paint and $\frac{1}{4}$ of it on art paper. How much money does he have left? $5.00
16. James ate $\frac{3}{8}$ of a pizza. Joyce ate $\frac{1}{4}$ of the pizza. What fraction of the pizza did they eat together? $\frac{5}{8}$ of the pizza
17. Chaka drank $\frac{3}{4}$ of a glass of lemonade. Shana drank $\frac{7}{8}$ of a glass of lemonade. Who drank more lemonade? How much more? Shana $\frac{1}{8}$ of a glass more
18. There was a party in Mr. Spector's class. Jonelle brought $\frac{1}{2}$ of the cookies and Raya brought $\frac{1}{3}$ of the cookies. Who brought more cookies? Jonelle

292 UNIT 11 LESSON 18 Explore Improper Fractions and Mixed Numbers

Homework and Remembering page 292

Home or School Activity

 Language Arts Connection

Mixed Number Who Am I? Have students make up a *Who Am I?* description for a mixed number or an improper fraction. It might be possible to have more than one correct answer. Collect the descriptions and then play *Who Am I?* by splitting the class into teams. The first team that answers correctly earns a point. Continue playing until one team has scored 5 points.

I am a mixed number with a value greater than 5 but less than 6. My denominator is 8. My numerator is less than 6 but greater than 4. Who am I?

Introduce Division with Remainders

Lesson Objectives

- Explore division with remainders.
- Understand and apply the term *remainder*.

Vocabulary
division
remainder
count-by

The Day at a Glance

Today's Goals	Materials	
1 Teaching the Lesson A1: Solve division word problems with remainders. A2: Find the answer to divisions with remainders. **2 Going Further** ► Differentiated Instruction **3 Homework and Spiral Review**	**Lesson Activities** Student Activity Book pp. 449–450 or Student Hardcover Book pp. 449–450 and Activity Workbook p. 213 (includes Class Write on Sheet) Homework and Remembering pp. 293–294 *A Remainder of One* by Elinor J. Pinczex (Houghton Mifflin, 1995)	**Going Further** Activity Cards 11-19 Multiplication Table (TRB M50) Homework and Remembering p. 293 Index cards Number cubes labeled 2, 3, 4, 5, 6 and 8 MathBoard materials Spinner G (TRB M143) Paper clips Counters Math Journals

Use Math Talk today!

Keeping Skills Sharp

Quick Practice — 5 MINUTES

Goal: Identify 6s count-bys just under a number. Identify the difference between the numbers.

Just Under Count-Bys Have a **Student Leader** say a number that is not a 6s count-by, such as 57. Have students say the 6s count-by that is nearest to, but less than that number. 54 Then have students calculate the difference between the count-by and the number. 3 Repeat with another number that is not a 6s count-by.

Daily Routines

Homework Review Let students work together to check their work.

Nonroutine Problem In a box of crayons, $\frac{1}{6}$ are purple, $\frac{2}{3}$ are orange, and 2 are blue. How many crayons are in the box? 12 crayons

Whole Box of Crayons

1/6 Purple | 2/3 Orange | 2 Blue

1 Teaching the Lesson

Activity 1

Introduction to Division with Remainders

 25 MINUTES

Goal: Solve division word problems with remainders.

Materials: Student Activity Book or Hardcover Book p. 449

 **NCTM Standards:**
Number and Operations
Problem Solving

Teaching Note

What to Expect from Students The concept of division with remainders further emphasizes the connection between mixed numbers and division, so it is presented at this time. While some students may grasp the concepts of division and remainders, not all students at this grade level are expected to fully master them at this time.

Alternate Approach

Counters Students who are having difficulty grasping the concept of a remainder may find modeling the division with counters helpful.

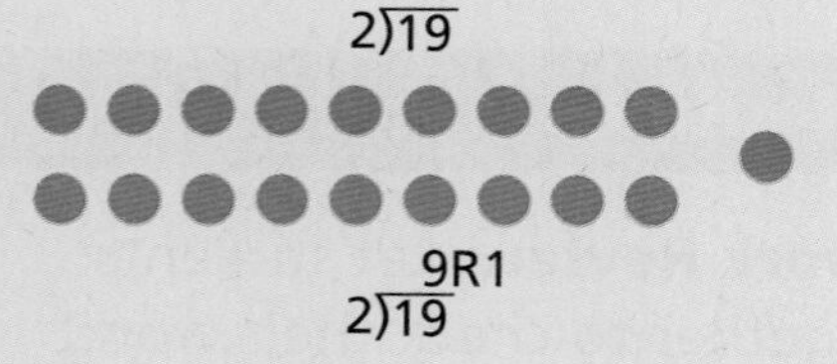

English Language Learners

Provide support with vocabulary for the word problems on Student Activity Book page 449.

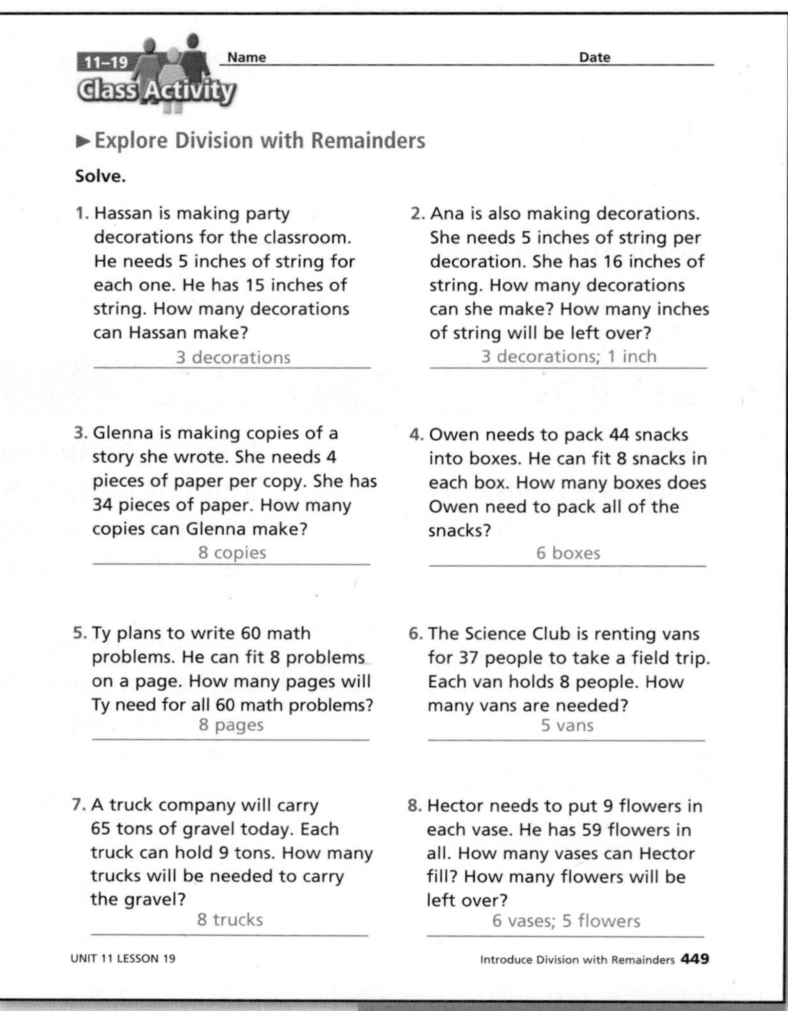

11–19 Class Activity

Name Date

▶ Explore Division with Remainders

Solve.

1. Hassan is making party decorations for the classroom. He needs 5 inches of string for each one. He has 15 inches of string. How many decorations can Hassan make? 3 decorations
2. Ana is also making decorations. She needs 5 inches of string per decoration. She has 16 inches of string. How many decorations can she make? How many inches of string will be left over? 3 decorations; 1 inch
3. Glenna is making copies of a story she wrote. She needs 4 pieces of paper per copy. She has 34 pieces of paper. How many copies can Glenna make? 8 copies
4. Owen needs to pack 44 snacks into boxes. He can fit 8 snacks in each box. How many boxes does Owen need to pack all of the snacks? 6 boxes
5. Ty plans to write 60 math problems. He can fit 8 problems on a page. How many pages will Ty need for all 60 math problems? 8 pages
6. The Science Club is renting vans for 37 people to take a field trip. Each van holds 8 people. How many vans are needed? 5 vans
7. A truck company will carry 65 tons of gravel today. Each truck can hold 9 tons. How many trucks will be needed to carry the gravel? 8 trucks
8. Hector needs to put 9 flowers in each vase. He has 59 flowers in all. How many vases can Hector fill? How many flowers will be left over? 6 vases; 5 flowers

UNIT 11 LESSON 19 Introduce Division with Remainders 449

Student Activity Book page 449

▶ Explore Division with Remainders WHOLE CLASS

Math Talk As a class, use **Solve and Discuss** to work through problems 1 and 2. Direct students' attention to problem 1 on Student Book page 449. Ask a volunteer to read it aloud for the class to solve.

- How can we solve the problem? Possible answer: Hassan needs 5 inches of string for each decoration. If we divide 15 by 5, the answer is 3. Hassan can make 3 decorations

Next, have a volunteer read aloud problem 2 on Student Book page 449 and repeat the same process as above. They should see that the division does not work out evenly as it did in problem 1.

- How is this problem different from the first problem? Possible answer: We can't divide 16 evenly by 5. We need to figure out the number of decorations we can make *and* how much string will be left over.

Put this drawing on the board. Have students discuss how they can use it to solve the problem.

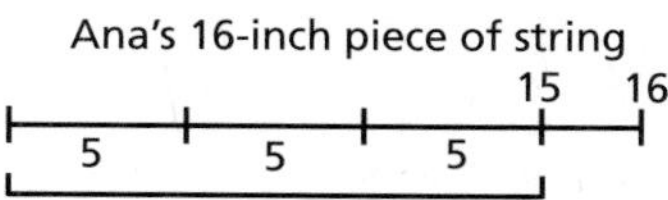

- How does this drawing help solve the problem? It shows that there are three 5-inch pieces of string and 1 inch left over.
- What is the answer? Ana can make 3 decorations. She will have 1 inch of string left over.

Explain that a *remainder* is an amount left over when we divide.

Show the division needed to solve problem 2 using standard math notation.

$5\overline{)16}$

- What is the count-by of 5 that is closest to, but less than, 16? 15 How many count-bys of 5 is that? 3

$$\begin{array}{r} 3 \\ 5\overline{)16} \\ 15 \end{array}$$

Write the 3 above the bar over the 6 and the 15 under 16.

- What is the difference between 16 and 15? 1

$$\begin{array}{r} 3\text{ R}1 \\ 5\overline{)16} \\ -15 \\ \hline 1 \end{array}$$

Write a subtraction sign next to 15, draw a bar under 15, subtract, and write 1.

What does the remainder of 1 tell us? There was 1 inch of string left over.

Point out that problem 2 is a *left-overs* division problem. Explain that left-overs are objects that cannot be used in the context of the problem. For example, Ana had extra string that could not be used to hang decorations. Explain that in these kinds of problems, the answer to the question will be the whole number answer without the *left-over* part.

Use **Solve and Discuss** to complete the page. Have volunteers explain how they solved the problem and write the division using standard math notation on the board.

Point out that problems 4–7 are *another whole* division problems. In this type of problem, the left-over objects require another whole to be added to the whole number answer. In problem 6, for example, an extra van must be rented for the people who do not fit in the filled vans. Students must remember to add another whole to take care of the remainder.

The Learning Classroom

Building Concepts Division with remainders is not like rounding. With rounding, you always round up if the answer is half or more. With division, the answer and what you do with the left-overs depends on the situation. The answer to the problem may be the whole number in the division answer or the whole number plus another whole. It does not depend on how many left-overs there are. Make sure your students pay attention to what each question is asking so that they know what to do with the remainder in each case.

Teaching Note

Math Background A third meaning of remainders—fractional parts—will be introduced in the next lesson. This interpretation involves dividing the remainder equally. If 2 people share 5 apples, for example, each person gets 2 whole apples, and $\frac{1}{2}$ of the remaining apple, or $2\frac{1}{2}$ apples.

Teaching Note

Watch For! Make sure students pay close attention to place value when dividing. Make sure students do **not** do the following:

$$\begin{array}{l} \;\;\;3\text{ R}1 \\ 5\overline{)16} \\ -\,15 \\ \;\;\;\;1 \end{array}$$

Having students work on grid paper helps them align their place values.

Activity 2

Practice Standard Math Notation for Divisions

 20 MINUTES

Goal: Find the answer to divisions with remainders.

Materials: Student Activity Book or Hardcover Book p. 450 and Activity Workbook p. 213 (includes special format)

 **NCTM Standards:**
Number and Operations
Problem Solving

Class Management

Students who take longer to solve the problems on the board can catch up to the class by only solving the odd-numbered exercises on Student Book page 450 and finishing the even-numbered exercises as homework or for extra credit.

Ongoing Assessment

Have students solve the following word problem by showing their work in standard math notation. Janine is putting 27 crackers in 6 lunchboxes. How many crackers go in each lunchbox? How many crackers will be left over?

11–19 Class Activity

Name ______ Date ______

▶ Practice Dividing with Remainders

Write the answer.

9. 3)17 5 R2	10. 6)26 4 R2	11. 8)27 3 R3	12. 7)39 5 R4
13. 6)40 6 R4	14. 9)56 6 R2	15. 5)48 9 R3	16. 2)15 7 R1
17. 5)33 6 R3	18. 8)45 5 R5	19. 7)44 6 R2	20. 3)29 9 R2
21. 4)30 7 R2	22. 9)71 7 R8	23. 3)31 10 R1	24. 8)63 7 R7
25. 2)17 8 R1	26. 4)27 6 R3	27. 5)37 7 R2	28. 6)56 9 R2
29. 7)54 7 R5	30. 8)54 6 R6	31. 9)73 8 R1	32. 10)55 5 R5

450 UNIT 11 LESSON 19 Introduce Division with Remainders

Student Activity Book page 450

▶ Practice Dividing with Remainders INDIVIDUALS

Refer students to Student Book page 450. Ask a volunteer to come to the board and use the standard math notation to find the answer to exercise 9 as students complete it at their seats.

- What is the count-by of 3 that is closest to, but less than, 17? 15 How many count-bys of 3 is that? 5

$$\begin{array}{r} 5 \\ 3\overline{)17} \\ \underline{15} \end{array}$$

- What is the difference between 17 and 15? 2
- What is the remainder? 2 What does it tell us? There is 2 left over after dividing 17 into equal groups of 3.

$$\begin{array}{r} 5\text{ R2} \\ 3\overline{)17} \\ \underline{-15} \\ 2 \end{array}$$

Repeat for exercises 10–16 asking other volunteers to explain and show their work on the board. Then have students complete the page on their own.

2 Going Further

Differentiated Instruction

Intervention — Activity Card 11-19

Just Under Count-Bys — Activity Card 11-19

Work: In pairs

Use:

- Homework and Remembering page 293
- TRB M50 (Multiplication Table)

1. **Work Together** Complete the divisions on Homework and Remembering page 293.
2. Use the Multiplication Table to help you find the count-by of each divisor that gives you a number close to but less than the dividend.

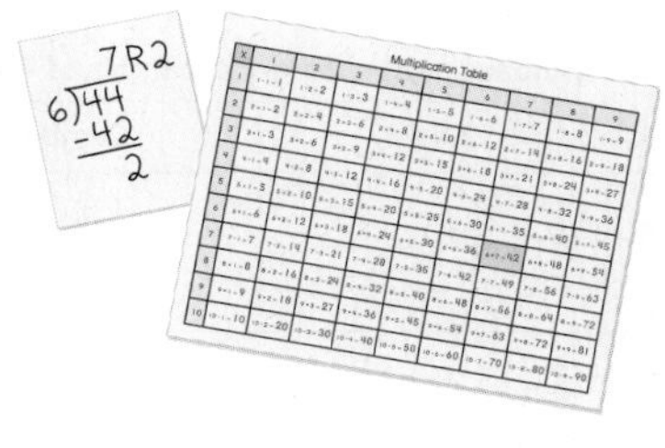

Unit 11, Lesson 19

Activity Note Have students check their work by noting whether the remainder is less than the divisor.

Math Writing Prompt

Make a Drawing Can you evenly divide 18 stickers among 4 people? Make a drawing to explain your thinking.

Software Support

Warm Up 13.25

On Level — Activity Card 11-19

Write Your Own — Activity Card 11-19 

Work: In pairs

Use:

- 10 Index cards
- Number cube labeled 2, 3, 4, 5, 6, 8
- MathBoard materials

1. **Work Together** Label 10 cards with a two-digit number less than 30. Shuffle the cards and put them face down.
2. Each partner draws a card and tosses the number cube. Then write a division on your MathBoard, dividing the number on the card by the number on the cube.

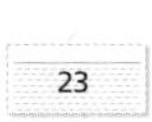

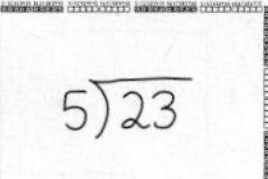

3. Trade MathBoards with your partner. Complete the division.
4. **Think** How can you check your work?
5. Repeat with other divisions.

Unit 11, Lesson 19

Activity Note Have students repeat the activity five times. After each round, students should check their work, making sure that each remainder is less than the divisor.

Math Writing Prompt

Analyze How can you use count-bys to divide? Use an example to explain your thinking.

Software Support

The Number Games: Up, Up, and Array, Level L

Challenge — Activity Card 11-19

Remainder Race — Activity Card 11-19

Work: In pairs

Use:

- TRB M143 (Spinner G)
- Paper clips
- 2 counters

1. **Work Together** Make a chart for the numbers 10–90 and the spinner shown below. Place both counters on the number 10 to begin the race.

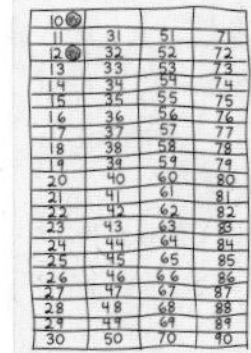

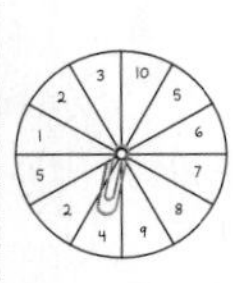

2. Take turns spinning and dividing the number that your counter is on by the number you spin. On the chart move the number of spaces in the remainder.
3. The first player to land on 90 wins the race.

Unit 11, Lesson 19

Activity Note To shorten the time needed to play the game, the rules can be revised to allow a player to win by landing on 90 or beyond that last space.

Math Writing Prompt

Explain Your Thinking If you are dividing something by 5, can you have a remainder of 6 things? Explain your thinking.

Software Support

Course II: Module 2: Unit 3: Meaning of Division

3 Homework and Spiral Review

Goal: Additional Practice

✓ Include students' completed Homework page as part of their portfolios.

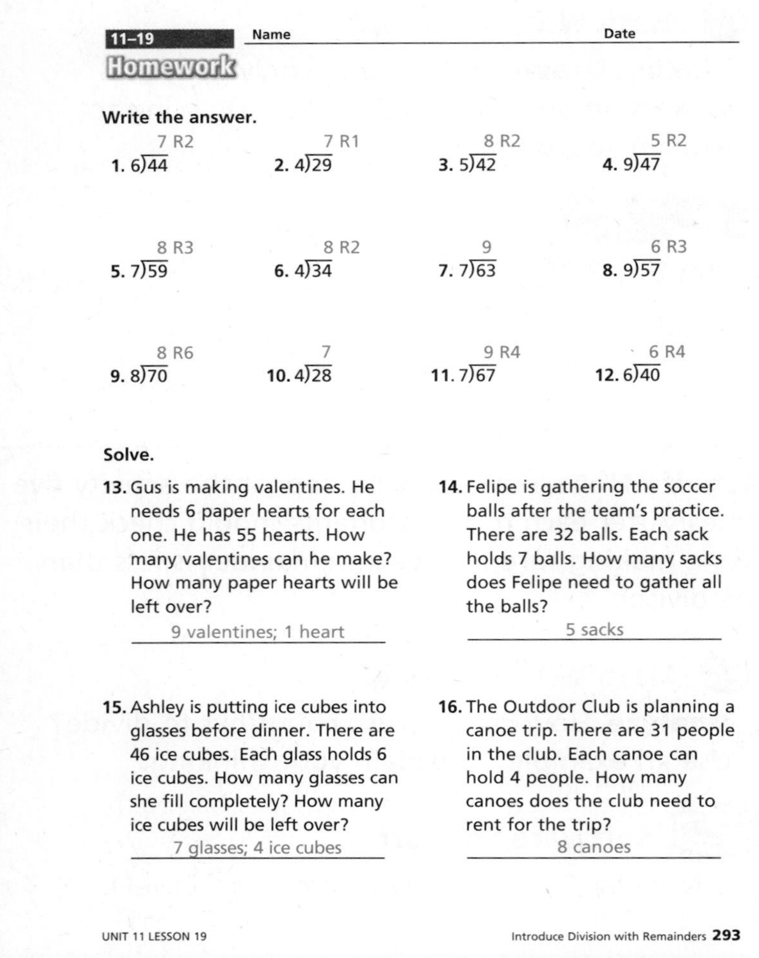

11–19 Homework   Name ________ Date ________

Write the answer.

1. $6\overline{)44}$ 7 R2
2. $4\overline{)29}$ 7 R1
3. $5\overline{)42}$ 8 R2
4. $9\overline{)47}$ 5 R2
5. $7\overline{)59}$ 8 R3
6. $4\overline{)34}$ 8 R2
7. $7\overline{)63}$ 9
8. $9\overline{)57}$ 6 R3
9. $8\overline{)70}$ 8 R6
10. $4\overline{)28}$ 7
11. $7\overline{)67}$ 9 R4
12. $6\overline{)40}$ 6 R4

Solve.

13. Gus is making valentines. He needs 6 paper hearts for each one. He has 55 hearts. How many valentines can he make? How many paper hearts will be left over?
9 valentines; 1 heart

14. Felipe is gathering the soccer balls after the team's practice. There are 32 balls. Each sack holds 7 balls. How many sacks does Felipe need to gather all the balls?
5 sacks

15. Ashley is putting ice cubes into glasses before dinner. There are 46 ice cubes. Each glass holds 6 ice cubes. How many glasses can she fill completely? How many ice cubes will be left over?
7 glasses; 4 ice cubes

16. The Outdoor Club is planning a canoe trip. There are 31 people in the club. Each canoe can hold 4 people. How many canoes does the club need to rent for the trip?
8 canoes

UNIT 11 LESSON 19   Introduce Division with Remainders 293

Homework and Remembering page 293

Goal: Spiral Review

This Remembering page would be appropriate anytime after today's lesson.

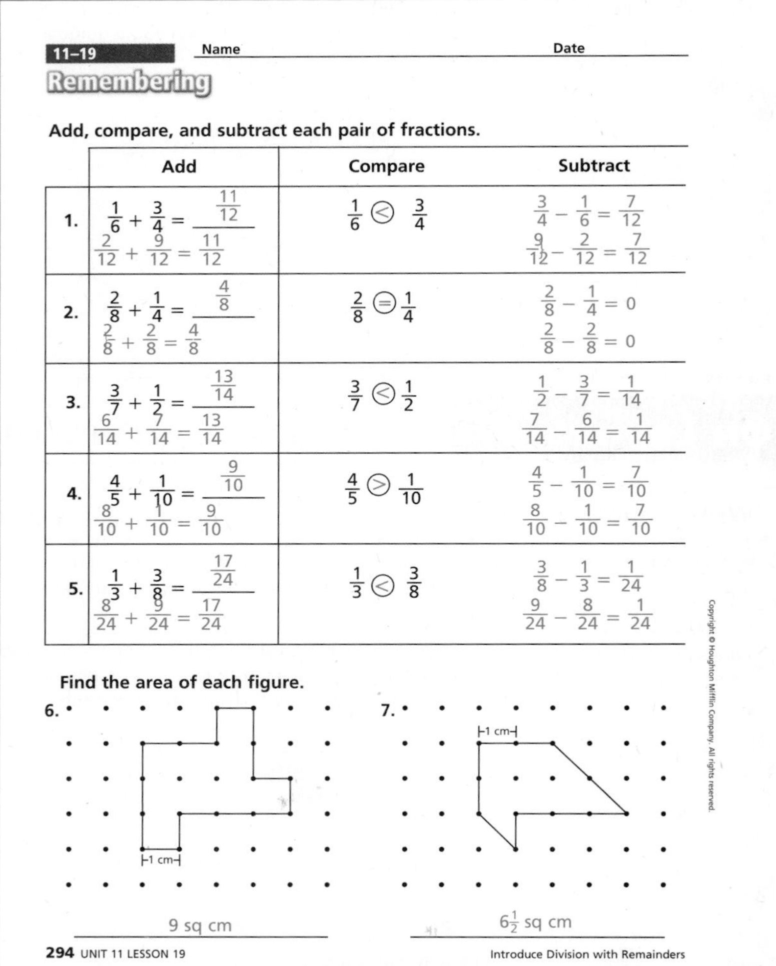

11–19 Remembering   Name ________ Date ________

Add, compare, and subtract each pair of fractions.

	Add	Compare	Subtract
1.	$\frac{1}{6}+\frac{3}{4}=\frac{11}{12}$; $\frac{2}{12}+\frac{9}{12}=\frac{11}{12}$	$\frac{1}{6} < \frac{3}{4}$	$\frac{3}{4}-\frac{1}{6}=\frac{7}{12}$; $\frac{9}{12}-\frac{2}{12}=\frac{7}{12}$
2.	$\frac{2}{8}+\frac{1}{4}=\frac{4}{8}$; $\frac{2}{8}+\frac{2}{8}=\frac{4}{8}$	$\frac{2}{8} = \frac{1}{4}$	$\frac{2}{8}-\frac{1}{4}=0$; $\frac{2}{8}-\frac{2}{8}=0$
3.	$\frac{3}{7}+\frac{1}{2}=\frac{13}{14}$; $\frac{6}{14}+\frac{7}{14}=\frac{13}{14}$	$\frac{3}{7} < \frac{1}{2}$	$\frac{1}{2}-\frac{3}{7}=\frac{1}{14}$; $\frac{7}{14}-\frac{6}{14}=\frac{1}{14}$
4.	$\frac{4}{5}+\frac{1}{10}=\frac{9}{10}$; $\frac{8}{10}+\frac{1}{10}=\frac{9}{10}$	$\frac{4}{5} > \frac{1}{10}$	$\frac{4}{5}-\frac{1}{10}=\frac{7}{10}$; $\frac{8}{10}-\frac{1}{10}=\frac{7}{10}$
5.	$\frac{1}{3}+\frac{3}{8}=\frac{17}{24}$; $\frac{8}{24}+\frac{9}{24}=\frac{17}{24}$	$\frac{1}{3} < \frac{3}{8}$	$\frac{3}{8}-\frac{1}{3}=\frac{1}{24}$; $\frac{9}{24}-\frac{8}{24}=\frac{1}{24}$

Find the area of each figure.

6. 1 cm — 9 sq cm

7. 1 cm — $6\frac{1}{2}$ sq cm

294 UNIT 11 LESSON 19   Introduce Division with Remainders

Homework and Remembering page 294

Home or School Activity

Literature Connection

A Remainder of One Read aloud Elinor J. Pinczes' book about dividing with remainders. As you read aloud each page, have students predict if Joe will march alone as a remainder.

Understand Remainders

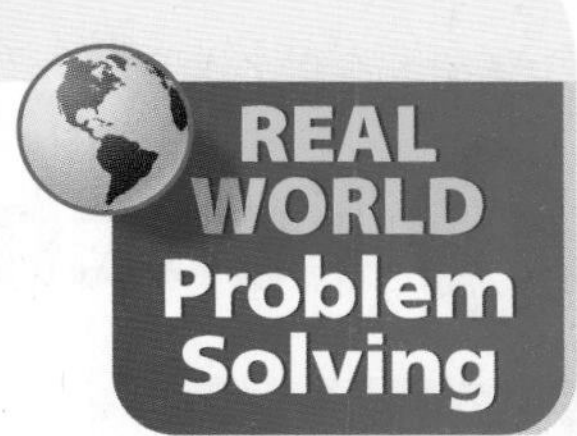

Lesson Objectives

- Write answers as a number plus a remainder or as mixed numbers.
- Solve word problems involving division with remainders.

Vocabulary	
division	mixed number
remainder	numerator
quotient	denominator

The Day at a Glance

Today's Goals	Materials	
1 Teaching the Lesson **A1:** Understand that remainders can be epxressed as fractions. **A2:** Solve division word problems and interpret the remainder to give the correct answer.	**Lesson Activities** Student Activity Book pp. 451–452 or Student Hardcover Book pp. 451–452 and Activity Workbook p. 214 (includes Class Write-on Sheets) Homework and Remembering pp. 295–296 Sentence Strips Two-Color Counters Sticky Notes Calculators	**Going Further** Activity Cards 11-20 Math Journals
2 Going Further ▸ Problem Solving Strategy: Estimate or Exact Answer ▸ Differentiated Instruction		
3 Homework and Spiral Review		

Use Math Talk today!

Keeping Skills Sharp

Quick Practice — 5 MINUTES

Goal: Identify 6s count-bys just under a given number. Identify the difference between the numbers.

Just Under Count-Bys Have a **Student Leader** say a number that is not a 6s count-by. Students respond with the 6s count-by that is nearest to, but less than that number. Then students calculate the difference between the count-by and the number. Repeat.

Leader: The nearest 6s count-by to 57 is what number?

Class: 54

Leader: What is the difference between the numbers? *Class:* 3

Daily Routines

Homework Review Have students share solutions with the class.

Act It Out Toby cut a strip of fabric into thirds. She kept one third and gave Mel one third. The last third she cut in half and gave each 3-inch piece to Clare and Tom. How long was the original strip of fabric? Use paper strips to act out the problem. 18 inches

1 Teaching the Lesson

Activity 1

Remainders as Fractions

 30 MINUTES

Goal: Understand that remainders can be expressed as fractions.

Materials: Student Activity Book or Hardcover Book p. 451 and Activity Workbook p. 214 (includes special format)

 **NCTM Standards:**
Number and Operations
Problem Solving

Teaching Note

Math Background The answer to a division can be given as a mixed number when the object being divided can be split or fractured into smaller equal parts. Cookies, sandwiches, pizzas, and other foods are examples of objects that can be easily fractured.

Four cousins wanted to share 9 cookies equally. How many cookies can each cousin get?

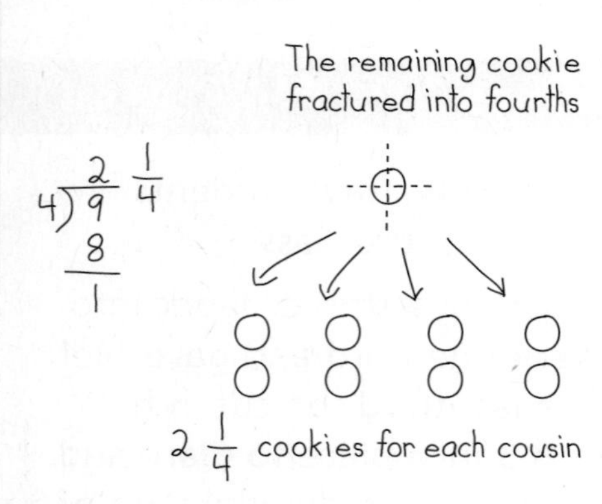

- Does anyone see a pattern in the way the fractions are formed in a mixed number answer? The top number in the fraction is the remainder in the division problem. And the bottom in the fraction is the number we divided by.

▶ Introduce Expressing the Remainder as a Fraction WHOLE CLASS

To introduce writing a quotient as a mixed number, have students use **Solve and Discuss** for the following problem.

The Soccer Club had a bake sale. Players are equally dividing the baked goods that no one bought. Omar and Rosita will divide the 11 brownies equally. How many brownies can each get?

$$\begin{array}{r} 5\text{ R}1 \\ 2\overline{)11} \\ -10 \\ \hline 1 \end{array}$$

Each person will get 5 brownies, because 2 times 5 equals 10. There will be 1 brownie left over.

If students do not suggest dividing the remaining brownie, explain that dividing it in half would be another way of solving the problem. Present this drawing to show how to fully divide the brownies.

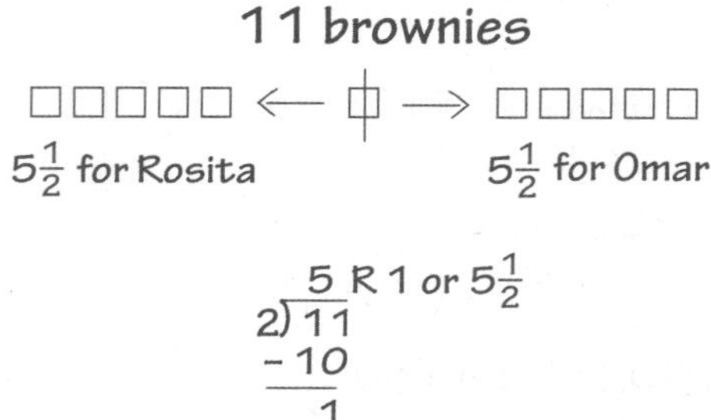

Omar and Rosita would each get $5\frac{1}{2}$ brownies. Explain that when you divide something like brownies, you can fracture the remainder into as many parts as you have groups.

- In the problem about brownies, how many groups are there? 2 How many times did we fracture the remainder? The remainder was fractured into 2 parts to make halves because we are dividing into 2 groups.

Write these three ways to write the division on the board.

$2\overline{)11}$ $\quad 11 \div 2 \quad$ $\frac{11}{2}$

- How would you write $\frac{11}{2}$ as a mixed number? $5\frac{1}{2}$

Write the following problem (as seen in the side column) and have students solve the problem expressing the answer as a mixed number and make a drawing to illustrate the answer. See the sample of student work.

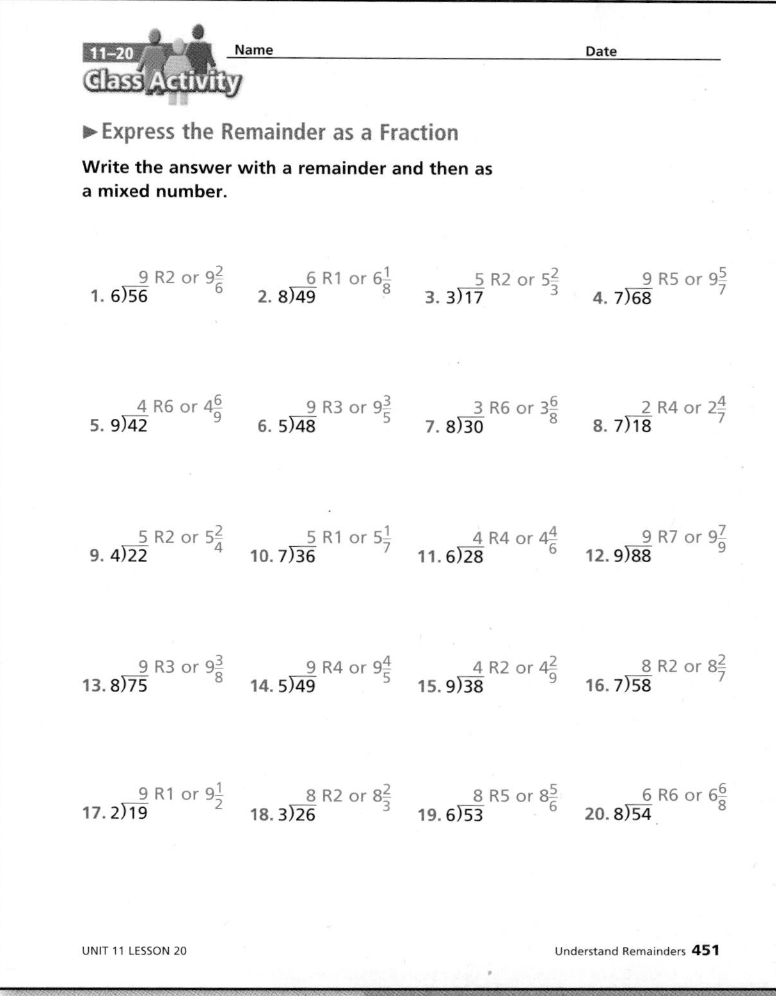

11–20 Class Activity

Name ________________ Date ________

▶ Express the Remainder as a Fraction

Write the answer with a remainder and then as a mixed number.

1. $6\overline{)56}$ 9 R2 or $9\frac{2}{6}$
2. $8\overline{)49}$ 6 R1 or $6\frac{1}{8}$
3. $3\overline{)17}$ 5 R2 or $5\frac{2}{3}$
4. $7\overline{)68}$ 9 R5 or $9\frac{5}{7}$
5. $9\overline{)42}$ 4 R6 or $4\frac{6}{9}$
6. $5\overline{)48}$ 9 R3 or $9\frac{3}{5}$
7. $8\overline{)30}$ 3 R6 or $3\frac{6}{8}$
8. $7\overline{)18}$ 2 R4 or $2\frac{4}{7}$
9. $4\overline{)22}$ 5 R2 or $5\frac{2}{4}$
10. $7\overline{)36}$ 5 R1 or $5\frac{1}{7}$
11. $6\overline{)28}$ 4 R4 or $4\frac{4}{6}$
12. $9\overline{)88}$ 9 R7 or $9\frac{7}{9}$
13. $8\overline{)75}$ 9 R3 or $9\frac{3}{8}$
14. $5\overline{)49}$ 9 R4 or $9\frac{4}{5}$
15. $9\overline{)38}$ 4 R2 or $4\frac{2}{9}$
16. $7\overline{)58}$ 8 R2 or $8\frac{2}{7}$
17. $2\overline{)19}$ 9 R1 or $9\frac{1}{2}$
18. $3\overline{)26}$ 8 R2 or $8\frac{2}{3}$
19. $6\overline{)53}$ 8 R5 or $8\frac{5}{6}$
20. $8\overline{)54}$ 6 R6 or $6\frac{6}{8}$

UNIT 11 LESSON 20 Understand Remainders 451

Student Activity Book page 451

▶ Express the Remainder as a Fraction INDIVIDUALS

Refer students to Student page 451. Work through exercise 1 together as a class writing the steps on the board as students give them.

- What is the count-by of 6 closest to but less than 56? 54 which is 9 × 6
- What is the difference between 56 and 54? 2
- Where should I write the remainder? Above the bar next to the 9.

$$\begin{array}{r} 9\text{ R }2 \text{ or } 9\frac{2}{6} \\ 6\overline{)56} \\ -54 \\ \hline 2 \end{array}$$

- How can you write the answer as a mixed number? Possible answer: Think 2 divided by 6 can be written $\frac{2}{6}$. So the answer is $9\frac{2}{6}$ or think of 56 ÷ 6 as the improper fraction, $\frac{56}{6}$, and write it as a mixed number.

Have students work individually to complete Student Book page 451. Students do not need to simplify the fraction remainders. Have students check their answers in pairs when they complete the page.

Class Management

While students do not need to write the fractional parts of their mixed number answers in simplest form, you might want to challenge students who finish early to do so.

English Language Learners

Make sure students understand *fracture*. Say: **In the brownie problem we *fractured* the last brownie.**

- **Beginning** Say: ***Fracture* means break into smaller equal parts.** Have students repeat.
- **Intermediate** Ask: **Does *fracture* mean break into smaller equal or unequal parts?** equal
- **Advanced** Say: ***Fracture* means break into smaller __.** equal parts

Activity 2

Word Problems with Remainders

 20 MINUTES

Goal: Solve division word problems and interpret the remainder to give the correct answer.

Materials: Student Activity Book or Hardcover Book p. 452

 **NCTM Standards:**
Number and Operations
Problem Solving

The Learning Classroom

Building Concepts Remind students that objects that can be easily split or fractured can be used to write division word problems with mixed number answers. Challenge students to identify three classroom objects that can be fractured. Ask them to explain how the objects might be used as the subjects of division word problems with mixed number answers.

Alternate Approach

Students may want to use counters or other countable objects to model the groups of cakes in the word problem. Remind students to use problem-solving strategies such as *make a model* or *draw a picture* to help them solve complicated division word problems.

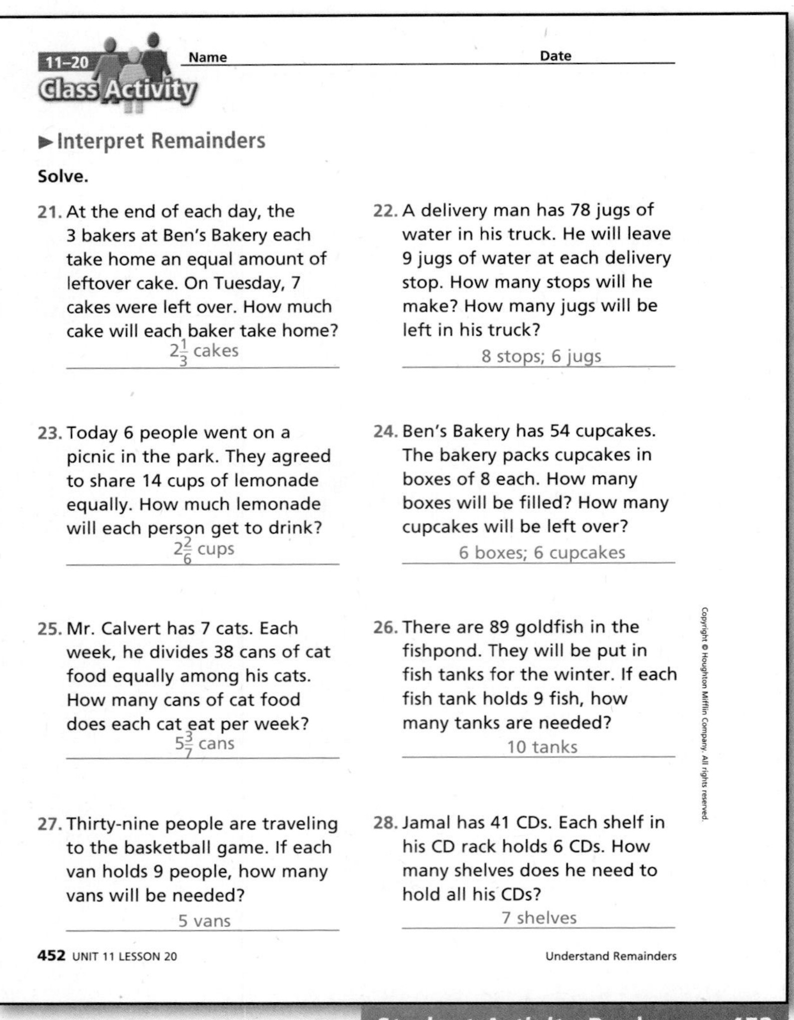

11–20 Class Activity   Name ____________   Date ____________

► Interpret Remainders

Solve.

21. At the end of each day, the 3 bakers at Ben's Bakery each take home an equal amount of leftover cake. On Tuesday, 7 cakes were left over. How much cake will each baker take home?
$2\frac{1}{3}$ cakes

22. A delivery man has 78 jugs of water in his truck. He will leave 9 jugs of water at each delivery stop. How many stops will he make? How many jugs will be left in his truck?
8 stops; 6 jugs

23. Today 6 people went on a picnic in the park. They agreed to share 14 cups of lemonade equally. How much lemonade will each person get to drink?
$2\frac{2}{6}$ cups

24. Ben's Bakery has 54 cupcakes. The bakery packs cupcakes in boxes of 8 each. How many boxes will be filled? How many cupcakes will be left over?
6 boxes; 6 cupcakes

25. Mr. Calvert has 7 cats. Each week, he divides 38 cans of cat food equally among his cats. How many cans of cat food does each cat eat per week?
$5\frac{3}{7}$ cans

26. There are 89 goldfish in the fishpond. They will be put in fish tanks for the winter. If each fish tank holds 9 fish, how many tanks are needed?
10 tanks

27. Thirty-nine people are traveling to the basketball game. If each van holds 9 people, how many vans will be needed?
5 vans

28. Jamal has 41 CDs. Each shelf in his CD rack holds 6 CDs. How many shelves does he need to hold all his CDs?
7 shelves

452 UNIT 11 LESSON 20   Understand Remainders

Student Activity Book page 452

► Interpret Remainders WHOLE CLASS

Refer students to the first problem on Student Book page 452.

- How would you solve problem 21? Divide 7 by 3
- Does it makes sense to give the answer as an amount plus a remainder, or "fracture" the remainder and give the answer as a mixed number? as a mixed number because a cake can be fractured

Then use **Solve and Discuss** to solve the problem. Have a volunteer go to the board to explain their work.

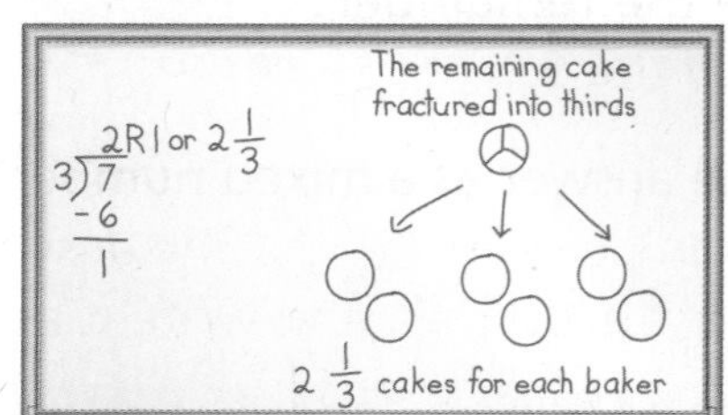

Use **Solve and Discuss** to solve problem 22. Discuss how the answer should be reported.

- A delivery man has 78 jugs of water in his truck. He will leave 9 jugs of water at each delivery stop. How many stops will he make? 8 How many jugs of water will be left over? 6 How do you know? 78 minus 72 equals 6
- How should we give the remainder? as the number of jugs left over Why not as a mixed number? because the question asked how many stops will be made; you cannot make part of a stop

Point out that this is the *left-over* type remainder answer that they were introduced to in the last lesson.

- What is a *left-over* type remainder answer? when the remainder cannot be used in the context of the problem

In the last lesson you were also introduced to the *another whole* type remainder.

- What is the *another whole* remainder? when the remainder needs another whole added to the whole number answer

In problem 21 we discovered a third type of remainder called a *fractional part* remainder.

- When do we give remainders as fractional parts? When we are talking about things that can be fractured and shared, such as things to eat, we write the answer as a whole number and a fractional part.
- What is a whole number and fractional part called? a mixed number

Depending on how well your class has understood how to interpret remainders, have students finish page 452 individually, in **Student Pairs**, or as a class using **Solve and Discuss**. If students work individually or in **Student Pairs**, they can write division word problems for a partner to solve if they finish early.

Teaching Note

Language and Vocabulary
Understanding the terms for the three types of remainders: left-over, another whole, and fraction is critical for English learners to explain how to interpret the remainder and check their understanding of what is being addressed in the classroom. Have students experiencing difficulty expressing themselves effectively practice explaining how to interpret the remainder with an English-speaking partner.

Ongoing Assessment

Have students divide 43 by 8 and write the answer as a mixed number.

2 Going Further

Problem Solving Strategy: Estimate or Exact Answer

Goal: Decide whether an estimate or exact answer is needed to solve a problem.

Materials: sentence strips, counters, sticky notes

 **NCTM Standards:**
Number and Operations
Problem Solving

Teaching Note

Math Background In some problem solving situations, it is not necessary for students to find an exact answer; instead, they can use strategies to make estimates and use words like *almost* or *about* to describe a number.

▶ Estimates and Exact Answers

SMALL GROUPS

Review the difference between an estimate and an exact answer with students. Explain to students that sometimes an estimate is fine, but other times, the same situation needs an exact number. Share the following situation to illustrate this point.

Suppose someone wants to roughly know how many students are in your school. Would you give an estimate or an exact number? estimate What if the principal was collecting data about attendance and needed to find out how many students were enrolled in the school. Would an estimate or an exact number be needed? exact number

Then, have **Small Groups** estimate the number of students in school. If you can access the real data, have groups compare their estimate with the exact number to see how close they were. You may want to have them brainstorm a list of real-life situations in which estimates or exact answers would be used.

Pass out the prepared sentence strips. Then, have **Small Groups** decide whether an estimate or an exact answer is needed for each of the following situations.

You're planning a party and you're trying to figure out how many invitations to make. How many people are coming to your party?

You're looking at a jar of jellybeans. How many jellybeans are in the jar?

You're looking at a picture in the newspaper of a crowd of people. How many people are in the picture?

Someone bought a drink and sandwich with a $5.00 bill at your deli. The total cost was $3.56. How much change do you owe them?

Allow each group to discuss their results and then have a person from each group present their situation and describe whether an exact answer or an estimate is appropriate. See the **Math Talk in Action** for a sample discussion.

Math Talk in Action

Let's look at a group that thought an exact answer was more appropriate than an estimate.

Marta: Our group was planning a party and we needed to find out how many people were coming so we could buy invitations. We thought we needed an exact number of guests so we could buy the right amount. We would need to know how many packages of invitations we needed to buy so we had enough.

Now let's look at a group who thought they could give an estimate instead of an exact answer.

Tony: Our group was looking at a picture in the newspaper of a crowd of people. We didn't have to know an exact number. We estimated there were a lot of people, probably in the thousands.

Differentiated Instruction

Extra Help Write the following on sticky notes: *exactly 20, about 20, more than 20,* and *less than 20.* Have students use counters to model each situation.

2 Going Further

Differentiated Instruction

Intervention — Activity Card 11-20

Division Tic-Tac-Toe

Activity Card 11-20 ●

Work: In pairs

Decide:

Who will be player X and who will be player O.

1. Copy the division problems below onto a 3-by-3 grid.

$3\overline{)16}$	$5\overline{)19}$	$6\overline{)20}$
$4\overline{)18}$	$7\overline{)23}$	$5\overline{)24}$
$6\overline{)31}$	$3\overline{)17}$	$8\overline{)29}$

2. Player X Choose a division problem on the grid and solve it. If you answer it correctly, then place an X on that square.
3. Player O Choose a problem on an unmarked square and solve it. Mark that square with an O if your answer is correct.
4. Take turns until one player makes tic-tac-toe or the game ends in a draw.

Unit 11, Lesson 20

Activity Note As students play the game, they should check each other's answers to the division problems before marking the grid.

Math Writing Prompt

Explain Your Thinking Explain why you can write the answer to this word problem as a mixed number: Four friends share 5 pizzas equally. How much pizza does each friend get?

Software Support

Warm Up 13.25

On Level — Activity Card 11-20

Class Picnic

Activity Card 11-20 ▲

Work: In pairs

1. Use the chart below and the number of students in your class to plan a class picnic.

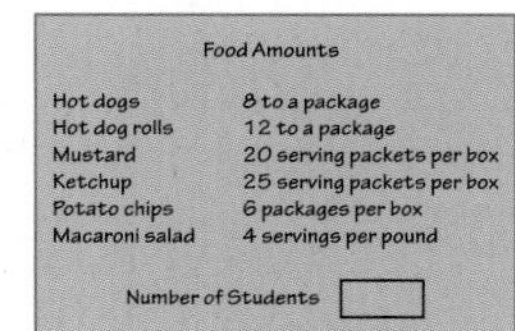

Food Amounts

Hot dogs	8 to a package
Hot dog rolls	12 to a package
Mustard	20 serving packets per box
Ketchup	25 serving packets per box
Potato chips	6 packages per box
Macaroni salad	4 servings per pound

Number of Students ☐

2. Decide how many packages of each type of food you need to buy. Be sure that everyone in the class has an equal amount of each item. Calculate how much will be left over.
3. Discuss Suppose one more student joins your class. How many more items will you need?

Unit 11, Lesson 20

Activity Note Students can extend the discussion to identify how many additional students would join the class before they would need to buy one more of each item.

Math Writing Prompt

Write Your Own Write a word problem that will have a mixed number answer.

Software Support

The Number Games: Up, Up, and Array, Level L

Challenge — Activity Card 11-20

Division Riddles

Activity Card 11-20 ■

Work: In pairs

1. Work Together Solve each riddle below.
   - I am less than 15 and greater than 10. Divide me by 5 and the remainder is 4. What number am I? 14
   - Divide me by 7 and the remainder is 2. I am a number between 10 and 20. What number am I? 16
2. Discuss What strategies did you use to solve each riddle?
3. Write your own riddle and trade with your partner to solve.
4. Check your partner's work.

Unit 11, Lesson 20

Activity Note Some students may use the strategy of guess and check to solve the riddles. Other students may recognize the relationship between remainders and multiples of the divisor to solve the riddle.

Math Writing Prompt

Work Backward Think of a number that is divided by 4 and equals $2\frac{3}{4}$. Explain how you can find that number.

DESTINATION Math®

Software Support

Course II: Module 2: Unit 3: Dividing by a 1-digit Number

3 Homework and Spiral Review

11–20 Homework **Goal:** Additional Practice

This Homework page provides practice in division.

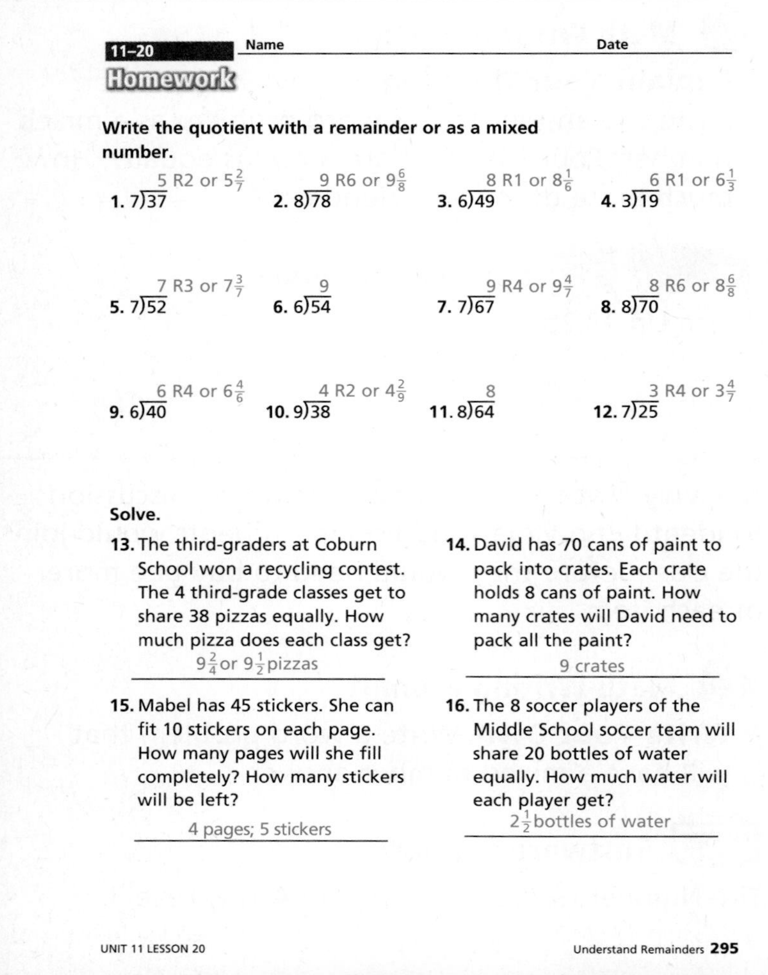

11–20 Homework Name ______ Date ______

Write the quotient with a remainder or as a mixed number.

1. $7\overline{)37}$ 5 R2 or $5\frac{2}{7}$
2. $8\overline{)78}$ 9 R6 or $9\frac{6}{8}$
3. $6\overline{)49}$ 8 R1 or $8\frac{1}{6}$
4. $3\overline{)19}$ 6 R1 or $6\frac{1}{3}$
5. $7\overline{)52}$ 7 R3 or $7\frac{3}{7}$
6. $6\overline{)54}$ 9
7. $7\overline{)67}$ 9 R4 or $9\frac{4}{7}$
8. $8\overline{)70}$ 8 R6 or $8\frac{6}{8}$
9. $6\overline{)40}$ 6 R4 or $6\frac{4}{6}$
10. $9\overline{)38}$ 4 R2 or $4\frac{2}{9}$
11. $8\overline{)64}$ 8
12. $7\overline{)25}$ 3 R4 or $3\frac{4}{7}$

Solve.

13. The third-graders at Coburn School won a recycling contest. The 4 third-grade classes get to share 38 pizzas equally. How much pizza does each class get?
$9\frac{2}{4}$ or $9\frac{1}{2}$ pizzas

14. David has 70 cans of paint to pack into crates. Each crate holds 8 cans of paint. How many crates will David need to pack all the paint?
9 crates

15. Mabel has 45 stickers. She can fit 10 stickers on each page. How many pages will she fill completely? How many stickers will be left?
4 pages; 5 stickers

16. The 8 soccer players of the Middle School soccer team will share 20 bottles of water equally. How much water will each player get?
$2\frac{1}{2}$ bottles of water

UNIT 11 LESSON 20 Understand Remainders **295**

Homework and Remembering page 295

11–20 Remembering **Goal:** Spiral Review

This Remembering page would be appropriate anytime after today's lesson.

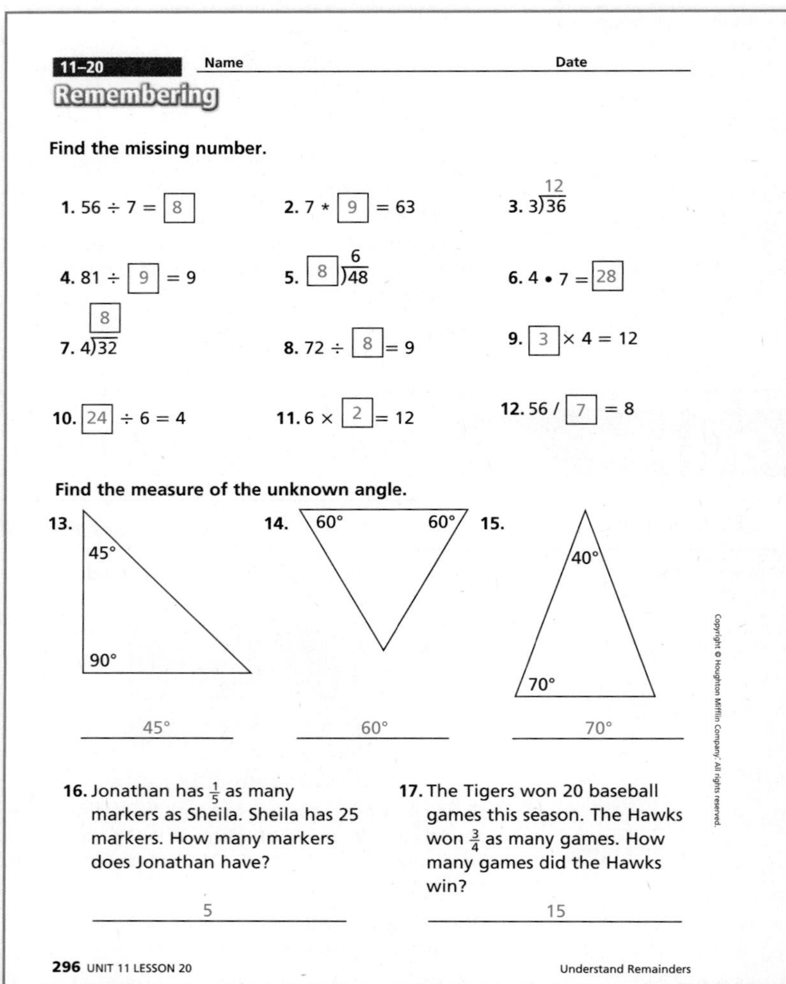

11–20 Remembering Name ______ Date ______

Find the missing number.

1. 56 ÷ 7 = [8]
2. 7 * [9] = 63
3. $3\overline{)36}$ [12]
4. 81 ÷ [9] = 9
5. $[8]\overline{)48}$ 6
6. 4 • 7 = [28]
7. $4\overline{)32}$ [8]
8. 72 ÷ [8] = 9
9. [3] × 4 = 12
10. [24] ÷ 6 = 4
11. 6 × [2] = 12
12. 56 / [7] = 8

Find the measure of the unknown angle.

13. 45°, 90° — 45°
14. 60°, 60° — 60°
15. 40°, 70° — 70°

16. Jonathan has $\frac{1}{5}$ as many markers as Sheila. Sheila has 25 markers. How many markers does Jonathan have?
5

17. The Tigers won 20 baseball games this season. The Hawks won $\frac{3}{4}$ as many games. How many games did the Hawks win?
15

296 UNIT 11 LESSON 20 Understand Remainders

Homework and Remembering page 296

Home or School Activity

Technology Connection

Use a Calculator Have students solve divisions with remainders using a calculator that shows remainders. Be sure that the calculator is set to show remainders (rather than decimals), and then have students practice with 15 ÷ 4, 18 ÷ 5, and 20 ÷ 3. After they practice, ask them to write and record the answers to ten of their own divisions, using the calculator to find the answers.

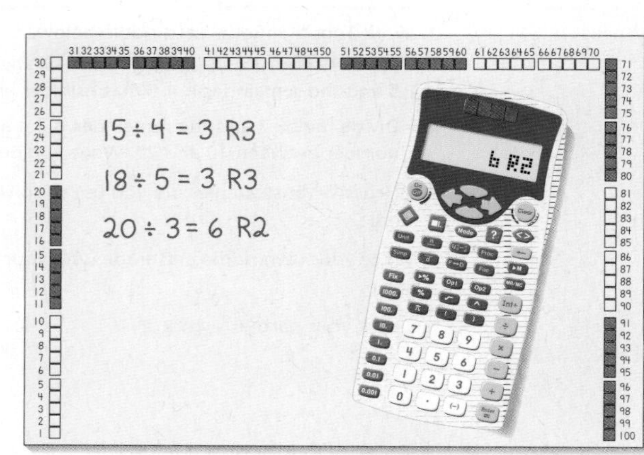

Practice Division with Remainders

Lesson Objectives

- Practice dividing with remainders.
- Solve word problems involving division with remainders.

Vocabulary
count-by
division
remainder
mixed number

The Day at a Glance

Today's Goals	Materials	
1 Teaching the Lesson **A1:** Solve division word problems with remainders. **A2:** Practice dividing with remainders.	**Lesson Activities** Student Activity Book pp. 453–454 or Student Hardcover Book pp. 453–454 Homework and Remembering pp. 297–298 Quick Quiz 5 (Assessment Guide) *The Great Divide* by Dayle Ann Dodds (Candlewick press, 1999)	**Going Further** Activity Cards 11-21 Inch Grid Paper (TRB M42) MathBoard materials Math Journals
2 Going Further ► Differentiated Instruction		
3 Homework and Spiral Review		

Use Math Talk today!

Keeping Skills Sharp

Quick Practice

Goal: Find 8s count-bys just under a given number. Find the difference between the numbers.

Just Under Count-Bys Have a **Student Leader** say a number that is not an 8s count-by. Students respond with the 8s count-by that is nearest to, but less than that number. Then students calculate the difference between the count-by and the number. Repeat. (See Unit 11 Lesson 20.)

Daily Routines

Homework Review Have students discuss the word problems from their homework. Encourage students to help each other understand and discuss how to solve the word problems.

Strategy Problem Tammy has a photo album that has the same number of pictures on each page. On Monday, she filled 5 pages with 10 photographs. By Tuesday, she has a total of 9 pages filled in all. How many photos did she include on Tuesday? 8 photos

1 Teaching the Lesson

Activity 1

Practice Solving Word Problems with Remainders

 **30 MINUTES**

Goal: Solve division word problems with remainders.

Materials: Student Activity Book or Hardcover Book p. 453

 **NCTM Standards:**
Number and Operations
Problem Solving

Teaching Note

What to Expect from Students Most students should be able to solve the problems on the page with speed and success, given the amount of practice they have had with division word problems. To maintain interest in the skill, you might want to challenge students to make a perfect score on the page.

English Language Learners

Draw pictures and ask simple questions to provide support with vocabulary for the word problems.

- **Beginning** Draw a *dresser* on the board. Say: **This is a *dresser*.** Point to a drawer. Say: **I put my clothes in the drawers.** Have students repeat.
- **Intermediate** Ask: **Are things at a grocery store on *shelves* or in *drawers*?** on shelves
- **Advanced** Ask: **Where do grocery stores keep cans? Where do people keep clothes? Where do girls keep jewelry?**

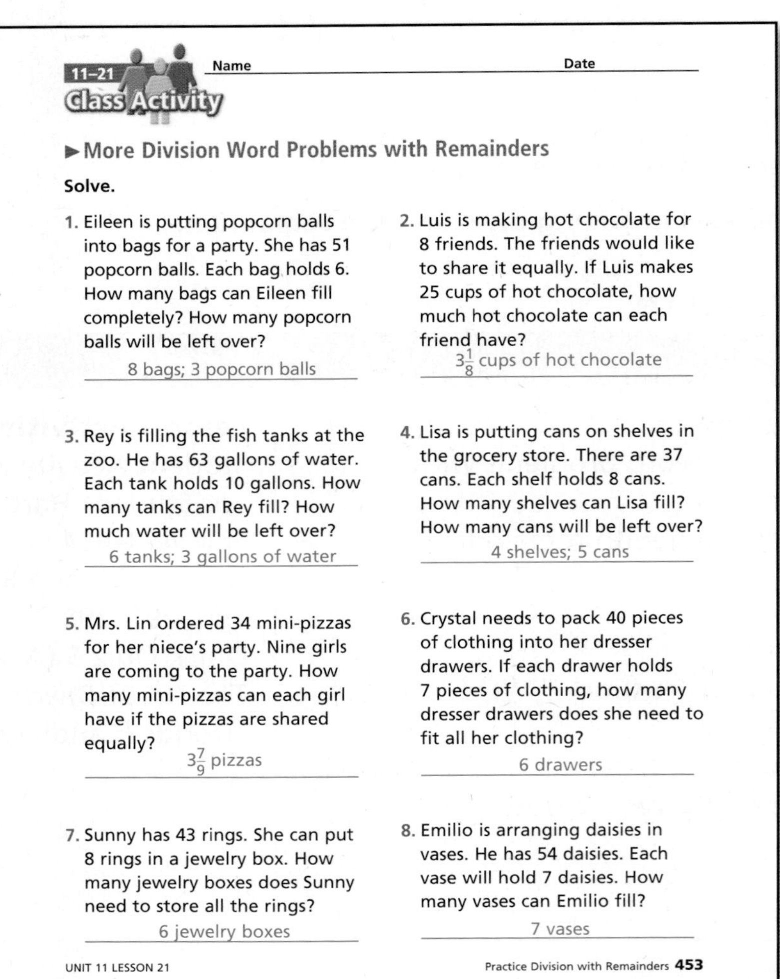
11–21 Class Activity   Name ____ Date ____

► More Division Word Problems with Remainders

Solve.

1. Eileen is putting popcorn balls into bags for a party. She has 51 popcorn balls. Each bag holds 6. How many bags can Eileen fill completely? How many popcorn balls will be left over?
8 bags; 3 popcorn balls

2. Luis is making hot chocolate for 8 friends. The friends would like to share it equally. If Luis makes 25 cups of hot chocolate, how much hot chocolate can each friend have?
$3\frac{1}{8}$ cups of hot chocolate

3. Rey is filling the fish tanks at the zoo. He has 63 gallons of water. Each tank holds 10 gallons. How many tanks can Rey fill? How much water will be left over?
6 tanks; 3 gallons of water

4. Lisa is putting cans on shelves in the grocery store. There are 37 cans. Each shelf holds 8 cans. How many shelves can Lisa fill? How many cans will be left over?
4 shelves; 5 cans

5. Mrs. Lin ordered 34 mini-pizzas for her niece's party. Nine girls are coming to the party. How many mini-pizzas can each girl have if the pizzas are shared equally?
$3\frac{7}{9}$ pizzas

6. Crystal needs to pack 40 pieces of clothing into her dresser drawers. If each drawer holds 7 pieces of clothing, how many dresser drawers does she need to fit all her clothing?
6 drawers

7. Sunny has 43 rings. She can put 8 rings in a jewelry box. How many jewelry boxes does Sunny need to store all the rings?
6 jewelry boxes

8. Emilio is arranging daisies in vases. He has 54 daisies. Each vase will hold 7 daisies. How many vases can Emilio fill?
7 vases

UNIT 11 LESSON 21   Practice Division with Remainders 453

Student Activity Book page 453

► More Division Word Problems with Remainders

WHOLE CLASS

Review the types of remainder problems that students worked with in previous lessons.

- What is a *left-over* type remainder? when the remainder cannot be used in the context of the problem
- What is the *another whole* remainder? when the remainder needs another whole added to the whole number answer
- What is a *fractional part* remainder? When we are talking about things that can be fractured, we write the answer as a whole number and a fractional part.

Have students think of examples of these types of problems.

Then refer students to Student Book page 453. Explain that all of the problems on the page involve division with remainders. Work together to solve the first 3 problems. Have several students work at the board while the rest of the students work at their seats.

Have a volunteer read aloud the first problem.

- What do you know? the number of popcorn balls and the number of balls that fit in each bag
- What do you want to find out? the number of bags you need and the number of balls that will be left over
- How can you find the number of bags? Possible answer: I used count-bys. 8 times 6 is 48. This is the 6s count-by closest to but less than 51. The answer is 8 bags.
- How can you find the number of balls left over? Possible answer: I found the difference between 51 and 48. There are 3 balls left over.

Repeat this type of questioning for problems 2 and 3.

Have students solve the rest of the problems individually or in pairs. While students work, walk around the room to monitor progress. Students who finish early can write word problems for a partner to solve.

Then have students finish the page, work as a class to classify each problem as a *left-over, another whole,* or *fractional parts* division problem. Students should conclude that 1, 3, 4, and 8 are left-over problems, 6 and 7 are another whole problems, and 2 and 5 are fractional parts problems.

▶ Check the Answer to a Division Problem

WHOLE CLASS

Then show students how they can check the answer to a division by multiplying the quotient by the divisor and adding the remainder. If the result is equal to the dividend, the answer to the division is correct.

$$8\overline{)77} = 9 \text{ R}5 \qquad \begin{array}{r} 77 \\ -72 \\ \hline 5 \end{array}$$

9	quotient
× 8	divisor
72	
+ 5	remainder
77	dividend

The Learning Classroom

Math Talk Rather than lead the discussion about the solutions to problems 2 and 3 on Student Book page 453, let Student Leaders prompt the students at the board about how they solved the division problems. Encourage the students at their desks to ask questions as well.

Ongoing Assessment

Have each student write one division with remainder problem, and trade with a partner and solve it. Have them identify what kind of problem it is.

Activity 2

Divide with Remainders

 20 MINUTES

Goal: Practice dividing with remainders.

Materials: Student Activity Book or Hardcover Book p. 454

 **NCTM Standards:**
Number and Operations
Problem Solving

Differentiated Instruction

Extra Help Using students' answers to the exercises as a guide, take note of students who have difficulty dividing by a particular divisor, such as 8 or 9. You can use a count-bys list for that number or a multiplication table to help them solve additional problems with that divisor.

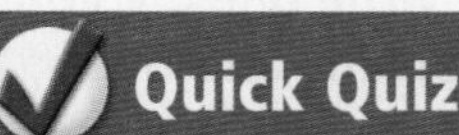

Quick Quiz

See Assessment Guide for Unit 11 Quick Quiz 3.

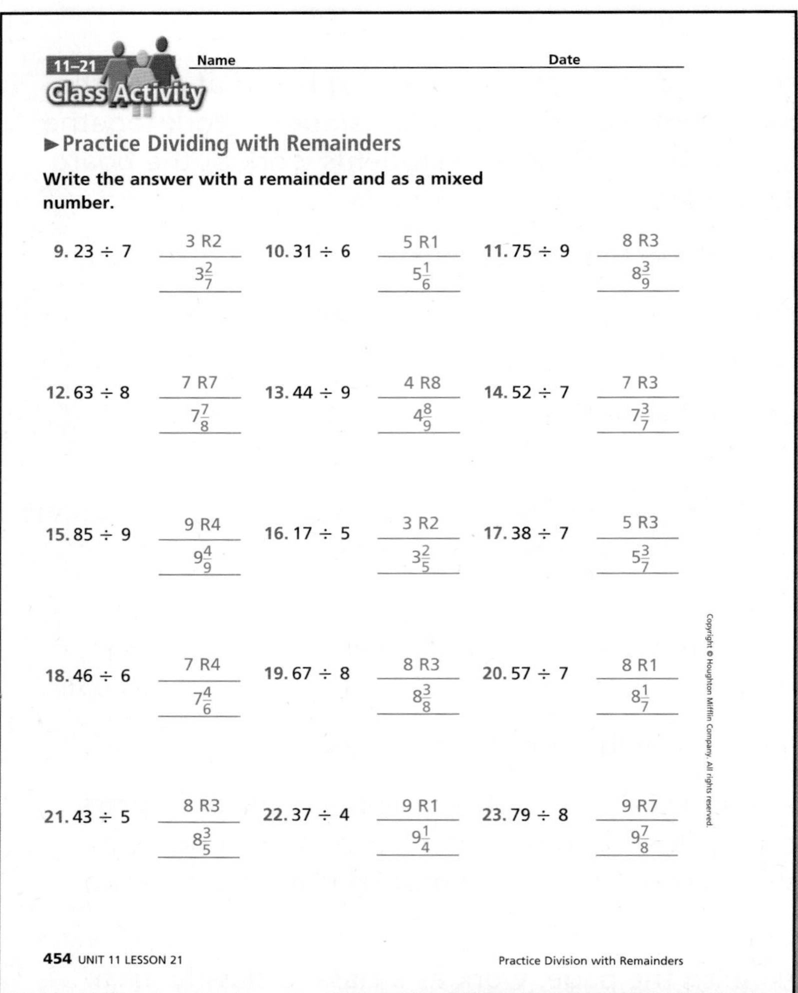

11–21 Class Activity

Name ______ Date ______

▶ Practice Dividing with Remainders

Write the answer with a remainder and as a mixed number.

9. 23 ÷ 7	3 R2 $3\frac{2}{7}$	10. 31 ÷ 6	5 R1 $5\frac{1}{6}$	11. 75 ÷ 9	8 R3 $8\frac{3}{9}$
12. 63 ÷ 8	7 R7 $7\frac{7}{8}$	13. 44 ÷ 9	4 R8 $4\frac{8}{9}$	14. 52 ÷ 7	7 R3 $7\frac{3}{7}$
15. 85 ÷ 9	9 R4 $9\frac{4}{9}$	16. 17 ÷ 5	3 R2 $3\frac{2}{5}$	17. 38 ÷ 7	5 R3 $5\frac{3}{7}$
18. 46 ÷ 6	7 R4 $7\frac{4}{6}$	19. 67 ÷ 8	8 R3 $8\frac{3}{8}$	20. 57 ÷ 7	8 R1 $8\frac{1}{7}$
21. 43 ÷ 5	8 R3 $8\frac{3}{5}$	22. 37 ÷ 4	9 R1 $9\frac{1}{4}$	23. 79 ÷ 8	9 R7 $9\frac{7}{8}$

454 UNIT 11 LESSON 21 Practice Division with Remainders

Student Activity Book page 454

▶ Practice Dividing with Remainders INDIVIDUALS

Refer students to Student Book page 454. Work through exercise 9 together as a class writing the steps on the board as students give them.

$$\begin{array}{r} 3 \text{ R2 or } 3\frac{2}{7} \\ 7\overline{)23} \\ -\,21 \\ \hline 2 \end{array}$$

- What is the count-by of 7 closest to but less than 23? 21 which is 3 × 7
- Where should I write the 3? above the 3
- What is the difference between 23 and 21? 2
- Where should I write the remainder? Above the bar next to the 3.
- How can you write the answer as a mixed number? Possible answers: Think 2 divided by 7 can be written $\frac{2}{7}$. So the answer is $3\frac{2}{7}$ or think of 23 ÷ 7 as the improper fraction, $\frac{23}{7}$ and write it as a mixed number.

Have them complete the page individually and then check their answers with a partner.

2 Going Further

Differentiated Instruction

Intervention — Activity Card 11-21

Remainder Tic-Tac-Toe

Activity Card 11-21 ●

Work: In pairs

Decide:

Who will be player X and player O.

1. Copy the tic-tac-toe board below.
2. Player X Choose a number on the board and decide if it can be divided by a 1-digit number with a remainder of 1. For example, 16 ÷ 5 = 3 R1. If you can find a divisor to give a remainder of 1, mark the square with an X.

16	22	43
31	25	19
33	29	26

3. Player O Take a turn and mark an O in the chosen square if the division gives the remainder 1.
4. Continue until one player makes tic-tac-toe or until the game ends in a draw.

Unit 11, Lesson 21

Activity Note Students can play the game again with the numbers 20, 17, 23, 14, 34, 29, 38, 44, and 32, trying to make quotients with a remainder of 2.

Math Writing Prompt

Investigate Math What is the greatest remainder you can have when the divisor is 6? How do you know?

Software Support

Warm Up 13.25

On Level — Activity Card 11-21

Cross Number Puzzle

Activity Card 11-21 ▲

Work: In pairs

Use:

- TRB M42 (Inch Grid paper)

1. On Your Own Outline a 4-by-4 grid as shown to the right.
2. Write division clues for 8 numbers. Then use the numbers to design your puzzle.
3. Shade the empty squares and write the clue numbers on the grid. Write the clues below your puzzle.
4. Exchange with your partner to solve.
5. Check your partner's work.

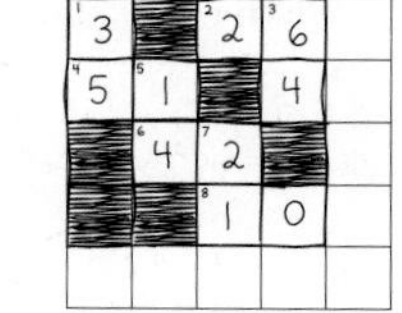

Across	Down
2. __ ÷ 4 = 6R2	1. __ ÷ 8 = 4R3
4. __ ÷ 8 = 6R3	3. __ ÷ 8 = 8
6. __ ÷ 7 = 6	5. __ ÷ 6 = 2R2
8. 22 ÷ 12 = 1R__	7. __ ÷ 3 = 7

Unit 11, Lesson 21

Activity Note Before students begin, use the example to point out characteristics of this puzzle such as how the numbers are oriented in the grid.

Math Writing Prompt

Explain Your Thinking A number divided by 5 has an answer of 4 R2. What is the dividend? Explain how you found it.

Software Support

The Number Games: Up, Up, and Array, Level L

Challenge — Activity Card 11-21

Number Substitution

Activity Card 11-21 ■

Work: On your own

Use:

- MathBoard materials

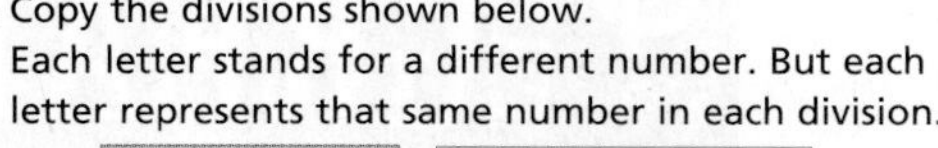

1. Copy the divisions shown below. Each letter stands for a different number. But each letter represents that same number in each division.

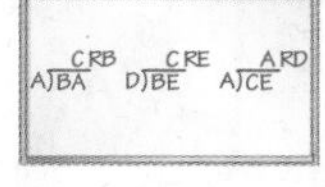

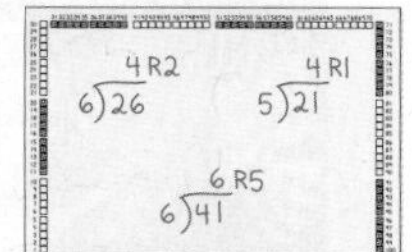

2. Replace each letter with a number that makes each division true. ***Hint:*** A = 6 and E = 1. B = 2; C = 4; D = 5
3. **Analyze** How can you use what you know about remainders to find the dividend in the third equation? A = 6; 6 × 6 = 36; the dividend CE must be between 36 and 42 because there is a remainder. E = 1, and only 41 has the digit 1 in the ones place.

Unit 11, Lesson 21

Activity Note One strategy for completing this activity is to begin with the third division and work with the hints to find other letter values.

Math Writing Prompt

Find the Pattern Suppose you divide a number, n, by 4 and the remainders in the answer is 1. What will the remainders be if you divide the next larger numbers, $n + 1$ and $n + 2$ by 4?

Software Support

Course II: Module 2: Unit 3: Meaning of Division

3 Homework and Spiral Review

Goal: Additional Practice

This Homework page provides practice in division with remainders.

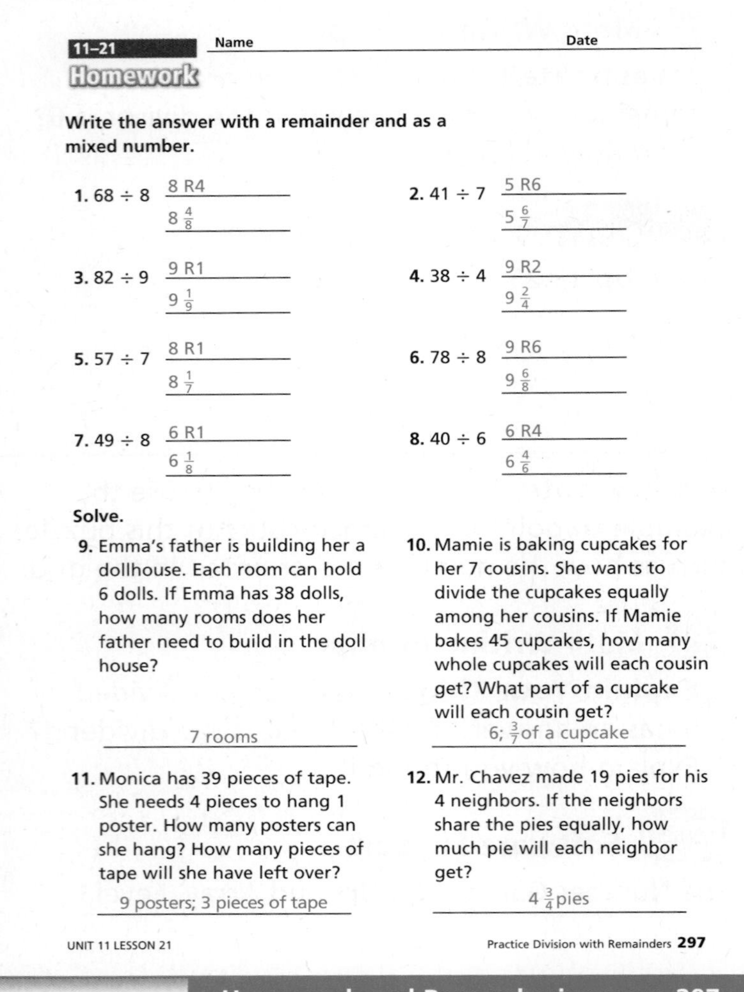

11–21 Name ______ Date ______

Homework

Write the answer with a remainder and as a mixed number.

1. 68 ÷ 8 8 R4 $8\frac{4}{8}$
2. 41 ÷ 7 5 R6 $5\frac{6}{7}$
3. 82 ÷ 9 9 R1 $9\frac{1}{9}$
4. 38 ÷ 4 9 R2 $9\frac{2}{4}$
5. 57 ÷ 7 8 R1 $8\frac{1}{7}$
6. 78 ÷ 8 9 R6 $9\frac{6}{8}$
7. 49 ÷ 8 6 R1 $6\frac{1}{8}$
8. 40 ÷ 6 6 R4 $6\frac{4}{6}$

Solve.

9. Emma's father is building her a dollhouse. Each room can hold 6 dolls. If Emma has 38 dolls, how many rooms does her father need to build in the doll house?
   7 rooms
10. Mamie is baking cupcakes for her 7 cousins. She wants to divide the cupcakes equally among her cousins. If Mamie bakes 45 cupcakes, how many whole cupcakes will each cousin get? What part of a cupcake will each cousin get?
   6; $\frac{3}{7}$ of a cupcake
11. Monica has 39 pieces of tape. She needs 4 pieces to hang 1 poster. How many posters can she hang? How many pieces of tape will she have left over?
   9 posters; 3 pieces of tape
12. Mr. Chavez made 19 pies for his 4 neighbors. If the neighbors share the pies equally, how much pie will each neighbor get?
   $4\frac{3}{4}$ pies

UNIT 11 LESSON 21 Practice Division with Remainders 297

Homework and Remembering page 297

Goal: Spiral Review

This Remembering page would be appropriate anytime after today's lesson.

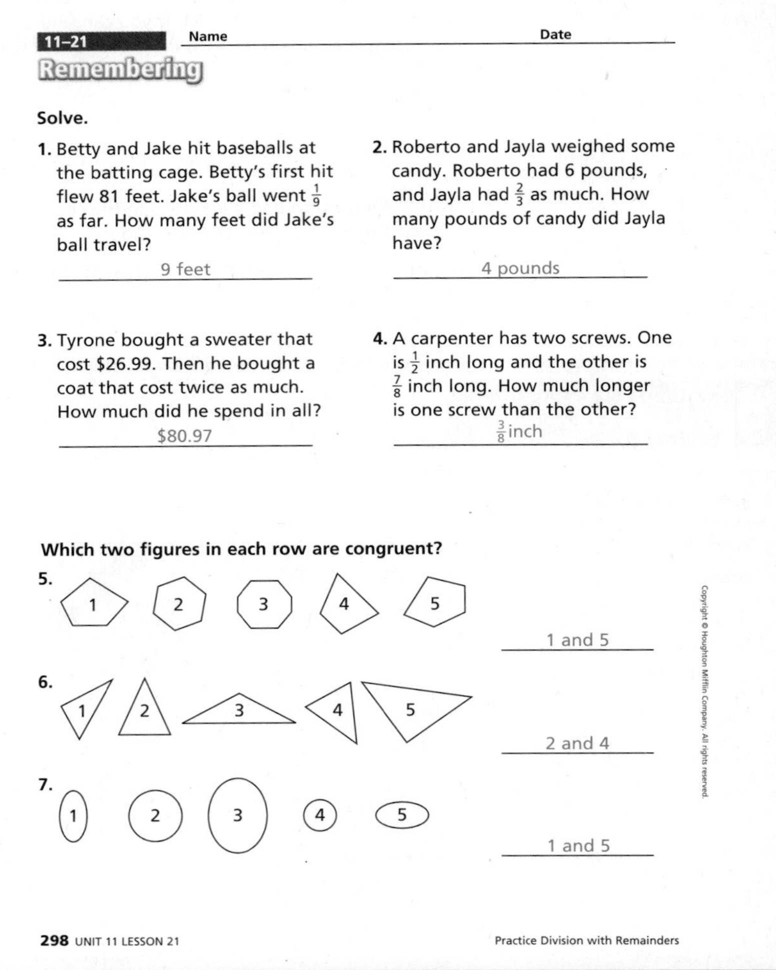

11–21 Name ______ Date ______

Remembering

Solve.

1. Betty and Jake hit baseballs at the batting cage. Betty's first hit flew 81 feet. Jake's ball went $\frac{1}{9}$ as far. How many feet did Jake's ball travel?
   9 feet
2. Roberto and Jayla weighed some candy. Roberto had 6 pounds, and Jayla had $\frac{2}{3}$ as much. How many pounds of candy did Jayla have?
   4 pounds
3. Tyrone bought a sweater that cost $26.99. Then he bought a coat that cost twice as much. How much did he spend in all?
   $80.97
4. A carpenter has two screws. One is $\frac{1}{2}$ inch long and the other is $\frac{7}{8}$ inch long. How much longer is one screw than the other?
   $\frac{3}{8}$ inch

Which two figures in each row are congruent?

5. 1 2 3 4 5 — 1 and 5
6. 1 2 3 4 5 — 2 and 4
7. 1 2 3 4 5 — 1 and 5

298 UNIT 11 LESSON 21 Practice Division with Remainders

Homework and Remembering page 298

Home or School Activity

Literature Connection

The Great Divide Dayle Ann Dodds' book takes students on a division marathon. As you read aloud this story, have students model the division that occurs on the pages. This rhyming adventure will help reinforce division (with and without remainders) in an exciting and fun way.

UNIT 11 LESSON 22

Use Mathematical Processes

Lesson Objectives

- Apply mathematical concepts and skills in meaningful contexts.
- Reinforce the NCTM process skills embedded in this unit, and in previous units, with a variety of problem-solving situations.

The Day at a Glance

Today's Goals	Materials	
1 Teaching the Lesson **A1: Math Connections** Use geometric figures to make designs; describe designs made out of geometric shapes. **A2: Problem Solving** Identify spinners that are fair and spinners that are unfair; draw a spinner to meet given probability requirements. **A3: Reasoning and Proof** Find the fewest number of colors needed to color a map. **A4: Representation** Make an organized list to solve a problem. **A5: Communication** Use a process of elimination to find the correct answer for a problem.	**Lesson Activities** Student Activity Book pp. 455–456 or Hardcover Book pp. 455–456 Homework and Remembering pp. 299–300 Map of Northeastern United States (TRB M163) Crayons	**Going Further** Activity Cards 11-22 Counters Spinner C (TRB M61) Paper Clip Pencil Spinner E (TRB M132) Connecting Cubes (8 red, 8 blue, 8 yellow) Paper bags Math Journals
2 Going Further ▸ Differentiated Instruction		
3 Homework and Spiral Review		

123 Use Math Talk today!

Keeping Skills Sharp

Quick Practice / Daily Routines	
If you wish to include Quick Practice or a Daily Routine, choose content based on the needs of your class.	**Class Management** Select activities from this lesson that support important goals and objectives, or that help students prepare for state or district tests.

1 Teaching the Lesson

Activity 1

Connections

Connections: Math and Art

 45 MINUTES

Goals: Use geometric figures to make designs; describe designs made out of geometric shapes.

Materials: Student Activity Book page 455, crayons

 **NCTM Standards:**
Problem Solving
Connections
Communication
Representation

11-22 Class Activity

Name ______ Date ______

▶ Math and Art

The Ndebele people in Africa paint their houses with geometric figures.

On a separate piece of paper, draw a picture of a house. Color the house with geometric figures.

1. What figures did you use?
   Answers will vary. Check children's work.
2. How many of each figure did you use?
   Answers will vary. Check children's work.
3. Did you use parallel or perpendicular lines?
   Answers will vary. Check children's work.
4. What kind of angles did you use?
   Answers will vary. Check children's work.
5. Are any of the shapes in your design congruent?
   Answers will vary. Check children's work.
6. Is your design symmetrical?
   Answers will vary. Check children's work.

UNIT 11 LESSON 22 Use Mathematical Processes 455

Student Activity Book page 455

Teaching Note

The Ndebele Tribe Have students do research on the Internet or in books to learn more about the Ndebele tribe of Africa.

▶ Discuss Ndebele Houses

Math Talk 

Task 1 Introduce the activity to the class.

Tell students that the Ndebele tribe lives in Africa and that they decorate their houses with geometric figures. Have students look at the top of their Student Book page to see a picture of one of the houses.

- What geometric figures do you see in the picture? Have students list the figures that they see.
- Do you see any parallel or perpendicular lines? Have students describe parallel and perpendicular lines that they see.
- What kind of angles do you see? Have students talk about the kinds of angles they see.
- Do you see any figures that are congruent? Have students point to figures that are congruent.
- Is their symmetry in the design? Have students show parts of the design that are symmetrical.

▶ Discuss Student Designs

Math Talk 

Task 2 When students have completed the activity, discuss their designs.

Have students show their designs to each other. Use the questions above to help students talk about their designs.

Activity 2

Problem Solving

The Great Game Company

 45–90 MINUTES

Goals: Identify spinners that are fair and spinners that are unfair; draw a spinner to meet given probability requirements.

Materials: Student Activity Book page 456

 **NCTM Standards:**
Problem Solving
Reasoning and Proof
Connections
Communication
Representation

Name Date

▶ The Great Game Company

The Great Game Company has asked you to help them with the spinners they make for games.

7. The company wants a fair spinner where it will be equally likely to get red, blue, or green. Which of the spinners below are fair? Which are unfair? Explain.

Spinner A 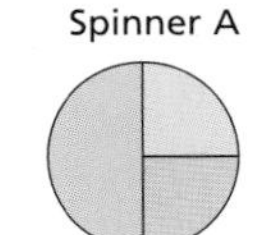 Spinner B 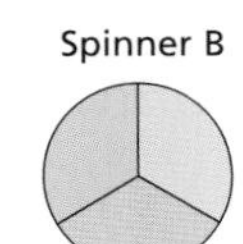 Spinner C 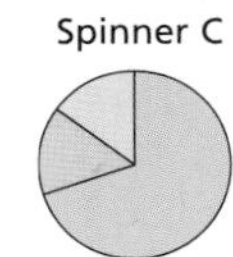

Spinner B is a fair spinner because each section is $\frac{1}{3}$ of the circle.
With both Spinners A and C there is a much greater chance of getting green than blue or red. So Spinners A and C are unfair.

8. The company wants a spinner where it is impossible to get blue and where it is more likely for a player to get red than green. Design a spinner for them. Answers will vary. sample:

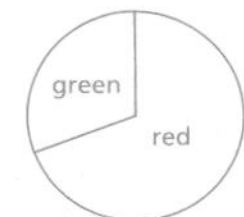

456 UNIT 11 LESSON 22 Use Mathematical Processes

Student Activity Book page 456

▶ What Makes a Fair Spinner? Math Talk 

Task 1 Begin with whole class discussion.

▶ Have you ever played games where you used a spinner? Allow students to share their experiences using spinners in games.

▶ What makes a spinner fair? A spinner is fair if there is an equal chance of getting each possibility.

Tell students that The Great Game Company needs some help with their spinners and that they are going to help them.

▶ Share Spinner Designs Math Talk 

Task 2 When students have completed the activity, discuss the exercises.

▶ Which Spinner is fair in exercise 7? Why is it fair? Spinner B is fair because there is an equal chance of getting each color.

▶ Which Spinners are unfair in exercise 7? Why are they unfair? Spinners A and C are unfair because with both spinners there is a much greater chance of getting green than the other colors.

▶ What does the spinner you designed for exercise 8 look like? Allow students to share their spinner designs. Have them analyze each design to see if it meets the requirements.

English Language Learners

Write *fair* on the board. Draw 2 children, each holding 3 cookies. Ask: **Do they have the same number of cookies?** yes

- **Beginning** Say: **This is fair.** Draw a child with no cookies. Ask: **Is this *fair*?** no
- **Intermediate and Advanced** Ask: **Is this *fair*?** yes Draw a child with no cookies. Say: **This isn't __.** fair Have students tell how to make the situation fair.

Activity 3

Reasoning and Proof

Color the Map

 15 MINUTES

Goal: Find the fewest number of colors needed to color a map.

Materials: Map of Northeastern United States (TRB M163), crayons

 **NCTM Standards:**
Problem Solving
Reasoning and Proof
Connections
Representation

Color the map of the Northeastern United States so that the colors of states that are next to each other are not the same. Use as few different colors as possible. How many colors did you use? Look at the results of the students. They should be able to do this with 4 different colors.

Hold a whole-class discussion of the problem.

- ► How many different colors did you use? Have students share their results.
- ► What do you think is the fewest number of colors you can use? You might want to tell students that mathematicians have found that the fewest number of colors is 4.

Activity 4

Representation

Marbles in a Bag

 15 MINUTES

Goal: Make an organized list to solve a problem.

 **NCTM Standards:**
Problem Solving
Reasoning and Proof
Representation

There are 4 marbles in a bag. One marble is yellow, one is red, one is blue, and one is green.

How many ways can you choose 2 marbles if the order doesn't matter? List the ways. 10 ways: YY, YR, YB, YG, RR, RB, RG, BB, BG, GG

How many ways can you choose 2 marbles if the order does matter? List the ways. 16 ways: YY, YR, RY, YB, BY, YG, GY, RR, RB, BR, RG, GR, BB, BG, GB, GG

Discuss the problem with the class.

- ► When order didn't matter how did you keep track of what was in the list so you knew you were not counting the same thing more than once? Answers will vary. Sample: I listed all the possible ways where yellow was first. Then I did the same for red but didn't list the red yellow combination since that had already been counted. Repeat for blue and then green.

Activity 5

Communication

Mio's Number

 15 MINUTES

Goal: Use a process of elimination to find the correct answer for a problem.

 **NCTM Standards:**
Problem Solving
Reasoning and Proof
Communication

Mio is thinking of one of these numbers: 76, 174, 176, 195. It has three digits. It is even and between 175 and 177. Use a process of elimination to find the number Mio is thinking of. 176

Hold a whole-class discussion of the problem.

- ► How did you use a process of elimination to arrive at the answer? Since the number has 3 digits you can eliminate 76. Since the number is even you can eliminate 195. Since the number is between 175 and 177 you can eliminate 174. The number left is 176 which meets all of the requirements.

2 Going Further

Differentiated Instruction

Intervention

Activity Card 11-22

Fractions of 12 — Activity Card 11-22 ●

Work: In pairs

Use:

- 50 counters
- Spinner C (TRB M61)
- Paper clip
- Pencil

1. Make a spinner that is divided into fourths. Label the sections: $\frac{1}{2}$, $\frac{1}{3}$, $\frac{1}{4}$, $\frac{1}{6}$. Place 12 counters between you.

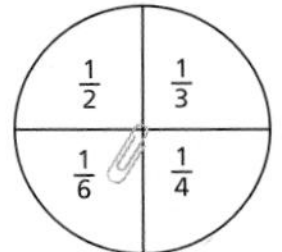

2. In turn, spin the spinner. Take that fraction of 12 counters.
3. Replenish the group of counters so there are 12 after each turn.
4. Play until one student has at least 15 counters.
5. **Analyze** What is the best fraction to spin? Why?
   $\frac{1}{2}$ is the best fraction to spin; it is the greatest fraction; $\frac{1}{2} = \frac{6}{12}$, $\frac{1}{3} = \frac{4}{12}$, $\frac{1}{4} = \frac{3}{12}$, $\frac{1}{6} = \frac{2}{12}$.

Unit 11, Lesson 22

Activity Note Have students review equivalent fractions for $\frac{1}{2}$, $\frac{1}{3}$, $\frac{1}{6}$, $\frac{1}{4}$. They can also use the fraction strips from Lesson 14 as an aid.

Math Writing Prompt

Explain Your Thinking What is $\frac{1}{4}$ of 20 counters? Show with pictures and explain.

Software Support

Warm Up 6.08

On Level

Activity Card 11-22

More Fractions of 12 — Activity Card 11-22 ▲

Work: In pairs

Use:

- 50 counters
- Spinner E (TRB M132)
- Paper clip
- Pencil

1. Make a spinner that is divided into eighths. Label the sections: $\frac{1}{2}$, $\frac{1}{3}$, $\frac{2}{3}$, $\frac{1}{4}$, $\frac{3}{4}$, $\frac{1}{6}$, $\frac{5}{6}$, $\frac{1}{12}$

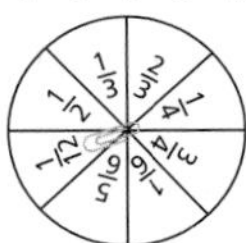

2. In turn, spin the spinner. Take that fraction of 12 counters.
3. Replenish the group of counters so there are 12 after each turn.
4. Play until one student has at least 15 counters.
5. **Analyze** What is a better spin, $\frac{2}{3}$ or $\frac{5}{6}$? Why?
   $\frac{5}{6}$ is a better spin; $\frac{2}{3} = \frac{4}{6}$, and $\frac{5}{6}$ is greater than $\frac{4}{6}$.

Unit 11, Lesson 22

Activity Note Remind students to find a common denominator for the fractions on the spinner.

Math Writing Prompt

Draw a Picture What is $\frac{5}{6}$ of 18 counters? Show with pictures and explain.

Software Support

Fraction Action: Number Line Mine, Level L

Challenge

Activity Card 11-22

Make a Circle Graph — Activity Card 11-22 ■

Work: In pairs

Use:

- Connecting cubes: 8 red, 8 blue, 8 yellow
- Paper bag
- Spinner E (TRB M132)

1. Pick 8 cubes out of a bag.
2. Make a circle graph to show what you picked.

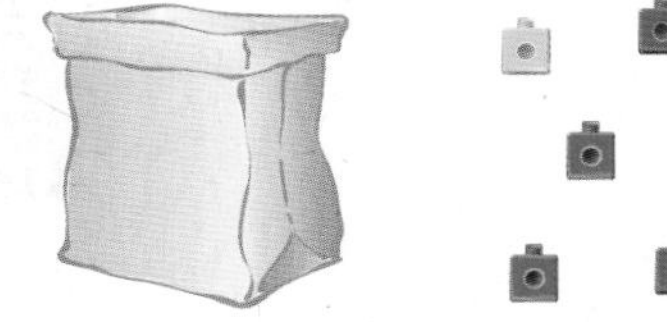

3. **Analyze** Tell what fraction of the graph each color is.
4. **Extend** Select 16 cubes from 12 red, 12 blue, and 12 yellow cubes in the bag. Make a circle graph to show your results.

Unit 11, Lesson 22

Activity Note Students can divide TRB M132 into twelfths to make their circle graphs for the Extend.

Math Writing Prompt

A Circle Graph Suppose you picked 6 cubes out of a bag and you wanted to make a circle graph to show what you picked. What fractions would you divide the circle graph into? Explain.

Software Support

Course II: Module 2: Unit 3: Fractional Parts

3 Homework and Spiral Review

Goal: Additional Practice

✓ Include student's completed Homework page as part of their portfolios.

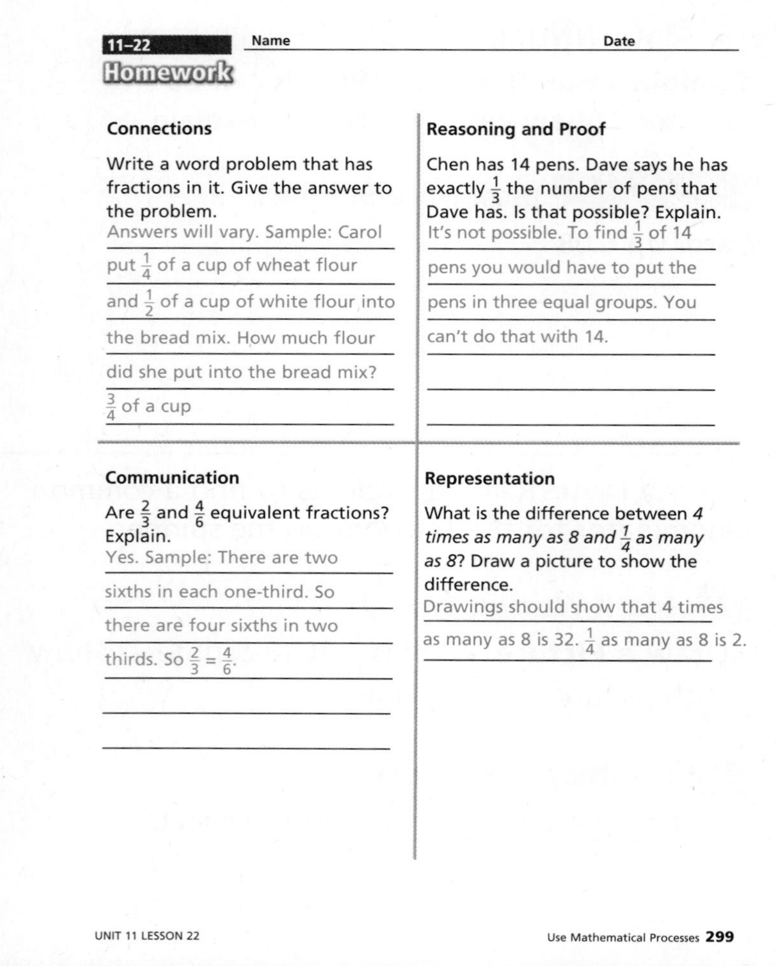

11–22 Homework Name ______ Date ______

Connections

Write a word problem that has fractions in it. Give the answer to the problem.

Answers will vary. Sample: Carol put $\frac{1}{4}$ of a cup of wheat flour and $\frac{1}{2}$ of a cup of white flour into the bread mix. How much flour did she put into the bread mix? $\frac{3}{4}$ of a cup

Reasoning and Proof

Chen has 14 pens. Dave says he has exactly $\frac{1}{3}$ the number of pens that Dave has. Is that possible? Explain.

It's not possible. To find $\frac{1}{3}$ of 14 pens you would have to put the pens in three equal groups. You can't do that with 14.

Communication

Are $\frac{2}{3}$ and $\frac{4}{6}$ equivalent fractions? Explain.

Yes. Sample: There are two sixths in each one-third. So there are four sixths in two thirds. So $\frac{2}{3} = \frac{4}{6}$.

Representation

What is the difference between *4 times as many as 8 and $\frac{1}{4}$ as many as 8*? Draw a picture to show the difference.

Drawings should show that 4 times as many as 8 is 32. $\frac{1}{4}$ as many as 8 is 2.

UNIT 11 LESSON 22 Use Mathematical Processes 299

Homework and Remembering page 299

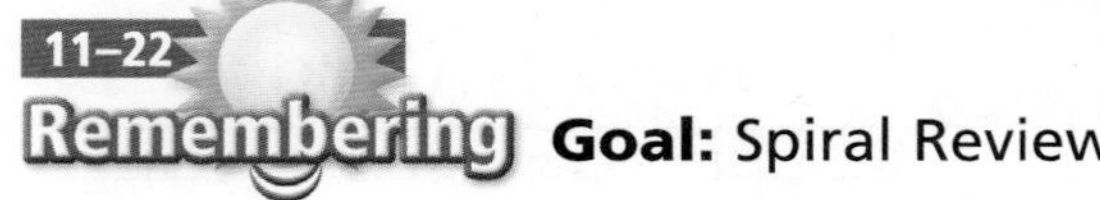

Goal: Spiral Review

This Remembering page would be appropriate anytime after today's lesson.

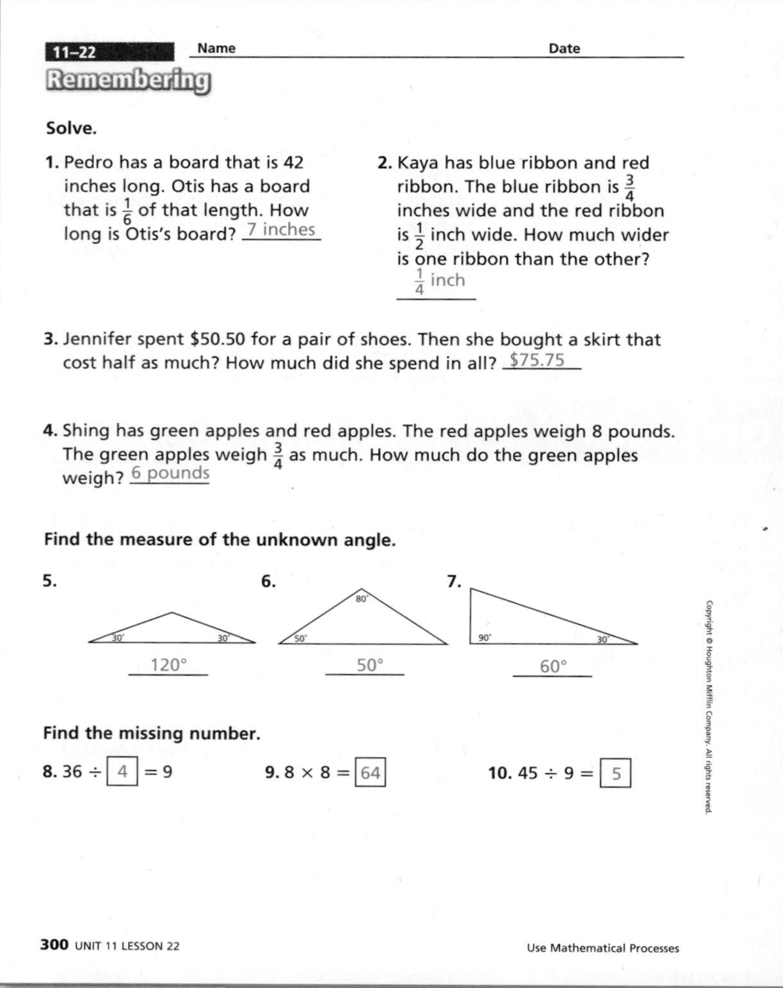

11–22 Remembering Name ______ Date ______

Solve.

1. Pedro has a board that is 42 inches long. Otis has a board that is $\frac{1}{6}$ of that length. How long is Otis's board? 7 inches

2. Kaya has blue ribbon and red ribbon. The blue ribbon is $\frac{3}{4}$ inches wide and the red ribbon is $\frac{1}{2}$ inch wide. How much wider is one ribbon than the other? $\frac{1}{4}$ inch

3. Jennifer spent $50.50 for a pair of shoes. Then she bought a skirt that cost half as much? How much did she spend in all? $75.75

4. Shing has green apples and red apples. The red apples weigh 8 pounds. The green apples weigh $\frac{3}{4}$ as much. How much do the green apples weigh? 6 pounds

Find the measure of the unknown angle.

5. 30°, 30° — 120°

6. 80°, 50° — 50°

7. 90°, 30° — 60°

Find the missing number.

8. 36 ÷ [4] = 9

9. 8 × 8 = [64]

10. 45 ÷ 9 = [5]

300 UNIT 11 LESSON 22 Use Mathematical Processes

Homework and Remembering page 300

Home or School Activity

Real-World Connection

Make a Circle Graph Have students make a circle graph that shows how they spend their time on a school day. They would want to include time eating, sleeping, being in school, playing, etc. You might want to have the students use M129 (Fraction of a Day) in the TRB.

Unit Review and Test

Lesson Objective

- **Assess student progress on unit objectives.**

The Day at a Glance

Today's Goals	Materials
1 Assessing the Unit ▶ Assess student progress on unit objectives. ▶ Use activities from unit lessons to reteach content. **2 Extending the Assessment** ▶ Use remediation for common errors. There is no homework assignment on a test day.	Unit 11 Test, Student Activity Book pp. 457–460 or Student Hardcover Book pages 457–460 and Activity Workbook pp. 215–218 Unit 11 Test, Form A or B, Assessment Guide pages (optional) Unit 11 Performance Assessment, Assessment Guide pages (optional)

Keeping Skills Sharp

Quick Practice — 5 MINUTES	
Goal: Review any skills you choose to meet the needs of your class. If you are doing a unit review day, use any of the Quick Practice activities that provide support for your class. If this is a test day, omit Quick Practice.	**Review and Test Day** You may want to choose a quiet game or other activity (reading a book or working on homework for another subject) for students who finish early.

1 Assessing the Unit

Assess Unit Objectives

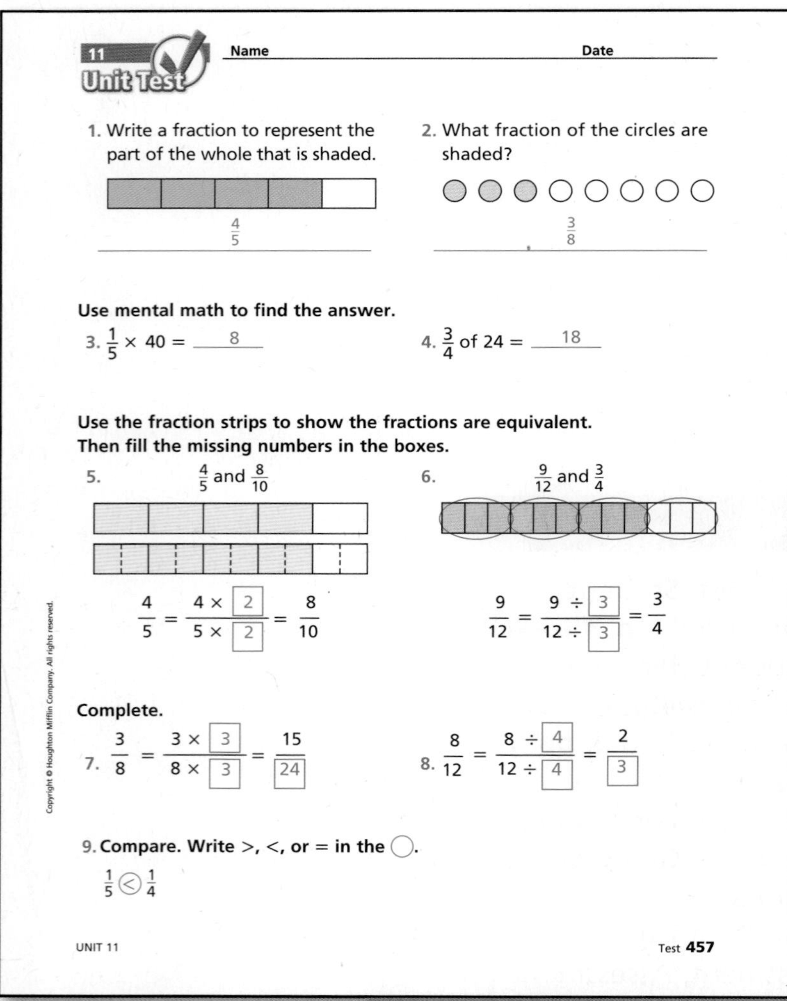

11 Unit Test Name Date

1. Write a fraction to represent the part of the whole that is shaded.

$\frac{4}{5}$

2. What fraction of the circles are shaded?

$\frac{3}{8}$

Use mental math to find the answer.

3. $\frac{1}{5} \times 40 =$ 8

4. $\frac{3}{4}$ of 24 = 18

Use the fraction strips to show the fractions are equivalent. Then fill the missing numbers in the boxes.

5. $\frac{4}{5}$ and $\frac{8}{10}$

$\frac{4}{5} = \frac{4 \times \boxed{2}}{5 \times \boxed{2}} = \frac{8}{10}$

6. $\frac{9}{12}$ and $\frac{3}{4}$

$\frac{9}{12} = \frac{9 \div \boxed{3}}{12 \div \boxed{3}} = \frac{3}{4}$

Complete.

7. $\frac{3}{8} = \frac{3 \times \boxed{3}}{8 \times \boxed{3}} = \frac{15}{\boxed{24}}$

8. $\frac{8}{12} = \frac{8 \div \boxed{4}}{12 \div \boxed{4}} = \frac{2}{\boxed{3}}$

9. **Compare. Write >, <, or = in the ○.**

$\frac{1}{5} < \frac{1}{4}$

Student Activity Book page 457

11 Unit Test Name Date

Use the spinner to answer exercises 10a. and 10b.

10. a. Describe the probability of spinning red on the spinner using one of these words: likely, unlikely, equally likely, certain, or impossible.

likely

b. Write the probability of spinning blue in two ways.

2 out of 8 or $\frac{2}{8}$

Complete.

11. a. Suppose you pull a marble out of the bag 20 times and return it to the bag each time. Which color marble do you predict will be pulled out most often?

black

b. What are all the possible outcomes when you toss 2 coins? Use H for heads and T for tails to make an organized list.

HH HT TH TT

Student Activity Book page 458

45 MINUTES (more if schedule permits)

Goal: Assess student progress on unit objectives.

Materials: Student Activity Book pp. 457–460 or Hardcover Book pp. 457–460 and Activity Workbook pp. 215–218; Assesment Guide (optional)

▶ Review and Assessment

If your students are ready for assessment on the unit objectives, you may use either the test on the Student Activity Book pages or one of the forms of the Unit 11 Test in the Assessment Guide to assess student progress.

The chart at the right lists the test items, the unit objectives they cover, and the lesson activities in which the objective is covered in this unit. You may revisit these activities with students who do not show mastery of the objectives.

Unit Test Items	Unit Objectives Tested	Activities to Use for Reteaching
1, 2	**11.1** Write a fraction to represent a part of a whole and a part of a set.	Lesson 1, Activity 3 Lesson 2, Activity 2
3, 4	**11.2** Find a fraction of a number.	Lesson 3, Activity 1 Lesson 6, Activity 1
10–11	**11.3** Express the probability of an event and use it to make predictions.	Lesson 8, Activity 1 Lesson 8, Activity 2 Lesson 8, Activity 3 Lesson 8, Activity 4
5–8, 12–13	**11.4** Write equivalent fractions and decimals.	Lesson 9, Activity 1 Lesson 11, Activity 1 Lesson 12, Activity 1 Lesson 13, Activity 1 Lesson 17, Activity 1, 2, 3

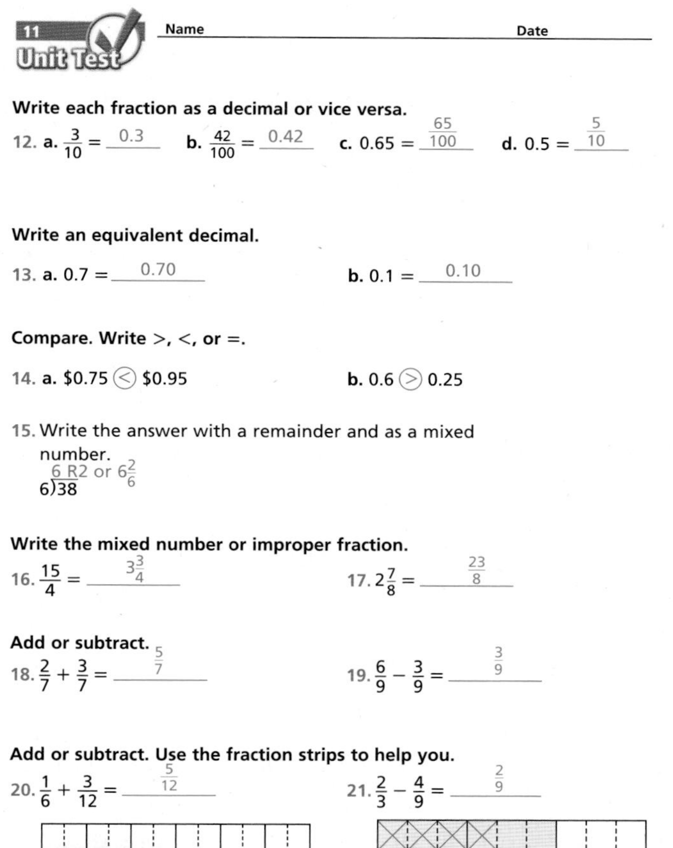

11 Unit Test Name Date

Write each fraction as a decimal or vice versa.

12. a. $\frac{3}{10}$ = 0.3 b. $\frac{42}{100}$ = 0.42 c. 0.65 = $\frac{65}{100}$ d. 0.5 = $\frac{5}{10}$

Write an equivalent decimal.

13. a. 0.7 = 0.70 b. 0.1 = 0.10

Compare. Write >, <, or =.

14. a. $0.75 < $0.95 b. 0.6 > 0.25

15. Write the answer with a remainder and as a mixed number.
$6\overline{)38}$ 6 R2 or $6\frac{2}{6}$

Write the mixed number or improper fraction.

16. $\frac{15}{4}$ = $3\frac{3}{4}$ 17. $2\frac{7}{8}$ = $\frac{23}{8}$

Add or subtract.

18. $\frac{2}{7} + \frac{3}{7}$ = $\frac{5}{7}$ 19. $\frac{6}{9} - \frac{3}{9}$ = $\frac{3}{9}$

Add or subtract. Use the fraction strips to help you.

20. $\frac{1}{6} + \frac{3}{12}$ = $\frac{5}{12}$ 21. $\frac{2}{3} - \frac{4}{9}$ = $\frac{2}{9}$

UNIT 11 Test 459

Student Activity Book page 459

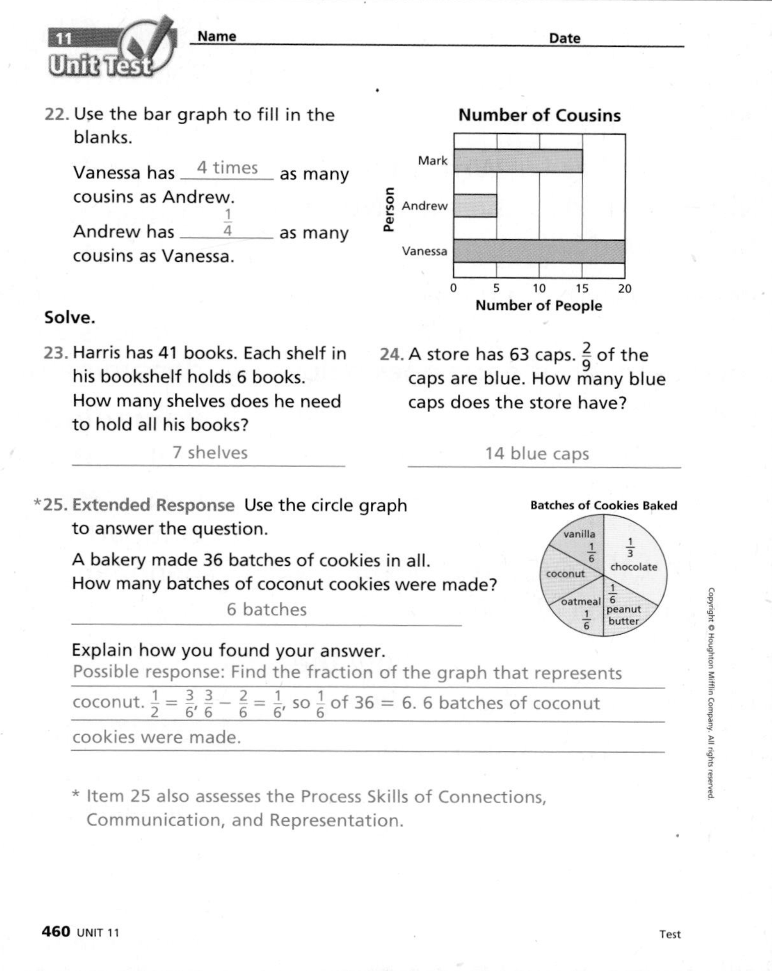

11 Unit Test Name Date

22. Use the bar graph to fill in the blanks.

Vanessa has 4 times as many cousins as Andrew.

Andrew has $\frac{1}{4}$ as many cousins as Vanessa.

Solve.

23. Harris has 41 books. Each shelf in his bookshelf holds 6 books. How many shelves does he need to hold all his books?

7 shelves

24. A store has 63 caps. $\frac{2}{9}$ of the caps are blue. How many blue caps does the store have?

14 blue caps

*25. **Extended Response** Use the circle graph to answer the question.

A bakery made 36 batches of cookies in all. How many batches of coconut cookies were made?

6 batches

Explain how you found your answer.

Possible response: Find the fraction of the graph that represents coconut. $\frac{1}{2} = \frac{3}{6}$, $\frac{3}{6} - \frac{2}{6} = \frac{1}{6}$, so $\frac{1}{6}$ of 36 = 6. 6 batches of coconut cookies were made.

* Item 25 also assesses the Process Skills of Connections, Communication, and Representation.

460 UNIT 11 Test

Student Activity Book page 460

Unit Test Items	Unit Objectives Tested	Activities to Use for Reteaching
9, 14	**11.5** Compare fractions and decimals.	Lesson 15, Activity 2 Lesson 16, Activity 2 Lesson 17, Activity 4
18–21	**11.6** Add and subtract fractions made from the same unit fractions and fractions made from different unit fractions.	Lesson 14, Activity 1 Lesson 15, Activity 1
16, 17	**11.7** Write an improper fraction as a mixed number and vice versa.	Lesson 18, Activity 3
15, 23	**11.8** Divide 2-digit numbers to 90 by 1-digit numbers and interpret remainders.	Lesson 19, Activity 1 Lesson 20, Activity 2 Lesson 21, Activity 1
22, 24–25	**11.9** Use fractions to solve problems, compare data on a bar graph, and to interpret circle graphs.	Lesson 4, Activity 1 Lesson 5, Activity 1 Lesson 7, Activity 2

▶ Assessment Resources

Form A Free Response Test (Assessment Guide)

Form B Multiple-Choice Test (Assessment Guide)

Performance Assessment (Assessment Guide)

▶ Portfolio Assessment

Teacher-selected Items for Student Portfolios:

- Homework, Lessons 5, 7, 11, 15, 16, 19, and 22
- Class Activity work, Lessons 2, 4, 6, 12, 14, 16, 20, and 22

Student-selected Items for Student Portfolios:

- Favorite Home or School Activity
- Best Writing Prompt

2 Extending the Assessment

Common Errors

Activities for Remediation

Unit Objective 11.1

Write a fraction to represent a part of a whole and part of a set.

Common Error: Writes the Number Shaded Over the Number Not Shaded

Remediation Remind students that the number that tells the total number of parts goes below the fraction bar and the number of unit fractions goes above the fraction bar.

Unit Objective 11.2

Find a fraction of a number.

Common Error: Finds Only the Unit Fraction of the Number

Remediation Have students circle the numerator in the fraction to remind them to find how many in that number of unit fractions.

Unit Objective 11.4

Write equivalent fractions and decimals.

Common Error: Cannot Write Equivalent Fractions

Students may have difficulty finding equivalent fractions when one denominator is not a multiple of the other.

Remediation Review how to use the gameboard for halves and thirds or the fractions strip sheet to find what unit fractions both fractions can be made from.

Unit Objective 11.5

Compare fractions and decimals.

Common Error: Compares Numerators of Unlike Fractions

Students may compare the numerators of unlike fractions without finding equivalent fractions with the same denominator first.

Remediation Have students highlight the denominators of each fraction before they begin comparing. Remind students if the denominators are not the same they need to write equivalent fractions before they compare.

Unit Objective 11.6

Add and subtract fractions made from the same unit fractions and fractions made from different unit fractions.

Common Error: Adds the Denominators When Adding Fractions Made From Different Unit Fractions

Remediation Have students use fraction strips under a whole strip to visualize that their answer is too small and that the fractions must be made from the same unit fractions before they can be added.

Unit Objective 11.7

Write an improper fraction as a mixed number and vice versa.

Common Error: Renames Improper Fractions as a Whole Number and an Improper Fraction

Students may not completely group all the fraction parts into wholes.

Remediation Have students draw a number of whole circles divided into the equal parts shown by the denominator of the improper fraction. Then shade the circles to represent the improper fraction.

Unit Objective 11.8

Divide 2-digit numbers to 90 by 1-digit numbers and interpret remainders.

Common Error: Remainder is Greater Than the Divisor

Students may not compare the remainder with the divisor to be sure it is less than the divisor.

Remediation Remind students to always compare the remainder with the divisor. If the remainder is greater, one or more equal groups can be made.

Unit Objective 11.9

Use fractions to solve problems, compare data on a bar graph, and to interpret circle graphs.

Common Error: Finds Incorrect Values for Fractional Parts of a Circle Graph

Students may not use the correct fraction of the circle to find the value of that section.

Remediation Remind students that all parts of the circle always add up to 1 whole. Tell them to compare the parts of the circle with each other to help decide what part of the whole each section represents.

Three-Dimensional Figures

IN UNIT 12, students continue to develop their knowledge of three-dimensional figures. Activities include building from nets, naming, and describing prisms, cones, pyramids, and cylinders. Students apply their knowledge of solid figures to designing a package and to sorting solid figures according to their own sorting rule. In the final lesson of the unit, students investigate the relationship between a circle and a sphere.

Skills Trace

Grade 2	Grade 3	Grade 4
• Identify and describe cubes, rectangular prisms, cones, square pyramids, cylinders, and spheres. • Draw 2-D views from 3-D models. • Explore the volume of 3-D shapes by counting cubic units.	• Identify and describe cubes, various prisms, cones, various pyramids, cylinders, and spheres. • Draw 2-D views from 3-D models. • Estimate and find the volume of objects by counting cubes.	• Identify and describe cubes, various prisms, cones, various pyramids, cylinders, and spheres. • Draw 2-D views from 3-D models, and justify drawings. • Estimate and explore the volume of objects by counting cubes, and then calculate the volume using formulas.

Unit 12 Contents

Big Idea **Properties of Three-Dimensional Figures**

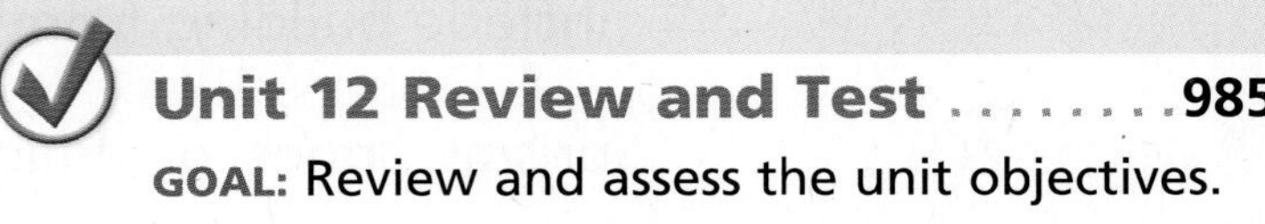

Unit 12 Assessment

Unit Objectives Tested	Unit Test Items	Lessons
12.1 Identify and describe cubes, prisms, cones, pyramids, cylinders, and spheres.	1, 3–10	1, 3–5
12.2 Draw 2-D views from 3-D models.	2	2

Assessment and Review Resources

Formal Assessment

Student Activity Book

- Unit Review and Test (pp. 473–474)

Assessment Guide

- Quick Quiz (p. A120)
- Test A–Open Response (pp. A121–A122)
- Test B–Multiple Choice (pp. A123–A124)
- Performance Assessment (pp. A125–A127)

Test Generator CD-ROM

- Open Response Test
- Multiple Choice Test
- Test Bank Items

Informal Assessment

Teacher Edition

- Ongoing Assessment (in every lesson)
- Math Talk (in every lesson)
- Portfolio Suggestions (p. 987)

Math Talk

- Math Talk in Action (p. 961)
- Solve and Discuss (pp. 964, 975)
- Student Pairs (pp. 953, 958, 961, 962)
- Small Groups (pp. 958, 959, 962, 964)
- In Activities (pp. 954, 969, 970, 976, 981)

Review Opportunities

Homework and Remembering

- Review of recently taught topics
- Spiral review

Teacher Edition

- Unit Review and Test (pp. 985–988)

Test Generator CD-ROM

- Custom review sheets

Planning Unit 12

NCTM Curriculum Focal Points and Connections Key: **1.** Number and Operations and Algebra **2.** Number and Operations **3.** Geometry **4.** Algebra **5.** Measurement **6.** Data Analysis **7.** Number and Operations

Lesson NCTM Focal Points NCTM Standards	Resources	Materials for Lesson Activities	Materials for Going Further
12-1 **Explore Cubes** NCTM Focal Point: 3.2 NCTM Standards: 3, 8	TE pp. 951–956 SAB pp. 460A–462 H&R pp. 301–302 AC 12-1 MCC 45	Scissors Tape	Clay Straws Wooden cubes Paint Paint brushes Aluminum foil Dental floss Math Journals
12-2 **Two-Dimensional Pictures of Three-Dimensional Buildings** NCTM Standards: 3, 4, 9, 10	TE pp. 957–966 SAB pp. 463–468 H&R pp. 303–304 AC 12-2 MCC 46	Cubes made from Lesson 1 ✓ Centimeter or inch cubes ✓ Connecting Cubes (optional)	Cubes made in Lesson 1 Rectangular boxes Calculators Rulers Yardsticks ✓ Centimeter Cubes Centimeter-Grid Paper (TRB M31) *Counting on Frank*, by Rod Clement Math Journals
12-3 **Explore Prisms, Cylinders, and Pyramids** NCTM Focal Point: 3.2 NCTM Standards: 3, 8, 10	TE pp. 967–972 SAB pp. 468A–468F H&R pp. 305–306 AC 12-3 MCC 47	Scissors Tape	✓ Pattern blocks Paper bag 3-D solids ✓ Rulers Scissors Tape Math Journals

Resources/Materials Key: TE: Teacher Edition SAB: Student Activity Book H&R: Homework and Remembering AC: Activity Cards MCC: Math Center Challenge AG: Assessment Guide ✓: Grade 3 kits TRB: Teacher's Resource Book

Lesson NCTM Focal Points NCTM Standards	Resources	Materials for Lesson Activities	Materials for Going Further
12-4 **Explore Cones** NCTM Focal Point: 3.2 NCTM Standards: 3, 9, 10	TE pp. 973–978 SAB pp. 468G–470 H&R pp. 307–308 AC 12-4 MCC 48	Scissors Tape 3-D figures Inch-Grid Paper (TRB M42) ✓ Rulers Colored pencils Various packages	Cardboard packages Scissors Tape Collection of 3-D shapes Venn Diagram (TRB M29) Cans Math Journals
12-5 **Explore Circles and Spheres** NCTM Focal Point: 3.2 NCTM Standards: 3, 4, 9	TE pp. 979–984 SAB pp. 471–472 H&R pp. 309–310 AC 12-5 AG Quick Quiz	String Paper clips ✓ Rulers Examples of spheres	Clay Dental floss ✓ Rulers Cans Math Journals
✓ Unit Review and Test	TE pp. 985–988 SAB pp. 473–474 AG Unit 12 Tests		

Hardcover Student Book

- Together, the Hardcover Student Book and its companion Activity Workbook contain all of the pages in the consumable Student Activity Book.

Manipulatives and Materials

- Essential materials for teaching *Math Expressions* are available in the Grade 3 kits. These materials are indicated by a ✓ in these lists. At the front of this Teacher Edition is more information about kit contents, alternatives for the materials, and use of the materials.

Independent Learning Activities

Ready-Made Math Challenge Centers

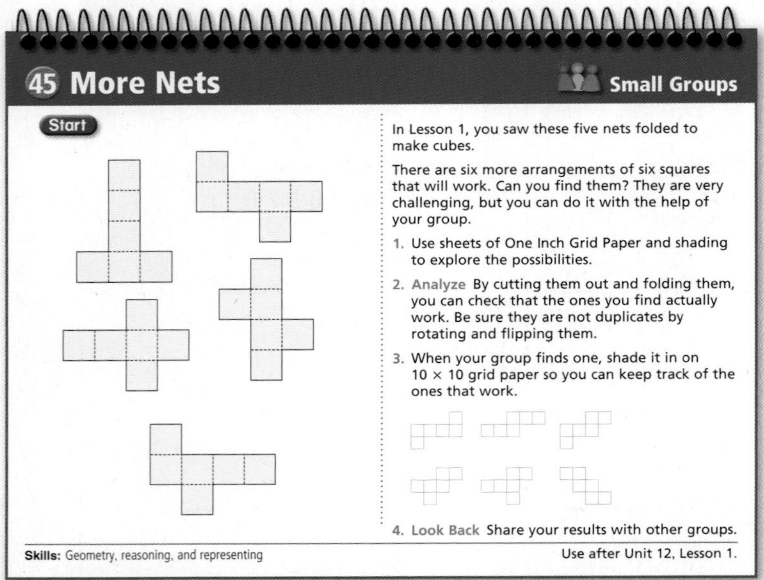

45 More Nets — Small Groups

Start

In Lesson 1, you saw these five nets folded to make cubes.

There are six more arrangements of six squares that will work. Can you find them? They are very challenging, but you can do it with the help of your group.

1. Use sheets of One Inch Grid Paper and shading to explore the possibilities.
2. **Analyze** By cutting them out and folding them, you can check that the ones you find actually work. Be sure they are not duplicates by rotating and flipping them.
3. When your group finds one, shade it in on 10 × 10 grid paper so you can keep track of the ones that work.
4. **Look Back** Share your results with other groups.

Skills: Geometry, reasoning, and representing — Use after Unit 12, Lesson 1.

Grouping Small Groups

Materials Scissors, tape, Inch Grid Paper (TRB M42), 10 × 10 Grid (TRB M43)

Objective Students find arrangements of squares that fold into cubes.

Connections Geometry and Reasoning

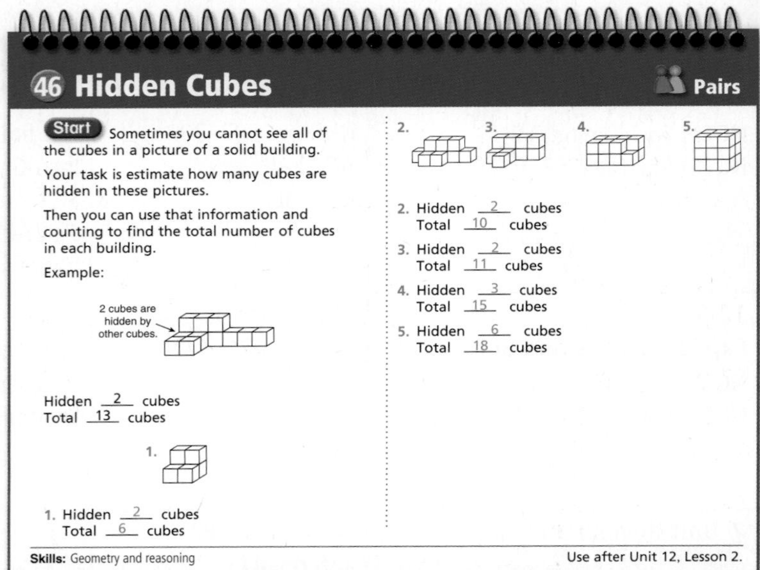

46 Hidden Cubes — Pairs

Start Sometimes you cannot see all of the cubes in a picture of a solid building.

Your task is estimate how many cubes are hidden in these pictures.

Then you can use that information and counting to find the total number of cubes in each building.

Example:

Hidden 2 cubes
Total 13 cubes

1. Hidden 2 cubes
Total 6 cubes

2. Hidden 2 cubes
Total 10 cubes

3. Hidden 2 cubes
Total 11 cubes

4. Hidden 3 cubes
Total 15 cubes

5. Hidden 6 cubes
Total 18 cubes

Skills: Geometry and reasoning — Use after Unit 12, Lesson 2.

Grouping Pairs

Materials Cubes (optional)

Objective Students visualize hidden cubes to find the cubes in an illustration of cube buildings.

Connections Geometry and Representation

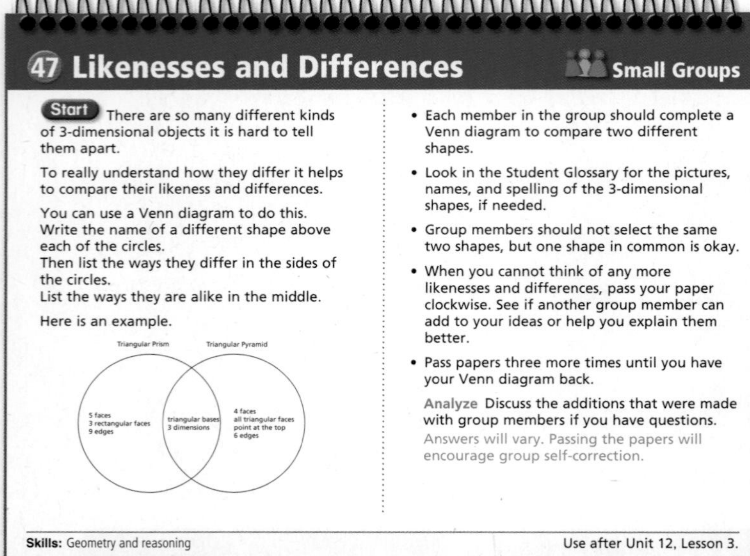

47 Likenesses and Differences — Small Groups

Start There are so many different kinds of 3-dimensional objects it is hard to tell them apart.

To really understand how they differ it helps to compare their likeness and differences.

You can use a Venn diagram to do this. Write the name of a different shape above each of the circles. Then list the ways they differ in the sides of the circles. List the ways they are alike in the middle.

Here is an example.

- Each member in the group should complete a Venn diagram to compare two different shapes.
- Look in the Student Glossary for the pictures, names, and spelling of the 3-dimensional shapes, if needed.
- Group members should not select the same two shapes, but one shape in common is okay.
- When you cannot think of any more likenesses and differences, pass your paper clockwise. See if another group member can add to your ideas or help you explain them better.
- Pass papers three more times until you have your Venn diagram back.

Analyze Discuss the additions that were made with group members if you have questions.

Answers will vary. Passing the papers will encourage group self-correction.

Skills: Geometry and reasoning — Use after Unit 12, Lesson 3.

Grouping Small Groups

Materials 3-dimensional models (optional)

Objective Students compare the attributes of 3-dimensional shapes.

Connections Geometry and Communication

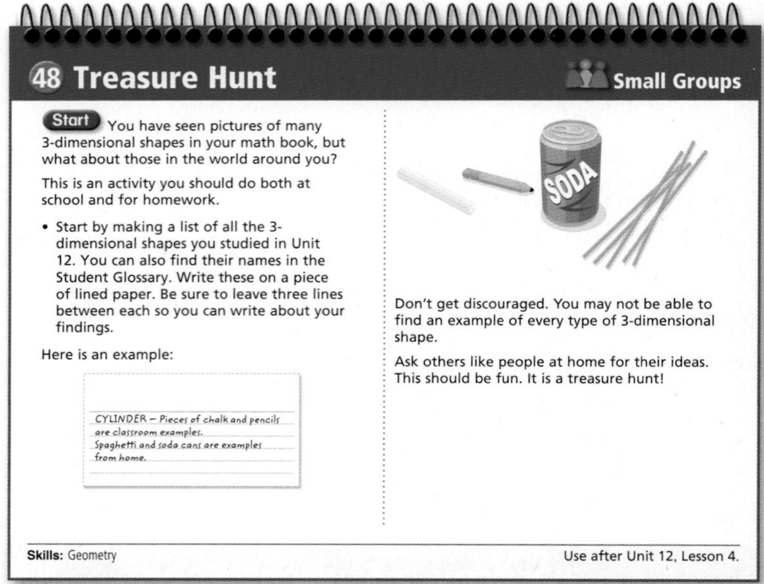

48 Treasure Hunt — Small Groups

Start You have seen pictures of many 3-dimensional shapes in your math book, but what about those in the world around you?

This is an activity you should do both at school and for homework.

- Start by making a list of all the 3-dimensional shapes you studied in Unit 12. You can also find their names in the Student Glossary. Write these on a piece of lined paper. Be sure to leave three lines between each so you can write about your findings.

Here is an example:

CYLINDER – Pieces of chalk and pencils are classroom examples. Spaghetti and soda cans are examples from home.

Don't get discouraged. You may not be able to find an example of every type of 3-dimensional shape.

Ask others like people at home for their ideas. This should be fun. It is a treasure hunt!

Skills: Geometry — Use after Unit 12, Lesson 4.

Grouping Small Groups

Materials Real-world 3-dimensional shapes

Objective Students identify real-world examples of 3-dimensional shapes.

Connections Geometry and Real World

Ready-Made Math Resources

Technology — Tutorial, Practice, and Intervention

Use online, individualized intervention and support to bring students to proficiency.

Help students practice skills and apply concepts through exciting math adventures.

Extend and enrich students' understanding of skills and concepts through engaging, interactive lessons and activities.

Visit **Education Place**®
www.eduplace.com

Visit www.eduplace.com/mx2t/ and find family, teacher, and student materials, activities, games, and more.

Literature Link

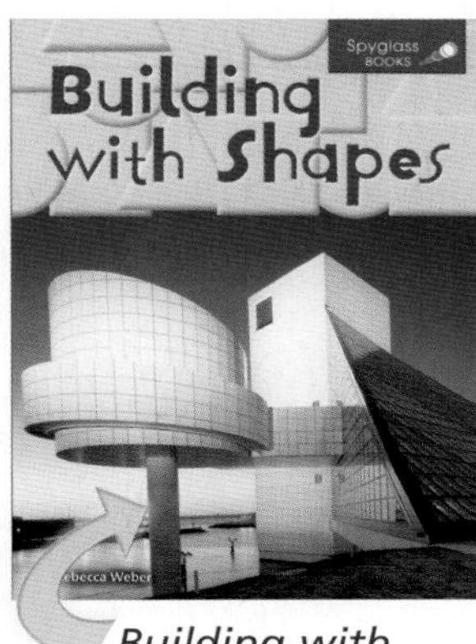

Building with Shapes

Building with Shapes

You enjoyed this book in Unit 8 where it served to discuss the names of shapes and line segmentation. This time, look at the exterior, or perimeter, of each shape in the book. How could the area inside those shapes be determined? Which shapes would be the easiest in terms of area to measure? Which would be the most difficult?

Unit 12 Teaching Resources

Differentiated Instruction

Individualizing Instruction		
	Level	Frequency
Activities	• Intervention • On Level • Challenge	All 3 in every lesson
	Level	Frequency
Math Writing Prompts	• Intervention • On Level • Challenge	All 3 in every lesson
Math Center Challenges	For advanced students	
	4 in every unit	

Reaching All Learners		
English Language Learners	Lessons	Pages
	1, 2, 3, 4, 5	951, 957, 967, 973, 979
Extra Help	Lesson	Page
	2	961
Alternate Approach	Lesson	Page
	2	960

Strategies for English Language Learners

Present this problem to all students. Offer the different levels of support to meet students' levels of language proficiency.

Objective To review two-dimensional figures

Problem Give students several different cut-out circles, squares, triangles, and rectangles. Ask: **What type of figure is this? Is it two-dimensional? What are the two dimensions?**

Newcomer

- Say: **Let's sort the figures.** Have students sort the figures into alike groups. Say: **Let's name the figures.**
- Say: **These are two-dimensional figures.** Have students repeat.

Beginning

- Say: **Let's sort the figures.** Have students sort the figures into alike groups. Have students name the figures.
- Say: **These are two-dimensional figures.** Ask: **Do they have 2 dimensions?** yes

Intermediate

- Have students sort the figures into alike groups. Have students name the figures.
- Say: **Are these two-dimensional figures?** yes **Are the dimensions length and width?** yes

Advanced

- Have students sort the figures into like groups and name the figures.
- Have students identify what makes the figures two-dimensional.

Connections

Real-World Connection
Lesson 2, page 966

Social Studies Connection
Lesson 3, page 972

Art Connection
Lesson 4, page 978

Sports Connection
Lesson 5, page 984

Putting Research into Practice for Unit 12

From Current Research: Spatial Sense

Much of the work students do with three-dimensional shapes involves visualization. By representing three-dimensional shapes in two dimensions and constructing three-dimensional shapes from two-dimensional representations, students learn about the characteristics of shapes. For example, in order to determine if the two-dimensional shape is a net that can be folded into a cube, students need to pay attention to the number, shape, and relative positions of its faces.

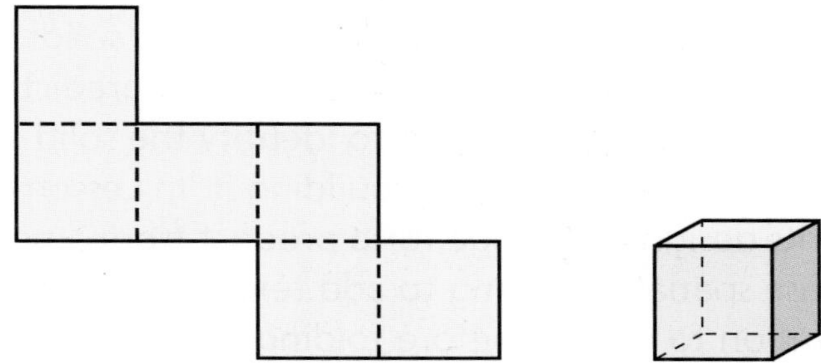

Students should become experienced in using a variety of representations for three-dimensional shapes, for example, making a freehand drawing of a cylinder or cone or constructing a building out of cubes from a set of views (for example, front, top, and side) like those shown below.

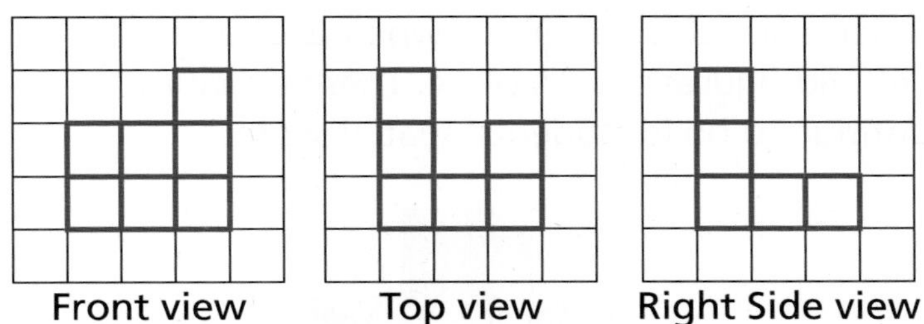

National Council of Teachers of Mathematics. *Principles and Standards for School Mathematics.* Reston: NCTM, 2000. 168.

Other Useful References: Three-Dimensional Geometry

Burton, Grace, Douglas Clements, Terrence Coburn, John Del Grande, John Firkins, Jeane Joyner, Miriam A. Leiva, Mary M. Lindquist, and Lorna Morrow. *Third Grade Book: Addenda Series, Grades K–6.* Reston: NCTM, 1992. 26–30.

Del Grande, John, and Lorna J. Morrow. *Geometry and Spatial Sense: Addenda Series, Grades K–6.* Reston: NCTM, 1993.

Gavin, M. Katherine, Louise P. Belkin, Ann Marie Spinelli, and Judy St. Marie. *Navigating Through Geometry in Grades 3–5 (with CD-ROM).* Reston: NCTM, 2001.

Senechal, Marjorie. "Shape." *On the Shoulders of Giants: New Approaches to Numeracy.* National Research Council. Washington: National Academy Press, 1990.

Build 3-D Figures From Nets

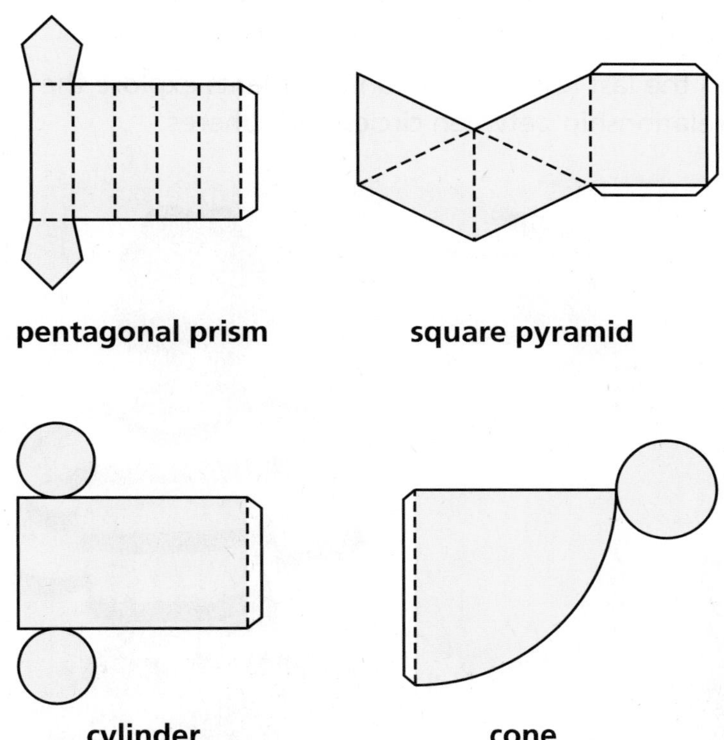

Getting Ready to Teach Unit 12

In this unit, students will continue to develop their knowledge of three-dimensional figures. Students use this knowledge as they sort and classify 3-D objects and apply their learning to real-word situations.

Three-Dimensional Solid Figures

Lessons 1, 3, 4, and 5

In the previous grade, students named and described cubes, rectangular prisms, cylinders, cones, pyramids, and spheres. They traced their faces and counted edges, vertices, and faces and observed if they stack, roll, or slide to help identify, sort, and classify these solid figures.

In this grade, students further develop their conceptual understanding of three-dimensional or solid figures by building them from nets. They name prisms from the shapes of their bases and identify if three-dimentional figures have parallel bases (stack), if they have flat surfaces (slide), or curved surfaces (roll). Using the attributes of solid figures they have observed, they compare solid figures and sort them according to their own sorting rules.

In the last lesson of the unit, students explore the relationship between circles and spheres.

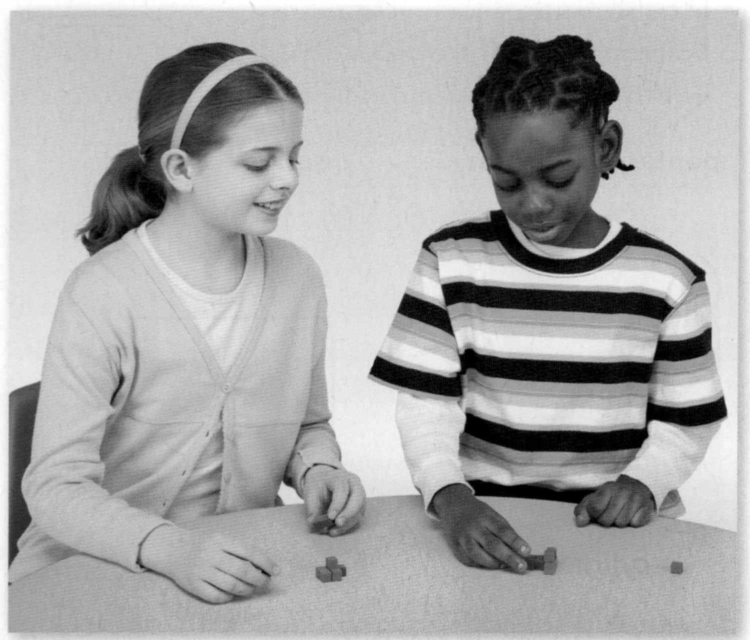

Spatial Sense

Lessons 1, 2, 3, 4, and 5

Students will develop their spatial sense through observations of the relationships between two-dimensional faces, views, and nets and three-dimensional objects. They observe the faces of three-dimensional solids, identifying their two-dimensional shapes and counting them, and they build three-dimensional solids from nets. After building solids from nets, they apply their spatial sense to predict if a net will form a cube, and to identify the solid a net will form before they try building it. In Lesson 4, students design a package for a product from a net. They use spatial reasoning to add text in the correct orientation to the net before folding it.

In the previous grade, students built rectangular prisms from cubes and drew them from the front, side, and top views. In this unit, students make three-dimensional buildings from cubes and draw them from front, back, right, left, and top views. They also create three-dimensional buildings from two-dimensional drawings. Throughout the unit, students sketch different viewpoints of each of the solid figures they explore. These activities continue to build students' spatial sense.

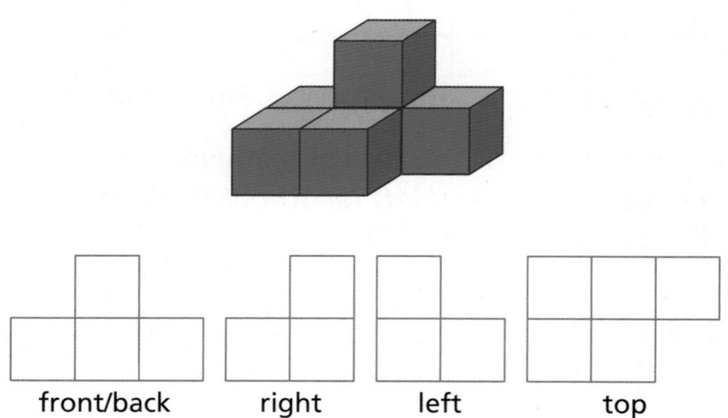

Explore Cubes

Lesson Objectives

- Identify and draw two-dimensional nets that will form cubes.
- Identify and count faces, edges, and vertices of cubes.

Vocabulary

cube	solid figures
net	face
two-dimensional	edge
plane figures	vertex
three-dimensional	

The Day at a Glance

Today's Goals	Materials	
1 Teaching the Lesson **A1:** Fold a net to form a cube and identify attributes of a cube. **A2:** Predict if a net will form a cube. **2 Going Further** ▶ Differentiated Instruction **3 Homework and Spiral Review**	**Lesson Activities** Student Activity Book pp. 460A–462 or Activity Workbook pp. 223–230 (includes Cut-Outs, Family Letter) Homework and Remembering pp. 301–302 A cube made from a net like the one on Student Activity Book page 460A Scissors Tape	**Going Further** Activity Cards 12-1 Clay Short Straws equal length Wooden Cubes Paint and paintbrushes Aluminum Foil Dental Floss Math Journals

Use Math Talk today!

Keeping Skills Sharp

Daily Routines

Symmetry Draw a figure that is symmetric. Explain your choice. Possible answer:

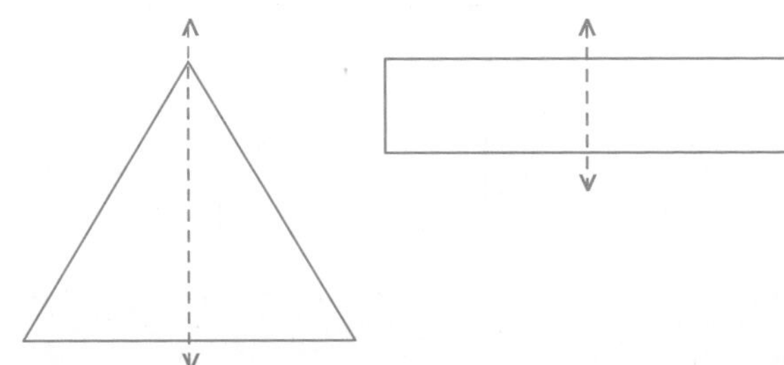

When folded, both halves are equal.

English Language Learners

Show a paper square and a cube. Write *cube* and *three-dimensional* on the board.

- **Beginning** Say: **A *square* is flat. A *cube* is three-dimensional.** Have students repeat.
- **Intermediate** Ask: **Is a *square* flat?** yes **Is a *cube* flat?** no Say: **A cube is three-___.** dimensional
- **Advanced** Have students tell how a *square* and a *cube* are different.

1 Teaching the Lesson

Activity 1

Build Cubes

 30 MINUTES

Goal: Fold a net to form a cube and identify attributes of a cube.

Materials: Student Activity Book pp. 460A–460B or Activity Workbook pp. 219–224, scissors, tape, cube made from net on Student Activity Book p. 460A or Activity Workbook p. 219 (includes cut-outs)

 **NCTM Standards:**
Geometry
Connections

▶ Make a Cube WHOLE CLASS

Before the lesson, make a cube using a net like the first net on Student Activity Book page 460A or Activity Book page 219. Begin the lesson by showing the cube to the class. Explain that the cube was made from a pattern called a *net*. Unfold the cube to show the class the net you used.

Have students cut out the first net on the solid lines on Student Activity Book page 460A or Activity Book page 219. Ask them to fold on the dashed lines and use the tabs to tape the net to form a cube while you do the same with your display net. They will use the other nets on this page in Activity 2 of this lesson.

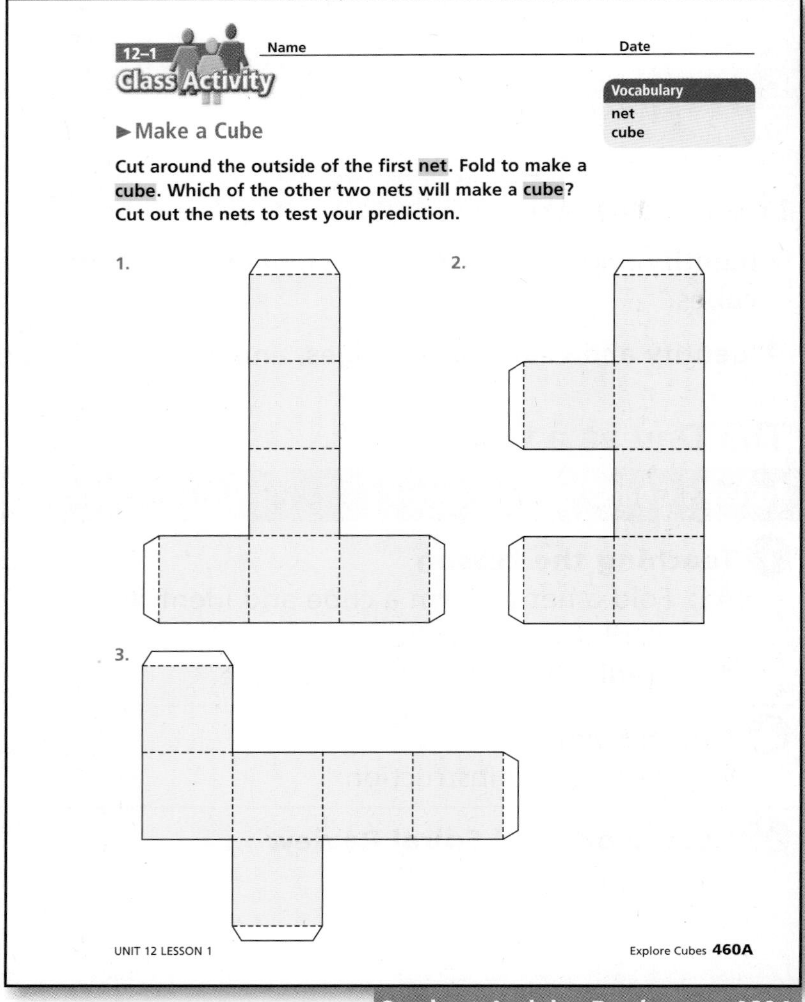

12–1 Class Activity   Name   Date

Vocabulary
net
cube

▶ Make a Cube

Cut around the outside of the first **net**. Fold to make a **cube**. Which of the other two nets will make a **cube**? Cut out the nets to test your prediction.

1.

2.

3.

UNIT 12 LESSON 1   Explore Cubes **460A**

Student Activity Book page 460A

▶ Three-Dimensional Figures WHOLE CLASS

Explain the concepts of two-dimensional figures and three-dimensional figures.

- Any figure that is flat and has 2 dimensions (length and width) is two-dimensional. The net for a cube is two-dimensional.

Have students list some figures that are two-dimensional. Possible answers: square; circle; triangle

Tell students that figures that have two dimensions are called *plane figures.*

- When you cut out a net and folded it, you made a cube that is three-dimensional. The cube is three-dimensional because it has three dimensions (length, width, and height).

Have students name some objects in the classroom that are three-dimensional. Possible answers: pencil, book, desk, bookcase, students

Figures that have three dimensions are *solid figures.*

Plane Figures   Solid Figures

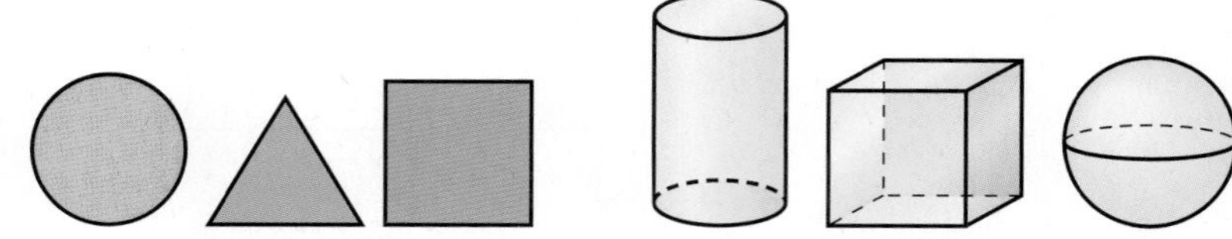

 **Class Management**

Looking Ahead Students will need the cubes they make in this lesson to build three-dimensional models in Lesson 2. Designate a place for students to store them.

▶ Faces, Edges, and Vertices WHOLE CLASS

Discuss with the class the features of a cube. Tell students that each flat surface on a cube is called a *face*.

- What shape are the faces? square
- How many faces does a cube have? 6

Explain that a cube's edges are the places where two faces meet.

- How many edges does a cube have? 12

Explain that a cube's vertices are the places where three edges meet.

- How many vertices does a cube have? 8

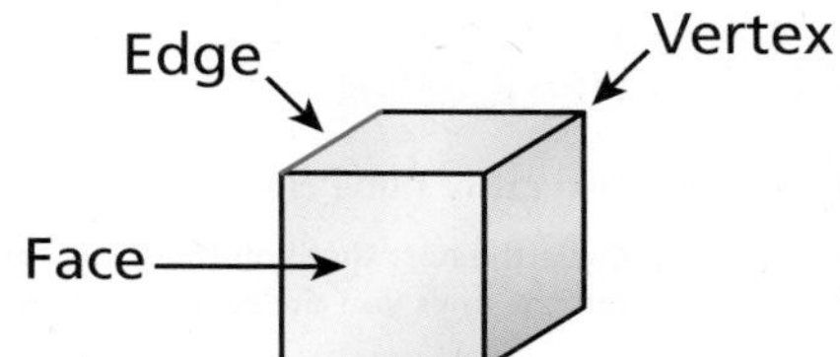

If necessary, students can mark the parts of a cube with a pencil to keep track as they count.

Activity 2

Recognize Nets for Cubes

 **30 MINUTES**

Goal: Predict if a net will form a cube.

Materials: Student Activity Book pp. 460A–460F or Activity Workbook pp. 219–224, scissors, tape

 **NCTM Standards:**
Geometry Connections

▶ Test Predictions PAIRS

Have students return to Student Activity Book page 460A or Activity Workbook p. 219 and cut out the second and third nets. Ask **Student Pairs** to predict whether these nets will fold into cubes and to explain their predictions. Students might mention the following:

- Each net has six squares that will make the six faces of a cube.
- I can visualize how the net in exercise 3 will fold up.
- The net in exercise 2 has two squares on the left which might overlap.

Invite students to try to fold the two nets into cubes and to discuss their predictions and observations.

- The net in exercise 2 will not form a cube because two of the faces will overlap.
- The net in exercise 2 has two squares on one side.
- The net in exercise 3 has one square on the left and one on the right.

Have students unfold the net that doesn't form a cube.

- Where could you move one square so the net will form a cube?
- Cut and tape the square in that location and test your net. One possible net is shown below.

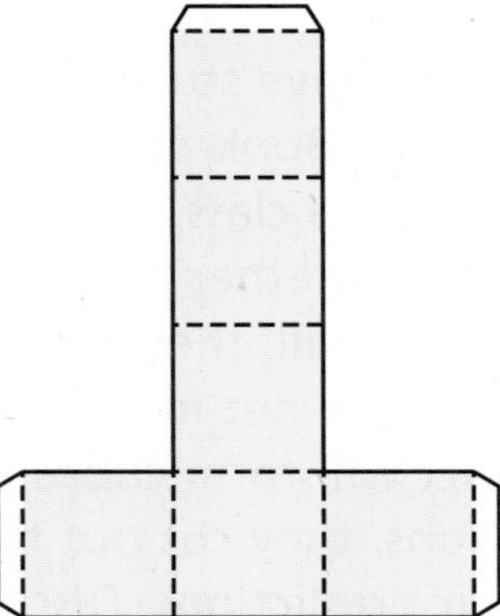

Class Management

Looking Ahead In Lesson 4 of this unit, students will need various empty, clean packages in the shapes of prisms, cylinders, and cones. Encourage students to bring in these packages throughout the unit.

Activity continued ▶

▶ Identify Cube Nets PAIRS

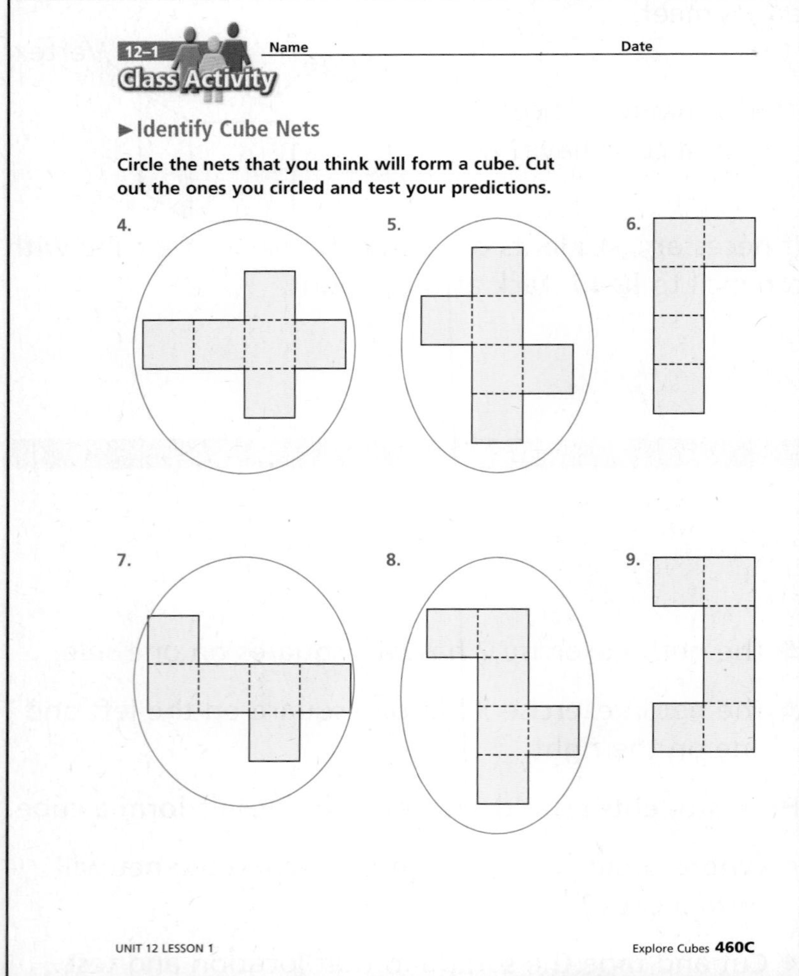
12–1 Class Activity Name Date

▶ Identify Cube Nets

Circle the nets that you think will form a cube. Cut out the ones you circled and test your predictions.

4. 5. 6.

7. 8. 9.

UNIT 12 LESSON 1 Explore Cubes **460C**

Student Activity Book page 460C

Math Talk Next, have students look at the nets on Student Activity Book page 460C or Activity Workbook page 219. As a class, discuss the net in exercise 4 and predict whether it will form a cube. If students predict that it will, they circle the net. Ask students to consider each net in exercises 5–9 and circle the ones they predict will form cubes. Once they have made their predictions, they cut out the ones they circled and test their predictions. Discuss what students learned from their predictions.

Differentiated Instruction

Extra Help For quick reference, have students begin a page in their notebooks with a drawing of a cube made from a net and its name. Students should continue to add to this page drawings and names of the 3-dimensional figures that they make from nets in this unit.

▶ Create a Cube Net INDIVIDUALS

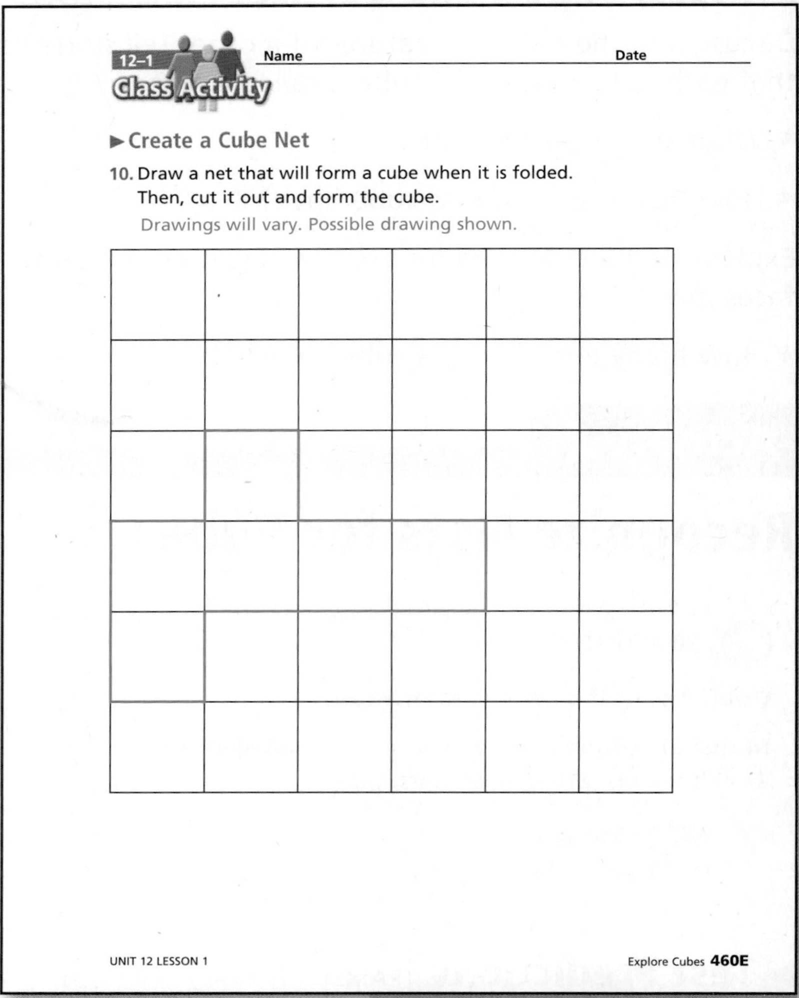
12–1 Class Activity Name Date

▶ Create a Cube Net

10. Draw a net that will form a cube when it is folded. Then, cut it out and form the cube.

Drawings will vary. Possible drawing shown.

UNIT 12 LESSON 1 Explore Cubes **460E**

Student Activity Book page 460E

Have students draw a net for a cube in exercise 10 on Student Activity Book page 460E or Activity Workbook page 223.

Ongoing Assessment

Draw these two nets on the board:

Have students predict whether or not each of these nets will form a cube and tell why they think so. If a net cannot form a cube, ask students to describe how they could change it so that it will form a cube.

Intervention

Activity Card 12-1

Straw Cube — Activity Card 12-1

Work: In pairs

Use:
- Clay
- 12 short straws of equal length

1. Work Together Make a cube from clay and straws. Begin by making 8 balls of clay.
2. Make a square by connecting four straws with four balls of clay. Make another square to match the first one.

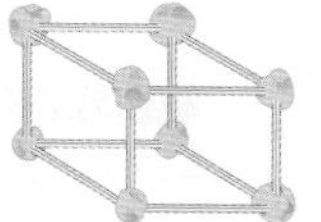

3. Connect both squares with straws to make a cube.
4. Copy and complete the statement below. Use your model to help you.

A cube has__ faces, __edges, and__vertices. 6; 12; 8

Unit 12, Lesson 1

Activity Note If time allows, have students dip their straw cube into a bowl of soapy water. When they lift out the cubes, have them count the faces.

Math Writing Prompt

Explain Your Thinking Is a square a two-dimensional or three-dimensional figure? Explain.

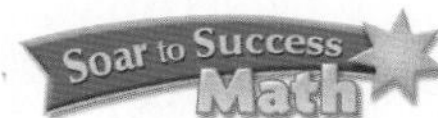

Software Support

Warm Up 36.02

On Level

Activity Card 12-1

Paint with Cubes — Activity Card 12-1

Work: In pairs

Use:
- Wooden cubes
- Paint and paintbrushes
- Aluminum foil

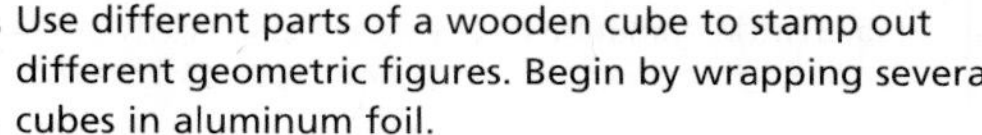

1. Use different parts of a wooden cube to stamp out different geometric figures. Begin by wrapping several cubes in aluminum foil.
2. Paint one face of the cube and press it onto a sheet of paper. What figure do you see? square

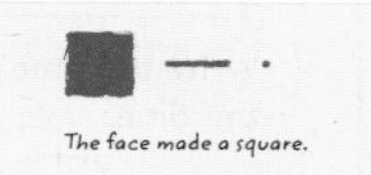

3. Paint a single edge of another cube and press it against the sheet of paper. What figure do you see now? line segment
4. What figure can you make by painting and stamping a single vertex? Use a cube to test your prediction. Point
5. Analyze Can you make any other shapes with a cube? Why or why not? No, every edge and face are the same.

Unit 12, Lesson 1

Activity Note Extend the activity by having students mark each face, edge, and vertex of a wooden cube with paint as they count the total number of each.

Math Writing Prompt

Make a Drawing Make a sketch of a net for a cube. How many squares does a net for a cube have? Why?

Software Support

Ice Station Exploration: Frozen Solids, Level G

Challenge

Activity Card 12-1

Cut Cubes — Activity Card 12-1

Work: In pairs

Use:
- Clay
- Dental floss

1. Make predictions about the faces of figures that are formed when you cut a cube in different directions.
2. First make two clay cubes. If you cut one cube horizontally, what will be the shapes of the faces of the two new figures? Use dental floss to cut the cube and test your predictions. Squares and rectangles

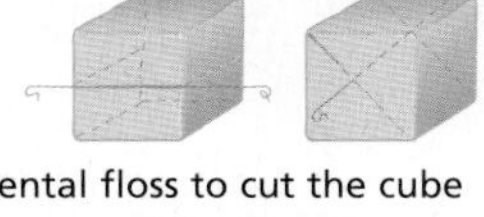

3. Repeat the activity with the second cube. If you cut the cube diagonally, what will be the shapes of the faces of the two new figures? Cut the cube to test your predictions. Triangles, squares, and rectangles

Unit 12, Lesson 1

Activity Note After students have completed the activity, discuss why it is impossible to create other figures by cutting the cubes along different horizontal or diagonal lines.

Math Writing Prompt

Use Reasoning Can you cut a cube so it will form several cubes? Explain.

Software Support

Course II: Module 3: Unit 1: Volume

3 Homework and Spiral Review

Goal: Additional Practice

This Homework page allows students to predict which nets will make cubes and test their predictions.

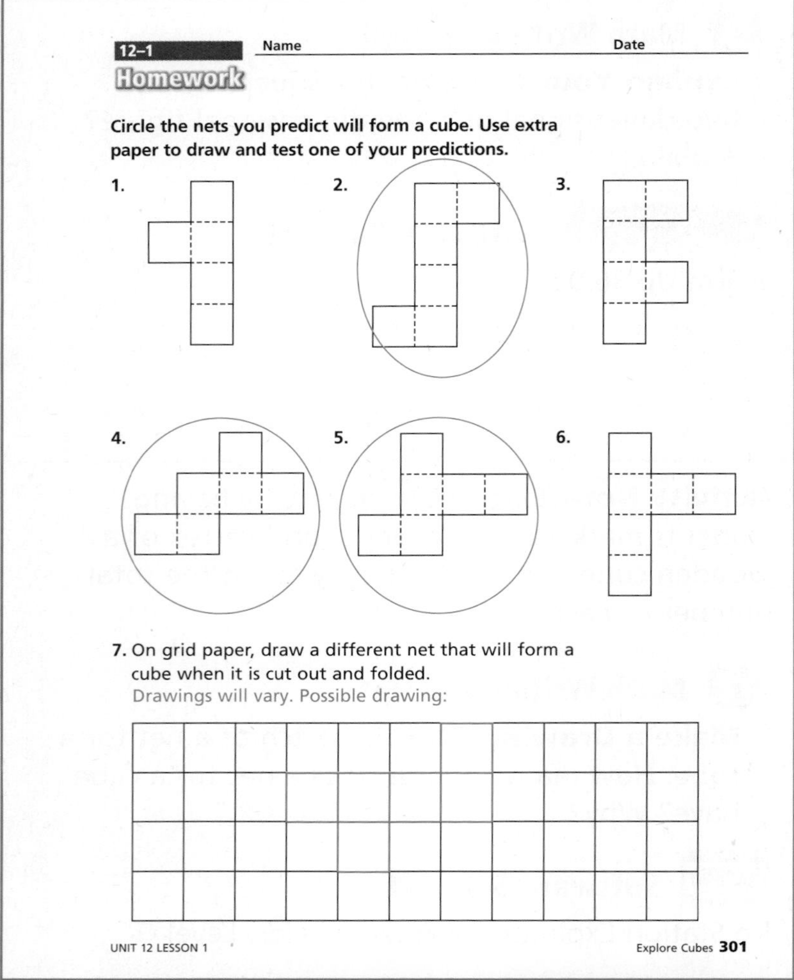

12–1 **Homework** Name ______ Date ______

Circle the nets you predict will form a cube. Use extra paper to draw and test one of your predictions.

1. 2. 3.

4. 5. 6.

7. On grid paper, draw a different net that will form a cube when it is cut out and folded.
Drawings will vary. Possible drawing:

UNIT 12 LESSON 1 Explore Cubes **301**

Homework and Remembering page 301

Goal: Spiral Review

This Remembering page would be appropriate anytime after today's lesson.

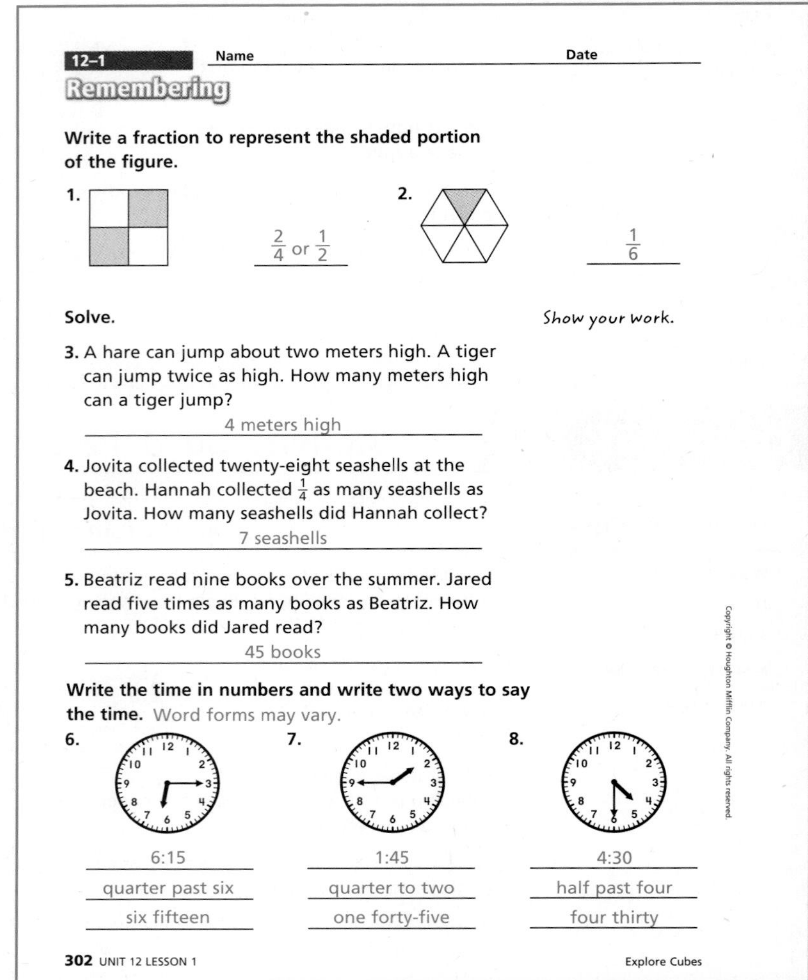

12–1 **Remembering** Name ______ Date ______

Write a fraction to represent the shaded portion of the figure.

1. $\frac{2}{4}$ or $\frac{1}{2}$

2. $\frac{1}{6}$

Solve. *Show your work.*

3. A hare can jump about two meters high. A tiger can jump twice as high. How many meters high can a tiger jump?
4 meters high

4. Jovita collected twenty-eight seashells at the beach. Hannah collected $\frac{1}{4}$ as many seashells as Jovita. How many seashells did Hannah collect?
7 seashells

5. Beatriz read nine books over the summer. Jared read five times as many books as Beatriz. How many books did Jared read?
45 books

Write the time in numbers and write two ways to say the time. Word forms may vary.

6. 6:15 — quarter past six — six fifteen

7. 1:45 — quarter to two — one forty-five

8. 4:30 — half past four — four thirty

302 UNIT 12 LESSON 1 Explore Cubes

Homework and Remembering page 302

Home and School Connection

Family Letter Have students take home the Family Letter on Student Activity Book page 461 or Activity Workbook page 225. A Spanish translation of this letter is on the following page. This letter explains how the concept of three-dimensional figures is developed in *Math Expressions.* It gives parents and guardians a better understanding of the learning that goes on in math class and creates a bridge between school and home.

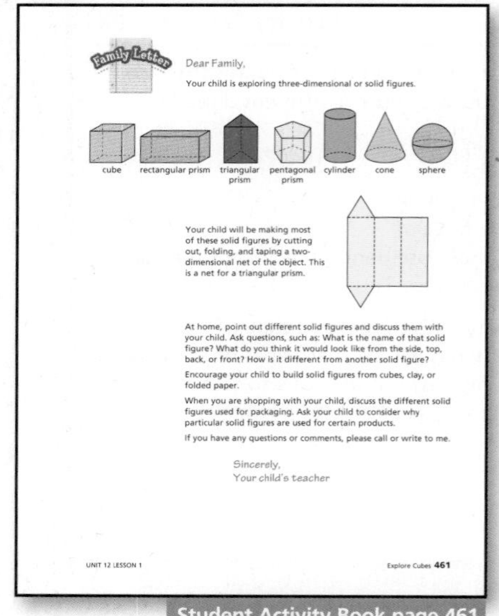

Family Letter

Dear Family,

Your child is exploring three-dimensional or solid figures.

cube, rectangular prism, triangular prism, pentagonal prism, cylinder, cone, sphere

Your child will be making most of these solid figures by cutting out, folding, and taping a two-dimensional net of the object. This is a net for a triangular prism.

At home, point out different solid figures and discuss them with your child. Ask questions, such as: What is the name of that solid figure? What do you think it would look like from the side, top, back, or front? How is it different from another solid figure?

Encourage your child to build solid figures from cubes, clay, or folded paper.

When you are shopping with your child, discuss the different solid figures used for packaging. Ask your child to consider why particular solid figures are used for certain products.

If you have any questions or comments, please call or write to me.

Sincerely,
Your child's teacher

UNIT 12 LESSON 1 Explore Cubes **461**

Student Activity Book page 461

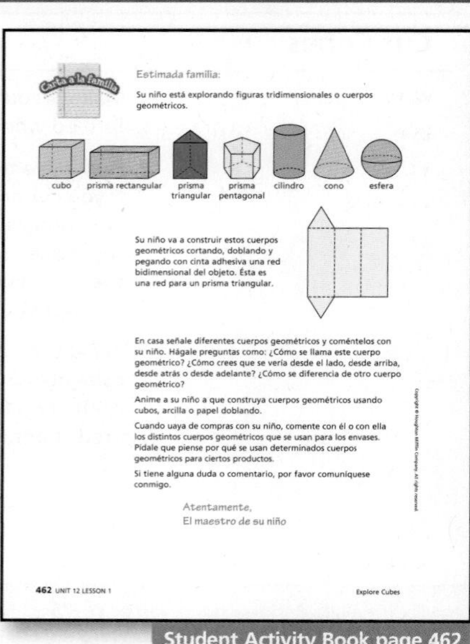

Carta a la familia

Estimada familia:

Su niño está explorando figuras tridimensionales o cuerpos geométricos.

cubo, prisma rectangular, prisma triangular, prisma pentagonal, cilindro, cono, esfera

Su niño va a construir estos cuerpos geométricos cortando, doblando y pegando con cinta adhesiva una red bidimensional del objeto. Ésta es una red para un prisma triangular.

En casa señale diferentes cuerpos geométricos y coméntelos con su niño. Hágale preguntas como: ¿Cómo se llama este cuerpo geométrico? ¿Cómo crees que se vería desde el lado, desde arriba, desde atrás o desde adelante? ¿Cómo se diferencia de otro cuerpo geométrico?

Anime a su niño a que construya cuerpos geométricos usando cubos, arcilla o papel doblando.

Cuando uaya de compras con su niño, comente con él o con ella los distintos cuerpos geométricos que se usan para los envases. Pídale que piense por qué se usan determinados cuerpos geométricos para ciertos productos.

Si tiene alguna duda o comentario, por favor comuníquese conmigo.

Atentamente,
El maestro de su niño

462 UNIT 12 LESSON 1 Explore Cubes

Student Activity Book page 462

Two-Dimensional Pictures of Three-Dimensional Buildings

Lesson Objective

- **Recognize that two-dimensional pictures can represent three-dimensional objects.**

Vocabulary

two-dimensional
three-dimensional
volume
cubic unit

The Day at a Glance

Today's Goals	Materials	
1 Teaching the Lesson **A1:** Build three-dimensional models from drawings. **A2:** Identify and draw different views of three-dimensional objects.	**Lesson Activities** Student Activity Book pp. 463–468 or Student Hardcover Book pp. 463–468 and Activity Workbook pp. 231–234 (includes Family Letter and Grids) Homework and Remembering pp. 303–304 Cubes made in Lesson 1 Centimeter cubes or inch cubes Connecting cubes (optional)	**Going Further** Activity Cards 12-2 Cubes made in Lesson 1 Rectangular boxes Calculators Rulers Yardsticks Centimeter cubes Centimeter Grid Paper (TRB M31) *Counting on Frank,* by Rod Clement Math Journals
2 Going Further ► Math Connection: Volume of Solid Figures ► Extension: Estimating Volume ► Differentiated Instruction		
3 Homework and Spiral Review		

Use **Math Talk** today!

Keeping Skills Sharp

Daily Routines

Homework Review Let students work together to check their work. Initially, pair less able students with more able students. Remind students to use what they know about helping others.

Logic Problems Use *all, some*, or *no* to complete each sentence.

1. If all spheres are shaped like a ball, then ____ circles are spheres. no
2. If all polygons are closed plane figures made up of line segments, than ____ scalene triangles are polygons. all

English Language Learners

Show a model of a cube building. Write *view* on the board.

- **Beginning** Say: **A *view* is how an object looks from one of the sides.** Have students repeat.
- **Intermediate** Ask: **Is the top *view* the same as the bottom *view*?** yes Say: **Is the right view the same as the top view?** no
- **Advanced** Have students tell how the top *view* and right *view* of the model are different.

1 Teaching the Lesson

Activity 1

Make Cube Models

 20 MINUTES

Goal: Build three-dimensional models from drawings.

Materials: Cubes made in Lesson 1, Student Activity Book or Hardcover Book p. 463, centimeter cubes or inch cubes

 **NCTM Standards:**
Geometry
Representation
Connections

▶ Make a Building SMALL GROUPS

Have students work in **Small Groups** of four to combine the cubes they made in Lesson 1. They will use eight or fewer cubes to make a building. Ask them to look closely at their building and think about what a drawing of their building might look like.

- Can you see all of the cubes you used to make the building? No; some of the cubes on the bottom and in the back are hidden by other cubes.
- How do you think you could make a drawing look three-dimensional? Answers will vary.

▶ Cube Models From Drawings PAIRS

Together, look at the first drawing on Student Book page 463 and discuss how many cubes make up the building.

- How many cubes are in the bottom level? 6
- How do you know? You can see 5 cubes and you can tell that there is 1 more hidden under the second level.
- How do we know there are cubes hidden under the second level? There must be cubes holding the second level up.
- How many cubes are in the second level? 4
- How many cubes were used to make this building? 10

Then have **Student Pairs** use centimeter or inch cubes to make a model of the building in exercise 1 and compare their models with those of their classmates.

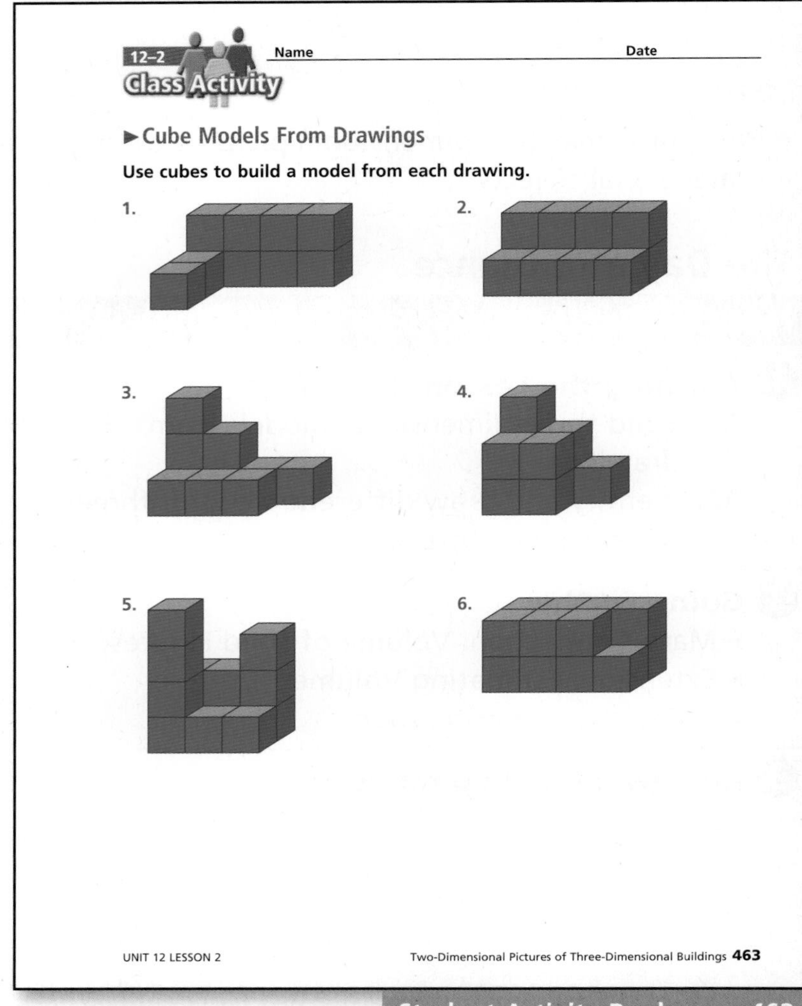
12–2 Class Activity Name Date

▶ Cube Models From Drawings

Use cubes to build a model from each drawing.

1.

2.

3.

4.

5.

6.

UNIT 12 LESSON 2 Two-Dimensional Pictures of Three-Dimensional Buildings **463**

Student Activity Book page 463

Next, have students build a model for exercise 2.

- How did you build your model?
- What did you have to think about to make your model look like the picture?

Ask students to follow the same process to model the drawings in exercises 3–6.

Class Management

You may want to check your state or district curriculum to see if this objective is required. If it is not, you may want to spend more time on other lessons and activities that are required.

Activity 2

Recognize Views of Buildings

 **20 MINUTES**

Goal: Identify and draw different views of three-dimensional objects.

Materials: Student Activity Book or Hardcover Book pp. 464–468 and Activity Workbook pp. 227–230 (includes grids and special formats), cubes made in Lesson 1 (3 per student), connecting cubes (optional)

 **NCTM Standards:**
Geometry
Representation
Connections

▶ Views of Three-Dimensional Objects

SMALL GROUPS

Have students work in **Small Groups** of three. Refer them to Student Book page 464 and have them use cubes and follow the instructions to build the model shown in exercise 7. Encourage students to look at this model from different perspectives to become familiar with the various views.

Ask students to turn their sheet of paper so the side marked *front* is facing them. Then have them look at the model to see the square faces of the cubes.

- How many square faces do you see? 3
- How many square faces do you see in the bottom row? 2
- How many square faces do you see in the top row? 1
- Which of the drawings represents the front view of the model? the first one

Have students view their model in the same way from each of the sides and label the drawings in exercise 8 as *front, back, right,* and *left.* Discuss with students that the drawings of the left and right views are mirror images of each other, as are the front and back views.

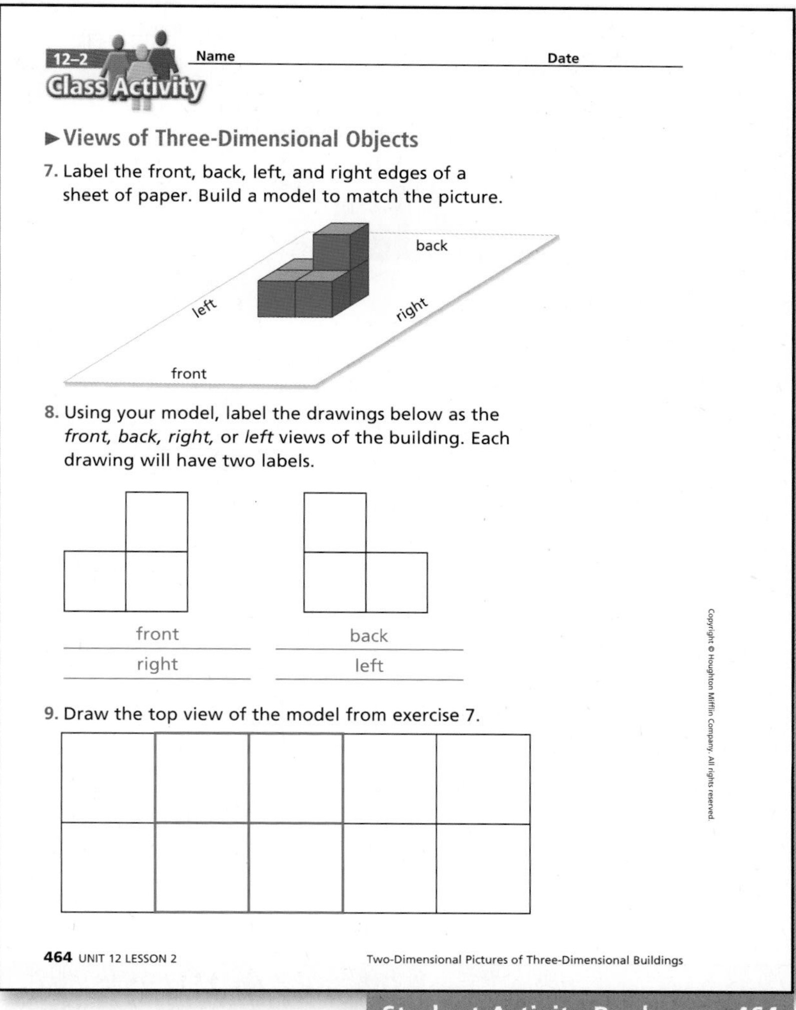

12–2 Class Activity Name Date

▶ Views of Three-Dimensional Objects

7. Label the front, back, left, and right edges of a sheet of paper. Build a model to match the picture.

8. Using your model, label the drawings below as the *front, back, right,* or *left* views of the building. Each drawing will have two labels.

9. Draw the top view of the model from exercise 7.

464 UNIT 12 LESSON 2 Two-Dimensional Pictures of Three-Dimensional Buildings

Student Activity Book page 464

Next, explain that their model also has a top view. This view shows the shape of the base of the model. Have students look at their model from above and draw what they see.

- What is the shape of the top view of this building? a two-by-two square

1 Teaching the Lesson (continued)

Next, have students build the model in exercise 10 on Student Book page 465, and then complete exercises 11 and 12.

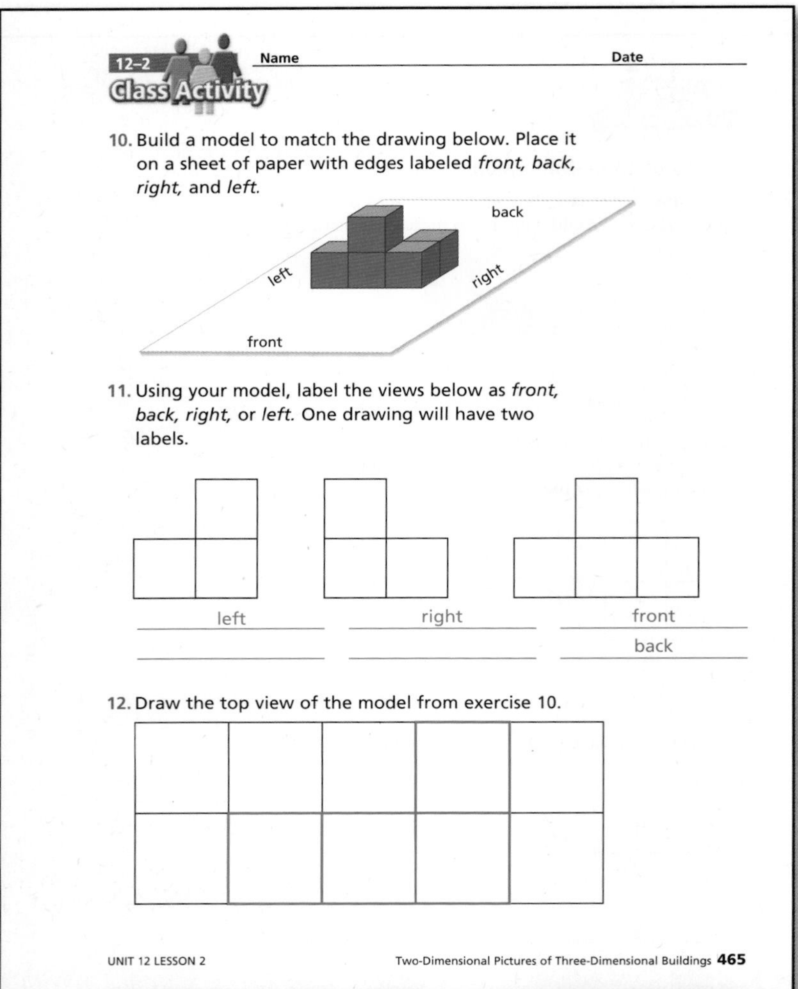

12–2 Class Activity

Name ______ Date ______

10. Build a model to match the drawing below. Place it on a sheet of paper with edges labeled *front, back, right,* and *left.*

11. Using your model, label the views below as *front, back, right,* or *left.* One drawing will have two labels.

left ______   right ______   front / back

12. Draw the top view of the model from exercise 10.

UNIT 12 LESSON 2   Two-Dimensional Pictures of Three-Dimensional Buildings 465

Student Activity Book page 465

Alternate Approach

Number Cubes Some students may need to color the faces of the cubes to help them visualize the different views of the models. To visualize the drawing in exercise 10, have students build the model and then place the blank, round stickers on the outside faces. Then they should color top, right, left, and back cubes a different color. The colors will help them draw the front, back, top, right, and left views.

Finally, have students complete exercises 13–15 on Student Book page 466.

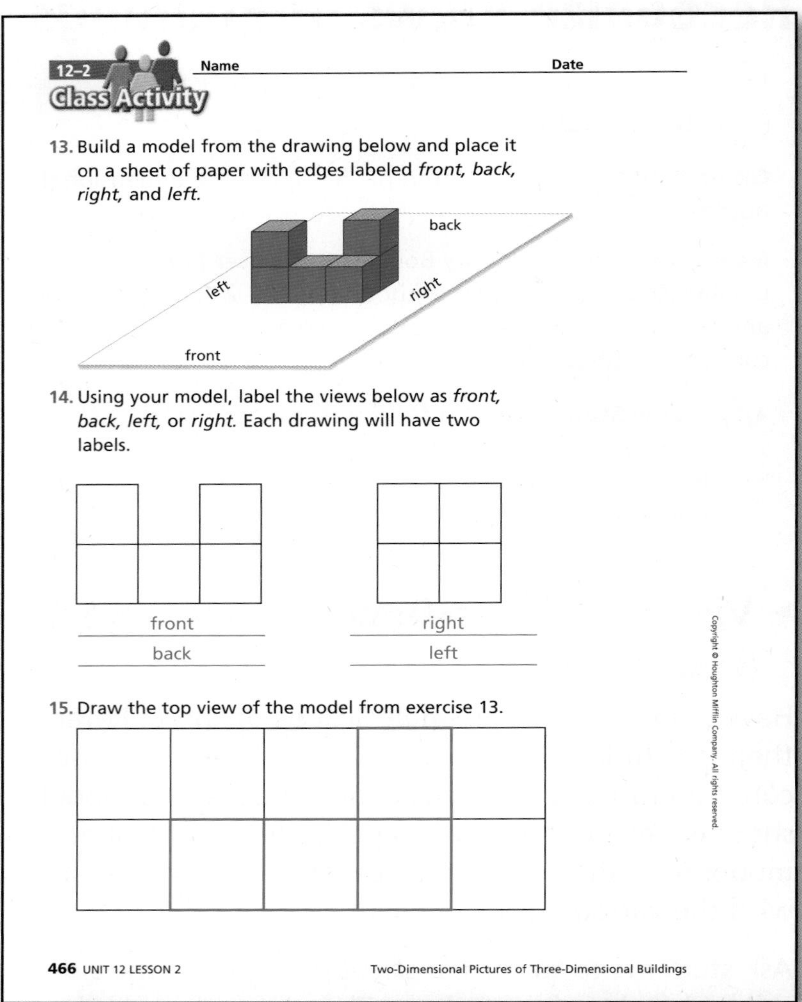

12–2 Class Activity

Name ______ Date ______

13. Build a model from the drawing below and place it on a sheet of paper with edges labeled *front, back, right,* and *left.*

14. Using your model, label the views below as *front, back, left,* or *right.* Each drawing will have two labels.

front / back   right / left

15. Draw the top view of the model from exercise 13.

466 UNIT 12 LESSON 2   Two-Dimensional Pictures of Three-Dimensional Buildings

Student Activity Book page 466

Ongoing Assessment

Ask students to make a model with 8 cubes. Ask them to draw the top, front, back, right, and left views.

▶ Make Models From Views PAIRS

Tell students that if they know the *top, front, back, right,* and *left* side views, they can often create a corresponding model.

Have **Student Pairs** complete exercises 16 and 17 on Student Book page 467. Circulate while they work and check that their work is correct and offer help where needed.

Tell students that sometimes one set of views can correspond to more than one model. Have students work in pairs to make a cube model with two rows of three cubes on the bottom and two rows of three cubes on top. Ask them to draw the front, back, top, right, and left views. Then have them remove one cube from the top and draw the same views. Ask them to compare the two sets of drawings.

 Math Talk in Action

Dipak: Why are all of the views similar?

Kenesha: We removed the cube from the top layer, but the cube in the first layer still shows. So, when you look at the model from any view, the faces of that cube show just like the cube above it would have.

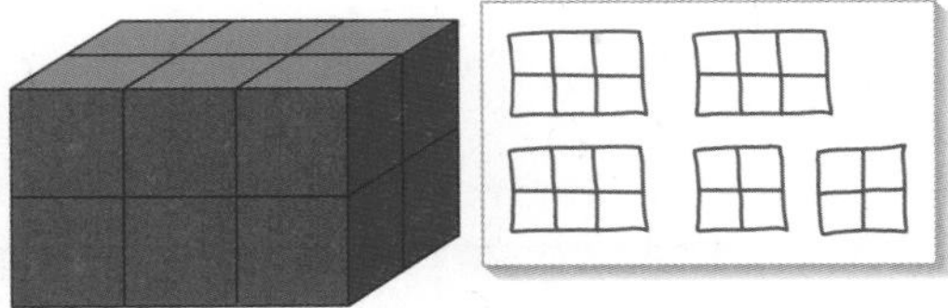

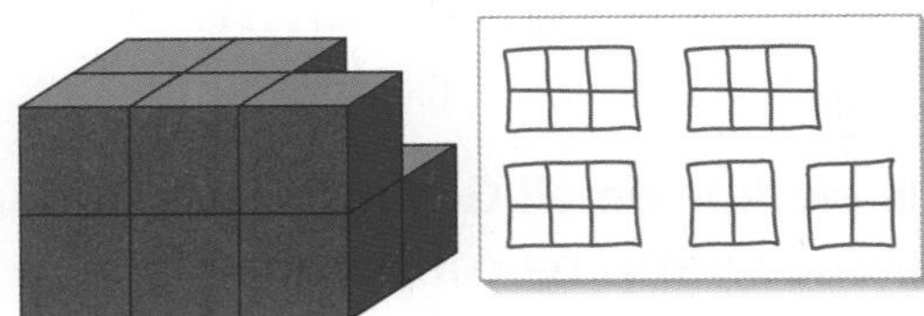

Have students who experience difficulty work with a **Helping Partner.**

Teaching Note

What to Expect From Students Most students will have to use a trial-and-error method to have success with these three-dimensional buildings. Encourage them to attempt a building based on the drawings, to look at their buildings from the different views, and to compare what they see with the drawings. They should then modify their buildings if necessary and again check their views against the drawings.

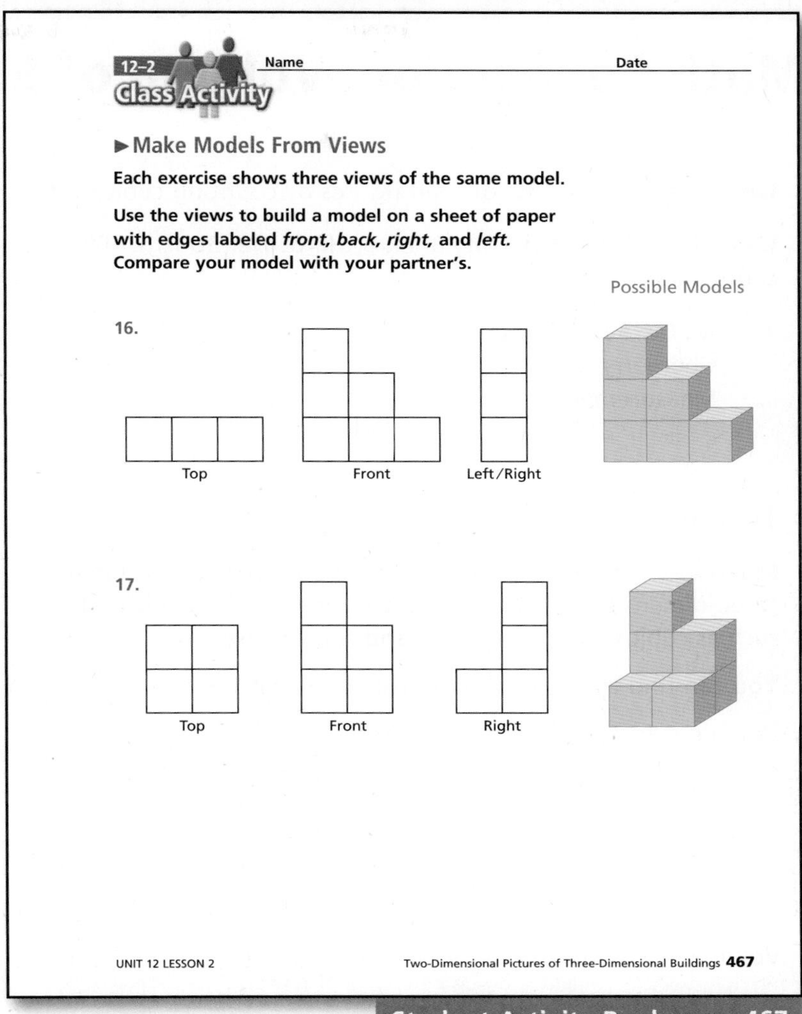

12–2 Class Activity Name Date

▶ Make Models From Views

Each exercise shows three views of the same model.

Use the views to build a model on a sheet of paper with edges labeled *front, back, right,* and *left.* Compare your model with your partner's.

Possible Models

16.

17.

UNIT 12 LESSON 2 Two-Dimensional Pictures of Three-Dimensional Buildings **467**

Student Activity Book page 467

Differentiated Instruction

Extra Help Students who are experiencing difficulty building the models with centimeter cubes can try using connecting cubes to build their models. When students use the connecting cubes, their buildings won't fall apart if they turn them to see the different viewpoints.

2 Going Further

Math Connection: Volume of Solid Figures

Goal: Find the volume of solid figures by counting cubic units.

Materials: Student Activity Book or Hardcover Book p. 468, cubes made in Lesson 1

 **NCTM Standards:**
Geometry
Measurement

Teaching Note

Math Background Volume is the amount of space inside a three-dimensional figure. Volume is measured in cubic units such as cubic centimeters (cm^3) and cubic inches ($in.^3$).

You can find the volume of a prism with this formula:

Volume = length × width × height

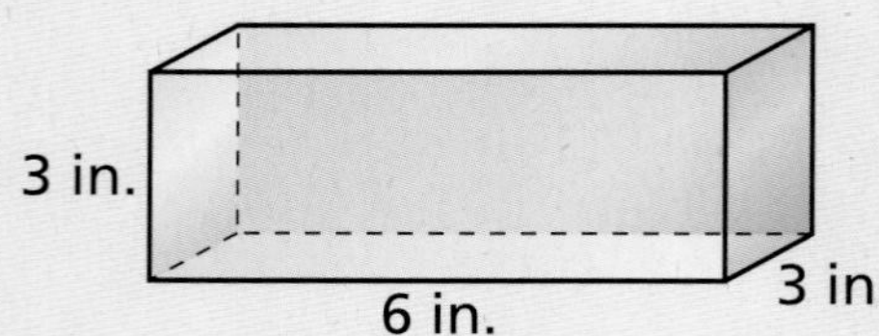

Volume = $3 \times 3 \times 6 = 54$ or 54 cubic inches ($in.^3$)

▶ Volume of 3-D Objects PAIRS

Hold up a paper cube from Lesson 1. Tell students that the cube occupies a certain amount of space or volume. Explain that it can be used as a unit to measure the volume of larger three-dimensional objects.

Have students look at the drawing in exercise 1 on Student Book page 468. Ask **Student Pairs** to model the drawing. Then have them count the number of cubes they used to make the figure. Tell them that the number of cubes, 8, is the volume in cubic units.

Have students complete exercises 2–6 in pairs. Encourage students to find the volume of each by counting cubes and hidden cubes in the drawings first and then by making models to check.

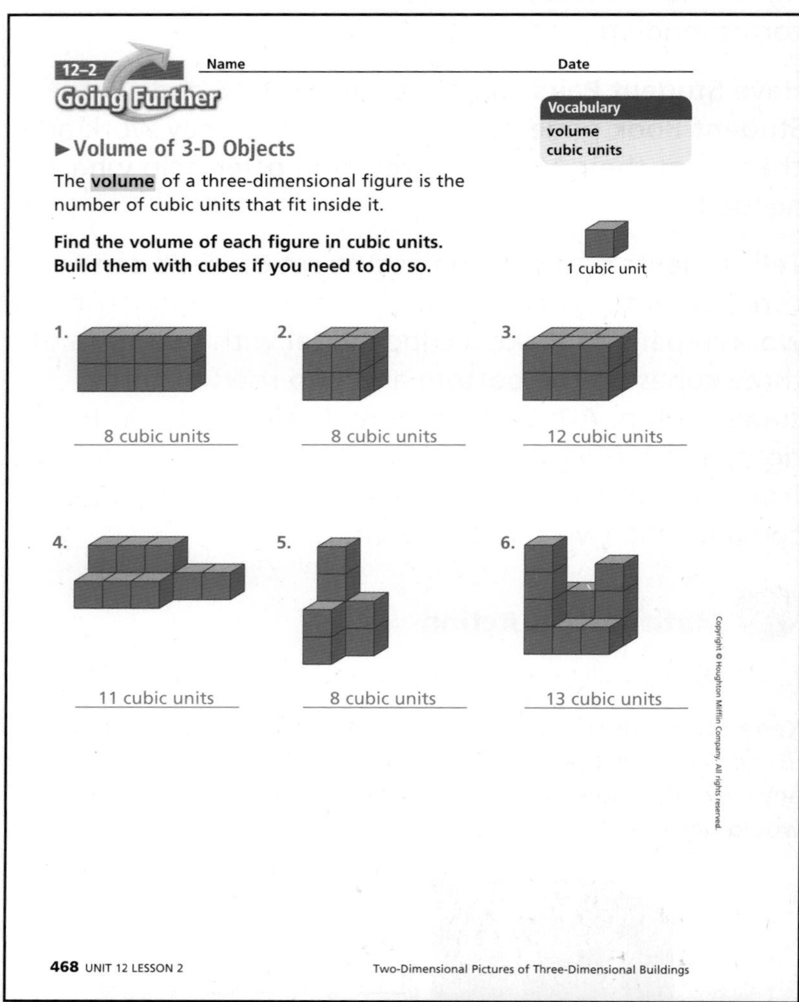

12–2 Going Further Name Date

Vocabulary
volume
cubic units

▶ Volume of 3-D Objects

The **volume** of a three-dimensional figure is the number of cubic units that fit inside it.

Find the volume of each figure in cubic units. Build them with cubes if you need to do so.

1 cubic unit

1. 8 cubic units
2. 8 cubic units
3. 12 cubic units
4. 11 cubic units
5. 8 cubic units
6. 13 cubic units

Copyright © Houghton Mifflin Company. All rights reserved.

468 UNIT 12 LESSON 2 Two-Dimensional Pictures of Three-Dimensional Buildings

Student Activity Book page 468

▶ Find a Formula for Volume

SMALL GROUPS

Have students work in **Small Groups**. Have students make a larger cube with the cubes they made in Lesson 1 that has 4 cubes on the bottom and 4 cubes on the top.

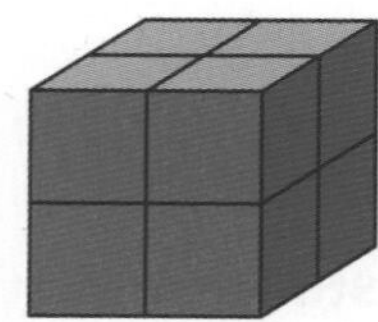

- How many cubes did you use? 8
- How could you describe the dimensions of the cube? Possible response: 2 cubes across, 2 cubes back, and 2

Have students remove the top layer.

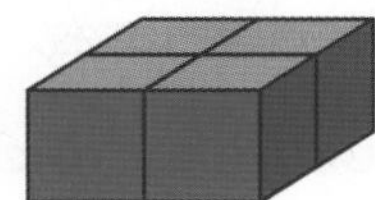

- How could you find the number of cubes in the bottom layer without counting? Multiply 2 × 2.

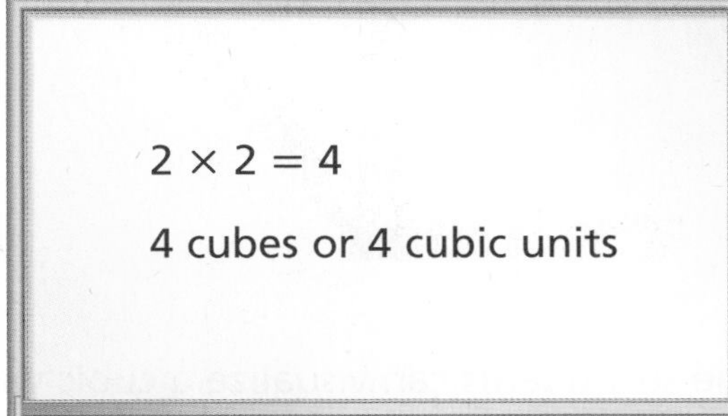

Put the top layer of cubes back on.

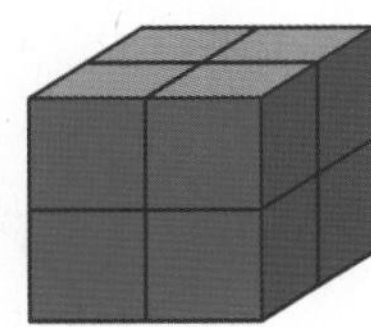

- How could you find the number of cubes in both layers without counting? Multiply the number in the bottom layer by 2

Write the following on the board.

$2 \times 2 = 4 \qquad 4 \times 2 = 8$

8 cubes or 8 cubic units or
8 cubic inches

- What formula in words could you write to find the volume? length × width × height

Write the following on the board:

length × width × height = volume
2 × 2 × 2 = 8
8 cubes or 8 cubic inches

Use the inch cubes to build the following prisms. Have the students use the formula to find the volumes and express their answers in cubic inches.

1.

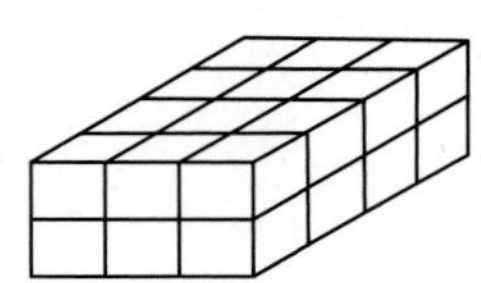

24 cubic inches

2.

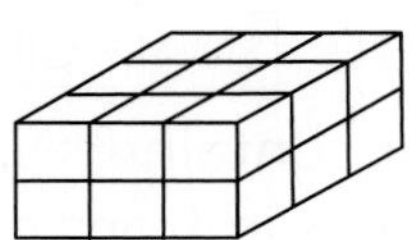

18 cubic inches

3.

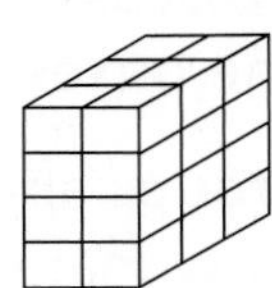

24 cubic inches

4.

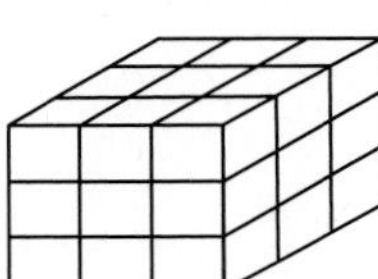

27 cubic inches

5.

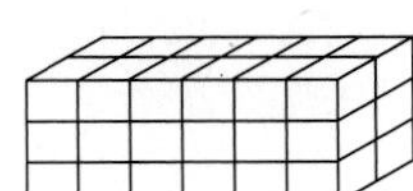

36 cubic inches

Extension: Estimating Volume

Goal: Estimate volume of solid figures

Materials: cubes from Lesson 1, rectangular boxes with length, width, and height under 12 inches, calculators, 3 rulers, 3 yard sticks

✓ **NCTM Standards:**
Geometry
Measurement

► Estimate Volume SMALL GROUPS

Place several rectangular containers with length, width, and height under 12 inches in front of the class. Each container should be numbered. Then have a student volunteer put the containers in order from greatest to least volume. Use **Solve and Discuss** to see if the class agrees with the order that the boxes are arranged.

Divide students into **Small Groups** and give them each a box. Have them estimate how many inch cubes will fit in the box and record their estimate. Then have them fill the length and width of the bottom layer of the box with inch cubes and have them stack cubes to show the height.

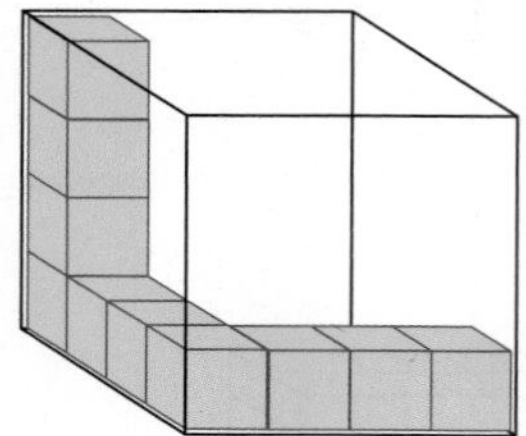

Once all groups have recorded their estimates, have the class revisit the order that the boxes were in. Students can calculate the number needed to check their estimates by calculating the number needed in the bottom layer and multiply that number by the number of layers.

Students can also use the formula for volume and a calculator to check their estimates.

Next have students visualize a cubic foot by placing one ruler as the length, another as the width, and another as the height.

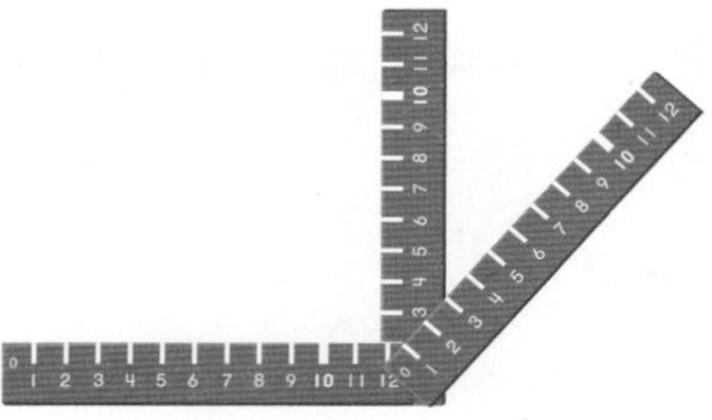

Do the same so students can visualize a cubic yard.

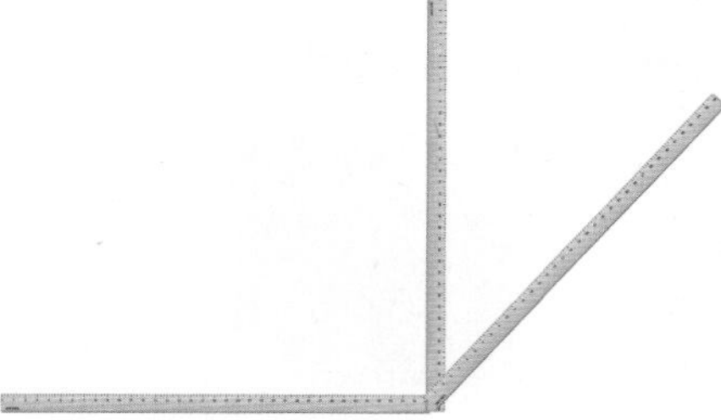

Challenge students to estimate the volume of 3-dimensional prisms in the classroom and the classroom itself using the appropriate size cubic unit. Then have them measure the length, width, and height of the 3-dimensional object to the nearest unit. Students can check their estimates using the formula for volume and a calculator.

If time allows, have students also try to estimate the volume of 3-dimensional figures in the classroom that are not prisms such as a glass and a milk jug.

Intervention — Activity Card 12-2

Draw Views
Activity Card 12–2 ●

Work: In pairs

Use:

- 6 Centimeter cubes
- TRB M31 (Centimeter-Grid Paper)

Decide:

Who will be Student 1 and who will be Student 2 for the first round.

1. Student 1: Build a three-dimensional shape using 6 centimeter cubes.

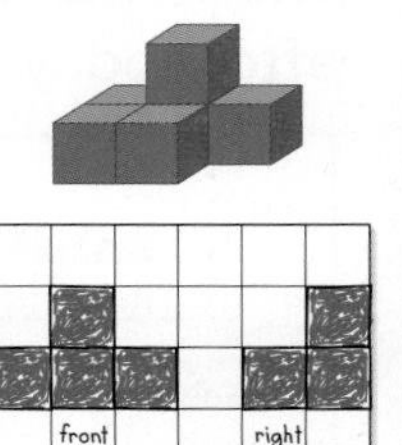

2. Student 2: Use grid paper to sketch four views of the shape. Label the sketches *top, front, right,* and *left,* as shown in the drawings of the shape on the right.

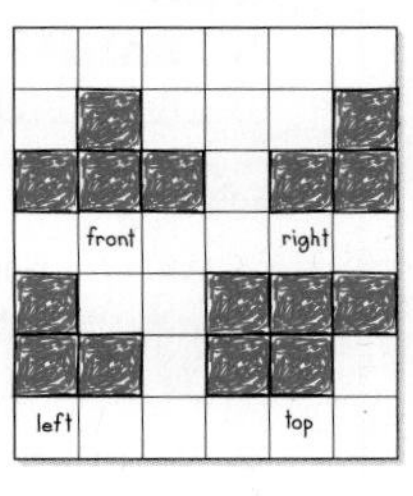

3. Think How many faces do you see from the top of your shape? How many faces do you see from each side?
4. Change roles and repeat the activity building a different shape.

Unit 12, Lesson 2

Activity Note Counting faces on each layer of a side will help students make accurate sketches of views and visualize the side from the correct perspective.

Math Writing Prompt

Explain Your Thinking Simon looked at a drawing of a cube building and said there were four cubes on top and two on the bottom. Bao said there were four cubes on top and four cubes on the bottom. Who is correct? Explain.

Software Support

Warm Up 36.18

On Level — Activity Card 12-2

Identical Views
Activity Card 12–2 ▲

Work: In pairs

Use:

- 15 centimeter cubes

1. Use two or more cubes to make a three-dimensional shape that has the same view from the top, front, back, left, and right.
2. Work Together Sketch each view to be sure that each face is the same.
3. Analyze Is there another shape that you could make with 15 cubes or less that has the same view from all sides and from the top? If so, make the shape. If not, tell how many cubes you would need to make another shape with identical views. no; you would need 27 cubes.

Unit 12, Lesson 2

Activity Note Only cubes with square faces will have identical views on all sides. After students have completed the activity, discuss how the symmetrical properties of the cube create identical views.

Math Writing Prompt

Predict and Verify Is the top view of a cube building always the same as the bottom view? Make models using cubes to test your answer. Describe what you discover.

Software Support

Ice Station Exploration: Frozen Solids, Level M

Challenge — Activity Card 12-2

Home Sweet Home
Activity Card 12–2 ■

Work: On your own

Use:

- Calculator
- *Counting on Frank*, by Rod Clement (optional)

1. In the book, *Counting on Frank*, the narrator says that 10 humpback whales would fit into the size of his house.
2. Use the facts and clues about the average size of a humpback whale to find about how large the house is.
3. If you have more time, read the rest of the picture book.

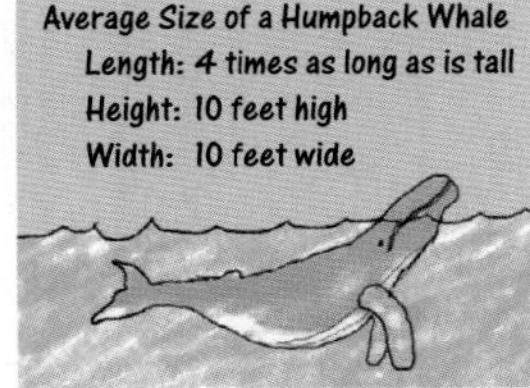

Unit 12, Lesson 2

Activity Note Encourage students to use what they know about mental math to help them with double-digit multiplication to find the volume.

Math Writing Prompt

Make a Drawing Two cube models have a volume of six cubic units. Must they have the same shape? Explain why or why not. Include a diagram in your answer.

Software Support

Course II: Module 3: Unit 1: Volume

3 Homework and Spiral Review

Goal: Additional Practice

For homework, students label and draw views of cube models.

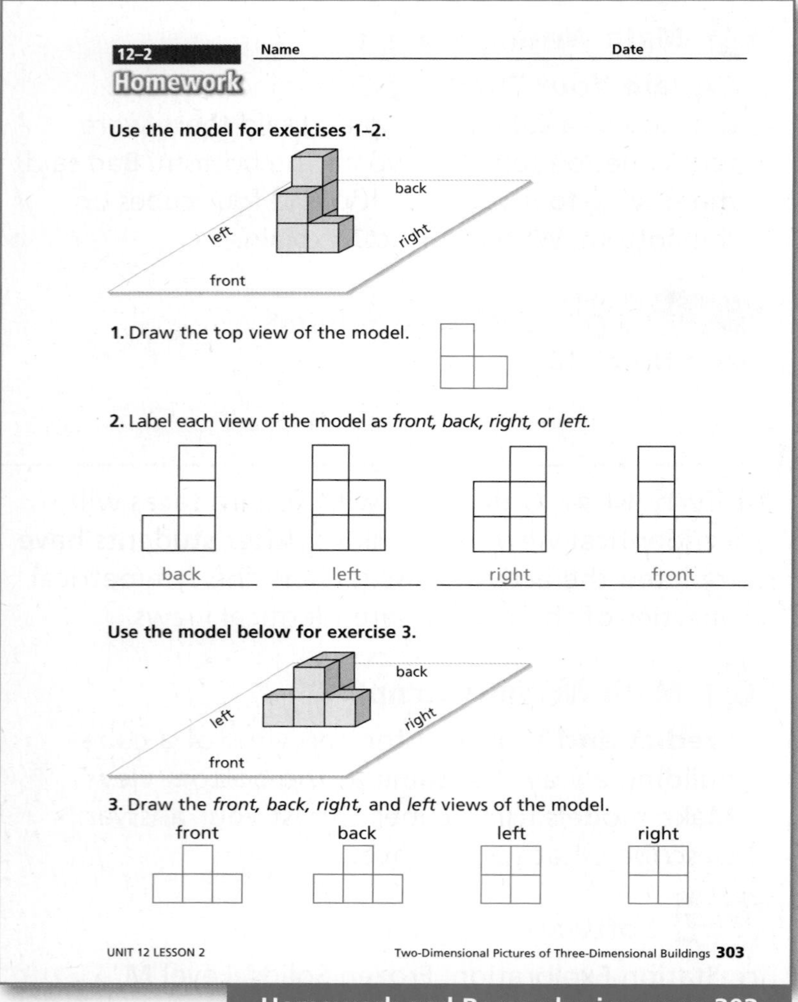

12–2 Homework Name ____ Date ____

Use the model for exercises 1–2.

back, left, right, front

1. Draw the top view of the model.

2. Label each view of the model as *front, back, right,* or *left.*

back — left — right — front

Use the model below for exercise 3.

back, left, right, front

3. Draw the *front, back, right,* and *left* views of the model.

front — back — left — right

UNIT 12 LESSON 2 — Two-Dimensional Pictures of Three-Dimensional Buildings 303

Homework and Remembering page 303

12–2 Remembering **Goal:** Spiral Review

This Remembering page would be appropriate anytime after today's lesson.

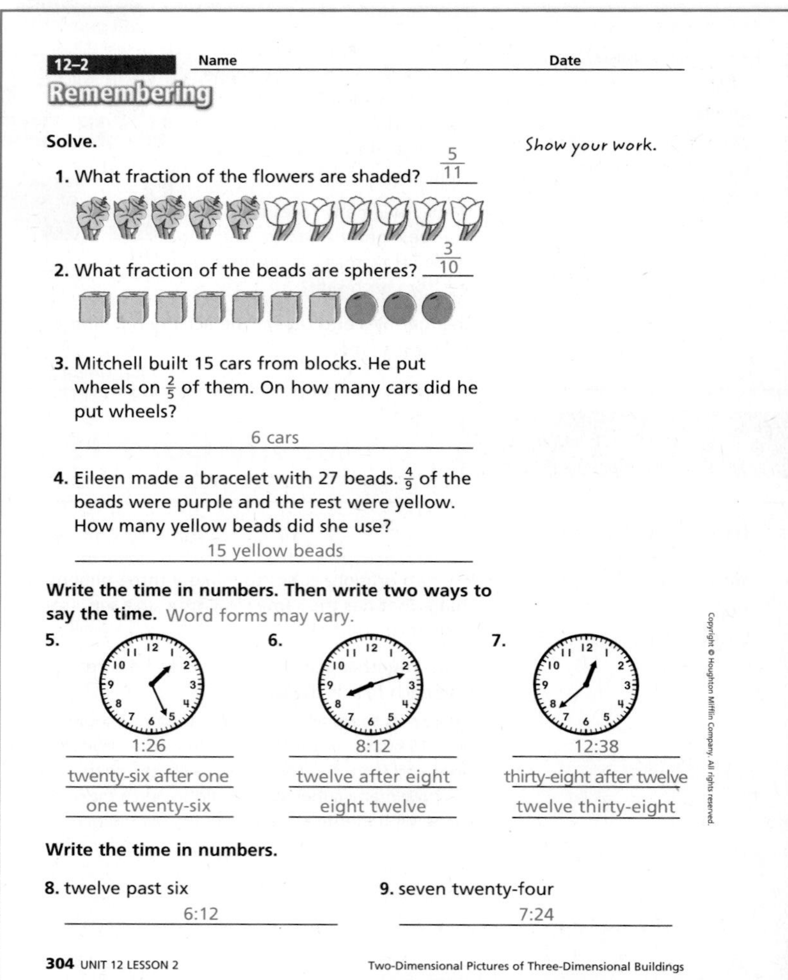

12–2 Remembering Name ____ Date ____

Solve. *Show your work.*

1. What fraction of the flowers are shaded? $\frac{5}{11}$

2. What fraction of the beads are spheres? $\frac{3}{10}$

3. Mitchell built 15 cars from blocks. He put wheels on $\frac{2}{5}$ of them. On how many cars did he put wheels?
   6 cars

4. Eileen made a bracelet with 27 beads. $\frac{4}{9}$ of the beads were purple and the rest were yellow. How many yellow beads did she use?
   15 yellow beads

Write the time in numbers. Then write two ways to say the time. Word forms may vary.

5. 1:26 — twenty-six after one — one twenty-six

6. 8:12 — twelve after eight — eight twelve

7. 12:38 — thirty-eight after twelve — twelve thirty-eight

Write the time in numbers.

8. twelve past six — 6:12

9. seven twenty-four — 7:24

304 UNIT 12 LESSON 2 — Two-Dimensional Pictures of Three-Dimensional Buildings

Copyright © Houghton Mifflin Company. All rights reserved.

Homework and Remembering page 304

Home or School Activity

Real-World Connection

A Two-Dimensional Plan People who sew often begin by cutting fabric from two-dimensional pattern pieces. Woodworkers often draw two-dimensional plans before making three-dimensional objects.

Students select a three-dimensional object at home or in school and make a pattern or a plan for creating the object.

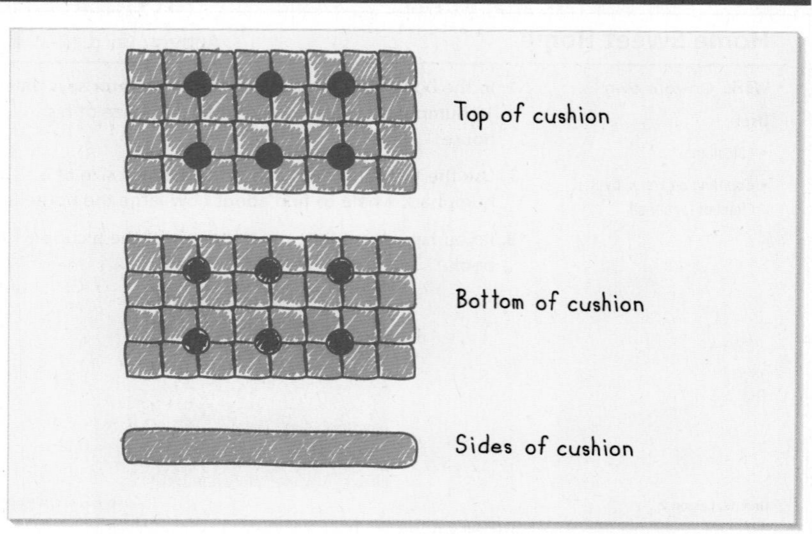

Explore Prisms, Cylinders, and Pyramids

Lesson Objectives

- Make prisms, cylinders, and pyramids from nets.
- Identify characteristics of prisms, cylinders, and pyramids.

Vocabulary

prism	rectangular prism
base	cylinder
triangular prism	circumference
square prism	pyramid
net	

The Day at a Glance

Today's Goals	Materials: Lesson Activities	Materials: Going Further
1 Teaching the Lesson **A1:** Build, name, and describe a variety of prisms. **A2:** Build, name, and describe a cylinder and a pyramid. **2 Going Further** ► Differentiated Instruction **3 Homework and Spiral Review**	Student Activity Book pp. 468A–468F or Activity Workbook pp. 235–240 (includes Nets for Figures) Homework and Remembering pp. 305–306 Scissors Tape	Activity Cards 12-3 Square Pattern Blocks Triangle Pattern Blocks Paper bag Rectangular prism Square prism Square Pyramid Cylinder Cube Ruler Scissors Tape Math Journals

Use Math Talk today!

Keeping Skills Sharp

Daily Routines

Homework Review Ask students to place their homework at the corner of their desks. As you circulate, check that student completed the assignment and see whether any problem caused difficulty for many students.

Estimation The teacher is planning a field trip. She knows 36 students and 4 teachers are going. Each bus holds 21 people. Should the teacher estimate the number of busses needed for the trip? Explain why or why not. If not, give the exact number of busses needed. Should not estimate, because students may be left behind if her estimate is too low; 2 busses will be needed.

English Language Learners

Draw an example of a prism on the board. Write *prism*.

- **Beginning** Say: **A *prism* is a three-dimensional figure.** Have students repeat.
- **Intermediate** Ask: **Is a *prism* flat?** no **Is a *prism* a three-dimensional figure?** yes
- **Advanced** Have students tell what makes *prism* a three-dimensional figure.

Teaching the Lesson

Activity 1

Build Prisms

 30 MINUTES

Goal: Build, name, and describe a variety of prisms.

Materials: Student Activity Book pp. 468A–468D or Activity Workbook pp. 231–234, scissors, tape

 **NCTM Standards:**
Geometry
Connections
Representation

► Prism Nets WHOLE CLASS

Have students look at the net in exercise 1. Explain that this is a net for a type of three-dimensional figure called a *prism*.

- A prism is a solid figure whose two parallel bases are congruent and whose faces are rectangles.
- A right prism is a solid shape with two parallel faces that are congruent polygons and other faces that are rectangles.

Have students cut out, and tape the net together. Remind students to cut along the solid lines and fold along the dashed lines.

Tell students that each flat surface of the prism is called a *face*. Ask students to describe the faces. Be sure to elicit that the prism has two faces that are triangles and three that are rectangles. Tell students that the two triangular faces are called *bases*. Point out that in a prism there are two parallel bases.

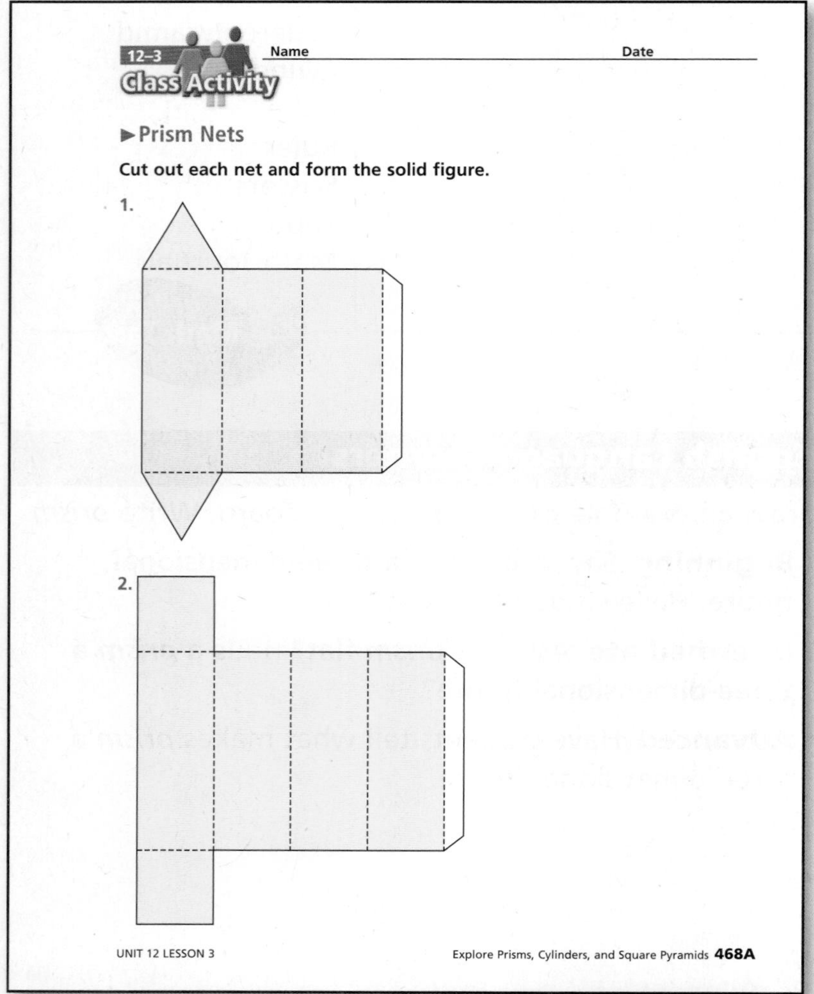
12-3
Class Activity
Name Date

► Prism Nets

Cut out each net and form the solid figure.

1.

2.

UNIT 12 LESSON 3 Explore Prisms, Cylinders, and Square Pyramids 468A

Student Activity Book page 468A

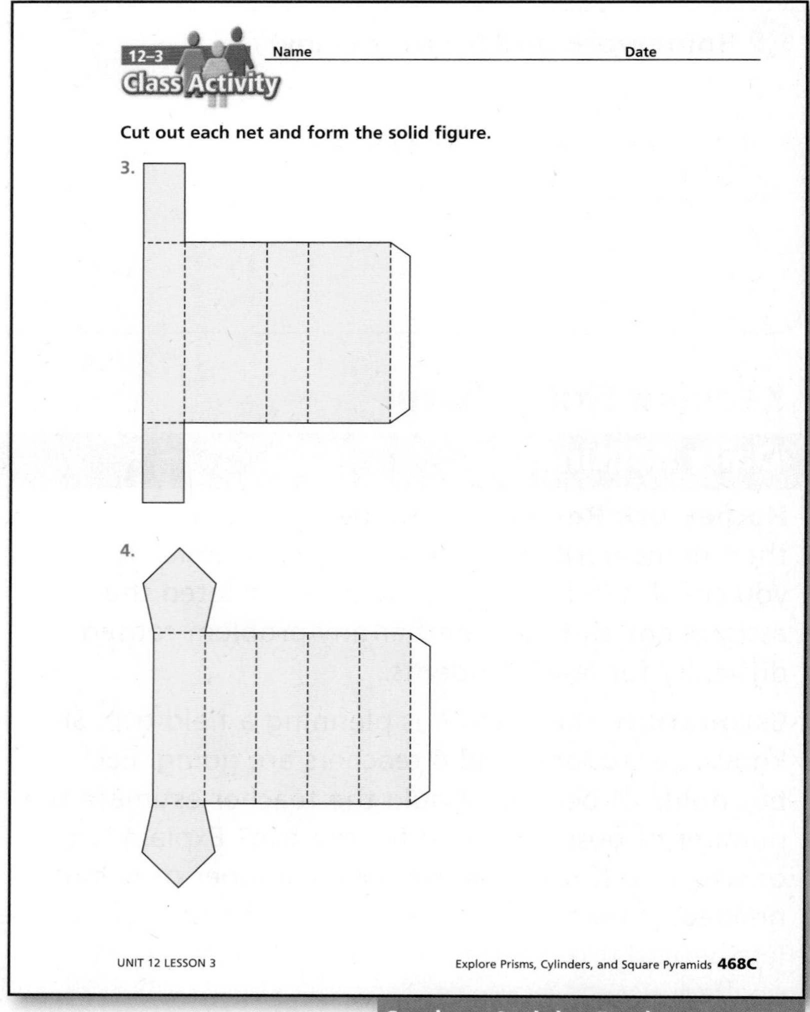
12-3
Class Activity
Name Date

Cut out each net and form the solid figure.

3.

4.

UNIT 12 LESSON 3 Explore Prisms, Cylinders, and Square Pyramids 468C

Student Activity Book page 468C

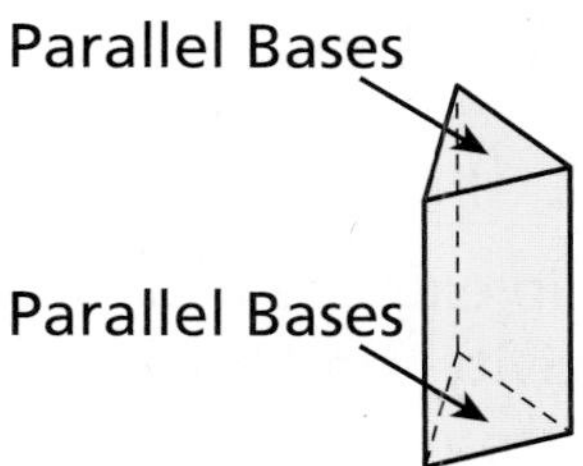

Explain that a prism is named according to the shape of its base.

- What shape is the base? triangle

Have students stand their prism on one of its bases. Explain that the height of the prism is how tall it is when it stands on one of its bases.

Have students predict what type of prisms nets 2, 3, and 4 on Student Activity Book pages 468A and 468C or Activity Workbook pages 231 and 233 will make. Ask them to cut out, fold, and assemble the nets to test their predictions.

Class Management

Looking Ahead Remind students to bring in any empty, clear packages for Lesson 4.

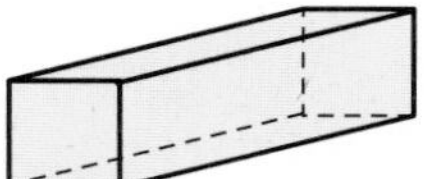 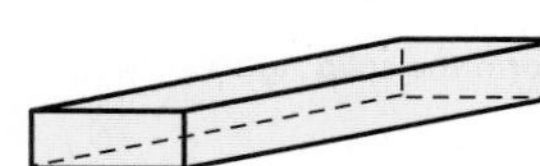 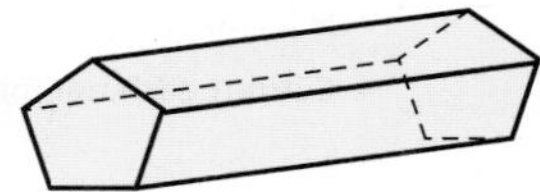

 **Math Talk** Discuss the characteristics of each prism.

- How many faces does this prism have?
- What shape is each face?
- Which of the faces on this prism do you think are the bases?
- What do you think this solid figure is called?
- How many edges does this prism have?
- How many vertices does this prism have?

Ask students to name some real-world objects that are shaped like each prism.

Views of Prisms Have students place each prism on its base and note the front, top, and side views. Ask students to describe what they notice about each view; for example, that all of the side views are rectangles, but the top views vary according to the name of the type of prism.

Display students' prisms for reference during the rest of the unit.

Activity 2

Build Cylinders and Pyramids

 **30 MINUTES**

Goal: Build, name, and describe a cylinder and a pyramid.

Materials: Student Activity Book p. 468E or Activity Workbook p. 235, scissors, tape

 **NCTM Standards:**
Geometry
Connections
Representation

► Cylinder Net INDIVIDUALS

Have students look at the net in exercise 5 on Student Activity Book page 468E or Activity Workbook page 239.

Have students predict what figure the net will make. Then have them cut and fold the net to form the figure.

Tell students that the solid figure is called a *cylinder*.

Math Talk Use the following questions to discuss the cylinder.

- How many bases does the cylinder have? 2
- What are the shapes of the bases? circles
- Are the bases parallel to each other? yes
- How would you describe the other surface? It is a curved surface.

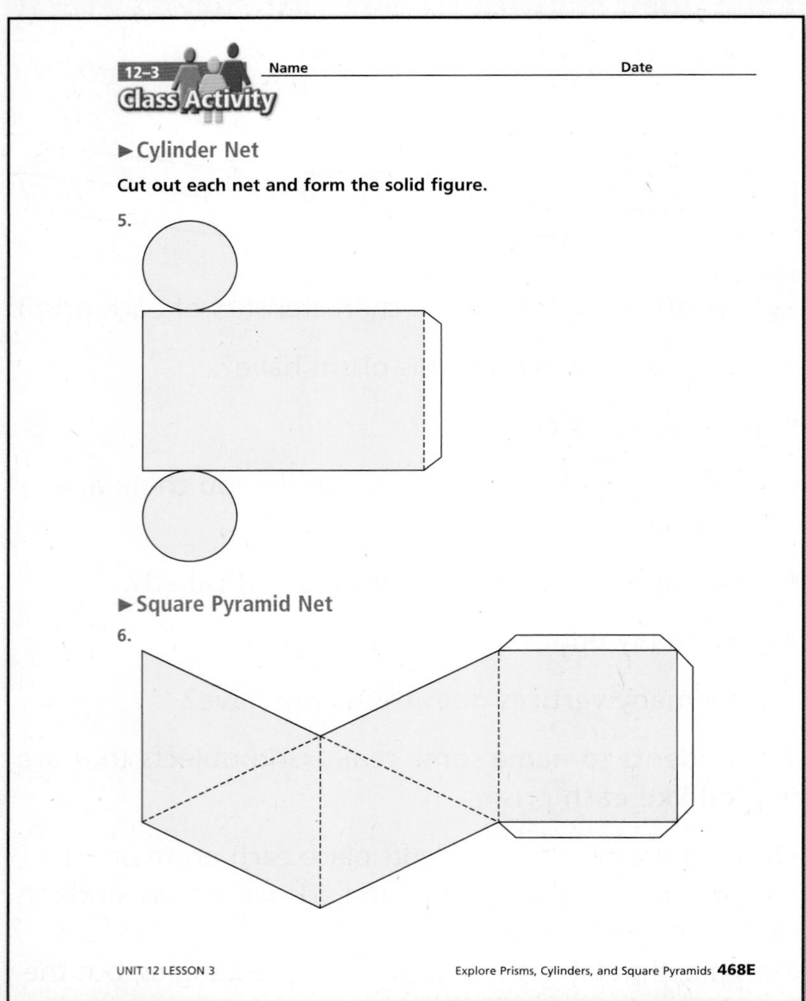

12-3 Class Activity Name Date

► Cylinder Net

Cut out each net and form the solid figure.

5.

► Square Pyramid Net

6.

UNIT 12 LESSON 3 Explore Prisms, Cylinders, and Square Pyramids **468E**

Student Activity Book page 468E

Ask students to name some real-world objects that are shaped liked cylinders. Possible responses: tennis ball, canisters, coffee cans, soup cans

Refer students to the display of prisms.

- How are prisms and cylinders the same? They both have parallel bases.
- How are they different? Possible answers: Cylinders have circular bases while prisms have bases with straight sides. A cylinder has one curved surface while prisms have rectangular or square sides.

Take apart and then remake one of the cylinders. Ask students to observe how the rectangle that is wrapped around the circular base is related to the perimeter of the circular bases.

- How does the length of the side of the rectangle on the net compare to the perimeter of the circular bases? They are equal.

Views of Cylinders Have students place their cylinder on one base and note its top view. Students will notice that the top view is a circle.

Display students' cylinders for reference.

► Square Pyramid Net INDIVIDUALS

Have students look at the net in exercise 6 on Student Activity Book page 468E or Activity Workbook page 235 and discuss how it is different from the nets they worked with in Activity 1. Then have them cut, fold, and assemble the figure.

Tell students that the figure is called a *square pyramid.*

Math Talk Use the following questions to discuss the square pyramid.

- How many faces does a square pyramid have? 5
- How many bases does it have? 1
- How many edges does it have? 8
- How many vertices does it have? 5

Ask students to name some real-world objects that are shaped like square pyramids. Possible responses: the pyramids in Egypt, gift box

- How is a pyramid different from the prisms you made? Prisms all had two parallel bases; a pyramid only has one base. The faces on a pyramid are triangles instead of rectangles. The faces of a pyramid meet to form a vertex.

Views of Pyramids Have students place their pyramid on its base and note the front, top, and side views. Discuss the various views. Students may notice that all of the side views of the square pyramid are triangles, but the top view is a square.

Display students' square pyramids for reference.

Ongoing Assessment

Display several prisms, a cylinder, and a pyramid. Ask students to name each solid figure, describe their faces, and identify the number of faces, bases, edges, and vertices.

2 Going Further

Differentiated Instruction

Intervention — Activity Card 12-3

Build Prisms

Activity Card 12–3 ●

Work: In pairs

Use:

- 5 square pattern blocks
- 5 triangle pattern blocks

1. Make a stack of square pattern blocks. What is the name of the prism you have made? What is the shape of the base of the prism? Square prism; square

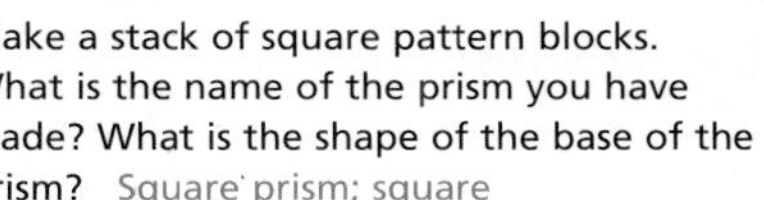

2. Now make a stack of triangular pattern blocks. What is the name of the prism you have made? What is the name of its base? Triangular prism; triangle base
3. **Analyze** How do you know which face is the base of a prism? What other shapes do you see on the faces of the prisms you made? A prism has two parallel bases that match. The remaining faces are rectangles. So each base of a square prism is a square; each base of a triangular prism is a triangle.

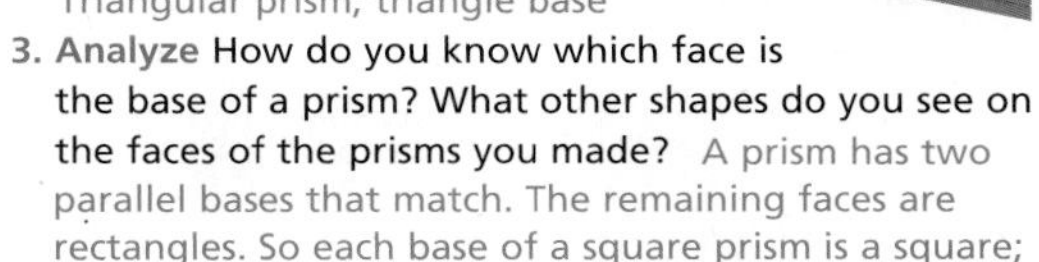

Unit 12, Lesson 3

Activity Note Before beginning this activity, ask students to describe a prism and tell how many bases it has. After completing the activity, students should compare and contrast the two prisms they made.

Math Writing Prompt

Make a Drawing Describe four objects that are prisms. Tell how each object is used. Make a drawing of one base on each object. Name the type of prism that describes each object.

Software Support

Warm Up 36.19

On Level — Activity Card 12-3

Hidden Solid Objects

Activity Card 12–3 ▲

Work: In pairs

Use:

- Paper bag
- Rectangular prism
- Square prism
- Square pyramid
- Cylinder
- Cube

Decide:

Who will be Student 1 and who will be Student 2 for the first round.

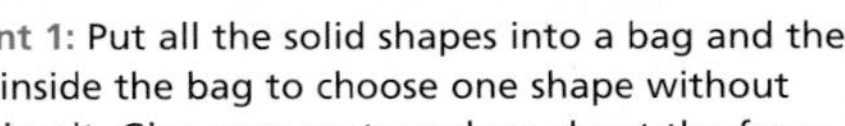

1. **Student 1:** Put all the solid shapes into a bag and then reach inside the bag to choose one shape without removing it. Give your partner clues about the faces and vertices of the solid.
2. **Student 2:** After hearing each clue, try to guess the shape of the solid. Then remove the solid from the bag to check your guess.
3. Switch roles and repeat the activity.

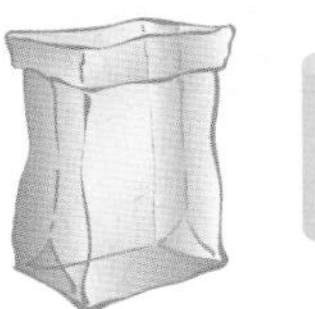

Unit 12, Lesson 3

Activity Note Students must first identify solids by touch in this activity. Suggest using clues such as the following: "The solid figure has five faces. Exactly one face is a square. The other faces are triangles."

Math Writing Prompt

Make a Comparison How are rectangular prisms and cylinders alike? How are they different?

Software Support

Shapes Ahoy: Undersea 3D, Level C

Challenge — Activity Card 12-3

Different Nets, Same Prism

Activity Card 12–3 ■

Work: In pairs

Use:

- Ruler
- Scissors
- Tape

1. **Work Together** Make three different nets for a triangular prism.

   Use a ruler to measure and draw each face and base. Then cut out the nets and tape them into solid shapes.

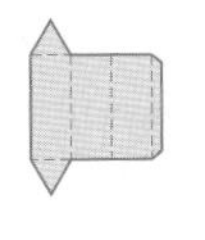

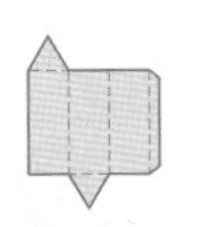

2. How many faces does each net have, including the bases? 5
3. What is the shape of each base? Triangle
4. **Discuss** Are there more than three ways to make a net for a triangular prism? How do you know? Yes, because the bases can be positioned in more than 3 ways on the net.

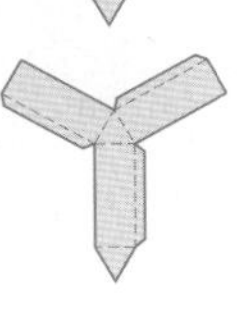

Unit 12, Lesson 3

Activity Note Challenge students to create more than three nets for a triangular prism if time allows. Repositioning the bases will result in different nets.

Math Writing Prompt

Predict and Verify Kalil is stacking square pattern blocks to make a three-dimensional object. Can he make a square prism that is not a cube? Explain why or why not. Use pattern blocks to verify your prediction.

Software Support

Course II: Module 3: Unit 1: Volume

3 Homework and Spiral Review

12–3 Homework **Goal:** Additional Practice

✓ Include students' completed Homework page as part of their portfolios.

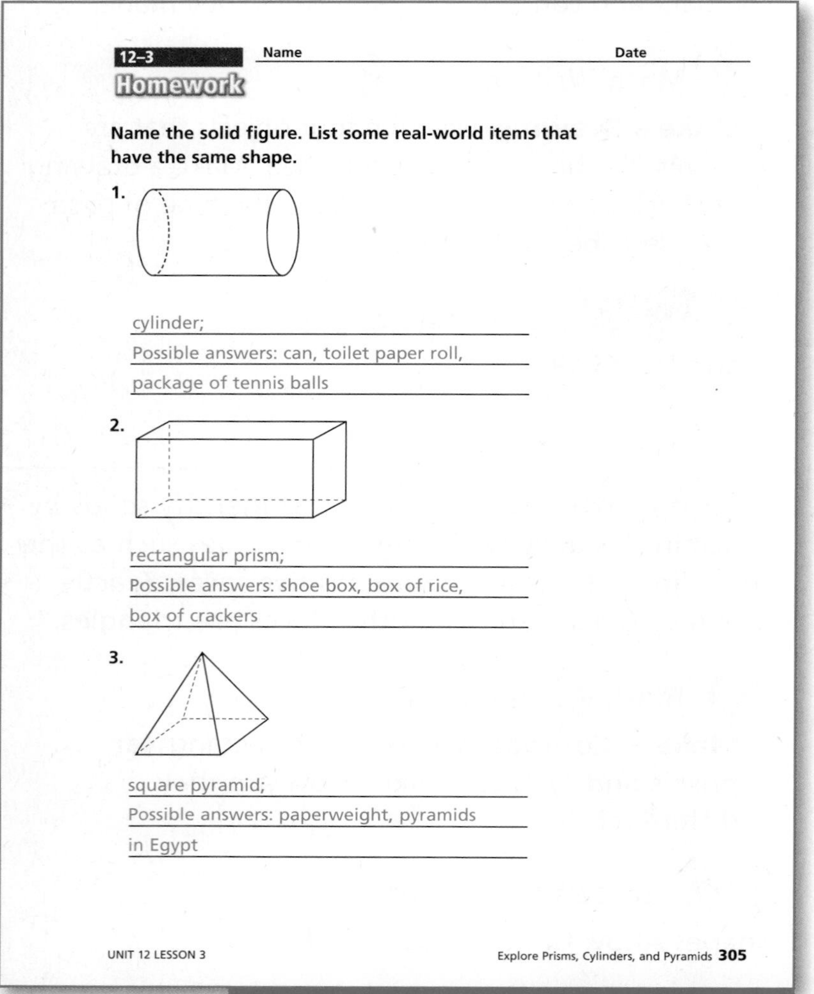

12–3 Homework Name Date

Name the solid figure. List some real-world items that have the same shape.

1. cylinder; Possible answers: can, toilet paper roll, package of tennis balls

2. rectangular prism; Possible answers: shoe box, box of rice, box of crackers

3. square pyramid; Possible answers: paperweight, pyramids in Egypt

UNIT 12 LESSON 3 Explore Prisms, Cylinders, and Pyramids 305

Homework and Remembering page 305

12–3 Remembering **Goal:** Spiral Review

This Remembering page would be appropriate anytime after today's lesson.

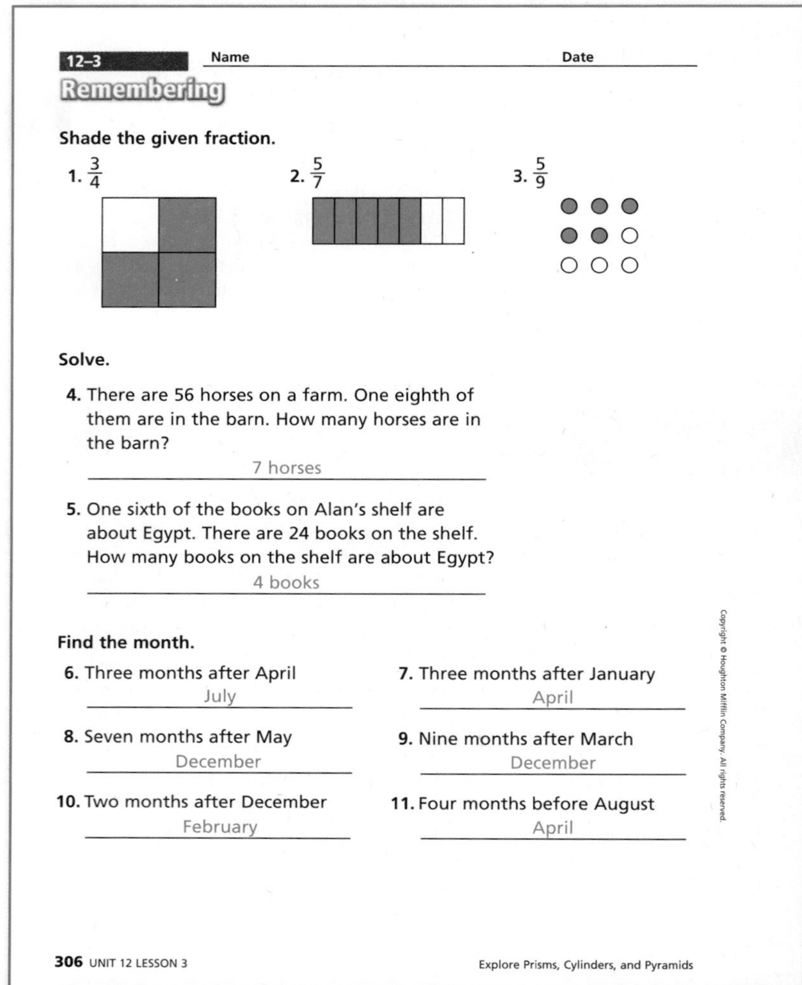

12–3 Remembering Name Date

Shade the given fraction.

1. $\frac{3}{4}$ 2. $\frac{5}{7}$ 3. $\frac{5}{9}$

Solve.

4. There are 56 horses on a farm. One eighth of them are in the barn. How many horses are in the barn? 7 horses

5. One sixth of the books on Alan's shelf are about Egypt. There are 24 books on the shelf. How many books on the shelf are about Egypt? 4 books

Find the month.

6. Three months after April July
7. Three months after January April
8. Seven months after May December
9. Nine months after March December
10. Two months after December February
11. Four months before August April

306 UNIT 12 LESSON 3 Explore Prisms, Cylinders, and Pyramids

Homework and Remembering page 306

Home or School Activity

Social Studies Connection

Buildings with Solid Figures Have students research solid figures used in architecture. Encourage them to research buildings from different time periods and cultures. For example, the pyramids of ancient Egypt are square pyramids. Some skyscrapers are rectangular prisms. Invite students to present drawings or photographs of the buildings and to identify the names of the solid figures in their structures.

This French castle is made up of cylinders, triangular prisms, and rectangular prisms.

Explore Cones

Lesson Objectives

- Make a cone from a net.
- Sort 3-D figures.
- Design a package for a product.

Vocabulary
cone
cylinder

The Day at a Glance

Today's Goals	Materials	
1 Teaching the Lesson **A1:** Build, name, and describe a cone and compare it to other solid figures. **A2:** Sort solid figures. **A3:** Design a package for a product.	**Lesson Activities** Student Activity Book pp. 468G–470 or Student Hardcover Book pp. 469–470 and Activity Workbook pp. 241–242 (includes Nets for Figures) Homework and Remembering pp. 307–308 Scissors Tape 3-D figures Inch Grid Paper (TRB M42) Rulers Colored pencils Various packages	**Going Further** Activity Cards 12-4 Cardboard packages Scissors Tape Venn Diagram (TRB M29) Several different three-dimensional shapes Cans Math Journals
2 Going Further ▸ Differentiated Instruction		
3 Homework and Spiral Review		

Use Math Talk today!

Keeping Skills Sharp

Daily Routines	English Language Learners
Homework Review Ask students if they had difficulty with any part of the homework. Plan to set aside some time to work with students needing extra help. **Perimeter** Hoi wants to put a tile border around his floor. The floor is a square. Each side has a length of 8 feet. How many feet of tile border does Hoi need? 32 feet	Show an example of a cone. Write *cone* on the board. • **Beginning** Say: **A *cone* is a three-dimensional figure with a circle base.** Have students repeat. • **Intermediate** Ask: **Is a *cone* a three-dimensional figure?** yes **Does it have a triangle base?** no **Does it have a circle base?** yes • **Advanced** Have students tell what type of figure a *cone* is and what type of base a *cone* has.

1 Teaching the Lesson

Activity 1

Build Cones

 **20 MINUTES**

Goal: Build, name, and describe a cone and compare it to other solid figures.

Materials: Student Activity Book pp. 468G–468H or Activity Workbook pp. 237–238, scissors, tape

 **NCTM Standards:**
Geometry
Connections
Representation

▶ Build a Cone WHOLE CLASS

Refer students to Student Activity Book page 468G or Activity Workbook p. 237. Then have students cut out, and tape the net together.

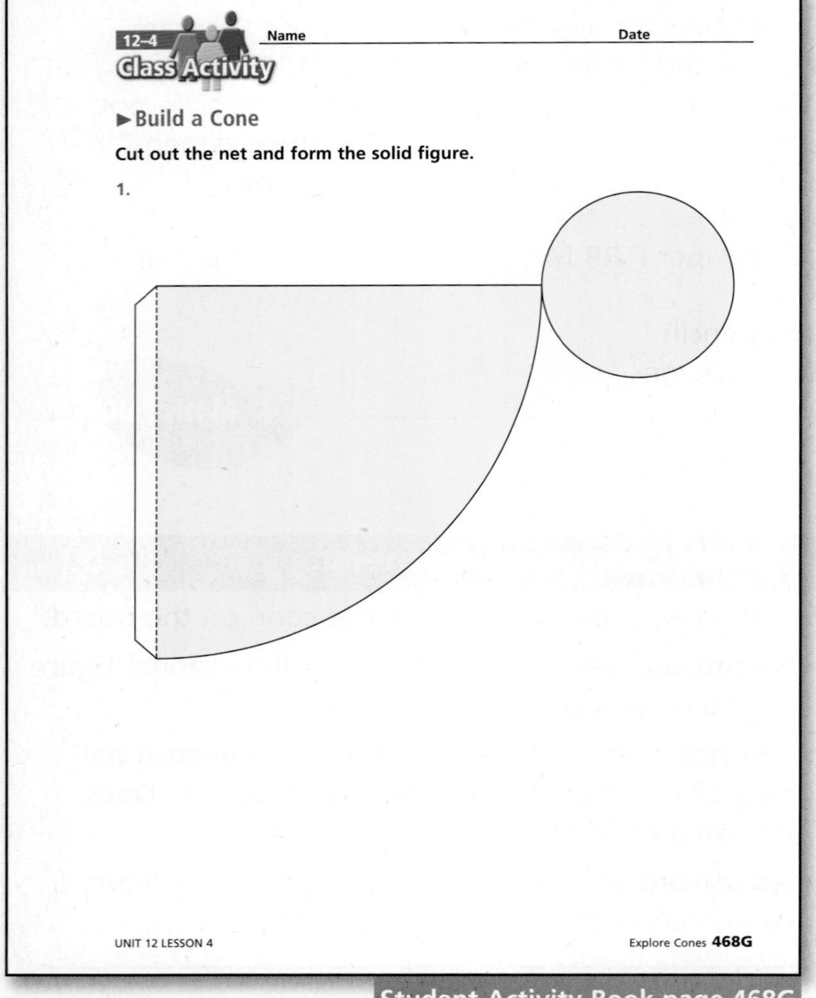
12–4 Class Activity Name Date

▶ Build a Cone

Cut out the net and form the solid figure.

1.

UNIT 12 LESSON 4 Explore Cones **468G**

Student Activity Book page 468G

- Does anyone know what this solid figure is called? a *cone*
- How many bases does a cone have? 1
- What is the shape of the base? a circle
- Describe the other surface. It is a curved surface that makes a point at the top.

Tell students that the point on a cone is called a vertex.

Have students compare a cone to other solid figures.

- How is this solid figure like a cylinder? Possible answer: It has a circular base.
- How is it different from a cylinder? Possible answers: It only has one base. It does not have parallel bases. It comes to a point at the top.
- How is this solid figure different from the prisms you made? Possible answers: It does not have rectangular faces. It has only one base. It has a curved surface.

Discuss how the circular base is related to the length of the curved part of the net. Show how the curved side wraps around the circumference of the circle by taking a cone apart and putting it back together again.

Ask students to name some real-world objects that are shaped like cones. Possible answers: ice-cream cones, pylons

Views of Cones Have students place their cone on its base and note the top view. Ask students to describe what they notice. The top view is a circle.

Display students' cones for reference during the rest of the unit.

Teaching Note

Math Background Be aware that opinions may vary as to whether a cone has a vertex. *Math Expressions* calls where a cone comes to a point, a vertex.

Activity 2

Sort Solid Figures

 **20 MINUTES**

Goal: Sort solid figures.

Materials: 3-D figures, Student Activity Book or Hardcover Book p. 469

 **NCTM Standards:**
Geometry
Connections
Representation

▶ Discuss Sorting Rules

WHOLE CLASS **Math Talk** 

Display a collection of 3-D figures including a cube, a square pyramid, a rectangular prism, a triangular prism, a cone, and a cylinder. If you do not have three-dimensional figures, have students refer to the figures at the top of Student Book page 469. Tell students that the solid figures can be sorted according to a sorting rule. Ask them to help you sort the figures according to the rule "solid figures that have at least one rectangular face and solid figures that don't have any."

- Which solid figures have at least one rectangular face? cube, square pyramid, triangular prism, rectangular prism
- Which solid figures don't have any rectangular faces? cone, cylinder

Next, ask students to help you sort the figures according to the sorting rule "solid figures that have parallel bases and solid figures that don't."

- Which solid figures have parallel bases? cube, triangular prism, rectangular prism, cylinder
- Which solid figures don't have parallel bases? square pyramid, cone
- What are some other attributes that could be used to sort these solid figures? Possible answers: size, number of edges, number of faces, number of vertices, curved or flat faces, shapes of faces

Have students sort the solid figures using one of the other attributes and discuss as a class.

▶ Sort 3-D Figures

WHOLE CLASS

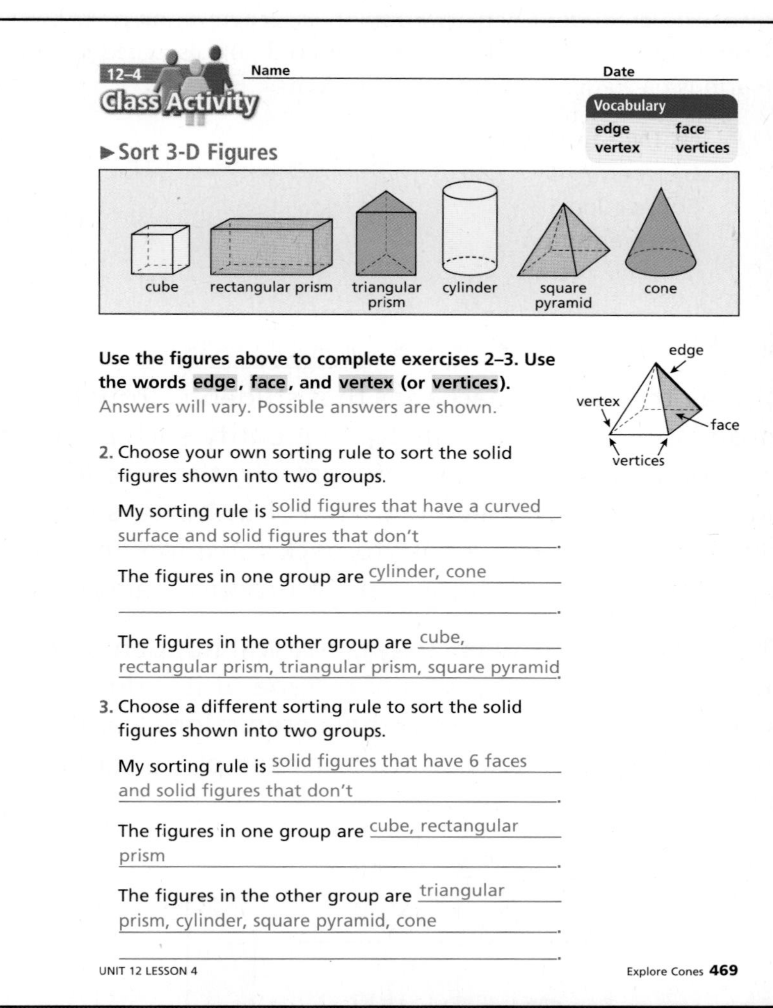

12-4 Class Activity Name Date

Vocabulary: edge, face, vertex, vertices

▶ Sort 3-D Figures

cube, rectangular prism, triangular prism, cylinder, square pyramid, cone

Use the figures above to complete exercises 2–3. Use the words edge, face, and vertex (or vertices).
Answers will vary. Possible answers are shown.

2. Choose your own sorting rule to sort the solid figures shown into two groups.
My sorting rule is solid figures that have a curved surface and solid figures that don't.
The figures in one group are cylinder, cone.
The figures in the other group are cube, rectangular prism, triangular prism, square pyramid.

3. Choose a different sorting rule to sort the solid figures shown into two groups.
My sorting rule is solid figures that have 6 faces and solid figures that don't.
The figures in one group are cube, rectangular prism.
The figures in the other group are triangular prism, cylinder, square pyramid, cone.

UNIT 12 LESSON 4 Explore Cones 469

Student Activity Book page 469

Ask students to complete exercises 2 and 3 on Student Book page 469. If students have difficulty sorting the figures on Student Book page 469, have them use three-dimensional solid figures. Have several students present their sorting rules and groupings.

Activity 3

Create Packages From Nets

20 MINUTES

Goal: Design a package for a product.

Materials: Student Activity Book or Hardcover Book p. 470, Inch-Grid Paper (TRB M42), rulers, colored pencils, scissors, tape, various packages collected from students

NCTM Standards:
Geometry
Connections
Representation

► Explore Packages WHOLE CLASS

Display the various packages that students brought into school. Have students try to identify each package as a solid figure. Together, discuss why those solid figures might have been chosen. For instance, shapes with parallel bases are easy to pack for shipping while a pyramid package might make a product stand out.

Then ask students what they think will happen if you cut apart the solid figure along some of its edges. After students have shared their predictions, carefully cut open a rectangular prism (for example, a cereal box).

Make sure students see that the two-dimensional object is a net of a rectangular prism. As time allows, challenge student volunteers to put together the cereal box by taping the net together, forming a rectangular prism.

► Packages INDIVIDUALS

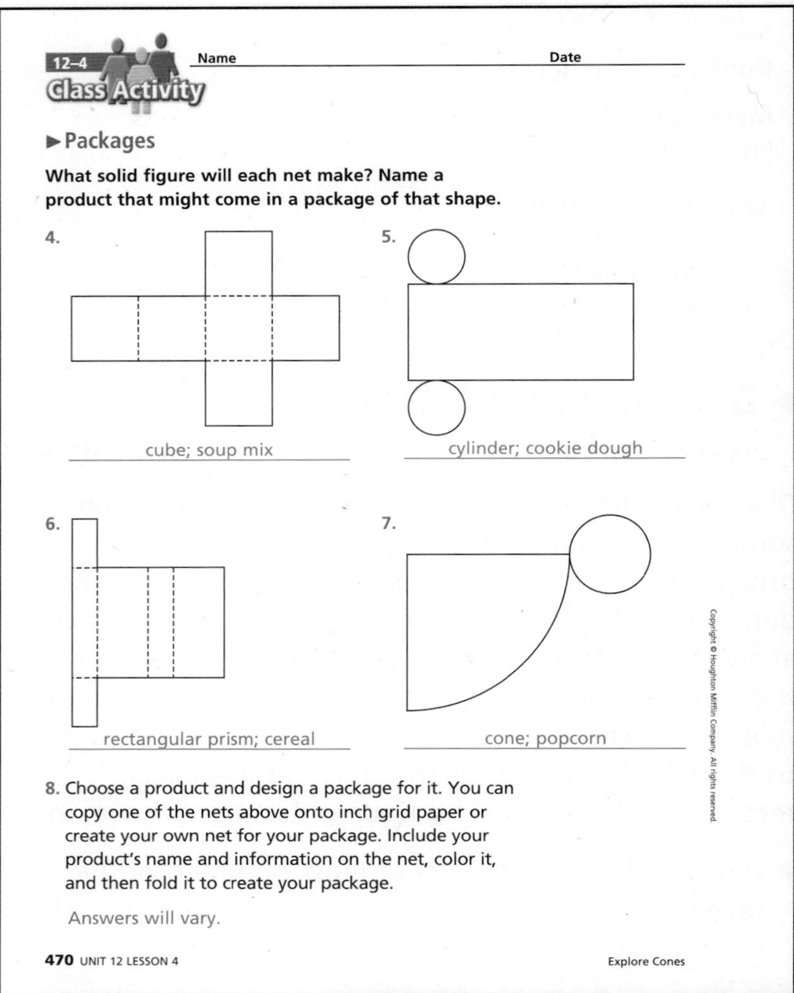
12–4 Class Activity Name Date

► Packages

What solid figure will each net make? Name a product that might come in a package of that shape.

4. cube; soup mix

5. cylinder; cookie dough

6. rectangular prism; cereal

7. cone; popcorn

8. Choose a product and design a package for it. You can copy one of the nets above onto inch grid paper or create your own net for your package. Include your product's name and information on the net, color it, and then fold it to create your package.

Answers will vary.

470 UNIT 12 LESSON 4 Explore Cones

Student Activity Book page 470

Have students complete exercises 4–7. Then have them complete exercise 8 to design a package for a product.

Math Talk Have students share their packages and explain why they chose that 3-D figure. In their explanations, have students list other objects that are seen daily that look like each 3-D figure. This will prove comprehension of the characteristics of each 3-D figure students have learned thus far.

2 Going Further

Differentiated Instruction

Intervention Activity Card 12-4

Nets in the Real World

Activity Card 12–4

Work: In pairs
Use:
- Cardboard packages
- Scissors
- Tape

1. On Your Own Choose a cardboard package and make a cut along one of the edges. Continue cutting edges until the package lies flat and forms a net.

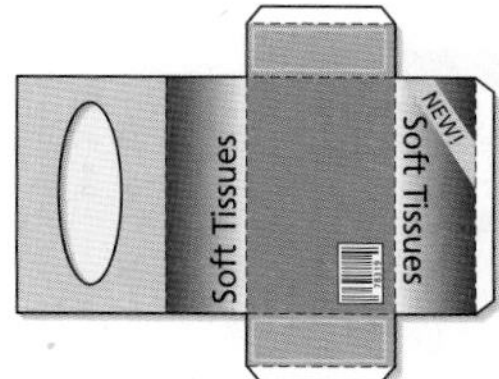

2. Exchange nets with your partner. Use tape to form the net into the original three-dimensional shape.

Unit 12, Lesson 4

Activity Note Students should only cut along the edges of the packages. Tell students not to cut off any parts of the package, so that the resulting net is complete.

Math Writing Prompt

Explain Your Thinking Leila made a net for a triangular prism. She drew two triangles and four rectangles. Explain whether her net will work.

Software Support

Warm Up 36.13

On Level Activity Card 12-4

Venn Diagrams

Activity Card 12–4

Work: In pairs
Use:
- TRB M29 (Venn Diagram)
- Several different three-dimensional shapes, such as cylinders, prisms, cones, and pyramids

1. Use a Venn Diagram to sort a collection of three-dimensional shapes. Choose attributes that you can use to describe the shapes.
2. Think How many edges, vertices, or faces does each shape have? Do some shapes have curved faces?
3. Discuss Is there a way to sort the shapes by describing only their bases?
4. Choose an attribute for each part of the Venn Diagram. Label the Venn Diagram and then sort the shapes. Share your results with other groups.

Unit 12, Lesson 4

Activity Note One way to categorize shapes is to use the labels *parallel bases* and *curved surfaces*. The cylinder has both of these attributes, and the square pyramid has neither one.

Math Writing Prompt

Use Reasoning You are making a package for a product that will be shipped to stores. Will you choose a cone or a rectangular prism for the package? Explain your choice.

Software Support

Shapes Ahoy: Undersea 3D, Level F

Challenge Activity Card 12-4

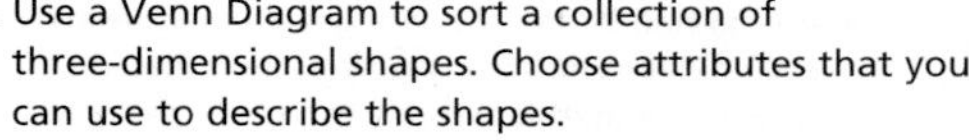

Compare and Contrast Packages

Activity Card 12–4

Work: In pairs
Use:
- Cardboard packages
- Cans

1. Choose two packages. Then discuss how the shapes are alike and how they are different.
2. Write a paragraph to compare and contrast both packages. Include as many attributes of each shape as you can. Use words like *cylinder, base, face, edge, vertex, surface,* and *prism.*
3. Share your work with other groups.
4. Analyze What attributes can be added to another group's paragraph?

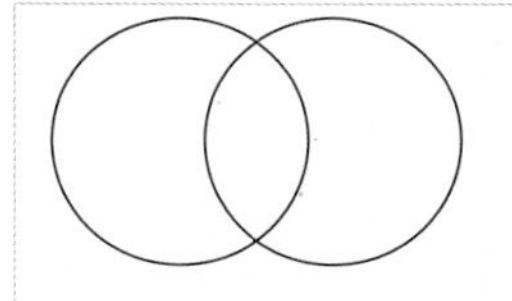

Unit 12, Lesson 4

Activity Note Encourage students to use topic sentences, details, and a closing sentence when they write their compare and contrast paragraph.

Math Writing Prompt

Draw a Picture Describe a hexagonal prism. What shape is the base? What shape are the faces? How many edges are there? Draw a sketch of a net for a hexagonal prism.

DESTINATION Math® **Software Support**

Course II: Module 3: Unit 1: Volume

3 Homework and Spiral Review

Goal: Additional Practice

This Homework page allows students to practice drawing nets and identifying solid figures.

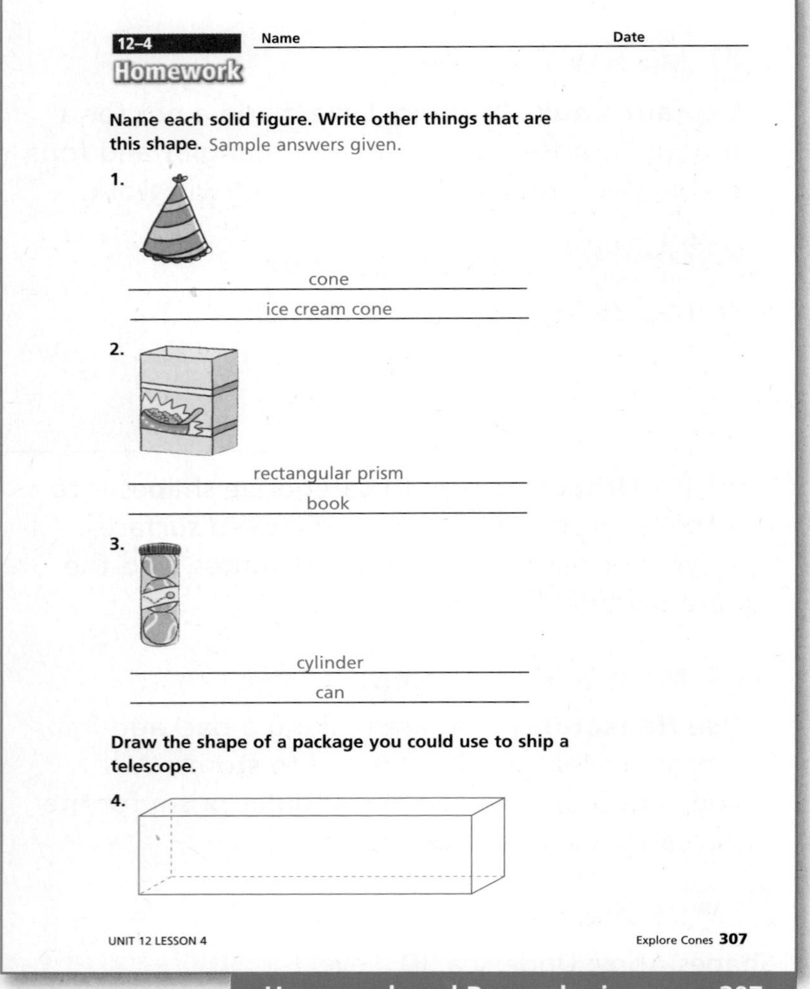

12–4 Homework Name ______ Date ______

Name each solid figure. Write other things that are this shape. Sample answers given.

1. cone
   ice cream cone

2. rectangular prism
   book

3. cylinder
   can

Draw the shape of a package you could use to ship a telescope.

4.

UNIT 12 LESSON 4 Explore Cones **307**

Homework and Remembering page 307

Goal: Spiral Review

This Remembering page would be appropriate anytime after today's lesson.

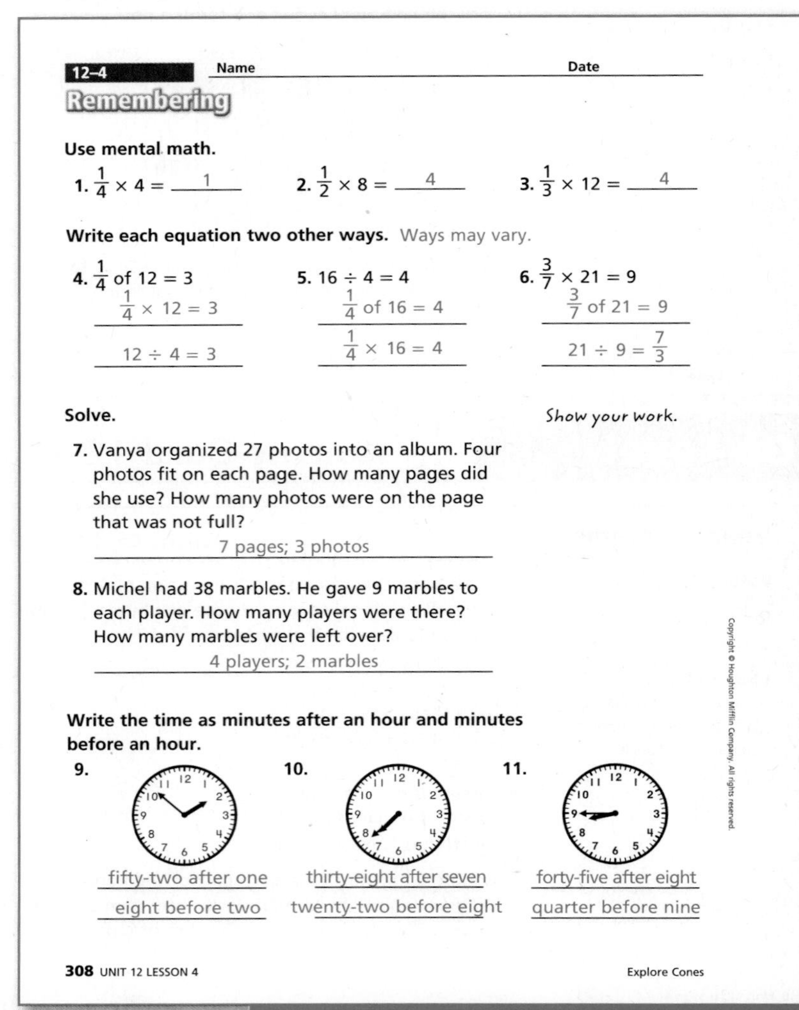

12–4 Remembering Name ______ Date ______

Use mental math.

1. $\frac{1}{4} \times 4 =$ 1
2. $\frac{1}{2} \times 8 =$ 4
3. $\frac{1}{3} \times 12 =$ 4

Write each equation two other ways. Ways may vary.

4. $\frac{1}{4}$ of $12 = 3$
   $\frac{1}{4} \times 12 = 3$
   $12 \div 4 = 3$
5. $16 \div 4 = 4$
   $\frac{1}{4}$ of $16 = 4$
   $\frac{1}{4} \times 16 = 4$
6. $\frac{3}{7} \times 21 = 9$
   $\frac{3}{7}$ of $21 = 9$
   $21 \div 9 = \frac{7}{3}$

Solve. *Show your work.*

7. Vanya organized 27 photos into an album. Four photos fit on each page. How many pages did she use? How many photos were on the page that was not full?
   7 pages; 3 photos

8. Michel had 38 marbles. He gave 9 marbles to each player. How many players were there? How many marbles were left over?
   4 players; 2 marbles

Write the time as minutes after an hour and minutes before an hour.

9. fifty-two after one
   eight before two
10. thirty-eight after seven
    twenty-two before eight
11. forty-five after eight
    quarter before nine

308 UNIT 12 LESSON 4 Explore Cones

Homework and Remembering page 308

Home or School Activity

Art Connection

Photo Cube Students create a themed photo cube using cutout photographs from magazines and newspapers. They trace or sketch a cube net on paper and paste the photos to each square of the net. Then they cut out and assemble the net. Some students may make their photo display using a different solid figure.

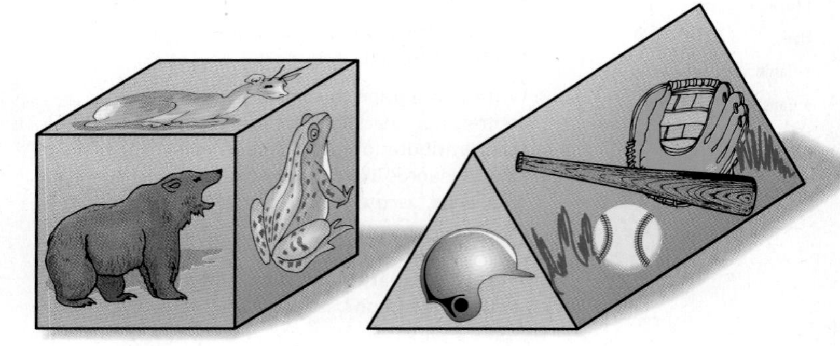

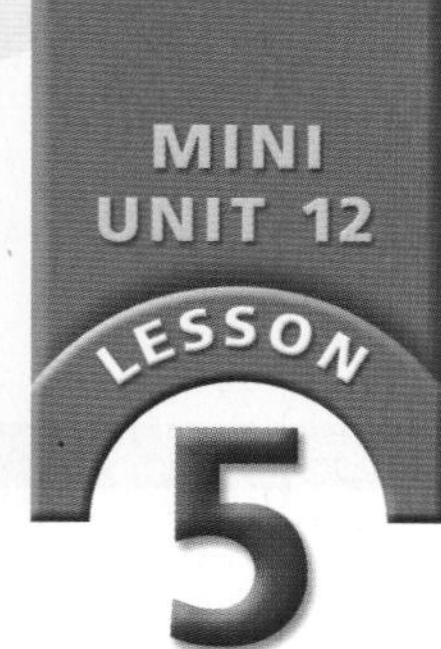

Explore Circles and Spheres

Lesson Objectives

- Draw a circle and label a radius and diameter in it.
- Find the circumference of a circle using string.
- Recognize the relationship between a circle and a sphere.

Vocabulary
circle
radius
diameter
circumference
sphere

The Day at a Glance

Today's Goals	Materials	
1 Teaching the Lesson **A1:** Identify circles and parts of circles. **A2:** Identify spheres and parts of spheres.	**Lesson Activities** Student Activity Book pp. 471–472 or Student Hardcover Book pp. 471–472 Homework and Remembering pp. 309–310 Quick Quiz (Assessment Guide) String Paper clips Examples of spheres Rulers	**Going Further** Activity Cards 12-5 Clay Dental Floss Rulers Cans Math Journals
2 Going Further ▸ Differentiated Instruction		
3 Homework and Spiral Review		

Use Math Talk today!

Keeping Skills Sharp

Daily Routines

Homework Review Have students discuss the errors from their homework. Encourage students to help each other understand how to correct these errors.

Strategy Problem Three students can sit on each of the two long sides of the rectangular picnic table. One student can sit at each end of the table. How many students could be seated if three tables were connected end to end? Make a drawing to help you solve the problem. 20 students;

	3 students	3 students	3 students	
1 student				1 student
	3 students	3 students	3 students	

English Language Learners

Model a paper circle and a ball. Write *circle* and *sphere* on the board.

- **Beginning** Ask: **Is a *circle* flat?** yes **Is a *sphere* flat?** no **Is a *sphere* three-dimensional?** yes
- **Intermediate** Ask: **Which is flat, the *circle* or the *sphere*?** circle Say: **The *sphere* is __.** three-dimensional
- **Advanced** Have students tell how a *circle* and a *sphere* are alike and different.

1 Teaching the Lesson

Activity 1

Explore Circles

 **30 MINUTES**

Goal: Identify circles and parts of circles.

Materials: string, Student Activity Book or Hardcover Book p. 471, paper clips (2 per pair), rulers, string

 **NCTM Standards:**
Geometry
Measurement
Connections

▶ Walk a Circle WHOLE CLASS

Invite two volunteers to the front of the room. Have each hold the opposite end of a piece of string and pull it tight. Ask one student to walk around the other while holding the string straight and tight the whole time. The student in the middle must rotate to keep facing the walking student.

- What figure is the walking student making? a circle
- If they don't keep the string tight, will they still make a circle? Why? No; the distance between has to be the same all the time to make a circle.

Have other pairs of students make circles of different sizes using strings of different lengths.

- Why are the circles we made different sizes? The strings are different lengths.

Draw a circle on the board using a piece of string and a dry-erase marker or chalk. Tie one end of the string around the marker. Hold the center end of the string to the board as you draw the circle around it.

Explain that the piece of string forms the radius of the circle and that the radius is what determines the size of the circle. Draw and label a radius on the circle on the board.

Then explain that the diameter of a circle is the length of a line segment that goes from one side of the circle to the other and passes through the center. Draw and label a diameter, which does not include the radius you already drew, on the circle on the board.

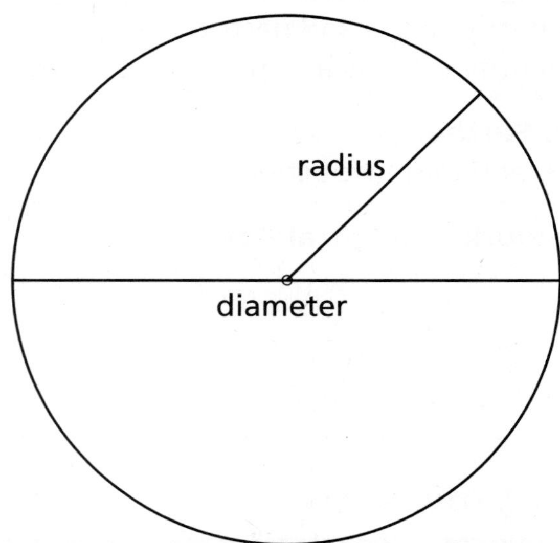

- How many radii make up a diameter? 2
- How do you know? It would take one radius to go from the side of a circle to the center and one more to go from the center to the other side.

Ask students which of the solid figures they built earlier in the unit had bases that were circles. cylinders, cones

▶ Characteristics of a Circle WHOLE CLASS

Have students complete exercise 1 on Student Book page 471. Students hold a pencil point inside the end of each paper clip. One pencil is the center and the other moves around to make a circle. Students can help each other by holding the paper still, if needed.

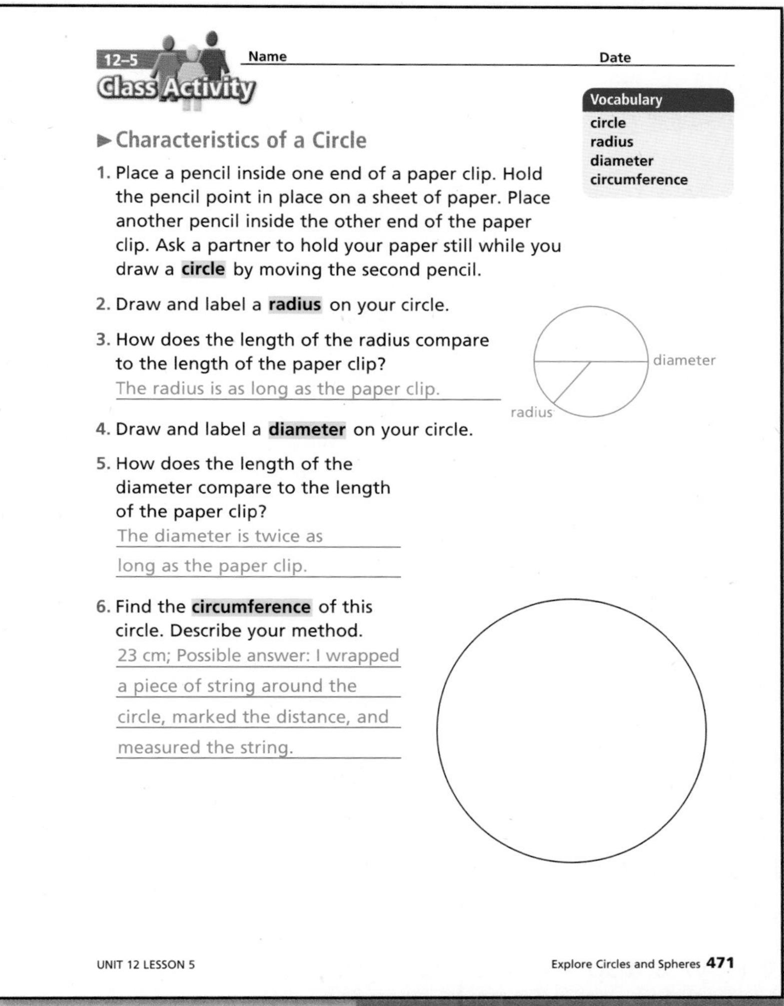

12-5 Class Activity

Name ______________________ Date ____________

Vocabulary
circle
radius
diameter
circumference

▶ Characteristics of a Circle

1. Place a pencil inside one end of a paper clip. Hold the pencil point in place on a sheet of paper. Place another pencil inside the other end of the paper clip. Ask a partner to hold your paper still while you draw a **circle** by moving the second pencil.
2. Draw and label a **radius** on your circle.
3. How does the length of the radius compare to the length of the paper clip? The radius is as long as the paper clip.
4. Draw and label a **diameter** on your circle.
5. How does the length of the diameter compare to the length of the paper clip? The diameter is twice as long as the paper clip.
6. Find the **circumference** of this circle. Describe your method. 23 cm; Possible answer: I wrapped a piece of string around the circle, marked the distance, and measured the string.

UNIT 12 LESSON 5 Explore Circles and Spheres **471**

Student Activity Book page 471

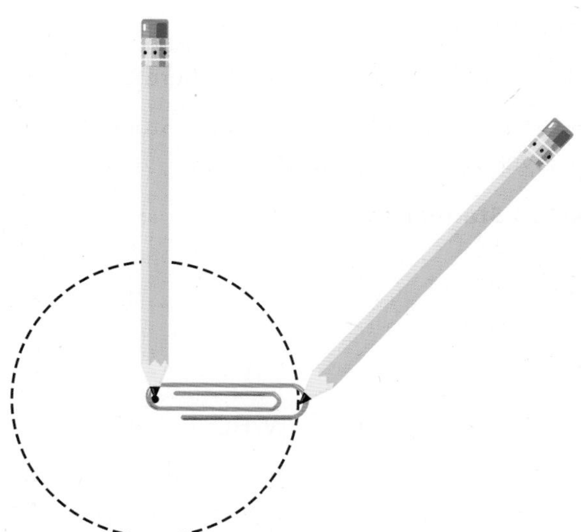

Math Talk Be sure students use a ruler to complete exercises 2 and 4. After students complete exercises 2–5, discuss their answers as a class.

- What is the relationship between the radius and diameter and the length of the paper clip? The radius is as long as the paper clip, and the diameter is twice as long.
- Ask students what the word *perimeter* means. the distance around a figure or object

Before students complete exercise 6, explain that the perimeter of a circle is called its *circumference*.

Ask students to suggest ideas for finding the circumference of a circle. Possible answers: Wrap a string around the circle, mark the distances, then measure the string; cut out the circle, roll it along a line, mark the beginning and end points, and measure the line segment.

Have students complete exercise 6, and then discuss their answers.

Ongoing Assessment

Ask students to sketch a circle and label a diameter and a radius in it.

1 Teaching the Lesson (continued)

Activity 2

Explore Spheres

 **30 MINUTES**

Goal: Identify spheres and parts of spheres.

Materials: examples of spheres, string, Student Activity Book or Hardcover Book p. 472, rulers

 **NCTM Standards:**
Geometry
Measurement
Connections

▶ Create a Sphere WHOLE CLASS

Show students some examples of spheres. Explain that a sphere is a solid figure shaped like a ball. Ask them for examples, and list them on the board.

Spheres	
basketball	globe
tennis ball	gumball
soccer ball	meatball
marble	softball

Repeat the demonstration from Activity 1, where two students show a circle using a piece of string. Explain that to make a sphere, the string, or radius, can go in every direction. Have the student in the center remain still, but ask the other student to pull the string in many directions, up and down, always keeping the string tight, to create a sphere.

Explain that a sphere has a center point, and every point on the surface of the sphere is an equal distance away from the center. This distance is the radius of the sphere.

Have students answer question 7 on Student Book page 472. Discuss their answers.

- How is a sphere similar to a circle? Possible answers: It has a round shape; both have a center point; the radii of both go from the center of the figure to the side.

▶ Characteristics of a Sphere WHOLE CLASS

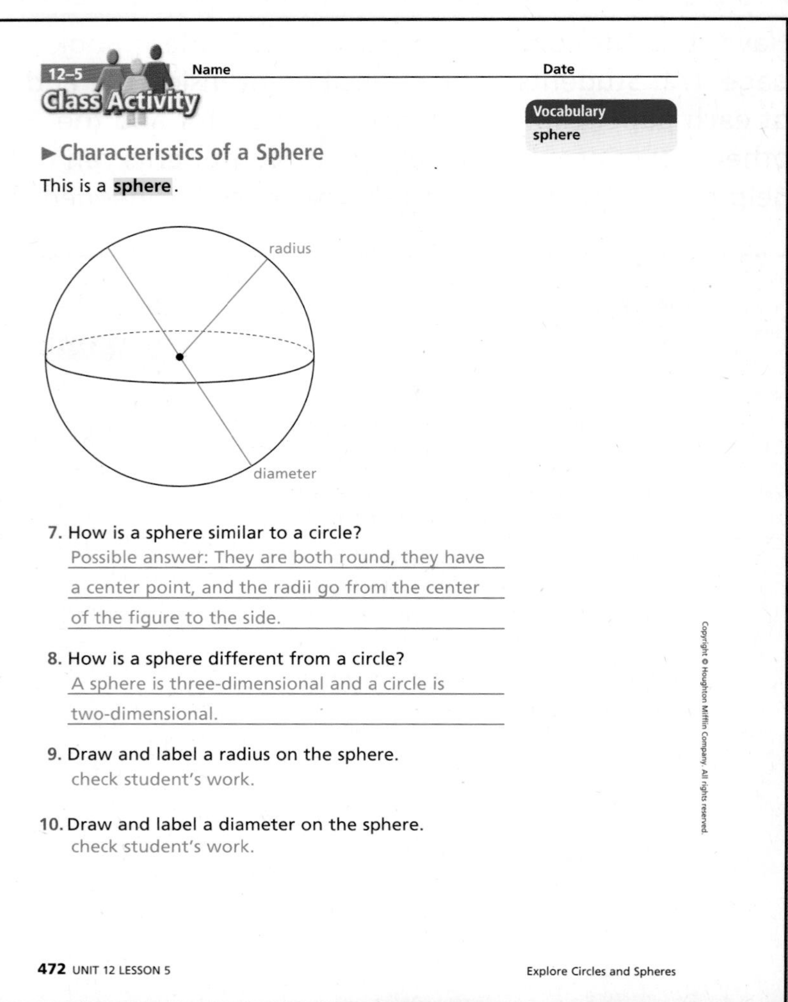
12–5 Class Activity Name Date

Vocabulary
sphere

▶ Characteristics of a Sphere

This is a **sphere**.

7. How is a sphere similar to a circle?
Possible answer: They are both round, they have a center point, and the radii go from the center of the figure to the side.

8. How is a sphere different from a circle?
A sphere is three-dimensional and a circle is two-dimensional.

9. Draw and label a radius on the sphere.
check student's work.

10. Draw and label a diameter on the sphere.
check student's work.

472 UNIT 12 LESSON 5 Explore Circles and Spheres

Student Activity Book page 472

Have students answer question 8. Discuss their answers.

- How is a sphere different from a circle? A sphere is three-dimensional and a circle is two-dimensional.

Ask students to use a ruler to complete exercises 9 and 10. Check their drawings.

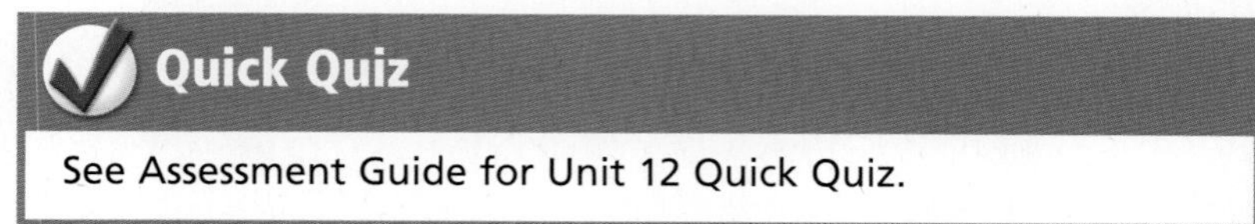
Quick Quiz

See Assessment Guide for Unit 12 Quick Quiz.

Intervention Activity Card 12-5

Cut a Sphere
Activity Card 12–5

Work: In pairs
Use:
- Clay
- Dental floss

1. Make a clay ball. Then cut it in half using dental floss.
2. What is the shape of the face that you see on each piece of the ball? circle

3. Use a pencil to carve a diameter on one shape. Then carve a radius on the other shape.
4. **Discuss** In how many different ways could you cut the ball in half? In how many different ways could you carve a radius and a diameter? There are an infinite number of ways for each activity.

Unit 12, Lesson 5

Activity Note Before beginning the activity, have students define the diameter and the radius of a circle.

Math Writing Prompt

Make a Drawing How does the length of the radius of a circle compare to the length of its diameter? Make a drawing to help you show the relationship.

Software Support

Warm Up 36.19

On Level Activity Card 12-5

Sphere Slices
Activity Card 12–5

Work: In pairs
Use:
- Clay
- Dental floss

1. Make a clay sphere. Then slice off pieces of it using dental floss.

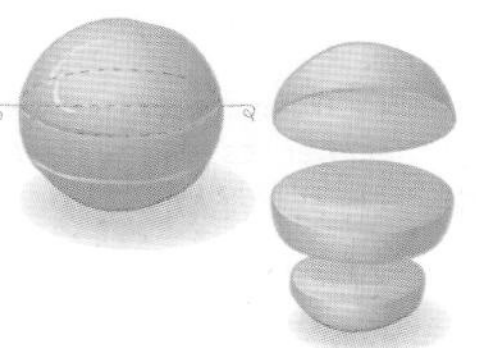

2. What is the shape of the face on each slice that you make? a circle
3. **Discuss** Is it possible to make any other shape by cutting a sphere in this way? If so, what shape can you make? No other shape is possible.

Unit 12, Lesson 5

Activity Note Have students compare and contrast the attributes of the slices that they make. All slices have circular faces but not all will show the center of both the circle and the sphere.

Math Writing Prompt

Use Reasoning Tiwa says the face of a sphere is a circle. Rida says a sphere doesn't have a face. Who is correct? Explain your choice.

Software Support

Shapes Ahoy: Undersea 3D, Level G

Challenge Activity Card 12-5

Find the Center of a Circle
Activity Card 12–5

Work: On your own
Use:
- Ruler
- Can

1. Using a can, trace a circle on a sheet of paper. Use a ruler to find the longest possible line that you can draw across the circle. The longest line is the diameter, which passes through the center.
2. Now draw another line through the center of the circle that is perpendicular to the first line. What do you notice about the intersection point? It is at the center of the circle.
3. Draw another circle and then draw two diameters that are not perpendicular.
4. **True or False?** The intersection of any two diameters of a circle is the center of the circle. Justify your answer. True, because every diameter passes exactly through the center.

Unit 12, Lesson 5

Activity Note To ensure that lines are perpendicular, students can use the corner of a piece of paper to make a right angle. By measuring the first diameter, they can ensure that each line represents a diameter.

Math Writing Prompt

Investigate Math List the solid figures with faces that are circles and have curved surfaces. Which has a curved surface but does not have a face that is a circle?

DESTINATION Math **Software Support**

Course II: Module 2: Unit 3: Fractional Parts

3 Homework and Spiral Review

12–5 Homework **Goal:** Additional Practice

This Homework page allows students to identify and compare the characteristics of circles and spheres.

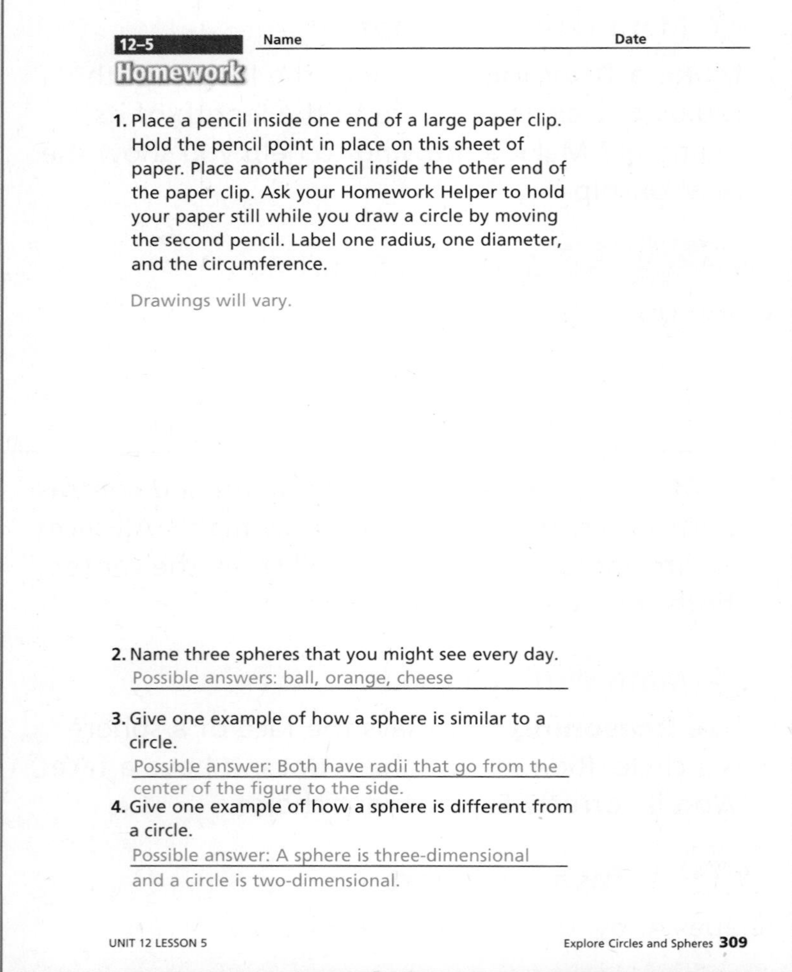

12–5 Homework Name ____ Date ____

1. Place a pencil inside one end of a large paper clip. Hold the pencil point in place on this sheet of paper. Place another pencil inside the other end of the paper clip. Ask your Homework Helper to hold your paper still while you draw a circle by moving the second pencil. Label one radius, one diameter, and the circumference.

   Drawings will vary.

2. Name three spheres that you might see every day.
   Possible answers: ball, orange, cheese
3. Give one example of how a sphere is similar to a circle.
   Possible answer: Both have radii that go from the center of the figure to the side.
4. Give one example of how a sphere is different from a circle.
   Possible answer: A sphere is three-dimensional and a circle is two-dimensional.

UNIT 12 LESSON 5 Explore Circles and Spheres **309**

Homework and Remembering page 309

12–5 Remembering **Goal:** Spiral Review

This Remembering page would be appropriate anytime after today's lesson.

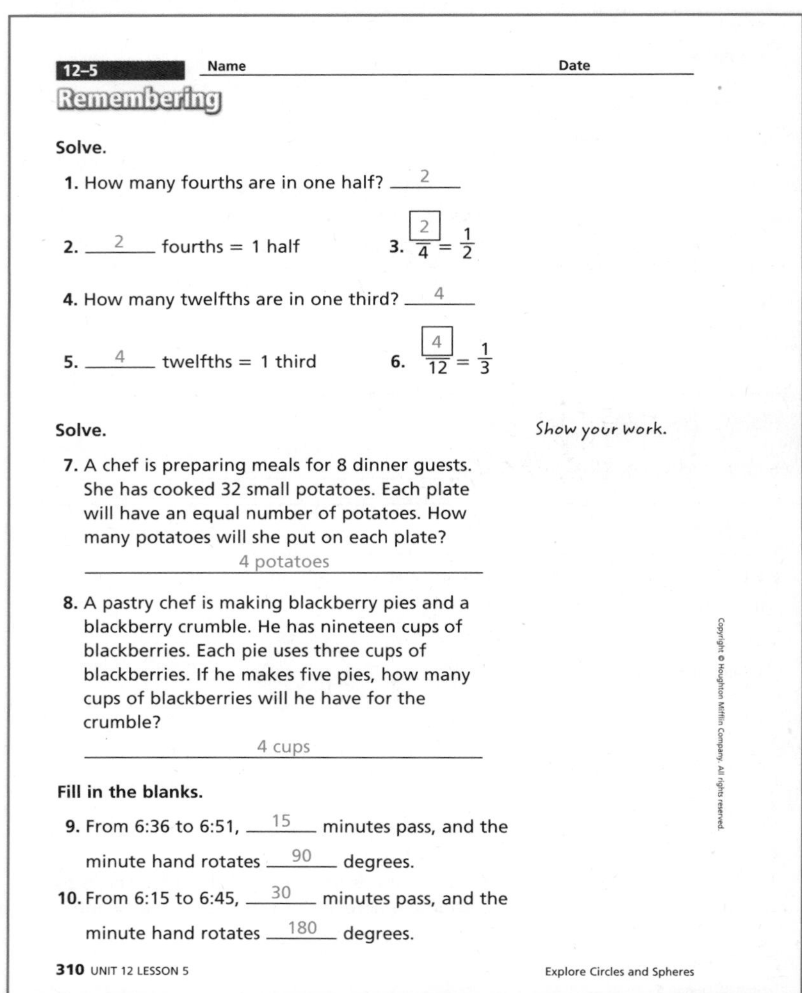

12–5 Remembering Name ____ Date ____

Solve.

1. How many fourths are in one half? 2
2. 2 fourths = 1 half
3. $\frac{\boxed{2}}{4} = \frac{1}{2}$
4. How many twelfths are in one third? 4
5. 4 twelfths = 1 third
6. $\frac{\boxed{4}}{12} = \frac{1}{3}$

Solve. *Show your work.*

7. A chef is preparing meals for 8 dinner guests. She has cooked 32 small potatoes. Each plate will have an equal number of potatoes. How many potatoes will she put on each plate?
   4 potatoes
8. A pastry chef is making blackberry pies and a blackberry crumble. He has nineteen cups of blackberries. Each pie uses three cups of blackberries. If he makes five pies, how many cups of blackberries will he have for the crumble?
   4 cups

Fill in the blanks.

9. From 6:36 to 6:51, 15 minutes pass, and the minute hand rotates 90 degrees.
10. From 6:15 to 6:45, 30 minutes pass, and the minute hand rotates 180 degrees.

310 UNIT 12 LESSON 5 Explore Circles and Spheres

Homework and Remembering page 310

Home or School Activity

Sports Connection

What Figure Is It? Have students list pieces of sports equipment that are made from solid figures they have studied. Have them identify the solid figure.

Baseball: sphere
Hockey puck: cylinder
Pylon: cone
Diving board: rectangular prism
Basketball: sphere
Package of tennis balls: cylinder

Unit Review and Test

Lesson Objective

- **Assess student progress on unit objectives.**

The Day at a Glance

Today's Goals	Materials
1 Assessing the Unit ▸ Assess student progress on unit objectives. ▸ Use activities from unit lessons to reteach content. **2 Extending the Assessment** ▸ Use remediation for common errors. There is no homework assignment on a test day.	Unit 12 Test, Student Activity Book pp. 473–474 or Hardcover Book pages 473–474 and Activity Workbook pp. 239–240 Unit 12 Test, Form A or B, Assessment Guide (optional) Unit 12 Performance Assessment, Assessment Guide (optional)

Keeping Skills Sharp

Daily Routines 5 MINUTES	
If you are doing a unit review day, go over the homework. If this is a test day, omit the homework review.	**Review and Test Day** You may want to choose a quiet game or other activity (reading a book or working on homework for another subject) for students who finish early.

1 Assessing the Unit

Assess Unit Objectives

45 MINUTES (more if schedule permits)

Goal: Assess student progress on unit objectives.

Materials: Student Activity Book pp. 473–474 or Hardcover Book pp. 473–474 and Activity Workbook pp. 239–240; Assessment Guide Unit 12 Test Form A or B (optional); Unit 12 Performance Assessment (optional)

▶ Review and Assessment

If your students are ready for assessment on the unit objectives, you may use either the test on the Student Activity Book pages or one of the forms of the Unit 12 Test in the Assessment Guide to assess student progress.

If you feel that students need some review first, you may use the test on the Student Book pages as a review of unit content, and then use one of the forms of the Unit 12 Test in the Assessment Guide to assess student progress.

To assign a numerical score for all of these test forms, use 10 points for each question.

You may also choose to use the Unit 12 Performance Assessment. Scoring for that assessment can be found in its rubric in the Assessment Guide.

▶ Reteaching Resources

The chart lists the test items, the unit objectives they cover, and the lesson activities in which the objective is covered in this unit. You may revisit these activities with students who do not show mastery of the objectives.

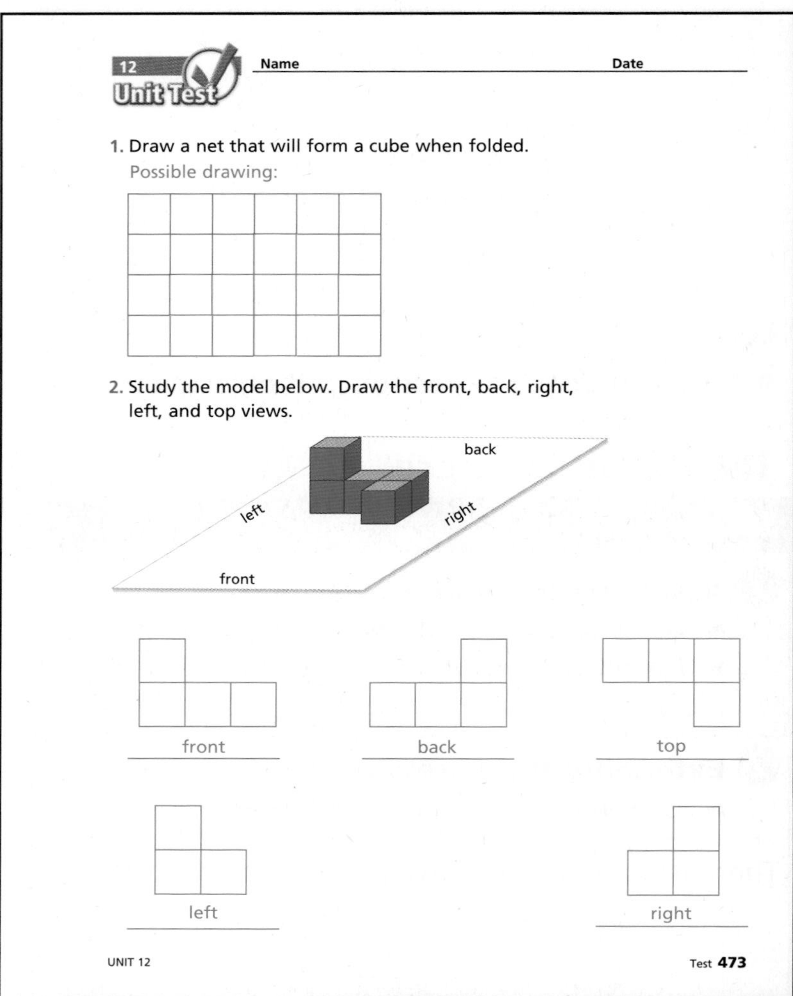
12 Unit Test
Name Date

1. Draw a net that will form a cube when folded.
Possible drawing:

2. Study the model below. Draw the front, back, right, left, and top views.

UNIT 12 Test 473

Student Activity Book page 473

Unit Test Items	Unit Objectives Tested	Activities to Use for Reteaching
1, 3–10,	**12.1** Identify and describe cubes, prisms, cones, pyramids, cylinders, and spheres.	Lesson 1, Activities 1 and 2 Lesson 3, Activities 1 and 2 Lesson 4, Activity 1 Lesson 5, Activity 2
2	**12.2** Draw 2-D views from 3-D models.	Lesson 2, Activities 1 and 2

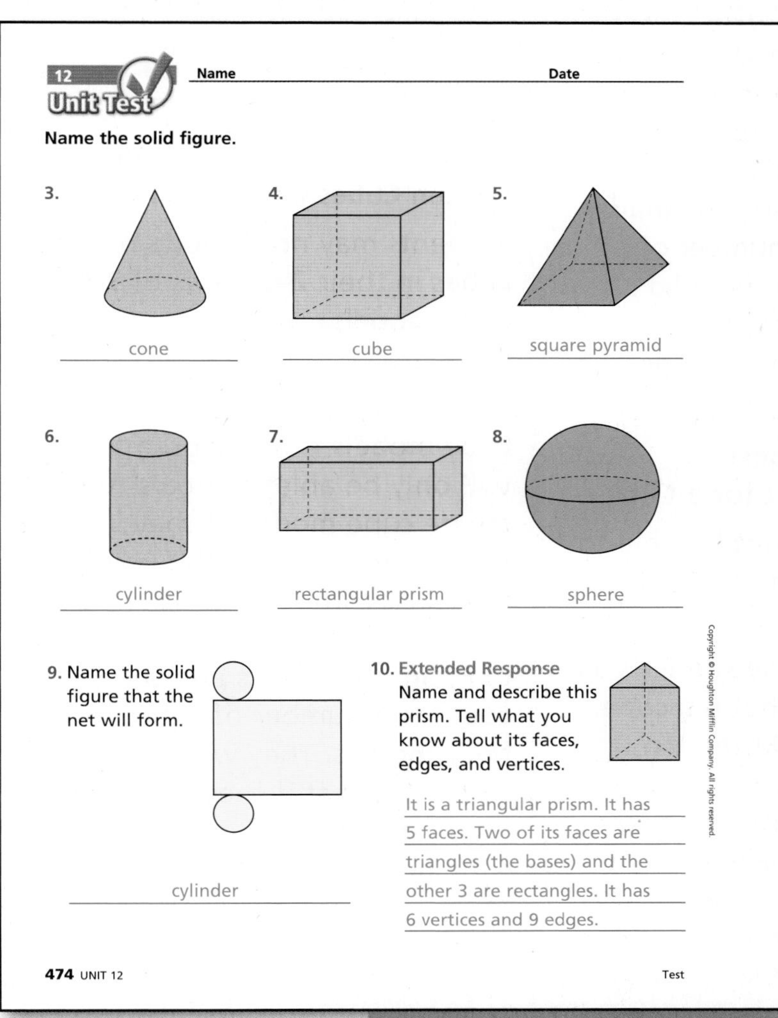

12 Unit Test Name ________ Date ________

Name the solid figure.

3. cone

4. cube

5. square pyramid

6. cylinder

7. rectangular prism

8. sphere

9. Name the solid figure that the net will form.

cylinder

10. Extended Response
Name and describe this prism. Tell what you know about its faces, edges, and vertices.

It is a triangular prism. It has 5 faces. Two of its faces are triangles (the bases) and the other 3 are rectangles. It has 6 vertices and 9 edges.

474 UNIT 12 Test

Student Activity Book page 474

▶ Assessment Resources

Free Response Tests
Unit 12 Test, Student Activity Book pages 473–474
Unit 12 Test, Form A, Assessment Guide

Extended Response Item
The last item in the Student Activity Book test and in the Form A test will require an extended response as an answer.

Multiple Choice Test
Unit 12 Test, Form B, Assessment Guide

Performance Assessment
Unit 12 Performance Assessment, Assessment Guide
Unit 12 Performance Assessment Rubric, Assessment Guide

▶ Portfolio Assessment

Teacher-selected Items for Student Portfolios:

- Homework, Lesson 3
- Class Activity work, Lessons 1, 2, 4

Student-selected Items for Student Portfolios:

- Favorite Home or School Activity
- Best Writing Prompt

2 Extending the Assessment

Common Errors

Activities for Remediation

Unit Objective 12.1

Identify and describe cubes, prisms, cones, pyramids, cylinders, and spheres.

Common Error: Doesn't Correctly Identify the 2-D Shapes of Faces on Solid Figures

Some students may not correctly describe faces of solid figures.

Remediation Provide students with a collection of solid figures and large sheets of paper. For each solid, have them trace all of the faces. Suggest they use a system like placing a piece of tape on each face after tracing it to ensure they don't miss any faces. Ask them to name the 2-D figures drawn from the faces.

Common Error: Incorrectly Names Real-World Solid Figures

Some students may not correctly name real-world solid figures.

Remediation Choose various items in the classroom that represent solid figures, such as books, dry-erase markers, erasers, and so on. Ask students to describe each item you chose and name the solid figure it models.

Common Error: Provides Incomplete Descriptions of Solid Figures

Some students may not include shapes of faces and number of faces, edges, and vertices when describing solid figures.

Remediation Collect samples of various solid figures and use them for a discussion. Work together to develop a description of each figure that includes identifying the shapes of the faces and the number of edges and vertices on the solid figure. Have students write the characteristics of each solid figure in their Math Journals.

Common Error: Doesn't Correctly Draw a Net for a Cube

Some students may not be able to visualize what solid figure a net will make.

Remediation Provide students a cardboard package that is a cube. Have them cut and flatten the package into a net. Tell them to cut along the edges (where two faces meet) and to make only enough cuts to flatten the package. Ask them to make sketches of the flattened package and then to fold the package into its original shape. Ask them to name the shapes and locations of the two-dimensional figures on the nets and where they are located in the corresponding solid figure.

Unit Objective 12.2

Draw 2-D views from 3-D models.

Common Error: Doesn't Visualize Hidden Cubes in 2-D Views

Students may not include hidden cubes in their 2-D views of 3-D cube models.

Remediation Provide students with plenty of experience making cube models from diagrams. They will only be able to successfully create cube models if they include the hidden cubes of the lower levels. Ask students to count the number of cubes they think a diagram represents and then count the number of cubes in their models. They will begin to recognize that if they see a cube on a top level, there must be a cube beneath it.

Measurement

THE GOAL FOR UNIT 13 is to extend students' measurement skills for length, capacity, and weight in the customary system and length, capacity, and mass in the metric system. How to read temperature in degrees Fahrenheit and degrees Celsius is also reviewed. This unit's division review focuses on "measurement division," in which equal groups of units are made. Students also review dividing with remainders, adding and subtracting fractions, converting improper fractions and mixed numbers, and solving word problems, all within measurement contexts.

Skills Trace

Grade 2	Grade 3	Grade 4
• Estimate and measure length to the nearest inch. • Estimate and measure perimeter, capacity, weight, and mass. • Convert measurements within the same system.	• Estimate and measure length to the nearest $\frac{1}{4}$ inch. • Estimate and measure perimeter, area, capacity, weight, and mass. • Convert measurements within the same system. • Read and compare temperatures in degrees Fahrenheit and degrees Celsius. • Solve problems involving customary and metric measurements, including mixed units within the same system.	• Estimate and measure length with precision. • Estimate and measure perimeter, area, capacity, weight, and mass. • Convert measurements within the same system. • Review temperature and connect it to integers on a number line. • Add and subtract units of length and time that require regrouping.

Unit 13 Contents

Unit 13 Assessment

Unit Objectives Tested	Unit Test Items	Lessons
13.1 Estimate and measure length to the nearest $\frac{1}{4}$-inch and the nearest centimeter; estimate perimeter and area.	1–2, 17	1, 3–4, 7
13.2 Convert measurements within the Customary System and within the Metric System.	3–14	2, 3, 5–6, 8–9
13.3 Read temperature in degrees Fahrenheit and degrees Celsius.	16	10
13.4 Solve problems involving customary or metric measurements.	15, 18–20	4, 6

Assessment and Review Resources

Formal Assessment

Student Activity Book

- Unit Review and Test (pp. 507–508)

Assessment Guide

- Quick Quizzes (pp. A128–A129, A130)
- Test A–Open Response (pp. A131–A132)
- Test B–Multiple Choice (pp. A133–A135)
- Performance Assessment (pp. A136–A138)

Test Generator CD-ROM

- Open Response Test
- Multiple Choice Test
- Test Bank Items

Informal Assessment

Teacher Edition

- Ongoing Assessment (in every lesson)
- Quick Practice (in every lesson)
- Portfolio Suggestions (p. 1077)

Math Talk

- Math Talk in Action (pp. 1026, 1060)
- Solve and Discuss (pp. 999, 1036, 1054, 1056)
- Student Pairs (pp. 1023, 1025, 1026, 1070)
- Small Groups (pp. 990, 1004, 1016, 1057)

  Helping Partners (pp. 1023, 1026, 1036)
- Scenarios (p. 991)
- In Activities (pp. 991, 993, 1009, 1017, 1040, 1046, 1052, 1064, 1065, 1070, 1071)

Review Opportunities

Homework and Remembering

- Review of recently taught topics
- Spiral Review

Teacher Edition

- Unit Review and Test (pp. 1075–1078)

Test Generator CD-ROM

- Custom Review Sheets

Planning Unit 13

NCTM Curriculum Focal Points and Connections Key: **1.** Number and Operations and Algebra **2.** Number and Operations **3.** Geometry **4.** Algebra **5.** Measurement **6.** Data Analysis **7.** Number and Operations

Lesson NCTM Focal Points NCTM Standards	Resources	Materials for Lesson Activities	Materials for Going Further
13-1 **Customary Units of Length** NCTM Focal Point: 5.1 NCTM Standards: 4, 8, 10	TE pp. 989–996 SAB pp. 475–478 H&R pp. 311–312 AC 13-1	Pencils of different lengths ✓ Inch ruler or meter sticks Scissors Tape Inch, $\frac{1}{2}$ Inch, and $\frac{1}{4}$ Rulers (TRB M144) ✓ MathBoard materials	$\frac{1}{4}$ Inch Rulers (TRB M144) Index cards Math Journals
13-2 **Inches, Feet, and Yards** NCTM Focal Points: 5.1, 5.3, 5.4 NCTM Standards: 1, 4, 8, 10	TE pp. 997–1002 SAB pp. 479–480 H&R pp. 313–314 AC 13-2 MCC 49	Yardsticks ✓ Inch Rulers	Yardstick Inch rulers (TRB M144) Math Journals
13-3 **Centimeters, Decimeters, and Meters** NCTM Focal Point: 7.5 NCTM Standards: 1, 4, 8, 10	TE pp. 1003–1012 SAB pp. 481–484 H&R pp. 315–316 AC 13-3 MCC 50	✓ MathBoard materials Meter sticks ✓ Centimeter rulers Scissors	Meter sticks Index cards ✓ Centimeter Rulers Boxes of spaghetti Calculator Math Journals
13-4 **Add Lengths** NCTM Focal Point: 5.1 NCTM Standards: 1, 3, 4, 8, 10	TE pp. 1013–1020 SAB pp. 485–486 H&R pp. 317–318 AC 13-4 AG Quick Quiz 1	✓ Inch Rulers Inch Grid Paper (TRB M42) Centimeter Grid Paper (TRB M31) ✓ Rulers Geoboards or Dot Array on MathBoard Rubber bands or dry erase markers	Zig Zag (TRB M145) String ✓ Inch Rulers Tape Scissors Math Journals
13-5 **Customary Units of Capacity** NCTM Standards: 1, 4, 6, 7	TE pp. 1021–1030 SAB pp. 487–490 H&R pp. 319–320 AC 13-5 MCC 51	Milk cartons (various sizes) Water or rice Various containers (different to milk) Sticky notes Bucket *Room for Ripley* by stuart J. Murphy	Drawing paper Containers (cup, pint, quart, half-gallon, gallon) Rice or water Chart paper Math Journals
13-6 **Metric Units of Capacity** NCTM Focal Point: 1.9 NCTM Standards: 1, 4, 6, 9	TE pp. 1031–1038 SAB pp. 491–492 H&R pp. 321–322 AC 13-6	Eye dropper or thimble 1-liter bottle Containers Sticky notes Water or rice	Metric measurement cups Centimeter cubes Clear containers Water 1-liter water bottle Math Journals
13-7 **Improper Fractions and Mixed Numbers in Measurement** NCTM Focal Point: 2.5 NCTM Standards: 1, 4, 6, 7	TE pp. 1039–1044 SAB pp. 493–494 H&R pp. 323–324 AC 13-7	None	Index cards Math Journals

Resources/Materials Key: TE: Teacher Edition SAB: Student Activity Book H&R: Homework and Remembering AC: Activity Cards MCC: Math Center Challenge AG: Assessment Guide ✓: Grade 3 kits TRB: Teacher's Resource Book

Lesson NCTM Focal Points NCTM Standards	Resources	Materials for Lesson Activities	Materials for Going Further
13-8 **Measurement Equivalencies and Fractions** NCTM Standards: 1, 2, 4, 8	TE pp. 1045–1050 SAB pp. 495–496 H&R pp. 325–326 AC 13-8	*How Tall, How Short, How Faraway* by David A. Adler	Containers (cup, pint, quart, half gallon, gallon) Water or rice ✓ Rulers Index cards Measuring cups Chart paper Markers Math Journals
13-9 **Customary Units of Weight and Metric Units of Mass** NCTM Standards: 1, 2, 4, 8	TE pp. 1051–1062 SAB pp. 497–502 H&R pp. 327–328 AC 13-9 MCC 52 AG Quick Quiz 2	Football and 10 pennies (optional) Balance scale Spring scale gram and kilogram units of mass Large paper clip and sneaker (optional) ✓ Connecting Cube Building Big Bridges David Macauley	Spring scale ✓ MathBoard materials *Who Sank the Boat?* by Pamela Allen Aluminum foil Small objects Sink or large bucket Water Math Journals
13-10 **Temperature** NCTM Standards: 4, 8, 10	TE pp. 1063–1068 SAB pp. 503–504 H&R pp. 329–330 AC 13-10 MCC 52	Transparency of Student Activity Book p. 503 (optional) Overhead projector (optional) Outdoor thermometer (Celsius and Fahrenheit)	Magazines Glue Sticky notes Scissors Math Journals
13-11 **Use Mathematical Processes** NCTM Focal Points: 1.9, 3.1, 5.1, 6.2 NCTM Standards: 1, 7, 8, 9, 10	TE pp. 1069–1074 SAB pp. 505–506 H&R pp. 331–332 AC 13-11	✓ Counters ✓ Pattern Black (hexagon) Grid paper Yardstick	✓ Number Cube ✓ Rules Math Journals
✓ Unit Review and Test	TE pp. 1075–1078 SAB pp. 507–508 AG Unit 13 Tests		

Hardcover Student Book

- Together, the Hardcover Student Book and its companion Activity Workbook contain all of the pages in the consumable Student Activity Book.

Manipulatives and Materials

- Essential materials for teaching *Math Expressions* are available in the Grade 3 kits. These materials are indicated by a ✓ in these lists. At the front of this Teacher Edition is more information about kit contents, alternatives for the materials, and use of the materials.

Independent Learning Activities

Ready-Made Math Challenge Centers

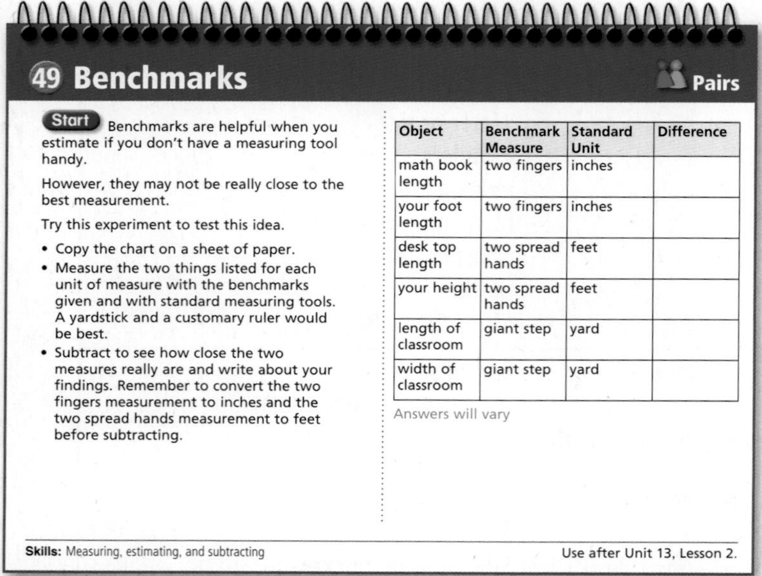

49 Benchmarks — Pairs

Start Benchmarks are helpful when you estimate if you don't have a measuring tool handy.

However, they may not be really close to the best measurement.

Try this experiment to test this idea.

- Copy the chart on a sheet of paper.
- Measure the two things listed for each unit of measure with the benchmarks given and with standard measuring tools. A yardstick and a customary ruler would be best.
- Subtract to see how close the two measures really are and write about your findings. Remember to convert the two fingers measurement to inches and the two spread hands measurement to feet before subtracting.

Object	Benchmark Measure	Standard Unit	Difference
math book length	two fingers	inches	
your foot length	two fingers	inches	
desk top length	two spread hands	feet	
your height	two spread hands	feet	
length of classroom	giant step	yard	
width of classroom	giant step	yard	

Answers will vary

Skills: Measuring, estimating, and subtracting

Use after Unit 13, Lesson 2.

Grouping Pairs

Materials Ruler, yardstick

Objective Students compare the difference between benchmark and standard measurements.

Connections Measurement and Estimation

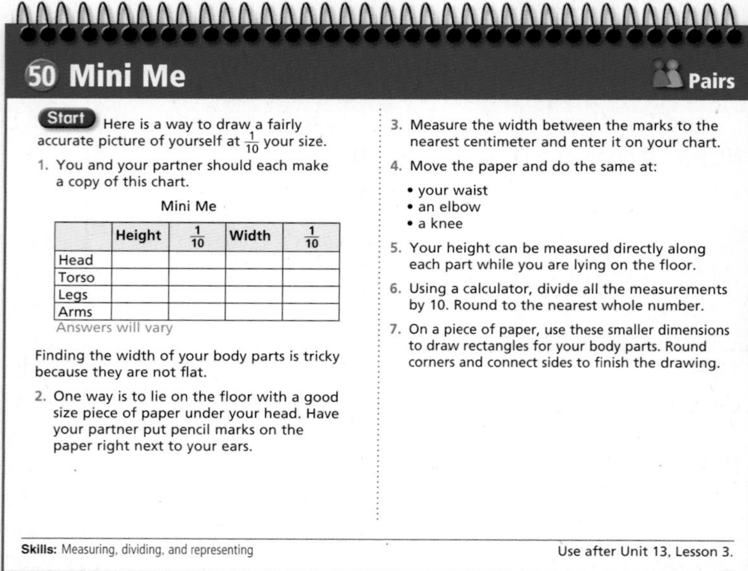

50 Mini Me — Pairs

Start Here is a way to draw a fairly accurate picture of yourself at $\frac{1}{10}$ your size.

1. You and your partner should each make a copy of this chart.

Mini Me

	Height	$\frac{1}{10}$	Width	$\frac{1}{10}$
Head				
Torso				
Legs				
Arms				

Answers will vary

Finding the width of your body parts is tricky because they are not flat.

2. One way is to lie on the floor with a good size piece of paper under your head. Have your partner put pencil marks on the paper right next to your ears.
3. Measure the width between the marks to the nearest centimeter and enter it on your chart.
4. Move the paper and do the same at:
   - your waist
   - an elbow
   - a knee
5. Your height can be measured directly along each part while you are lying on the floor.
6. Using a calculator, divide all the measurements by 10. Round to the nearest whole number.
7. On a piece of paper, use these smaller dimensions to draw rectangles for your body parts. Round corners and connect sides to finish the drawing.

Skills: Measuring, dividing, and representing

Use after Unit 13, Lesson 3.

Grouping Pairs

Materials Large sheets of paper, metric tape measures or meter sticks

Objective Students draw a scale model of their bodies.

Connections Measurement and Representation

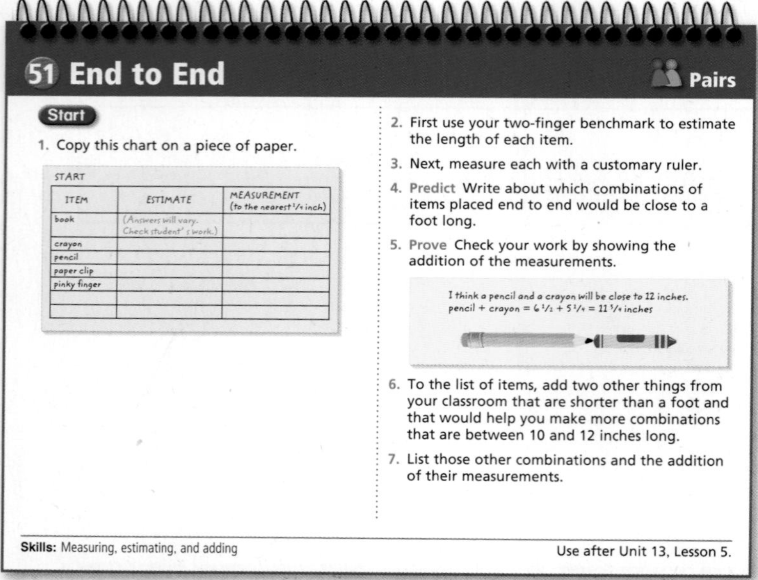

51 End to End — Pairs

Start

1. Copy this chart on a piece of paper.

START

ITEM	ESTIMATE	MEASUREMENT (to the nearest 1/4 inch)
book	(Answers will vary. Check student's work.)	
crayon		
pencil		
paper clip		
pinky finger		

2. First use your two-finger benchmark to estimate the length of each item.
3. Next, measure each with a customary ruler.
4. **Predict** Write about which combinations of items placed end to end would be close to a foot long.
5. **Prove** Check your work by showing the addition of the measurements.

I think a pencil and a crayon will be close to 12 inches.
pencil + crayon = $6\frac{1}{2} + 5\frac{1}{4} = 11\frac{3}{4}$ inches

6. To the list of items, add two other things from your classroom that are shorter than a foot and that would help you make more combinations that are between 10 and 12 inches long.
7. List those other combinations and the addition of their measurements.

Skills: Measuring, estimating, and adding

Use after Unit 13, Lesson 5.

Grouping Pairs

Materials Quarter inch ruler

Objective Students estimate, measure and add lengths to the nearest $\frac{1}{4}$ inch.

Connections Measurement and Estimation

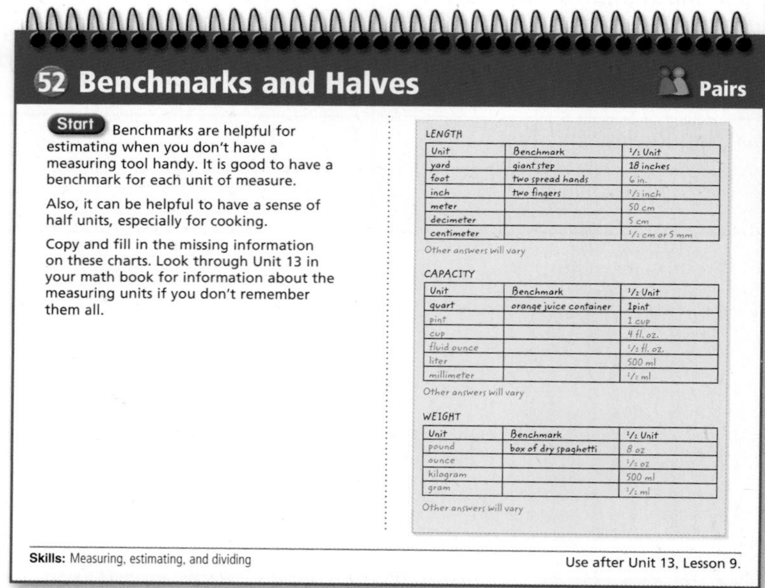

52 Benchmarks and Halves — Pairs

Start Benchmarks are helpful for estimating when you don't have a measuring tool handy. It is good to have a benchmark for each unit of measure.

Also, it can be helpful to have a sense of half units, especially for cooking.

Copy and fill in the missing information on these charts. Look through Unit 13 in your math book for information about the measuring units if you don't remember them all.

LENGTH

Unit	Benchmark	1/2 Unit
yard	giant step	18 inches
foot	two spread hands	6 in.
inch	two fingers	1/2 inch
meter		50 cm
decimeter		5 cm
centimeter		1/2 cm or 5 mm

Other answers will vary

CAPACITY

Unit	Benchmark	1/2 Unit
quart	orange juice container	1pint
pint		1 cup
cup		4 fl. oz.
fluid ounce		1/2 fl. oz.
liter		500 ml
millimeter		1/2 ml

Other answers will vary

WEIGHT

Unit	Benchmark	1/2 Unit
pound	box of dry spaghetti	8 oz
ounce		1/2 oz
kilogram		500 ml
gram		1/2 ml

Other answers will vary

Skills: Measuring, estimating, and dividing

Use after Unit 13, Lesson 9.

Grouping Pairs

Materials Student book

Objective Students identify benchmarks for different measurement units and determine the value of half units.

Connections Measurement and Computation

Ready-Made Math Resources

Technology — Tutorials, Practice, and Intervention

Use online, individualized intervention and support to bring students to proficiency.

Help students practice skills and apply concepts through exciting math adventures.

Extend and enrich students' understanding of skills and concepts through engaging, interactive lessons and activities.

Visit **Education Place**®
www.eduplace.com

Visit www.eduplace.com/mx2t/ and find family, teacher, and student materials, activities, games, and more.

Literature Links

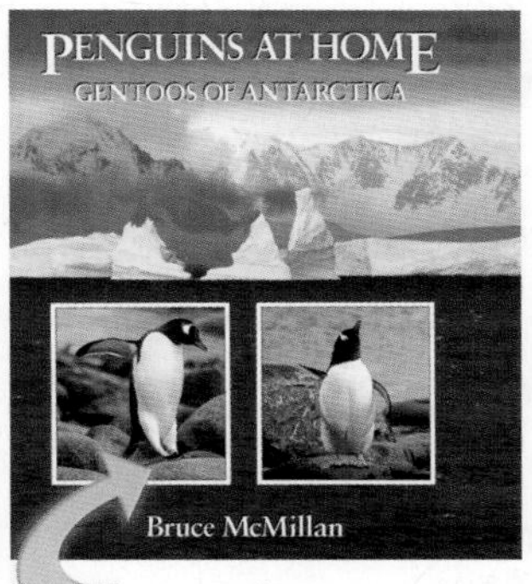

Penguins at Home
Gentoos of Antarctica

Penguins at Home Gentoos of Antarctica
Learn the height of a penguin, how deep they can dive, or how much distance is required between their nests to name but a few facts in this fascinating book by Bruce McMillan.

Literature Connections

- *Room for Ripley,* by Stuart J. Murphy, illustrated by Sylvie Wickstrom (HarperTrophy, 1999)
- *How Tall, How Short, How Faraway?,* by David A. Adler, illustrated by Nancy Tobin (Holiday House, 2000)

Unit 13 Teaching Resources

Differentiated Instruction

Individualizing Instruction		
	Level	**Frequency**
Activities	• Intervention • On Level • Challenge	All 3 in every lesson
	Level	**Frequency**
Math Writing Prompts	• Intervention • On Level • Challenge	All 3 in every lesson
Math Center Challenges	For advanced students	
	4 in every unit	

Reaching All Learners		
	Lessons	**Pages**
English Language Learners	1, 2, 3, 4, 5, 6, 7, 8, 9, 10, 11	990, 999, 1005, 1016, 1023, 1033, 1041, 1047, 1052, 1066, 1070
	Lessons	**Pages**
Extra Help	1, 2, 3, 4, 5, 7, 8	991, 999, 1006, 1008, 1014, 1024, 1041, 1046, 1053, 1054
	Lessons	**Pages**
Advanced Learners	1, 4, 10	990, 994, 1018, 1066
	Lessons	**Pages**
Alternate Approach	1, 2, 3	998, 1000, 1005

Strategies for English Language Learners

Present this problem to all students. Offer the different levels of support to meet students' levels of language proficiency.

Objective To review the terms for measurement and the tools used for measuring.

Problem Model the uses of a ruler and a scale. Write *ruler* and *scale* on the board. Have students identify which tool is used to measure length and weight.

Newcomer

- Model measuring the *length* of a book with the *ruler*. Say: **We measure *length* with a *ruler*. This book is ___ inches long.** Have students repeat.
- Continue with *weight.*

Beginning

- Model measuring with the ruler. Ask: **Do I use the *ruler* to measure *weight*?** no ***Length*?** yes
- Continue with *weight.*

Intermediate

- Model measuring with the ruler. Ask: **What measuring tool is this?** ruler **Do I use a ruler to measure *length* or *weight*?** length
- Continue with *weight.*

Advanced

- Hold up a book. Say: **I want to measure the length of this book.** Ask: **Which measuring tool do I use?** ruler
- Continue with *weight.*

Connections

Art Connections
Lesson 2, page 1002
Lesson 4, page 1020

Math-to-Math Connection
Lesson 10, page 1068

Music Connection
Lesson 6, page 1038

Physical Education Connection
Lesson 3, page 1012

Real-World Connection
Lesson 7, page 1044

Technology Connection
Lesson 9, page 1062

Literature Connections
Lesson 5, page 1030
Lesson 8, page 1050

Math Background

Putting Research into Practice for Unit 13

From our Curriculum Research Project: Measurement

In this unit, students will learn to focus on and measure various attributes of objects. They will learn the tools and processes for measuring length, capacity, weight, mass, and temperature. Students will use both customary and metric units of measure. They will also discuss reasonable units to use for making various measurements. A large part of understanding the various units used for a particular attribute is converting between units of measure, such as number of pints in a quart. Students will compare units and convert between them within each system of measure.

This unit serves in many ways as a consolidation of mathematical topics in this volume. Division, in particular, plays a large role, when students convert between units. For example, to convert 16 feet to yards, students divide 16 by 3 to get 5 with a remainder of 1. So there are 5 yards in 16 feet with 1 foot left over. Other mathematical topics student apply in this unit are adding and subtracting fractions and converting between improper fractions and mixed numbers.

–Karen Fuson, Author
Math Expressions

From Current Research: Length Measurement

Proficiency in the measurement of length requires the learner to restructure space so that he or she "sees" a count of n adjacent unit lengths as representing a distance of n units. Children need to recognize the need for identical units, and they need to understand that a unit can be partitioned into smaller units ... When the number line is used as a pedagogical tool, efforts must be made to be sure that students understand that they are counting lengths, not the endpoints where the numbers are.

National Research Council. "Developing Proficiency with Whole Numbers." *Adding It Up: Helping Children Learn Mathematics.* Washington, D.C.: National Academy Press, 2001. 281–282.

Other Useful References: Measurement

Carpenter, T.P., and R. Lewis. "The Development of the Concept of a Standard Unit of Measure in Young Children." *Journal for Research in Mathematics Education,* 7 (1976): 53–64.

Hiebert, J. "Units of Measure: Results and Implications from National Assessment." *Arithmetic Teacher,* 28 (1981): 38–43.

Getting Ready to Teach Unit 13

In this unit, students extend their measurement and estimation skills for length, capacity, weight, and mass in both measurement systems. Students also learn how to read and compare temperatures in both Fahrenheit and Celsius.

Measurement Units

Length

Lessons 1, 2, 3, and 7

Students estimate, measure, and draw lengths using customary units of inches, feet, and yards. They also estimate and measure lengths using metric units of centimeters, decimeters, and meters. Students will measure length to a nearest unit, such as nearest inch, half-inch, or quarter-inch. They will learn how to choose an appropriate length unit. Students will also find and use measurement benchmarks, such as a small paper clip is about 1 inch long, to help them visualize the size of units. Students will also convert between units and use their knowledge of multiplication and division to help with these conversions.

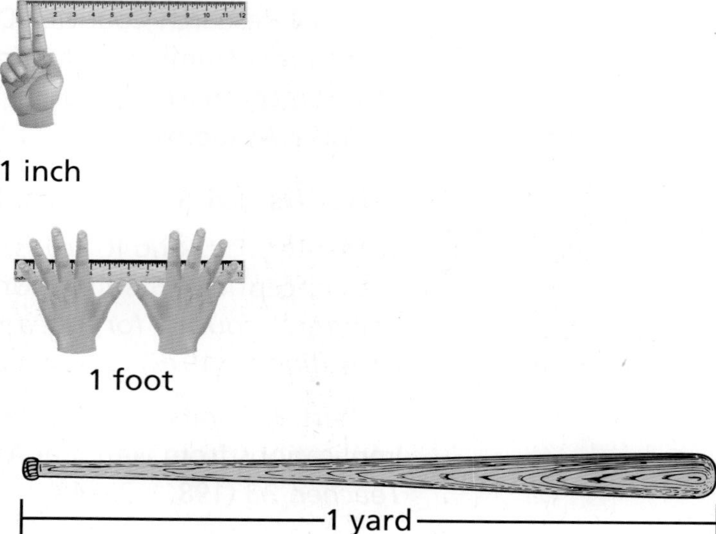

Add Lengths

Lesson 4

Students gain experience in adding customary units of length. They add whole numbers and mixed numbers with like and unlike denominators.

Addition	Description
1 in. + $1\frac{1}{4}$ in.	Whole number plus a mixed number
$1\frac{3}{4}$ in. + $1\frac{1}{4}$ in.	Mixed number plus a mixed number with the same denominators.
$1\frac{1}{2}$ in. + $1\frac{1}{4}$ in.	Mixed number plus a mixed number with different denominators.

Capacity
Lessons 5 and 6

Students will be presented with customary units of capacity using the "milk standard." They will see milk cartons labeled with their capacities, or how much they can hold: 1 cup, 1 pint, 1 quart, half-gallon, 1 gallon. We ask students to examine and predict how the sizes of containers relate to each other. They also use rice or water to fill and compare capacities of the containers. Students state each comparison in an equation in two ways to help with conversions.

Capacity Conversions	
1 cup = $\frac{1}{2}$ pint	1 pint = 2 cups
1 pint = $\frac{1}{2}$ quart	1 quart = 2 pints
1 quart = $\frac{1}{2}$ half-gallon	1 half-gallon = 2 quarts
1 half-gallon = $\frac{1}{2}$ gallon	1 gallon = 2 half-gallons

Weight and Mass
Lesson 9

Students find benchmarks for ounces, pounds, grams, and kilograms. They estimate the weight or mass of an object. Students choose an appropriate unit to use to measure the weight or mass of an object. They convert between pounds and ounces and between grams and kilograms.

Benchmarks for 1 Pound, 1 Ounce, 1 Kilogram, and 1 Gram

One pound (1 lb):
box of butter

One ounce (1 oz):
slice of cheese

One kilogram (1 kg):
textbook

One gram (1 g):
paper clip

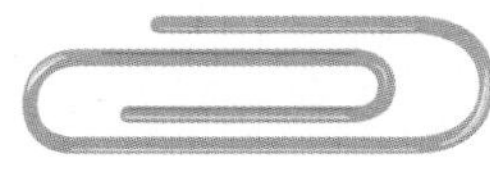

Temperature
Lesson 10

Students read temperature in degrees Fahrenheit and Celsius. Students also establish benchmarks for warm and cold temperatures, and estimate temperature in various situations.

Patterns

Using Patterns to Help Find Relationships Between Units of Measurement

Lessons 2, 3, 5, 6, 8, and 9

We continue to encourage students to use patterns in this unit to help with converting between units. We use tables to help students find relationships between units of measurement. Once students know the relative relationship between units, for example, 2 pints = 1 quart, they can use patterns, including doubling, multiplications, and divisions they know to help them find other equivalents.

Pints	2	4	1
Quarts	1	2	$\frac{1}{2}$

Problem Solving

In *Math Expressions* a research-based, algebraic problem-solving approach that focuses on problem types is used: understand the situation, represent the situation with a math drawing or an equation, solve the problem, and see that the answer makes sense. In this unit students solve problems involving measurement.

Use Mathematical Processes

Lesson 11

The NCTM process skills of problem solving, reasoning and proof, communication, connections, and representation are interwoven through all lessons throughout the year. The last lesson of this unit allows students to extend their use of mathematical processes to other situations.

NCTM Process Skill	Activity and Goal
Representation	1: Show that hexagons can tessellate. 2: Record data in a table and a bar graph. 4: Design card on a net that will fold into a cube.
Communication	1: Discuss which shapes cover the space better. 2: Discuss results of shadow comparisons. 4: Share cube designs. 5: Discuss the solution to a story problem.
Connections	1: Math and Science: Honeycomb Structure and Hexagons
Reasoning and Proof	1: Support or disprove that hexagons cover the space without holes. 3: Use examples to support that a triangle can have only one obtuse angle.
Problem Solving	2: Solve problems involving measurement. 5: Solve a problem that involves division with a remainder.

Customary Units of Length

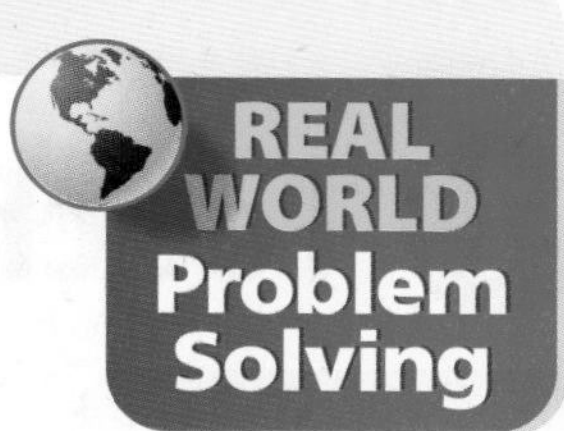

Lesson Objectives

- **Measure length with non-standard units.**
- **Discuss units of measurement and measuring tools.**
- **Measure length in inches, half-inches, and quarter-inches with rulers.**
- **Draw line segments to a specified length.**

Vocabulary
inch (in.)
foot (ft)
ruler

The Day at a Glance

Today's Goals	Materials	
1 Teaching the Lesson **A1:** Measure with non-standard and standard units. **A2:** Discuss units and tools of measurement. **A3:** Assemble, discuss, and use rulers. **A4:** Use rulers to draw line segments to a given number of inches.	**Lesson Activities** Student Activity Book pp. 475–478 or Student Hardcover Book pp. 475–478 and Activity Workbook pp. 241–242 (includes Family Letter) Homework and Remembering pp. 311–312 Pencils Inch Rulers or meter sticks Inch Rulers (TRB M144) Scissors Tape MathBoard materials	**Going Further** Activity Cards 13-1 Inch rulers (TRB M144) Index cards Math Journals
2 Going Further ▶ Differentiated Instruction		
3 Homework and Spiral Review		

Use **Math Talk** *today!*

Keeping Skills Sharp

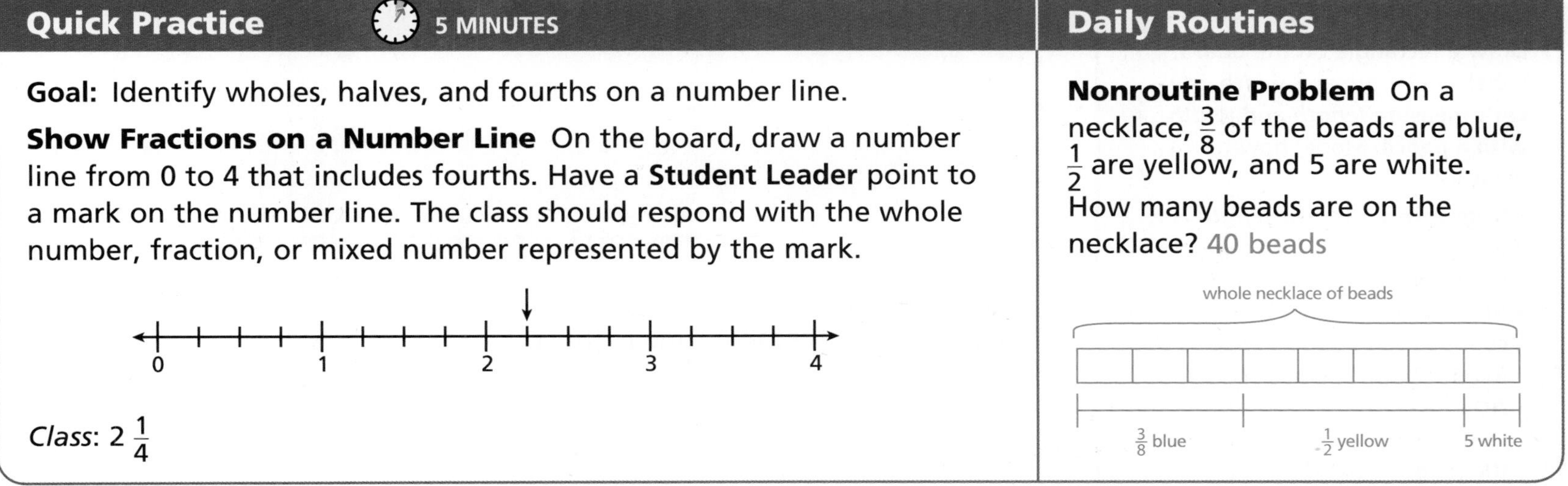

Quick Practice — 5 MINUTES

Goal: Identify wholes, halves, and fourths on a number line.

Show Fractions on a Number Line On the board, draw a number line from 0 to 4 that includes fourths. Have a **Student Leader** point to a mark on the number line. The class should respond with the whole number, fraction, or mixed number represented by the mark.

Class: $2\frac{1}{4}$

Daily Routines

Nonroutine Problem On a necklace, $\frac{3}{8}$ of the beads are blue, $\frac{1}{2}$ are yellow, and 5 are white. How many beads are on the necklace? 40 beads

1 Teaching the Lesson

Activity 1

Non-Standard Units of Measurement

 **15 MINUTES**

Goal: Measure with non-standard and standard units.

Materials: Pencils of different lengths, inch rulers or meter sticks

 **NCTM Standards:**
Measurement
Communication
Representation

Differentiated Instruction

Advanced Learners Some students may want to record fractions of pencil lengths instead of recording to the nearest whole pencil length. For example, they might record *about* $4\frac{1}{2}$ *pencil lengths* instead of *about 5 pencil lengths.*

Class Management

If students do not have individual desks, you could have them measure work tables that are the same size.

English Language Learners

Draw a rectangle on the board. Label the *length* and *width*. Say: **Let's measure *length* and *width* with a pencil.** Model how to measure.

- **Beginning** Say: **The *length* is X pencils.** Have students repeat. Continue with *width*.
- **Intermediate** Have students count as you measure. Ask: **Is the *length/width* X pencils?** yes
- **Advanced** Have students tell the steps for measuring. Ask: **What is the *length/width*?**

▶ Use Pencils as Units SMALL GROUPS

Divide students into **Small Groups** of 3 or 4. Give each group a pencil. Each group's pencil should be a different length. Draw the table below on the board to record each group's estimate of the width of a desk in pencil lengths. Ask students: About how many pencils long do you think the width of a desk is? Make sure that every group is using the same definition for the *width* of their desk.

Group Number	Estimate of Desk Width (in pencil lengths)	Actual Desk Width (in pencil lengths)	Desk Width (in inches)
1			
2			
3			
4			
5			

Explain that each group should use the pencil to measure the width of a student desk. Demonstrate and explain how to measure using a pencil as a unit:

- Align one end of the pencil with one end of the desk.
- Place your finger at the other end of the pencil. Move the back end of the pencil to the point your finger is marking.
- Continue until you come to the end of the desk. Make sure you keep track of how many pencil lengths you have used.

For each group, record the actual measure of the desk width, in pencil lengths, in the table shown above.

- Why are the measurements in pencils different for each group? Each group has a different-sized pencil.

Math Talk Give students another scenario involving non-standard units. For example,

- Suppose a class is decorating their room for a party. They want to hang streamers that are all the same length. The teacher asks the students to cut streamers 4 pencils long. Would the lengths be the same? No
- Why not? Possible answer: The pencils would not all be the same length, so 4 pencil lengths would be different for each student.
- How could the teacher make sure the streamers come out the same length? Possible answer: She could have each student use the same length object to measure the streamers.

Now give each group an inch ruler and explain that the lengths shown on the rulers are standard units of measurement. Each group will now be measuring with units of the same length, rather than units of different length, as they did with the pencils.

- If the teacher had asked students to cut streamers 4 inches long, instead of 4 pencils long, would the streamers be the same length or different lengths? They would be the same length.

Have each group measure the width of a student desk in inches, using the ruler. Record the measurements in the table you drew on the board previously in this lesson. Verify and discuss the fact that the measurements are the same. If any measurement is significantly different, have that group remeasure.

Differentiated Instruction

Extra Help Students may need to review how to measure with a ruler. If students are using rulers:

- ▶ Align the 0 mark of the ruler with one end of the desk.
- ▶ If the width of the desk is longer than the ruler, place a finger on the desk to mark the end of the ruler.
- ▶ Place the 0 mark of the ruler where your finger is.
- ▶ Repeat until you come to the end of the desk.
- ▶ Record how many ruler lengths (feet) you used.
- ▶ Record any extra inches.

Activity 2

Discuss Measurement

▶ Discuss Units and Tools of Measurement WHOLE CLASS

Math Talk Discuss different ways objects can be measured.

- Name something you have measured at home, or something someone you know has measured. the length of a room

15 MINUTES

Goal: Discuss units and tools of measurement

Materials: Rulers or meter sticks

NCTM Standards:
Measurement
Communication
Representation

Activity continued ▶

1 Teaching the Lesson (continued)

Teaching Note

Math Background Before units of length became standardized in the metric and customary systems, parts of the body were often used as units of measurement. One of the first documented examples of a unit of length is the *cubit,* used in Egypt. The cubit was the length of the arm from the elbow to the outstretched fingertips.

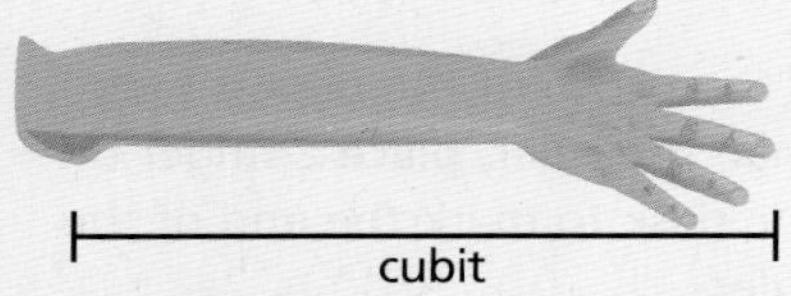

Some other units used before units were standardized:

Digit: top of index finger where it bends

Palm: width of palm

Span: length across the tip of pinkie finger to thumb

Differentiated Instruction

English Learners Remind students that many words in English have more than one meaning. For example, in addition to its mathematical meaning, *feet* can refer to what you use for walking. A *yard* is not only a unit of measure, but the ground outside a house.

Discuss situations in which someone might measure something.

- Suppose a truck carrying a huge tank of milk were parked in the parking lot. What measurements would tell us about this truck? Possible responses: the length and width of the truck, the weight of the truck, how much milk the tank holds.

Make a list on the board of students' suggestions. Some examples are shown below. Using the list you made on the board, discuss the tools you might use for each measurement. Some examples are shown below.

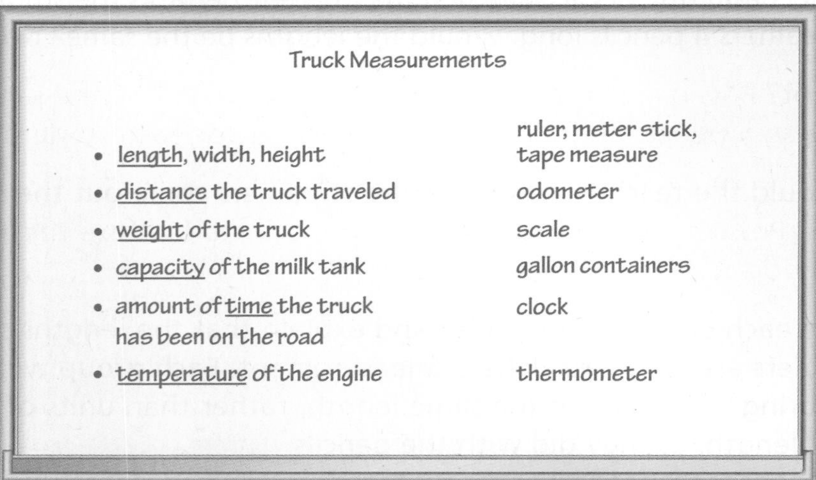

Now move the discussion toward *units* of measurement. On the board, make a chart like the one shown below. Have students list units that are used to measure length, weight, time, temperature, capacity, and any other measurable attributes that are suggested. Note that this exercise is only to *introduce* units that students will study more closely later. It is not necessary that students list all the units given in the sample chart below. Also, it is not necessary to discuss measurement equivalencies or conversions at this point.

Length (height, perimeter, distance, etc.)	Weight	Capacity	Time	Temperature
inches	ounces	cups	seconds	degrees Fahrenheit
feet	pounds	pints	minutes	degrees Celsius
yards	tons	quarts	hours	
centimeters	grams	gallons	days	
meters	kilograms	milliliters	weeks	
decimeters		liters	months	
miles		teaspoons	years	
kilometers		tablespoons	decades	
			centuries	

Activity 3

Measure with Rulers

▶ Assemble and Discuss Rulers

WHOLE CLASS

Math Talk 

Distribute Inch Rulers (TRB M144), scissors, and tape to each student. First, have students assemble the 4 versions of the inch rulers. They will need to attach the second section of the rulers with the first parts of the rulers on the tab. Then, discuss the 4 different versions of the inch ruler asking them questions about the different marks. This will provide an opportunity to review fractions.

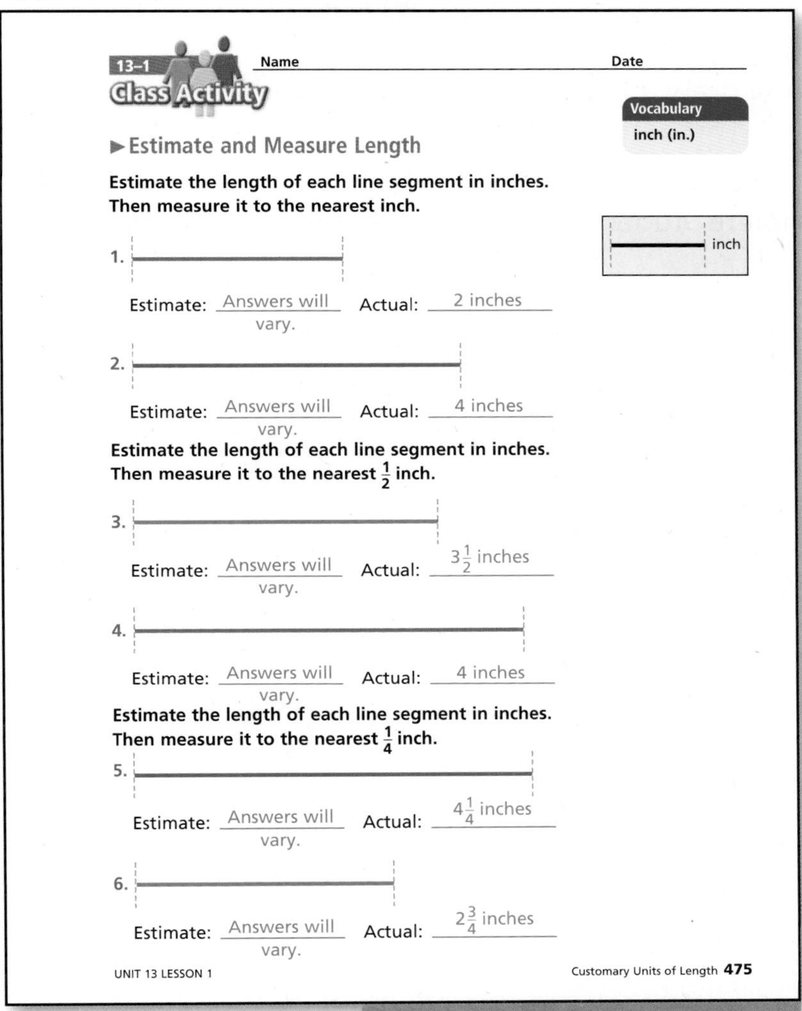

13–1 Class Activity

Name ______ Date ______

Vocabulary: inch (in.)

▶ Estimate and Measure Length

Estimate the length of each line segment in inches. Then measure it to the nearest inch.

1. Estimate: Answers will vary. Actual: 2 inches

2. Estimate: Answers will vary. Actual: 4 inches

Estimate the length of each line segment in inches. Then measure it to the nearest $\frac{1}{2}$ inch.

3. Estimate: Answers will vary. Actual: $3\frac{1}{2}$ inches

4. Estimate: Answers will vary. Actual: 4 inches

Estimate the length of each line segment in inches. Then measure it to the nearest $\frac{1}{4}$ inch.

5. Estimate: Answers will vary. Actual: $4\frac{1}{4}$ inches

6. Estimate: Answers will vary. Actual: $2\frac{3}{4}$ inches

UNIT 13 LESSON 1 Customary Units of Length 475

Student Activity Book page 475

▶ Estimate and Measure Length

WHOLE CLASS

Have students use the Inch, $\frac{1}{2}$-inch, and $\frac{1}{4}$-inch rulers to estimate and then measure classroom objects to the nearest foot, inch, half-inch, and quarter-inch. Discuss which measurements are more accurate. Then have students estimate (use the visual of 1 inch shown on the page) and measure the line segments on Student Book page 475 using their rulers. Discuss the rule of rounding up when a measurement comes at the halfway point between two marks on the ruler. For example, when measuring to the nearest inch, $3\frac{1}{2}$ inches rounds to 4 inches. When measuring to the nearest half-inch, $3\frac{1}{4}$ inches rounds to $3\frac{1}{2}$ inches.

 **15 MINUTES**

Goal: Assemble, discuss, and use rulers.

Materials: Inch Rulers (TRB M144), scissors, tape, Student Activity Book page 507

 **NCTM Standards:**
Measurement
Communication
Representation

Class Management

You may want to photocopy Inch Rulers (TRB M144) on cardstock to make these rulers more durable.

Teaching Note

Language and Vocabulary
Students may need help with the correct language to use when discussing measurements. As you look over Student Book page 475, discuss how to say the measurements, for example, "three and a half inches" and "two and three fourths inches."

1 Teaching the Lesson (continued)

Activity 4

Draw Line Segments

 15 MINUTES

Goal: Use rulers to draw line segments to a given number of inches.

Materials: Inch, $\frac{1}{2}$-Inch, and $\frac{1}{4}$-Inch Rulers (from TRB M144), Student Activity Book or Hardcover book p. 476, MathBoard materials

 **NCTM Standards:**
Measurement
Communication
Representation

Differentiated Instruction

Advanced Learners Some students may be ready to draw a line segment and then draw a line segment that is shorter than the original. For example,

Student Leader: Draw a line segment that is $6\frac{1}{4}$ inches long.
Students draw this length.
Student Leader: Now draw a line segment that is $3\frac{1}{2}$ inches shorter.

You may want to discuss how drawing these segments relates to addition and subtraction, and the Draw a Picture problem-solving strategy.

 Ongoing Assessment

Ask students the following:

Suppose you are measuring a string to the nearest half-inch. The string measures between the $5\frac{3}{4}$-Inch mark and the 6-inch mark. What measurement will you record?

▶ Follow Directions to Draw Line Segments

WHOLE CLASS

Have students practice drawing line segments of different lengths on their MathBoards. Students may choose lengths to draw on their own, or you might have a Student Leader give a length and then give instructions how to draw the line segment.

Student Leader: Draw a line segment that is $5\frac{1}{2}$ inches long.
Students draw this length.
Student Leader: Now draw a line segment that is $3\frac{1}{4}$ inches.

▶ Draw Line Segments WHOLE CLASS

Have students complete Student Book page 476 using their Inch, $\frac{1}{2}$-Inch, and $\frac{1}{4}$-Inch rulers.

13–1 Class Activity Name ______ Date ______

▶ Draw Line Segments

Draw a line segment that has the given length. Check students' work.

7. 5 inches

8. $4\frac{1}{2}$ inches

9. $4\frac{3}{4}$ inches

10. $3\frac{1}{4}$ inches

11. 2 inches

12. $1\frac{1}{4}$ inches

13. $1\frac{1}{2}$ inches

14. $3\frac{3}{4}$ inches

15. Draw a rectangle that is 1 inch wide and 3 inches long.

Student Activity Book page 476

Intervention — Activity Card 13-1

Locate Measurements on a Ruler
Activity Card 13-1 ●

Work: In pairs

Use:
- $\frac{1}{4}$-inch ruler or TRB M144 ($\frac{1}{4}$-inch Ruler)

1. Look at the ruler below. What interval does each tic mark on the ruler represent? $\frac{1}{4}$ inch
2. What measurement is shown on the ruler? $1\frac{3}{4}$ inches

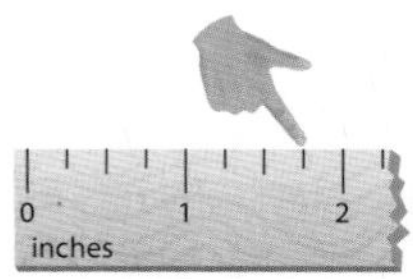

3. Take turns. Use your ruler to answer the questions below.
   - Where is 5 inches on the ruler?
   - Where is $4\frac{1}{2}$ inches on the ruler?
   - Where is $3\frac{1}{4}$ inches on the ruler?
   - Where is $2\frac{3}{4}$ inches on the ruler?

Unit 13, Lesson 1

Activity Note Students should justify each answer they give by counting the $\frac{1}{4}$-inch intervals. Continue the activity as needed to build student confidence with quarter-inch measurements.

Math Writing Prompt

You Decide Christopher wants to measure the length of his classroom. Should he use a paper clip, a ruler, or a shoe to measure the length? Explain your thinking.

Software Support

Warm Up 38.12

On Level — Activity Card 13-1

Estimate and Compare
Activity Card 13-1 ▲

Work: In pairs

Use:
- $\frac{1}{4}$-inch ruler or TRB M144 ($\frac{1}{4}$-inch Ruler)

1. Choose a classroom object to measure.
2. **On Your Own** Create a chart like the one shown to the right. Record the object you have chosen and your estimate of its length.

Object	Estimate of Length	Actual Length
Piece of chalk	3 inches	$3\frac{1}{2}$ inches
Fish tank	1 foot, 2 inches	1 foot, 6 inches
Stapler		

3. **Work Together** Measure the length of the object to the nearest $\frac{1}{4}$-inch and record the actual measurement.
4. The student whose estimate is closer to the actual measurement wins one point. Continue the activity until one student wins five points.

Unit 13, Lesson 1

Activity Note Make sure that students agree on which side of each object they are estimating and measuring length. After completing the activity, have students discuss their estimation strategies.

Math Writing Prompt

Explain Your Thinking Suppose you wanted to find the closest measurement to the actual length of a pencil. Would you measure the pencil to the nearest inch, half-inch, or quarter-inch? Explain.

Software Support

Ice Station Exploration: Linear Lab, Level F

Challenge — Activity Card 13-1

Draw Shapes
Activity Card 13-1 ■

Work: In pairs

Use:
- Two $\frac{1}{4}$-inch rulers or TRB M144 ($\frac{1}{4}$-inch Ruler)
- Math Journals
- Index cards

1. **On Your Own** In your Math Journal use a ruler to draw each figure listed below with the correct perimeter. Remember: a rectangle and a square each have four right angles. Use an index card to help you form right angles.

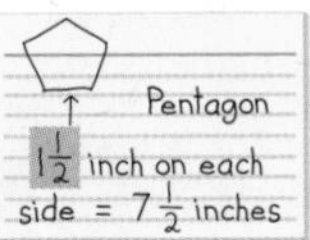

   - Pentagon (5 sides); Perimeter: $7\frac{1}{2}$ inches
   - Rectangle; Perimeter: 6 inches
   - Square; Perimeter: 5 inches
   - Triangle; Perimeter: $9\frac{3}{4}$ inches
   - Hexagon (6 sides); Perimeter: 3 inches
2. Exchange Math Journals with your partner. Use your ruler to check your partner's work.

Unit 13, Lesson 1

Activity Note The triangle, pentagon, and hexagon need not be equilateral. However, one strategy is to divide the perimeter by the number of sides to find the measure for each side.

Math Writing Prompt

Number Sense Draw what you think a ruler with eighths marks looks like. Label the $\frac{3}{8}$ mark. Explain why it should go there.

DESTINATION Math® **Software Support**

Course II: Module 4: Unit 1: Number Patterns and Properties

Homework and Spiral Review

13–1 Homework **Goal:** Additional Practice

Include students' completed Homework page as part of their portfolios.

13–1 Remembering **Goal:** Spiral Review

This Remembering page would be appropriate anytime after today's lesson.

13–1 Name ________ Date ________

Homework

Estimate the length of each line segment in inches. Then measure it to the nearest inch.

1 inch

1. Estimate: Answers will vary. Actual: 3 inches

Estimate the length of each line segment in inches. Then measure it to the nearest $\frac{1}{2}$ inch.

2. Estimate: Answers will vary. Actual: $2\frac{1}{2}$ inches

Estimate the length of each line segment. Then measure it to the nearest $\frac{1}{4}$ inch.

3. Estimate: Answers will vary. Actual: $1\frac{1}{4}$ inch

4. Estimate: Answers will vary. Actual: 5 inches

Draw a line segment that has the given length. Check students' work.

5. 4 inches

6. $3\frac{1}{4}$ inches

7. $4\frac{1}{2}$ inches

8. $\frac{3}{4}$ inch

9. Marta wants to make 4 necklaces that are the same length. She asks her friends to cut the string for the necklaces 15 paper clips long. Would all the lengths be the same? Explain your thinking.
No; The lengths won't all be the same because paper clips can be different sizes.

UNIT 13 LESSON 1 Customary Units of Length **311**

Homework and Remembering page 311

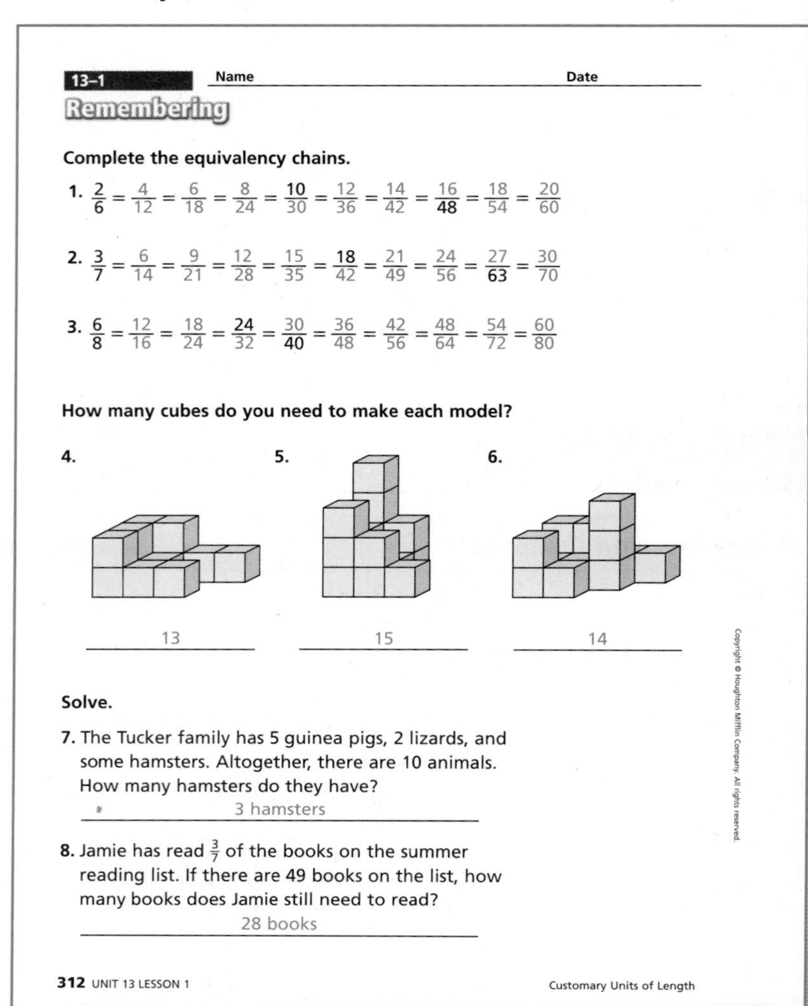

13–1 Name ________ Date ________

Remembering

Complete the equivalency chains.

1. $\frac{2}{6} = \frac{4}{12} = \frac{6}{18} = \frac{8}{24} = \frac{10}{30} = \frac{12}{36} = \frac{14}{42} = \frac{16}{48} = \frac{18}{54} = \frac{20}{60}$

2. $\frac{3}{7} = \frac{6}{14} = \frac{9}{21} = \frac{12}{28} = \frac{15}{35} = \frac{18}{42} = \frac{21}{49} = \frac{24}{56} = \frac{27}{63} = \frac{30}{70}$

3. $\frac{6}{8} = \frac{12}{16} = \frac{18}{24} = \frac{24}{32} = \frac{30}{40} = \frac{36}{48} = \frac{42}{56} = \frac{48}{64} = \frac{54}{72} = \frac{60}{80}$

How many cubes do you need to make each model?

4. 13

5. 15

6. 14

Solve.

7. The Tucker family has 5 guinea pigs, 2 lizards, and some hamsters. Altogether, there are 10 animals. How many hamsters do they have?
3 hamsters

8. Jamie has read $\frac{3}{7}$ of the books on the summer reading list. If there are 49 books on the list, how many books does Jamie still need to read?
28 books

312 UNIT 13 LESSON 1 Customary Units of Length

Homework and Remembering page 312

Home and School Connection

Family Letter Have children take home the Family Letter on Student Book page 477. A Spanish translation of this letter is on the following page in the Student Book. This letter explains how the concept of measurement is developed in *Math Expressions*. It gives parents and guardians a better understanding of the learning that goes on in math class and creates a bridge between school and home.

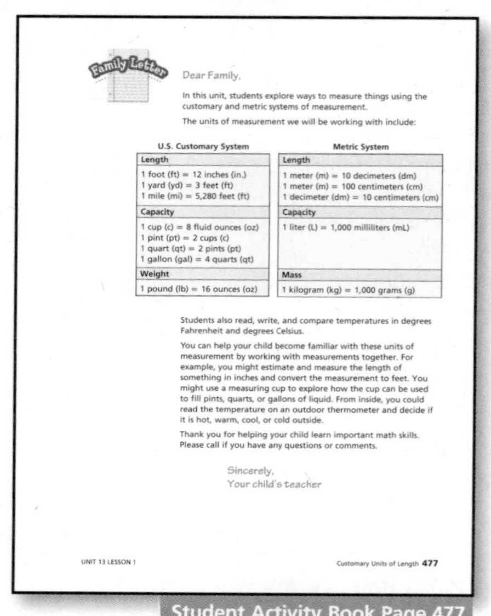

Family Letter

Dear Family,

In this unit, students explore ways to measure things using the customary and metric systems of measurement.

The units of measurement we will be working with include:

U.S. Customary System	Metric System
Length	**Length**
1 foot (ft) = 12 inches (in.) 1 yard (yd) = 3 feet (ft) 1 mile (mi) = 5,280 feet (ft)	1 meter (m) = 10 decimeters (dm) 1 meter (m) = 100 centimeters (cm) 1 decimeter (dm) = 10 centimeters (cm)
Capacity	**Capacity**
1 cup (c) = 8 fluid ounces (oz) 1 pint (pt) = 2 cups (c) 1 quart (qt) = 2 pints (pt) 1 gallon (gal) = 4 quarts (qt)	1 liter (L) = 1,000 milliliters (mL)
Weight	**Mass**
1 pound (lb) = 16 ounces (oz)	1 kilogram (kg) = 1,000 grams (g)

Students also read, write, and compare temperatures in degrees Fahrenheit and degrees Celsius.

You can help your child become familiar with these units of measurement by working with measurements together. For example, you might estimate and measure the length of something in inches and convert the measurement to feet. You might use a measuring cup to explore how the cup can be used to fill pints, quarts, or gallons of liquid. From inside, you could read the temperature on an outdoor thermometer and decide if it is hot, warm, cool, or cold outside.

Thank you for helping your child learn important math skills. Please call if you have any questions or comments.

Sincerely,
Your child's teacher

UNIT 13 LESSON 1 Customary Units of Length **477**

Student Activity Book Page 477

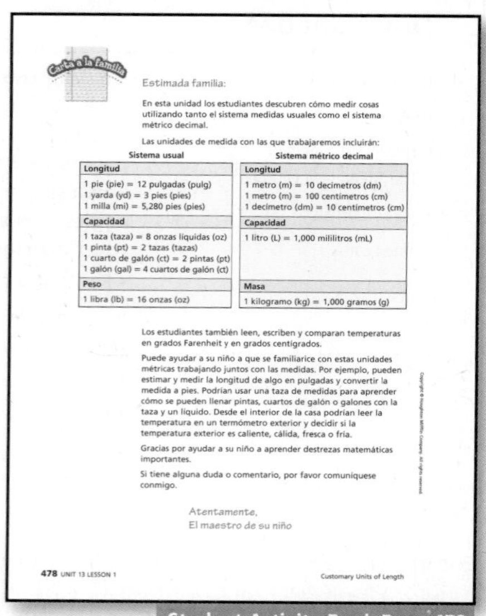

Carta a la familia

Estimada familia:

En esta unidad los estudiantes descubren cómo medir cosas utilizando tanto el sistema medidas usuales como el sistema métrico decimal.

Las unidades de medida con las que trabajaremos incluirán:

Sistema usual	Sistema métrico decimal
Longitud	**Longitud**
1 pie (pie) = 12 pulgadas (pulg) 1 yarda (yd) = 3 pies (pies) 1 milla (mi) = 5,280 pies (pies)	1 metro (m) = 10 decimetros (dm) 1 metro (m) = 100 centímetros (cm) 1 decímetro (dm) = 10 centímetros (cm)
Capacidad	**Capacidad**
1 taza (taza) = 8 onzas líquidas (oz) 1 pinta (pt) = 2 tazas (tazas) 1 cuarto de galón (ct) = 2 pintas (pt) 1 galón (gal) = 4 cuartos de galón (ct)	1 litro (L) = 1,000 mililitros (mL)
Peso	**Masa**
1 libra (lb) = 16 onzas (oz)	1 kilogramo (kg) = 1,000 gramos (g)

Los estudiantes también leen, escriben y comparan temperaturas en grados Farenheit y en grados centígrados.

Puede ayudar a su niño a que se familiarice con estas unidades métricas trabajando juntos con las medidas. Por ejemplo, pueden estimar y medir la longitud de algo en pulgadas y convertir la medida a pies. Podrían usar una taza de medidas para aprender cómo se pueden llenar pintas, cuartos de galón o galones con la taza y un líquido. Desde el interior de la casa podrían leer la temperatura en un termómetro exterior y decidir si la temperatura exterior es caliente, cálida, fresca o fría.

Gracias por ayudar a su niño a aprender destrezas matemáticas importantes.

Si tiene alguna duda o comentario, por favor comuníquese conmigo.

Atentamente,
El maestro de su niño

478 UNIT 13 LESSON 1 Customary Units of Length

Student Activity Book Page 478

Inches, Feet, and Yards

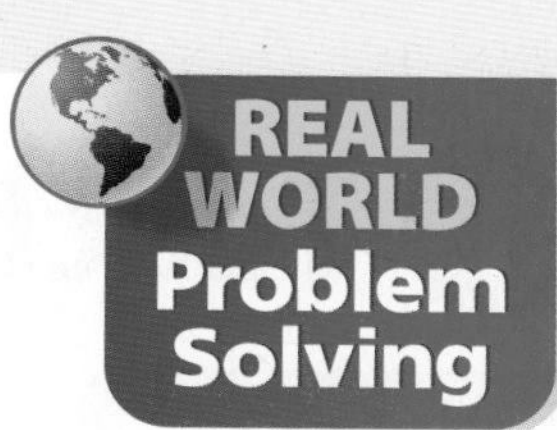

Lesson Objectives

- Convert between yards, feet, and inches.
- Find benchmarks for inch, foot, yard, and mile.
- Choose the appropriate customary units of length.

Vocabulary
foot
yard
mile
benchmark

The Day at a Glance

Today's Goals	Materials	
1 Teaching the Lesson **A1:** List units of length and convert between inches, feet, and yards. **A2:** Determine benchmarks for yards, feet, inches, and miles. Choose appropriate units of measure. **2 Going Further** ▸ Differentiated Instruction **3 Homework and Spiral Review**	**Lesson Activities** Student Activity Book pp. 479–480 or Student Hardcover Book pp. 479–480 Homework and Remembering pp. 313–314 Yardsticks Inch Rulers (TRB M144)	**Going Further** Activity Cards 13-2 Yardsticks Inch Rulers (TRB M144) Math Journals

Use **Math Talk** *today!*

Keeping Skills Sharp

Quick Practice — 5 MINUTES

Goal: Review multiplying and dividing by 3 and 12.

Materials: pointer

Multiply and Divide by 3 and 12 On the board write the numbers 1 through 12. Next to this, write some multiples of 12. The first list will be multiplied by 3 or 12. The second list will be divided by 3 or 12.

Have a **Student Leader** point to a number in the multiplication section and specify whether students should multiply by 3 or by 12. After the leader gets a correct response, have the leader then point to a number in the division section and say whether it should be divided by 3 or 12. Repeat several times.

Daily Routines

Homework Review Let students work together to check their work. Remind students to use what they know about helping others.

Calendar Dina has basketball practice from September 2 to November 2. She has swimming practice from March 15 to June 15. Which practice lasts longer? How much longer? swimming practice; 1 month longer.

1 Teaching the Lesson

Activity 1

Convert Customary Units of Length

 **30 MINUTES**

Goal: List units of length and convert between inches, feet, and yards.

Materials: Yardsticks, Inch Rulers (TRB M144), Student Activity Book or Hardcover Book p. 479

 **NCTM Standards:**
Number and Operations
Measurement
Communication
Representation

 Class Management

If you don't have a yardstick in your classroom, students may make yardsticks. Have students line up three rulers from Lesson 1 end to end. Tape the rulers together to make a yardstick.

Differentiated Instruction

Extra Help To help students remember the conversions, display the following rulers in the classroom for all to see. Attach a 12-inch ruler to a sneaker so students can see there are "12 inches in 1 foot." Also, attach 3 sneakers to a yardstick to help students remember there are "3 feet in 1 yard."

 Alternate Approach

If students are having difficulty converting, you might suggest they use their Inch Rulers from Lesson 1 to model a few exercises. For exercise 1, students may lay down the Inch Ruler to represent a foot and then use the $\frac{1}{2}$-inch ruler to show 3 more inches for a total of 15 inches.

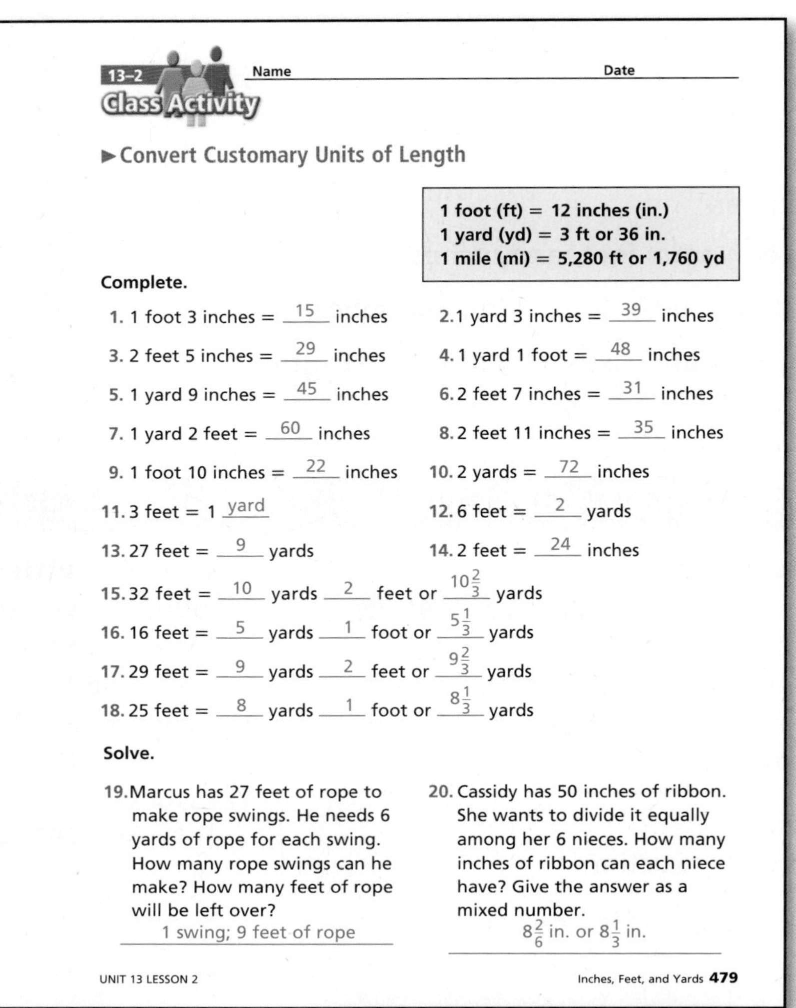

13–2 Class Activity   Name ____________ Date ________

▶ Convert Customary Units of Length

1 foot (ft) = 12 inches (in.)
1 yard (yd) = 3 ft or 36 in.
1 mile (mi) = 5,280 ft or 1,760 yd

Complete.

1. 1 foot 3 inches = 15 inches
2. 1 yard 3 inches = 39 inches
3. 2 feet 5 inches = 29 inches
4. 1 yard 1 foot = 48 inches
5. 1 yard 9 inches = 45 inches
6. 2 feet 7 inches = 31 inches
7. 1 yard 2 feet = 60 inches
8. 2 feet 11 inches = 35 inches
9. 1 foot 10 inches = 22 inches
10. 2 yards = 72 inches
11. 3 feet = 1 yard
12. 6 feet = 2 yards
13. 27 feet = 9 yards
14. 2 feet = 24 inches
15. 32 feet = 10 yards 2 feet or $10\frac{2}{3}$ yards
16. 16 feet = 5 yards 1 foot or $5\frac{1}{3}$ yards
17. 29 feet = 9 yards 2 feet or $9\frac{2}{3}$ yards
18. 25 feet = 8 yards 1 foot or $8\frac{1}{3}$ yards

Solve.

19. Marcus has 27 feet of rope to make rope swings. He needs 6 yards of rope for each swing. How many rope swings can he make? How many feet of rope will be left over?
1 swing; 9 feet of rope

20. Cassidy has 50 inches of ribbon. She wants to divide it equally among her 6 nieces. How many inches of ribbon can each niece have? Give the answer as a mixed number.
$8\frac{2}{6}$ in. or $8\frac{1}{3}$ in.

UNIT 13 LESSON 2   Inches, Feet, and Yards **479**

Student Activity Book page 479

▶ Convert Customary Units of Length WHOLE CLASS

Ask students to name all the customary units of length they can recall. Write the units on the board in order of increasing size.

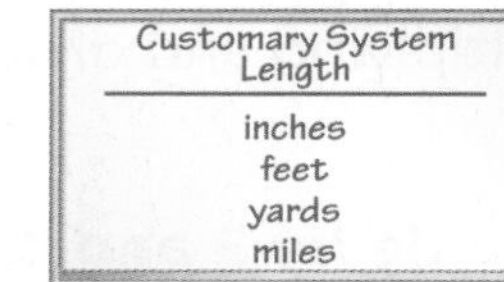

Show students a yardstick. Have three students bring their Inch rulers (they may use any version from Lesson 1 or a regular inch ruler) to the front of the class, and demonstrate that three feet fit in one yard.

As a class, make a list on the board to describe the relationship among inches, feet, and yards:

12 inches = 1 foot
3 feet = 1 yard
36 inches = 1 yard

Refer students to Student Book page 479. Work through the first three exercises as a class. For exercises 1 and 2, make sure students know they must add extra inches after converting 1 foot to 12 inches and 1 yard to 36 inches.

Help students understand that they must multiply, then add, in exercise 3 to find the number of inches:

- For exercise 3, how do we find how many inches are in 2 feet? Multiply the number of feet by 12.
- How do we find the total number of inches? Add the number of inches in 2 feet and 5 more inches.

Have students complete exercises 4–12. Then check together as a class. Then work together to complete exercises 13–15.

- For exercise 13, how can we find how many yards are in 27 feet? Divide the number of feet by 3.
- For exercise 15, how can we find how many yards are in 32 feet? Divide the number of feet by 3.
- How many yards are there in 32 feet? How many are left over? 10 yards; 2 feet left over.
- For exercise 16, how many yards are in 16 feet? How many are left over? 5 yards; 1 foot.
- How would we write 1 foot as a fraction of a yard? 1 foot is $\frac{1}{3}$ of a yard.
- So how would we write 5 yards, 1 foot as yards? $5\frac{1}{3}$ yards

Have students complete exercises 17–18. Then check together.

123 **Math Talk** Using **Solve and Discuss**, solve problems 19 and 20. Problem 19 includes conversion from yards to feet. Problem 20 does not include conversion, but requires writing a remainder as a fraction.

Summarize when to multiply and when to divide when converting units of length.

- When we convert from larger units to smaller units, do we multiply or divide? multiply
- When we convert from smaller units to larger units, do we divide or multiply? divide

Teaching Note

What to Expect from Students Students may not finish all the problems on Student Book page 479 during class; the main goal is for students to receive a solid introduction so they can complete similar exercises for homework.

Differentiated Instruction

Extra Help If students are having trouble finding a mixed number for yards in exercises 15–18, you might use a visual to help them. For exercise 16, there is 1 foot left over after making 5 yards from 16 feet. Show them a yardstick and a ruler, and demonstrate that the ruler makes up $\frac{1}{3}$ of the yardstick. So, 1 foot is $\frac{1}{3}$ of a yard.

Teaching Note

Measuring in the Real World Make sure students understand how every-day objects can be measured in mixed units (for example, feet and inches, yards and feet, yards and inches, and so on). Have students measure their heights with yardsticks and inch rulers to demonstrate how height can be expressed in mixed units. For example, 4 ft 2 in.

English Language Learners

Write *abbreviation, in., ft,* and *yd* on the board. Point and say: **An *abbreviation* is a shorter, faster way to write something. These mean *inches, feet,* and *yards*.** Have students repeat.

Activity 2

Establishing Benchmarks and Choosing Units

 25 MINUTES

Goal: Determine benchmarks for yards, feet, inches, and miles. Choose appropriate units of measure.

Materials: Yardsticks, Inch Rulers (TRB M144), Student Activity Book or Hardcover Book p. 480

 **NCTM Standards:**
Number and Operations
Measurement
Communication
Representation

Alternate Approach

You might want to allow students to take their rulers around the room, looking for objects that are about 1 inch, 1 foot, and 1 yard long. This will help them find benchmarks, and familiarize students with these standard lengths.

inch
width of a quarter
length of a small paperclip

foot
length of a sheet of paper
width of a computer screen

yard
a baseball bat
the height of a doorknob

Ongoing Assessment

Use this problem to see if students can convert units of length. Have students solve the following:

► Rachel will be allowed to sit in a car without a booster seat when she is 4 feet 9 inches tall. How many inches tall will she be?
57 inches

13–2 Class Activity   Name ______ Date ______

Vocabulary
inch
foot
yard
mile

► Find Benchmarks

Write the answer.

21. This line segment is 1 **inch** long.
Put two fingers on the line segment. Then hold up your fingers. Write the name of an object that is about 1 inch (or two finger widths) long.
Possible answer: small paper clip

22. One **foot** is equal to 12 inches. Spread both hands on a ruler to show 1 foot. Write the name of an object that is about 1 foot (or both hands) long.
Possible answer: book

23. One **yard** is equal to 3 feet or 36 inches. How many 12-inch lengths are in 1 yard? Write the name of an object that is about 1 yard long.
three 12-inch lengths; Possible answer: the width of a door

24. One **mile** is 5,280 feet or 1,760 yards. In describing a long distance, why would it make sense to use miles instead of feet or yards?
Possible answer: There would be so many feet or yards it would be difficult to count the units.

► Choose Appropriate Units

Choose the unit you would use to measure each. Write *inch, foot, yard,* or *mile.* Possible answers:

25. the width of a piece of notebook paper inch
26. the length of a classroom board foot or yard
27. the height of the school foot or yard
28. the distance you travel to school mile

480 UNIT 13 LESSON 2   Inches, Feet, and Yards

Student Activity Book page 480

► Find Benchmarks WHOLE CLASS

Explain that a benchmark can help you estimate the length of an object or a distance. For example, if you know that a small paperclip is about 1 inch long, then you can estimate the length of a caterpillar by thinking about how many paperclips long the caterpillar is.

Brainstorm with students to find benchmarks for inch, foot, yard, and mile.

List their benchmarks on the board. See the side column for sample responses. Then, have students complete exercises 21–24 on Student Book page 480.

► Choose Appropriate Units WHOLE CLASS

Have students name objects or distances that could reasonably be measured by the units *inch, foot, yard,* and *mile.* Then have students complete exercises 25–28.

2 Going Further

Differentiated Instruction

Intervention — Activity Card 13-2

Estimate Lengths

Activity Card 13-2 ●

Work: In pairs

Use:

- Yardstick
- TRB M144 (Inch Ruler)
- Math Journals

1. Make a list of five objects in the classroom.
2. On Your Own Estimate the length of each object in feet and inches. Record your estimates in your Math Journal.
3. Work Together Measure each object, using a ruler or yardstick. Record each measurement in feet and inches in your Math Journal.

Object	Estimate (in inches)	Actual Length (in inches)	Who came closer?
Class board	8 feet = 96 inches	6 feet 6 inches = 78 inches	Jason
Beanbag chair			
Teacher's desk			
Window			
Fish tank			

4. Does one strategy give a closer estimate? Explain.

Unit 13, Lesson 2

Activity Note Encourage students to develop benchmarks to use in making their estimates. Have them share their strategies with their classmates after completing the activity.

Math Writing Prompt

Estimation Laura and Mai see a bird in a tree. Laura estimates the tree is 4 inches high. Mai estimates the tree is 4 yards high. Explain who you think is correct and why.

Software Support

Warm Up 38.13

On Level — Activity Card 13-2

My Robot

Activity Card 13-2 ▲

Work: In pairs

Use:

- Ruler or yardstick

Decide:

Who will be Student 1 and who will be Student 2 for the first round.

1. Play a game with robots and measurements.
2. Student 1: Give the height of an imaginary robot using inches, feet and inches, or yards and inches.

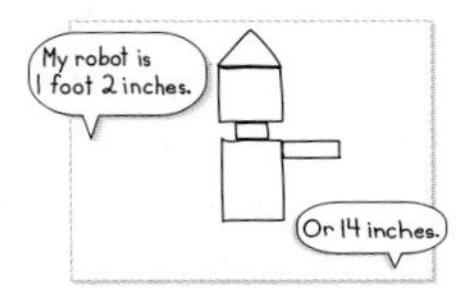

3. Student 2: Give the same height using a different unit or units of measurement.
4. Work Together Use a ruler or yardstick to check if both measurements are the same. If the measurements are the same, Student 2 draws a part of a robot.
5. Continue the activity, switching roles for each round, until each robot is complete.

Unit 13, Lesson 2

Activity Note Suggest that students make a list of customary conversions before beginning the activity. Encourage students to repeat the activity for at least 6 rounds if time permits.

Math Writing Prompt

Real-World Application Explain when it would make sense to use inches to measure length. Explain when it would make sense to use yards to measure length.

Software Support

The Number Games: Tiny's Think Tank, Level M

Challenge — Activity Card 13-2

You're the Architect

Activity Card 13-2 ■

Work: On your own

Use:

- TRB M144 (Inch Ruler)

1. Use a ruler and the information given below to draw a design for the front of a house. Label each measurement on your completed drawing.

House is a 4 in. × 6 in. rectangle. Design your own roof. The chimney has a perimeter of 4 inches.

Door is a 2 in. × 3 in. rectangle, with the knob $1\frac{1}{2}$ in. high.

There are 3 square windows in the house. There is $\frac{1}{4}$ in. space between each window.

2. Exchange papers with a classmate to compare and check each other's work.

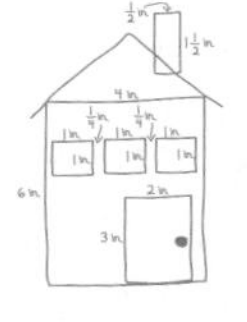

Unit 13, Lesson 2

Activity Note Tell students that the perimeter of the chimney refers to the face of the chimney that is visible from the front of the house. The roof can be any shape, and the windows should align.

Math Writing Prompt

Number Sense Explain how you would find how many yards are in 2 miles, if there are 5,280 feet in one mile.

Software Support

Course II: Module 3: Unit 1: Area

3 Homework and Spiral Review

Goal: Additional Practice

✓ This Homework page provides practice in converting customary units of length.

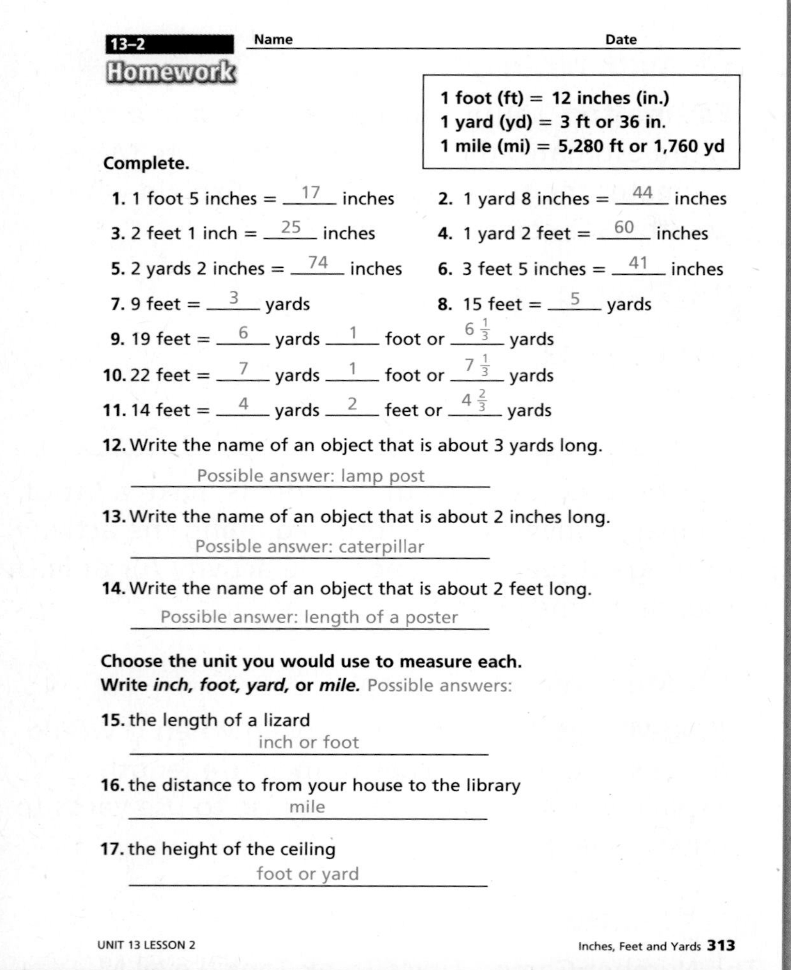

13–2 **Homework** Name ______ Date ______

1 foot (ft) = 12 inches (in.)
1 yard (yd) = 3 ft or 36 in.
1 mile (mi) = 5,280 ft or 1,760 yd

Complete.

1. 1 foot 5 inches = 17 inches
2. 1 yard 8 inches = 44 inches
3. 2 feet 1 inch = 25 inches
4. 1 yard 2 feet = 60 inches
5. 2 yards 2 inches = 74 inches
6. 3 feet 5 inches = 41 inches
7. 9 feet = 3 yards
8. 15 feet = 5 yards
9. 19 feet = 6 yards 1 foot or $6\frac{1}{3}$ yards
10. 22 feet = 7 yards 1 foot or $7\frac{1}{3}$ yards
11. 14 feet = 4 yards 2 feet or $4\frac{2}{3}$ yards
12. Write the name of an object that is about 3 yards long.
    Possible answer: lamp post
13. Write the name of an object that is about 2 inches long.
    Possible answer: caterpillar
14. Write the name of an object that is about 2 feet long.
    Possible answer: length of a poster

Choose the unit you would use to measure each. Write *inch, foot, yard,* or *mile.* Possible answers:

15. the length of a lizard
    inch or foot
16. the distance to from your house to the library
    mile
17. the height of the ceiling
    foot or yard

UNIT 13 LESSON 2 Inches, Feet and Yards **313**

Homework and Remembering page 313

Goal: Spiral Review

This Remembering page would be appropriate anytime after today's lesson.

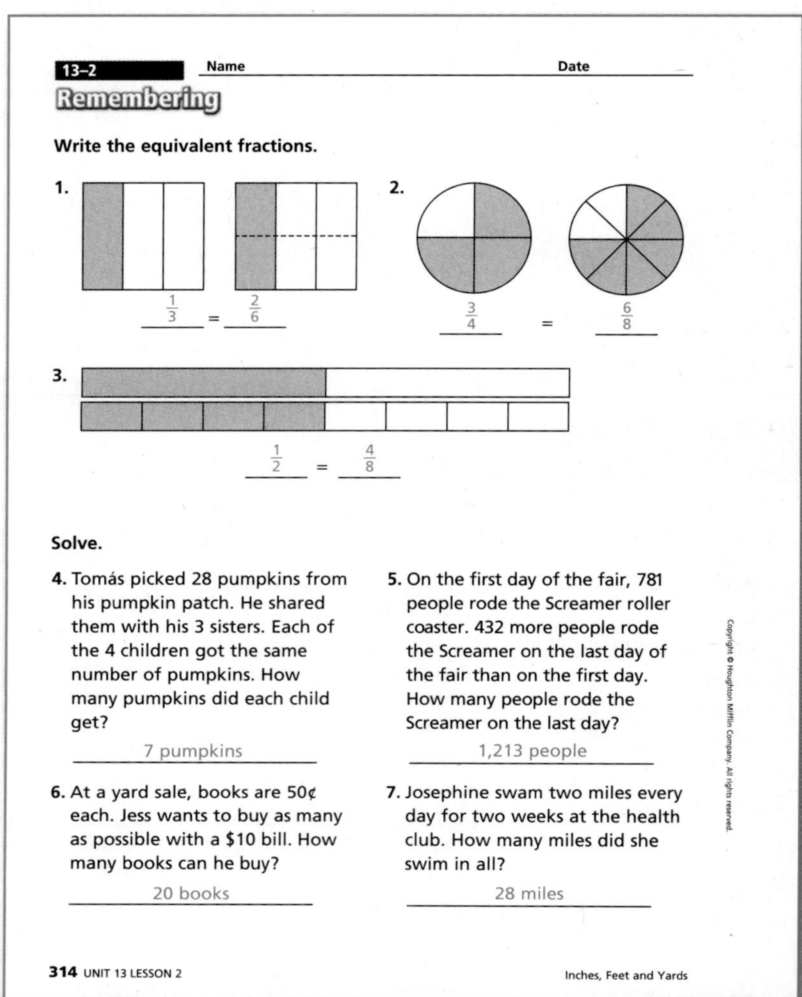

13–2 **Remembering** Name ______ Date ______

Write the equivalent fractions.

1. $\frac{1}{3}$ = $\frac{2}{6}$
2. $\frac{3}{4}$ = $\frac{6}{8}$
3. $\frac{1}{2}$ = $\frac{4}{8}$

Solve.

4. Tomás picked 28 pumpkins from his pumpkin patch. He shared them with his 3 sisters. Each of the 4 children got the same number of pumpkins. How many pumpkins did each child get?
   7 pumpkins
5. On the first day of the fair, 781 people rode the Screamer roller coaster. 432 more people rode the Screamer on the last day of the fair than on the first day. How many people rode the Screamer on the last day?
   1,213 people
6. At a yard sale, books are 50¢ each. Jess wants to buy as many as possible with a $10 bill. How many books can he buy?
   20 books
7. Josephine swam two miles every day for two weeks at the health club. How many miles did she swim in all?
   28 miles

314 UNIT 13 LESSON 2 Inches, Feet and Yards

Homework and Remembering page 314

Home or School Activity

Art Connection

Yards of Designs Have students measure one yard of string or ribbon with a yardstick or an inch ruler (3 feet = 1 yard). Then have them arrange their ribbon or string into an object without cutting the ribbon or string. Display students' yard designs on a bulletin board.

This art activity can also facilitate a classroom discussion on differences and similarities, or how people can have different interpretations of the same thing.

Yards of Design

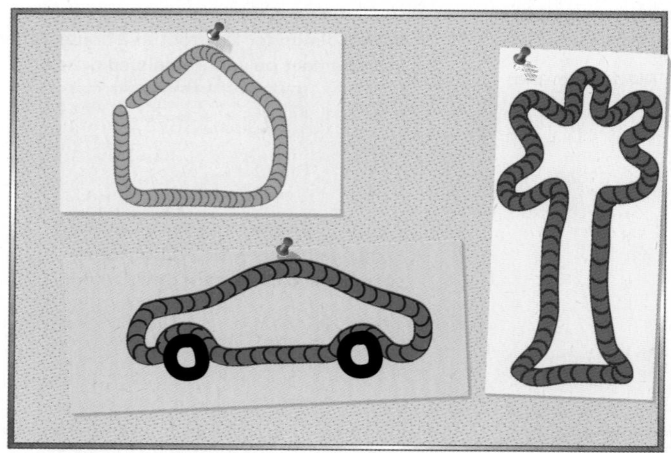

Centimeters, Decimeters, and Meters

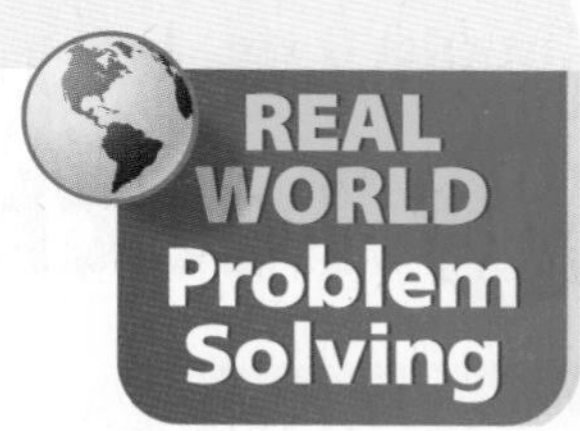

Lesson Objectives

- Measure classroom objects to the nearest meter, decimeter, and centimeter.
- Convert among centimeters, decimeters, and meters.
- Discuss benchmarks for centimeters, decimeters, and meters.
- Choose the appropriate metric unit of length.

Vocabulary

centimeter (cm)
decimeter (dm)
meter (m)
kilometer (km)

The Day at a Glance

Today's Goals	Materials	
1 Teaching the Lesson **A1:** Discuss metric units of length and use a meter stick to measure classroom objects. **A2:** Use function tables to convert metric units of length. **A3:** Find benchmarks for metric units of length and choose an appropriate unit of metric length for measuring objects. **2 Going Further** ▸ Differentiated Instruction **3 Homework and Spiral Review**	**Lesson Activities** Student Activity Book pp. 481–484 or Student Hardcover Book pp. 481–484 and Activity Workbook pp. 243–245 (includes tables) Homework and Remembering pp. 315–316 Scissors Meter sticks Centimeter ruler (TRB M26) MathBoard Materials	**Going Further** Activity Cards 13-3 Meter Sticks Index cards Centimeter Rulers Box of Spaghetti Calculator Math Journals

Use Math Talk today!

Keeping Skills Sharp

Quick Practice — 5 MINUTES

Goal: Review multiplying and dividing by 10 and 100.

Multiply and Divide by 10 and 100 Write the numbers 1 through 12 on the board. In a second list, write the first nine multiples of 10 and in a third list, the first ten multiples of 100.

Have a **Student Leader** point to a number in the multiplication section and say to multiply by 10 or 100. Then have the leader point to a number in a division section and say what to divide by. The numbers in the second list are to be divided by 10 and in the third list, divided by 10 or 100.

Daily Routines

Homework Review Have students explain how they found their errors.

Equations Greg bought 4 packs of markers with the same number of markers in each pack. He bought a total of 48 markers. How many markers were in each pack? Write a solution equation. 12 markers per pack; 48 markers ÷ 4 packs = □

1 Teaching the Lesson

Activity 1

Metric Units of Length

20 MINUTES

Goal: Discuss metric units of length and use a meter stick to measure classroom objects.

Materials: MathBoard materials, meter sticks, centimeter rulers or Centimeter Ruler (TRB M26), scissors, Student Activity Book or Hardcover Book page 481 and Activity Workbook page 243 (includes table).

NCTM Standards:
Measurement
Communication
Representation

Teaching Note

Math Background The metric system is based on powers of 10. The prefixes tell what relationship the unit has to the base unit. In metric length, the base unit is the meter. All linear measurements are related to the meter. The **centi**meter is one hundredth of a meter. The **deci**meter is one tenth of a meter. The **kilo**meter is 1,000 times a meter.

Metric Prefixes					
kilo	hecto	deka	deci	centi	milli
1,000	100	10	0.1	0.01	0.001

▶ Introduce Metric Units of Length WHOLE CLASS

Remind students that they have already worked with centimeters in Unit A. Have them take out their MathBoards and look at the space between the dots on their dot arrays. This space is 1 centimeter.

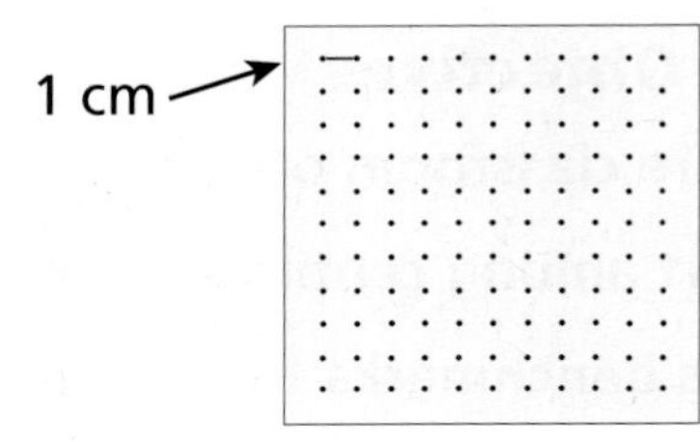

Ask students to name all the units they can for metric units of length. Make a list on the board in order of increasing size.

Metric Length System
centimeters
decimeters
meters
kilometers

Show students a meter stick. Have a student point out where 10 centimeters lies on the meter stick. Tell students this is 1 decimeter.

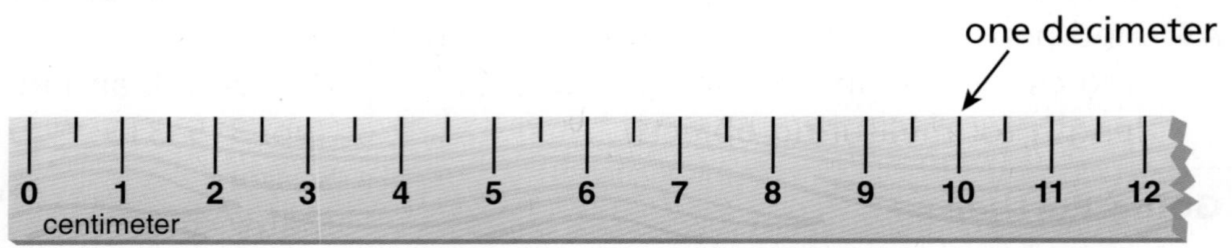

- How many centimeters are on the meter stick? 100
- How many decimeters are on the meter stick? 10

▶ Measure to the Nearest Centimeter, Decimeter, and Meter SMALL GROUPS

Divide students into **Small Groups** of 3 or 4. Give each **Small Group** a meter stick and have them estimate and measure classroom objects to the nearest centimeter, decimeter, and meter and record their results. Have students make and complete a table like the one below to record their results.

Classroom Object to Measure in m, dm, or cm	Estimate of Length	Actual Length
Length of pencil (cm)		
Width of desk (dm)		
Length of classroom (m)		

13–3 Class Activity Name Date

Vocabulary
centimeter (cm)

► Estimate and Measure Length

Estimate the length of each line segment in centimeters. Then measure it to the nearest centimeter.

1 cm

1. Estimate: Answers will vary. Actual: 3 cm
2. Estimate: Answers will vary. Actual: 5 cm
3. Estimate: Answers will vary. Actual: 5 cm
4. Estimate: Answers will vary. Actual: 8 cm
5. Estimate: Answers will vary. Actual: 6 cm
6. Estimate the length of these items in your classroom. Then measure to the nearest centimeter. Record your information in the chart. Check students' tables.

	Estimate (cm)	Actual (cm)
pair of scissors		
gluestick		
pencil		
marker		

UNIT 13 LESSON 3 Centimeters, Decimeters, and Meters **481**

Student Activity Book page 481

► Estimate and Measure Length WHOLE CLASS

Refer students to Student Book page 481. Students will need a centimeter ruler to complete this page. If students do not have centimeter rulers, have them use Centimeter Rulers (TRB M26).

Be sure students understand that they need to estimate the length of the segment first in centimeters. Then they will measure to the nearest centimeter. Remind students that when a measurement is halfway or more than halfway between two centimeters, round up. When it is less than halfway, round down.

- What is the measure of a line segment that measures more than halfway to 6 centimeters? 6 cm
- What is the measure of a line segment than measures less than halfway to 6 cm? 5 cm

Have students complete the page.

Alternate Approach

Students may choose objects to measure in the classroom that are different from those listed in the table. They should, however, measure one object to the nearest centimeter, one to the nearest decimeter, and one to the nearest meter.

English Language Learners

Write *estimate* on the board. Draw a line about 10 cm long on the board. Say: **I *estimate* this line is 10 centimeters.**

- **Beginning** Say: **I did not measure. I do not know exactly.** Ask: **Is an *estimate* a good guess?** yes
- **Intermediate** Ask: **Is an *estimate* a good guess or an exact answer?** good guess
- **Advanced** Ask: **Do I know for certain?** no Say: **An *estimate* is a good __.** guess Ask: **What do I do to get an exact answer?** measure

Class Management

You may wish to make a transparency of the page and have volunteers use a transparent ruler to show how they estimated and measured each line segment.

Activity 2

Convert Between Metric Units of Length

 **20 MINUTES**

Goal: Use function tables to convert metric units of length.

Materials: Meter stick, Student Activity Book or Hardcover Book pp. 482–483 and Activity Workbook pp. 244–245 (includes tables)

 **NCTM Standards:**
Number and Operations
Measurement
Communication
Representation

Differentiated Instruction

Extra Help Display a meter stick at the front of the class with centimeters and decimeters labeled as a visual aid. This may help students to form a mental picture of the measurement as they do conversions; for example, it may help them to put together 3 meter sticks mentally to make 300 centimeters. This activity is excellent for **English learners** because it involves working with a visual.

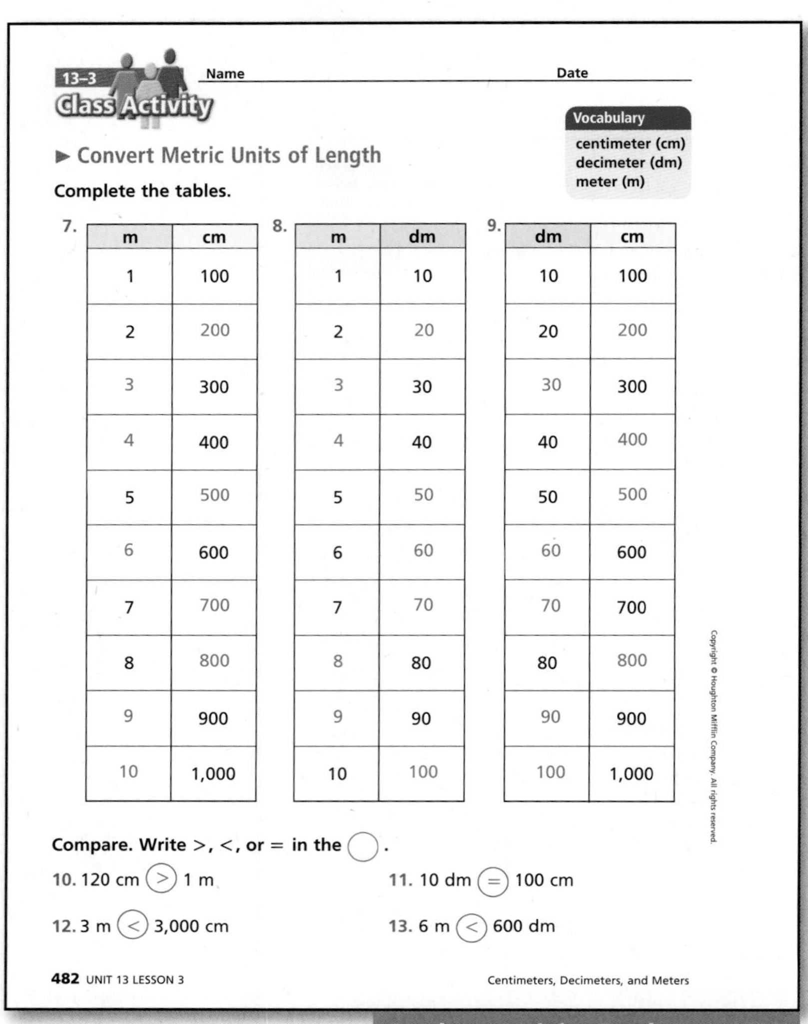

13–3 Class Activity

Name ______ Date ______

Vocabulary
centimeter (cm)
decimeter (dm)
meter (m)

▸ Convert Metric Units of Length

Complete the tables.

7.

m	cm
1	100
2	200
3	300
4	400
5	500
6	600
7	700
8	800
9	900
10	1,000

8.

m	dm
1	10
2	20
3	30
4	40
5	50
6	60
7	70
8	80
9	90
10	100

9.

dm	cm
10	100
20	200
30	300
40	400
50	500
60	600
70	700
80	800
90	900
100	1,000

Compare. Write $>$, $<$, or $=$ in the ◯.

10. 120 cm ($>$) 1 m
11. 10 dm ($=$) 100 cm
12. 3 m ($<$) 3,000 cm
13. 6 m ($<$) 600 dm

482 UNIT 13 LESSON 3 Centimeters, Decimeters, and Meters

Student Activity Book page 482

▸ Convert Metric Units of Length WHOLE CLASS

Ask students to think about how metric units are based on groups of ten. Using a meter stick, point out that there are 100 centimeters in a meter.

Examine the first function table as a class. Review that a function table shows the relationship between two sets of numbers.

- What do the numbers 100 and 1 tell us in the first row of the table? There are 100 centimeters in 1 meter
- How is the number in the first column related to the number in the second column? Multiply the first column number by 100 to get the second column number.

Have students complete exercise 7. Then have student volunteers give their answers and explain how they got them.

Then ask a volunteer to point out a decimeter on a meter stick. Have students skip count to show the number of decimeters in a meter.

- How many decimeters in 2 m? 20 dm

Have students complete the function table in exercise 8. Then check the answers together.

Hold up the meter stick and have a volunteer use the meter stick to show that 10 dm = 100 cm. Ask students:

- If 10 decimeters equals 100 centimeters, or this whole meter stick, then how many decimeters are in 200 centimeters, or two whole meter sticks? 20 decimeters
- How many decimeters in 3 whole meter sticks, or 300 centimeters? 30 decimeters

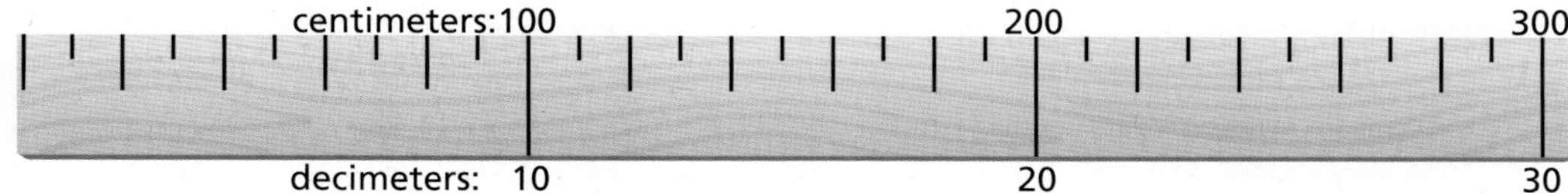

Have students complete the function table in exercise 9. Then check the answers together.

Then work through exercise 10 together.

- What do you need to do to compare these units? Convert the measurement in centimeters to meters or convert the measurement in meters to centimeters.
- How many centimeters in 1 meter? 100
- What sign will you write in the circle? the greater than sign

Have students work in helping pairs to complete exercises 11–13.

For exercise 14 on Student Book page 483, you might have students skip count by tens on the meter stick to find the first few rows of the table.

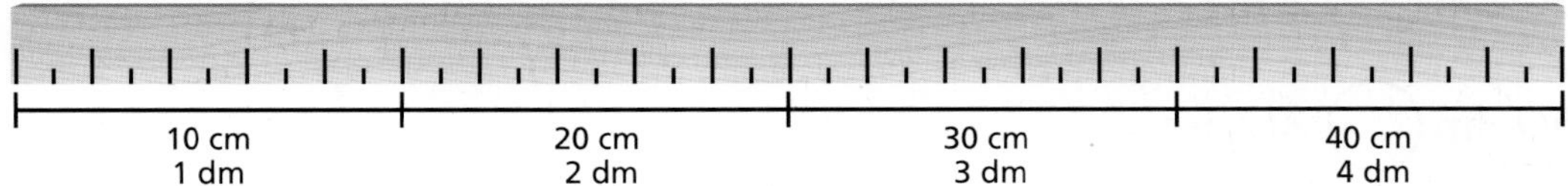

Invite a Student Leader to skip count centimeters by 10, while the class gives decimeters and fills in the table.

The Learning Classroom

Building Concepts Remind students they can fill in the function tables by finding a pattern. Work with them to make sure they can identify the correct pattern for each table. If they use this strategy, help them to also understand how the units are related on the meter stick.

Activity continued ▶

Differentiated Instruction

Extra Help If students are struggling with completing the tables because they are having difficulty multiplying by 10 or 100, you might suggest they try repeated addition. To find the number of decimeters in 4 meters, they can add 10 dm + 10 dm + 10 dm + 10 dm = 40 dm.

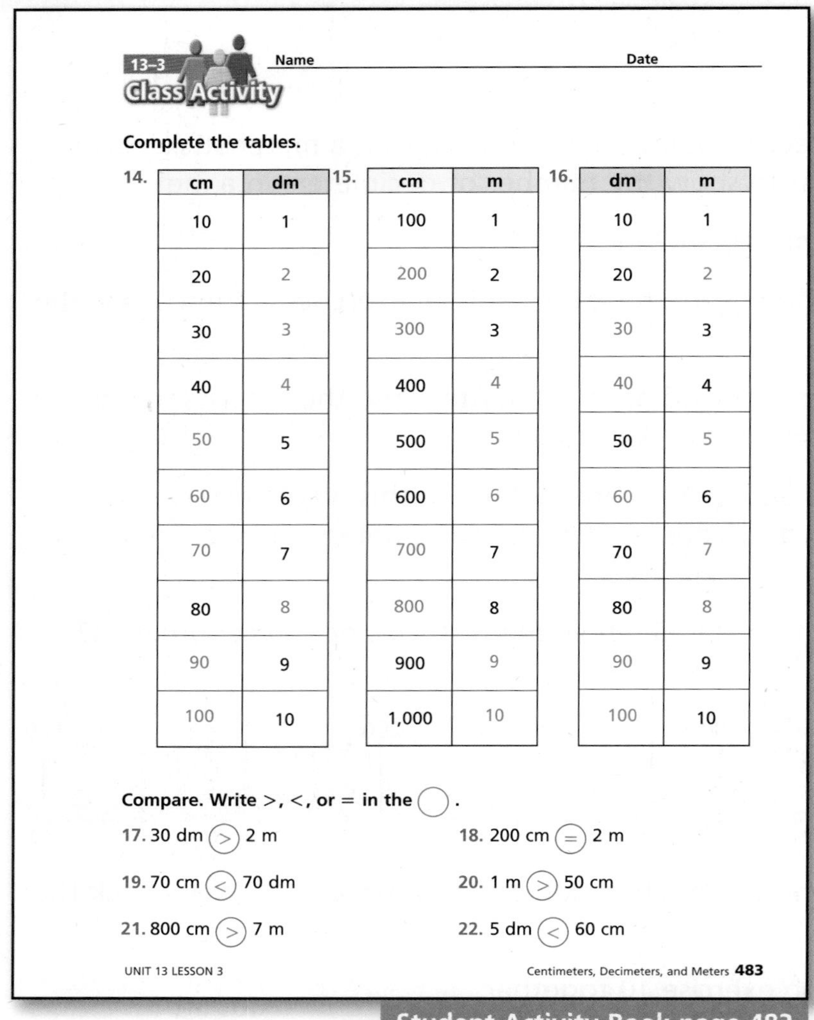

13-3 Class Activity

Name ____________ Date ____________

Complete the tables.

14.

cm	dm
10	1
20	2
30	3
40	4
50	5
60	6
70	7
80	8
90	9
100	10

15.

cm	m
100	1
200	2
300	3
400	4
500	5
600	6
700	7
800	8
900	9
1,000	10

16.

dm	m
10	1
20	2
30	3
40	4
50	5
60	6
70	7
80	8
90	9
100	10

Compare. Write >, <, or = in the ◯.

17. 30 dm (>) 2 m
18. 200 cm (=) 2 m
19. 70 cm (<) 70 dm
20. 1 m (>) 50 cm
21. 800 cm (>) 7 m
22. 5 dm (<) 60 cm

UNIT 13 LESSON 3 Centimeters, Decimeters, and Meters **483**

Student Activity Book page 483

Have students complete the function tables in exercises 15 and 16 and check their answers together. Then work through exercise 17 together.

- What do you need to do to compare these units? Convert the measurement in meters to decimeters or convert the measurement in decimeters to meters.
- How many decimeters in 2 meters? 20

Write the following on the board:

30 dm ◯ 2 m

30 dm ◯ 20 dm

What sign will you write in the circles? the greater than sign

Have students work in helping pairs to complete exercises 18–22.

Activity 3

Established Benchmarks and Choose Units

▶ Discuss Benchmarks for Metric Units of Length

WHOLE CLASS

Math Talk

Review the list of metric measurements of length that you wrote on the board earlier in this lesson.

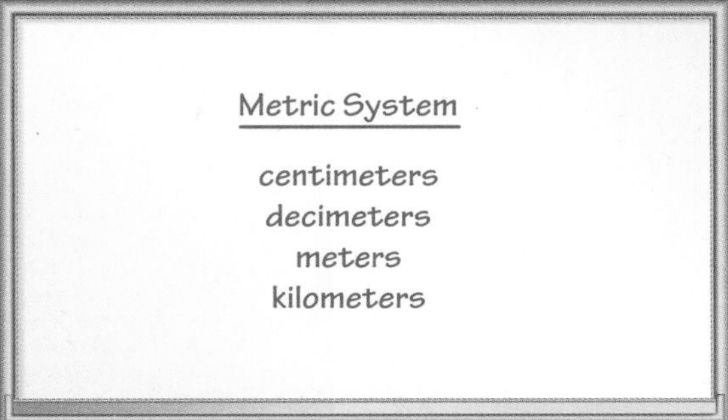

Review the meaning of *benchmark.*

- A benchmark can help you estimate the length of an object or a distance.

Display the meter stick, and work with students to find benchmarks for a centimeter, decimeter, and meter. Some examples are shown below.

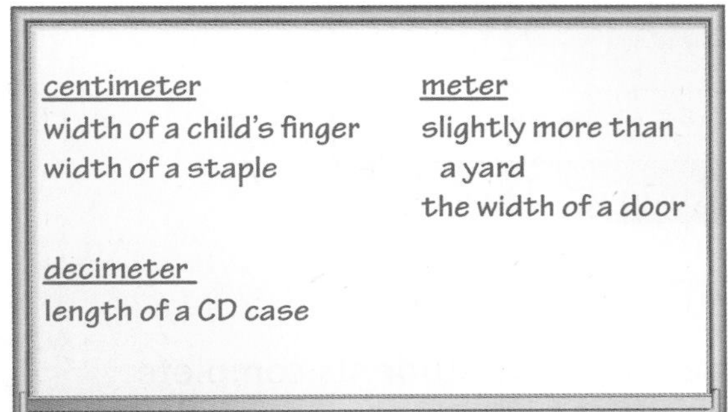

Introduce the idea that a kilometer is the distance students can walk in about 10 minutes.

Ask students to name objects in the classroom they would measure in centimeters, then use the benchmark to estimate the measure of that object. Repeat for meter and decimeter.

15 MINUTES

Goal: Find benchmarks for metric units of length and choose an appropriate unit of metric length for measuring objects.

Materials: Meter stick, Student Activity Book or Hardcover Book p. 484

NCTM Standards:
Measurement
Communication
Representation

Teaching Note

Measuring in the Real World Make sure students understand how every-day objects can be measured in mixed units (for example, meters and centimeters and so on). Encourage students to measure objects in the classroom with meter sticks and centimeter rulers to demonstrate how objects can have both units of length in their measurements. For example, the width of the doorway is 2 m 3 cm. In later grades, mixed metric measurements will be written as decimals.

Ongoing Assessment

Ask students to explain how centimeters, decimeters, and meters are related.

Activity continued ▶

Teaching Note

Math Background It is important that students understand that a centimeter is not the rough equivalent of an inch. When finding a benchmark for a centimeter, show students a ruler with centimeters and inches, and point out that a centimeter is less than half of an inch.

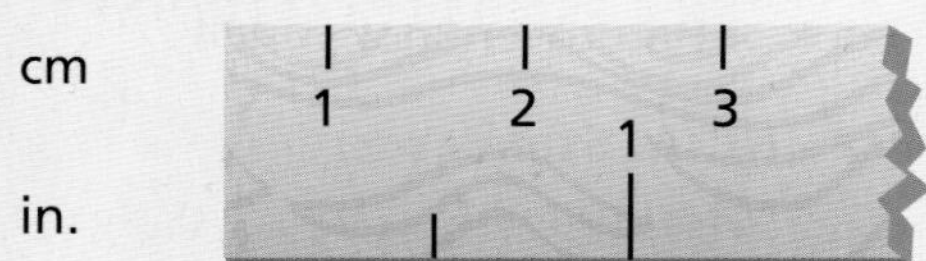

State Standards

If your state requires an understanding of the relationships between yards and meters and miles and kilometers, take this opportunity to compare the benchmarks for yards and miles students used in Lesson 2 with the benchmarks students used in this lesson for meters and kilometers. For example, if students used the height of a door knob for a yard, have a volunteer show how high a meter is in comparison. If a person can walk a kilometer in 10 minutes, then it would take them half again that time or about 15 minutes to walk a mile. Then estimate lengths and distances in both systems using benchmarks and compare the results.

13-3 Class Activity Name ______ Date ______

Vocabulary
centimeter (cm)
decimeter (dm)
meter (m)
kilometer (km)

▶ Find Benchmarks

23. This line segment is 1 **centimeter** long. Use your little finger to show 1 centimeter. Write an object that is about 1 cm (or your little finger width) long.
Possible answer: width of a staple

24. One **decimeter** is equal to 10 cm. This line segment is 1 decimeter long. Spread your hand to show 1 decimeter. Write an object that is about 1 dm (or your hand spread out) long.
Possible answer: small tape dispenser

25. One **meter** is equal to 100 cm. How many decimeters are in one meter? Write an object or distance that is about 1 meter long.
10 dm; Possible answer: the height of a doorknob

26. One **kilometer** is 1,000 meters. It takes you about 10 minutes to walk a kilometer. Write the name of a place that is about 1 km from your house.
Answers will vary.

▶ Choose the Appropriate Unit

Choose the unit you would use to measure each. Write *centimeter, decimeter, meter,* or *kilometer.* Possible answers:

27. the width of your classroom meter
28. the distance you fly on an airplane kilometer
29. the length of a pencil centimeter or decimeter
30. the length of your fingernail centimeter

484 UNIT 13 LESSON 3 Centimeters, Decimeters, and Meters

Student Activity Book page 484

▶ Find Benchmarks INDIVIDUALS

Refer students to Student Book page 484. Have students complete exercises 23–26. Then have volunteers explain their answers.

▶ Choose the Appropriate Unit SMALL GROUPS

Ask students:

- Which unit would you use to measure the length of a marker? Possible answer: centimeters
- Which unit would you use to measure the length of a stadium? Possible answer: meters
- Which unit would you use to measure the width of your desk? Possible answer: centimeters or decimeters
- Which unit would you use to measure the distance you could walk in half an hour? Possible answer: kilometers

Then have students complete exercises 27–30.

2 Going Further

Differentiated Instruction

Intervention — Activity Card 13-3

Metric Measurement — Activity Card 13-3 ●

Work: In pairs

Use:

- Meter stick

Decide:

Who will be Student 1 and who will be Student 2 for the first round.

1. **Student 1:** Use the meter stick to draw a line segment that is evenly divisible by 10; for example, 60 centimeters or 90 centimeters.
2. **Student 2:** Estimate the length of the line segment that your partner drew. Use the meter stick to measure the segment in centimeters and again in decimeters. Record each measurement. Have your partner to check your work.

   Estimate: ______ cm
   Actual: ______ cm
   ______ dm

3. Change roles and repeat the activity. Each time, draw a line segment with a length that is divisible by 10.

Unit 13, Lesson 3

Activity Note Encourage students to develop benchmarks to help them estimate line segments. Have students recall how to convert centimeters to decimeters before beginning the activity.

Math Writing Prompt

Reasonable Answer Would you measure the distance between two towns in centimeters, meters, kilometers, or decimeters? Explain why you chose that unit of length.

Software Support

Warm Up 38.14

On Level — Activity Card 13-3

Make 5 Meters — Activity Card 13-3 ▲

Work: In pairs

Use:

- Math Journals
- 8 Index cards

1. Make a set of 8 index cards labeled with the distances shown below. Place them in a stack face down.

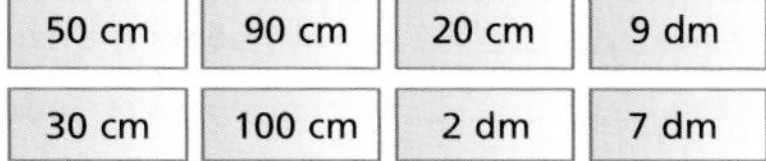

50 cm	90 cm	20 cm	9 dm
30 cm	100 cm	2 dm	7 dm

2. Take turns choosing a card and adding the distance to your total. Then return the card to the bottom of the stack. 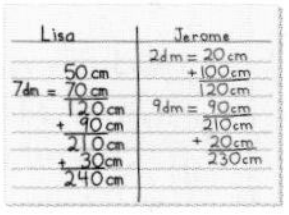
3. The first player to reach a total of 5 meters wins.

Unit 13, Lesson 3

Activity Note Students will probably find it easier to translate decimeters into centimeters before adding. Have students also recall how to convert centimeters to meters before beginning the activity.

Math Writing Prompt

Math-to-Math Connections How are a centimeter and a meter similar to an inch and a foot? How are they different?

Software Support

The Number Games: Tiny's Think Tank, Level Q

Challenge — Activity Card 13-3

Meters of Spaghetti — Activity Card 13-3 ■

Work: In small groups

Use:

- Meter sticks
- Centimeter rulers
- Box of spaghetti
- Calculator

1. **Work Together** Imagine laying all the spaghetti in a box end to end. Estimate how many meters long all the spaghetti in a box would be. 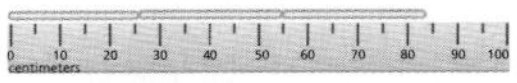
2. Discuss which strategies you could use to make your estimate. Is it possible to measure each piece of spaghetti? Is there a way to estimate a total by measuring just one piece? Would it help to know how many pieces equal one meter?
3. Compare your estimate with those of other groups.
4. **Analyze** Determine the strategy that each group used and decide which one was the best to use.

Unit 13, Lesson 3

Activity Note Students might measure one piece of spaghetti and multiply it by the number in the box, or they might determine how many equal one meter and divide the number of pieces by that amount.

Math Writing Prompt

You Decide Which units of measurement are easier for you to convert, customary units or metric units? Explain.

DESTINATION Math® **Software Support**

Course II: Module 4: Unit 1: Number Patterns and Properties

Homework and Spiral Review

13–3 **Homework** **Goal:** Additional Practice

This Homework page provides practice in using and converting metric units of length.

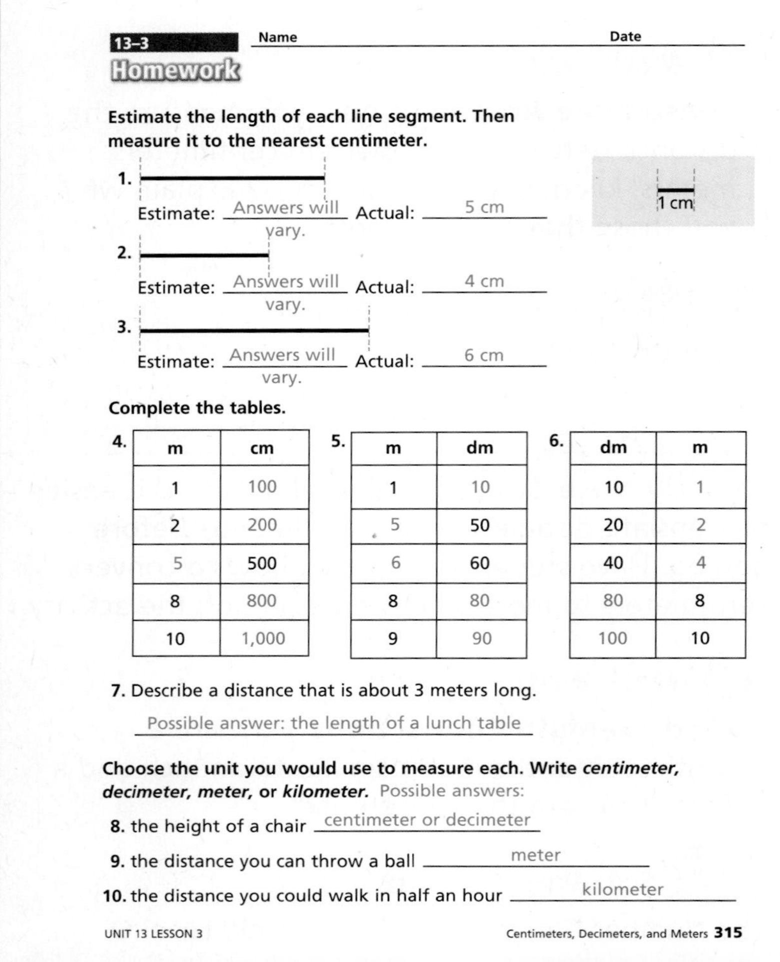

13–3 **Homework** Name ____ Date ____

Estimate the length of each line segment. Then measure it to the nearest centimeter.

1. Estimate: Answers will vary. Actual: 5 cm

1 cm

2. Estimate: Answers will vary. Actual: 4 cm

3. Estimate: Answers will vary. Actual: 6 cm

Complete the tables.

4.

m	cm
1	100
2	200
5	500
8	800
10	1,000

5.

m	dm
1	10
5	50
6	60
8	80
9	90

6.

dm	m
10	1
20	2
40	4
80	8
100	10

7. Describe a distance that is about 3 meters long.
Possible answer: the length of a lunch table

Choose the unit you would use to measure each. Write *centimeter*, *decimeter*, *meter*, or *kilometer*. Possible answers:

8. the height of a chair centimeter or decimeter
9. the distance you can throw a ball meter
10. the distance you could walk in half an hour kilometer

UNIT 13 LESSON 3 Centimeters, Decimeters, and Meters **315**

Homework and Remembering page 315

13–3 **Remembering** **Goal:** Spiral Review

This Remembering page would be appropriate anytime after today's lesson.

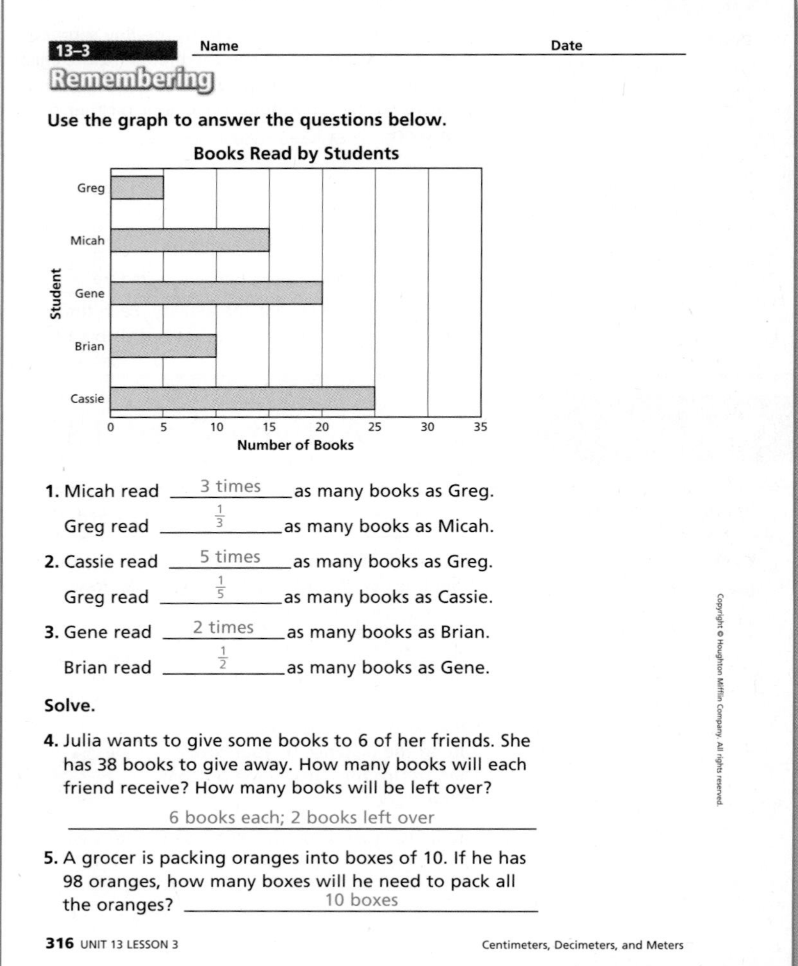

13–3 **Remembering** Name ____ Date ____

Use the graph to answer the questions below.

1. Micah read 3 times as many books as Greg.
   Greg read $\frac{1}{3}$ as many books as Micah.
2. Cassie read 5 times as many books as Greg.
   Greg read $\frac{1}{5}$ as many books as Cassie.
3. Gene read 2 times as many books as Brian.
   Brian read $\frac{1}{2}$ as many books as Gene.

Solve.

4. Julia wants to give some books to 6 of her friends. She has 38 books to give away. How many books will each friend receive? How many books will be left over?
   6 books each; 2 books left over
5. A grocer is packing oranges into boxes of 10. If he has 98 oranges, how many boxes will he need to pack all the oranges? 10 boxes

316 UNIT 13 LESSON 3 Centimeters, Decimeters, and Meters

Homework and Remembering page 316

Home or School Activity

Physical Education Connection

Olympic Distances Running races in the Olympics are measured in metric units of length. In the 2004 Olympics in Athens, Greece, Lauryn Williams ran the 100-meter dash in a little less than 11 seconds. She placed second in the race.

Use a meter stick to mark off 100 meters. Have a friend time you using a stopwatch or the second hand of a watch. How fast can you run the 100-meter dash? How does your time compare with Lauryn Williams's time?

Add Lengths

Lesson Objectives

- Measure sides of figures to the nearest quarter inch.
- Add measurements to find perimeter.
- Add customary lengths in inches, half inches, and quarter inches.
- Estimate perimeter and area.

Vocabulary
perimeter
area

The Day at a Glance

Today's Goals	Materials	
1 Teaching the Lesson A1: Measure perimeter to the nearest quarter-inch. A2: Estimate Perimeter in inches. A3: Estimate Area in square inches and square centimeters. A4: Add lengths in fractions of inches. **2 Going Further** ► Differentiated Instruction **3 Homework and Spiral Review**	**Lesson Activities** Student Activity Book pp. 485–486 or Student Hardcover Book pp. 485–486 Homework and Remembering pp. 317–318 Quick Quiz 1 Inch Rulers (TRB M144) Inch Grid Paper (TRB M42) Centimeter Grid Paper (TRB M31) Centimeter Rulers Geoboards or Dot Array on Mathboard Rubber bands or dry erase markers	**Going Further** Activity Cards 13-4 Zig Zag (TRB M145) String Inch Rulers Tape Scissors Math Journals

Use Math Talk today!

Keeping Skills Sharp

Quick Practice (5 MINUTES)

Goal: Find equivalent fractions.

Equivalence Chains Have a **Student Leader** write a fraction on the board. As volunteers take turns identifying the equivalent fractions for the fraction in order (up to $\frac{10 \times \text{numerator}}{10 \times \text{denominator}}$), the **Student Leader** writes the fractions on the board as an equivalence chain. (See Unit 11 Lesson 13.)

Daily Routines

Homework Review Set aside time to work with students needing extra help.

Nonroutine Problem Two shirts cost $24 in all. One shirt costs twice as much as the other shirt. How much does each shirt cost? Explain how you found your answer. $16 and $8; $24 \div 3 = 8$; $24 - 8 = 16$

$24 in all
first shirt
2 times the cost of the first shirt

1 Teaching the Lesson

Activity 1

Add to Find Perimeter

 30 MINUTES

Goal: Measure perimeter to the nearest quarter-inch.

Materials: Rulers or Inch Rulers (TRB M144), Student Activity Book or Hardcover Book p. 485

 **NCTM Standards:**
Number and Operations
Measurement
Communication
Representation

Differentiated Instruction

Extra Help To reinforce the connection between improper fractions and mixed numbers, count off the unit fractions on a ruler and look at the corresponding mixed number. For example to reinforce that $\frac{5}{4} = 1\frac{1}{4}$ you might count off 5 fourth marks on the ruler.

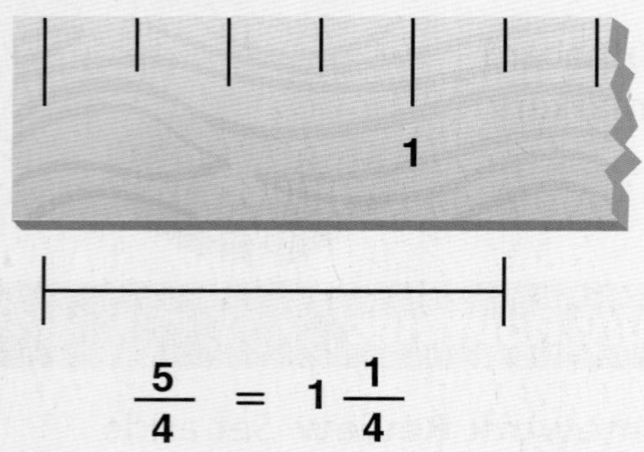

Teaching Note

Watch For! Some students may still not be clear about how to record measurements to the nearest quarter inch. They may be confused about recording a measurement that falls nearest a one-half mark. Point out the quarter-inch marks on a ruler. Help students understand that the $\frac{1}{2}$ mark is also the $\frac{2}{4}$ mark.

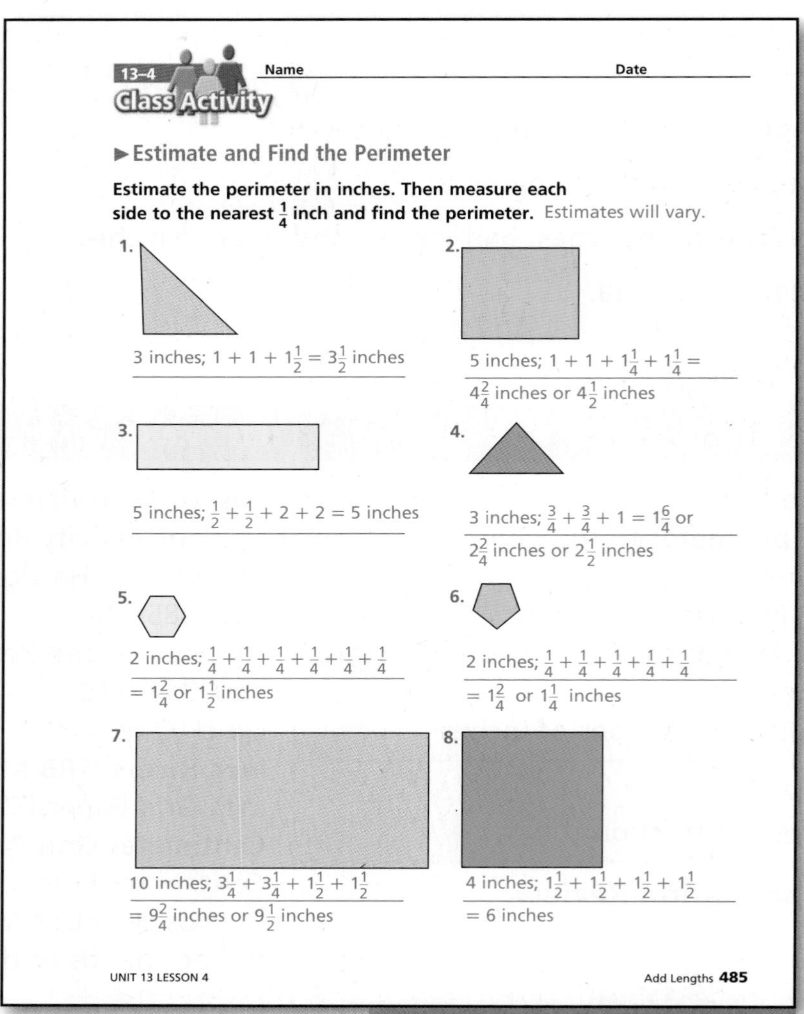

13–4 Class Activity

Name Date

▶ Estimate and Find the Perimeter

Estimate the perimeter in inches. Then measure each side to the nearest $\frac{1}{4}$ inch and find the perimeter. Estimates will vary.

1. 3 inches; $1 + 1 + 1\frac{1}{2} = 3\frac{1}{2}$ inches

2. 5 inches; $1 + 1 + 1\frac{1}{4} + 1\frac{1}{4} = 4\frac{2}{4}$ inches or $4\frac{1}{2}$ inches

3. 5 inches; $\frac{1}{2} + \frac{1}{2} + 2 + 2 = 5$ inches

4. 3 inches; $\frac{3}{4} + \frac{3}{4} + 1 = 1\frac{6}{4}$ or $2\frac{2}{4}$ inches or $2\frac{1}{2}$ inches

5. 2 inches; $\frac{1}{4} + \frac{1}{4} + \frac{1}{4} + \frac{1}{4} + \frac{1}{4} + \frac{1}{4} = 1\frac{2}{4}$ or $1\frac{1}{2}$ inches

6. 2 inches; $\frac{1}{4} + \frac{1}{4} + \frac{1}{4} + \frac{1}{4} + \frac{1}{4} = 1\frac{2}{4}$ or $1\frac{1}{4}$ inches

7. 10 inches; $3\frac{1}{4} + 3\frac{1}{4} + 1\frac{1}{2} + 1\frac{1}{2} = 9\frac{2}{4}$ inches or $9\frac{1}{2}$ inches

8. 4 inches; $1\frac{1}{2} + 1\frac{1}{2} + 1\frac{1}{2} + 1\frac{1}{2} = 6$ inches

UNIT 13 LESSON 4 Add Lengths 485

Student Activity Book page 485

▶ Estimate and Find the Perimeter WHOLE CLASS

On the board, draw a rectangle with the sides labeled as shown.

$3\frac{1}{2}$ feet, $4\frac{1}{2}$ feet

Ask for volunteers to explain how to find the perimeter of the figure.

$$\text{Perimeter: } 3\tfrac{1}{2}\text{ feet} + 3\tfrac{1}{2}\text{ feet} + 4\tfrac{1}{2}\text{ feet} + 4\tfrac{1}{2}\text{ feet} = 14 + \tfrac{4}{2} = 14 + 2 = 16\text{ feet}$$

Summarize that to add mixed numbers, first add the whole numbers and then add the fractions. If the sum of the fractions is an improper fraction, write it as a whole or mixed number and add it to the sum of the whole numbers.

Have students complete Student Book page 485.

Activity 2

Estimate Perimeter

▶ Estimate Perimeter of Real-World Objects

SMALL GROUPS

Ask for Ideas To estimate the perimeter of the figures on Student Book page 485, what did you need to know? The approximate length of each side.

- How did you estimate the length of each? Possible response: Used two fingers as an estimate for an inch. Then estimated the number of "two finger" lengths around the figure.

Small Groups should find three objects in the classroom that they can estimate and measure the perimeter of (for example, a book, a piece of paper, the top of a pencil case, and so on).

Once students have gathered their objects, they should visualize their inch referent and estimate the perimeter of each object. Remind students how to find the perimeter of an object. Add up all the lengths of the sides.

Students can check their estimates by measuring with the side of the squares or by using an inch or centimeter ruler. Have students discuss how close their estimates were to the actual measurements.

 **15 MINUTES**

Goal: Estimate perimeter in inches

Materials: Inch Grid Paper (TRB M42), inch and centimeter rulers

 **NCTM Standards:**
Number and Operations
Measurement

Activity 3

Estimate Area

▶ Relative Size of a Square Inch and Square Centimeter

SMALL GROUPS

Ask for Ideas In Unit 8 you found the area of figures and real-world objects in square centimeters.

- What is area? Area is the number of square units that covers the flat surface of a figure or object.
- How could you estimate the area of a book's cover in square units? Possible response: Visualize about how many square units would fit on the surface.

Pass out Inch Grid Paper to half of the students and Centimeter Grid Paper to the other half of the class. Then have groups cut out one square from their papers. Explain that each of these squares represents a square unit. Some groups have a square inch and others have a square

Activity continued ▶

 **15 MINUTES**

Goal: Establish a referent for a square inch; Estimate area in square inches and square centimeters.

Materials: Inch Grid Paper (TRB M42), Centimeter Grid Paper (TRB M31), Inch and Centimeter Rulers, objects from Activity 2, geoboards or Dot Array on MathBoard, rubber bands or dry erase markers

 **NCTM Standards:**
Number and Operations
Geometry
Measurement

English Language Learners

Draw a line about 10 in. long on the board. Measure it with your thumb. Write and say: **This line is *about* 10 inches long.**

- **Beginning** Ask: **Is the measurement exact?** no **Is it an *estimate*?** yes
- **Intermediate** Ask: **Does *about* mean the measurement is exact or an *estimate*?** estimate
- **Advanced** Say: **The measurement is not __.** exact **It is an __.** estimate

centimeter. Have groups explore the classroom to find things that take up an area of one square inch or one square centimeter so they can develop a personal referent to help them estimate area. Have students share what they might use as a personal referent for a square inch or square centimeter. (Examples: square inch: postage stamp, quarters; square centimeter: sticker, head of thumb tack).

▶ Estimate Area of Real World Objects SMALL GROUPS

For this activity, groups should continue to use the three objects they used from Activity 2. (For example, a book, a piece of paper, the top of a pencil case, and so on). Make sure all **Small Groups** have inch grid and centimeter grid paper to check their estimates.

Students should look at their objects and estimate the area of each object. Remind students that the area is how many square units will fit on top of the surface of an object. Have students share the different ways they estimated the area and discuss the methods as a class.

Students can check their estimates by placing inch squares or centimeter squares on top of the object. Have students discuss how close their estimates were to the actual measurements. Point out to students that a whole square may not fit evenly on the object and sometimes students may have to visualize parts of squares making up a whole square.

▶ Estimate Area on the Geoboard SMALL GROUPS

As time allows, have **Small Groups** investigate and estimate the area of non-rectangular shapes on the geoboard or Dot Array of their MathBoards. Challenge students to make various shapes and use different strategies to estimate the area.

Use the following discussion points to help students with estimating.

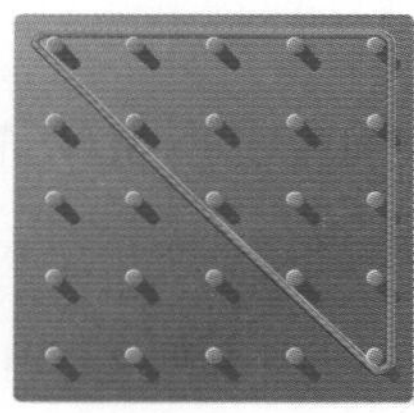

- There are 6 whole squares.
- There are 4 half squares which make two whole squares.
- 4 plus 6 is 10.
- So, the area is about 10 square units.

Activity 4

Practice Adding Customary Lengths

▶ Add Customary Units of Length WHOLE CLASS

Write the following exercises on the board.

A. 1 in. + $1\frac{1}{4}$ in.

B. $1\frac{3}{4}$ in. + $1\frac{1}{4}$ in.

C. $1\frac{1}{2}$ in. + $1\frac{1}{4}$ in.

Math Talk Discuss how the exercises on the board are different. Make sure the following points are made.

- Exercise A is a whole number plus a mixed number.
- Exercise B is a mixed number plus a mixed number with the same denominators.
- Exercise C is a mixed number plus a mixed number with different denominators.

Then have the students solve the first exercise in pairs. Discuss methods and answers as a class.

- What numbers did you add first? Possible answer: add the whole numbers; 1 + 1 = 2.
- What was your next step? Add the fractional part; 2 in. + $\frac{1}{4}$ in. = $2\frac{1}{4}$.

Move to the second exercise on the board. Again, have the students find the sum in pairs. Discuss methods and answers as a class.

- What numbers did you add first? Possible answer: $\frac{3}{4} + \frac{1}{4} = \frac{4}{4}$ or 1.
- What did you do next? Add the whole numbers, then add the sum to the sum of the fractional part. 1 + 1 = 2; 2 + 1 = 3

You may wish to have students draw line segments to "prove" their answers. For example, a student volunteer draws a $1\frac{3}{4}$-inch line using a ruler, then adds a $1\frac{1}{4}$-inch line segment to one end of the first line segment. The student then measures the whole segment. The sum should match the length of the line segment.

Activity continued ▶

30 MINUTES

Goal: Add lengths in fractions of inches.

Materials: Student Activity Book or Hardcover Book p. 486

NCTM Standards:
Number and Operations
Measurement
Communication
Representation

Ongoing Assessment

Ask students to explain how they can find the perimeter of a sheet of paper that is $8\frac{1}{2}$ inches by 11 inches.

Teaching the Lesson (continued)

Differentiated Instruction

Advanced Learners The exercises on Student Book page 486 include adding halves and fourths. If you feel some students are ready, you might write some similar exercises on the board using eighths or sixteenths and have them work on them individually or in groups. For example,

$8\frac{1}{8}$ in. + $7\frac{5}{16}$ in. = ☐ $15\frac{7}{16}$ in.

or

$6\frac{1}{2}$ in. + $2\frac{1}{16}$ in. = ☐ $8\frac{9}{16}$ in.

Quick Quiz

See Assessment Guide for Unit 13 Quick Quiz 1.

Class Management

Looking Ahead Remind students to bring in empty, clean milk containers. You will need them in Lesson 5.

Finally, move to the third problem on the board. Have students work together or individually to find the sum. Discuss what extra step must be taken when addends have different denominators.

- What numbers did you add first? Possible answer: $\frac{1}{2}$ in. and $\frac{1}{4}$ in. = $\frac{3}{4}$ in.
- What did you have to do before you added the fractions? Rename $\frac{1}{2}$ in. as $\frac{2}{4}$ in.
- What was your next step? Add the whole numbers. Then add the sum to the fractional part. $1 + 1 = 2$; $2 + \frac{3}{4} = 2\frac{3}{4}$ inches

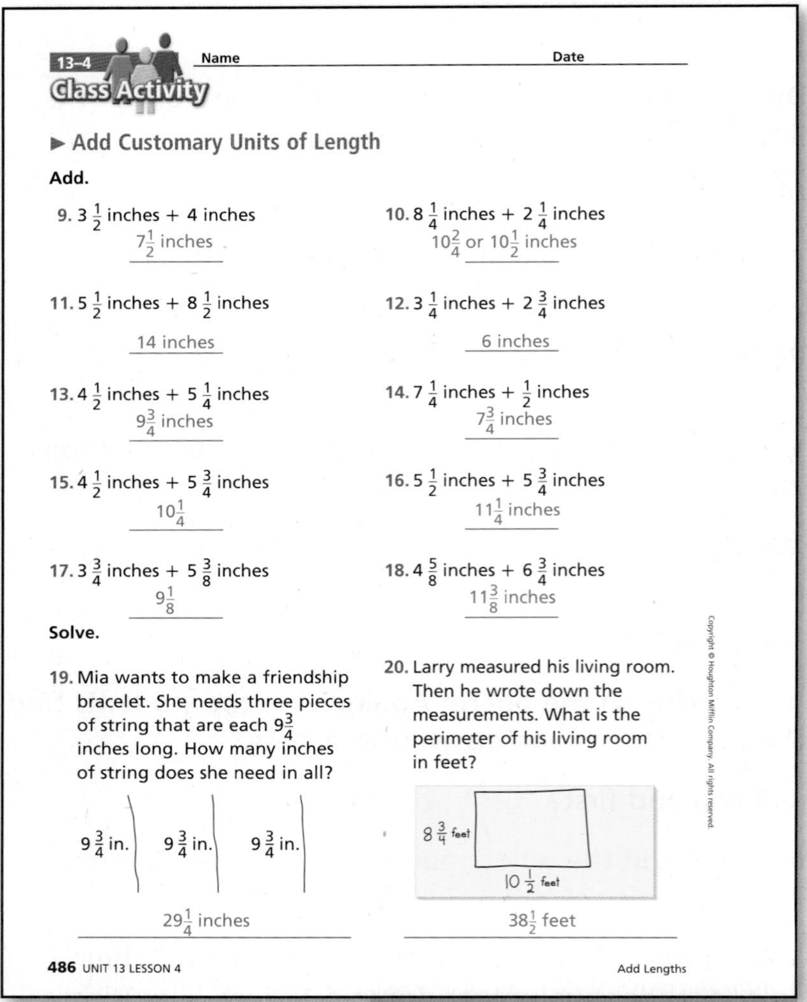

13–4 Class Activity Name Date

▶ Add Customary Units of Length

Add.

9. $3\frac{1}{2}$ inches + 4 inches $7\frac{1}{2}$ inches

10. $8\frac{1}{4}$ inches + $2\frac{1}{4}$ inches $10\frac{2}{4}$ or $10\frac{1}{2}$ inches

11. $5\frac{1}{2}$ inches + $8\frac{1}{2}$ inches 14 inches

12. $3\frac{1}{4}$ inches + $2\frac{3}{4}$ inches 6 inches

13. $4\frac{1}{2}$ inches + $5\frac{1}{4}$ inches $9\frac{3}{4}$ inches

14. $7\frac{1}{4}$ inches + $\frac{1}{2}$ inches $7\frac{3}{4}$ inches

15. $4\frac{1}{2}$ inches + $5\frac{3}{4}$ inches $10\frac{1}{4}$

16. $5\frac{1}{2}$ inches + $5\frac{3}{4}$ inches $11\frac{1}{4}$ inches

17. $3\frac{3}{4}$ inches + $5\frac{3}{8}$ inches $9\frac{1}{8}$

18. $4\frac{5}{8}$ inches + $6\frac{3}{4}$ inches $11\frac{3}{8}$ inches

Solve.

19. Mia wants to make a friendship bracelet. She needs three pieces of string that are each $9\frac{3}{4}$ inches long. How many inches of string does she need in all?

$9\frac{3}{4}$ in. $9\frac{3}{4}$ in. $9\frac{3}{4}$ in.

$29\frac{1}{4}$ inches

20. Larry measured his living room. Then he wrote down the measurements. What is the perimeter of his living room in feet?

$8\frac{3}{4}$ feet $10\frac{1}{2}$ feet

$38\frac{1}{2}$ feet

486 UNIT 13 LESSON 4 Add Lengths

Student Activity Book page 486

Refer students to Student Book page 486. Have students complete the page in pairs. As students complete the page, walk around the room and monitor their progress.

2 Going Further

Differentiated Instruction

Intervention

Activity Card 13-4

Zig Zag

Activity Card 13-4

Work: In pairs

Use:

- TRB M145 (Zig Zag)
- String
- Inch Rulers
- Tape
- Scissors

1. **Work Together** Estimate the total length of the zig zag line segment in Exercise 1 and record your estimate.
2. Now measure each line segment to find the actual total length of the zig zag line segment. Record the length that you measured.

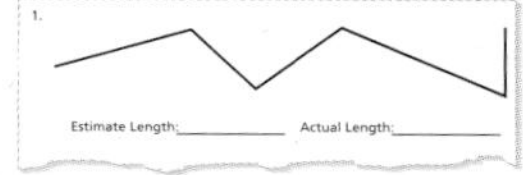

3. Check your work by taping a string along each segment of the zig zag from beginning to end. Cut the string at the end of the last segment. Remove the string and measure its length.
4. **Analyze** How close was your estimate to the actual length?

Unit 13, Lesson 4

Activity Note This activity will work best if the string that is used to check measurements does not stretch when pulled tight. If time allows, challenge students to try exercises 2 and 3.

Math Writing Prompt

Explain Your Thinking Explain the steps you would take to find the perimeter of a square where each side is $1\frac{3}{4}$ inches.

Software Support

Warm Up 38.12

On Level

Activity Card 13-4

Find the Missing Sides

Activity Card 13-4

Work: In pairs

1. Look at the three figures shown at the right. The first figure is called a pentagon because it has 5 sides. The second figure is called a hexagon because it has 6 sides. The third figure is called an octagon because it has 8 sides.

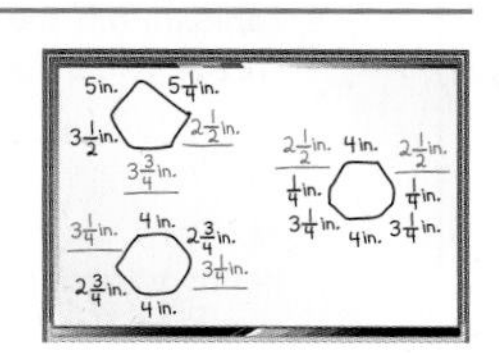

2. The perimeter of each figure is 20 inches. Work together to find possible lengths for the missing measures on each figure.
3. **Think** What strategies did you use to find the missing measures? Share your ideas with others.

Unit 13, Lesson 4

Activity Note Some students may use the strategy of counting on to 20 after finding the sum of the given measures. There are an infinite number of possible pairs of measures that will complete each figure.

Math Writing Prompt

Error Analysis Elise added $5\frac{3}{4}$ inches + $7\frac{3}{8}$ inches and said that $12\frac{6}{12}$ was the answer. Is that correct? Explain your thinking.

Software Support

Ice Station Exploration: Polar Planes, Level P

Challenge

Activity Card 13-4

Make Octagons

Activity Card 13-4

Work: In pairs

Use:

- Ruler
- String (50 inches long)
- Scissors

1. Look at the problem below.

   Mrs. Chin has 50 feet of fencing to put around her garden. The garden will be shaped like an octagon. How can she arrange the fencing?

2. **Work Together** Use the string to show how to arrange the fence. Let one inch of string equal one foot of fencing. Draw an octagon showing your string design. Label the length for each of the 8 sides.

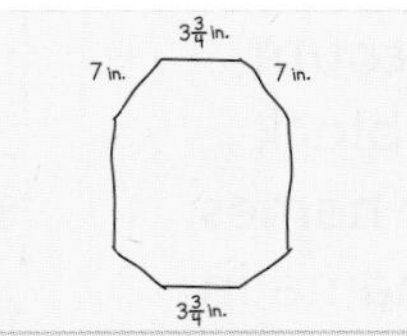

3. Use mixed numbers as the length for at least 2 sides. Do not make more than 2 sides the same length.

Unit 13, Lesson 4

Activity Note Students will not be able to draw the octagons to scale, but their drawings should be a reasonable approximation of the model they made with their string, including the measurement labels.

Math Writing Prompt

Number Sense When you add fractions, is the sum always a fraction? Explain.

DESTINATION Math®

Software Support

Course II: Module 3: Unit 1: Area

3 Homework and Spiral Review

13–4 Homework **Goal:** Additional Practice

This Homework page provides practice in adding fractional lengths.

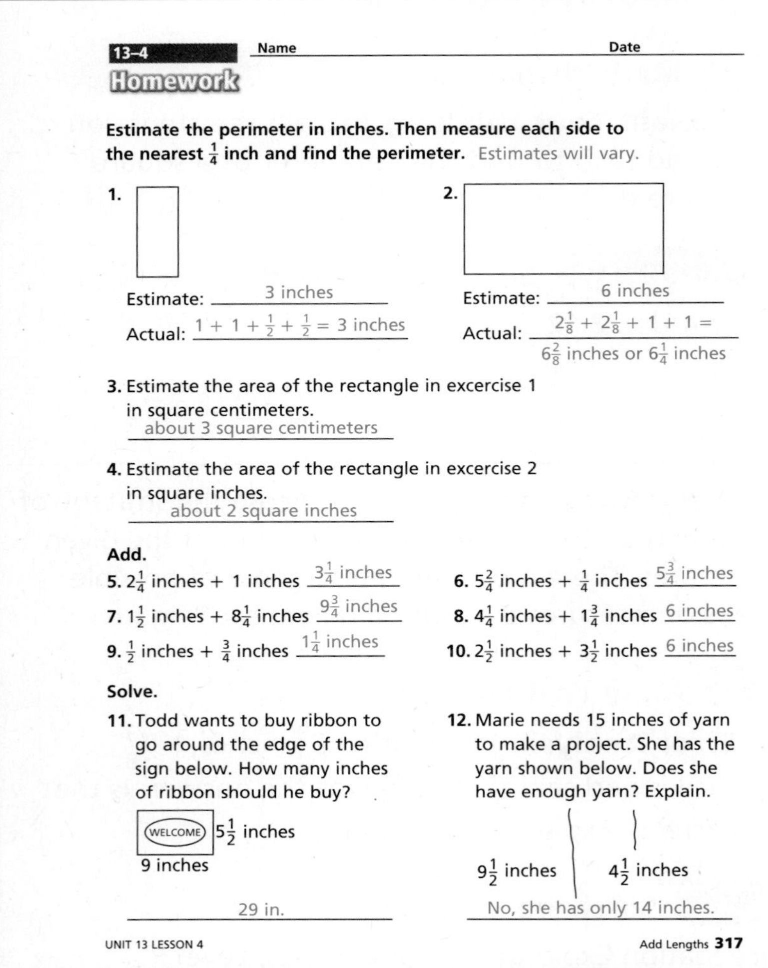

13–4 Homework

Name ____ Date ____

Estimate the perimeter in inches. Then measure each side to the nearest $\frac{1}{4}$ inch and find the perimeter. Estimates will vary.

1\. Estimate: 3 inches
Actual: $1 + 1 + \frac{1}{2} + \frac{1}{2} = 3$ inches

2\. Estimate: 6 inches
Actual: $2\frac{1}{8} + 2\frac{1}{8} + 1 + 1 =$ $6\frac{2}{8}$ inches or $6\frac{1}{4}$ inches

3\. Estimate the area of the rectangle in excercise 1 in square centimeters.
about 3 square centimeters

4\. Estimate the area of the rectangle in excercise 2 in square inches.
about 2 square inches

Add.

5\. $2\frac{1}{4}$ inches + 1 inches $3\frac{1}{4}$ inches

6\. $5\frac{2}{4}$ inches + $\frac{1}{4}$ inches $5\frac{3}{4}$ inches

7\. $1\frac{1}{2}$ inches + $8\frac{1}{4}$ inches $9\frac{3}{4}$ inches

8\. $4\frac{1}{4}$ inches + $1\frac{3}{4}$ inches 6 inches

9\. $\frac{1}{2}$ inches + $\frac{3}{4}$ inches $1\frac{1}{4}$ inches

10\. $2\frac{1}{2}$ inches + $3\frac{1}{2}$ inches 6 inches

Solve.

11\. Todd wants to buy ribbon to go around the edge of the sign below. How many inches of ribbon should he buy?
WELCOME $5\frac{1}{2}$ inches
9 inches
29 in.

12\. Marie needs 15 inches of yarn to make a project. She has the yarn shown below. Does she have enough yarn? Explain.
$9\frac{1}{2}$ inches $4\frac{1}{2}$ inches
No, she has only 14 inches.

UNIT 13 LESSON 4 Add Lengths 317

Homework and Remembering page 317

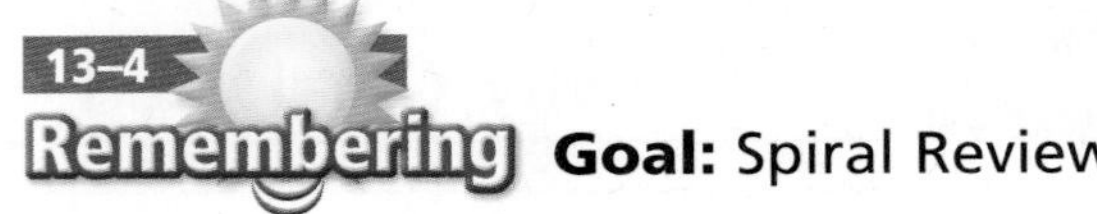

13–4 Remembering **Goal:** Spiral Review

This Remembering page would be appropriate anytime after today's lesson.

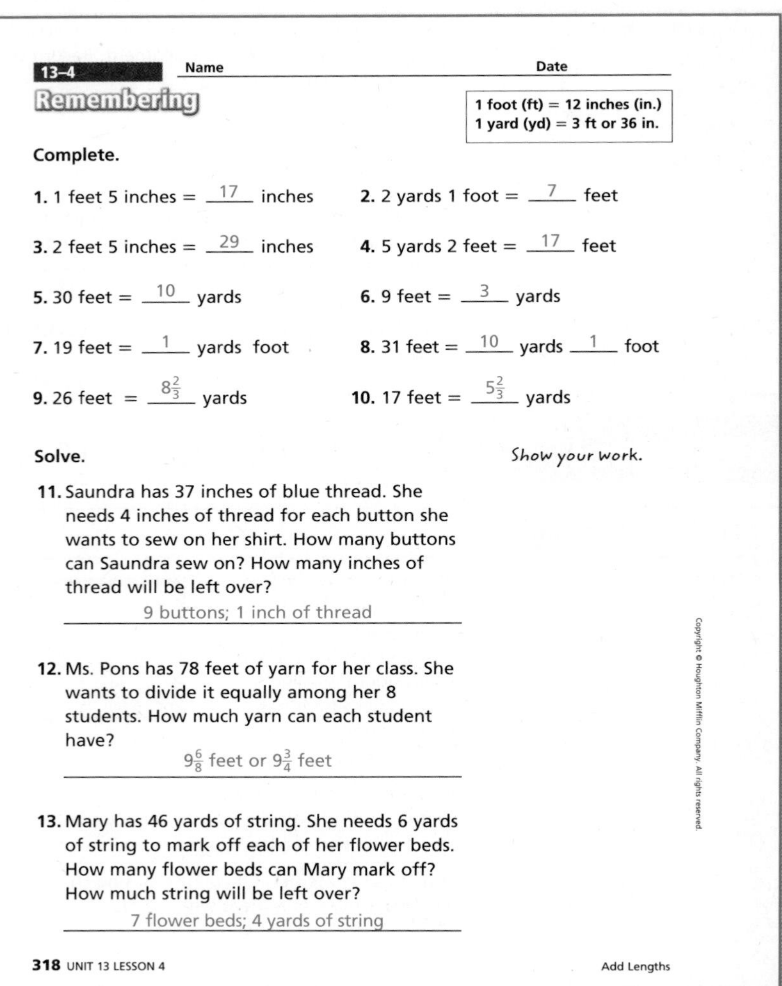

13–4 Remembering

Name ____ Date ____

1 foot (ft) = 12 inches (in.)
1 yard (yd) = 3 ft or 36 in.

Complete.

1\. 1 feet 5 inches = 17 inches

2\. 2 yards 1 foot = 7 feet

3\. 2 feet 5 inches = 29 inches

4\. 5 yards 2 feet = 17 feet

5\. 30 feet = 10 yards

6\. 9 feet = 3 yards

7\. 19 feet = ____ yards 1 foot

8\. 31 feet = 10 yards 1 foot

9\. 26 feet = $8\frac{2}{3}$ yards

10\. 17 feet = $5\frac{2}{3}$ yards

Solve. *Show your work.*

11\. Saundra has 37 inches of blue thread. She needs 4 inches of thread for each button she wants to sew on her shirt. How many buttons can Saundra sew on? How many inches of thread will be left over?
9 buttons; 1 inch of thread

12\. Ms. Pons has 78 feet of yarn for her class. She wants to divide it equally among her 8 students. How much yarn can each student have?
$9\frac{6}{8}$ feet or $9\frac{3}{4}$ feet

13\. Mary has 46 yards of string. She needs 6 yards of string to mark off each of her flower beds. How many flower beds can Mary mark off? How much string will be left over?
7 flower beds; 4 yards of string

318 UNIT 13 LESSON 4 Add Lengths

Homework and Remembering page 318

Home or School Activity

Art Connection

Name That Perimeter Have students write out their names in block letters on Centimeter-Grid Paper (TRB M31). Have students count each unit as $\frac{1}{2}$-inch instead of a centimeter unit. After their block lettering is complete, have them find the perimeter of their names. If time allows, challenge students to find the area of their name in $\frac{1}{2}$-square inches by counting $\frac{1}{2}$ units. Point out that the area of each block is $\frac{1}{2}$-square inch.

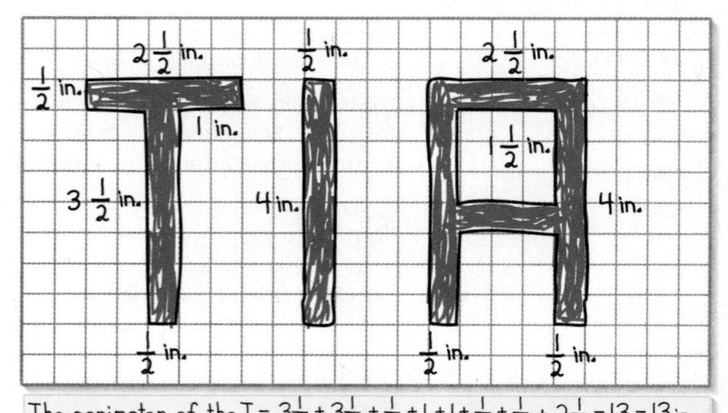

The perimeter of the T = $3\frac{1}{2} + 3\frac{1}{2} + \frac{1}{2} + 1 + 1 + \frac{1}{2} + \frac{1}{2} + 2\frac{1}{2} = 13 = 13$ in.
The perimeter of the I = $\frac{1}{2} + \frac{1}{2} + 4 + 4 = 9 = 9$ in.
The perimeter of the A = $2\frac{1}{2} + 4 + 4 + \frac{1}{2} + \frac{1}{2} + 1\frac{1}{2} + 1\frac{1}{2} + 1\frac{1}{2} + 1\frac{1}{2} + 1\frac{1}{2} + 1\frac{1}{2} + 1\frac{1}{2} = 22 = 22$ in.
The perimeter of my name is $13 + 9 + 22 = 44$ in.

Customary Units of Capacity

Vocabulary
capacity
cup (c)
pint (pt)
quart (qt)
gallon (gal)

Lesson Objectives

- Discover relationships among cups, pints, quarts, half-gallons, and gallons.
- Establish benchmarks for capacity and choose units for measuring capacity.
- Estimate capacity.

The Day at a Glance

Today's Goals	Materials	
1 Teaching the Lesson **A1:** Fill and compare various sizes of milk cartons. **A2:** Complete tables relating customary units of capacity. **A3:** Establish benchmarks for capacity and choose customary units for measuring capacity. **A4:** Estimate capacity.	**Lesson Activities** Student Activity Book pp. 487–490 or Student Hardcover Book pp. 487–490 and Activity Workbook p. 246 (includes table) Homework and Remembering pp. 319–320 Milk cartons of various sizes Water or rice Various containers (different to milk) Sticky notes Bucket *Room for Ripley* by Stuart J. Murphy (HarperTrophy, 1999)	**Going Further** Activity Cards 13-5 Drawing Paper Containers (cup, pint, quart, half-gallon, gallon) Rice or Water Chart Paper Math Journals
2 Going Further ► Differentiated Instruction		
3 Homework and Spiral Review		

Use Math Talk today!

Keeping Skills Sharp

Quick Practice — 5 MINUTES

Goal: Practice "as many as" comparisons with 2s, 4s, and 8s.

Comparison Chant The class is divided into two groups. The **Student Leader** writes 2, 4, or 8 and one of its count-bys on the board. The leader asks one group to compare the first number to the second, and then asks the second group to compare the second number to the first.

Leader: Group 1, compare 4 to 20. Group 2, compare 20 to 4.

Group 1: 4 is $\frac{1}{5}$ as many as 20.

Group 2: 20 is 5 times as many as 4.

Daily Routines

Homework Review While checking that the assignment was completed, see if a problem(s) caused difficulty.

Act It Out Rhonda cut one string into two equal pieces. Next she cut 11 inches off one piece. That gave her a piece of string that was 29 inches long. How long was the whole piece of string? Use paper strips to act out the problem.

80 inches

first equalpiece
second equal piece
29 in.
11 in.

1 Teaching the Lesson

Activity 1

Introduce Capacity

 15 MINUTES

Goal: Fill and compare various sizes of milk cartons.

Materials: Collected milk cartons, water or rice (1 gallon), Student Activity Book or Hardcover Book p. 487

 **NCTM Standards:**
Number and Operations
Measurement
Problem Solving

The Learning Classroom

Building Concepts Students will likely be familiar with containers and their capacities from their everyday experiences. Some students may have difficulty identifying the appropriate capacity names and their related sizes of containers. In this lesson, students will have an opportunity to measure the capacity of various-sized containers, identify the units, and build referents for the various standard units of capacity. Whenever you can, reinforce the vocabulary term *capacity* defining it as how much a container can hold.

▶ Measuring with Units of Capacity WHOLE CLASS

In preparation for this activity, cut the tops off any milk cartons that were collected. Also, be sure the sizes of the cartons are clearly marked. You may wish to label the containers with large labels saying "1 cup," "1 pint," "1 quart," "$\frac{1}{2}$-gallon," and "1 gallon."

Arrange a set of milk containers in order of increasing or decreasing size in a place where students can see them.

Allow students to examine the containers firsthand. Ask students to predict how the sizes of containers relate to each other and state each comparison in an equation in two ways. Possible response: 2 pints = 1 quart and 1 pint = $\frac{1}{2}$ quart. Write students' predictions and comparisons on the board.

To verify the relationship between cups and pints, have a student fill the 1-cup milk container with rice or water. Then have them see how many times the cup's contents can be poured into each container. Do the same for the other amounts: count the number of times the pint's contents can fit into the quart, the number of times the quart's contents fit into the half-gallon, and the number of times the half-gallon's contents fit into the gallon.

2 cups = 1 pint	2 pints = 1 quart	2 quarts = $\frac{1}{2}$ gallon	2 half-gallons = 1 gallon
4 cups = 1 quart	4 pints = $\frac{1}{2}$ gallon	4 quarts = 1 gallon	
8 cups = $\frac{1}{2}$ gallon	8 pints = 1 gallon		
16 cups = 1 gallon			

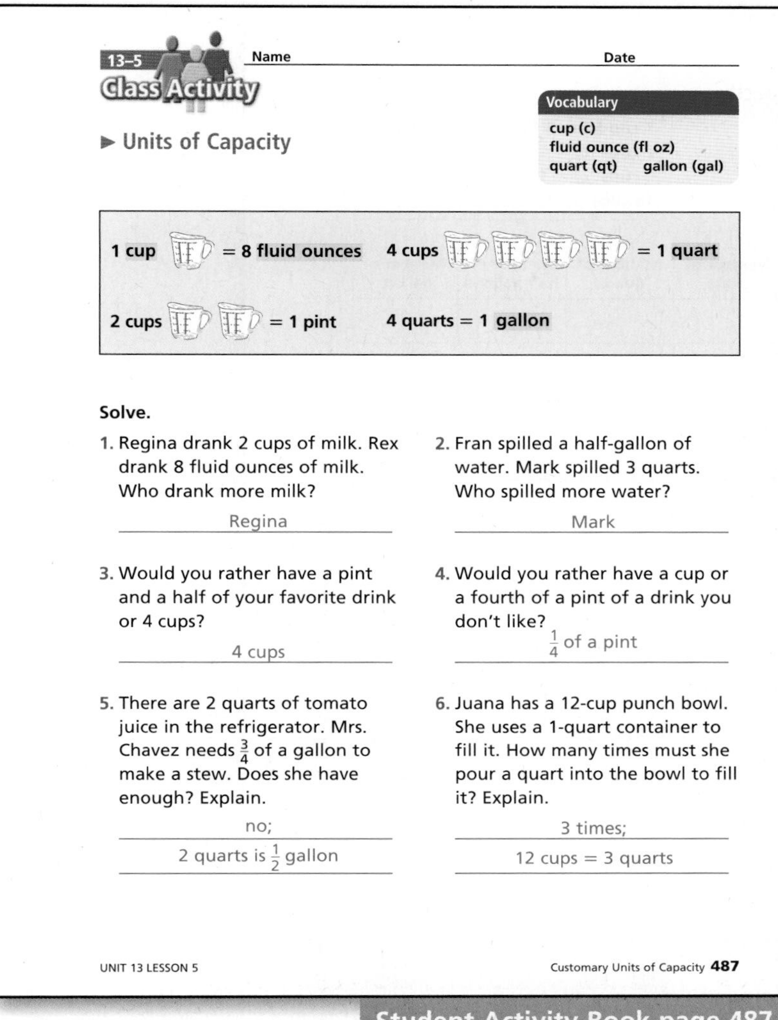

13–5 Class Activity

Name ______ Date ______

▶ Units of Capacity

Vocabulary
cup (c)
fluid ounce (fl oz)
quart (qt) gallon (gal)

1 cup = 8 fluid ounces
4 cups = 1 quart
2 cups = 1 pint
4 quarts = 1 gallon

Solve.

1. Regina drank 2 cups of milk. Rex drank 8 fluid ounces of milk. Who drank more milk?
Regina

2. Fran spilled a half-gallon of water. Mark spilled 3 quarts. Who spilled more water?
Mark

3. Would you rather have a pint and a half of your favorite drink or 4 cups?
4 cups

4. Would you rather have a cup or a fourth of a pint of a drink you don't like?
$\frac{1}{4}$ of a pint

5. There are 2 quarts of tomato juice in the refrigerator. Mrs. Chavez needs $\frac{3}{4}$ of a gallon to make a stew. Does she have enough? Explain.
no;
2 quarts is $\frac{1}{2}$ gallon

6. Juana has a 12-cup punch bowl. She uses a 1-quart container to fill it. How many times must she pour a quart into the bowl to fill it? Explain.
3 times;
12 cups = 3 quarts

UNIT 13 LESSON 5 Customary Units of Capacity 487

Student Activity Book page 487

▶ Units of Capacity PAIRS

Have **Student Pairs** examine the measurement representations and equivalencies on Student Book page 487. Have students discuss the relationships shown. Encourage students to use varied comparison language. Emphasize the two ways that the equivalencies can be written: in whole numbers (2 cups = 1 pint) or with fractions (1 cup = $\frac{1}{2}$ pint).

Divide the class into **Helping Pairs**. Have partners work together to solve problems 1–6 on Student Book page 487. While students work, walk around the room to monitor progress. Follow up by discussing answers and reasoning as a class.

English Language Learners

Write *Units of Capacity, fl oz, c, pt, qt,* and *gal* on the board. Ask: **Are these *abbreviations* for *units of capacity*?** yes

- **Beginning** Model containers for each unit, identify them, and point to the abbreviation. Have students repeat.
- **Intermediate** Hold up a *cup*. Ask: **Is this a *fluid ounce* or a *cup*?** cup **Is the abbreviation *c* or *qt*?** c Continue with other units.
- **Advanced** Model containers. Have students identify the units and abbreviations.

Ongoing Assessment

Ask questions such as the following:

▶ One cup is *how many times* the size of a pint?

▶ Which unit is 4 times as many as a cup?

Activity 2

Convert Between Customary Units of Capacity

 15 MINUTES

Goal: Complete tables relating customary units of capacity.

Materials: Student Activity Book or Hardcover Book p. 488 and Activity Workbook p. 246 (includes table)

 **NCTM Standards:**
Number and Operations
Measurement
Reasoning and Proof

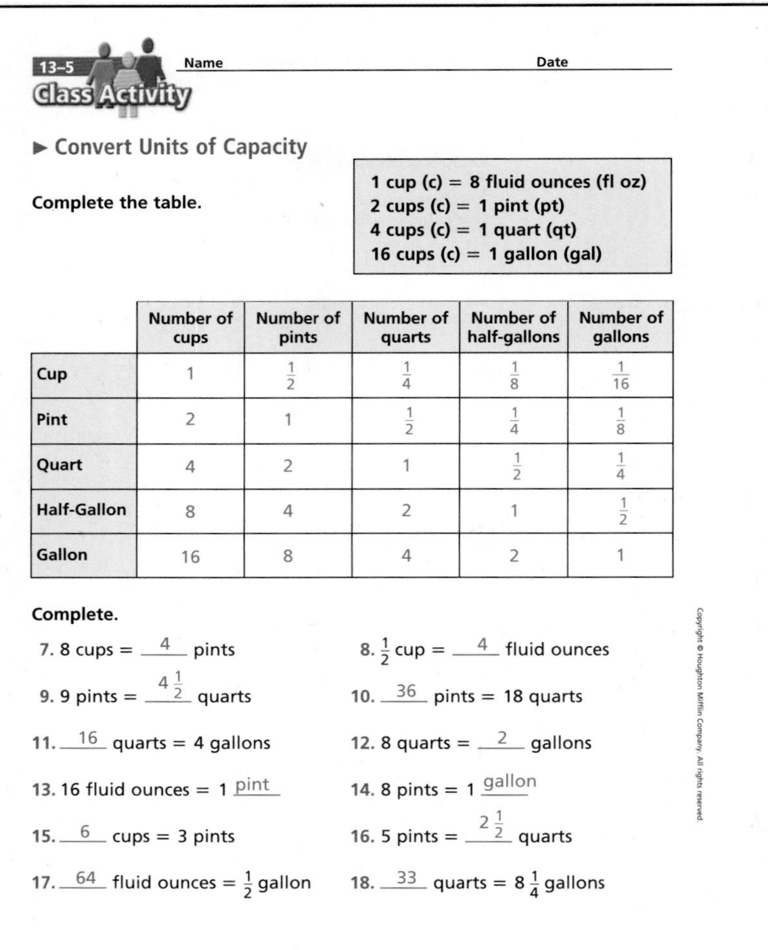

13–5 Class Activity Name Date

▶ Convert Units of Capacity

Complete the table.

1 cup (c) = 8 fluid ounces (fl oz)
2 cups (c) = 1 pint (pt)
4 cups (c) = 1 quart (qt)
16 cups (c) = 1 gallon (gal)

	Number of cups	Number of pints	Number of quarts	Number of half-gallons	Number of gallons
Cup	1	$\frac{1}{2}$	$\frac{1}{4}$	$\frac{1}{8}$	$\frac{1}{16}$
Pint	2	1	$\frac{1}{2}$	$\frac{1}{4}$	$\frac{1}{8}$
Quart	4	2	1	$\frac{1}{2}$	$\frac{1}{4}$
Half-Gallon	8	4	2	1	$\frac{1}{2}$
Gallon	16	8	4	2	1

Complete.

7. 8 cups = 4 pints
8. $\frac{1}{2}$ cup = 4 fluid ounces
9. 9 pints = $4\frac{1}{2}$ quarts
10. 36 pints = 18 quarts
11. 16 quarts = 4 gallons
12. 8 quarts = 2 gallons
13. 16 fluid ounces = 1 pint
14. 8 pints = 1 gallon
15. 6 cups = 3 pints
16. 5 pints = $2\frac{1}{2}$ quarts
17. 64 fluid ounces = $\frac{1}{2}$ gallon
18. 33 quarts = $8\frac{1}{4}$ gallons

488 UNIT 13 LESSON 5 Customary Units of Capacity

Student Activity Book page 488

▶ Convert Units of Capacity WHOLE CLASS

In this activity, students complete a table to relate different customary units of capacity.

Fill in the table as a class. Continue practicing fraction, division, and multiplication language.

- How many pints are in 1 cup? $\frac{1}{2}$ pint How many quarts are in 1 cup? $\frac{1}{4}$ quart A cup is what fraction of a quart? $\frac{1}{4}$ One quart is how many times the size of a cup? 4 times
- What patterns do you see in the table? Each measure is twice the size of the next smaller measure. Each measure is half the size of the next larger measure.

Have students complete exercises 7–18 in helping pairs.

Differentiated Instruction

Extra Help Some students may have difficulty with the fraction-related language used for comparing units. Model how to use the number of smaller units in the larger unit to help with the fraction-related language. For example, to find how many quarts that 1 cup is, ask:

▶ How many cups are there in 1 quart? 4 cups

▶ Then 4, is the denominator to use for your fraction, and the numerator is 1. The fraction, $\frac{1}{4}$, means 1 part of 4 parts in the whole.

Activity 3

Establish Benchmarks and Choose Units

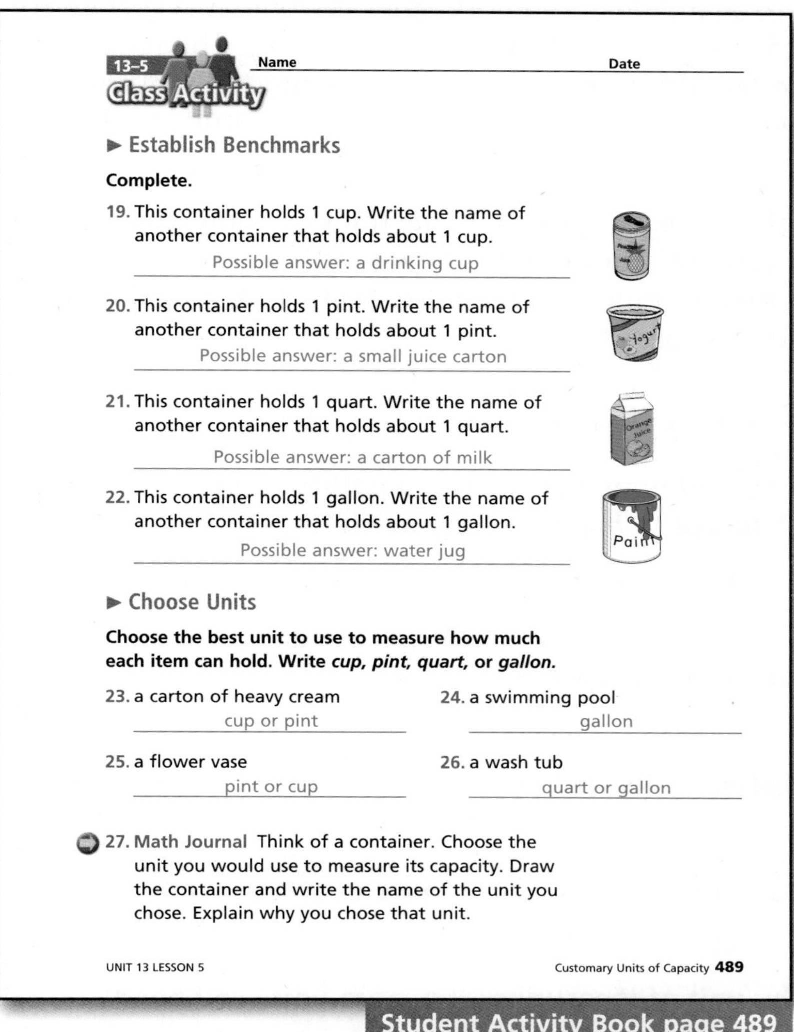

13–5 Class Activity

Name Date

► Establish Benchmarks

Complete.

19. This container holds 1 cup. Write the name of another container that holds about 1 cup.
Possible answer: a drinking cup

20. This container holds 1 pint. Write the name of another container that holds about 1 pint.
Possible answer: a small juice carton

21. This container holds 1 quart. Write the name of another container that holds about 1 quart.
Possible answer: a carton of milk

22. This container holds 1 gallon. Write the name of another container that holds about 1 gallon.
Possible answer: water jug

► Choose Units

Choose the best unit to use to measure how much each item can hold. Write *cup, pint, quart,* or *gallon.*

23. a carton of heavy cream
cup or pint

24. a swimming pool
gallon

25. a flower vase
pint or cup

26. a wash tub
quart or gallon

27. Math Journal Think of a container. Choose the unit you would use to measure its capacity. Draw the container and write the name of the unit you chose. Explain why you chose that unit.

UNIT 13 LESSON 5 Customary Units of Capacity **489**

Student Activity Book page 489

► Establish Benchmarks PAIRS

Have **Student Pairs** name units they have used to measure capacity (how much a container can hold). List the units on the board, including: cup, gallon, pint, quart. Then have students order the units from smallest to largest.

Review the meaning of benchmarks.

- A benchmark can help you estimate how much or how many.

Direct students' attention to exercises 19–22 on Student Book page 489. Have students work in pairs to brainstorm benchmark containers for cup, pint, quart, and gallon.

Activity continued ►

15 MINUTES

Goal: Establish benchmarks for capacity and choose customary units for measuring capacity.

Materials: Student Activity Book or Hardcover Book p. 489

NCTM Standards:
Number and Operations
Measurement
Reasoning and Proof

 Teaching the Lesson (continued)

Class Management

Since students will be completing their work on choosing a container and measuring its capacity on their own in exercise 27, make sure to schedule some time to allow students to share their work. Some students will benefit from looking at various capacity containers.

▶ Choose Units PAIRS

Ask **Student Pairs** to share ideas about whether it would make sense to use a gallon unit to measure how much a mug can hold. Then ask them if it makes sense to use a cup unit to measure how much a fuel truck can hold. Then have them complete exercises 23–26 on Student Book page 489.

Before completing exercise 27, have students think of some objects they could measure for capacity, for example, how much water a bathtub can hold, how much juice a thermos can hold. See **Math Talk in Action** for a sample classroom discussion.

 Math Talk in Action

Suppose we want to find how much water a bathtub can hold. Would a cup be a good unit to use to measure how much?

Jeremy: No, because it's so small and it would take a long time to measure.

What unit might be better to use?

Keiko: A quart.

Ok. Are there any other units that might be good to use?

Elisa: A gallon.

Would the bathtub hold more gallons or more quarts of water?

Elisa: More quarts. Quarts are smaller than qallons.

Yes. The smaller the unit of measuring, the more units you need.

Have students work in pairs and choose two objects. They should discuss which measurement unit would be best to use to measure how much their object can hold. Discuss some units, such as the standardized cup, pint, quart, and gallon, as well as nonstandard units, such as drop, ladle, and bucket. Have them think about which unit would make sense.

- Is a cup a good unit to use to measure how much a bathtub can hold? Why or why not?

Ask students to complete exercise 27 and have pairs of students share their responses. Encourage the class to ask each other questions.

Have students who have difficulty work with a **Helping Partner**.

Activity 4

Estimate Capacity

▶ Review Capacity with Containers WHOLE CLASS

Use the milk containers from the beginning of the lesson. Remove the measurement labels and challenge students to re-label the containers again with the correct measurements and put them in the correct order of size. Review the relationships between the containers. For example, ask students:

- How many pints of water can fit into a quart container? 2
- How many cups of water can fit into a gallon? 16 cups

Now, have students look at different containers (do not place them in order of size) and have them use what they know about the milk containers to estimate which container they think will hold a *cup*, a *pint*, a *quart*, and a *gallon* of water. Have them write their estimates on sticky notes and then arrange the containers from smallest to largest.

 **15 MINUTES**

Goal: Estimate customary units of capacity.

Materials: Milk containers from activity 1, 4 new containers that measure cup, pint, quart, and gallon, sticky notes, bucket, Student Activity or Hardcover Book p. 490

 **NCTM Standard:**
Measurement

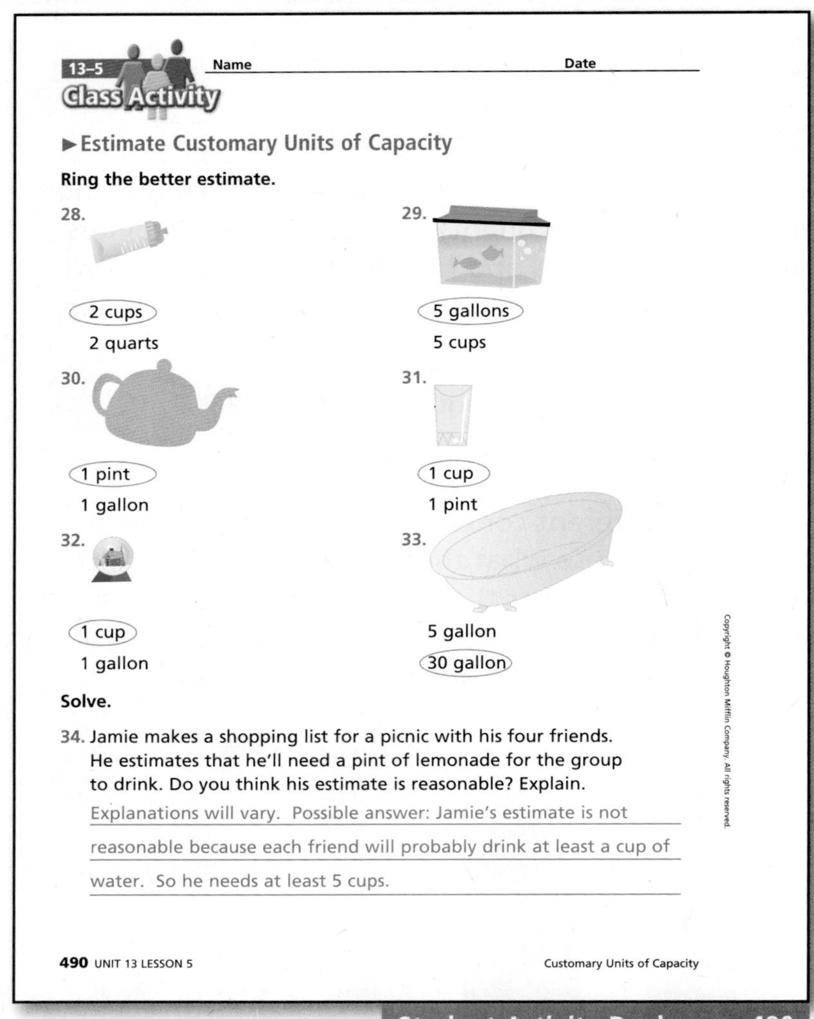

13-5 Class Activity Name Date

► Estimate Customary Units of Capacity

Ring the better estimate.

28. (2 cups) / 2 quarts

29. (5 gallons) / 5 cups

30. (1 pint) / 1 gallon

31. (1 cup) / 1 pint

32. (1 cup) / 1 gallon

33. 5 gallon / (30 gallon)

Solve.

34. Jamie makes a shopping list for a picnic with his four friends. He estimates that he'll need a pint of lemonade for the group to drink. Do you think his estimate is reasonable? Explain.

Explanations will vary. Possible answer: Jamie's estimate is not reasonable because each friend will probably drink at least a cup of water. So he needs at least 5 cups.

Copyright © Houghton Mifflin Company. All rights reserved.

490 UNIT 13 LESSON 5 Customary Units of Capacity

Student Activity Book page 490

Ongoing Assessment

- Select a container to measure its capacity.
- Ask students to name a unit that would be practical to measure how much the container can hold.

► Estimate Customary Units of Capacity INDIVIDUALS

To prepare students for choosing the better estimate of capacity on Student Book page 490, show students a bucket and have them estimate how many cups, pints, and so on can fit in the bucket. For example, ask students if they think it is a good estimate that the bucket would hold 50 cups of water or 50 gallons of water, and so on.

Have students complete exercises 28–34 on Student Book page 490 and discuss the students' estimates as a class.

Going Further

Differentiated Instruction

Intervention — Activity Card 13-5

List Benchmarks for Capacity — Activity Card 13-5

Work: In pairs
Use:
- Drawing paper

1. **Work Together** Make a list of benchmarks for units of capacity. List a benchmark for each of the following units: cup, pint, quart, gallon. Then draw a picture of each benchmark in your list.
2. **Think** A cup is about the size of one adult's closed hand. So two smaller closed hands might also equal the capacity of a cup.

Unit	My Benchmark
1 cup	2 of my closed hands
1 pint	
1 quart	
1 gallon	

3. Choose containers for products that you can find at home or at the grocery store to use as benchmarks for the remaining units in your list. Share your work with your class.

Unit 13, Lesson 5

Activity Note Dairy product containers for milk, ice cream, yogurt, and cottage cheese can represent benchmarks for common units of capacity. A large can of paint can also represent a gallon benchmark.

Math Writing Prompt

Explain Your Thinking Roberto is very thirsty after his bike ride. Should he drink 1 fluid ounce or 1 cup of water? Explain.

Software Support

Warm Up 40.05

On Level — Activity Card 13-5

Act Out Capacity Comparisons — Activity Card 13-5

Work: In pairs
Use:
- Containers (cup, pint, quart, half-gallon, gallon)
- Rice or water

1. Use containers and rice or water to act out each situation described below.
2. **Think** How many cups are in each pint? How many quarts are in a gallon?
   2 c = 1 pt; 4 qt = 1 gal

Wendy has 1 cup of juice. Janie has 1 pint of juice. Wendy has ☐ as many cups of juice as Janie has. Wendy has ☐ pint of juice. $\frac{1}{2}$; $\frac{1}{2}$

Juan bought 1 gallon of milk for his family. Ronny bought 1 quart of milk for his family. Ronny bought ☐ as many gallons of milk as Juan did. Ronny has ☐ gallon of milk. $\frac{1}{4}$; $\frac{1}{4}$

3. Use what you observe to find and record the missing information in each description.
4. **Extend** Write your own word problem for your partner to solve.

Unit 13, Lesson 5

Activity Note To reinforce the relationships among the units, have students pour the smaller capacity container into the larger one as many times as it takes to fill the larger container.

Math Writing Prompt

Reasoning Devon said that he drinks 2 gallons of milk every day. Do you think this is correct? Explain your thinking.

Software Support

The Number Games: Tiny's Think Tank, Level N

Challenge — Activity Card 13-5

Measurements in Recipes — Activity Card 13-5

Work: In pairs
Use:
- Chart paper

1. The paper below lists the different juices that Dora needs to make 26 cups of punch. But the paper is torn, so the amount for each type of juice is missing.

CH RECIPE
qt orange juice
pt pineapple juice
c lemonade
pt strawberry juice

2. **Work Together** Find out how much of each juice Dora should buy to make 26 cups of punch. Answers will vary. Possible answer: 2 qt orange; 2 pt pineapple; 6 c lemonade; 4 pt strawberry
3. Compare your recipe with those of other groups. What strategies did you use to find the missing measurements?

Unit 13, Lesson 5

Activity Note Tell students that the recipe uses only whole unit amounts. Students may wish to convert each unit into cups to make it easier to find multiples of each unit that together equal 26 cups.

Math Writing Prompt

Summarize Can containers with different shapes have the same capacity? Explain.

DESTINATION Math® **Software Support**

Course II: Module 3: Unit 1: Volume

 Homework and Spiral Review

13–5 **Homework** **Goal:** Additional Practice

This Homework page provides practice in converting customary units of capacity.

13–5 **Remembering** **Goal:** Spiral Review

This Remembering page would be appropriate anytime after today's lesson.

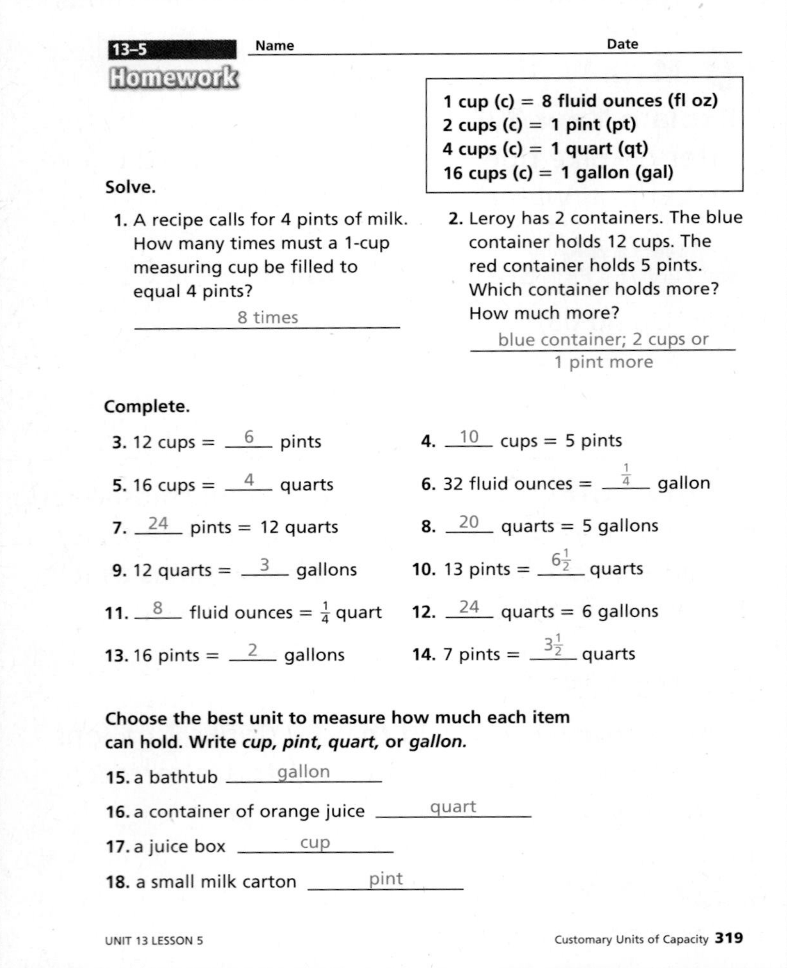

13–5 **Homework** Name ______ Date ______

> **1 cup (c) = 8 fluid ounces (fl oz)**
> **2 cups (c) = 1 pint (pt)**
> **4 cups (c) = 1 quart (qt)**
> **16 cups (c) = 1 gallon (gal)**

Solve.

1. A recipe calls for 4 pints of milk. How many times must a 1-cup measuring cup be filled to equal 4 pints? 8 times

2. Leroy has 2 containers. The blue container holds 12 cups. The red container holds 5 pints. Which container holds more? How much more? blue container; 2 cups or 1 pint more

Complete.

3. 12 cups = 6 pints
4. 10 cups = 5 pints
5. 16 cups = 4 quarts
6. 32 fluid ounces = $\frac{1}{4}$ gallon
7. 24 pints = 12 quarts
8. 20 quarts = 5 gallons
9. 12 quarts = 3 gallons
10. 13 pints = $6\frac{1}{2}$ quarts
11. 8 fluid ounces = $\frac{1}{4}$ quart
12. 24 quarts = 6 gallons
13. 16 pints = 2 gallons
14. 7 pints = $3\frac{1}{2}$ quarts

Choose the best unit to measure how much each item can hold. Write *cup, pint, quart,* or *gallon.*

15. a bathtub gallon
16. a container of orange juice quart
17. a juice box cup
18. a small milk carton pint

UNIT 13 LESSON 5 Customary Units of Capacity **319**

Homework and Remembering page 319

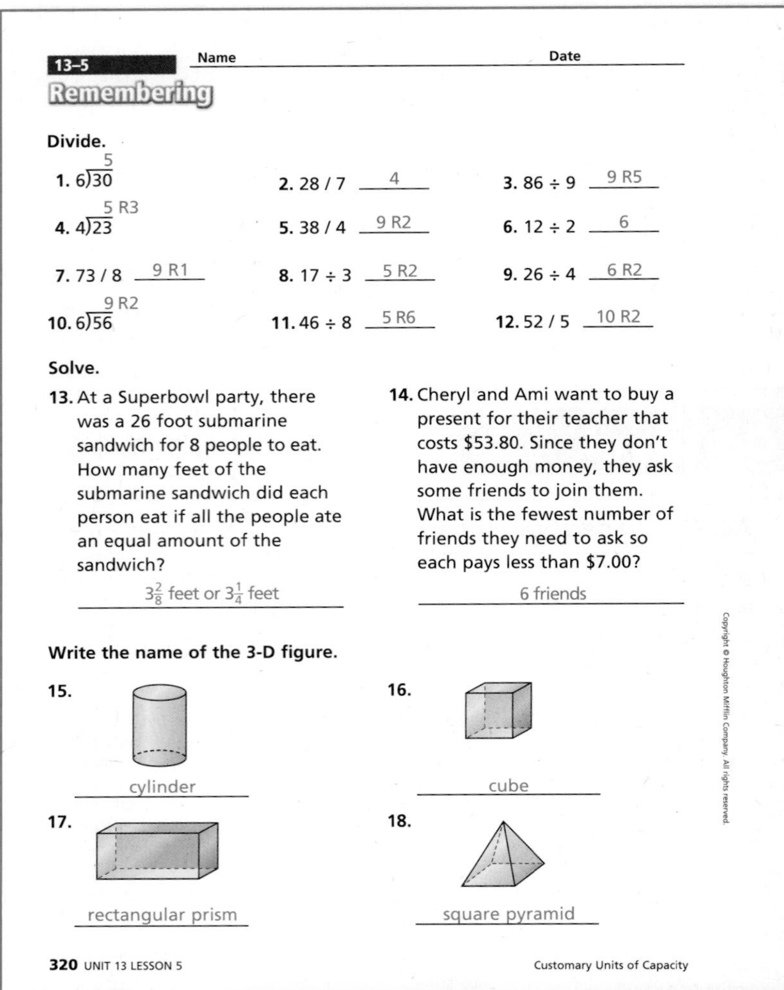

13–5 **Remembering** Name ______ Date ______

Divide.

1. $6\overline{)30}$ 5
2. 28 / 7 4
3. 86 ÷ 9 9 R5
4. $4\overline{)23}$ 5 R3
5. 38 / 4 9 R2
6. 12 ÷ 2 6
7. 73 / 8 9 R1
8. 17 ÷ 3 5 R2
9. 26 ÷ 4 6 R2
10. $6\overline{)56}$ 9 R2
11. 46 ÷ 8 5 R6
12. 52 / 5 10 R2

Solve.

13. At a Superbowl party, there was a 26 foot submarine sandwich for 8 people to eat. How many feet of the submarine sandwich did each person eat if all the people ate an equal amount of the sandwich? $3\frac{2}{8}$ feet or $3\frac{1}{4}$ feet

14. Cheryl and Ami want to buy a present for their teacher that costs $53.80. Since they don't have enough money, they ask some friends to join them. What is the fewest number of friends they need to ask so each pays less than $7.00? 6 friends

Write the name of the 3-D figure.

15. cylinder
16. cube
17. rectangular prism
18. square pyramid

320 UNIT 13 LESSON 5 Customary Units of Capacity

Homework and Remembering page 320

Home or School Activity

 Literature Connection

Room for Ripley Read aloud Stuart J. Murphy's book about a young boy who needs to find out how much water he needs for his fishbowl. Before reading the story, show a picture of Carlos' fish bowl and have the students predict the unit of measurement (cup, pint, or half gallon) they think Carlos should use to fill his fish tank.

Metric Units of Capacity

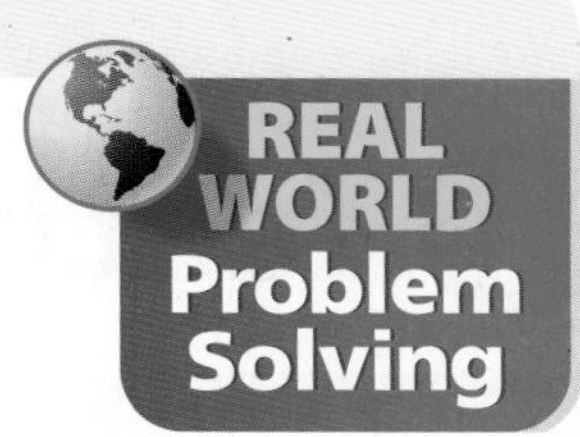

Lesson Objectives

- Become familiar with metric units of capacity. Select reasonable metric units for various measurement tasks.
- Convert metric units of capacity.
- Estimate capacity.
- Solve word problems involving capacity.

Vocabulary	
liter (L)	pint (pt)
milliliter (mL)	quart (qt)
capacity	half-gallon
cup (c)	gallon (gal)

The Day at a Glance

Today's Goals	Materials	
1 Teaching the Lesson **A1:** Learn and convert basic metric units of capacity and discuss their uses. **A2:** Estimate capacity in liters and millileters. **A3:** Solve capacity word problems involving customary and metric units of measurement. **2 Going Further** ▸ Differentiated Instruction **3 Homework and Spiral Review**	**Lesson Activities** Student Activity Book pp. 491–492 or Student Hardcover Book pp. 491–492 Homework and Remembering pp. 321–322 Eye dropper or thimble 1-liter water bottle Three containers (for example a bucket, a water bottle, and a cup) Sticky notes Water or rice	**Going Further** Activity Cards 13-6 Water Containers, various-sized cups, cartons Metric measurement cups Centimeter cubes Small, clear containers 1-liter water bottle Math Journals

Use Math Talk today!

Keeping Skills Sharp

Quick Practice — 5 MINUTES

Goal: Identify 6s and 7s count-bys just under a number. Identify the difference between the numbers.

Just Under Count-Bys Have a **Student Leader** lead this activity for 6s and 7s. (See Unit 11 Lesson 20.)

Strategy Problem The store uses soup cans to make displays. The first display uses 45 cans. The second uses 51 cans. The third uses 57 cans. If the pattern continues, how many cans are in the fourth display? 63 cans

Daily Routines

Homework Review Let students work together to check their work. Remind students to use what they know about helping others.

45 → +6 → 51 → +6 → 57 → +6 → 63

1 Teaching the Lesson

Activity 1

Liters and Milliliters

 15 MINUTES

Goal: Learn and convert basic metric units of capacity and discuss their uses.

Materials: Student Activity Book or Hardcover Book p. 491, eye dropper or thimble, 1-liter bottle

 **NCTM Standards:**
Number and Operations
Measurement
Connections

Teaching Note

State Standards If your state requires an understanding of the relationship between quarts and liters, use this opportunity to compare the benchmarks used for quarts in lesson 5 with the benchmarks used for a liter in this lesson. Students should note that a liter is slightly more than a quart. Then estimate the capacity of some containers in quarts and then in liters and compare the results.

► Introduce Metric Units of Capacity WHOLE CLASS

Ask students to list the customary units of capacity that they have worked with. Write the units on the board in order of increasing size. In a separate column, list milliliters and liters.

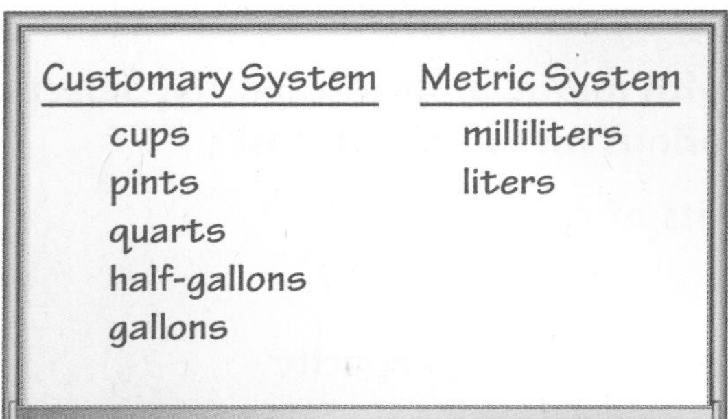

Briefly discuss the approximate sizes of the metric units. Show an eye dropper or thimble as an example of a container that holds about 1 milliliter. Show a liter bottle of water as an example of a container that holds 1 liter. Tell students that a 1 liter container holds 1,000 milliliters.

Ask which units would be useful for measuring very small, small, medium, and large amounts. As students respond, ask them to clarify each time whether the unit in question is metric or customary.

Suggest a few things to measure (for example, a dose of medicine, lemonade for a class picnic, and gasoline), and have students explain which unit in each system would be best to measure in.

Divide the class into groups of three. Have the groups note things that could be reasonably measured by metric units in the chart. Follow up by having groups share the things they noted for the units.

► Convert Metric Units of Capacity WHOLE CLASS

Direct students' attention to Student Book page 491. Do the first two conversions as a class and then have students complete exercises 3–6 independently.

► Benchmarks for a Liter and Milliliter WHOLE CLASS

Review the meaning of benchmarks: *A benchmark can help you estimate how much or how many.* Brainstorm with students to find benchmarks for liter and milliliter (for example, the size of a quart of milk carton and a thimble). Direct students' to exercises 7 and 8 on Student Book page 491. Have them record their own benchmarks for liter and milliliter here.

13–6 Class Activity

Name Date

Vocabulary
liter (L)
milliliter (mL)

► Convert Metric Units of Capacity

1 liter (L) = 1,000 milliliters (mL)

Complete.

1. 2 L = 2,000 mL
2. 15,000 mL = 15 L
3. $\frac{1}{2}$ L = 500 mL
4. $\frac{1}{4}$ L = 250 mL
5. 4 L = 4,000 mL
6. 4,000 mL = 4 L

► Benchmarks for a Liter and a Milliliter

Write the answer.

7. This bottle holds 1 **liter**.

Name another container that holds about 1 liter.
Possible answer: a thermos

8. This eyedropper holds 1 **milliliter**.

Name another container that holds about 1 milliliter.
Possible answer: a baby spoon

► Choose the Appropriate Unit

Choose the unit you would use to measure the capacity of each. Write *mL* or *L*.

9. a kitchen sink L
10. a soup spoon mL
11. a teacup mL
12. a washing machine L

Circle the better estimate.

13. a juice container (1 L) 1 mL
14. a bowl of soup 500 L (500 mL)

UNIT 13 LESSON 6 Metric Units of Capacity **491**

Student Activity Book page 491

► Choose the Appropriate Unit WHOLE CLASS

Share the following situations with students. Have them discuss the units of measurement they would use.

- Does it make sense to use a liter unit to measure how much a spoon can hold?
- Does it make sense to use a milliliter unit to measure how much a bathtub can hold?

Then have them complete exercises 9–14 on Student Book page 491.

Teaching Note

Math Background It is not necessary to discuss specific conversions between the two systems, but it would be useful for students to recognize that a liter is about the size of a quart, and that milliliters are much smaller than cups. (There are about 237 milliliters in 1 cup; there are about 5 milliliters in 1 teaspoon.)

English Language Learners

Write *Metric Units of Capacity, L,* and *mL* on the board. Ask: **Are *L* and *ml* abbreviations for *Metric Units of Capacity*?** yes

- **Beginning** Point to and identify each abbreviation. Have students repeat.
- **Intermediate** Ask: **Are metric units a different system?** yes **Is mL the abbreviation for liter or milliliter?** milliliter Say: **L is the abbreviation for __.** liter
- **Advanced** Have students identify each abbreviation.

Teaching Note

Measuring in the Real World Make sure students understand how every-day objects can be measured in mixed units, for example, liters and milliliters and so on. In later grades, students will express mixed metric units of capacity as a decimal.

Activity 2

Estimate Capacity

 15 MINUTES

Goal: Estimate metric units of capacity.

Materials: Three containers (for example a bucket, a water bottle, and a cup), sticky notes, water (or rice)

 **NCTM Standard:** Measurement

▶ Estimate Metric Units of Capacity WHOLE CLASS

Review benchmarks of a liter and milliliter with students. Hold up a spoon and a 1-liter clear water bottle so they visulaize the size of a liter and milliliter.

Then show students three different containers (for example, a coffee cup or mug, a juice container, and a bucket) and label them A, B, and C.

Write the following chart on the board and have students estimate whether the container will hold more or less than a liter of water.

Container	Estimate (More or Less than 1 Liter)	Actual (More or Less than 1 Liter)
A		
B		
C		

Have student volunteers test their predictions and estimates by filling the contents of the liter container into containers A, B, and C.

In the example shown here, students should realize the following points:

- Container A will hold more than one liter.
- Container B will hold less than one liter.
- Container C will hold less than one liter.

Challenge students to then estimate how may liters would fit into the bucket, or how many milliliters they think would fill the cup, and so on.

▶ Choose the Better Estimate WHOLE CLASS

Write the following on the board and have the class choose the better estimate. Have students explain why they chose that estimate.

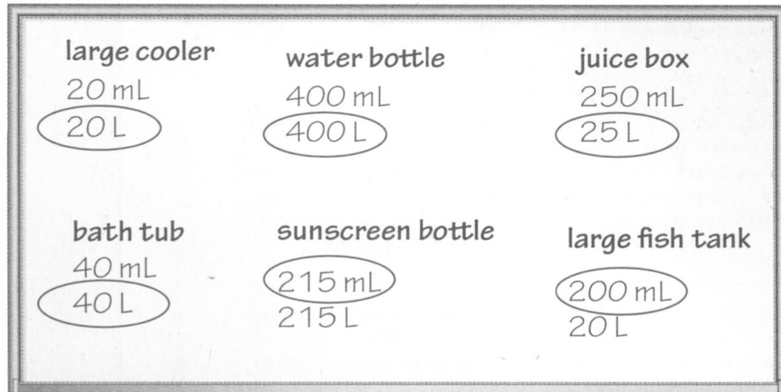

As time allows, share the following word problem with students and have them explain their thinking and math reasoning.

> Batai knows it's important to drink a lot of water to keep healthy. He keeps track of his daily water intake. He wrote that he drank 4 milliliters of water during the day. Do you think he's correct?

Students should realize that Batai probably meant that he drank 4 liters of water since 4 milliliters of water would only be about 4 teaspoons of water.

Activity 3

Capacity Word Problems

 **20 MINUTES**

Goal: Solve capacity word problems involving customary and metric units of measurement.

Materials: Student Activity Book or Hardcover Book p. 492

 **NCTM Standards:**
Number and Operations
Measurement
Problem Solving

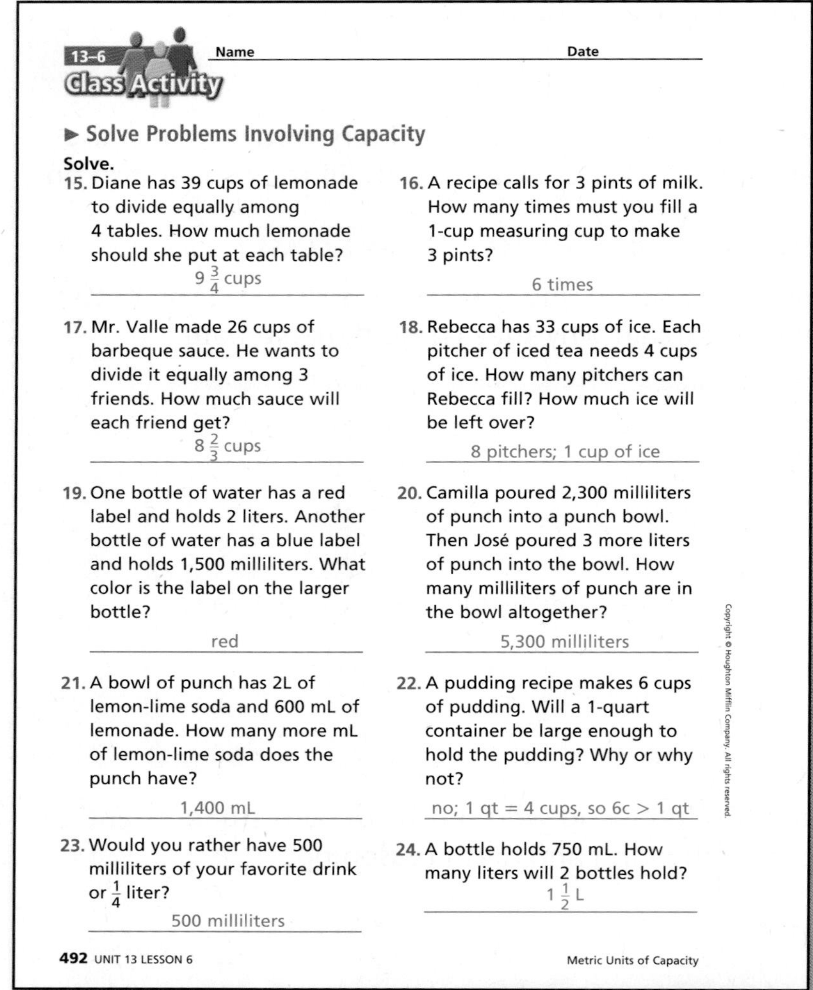

13–6 Class Activity Name Date

▶ Solve Problems Involving Capacity

Solve.

15. Diane has 39 cups of lemonade to divide equally among 4 tables. How much lemonade should she put at each table? $9\frac{3}{4}$ cups

16. A recipe calls for 3 pints of milk. How many times must you fill a 1-cup measuring cup to make 3 pints? 6 times

17. Mr. Valle made 26 cups of barbeque sauce. He wants to divide it equally among 3 friends. How much sauce will each friend get? $8\frac{2}{3}$ cups

18. Rebecca has 33 cups of ice. Each pitcher of iced tea needs 4 cups of ice. How many pitchers can Rebecca fill? How much ice will be left over? 8 pitchers; 1 cup of ice

19. One bottle of water has a red label and holds 2 liters. Another bottle of water has a blue label and holds 1,500 milliliters. What color is the label on the larger bottle? red

20. Camilla poured 2,300 milliliters of punch into a punch bowl. Then José poured 3 more liters of punch into the bowl. How many milliliters of punch are in the bowl altogether? 5,300 milliliters

21. A bowl of punch has 2L of lemon-lime soda and 600 mL of lemonade. How many more mL of lemon-lime soda does the punch have? 1,400 mL

22. A pudding recipe makes 6 cups of pudding. Will a 1-quart container be large enough to hold the pudding? Why or why not? no; 1 qt = 4 cups, so 6c > 1 qt

23. Would you rather have 500 milliliters of your favorite drink or $\frac{1}{4}$ liter? 500 milliliters

24. A bottle holds 750 mL. How many liters will 2 bottles hold? $1\frac{1}{2}$ L

492 UNIT 13 LESSON 6 Metric Units of Capacity

Student Activity Book page 492

▶ Solve Problems Involving Capacity INDIVIDUALS

Direct students' attention to problems 15–24 on Student Book page 494. Point out that some equivalencies will not be even, and they will need to divide and decide how to deal with the remainder. Tell students that these answers should be in the form of mixed numbers.

Math Talk Once most of the students have completed the first problem, use **Solve and Discuss** and have volunteers explain how they solved the problem. Continue this procedure for the rest of the problems.

Have struggling students work with a **Helping Partner**.

Ongoing Assessment

Have students solve this problem:

- Jin had a 1-liter bottle of water. He drank half of the water. How many milliliters does he have left?

2 Going Further

Differentiated Instruction

Intervention — Activity Card 13-6

How Many Milliliters? Activity Card 13-6

Work: In pairs

Use:

- Metric measurement cup
- 50 centimeter cubes
- Several small, clear containers
- Water

1. A centimeter cube holds 1 milliliter of water. Use the centimeter cubes to help you estimate the capacity of other containers.
2. **Work Together** Choose a clear rectangular container and estimate how many milliliters of water it can hold. Record your estimate. Then fill the rectangular container with as many centimeter cubes as possible.
3. **Compare** How does your estimate compare to the number of centimeter cubes that fill the container?

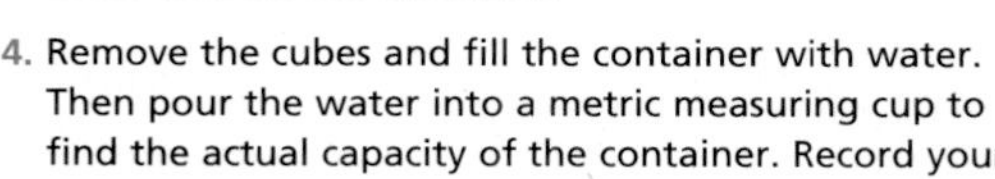

4. Remove the cubes and fill the container with water. Then pour the water into a metric measuring cup to find the actual capacity of the container. Record your results. Compare with your estimate.

Unit 13, Lesson 6

Activity Note This activity works best with rectangular containers. Repeat the activity as time allows. Have students discuss the strategies that they used to estimate the capacity of each container.

Math Writing Prompt

Representation One centimeter cube holds 1 milliliter of water. How many centimeter cubes hold 1 liter of water? Explain how you know.

Software Support

Warm Up 40.09

On Level — Activity Card 13-6

Finding 1-Liter Containers Activity Card 13-6

Work: In pairs

Use:

- 1-liter water bottle
- Water
- Containers (various sizes)

1. Find two containers that you think each hold about 1 liter of water.
2. Measure the capacity of each container by filling it with water from the 1-liter water bottle.

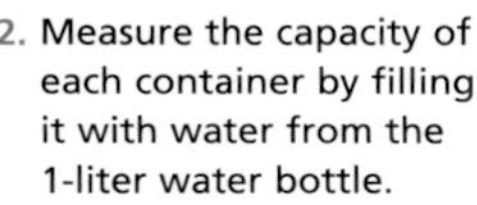

3. **Compare** How does your estimate compare with the actual measurement?
4. Choose another container and estimate its capacity in liters. Check your estimate again.
5. **Think** Does the shape of a container make it harder or easier to estimate its capacity? What strategies can you use to make a closer estimate?

Unit 13, Lesson 6

Activity Note The 1-liter bottle will give students a measurement that is accurate to the nearest liter. Students can express a closer measurement using fractions of a liter to compare with their estimate.

Math Writing Prompt

Explain Your Thinking A container holds $2\frac{1}{2}$ L. Another container holds 2,200 mL. Which container has the greater capacity? Explain.

Software Support

The Number Games: Tiny's Think Tank, Level N

Challenge — Activity Card 13-6

More Units of Capacity Activity Card 13-6

Work: In pairs

1. The measurements below were used in England in the 1700s. How many English gallons were equal to the English barrel? 36

9 gallons = 1 firkin
2 firkins = 1 kilderkin
2 kilderkins = 1 barrel
$1\frac{1}{2}$ barrels = 1 hogshead
$1\frac{1}{3}$ hogshead = 1 puncheon
2 hogsheads = 1 pipe
2 pipes = 1 tun

2. Use the English units to write five conversion problems. Exchange with other pairs to solve.

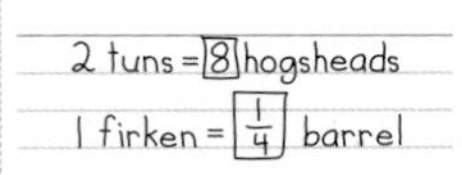

Unit 13, Lesson 6

Activity Note Have students solve their own conversion problems then exchange with other students. Have students justify any answers that differ.

Math Writing Prompt

Connected Math Washing dishes by hand uses about 30 L of water, using the dishwasher about 40,000 mL, brushing your teeth about 10 L. Explain how to make a bar graph of the data and make the graph.

Software Support

Course II: Module 3: Unit 1: Volume

3 Homework and Spiral Review

Goal: Additional Practice

This Homework page provides practice in converting metric units of capacity.

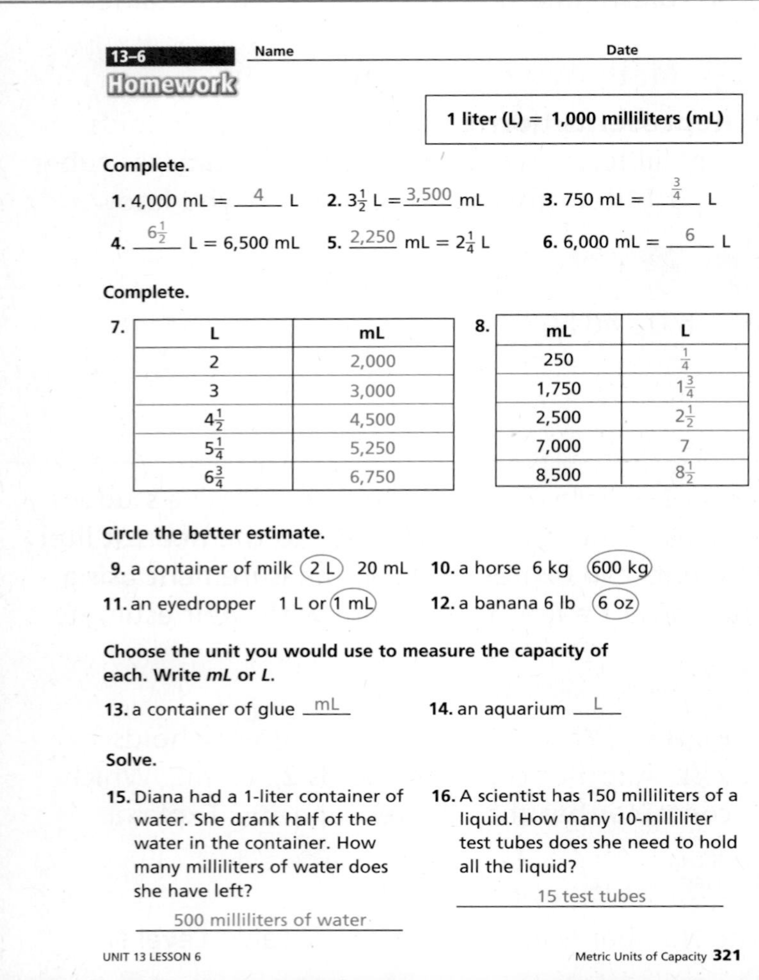

13–6 Homework Name ______ Date ______

1 liter (L) = 1,000 milliliters (mL)

Complete.

1. 4,000 mL = 4 L
2. $3\frac{1}{2}$ L = 3,500 mL
3. 750 mL = $\frac{3}{4}$ L
4. $6\frac{1}{2}$ L = 6,500 mL
5. 2,250 mL = $2\frac{1}{4}$ L
6. 6,000 mL = 6 L

Complete.

7.

L	mL
2	2,000
3	3,000
$4\frac{1}{2}$	4,500
$5\frac{1}{4}$	5,250
$6\frac{3}{4}$	6,750

8.

mL	L
250	$\frac{1}{4}$
1,750	$1\frac{3}{4}$
2,500	$2\frac{1}{2}$
7,000	7
8,500	$8\frac{1}{2}$

Circle the better estimate.

9. a container of milk (2 L) 20 mL
10. a horse 6 kg (600 kg)
11. an eyedropper 1 L or (1 mL)
12. a banana 6 lb (6 oz)

Choose the unit you would use to measure the capacity of each. Write *mL* or *L*.

13. a container of glue mL
14. an aquarium L

Solve.

15. Diana had a 1-liter container of water. She drank half of the water in the container. How many milliliters of water does she have left?
500 milliliters of water
16. A scientist has 150 milliliters of a liquid. How many 10-milliliter test tubes does she need to hold all the liquid?
15 test tubes

UNIT 13 LESSON 6 Metric Units of Capacity **321**

Homework and Remembering page 321

Goal: Spiral Review

This Remembering page would be appropriate anytime after today's lesson.

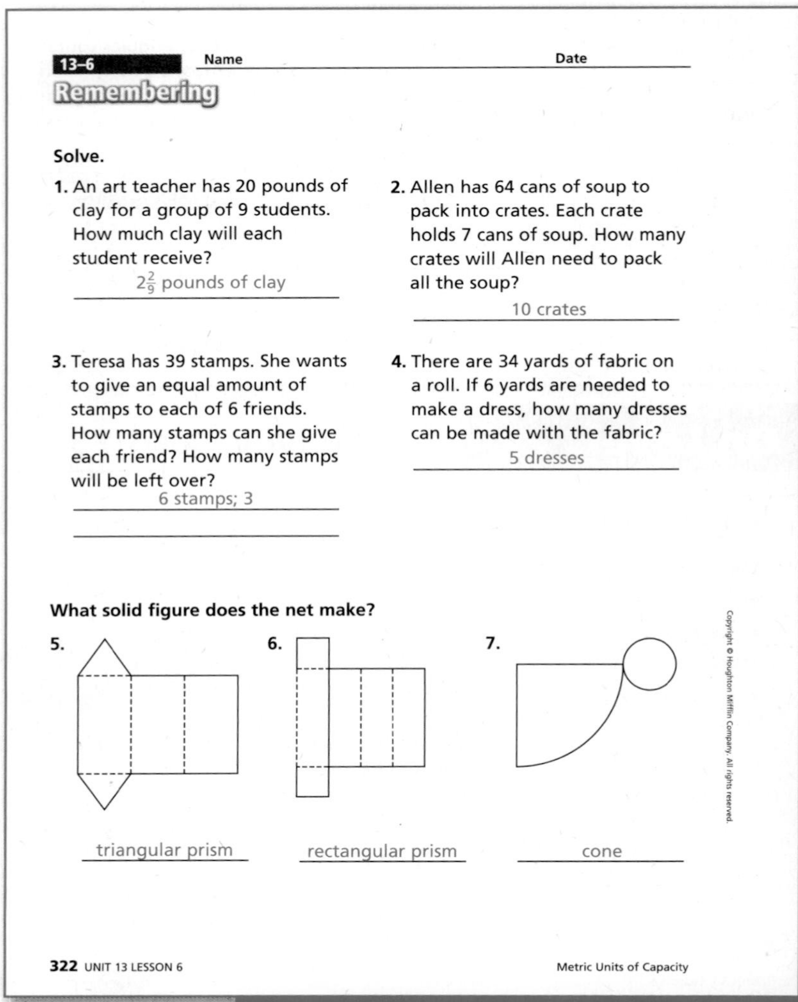

13–6 Remembering Name ______ Date ______

Solve.

1. An art teacher has 20 pounds of clay for a group of 9 students. How much clay will each student receive?
$2\frac{2}{9}$ pounds of clay
2. Allen has 64 cans of soup to pack into crates. Each crate holds 7 cans of soup. How many crates will Allen need to pack all the soup?
10 crates
3. Teresa has 39 stamps. She wants to give an equal amount of stamps to each of 6 friends. How many stamps can she give each friend? How many stamps will be left over?
6 stamps; 3
4. There are 34 yards of fabric on a roll. If 6 yards are needed to make a dress, how many dresses can be made with the fabric?
5 dresses

What solid figure does the net make?

5. triangular prism
6. rectangular prism
7. cone

322 UNIT 13 LESSON 6 Metric Units of Capacity

Homework and Remembering page 322

Home or School Activity

Music Connection

Bottle Xylophone Each note in music has a specific sound. A series of notes that increases in pitch at regular intervals is called a musical scale. Have students fill glass containers with different amounts of water. Once the bottles are set up, have students predict which bottle will make the highest or lowest sound. Then have them tap each bottle with a spoon and arrange them by pitch into a musical scale of bottles.

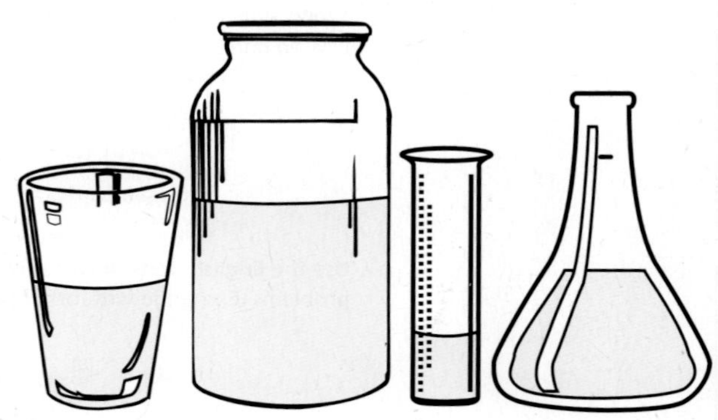

Improper Fractions and Mixed Numbers in Measurement

Lesson Objectives

- **Convert improper fractions to mixed numbers and mixed numbers to improper fractions.**
- **Visualize fractions and mixed numbers as lengths.**

Vocabulary
improper fraction
mixed number
cup

The Day at a Glance

Today's Goals	Materials	
1 Teaching the Lesson **A1:** Convert improper fractions to whole numbers or mixed numbers. **A2:** Identify fractions of an inch on a ruler.	**Lesson Activities** Student Activity Book pp. 493–494 or Student Hardcover Book pp. 493–494 Homework and Remembering pp. 323–324	**Going Further** Activity Cards 13-7 Index Cards Math Journals
2 Going Further ▶ Differentiated Instruction		
3 Homework and Spiral Review		

Use **Math Talk** today!

Keeping Skills Sharp

Quick Practice — 5 MINUTES

Goal: Identify 8s and 9s count-bys just under a number. Identify the difference between the numbers.

Just Under Count-Bys Have a **Student Leader** lead this activity for 8s and 9s. (See Unit 11 Lesson 21.)

Leader: The nearest 9s count-by *just under* 57 is?
Class: 54! (54 ÷ 9 = 6)

Leader: What's the difference between 54 and 57?
Class: 3! (57 ÷ 9 = 6 R3)

Daily Routines

Homework Review Send students to the board to share their solutions for problems 13 and 14. Have each student at the board explain his/her solution. Encourage the rest of the class to ask clarifying questions and make comments.

Elapsed Time Ted has swimming practice from 3:15 P.M. to 4:45 P.M. Then, he has a clarinet lesson at 5:30 P.M. It takes Ted 20 minutes to get from swimming to his lesson. If swimming practice runs late 25 minutes, will Ted be on time for his clarinet lesson? Explain.
Yes; 25 minutes past 4:45 P.M. is 5:10 P.M. 20 minutes past 5:10 P.M. is 5:30 P.M., the start of the lesson.

1 Teaching the Lesson

Activity 1

Improper Fractions, Mixed Numbers, and Whole Numbers in Measurements

 25 MINUTES

Goal: Convert improper fractions to whole numbers or mixed numbers.

Materials: Student Activity Book or Hardcover Book p. 493

 **NCTM Standards:**
Number and Operations
Measurement

The Learning Classroom

Building Concepts This activity reviews converting improper fractions and mixed numbers. If your class skipped the improper fraction and mixed number sections in Unit 6, this activity can serve as an introduction. You may wish to supplement the lesson with drawings if you are covering this topic for the first time with your class (see Unit 6 Lesson 17).

Teaching Note

Language and Vocabulary You may need to continually reinforce the definitions of the key vocabulary terms used in this lesson. An *improper fraction* is a fraction that is greater than or equal to 1. The numerator in an improper fraction is greater than or equal to the denominator. Some examples of improper fractions are: $\frac{3}{3}$ and $\frac{5}{4}$. A *mixed number* is a number containing a whole number part and a fractional part. Some examples of mixed numbers are $1\frac{1}{2}$ and $2\frac{3}{4}$. To simplify an improper fraction means to convert it into a whole number or a mixed number. Some examples of simplifying are $\frac{8}{4} = 2$ and $\frac{7}{2} = 3\frac{1}{2}$.

▶ Review Simplifying Improper Fractions WHOLE CLASS

Write these fractions on the board:

$$\frac{1}{1} \quad \frac{2}{2} \quad \frac{3}{3} \quad \frac{4}{4} \quad \frac{5}{5}$$

- Are all these fractions equivalent? How do you know? Yes, they are all equal to 1.

Write these fractions on the board:

$$\frac{2}{1} \quad \frac{4}{2} \quad \frac{6}{3} \quad \frac{8}{4} \quad \frac{10}{5}$$

Have students simplify the fractions. Check answers and discuss the results.

- What do you notice about your answers? These fractions are all equal to whole numbers.
- Are all these fractions equivalent? How do you know? Yes, they are all equal to 2.
- How did you change these fractions to a whole number? Possible answers: Think how many parts are in one whole. How many wholes can be made from the number of parts? Or divide the numerator by the denominator.

Ask a volunteer to come to the board and explain how to simplify one of the improper fractions above.

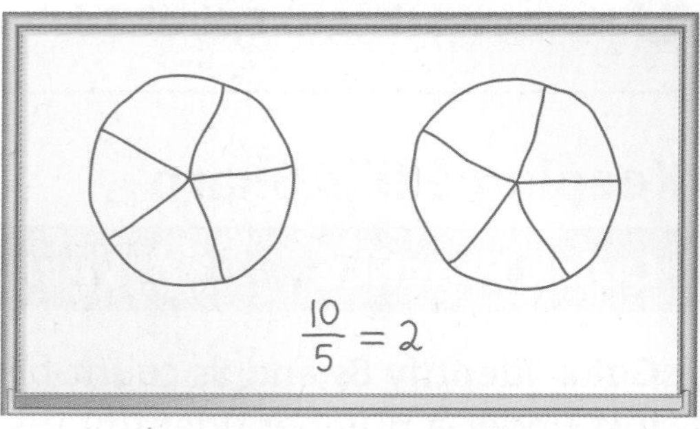

Write these fractions on the board:

$$\frac{3}{2} \quad \frac{4}{2} \quad \frac{6}{4} \quad \frac{5}{2} \quad \frac{8}{3} \quad \frac{9}{3}$$

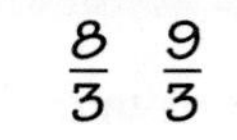 **Math Talk** Discuss which fractions represent whole numbers and which represent mixed numbers. Ask students to explain the difference between the two kinds of fractions.

- Which of these fractions represent whole numbers? $\frac{4}{2}$ and $\frac{9}{3}$ represent whole numbers because you can divide 4 evenly by 2, and 9 evenly 3.
- Why do the other fractions represent mixed numbers? Because you can't evenly divide the numerator by the denominator.

Have students simplify these fractions. Check answers and reasoning. Discuss how simplifying some of these fractions is like solving division with remainder problems in which you give the answer as a mixed number.

- How much is $\frac{3}{2}$? $1\frac{1}{2}$ How do you know? Three divided by 2 equals $1\frac{1}{2}$.

Now review writing mixed numbers as improper fractions. Discuss converting $1\frac{1}{2}$ to $\frac{3}{2}$. All students should find the student explanation given below very accessible. Some students may propose multiplying the 1 whole by 2, and then adding the 1 from $\frac{1}{2}$, to find out how many halves there are. That is fine, so long as students understand the concept behind the algorithm.

- How could we figure out that $1\frac{1}{2}$ equals $\frac{3}{2}$? We could rename the 1 whole as $\frac{2}{2}$. Then we could add $\frac{2}{2}$ to $\frac{1}{2}$. Two-halves plus $\frac{1}{2}$ equals $\frac{3}{2}$.

▶ Use Improper Fractions and Mixed Numbers in Measurements WHOLE CLASS

13-7 Class Activity

Name ____ Date ____

▶ Use Improper Fractions and Mixed Numbers in Measurements

Write the improper fraction or mixed number for each measurement.

1. $\frac{7}{2}$ c = $3\frac{1}{2}$ c	2. $\frac{9}{5}$ L = $1\frac{4}{5}$ L	3. $\frac{18}{4}$ m = $4\frac{2}{4}$ m or $4\frac{1}{2}$ m
4. $1\frac{3}{8}$ qt = $\frac{11}{8}$ qt	5. $1\frac{3}{4}$ ft = $\frac{7}{4}$ ft	6. $3\frac{2}{3}$ gal = $\frac{11}{3}$ gal
7. $4\frac{1}{2}$ in. = $\frac{9}{2}$ in.	8. $\frac{16}{7}$ pt = $2\frac{2}{7}$ pt	9. $3\frac{7}{8}$ c = $\frac{31}{8}$ c
10. $2\frac{5}{6}$ mi = $\frac{17}{6}$ mi	11. $3\frac{1}{3}$ yd = $\frac{10}{3}$ yd	12. $\frac{19}{12}$ ml = $1\frac{7}{12}$ ml
13. $\frac{17}{9}$ km = $1\frac{8}{9}$ km	14. $2\frac{1}{4}$ in. = $\frac{9}{4}$ in.	15. $\frac{21}{5}$ qt = $4\frac{1}{5}$ qt

UNIT 13 LESSON 7 Improper Fractions and Mixed Numbers in Measurements 493

Student Activity Book page 493

Direct students' attention to Student Book page 493. Complete the first few exercises as a class. Be sure everyone understands what to do. Then have students complete the rest of the exercises individually or in pairs. Follow up by checking answers as a class.

Differentiated Instruction

Extra Help Some students may have difficulty finding the correct answer when simplifying an improper fraction. Tell the students they should check the answer by changing the whole number part of the answer to an improper fraction. Tell them to use the denominator from the answer. For example, for an answer of $2\frac{2}{3}$ when simplifying $\frac{8}{3}$, say, *"2 is equal to how many thirds?"* Model writing the answer: $2 = \frac{6}{3}$. Now show how to add the fraction part of the mixed number: $\frac{6}{3} + \frac{2}{3} = \frac{8}{3}$. If the answer matches the original improper fraction. The mixed number is correct.

English Language Learners

Write *simplify* and *convert* on the board. Write $\frac{2}{4} = \frac{1}{2}$ and $2\frac{1}{4} = \frac{9}{4}$.

- **Beginning** Ask: **Did I *convert* $\frac{2}{4}$ to $\frac{1}{2}$?** no **Did I simplify?** yes **Did I *convert* $2\frac{1}{4}$?** yes
- **Intermediate and Advanced** Ask: **Did I *convert* or *simplify* $\frac{2}{4}$?** simplify **What did I do to $2\frac{1}{4}$?** convert **Does convert mean change from a mixed number to an improper fraction?** yes

Ongoing Assessment

- ▶ What is one example of an improper fraction that is a whole number?
- ▶ What steps do you use to simplify the improper fraction, $\frac{5}{2}$?

Activity 2

Rulers as Number Lines

 25 MINUTES

Goal: Identify fractions of an inch on a ruler.

Materials: Student Activity Book or Hardcover Book p. 494

 **NCTM Standards:**
Number and Operations
Measurement
Problem Solving
Reasoning and Proof

The Learning Classroom

Building Concepts Previous to this activity, students have been writing just a fraction, for example, $\frac{1}{4}$, in response to exercises in which they identify, add, or subtract fractions. In the exercises on page 526 of the Student Activity Book, students need to include the unit of measurement in their answer (*inch* or *in.*). Explain to students that when they are working with measurements, it is important to use unit labels in their responses. Three fourths of an inch is very different from three fourths of a circle.

► If you had only a $\frac{1}{4}$-cup measuring cup, how many $\frac{1}{4}$-cups would you need for $2\frac{1}{4}$ cups milk?

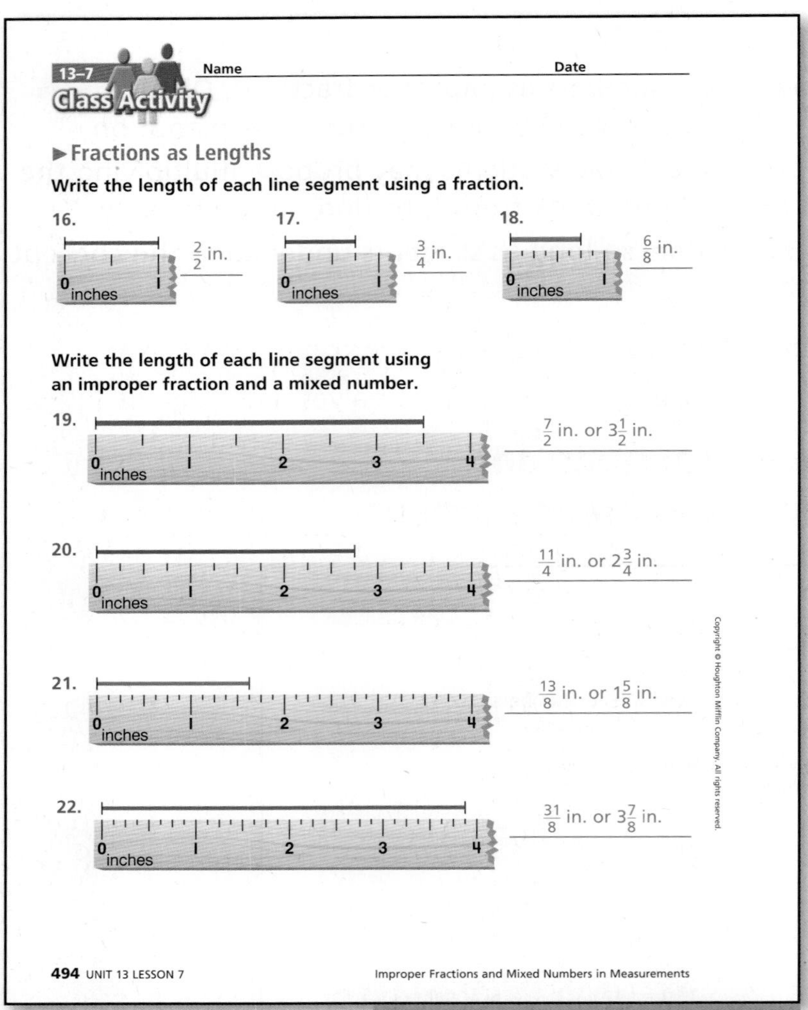
13–7 Class Activity Name Date

► Fractions as Lengths

Write the length of each line segment using a fraction.

16. $\frac{2}{2}$ in.

17. $\frac{3}{4}$ in.

18. $\frac{6}{8}$ in.

Write the length of each line segment using an improper fraction and a mixed number.

19. $\frac{7}{2}$ in. or $3\frac{1}{2}$ in.

20. $\frac{11}{4}$ in. or $2\frac{3}{4}$ in.

21. $\frac{13}{8}$ in. or $1\frac{5}{8}$ in.

22. $\frac{31}{8}$ in. or $3\frac{7}{8}$ in.

494 UNIT 13 LESSON 7 Improper Fractions and Mixed Numbers in Measurements

Student Activity Book page 494

► Fractions as Lengths WHOLE CLASS

Have students look at Student Book page 494. Work through exercises 16–18 with students. For each exercise, make sure students understand what fraction each tick mark within each inch represents.

Next, have students look at exercise 19. Have a volunteer give a suggestion for the length of the line segment as a mixed number.

- How many whole inches are in the line segment? 3
- What fraction of an inch more is the length of the line segment? $\frac{1}{2}$ inch

Now have a student give the length of the line segment as an improper fraction.

- How many half inches long is the line segment? 7
- How can you write seven halves as a fraction? $\frac{7}{2}$

Work with students to complete the exercises on this page.

2 Going Further

Differentiated Instruction

Intervention — Activity Card 13-7

Fraction Equivalents — Activity Card 13-7 ●

Work: In pairs

Use:
- Index cards

1. Make a set of index cards like the ones shown below. Then shuffle the cards and place them face down in a 6-by-3 grid to play a fraction game.

$\frac{5}{4}$	$1\frac{5}{6}$	$\frac{3}{2}$	$1\frac{1}{2}$	$1\frac{3}{4}$	$1\frac{2}{3}$
$\frac{7}{4}$	$\frac{5}{3}$	$1\frac{2}{5}$	$1\frac{1}{3}$	$\frac{8}{3}$	$\frac{9}{4}$
$2\frac{2}{3}$	$2\frac{1}{4}$	$\frac{4}{3}$	$\frac{11}{6}$	$1\frac{1}{4}$	$\frac{7}{5}$

2. Take turns. Turn over two cards and decide if the cards show an improper fraction and its matching mixed number.
3. If the cards match, keep the cards. Otherwise, return the cards face down in the same position.
4. Continue taking turns until all the cards are matched. The player with the greater number of matches wins.

Unit 13, Lesson 7

Activity Note Encourage students to draw models of the fractions to help them find matches.

Math Writing Prompt

Explain Your Thinking Choose any mixed number. Change it to an improper fraction. Write the steps you used.

Software Support

Warm Up 9.29

On Level — Activity Card 13-7

Match the Measurements — Activity Card 13-7 ▲

Work: In pairs

1. Choose numbers to complete each story below.

Choose from these numbers:

$\frac{7}{4}$ $\frac{2}{3}$ $\frac{3}{2}$ $\frac{5}{2}$ $\frac{4}{4}$ $\frac{3}{3}$

Marci measured some oatmeal using a quarter-cup measure. She measured almost 2 cups in all. The total measurement of the oatmeal was ______ cups. $\frac{7}{4}$

Gregory measured almost 3 cups of flour for a bread recipe. He used a half-cup measure. The total measurement of the flour was ______ cups. $\frac{5}{2}$

Milton used a third-cup measure to measure some honey for a cake recipe. He measured exactly 1 cup in all. The total amount of honey he used was ______ cup(s). $\frac{3}{3}$

2. Record your work and discuss your strategies.

Unit 13, Lesson 7

Activity Note Be sure that students understand the significance of the size of the measuring cup. To solve the first problem, students need to find the greatest quarter-cup measure that is less than 2 cups.

Math Writing Prompt

Use a Number Line Create a number line from 0 to 5 and locate points at $\frac{5}{4}$, $\frac{13}{4}$, $\frac{5}{2}$, $\frac{19}{4}$, and $\frac{7}{4}$. Explain how you located each point.

Software Support

Fraction Action: Number Line Mine, Level F

Challenge — Activity Card 13-7

Logical Reasoning — Activity Card 13-7 ■

Work: On your own

1. Read the problem below. Use logical reasoning to help you solve the problem.

5 different students are the following heights:

55 inches, $4\frac{1}{4}$ feet, $4\frac{1}{12}$ feet, 52 inches, and 4 feet.

Martha is the tallest. Deacon is exactly 4 feet tall. Zahara is next to the shortest. Brent is 2 inches taller than Zahara. Cassandra is taller than Zahara. How tall is each person?

Martha: 55 in.; Deacon: 4 ft; Brent: $4\frac{1}{4}$ ft; Zahara: $4\frac{1}{12}$ ft; Cassandra: 52 in.

2. Make a chart to help you organize your thinking.
3. **Analyze** How can you use equivalent measures to make it easier to solve the problem? Changing all measurements to inches makes it easier to compare and order the heights.

Unit 13, Lesson 7

Activity Note Suggest that students use a chart to record what they know about each student's height. The information given in the problem allows the elimination of one or more heights for each student.

Math Writing Prompt

Connected Math We spent $2\frac{1}{2}$ hours in Adventure Castle, ate lunch for 45 minutes, waited $1\frac{1}{2}$ hours in line, and took a 15-minute ride. Explain how to find the total time spent.

Software Support

Course II: Module 4: Unit 1: Number Patterns and Properties

3 Homework and Spiral Review

Goal: Additional Practice

This Homework page provides practice in solving comparison problems involving multiplication and division.

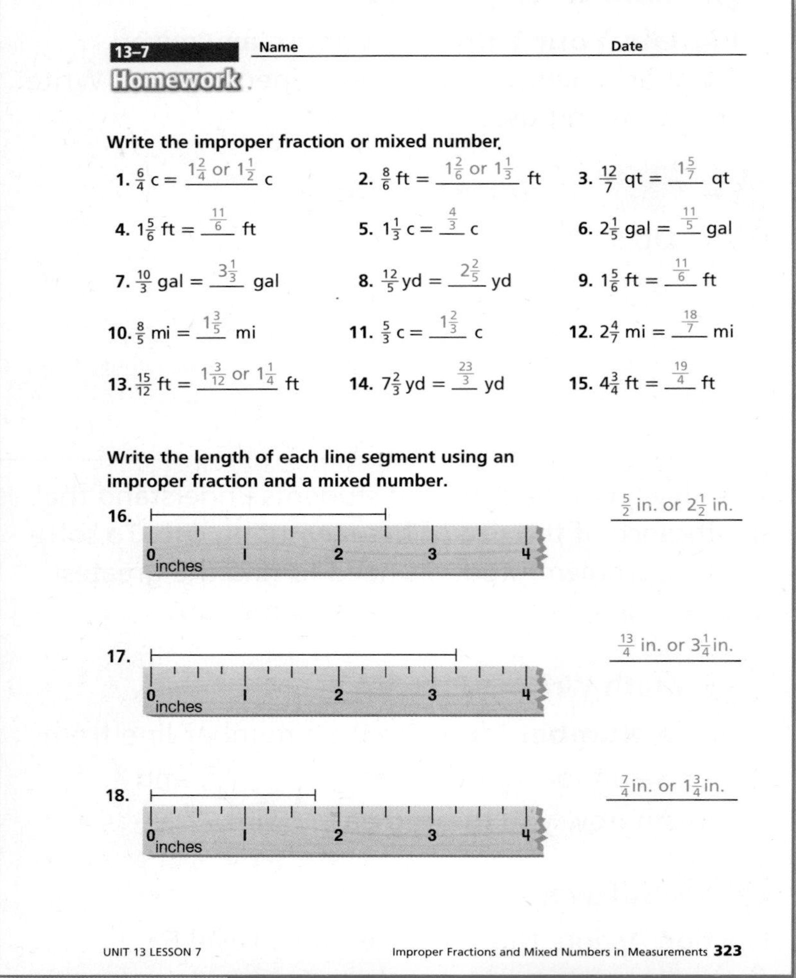

13–7 Homework Name Date

Write the improper fraction or mixed number.

1. $\frac{6}{4}$ c = $1\frac{2}{4}$ or $1\frac{1}{2}$ c
2. $\frac{8}{6}$ ft = $1\frac{2}{6}$ or $1\frac{1}{3}$ ft
3. $\frac{12}{7}$ qt = $1\frac{5}{7}$ qt
4. $1\frac{5}{6}$ ft = $\frac{11}{6}$ ft
5. $1\frac{1}{3}$ c = $\frac{4}{3}$ c
6. $2\frac{1}{5}$ gal = $\frac{11}{5}$ gal
7. $\frac{10}{3}$ gal = $3\frac{1}{3}$ gal
8. $\frac{12}{5}$ yd = $2\frac{2}{5}$ yd
9. $1\frac{5}{6}$ ft = $\frac{11}{6}$ ft
10. $\frac{8}{5}$ mi = $1\frac{3}{5}$ mi
11. $\frac{5}{3}$ c = $1\frac{2}{3}$ c
12. $2\frac{4}{7}$ mi = $\frac{18}{7}$ mi
13. $\frac{15}{12}$ ft = $1\frac{3}{12}$ or $1\frac{1}{4}$ ft
14. $7\frac{2}{3}$ yd = $\frac{23}{3}$ yd
15. $4\frac{3}{4}$ ft = $\frac{19}{4}$ ft

Write the length of each line segment using an improper fraction and a mixed number.

16. $\frac{5}{2}$ in. or $2\frac{1}{2}$ in.
17. $\frac{13}{4}$ in. or $3\frac{1}{4}$ in.
18. $\frac{7}{4}$ in. or $1\frac{3}{4}$ in.

UNIT 13 LESSON 7 Improper Fractions and Mixed Numbers in Measurements 323

Homework and Remembering page 323

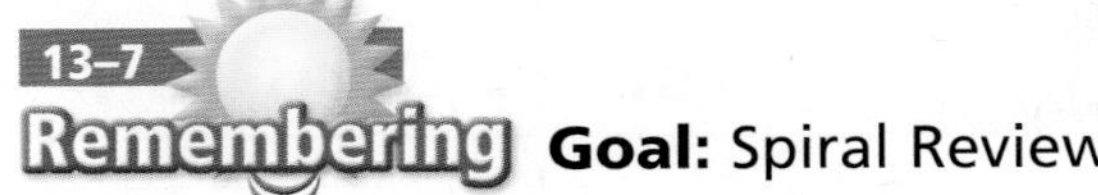

Goal: Spiral Review

This Remembering page would be appropriate anytime after today's lesson.

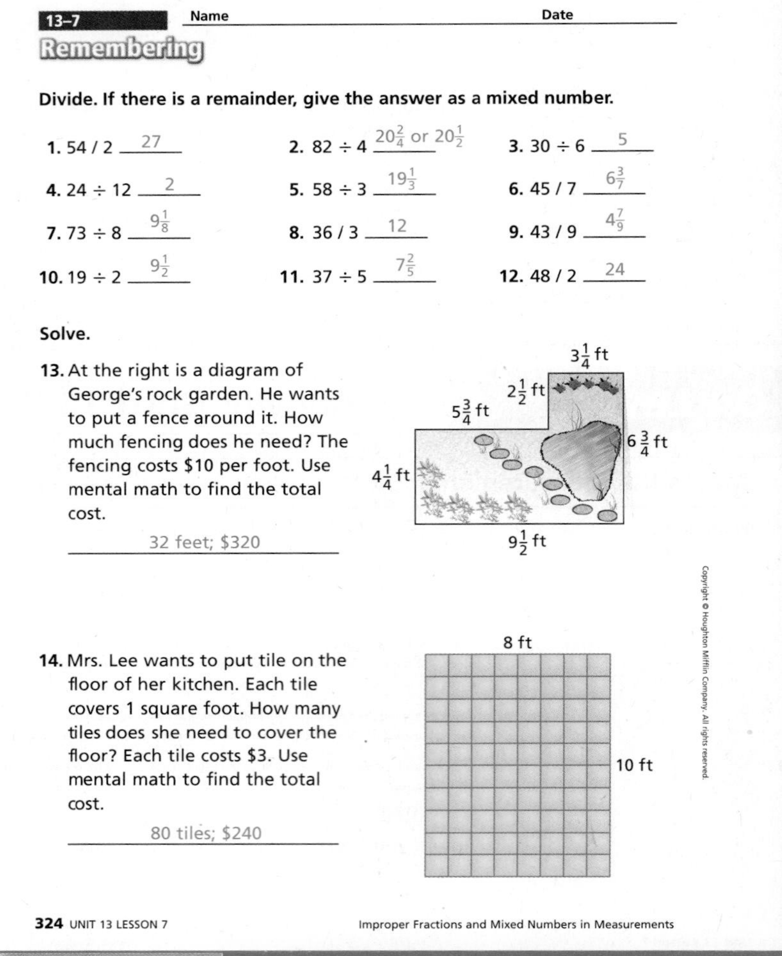

13–7 Remembering Name Date

Divide. If there is a remainder, give the answer as a mixed number.

1. 54 / 2 27
2. 82 ÷ 4 $20\frac{2}{4}$ or $20\frac{1}{2}$
3. 30 ÷ 6 5
4. 24 ÷ 12 2
5. 58 ÷ 3 $19\frac{1}{3}$
6. 45 / 7 $6\frac{3}{7}$
7. 73 ÷ 8 $9\frac{1}{8}$
8. 36 / 3 12
9. 43 / 9 $4\frac{7}{9}$
10. 19 ÷ 2 $9\frac{1}{2}$
11. 37 ÷ 5 $7\frac{2}{5}$
12. 48 / 2 24

Solve.

13. At the right is a diagram of George's rock garden. He wants to put a fence around it. How much fencing does he need? The fencing costs $10 per foot. Use mental math to find the total cost.
32 feet; $320

$3\frac{1}{4}$ ft, $2\frac{1}{2}$ ft, $5\frac{3}{4}$ ft, $6\frac{3}{4}$ ft, $4\frac{1}{4}$ ft, $9\frac{1}{2}$ ft

14. Mrs. Lee wants to put tile on the floor of her kitchen. Each tile covers 1 square foot. How many tiles does she need to cover the floor? Each tile costs $3. Use mental math to find the total cost.
80 tiles; $240

8 ft, 10 ft

Copyright © Houghton Mifflin Company. All rights reserved.

324 UNIT 13 LESSON 7 Improper Fractions and Mixed Numbers in Measurements

Homework and Remembering page 324

Home or School Activity

Real-World Connection

Fraction Flapjacks Give students the recipe for Fraction Flapjacks (pancakes). Students should figure out the measurements to make the recipe yield enough pancakes for each child in the class to have at least 2 pancakes. Students should record measurements in a new recipe and explain what might happen if their measurements are not correct.

Fraction Flapjacks

$1\frac{1}{3}$ c flour
3 tsp baking powder
$\frac{1}{2}$ tsp salt
3 tbsp sugar
1 egg
$1\frac{1}{4}$ c milk
3 tbsp melted butter or vegetable oil
$\frac{1}{4}$ tsp vanilla

Stir flour, baking powder, salt, and sugar together. Beat egg and add milk. Pour into dry ingredients. Add butter and vanilla. Stir quickly until ingredients are mixed and batter is still lumpy. Drop by 1/4 cups on hot griddle. Cook the pancakes until they are filled with bubbles and golden brown. Turn and brown the other side. Serve as hot as possible!
Yield: 12 pancakes

Measurement Equivalencies and Fractions

Vocabulary	
inch (in.)	**cup (c)**
foot (ft)	**pint (pt)**
yard (yd)	**quart (qt)**
centimeter (cm)	**gallon (gal)**
meter (m)	

Lesson Objective

- **Convert measurements of length and capacity involving fractions.**

The Day at a Glance

Today's Goals	Materials	
1 Teaching the Lesson **A:** Convert customary and metric measurements of length and capacity. **2 Going Further** ▸ Differentiated Instruction **3 Homework and Spiral Review**	**Lesson Activities** Student Activity Book pp. 495–496 or Student Hardcover Book pp. 495–496 and Activity Workbook p. 247 (includes table) Homework and Remembering pp. 325–326 *How Tall, How Short, How Far Away* by David A. Adler (Holiday House, 2000)	**Going Further** Activity Cards 13-8 Cup, pint, quart, and gallon containers Water or rice Inch Ruler Index cards labeled 2, 3, 4, 6 and 12 Chart paper Empty gallon milk container Measuring Cups Markers Math Journals

Use Math Talk today!

Keeping Skills Sharp

Quick Practice — 5 MINUTES	Daily Routines
Goal: Identify 6s, 7s, 8s, and 9s count-bys just under a number. Identify the difference between the numbers. **Just Under Count-Bys** Have a **Student Leader** lead this activity for 6s, 7s, 8s, and 9s. (See Unit 13 Lesson 6.)	**Homework Review** Have students explain how they found their errors. **Perimeter** Kelly placed 24 feet of fencing around her garden. Her garden is shaped like a rectangle that has a length of 5 ft. What is the width of her garden? 7 feet

1 Teaching the Lesson

Activity 1

Convert Measurements

55 MINUTES

Goal: Convert customary and metric measurements of length and capacity.

Materials: Student Activity Book or Hardcover Book pp. 495–496 and Activity Workbook p. 247 (includes table)

NCTM Standards:
Number and Operations
Algebra
Measurement
Communication

Differentiated Instruction

Extra Help Some students may have difficulty thinking about fractions of a unit. If students are converting inches to feet, you might have them draw a picture of a number of inches in a foot, and circle the number of inches specified. This will give them a concrete model of the conversion. For example:

How many feet are 4 inches?
- Draw the total amount of inches in one foot.
- Circle the number of inches we are talking about.

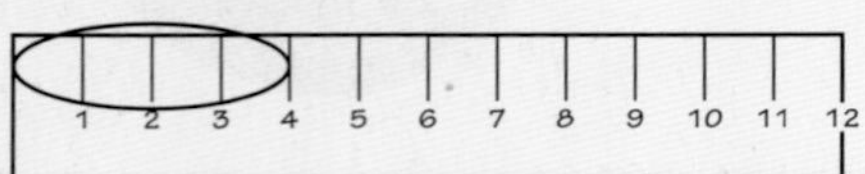

Number of inches we are talking about. → $\frac{4}{12} = \frac{1}{3}$ foot
12 inches in 1 foot. →

This hands-on visual activity is excellent for **English learners**.

▶ Discuss Measurement Equivalencies

WHOLE CLASS

Math Talk

In this lesson, students will practice converting measurements of length and measurements of capacity. Begin the lesson by making a table on the board to review linear equivalencies. Have the class help you fill in the table. Include metric and customary units.

Length		Capacity	
1 yard (yd)	= 3 feet (ft)	1 gallon (gal)	= 16 cups (c)
1 foot (ft)	= 12 inches (in.)	1 gallon (gal)	= 4 quarts (qt)
1 centimeter (cm)	= 10 millimeters (mm)	1 quart (qt)	= 2 pints (pt)
1 decimeter (dm)	= 10 centimeters (cm)	1 pint (pt)	= 2 cups (c)
1 meter (m)	= 100 centimeters (cm)	1 liter (L)	= 1,000 milliliters (mL)
1 kilometer (km)	= 1,000 meters (m)		

As a class, do a few conversions using the table you created. Use only whole-number conversions. For example, ask:

- There are 4 quarts in a gallon. How many gallons are 8 quarts? 2 gallons
- There are 3 feet in one yard. How many yards are 12 feet? 4 yards

When students seem comfortable with this task, tell them that sometimes when they find equivalent values for measurements they will need to use fractions. Give students a few examples and discuss each answer. For example, you might ask the following:

- There are 12 inches in one foot. How much of a foot is 6 inches? $\frac{1}{2}$ foot
- There are 16 cups in one gallon. How much of a gallon is 8 cups? $\frac{1}{2}$ gallon
- How much of a gallon is 4 cups? $\frac{4}{16}$ or $\frac{1}{4}$ gallon

You might draw a picture on the board if students have trouble with a conversion.

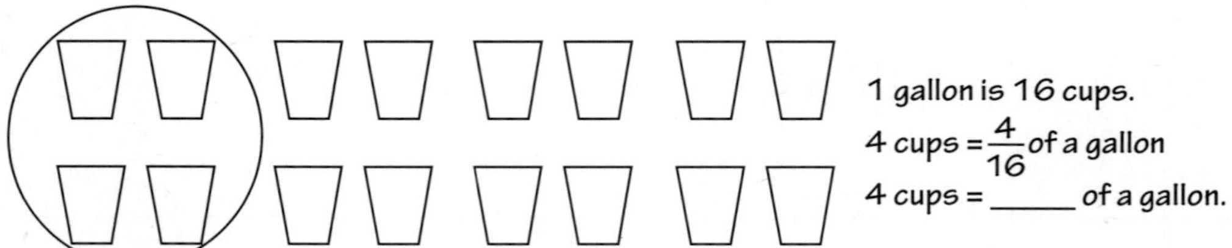

▶ Review Measurement Equivalencies WHOLE CLASS

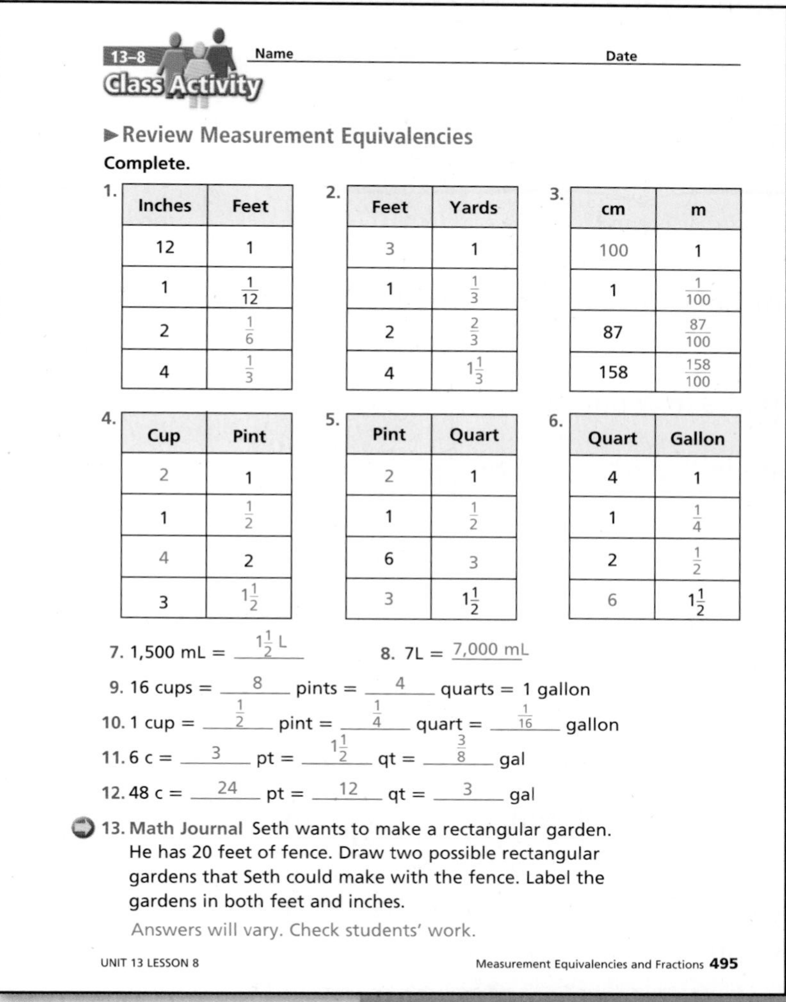

13–8 Class Activity Name Date

▶ Review Measurement Equivalencies

Complete.

1.

Inches	Feet
12	1
1	$\frac{1}{12}$
2	$\frac{1}{6}$
4	$\frac{1}{3}$

2.

Feet	Yards
3	1
1	$\frac{1}{3}$
2	$\frac{2}{3}$
4	$1\frac{1}{3}$

3.

cm	m
100	1
1	$\frac{1}{100}$
87	$\frac{87}{100}$
158	$\frac{158}{100}$

4.

Cup	Pint
2	1
1	$\frac{1}{2}$
4	2
3	$1\frac{1}{2}$

5.

Pint	Quart
2	1
1	$\frac{1}{2}$
6	3
3	$1\frac{1}{2}$

6.

Quart	Gallon
4	1
1	$\frac{1}{4}$
2	$\frac{1}{2}$
6	$1\frac{1}{2}$

7. 1,500 mL = $1\frac{1}{2}$ L

8. 7L = 7,000 mL

9. 16 cups = 8 pints = 4 quarts = 1 gallon

10. 1 cup = $\frac{1}{2}$ pint = $\frac{1}{4}$ quart = $\frac{1}{16}$ gallon

11. 6 c = 3 pt = $1\frac{1}{2}$ qt = $\frac{3}{8}$ gal

12. 48 c = 24 pt = 12 qt = 3 gal

13. Math Journal Seth wants to make a rectangular garden. He has 20 feet of fence. Draw two possible rectangular gardens that Seth could make with the fence. Label the gardens in both feet and inches.

Answers will vary. Check students' work.

UNIT 13 LESSON 8 Measurement Equivalencies and Fractions 495

Student Activity Book page 495

Have students look at Student Book page 495. Tell students they will use fractions to rename inches as feet in the first table. While students look at the first table, ask them to explain why 1 inch is the same as $\frac{1}{12}$ foot. There are 12 inches in 1 foot, so 1 inch is $\frac{1}{12}$ of a foot.

Move to the next row of the table, and ask students to find a fraction of a foot for 2 inches. Most students will answer $\frac{2}{12}$. Write this fraction on the board and review how to simplify to $\frac{1}{6}$.

Activity continued ▶

The Learning Classroom

Building Concepts Have students write a rule to complete the function tables. For example, they may see the first row of the second table and use that rule for the rest of the table: "divide each number of feet by 3."

English Language Learners

Write *function table* and have students look at Student Book page 495.

- **Beginning** Say: **These are *function tables*. They help us convert units.** Have students repeat.
- **Intermediate** Ask: **Do these tables help us convert units?** yes **Are they *function tables*?** yes
- **Advanced** Ask: **What kind of tables are these?** function tables **What do they help us do?** convert units

Teaching the Lesson (continued)

Class Management

Have students bring in old magazines or newspapers. They will need to cut weather scenes from them for the Intervention and On-Level Differentiated Instruction activities in Lesson 10.

Ongoing Assessment

Ask students to do the following:

- ► List the customary units of length in order from smallest to largest.
- ► List the customary units of capacity in order from smallest to largest.

As a class or in small groups, complete all the tables on Student Book page 495. In exercise 2, in the last row of the table, students must give their first answer in mixed number form. Go through this conversion with students. An example of a solution is shown below.

How many yards is 4 feet?

3 feet in 1 yard ⟶ $\frac{4}{3}$ yards = $1\frac{1}{3}$ yards

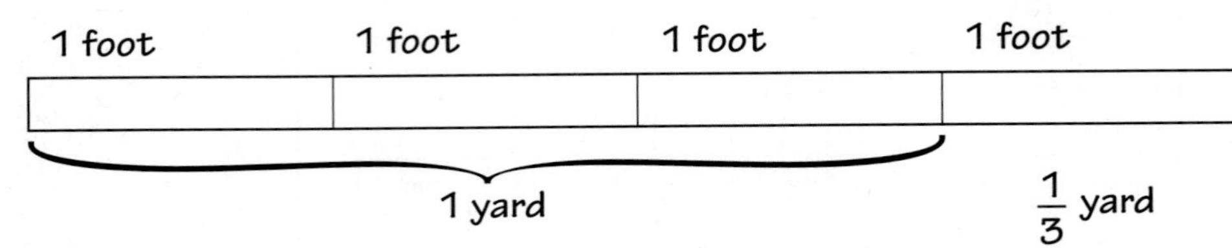

Similarly, you might help the class solve the last row in exercise 4. For example:

How many pints in 3 cups?

2 cups in 1 pint ⟶ $\frac{3}{2}$ pints = $1\frac{1}{2}$ pints

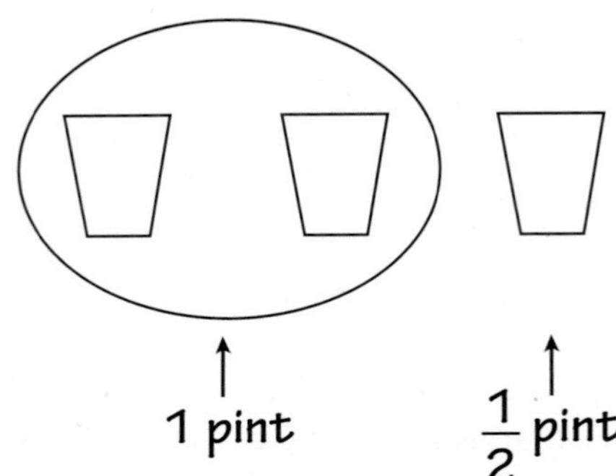

In small groups, have students discuss how they solved problem 13 and then share the diagrams of Seth's garden.

- How did you find the measure of the sides of a rectangle with a perimeter of 20 feet? The measure of two adjacent sides need to have a sum of $\frac{1}{2}$ of 20 or 10. So think what numbers will give a sum of 10. (1 + 9, 2 + 8, 3 + 7, 4 + 6) So the rectangles could be 1 by 9, 2 by 8, 3 by 7, or 4 by 6.
- How did you decide which dimensions to use? Possible answer: I used a 3 by 7 and a 4 by 6 because those sizes will have the greatest area.

2 Going Further

Differentiated Instruction

Intervention — Activity Card 13-8

Fill a Gallon — Activity Card 13-8 ●

Work: In small groups

Use:
- Cup, pint, quart, half-gallon, and gallon containers
- Water or rice

1. Follow the instructions below to fill the gallon container. Use a combination of cups, pints, quarts, and half-gallon measures.
   - Fill the cup 4 times.
   - Fill the pint container 2 times.
   - Fill a third type of container 2 times.

2. Discuss Which type of container did you choose after using the cup and the pint? Explain. Quart, because 4 cups + 2 pints = 2 quarts, and 4 quarts = 1 gallon

Unit 13, Lesson 8

Activity Note After students have correctly filled the gallon container, have them make up their own instructions. They can challenge other students to fill a gallon using different combinations of units.

Math Writing Prompt

Find the Error Jack says that 1 quart equals $\frac{1}{3}$ gallon. Is he correct? Explain.

Software Support

Warm Up 40.06

On Level — Activity Card 13-8

Snail Race — Activity Card 13-8 ▲

Work: In pairs

Use:
- Inch rulers
- Index cards labeled 2, 3, 4, 6, and 12
- Chart paper

Decide:

Who will begin the first round.

1. Play the Snail Race game. Shuffle the index cards and place them face down in a pile.
2. Begin the first round. Choose the top card from the pile. Use the number to complete the sentence below and answer the question. Then use your ruler to draw a line to match the number of inches your snail traveled.

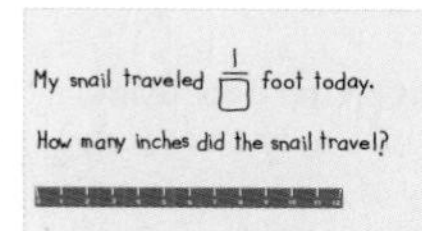

3. Take turns and continue the game. Draw the next card to find another distance for a snail to travel. The first player whose snail reaches 36 inches, or 1 yard wins.

Unit 13, Lesson 8

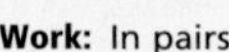

Activity Note Students may find it helpful to rename fractions as twelfths and then use the numerator as the number of inches.

Math Writing Prompt

Explain Your Thinking Explain how to convert a number of yards to inches. Give an example.

Software Support

Fraction Action: Number Line Mine, Level L

Challenge — Activity Card 13-8

Estimate Capacity — Activity Card 13-8 ■

Work: In pairs

Use:
- Empty gallon milk container
- Measuring cups
- Markers
- Water or rice

1. Use what you know about fractions to estimate measures on the gallon container.

   Use a marker to label three lines showing $\frac{1}{8}$ gallon, $\frac{1}{2}$ gallon, and $\frac{3}{4}$ gallon.
2. How many cups are in $\frac{1}{8}$ gal? $\frac{1}{2}$ gal? $\frac{3}{4}$ gal? 2 cups; 8 cups; 12 cups
3. Test the accuracy of your estimates by pouring the correct number of cups of water or rice into the gallon container.
4. Discuss What strategy did you use to make your estimates. Did you overestimate or underestimate each measure?

Unit 13, Lesson 8

Activity Note Students should think of other fractional values for the gallon container, challenge each other to estimate where that measure is on the container, and then check their estimates.

Math Writing Prompt

Number Sense Judy had 1 yard of ribbon. She cut a piece of ribbon $1\frac{3}{4}$ feet long. Did she have more or less than $\frac{1}{2}$ yard of ribbon left? Explain.

DESTINATION Math® **Software Support**

Course II: Module 3: Unit 1: Volume

Homework and Spiral Review

13–8 **Homework** **Goal:** Additional Practice

Include students' completed Homework page as part of their portfolios.

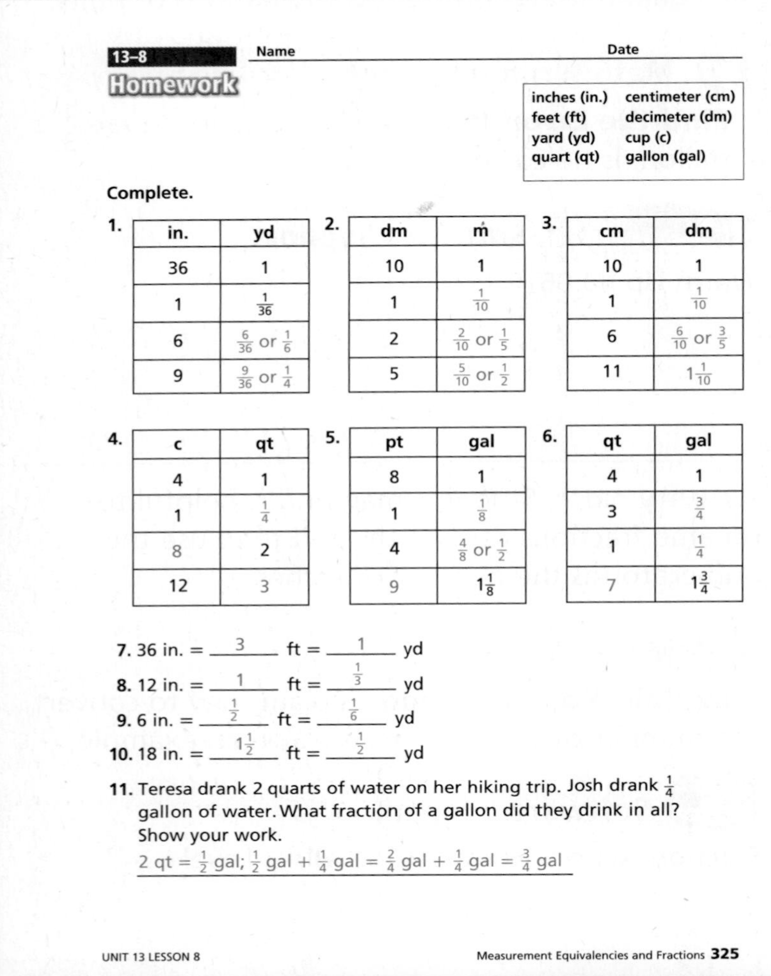

13–8 Homework Name ______ Date ______

inches (in.)	centimeter (cm)
feet (ft)	decimeter (dm)
yard (yd)	cup (c)
quart (qt)	gallon (gal)

Complete.

1.

in.	yd
36	1
1	$\frac{1}{36}$
6	$\frac{6}{36}$ or $\frac{1}{6}$
9	$\frac{9}{36}$ or $\frac{1}{4}$

2.

dm	m
10	1
1	$\frac{1}{10}$
2	$\frac{2}{10}$ or $\frac{1}{5}$
5	$\frac{5}{10}$ or $\frac{1}{2}$

3.

cm	dm
10	1
1	$\frac{1}{10}$
6	$\frac{6}{10}$ or $\frac{3}{5}$
11	$1\frac{1}{10}$

4.

c	qt
4	1
1	$\frac{1}{4}$
8	2
12	3

5.

pt	gal
8	1
1	$\frac{1}{8}$
4	$\frac{4}{8}$ or $\frac{1}{2}$
9	$1\frac{1}{8}$

6.

qt	gal
4	1
3	$\frac{3}{4}$
1	$\frac{1}{4}$
7	$1\frac{3}{4}$

7. 36 in. = 3 ft = 1 yd
8. 12 in. = 1 ft = $\frac{1}{3}$ yd
9. 6 in. = $\frac{1}{2}$ ft = $\frac{1}{6}$ yd
10. 18 in. = $1\frac{1}{2}$ ft = $\frac{1}{2}$ yd
11. Teresa drank 2 quarts of water on her hiking trip. Josh drank $\frac{1}{4}$ gallon of water. What fraction of a gallon did they drink in all? Show your work.
2 qt = $\frac{1}{2}$ gal; $\frac{1}{2}$ gal + $\frac{1}{4}$ gal = $\frac{2}{4}$ gal + $\frac{1}{4}$ gal = $\frac{3}{4}$ gal

UNIT 13 LESSON 8 Measurement Equivalencies and Fractions 325

Homework and Remembering page 325

13–8 **Remembering** **Goal:** Spiral Review

This Remembering page would be appropriate anytime after today's lesson.

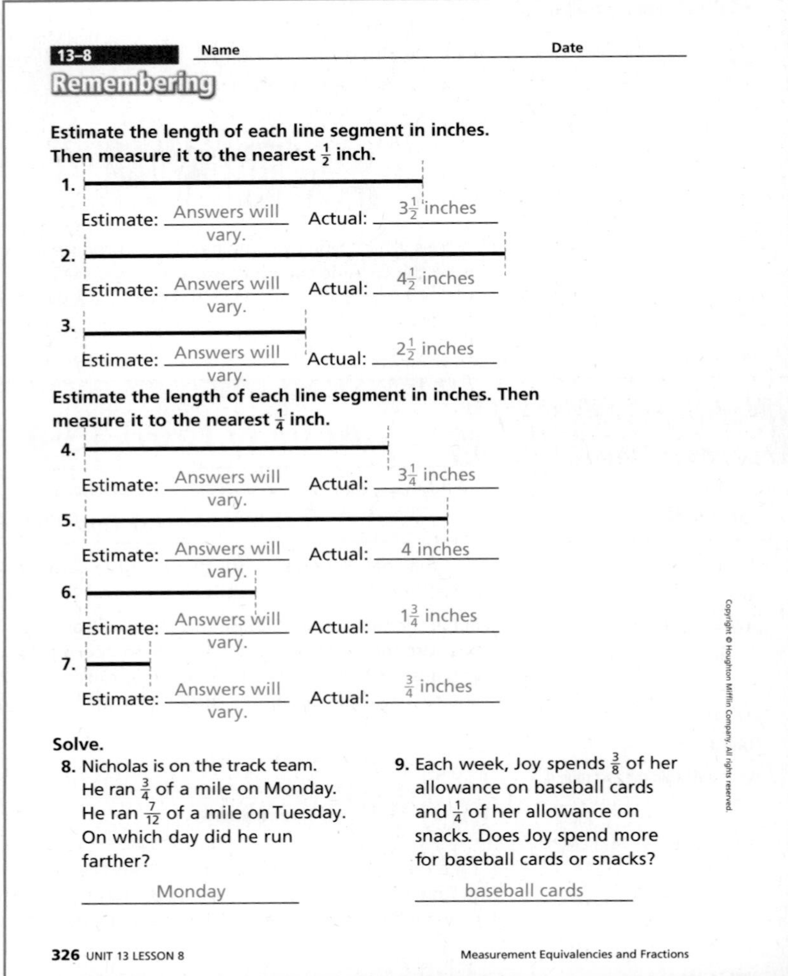

13–8 Remembering Name ______ Date ______

Estimate the length of each line segment in inches. Then measure it to the nearest $\frac{1}{2}$ inch.

1. Estimate: Answers will vary. Actual: $3\frac{1}{2}$ inches
2. Estimate: Answers will vary. Actual: $4\frac{1}{2}$ inches
3. Estimate: Answers will vary. Actual: $2\frac{1}{2}$ inches

Estimate the length of each line segment in inches. Then measure it to the nearest $\frac{1}{4}$ inch.

4. Estimate: Answers will vary. Actual: $3\frac{1}{4}$ inches
5. Estimate: Answers will vary. Actual: 4 inches
6. Estimate: Answers will vary. Actual: $1\frac{3}{4}$ inches
7. Estimate: Answers will vary. Actual: $\frac{3}{4}$ inches

Solve.

8. Nicholas is on the track team. He ran $\frac{3}{4}$ of a mile on Monday. He ran $\frac{7}{12}$ of a mile on Tuesday. On which day did he run farther?
Monday
9. Each week, Joy spends $\frac{3}{8}$ of her allowance on baseball cards and $\frac{1}{4}$ of her allowance on snacks. Does Joy spend more for baseball cards or snacks?
baseball cards

326 UNIT 13 LESSON 8 Measurement Equivalencies and Fractions

Homework and Remembering page 326

Home or School Activity

Literature Connection

How Tall, How Short, How Faraway For a historical perspective on measurement, read aloud David Adler's book. Adler explains how measurement systems developed in ancient Egypt and Rome, how they became standardized, and describes the origin of the metric system.

UNIT 13 LESSON 9

Customary Units of Weight and Metric Units of Mass

Lesson Objectives

- Find benchmarks for ounces, pounds, grams, and kilograms.
- Estimate the weight or mass of an object.
- Choose the appropriate unit to measure weight or mass of an object.
- Convert between pounds and ounces and between grams and kilograms.

Vocabulary
pound (lb)
ounce (oz)
gram (g)
kilogram (kg)

The Day at a Glance

Today's Goals	Materials	
1 Teaching the Lesson **A1:** Establish benchmarks for ounces and pounds, estimate the weight of objects, choose appropriate units, and convert between ounces and pounds. **A2:** Establish benchmarks for grams and kilograms, estimate the mass of objects, choose appropriate units, and convert between grams and kilograms.	**Lesson Activities** Student Activity Book pp. 497–502 or Student Hardcover Book pp. 497–502 and Activity Workbook pp. 248–249 (includes tables) Homework and Remembering pp. 327–328 Football, 10 pennies, large paperclip, sneaker (optional) Balance scale Spring scale Gram and kilogram units of mass Connecting Cubes *Building Big Bridges* David Macauley (WGBH, 2000)	**Going Further** Student Activity Book p. 502 or Student Hardcover Book p. 502 Activity Cards 13-9 Water Spring scale Aluminum foil Sink or large bucket *Who Sank the Boat?* by Pamela Allen (Paper Star, 1996) ✓ MathBoard materials Various small objects Math Journals
2 Going Further ► Math Connection: Addition and Subtraction with Mixed Units ► Differentiated Instruction		
3 Homework and Spiral Review		

Use Math Talk today!

Keeping Skills Sharp

Quick Practice — 5 MINUTES	Daily Routines	
Goal: Identify 6s, 7s, 8s, and 9s count-bys just under a number. Identify the difference between the numbers. **Just Under Count-Bys** (See Unit 13 Lesson 6.)	**Homework Review** Take time to work with students needing extra help with the homework.	**Strategy Problem** Pablo cut string into 4 equal pieces. Then, he cut each piece in half. Now, each piece has a 2-inch length. What was the length of the whole string? 16 inches whole piece of string 2 in. 2 in.

1 Teaching the Lesson

Activity 1

Customary Units of Weight

 20 MINUTES

Goal: Establish benchmarks for ounces and pounds, choose appropriate units, and convert between ounces and pounds.

Materials: Football and 10 pennies (optional), Student Activity Book or Hardcover Book pp. 497–498 and Activity Workbook p. 252 (includes tables)

 **NCTM Standards:**
Number and Operations
Algebra
Measurement
Communication

Teaching Note

Language and Vocabulary You might choose to discuss the difference between *ounces* and *fluid ounces*. A container of milk might list fluid ounces. A fluid ounce is a unit of capacity. An ounce is a unit of weight.

1 cup = 8 fluid ounces

English Language Learners

Draw a *scale* on the board.

- **Beginning** Say: **This is a scale. Do we use *scales* to measure *weight*?** yes
- **Intermediate** Point to the scale. Ask: **What is this?** scale Say: **We use *scales* to measure __.** weight
- **Advanced** Have students identify the *scale* and tell what it measures.

▶ Benchmarks for Pounds and Ounces WHOLE CLASS

Math Talk Ask students to think of situations in which they or someone they know needed to weigh something. Students might mention getting weighed at the doctor or weighing bananas at the grocery store. What is measured when we weigh something? how heavy the object is

- What tool do we usually use to weigh something? a scale
- What units are used when we weigh something? pounds, ounces, tons

Tell students that in this activity, they will work with pounds and ounces. On the board, write:

16 ounces = 1 pound

Students may need to feel what 1 pound and 1 ounce feels like. Pass around a football (1 lb) and 10 pennies (1 oz), so students can feel the difference in weight. You might also weigh the two objects using a balance scale so students can see how a pound is heavier and an ounce is lighter.

With the class, brainstorm to find benchmarks for a pound and an ounce. Write notes on the board. At this point, introduce the abbreviations for pound (lb) and ounce (oz).

Ask the following questions:

- What objects can we think of that weigh about one pound? Answers will vary. Possible response: box of butter
- What objects can we think of that weigh about one ounce? Answers will vary. Possible response: slice of cheese

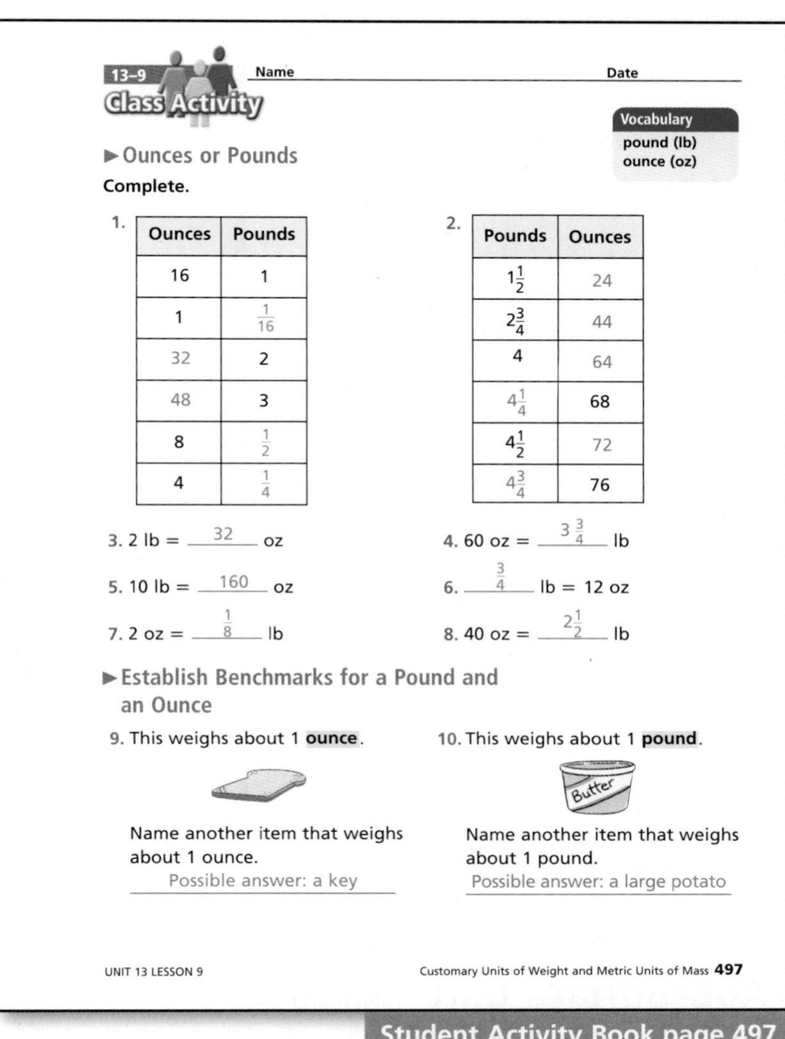

13–9 Class Activity

Name Date

Vocabulary
pound (lb)
ounce (oz)

▶ Ounces or Pounds

Complete.

1.

Ounces	Pounds
16	1
1	$\frac{1}{16}$
32	2
48	3
8	$\frac{1}{2}$
4	$\frac{1}{4}$

2.

Pounds	Ounces
$1\frac{1}{2}$	24
$2\frac{3}{4}$	44
4	64
$4\frac{1}{4}$	68
$4\frac{1}{2}$	72
$4\frac{3}{4}$	76

3. 2 lb = 32 oz
4. 60 oz = $3\frac{3}{4}$ lb
5. 10 lb = 160 oz
6. $\frac{3}{4}$ lb = 12 oz
7. 2 oz = $\frac{1}{8}$ lb
8. 40 oz = $2\frac{1}{2}$ lb

▶ Establish Benchmarks for a Pound and an Ounce

9. This weighs about 1 **ounce**.

Name another item that weighs about 1 ounce.
Possible answer: a key

10. This weighs about 1 **pound**.

Butter

Name another item that weighs about 1 pound.
Possible answer: a large potato

UNIT 13 LESSON 9 Customary Units of Weight and Metric Units of Mass **497**

Student Activity Book page 497

▶ Ounces or Pounds WHOLE CLASS

Have students look at exercises 1–8 on Student Book page 497. Work through the first few conversions with the class and make sure students understand how to write ounces as a fraction of a pound and how to write a mixed number of pounds as ounces.

▶ Establish Benchmarks for a Pound and an Ounce INDIVIDUALS

Remind students when they come to exercises 9 and 10, they should think about the benchmarks they brainstormed as a class and the objects they found that weighed about one pound and the objects they found that weighed about one ounce.

Activity continued ▶

Differentiated Instruction

Extra Help Students might want to make a drawing to help them complete the exercises. For example, to complete exercise 3 students might draw 2 circles to show 2 pounds, and then below each circle draw 16 dots to show how many ounces are in each pound. They can then count the dots to find how many ounces are in 2 pounds.

Teaching Note

Measuring in the Real World Make sure students understand how every-day objects can be measured in mixed units (for example, pounds and ounces and so on). Encourage students to weigh objects in the classroom with spring scales to demonstrate how objects can use both units. For example, a book weighs 1 lb 6 ounces.

Differentiated Instruction

Extra Help Remind students that the weight of a slice of bread is measured in ounces and the weight of a brick is measured in pounds. Encourage students to think about the weight of an object and decide if they should measure it in bricks or slices of bread.

Teaching Note

Math Background Weight is the measure of the gravitational force by which an object is attracted to another object. On Earth, that object is the Earth itself. The weight of an object changes with its distance from Earth's center; this is why an astronaut seems "weightless" in outer space. Weight is measured with spring or platform scales.

Mass is the measure of the amount of matter in an object; it does not change with the object's position. When a balance scale is used to compare two objects, it is their masses that are being compared.

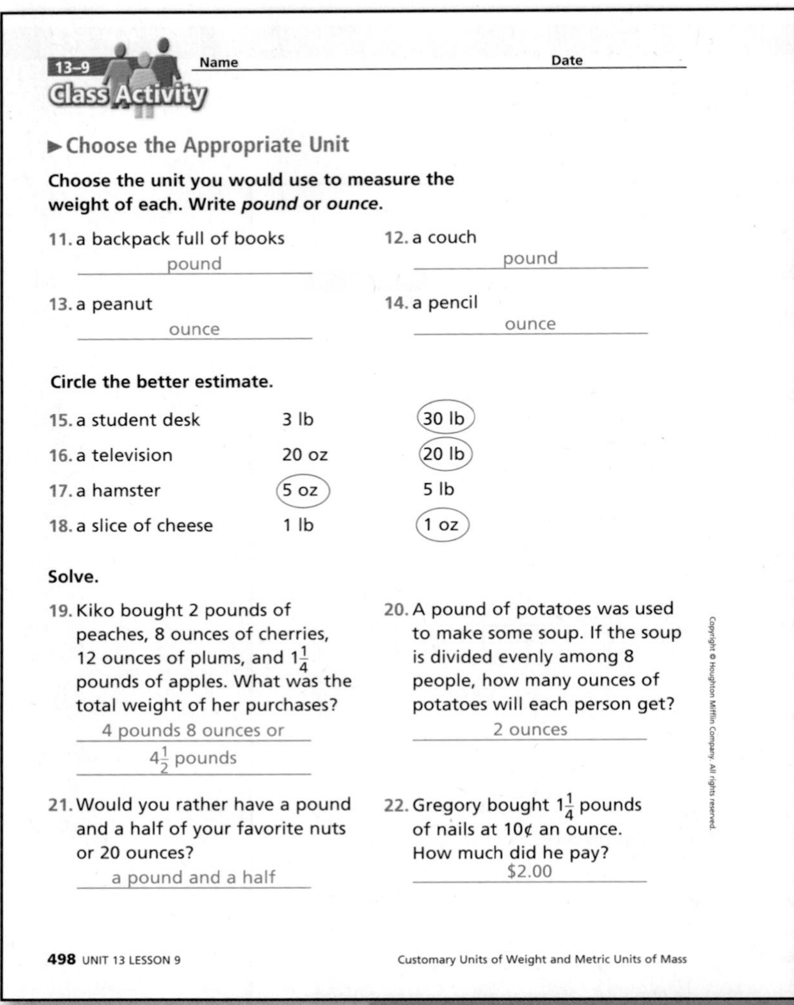

13–9 Class Activity Name Date

▶ Choose the Appropriate Unit

Choose the unit you would use to measure the weight of each. Write *pound* or *ounce*.

11. a backpack full of books pound
12. a couch pound
13. a peanut ounce
14. a pencil ounce

Circle the better estimate.

15. a student desk 3 lb (30 lb)
16. a television 20 oz (20 lb)
17. a hamster (5 oz) 5 lb
18. a slice of cheese 1 lb (1 oz)

Solve.

19. Kiko bought 2 pounds of peaches, 8 ounces of cherries, 12 ounces of plums, and $1\frac{1}{4}$ pounds of apples. What was the total weight of her purchases? 4 pounds 8 ounces or $4\frac{1}{2}$ pounds

20. A pound of potatoes was used to make some soup. If the soup is divided evenly among 8 people, how many ounces of potatoes will each person get? 2 ounces

21. Would you rather have a pound and a half of your favorite nuts or 20 ounces? a pound and a half

22. Gregory bought $1\frac{1}{4}$ pounds of nails at 10¢ an ounce. How much did he pay? $2.00

498 UNIT 13 LESSON 9 Customary Units of Weight and Metric Units of Mass

Student Activity Book page 498

▶ Choose the Appropriate Unit INDIVIDUALS

As students work through exercises 11–18, it may help them to have a weight referent on their desk. For example, if students use a standard size textbook, it is probably about 2 pounds. They may want to lift this occasionally to give an idea of how much the book weighs in comparison to a student desk or a television.

Use **Solve and Discuss** to complete problems 19–22 as a class. Remind students that all measurements need to be in a common unit to add, subtract, or compare them.

Activity 2

Metric Units of Mass

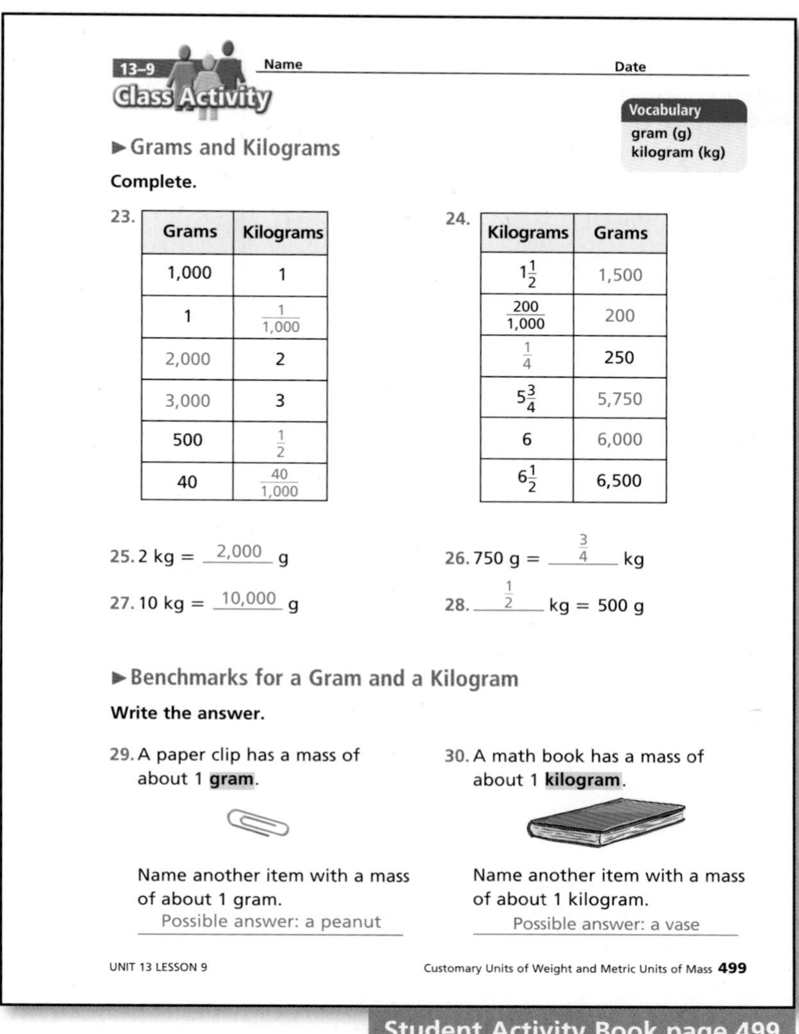

13–9 Class Activity

Name ____________ Date ____________

Vocabulary
gram (g)
kilogram (kg)

► Grams and Kilograms

Complete.

23.

Grams	Kilograms
1,000	1
1	$\frac{1}{1,000}$
2,000	2
3,000	3
500	$\frac{1}{2}$
40	$\frac{40}{1,000}$

24.

Kilograms	Grams
$1\frac{1}{2}$	1,500
$\frac{200}{1,000}$	200
$\frac{1}{4}$	250
$5\frac{3}{4}$	5,750
6	6,000
$6\frac{1}{2}$	6,500

25. 2 kg = 2,000 g

26. 750 g = $\frac{3}{4}$ kg

27. 10 kg = 10,000 g

28. $\frac{1}{2}$ kg = 500 g

► Benchmarks for a Gram and a Kilogram

Write the answer.

29. A paper clip has a mass of about 1 **gram**.

Name another item with a mass of about 1 gram.
Possible answer: a peanut

30. A math book has a mass of about 1 **kilogram**.

Name another item with a mass of about 1 kilogram.
Possible answer: a vase

UNIT 13 LESSON 9 Customary Units of Weight and Metric Units of Mass 499

Student Activity Book page 499

► Grams and Kilograms WHOLE CLASS

On the board, write: *1,000 grams = 1 kilogram*

Refer students to exercises 23–28 on Student Book page 499. Go through the first few conversions as a class. Then have students complete the exercises.

► Benchmarks for a Gram and a Kilogram

INDIVIDUALS

Direct students attention to the benchmarks for gram and kilogram in exercises 29 and 30. You may want to pass around a large paper clip (1 g) and a sneaker (1 kg), so the class can feel the difference between a gram and a kilogram.

Activity continued ►

 **20 MINUTES**

Goal: Establish benchmarks for grams and kilograms, estimate the mass of objects, choose appropriate units, and convert between grams and kilograms.

Materials: Large paper clip, and sneaker (optional), balance scale, Student Activity Book or Hardcover Book pp. 499–500 and Activity Workbook p. 253 (includes tables)

 **NCTM Standards:**
Number and Operations
Algebra
Measurement
Communication

Teaching Note

State Standards If your state requires an understanding of the relationship between pounds and kilograms, use this opportunity to compare benchmarks used for a pound with the benchmarks used for a kilogram. Students should note that a kilogram is slightly more than 2 pounds. Then estimate the weight in pounds and mass in kilograms of some objects. Compare the results.

Teaching Note

Measuring in the Real World Make sure students understand how every-day objects can be measured in mixed units, for example, kilograms and grams and so on. For example the package weighs 2 kilograms, 80 grams. In later grades mixed metric measurements will be expressed as decimals.

Ongoing Assessment

Ask students to think of an object whose mass is greater than 1 kilogram but less than 5 kilograms.

13–9 Class Activity Name ____ Date ____

▶ Choose the Appropriate Unit

Choose the unit you would use to measure the mass of each. Write *gram* or *kilogram*.

31. an elephant — kilogram
32. a crayon — gram
33. a stamp — gram
34. a dog — kilogram

Circle the better estimate.

35. a pair of sunglasses	(150 g)	150 kg
36. a horse	6 kg	(600 kg)
37. a watermelon	40 g	(4 kg)
38. a quarter	500 g	(5 g)

Solve.

39. The mass of a small penguin is 1 kilogram 800 grams. How many grams less than 2 kilograms is that? — 200 g

40. Would you rather have $\frac{1}{2}$ kilogram or 400 grams of your favorite candy? — $\frac{1}{2}$ kg

41. Rolls of coins are sometimes weighed to check how many are inside. A penny weighs about 3 g. About how many grams would a dollar's worth of pennies weigh? — about 300 g

42. Jenna wants to put 200 grams of peanuts in each of 5 small cups for party favors. Would a 1-kg bag of peanuts be enough to fill the cups? Explain. — yes; 200 + 200 + 200 + 200 + 200 = 1000 or 1,000 g, 1000 g = 1kg

500 UNIT 13 LESSON 9 Customary Units of Weight and Metric Units of Mass

Student Activity Book page 500

▶ Choose the Appropriate Unit INDIVIDUALS

Before students work through exercises 31–38, it may help to tell them that 1 kilogram is equal to a little more than 2 pounds. Since students have had more experience with weight references in pounds, it may help them to compare a kilogram with a weight they are familiar with.

Use **Solve and Discuss** to complete problems 39–42 as a class.

Activity 3

Estimate Weight and Mass

▶ Estimate Weight SMALL GROUPS

As time allows have **Small Groups** go around the classroom and find at least three objects that weigh about 1 pound. Once all groups have found their objects, have groups present their findings to the class. Encourage other groups to question the group's weight estimates and have members of the group explain why their group estimated that way. Once all groups have shared their estimates and strategies, have groups test their estimates by weighing the objects on a spring or platform scale.

Then have groups repeat the activity, but this time have groups find objects that they think weigh about an ounce. Students should share their findings and test their estimates by weighing the objects on a spring or platform scale.

▶ Estimate Mass WHOLE CLASS

Have students hold a medium size hardcover book and go around the classroom and find objects they think weigh about a kilogram. Once all groups have found their objects, have groups present their findings to the class. Encourage other groups to question the group's mass estimates and have members of the group explain why their group estimated that way. Once all groups have shared, have groups test their estimates by weighing the objects on a balance scale or pan balance.

Then have groups repeat the activity, but this time have groups find objects that they think weigh about a gram. Have them hold a paper clip or connecting cube to feel what a gram feels like. Students should share their findings and test their estimates by weighing the objects on a balance scale or pan balance.

 **20 MINUTES**

Goal: Estimate weight and mass.

Materials: sneaker or hard cover book, paper clip or connecting cube, spring scale, balance scale, gram and kilogram units of mass, Student Activity Book or Hardcover Book p. 501

 **NCTM Standard:**
Measurement

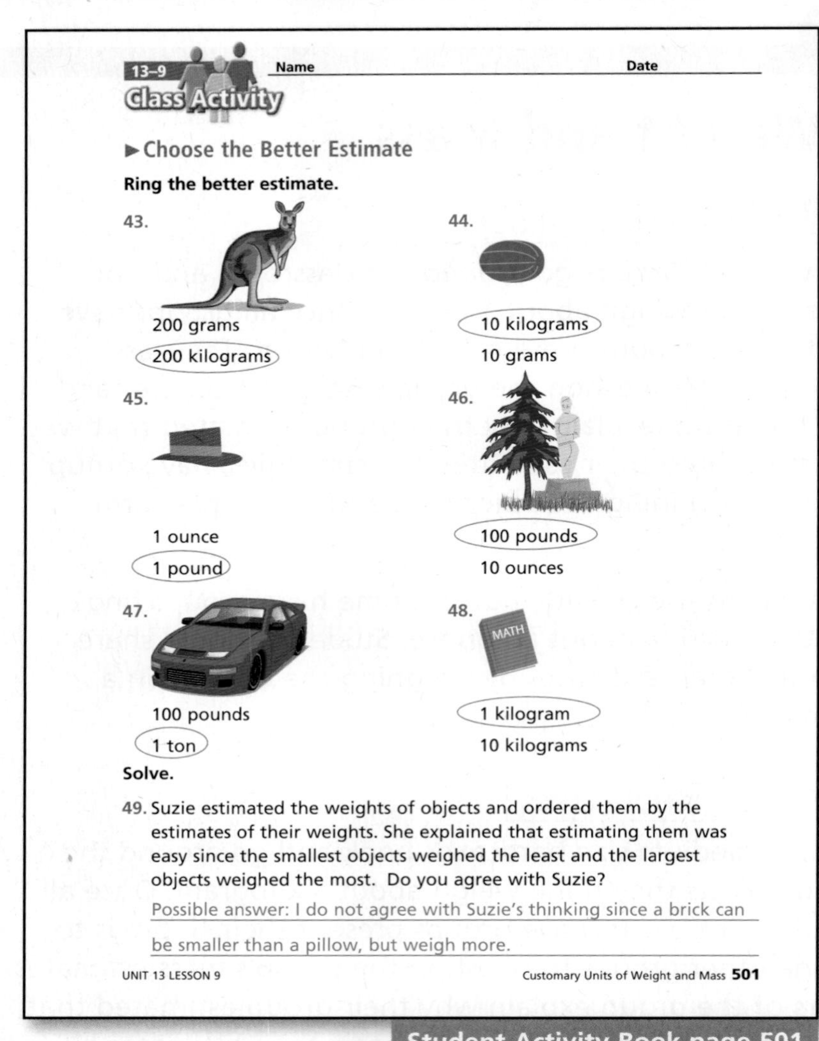
13–9 Class Activity

Name Date

▶ Choose the Better Estimate

Ring the better estimate.

43. 200 grams / (200 kilograms)

44. (10 kilograms) / 10 grams

45. 1 ounce / (1 pound)

46. (100 pounds) / 10 ounces

47. 100 pounds / (1 ton)

48. (1 kilogram) / 10 kilograms

Solve.

49. Suzie estimated the weights of objects and ordered them by the estimates of their weights. She explained that estimating them was easy since the smallest objects weighed the least and the largest objects weighed the most. Do you agree with Suzie?

Possible answer: I do not agree with Suzie's thinking since a brick can be smaller than a pillow, but weigh more.

UNIT 13 LESSON 9 Customary Units of Weight and Mass **501**

Student Activity Book page 501

▶ Choose the Better Estimate INDIVIDUALS

Have students complete exercises 43–49 individually and then have them discuss their estimates as a class. As time allows, have students share their explanations and reasoning for problem 49.

2 Going Further

Math Connection: Addition and Subtraction with Mixed Units

Goal: Add and subtract measurements with mixed units within the same system.

Materials: Student Activity Book or Hardcover Book page 502

NCTM Standards:
Measurement
Number and Operations

▶ Review Converting Measurements

Write this conversion table on chart paper for student reference while reviewing how to convert and completing Student Book page 502.

Measurement Conversion Chart

Length	Capacity	Weight/Mass	Time
1 ft = 12 in.	1 c = 8 fl oz	1 lb = 16 oz	1 min = 60 sec
1 yd = 3ft. or 36 in.	1 pt = 2 c	1 kg = 1,000 g	1 hr = 60 min
1 m = 100 cm	1 qt = 4c		1 day = 24 hr
1 dm = 10 cm	1 L = 1,000 mL		

Ask for ideas Ask students to give examples of when they converted measurements and explain what they did. Students should mention the following:

- In word problems when adding measurements in different units such as 27 ft + 7 yards, I converted units so units are the same: 9 yards + 7 yards = 16 yards.
- To compare measurements such as 120 cm and 1 m, change units so they are the same. 1 m = 100 cm so 120 cm > than 1 m.

Another example of when you may need to convert is when you need to simplify a measurement. Write the following on the board and ask volunteers to explain how to simplify the measurements.

5 ft 16 in.	2 gal 9 qt	3 lb 18 oz
3 yd 8ft	1 pt 3c	1 kg 1,500 g
1hr 70 min	2 days 25 h	2L 2,000 mL

Activity continued ▶

Math Talk in Action

Can anyone try solve this problem? 3 feet 2 inches – 2 feet 8 inches

Mitchell: Since you can't take 8 inches from 2 inches, you need to rename the measurement. I will convert to inches and then subtract. 38 inches minus 32 inches is 6 inches.

Can anyone think of another way to rename the measurement but still use feet and inches?

Sophie: You would set it up like subtraction when you borrow. When you borrow though you are borrowing a 12 for 12 inches in a foot, not a ten or 100 like when you borrow with numbers. So, you would change 3 ft 2 in. to 2 ft 14 inches and then subtract 2 ft 8 in., which gives you 6 inches.

Then ask students how they would subtract 2 ft 8 in. from 3 ft 2 in. See **Math Talk in Action** in side column for a sample discussion.

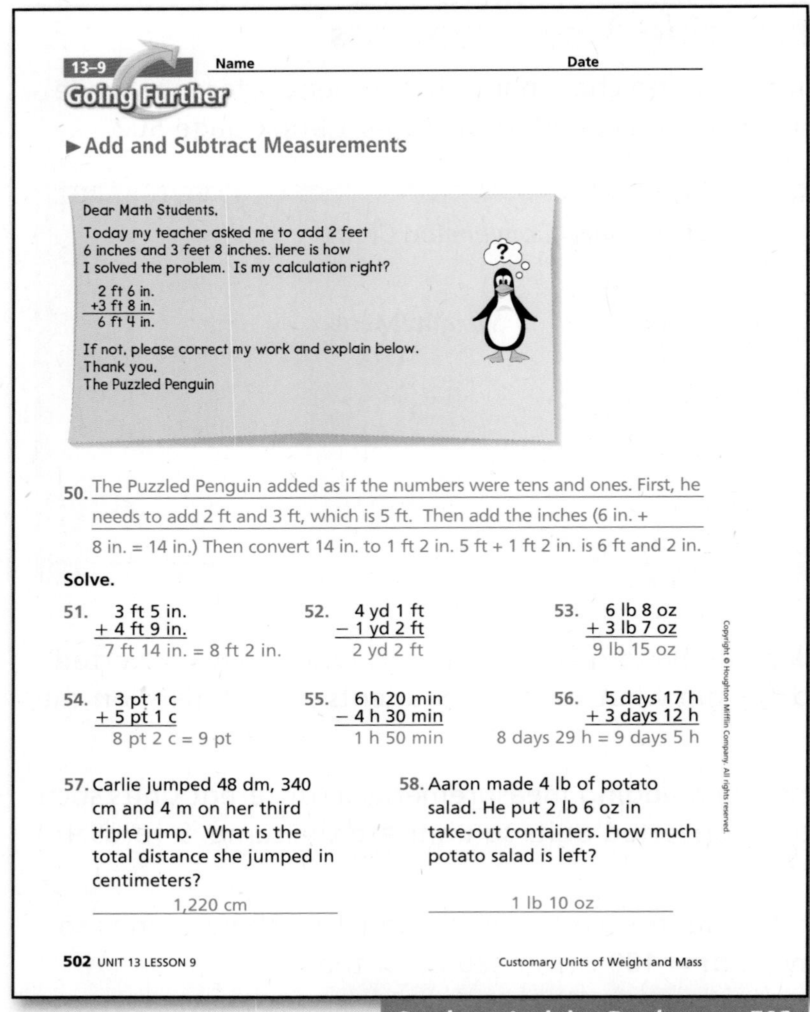

13–9 Going Further   Name ____ Date ____

► Add and Subtract Measurements

Dear Math Students,
Today my teacher asked me to add 2 feet 6 inches and 3 feet 8 inches. Here is how I solved the problem. Is my calculation right?

2 ft 6 in.
+3 ft 8 in.
6 ft 4 in.

If not, please correct my work and explain below.
Thank you,
The Puzzled Penguin

50. The Puzzled Penguin added as if the numbers were tens and ones. First, he needs to add 2 ft and 3 ft, which is 5 ft. Then add the inches (6 in. + 8 in. = 14 in.) Then convert 14 in. to 1 ft 2 in. 5 ft + 1 ft 2 in. is 6 ft and 2 in.

Solve.

51. 3 ft 5 in. + 4 ft 9 in. = 7 ft 14 in. = 8 ft 2 in.

52. 4 yd 1 ft − 1 yd 2 ft = 2 yd 2 ft

53. 6 lb 8 oz + 3 lb 7 oz = 9 lb 15 oz

54. 3 pt 1 c + 5 pt 1 c = 8 pt 2 c = 9 pt

55. 6 h 20 min − 4 h 30 min = 1 h 50 min

56. 5 days 17 h + 3 days 12 h = 8 days 29 h = 9 days 5 h

57. Carlie jumped 48 dm, 340 cm and 4 m on her third triple jump. What is the total distance she jumped in centimeters?
1,220 cm

58. Aaron made 4 lb of potato salad. He put 2 lb 6 oz in take-out containers. How much potato salad is left?
1 lb 10 oz

502 UNIT 13 LESSON 9   Customary Units of Weight and Mass

Student Activity Book page 502

► Add and Subtract Measurements

Then have students independently complete the rest of Student Book page 502.

Activity continued ►

2 Going Further

Differentiated Instruction

Intervention — Activity Card 13-9

Use a Scale — Activity Card 13-9 ●

Work: In small groups

Use:
- Spring scale
- MathBoard materials

1. Copy the table below on your MathBoard.

Object	Estimated Weight	Actual Weight

2. Work Together Estimate and then find the actual weight of objects in your classroom using a spring scale. Record your results.
3. Discuss Does making more estimates improve your ability to make a closer estimate? Why or why not?

Unit 13, Lesson 9

Activity Note Help students understand how to place the weights on one side of the scale and the object on the other side to balance it.

Math Writing Prompt

Explain Your Thinking How do you know which side of a balance scale has the lighter object or objects on it? Use an example to explain your thinking.

Software Support

Warm Up 39.06

On Level — Activity Card 13-9

Pack a Backpack — Activity Card 13-9 ▲

Work: In pairs

Use:
- Math Journal

1. Pretend that you are preparing for a desert hike. You are limited to 5 pounds of gear in your backpack. Which supplies from the list below will you choose?

2 bottles of water	24 ounces each
map of desert	4 ounces
compass	12 ounces
4 cans of tuna	8 ounces each
umbrella	8 ounces
a favorite book	16 ounces
matches	4 ounces
gloves	9 ounces
sunscreen	20 ounces

2. Analyze Calculate the total weight of your gear and explain how you made your choices.

Unit 13, Lesson 9

Activity Note Any solution that comes to 5 pounds is acceptable. Students may choose to add fractions of a pound or to find how many ounces in 5 pounds (80) and add ounces.

Math Writing Prompt

Think About It If 10 apples weigh about the same as 2 textbooks, how many textbooks weigh about the same as 25 apples? Explain your thinking.

Software Support

The Number Games: Tiny's Think Tank, Level O

Challenge — Activity Card 13-9

Sink the Boat — Activity Card 13-9 ■

Work: In small groups

Use:
- *Who Sank the Boat* by Pamela Allen (Paper Star, 1996)
- Aluminum foil
- Scale
- Various small objects
- Water
- Large bucket or sink

1. Read Pamela Allen's book *Who Sank the Boat* about five animals taking a boat ride.

   Discuss How did the weight of each animal and the order in which the animals entered the boat determine the outcome?
2. Make a boat out of aluminum foil and float it in a bucket or sink of water. Weigh several small objects and arrange them in order of weight. Predict when the boat will sink before you add the objects one-by-one to your boat.
3. Analyze Was your prediction correct? Will the outcome change if you reorder the objects and load the boat again? Try it and see.

Unit 13, Lesson 9

Activity Note Finding the total weight of the objects that sank the boat will help students decide the number of objects that will allow the boat to stay afloat.

Math Writing Prompt

More Than One Answer Four puppies together weigh the same as their mother. If the total weight for all the dogs is 32 pounds, how much could each dog weigh?

DESTINATION Math® **Software Support**

Course II: Module 4: Unit 1: Number Patterns and Properties

Homework and Spiral Review

13–9 Homework **Goal:** Additional Practice

✓ Include students' completed Homework page as part of their portfolios.

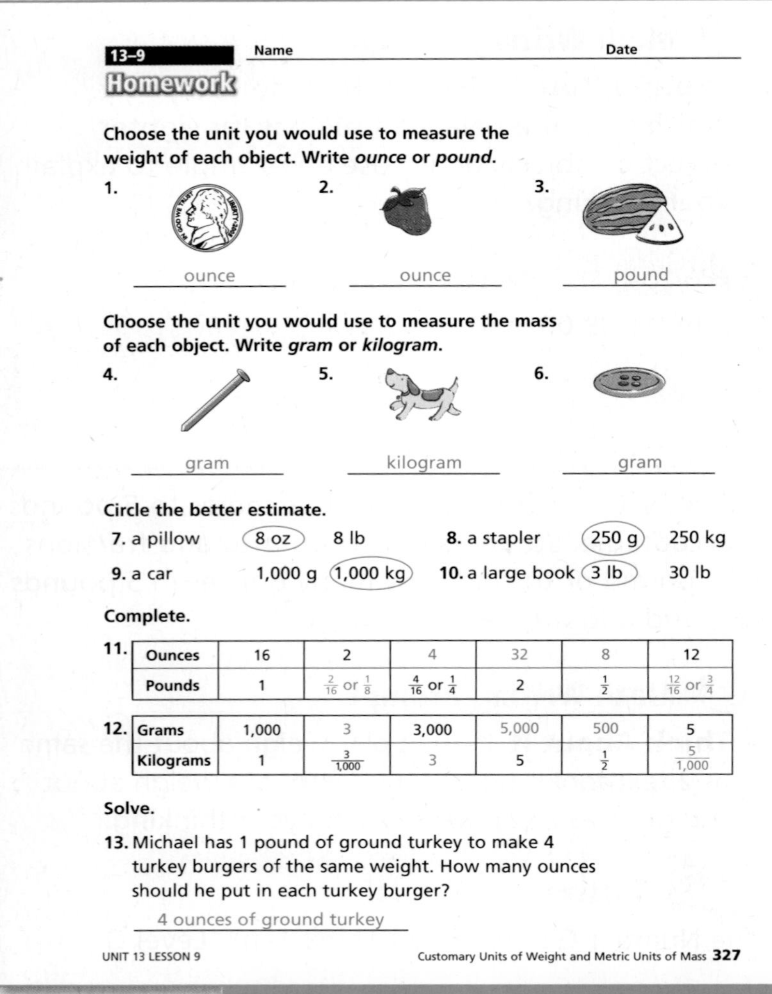

13–9 Homework Name ____________ Date ____________

Choose the unit you would use to measure the weight of each object. Write *ounce* or *pound*.

1. ounce
2. ounce
3. pound

Choose the unit you would use to measure the mass of each object. Write *gram* or *kilogram*.

4. gram
5. kilogram
6. gram

Circle the better estimate.

7. a pillow (8 oz) 8 lb
8. a stapler (250 g) 250 kg
9. a car 1,000 g (1,000 kg)
10. a large book (3 lb) 30 lb

Complete.

11.

Ounces	16	2	4	32	8	12
Pounds	1	$\frac{2}{16}$ or $\frac{1}{8}$	$\frac{4}{16}$ or $\frac{1}{4}$	2	$\frac{1}{2}$	$\frac{12}{16}$ or $\frac{3}{4}$

12.

Grams	1,000	3	3,000	5,000	500	5
Kilograms	1	$\frac{3}{1,000}$	3	5	$\frac{1}{2}$	$\frac{5}{1,000}$

Solve.

13. Michael has 1 pound of ground turkey to make 4 turkey burgers of the same weight. How many ounces should he put in each turkey burger?
4 ounces of ground turkey

UNIT 13 LESSON 9 Customary Units of Weight and Metric Units of Mass 327

Homework and Remembering page 327

13–9 Remembering **Goal:** Spiral Review

This Remembering page would be appropriate anytime after today's lesson.

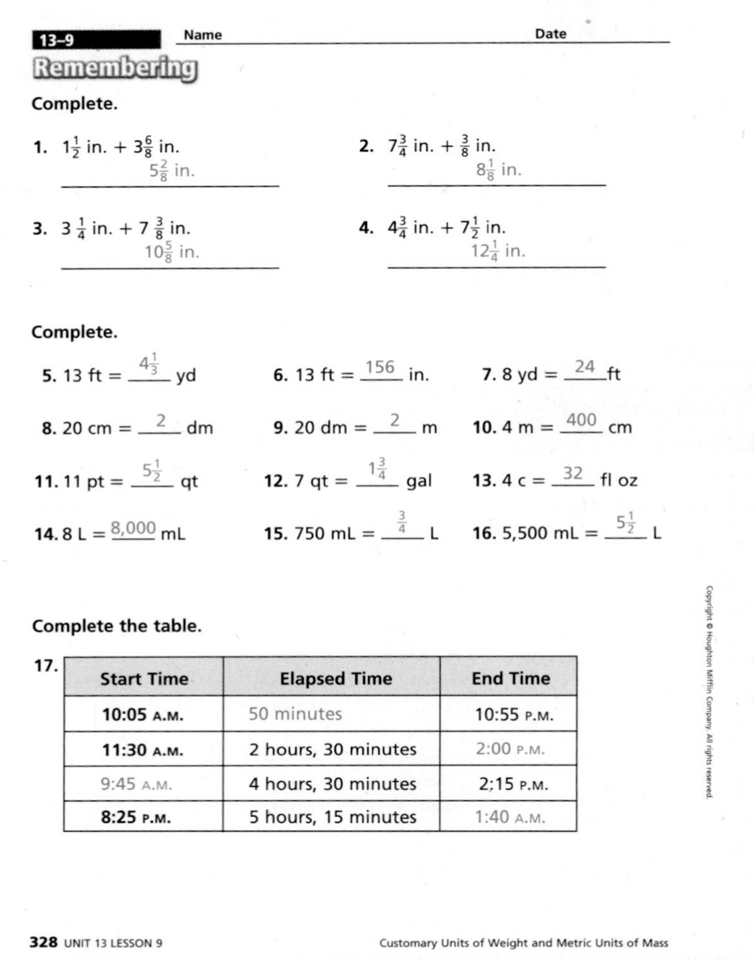

13–9 Remembering Name ____________ Date ____________

Complete.

1. $1\frac{1}{2}$ in. + $3\frac{6}{8}$ in. $5\frac{2}{8}$ in.
2. $7\frac{3}{4}$ in. + $\frac{3}{8}$ in. $8\frac{1}{8}$ in.
3. $3\frac{1}{4}$ in. + $7\frac{3}{8}$ in. $10\frac{5}{8}$ in.
4. $4\frac{3}{4}$ in. + $7\frac{1}{2}$ in. $12\frac{1}{4}$ in.

Complete.

5. 13 ft = $4\frac{1}{3}$ yd
6. 13 ft = 156 in.
7. 8 yd = 24 ft
8. 20 cm = 2 dm
9. 20 dm = 2 m
10. 4 m = 400 cm
11. 11 pt = $5\frac{1}{2}$ qt
12. 7 qt = $1\frac{3}{4}$ gal
13. 4 c = 32 fl oz
14. 8 L = 8,000 mL
15. 750 mL = $\frac{3}{4}$ L
16. 5,500 mL = $5\frac{1}{2}$ L

Complete the table.

17.

Start Time	Elapsed Time	End Time
10:05 A.M.	50 minutes	10:55 P.M.
11:30 A.M.	2 hours, 30 minutes	2:00 P.M.
9:45 A.M.	4 hours, 30 minutes	2:15 P.M.
8:25 P.M.	5 hours, 15 minutes	1:40 A.M.

328 UNIT 13 LESSON 9 Customary Units of Weight and Metric Units of Mass

Homework and Remembering page 328

Home or School Activity

Technology Connection

Build a Bridge Have students watch David Macaulay's video, *Building Big.* Students will meet architects who engineered world-famous bridges. As students learn characteristics of a well-built bridge, challenge students to build a bridge out of spaghetti, toothpicks, popsicle sticks, or straws. Have them predict which bridge will hold the most amount of weight, and then test their predictions.

Temperature

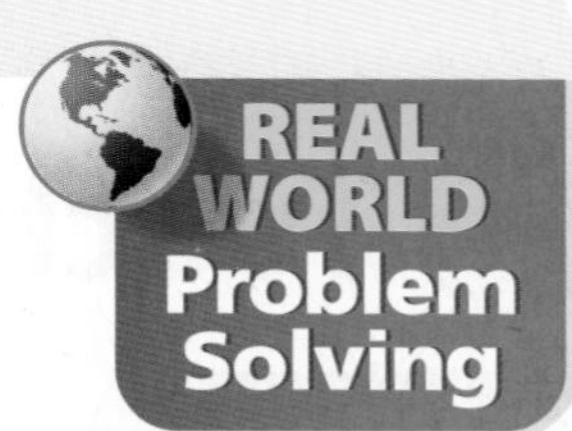

Lesson Objectives

- Read temperatures in degrees Fahrenheit and degrees Celsius on a thermometer.
- Discuss warm and cold benchmarks.
- Estimate temperatures in degrees Fahrenheit and degrees Celsius.

Vocabulary

degrees Fahrenheit (°F)
degrees Celsius (°C)

The Day at a Glance

Today's Goals	Materials	
1 Teaching the Lesson **A1:** Read temperatures in degrees Fahrenheit on a thermometer, discuss warm and cold benchmarks in degrees Fahrenheit, and estimate temperatures in degrees Fahrenheit. **A2:** Read temperatures in degrees Celsius on a thermometer, discuss warm and cold benchmarks in degrees Celsius, and estimate temperatures in degrees Celsius.	**Lesson Activities** Student Activity Book pp. 503–504 or Student Hardcover Book pp. 503–504 Homework and Remembering pp. 329–330 Transparency of Student Activity Book page 503 and overhead projector (optional) Outdoor thermometer (optional) Quick Quiz 2	**Going Further** Activity Cards 13-10 Magazines Scissors, Glue, Sticky notes Math Journals
2 Going Further ▸ Differentiated Instruction		
3 Homework and Spiral Review		

Use Math Talk today!

Keeping Skills Sharp

Quick Practice — 5 MINUTES	Daily Routines
Goal: Review finding numbers on a number line. **Number Lines** On the board, draw a number line from 0 to 20 with tick marks every two numbers and the labels 0, 10, and 20. 0 10 20 Have a **Student Leader** say a whole number between 0 and 20 and then ask a volunteer to locate this number on the number line.	**Homework Review** Have students discuss and help each other resolve difficulties from the homework. **Area** Marcus laid 48 square feet of carpet on his floor. The floor is a rectangle that has a width of 6 feet. What is the length of the floor? 8 feet

1 Teaching the Lesson

Activity 1

Degrees Fahrenheit

25 MINUTES

Goal: Read temperatures in degrees Fahrenheit on a thermometer, discuss warm and cold benchmarks in degrees Fahrenheit, and estimate temperatures in degrees Fahrenheit.

Materials: Student Activity Book or Hardcover Book p. 503, Transparency of Student Activity Book page 503 and overhead projector (optional), outdoor thermometer (optional)

NCTM Standards:
Measurement
Communication
Representation

Class Management

You may want to make a transparency of Student Book page 503 for use in this lesson.

Teaching Note

Math Background You may want to explain to students that in a mercury or alcohol thermometer, the liquid inside expands as it is heated and contracts as it is cooled, causing the column of liquid to rise or fall.

The Learning Classroom

Building Concepts If you have an outdoor thermometer, you might bring the class outside to read it, or have a few volunteers read it through the window. If you go outside, have students predict what they think the temperature is before reading the thermometer.

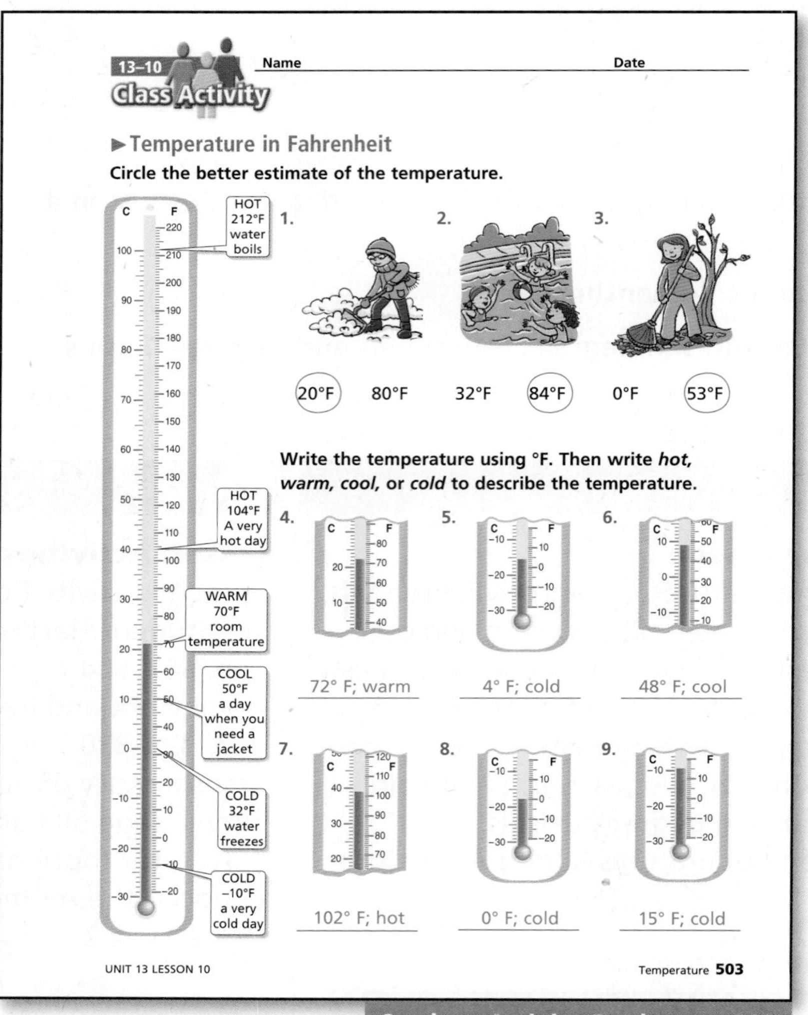

13–10 Class Activity Name Date

▶ Temperature in Fahrenheit

Circle the better estimate of the temperature.

HOT 212°F water boils

HOT 104°F A very hot day

WARM 70°F room temperature

COOL 50°F a day when you need a jacket

COLD 32°F water freezes

COLD −10°F a very cold day

1. 20°F 80°F

2. 32°F 84°F

3. 0°F 53°F

Write the temperature using °F. Then write *hot*, *warm*, *cool*, or *cold* to describe the temperature.

4. 72° F; warm

5. 4° F; cold

6. 48° F; cool

7. 102° F; hot

8. 0° F; cold

9. 15° F; cold

UNIT 13 LESSON 10 Temperature 503

Student Activity Book page 503

▶ Discuss Temperature in Fahrenheit

WHOLE CLASS

Math Talk 

Direct students to Student Book page 503 and point out the thermometer. Ask the following questions: What kind of measurement is a thermometer used for? temperature Have you ever measured the temperature of something? outside temperature; body temperature

- What is measured when we find the temperature of something? how hot or cold something is
- What units are used when we find temperature? degrees Fahrenheit or degrees Celsius

In this activity, students will learn about degrees Fahrenheit, so they will only use the °F side of the thermometer. Point out 65 degrees Fahrenheit on the thermometer, and show students the abbreviation on the board: 65°F

- What is the temperature at which water boils? 212°F Point to this on the thermometer or on the overhead transparency.
- Does anyone know what normal body temperature is for someone who is not sick. Around 98°F or 99°F Have a student mark and label this on the thermometer.

Finally, if you have a thermostat in your room, ask students to predict what the temperature is in the room. Write predictions on the board, then check the temperature. Mark and label this temperature on the thermometer. Discuss how close students' estimates were.

▶ Temperature in Fahrenheit WHOLE CLASS

Direct students to Student Book page 503. Remind students that they will use the Fahrenheit side of the thermometer for this page. Discuss the benchmarks that you have not already reviewed in class. For example, you could talk about how a 50-degree day might feel. Have students estimate the temperature in various situations shown in exercises 1–3. Then have them read the thermometers and complete exercises 4–9.

Teaching Note

Math Background Daniel Fahrenheit (1686–1736) decided he wanted 180 degrees between freezing and boiling. So he put a mercury thermometer in ice and marked the level of mercury as 32 degrees. Then he put the thermometer in boiling water and marked the level of mercury as 212 degrees, 180 degrees higher than freezing. This is how the Fahrenheit scale came about. Fahrenheit scales usually show a mark for each 2°. If reading such scales is important for your students, please draw some parts of a scale on the board and have students practice reading them.

Activity 2

Degrees Celsius

▶ Discuss Temperature in Celsius

WHOLE CLASS

Math Talk 

Tell students that in this activity, they will learn about degrees Celsius. Point out 20 degrees Celsius on the thermometer on Student Book page 503, and show students the abbreviation on the board: 20°C

Discuss some temperature benchmarks with students. The benchmarks will already be marked on the Fahrenheit side. Students will just need to find and mark these temperatures on the Celsius side of the scale. Ask:

- What is the temperature at which water freezes in degrees Celsius? 0°C
- Is the measurement in °C higher or lower than in °F. lower
- What is the temperature at which water boils in degrees Celsius? 100°C
- What is the temperature of a healthy body in degrees Celsius? 37°C
- Is the measurement in °C higher or lower than in °F. lower
- What is the temperature of the room in degrees Celsius? Answers will vary.
- Which scale is farther apart between tens? The Celsius Scale

Activity continued ▶

 **25 MINUTES**

Goal: Read temperatures in degrees Celsius on a thermometer, discuss warm and cold benchmarks in degrees Celsius, and estimate temperatures in degrees Celsius.

Materials: Student Activity Book or Hardcover Book p. 504

 **NCTM Standards:**
Measurement
Communication
Representation

The Learning Classroom

Building Concepts To give a better sense of the Celsius scale, you might want to use an outdoor thermometer that includes degrees Celsius. Have students estimate what they think the temperature might be in degrees Celsius, and then check it on the thermometer.

Differentiated Instruction

Advanced Learners Some students may be interested in discussing boiling and freezing points of liquids other than water. Mercury, for example, boils at 357°C and freezes at −39°C.

Ongoing Assessment

Have students write three of their own temperatures in degrees Fahrenheit and write *hot, warm, cool,* or *cold* to describe the temperatures.

Quick Quiz

See Assessment Guide for Unit 13 Quick Quiz 2.

English Language Learners

Draw an ice cube and a pot of boiling water on the board. Point to each.

- **Beginning** Say: **Very cold water becomes ice. It *freezes*. Very hot water bubbles. It *boils*.** Have students repeat.
- **Intermediate** Say: **When water turns to ice, it is __.** freezing **Water *boils* when it's very __.** hot
- **Advanced** Have student tell what happens when water gets very cold and very hot.

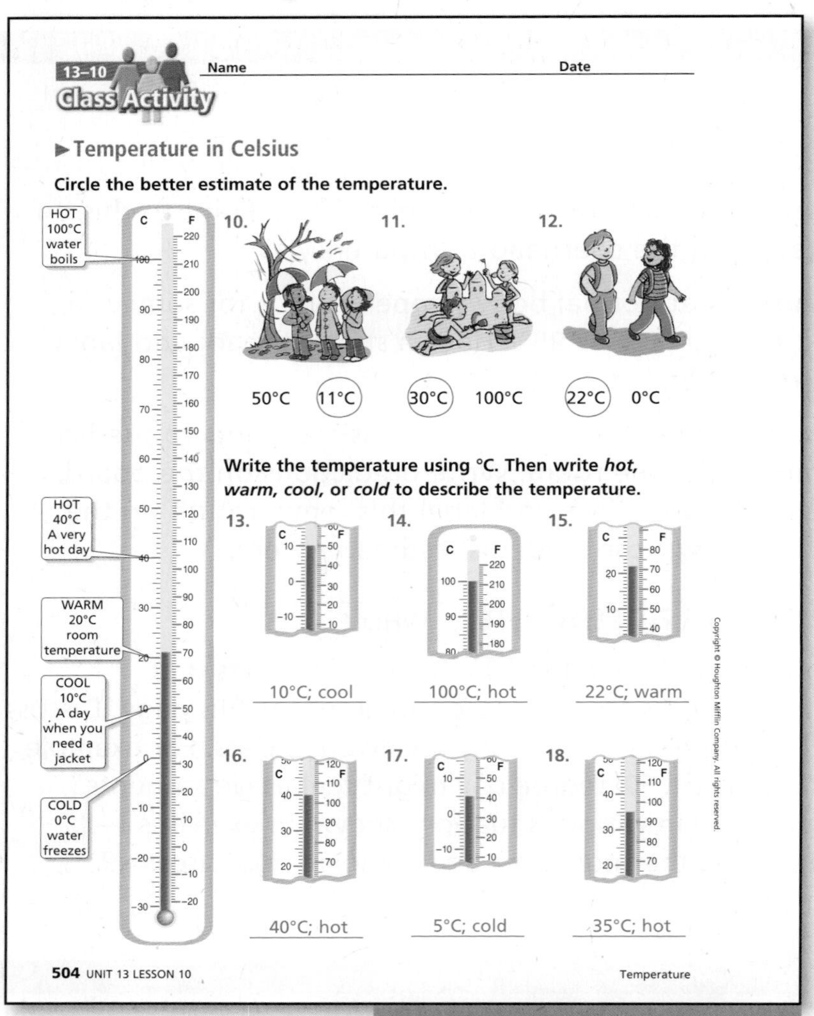

13–10 Class Activity Name Date

▶ Temperature in Celsius

Circle the better estimate of the temperature.

10. 50°C (11°C)
11. (30°C) 100°C
12. (22°C) 0°C

Write the temperature using °C. Then write *hot, warm, cool,* or *cold* to describe the temperature.

13. 10°C; cool
14. 100°C; hot
15. 22°C; warm
16. 40°C; hot
17. 5°C; cold
18. 35°C; hot

504 UNIT 13 LESSON 10 Temperature

Student Activity Book page 504

▶ Temperature in Celsius WHOLE CLASS

Have students look at Student Book page 504. Point out the Celsius scale and benchmarks on the left side. Be sure students understand that 100°C is as hot as 212°F, and that a *warm* day is 20°C. Some students might notice that negative temperatures are shown on the thermometer. You might point out that on the Fahrenheit scale, the temperature must drop far below freezing to be in negative numbers. Have students practice estimating and reading temperatures in degrees Celsius by completing exercises 10–18.

2 Going Further

Differentiated Instruction

Intervention Activity Card 13-10

Guess My Temperature

Activity Card 13-10 ●

Work: In pairs

Use:

- Magazines
- Scissors
- Glue
- Sticky notes

1. On Your Own Find at least three weather scenes from a magazine. Attach them to a sheet of paper. Write an appropriate Fahrenheit temperature under the picture of each scene. Then cover it with a sticky note.

2. Trade papers with your partner and try to guess the temperature for each picture. Write your guess on the sticky note. Then compare it to the temperature written under the note.
3. Discuss Can you justify both temperatures for each picture? Why or why not?

Unit 13, Lesson 10

Activity Note Discuss with students an appropriate range of Fahrenheit temperatures for each picture that they have chosen.

Math Writing Prompt

Explain Your Thinking On a warm day, the thermometer reads 20°. Is the thermometer showing Fahrenheit or Celsius? Explain how you know.

Software Support

Warm Up 49.02

On Level Activity Card 13-10

Weather Collage

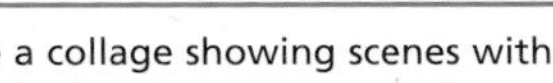

Activity Card 13-10 ▲

Work: In small groups

Use:

- Magazines
- Scissors
- Glue

1. Work Together Make a collage showing scenes with different Celsius temperatures.
2. Write at least three different Celsius temperatures, one for a cold day, one for a warm day, and one for a hot day. Then look in magazines to find pictures to match each temperature.
3. Cut out the pictures and glue them onto your collage with the correct temperature label under each one.

Unit 13, Lesson 10

Activity Note Discuss with students an appropriate range of Celsius temperatures for each picture that they have chosen.

Math Writing Prompt

Investigate Math Sue Jung is going away on a trip. It is 20°C where she is going. Describe what kind of clothes she should pack. Explain your thinking.

Software Support

The Number Games: Tiny's Think Tank, Level P

Challenge Activity Card 13-10

Temperatures Below Zero

Activity Card 13-10 ■

Work: In pairs

Use:

- Student Activity Book page 504
- Math Journals

1. Read the story below.
   - Madeline checked the temperature in the morning. It was 6°C.
   - By noon the temperature had climbed 2 degrees Celsius.
   - But after noon, the temperature dropped 5 degrees Celsius.
   - Freezing rain started at 3 P.M. The temperature dropped 4 more degrees Celsius by 4 P.M.
2. Use the thermometer on Student Activity Book page 504 as a number line. What was the temperature at 4 P.M.? −1°C
3. Write your own temperature story about temperatures below zero. Share your story with your partner to find the final temperature.

Unit 13, Lesson 10

Activity Note Suggest that students make a diagram that shows each intermediate temperature as the weather warms and then cools towards afternoon.

Math Writing Prompt

Number Sense When you read a thermometer, does each mark always equal one degree? Explain.

DESTINATION Math® **Software Support**

Course II: Module 3: Unit 2: Temperature

3 Homework and Spiral Review

13–10 Homework **Goal:** Additional Practice

This Homework page provides practice in reading thermometers.

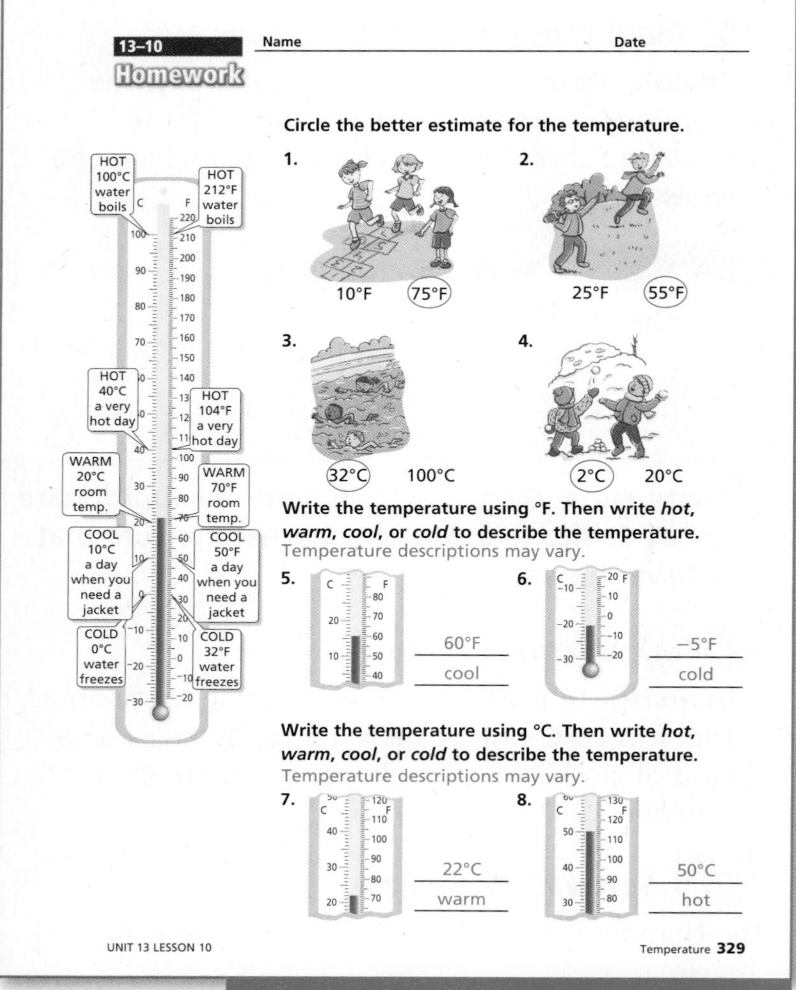

13–10 Homework

Name ____________ Date ____________

Circle the better estimate for the temperature.

1. 10°F (75°F)
2. 25°F (55°F)
3. (32°C) 100°C
4. (2°C) 20°C

Write the temperature using °F. Then write *hot*, *warm*, *cool*, or *cold* to describe the temperature.

Temperature descriptions may vary.

5. 60°F cool
6. −5°F cold

Write the temperature using °C. Then write *hot*, *warm*, *cool*, or *cold* to describe the temperature.

Temperature descriptions may vary.

7. 22°C warm
8. 50°C hot

UNIT 13 LESSON 10 Temperature 329

Homework and Remembering page 329

13–10 Remembering **Goal:** Spiral Review

This Remembering page would be appropriate anytime after today's lesson.

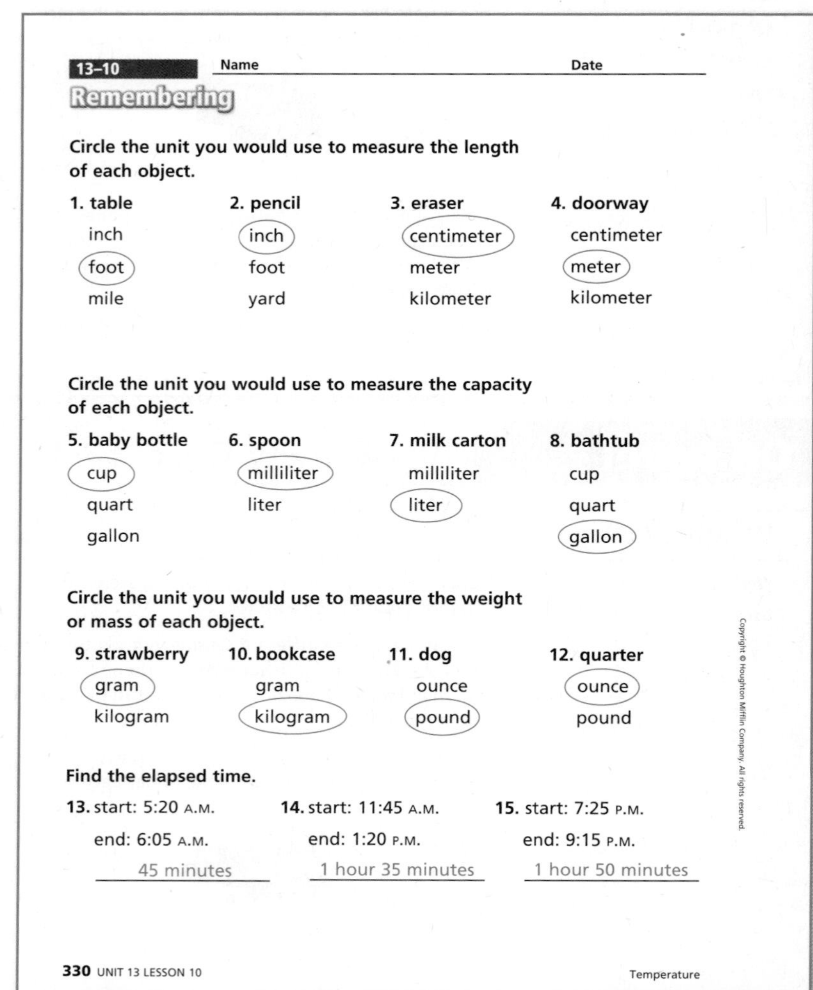

13–10 Remembering

Name ____________ Date ____________

Circle the unit you would use to measure the length of each object.

1. table: inch, (foot), mile
2. pencil: (inch), foot, yard
3. eraser: (centimeter), meter, kilometer
4. doorway: centimeter, (meter), kilometer

Circle the unit you would use to measure the capacity of each object.

5. baby bottle: (cup), quart, gallon
6. spoon: (milliliter), liter
7. milk carton: milliliter, (liter)
8. bathtub: cup, quart, (gallon)

Circle the unit you would use to measure the weight or mass of each object.

9. strawberry: (gram), kilogram
10. bookcase: gram, (kilogram)
11. dog: ounce, (pound)
12. quarter: (ounce), pound

Find the elapsed time.

13. start: 5:20 A.M. end: 6:05 A.M. 45 minutes
14. start: 11:45 A.M. end: 1:20 P.M. 1 hour 35 minutes
15. start: 7:25 P.M. end: 9:15 P.M. 1 hour 50 minutes

330 UNIT 13 LESSON 10 Temperature

Homework and Remembering page 330

Home or School Activity

Math-to-Math Connection

How Hot Is Honolulu? For one week, have students record temperatures for various cities in the United States or in the world. Have students display their data in a line graph to show how the temperatures changed over the week. Students can compare and discuss their line graphs with other students.

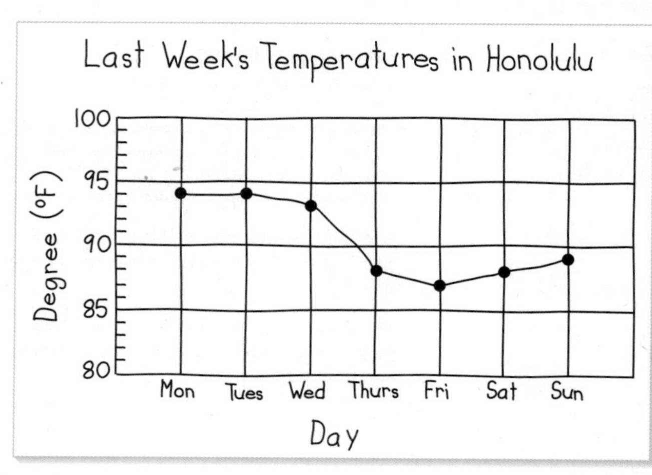

Use Mathematical Processes

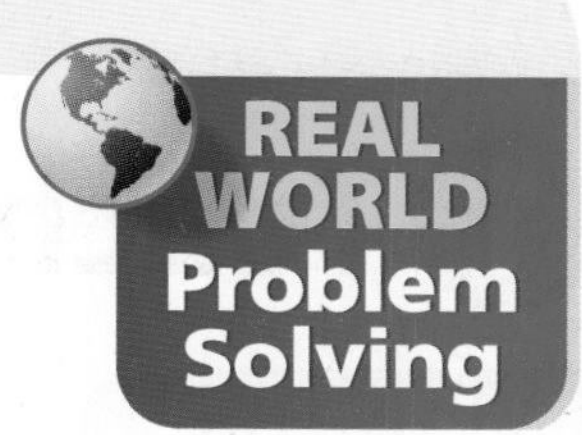

Lesson Objectives

- Apply mathematical concepts and skills in meaningful contexts.
- Reinforce the NCTM process skills embedded in this unit, and in previous units, with a variety of problem-solving situations.

The Day at a Glance

Today's Goals	Materials	
1 Teaching the Lesson **Science Connection** Identify which shape better, covers a surface circles or hexagons; show that you can surround one hexagon with 6 hexagons and there will not be any holes. **Problem Solving** Make a prediction; collect data to answer a question; record data in a table and bar graph; write about the results. **Reasoning and Proof** Use examples to support that a triangle can have at most one obtuse angle. **Representation** Draw a net for a cube; put text and images on the net correctly so they go the right way when the net is folded into a cube. **Communication** Solve a story problem that involves division with a remainder.	**Lesson Activities** Student Activity Book (pp. 505–506) Homework and Remembering (pp. 331–332) Circular counters Pattern Block hexagon Grid paper Yardstick	**Going Further** Activity Cards 13-11 Number cube with numbers 1–6 Rulers (TRB M144) Math Journals
2 Going Further ► Differentiated Instruction		
3 Homework and Spiral Review		

Use Math Talk today!

Keeping Skills Sharp

Quick Practice / Daily Routines	
If you wish to include Quick Practice or a Daily Routine, choose content based on the needs of your class.	**Class Management** Select activities from this lesson that support important goals and objectives, or that help students prepare for state or district tests.

1 Teaching the Lesson

Activity 1

Connections

Math and Science

 45 MINUTES

Goals: Identify which shape better covers a surface circles or hexagons; show that you can surround one hexagon with 6 hexagons and there will not be any holes.

Materials: Student Activity Book page 505, circular counters, Pattern Block hexagon

 **NCTM Standards:**

Problem Solving
Communication
Reasoning and Proof
Connections
Representation

13–11 Class Activity Name Date

▶ Math and Science

Bees store the honey they make in a structure called honeycomb. The bees need the honey that is stored for food during the winter. The best thing for the bees is to have as much space as possible to store the honey.

1. Cover a piece of paper with circular counters. Cover the same size piece of paper with pattern block hexagons. Do the circles cover the page completely?
   No. There are spaces between the circles.
   Do the hexagons cover the page completely?
   Yes. There are no spaces between the hexagons.
2. The honeycomb is made out of hexagons. Why does the hexagon work better for the bees than the circle?
   There is wasted space between the circles. There are no spaces between the hexagons. So all of the space can be used for storage.
3. You can surround 1 hexagon with 6 hexagons and there won't be any holes. Use pattern blocks to support or disprove the statements.
   My model shows there is one hexagon surrounded by 6 hexagons and there are no holes.

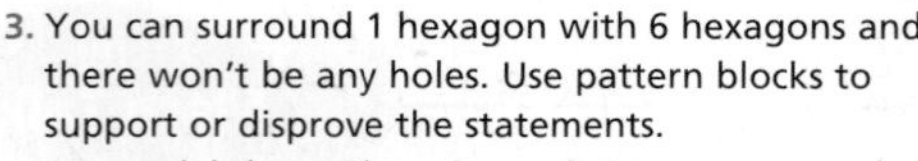

UNIT 13 LESSON 11 Use Mathematical Processes 505

Student Activity Book page 505

▶ Discuss the Information

Task 1 Have students read the paragraph about bees at the top of the page. Discuss the information as a class and ask questions such as:

- Have you ever seen a beehive? Have students share their experiences.
- Have you ever seen honeycomb? What is the shape of the cells in the honeycomb? Have students share their experiences.

▶ Make Tesselations

Task 2 Have **Student Pairs** complete the activity. Then ask questions such as:

- Which shape covered the space better, the circle or the hexagon? hexagon
- Why is a hexagon a better choice for the honeycomb structure than a circle? With the circle there is wasted space. There is no wasted space with the hexagon.
- How did you support or disprove that you can surround 1 hexagon with 6 hexagons and there won't be any holes? Allow students to show what happened when they surrounded 1 hexagon with 6 hexagons.

English Language Learners

Make sure students can identify and describe a hexagon. Help them compare it to a circle.

Draw both shapes on the board.

- **Beginning** Point and ask: **Does a circle have straight sides?** no **Does a *hexagon have straight sides*?** yes **How many sides does a *hexagon* have?** 6 sides
- **Intermediate and Advanced** Ask: **Which shape has straight sides?** hexagon **Which shape is better for building something?** hexagon

Activity 2

Problem Solving

Measurement

 **60 MINUTES**

Goals: Make a prediction; collect data to answer a question; record data in a table and bar graph; write about the results.

Materials: Student Activity Book page, grid paper, yardstick

 **NCTM Standards:**

Problem Solving
Connections
Communication
Representation

13–11 Class Activity Name Date

▶ Shadows

4. If you measured the shadow of a yardstick at different times of the day, do you think the shadow would always be the same length or would it be different? Make a prediction.
Answers will vary. Sample: I think it would be different because sometimes my shadow is short and other times it is long.

5. Measure the length of the shadow of a yardstick at four different times of the day. Put the yardstick at the same spot each time. Record the shadow lengths in the table below. Answers will vary. Check children's work.

Time of Day	Length of Shadow of Yardstick

6. On a separate piece of paper, make a bar graph that shows the length of the shadow at different times of the day.
Answers will vary. Check children's work.

7. Write about what you found out. Compare what you found out to what you predicted in exercise 4.
Answers will vary. Sample: I found that the shadow gets shorter and shorter and then it starts getting longer and longer. I predicted the shadow would be different lengths at different times of the day and it was.

506 UNIT 13 LESSON 11 Use Mathematical Processes

Student Activity Book page 506

Teaching Note

More Shadow Activities Have students measure the shadow at the same time of day at four different times of the year. Have them compare the results. They will find that the shadows are shorter in summer than in winter. Bring out in a discussion that the length of a shadow depends on the time of day and the position of the sun at different times of the year.

▶ Measure Shadows

Math Talk 

Task 1 Begin with whole class discussion of shadows. In this activity, students are going to measure the shadow of a yardstick. Choose a sunny day for doing the activity so the shadow will be very clear. Choose a location such as the playground for the activity. Choose four times spaced out during the day to measure the shadow.

- Does the length of a shadow change throughout the day? Answers will vary. Allow students to share their thoughts.

▶ Compare Shadow Lengths

Task 2 Tell students that they are going to measure the length of the shadow of a yardstick four different times during the day to find out what happens to the length of the shadow. Put students in groups of 3 so that one student can hold the yardstick, one student can measure the shadow, and one student can record the results. Students should measure at the same place each time. Remind students not to look directly at the sun during this activity so they don't hurt their eyes.

▶ Find a Pattern with Shadows

Math Talk 

Task 3 When students have completed the activity, discuss the results. Ask questions such as:

- What happened to the shadow during the day? Answers will vary. sample: The shadow got shorter and shorter. The shadow was very short around noon. Then the shadow got longer and longer.

Activity 3

Reasoning and Proof

A Statement About Triangles

 **15 MINUTES**

Goal: Use examples to support that a triangle can have at most one obtuse angle.

 **NCTM Standards:**
Problem Solving
Reasoning and Proof
Communication
Representation

Support or disprove the statement using examples.
A triangle can have at most one obtuse angle.
Students should have drawn triangles with an obtuse angle and pointed out that the other two angles are acute angles.

Hold a whole-class discussion of the problem.

- Did you support or disprove the statement? Support
- What examples did you use to support the statement? Have students show each other the examples they used to support the statement.
- Some students may use the sum of the angle measures of a triangle to prove the statement is true. Possible answer: An obtuse is angle than 90°. If you subtract an angle, for example 92°, from 180°, the difference is 88°. If you divide 88° by 2, the result is 44°. This proves that there can only be 1 obtuse angle in a triangle.

Activity 4

Representation

A Birthday Cube

 **15 MINUTES**

Goal: Draw a net for a cube; put text and images on the net correctly so they go the right way when the net is folded into a cube.

 **NCTM Standards:**
Problem Solving
Connections
Representation
Communication

Design a birthday card on a net that will fold into a cube with images on so that they go the right way when the card is folded into a cube. Check student's work.

Discuss the problem with the class.

- What does your birthday card design look like before it is folded and after it is folded? Have students show their design before it is folded and after it is folded.
- How many different arrangements of squares will work? There are 11 nets of a cube and these are the arrangements of squares that will work. See how many of the nets of a cube the students used.

Activity 5

Communication

Lupe's Photo Album

 **15 MINUTES**

Goal: Solve a story problem that involves division with a remainder.

NCTM Standards:
Problem Solving
Connections
Communication

Lupe is putting a photograph in her photo album. Each page can hold four photographs. Lupe has 34 photographs. How many pages will she need? Explain.
When you divide 34 by 4 you get 8 R2. Lupe needs another page for the two remaining photos.

Hold a whole-class discussion of the problem.

- Since 34 divided by 4 is 8 with a remainder of 2, why isn't the answer to this problem 8? If Lupe had just 8 pages, she would not have a page for the 2 photos represented by the remainder. She needs a page for those photos so she needs 9 pages.

Intervention

Activity Card 13-11

Move Forward by $\frac{1}{2}$ Inches Activity Card 13-11

Work: In pairs

Use:

- Number cube with numbers 1–6
- Rulers (TRB M144)

Decide:

Who will be Student 1 and who will be Student 2 for the first round.

1. Each player makes a $\frac{1}{2}$-inch ruler.
2. Student 1: Roll the number cube. Start at 0 on the ruler. Move the number of $\frac{1}{2}$ inches that is on the number cube. Put a mark where you land.

3. Student 2: Do the same as Student 1.
4. Take turns. Whoever gets to 12 inches first wins.

Unit 13, Lesson 11

Activity Note Students practice the process skill of representation. They also apply what they learned about fractions and measurement.

Math Writing Prompt

Explain Your Thinking Suppose you are on 10 inches and you want to get to 12 inches or beyond in your next turn. What is the least number that can show up on the number cube to do that? Explain.

Software Support

Warm Up 38.12

On Level

Activity Card 13-11

Move Forward by $\frac{1}{4}$ Inches Activity Card 13-11

Work: In pairs

Use:

- Number cube with numbers 1–6
- Rulers (TRB M144)

Decide:

Who will be Student 1 and who will be Student 2 for the first round.

1. Each player makes a $\frac{1}{4}$-inch ruler.
2. Student 1: Roll the number cube. Start at 0 on the ruler. Move the number of $\frac{1}{4}$ inches that is on the number cube. Put a mark where you land.

3. Student 2: Do the same as Student 1.
4. Take turns. Whoever gets to 12 inches first wins.

Unit 13, Lesson 11

Activity Note Students practice the process skill of representation. They also apply what they learned about fractions and measurement in this unit.

Math Writing Prompt

Explain Your Thinking Suppose you are on $10\frac{1}{2}$ inches and you want to get to 12 inches or beyond in your next turn. What is the least number that can show up on the number cube to do that? Explain.

Software Support

Ice Station Exploration: Linear Lab, Level F

Challenge

Activity Card 13-11

Move Backward by $\frac{1}{4}$ Inches Activity Card 13-11

Work: In pairs

Use:

- Number cube with numbers 1–6
- Rulers (TRB M144)

Decide:

Who will be Student 1 and who will be Student 2 for the first round.

1. Each player makes a $\frac{1}{4}$-inch ruler.
2. Student 1: Roll the number cube. Start at 12 inches on the ruler. Move backward the number of $\frac{1}{4}$ inches that is on the number cube. Put a mark where you land.

3. Student 2: Do the same as Student 1.
4. Take turns. Whoever gets to 0 inches first wins.

Unit 13, Lesson 11

Activity Note Students practice the process skill of representation. They also apply what they learned about fractions and measurement.

Math Writing Prompt

Investigate Math Suppose you are on $1\frac{1}{4}$ inches and you want to get to 0 inches or beyond in your next turn. What is the least number that can show up on the number cube to do that? Explain.

Software Support

Course II: Module 2: Unit 3: Fractional Parts

Homework and Spiral Review

13–11 **Homework** **Goal:** Additional Practice

✓ Include students' completed Homework page as part of their portfolios.

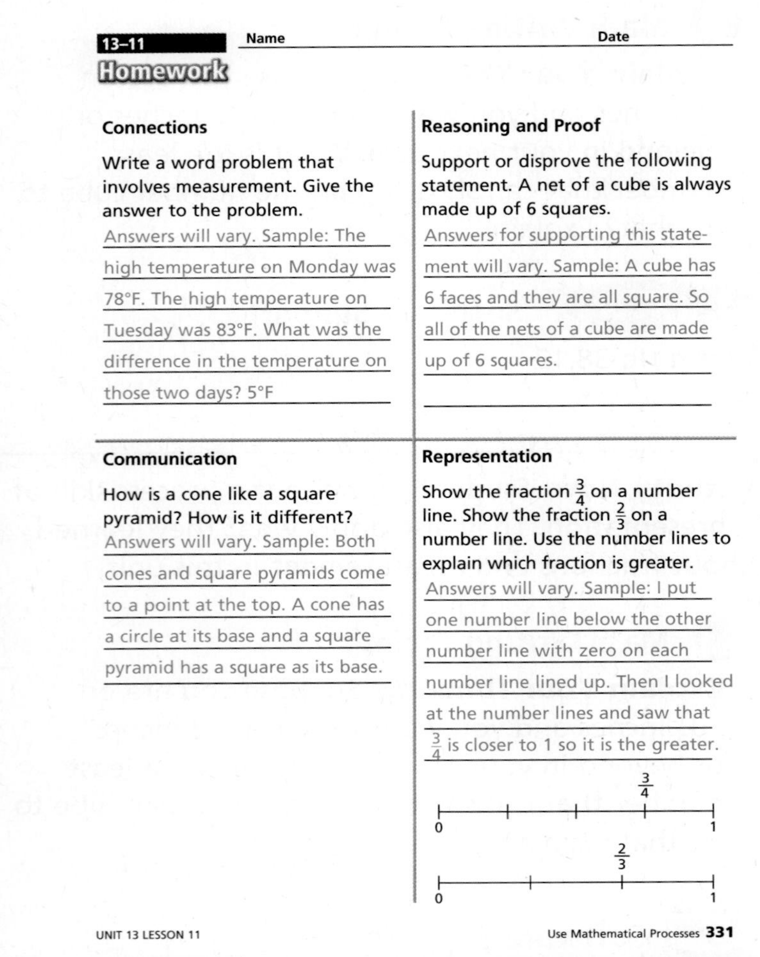

13–11 Name ______ Date ______

Homework

Connections

Write a word problem that involves measurement. Give the answer to the problem.

Answers will vary. Sample: The high temperature on Monday was 78°F. The high temperature on Tuesday was 83°F. What was the difference in the temperature on those two days? 5°F

Reasoning and Proof

Support or disprove the following statement. A net of a cube is always made up of 6 squares.

Answers for supporting this statement will vary. Sample: A cube has 6 faces and they are all square. So all of the nets of a cube are made up of 6 squares.

Communication

How is a cone like a square pyramid? How is it different?

Answers will vary. Sample: Both cones and square pyramids come to a point at the top. A cone has a circle at its base and a square pyramid has a square as its base.

Representation

Show the fraction $\frac{3}{4}$ on a number line. Show the fraction $\frac{2}{3}$ on a number line. Use the number lines to explain which fraction is greater.

Answers will vary. Sample: I put one number line below the other number line with zero on each number line lined up. Then I looked at the number lines and saw that $\frac{3}{4}$ is closer to 1 so it is the greater.

$\frac{3}{4}$ (number line from 0 to 1)

$\frac{2}{3}$ (number line from 0 to 1)

UNIT 13 LESSON 11 Use Mathematical Processes **331**

Homework and Remembering page 331

13–11 **Remembering** **Goal:** Spiral Review

This Remembering page would be appropriate anytime after today's lesson.

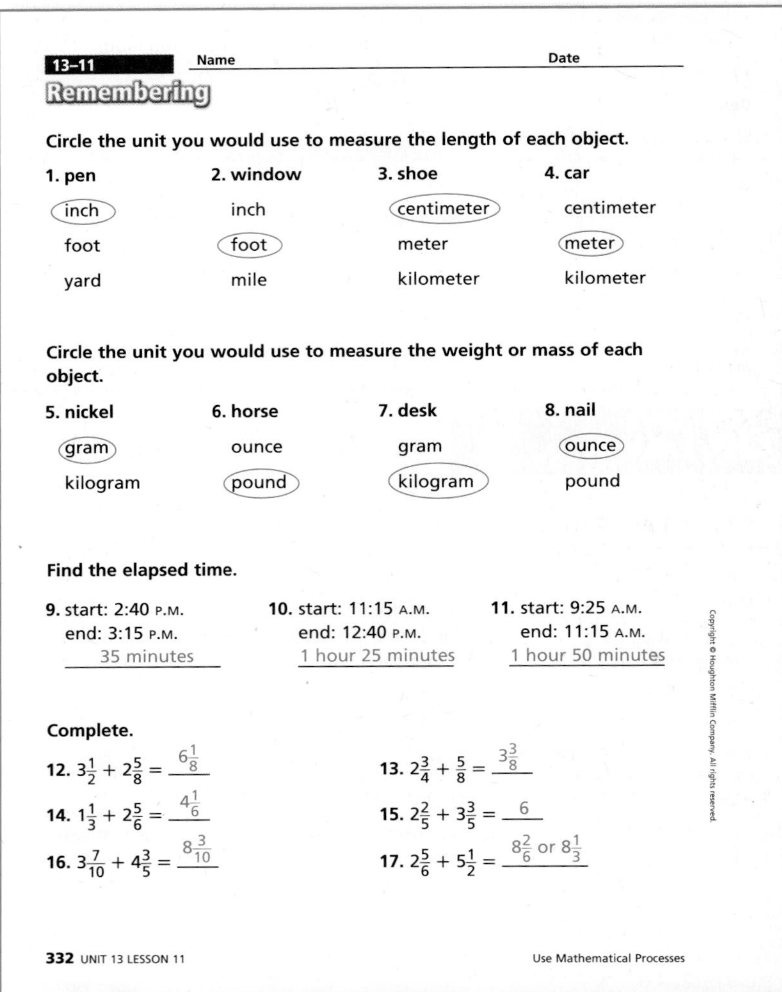

13–11 Name ______ Date ______

Remembering

Circle the unit you would use to measure the length of each object.

1. pen	**2. window**	**3. shoe**	**4. car**
(inch)	inch	(centimeter)	centimeter
foot	(foot)	meter	(meter)
yard	mile	kilometer	kilometer

Circle the unit you would use to measure the weight or mass of each object.

5. nickel	**6. horse**	**7. desk**	**8. nail**
(gram)	ounce	gram	(ounce)
kilogram	(pound)	(kilogram)	pound

Find the elapsed time.

9. start: 2:40 P.M. end: 3:15 P.M. — 35 minutes

10. start: 11:15 A.M. end: 12:40 P.M. — 1 hour 25 minutes

11. start: 9:25 A.M. end: 11:15 A.M. — 1 hour 50 minutes

Complete.

12. $3\frac{1}{2} + 2\frac{5}{8} = 6\frac{1}{8}$

13. $2\frac{3}{4} + \frac{5}{8} = 3\frac{3}{8}$

14. $1\frac{1}{3} + 2\frac{5}{6} = 4\frac{1}{6}$

15. $2\frac{2}{5} + 3\frac{3}{5} = 6$

16. $3\frac{7}{10} + 4\frac{3}{5} = 8\frac{3}{10}$

17. $2\frac{5}{6} + 5\frac{1}{2} = 8\frac{2}{6}$ or $8\frac{1}{3}$

332 UNIT 13 LESSON 11 Use Mathematical Processes

Homework and Remembering page 332

Home or School Activity

Real-World Connection

What's the Temperature? Have students take the temperature outside every hour for a day. Have them record the change over time on a line graph.

Unit Review and Test

Lesson Objective

- **Assess student progress on unit objectives.**

The Day at a Glance

Today's Goals	Materials
1 Assessing the Unit ► Assess student progress on unit objectives. ► Use activities from unit lessons to reteach content.	Unit 13 Test, Student Activity Book or Hardcover Book pp. 507–508 Unit 13 Test, Form A or B, Assessment Guide (optional) Unit 13 Performance Assessment, Assessment Guide (optional)
2 Extending the Assessment ► Use remediation for common errors.	
There is no homework assignment on a test day.	

Keeping Skills Sharp

Quick Practice — 5 MINUTES	
Goal: Review any skills you choose to meet the needs of your students. If you are doing a unit review day, use any of the Quick Practice activities that provide support for your students. If this is a test day, omit Quick Practice.	**Review and Test Day** You may want to choose a quiet game or other activity (reading a book or working on homework for another subject) for students who finish early.

1 Assessing the Unit

Assess Unit Objectives

45 MINUTES (more if schedule permits)

Goal: Assess student progress on unit objectives.

Materials: Student Activity Book or Hardcover Book pp. 507–508; Assessment Guide Unit 13 Test Form A or B (optional); Assessment Guide Unit 13 Performance Assessment (optional)

▶ Review and Assessment

If your students are ready for assessment on the unit objectives, you may use either the test on the Student Book pages or one of the forms of the Unit 13 Test in the Assessment Guide to assess student progress.

If you feel that students need some review first, you may use the test on the Student Book pages as a review of unit content, and then use one of the forms of the Unit 13 Test in the Assessment Guide to assess student progress.

To assign a numerical score for all of these test forms, use 5 points for each question.

You may also choose to use the Unit 13 Performance Assessment. Scoring for that assessment can be found in its rubric in the Assessment Guide.

▶ Reteaching Resources

The chart at the right lists the test items, the unit objectives they cover, and the lesson activities in which the objective is covered in this unit. You may revisit these activities with students who do not show mastery of the objectives.

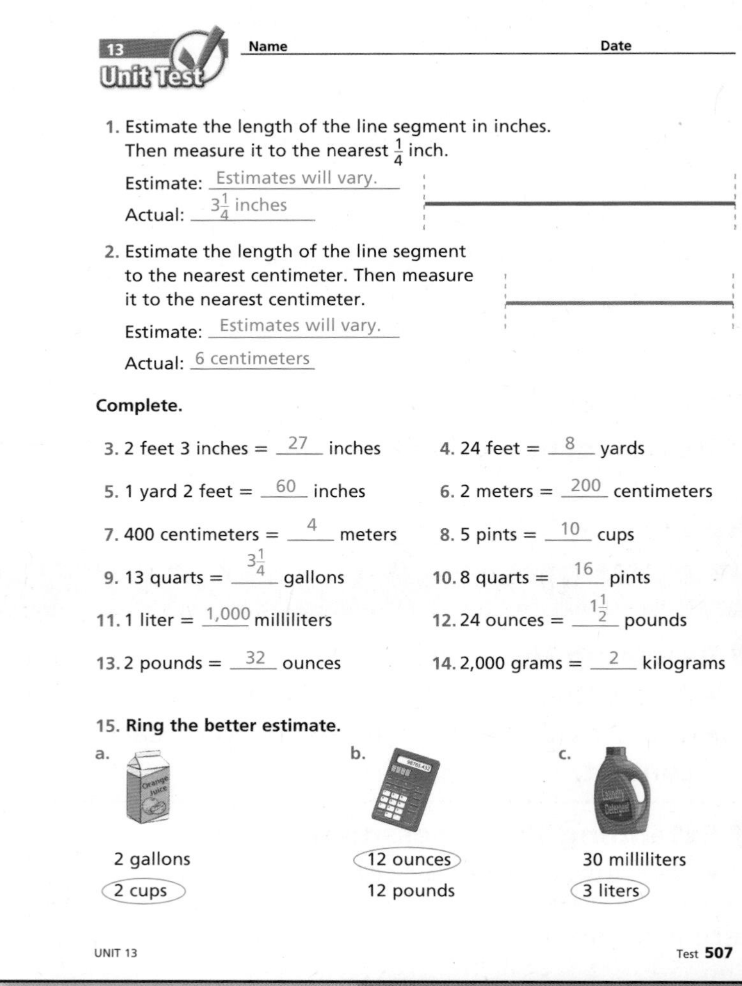

13 Unit Test

Name ______ Date ______

1. Estimate the length of the line segment in inches. Then measure it to the nearest $\frac{1}{4}$ inch.
Estimate: Estimates will vary.
Actual: $3\frac{1}{4}$ inches

2. Estimate the length of the line segment to the nearest centimeter. Then measure it to the nearest centimeter.
Estimate: Estimates will vary.
Actual: 6 centimeters

Complete.

3. 2 feet 3 inches = 27 inches
4. 24 feet = 8 yards
5. 1 yard 2 feet = 60 inches
6. 2 meters = 200 centimeters
7. 400 centimeters = 4 meters
8. 5 pints = 10 cups
9. 13 quarts = $3\frac{1}{4}$ gallons
10. 8 quarts = 16 pints
11. 1 liter = 1,000 milliliters
12. 24 ounces = $1\frac{1}{2}$ pounds
13. 2 pounds = 32 ounces
14. 2,000 grams = 2 kilograms

15. **Ring the better estimate.**

a. 2 gallons / (2 cups)

b. (12 ounces) / 12 pounds

c. 30 milliliters / (3 liters)

UNIT 13 Test 507

Student Activity Book page 507

Unit Test Items	Unit Objectives Tested	Activities to Use for Reteaching
1–2, 17	**13.1** Estimate and measure length to the nearest $\frac{1}{4}$-inch and the nearest centimeter; estimate perimeter and area.	Lesson 1, Activity 4 Lesson 3, Activity 1 Lesson 4, Activities 2-3 Lesson 7, Activity 2
3–14	**13.2** Convert measurements within the Customary System and within the Metric System.	Lesson 2, Activity 1 Lesson 3, Activity 2 Lesson 5, Activity 2 Lesson 6, Activity 1 Lesson 8, Activity 1 Lesson 9, Activities 1-2

Name ______ Date ______

16. Write the temperature. Then write *hot, warm, cool,* or *cold* to describe the temperature.

a. b.

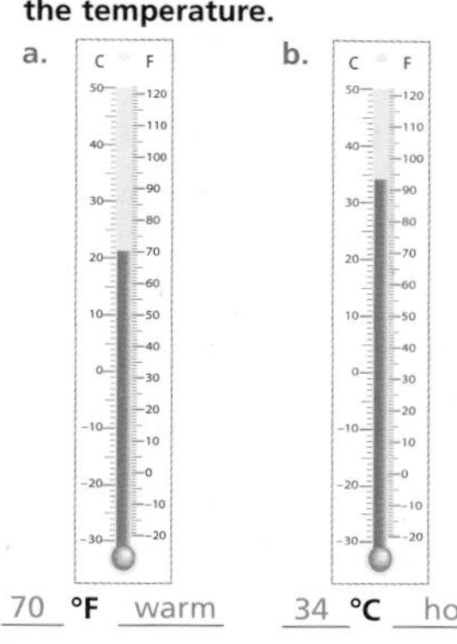

70 °F warm   34 °C hot

17. Use the rectangle around 17a.–c. to complete 17a.–c.
Estimates may vary.

a. Estimate the perimeter in inches. about 12 inches

b. Find the actual perimeter in inches. 12 inches

c. Estimate the area in square inches. about 9 sq inches

Solve.

18. Bert has 56 gallons of water for the pet shop's fish tanks. Each tank holds 6 gallons of water. How many tanks can Bert fill? How much water will be left?
9 tanks; 2 gallons

19. A ten-gallon fish tank needs to have half of its water replaced every two weeks. How many quarts of water need to be replaced every two weeks?
20 quarts of water

*20. **Extended Response** A loaf of bread has 40 slices. Each slice weighs 1 ounce. How many pounds does the loaf of bread weigh? Explain how you found the answer.
$2\frac{1}{2}$ pounds; 40 slices weigh 40 ounces. 16 + 16 + 8 = 40, so 40 ounces equals $2\frac{1}{2}$ pounds.

*Item 20 also assesses the process skills of Connections, Communication, and Reasoning and Proof.

508 UNIT 13   Test

Student Activity Book page 508

Unit Test Items	Unit Objectives Tested	Activities to Use for Reteaching
16	**13.3** Read temperature in degrees Fahrenheit and degrees Celsius.	Lesson 10, Activities 1–2
15, 18–20	**13.4** Solve problems involving customary or metric measurements.	Lesson 4, Activity 1 Lesson 6, Activity 2

▶ Assessment Resources

Free Response Tests
Unit 13 Test, Student Book pages 507–508
Unit 13 Test, Form A, Assessment Guide

Extended Response Item
The last item in the Student Book test and in the Form A test will require an extended response as an answer.

Multiple Choice Test
Unit 13 Test, Form B, Assessment Guide

Performance Assessment
Unit 13 Performance Assessment, Assessment Guide
Unit 13 Performance Assessment Rubric, Assessment Guide

▶ Portfolio Assessment

Teacher-selected Items for Student Portfolios:

- Homework, Lessons 1, 8, 9, and 11
- Class Activity work, Lessons 5, 6, 10, and 11

Student-selected Items for Student Portfolios:

- Favorite Home or School Activity
- Best Writing Prompt

2 Extending the Assessment

Common Errors

Activities for Remediation

Unit Objective 13.1

Estimate and measure length to the nearest $\frac{1}{4}$-inch and the nearest centimeter; estimate perimeter and area.

Common Error: Uses a Ruler Incorrectly

Students may have difficulty using a ruler correctly.

Remediation Make sure students know where 0 is on their ruler and how to align it on the line segment they are measuring.

Common Error: Measures to the Nearest Inch, Half-Inch, or Quarter-Inch Incorrectly

Students may not understand how to identify the half-way marks for each unit.

Remediation Use an overhead transparency with a transparent ruler. Point out the just under marks and just over marks that students need to use to measure to the nearest inch, half-inch and quarter-inch. Then draw a line segment that is 3 in., just under $3\frac{1}{2}$ in., and just over $2\frac{1}{2}$ in. so students can see the range of lengths that measure to the nearest inch. Draw line segments to show the range for line segments that measure $4\frac{1}{2}$ in. to the nearest $\frac{1}{2}$-inch and for line segments that measure $1\frac{1}{4}$ in. to the nearest $\frac{1}{4}$-inch.

Unit Objective 13.2

Convert measurements within the Customary System and within the Metric System.

Common Error: Does not Apply the Correct Operation When Making Conversions

Students may not understand when to multiply or divide to convert units of measurement.

Remediation Remind students that division or repeated subtraction is used to change from smaller units to larger units, and multiplication or repeated addition is used to convert from larger units to smaller units.

Common Error: Converts Customary Units of Length, Capacity, or Weight Incorrectly

Students may have difficulty converting units because they do not use the correct equivalent relationships between the units.

Remediation Use models to demonstrate unit conversions and then have students create conversion charts. For example, point out the inches and feet on a yardstick to demonstrate length conversions. To demonstrate capacity conversions, have students pour rice or water from a one-cup container into a pint container; they will see that they have to pour 2 cups to fill the pint. Similarly, demonstrate pints to quarts and quarts to gallons. Show 16 oz = 1 lb on a scale.

Unit Objective 13.3

Read temperature in degrees Fahrenheit and degrees Celsius.

Common Error: Reads a Thermometer Incorrectly

Some students may misinterpret or miscount the thermometer scale.

Remediation Have students skip count between marked units to be sure they understand how many degrees the marks represent.

Unit Objective 13.4

Solve problems involving customary or metric measurements.

Common Error: Forgets to Convert Units

Students try to solve problems that involve different units of measurement without converting them to a common unit.

Remediation Have students use a highlighter to mark the measurement units in a problem.

Directions and Locations

IN UNIT 14, students are introduced to coordinate grids. Students first follow directions, describe routes, and make maps on grids. Next, they use ordered pairs to locate and identify points on coordinate grids. Activities include plotting and joining points to draw rectangles, and completing figures by naming and plotting ordered pairs. In the final activity of the unit, students measure the length of line segments drawn on coordinate grids using the distance between adjacent lines as a unit.

Skills Trace

Grade 2	Grade 3	Grade 4
• Name and graph ordered pairs on a coordinate grid. • Use ordered pairs on a coordinate grid to locate objects.	• Find locations given directions (*up*, *down*, *left*, and *right*). • Describe routes between locations on maps and grids, including finding the shortest route between two locations. • Use ordered pairs to locate points, and name ordered pairs for points on a coordinate grid. • Identify parallel and perpendicular line segments and lines on the coordinate grid.	• Use ordered pairs to read and plot points on the coordinate plane. • Draw simple figures in the coordinate plane, and determine the length of the sides of the figures. • Use ordered pairs from a function table to graph an equation on the coordinate plane.

Unit 14 Contents

Big Idea **Name and Plot Points Coordinate Grids**

Planning Unit 14

NCTM Curriculum Focal Points and Connections Key: **1.** Number and Operations and Algebra **2.** Number and Operations **3.** Geometry **4.** Algebra **5.** Measurement **6.** Data Analysis **7.** Number and Operations

Lesson NCTM Focal Points NCTM Standards	Resources	Materials for Lesson Activities	Materials for Going Further
14-1 **Directions and Maps** NCTM Standards: 3, 4, 10	TE pp. 1079–1084 SAB pp. 509–514 H&R pp. 333–334 AC 14-1 MCC 53	Transparency of Student Activity Book p. 509 Overhead projector	Masking tape Inch Grid Paper (TRB M42) ✓ Two-color counters ✓ Number Cubes Math Journals
14-2 **Locate Points on a Coordinate Grid** NCTM Standards: 3, 9, 10	TE pp. 1085–1090 SAB pp. 515–518 H&R pp. 335–336 AC 14-2 MCC 54	Transparency of Student Activity Book pp. 515–517 Overhead projector ✓ Rulers Coordinate Grid (TRB M148)	Masking tape Sticky notes Coordinate Grid (TRB M148) Math Journals
14-3 **Explore Line Segments and Figures on a Coordinate Grid** NCTM Focal Points: 3.1, 3.2 NCTM Standards: 3, 4, 10	TE pp. 1091–1096 SAB pp. 519–522 H&R pp. 337–338 AC 14-3 MCC 55, 56 AG Quick Quiz	Transparency of Coordinate Grid (TRB 148) (optional) Overhead projector (optional) Coordinate Grid (TRB M148) ✓ Rulers	Coordinate Grid (TRB M148) Centimeter Grid Paper (TRB M31) Math Journals
✓ **Unit Review and Test**	TE pp. 1097–1100 SAB pp. 523–524 AG Unit 14 Tests		

Resources/Materials Key: TE: Teacher Edition SAB: Student Activity Book H&R: Homework and Remembering AC: Activity Cards MCC: Math Center Challenge AG: Assessment Guide ✓: Grade 3 kits TRB: Teacher's Resource Book

NCTM Standards and Expectations Key: 1. Number and Operations 2. Algebra 3. Geometry 4. Measurement 5. Data Analysis and Probability 6. Problem Solving 7. Reasoning and Proof 8. Communication 9. Connections 10. Representation

Hardcover Student Book

- Together, the Hardcover Student Book and its companion Activity Workbook contain all of the pages in the consumable Student Activity Book.

Manipulatives and Materials

- Essential materials for teaching *Math Expressions* are available in the Grade 3 kits. These materials are indicated by a ✓ in these lists. At the front of this Teacher Edition is more information about kit contents, alternatives for the materials, and use of the materials.

Independent Learning Activities

Ready-Made Math Challenge Centers

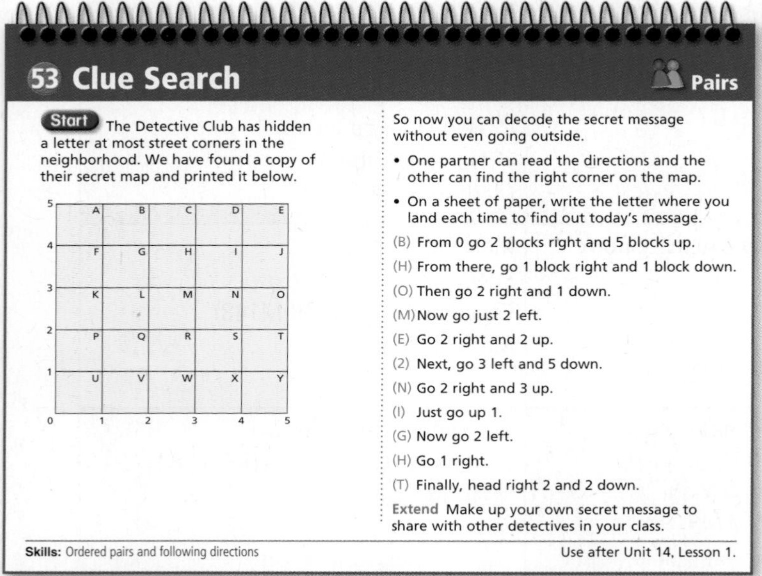

Grouping Pairs

Materials Hundred Grid (TRB M148)

Objective Students follow directions and describe locations on a map.

Connections Geometry and Communication

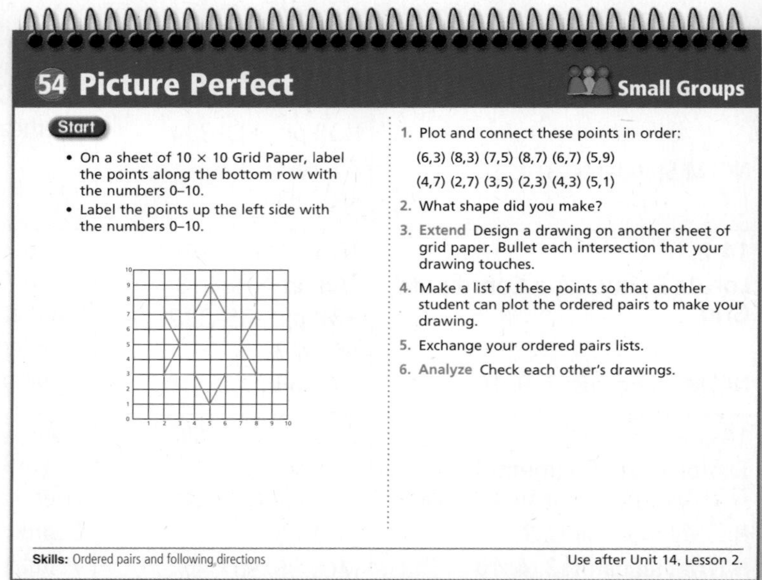

Grouping Small Groups

Materials 10 × 10 Grid (TRB M43)

Objective Students visualize a quadrilateral on a grid and use strategy to guess the coordinates of its vertices.

Connections Geometry and Reasoning

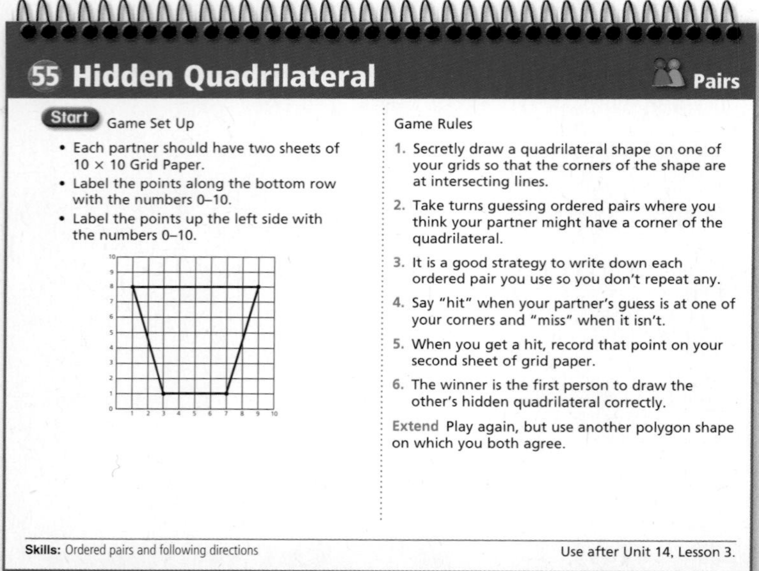

Grouping Pairs

Materials 10 × 10 Grid (TRB M43)

Objective Students use and name ordered pairs on a coordinate grid.

Connections Geometry and Representation

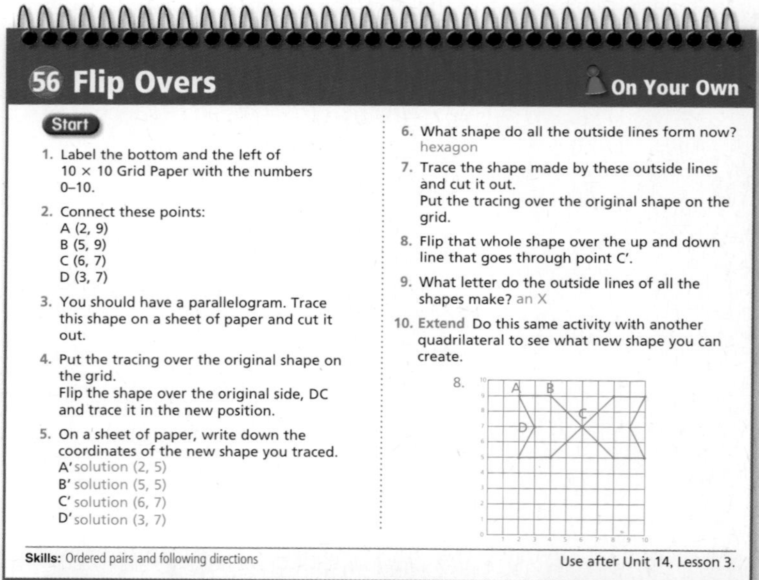

Grouping Individuals

Materials Scissors, 10 × 10 Grid (TRB M43)

Objective Students locate points on a grid and reflect shapes over lines of symmetry.

Connections Geometry and Representation

Ready-Made Math Resources

Technology — Tutorial, Practice, and Intervention

Use online, individualized intervention and support to bring students to proficiency.

Help students practice skills and apply concepts through exciting math adventures.

Extend and enrich students' understanding of skills and concepts through engaging, interactive lessons and activities.

Visit **Education Place**®
www.eduplace.com

Visit www.eduplace.com/mx2t/ and find family, teacher, and student materials, activities, games, and more.

Literature Link

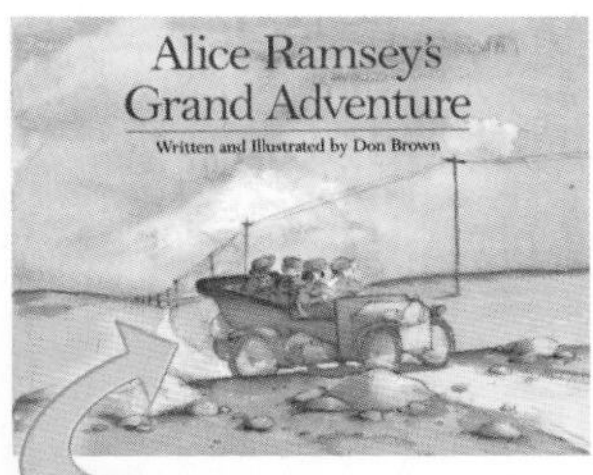

Alice Ramsey's Grand Adventure

Alice Ramsey's Grand Adventure

Alice, a friend, and two sisters-in-law travel cross country in this tale by Don Brown, set in 1909. Unlike travel today, for Alice there were no road signs and the roads were poor. The only aid Alice had was a Blue Book, a guide which contained directions such as "Turn left at the red barn with the yellow silo." In a day of Global Positioning Systems, this tale is bound to amaze your students as to how different it once was to find your way anywhere!

Unit 14 Assessment

Unit Objectives Tested	Unit Test Items	Lessons
14.1 Find locations given directions (up, down, left, and right) and describe routes between locations on maps and grids.	1–4	1
14.2 Use ordered pairs to locate points and name ordered pairs for points on a coordinate grid.	5–10	2, 3

Assessment and Review Resources

Formal Assessment

Student Activity Book

- Unit Review and Test (pp. 523–524)

Assessment Guide

- Quick Quiz (p. A139)
- Test A-Open Response (pp. A140–A142)
- Test B-Multiple Choice (pp. A143–A145)
- Performance Assessment (pp. A146–A148)

Test Generator CD-ROM

- Open Response Test
- Multiple Choice Test
- Test Bank Items

Informal Assessment

Teacher Edition

- Ongoing Assessment (in every lesson)
- Math Talk (in every lesson)
- Portfolio Suggestions (p. 1099)

Math Talk

- Math Talk in Action (p. 1093)
- Student Pairs (pp. 1081, 1086, 1087, 1093)
  Helping Partners (pp. 1082, 1093)
- In Activities (pp. 1081, 1088)

Review Opportunities

Homework and Remembering

- Review of recently taught topics
- Spiral Review

Teacher Edition

- Unit Review and Test (pp. 1097–1100)

Test Generator CD-ROM

- Custom Review Sheets

Unit 14 Teaching Resources

Differentiated Instruction

Individualizing Instruction		
	Level	Frequency
Activities	• Intervention • On Level • Challenge	All 3 in every lesson
	Level	Frequency
Math Writing Prompts	• Intervention • On Level • Challenge	All 3 in every lesson
Math Center Challenges	For advanced students	
	4 in every unit	

Reaching All Learners		
English Language Learners	Lessons	Pages
	1, 2, 3	1079, 1085, 1091
Extra Help	Lesson	Page
	2	1086

Strategies for English Language Learners

Present this problem to all students. Offer the different levels of support to meet students' levels of language proficiency.

Objective To review direction words right, left, up, and down

Problem Give students 9 colored cubes: 1 black, 2 red, 2 yellow, 2 green, and 2 blue. Direct students to place the cubes as follows:

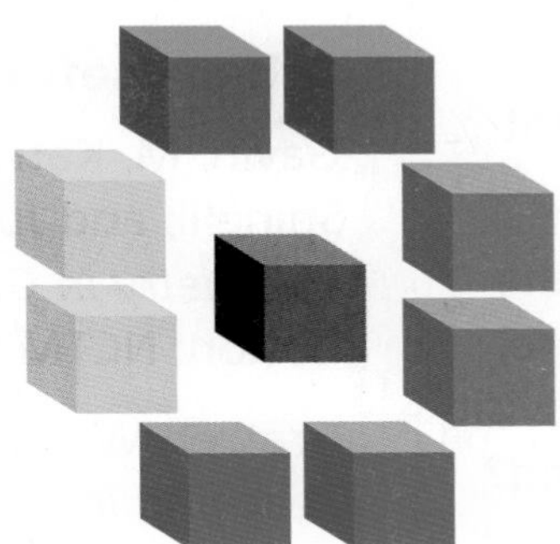

Newcomer

- Say: **Red is on the right.** Have students repeat. Continue with other colors.

Beginning

- Ask: **Is red is on the right or left?** right Continue with other colors.

Intermediate

- Ask: **Which cubes are on the right?** red **Which cubes are on the left?** yellow **Which cubes are above the black cube?** green **Which cubes are below the black cube?** blue

Advanced

- Have children identify the location of the cubes in relation to the black cube.

Connections

Social Studies Connection
Lesson 2, page 1090

Language Arts Connection
Lesson 3, page 1096

Putting Research into Practice for Unit 14

From Current Research: Coordinate Geometry

In grades 3–5, the ideas about location, direction, and distance that were introduced in pre-kindergarten through grade 2 can be developed further.

- Students can give directions for moving from one location to another in their classroom, school, or neighborhood
- Use maps and grids
- Learn to locate points, create paths, and measure distances within a coordinate system

Students can first navigate on grids by using landmarks. For example, the map in the figure below can be used to explore questions like these:

- What is the shortest possible route from the school to the park along the streets (horizontal and vertical lines of the grid)? How do you know?
- Can there be several different "shortest paths," all of the same length? If so, how many different "shortest paths" are there?
- What if you need to start at the school, go to the park to pick up your little sister, stop at the store, and visit the library—in what order should you visit these locations to minimize the distance traveled?

In this activity, students are using grids and developing fundamental ideas and strategies for navigating the grid, a part of discrete mathematics.

Students at this level also should learn how to use two numbers to name points on a coordinate grid and should realize that a pair of numbers corresponds to a particular point on the grid.

Using coordinates, they can specify paths between locations and examine the symmetry, congruence, and similarity of shapes drawn on the grid. They can also explore methods for measuring the distance between locations on the grid. As students' ideas about the number system expand to include negative numbers, they can work in all four quadrants of the Cartesian plane.

National Council of Teachers of Mathematics. *Principles and Standards for School Mathematics.* Reston: NCTM, 2000. 166.

Other Useful References: Maps

Gavin, M. Katherine, Louise P. Belkin, Ann Marie Spinelli, and Judy St. Marie. *Navigating through Geometry in Grades 3–5* (with CD-ROM) (Chapter 2). Reston: NCTM, 2001.

Gratzer, William. "Maps and Algebra." *Mathematics Teaching in the Middle School* 8.6 (Feb. 2003): 300.

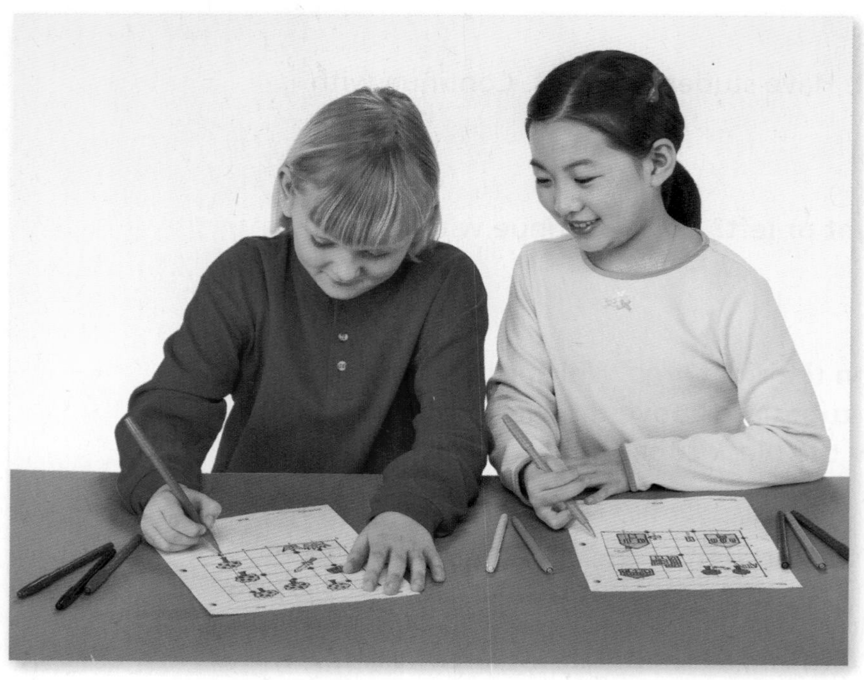

Getting Ready to Teach Unit 14

Students are introduced to the coordinate grid as they follow directions, describe routes, make maps, and draw figures. These activities allow students to develop their spatial sense and help build algebraic reasoning skills.

Directions and Solving Equations

Lesson 1

Students follow directions up, down, right, and left to locate features on grids. They also describe routes on grids. These activities help prepare students for later work with coordinate geometry as they use a starting point (input), a coordinate number, and an ending point.

Coordinate Geometry

Lesson 2

Students are introduced to ordered pairs. They first learn how to use ordered pairs to identify features on a coordinate grid and then they write ordered pairs naming points on coordinate grids. These skills provide the foundation for later work in coordinate geometry and algebra when students do transformations and plot equations on coordinate grids.

Algebraic Reasoning

Lesson 3

Students draw rectangles on grids. To do so, they follow instructions that involve a mathematical relationship between the lengths of two sides of a rectangle: for instance, they are asked to draw a rectangle with a length that is 2 units longer than its width. These exercises help to build students' algebraic reasoning: they must reason that they can choose the width (variable) and then add 2 to the width to find the length (equation).

Measurement

Lesson 3

Students use the grid lines to measure the length of line segments on coordinate grids. These activities reinforce the concept of linear measurement as counting adjacent, non-overlapping units, and prepare students for work with maps and scales in subsequent grades, in Social Studies, and in real-world applications. Using grids for linear measurement also prepares students for the area measurement work they will do in subsequent grades.

Spatial Sense

Lessons 1, 2, and 3

Students develop their spatial sense by exploring coordinate grids. Activities include creating maps, identifying points on maps, and navigating between places on maps. They also plot ordered pairs to make a picture on a grid.

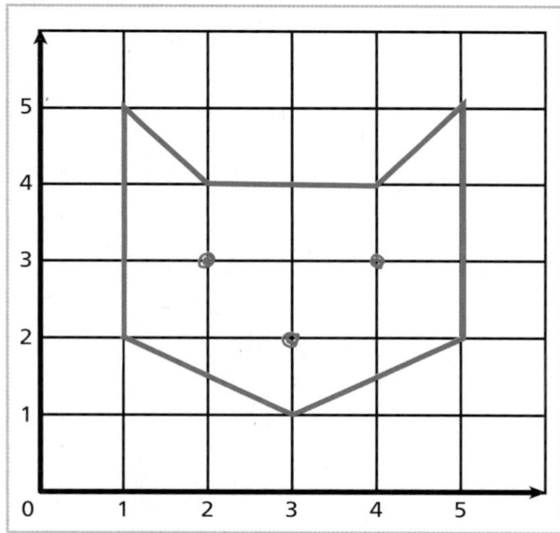

Students use spatial sense to visualize how to complete geometric figures by plotting missing points on coordinate grids.

Directions and Maps

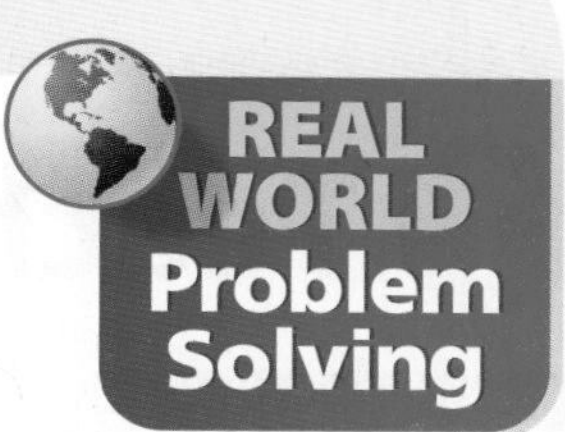

Lesson Objectives

- Follow up, down, right, and left directions on a grid.
- Describe movements on a grid.
- Make a map on a grid.

Vocabulary
map
route

The Day at a Glance

Today's Goals	Materials	
1 Teaching the Lesson **A1:** Use a grid map. **A2:** Make a map on a grid and describe routes on the map. **2 Going Further** ▸ Differentiated Instruction **3 Homework and Spiral Review**	**Lesson Activities** Student Activity Book pp. 509–514 or Student Hardcover Book pp. 509–514 and Activity Workbook pp. 250–252 (includes Grid and Family Letter) Homework and Remembering pp. 333–334 Transparency of Student Book p. 509 and overhead projector	**Going Further** Activity Cards 14-1 Masking tape Inch Grid Paper (TRB M42) Two-color counters Number cubes Math Journals

Use Math Talk today!

Keeping Skills Sharp

Daily Routines

Logic Problems Use *all*, *some*, or *no* to complete each sentence.

1. If all figures that are flat and have 2 dimensions are two-dimensional, then ____ nets of three-dimensional figures are two-dimensional. all

2. If all prisms are solid figures whose two parallel bases are congruent and whose faces are rectangles, then ____ prisms are cubes. some

English Language Learners

Draw a map of how to get from the classroom to the drinking fountain on the board. Write *map*.

- **Beginning** Say: **A *map* shows how to get from one place to another.** Have students repeat.
- **Intermediate** Ask: **Does a *map* show people on it?** no **Does a map show places?** yes **Does a *map* show how to get from one place to another?** yes
- **Advanced** Have students tell what a map is used for.

1 Teaching the Lesson

Activity 1

Map Directions

 30 MINUTES

Goal: Use a grid map.

Materials: Student Activity Book or Hardcover Book pp. 509–510, transparency of Student Activity Book or Hardcover Book p. 509, overhead projector

 **NCTM Standards:**
Geometry
Measurement
Representation

▶ Read a Map WHOLE CLASS

Have students refer to the map of a neighborhood on Student Book page 509.

Use a transparency of Student Book page 509 or draw a grid on the board and add arrows showing how to move on a map—up, down, right, and left along a line segment.

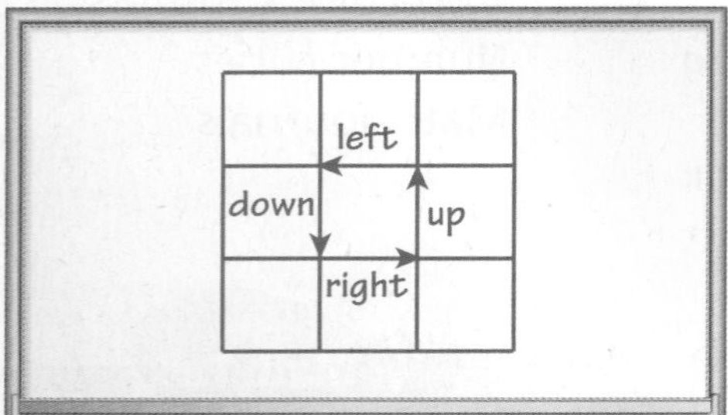

Point out that the distance between two line segments on the grid is 1 block. To give students practice reading the map, ask the following questions:

- How far is the arena from the post office taking the shortest route? 4 blocks
- How far is the recreation center from Pierre's house? 2 blocks
- Is the post office or the movie theater closer to the library? post office
- How much closer is the post office to the library than the movie theater to the library? 1 block

Have students complete exercises 1–3 on their own. When they are finished, discuss their answers.

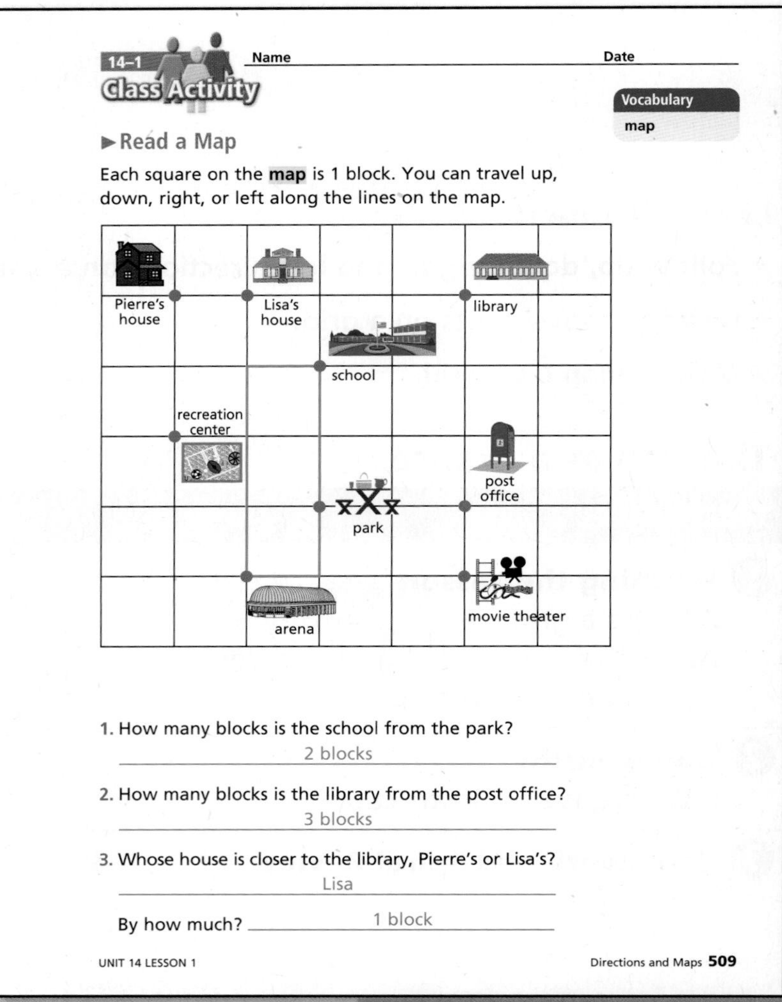
14–1 Class Activity Name Date

Vocabulary
map

▶ Read a Map

Each square on the **map** is 1 block. You can travel up, down, right, or left along the lines on the map.

1. How many blocks is the school from the park? 2 blocks
2. How many blocks is the library from the post office? 3 blocks
3. Whose house is closer to the library, Pierre's or Lisa's? Lisa

By how much? 1 block

UNIT 14 LESSON 1 Directions and Maps **509**

Student Activity Book page 509

Teaching Note

Math Background Some students may be familiar with real maps that have letters and numbers labeling the grid lines. On these maps, the letters and numbers are used as a reference to locate the city or place nearby. At this grade level, however, students work with maps where locations appear at the intersection of grid lines. This setup helps prepare students for later work with coordinate grids.

▶ Follow Directions PAIRS

Once again, direct students' attention to the map on Student Book page 509. Remind them that they can travel on the map by going up, down, right, or left along a line segment.

Have students work in pairs using the map on the transparency of Student Book page 509 or one student's map.

Ask the following questions.

- If you start at Lisa's house and walk right 3 blocks, where will you be? library
- If you start at the post office and walk left 2 blocks, where will you be? park
- If you start at the school and walk down 2 blocks, where will you be? park
- If you start at the recreation center and go up 2 blocks, where will you be? Pierre's house

Have students complete exercises 4–7 on Student Book page 510. When they are finished, invite volunteers to show how they moved on the map.

▶ Describe Routes PAIRS

Tell **Student Pairs** that they can create routes between locations on the map by traveling up, down, right, and left. Have **Student Pairs** identify two routes from Lisa's house to the movie theater.

- If I want to go from Lisa's house to the movie theater what route can I take? Possible answer: 2 blocks right, 4 blocks down, 1 block right
- Is there another route I can take? Possible answer: 3 blocks down, 3 blocks right, 1 block down
- Which is the shortest route? They are both the same distance.

Ask **Student Pairs** to complete exercises 8–13.

Math Talk After they have completed the exercises, invite volunteers to share their routes. As a class, discuss how they know that these routes are correct.

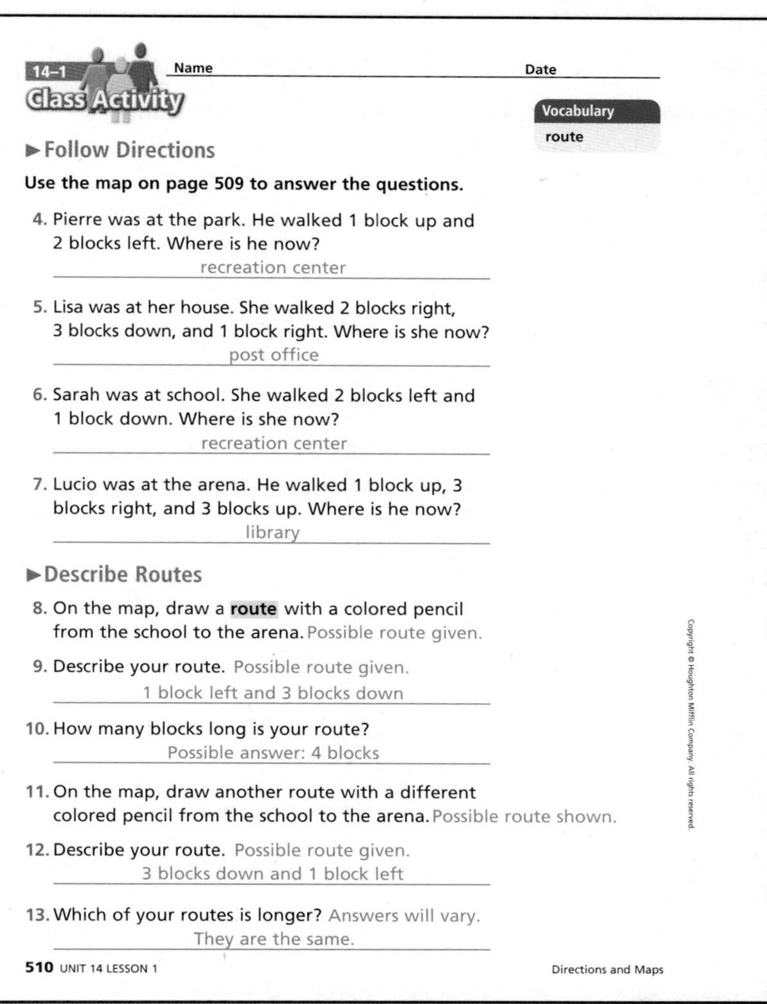

14–1 Class Activity Name ____ Date ____

Vocabulary: route

▶ Follow Directions

Use the map on page 509 to answer the questions.

4. Pierre was at the park. He walked 1 block up and 2 blocks left. Where is he now? recreation center
5. Lisa was at her house. She walked 2 blocks right, 3 blocks down, and 1 block right. Where is she now? post office
6. Sarah was at school. She walked 2 blocks left and 1 block down. Where is she now? recreation center
7. Lucio was at the arena. He walked 1 block up, 3 blocks right, and 3 blocks up. Where is he now? library

▶ Describe Routes

8. On the map, draw a **route** with a colored pencil from the school to the arena. Possible route given.
9. Describe your route. Possible route given. 1 block left and 3 blocks down
10. How many blocks long is your route? Possible answer: 4 blocks
11. On the map, draw another route with a different colored pencil from the school to the arena. Possible route shown.
12. Describe your route. Possible route given. 3 blocks down and 1 block left
13. Which of your routes is longer? Answers will vary. They are the same.

Student Activity Book page 510

Challenge students to place a new location on their maps. For example, a supermarket, then have **Student Pairs** to find the shortest route from different locations on the map.

Ongoing Assessment

Ask students to do the following:

- ▶ Describe two routes of the same length from the recreation center to the arena.
- ▶ Lisa wants to go from her house to the post office to mail some letters and then to the library to finish her homework. Describe two different routes she can take.

Activity 2

Create a Map

 30 MINUTES

Goal: Make a map on a grid and describe routes on the map.

Materials: Student Activity Book or Hardcover Book pp. 511–512 and Activity Workbook p. 250 (includes grid)

 **NCTM Standards:**
Geometry
Measurement
Representation

▶ Make a Map INDIVIDUALS

Have students work independently to complete exercise 14, making a map of an amusement park.

14–1 Class Activity Name Date

▶ Make a Map

14. Draw a map of an amusement park. Include a waterfall, treasure chest, bumper cars, a snack bar, and other places such as raging rapids, scrambler, pirates cove, or sunken ship. Place each point for the place where two grid lines intersect on the map.
Check students' work.

UNIT 14 LESSON 1 Directions and Maps 511

Student Activity Book page 511

▶ Use Your Map PAIRS

14–1 Class Activity Name Date

▶ Use Your Map

Use the map you created on page 511 to complete the following.

15. Draw a route on your map with a colored pencil from the snack bar to the bumper cars. Check students' grids.

16. Describe this route.
Answers will vary.

17. Draw a route on your map with a different colored pencil from the snack bar to the water fall. Check students' grids.

18. Describe this route.
Answers will vary.

19. Which place is further from the snack bar, the bumper cars or the waterfall?
Answers will vary.

Choose two places on your map.

20. Name the two places and describe a route from one to the other.
Answers will vary.

21. Describe a different route from one place to the other.
Answers will vary.

22. Is the second route longer, shorter, or equal in distance to your first route?
Answers will vary.

512 UNIT 14 LESSON 1 Directions and Maps

Student Activity Book page 512

Have one student complete exercises 15–22 on Student Book page 512 using his or her partner's map. The other student checks his or her partner's work as it is completed. Then students switch roles. In exercises 19 and 22, students can find the length of the routes by counting blocks on their maps. Have students who experience difficulty check their answers with a **Helping Partner**.

2 Going Further

Intervention — Activity Card 14-1

Walk on a Grid — Activity Card 14–1 ●

Work: In pairs

Use:
- Masking tape

Decide:
Who will be Student 1 and who will be Student 2 for the first round.

1. **Work Together** Make a 5 by 5 grid on the floor with masking tape.
2. **Student 1:** Choose a starting point where two lines intersect and stand on the grid.
3. **Student 2:** Choose an end point. Give your partner directions to reach the point such as "Walk 2 units up. Walk 3 units to the right." Then give directions to return to the starting point.
4. Exchange roles and repeat the activity.

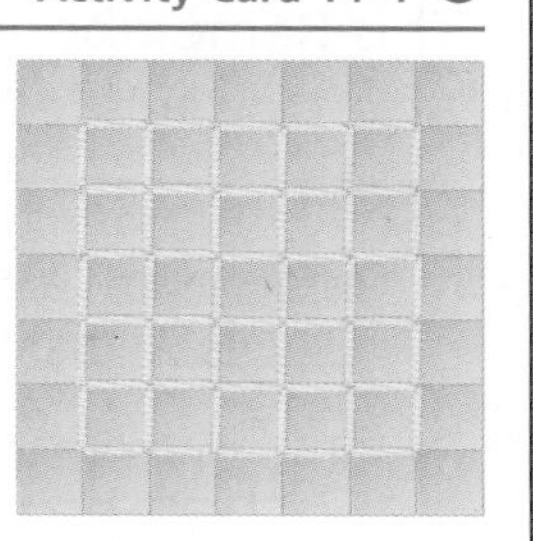

Unit 14, Lesson 1

Activity Note Challenge students to give three-step instructions to travel to a number of places on the grid and then give directions to return to the starting point.

Math Writing Prompt

Explain Your Thinking You are making a treasure hunt for a party. You want to make a map showing where each item is hidden. Will you make the map on a grid or not? Explain your choice.

Software Support

Warm Up 34.05

On Level — Activity Card 14-1

Race to the Happy Face — Activity Card 14–1 ▲

Work: In pairs

Use:
- TRB M42 (Inch Grid Paper)
- 2 two-color counters
- 2 number cubes labeled 1–6

1. **Work Together** Choose a point on the grid where two lines intersect and draw a happy face. Place your counter at the lower left corner of the grid.
2. Take turns. Roll two number cubes. Move your counter left or right using the number on one cube and up or down using the number on the other.
3. Continue for three rounds. The player whose counter is closer to the happy face wins the race.

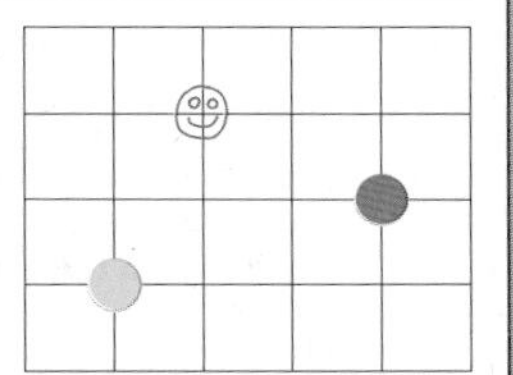

Unit 14, Lesson 1

Activity Note Suggest that students use a grid that measures at least 10 by 10 to accommodate significant movement in all directions.

Math Writing Prompt

Explain a Method Explain how to find the length, in units, of a route on a grid.

Software Support

The Number Games: ArachnaGraph, Level G

Challenge — Activity Card 14-1

Where Was Your Starting Point? — Activity Card 14–1 ■

Work: In pairs

Use:
- TRB M42 (Inch Grid Paper)

Decide:
Who will be Student 1 and who will be Student 2 for the first round.

1. **Work Together** Make a map of a park on grid paper. Include features such as a bench, swing, fountain, slide, pond, and sandbox.
2. **Student 1:** Describe a route to one of the features in your park. Do not tell your partner where your starting point is.
3. **Student 2:** Work backwards to find the starting point.
4. Switch roles and repeat the activity.
5. **Analyze** Does the order matter when you reverse each direction to the starting point? no

I ended up at the swing. To get there I walked 3 units right and 2 units down. Where did I start?

Unit 14, Lesson 1

Activity Note If time permits, challenge students to find at least three ways to move from the starting point to the ending point.

Math Writing Prompt

Show Your Thinking Sam described two different routes between two places on a map. He says that different routes are always different lengths. Do you agree or disagree? Include a picture in your answer.

DESTINATION Math® **Software Support**

Course II: Module 3: Unit 1: Area

3 Homework and Spiral Review

Goal: Additional Practice

This Homework page allows students to practice locating places and describing routes on a map.

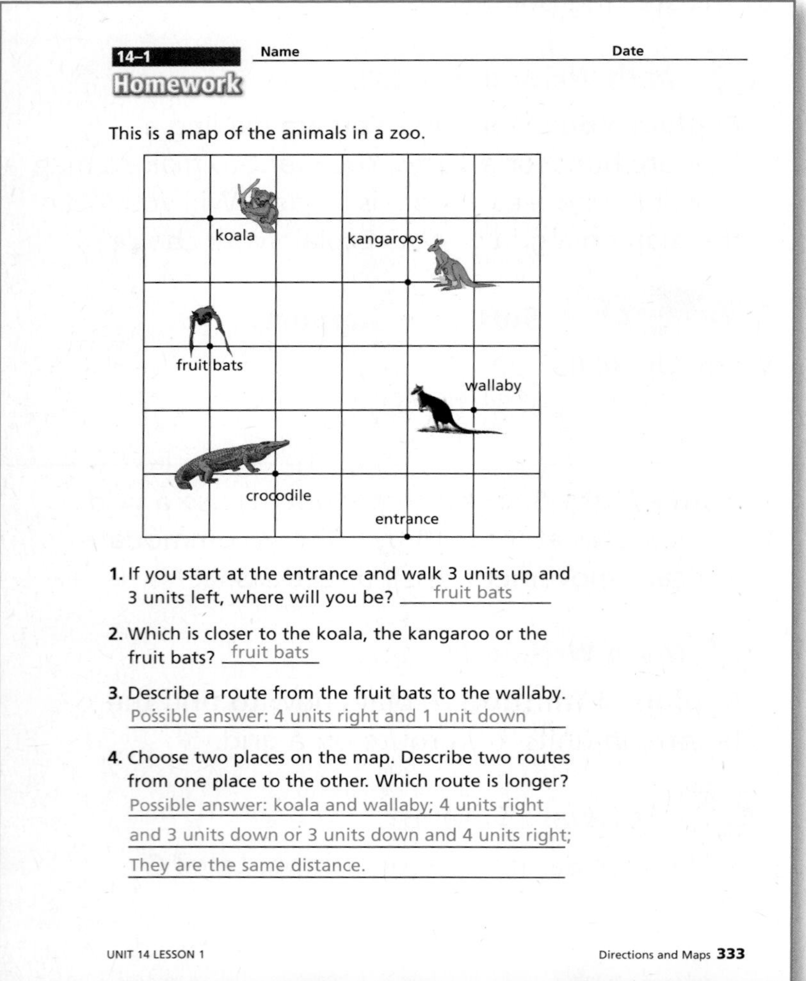

14–1 Homework   Name ______ Date ______

This is a map of the animals in a zoo.

1. If you start at the entrance and walk 3 units up and 3 units left, where will you be? fruit bats
2. Which is closer to the koala, the kangaroo or the fruit bats? fruit bats
3. Describe a route from the fruit bats to the wallaby. Possible answer: 4 units right and 1 unit down
4. Choose two places on the map. Describe two routes from one place to the other. Which route is longer? Possible answer: koala and wallaby; 4 units right and 3 units down or 3 units down and 4 units right; They are the same distance.

UNIT 14 LESSON 1   Directions and Maps 333

Homework and Remembering page 333

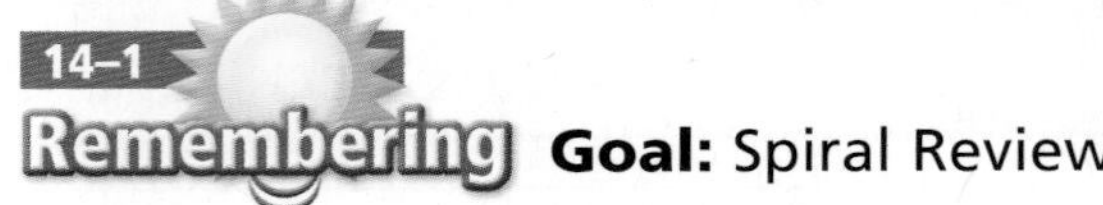

Goal: Spiral Review

This Remembering page would be appropriate anytime after today's lesson.

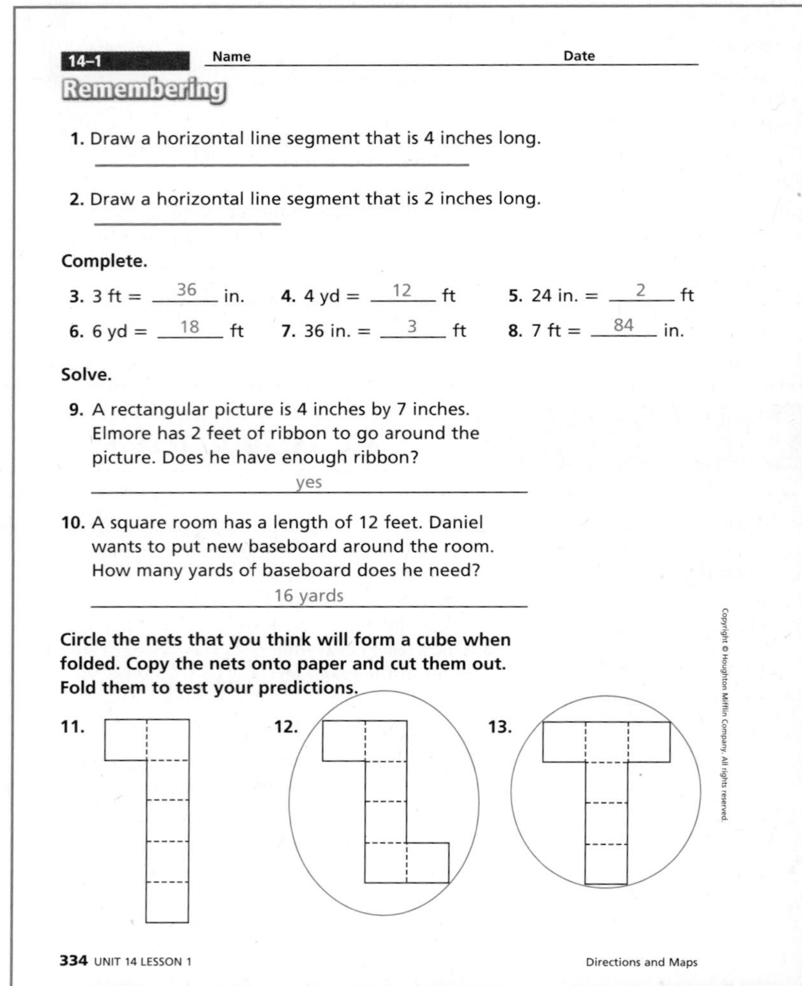

14–1 Remembering   Name ______ Date ______

1. Draw a horizontal line segment that is 4 inches long.
2. Draw a horizontal line segment that is 2 inches long.

Complete.

3. 3 ft = 36 in.
4. 4 yd = 12 ft
5. 24 in. = 2 ft
6. 6 yd = 18 ft
7. 36 in. = 3 ft
8. 7 ft = 84 in.

Solve.

9. A rectangular picture is 4 inches by 7 inches. Elmore has 2 feet of ribbon to go around the picture. Does he have enough ribbon? yes
10. A square room has a length of 12 feet. Daniel wants to put new baseboard around the room. How many yards of baseboard does he need? 16 yards

Circle the nets that you think will form a cube when folded. Copy the nets onto paper and cut them out. Fold them to test your predictions.

11. 12. 13.

334 UNIT 14 LESSON 1   Directions and Maps

Homework and Remembering page 334

Home and School Connection

Family Letter Have students take home the Family Letter on Student Book page 513 or Activity Workbook p. 251. A Spanish translation of this letter is on the following page. This letter explains how the concept of coordinate grids is developed in *Math Expressions.* It gives parents and guardians a better understanding of the learning that goes on in math class and creates a bridge between school and home.

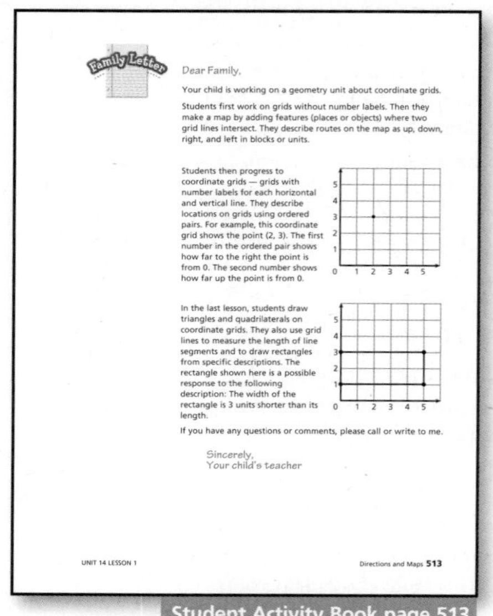

Family Letter

Dear Family,

Your child is working on a geometry unit about coordinate grids.

Students first work on grids without number labels. Then they make a map by adding features (places or objects) where two grid lines intersect. They describe routes on the map as up, down, right, and left in blocks or units.

Students then progress to coordinate grids — grids with number labels for each horizontal and vertical line. They describe locations on grids using ordered pairs. For example, this coordinate grid shows the point (2, 3). The first number in the ordered pair shows how far to the right the point is from 0. The second number shows how far up the point is from 0.

In the last lesson, students draw triangles and quadrilaterals on coordinate grids. They also use grid lines to measure the length of line segments and to draw rectangles from specific descriptions. The rectangle shown here is a possible response to the following description: The width of the rectangle is 3 units shorter than its length.

If you have any questions or comments, please call or write to me.

Sincerely,
Your child's teacher

UNIT 14 LESSON 1   Directions and Maps 513

Student Activity Book page 513

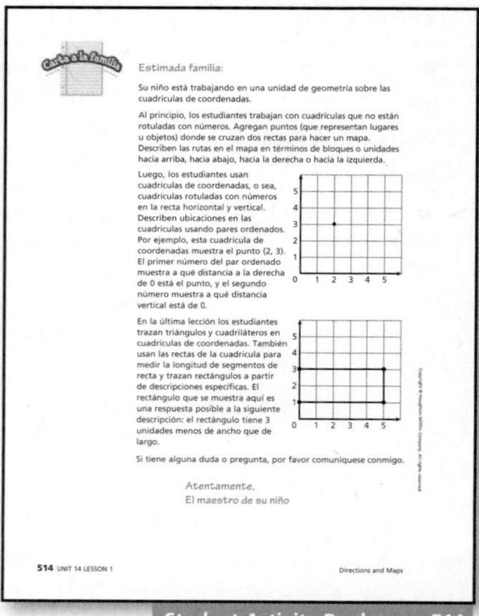

Carta a la familia

Estimada familia:

Su niño está trabajando en una unidad de geometria sobre las cuadrículas de coordenadas.

Al principio, los estudiantes trabajan con cuadrículas que no están rotuladas con números. Agregan puntos (que representan lugares u objetos) donde se cruzan dos rectas para hacer un mapa. Describen las rutas en el mapa en términos de bloques o unidades hacia arriba, hacia abajo, hacia la derecha o hacia la izquierda.

Luego, los estudiantes usan cuadrículas de coordenadas, o sea, cuadrículas rotuladas con números en la recta horizontal y vertical. Describen ubicaciones en las cuadrículas usando pares ordenados. Por ejemplo, esta cuadrícula de coordenadas muestra el punto (2, 3). El primer número del par ordenado muestra a qué distancia a la derecha de 0 está el punto, y el segundo número muestra a qué distancia vertical está de 0.

En la última lección los estudiantes trazan triángulos y cuadriláteros en cuadrículas de coordenadas. También usan las rectas de la cuadrícula para medir la longitud de segmentos de recta y trazan rectángulos a partir de descripciones específicas. El rectángulo que se muestra aquí es una respuesta posible a la siguiente descripción: el rectángulo tiene 3 unidades menos de ancho que de largo.

Si tiene alguna duda o pregunta, por favor comuníquese conmigo.

Atentamente,
El maestro de su niño

514 UNIT 14 LESSON 1   Directions and Maps

Student Activity Book page 514

Locate Points on a Coordinate Grid

Lesson Objectives

- Use ordered pairs to locate points on a grid.
- Name ordered pairs for points on a grid.
- Solve problems using ordered pairs.
- Draw rectangles by joining points on a grid.

Vocabulary
coordinate grid
ordered pair

The Day at a Glance

Today's Goals	Materials	
1 Teaching the Lesson **A1:** Locate and identify points on a coordinate grid. **A2:** Connect points on a coordinate grid to make a rectangle. **2 Going Further** ▸ Differentiated Instruction **3 Homework and Spiral Review**	**Lesson Activities** Student Activity Book pp. 515–518 or Student Hardcover Book pp. 515–518 and Activity Workbook p. 253–254 (includes Special Format) Homework and Remembering pp. 335–336 Transparency of Student Book pp. 515–517 and overhead projector	**Going Further** Activity Cards 14-2 Masking tape Sticky notes Coordinate Grid (TRB M148) Math Journals

Use Math Talk today!

Keeping Skills Sharp

Daily Routines

Homework Review If students give incorrect answers, have them explain how they found the answers. This can help you determine whether the error is conceptual or procedural.

Strategy Problem Dexter puts up a 24-foot-long fence to make a rectangular area for his pets to play in. He divides the rectangle into 3 equal squares all in one row. The side of each square is 3 feet long. What is the area of the section? 27 square feet

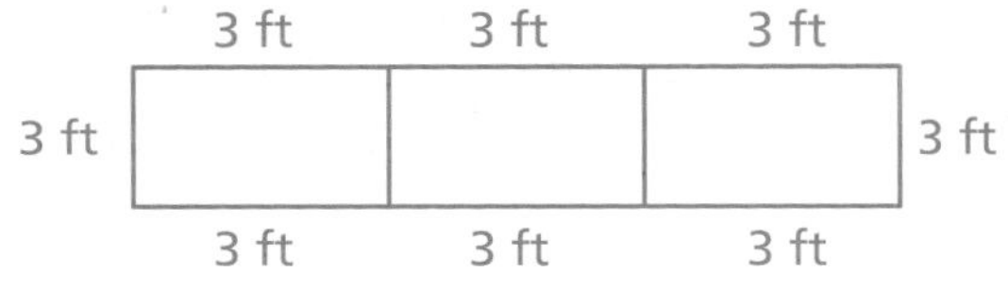

English Language Learners

Draw a 5 × 5 coordinate grid on the board. Plot a point at (3, 4). Write (3, 4) and *ordered pair*.

- **Beginning** Say: **An *ordered pair* describes a location on a grid.** Have students repeat. Ask: **Is (3, 4) an ordered pair?** yes
- **Intermediate** Say: **(3, 4) is an *ordered* __.** pair **An *ordered pair* describes a location on a __.** grid
- **Advanced** Have students identify the ordered pair and tell what it describes on the grid.

1 Teaching the Lesson

Activity 1

Ordered Pairs

 35 MINUTES

Goal: Locate and identify points on a coordinate grid.

Materials: Student Activity Book or Hardcover Book pp. 515–517, transparency of Student Activity Book or Hardcover Book pp. 515–517, overhead projector

 **NCTM Standards:**
Geometry Representation

▶ Coordinate Grids WHOLE CLASS

Refer students to the coordinate grid on Student Book page 515. Explain that a coordinate grid can be used to name the exact location of a point on a grid.

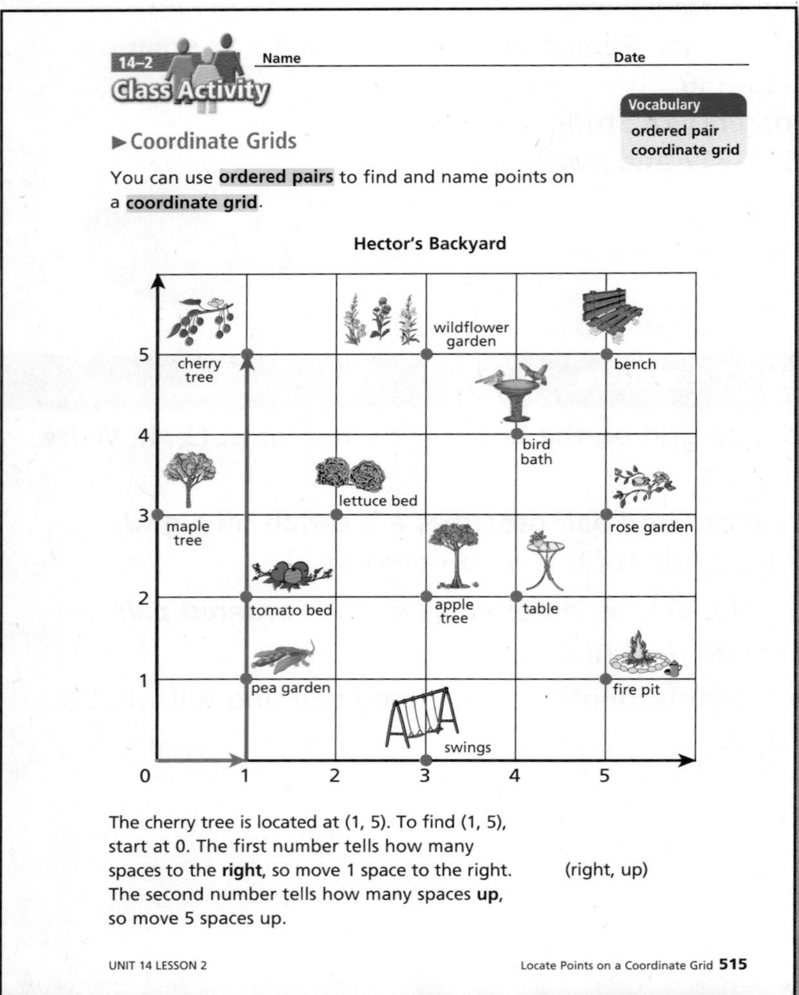

Student Activity Book page 515

Use the transparency of the grid on Student Book page 515 or hold up the grid that shows the map of Hector's backyard. Explain that when you work with a coordinate grid, you always start at 0. Show students that to travel to the cherry tree, you begin at 0 and move to the right 1 unit, then move up 5 units.

- How many units to the right of 0 did we move? 1 unit
- How many units up is the cherry tree? 5 units

Write "cherry tree" on the board, and beside it write the ordered pair (1, 5).

Invite students to look carefully at the coordinate grid.

- What does this map show? the things in Hector's backyard
- Look at the numbers along the side and bottom of the grid. How can you describe them? Both sets of numbers start with the same 0 and increase by ones.
- How can you describe the grid lines? They are horizontal and vertical line segments that cross. They are equally spaced.
- Where are the backyard places located on this coordinate grid? at the intersection of 2 line segments

▶ Locate Points PAIRS

Explain that we move right for the first number in an ordered pair and up for the second number in the ordered pair.

Write the ordered pair (2, 3) on the board. Tell **Student Pairs** that this pair of numbers describing the location of a point is called an *ordered pair*.

Differentiated Instruction

Extra Help Have students working in pairs practice plotting points verbally. Student A says: Plot the point with the ordered pair five, two. While finding the point, Student B says: Move five units to the right, move two units up. The coordinates are five, two.

- Which number comes first in the ordered pair? 2
- What does this number tell us? The number tells how far to the right of 0 the point is.
- What does the second number tell us? The number tells how far up from 0 the point is.
- What is located at (2, 3)? the lettuce bed

Have students complete exercises 1–6 on Student Book page 516 with a partner. When they are finished, have volunteers show how they found each location.

▶ Write Ordered Pairs PAIRS

Look together at Student Book page 516. Explain to students that to write an ordered pair for a point, count the number of lines from 0 traveling right to the point. This is the first number of the ordered pair. Then count the number of lines traveling up to the point. This is the second number of the ordered pair.

Have **Student Pairs** complete exercises 7–13. When they are finished, have volunteers show how they found the ordered pair for the location.

▶ Solve Problems with Ordered Pairs

INDIVIDUALS

Have students complete exercises 14–18 on Student Book page 517. Exercises 16 and 17 introduce ordered pairs that include 0. When students are finished, discuss their answers as a class.

14–2 Class Activity Name ____ Date ____

▶ Locate Points

Hector's Backyard

Use each ordered pair to find places in Hector's backyard. Name what you find at each point.

1. (3, 5) wildflower garden
2. (4, 2) table
3. (1, 2) tomato bed
4. (5, 5) bench
5. (3, 0) swings
6. (0, 3) maple tree

▶ Write Ordered Pairs

Write the ordered pair for the location of each place in Hector's backyard.

7. lettuce bed (2, 3)
8. rose garden (5, 3)
9. fire pit (5, 1)
10. bird bath (4, 4)
11. apple tree (3, 2)
12. maple tree (0, 3)
13. Draw a new place at the intersection of two grid lines on the map of Hector's backyard. Write the ordered pair for its location. (____, ____)
Check students' grids. Answers will vary.

516 UNIT 14 LESSON 2 Locate Points on a Coordinate Grid

Student Activity Book page 516

14–2 Class Activity Name ____ Date ____

▶ Solve Problems With Ordered Pairs

Use the coordinate grid below for exercises 14–18.

Fair Ground

14. Larry went to the fair with his sister, Marissa. First they went to (1, 2). Where did they go first?
roller coaster
15. Larry and Marissa went to (3, 4). What is located at (3, 4)?
science exhibit
16. In the afternoon, Larry went to the home exhibit and Marissa went to the Ferris wheel. Write the ordered pairs for each location.
home exhibit (0, 4) Ferris wheel (2, 0)
17. What do the points for the Ferris wheel and home exhibit have in common?
They are on an axis.
18. Larry said he would meet Marissa at the horse barn at (5, 4). What mistake did he make? What is the correct ordered pair?
He mixed up the numbers in the ordered pair; (4, 5).

UNIT 14 LESSON 2 Locate Points on a Coordinate Grid 517

Student Activity Book page 517

Activity 2

Plot a Picture

 **25 MINUTES**

Goal: Connect points on a coordinate grid to make a rectangle.

Materials: Ruler, Coordinate Grid (TRB M148), Student Activity Book or Hardcover Book p. 518

✓ **NCTM Standards:**
Geometry
Representation
Connections

▶ Picture on a Grid WHOLE CLASS

Write the following ordered pairs on the board. (4, 4), (5, 5), (5, 2) (3, 1) (1, 2) (1, 5) (2, 4)

Have students use Coordinate Grid (TRB M148) to plot the ordered pairs and connect them in the order listed. Then connect the last point to the first point to make a picture.

Next have them plot these three points for two eyes and a nose. (2, 3), (4, 3), (3, 2)

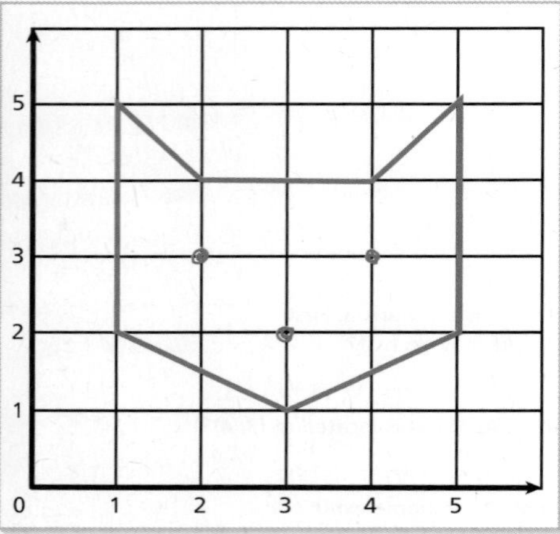

- What animal did you make? a fox or raccoon

Math Talk As a class, discuss if the order in which the points are plotted affects the drawing. Ask students what does affect the drawing on a grid. No; The order in which the points are connected Discuss what must happen to the last point in order to complete the picture. The last point must be connected to the first point.

Name ____________ Date ____________

▶ Figures on Grids

Use the coordinate grid below for exercises 19–22.

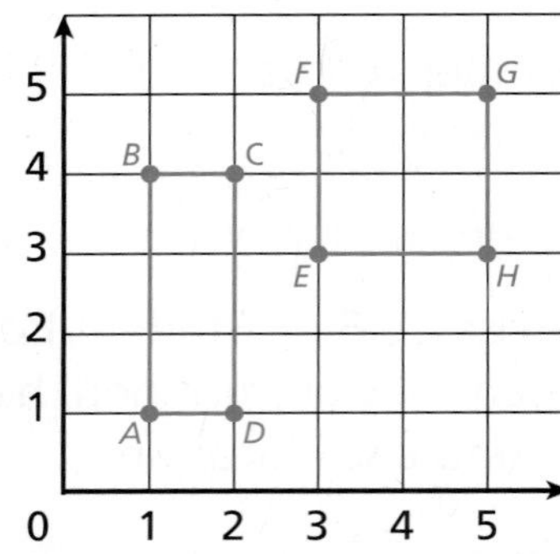

19. Graph each ordered pair. Label the point with the given letter. Check students' grids.
Point *A* (1, 1), Point *B* (1, 4), Point *C* (2, 4), Point *D* (2, 1)

20. Draw a line segment to connect the points in order that you marked for exercise 19. Name the figure you drew.
Possible answer: rectangle

21. Graph each ordered pair. Label the point with the given letter. Check students' grids.
Point *E* (3, 3), Point *F* (3, 5), Point *G* (5, 5), Point *H* (5, 3)

22. Draw a line segment to connect the points in order that you marked for exercise 21. Name the figure you drew.
Possible answer: square

518 UNIT 14 LESSON 2 Locate Points on a Coordinate Grid

Student Activity Book page 518

▶ Figures on Grids INDIVIDUALS

Have students complete exercises 19–22 on Student Book page 518.

 **Ongoing Assessment**

Ask these questions about the map on Student Activity Book page 545:

- ▶ What is the ordered pair for the location of the snack stand?
- ▶ Odessa went to an exhibit at (3, 4) and then she went to an exhibit at (5, 3). Which exhibit did she see first, the science, garden, or home exhibit? Which exhibit did she see next?

2 Going Further

Differentiated Instruction

Intervention

Activity Card 14-2

Where Are You? Activity Card 14–2

Work: In pairs

Use:

- Masking tape
- Sticky notes

Decide:

Who will be Student 1 and who will be Student 2 for the first round.

1. **Work Together** Make a large 5-by-5 coordinate grid on the floor using masking tape. Label each vertical and horizontal grid line with numbers written on sticky notes.
2. **Student 1:** Stand on a point on the grid and name the location using an ordered pair.
3. **Student 2:** Call out a new location. As your partner moves to that location along the grid lines, record the route that your partner uses.
4. Change roles and repeat the activity.

Unit 14, Lesson 2

Activity Note Be sure that students correctly identify the horizontal and the vertical axes of the grid before they begin the activity. Remind them to begin at (0, 0) to identify each ordered pair.

Math Writing Prompt

Explain Your Thinking Lao drew a map of his room using a coordinate grid. Explain how he can describe the location of his bed.

Soar to Success Math **Software Support**

Warm Up 34.14

On Level

Activity Card 14-2

Write a Word Problem Activity Card 14–2

Work: In pairs

Use:

- TRB M148 (Coordinate Grid)

1. **Work Together** Draw different shapes at several points on a coordinate grid.
2. **On Your Own** Write a word problem using the ordered pairs that locate each shape.
3. Exchange problems with your partner to solve.
4. **Explain** Is it important to name the coordinates of a point in a certain order? Why or why not?

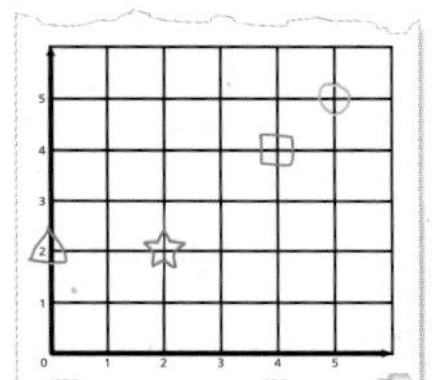

Clues to my figure:
The first number in the ordered pair is the same as the second number. Both numbers are even and greater than two.
What is the figure and where is it located?

square; (4,4)

Unit 14, Lesson 2

Activity Note Before writing their word problems, students should identify the coordinates of each shape drawn on the grid. Then they can use number sense to write clues identifying a location and shape.

Math Writing Prompt

You Decide Are (2, 3) and (3, 2) the same point on a grid? Explain why or why not.

Software Support

The Number Games: ArachnaGraph, Level G

Challenge

Activity Card 14-2

Describe Routes Activity Card 14–2

Work: On your own

Use:

- TRB M148 (Coordinate Grid)

1. Use the coordinate grid to draw a map of a place that you know. Draw pictures at points on the map to show several landmarks. Mark a walking path that connects several of these landmarks.
2. Use the map and the ordered pairs for each location along the path to describe your walk.
3. Exchange maps with another student and write a description of another walk that you could take.

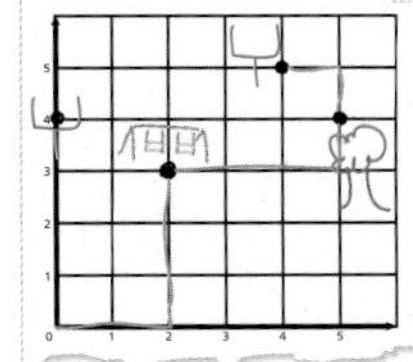

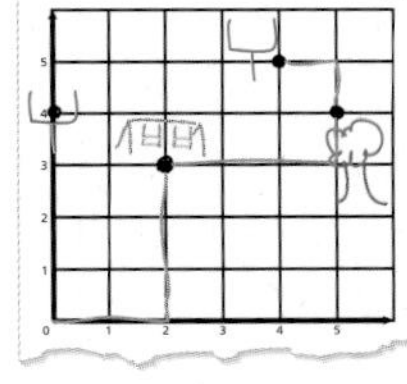

At recess I walked to the swings at (2,3). Then I walked right and up to the oak tree at (5,4). I walked up and left to a goal post at (4,5).

Unit 14, Lesson 2

Activity Note As a variation on the activity, have students draw a compass on the grid and use north, south, east, and west directions in their description of the walking paths.

Math Writing Prompt

Show Your Thinking Can both numbers in an ordered pair be the same? Explain why or why not. Draw a coordinate grid to support your answer.

DESTINATION Math **Software Support**

Course II: Module 3: Unit 1: Area

Homework and Spiral Review

14–2 Homework **Goal:** Additional Practice

✓ Include students' completed Homework page as part of their portfolios.

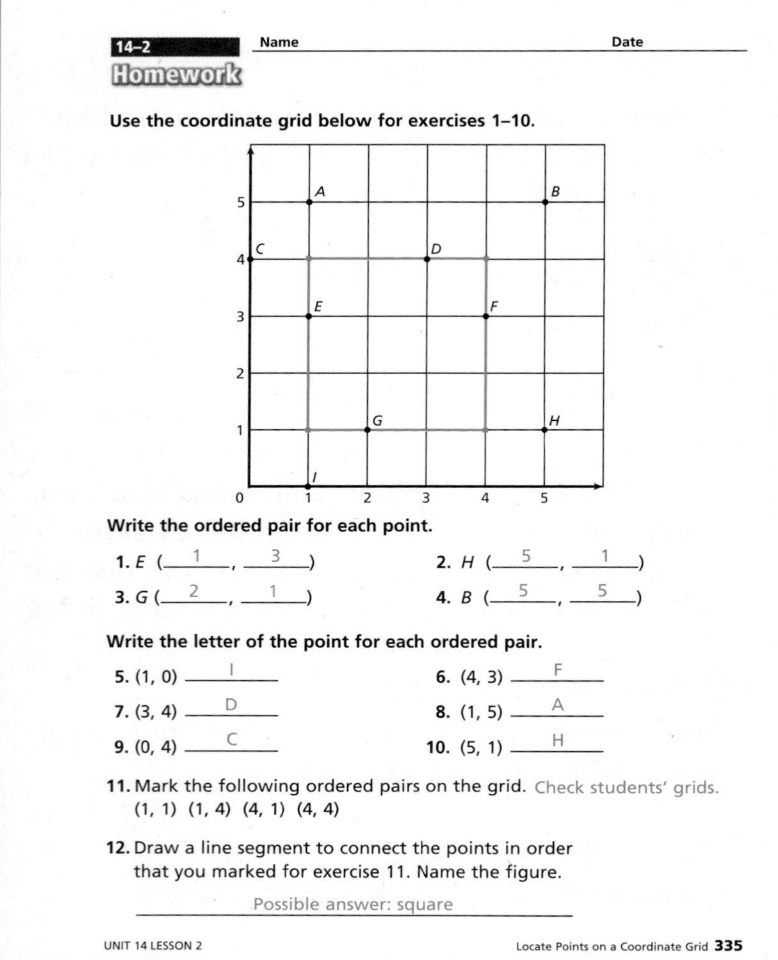

14–2 Homework Name Date

Use the coordinate grid below for exercises 1–10.

Write the ordered pair for each point.

1. *E* (1, 3)
2. *H* (5, 1)
3. *G* (2, 1)
4. *B* (5, 5)

Write the letter of the point for each ordered pair.

5. (1, 0) I
6. (4, 3) F
7. (3, 4) D
8. (1, 5) A
9. (0, 4) C
10. (5, 1) H

11. Mark the following ordered pairs on the grid. Check students' grids.
(1, 1) (1, 4) (4, 1) (4, 4)

12. Draw a line segment to connect the points in order that you marked for exercise 11. Name the figure.
Possible answer: square

UNIT 14 LESSON 2 Locate Points on a Coordinate Grid 335

Homework and Remembering page 335

14–2 Remembering **Goal:** Spiral Review

This Remembering page would be appropriate anytime after today's lesson.

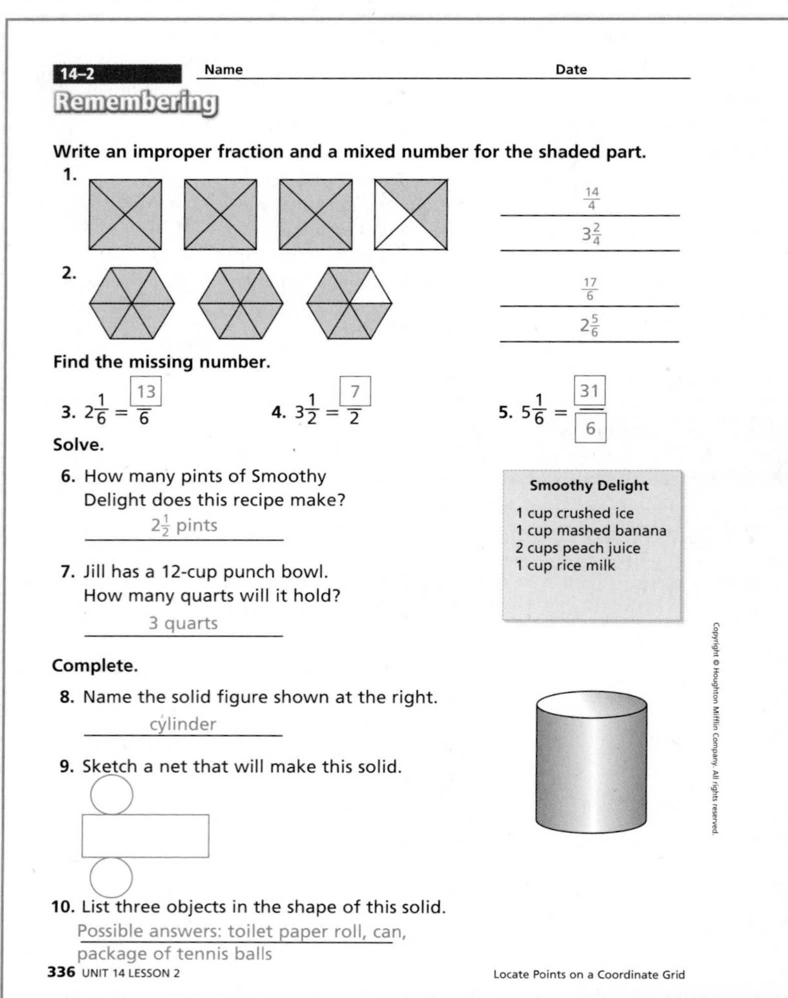

14–2 Remembering Name Date

Write an improper fraction and a mixed number for the shaded part.

1. $\frac{14}{4}$ $3\frac{2}{4}$

2. $\frac{17}{6}$ $2\frac{5}{6}$

Find the missing number.

3. $2\frac{1}{6} = \frac{13}{6}$
4. $3\frac{1}{2} = \frac{7}{2}$
5. $5\frac{1}{6} = \frac{31}{6}$

Solve.

6. How many pints of Smoothy Delight does this recipe make?
$2\frac{1}{2}$ pints

7. Jill has a 12-cup punch bowl. How many quarts will it hold?
3 quarts

Smoothy Delight
1 cup crushed ice
1 cup mashed banana
2 cups peach juice
1 cup rice milk

Complete.

8. Name the solid figure shown at the right.
cylinder

9. Sketch a net that will make this solid.

10. List three objects in the shape of this solid.
Possible answers: toilet paper roll, can, package of tennis balls

336 UNIT 14 LESSON 2 Locate Points on a Coordinate Grid

Copyright © Houghton Mifflin Company. All rights reserved.

Homework and Remembering page 336

Home or School Activity

Social Studies Connection

Make a Map Invite students to make a map on Coordinate Grid (TRB M148). They can make a map of their bedroom, home, neighborhood, or another location of their choice. Remind them to place a point for each item they are including at the intersection of two grid lines. Have students exchange maps and write the ordered pair for each item.

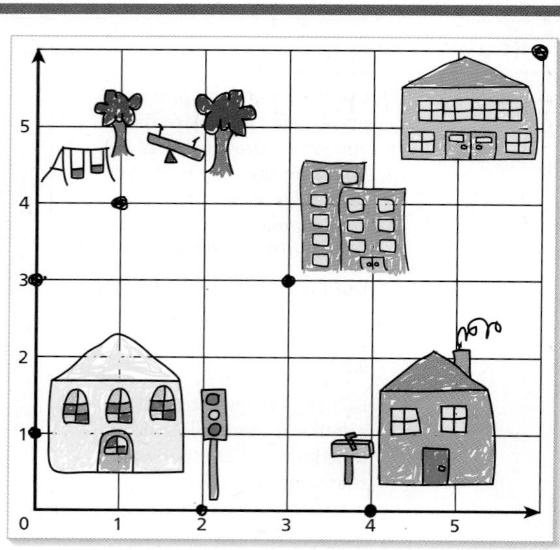

Explore Line Segments and Figures on a Coordinate Grid

Lesson Objectives

- Visualize how to complete plane figures on a coordinate grid.
- Describe the location of points on a grid using ordered pairs.
- Use grid lines on a coordinate grid to measure the length of line segments.

Vocabulary
coordinate grid
ordered pair

The Day at a Glance

Today's Goals	Materials	
1 Teaching the Lesson **A1:** Complete figures on a coordinate grid by naming a missing ordered pair. **A2:** Measure the length of line segments on a coordinate grid.	**Lesson Activities** Student Activity Book pp. 519–522 or Student Hardcover Book pp. 519–522 and Activity Workbook pp. 255–258. Homework and Remembering pp. 337–338 Quick Quiz (Assessment Guide) Rulers Coordinate Grid (TRB M148) Overhead projector and Transparency of Coordinate Grid (TRB M148) (optional)	**Going Further** Activity Cards 14-3 Coordinate Grid (TRB M148) Centimeter Grid Paper (TRB M31) Math Journals
2 Going Further ▶ Differentiated Instruction		
3 Homework and Spiral Review		

Use **Math Talk** today!

Keeping Skills Sharp

Daily Routines

Homework Review Let students work together to check their work. Remind students to use what they know about helping others.

Strategy Problem Lucas bought 2 boxes of pasta for \$1.39 each and one pound of zucchini for \$0.69. He gave the cashier \$5.00. How much change did he receive? Explain how using rounded costs can help you solve the problem. \$1.53; Possible answer: Using rounded costs helps me focus on which operations to use.

English Language Learners

Draw a 5 × 5 coordinate grid on the board. Plot 3 points to make a triangle. Write *point*.

- **Beginning** Say: **A *point* is a location of an ordered pair.** Have students repeat.
- **Intermediate** Ask: **Are there any *points* plotted on the grid?** yes **How many *points* have been plotted?** 3 points
- **Advanced** Have students identify the *points* that have been plotted on the grid.

1 Teaching the Lesson

Activity 1

Draw Triangles and Quadrilaterals on a Grid

 30 MINUTES

Goal: Complete figures on a coordinate grid by naming a missing ordered pair.

Materials: Rulers (1 per student), transparency of Coordinate Grid (TRB M148) and overhead projector (optional), Student Activity Book or Hardcover Book pp. 519–520.

 **NCTM Standards:**
Geometry
Representation

▶ Triangles on Coordinate Grids

WHOLE CLASS

14–3 Class Activity Name ________ Date ________

▶ Triangles on Coordinate Grids

1. Mark a point on this coordinate grid to form the third vertex of a right triangle. Join the three points with line segments to make a right triangle. Possible drawing:
2. Write the ordered pair for each vertex.
(1, 5) (4, 5) (1, 3)

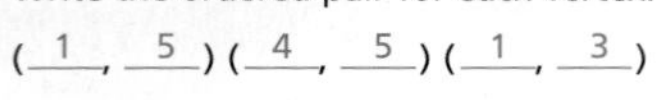

3. Mark a point on this coordinate grid to form the third vertex of an obtuse triangle. Join the three points to make an obtuse triangle. Possible drawing:
4. Write the ordered pair for each vertex.
(3, 4) (5, 3) (5, 1)

5. Draw a triangle on this coordinate grid. Place each vertex at the intersection of two grid lines. Possible drawing:
6. Write the ordered pair for each vertex.
(1, 2) (3, 4) (5, 2)

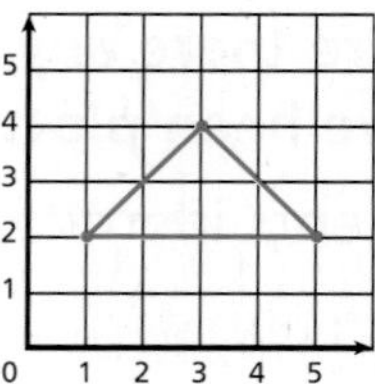

UNIT 14 LESSON 3 Explore Line Segments and Figures on a Coordinate Grid 519

Student Activity Book page 519

Distribute Coordinate Grid (TRB M148). Display an overhead transparency of TRB M148 or draw a large 5-by-5 coordinate grid on the board. Mark a point at (1, 0) and another point at (4, 0). Ask students to do the same on their grids.

Mark a third point at (1, 4). Then have students connect the three points to form a triangle with a ruler.

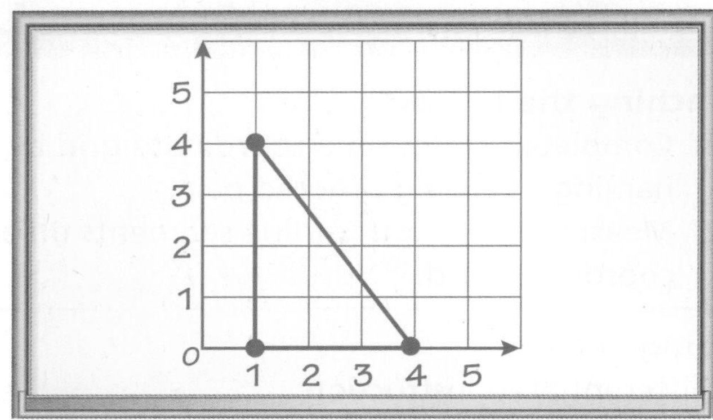

- What type of triangle did I make? right triangle
- How do you know? Possible answer: It has a right angle.

Ask students to draw a third point on their coordinate grid to form a different right triangle. Have them use a ruler to join the points. Invite them to hold up their triangles so they can see the various possibilities.

Ask several students to give the ordered pair for the third point of their triangle. Possible answers: (1, 1), (1, 2), (1, 3), (1, 5), (4, 1), (4, 2), (4, 3), (4, 4), (4, 5)

Review the definitions of obtuse triangle and acute triangle.

Then have students erase their right triangles, leaving the two original points they drew on their grids and ask the following questions:

- Can you draw a third point to form an obtuse triangle? yes
- Name an ordered pair that will form an obtuse triangle. Possible answers: (0, 1), (0, 2), (0, 3), (0, 4), (0, 5), (5, 1), (5, 2), (5, 3), (5, 4), (5, 5)

- Can you draw a third point to form an acute triangle? yes
- Name an ordered pair that will form an acute triangle. Possible answers: (2, 1), (2, 2), (2, 3), (2, 4), (2, 5), (3, 1), (3, 2), (3, 3), (3, 4), (3, 5)

Ask students to complete exercises 1–6 on Student Book page 519.

▶ Quadrilaterals on Coordinate Grids

PAIRS

Explain to students that they will now have a chance to draw parallel and perpendicular line segments on coordinate grids to form quadrilaterals. You may want to review the characteristics of different quadrilaterals.

Ask **Student Pairs** to complete exercises 7–12 on Student Activity Book page 520.

When students have finished, ask volunteers to draw their quadrilaterals on the board and identify the perpendicular line segments and parallel line segments.

Math Talk in Action

Jun: How do we place the fourth point in Exercise 7?

Anil: Each side of the square is 3 spaces. Count 3 spaces down from (4, 4). Stop at (4, 1). How do we place the fourth point in Exercise 9?

Jun: Move 2 spaces up from (4, 3). Stop at (4, 5).

14–3 Class Activity Name Date

▶ Quadrilaterals on Coordinate Grids

7. Mark a point on this coordinate grid to form the fourth vertex of a square. Join the four points with line segments to make a square.

8. Write the ordered pair for each vertex.

(1, 1) (1, 4)
(4, 1) (4, 4)

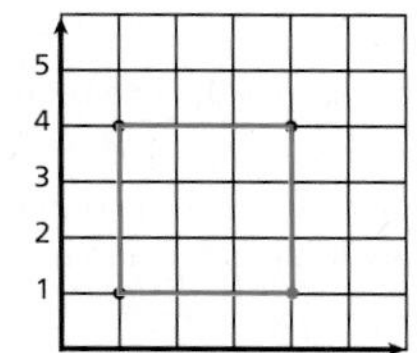

9. Mark a point on this coordinate grid to form the fourth vertex of a parallelogram. Join the four points to make a parallelogram. Possible drawing:

10. Write the ordered pair for each vertex.

(2, 2) (2, 4)
(4, 3) (4, 5)

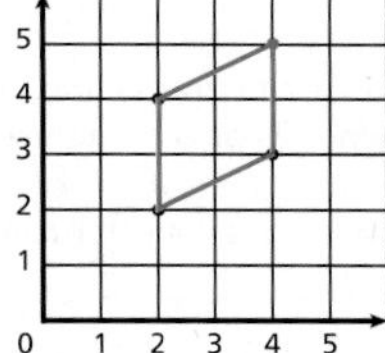

11. Draw a quadrilateral on this coordinate grid. Place each vertex at the intersection of two grid lines. Possible drawing:

12. Write the ordered pair for each vertex.

(1, 3) (1, 5)
(5, 3) (5, 5)

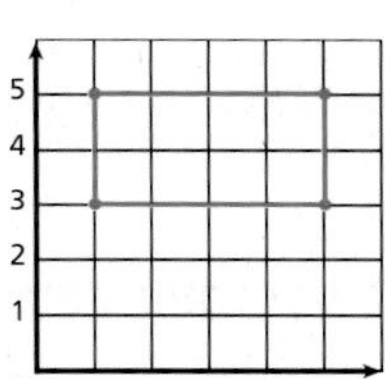

520 UNIT 14 LESSON 3 Explore Line Segments and Figures on a Coordinate Grid

Student Activity Book page 520

Activity 2

Lengths of Line Segments

30 MINUTES

Goal: Measure the length of line segments on a coordinate grid.

Materials: Coordinate Grid (TRB M148), overhead projector and transparency of Coordinate Grid (TRB M148), Student Activity Book or Hardcover Book pp. 521–522 and Activity Book pp. 257–258.

NCTM Standards:
Geometry Measurement Representation

▶ Distance Between Points

INDIVIDUALS

Distribute Coordinate Grid (TRB M148). Display an overhead transparency of TRB M148 or draw a large 5-by-5 coordinate grid on the board. Mark a point at (1, 2) and another point at (4, 2). Join the two points with a line segment. Ask students to do the same on their grids. You may want to have struggling students work with a **Helping Partner** for this activity.

Activity continued ▶

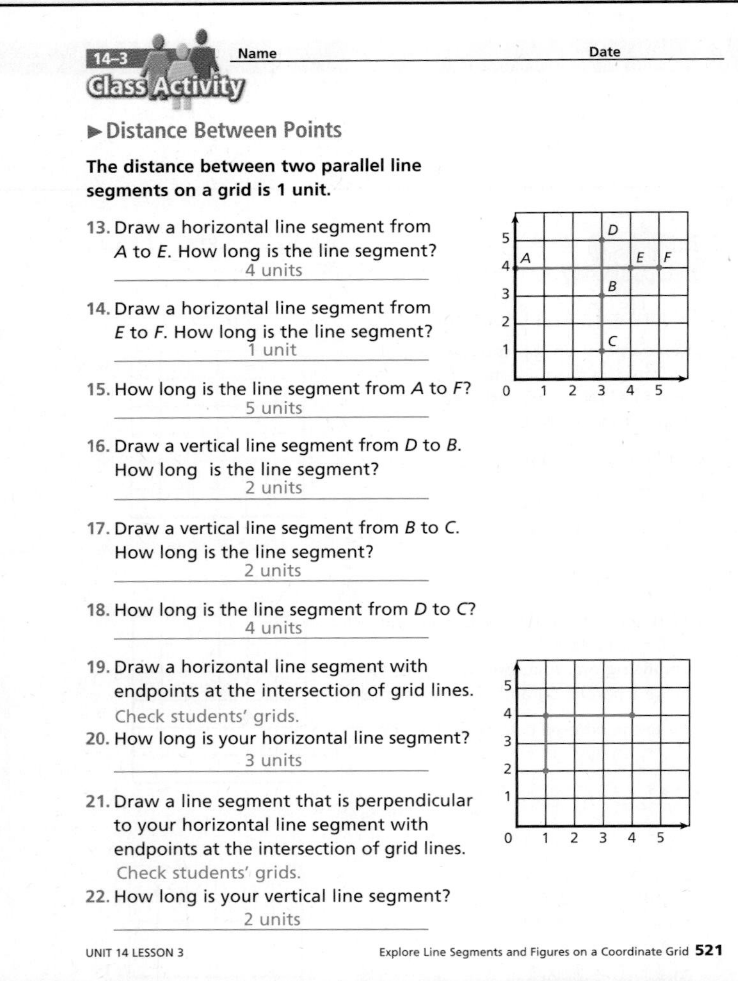

14–3 Class Activity Name Date

▶ Distance Between Points

The distance between two parallel line segments on a grid is 1 unit.

13. Draw a horizontal line segment from *A* to *E*. How long is the line segment? 4 units
14. Draw a horizontal line segment from *E* to *F*. How long is the line segment? 1 unit
15. How long is the line segment from *A* to *F*? 5 units
16. Draw a vertical line segment from *D* to *B*. How long is the line segment? 2 units
17. Draw a vertical line segment from *B* to *C*. How long is the line segment? 2 units
18. How long is the line segment from *D* to *C*? 4 units
19. Draw a horizontal line segment with endpoints at the intersection of grid lines. Check students' grids.
20. How long is your horizontal line segment? 3 units
21. Draw a line segment that is perpendicular to your horizontal line segment with endpoints at the intersection of grid lines. Check students' grids.
22. How long is your vertical line segment? 2 units

UNIT 14 LESSON 3 Explore Line Segments and Figures on a Coordinate Grid **521**

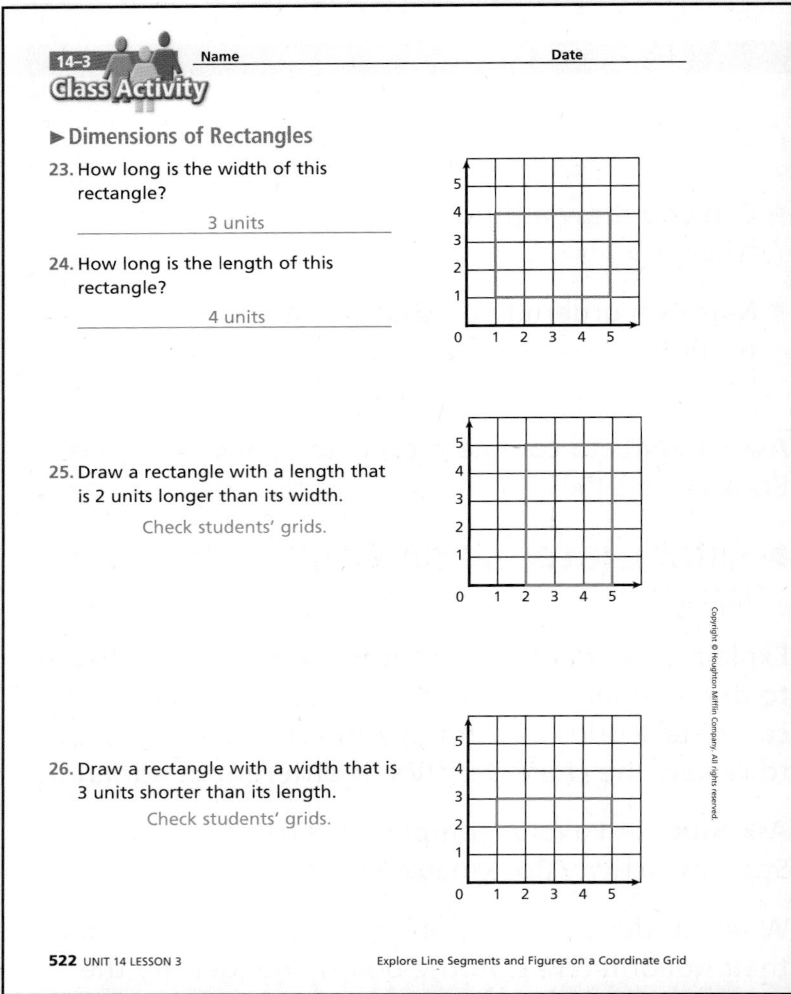

14–3 Class Activity Name Date

▶ Dimensions of Rectangles

23. How long is the width of this rectangle? 3 units
24. How long is the length of this rectangle? 4 units
25. Draw a rectangle with a length that is 2 units longer than its width. Check students' grids.
26. Draw a rectangle with a width that is 3 units shorter than its length. Check students' grids.

522 UNIT 14 LESSON 3 Explore Line Segments and Figures on a Coordinate Grid

Student Activity Book page 521

Student Activity Book page 522

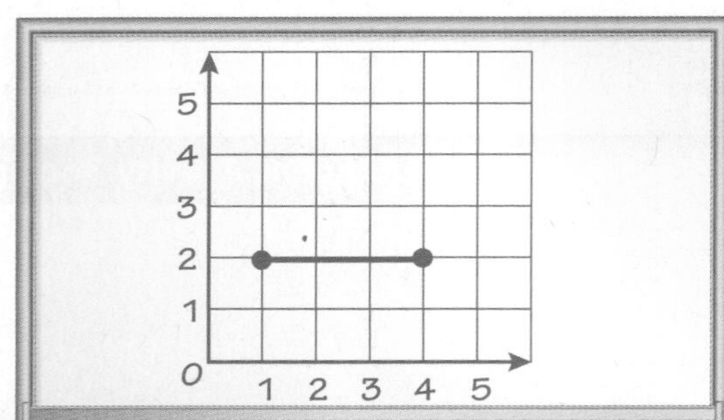

- How can I use the grid to find the length of this horizontal line segment? Count the units between the two endpoints.
- What is the length of this line segment? 3 units

Have students complete exercises 13–22 on Student Book page 521 on their own.

▶ Dimensions of Rectangles INDIVIDUALS

Ask students to complete exercises 23–26 on Student Book page 522.

Quick Quiz

See Assessment Guide for Unit 14 Quick Quiz.

Ongoing Assessment

Ask students to use Coordinate Grid (TRB M148) to complete the following exercises:

- ▶ Draw a rectangle with a width that is 4 units shorter than its length. Write the ordered pair for each vertex.
- ▶ Draw a right triangle. Write the ordered pair for each vertex.

2 Going Further

Differentiated Instruction

Intervention — Activity Card 14-3

Draw a Quadrilateral

Activity Card 14–3

Work: In pairs

Use:

- 2 TRB M148 (Coordinate Grid)

1. **On Your Own** Draw a quadrilateral of your choice on a coordinate grid.
2. Write the ordered pair for each vertex on a separate sheet of paper.
3. Exchange lists of ordered pairs with your partner. Use the list to draw your partner's quadrilateral on your grid.
4. **Analyze** How can you use the grid drawings to demonstrate the properties of the quadrilaterals?

Answers will vary. Right angles, congruent angles and lines, and parallel and perpendicular lines can be identified on the grid.

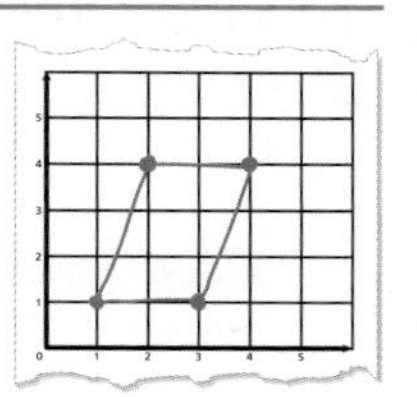

The vertices of my parallelogram are at (1,1) (3,1) (2,4) (4,4).

Unit 14, Lesson 3

Activity Note To make the activity more challenging, have students exchange lists of coordinates without naming the quadrilateral. Repeat the activity as time allows.

Math Writing Prompt

You Decide Rupa drew a rectangle on a coordinate grid. Nancy wants to draw the same rectangle on her grid. How many ordered pairs does Rupa need to list for Nancy? Explain.

Software Support

Warm Up 34.15

On Level — Activity Card 14-3

Draw Obtuse Triangles

Activity Card 14–3

Work: In pairs

Use:

- 6 TRB M148 (Coordinate Grid)
- a square corner (a piece of paper, an index card, or an envelope)

1. **Work Together** Draw an obtuse triangle on the coordinate grid. First mark and connect points at (1, 0), and (1, 5). Then locate all possible points for the third vertex of the triangle.
2. Draw the triangles. Name the ordered pairs for the third vertex.
3. Repeat the activity to make acute triangles. Using the same two points, locate and name all possible points for the third vertex.

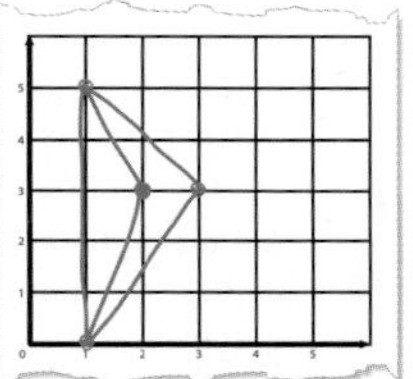

We can make an obtuse triangle using these ordered pairs for the third point: (2,1) (2,2) (2,3) (3,2) (3,3) and (2,4).

Unit 14, Lesson 3

Activity Note Have students use the square corner to check for right angles and to decide if they have an obtuse angle or all acute angles in their triangles.

Math Writing Prompt

Explain a Method Harris wants to find the length of a line segment on a grid with endpoints at (0, 2) and (5, 2). Explain how he can do it.

Software Support

The Number Games: ArachnaGraph, Level G

Challenge — Activity Card 14-3

Plot a Boat

Activity Card 14–3

Work: In pairs

Use:

- 2 TRB M31 (Centimeter Grid Paper)

1. **On Your Own** Make a 10-by-10 coordinate grid on centimeter grid paper. Use line segments to draw the outline of a sailboat on the grid. Mark each point where two or more line segments meet.
2. Write instructions for your partner to recreate your sailboat on a blank grid. Use the ordered pairs of the points you marked along the outline of your boat.
3. **Analyze** Is there any other way to describe the outline of your boat accurately?

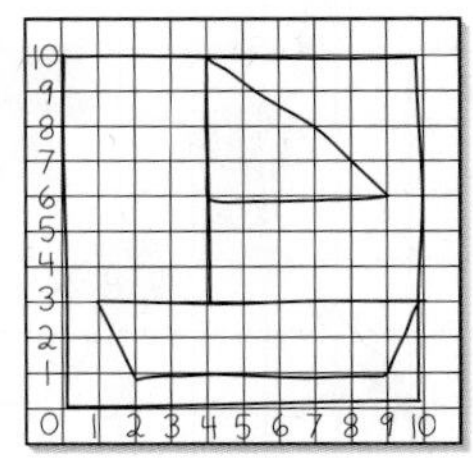

Unit 14, Lesson 3

Activity Note Some students might use the location of the boat relative to the axes of the grid to describe its outline. They could also use the lengths of the line segments as part of the description.

Math Writing Prompt

Predict and Verify Jamil drew a point at (1, 1) and at (4, 1). What kinds of triangles can he make with a third point? Mark the two points and check your predictions.

Software Support

Course II: Module 3: Unit 1: Area

Homework and Spiral Review

14–3 Homework **Goal:** Additional Practice

For Homework, students draw rectangles and quadrilaterals on coordinate grids.

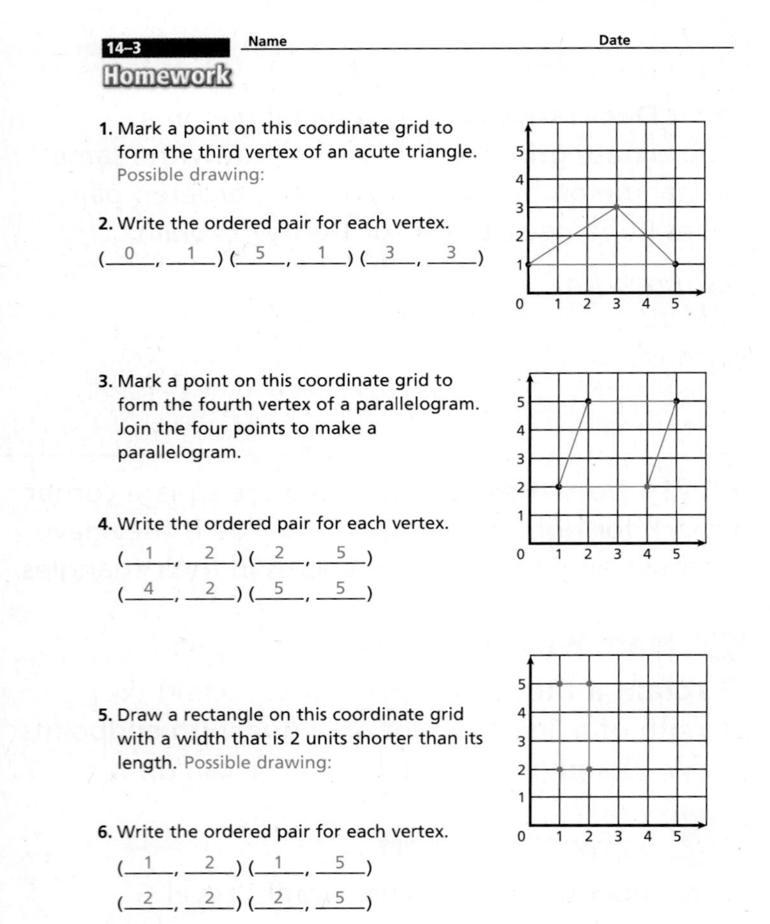

14–3 Homework Name ______ Date ______

1. Mark a point on this coordinate grid to form the third vertex of an acute triangle. Possible drawing:
2. Write the ordered pair for each vertex.
(0, 1) (5, 1) (3, 3)
3. Mark a point on this coordinate grid to form the fourth vertex of a parallelogram. Join the four points to make a parallelogram.
4. Write the ordered pair for each vertex.
(1, 2) (2, 5)
(4, 2) (5, 5)
5. Draw a rectangle on this coordinate grid with a width that is 2 units shorter than its length. Possible drawing:
6. Write the ordered pair for each vertex.
(1, 2) (1, 5)
(2, 2) (2, 5)

UNIT 14 LESSON 3 Explore Line Segments and Figures on a Coordinate Grid **337**

Homework and Remembering page 337

14–3 Remembering **Goal:** Spiral Review

This Remembering page would be appropriate anytime after today's lesson.

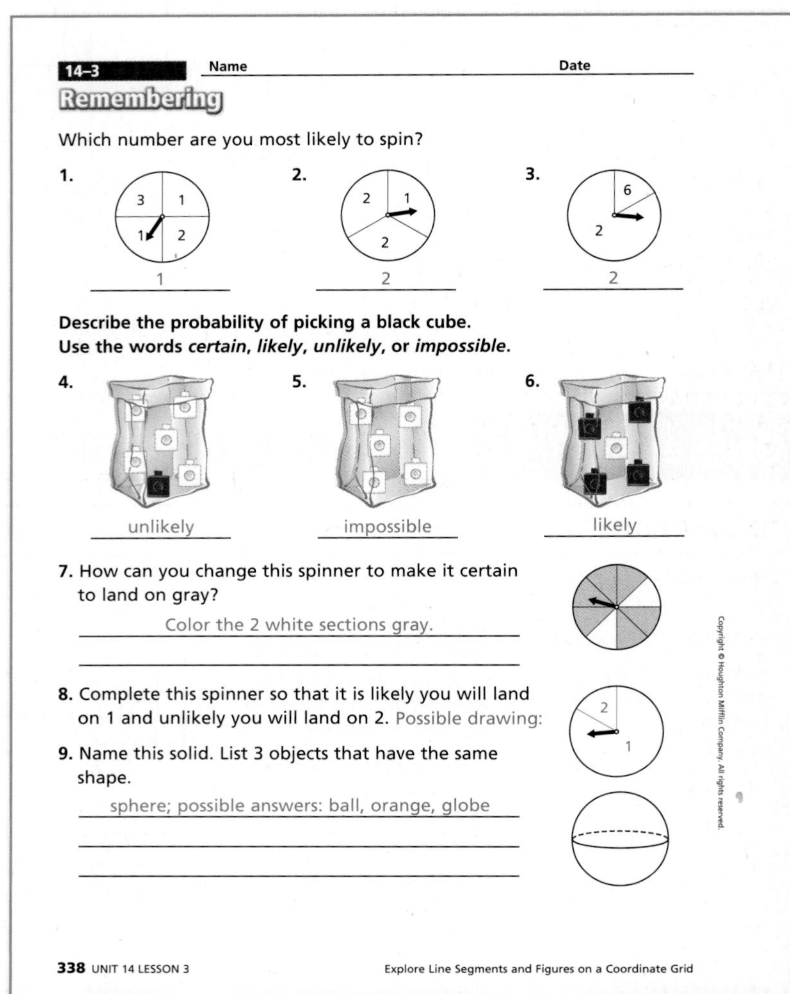

14–3 Remembering Name ______ Date ______

Which number are you most likely to spin?

1. 1
2. 2
3. 2

Describe the probability of picking a black cube. Use the words *certain, likely, unlikely,* or *impossible*.

4. unlikely
5. impossible
6. likely
7. How can you change this spinner to make it certain to land on gray?
Color the 2 white sections gray.
8. Complete this spinner so that it is likely you will land on 1 and unlikely you will land on 2. Possible drawing:
9. Name this solid. List 3 objects that have the same shape.
sphere; possible answers: ball, orange, globe

338 UNIT 14 LESSON 3 Explore Line Segments and Figures on a Coordinate Grid

Homework and Remembering page 338

Home or School Activity

Language Arts Connection

Treasure Map Invite students to make a treasure map on a coordinate grid. Their map should include at least three different hidden treasures. Have them write a story to accompany the map.

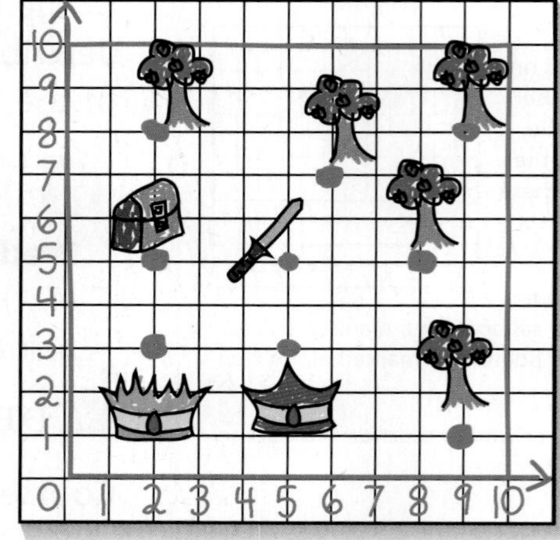

A long time ago, a king, a queen, and their two children lived in a castle. One day a group of knights came to visit the king...

Unit Review and Test

Lesson Objective

- **Assess student progress on unit objectives.**

The Day at a Glance

Today's Goals	Materials
1 Assessing the Unit ► Assess student progress on unit objectives. ► Use activities from unit lessons to reteach content. **2 Extending the Assessment** ► Use remediation for common errors. There is no homework assignment on a test day.	Unit 14 Test, Student Activity Book or Hardcover Book pp. 523–524 Unit 14 Test, Form A or B, Assessment Guide (optional) Unit 14 Performance Assessment, Assessment Guide (optional)

Keeping Skills Sharp

Daily Routines 5 MINUTES	
If you are doing a unit review day, go over the homework. If this is a test day, omit the homework review.	**Review and Test Day** You may want to choose a quiet game or other activity (reading a book or working on homework for another subject) for students who finish early.

Assessing the Unit

Assess Unit Objectives

45 MINUTES (more if schedule permits)

Goal: Assess student progress on unit objectives.

Materials: Student Activity Book or Hardcover Book pp. 523–524; Assessment Guide Unit 14 Form A and B (optional); Unit 14 Performance Assessment (optional)

▶ Review and Assessment

If your students are ready for assessment on the unit objectives, you may use either the test on the Student Book pages or one of the forms of the Unit 14 Test in the Assessment Guide to assess student progress.

If you feel that students need some review first, you may use the test on the Student Book pages as a review of unit content, and then use one of the forms of the Unit 14 Test in the Assessment Guide to assess student progress.

To assign a numerical score for all of these test forms, use 10 points for each question.

You may also choose to use the Unit 14 Performance Assessment. Scoring for that assessment can be found in its rubric in the Assessment Guide.

▶ Reteaching Resources

The chart lists the test items, the unit objectives they cover, and the lesson activities in which the objective is covered in this unit. You may revisit these activities with students who do not show mastery of the objectives.

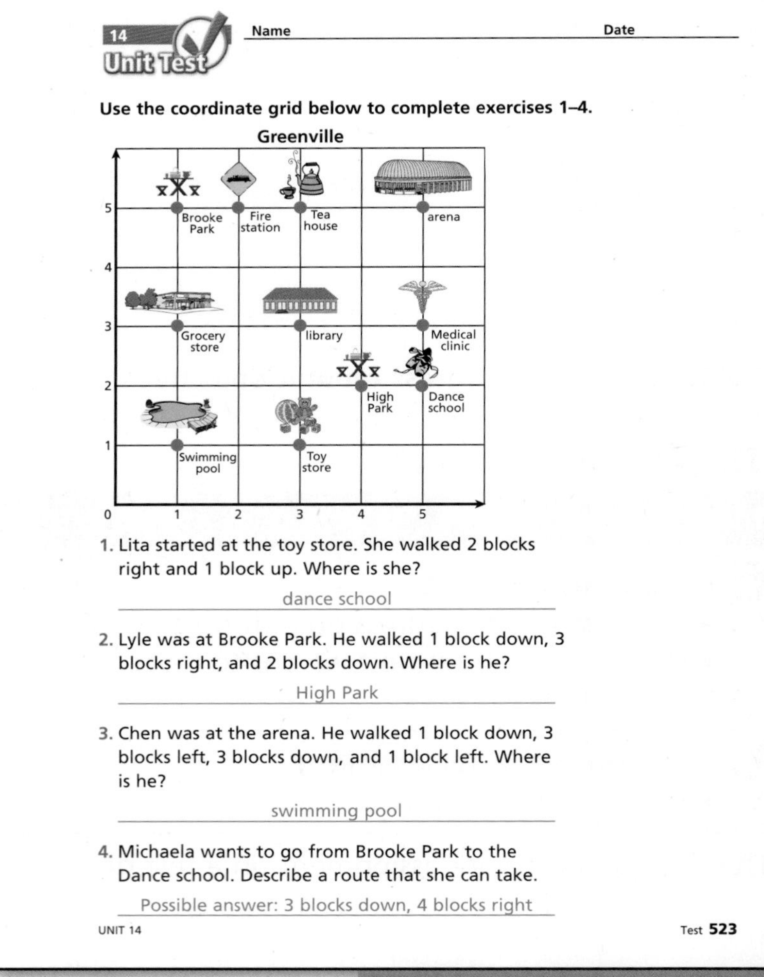

14 Unit Test

Name ________ Date ________

Use the coordinate grid below to complete exercises 1–4.

Greenville

1. Lita started at the toy store. She walked 2 blocks right and 1 block up. Where is she?
   dance school

2. Lyle was at Brooke Park. He walked 1 block down, 3 blocks right, and 2 blocks down. Where is he?
   High Park

3. Chen was at the arena. He walked 1 block down, 3 blocks left, 3 blocks down, and 1 block left. Where is he?
   swimming pool

4. Michaela wants to go from Brooke Park to the Dance school. Describe a route that she can take.
   Possible answer: 3 blocks down, 4 blocks right

UNIT 14 Test **523**

Student Activity Book page 523

Unit Test Items	Unit Objectives Tested	Activities to Use for Reteaching
1–4	**14.1** Find locations given directions (up, down, left, and right) and describe routes between locations on maps and grids.	Lesson 1, Activity 1
5–10	**14.2** Use ordered pairs to locate points and name ordered pairs for points on a coordinate grid.	Lesson 2, Activity 1 Lesson 3, Activity 1

14 Unit Test Name Date

Use the coordinate grid below to complete exercises 5–10.

Name the animals you find at the point for each ordered pair.

5. (1, 2) sea lions

6. (5, 0) orca whales

Write the ordered pair for the location of the animals.

7. Sharks (5 , 3)

8. Dolphins (3 , 5)

9. Mato went to the aquarium. The first place he went to was at (5, 5). Which place did he go to first?

beluga whales

Aquarium

Dolphins, Beluga whales, Otters, Sharks, Sea lions, Harbor seals, Orca whales

0 1 2 3 4 5

10. Extended Response After watching the sea lions being fed, Mato went to see the otters and the harbor seals. Write the ordered pair for each animal.

otters (2 , 4) harbor seals (4 , 2)

What is the order of the numbers in an ordered pair? Why does the order matter? Use the example of the otters and harbor seals in your explanation.

The first number tells you how many spaces to the right of 0 to move. The second number tells you how many spaces up. If you do not follow the correct order, you will be at the wrong point. For example, if you wrote the ordered pair for the otters in the wrong order, you would be writing the ordered pair for the harbor seals.

524 UNIT 14 Test

Student Activity Book page 524

▶ Assessment Resources

Free Response Tests

Unit 14 Test, Student Book pages 523–524
Unit 14 Test, Form A, Assessment Guide

Extended Response Item

The last item in the Student Activity Book test and in the Form A test will require an extended response as an answer.

Multiple Choice Test

Unit 14 Test, Form B, Assessment Guide

Performance Assessment

Unit 14 Performance Assessment, Assessment Guide
Unit 14 Performance Assessment Rubric, Assessment Guide

▶ Portfolio Assessment

Teacher-selected Items for Student Portfolios:

- Homework, Lesson 2
- Class Activity work, Lessons 1, 3

Student-selected Items for Student Portfolios:

- Favorite Home or School Activity
- Best Writing Prompt

② Extending the Assessment

Common Errors

Activities for Remediation

Unit Objective 14.1

Find locations given directions (up, down, left, and right) and describe routes between locations on maps and grids.

Common Error: Has Difficulty Following Directions Left, Right, Up, and Down

Some students have difficulty following directions left, right, up, and down.

Remediation Play "Someone Says" with students. Have them stand and follow such directions as "Someone says walk two steps right. Someone says walk three steps up. Someone says walk one step back."

Common Error: Includes Diagonal Paths When Describing Routes

Some students may not limit their movements on a grid to left, right, up, and down.

Remediation Tell students to think of the lines on coordinate grids as being like horizontal and vertical streets. Students can only travel along the streets in one direction at a time and they can't take diagonal shortcuts.

Unit Objective 14.2

Use ordered pairs to locate points and name ordered pairs for points on a coordinate grid.

Common Error: Thinks Ordered Pairs Refer to the Spaces Between Grid Lines Rather Than the Intersections of Grid Lines

Some students may think ordered pairs refer to the spaces between grid lines like on maps they may have seen, instead of intersections of grid lines.

Remediation Tell students that ordered pairs are used to locate specific points, not spaces, on coordinate grids. Show students how to locate a point such as (3, 5) by following the vertical line labeled 3 up to the horizontal line labeled 5. Tell students (3, 5) is at the intersection of these two lines.

Common Error: Transposes Numbers in Ordered Pairs

Some students may transpose numbers in ordered pairs.

Remediation Draw a coordinate grid with the numbers on the vertical axis in one color and the numbers on the horizontal axis in a second color. Write ordered pairs for points on the grid using the corresponding colors. Have students observe how the numbers on the grid match the numbers in the ordered pairs. Tell students that in an ordered pair, the first number always shows the distance from 0 to the right, and the second number always shows the distance from 0 up. The ordered pair is (right, up).

If students have difficulty remembering that the order is right and then up, suggest they think of a plane taking off: it travels along the ground first before going up.

Common Error: Doesn't Start Counting at Zero When Naming Ordered Pairs

Some students may not correctly identify the numbers in an ordered pair because they aren't counting from 0.

Remediation Make a poster of a coordinate grid and write "START" at the (0, 0) point. Demonstrate how to write ordered pairs for points on the grid by counting the number of horizontal spaces from 0 to the right and then counting the number of vertical spaces up from 0.

Common Error: Doesn't Recognize That Points Located on an Axis Have Zero in the Ordered Pair

Some students may not readily name the ordered pair for features on the vertical or horizontal axis.

Remediation Point to the bottom left-hand side of the grid and ask students how many spaces to the right of 0 your finger is located (0). Then ask them how many spaces up from 0 your finger is located (0). Move your finger to the right to (2, 0) and ask how many spaces to the right you moved (2) and how many spaces up you moved (0). Tell them the ordered pair is (2, 0). Continue with other examples along the horizontal axis. Then move your finger to (0, 2). Ask how many spaces to the right from 0 your finger is (0). Ask how many spaces up from 0 your finger is (2). Tell students the ordered pair is (0, 2). Continue for other points along the vertical axis.

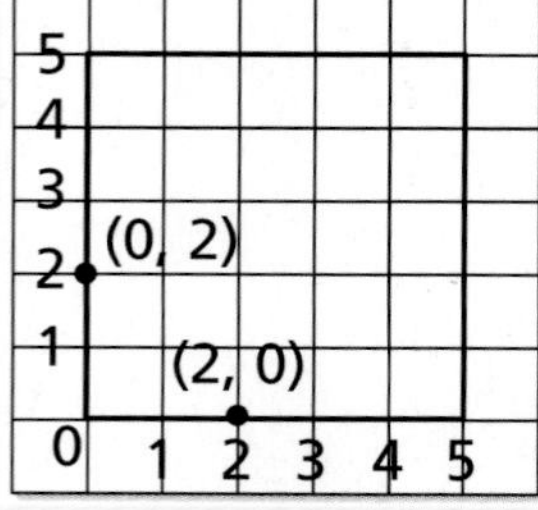

Extension Lessons

Some state standards include content that is not generally included at this grade level. In order to cover these standards, we have provided these extension lessons. Use them only if you need to cover this content.

Place Value Through Hundred Thousand

Lesson Objectives

- Identify and write numbers through hundred thousands.
- Compare and order numbers up to 10,000.
- Add, subtract, and compare with large numbers.

Vocabulary
standard form
word form

The Day at a Glance

Today's Goals	Materials	
1 Teaching the Lesson **A1:** Identify place value and read and write numbers through hundred thousands. **A2:** Compare and order numbers up to 10,000. Estimate, add, and subtract with numbers through hundred thousands.	**Lesson Activities** Student Activity Book pages 525–526 or Student Hardcover Book pages 525–526 Homework and Remembering pages 339–340 MathBoard materials	**Going Further** Activity Cards E-1 TRB M31 (Centimeter Grid Paper) Number Cubes Calculators (optional) Sticky notes (optional) MathBoard materials Math Journals
2 Going Further ► Differentiated Instruction		
3 Homework		

Use Math Talk today!

Keeping Skills Sharp

Quick Practice — 5 MINUTES

Because you may be using this lesson at any time during the year, no specific Quick Practice is recommended. Use any Quick Practice activity that meets your students' needs.

Daily Routines

Logic Problem A third grade class took a survey to find out where students prefer to swim. Use these clues to make a possible tally chart that could display the data.

- ► **Pool** was chosen most often.
- ► **Ocean** was chosen least often.
- ► **Lake** was chosen more often than river.

Possible tally chart.

Swimming Spots	Tally	Number
Pool	卌 卌 ||||	14
Lake	卌	5
Ocean	||	2
River	||||	4

1 Teaching the Lesson

Activity 1

Identify Place Value

20 MINUTES

Goal: Identify place value and read and write numbers through hundred thousands.

Materials: Student Activity Book or Hardcover Book page 525

NCTM Standards:
Number and Operations
Connections

Name ____________ Date ____________

Vocabulary
place value
standard form
word form

▶ **Identify Place Value Through Hundred Thousands**

To read and write numbers you need to understand **place value**.

1. What are the names of the places of a three-digit number?
hundreds, tens, and ones

Hundreds	Tens	Ones
2	3	5

2. How do we read and write 235 with words?
two hundred thirty-five

Hundred Thousands	Ten Thousands	Thousands	Hundreds	Tens	Ones
1	6	8	2	3	5

Write the value of the underlined digit.

3. 13,456 3,000
4. 190,765 700
5. 88,763 80,000
6. 4,567 60

▶ **Write Numbers Different Ways**

Standard form: 15,678 **Word form**: fifteen thousand, six hundred seventy-eight

Write each number in standard form.

7. six thousand, one hundred eight 6,108
8. six thousand eight 6,008
9. one hundred sixty six thousand, eighty 166,080

Write each number in word form.

10. 17,893 seventeen thousand, eight hundred ninety-three
11. 175,635 one hundred seventy five thousand, six hundred thirty-five

EXTENSION LESSON 1 Place Value Through Hundred Thousand 525

Student Activity Book page 525

Ask for Ideas Invite volunteers to make place value drawings on the board for the numbers 4,876 and 10,456. Ask other volunteers to share what they know about larger numbers beyond ten thousand and up through a hundred thousand.

▶ Identify Place Value Through Hundred Thousand WHOLE CLASS

Direct students' attention to Student Book page 525. Have them complete exercises 1 and 2.

Now have them look at the place value chart below exercise 2 and cover the Hundred Thousands and Ten Thousands places with their fingers. Have a volunteer read aloud the number. eight thousand, 2 hundred thirty-five.

Then have students just cover the Hundred Thousands place and read the number. sixty eight thousand, two hundred thirty-five

Repeat, reading the whole number. one hundred sixty-eight thousand, two hundred thirty-five.

Complete exercise 3 with students and have them work independently on exercises 4–6.

▶ Write Numbers Different Ways

INDIVIDUALS

Remind students that numbers can be written in different ways. Explain that in today's lesson, students will be focusing on *standard* and *word forms*. Have students look at the *standard form* example on Student Activity Book page 525 and read aloud the number. Have volunteers identify the value of each digit in the number.

1= 10,000 6= 600 8=8
5= 5,000 7= 70

Write 134,789 on the board and have students write the number in word form on their MathBoard. Then have students complete exercises 7–11 independently.

English Language Learners

Write 1,582 and *place value* on the board. Ask: **Does *place value* mean *ones, tens, hundreds,* or *thousands*?** yes

- **Beginning** Point and say: **2 is in the ones place.** Have students repeat. Continue with other places.
- **Intermediate and Advanced** Ask: **What number is in the *ones* place?** 2 Continue with other places.

Activity 2

Compare, Order, and Compute with Large Numbers

35 MINUTES

Goals: Compare and order numbers up to 10,000. Estimate, add, and subtract with numbers through hundred thousands.

Materials: Student Activity Book or Hardcover Book page 526, MathBoard materials

NCTM Standards:
Number and Operations
Problem Solving
Connections

E–1 Name ______ Date ______

Class Activity

Vocabulary
greater than >
less than <
equal =
greatest
least

► Compare and Order Numbers to 10,000

Discuss the problem below.

Jim has 24 trading cards and Hattie has 42 trading cards. Who has more trading cards? How do you know?

Write greater than (>), less than (<), or equal (=) to make each statement true.

12. 4,008 (<) 4,108
13. 2,356 (<) 2,563
14. 8,567 (<) 9,567
15. 3,989 (>) 3,899
16. 2,385 (=) 2,385
17. 3,235 (>) 2,350

Write each group of numbers in order from greatest to least.

18. 8,456 4,567 4,675
8,456 4,675 4,567

19. 3,465 3,654 3,546
3,654 3,546 3,465

► Add, Subtract, and Estimate with Large Numbers

Solve using any method. Use estimation to check that your results are reasonable.

20. 73,608 + 9,729 = 83,337

21. 33,756 − 13,897 = 19,859

22. Bob's town has a population of 13,226 people. Mia's town has 11,867 people. Tani's town has 33,569 people. How many people live in the three towns?
58,662 people

23. How many more people live in Tani's town than Bob's town?
20,343 people

526 EXTENSION LESSON 1 Place Value Through Hundred Thousand

Student Activity Book page 526

► Compare and Order Numbers to 10,000 WHOLE CLASS

Compare Discuss the problem at the top of Student Book page 526. Students should draw place value models or discuss how they know which number is greater.

Use the following questions to help students explain their thinking on comparing numbers.

- What makes the 2 larger in 24 than it is in 42? In 24, the 2 stands for 20 or 2 tens. In 42, the 2 stands for 2 or 2 ones.
- What makes 4 smaller in 24 than in 42? In 24 the 4 stands for 4 ones and in 42, the 4 stands for 40 or 4 tens.

Review inequality symbols with students and discuss how students can use the notation for *greater than* and *less than*.

- The smaller number is always at the closed (smaller) end of the symbol: $24 < 42$, or 24 is less than 42.
- The larger number is always at the open (larger) end of the symbol: $42 > 24$, or 42 is greater than 24.

Order Explain to students that when you compare numbers, you are comparing two numbers. When you have three or more numbers that you want to put in order from least to greatest, that is called *ordering*.

- Suppose Taylor has 56 cards. Put the number of cards that Taylor, Jim, and Hattie have in order from least to greatest and then greatest to least. 24, 42, 56; 56, 42, 24.

Have students complete exercises 12–19 independently.

► Add, Subtract, and Estimate with Large Numbers WHOLE CLASS

Addition Write the following addition problem on the board:

73,608 + 91,729

Ask three volunteers to the board and have each volunteer use a different method to solve the problem. 165,337 Have volunteers use the New Groups Below, New Groups Above, and Show All Totals methods.

Remind students to rewrite the problem vertically. Check to make sure they aligned all the place values correctly.

Students at their seats should use any method they wish and once students have completed the exercise, use the **Solve and Discuss** structure to discuss and compare the three methods.

Subtraction Write the following subtraction problem on the board.

156,402 − 80,169

Then have student volunteers rewrite the example vertically, solve the problem, and discuss the methods as a class. 76,233

Check Results Explain to students that they can check their subtraction with addition. Have a student volunteer show how to check their subtraction by adding 76,233 plus 80,169 to get 156,402.

Estimate Explain to students that they can also use estimation to see if their answer is close or reasonable. Write the addition example on the board.

$$\begin{array}{r} \mathbf{73{,}608} \\ \mathbf{+\ 91{,}729} \\ \hline \end{array}$$

Then have students round each number to the nearest ten thousand and add.

$$\begin{array}{r} \mathbf{70{,}000} \\ \mathbf{+\ 90{,}000} \\ \hline \mathbf{160{,}000} \end{array}$$

Students should compare their estimate with their answer to see if they are close. 160,000 is close to 165,337, so their answer seems reasonable.

Now have students use estimation with the subtraction example.

$$\begin{array}{r} \mathbf{156{,}402} \\ \mathbf{-\ 80{,}169} \\ \hline \end{array}$$

Have students round to the nearest ten thousand and subtract.

$$\begin{array}{r} \mathbf{160{,}000} \\ \mathbf{-\ 80{,}000} \\ \hline \mathbf{80{,}000} \end{array}$$

Students should compare their estimates with their answer to see if they are close. 80,000 is close to 76,233, so their answer is reasonable.

Have students solve problems 20–23 on Student Book page 526. Encourage students to use estimation to check if their answers are reasonable.

Ongoing Assessment

Have students solve the following problems. Encourage them to use estimation to check if their answer is reasonable.

$$\begin{array}{r} 36{,}456 \\ +\ 27{,}987 \\ \hline 64{,}443 \end{array} \qquad \begin{array}{r} 86{,}456 \\ -\ 12{,}899 \\ \hline 73{,}557 \end{array}$$

2 Going Further

Differentiated Instruction

Intervention — Activity Card E-1

Grid It

Activity Card E-1 ●

Work: In pairs

Use:

- Centimeter Grid Paper (TRB31)
- MathBoard materials

Decide:

Who will be Student 1 and who will be Student 2 first.

1. **Student 1:** Write an addition or subtraction problem horizontally on the MathBoard.
2. **Student 2:** Rewrite the problem vertically on grid paper. This will help you line up the numbers.
3. Both students check to see if the addition or subtraction was done correctly.
4. Switch roles and repeat the activity using different problems.

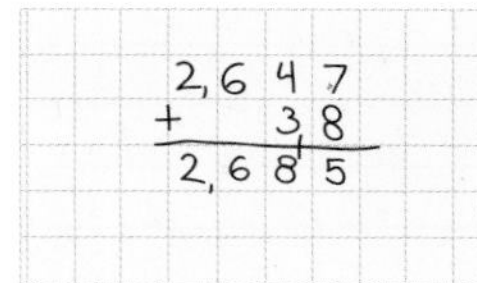

Extension, Lesson 1

Activity Note Provide TRB M31 (Centimeter Grid Paper) for students.

Math Writing Prompt

Explain Your Thinking Explain how you can tell that you will need to make a new ten when you add two numbers.

Software Support

Warm Up 10.33

On Level — Activity Card E-1

Roll a Sum

Activity Card E-1 ▲

Work: In pairs

Use:

- Number cube
- Calculators (optional)

Decide:

Who will be Student 1 and who will be Student 2.

1. **Student 1:** Roll a number cube. *Suppose you roll a 5.*
2. **Student 2:** Roll that many times to get an addend. In this example, you roll until you have a 5-digit number. *Suppose you roll 31,115.*
3. **Student 1:** Roll again. *Suppose you roll a 4.*
4. **Student 2:** Roll until you get a 4-digit number. *Suppose you roll 4,674.*
5. Both students add the two numbers and then compare answers. You can check your answers with a calculator.

Extension, Lesson 1

Activity Note Remind students to solve their problems on paper before checking their answers on the calculator.

Math Writing Prompt

You Decide Write a word problem that requires adding two 5-digit numbers, but has a 6 digit-answer. Explain how you chose your numbers.

Software Support

The Number Games: Tiny's Think Tank, Level A

Challenge — Activity Card E-1

Speed Addition

Activity Card E-1 ■

Work: In small groups

Use:

- Sticky note (optional)

Decide:

Who will be the Student Leader first. Every student will be the leader once.

1. **Student Leader:** Read this rule: Each addend must be 7 digits with exactly 3 zeros.
2. **Student Leader:** Write an addition example in column form and find the total. If you have sticky notes, cover your answer so the group can't see it.
3. **Student Leader:** Show the problem to the group and the first student who finds the correct answer gets a point.
4. Repeat with a new **Student Leader.**

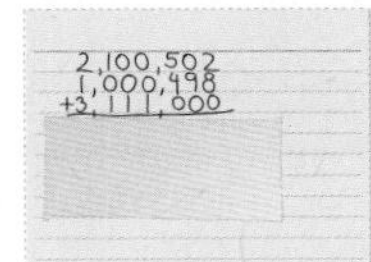

Extension, Lesson 1

Activity Note You may want to provide large sticky notes to students so they can cover their answers.

Math Writing Prompt

Reasoning If you add two different 6-digit numbers, what is the greatest possible total? What is the least possible total? Explain your answer.

DESTINATION Math® **Software Support**

Course II: Module 2: Unit 1: Estimating and Finding Differences within 9,999

3 Homework

Goal: Additional Practice

Because you may be using this lesson at any time during the year, no Spiral Review is included. Use this Homework page to provide students with additional practice.

E–1 Homework

Name ____ Date ____

Write the value of the underlined digit.

1. 98,765 700
2. 88,265 8,000
3. 9,506 6
4. 67,894 60,000

Write each number in standard form.

5. twenty five thousand, eight hundred thirty 25,830
6. ninety nine thousand, six hundred nine 99,609

Write each number in word form.

7. 8,013 eight thousand, thirteen
8. 13,456 thirteen thousand, four hundred fifty-six

Write greater than (>), less than (<), or equal (=) to make each statement true.

9. 8,652 (>) 8,562
10. 9,001 (<) 9,011

Write each group of numbers in order from least to greatest.

11. 567 2,346 765 — 567 765 2,346
11. 8,065 8,056 8,650 — 8,056 8,065 8,650

Solve using any method.

13. In a recent election, 17,285 people voted in one city and 26,122 voted in another city. How many people voted in both cities? 43,407 people
14. On Saturday, the baseball stadium had 36,004 fans at the game. On Sunday they had 28,990. How many more fans were at Saturday's game than at Sunday's game? 7,014 fans

EXTENSION LESSON 1 Place Value Through Hundred Thousand **339**

Homework and Remembering page 339

E–1 Homework

Name ____ Date ____

15. **Write the number 183,421 in word form. Then write the place value name of the digit 8.**

one hundred eighty-three thousand, four hundred twenty-one; The 8 is in the ten thousands place.

340 EXTENSION LESSON 1 Place Value Through Hundred Thousand

Homework and Remembering page 340

Home or School Activity

Language Arts Connection

Writing Numbers Review these rules for writing numbers in word form, and give examples:

- If the number is between 20 and 100, and you need two words, use a hyphen. (68 is sixty-eight.)
- Do not use the word "and" when writing whole numbers as words. (6,007 is six thousand, seven.)

Ask students to write some numbers in word form.

Number	Words
25	twenty-five
186	one hundred eighty-six
1,615	one thousand, six hundred fifteen
4,609	four thousand, six hundred nine
8,030	eight thousand, thirty

Multiplication Arrays

Vocabulary

product
array
Commutative Property of Multiplication
Associative Property of Multiplication
factor

Lesson Objective

- **Model a product of ones, ones and tens, and tens.**

The Day at a Glance

Today's Goals	Materials	
1 Teaching the Lesson **A1:** Model multiplication of tens and ones **A2:** Model multiplication of tens. **2 Going Further** ► Differentiated Instruction **3 Homework**	**Lesson Activities** Student Activity Book pages 527–530 or Student Hardcover Book pages 527–530 Homework and Remembering pages 341–342 MathBoard materials Base-ten blocks	**Going Further** Activity Cards E-2 TRB M31 (Centimeter Grid Paper) Two-color counters Math Journals

Use **Math Talk** today!

Keeping Skills Sharp

Quick Practice — 5 MINUTES

Because you may be using this lesson at any time during the year, no specific Quick Practice is recommended. Use any Quick Practice activity that meets your students' needs.

Daily Routines

Homework Review Let students work together to check their work. Remind students to use what they know about helping others.

Reasoning Can you draw a triangle with two right angles? Explain why or why not.

No. One right angle measures 90°. Two right angles have a total measure of 180° and the total sum of the measure of all three angles within one triangle is 180°. So, the sum would be greater than 180°.

1 Teaching the Lesson

Activity 1

Arrays of Ones and Tens

 25 MINUTES

Goal: Model multiplication of ones and tens.

Materials: Student Activity Book or Hardcover Book pages 527–528, MathBoard Materials, base-ten blocks

 **NCTM Standards:**
Number and Operations
Connections
Representation

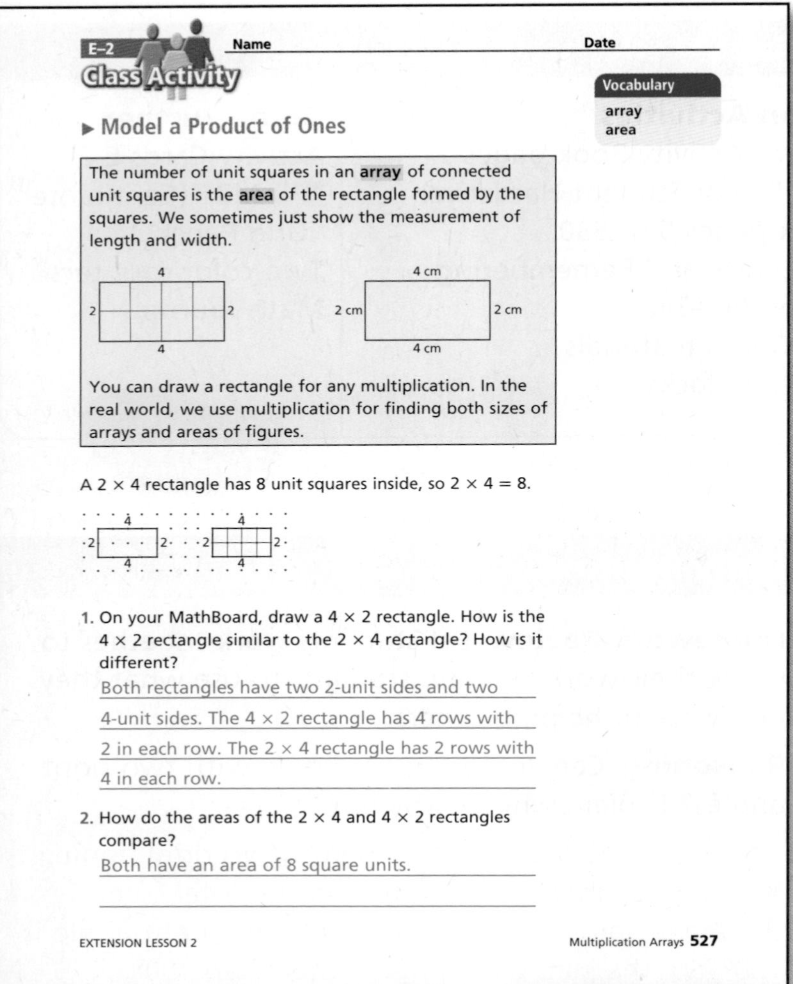

E-2 Class Activity

Name ______ Date ______

Vocabulary
array
area

▶ Model a Product of Ones

The number of unit squares in an **array** of connected unit squares is the **area** of the rectangle formed by the squares. We sometimes just show the measurement of length and width.

You can draw a rectangle for any multiplication. In the real world, we use multiplication for finding both sizes of arrays and areas of figures.

A 2×4 rectangle has 8 unit squares inside, so $2 \times 4 = 8$.

1. On your MathBoard, draw a 4×2 rectangle. How is the 4×2 rectangle similar to the 2×4 rectangle? How is it different?
Both rectangles have two 2-unit sides and two 4-unit sides. The 4×2 rectangle has 4 rows with 2 in each row. The 2×4 rectangle has 2 rows with 4 in each row.

2. How do the areas of the 2×4 and 4×2 rectangles compare?
Both have an area of 8 square units.

EXTENSION LESSON 2 Multiplication Arrays **527**

Student Activity Book page 527

Ask for Ideas Remind students how to count units and draw rectangles on the MathBoards. Have volunteers model different rectangles.

▶ Model a Product of Ones WHOLE CLASS

On their MathBoards, have students draw a 2×4 rectangle, and label the sides. Have them draw the eight unit squares inside.

Discuss how the rectangle shows that $2 \times 4 = 8$. To emphasize that this array is composed of units of 1, write the equation as $2 \times 4 \times 1 = 8$.

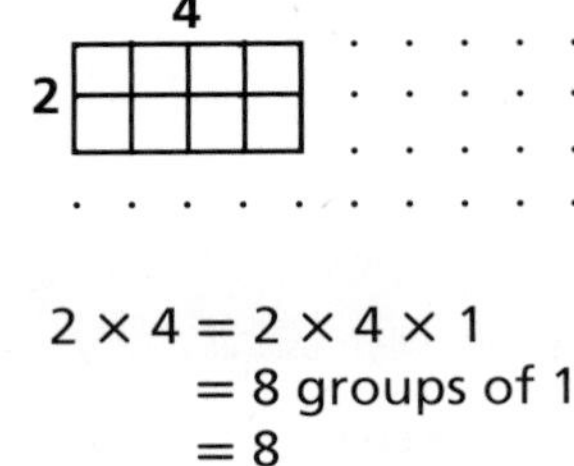

$$\begin{aligned} 2 \times 4 &= 2 \times 4 \times 1 \\ &= 8 \text{ groups of } 1 \\ &= 8 \end{aligned}$$

Teaching Note

Watch For! Students often make rectangles 1 unit too short on the length and width. They do this because they are counting the dots rather than the lengths. Be sure to point out that 2 represents 2 unit lengths and 4 represents 4 unit lengths.

The Learning Classroom

Math Talk Have students practice explaining one another's work in their own words. Begin by having a volunteer write his or her work on the board. Then as the students point to parts of the problem, another student identifies and explains the parts.

English Language Learners

Write *array, column*, and *row* on the board. Draw a 2×3 rectangle showing the *square units*.

- **Beginning** Point and ask: **Does the rectangle have 3 *columns*?** yes **Does it have 3 rows?** no **Does it have 2 rows?** yes **Is it a 2 × 3 *array*?** yes
- **Intermediate and Advanced** Ask: **What shape is this *array*?** rectangle Say: **It has 2 __** rows **and 3 __.** columns **The total *square* units is __.** 6 **The *area* is __.** 6 square units

▶ Review the Commutative Property

WHOLE CLASS

Have students draw a 4 × 2 rectangle. Discuss problems 1 and 2 on Student Book page 527.

- How is this rectangle similar to the 2 × 4 rectangle? Both have a 2-unit side and a 4-unit side.
- How is it different? It is turned, so the 2-unit side is on the bottom instead of the 4-unit side.
- How do the areas of the 2 × 4 and 4 × 2 rectangles compare? They are the same.

Write 2 × 4 = 4 × 2 on the board. Ask if anyone can remember which property tells us that the order of the factors in a multiplication does not change the product. The Commutative Property of Multiplication

▶ Model a Product of Ones and Tens

WHOLE CLASS

On their MathBoards have students draw a 2 × 40 rectangle and label its sides. Ask them how they could find the area of this rectangle. As each of the following possibilities arises, have students draw and label a new 2 × 40 rectangle.

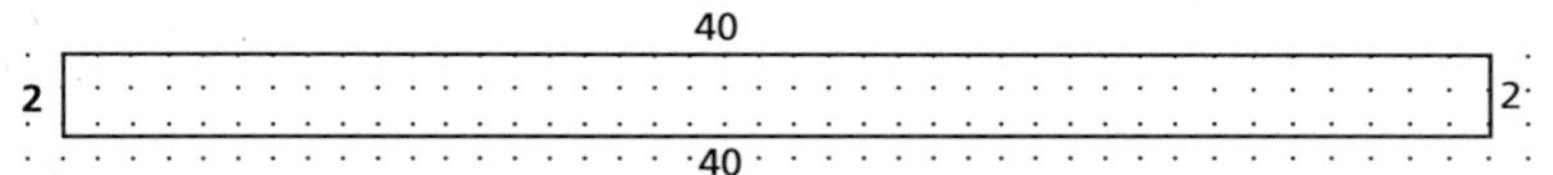

- Divide the rectangle *across* to show 2 groups of 40.

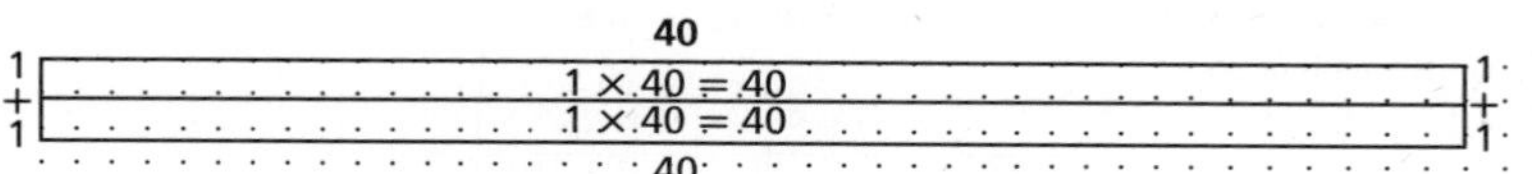

- Divide the rectangle *up-and-down* to show 4 groups of 20.

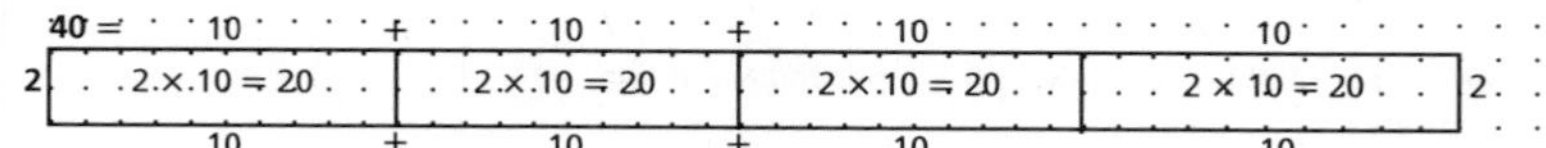

- Divide the rectangle both *across* and *up-and-down* to show 8 groups of 10. (Students need only label one of the inner rectangles.)

40 = 10 + 10 + 10 + 10

1 × 10 = 10	1 × 10 = 10	1 × 10 = 10	1 × 10 = 10
1 × 10 = 10	1 × 10 = 10	1 × 10 = 10	1 × 10 = 10

10 + 10 + 10 + 10

Teaching Note

MathBoards It may be easier and help if students use a plus sign to mark off ten dots on their Boards.

Activity continued ▶

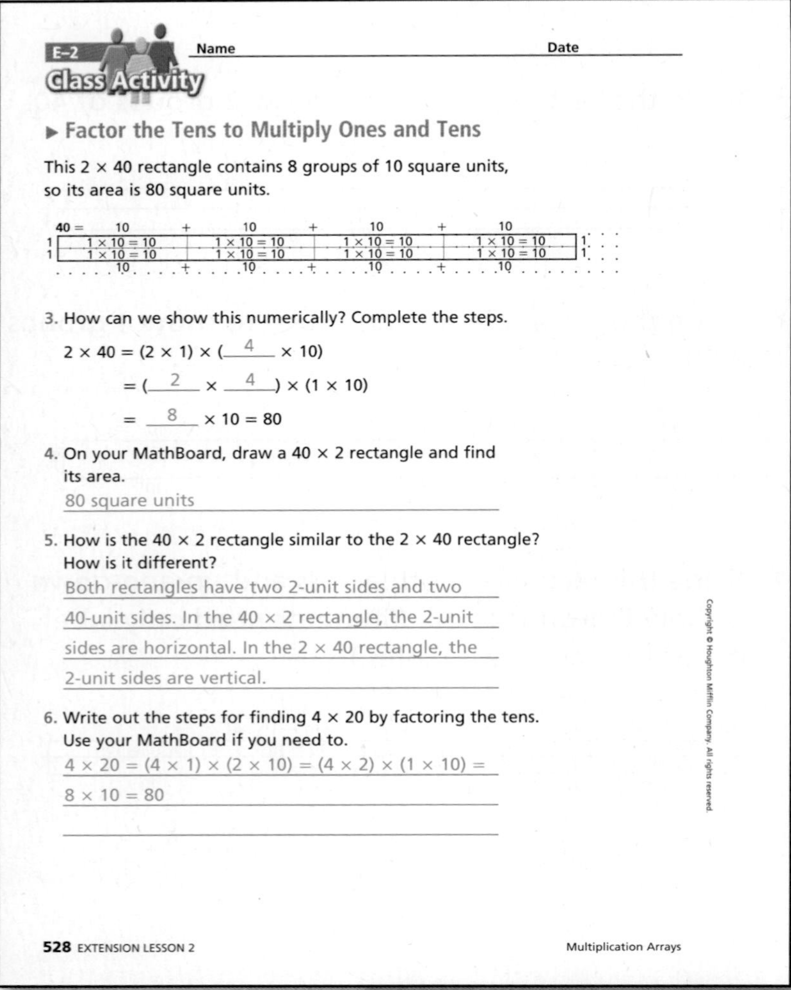

E-2 Class Activity

Name ______ Date ______

▸ Factor the Tens to Multiply Ones and Tens

This 2 × 40 rectangle contains 8 groups of 10 square units, so its area is 80 square units.

3. How can we show this numerically? Complete the steps.

$2 \times 40 = (2 \times 1) \times (\underline{4} \times 10)$

$= (\underline{2} \times \underline{4}) \times (1 \times 10)$

$= \underline{8} \times 10 = 80$

4. On your MathBoard, draw a 40 × 2 rectangle and find its area.

80 square units

5. How is the 40 × 2 rectangle similar to the 2 × 40 rectangle? How is it different?

Both rectangles have two 2-unit sides and two 40-unit sides. In the 40 × 2 rectangle, the 2-unit sides are horizontal. In the 2 × 40 rectangle, the 2-unit sides are vertical.

6. Write out the steps for finding 4 × 20 by factoring the tens. Use your MathBoard if you need to.

4 × 20 = (4 × 1) × (2 × 10) = (4 × 2) × (1 × 10) = 8 × 10 = 80

528 EXTENSION LESSON 2 Multiplication Arrays

Student Activity Book page 528

▸ Factor the Tens to Multiply Ones and Tens INDIVIDUALS

Have students turn to Student Book page 528. Explain that factoring the tens can help them find products such as 2 × 40. Have students complete exercise 3 in their books and then discuss the steps. Students should see that 2 × 40 becomes (2 × 4) × (1 × 10), or 8 groups of 1 × 10 rectangles.

You might discuss the properties involved in writing the steps in exercise 3. As discussed above, the Commutative Property allows us to change the order of the factors. The Associative Property lets us group the factors in different ways.

Have students complete exercises 4–6. Exercises 4 and 5 review the Commutative Property. Exercise 6 gives students more practice factoring the tens.

Teaching Note

What to Expect From Students
Some students may find the process of rewriting 2 × 40 as (2 × 4) × (1 × 10) to be tedious and unnecessary. Tell them that understanding this process will give them a strategy for solving more difficult products.

Alternate Approach

Base-Ten Blocks Have students model the multiplication (2 × 40) using base ten blocks.

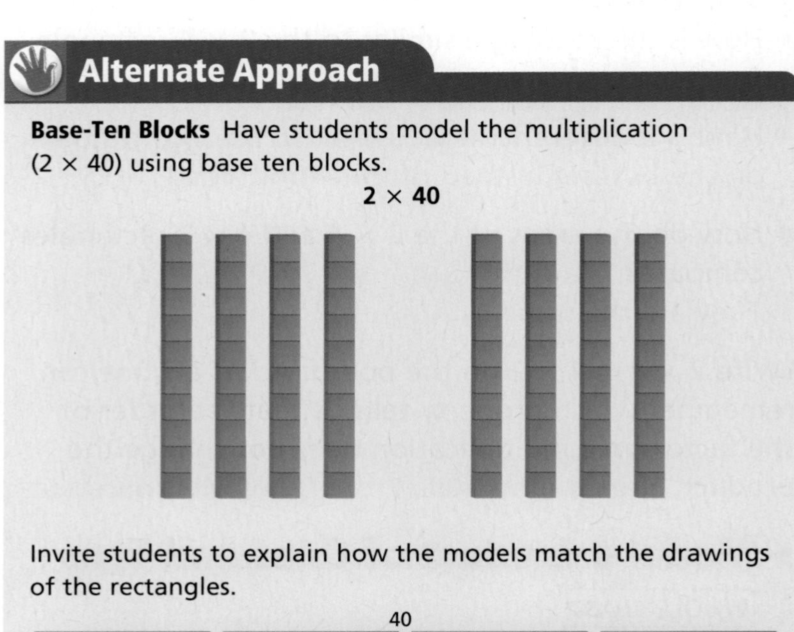

Invite students to explain how the models match the drawings of the rectangles.

Activity 2

Arrays of Hundreds

25 MINUTES

Goal: Model multiplication of tens.

Materials: Student Activity Book or Hardcover Book pages 529–530, MathBoard Materials

NCTM Standards:
Number and Operations
Connections
Representations

E–2 Class Activity

Name ________________ Date ________

▶ Model a Product of Tens

7. Find the area of this 20 × 40 rectangle by dividing it into 10-by-10 squares of 100.

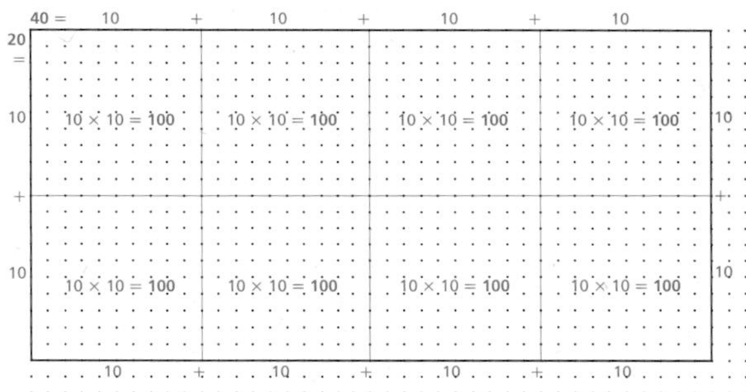

▶ Factor the Tens

8. Complete the steps to show your work in problem 7 numerically.

20 × 40 = (__2__ × 10) × (__4__ × 10)

= (__2__ × __4__) × (10 × 10)

= __8__ × 100

= 800

9. Is it true that 20 × 40 = 40 × 20? Explain how you know.
They are equal by the Commutative Property.

10. Write out the steps for finding 40 × 20 by factoring the tens. Use your MathBoard if you need to.
40 × 20 = (4 × 10) × (2 × 10) =
(4 × 2) × (10 × 10) = 8 × 100 = 800

EXTENSION LESSON 2 Multiplication Arrays **529**

Student Activity Book page 529

▶ Model a Product of Tens [WHOLE CLASS]

Refer students to the rectangle in exercise 7 on Student Book page 529 or have them draw a 20 × 40 rectangle on their MathBoards.

Have students divide this rectangle into an array of 10-by-10 squares.

- What value does each of these squares represent? 100
- How many groups of 100 are there? 8 What is the total area? 800

▶ Factor the Tens [INDIVIDUALS]

Explain that factoring the tens can help students find 20 × 40. Have students complete exercise 8, and then discuss the steps as a class.

Have students complete exercises 9 and 10.

The Learning Classroom

Helping Community When stronger math students finish their work early, let them help others who might be struggling. Many students enjoy the role of helping other students. In their "helper" role, students who might become bored challenge themselves as they explain math content to others.

Activity continued ▶

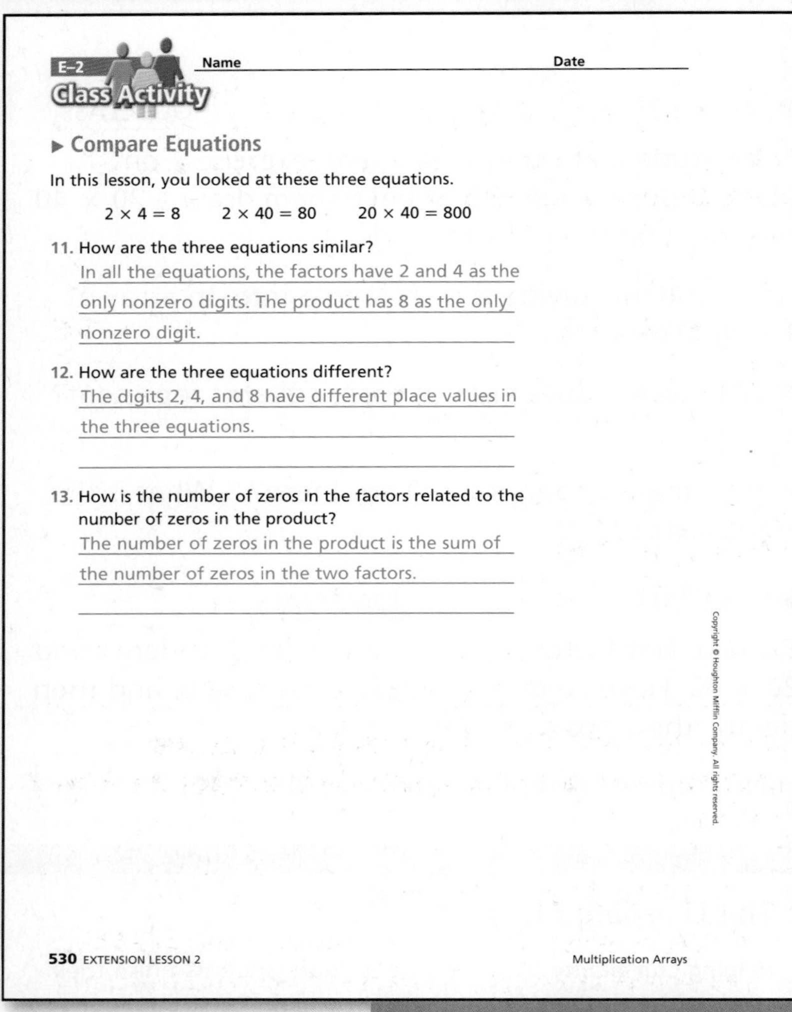
E-2 Class Activity

Name _______ Date _______

▶ Compare Equations

In this lesson, you looked at these three equations.

2 × 4 = 8   2 × 40 = 80   20 × 40 = 800

11. How are the three equations similar?
In all the equations, the factors have 2 and 4 as the only nonzero digits. The product has 8 as the only nonzero digit.

12. How are the three equations different?
The digits 2, 4, and 8 have different place values in the three equations.

13. How is the number of zeros in the factors related to the number of zeros in the product?
The number of zeros in the product is the sum of the number of zeros in the two factors.

Copyright © Houghton Mifflin Company. All rights reserved.

530 EXTENSION LESSON 2   Multiplication Arrays

Student Activity Book page 530

▶ Compare Equations INDIVIDUALS

Exercises 11–13 on Student Book page 530 review the equations students studied in this lesson. Have students complete the problems, and then discuss the answers as a class. Make sure students see that the total number of zeros in the factors is the same as the number of zeros in the product.

▶ Extend the Lesson PAIRS

As time allows, have pairs of students draw rectangles and compare these equations.

2×3

2×30

20×30

3×4

3×40

30×40

Ongoing Assessment

Have students draw a 4×7 rectangle and find its area. Then ask them to write out the steps for finding each of the following products:

4×70

40×70

2 Going Further

Differentiated Instruction

Intervention

Activity Card E-2

Make a Multiplication Chart Activity Card E-2

Work: On your own

Use:

- TRB M31 (Centimeter Grid Paper)

1. Copy the multiplication chart onto your grid paper.

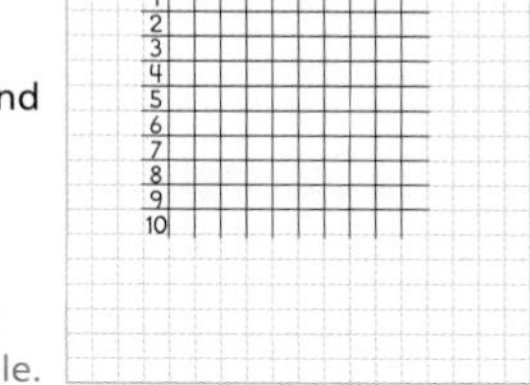

2. Draw a rectangle on the grid that is 4 units long and 3 units wide.
3. Think How can you use the rectangle to find the product of 4×3? Count squares inside the rectangle.
4. Fill in as many products as you can from memory. Draw rectangles for any products that you cannot remember.

Extension, Lesson 2

Activity Note Once students have completed their charts, have them work in pairs to check answers and discuss any discrepancies.

Math Writing Prompt

Describe a Pattern $6 \times 10 = 60$, $6 \times 100 = 600$, and $6 \times 1{,}000 = 6{,}000$

What pattern do you see?

Software Support

Warm Up 12.20

On Level

Activity Card E-2

Find Rectangles for Products Activity Card E-2

Work: On your own

Use:

- TRB M31 (Centimeter Grid Paper)

1. The diagram below shows two possible rectangles for the product 36. Copy them onto your grid paper.

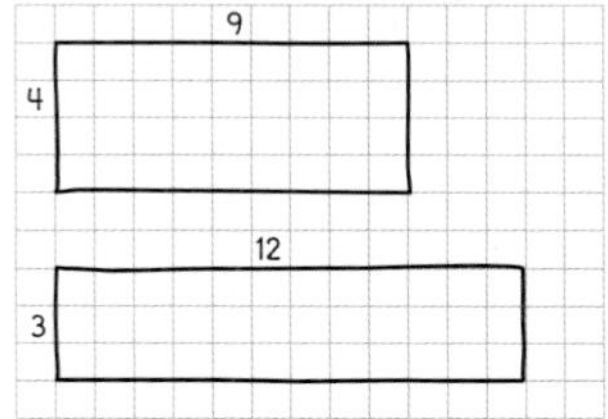

2. Find all other possible rectangles for 36.
3. Repeat the process to find all possible rectangles for 25 and 18.

Extension, Lesson 2

Activity Note Point out that 25 is a square number, so one of the possible rectangles is a 5-by-5 square.

Math Writing Prompt

Organization Skills How can you be sure that you have found all the rectangles for a number?

Software Support

Ice Station Exploration: Polar Planes, Level Q

Challenge

Activity Card E-2

Find Primes Activity Card E-2

Work: On your own

Use:

- Counters

1. The drawing below shows the arrays for the prime number 5. A prime number has exactly two possible arrays because it has exactly two factors.

2. Find all the numbers less than 50 that have exactly two arrays. Use counters if necessary. 2, 3, 5, 7, 11, 13, 17, 19, 23, 29, 31, 37, 41, 43, 47

Extension, Lesson 2

Activity Note Remind students that even numbers always have the factor 2. So even numbers greater than 2 cannot be prime numbers.

Math Writing Prompt

Reasoning Skills Do any numbers have an odd number of rectangular arrays? Explain.

DESTINATION Math **Software Support**

Course II: Module 2: Unit 2: Repeated Addition and Arrays

3 Homework

Goal: Additional Practice

Because you may be using this lesson at any time during the year, no Spiral Review is included. Use this Homework page to provide students with additional practice.

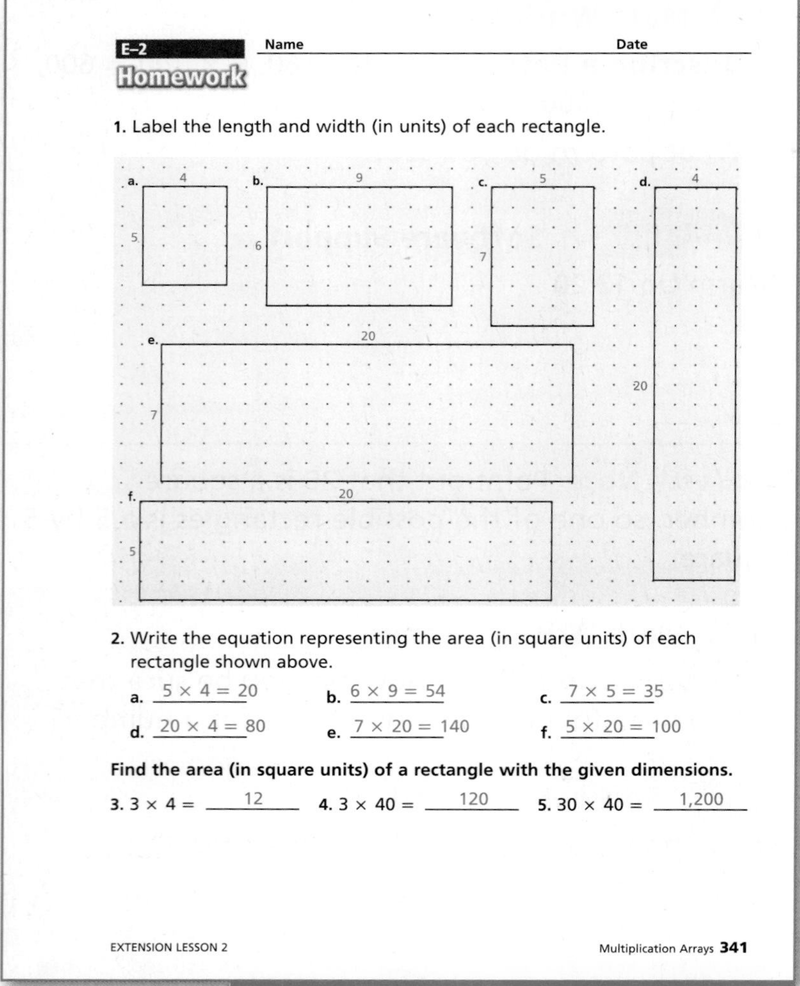

E–2 Homework

Name ______ Date ______

1. Label the length and width (in units) of each rectangle.

2. Write the equation representing the area (in square units) of each rectangle shown above.

a. 5 × 4 = 20 b. 6 × 9 = 54 c. 7 × 5 = 35

d. 20 × 4 = 80 e. 7 × 20 = 140 f. 5 × 20 = 100

Find the area (in square units) of a rectangle with the given dimensions.

3. 3 × 4 = 12 4. 3 × 40 = 120 5. 30 × 40 = 1,200

EXTENSION LESSON 2 Multiplication Arrays **341**

Homework and Remembering page 341

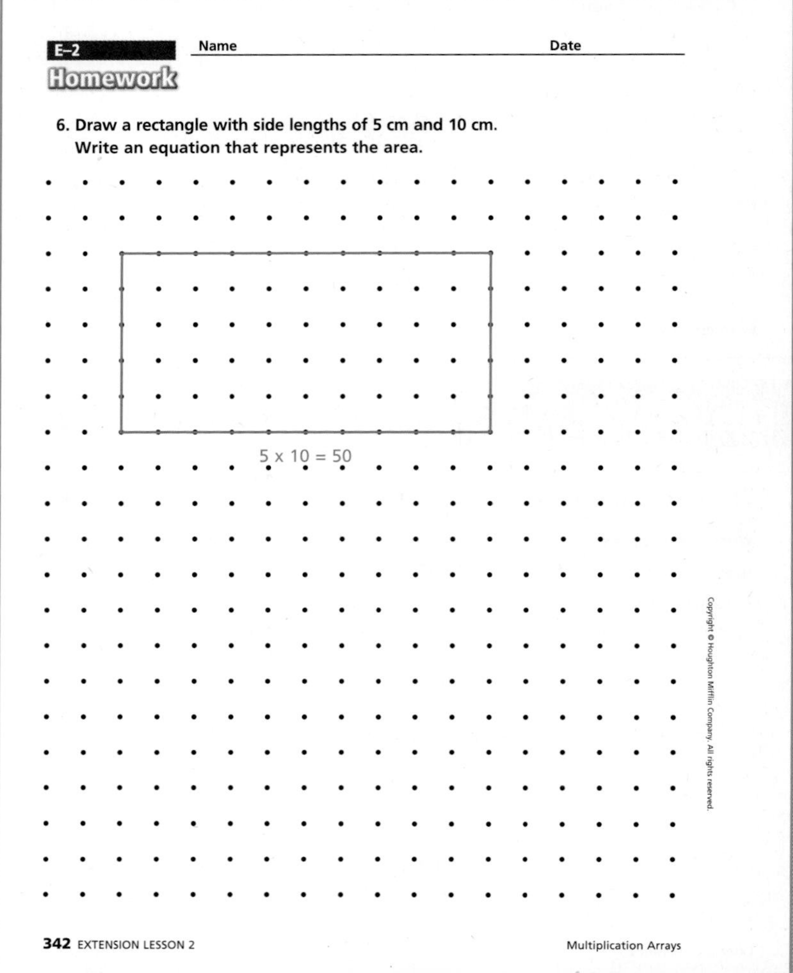

E–2 Homework

Name ______ Date ______

6. Draw a rectangle with side lengths of 5 cm and 10 cm. Write an equation that represents the area.

342 EXTENSION LESSON 2 Multiplication Arrays

Homework and Remembering page 342

Home or School Activity

Social Studies Connection

Congress Have students research how the number of United States senators is determined. Have students describe how they could use their skills for multiplying a one-digit number by a two-digit number to find this number. Ask them what information is needed to make this calculation.

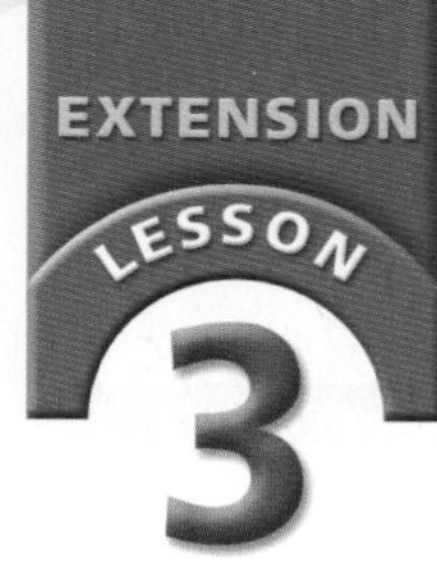

Mental Math and Multiplication with Tens

Lesson Objective

- **Understand patterns of multiplication with ones, tens and hundreds.**

Vocabulary

factor
product

Today's Goals	Materials	
1 Teaching the Lesson **A1:** Find numeric patterns in multiplication with ones and tens. **A2:** Solve multiplication problems mentally by factoring the tens.	**Lesson Activities** Student Activity Book pages 531–532 or Student Hardcover Book pages 531–532 Homework and Remembering pages 343–344	**Going Further** Activity Cards E-3 Base-ten blocks TRB M164 (Cross Number Grid) Math Journals
2 Going Further ▸ Differentiated Instruction		
3 Homework		

123 Use **Math Talk** today!

Keeping Skills Sharp

Quick Practice — 5 MINUTES

Because you may be using this lesson at any time during the year, no specific Quick Practice is recommended. Use any Quick Practice activity that meets your students' needs.

Daily Routines

Homework Review If students give incorrect answers, have them explain how they found the answers. This can help determine whether the error is conceptual or procedural.

Logic Problems Use *all, some*, or *no* to complete each sentence.

1. If all figures that are flat are two-dimensional, then _______ faces on a three-dimensional figure are two-dimensional. all
2. If all prisms are solid figures whose two parallel bases are congruent and whose faces are rectangles, then _______ cylinders are prisms. no

1 Teaching the Lesson

Activity 1

Review Multiplication With Tens

 30 MINUTES

Goal: Find numeric patterns in multiplication with ones and tens.

Materials: Student Activity Book or Hardcover Book pp. 531–532

 **NCTM Standards:**
Number and Operations
Connections

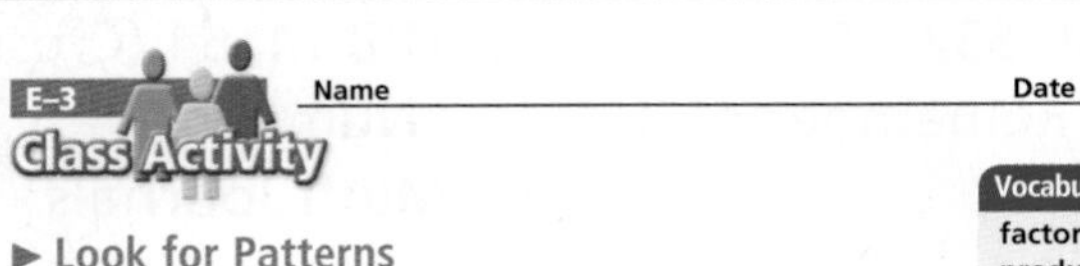

E-3 Class Activity Name Date

Vocabulary
factors
product

▶ Look for Patterns

Multiplying large numbers in your head is easier when you learn patterns of multiplication with tens.

Start with column A and look for the patterns used to get the expressions in each column. Complete the table.

Table 1

	A	B	C	D
	2 × 4	2 × 1 × 4 × 1	8 × 1	8
1.	2 × 40	2 × 1 × 4 × 10	8 × 10	80
2.	20 × 40	2 × 10 × 4 × 10	8 × 100	800

3. How are the expressions in column B different from the expressions in column A?
Answers will vary. Possible answer: In column B, we rewrite each factor as a one-digit number times a place value such as 1, 10, 100.

4. In column C, we see that each expression can be written as a number times a place value. Which of these **factors** gives more information about the size of the **product**?
the factor representing the place value

5. Why is 8 the first digit of the products in column D?
2 × 4 is 8

6. Why are there different numbers of zeros in the products in column D?
Answers will vary. Possible answer: because each product has a different number of factors of 10

EXTENSION LESSON 3 Mental Math and Multiplication with Tens 531

Student Activity Book page 531

Ask for Ideas Write the following exercises on the board. Have volunteers solve them.

2 + 4 20 + 40 200 + 400

Then discuss addition patterns they see and ask them to make generalizations for multiplication patterns. They will check their generalization in the next two activities.

▶ Look for Patterns WHOLE CLASS

Direct students to Table 1 on page 531 of the Student Book and have students complete Table 1.

When the class has completed the table, review the answers to exercises 1–2 and then use exercises 3–6 to discuss the table. Allow time for the students to record their answers to each exercise.

Ask a volunteer to show how to rearrange the factors in column B of the last row to get 8 × 100. 2 × 10 × 4 × 10 = (2 × 4) × (10 × 10) = 8 × 100

English Language Learners

Write *factor, product,* and *place value* on the board. Write 2 × 30 = 60 and 2 × 3 × 10 = 60.

- **Beginning** Point to each equation. Ask: **Are the *products* the same?** yes **Is 10 the *place value* of 30?** yes **Did I *factor* the first equation?** yes
- **Intermediate and Advanced** Have students identify the *products* and *factors*. Say: **The *place value* of 30 is __.** 10 **In the second equation I *factored* __.** 30

Activity continued ▶

Name ______ Date ______

E-3 Class Activity

▶ Compare Tables

Complete each table.

Table 2

	A	B	C	D
	4 × 3	4 × 1 × 3 × 1	12 × 1	12
7.	4 × 30	4 × 1 × 3 × 10	12 × 10	120
8.	40 × 30	4 × 10 × 3 × 10	12 × 100	1,200

Table 3

	A	B	C	D
	5 × 8	5 × 1 × 8 × 1	40 × 1	40
9.	5 × 80	5 × 1 × 8 × 10	40 × 10	400
10.	50 × 80	5 × 10 × 8 × 10	40 × 100	4,000

11. Why do the products in Table 2 have more digits than the products in Table 1?
Answers will vary. Possible answer: because 4 × 3 has a two-digit product, 12

12. Why are there more zeros in the products in Table 3 than those in Table 2?
Answers will vary. Possible answer: because 5 × 8 has a two-digit product that includes a zero, 40

532 EXTENSION LESSON 3 Mental Math and Multiplication with Tens

Student Activity Book page 532

▶ Compare Tables WHOLE CLASS

Have students complete Tables 2 and 3 (exercises 7–10) and exercises 11 and 12 on Student Book page 532. Make sure students understand that the difference from Table 1 to Table 2 is that the product of the non-zero digits has two digits instead of one. For a sample of classroom dialogue for exercise 11, see Math Talk in Action.

Exercise 12 asks students why there are more zeros in the products of Table 3. Make sure students understand that the pattern is the same. The pattern with the zeros only looks different because the product of the non-zero digits (5 × 8) includes a zero.

Ask students when and why they would encounter the pattern variation found in Table 3. If necessary, explain that they would encounter the variation when the non-zero digits are 5 and an even number. The product of the non-zero digits will end in zero, so the final product will have an "extra" zero.

The Learning Classroom

Building Concepts Discuss with students how helpful it is to factor the tens when multiplying tens. Students should see that multiplying one-digit numbers is easier to do in their head.

Math Talk in Action

How are Tables 1 and 2 different?

Kim: In Table 1, 2 is multiplied by 4. Then the product, 8, is multiplied by the product of the 10s. In Table 2, 4 is multiplied by 3. Then the product, 12, is multiplied by the product of the 10s.

Hannah: The answers in column D have one more digit in Table 2.

Jacob: The product of 2 × 4 has one digit but the product of 4 × 3 has two digits, so the answers in column D in Table 2 have one more digit than the answers in column D in Table 1.

1 Teaching the Lesson

Activity 2

Arrays of Ones and Tens

 25 MINUTES

Goal: Solve multiplication problems mentally by factoring the tens.

 **NCTM Standard:**
Number and Operations

► Practice Mental Math SMALL GROUPS

Have the students work in **Small Groups** or **Student Pairs** to solve the problems below and then discuss the number patterns.

9 × 2 and 9 × 20 18; 180

3 × 2 and 30 × 2 6; 60

6 × 8 and 60 × 80 48; 4,800

2 × 5 and 2 × 50 10; 100

9 × 5 and 90 × 50 45; 4,500

4 × 7 and 4 × 70 28; 280

7 × 3 and 70 × 30 21; 2,100

3 × 5 and 30 × 50 15; 1,500

Ask volunteers to share their thought processes.

Encourage all students to ask questions that will help everyone understand the factoring-the-tens method presented in the lesson. Discussing this method may help students internalize the process. Ask students how knowing their basic multiplications can help them find products involving tens numbers. I can multiply the non-zero digits and then multiply the tens. For example, in the first exercise, I know that 9 × 2 = 18. Then I just multiply the 10s.

Students who know their multiplications may be able to do these problems in their heads and will finish the exercises very quickly. Challenge these students to write a table for the products in the exercises. Have them classify each exercise as the pattern type found in Table 1, Table 2, or Table 3 on Student Book pages 531–532.

 **Ongoing Assessment**

Have students:

- ► choose a two-digit number ending in zero and multiply it by a one-digit number of their choice.
- ► indicate whether their pair of numbers is like the pairs in Table 1, Table 2, or Table 3.

The Learning Classroom

Helping Partners Initially, it is useful to model pair activities for students by contrasting effective and ineffective helping. For example, students need to help partners solve a problem their way, rather than doing the work for the partner. Helping pairs often foster learning in both students as the helper strives to adopt the perspective of the novice.

2 Going Further

Differentiated Instruction

Intervention — Activity Card E-3

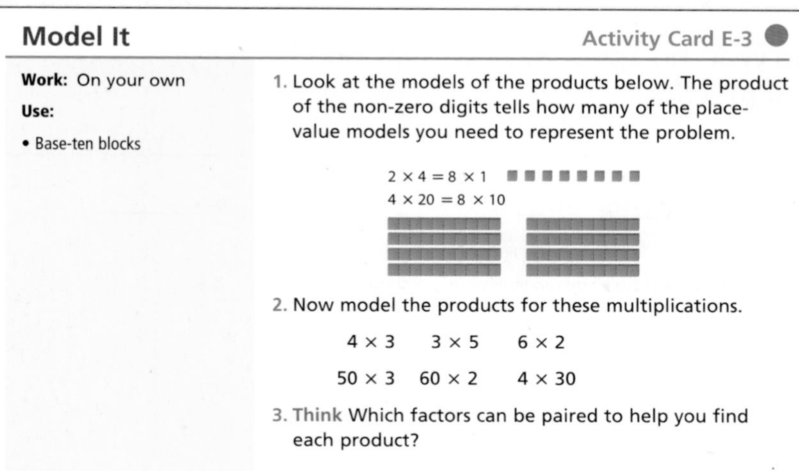

Model It — Activity Card E-3

Work: On your own

Use:

- Base-ten blocks

1. Look at the models of the products below. The product of the non-zero digits tells how many of the place-value models you need to represent the problem.

   2 × 4 = 8 × 1
   4 × 20 = 8 × 10

2. Now model the products for these multiplications.

   4 × 3   3 × 5   6 × 2

   50 × 3   60 × 2   4 × 30

3. **Think** Which factors can be paired to help you find each product?

Extension, Lesson 3

Activity Note Be sure that students make the connection between having a factor that is a multiple of 10 and using tens blocks to model the product.

Math Writing Prompt

Compare Products Describe how the products 2 × 3 and 20 × 3 are alike and how they are different.

Software Support

Warm Up 12.30

On Level — Activity Card E-3

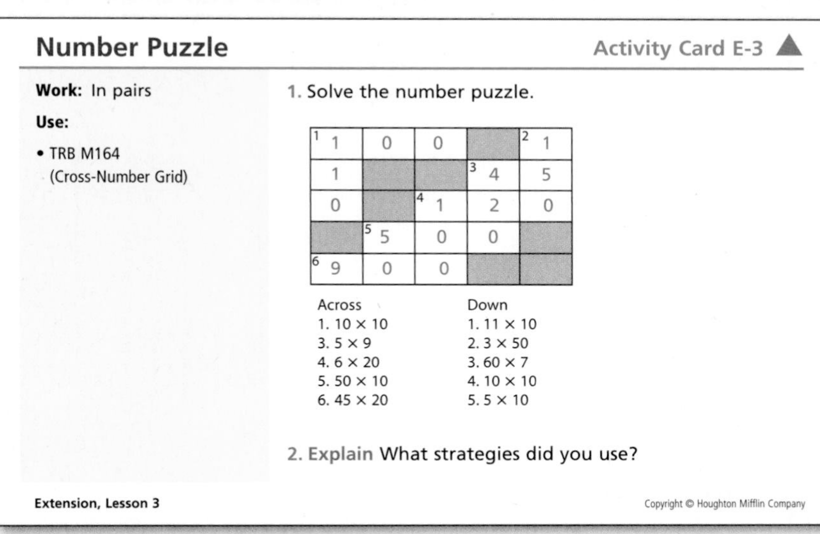

Number Puzzle — Activity Card E-3

Work: In pairs

Use:

- TRB M164 (Cross-Number Grid)

1. Solve the number puzzle.

(1) 1	0	0	■	(2) 1
1	■	■	(3) 4	5
0	■	(4) 1	2	0
■	(5) 5	0	0	■
(6) 9	0	0	■	■

Across
1. 10 × 10
3. 5 × 9
4. 6 × 20
5. 50 × 10
6. 45 × 20

Down
1. 11 × 10
2. 3 × 50
3. 60 × 7
4. 10 × 10
5. 5 × 10

2. **Explain** What strategies did you use?

Extension, Lesson 3

Activity Note Students who finish early can create their own multiplication number puzzle and exchange with another pair to solve.

Math Writing Prompt

Explain Your Thinking Explain how you would use the factor 10 to multiply 70 × 8 mentally.

Software Support

The Number Games: Up, Up, and Array, Level I

Challenge — Activity Card E-3

Work Backward — Activity Card E-3

Work: On your own

1. Copy the table below. Then complete the table, using the directions below. Each row has three products that are equal.

Column A	Column B	Column C
2 × 50	2 × 5 × 10	10 × 10
5 × 500	5 × 5 × 100	25 × 100
3 × 5	3 × 5 × 1	15 × 1

2. In Column B, write the product with three factors, one of which is 1, 10, or 100.
3. In Column A, write the product in Column B as the product of two factors, one of which is a multiple of 1, 10, 100.

Extension, Lesson 3

Activity Note Students who finish early can extend the activity by finding alternative equivalent products for Columns A and B.

Math Writing Prompt

Alternate Approaches Explain how you can rewrite the number 600 as a product of factors that include 10 or 100. Explain a strategy for finding five different ways of doing this.

DESTINATION Math® **Software Support**

Course II: Module 2: Unit 2: Finding Products less than 100

3 Homework

Goal: Additional Practice

Because you may be using this lesson at any time during the year, no Spiral Review is included. Use this Homework page to provide students with additional practice.

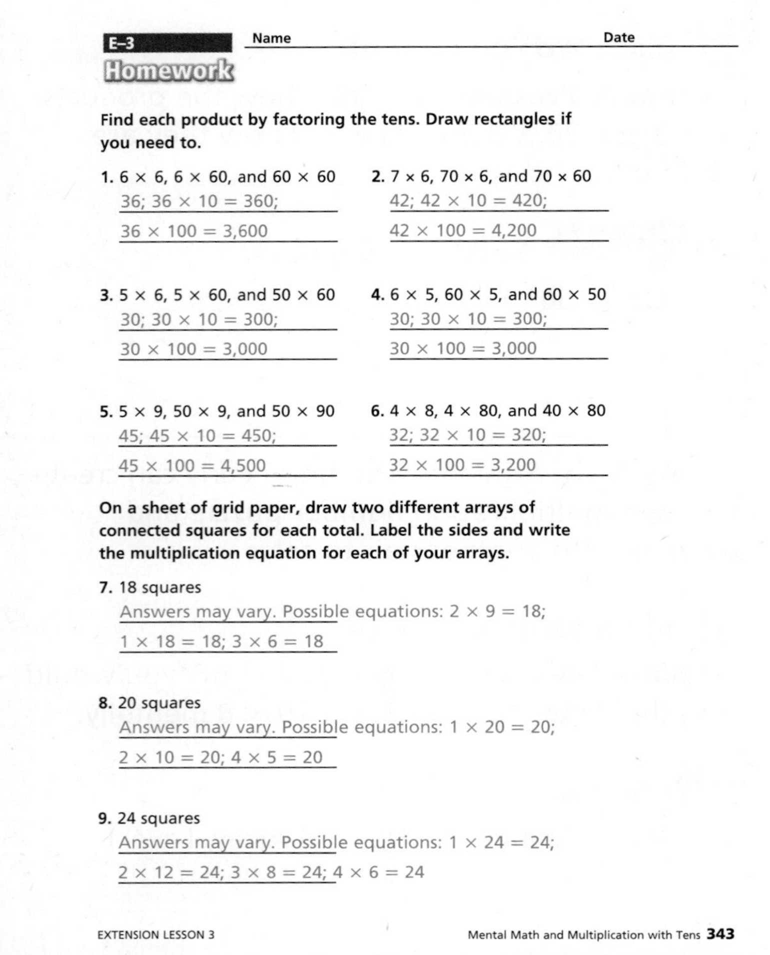

E-3 Homework Name ____ Date ____

Find each product by factoring the tens. Draw rectangles if you need to.

1. 6×6, 6×60, and 60×60
   36; $36 \times 10 = 360$;
   $36 \times 100 = 3{,}600$
2. 7×6, 70×6, and 70×60
   42; $42 \times 10 = 420$;
   $42 \times 100 = 4{,}200$
3. 5×6, 5×60, and 50×60
   30; $30 \times 10 = 300$;
   $30 \times 100 = 3{,}000$
4. 6×5, 60×5, and 60×50
   30; $30 \times 10 = 300$;
   $30 \times 100 = 3{,}000$
5. 5×9, 50×9, and 50×90
   45; $45 \times 10 = 450$;
   $45 \times 100 = 4{,}500$
6. 4×8, 4×80, and 40×80
   32; $32 \times 10 = 320$;
   $32 \times 100 = 3{,}200$

On a sheet of grid paper, draw two different arrays of connected squares for each total. Label the sides and write the multiplication equation for each of your arrays.

7. 18 squares
   Answers may vary. Possible equations: $2 \times 9 = 18$;
   $1 \times 18 = 18$; $3 \times 6 = 18$
8. 20 squares
   Answers may vary. Possible equations: $1 \times 20 = 20$;
   $2 \times 10 = 20$; $4 \times 5 = 20$
9. 24 squares
   Answers may vary. Possible equations: $1 \times 24 = 24$;
   $2 \times 12 = 24$; $3 \times 8 = 24$; $4 \times 6 = 24$

EXTENSION LESSON 3 Mental Math and Multiplication with Tens **343**

Homework and Remembering page 343

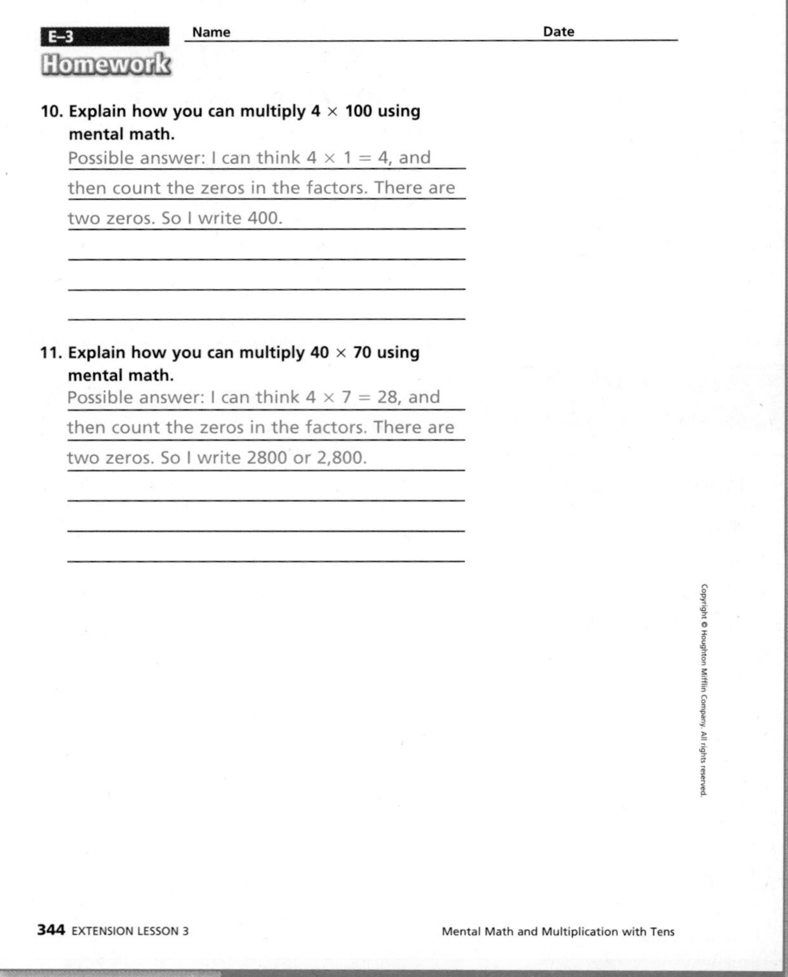

E-3 Homework Name ____ Date ____

10. **Explain how you can multiply 4×100 using mental math.**
    Possible answer: I can think $4 \times 1 = 4$, and then count the zeros in the factors. There are two zeros. So I write 400.
11. **Explain how you can multiply 40×70 using mental math.**
    Possible answer: I can think $4 \times 7 = 28$, and then count the zeros in the factors. There are two zeros. So I write 2800 or 2,800.

344 EXTENSION LESSON 3 Mental Math and Multiplication with Tens

Homework and Remembering page 344

Home or School Activity

Science Connection

Find Factor Pairs Tell students that the distance around the Earth is about 25,000 miles. The distance through the center of the Earth from the North Pole to the South Pole is about 8,000 miles. Have students find factor pairs that have a product of 25,000 and 8,000. There are several possibilities.

$25{,}000 = 10 \times 2{,}500$
$25{,}000 = 100 \times 250$
$25{,}000 = 1{,}000 \times 25$

$8{,}000 = 10 \times 800$
$8{,}000 = 100 \times 80$
$8{,}000 = 1{,}000 \times 8$

Model One-Digit by Two-Digit Multiplication

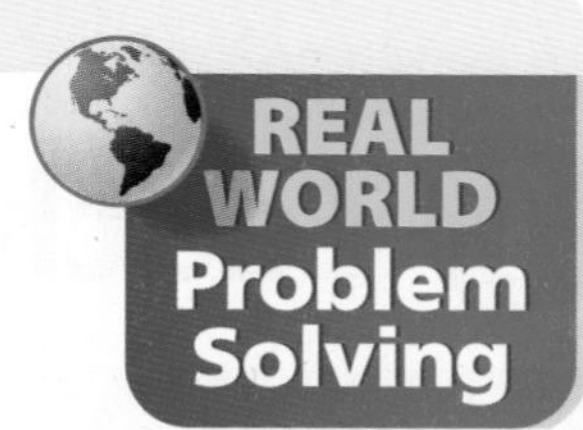

Vocabulary
area
square units

Lesson Objective

- **Represent one-digit by two-digit multiplication using area models.**

The Day at a Glance

Today's Goals	Materials	
1 Teaching the Lesson **A1:** Understand one-digit by two-digit multiplication. **A2:** Practice one-digit by two-digit multiplication.	**Lesson Activities** Student Activity Book pp. 533–534 or Student Hardcover Book pp. 533–534 Homework and Remembering pp. 345–346 MathBoard materials Base-ten blocks	**Going Further** Activity Cards E-4 *Match-Up* Game Cards (TRB M165–166) Math Journals
2 Going Further ► Differentiated Instruction		
3 Homework		

Use Math Talk today!

Keeping Skills Sharp

Quick Practice 5 MINUTES	Daily Routine
Because you may be using this lesson at any time during the year, no specific Quick Practice is recommended. Use any Quick Practice activity that meets your students' needs.	**Homework Review** Have students discuss any difficulties from their homework. Encourage students to help each other resolve these difficulties. **Estimation** At the concert, the students are seated in 9 rows. Each row seats 17 students. About how many students are seated at the concert? Explain how you found your answer. Possible answer: about 200 students; The question said about, so I rounded each number to the nearest ten, 10 and 20, and multiplied to find the estimated product.

1 Teaching the Lesson

Activity 1

Multiplication Modeling

 **30 MINUTES**

Goal: Understand one-digit by two-digit multiplication.

Materials: Student Activity Book or Hardcover Book p. 533, base-ten blocks (optional)

 **NCTM Standards:**
Number and Operations
Reasoning
Representation

E-4 **Class Activity** Name ________ Date ________

Vocabulary
area
square units

▶ **Explore the Area Model**

Copy this rectangle on your MathBoard.

20 + 6
3 | 3 × 20 = 60 | 3 × 6 = 18

1. How many **square units** of **area** are there in the tens part of the drawing? 60
2. What multiplication equation gives the area of the tens part of the drawing? 3 × 20 = 60 Write this equation in its rectangle.
3. How many square units of area are there in the ones part? 18
4. What multiplication equation gives the area of the ones part? 3 × 6 = 18 Write this equation in its rectangle.
5. What is the total of the two areas? 78
6. How do you know that 78 is the correct product of 3 × 26?
   Answers will vary.
7. Read problems A and B.
   A. Brad's photo album has 26 pages. Each page has 5 photos. How many photos are in Brad's album?
   B. Nick took 5 photos. Haley took 26 photos. How many more photos did Haley take than Nick?
   Which problem could you solve using the multiplication you just did? Explain why.
   Problem A; In problem A we are finding the total in 26 groups of 5. We find this by calculating 5 × 26.

EXTENSION LESSON 4 Model One-Digit by Two-Digit Multiplication 533

Student Activity Book page 533

▶ Explore the Area Model WHOLE CLASS

Refer students to the area model at the top of Student Book page 533. Use problems 1–6 to help students see that the model represents 3 × 26 = 78.

Here are some additional questions to help encourage discussion.

- How can you prove that there are 60 square units in the tens part of the drawing? Possible answers: Count 60 small squares or count 6 groups of 10 squares.
- How can you prove that there are 18 square units in the ones part of the drawing? Possible answer: Count the squares.
- How can you prove that there are 78 square units in the whole drawing? The large rectangle is made up of the two smaller rectangles and 60 + 18 = 78.
- How can you use repeated addition to check that 3 × 26 = 78? 26 + 26 + 26 = 78

If students are having difficulty visualizing the multiplication, you may want to use base-ten blocks. See the Alternate Approach.

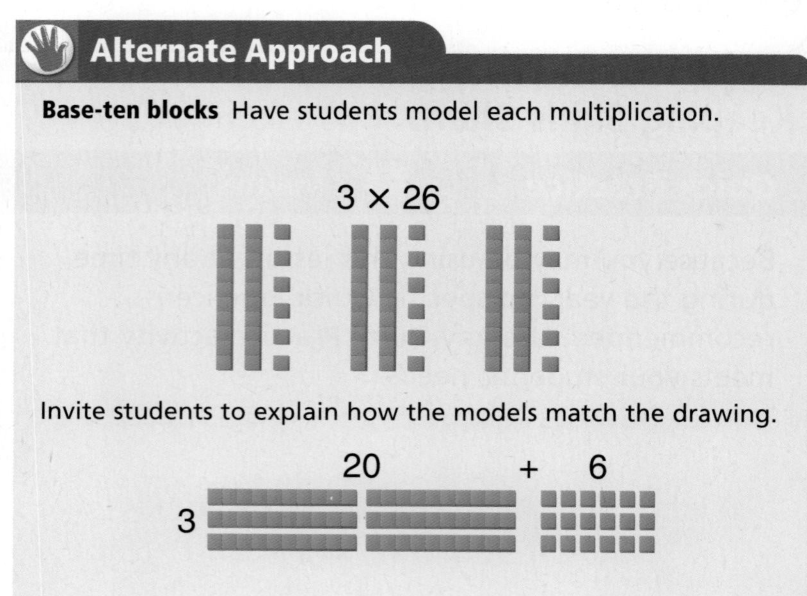

Math Talk Discuss problem 7. Encourage all students to ask questions so they understand that problem A can be solved by multiplying 26 by 5 and problem B can be solved by subtracting 5 from 26. Model questioning if needed.

- What is the problem situation for each problem? Problem A: Equal Groups; Problem B: Additive Comparison
- How can you represent each problem?

Encourage students to identify and discuss situations in which multiplication would help to solve a real-world problem. If time permits, have **Helping Partners** write and exchange multiplication problems about real situations (buying two or three of the same item, doubling a recipe, finding the area of a room, and so on).

The Learning Classroom

Building Concepts Why use the area method to teach multi-digit multiplication? The area method is the easiest method for students to use. By teaching it first, we build conceptual understanding for all students and provide a method that any student can use. We also encourage students to explore other methods. We then teach a research-based algorithm that is accessible to most students.

English Language Learners

Write *square unit* and *area* on the board. Draw a 4 × 6 rectangle on the board.

- **Beginning** Point and say: **This is 1 *square unit*.** Have students repeat. Ask: **How many *square units* are there?** 24 Ask: **Is the *area* 24 square units?** yes
- **Intermediate** Ask: **How many *square units* are in each row?** 6 **How many square units are in each column?** 4 **Is the *area* 4 × 6?** yes **What is the *area*?** 24 square units
- **Advanced** Have students tell about the *square units* and how to find the *area*.

Activity 2

Practice Multiplication

 **25 MINUTES**

Goal: Practice one-digit by two-digit multiplication.

Materials: Student Activity Book or Hardcover Book p. 534, MathBoard materials

 **NCTM Standards:**
Number and Operations
Problem Solving
Represenation

▶ Use Rectangles to Multiply WHOLE CLASS

Have students use their MathBoards (either side) to solve problems 8–15 on Student Book page 534. Ask volunteers to share their work. Encourage all students to ask questions that will help everyone understand the methods that were used. Model the questioning if needed.

- How did you label your rectangle?
- Why did you write 38 as 30 + 8?
- Why did you add the two products?

Math Talk Use problems 8–15 on Student Book page 534 to help students make connections.

- How might you find the product for exercise 9, using addition rather than multiplication? Why? Add 29 + 29 + 29. That is equal to 3 × 29.
- How would the rectangle for exercise 13 be different from the rectangle for exercise 14? The rectangle for exercise 14 would have only a tens part, not a ones part.
- How could you use your answer from exercise 10 to quickly find the answer to exercise 15? Add 28 to the answer to exercise 10.

Activity continued ▶

E-4 Class Activity

Name Date

▶ Use Rectangles to Multiply

Draw a rectangle for each problem on your MathBoard. Find the tens product, the ones product, and the total.

Check students' drawings.

8. 8 × 38
8 × 30 = 240
8 × 8 = 64
304

9. 3 × 29
3 × 20 = 60
3 × 9 = 27
87

10. 4 × 28
4 × 20 = 80
4 × 8 = 32
112

11. 5 × 46
5 × 40 = 200
5 × 6 = 30
230

12. 2 × 38
2 × 30 = 60
2 × 8 = 16
76

13. 3 × 28
3 × 20 = 60
3 × 8 = 24
84

14. 5 × 30
5 × 30 = 150
5 × 0 = 0
150

15. 5 × 28
5 × 20 = 100
5 × 8 = 40
140

Solve each problem.

Show your work.

16. Claudia's father planted 8 rows of tomatoes in his garden. Each row had 12 plants. How many tomato plants were in Claudia's father's garden?
96 tomato plants

17. The bakery can ice their cakes with chocolate, strawberry, or vanilla icing. The bakery has a total of 67 different ways to decorate iced cakes. How many different combinations of icing and decorations can the bakery make?
201 combinations

18. Complete this word problem. Then solve it.
Answers will vary.
_____ has _____ boxes of _____.
There are _____ _____ in each box.
How many _____ does _____
have altogether? _____

534 EXTENSION LESSON 4 Model One-Digit by Two-Digit Multiplication

Student Activity Book page 534

Use **Solve and Discuss** for problems 16–18. Have students work independently, using whatever method they like. Encourage questioning by the other students to clarify different strategies. Model questions as needed.

Differentiated Instruction

Special Needs For exercise 18, provide students with this word and number bank to help them complete the problem.

Markers
24
4
Batai

The Learning Classroom

Math Talk Review with the class what makes a good explanation.

1) Write your work so everyone can see it.
2) Talk loud enough for other students to hear.
3) Use a pointer to point to your work.
4) Say how you arrived at the answer, not just the answer.
5) Stand to the side of your work when you talk.

Ongoing Assessment

- Compare 4 × 30 and 4 × 37. How are they the same? How are they different?
- Describe in your own words how you would find the product of 2 × 21.

Intervention Activity Card E-4

Multiplication *Match-Up* Activity Card E-4 ●

Work: In pairs

Use:

- TRB M165–166 (*Match Up* Cards)
- Scissors

1. Cut out the 16 game cards, and place them face down in a rectangular array.
2. Take turns. Choose two cards. If the cards match a multiplication and a model, keep the cards. If the cards do not match, return them face down in the same positions.

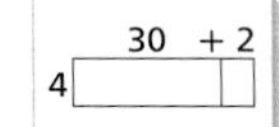

3. Continue playing until all cards are matched. The player with more cards wins the game.

Extension, Lesson 4

Activity Note If time allows, students can repeat the game with the same cards or use index cards to make up their own multiplications and models for a new game.

Math Writing Prompt

Understand Multiplication Explain how 3 × 21 and 21 + 21 + 21 are related.

Software Support

Warm Up 12.30

On Level Activity Card E-4

Create Word Problems Activity Card E-4 ▲

Work: In pairs

1. Write a word problem for each of the expressions below.

   2 × 25 25 – 2 2 + 25

2. Exchange problems with your partner to solve.
3. **Discuss** Is there more than one way to solve any of the word problems? How could you check each solution?

Extension, Lesson 4

Activity Note To reinforce multiplication concepts, select appropriate student problems to use for class discussion.

Math Writing Prompt

Explain Your Thinking Write a multiplication word problem for 4 × 35. Show a way to find the product. Use pictures, words, or symbols to explain your answer.

Software Support

The Number Games: Up, Up, and Array, Level J

Challenge Activity Card E-4

Work Backward Activity Card E-4 ■

Work: On your own

1. Find the one-digit by two-digit multiplication example that you can solve by using this addition. 37 × 3

$$\begin{array}{r} 90 \\ +21 \\ \hline 111 \end{array}$$

2. Find three one-digit by two-digit multiplication examples that you can solve by using this addition. 12 × 6; 36 × 2; 24 × 3

$$\begin{array}{r} 60 \\ +12 \\ \hline 72 \end{array}$$

3. **Analyze** Why is there only one possible multiplication for the first product? 21 has only 1 set of one-digit factors, 3 and 7.

Extension, Lesson 4

Activity Note Extend the activity by having students write a word problem for each multiplication that they write.

Math Writing Prompt

Investigate Math Suppose you know that 2 × 34 = 68. How does that help you to find 4 × 34? Explain your thinking.

Software Support

Course II: Module 2: Unit 2: Finding Products less than 100

3 Homework

Goal: Additional Practice

Because you may be using this lesson at any time during the year, no Spiral Review is included. Use this Homework page to provide students with additional practice.

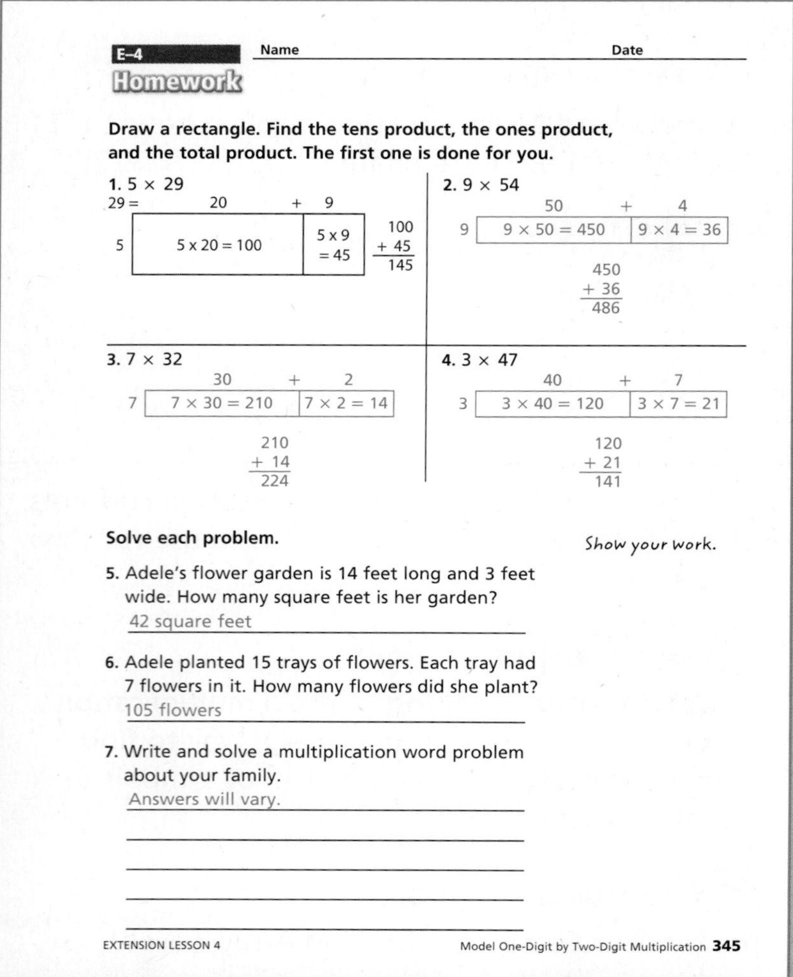

E–4 Homework Name ______ Date ______

Draw a rectangle. Find the tens product, the ones product, and the total product. The first one is done for you.

1. 5×29
   29 = 20 + 9
   5 | 5 x 20 = 100 | 5 x 9 = 45
   100 + 45 = 145

2. 9×54
   50 + 4
   9 | 9 × 50 = 450 | 9 × 4 = 36
   450 + 36 = 486

3. 7×32
   30 + 2
   7 | 7 × 30 = 210 | 7 × 2 = 14
   210 + 14 = 224

4. 3×47
   40 + 7
   3 | 3 × 40 = 120 | 3 × 7 = 21
   120 + 21 = 141

Solve each problem. *Show your work.*

5. Adele's flower garden is 14 feet long and 3 feet wide. How many square feet is her garden?
   42 square feet

6. Adele planted 15 trays of flowers. Each tray had 7 flowers in it. How many flowers did she plant?
   105 flowers

7. Write and solve a multiplication word problem about your family.
   Answers will vary.

EXTENSION LESSON 4 Model One-Digit by Two-Digit Multiplication 345

Homework and Remembering page 345

E–4 Homework Name ______ Date ______

8. Choose two factors that have a product of 104. Draw a quick picture to show that you are correct. You do not need to draw the area model actual size. Just make a sketch.

   Possible answer: $2 \times 52 = 104$
   50 + 2
   2 | 100 | 4
   100 + 4 = 104

346 EXTENSION LESSON 4 Model One-Digit by Two-Digit Multiplication

Homework and Remembering page 346

Home or School Activity

Science Connection

Estimate Area Explain to students that are going to plan a square garden with tomato plants 36 inches apart and 10 plants on each side of the garden. Students should draw a diagram to show size of the garden and determine the total number of plants needed. They should find the perimeter of the garden. Allow students to use dot paper to help them plan the garden. 100 plants; 1,296 in. There are 9 sections of 36 in. on one side.

$36 \times 9 = 324$

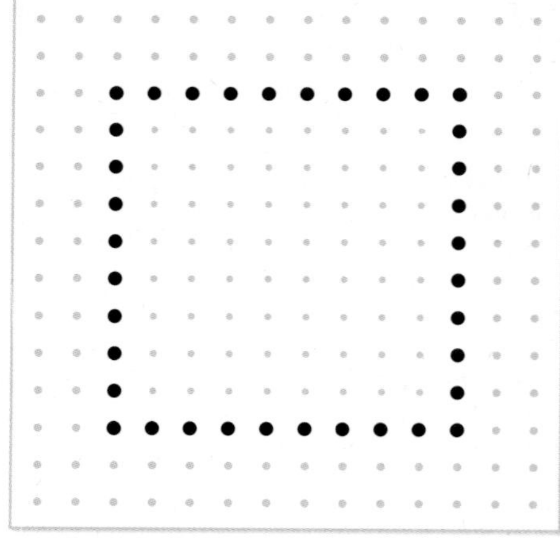

324
324
324
+ 324
1,296

Methods of One-Digit by Two-Digit Multiplication

Lesson Objectives

- Relate the area model of multiplication to numeric methods of multiplication.
- Practice one-digit by two-digit multiplication.

Vocabulary

Expanded Notation Method
Algebraic Notation Method

The Day at a Glance

Today's Goals	Materials	
1 Teaching the Lesson **A1:** Relate the area model for multiplication to numeric methods for multiplication. **A2:** Use expanded or algebraic notation to multiply a one-digit number by a two-digit number.	**Lesson Activities** Student Activity Book pp. 535–536 or Student Hardcover Book pp. 535–536 Homework and Remembering pp. 347–348	**Going Further** Activity Cards E-5 Play money Math Journals
2 Going Further ► Differentiated Instruction		
3 Homework		

Use Math Talk today!

Keeping Skills Sharp

Quick Practice 5 MINUTES	Daily Routine
Because you may be using this lesson at any time during the year, no specific Quick Practice is recommended. Use any Quick Practice activity that meets your students' needs.	**Homework Review** Send students to the board to show their solutions. Have each student explain his/her solution. Have the rest of the class ask clarifying questions and make comments. **Strategy Problem** Sarah spent \$5 from her savings to buy a book. Then, she spent half of her remaining savings when she paid \$9 for a shirt. How much money did Sarah have in savings before she bought the book and the shirt? \$23

1 Teaching the Lesson

Activity 1

Multiplication Methods

 25 MINUTES

Goal: Relate the area model for multiplication to numeric methods for multiplication.

Materials: Student Activity Book or Hardcover Book p. 535

 **NCTM Standards:**
Number and Operations
Representation
Communication

▶ Numeric Multiplication Methods

WHOLE CLASS

Create Word Problems for the Problem Write the problem 4 × 27 on the board. Ask the class to create word problems for these numbers. Tell them that they can use any kind of multiplication problem, not just areas. Emphasize that the area rectangle model can be used to solve any kind of multiplication situation.

Then tell students that you are going to show them two methods of multiplication that Grade 3 students find easy to understand and to do. Their job is to understand each method. Later they can choose which method they use, including any method they invent or already know as long as they can explain it.

Expanded Notation Method Demonstrate how to use the Expanded Notation Method to solve 4 × 27. Be sure students can relate each numerical step to a part of the drawing.

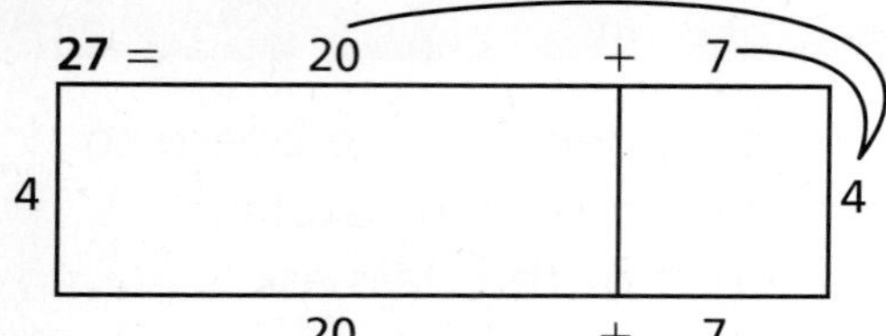

$$\begin{array}{r} 27 = 20 + 7 \\ \times\ 4 = \quad\ \ 4 \\ \hline 4 \times 20 = \ 80 \\ 4 \times \ 7 = \ 28 \\ \hline 108 \end{array}$$

Algebraic Notation Method Now demonstrate the Algebraic Notation Method. Be sure that students can connect each step of the Algebraic Notation Method to the corresponding part of the drawing.

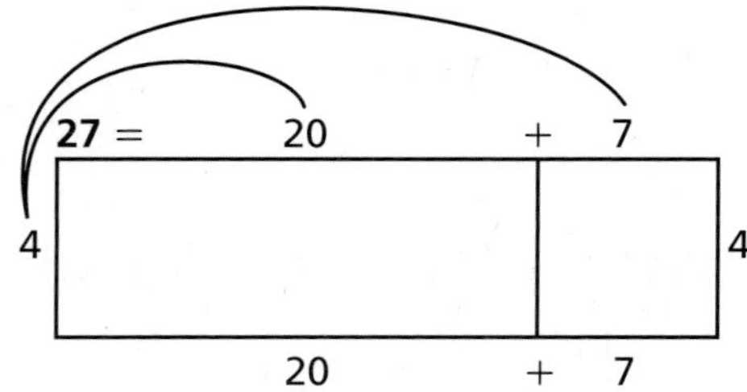

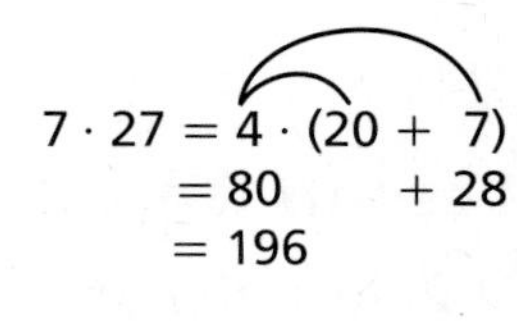

Tell students that we will call the method (Lesson 4) of drawing an *area model* and adding the areas of the sections the **Rectangle Sections Method**. Point out that students now know three multiplication methods—the Rectangle Sections Method, the Expanded Notation Method, and the Algebraic Notation Method

Teaching Note

Math Background This lesson uses the concept of place values and of breaking numbers into parts. The area model shows each place-value product as a rectangle. Each part of this area model needs to be related to the new numerical methods for today: Expanded Notation and Algebraic Notation. These methods just organize the writing of the two multiplications differently.

English Language Learners

Write *model* and *method* on the board. Draw and point to an *area model* for 5 × 16.

- **Beginning** Say: **An *area model* helps use visualize the situation.** Point to *method*. Say: **A *method* is how we find the answer.** Have students repeat.
- **Intermediate** Say: **This is an *area* __.** model Ask: **Is a *method* a way to solve a problem?** yes
- **Advanced** Ask: **What kind of *model* is this?** area model **What do we call a way to solve a problem?** method

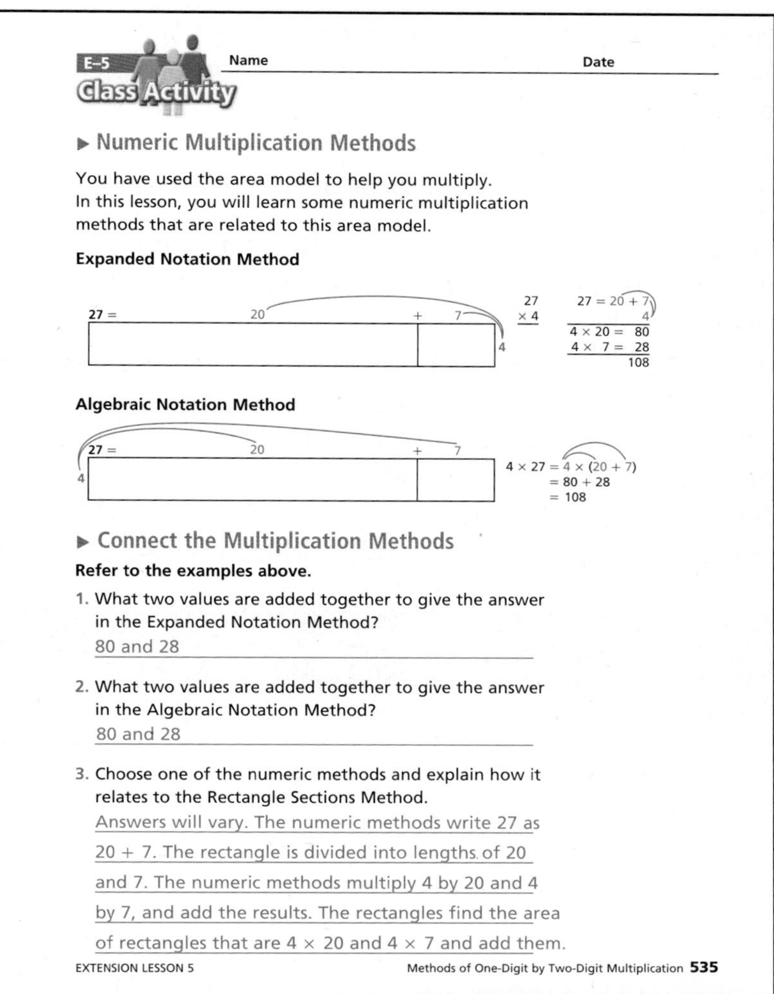

E-5 Class Activity

Name Date

▶ Numeric Multiplication Methods

You have used the area model to help you multiply. In this lesson, you will learn some numeric multiplication methods that are related to this area model.

Expanded Notation Method

Algebraic Notation Method

▶ Connect the Multiplication Methods

Refer to the examples above.

1. What two values are added together to give the answer in the Expanded Notation Method?
   80 and 28
2. What two values are added together to give the answer in the Algebraic Notation Method?
   80 and 28
3. Choose one of the numeric methods and explain how it relates to the Rectangle Sections Method.
   Answers will vary. The numeric methods write 27 as 20 + 7. The rectangle is divided into lengths of 20 and 7. The numeric methods multiply 4 by 20 and 4 by 7, and add the results. The rectangles find the area of rectangles that are 4 × 20 and 4 × 7 and add them.

EXTENSION LESSON 5 Methods of One-Digit by Two-Digit Multiplication **535**

Student Activity Book page 535

▶ Connect the Multiplication Methods

PAIRS

Summarize the two numeric methods by discussing the examples on Student Book page 535. Then have students work in **Student Pairs** to answer exercises 1–3.

Give students an opportunity to say which method they prefer and why. Try to make sure every method is represented as a method that someone prefers. It may be interesting and informative to make a bar chart to show the number of students who prefer each method.

Teaching Note

Math Background The students are using the Distributive Property of Multiplication over Addition when they multiply each number summed in the parentheses by the number outside the parentheses. This property is often referred to simply as the Distributive Property.

Math Talk in Action

Which method is your favorite?

Kari: I like to draw rectangles because it is easy to see how big each part is.

Maree: I prefer the Algebraic Notation Method because I like to have it all on one line.

Jordy: I prefer the Expanded Notation Method because I like to see the whole step for each part to be sure I get it right. When I show all my work in the expanded form, it is easier to see where I have made a mistake.

Activity 2

Practice Multiplication

 20 MINUTES

Goal: Use expanded or algebraic notation to multiply a one-digit number by a two-digit number.

Materials: Student Activity Book or Hardcover Book p. 536

 **NCTM Standards:**
Number and Operations

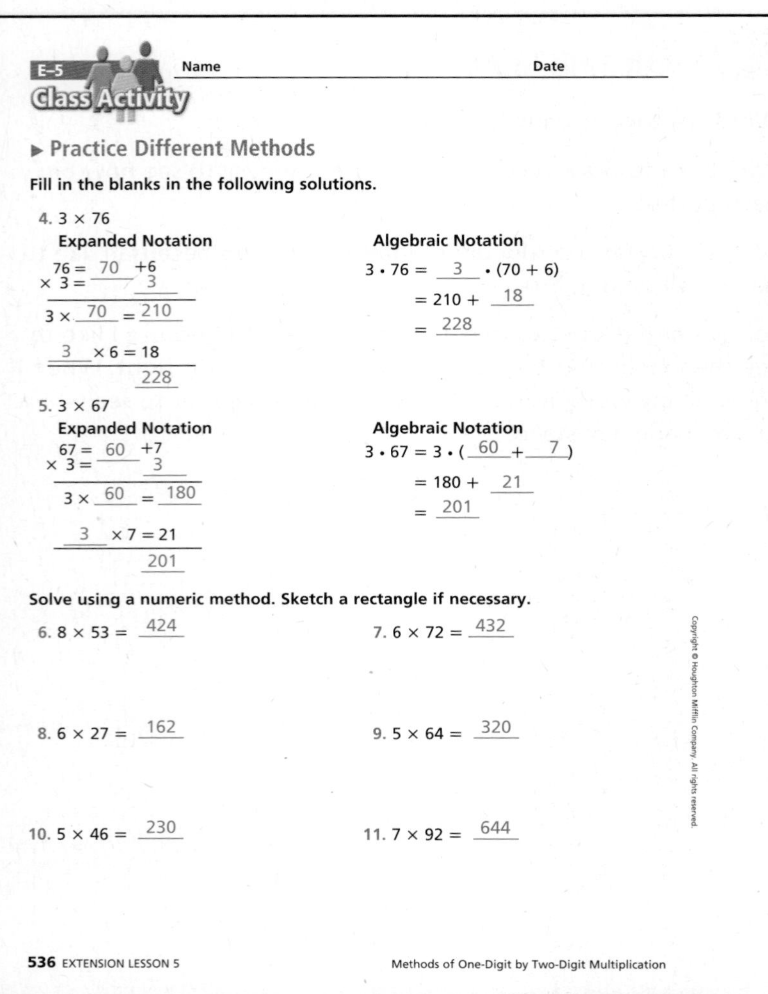

E-5 Class Activity Name Date

▸ Practice Different Methods

Fill in the blanks in the following solutions.

4. 3 × 76

Expanded Notation

76 = 70 + 6
× 3 = 3

3 × 70 = 210

3 × 6 = 18

228

Algebraic Notation

3 • 76 = 3 • (70 + 6)
= 210 + 18
= 228

5. 3 × 67

Expanded Notation

67 = 60 + 7
× 3 = 3

3 × 60 = 180

3 × 7 = 21

201

Algebraic Notation

3 • 67 = 3 • (60 + 7)
= 180 + 21
= 201

Solve using a numeric method. Sketch a rectangle if necessary.

6. 8 × 53 = 424

7. 6 × 72 = 432

8. 6 × 27 = 162

9. 5 × 64 = 320

10. 5 × 46 = 230

11. 7 × 92 = 644

536 EXTENSION LESSON 5 Methods of One-Digit by Two-Digit Multiplication

Student Activity Book page 536

▸ Practice Different Methods INDIVIDUALS

Have the students practice the Expanded Notation Method and Algebraic Notation Method by solving exercises 4 and 5 on page 536 of the Student Book. Then let them choose the numeric method that works best for them to find the products in exercises 6–11.

Students who are having difficulty with the new numeric methods, Expanded Notation and Algebraic Notation, should be encouraged to find the product using the Rectangle Sections Method. This numeric method organizes the multiplication and is sufficient for Grade 3. More advanced students may want to practice using both methods on page 536. They could choose one method for the even-numbered exercises and the other method for the odd-numbered exercises.

 **Ongoing Assessment**

Have the students use their favorite method to find 7 × 58.

2 Going Further

Differentiated Instruction

Intervention — Activity Card E-5

From Sum to Product — Activity Card E-5

Work: In pairs

1. Copy the two rectangles below.

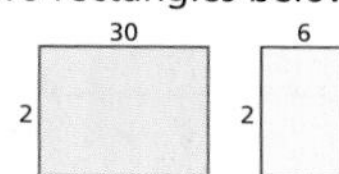

2. Write a multiplication equation for the area of each rectangle. Then find the sum of both areas.
   $2 \times 30 = 60$; $2 \times 6 = 12$; $60 + 12 = 72$
3. Work backward from the sum of the two areas to write a single multiplication equation for the sum. First, write each area as the product of two factors, as shown in the model. $2 \times 30 + 2 \times 6 = 72$
4. **Look Back** Which number appears in both products? Use that number to write a single product.
   $2 \times (30 + 6) = 72$; $2 \times 36 = 72$

Extension, Lesson 5

Activity Note Review the Distributive Property before students begin this activity.

Math Writing Prompt

Explain Your Thinking Explain how to use the Expanded Notation Method to solve 4×16.

Software Support

Warm Up 12.39

On Level — Activity Card E-5

Notation Game — Activity Card E-5

Work: In pairs

Use:

- 1 coin

Decide:

Who will be Student 1 and who will be Student 2.

1. **Student 1:** Write a one-digit by two-digit multiplication.
2. **Student 2:** Flip a coin to choose the method for solving the problem. For heads, use the Expanded Notation Method. For tails, use the Algebraic Notation Method. Find the product.

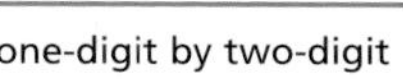

3. Exchange roles and repeat the activity twice.
4. **Analyze** Discuss each method. Which method do you prefer? Why?

Extension, Lesson 5

Activity Note To check answers, have the partner who created the problem solve it with the alternative method. Students can then compare answers and discuss.

Math Writing Prompt

Make Connections Draw an area model that represents the Algebraic Notation Method of finding the product 3×27.

Software Support

The Number Games: Up, Up, and Array, Level J

Challenge — Activity Card E-5

Work Backward — Activity Card E-5

Work: On your own

1. Copy each problem and find the sum.

300 + 20	210 + 15
40 + 16	110 + 15
500 + 25	320 + 10

2. For each sum, work backward to find a product that would use this sum in the Algebraic Notation Method.
   Answers will vary. Samples: $300 + 20 = 10 \times 32$ or 5×64
3. **Discuss** Explain to a friend how you found each product.

Extension, Lesson 5

Activity Note Challenge students to write as many products as they can for each sum, within a given time period.

Math Writing Prompt

Compare Methods Describe the differences between the Expanded Notation Method and the Algebraic Notation Method.

DESTINATION Math® **Software Support**

Course II: Module 4: Unit 1: Number Patterns and Properties

Homework

E–5 Homework Goal: Additional Practice

Because you may be using this lesson at any time during the year, no Spiral Review is included. Use this Homework page to provide students with additional practice

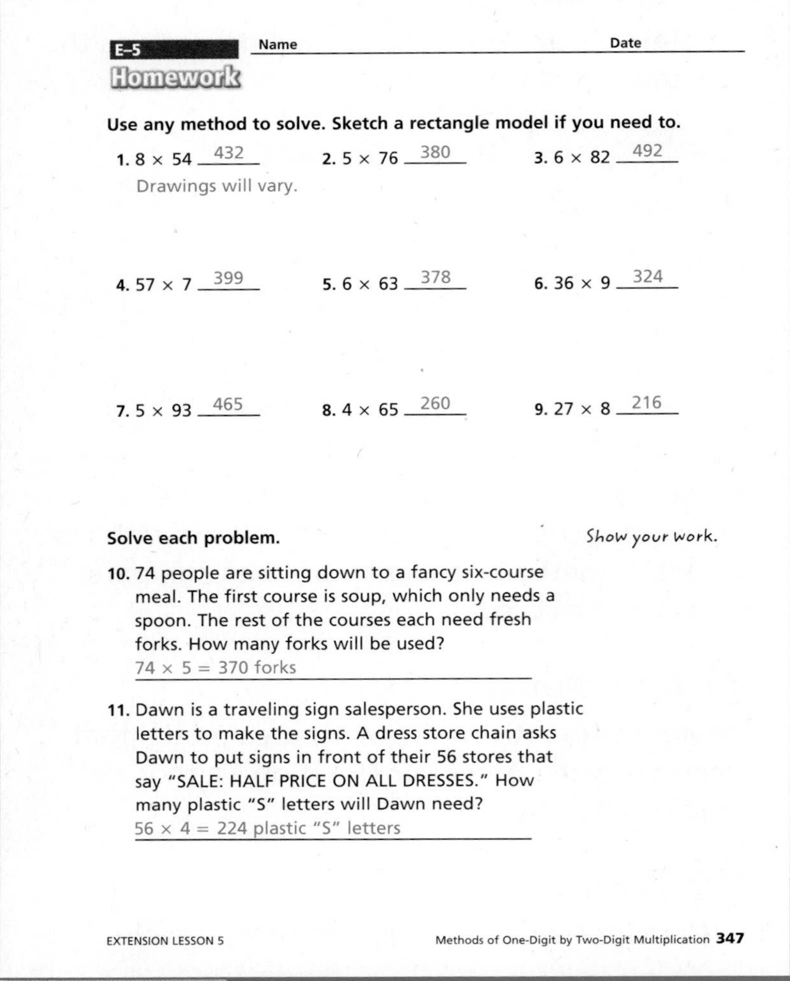

E–5 Homework Name ____________ Date ____________

Use any method to solve. Sketch a rectangle model if you need to.

1. 8 × 54 432 Drawings will vary.
2. 5 × 76 380
3. 6 × 82 492
4. 57 × 7 399
5. 6 × 63 378
6. 36 × 9 324
7. 5 × 93 465
8. 4 × 65 260
9. 27 × 8 216

Solve each problem. *Show your work.*

10. 74 people are sitting down to a fancy six-course meal. The first course is soup, which only needs a spoon. The rest of the courses each need fresh forks. How many forks will be used?
74 × 5 = 370 forks

11. Dawn is a traveling sign salesperson. She uses plastic letters to make the signs. A dress store chain asks Dawn to put signs in front of their 56 stores that say "SALE: HALF PRICE ON ALL DRESSES." How many plastic "S" letters will Dawn need?
56 × 4 = 224 plastic "S" letters

EXTENSION LESSON 5 Methods of One-Digit by Two-Digit Multiplication 347

Homework and Remembering page 347

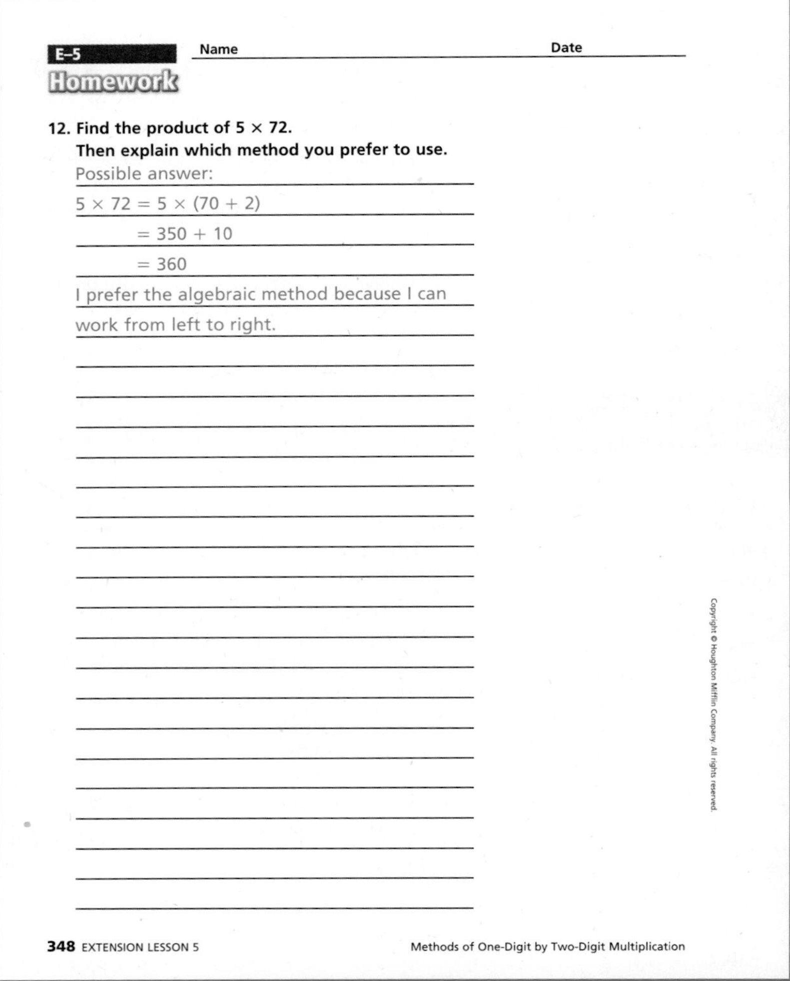

E–5 Homework Name ____________ Date ____________

12. Find the product of 5 × 72. Then explain which method you prefer to use.

Possible answer:
5 × 72 = 5 × (70 + 2)
= 350 + 10
= 360
I prefer the algebraic method because I can work from left to right.

348 EXTENSION LESSON 5 Methods of One-Digit by Two-Digit Multiplication

Homework and Remembering page 348

Home or School Activity

Literature Connection

The King's Chessboard Have students read the first few pages of this book written by David Birch (Puffin 1993, Illustrator Davis Grebu). Ask students to figure out on what day two-digit times one-digit multiplication is needed to find how much rice the wise man will be paid. Have students help the king by finding each day's payment. You might want to have a bulletin board showing each day's payment.

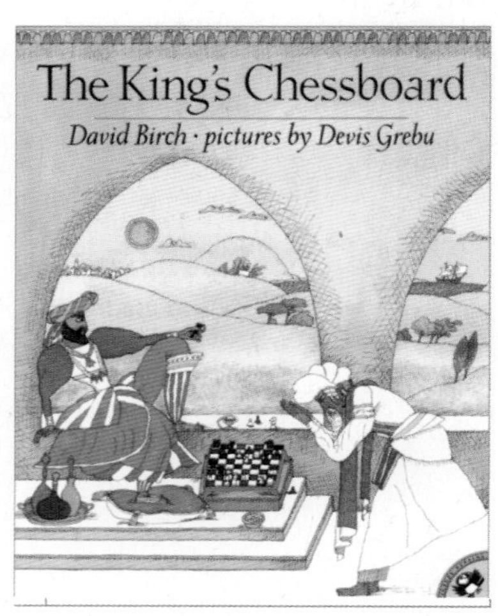

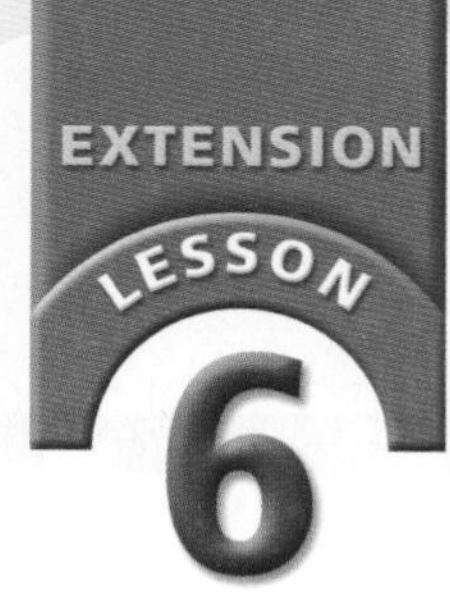

Discuss Different Methods of Multiplication

Vocabulary
Expanded Notation Method
Shortcut Method

Lesson Objective

- Compare and analyze methods of multiplication.

The Day at a Glance

Today's Goals	Materials	
1 Teaching the Lesson **A1:** Compare methods for multiplying a one-digit number by a two-digit number. **A2:** Practice multiplying with different methods.	**Lesson Activities** Student Activity Book pp. 537–538 or Student Hardcover Book pp. 537–538 Homework and Remembering pages 349–350	**Going Further** Activity Cards E-6 Math Journals
2 Going Further ▸ Differentiated Instruction		
3 Homework		

Use Math Talk today!

Keeping Skills Sharp

Quick Practice (5 MINUTES)	Daily Routines
Because you may be using this lesson at any time during the year, no specific Quick Practice is recommended. Use any Quick Practice activity that meets your students' needs.	**Homework Review** Ask students if they had difficulty with any part of the homework. Plan to set aside time to work with students needing extra help. **Mental Math** Calvin says he can use the answer to 4 × 4 to find the answer to 40 × 4, 40 × 40, and 400 × 400. Is this possible? If so, give the products. Explain. Yes; 16; 160; 1,600; 160,000; Count the zeros in the factors and insert this many zeros to the right of 16 for each product.

1 Teaching the Lesson

Activity 1

Compare Multiplication Methods

25 MINUTES

Goal: Compare methods for multiplying a one-digit number by a two-digit number.

Materials: Student Activity Book or Hardcover Book p. 537

NCTM Standards:
Number and Operations
Problem Solving
Communication

▶ Share Multiplication Methods

WHOLE CLASS

On the board, write 7 × 23 = ___. Then have students share any solution methods they know that have not been discussed on previous days. They should be able to relate their method to the area model.

E–6 Class Activity

Name ______ Date ______

▶ Compare Multiplication Methods

Compare these methods for solving 7 × 23.

Method A	Method B	Method C	Method D	Method E
23 = 20 + 3	23 = 20 + 3	23	23	[2]23
× 7 = 7	× 7 = 7	× 7	× 7	× 7
7 × 20 = 140	140	140	21	161
7 × 3 = 21	21	21	140	
161	161	161	161	

1. How are all the methods similar? List at least two similarities.
Answers will vary.

2. How are the methods different? List at least three differences.
Answers will vary.

▶ Analyze the Shortcut Method

Method E can be broken down into 2 steps.

Method E:	Step 1	Step 2
	[2]23	[2]23
	× 7	× 7
	1	161

3. Where are the products 140 and 21 from methods A–D?
Answers will vary. Possible answer: The 21 is shown by the rightmost 1 and the regrouped 2. The 140 is the 2 × 7 and is added to the regrouped 2 to make 16 (160).

EXTENSION LESSON 6 Discuss Different Methods of Multiplication 537

Student Activity Book page 537

▶ Compare Multiplication Methods

WHOLE CLASS

Send five students to the board. Have each student neatly copy one of the numeric methods shown onto the board. Be sure the methods are copied in the same order as on page 537 of the Student Book. Have the students describe each step of their method. Then have the class identify the changes in each succeeding method.

- Method A is the full Expanded Notation Method, including the tens and ones equations.

Teaching Note

What to Expect From Students
Comparing five methods at once is a task of greater complexity than students are used to at this level, and some students may struggle or stop working. Help students break down their comparisons into smaller parts. They may want to circle two methods at a time. Encourage students to discuss how they feel about comparing several methods at once and strategies they personally use for handling large or difficult tasks such as this one.

English Language Learners

Write *similar* and *different* on the board. Write methods A through E for solving 9 × 28 on the board. Guide students to compare the methods.

- **Beginning** Point and ask: **Are the partial products *similar* or *different*?** similar **Are the steps *similar*?** no **Are they *different*?** yes
- **Intermediate and Advanced**
Have students tell what is similar and different about the methods.

- Method B shows the Expanded Notation Method without the tens and ones equations, which can be done mentally.
- Method C drops writing the step of separating the tens and ones in 23 (done mentally) but still multiplies the tens before the ones (multiplying left to right).
- Method D multiplies the tens and ones separately but starts with the ones place. (The Expanded Notation Method can be done in either order.)
- Method E adds the tens and ones multiplications together as you go and writes them in the same row. You multiply by the ones first and write the tens value above the tens column in the top factor so you can add it to the tens multiplication (7×2 tens = 14 tens, plus the 2 tens from 7×3 is 16 tens).

Discuss exercises 1–2.

▶ Analyze the Shortcut Method

WHOLE CLASS

Discuss the two steps for Method E on Student Book page 537. Ask the following questions:

- Describe step 1 with place-value language. Possible answer: 7×3 ones = 21 ones. Write 1 in the ones column and write the 2 tens above the tens column.
- Describe step 2 with place-value language. Possible answer: 7×2 tens = 14 tens. Add the 2 tens from step 1 to make a total of 16 tens. Write 6 in the tens column and write 1 in the hundreds column.

Point out that the result is the same as with the Expanded Notation Method, but the Shortcut Method allows us to use fewer symbols. In step 1, we arrange the result of 7×3 differently. Before we wrote 21, but here we split 21 into 20 and 1. We place the 1 in the same position as before but the 20 gets placed as a 2 above the 2 in 23 so that it can be added to the product found in step 2. In step 2 we multiply 7×20 and add the 20 from step 1. By splitting the 21 and adding 20 to 140, we have streamlined the process.

Now have the class work in **Student Pairs** to answer exercise 3 on page 537.

Teaching Note

Math Background The Shortcut Method (Method E) is the common method currently taught in most schools in the United States. It is a complex method that is difficult for many third-graders, especially when multiplying a two-digit number by a two-digit number. For many students, it is a process that is memorized rather than understood. In this activity, we relate it to the Expanded Notation Method by first dropping steps and switching the order of multiplication from the highest place-value (tens in this case) to the lowest place value (ones in this case). The Shortcut Method is too difficult for many third-graders. It will be more of a focus in the upper grades.

Teaching Note

What to Expect from Students
Less-accomplished students may continue to use an area drawing and add the products outside the rectangle. We call this the Rectangle Sections Method. It helps students organize their thinking, and it generalizes well to two-digit by two-digit problems.

1 Teaching the Lesson

Activity 2

Practice Multiplication

 20 MINUTES

Goal: Practice multiplying with different methods.

Materials: Student Activity Book or Hardcover Book p. 538

 **NCTM Standard:**
Number and Operations

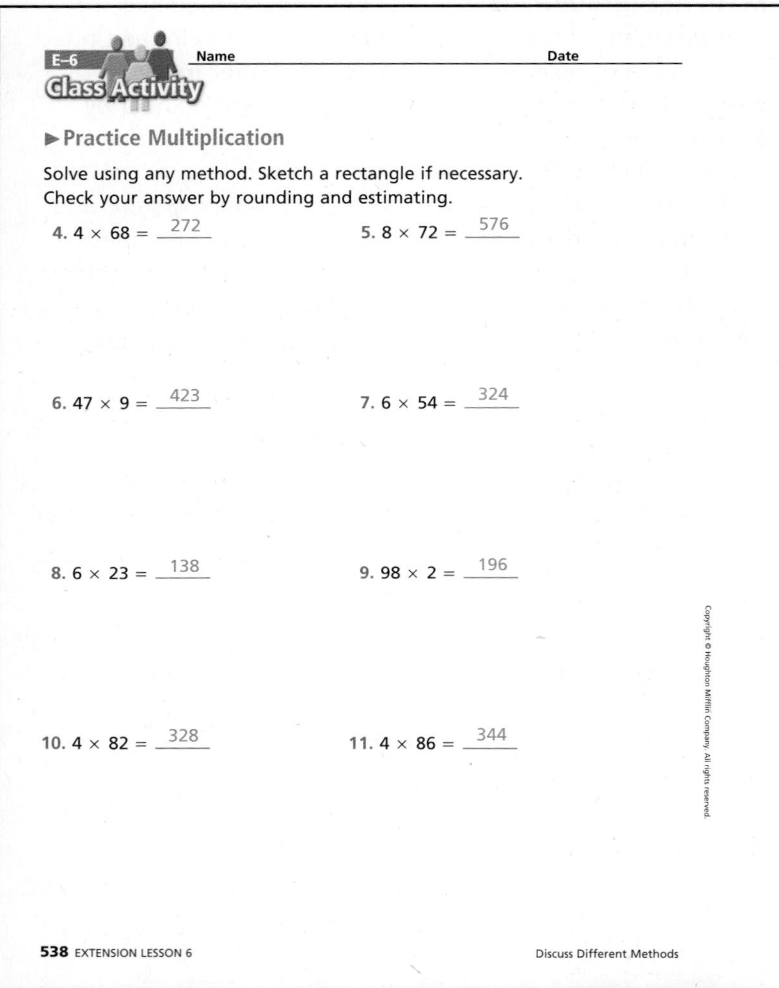

E-6 Class Activity

Name Date

▶ Practice Multiplication

Solve using any method. Sketch a rectangle if necessary.
Check your answer by rounding and estimating.

4. 4 × 68 = 272
5. 8 × 72 = 576
6. 47 × 9 = 423
7. 6 × 54 = 324
8. 6 × 23 = 138
9. 98 × 2 = 196
10. 4 × 82 = 328
11. 4 × 86 = 344

538 EXTENSION LESSON 6 Discuss Different Methods

Student Activity Book page 538

▶ Practice Multiplication PAIRS

Use **Solve and Discuss** for exercises 4–11 on Student Book page 538. Make sure a variety of solution methods are presented.

▶ Extend the Lesson PAIRS

Encourage students to make up similar multiplication exercises like the ones on Student Activity Book page 538. Each student should solve the exercises using any method they feel comfortable with. Once students are done, pairs should compare and discuss their solution methods.

The Learning Classroom

Math Talk Remind students of the **Solve and Discuss** structure of this program. Ask four or five students to go to the board and solve a problem, using any method they choose. The other students work on the same problem at their desks. Then the students at the board explain their methods. Students at their desks ask questions and assist each other in understanding the problem. Thus, students actually solve, explain, question, and justify. Usually only two or three students explain because classes do not like to sit through more explanations.

Ongoing Assessment

Have students use a numeric method to solve:

$$\begin{array}{r} 27 \\ \times\ 5 \\ \hline \end{array}$$

2 Going Further

Differentiated Instruction

Intervention — Activity Card E-6

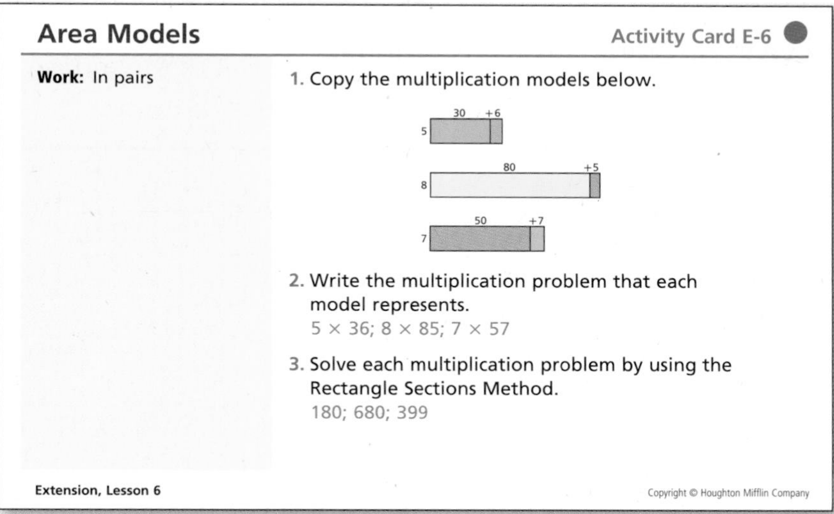
Area Models — Activity Card E-6 ●

Work: In pairs

1. Copy the multiplication models below.

2. Write the multiplication problem that each model represents.
   5 × 36; 8 × 85; 7 × 57
3. Solve each multiplication problem by using the Rectangle Sections Method.
   180; 680; 399

Extension, Lesson 6 Copyright © Houghton Mifflin Company

Activity Note If time permits, repeat the activity by having students draw their own area models and then exchange papers with a partner.

Math Writing Prompt

Choose a Method If you could only use one method for multiplying one-digit numbers by two-digit numbers, which method would you use? Explain.

Software Support

Warm Up 45.26

On Level — Activity Card E-6

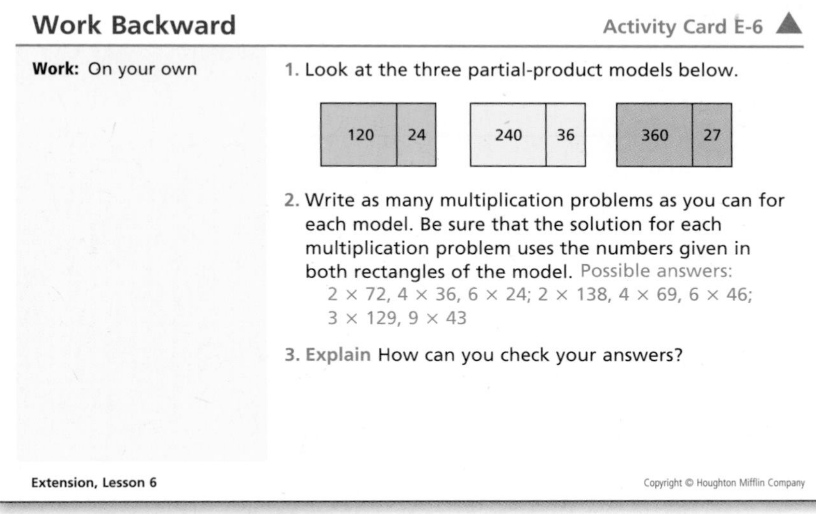
Work Backward — Activity Card E-6 ▲

Work: On your own

1. Look at the three partial-product models below.

120	24

240	36

360	27

2. Write as many multiplication problems as you can for each model. Be sure that the solution for each multiplication problem uses the numbers given in both rectangles of the model. Possible answers:
   2 × 72, 4 × 36, 6 × 24; 2 × 138, 4 × 69, 6 × 46; 3 × 129, 9 × 43
3. Explain How can you check your answers?

Extension, Lesson 6 Copyright © Houghton Mifflin Company

Activity Note If time permits, repeat the activity by having students draw their own rectangle models and then exchange papers with another student.

Math Writing Prompt

Explain Your Thinking Explain to another student how to use the Shortcut Method to solve 8 × 93.

Software Support

The Number Games: Up, Up, and Array, Level K

Challenge — Activity Card E-6

Multiplication Patterns — Activity Card E-6 ■

Work: In pairs

1. Find each of the following products. 80

   4 × 20 8 × 10 16 × 5

2. Discuss and record any patterns that you see. See below.
3. Generalize Write your own multiplication problems with a similar pattern for the following products.

   5 × 64 3 × 48

   10 × 32, 20 × 16, 40 × 8; 6 × 24, 12 × 12

2. The first factor in each problem is doubled from one product to the next. The second factor in each problem is reduced by half from one product to the next.

Extension, Lesson 6 Copyright © Houghton Mifflin Company

Activity Note To extend the activity, have students come up with other sets of products that have the same pattern.

Math Writing Prompt

Your Opinion Is it helpful to learn several methods for multiplying? Explain.

Software Support

Course II: Module 4: Unit 1: Number Patterns and Properties

3 Homework

E-6 Homework Goal: Additional Practice

Because you may be using this lesson at any time during the year, no Spiral Review is included. Use this Homework page to provide students with additional practice.

E-6 Homework Name ____ Date ____

Solve using any numeric method. Use rounding and estimating to see if your answer makes sense.

1. 82 × 6 492
2. 7 × 43 301
3. 9 × 38 342
4. 2 × 94 188
5. 4 × 68 272
6. 81 × 6 486
7. 35 × 9 315
8. 5 × 79 395
9. 2 × 74 148

Solve each problem. *Show your work.*

10. Describe how you solved one of the exercises above. Write at least two sentences.
Accept all answers that make sense.

11. Miranda wrote the full alphabet (26 letters) 6 times. How many letters did she write?
156 letters

12. Niko has 17 packs of bulletin-board cutouts. Each one contains 7 shapes. How many shapes does she have altogether?
119 shapes

EXTENSION LESSON 6 Discuss Different Methods of Multiplication 349

E-6 Homework Name ____ Date ____

13. **Explain how multiplication and addition are related.**
Possible answer: I use both addition and multiplication to find the total amount. For addition, the groups can be unequal. For multiplication, the groups must be equal. Repeated addition can be used to solve multiplication.

350 EXTENSION LESSON 6 Discuss Different Methods of Multiplication

Homework and Remembering page 349 **Homework and Remembering page 350**

Home or School Activity

Real-World Connection

Tell students that that are going to solve a problem about a bulletin board. Give them this problem.

If a bulletin board is 6 feet wide and 4 feet high, how many 9 in. by 12 in. sheets of construction paper are needed to cover the board? What is the area of the board? 32 sheets; 24 sq ft

Explain that the paper will be placed next to each other without gaps or overlaps.

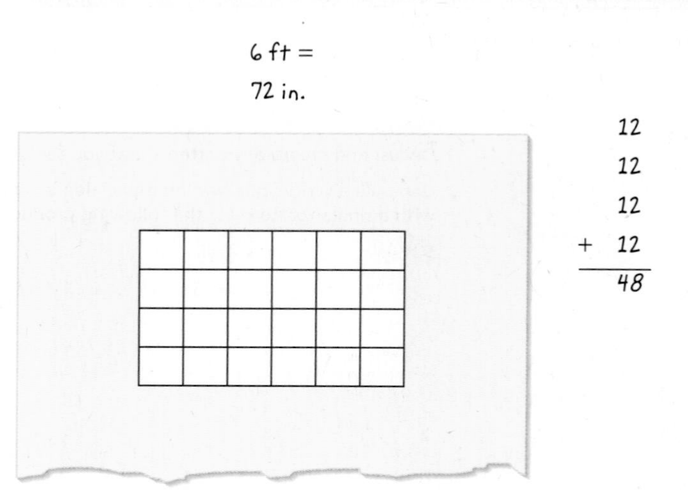

One-Digit by Three-Digit Multiplication

Lesson Objectives

- **Draw area models to represent the product of a one-digit number and a three-digit number.**
- **Use Numeric methods to multiply a one-digit number by a three-digit number.**

Vocabulary

Rectangles Sections Method
Expanded Notation Method
Algebraic Notation Method

The Day at a Glance

Today's Goals	Materials	
1 Teaching the Lesson **A1:** Model one-digit by three-digit multiplication. **A2:** Practice multiplication of one-digit numbers by three-digit numbers.	**Lesson Activities** Student Activity Book pp. 539–540 or Student Hardcover Book pp. 539–540 Homework and Remembering pages 351–352 Base-ten blocks MathBoard materials	**Going Further** Activity Cards E-7 *Go Fish* Game Cards (TRB M167) Scissors Math Journals
2 Going Further ► Differentiated Instruction		
3 Homework		

Use Math Talk today!

Keeping Skills Sharp

Quick Practice 5 MINUTES	Daily Routines
Because you may be using this lesson at any time during the year, no specific Quick Practice is recommended. Use any Quick Practice activity that meets your students' needs.	**Homework Review** Ask students to place their homework at the corner of their desks. Circulate during the Quick Practice and check that students completed the assignment, and see whether any problem caused difficulty for many students. **Strategy Problem** Teresa scored 26 points in 10 soccer games. In each game, she scored either 2 or 3 points. In how many games did she score 3 points? Explain how you found your answer. 6 games; Possible explanation: Guessed 5 games at 3 points and 5 games at 2 points, totaling 25 points < 26 points. So, I increased the 3-point games to 6 and decreased the 2-point games to 4.

1 Teaching the Lesson

Activity 1

Use the Area Model to Multiply Hundreds

 25 MINUTES

Goal: Model one-digit by three-digit multiplication.

Materials: Student Activity Book or Hardcover Book p. 539, MathBoard materials, base-ten blocks (optional)

 **NCTM Standards:**
Number and Operations
Representation
Communication

▶ Different Methods WHOLE CLASS

Explain to students that they will now solve 1-digit times 3-digit problems using each of the 3 methods they know: Rectangle Sections, Expanded Notation, and Algebraic Notation. You will be asking for volunteers to go to the board for each method. Tell students that everyone needs to draw rectangle sketches and relate each part of their sketch to each step of their numeric method. This helps everyone understand. Later, during the practice for Activity 2, students do not have to draw rectangles if they do not want to do so. At the end of the lesson, discuss any other methods students want to share.

▶ Discuss the Rectangle Sections Method

WHOLE CLASS

Math Talk 

Have some student volunteers draw rectangles showing 3 × 458 on the board as everyone else sketches on their MathBoards.

458 =	400	+ 50	+ 8	
3	3 × 400 = 1,200	3 × 50 = 150	3 × 8 = 24	3

$$\begin{array}{r} 1{,}200 \\ 150 \\ +\ 24 \\ \hline 1{,}374 \end{array}$$

Have students find the area of each section and then add to find the total area.

Discuss solutions relating each step inside the rectangle to the products added outside the rectangle. Be sure that listeners understand the steps for finding the product of 3 × 458 by using the Rectangle Sections Method.

- First multiply 3 × 400 = 1,200.
- Then multiply 3 × 50 = 150.
- Then multiply 3 × 8 = 24.
- Finally, add 1,200 + 150 + 24 = 1,374.

Teaching Note

What to Expect from Students As students work with the area model to show different methods of multiplying a one-digit number by a three-digit number, many may realize that the only difference in the methods is in the order of the steps. Some students may arrive at the correct conclusion that, in all three methods, you multiply the ones, tens, and hundreds and then add all three products to get the final product. This realization can help students to be successful when they work with the Shortcut Method, but the notation in the Shortcut Method is too difficult for many third-graders.

Alternate Approach

Base-Ten Blocks Have students model 3 × 458 using base-ten blocks.

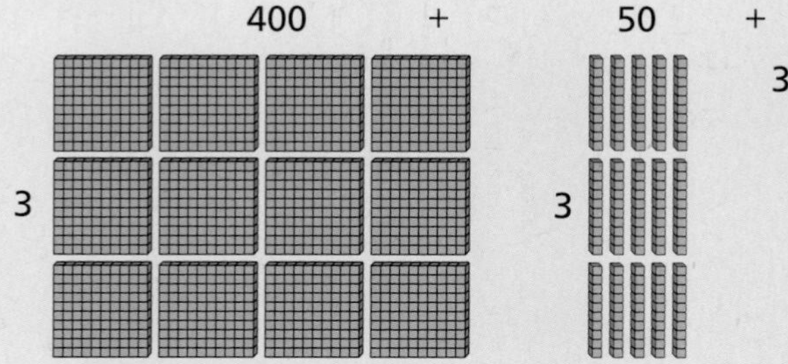

Ask students to explain how this base-ten model matches the area sketch.

English Language Learners

Write *expanded notation* and 362 = 300 + 60 + 2 on the board.

- **Beginning** Point and say: **This is *expanded notation.* We *expand* 362 into hundreds, tens, and ones.** Have students repeat.
- **Intermediate** Point to 362. Ask: **Is 3 in the hundreds place or tens place?** hundreds place **In *expanded notation,* do we show the place value of each number?** yes
- **Advanced** Ask: **How did I write 362?** in expanded notation **What does *expanded notation* show?** hundreds, tens, ones

▶ Discuss the Expanded Notation Method

WHOLE CLASS **Math Talk**

Have students go to the board to sketch a model and solve 3 × 458 using the Expanded Notation Method, while the other students work on their MathBoards. Have students add arcs to show the multiplications.

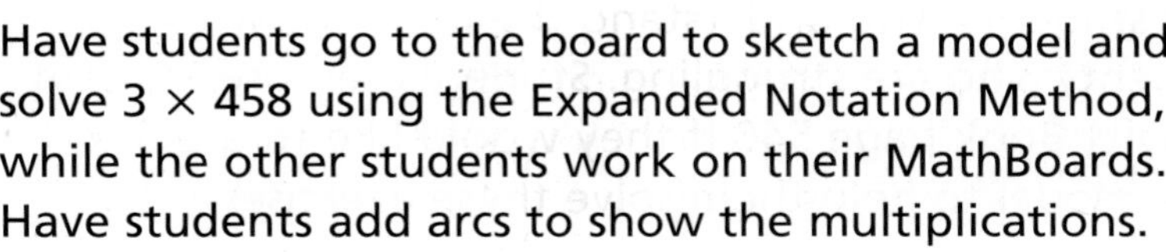

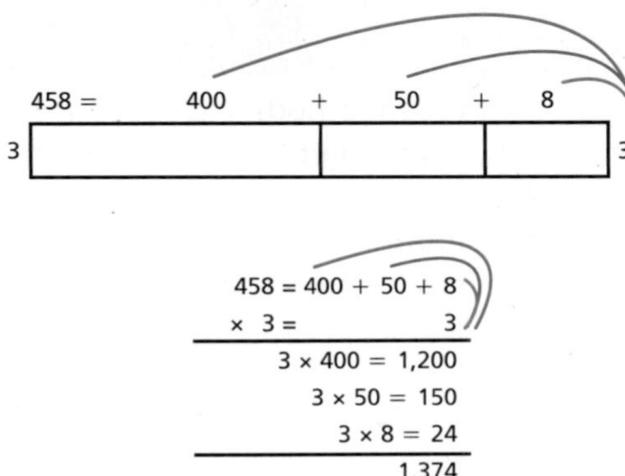

Have a student discussion of how each step in the Expanded Notation Method relates to each part of the rectangle model.

- Have someone summarize the Expanded Notation Method: What three steps are used in the Expanded Notation Method? You split 458 into hundreds, tens, and ones. Then you multiply each of the three place values by 3. Then you add the three products together.
- Then discuss as a class how the Expanded Notation Method is similar to the Rectangle Sections Method. They both use expanded notation of 458. They both multiply 3 × 400, 3 × 50, and 3 × 8. They both add the three products together at the end to find the final product.

▶ Discuss the Algebraic Notation Method

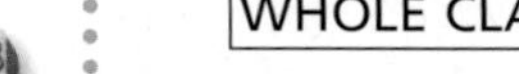
WHOLE CLASS **Math Talk** 

Invite some students to the board to sketch a model and solve 3 × 458 using the Algebraic Notation Method, while the rest of the class works on their MathBoards. Make sure the students add the arcs to show each multiplication. Have students explain their numeric steps and relate them to the model.

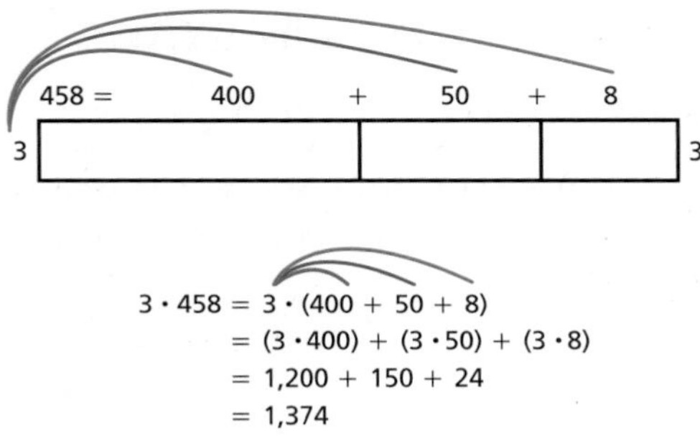

Make sure students see that 458 must again be written in expanded notation. Then, each addend is multiplied by 3. The process is the same but where things are written is different. Ask if anyone has another method they want to share and discuss it.

Activity 2

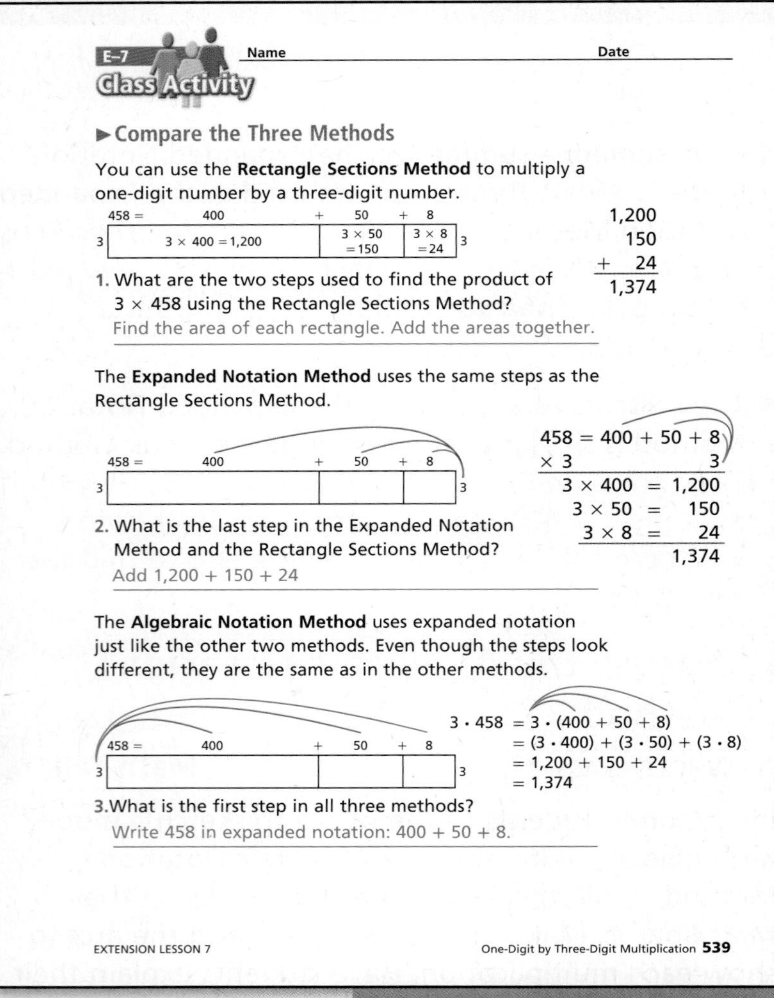

E-7 Class Activity Name Date

▶ Compare the Three Methods

You can use the **Rectangle Sections Method** to multiply a one-digit number by a three-digit number.

458 = 400 + 50 + 8

3 × 400 = 1,200 | 3 × 50 = 150 | 3 × 8 = 24

1,200
150
+ 24
1,374

1. What are the two steps used to find the product of 3 × 458 using the Rectangle Sections Method?
Find the area of each rectangle. Add the areas together.

The **Expanded Notation Method** uses the same steps as the Rectangle Sections Method.

458 = 400 + 50 + 8
× 3   3
3 × 400 = 1,200
3 × 50 = 150
3 × 8 = 24
1,374

2. What is the last step in the Expanded Notation Method and the Rectangle Sections Method?
Add 1,200 + 150 + 24

The **Algebraic Notation Method** uses expanded notation just like the other two methods. Even though the steps look different, they are the same as in the other methods.

3 • 458 = 3 • (400 + 50 + 8)
= (3 • 400) + (3 • 50) + (3 • 8)
= 1,200 + 150 + 24
= 1,374

3. What is the first step in all three methods?
Write 458 in expanded notation: 400 + 50 + 8.

EXTENSION LESSON 7   One-Digit by Three-Digit Multiplication 539

Student Activity Book page 539

▶ Compare the Three Methods

WHOLE CLASS

As a summary, have students answer questions 1–3 on Student Book page 539. See Math Talk in Action for possible discussion points.

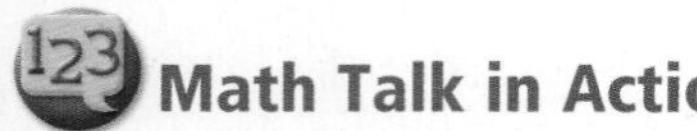

Math Talk in Action

What do the three methods have in common?

Steve: Somewhere in each method, you have to multiply 3 times 400, 3 times 50, and 3 times 8.

Mirella: In all of the methods, you have to add 1,200 + 150 + 24 to get your final answer.

Ahmed: Even though one of the methods is called The Expanded Notation Method, you really do expanded notation in all of the methods. You have to split 458 into 400 + 50 + 8 for all three.

Practice One-Digit by Three-Digit Multiplication

 25 MINUTES

Goal: Practice multiplication of one-digit numbers by three-digit numbers.

Materials: Student Activity Book or Hardcover Book page 540.

 **NCTM Standards:**
Number and Operations
Representation
Communication

▶ Practice Multiplication

PAIRS

Write the following on the board:

6 × 328 = 1,968   7 × 456 = 3,192

8 × 279 = 2,232   3 × 725 = 2,175

Have the students work in **Student Pairs** to multiply. Pair students who understand the methods with students who are struggling. Students can use Student Activity Book page 540 if they would like to use an area model to help them solve these exercises.

Ongoing Assessment

As students work with the methods and models of multiplying one-digit numbers by three-digit numbers, listen in as they explain their strategies to their partners. Listen for place-value language, expanded notation, and ideas about multiplying hundreds, tens, and ones by the single-digit factor.

2 Going Further

Differentiated Instruction

Intervention — Activity Card E-7

Use Expanded Notation
Activity Card E-7

Work: On your own

1. Look at the model of 2 × 143 below. How many times does the model show the expanded form of 143? Twice

100	40	3
100	40	3

2. Use the model to find the product of 2 × 143. 286
3. **Analyze** How could you change the model above to find the product of 4 × 143? add two more rectangles each showing 100 + 40 + 3; 572
4. Make models for 3 × 152 and 2 × 349. Then find each product. 456; 698

Extension, Lesson 7

Activity Note If time permits, have students draw their own Expanded Notation model and exchange papers with another student. Then have them identify the multiplication problem for the model.

Math Writing Prompt

Place Value Use place-value language to explain why 132 and 231 represent different numbers even though they have the same digits.

Software Support

Warm Up 12.37

On Level — Activity Card E-7

Go Fish
Activity Card E-7

Work: In pairs

Use:
- TRB M167 (*Go Fish* Game Cards)
- Scissors

1. Shuffle the cards. Each player takes 5 cards.
2. Take turns asking for a match. If your partner has your match, set the pair down. If there is no match, end your turn by drawing another card from the deck to match, if possible. The first player to have no cards left is the winner.

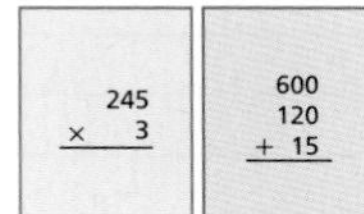

Extension, Lesson 7

Activity Note Extend the activity by having two pairs of students form a larger group, playing the game with 20 cards.

Math Writing Prompt

Word Problem Write a word problem for 3 × 471. Explain how to find the answer.

Software Support

The Number Games: Up, Up, and Array, Level J

Challenge — Activity Card E-7

Use Substitution
Activity Card E-7

Work: On your own

1. Look at the substitution shown below to evaluate the expression $n \times 4$ for $n = 6$.

$$n \times 4 = 6 \times 4 = 24$$

2. Find the value of the product $n \times 4$ for each value of n given. 28, 136, 500, 854

$n = 7$

$n = 34$

$n = 125$

$n = 216$

3. When $w = 115$ and $p = 3$, what is $w \times p$? 345

Extension, Lesson 7

Activity Note To extend the activity, have students write their own multiplication expressions and values for the variables and then exchange with partners to practice substitution.

Math Writing Prompt

Compare Explain why 3 • (200 + 10 + 8) is the same as (3 • 200) + (3 • 10) + (3 • 8).

DESTINATION Math® **Software Support**

Course II: Module 2: Unit 2: Repeated Addition and Arrays

3 Homework

Goal: Additional Practice

Because you may be using this lesson at any time during the year, no Spiral Review is included. Use this Homework page to provide students with additional practice.

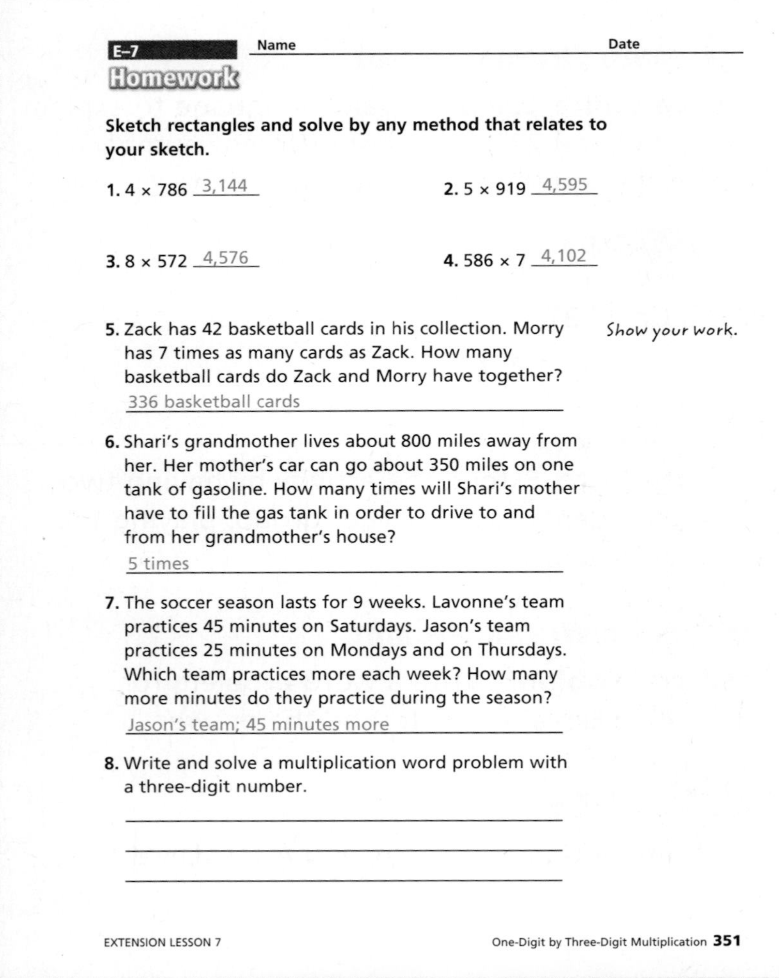

E-7 Homework Name ____________ Date ________

Sketch rectangles and solve by any method that relates to your sketch.

1. 4 × 786 3,144
2. 5 × 919 4,595
3. 8 × 572 4,576
4. 586 × 7 4,102

Show your work.

5. Zack has 42 basketball cards in his collection. Morry has 7 times as many cards as Zack. How many basketball cards do Zack and Morry have together?
336 basketball cards
6. Shari's grandmother lives about 800 miles away from her. Her mother's car can go about 350 miles on one tank of gasoline. How many times will Shari's mother have to fill the gas tank in order to drive to and from her grandmother's house?
5 times
7. The soccer season lasts for 9 weeks. Lavonne's team practices 45 minutes on Saturdays. Jason's team practices 25 minutes on Mondays and on Thursdays. Which team practices more each week? How many more minutes do they practice during the season?
Jason's team; 45 minutes more
8. Write and solve a multiplication word problem with a three-digit number.

EXTENSION LESSON 7 — One-Digit by Three-Digit Multiplication 351

Homework and Remembering page 351

E-7 Homework Name ____________ Date ________

9. **Explain how to multiply 4 × 382.**
Possible answer: I multiply 4 times the hundreds, then 4 times the tens, and finally 4 times the ones. Then I add the products to find the total amount.
$4 \times 300 = 1{,}200$
$4 \times 80 = 320$
$4 \times 2 = 8$
$1{,}200 + 320 + 8 = 1{,}528$

352 EXTENSION LESSON 7 — One-Digit by Three-Digit Multiplication

Homework and Remembering page 352

Home or School Activity

Social Studies Connection

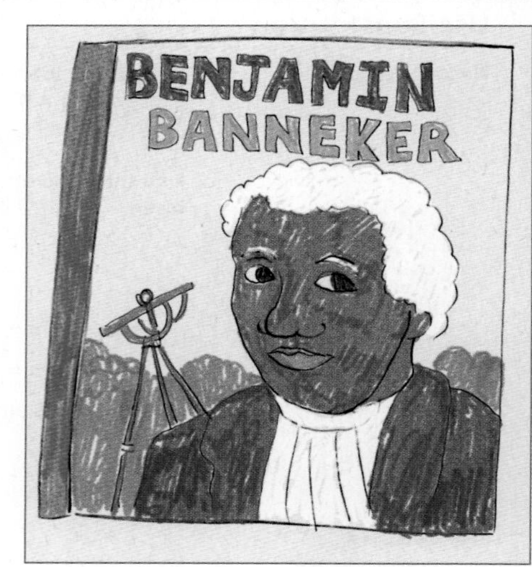

Benjamin Banneker Benjamin Banneker was a scientist and mathematician who lived from 1731–1806. He was the technical assistant in the first surveying of the Federal District, which is now Washington, D.C.

Surveyors determine the area of a region and the length of boundary lines. In Washington D.C., a city block is 264 feet.

Have students determine the length of seven city blocks in Washington, D.C. Have the students find the length of a block and a street in their town.

Practice One-Digit by Three-Digit Multiplication

Vocabulary
Shortcut Method

Lesson Objectives

- Multiply one-digit numbers by three-digit numbers.
- Use the Shortcut Method (the standard multiplication algorithm).

The Day at a Glance

Today's Goals	Materials	
1 Teaching the Lesson **A1:** Review different methods of multiplying one-digit numbers by three-digit numbers. **A2:** Use the Shortcut Method to multiply a one-digit number by a three-digit number.	**Lesson Activities** Student Activity Book pp. 541–542 or Student Hardcover Book pp. 541–542 Homework and Remembering pp. 353–354	**Going Further** Activity Cards E-8 Math Journals
2 Going Further ▸ Differentiated Instruction		
3 Homework		

Use Math Talk today!

Keeping Skills Sharp

Quick Practice 5 MINUTES	Daily Routines
Because you may be using this lesson at any time during the year, no specific Quick Practice is recommended. Use any Quick Practice activity that meets your students' needs.	**Homework Review** Let students work together to check their work. Initially, pair less able students with more able students. Remind students to use what they know about helping others. **Nonroutine Problem** Kyle ate $\frac{1}{5}$ of an orange. Oanh ate $\frac{1}{2}$ of the orange. How much of the orange did they eat together? $\frac{7}{10}$ of the orange

1 Teaching the Lesson

Activity 1

Review Different Methods

 **20 MINUTES**

Goal: Review different methods of multiplying one-digit numbers by three-digit numbers.

 **NCTM Standards:**
Number and Operations
Algebra
Representation
Communication

▶ Review Different Multiplication Methods WHOLE CLASS

Write 235 × 9 on the board and draw the corresponding area model.

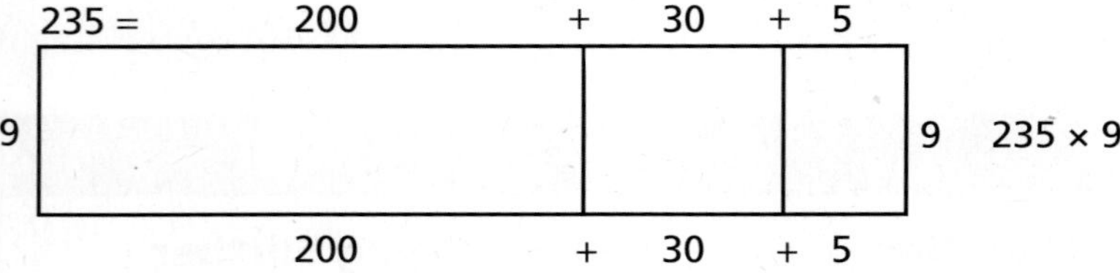

Have three students come to the board to each demonstrate one of the three methods to multiply a one-digit number by a three-digit number: Rectangle Sections Method, Expanded Notation Method, and Algebraic Notation Method.

For each method, the student should relate the numeric steps to the area model.

Rectangle Sections Method

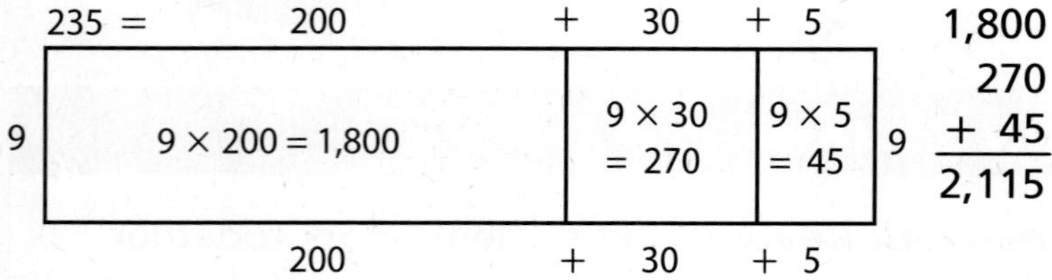

$$\begin{array}{r} 1{,}800 \\ 270 \\ +\ 45 \\ \hline 2{,}115 \end{array}$$

Students who are watching the students at the board should ask questions to clarify their understanding of the method. For example,

- Why did you multiply 9 × 30?
- How did you get 2,115 as the final answer?

Expanded Notation Method

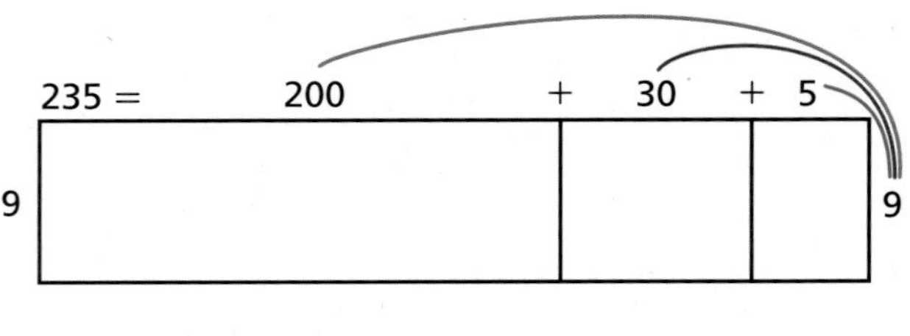

$$\begin{array}{r} 235 = 200 + 30 + 5 \\ \times\ 9 = \qquad\qquad\quad 9 \\ \hline 9 \times 200 = 1{,}800 \\ 9 \times 30 = \quad 270 \\ 9 \times 5 = \quad\ \ 45 \\ \hline 2{,}115 \end{array}$$

The Algebraic Notation Method

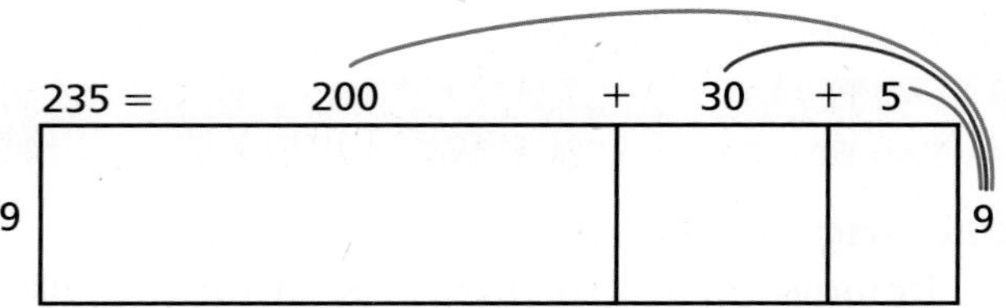

$$\begin{aligned} 9 \bullet 235 &= 9 \bullet (200 + 30 + 5) \\ &= (9 \bullet 200) + (9 \bullet 30) + (9 \bullet 5) \\ &= 1{,}800 + 270 + 45 \\ &= 2{,}115 \end{aligned}$$

When all methods have been presented, have students discuss how the methods are alike and how they are different.

Teaching Note

What to Expect from Students
These methods have been worked with extensively in previous lessons. Review the three methods only as needed by the students in your class. All students do not need to master all three methods. Each student should be proficient with at least one of the methods, although some students enjoy the challenge of mastering and explaining all three.

Activity 2

Use the Shortcut Method

 15 MINUTES

Goal: Use the Shortcut Method to multiply a one-digit number by a three-digit number.

Materials: Student Activity Book or Hardcover Book pp. 541–542

 **NCTM Standards:**

Number and Operations
Communication
Representation

E–8 Name ________ Date ________

▶ Compare Multiplication Methods

Look at the drawing and the five numeric solutions for 437 × 6.

	437 = 400	+ 30	+ 7
6	6 × 400 = 2,400	6 × 30 = 180	6 × 7 = 42

Method A	Method B	Method C	Method D	Method E
437 = 400 + 30 + 7	437 = 400 + 30 + 7	437	437	2 4 437
× 6 = 6	× 6 = 6	× 6	× 6	× 6
6 × 400 = 2,400	2,400	2,400	42	2,622
6 × 30 = 180	180	180	180	
6 × 7 = 42	42	42	2,400	
2,622	2,622	2,622	2,622	

1. How are the solutions similar? List at least two ways.
Answers will vary. Possible answers: The methods all arrive at the same final answer. They all involve adding together the same three partial products.

2. How are the solutions different?
List at least three comparisons between methods.
Answers will vary. Possible answers: Method C has the steps in a different order than Method D; Method A is similar to Method B, but shows the multiplication; Method E does not show the steps, but all other methods show adding three parts.

3. How do Methods A–D relate to the drawing? List at least two ways.
Answers will vary. Possible answers: The breakdown into expanded notation is the same. The final product is the same.

EXTENSION LESSON 8 Practice One-Digit by Three-Digit Multiplication **541**

Student Activity Book page 541

▶ Compare Multiplication Methods

WHOLE CLASS

Have a **Student Leader** draw a rectangle model for 6 × 437 on the board. Use **Solve and Discuss** to find the solution.

Direct the students to method A on page 541 in the Student Book. Method A is the full Expanded Notation Method, including the hundreds, tens, and ones equations. Discuss this method with the class.

- How do the equations in method A relate to the drawing? The equations and the drawing show all of the multiplying you have to do to find the final product.
- What four steps do you have to do in method A? You have to 1) multiply 6 × the hundreds, 2) multiply 6 × the tens, 3) multiply 6 × the ones, and 4) add all of those products together.

Ask students to look at method B. This is the Expanded Notation method without the hundreds, tens, and ones equations. Ask the students to notice what is different between methods A and B. In method B, we don't show the full place value equations. We just show the answers.

Have the students look at method C, which drops the step of separating 437 into hundreds, tens, and ones. Ask students to compare this method to method B. Ask the students what is not written but what is "understood" in method C. The expanded notation is not written but it is understood because 6 × the 4 in the hundreds place is 6 × 400 = 2,400, 6 × the 3 in the tens place is 6 × 30 = 180, and 6 × the 7 in the ones place is 42.

Have the students look at method D, which multiplies the ones first, then the tens, then the hundreds. Ask the students to describe what has changed in method D.

Direct students' attention to method E, which is the Shortcut method. Ask the students to identify the major changes that they see between methods D and E. It looks much shorter, it has some regrouped digits at the top, there are no visible "in-between" steps like adding 42, 180, and 2,400 to get the final total.

After the class discussion on these solutions, have students complete exercises 1–3.

Teaching Note

What to Expect from Students

Because there are many different methods to multiply a one-digit number by a three-digit number, students may not realize that all the methods involve the same steps, no matter how hidden they are. Help students to see that every multiplication of a one-digit number by a three-digit number will have the same four steps:

1) Multiply ones by ones.

2) Multiply ones by tens.

3) Multiply ones by hundreds.

4) Add all of the products.

E–8 Class Activity — Name ____ Date ____

► Analyze the Shortcut Method

Look at this breakdown of solution steps for Method E.

Step 1	Step 2	Step 3
1 363 × 5 5	3 1 363 × 5 15	3 1 363 × 5 1,815

4. Describe what happens in Step 1.
Answers will vary. Check students' explanations.

5. Describe what happens in Step 2.
Answers will vary. Check students' explanations.

6. Describe what happens in Step 3.
Answers will vary. Check students' explanations.

Practice the Shortcut Method on these problems.

7. 415 × 3 = 1,245

8. 768 × 9 = 6,912

9. 632 × 7 = 4,424

10. 349 × 6 = 2,094

542 EXTENSION LESSON 8 — Practice One-Digit by Three-Digit Multiplication

Student Activity Book page 542

► Analyze the Shortcut Method

WHOLE CLASS

Page 542 of the Student Book shows the steps involved in method E, the Shortcut Method.

Exercises 4–6 ask students to explain each step. Discuss the answers as a class. See a sample of classroom dialogue in the Math Talk in Action.

After the discussion, have students work in **Student Pairs** to complete exercises 7–10.

Math Talk in Action

Use place-value language to describe the Shortcut Method step-by-step.

Amanda: Step 1 is ones multiplication. I would multiply 5 × 3 ones = 15 ones. Write the 5 in the ones column below the 3 ones and 5 ones. Regroup 15 ones to make 1 ten and write a 1 above the 6, which is in the tens column.

Saul: In step 2, you do tens multiplication. 5 × 6 tens = 30 tens. Add the 1 ten from the ones multiplication to make a total of 31 tens. Write 1 in the tens column below the line. Regroup the 30 tens to make new hundreds. Write a 3 above the hundreds column.

Rachel: Step 3 is hundreds multiplication. Multiply 5 × 3 hundreds = 15 hundreds. Add the 3 hundreds from the tens multiplication step for a total of 18 hundreds. Write 8 in the hundreds column and one in the thousand.

English Language Learners

Write *method* and *shortcut* on the board.

- **Beginning** Ask: **Is a *method* a way to solve a problem?** yes **Is a *shortcut* a fast way?** yes **Are there fewer steps in a *shortcut*?** yes
- **Intermediate** Say: **The way we solve a problem is called a __.** method **A faster way to solve a problem is a __.** shortcut
- **Advanced** Have students tell the difference between a *method* and a *shortcut method.*

Intervention Activity Card E-8

You Decide Activity Card E-8

Work: On your own

1. The model below shows an area model for 2 × 347. Copy the model.

   300 + 40 + 7
   2
   300 + 40 + 7

2. Use any method to solve the multiplication.
3. Analyze How could you use addition to check your work? 347 + 347 = 694

Extension, Lesson 8

Activity Note Remind students how to use repeated addition to solve multiplication problems. Use multiple examples.

Math Writing Prompt

Another Way How can you use repeated addition to check the answer to 462 × 4 is correct? Show your work.

Software Support

Warm Up 12.37

On Level Activity Card E-8

Partial Products Activity Card E-8

Work: On your own

1. Copy the missing-digit puzzle below.

   2<u>3</u>7 = <u>200</u> + 30 + 7
   × 5 × 5
   1,000
   150
   35
   1,185

2. Each blank represents a missing digit. Complete the puzzle.
3. Explain What strategies did you use to find the missing digits?
4. Create your own missing-digits puzzle, and exchange it with another student to solve.

Extension, Lesson 8

Activity Note To extend the activity, have students create their own missing-digit puzzle and exchange it with another student.

Math Writing Prompt

Choose Your Method Describe the multiplication method that makes the most sense to you. Explain why.

Software Support

The Number Games: Up, Up, and Array, Level J

Challenge Activity Card E-8

Investigation Activity Card E-8

Work: On your own

1. Copy the multiplication puzzle below.

   □□□
   × □
   9 8 4

2. Each box represents a missing digit. There are 4 possible combinations of digits to complete the puzzle. Find as many combinations as you can. 123 × 8; 246 × 4; 492 × 2; 984 × 1
3. Explain What strategies did you use to find the missing digits?
4. Create your own multiplication puzzle, and exchange it with another student to solve.

Extension, Lesson 8

Activity Note Have students discuss any patterns they see in the four solutions. Then have them make up their own multiplication puzzle with four solutions for other students to solve.

Math Writing Prompt

Regrouping Explain why a 2 might be written above the tens column in a multiplication problem.

Software Support

Course II: Module 1: Unit 1: Comparing and Ordering

3 Homework

E–8 Homework **Goal:** Additional Practice

Because you may be using this lesson at any time during the year, no Spiral Review is included. Use this Homework page to provide students with additional practice.

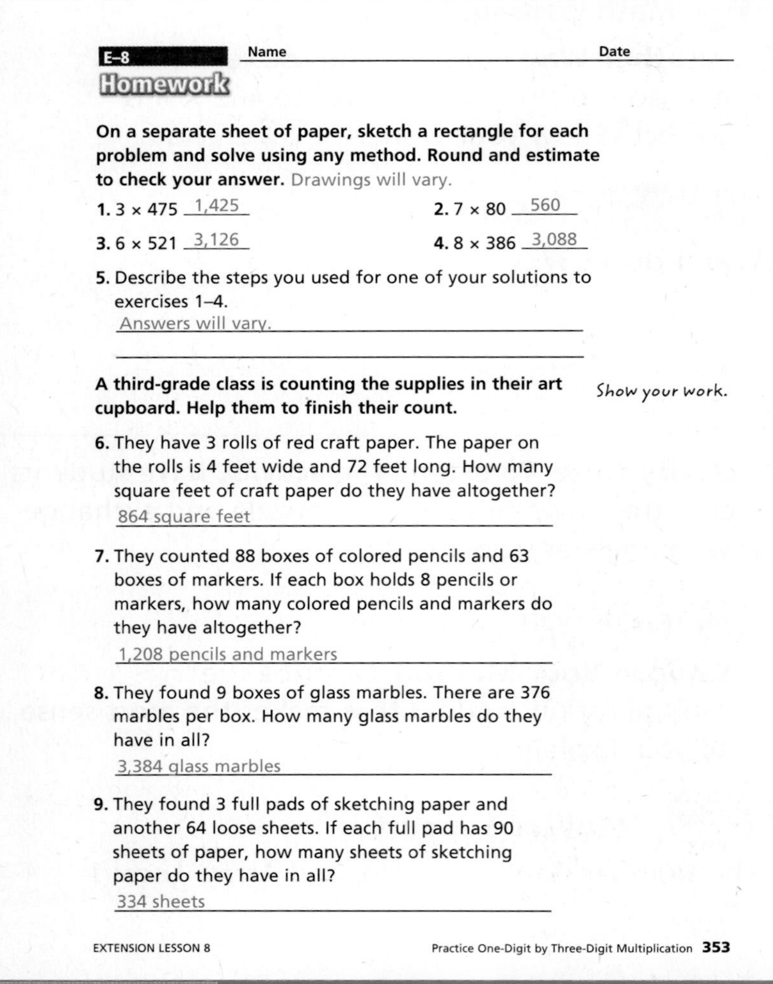

E–8 Homework Name Date

On a separate sheet of paper, sketch a rectangle for each problem and solve using any method. Round and estimate to check your answer. Drawings will vary.

1. 3 × 475 1,425

2. 7 × 80 560

3. 6 × 521 3,126

4. 8 × 386 3,088

5. Describe the steps you used for one of your solutions to exercises 1–4.
Answers will vary.

A third-grade class is counting the supplies in their art cupboard. Help them to finish their count.

Show your work.

6. They have 3 rolls of red craft paper. The paper on the rolls is 4 feet wide and 72 feet long. How many square feet of craft paper do they have altogether?
864 square feet

7. They counted 88 boxes of colored pencils and 63 boxes of markers. If each box holds 8 pencils or markers, how many colored pencils and markers do they have altogether?
1,208 pencils and markers

8. They found 9 boxes of glass marbles. There are 376 marbles per box. How many glass marbles do they have in all?
3,384 glass marbles

9. They found 3 full pads of sketching paper and another 64 loose sheets. If each full pad has 90 sheets of paper, how many sheets of sketching paper do they have in all?
334 sheets

EXTENSION LESSON 8 Practice One-Digit by Three-Digit Multiplication **353**

Homework and Remembering page 353

E–8 Homework Name Date

10. Write and solve a word problem using the factors 6 and 246.
Possible problem: There are 246 books on each shelf in the library. How many books are on six shelves?
6 × 246 = 1,476 books

354 EXTENSION LESSON 8 Practice One-Digit by Three-Digit Multiplication

Homework and Remembering page 354

Home or School Activity

Real-World Connection

Exact or Estimate Math is used in many different ways during the course of a day. Students can research by asking family members or friends when they use math. Have the students put their findings into two columns: *When an Exact Answer is Needed* and *When an Estimate Works.*

Then have them use their research to give a general description of when exact answers are needed and when estimates work.

When an Exact Answer is Needed	When an Estimate Works

Find the Unknown Factor

Vocabulary
dividend
divisor
quotient
factor

Lesson Objective

- **Understand real-world division situations.**

The Day at a Glance

Today's Goals	Materials	
1 Teaching the Lesson **A1:** Explore three different methods of division and understand real-world division situations. **2 Going Further** ▸ Differentiated Instruction **3 Homework**	**Lesson Activities** Student Activity Book pp. 543–544 or Student Hardcover Book pp. 543–544 Homework and Remembering pp. 355–356	**Going Further** Activity Cards E-9 Base-ten blocks Homework and Remembering p. 355 MathBoard materials Calculators (optional) Blank paper Math Journals

Use Math Talk today!

Keeping Skills Sharp

Quick Practice 5 MINUTES	Daily Routines
Because you may be using this lesson at any time during the year, no specific Quick Practice is recommended. Use any Quick Practice activity that meets your students' needs.	**Homework Review** Ask students to briefly describe some strategies they used in their homework. Sometimes you will find that students solve each problem correctly but use an inefficient strategy. **Reasoning** Rodrigo had 24 pens. He said that $\frac{1}{4}$ were red, $\frac{1}{4}$ were blue, $\frac{1}{4}$ were green, and $\frac{1}{4}$ were black. Can the pens be grouped like this? Explain. Yes; $\frac{1}{4}$ of 24 is 6. There are 4 groups of 6 in 24.

1 Teaching the Lesson

Activity 1

Divide Hundreds

50 MINUTES

Goal: Explore three methods of division and understand real-world division situations.

Materials: Student Activity Book pages 543–544

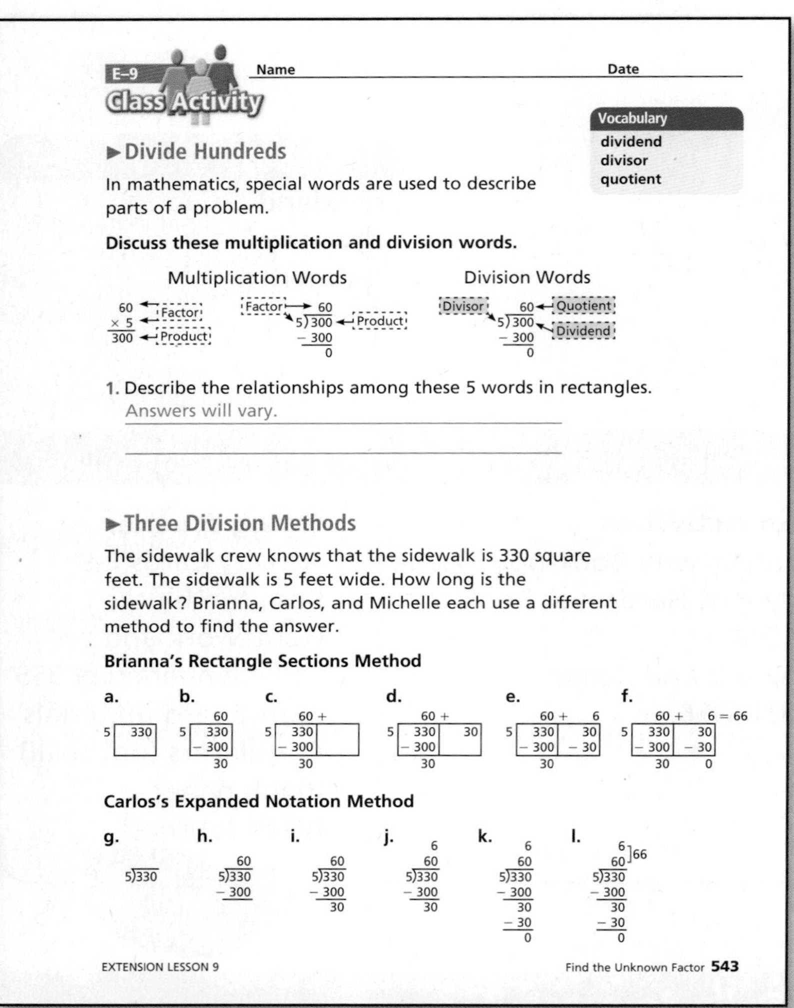

E–9 Class Activity

Name ____________ Date ____________

Vocabulary
dividend
divisor
quotient

▶ Divide Hundreds

In mathematics, special words are used to describe parts of a problem.

Discuss these multiplication and division words.

Multiplication Words: 60 ← Factor; × 5 ← Factor; 300 ← Product. Factor → 60; 5)300 ← Product; − 300; 0

Division Words: Divisor → 5)300; 60 ← Quotient; 300 ← Dividend; − 300; 0

1. Describe the relationships among these 5 words in rectangles.
Answers will vary.

▶ Three Division Methods

The sidewalk crew knows that the sidewalk is 330 square feet. The sidewalk is 5 feet wide. How long is the sidewalk? Brianna, Carlos, and Michelle each use a different method to find the answer.

Brianna's Rectangle Sections Method

a. 5 | 330
b. 60; 5 | 330 − 300 = 30
c. 60 +; 5 | 330 − 300 = 30 |
d. 60 +; 5 | 330 − 300 = 30 | 30
e. 60 + 6; 5 | 330 − 300 = 30 | 30 − 30
f. 60 + 6 = 66; 5 | 330 − 300 = 30 | 30 − 30 = 0

Carlos's Expanded Notation Method

g. 5)330
h. 60; 5)330; − 300
i. 60; 5)330; − 300; 30
j. 6; 60; 5)330; − 300; 30
k. 6; 60; 5)330; − 300; 30; − 30; 0
l. 6; 60]66; 5)330; − 300; 30; − 30; 0

EXTENSION LESSON 9 Find the Unknown Factor **543**

Student Activity Book page 543

Teaching Note

Language and Vocabulary *Math Expressions* will often use the multiplication terms *product* ÷ *factor* = *factor* for division (as opposed to *dividend* ÷ *divisor* = *quotient*) because the multiplication terms help students relate division to multiplication. Most students also find the multiplication words easier to say and remember. You should use the division terms as much as needed to satisfy your school's learning goals.

▶ Divide Hundreds WHOLE CLASS

Write on the board: 5)30 5)300

Ask students to give word-problem situations for both expressions.

Have students find solutions to the problems by relating them to multiplication. Write the related multiplications below the divisions and then write the division solutions.

Tell students that they will be using the solutions 30 ÷ 5 and 300 ÷ 5 to solve another problem, but first they must learn some division vocabulary to make the discussion easier.

Leave the solutions on the board. Label the parts of the multiplication and division problems as shown at the top of page 543 in the Student Activity Book. Discuss with the students how multiplication and division relate to each other.

- The two words that start with "d" are the main parts of the division problem. The *dividend* in division is the number that is divided. It is the *product* in multiplication. The *divisor* is the number that divides the dividend. It is one of the factors in multiplication.
- The *quotient* is the result of the division. It is the other factor in multiplication.
- While the order of the factors in multiplication does not affect the result, the divisor and quotient in division are *not* interchangeable. The divisor is the known factor in division, and the quotient is the unknown factor.

▶ Three Division Methods WHOLE CLASS

Have the students read the problem on Student Activity Book page 543.

- What type of division problem is it? area
- What operation is needed for the solution? 330 ÷ 5 or 5 × _____ = 330.

Ask students how this problem is related to the problems on the board. Then tell students that they will solve 330 ÷ 5 by solving 300 ÷ 5 and 30 ÷ 5.

Lead a discussion of the steps in each of the three long-division methods on pages 543 and 544, writing each step of each method on the board as you go. Elicit as much of the discussion as possible from the students.

Brianna's Rectangle Sections Method The general method is to find the unknown length of the rectangle, so we:

a. Draw the first rectangle section. Write the product inside the section and the known factor at the left side.

b. Ask, "5 times what tens number or multiple of ten gives an answer closest to 330 without going over?" $5 \times 60 = 300$ and $5 \times 70 = 350$, so 60 gives us the answer closest to 300 without going over. Write 60 at the top of the rectangle section. Multiply 5 by 60 and write the product, 300, under 330 inside the rectangle. Subtract 300 from 330 and write the difference, 30, below the first rectangle section.

c. Draw a second rectangle section to the right of the first section. Write a plus sign after the 60 between the two sections as you prepare to find the ones place of the unknown factor.

d. Write 30, the difference from the first section, inside the second section.

e. Ask, "5 times what number gives an answer closest to 30 without going over?" $5 \times 6 = 30$ Write 6 at the top of the second section. Multiply $5 \times 6 = 30$. Write 30 below the existing 30. Subtract 30 from 30 to get 0. Write 0, below the second rectangle section.

f. Add the quotients from each section. $60 + 6 = 66$. So, $330 \div 5 = 66$.

Carlos' Expanded Notation Method This method is like Brianna's Rectangle Sections Method but without the rectangle sections.

g. Write the problem using a standard long-division sign, with the known factor at the left and the product inside.

Teaching Note

Math Background This unit gives students three methods for long division.

Rectangle Sections Method The sections of the rectangle are built up, one section for each place value of the dividend. The process starts with the largest place value and ends with the ones place. The last step adds the section sub-quotients to find the final quotient.

Expanded Notation Method The rectangle drawing is replaced with the long-division bracket. Solving involves building the quotient place value by place value. However, the place-value sub-quotients are stacked one on top of the other with the place values aligned, starting with the largest place value and ending with the ones. The last step adds the sub-quotients to find the final quotient.

Digit-by-Digit Method This is a short version of the Expanded Notation Method. Some students may learn this method without understanding why it works. For this reason, students should be able to relate it to the Rectangle Sections and Expanded Notation methods, both of which show the place values. When students explain this method, they should be able to say the name of the place for each digit in the quotient.

English Language Learners

Write *remainder* on the board. Say: **A *remainder* is what is left over after dividing.** Have students repeat.

h. Ask, "5 times what tens number or multiple of ten gives an answer closest to 330 without going over?" Write 60 above the long-division sign. Multiply: $5 \times 60 = 300$. Write 300 under 330.

i. Subtract: $330 - 300 = 30$.

j. Ask, "5 times what number gives an answer closest to 30 without going over?" Write 6 in the ones place above 60.

k. Multiply: $5 \times 6 = 30$. Write 30 under 30, and subtract. $30 - 30 = 0$, so write 0 below the line.

l. Add: $60 + 6 = 66$. This means $330 \div 5 = 66$.

Activity continued ▶

E-9 Class Activity Name ______ Date ______

► Three Division Methods (Continued)

Michelle's Digit-by-Digit Method

m. $5\overline{)330}$

n. $5\overline{)330}$ with 6 above; − 30

o. $5\overline{)330}$ with 6 above; − 30; 3

p. $5\overline{)330}$ with 6 above; − 30; 30

q. $5\overline{)330}$ with 66 above; − 30; 30

r. $5\overline{)330}$ with 66 above; − 30; 30; − 30; 0

Answer the following questions. Answers will vary.

2. How are their methods alike?

3. How are their methods different?

4. What other methods do you know that could solve this problem?

5. How do the division methods relate to the multiplication methods below?

Rectangle Sections Method

	60 +	6	
5	60 × 5 = 300	5 × 6 = 30	300 + 30 = 330

Expanded Notation Method

66 = 60 + 6
5 = 5
5 × 60 = 300
5 × 6 = 30
330

544 EXTENSION LESSON 9 Find the Unknown Factor

Student Activity Book page 544

Michelle's Digit-by-Digit Method This method is like Carlos' Expanded Notation Method, but it omits the place-holder zeros so that the quotient can be built without adding the place-value parts at the end. Only one or two digits in the product are considered in each step.

m. Write the problem in standard long-division format.

n. Ask, "5 times what number gives an answer closest to 33 without going over?" Write 6 above the second 3 in 33. Multiply: 5 × 6 = 30. Write 30 under 33.

o. Subtract: 33 − 30 = 3.

p. Bring down the ones-place zero from the product, or dividend, to make the number large enough to divide by 5.

q. Ask, "5 times what number gives an answer closest to 30 without going over?" Write 6 above the 0 in 30.

r. Multiply: 5 × 6 = 30. Subtract 30 from 30. The difference is 0, so write 0 below the line.

Compare the Methods Have students discuss problem 2. Point out the following common features:

- build the unknown factor place-by-place, beginning with the largest place
- subtract each partial product from the part of the dividend that is being divided to find out how much remains that still needs to be divided
- write the unknown factor above the product with the place values aligned

Help students see how the solution to 330 ÷ 5 puts together the parts of the 300 ÷ 5 and 30 ÷ 5 problems. The Rectangle Sections Method clearly shows how the parts are used.

Have students discuss problem 3. They should identify the following differences:

- The Rectangle Sections and Expanded Notation methods both show the complete partial product (60), whereas the Digit-by-Digit method only shows the active digit (6), leaving the next smaller place value empty for the next part of the unknown factor.
- The Rectangle Sections and Expanded Notation methods each end by adding the place-value partial products, whereas the Digit-by-Digit Method is a build-as-you-go process that records one digit at a time.

Have students discuss problems 4 and 5 as a class. Encourage all the different methods of division to be explored. As you relate multiplication and division, the focus of the discussion should be on how division builds up the unknown factors of the multiplication place-by-place.

Ongoing Assessment

Have students use any method to find the following answers:

360 ÷ 5

420 ÷ 5

2 Going Further

Differentiated Instruction

Intervention

Activity Card E-9

Visualize Division — Activity Card E-9 

Work: In small groups

Use:

- Base-ten blocks
- Homework and Remembering page 355

1. Choose any problem to solve from your Homework page.
2. Model the division with base-ten blocks to help you find the quotient.
3. Look at the picture below to see how you would use base-ten blocks to divide 330 ÷ 5.
4. Hint You may have to ungroup hundreds into tens and ungroup tens into ones in order to divide into equal groups.

330 ÷ 5

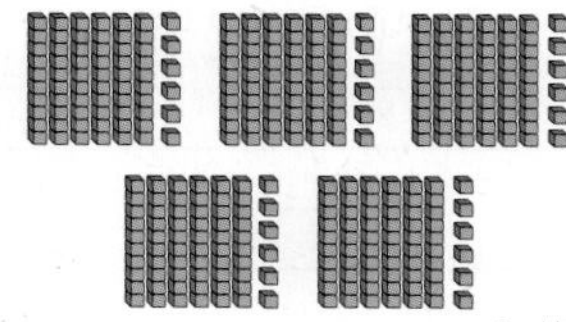

Extension, Lesson 9

Activity Note If you do not have enough base-ten blocks to use with small groups, encourage students to use place value drawings to represent the numbers.

 **Math Writing Prompt**

Justify Your Thinking Which of the three division methods from this lesson do you like best? Explain your choice with examples.

Software Support

Warm Up 13.28

On Level

Activity Card E-9

Check it Out! — Activity Card E-9

Work: In pairs

Use:

- MathBoard materials
- Calculator (optional)

Decide:

Who is Student 1 and who is Student 2.

1. Student 1: Write a division problem for your partner to solve. Make sure your dividend is a three-digit number, ends in 0, and your divisor is a 5.
2. Student 2: Use any method to solve the division problem.
3. Student 1: Check your partner's work with multiplication.
4. Students 1 and 2: Check your operations with a calculator.
5. Switch roles and repeat steps 1-4 again.

330 ÷ 5 = 66
66 × 5 = 330 ✓

Extension, Lesson 9

Activity Note Make sure students solve their problems on paper before using the calculator.

Math Writing Prompt

Make Connections Use the words *total* and *equal groups* to explain how multiplication and division are related.

Software Support

The Number Games: Up, Up, and Array, Level N

Challenge

Activity Card E-9

Real-World Estimation — Activity Card E-9

Work: In small groups

Use:

- blank paper

1. Brainstorm a list of times in which you think you would need to estimate a quotient.

Grocery store: Estimate the price of one item priced at 3 for a certain price.

Road trip: Given the total distance of a multi-day trip, estimate the distance you need to drive each day.

2. Write a word problem related to one of the examples. Make sure your dividend is a three-digit number, ends in 0, and your divisor is a 5.
3. Discuss Exchange papers and try and solve each other's word problems.

Extension, Lesson 9

Activity Note You may want to brainstorm a list collectively and display on chart paper for all groups to use in the activity.

 **Math Writing Prompt**

Write Definitions Write your own definitions for the words *dividend, divisor,* and *quotient.* Explain how these terms relate to *factor* and *product.* Use an example for each definition.

 DESTINATION Math® **Software Support**

Course II: Module 2: Unit 3: Dividing by a 1-digit Number

3 Homework

Goal: Additional Practice

Because you may be using this lesson at any time during the year, no Spiral Review is included. Use this Homework page to provide students with additional practice.

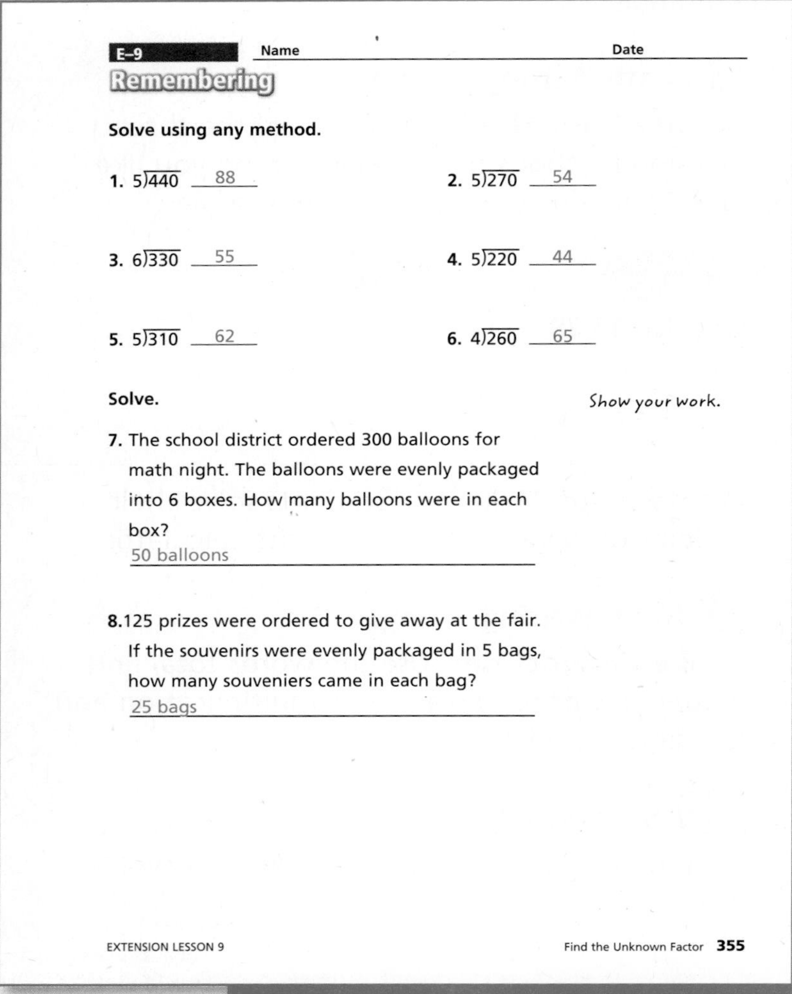

E–9 Remembering Name ______ Date ______

Solve using any method.

1. $5\overline{)440}$ 88
2. $5\overline{)270}$ 54
3. $6\overline{)330}$ 55
4. $5\overline{)220}$ 44
5. $5\overline{)310}$ 62
6. $4\overline{)260}$ 65

Solve. *Show your work.*

7. The school district ordered 300 balloons for math night. The balloons were evenly packaged into 6 boxes. How many balloons were in each box?
50 balloons

8. 125 prizes were ordered to give away at the fair. If the souvenirs were evenly packaged in 5 bags, how many souveniers came in each bag?
25 bags

EXTENSION LESSON 9 Find the Unknown Factor 355

Homework and Remembering page 355

E–9 Homework Name ______ Date ______

9. Explain how to solve this problem.
How many six-packs of juice do you need to have 360 juice boxes?
Draw a picture if you need to.

Accept any method students use to support their answer.
Possible answer: 60 six-packs of juice;
I can find a pattern. Add 60 for every 10 six-packs.
10 six-packs of juice = 60 juice boxes
20 six-packs of juice = 120 juice boxes
30 six-packs of juice = 180 juice boxes
40 six-packs of juice = 240 juice boxes
50 six-packs of juice = 300 juice boxes
60 six-packs of juice = 360 juice boxes

356 EXTENSION LESSON 9 Find the Unknown Factor

Homework and Remembering page 356

Home or School Activity

Language Arts Connection

Explain that the language of mathematics helps us understand a situation. Read this problem.

A car has a height of 72 in. A tricycle's handlebars are $\frac{1}{4}$ as high as the car. How high are the tricycle handlebars? 18 in.

Lead students to divide 72 by 4 to find the height of the handlebars. Have students find other comparisons and write an equation that represents the comparison.

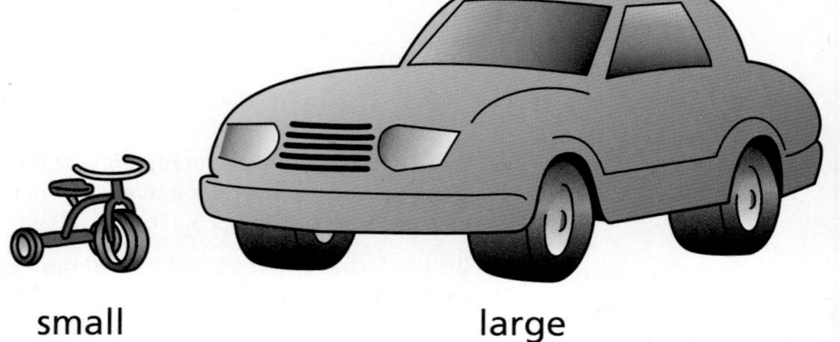

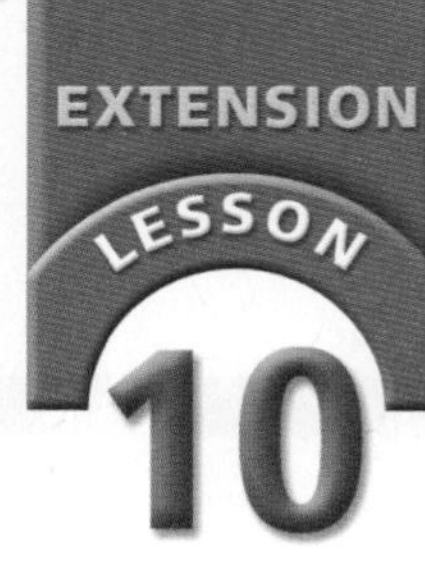

Estimate Products and Quotients

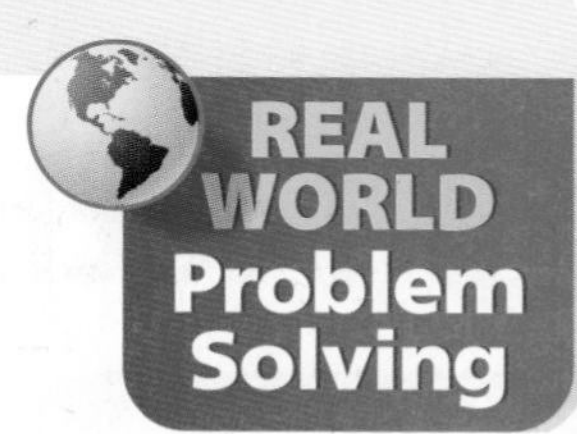

Vocabulary
- estimate
- product
- quotient
- rounding frames
- compatible numbers

Lesson Objectives

- **Use estimation and multiplication with tens to check products and solve real-world problems.**
- **Use various methods to estimate products and quotients.**

The Day at a Glance

Today's Goals	Materials	
1 Teaching the Lesson **A1:** Use the area model to round numbers and estimate products. **A2:** Use basic facts to estimate quotients.	**Lesson Activities** Student Activity Book pp. 545–546 or Student Hardcover Book pp. 545–546 Homework and Remembering pp. 357–358 MathBoard materials Colored pencils or markers (optional)	**Going Further** Activity Cards E-10 Math Journals
2 Going Further ▸ Differentiated Instruction		
3 Homework		

Use Math Talk today!

Keeping Skills Sharp

Quick Practice (5 MINUTES)	Daily Routines
Because you may be using this lesson at any time during the year, no specific Quick Practice is recommended. Use any Quick Practice activity that meets your students' needs.	**Homework Review** Ask students if they had difficulty with any part of the homework. Plan to set aside some time to work with students needing extra help. **Area** Tamara has 20 square feet that she would like to put a fence around. What is the length and width of the rectangle that would have the greatest perimeter? Explain how you found your answer. A rectangle with sides 10 feet by 2 feet; Possible explanation: I drew pictures of rectangles with areas of 20 square feet and added to find which had the greatest perimeter.

1 Teaching the Lesson

Activity 1

Estimate Products

 25 MINUTES

Goal: Use the area model to round numbers and estimate products.

Materials: Student Activity Book or Hardcover Book p. 545, MathBoard materials, colored pencils or markers (optional)

 **NCTM Standards:**
Number and Operations
Communication
Problem Solving

► Round to the Nearest Ten WHOLE CLASS

Write 68 on the Class MathBoard. Have students discuss what they remember about rounding by asking:

- Why do we sometimes round numbers? to make them easier to work with
- What do we do when we round a number to the nearest tens place? decide if the number is closer to the next higher ten or to the next lower ten

Write 70 above and 60 below 68. Underline the tens place to see the place to which we are rounding. Then ask:

70
<u>6</u>8
60

- Which digit tells which way to round? the ones place
- How do we decide which way to round? 5 and more gets changed to the next higher ten; 4 and less gets changed to zero
- What is the value of 68 rounded to the nearest tens place? 70 Circle 70.

70
6<u>8</u>
60

(70)
<u>6</u>8
60

Tell students that rounding can help them estimate products.

On the Class MathBoard, sketch four rectangles with a height of 3 and lengths of 70, 68, 63, and 60, and list the products they represent. Then have students draw these on their MathBoards.

Have students solve 3 × 70 and 3 × 60 first and write these equations in the rectangles. Tell students that the 3 × 70 and 3 × 60 rectangles are *rounding frames* for both 3 × 63 and 3 × 68. These rounding frames show the two tens products that the answers are between.

Next, show the lower rounding frame visually by breaking the 3 × 63 and 3 × 68 rectangles into two parts where one part is the lower frame (a 3 × 60 rectangle). Then extend each rectangle with a dashed line to show the upper frame (a 3 × 70 rectangle). Have students draw these frames on their MathBoard as well. Have them discuss how the products for 63 and 68 are between the product for the lower frame and the product for the upper frame.

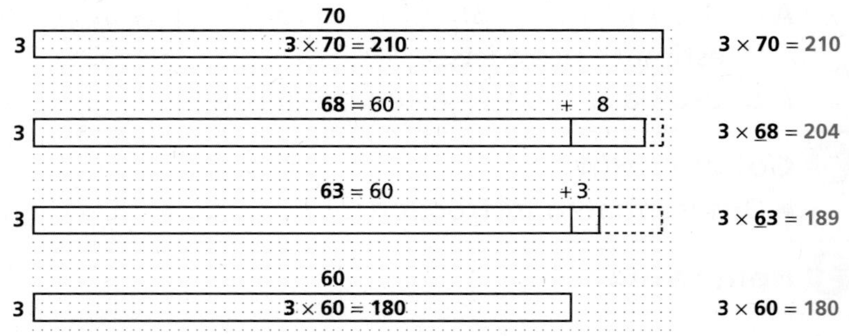

- Compare the 3 × 68 rectangle to the 3 × 70 and the 3 × 60 rectangles. Which one is it closer to? 3 × 70 So is 3 × 68 closer to 180 or 210? 210
- Compare the 3 × 63 rectangle to the 3 × 70 and the 3 × 60 rectangles. Which one is it closer to? 3 × 60 So is 3 × 63 closer to 180 or 210? 180

Have students find the products 3 × 63 and 3 × 68 to check their estimates. Discuss how both answers are between the frames of 180 and 210. Explain that rounding frames can be used to quickly check if an answer makes sense, but now we will just use numerical rounding frames instead of drawing the rectangles.

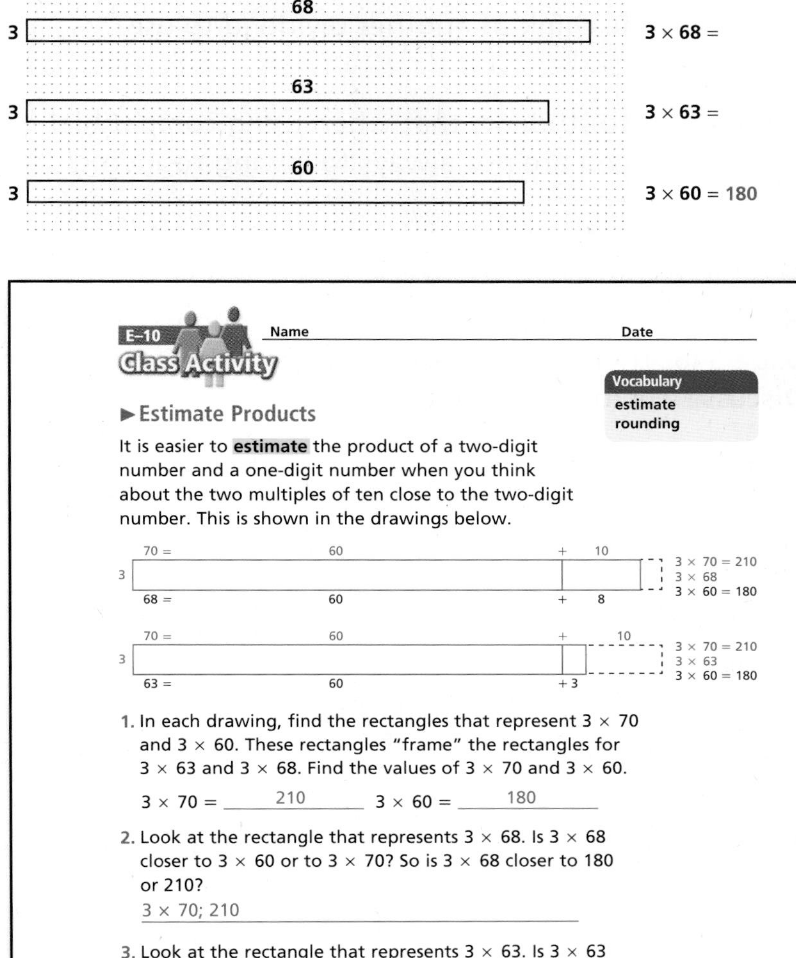

E–10 **Class Activity** Name Date

Vocabulary
estimate
rounding

► **Estimate Products**

It is easier to **estimate** the product of a two-digit number and a one-digit number when you think about the two multiples of ten close to the two-digit number. This is shown in the drawings below.

1. In each drawing, find the rectangles that represent 3 × 70 and 3 × 60. These rectangles "frame" the rectangles for 3 × 63 and 3 × 68. Find the values of 3 × 70 and 3 × 60.

   3 × 70 = 210 3 × 60 = 180

2. Look at the rectangle that represents 3 × 68. Is 3 × 68 closer to 3 × 60 or to 3 × 70? So is 3 × 68 closer to 180 or 210?

   3 × 70; 210

3. Look at the rectangle that represents 3 × 63. Is 3 × 63 closer to 3 × 60 or to 3 × 70? Is 3 × 63 closer to 180 or 210?

   3 × 60; 180

4. Explain how to use **rounding** to estimate the product of a one-digit number and a two-digit number.

   Answers will vary. Possible answer: Round the two-digit number to the nearest ten and multiply by the one-digit number.

EXTENSION LESSON 10 Estimate Products and Quotients **545**

Student Activity Book page 545

► Estimate Products INDIVIDUALS

Have students answer problems 1–4 on Student Book page 545 individually, and then review the answers with the class.

Have students discuss how they use rounding and estimation to check answers to multiplication problems.

Teaching Note

Quick Sketches Encourage students to move from drawing on the dot side of their MathBoards to making quick sketches on the white side. Some students may find it helpful to make sketches as shown. Students could also just show the number labels.

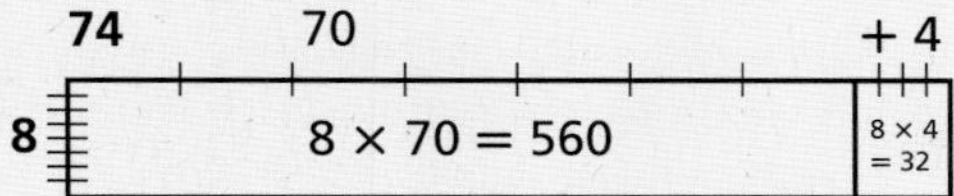

Ongoing Assessment

Have students estimate the following products:

► 42 × 7

► 68 × 3

Alternate Approach

Color Suggest that students use colored pencils or markers to highlight the 3 × 70 and 3 × 60 rounding frames, making them easier to recognize.

English Language Learners

Write 3 × 27, *round,* 3 × 30, and *estimate* on the board.

- **Beginning** Point and say: **We can *round* 27 and then multiply 3 × 30.** Ask: **Is the answer exact?** no **Is it an *estimate?*** yes
- **Intermediate** Say: **I *rounded* 27 to ____.** 30 Ask: **Will the answer be exact or an *estimate?*** estimate
- **Advanced** Ask: **Which number did I *round?*** 27 Say: **The answer won't be exact, it will be an ____.** estimate

Activity 2

Estimate Quotients

25 MINUTES

Goal: Use basic facts to estimate quotients.

Materials: Student Activity Book or Hardcover Book p. 546

NCTM Standards:
Number and Operations
Problem Solving

▶ Use Compatible Numbers to Estimate Real-World Situations WHOLE CLASS

Have students discuss when they may need to estimate quotients in everyday problem-solving situations. Encourage students to give examples of division problems that go along with the situation they describe.

For example:

- Shopping situations
- Driving distances
- Packaging items

Explain to students that when they estimate quotients, it is good to use compatible numbers. Compatible numbers are numbers that are easy to calculate in your head.

Write this example on the board:

$$8\overline{)350}$$

Use the following points to help students with estimation:

- Can you divide this evenly? no
- Which basic fact will help you estimate the quotient? $32 \div 8 = 4$
- Use multiples of tens to find a new dividend that can be easily divided by 8. 350 is close to 320 which can be evenly divided by 8. $320 \div 8 = 40$.
- Can anyone think of another dividend to use? $400 \div 8 = 50$
- Point out to students that when using compatible numbers, you are not always following rounding rules.

▶ Estimate Quotients INDIVIDUALS

Have students solve exercises 5–10 on Student Book page 546. Then have students use the **Solve and Discuss** structure to solve problem 11.

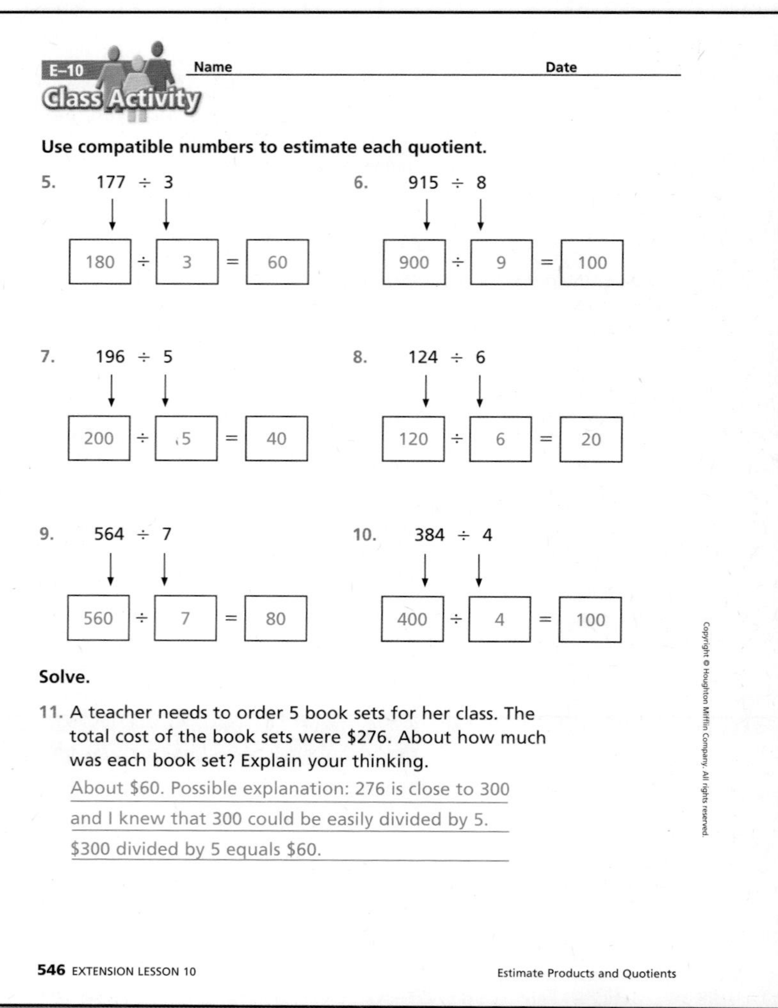
E-10 Class Activity   Name ______ Date ______

Use compatible numbers to estimate each quotient.

5. 177 ÷ 3 → 180 ÷ 3 = 60
6. 915 ÷ 8 → 900 ÷ 9 = 100
7. 196 ÷ 5 → 200 ÷ 5 = 40
8. 124 ÷ 6 → 120 ÷ 6 = 20
9. 564 ÷ 7 → 560 ÷ 7 = 80
10. 384 ÷ 4 → 400 ÷ 4 = 100

Solve.

11. A teacher needs to order 5 book sets for her class. The total cost of the book sets were $276. About how much was each book set? Explain your thinking.
About $60. Possible explanation: 276 is close to 300 and I knew that 300 could be easily divided by 5. $300 divided by 5 equals $60.

546 EXTENSION LESSON 10   Estimate Products and Quotients

Student Activity Book page 546

2 Going Further

Differentiated Instruction

Intervention — Activity Card E-10

Lower and Higher

Activity Card E-10 ●

Work: In pairs

1. Copy the table below. Complete the columns for *Nearest Ten Below* and *Nearest Ten Above*.

Nearest Ten Below	Number	Nearest Ten Above	Rounded Value
50	56	60	60
20	21	30	20
70	78	80	80
60	64	70	60
30	39	40	40

2. Make a rectangle model for each of the numbers in the table. Use the model to round each number. Complete the *Rounded Value* column.

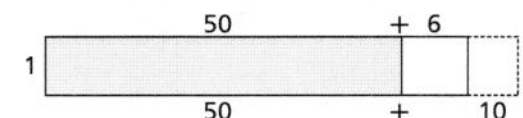

Extension, Lesson 10

Activity Note Ask the students to explain how the rectangle model helps them see how to round the number.

Math Writing Prompt

Explain Your Thinking Would 40 × 7 or 50 × 7 give you a better estimate of 47 × 7? Explain your answer.

Software Support

Warm Up 15.14

On Level — Activity Card E-10

Range of Estimates

Activity Card E-10 ▲

Work: In pairs

1. Look at the multiplication rectangles below.

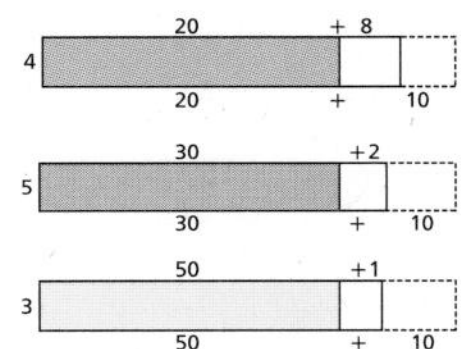

2. **On Your Own** Determine what product each model represents. Then decide what two products will show the range for the estimate. See below.
3. **Discuss** Explain your answers to your partner.

2. 4 × 28, 4 × 20, 4 × 30; 5 × 32, 5 × 30, 5 × 40; 3 × 51, 3 × 50, 3 × 60

Extension, Lesson 10

Activity Note Extend the activity by having students work together to choose multiplications and then draw estimate models for them.

Math Writing Prompt

Use Estimation There are 77 students who each need 3 books. Estimate how many books are needed. Explain whether your estimate is too high or too low.

Software Support

The Number Games: Up, Up, and Array, Level I

Challenge — Activity Card E-10

One-Digit Patterns

Activity Card E-10 ■

Work: On your own

1. The model below shows the difference between 4 × 50 and 4 × 40.

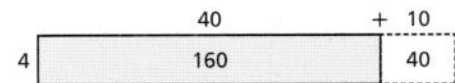

2. Create models to show the difference between each pair of products below.

   3 × 50 and 3 × 40 30

   5 × 50 and 5 × 40 50

3. **Analyze** What patterns do you see in the models? Use the patterns to find three pairs of products that have a difference of 60. Each difference is a multiple of 10 and the one-digit factor.

Extension, Lesson 10

Activity Note Pairs of products, such as 6 × 70 and 6 × 60, have a difference of 60. Challenge students to write products that have a difference that is not a multiple of 10, such as 25. 5 × 60 and 5 × 65

Math Writing Prompt

Write Your Own Write a word problem with an answer that could be estimated as 40 × 6.

Software Support

Course II: Module 4: Unit 1: Number Patterns and Properties

Homework

E–10 Homework **Goal:** Additional Practice

Because you may be using this lesson at any time during the year, no Spiral Review is included. Use this Homework page to provide students with additional practice.

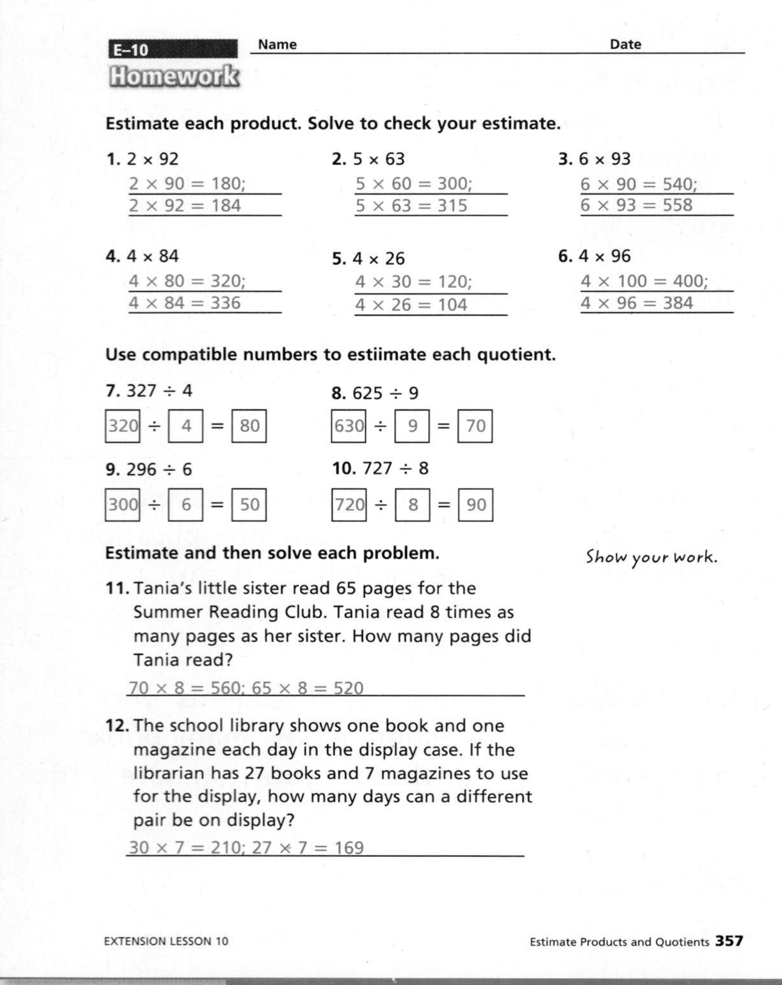

E–10 Homework

Name ____________ Date ____________

Estimate each product. Solve to check your estimate.

1. 2 × 92
$2 \times 90 = 180$;
$2 \times 92 = 184$

2. 5 × 63
$5 \times 60 = 300$;
$5 \times 63 = 315$

3. 6 × 93
$6 \times 90 = 540$;
$6 \times 93 = 558$

4. 4 × 84
$4 \times 80 = 320$;
$4 \times 84 = 336$

5. 4 × 26
$4 \times 30 = 120$;
$4 \times 26 = 104$

6. 4 × 96
$4 \times 100 = 400$;
$4 \times 96 = 384$

Use compatible numbers to estiimate each quotient.

7. 327 ÷ 4
320 ÷ 4 = 80

8. 625 ÷ 9
630 ÷ 9 = 70

9. 296 ÷ 6
300 ÷ 6 = 50

10. 727 ÷ 8
720 ÷ 8 = 90

Estimate and then solve each problem.

Show your work.

11. Tania's little sister read 65 pages for the Summer Reading Club. Tania read 8 times as many pages as her sister. How many pages did Tania read?
$70 \times 8 = 560$; $65 \times 8 = 520$

12. The school library shows one book and one magazine each day in the display case. If the librarian has 27 books and 7 magazines to use for the display, how many days can a different pair be on display?
$30 \times 7 = 210$; $27 \times 7 = 169$

EXTENSION LESSON 10 Estimate Products and Quotients **357**

Homework and Remembering page 357

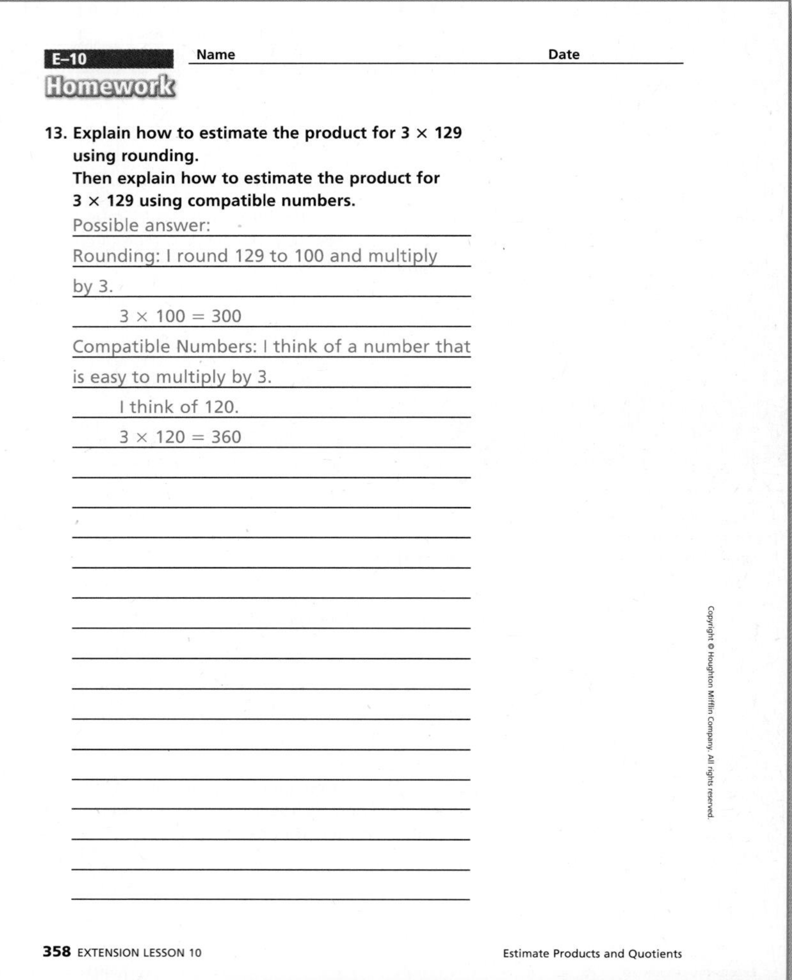

E–10 Homework

Name ____________ Date ____________

13. Explain how to estimate the product for 3 × 129 using rounding.
Then explain how to estimate the product for 3 × 129 using compatible numbers.

Possible answer:
Rounding: I round 129 to 100 and multiply by 3.
$3 \times 100 = 300$
Compatible Numbers: I think of a number that is easy to multiply by 3.
I think of 120.
$3 \times 120 = 360$

358 EXTENSION LESSON 10 Estimate Products and Quotients

Homework and Remembering page 358

Home or School Activity

Math-to-Math Connection

Consumer Math Estimating can be a useful tool when shopping. Have students select an item in a newspaper ad or catalog that they want to buy. Have them estimate the cost of purchasing three of these items. Then have them calculate the exact price.

Different Ways to Solve a Problem

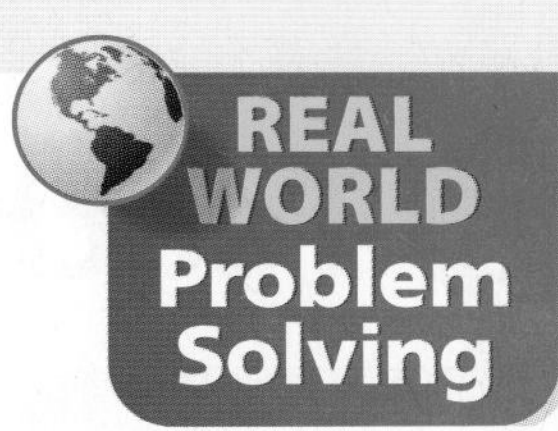

Lesson Objectives

- **Model repeated addition and subtraction.**
- **Choose the operation to use to solve a world problem.**
- **Compare methods and find the most efficient method to choose.**

The Day at a Glance

Today's Goals	Materials	
1 Teaching the Lesson **A1:** Decide which operation to use to solve a word problem and decide which method is most efficient. **2 Going Further** ► Differentiated Instruction **3 Homework**	**Lesson Activities** Student Activity Book pp. 547–548 or Student Hardcover Book pp. 547–548 Homework and Remembering pages 359–360 MathBoard materials	**Going Further** Activity Cards E-11 Game Cards (TRB M25) Two-color counters Hundred Chart (TRB M34) Number Cubes Mathboard materials Math Journals

Use Math Talk today!

Keeping Skills Sharp

Quick Practice (5 MINUTES)	Daily Routines
Because you may be using this lesson at any time during the year, no specific Quick Practice is recommended. Use any Quick Practice activity that meets your students' needs.	**Homework Review** Ask students to place their homework at the corner of their desks. As you circulate during the Quick Practice, check that students completed the assignment, and see whether any problem caused difficulty for many students. **Strategy Problem** Jack created an art piece using marbles. The first row of the art piece has 1 marble. The second row has 3 marbles. The third row has 6 marbles. The fourth row has 10 marbles. If the pattern continues, how many marbles will be in the eighth row? Explain. 36 marbles

1 Teaching the Lesson

Activity 1

Choose the Operation

 **55 MINUTES**

Goal: Decide which operation to use to solve a word problem and decide which method is most efficient.

Materials: Student Activity Book and Hardcover Book pp. 547–548, MathBoard materials

 **NCTM Standards:**
Number and Operations
Problem Solving
Connections

▶ Model Multiplication WHOLE CLASS

Review with students the different ways to model multiplication with this word problem. Write the following on the board:

Kim has 3 strips of stickers. There are 5 stickers on each strip. How many stickers does Kim have in all? 15 stickers

Have students solve this problem on their MathBoards. Circulate around the room, looking for different methods. Have volunteers share their thinking with the class. Make sure the following methods are shown:

Equal Groups

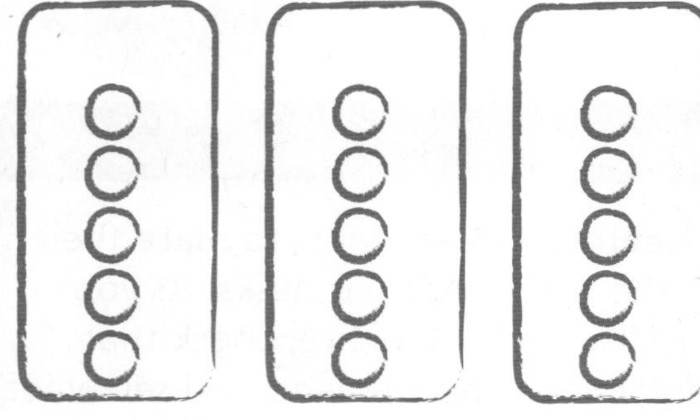

Repeated Addition
$5 + 5 + 5 = 15$

Multiplication
$3 \times 5 = 15$ or $5 \times 3 = 15$

Math Talk

Discuss with students which method they liked using most and have them explain why. Also have them discuss which method is the most efficient, or quickest, to use.

▶ Model Division WHOLE CLASS

Review with students the different ways to model division with this word problem. Write the following on the board:

Alvin brought 15 peaches home. He divided them equally into 5 paper bags. How many peaches did he put in each bag? 3 peaches

Have students solve this problem on their MathBoards. Circulate around the room, looking for different methods. Have volunteers share their thinking with the class. Make sure the following methods are shown:

Equal Groups

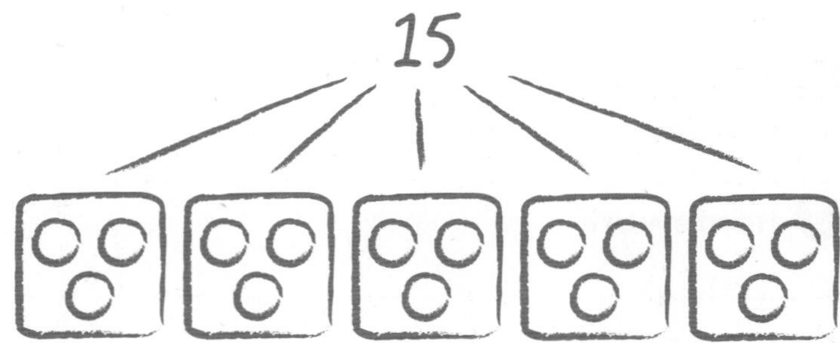

Repeated Subtraction
$15 - 5 = 10$

$10 - 5 = 5$

$5 - 5 = 0$

Division
$\frac{15}{5}$ is 3 or $15 \div 5 = 3$ or $5\overline{)15}$ is 3

Math Talk

Discuss with students which method they liked using most and have them explain why. Also have them discuss which method is the most efficient, or quickest, to use.

▶ The Puzzled Penguin INDIVIDUALS

Have a volunteer read aloud the Puzzled Penguin problem. Then have students solve exercise 1 independently on Student Activity Book page 547 and have volunteers share their explanations.

Once explanations have been shared, encourage students to complete the rest of the page on their own. Then discuss the results as a class and have students share their drawings for exercise 2.

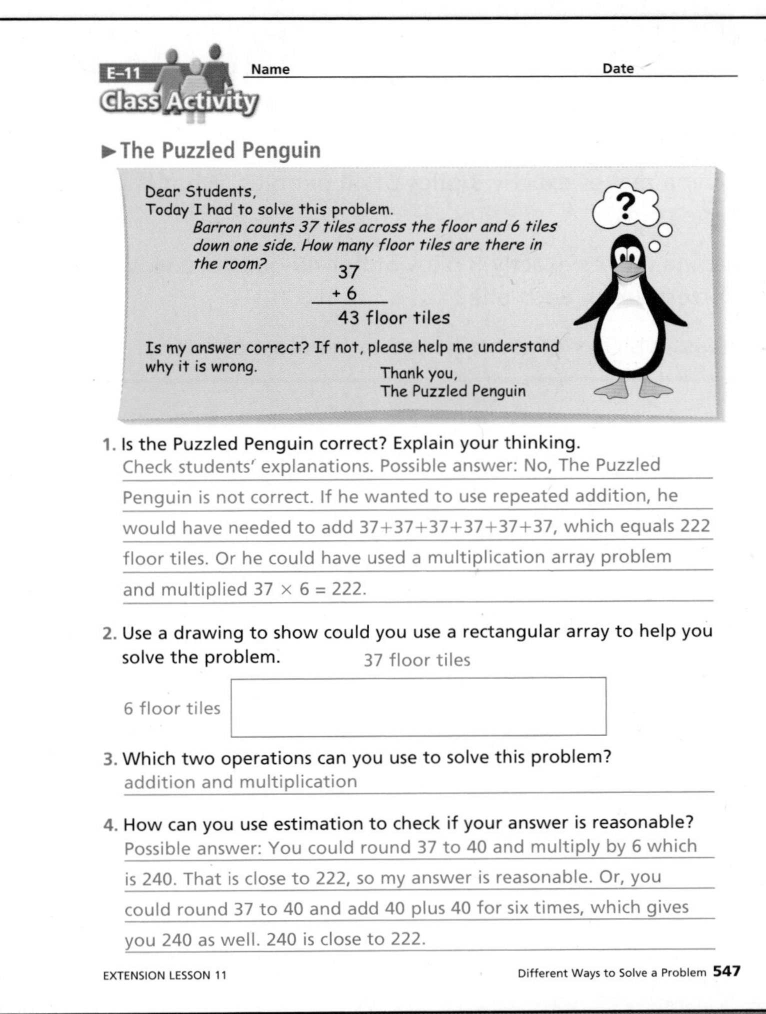

E-11 Class Activity Name Date

▶ The Puzzled Penguin

Dear Students,
Today I had to solve this problem.
Barron counts 37 tiles across the floor and 6 tiles down one side. How many floor tiles are there in the room?

$$\begin{array}{r} 37 \\ +\ 6 \\ \hline 43 \end{array}$$ floor tiles

Is my answer correct? If not, please help me understand why it is wrong.
Thank you,
The Puzzled Penguin

1. Is the Puzzled Penguin correct? Explain your thinking.
Check students' explanations. Possible answer: No, The Puzzled Penguin is not correct. If he wanted to use repeated addition, he would have needed to add 37+37+37+37+37+37, which equals 222 floor tiles. Or he could have used a multiplication array problem and multiplied 37 × 6 = 222.

2. Use a drawing to show could you use a rectangular array to help you solve the problem.
37 floor tiles
6 floor tiles

3. Which two operations can you use to solve this problem?
addition and multiplication

4. How can you use estimation to check if your answer is reasonable?
Possible answer: You could round 37 to 40 and multiply by 6 which is 240. That is close to 222, so my answer is reasonable. Or, you could round 37 to 40 and add 40 plus 40 for six times, which gives you 240 as well. 240 is close to 222.

EXTENSION LESSON 11 Different Ways to Solve a Problem 547

Student Activity Book page 547

Math Talk

Encourage students to also discuss whether they think repeated addition or multiplication is the most efficient way to solve the problem. Most students should see that multiplication is quicker, but repeated addition is an effective method to use if they cannot figure out how to multiply correctly.

English Language Learners

Write *efficient* on the board. Model a calculator. Say: **I have to do a lot of addition and multiplication.**

- **Beginning** Say: **A calculator is fast and correct. It is *efficient.*** Have students repeat.
- **Intermediate** Ask: **Which is faster, a calculator or solving on paper?** calculator **Which is more *efficient?*** calculator
- **Advanced** Have students tell the difference between using a calculator or solving on paper.

Activity continued ▶

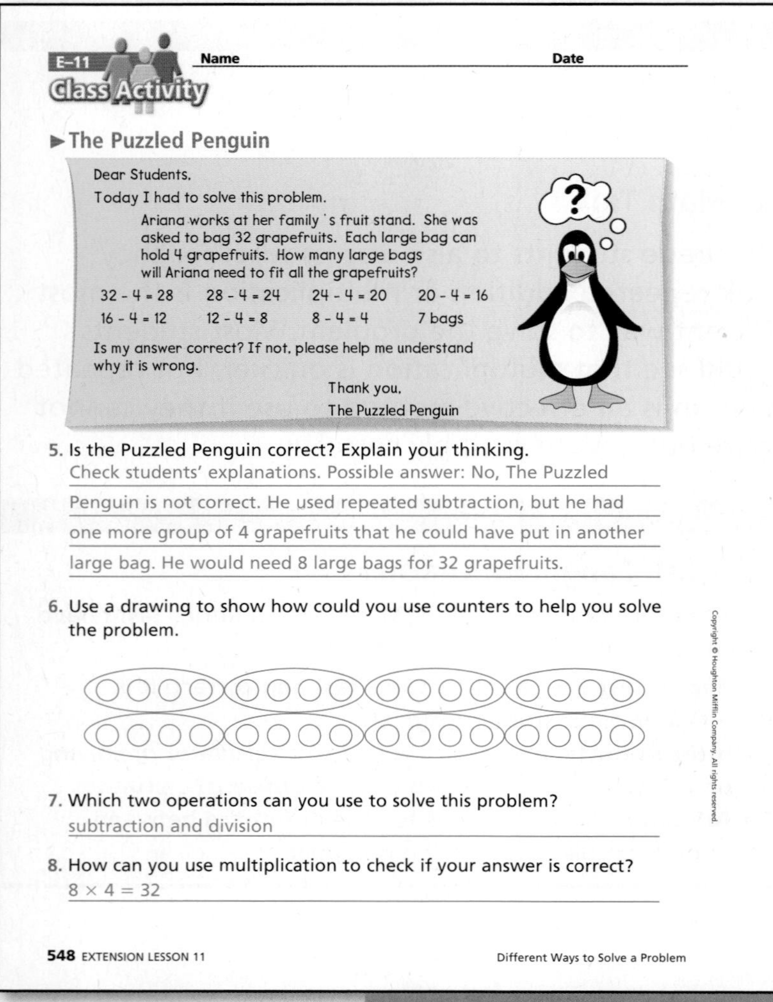
E-11 Class Activity

Name ______ Date ______

▶ The Puzzled Penguin

Dear Students,

Today I had to solve this problem.

Ariana works at her family's fruit stand. She was asked to bag 32 grapefruits. Each large bag can hold 4 grapefruits. How many large bags will Ariana need to fit all the grapefruits?

32 - 4 = 28   28 - 4 = 24   24 - 4 = 20   20 - 4 = 16

16 - 4 = 12   12 - 4 = 8   8 - 4 = 4   7 bags

Is my answer correct? If not, please help me understand why it is wrong.

Thank you,

The Puzzled Penguin

5. Is the Puzzled Penguin correct? Explain your thinking.
Check students' explanations. Possible answer: No, The Puzzled Penguin is not correct. He used repeated subtraction, but he had one more group of 4 grapefruits that he could have put in another large bag. He would need 8 large bags for 32 grapefruits.

6. Use a drawing to show how could you use counters to help you solve the problem.

7. Which two operations can you use to solve this problem?
subtraction and division

8. How can you use multiplication to check if your answer is correct?
$8 \times 4 = 32$

Copyright © Houghton Mifflin Company. All rights reserved.

548 EXTENSION LESSON 11   Different Ways to Solve a Problem

Student Activity Book page 548

▶ The Puzzled Penguin INDIVIDUALS

Have a volunteer read aloud the Puzzled Penguin problem. Then have students solve exercise 5 independently on Student Book page 548 and have volunteers share their explanations.

Once explanations have been shared, encourage students to complete the rest of the page on their own. Then discuss the results as a class and have students share their drawings for exercise 6.

▶ Create Your Own Word Problems

PAIRS

As time allows, have pairs of students write their own word problems for their partners to solve. Students should discuss their answers and discuss the methods and operations used to solve the word problems. Encourage students to continually discuss which method they think is the most efficient to use.

Math Talk

Encourage students to also discuss whether they think repeated subtraction or division is the most efficient way to solve the problem. Most students should see that division is quicker, but repeated subtraction is an effective method to use if they cannot figure out how to divide correctly. When students are dealing with division situations that have left-overs or remainders, repeated subtraction clearly shows how many are left over as well.

Ongoing Assessment

Have students solve these word problems using any operation they choose.

Rachina makes exactly 3 piles of 40 pennies. What is the value of the coins?

Rachina makes exactly 8 piles of her 40 quarters. How may quarters are in each pile?

Discuss which methods seemed to be most efficient.

2 Going Further

Differentiated Instruction

Intervention Activity Card E-11

Compare 2 and 5

Activity Card E-11

Work: In pairs

Use:

- 2 number cubes (labeled 1-6)
- MathBoard materials
- Two-color counters

Decide:

Who is Student 1 and who is Student 2.

1. **Student 1:** Roll both number cubes to create a two-digit number. That is your dividend (for example 16).
2. **Student 2:** You divide that number by 2. You can use counters, division, or repeated subtraction to help you solve. (for example $16 \div 2 = 8$)
3. **Student 1:** You divide that number by 5. You can use counters, division, or repeated subtraction to help you solve. $16 \div 5$ is 3 with one left over.
4. If your problem can be divided evenly, you get a point.
5. Switch roles and continue steps 1–4 for five turns. The student with more points wins!

2) 16

Extension, Lesson 11

Activity Note You may want to encourage students to model repeated subtraction on a number line.

Math Writing Prompt

Explain Your Thinking Susan had a box of muffins with 4 rows of 6 muffins. Explain how to use repeated addition and multiplication to describe how many muffins were in the box.

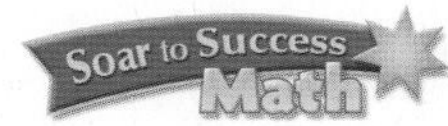

Software Support

Warm Up 13.10

On Level Activity Card E-11

Product Derby

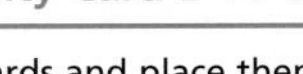

Activity Card E-11

Work: In pairs

Use:

- Two sets of TRB M25 (Game Cards)
- Two-color counters
- TRB M34 (Hundred Chart)

Decide:

Who is Student 1 (red counter) and who is Student 2 (yellow counter).

1. **Student 1:** Shuffle each set of Game Cards and place them face down in two piles.
2. **Student 2:** Turn over the top two cards and multiply the numbers (for example, $6 \times 3 = 18$). Use repeated addition or multiplication to solve. If the product is available on the Hundred Chart, cover the number with your color counter.
3. **Student 1:** Turn over the next two cards and multiply the numbers (for example, $5 \times 5 = 25$). Cover the product number. If the product is already covered, play continues with the next player.
4. Continue until all cards have been used. The player with more counters on the board wins!

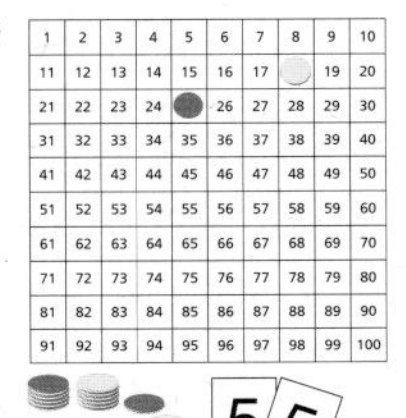

1	2	3	4	5	6	7	8	9	10
11	12	13	14	15	16	17		19	20
21	22	23	24		26	27	28	29	30
31	32	33	34	35	36	37	38	39	40
41	42	43	44	45	46	47	48	49	50
51	52	53	54	55	56	57	58	59	60
61	62	63	64	65	66	67	68	69	70
71	72	73	74	75	76	77	78	79	80
81	82	83	84	85	86	87	88	89	90
91	92	93	94	95	96	97	98	99	100

Extension, Lesson 11

Activity Note Provide students with the Hundred Chart (TRB M34).

Math Writing Prompt

You Decide When solving word problems, explain which method you like to use: repeated addition, repeated subtraction, multiplication, or division.

Software Support

Fraction Action: Number Line Mine, Level D

Challenge Activity Card E-11

Product or Quotient Derby

Activity Card E-11

Work: In pairs

Use:

- Two sets of TRB M25 (Game Cards)
- Two-color counters
- TRB M34 (Hundred Chart)

Decide:

Who is Student 1 (red counter) and who is Student 2 (yellow counter).

1. **Student 1:** Shuffle each set of Game Cards and place them face down in two piles.
2. **Student 2:** Turn over the top two cards and multiply or divide the numbers (for example, $6 \times 3 = 18$ or $6 \div 3 = 2$). If the product or the quotient is available on the Hundred Chart, cover the number with your color counter.
3. **Student 1:** Turn over the next two cards. Repeat the above steps. If the product or quotient is already covered, play continues with your partner.
4. Continue until all cards have been used. The player with more counters on the board wins!

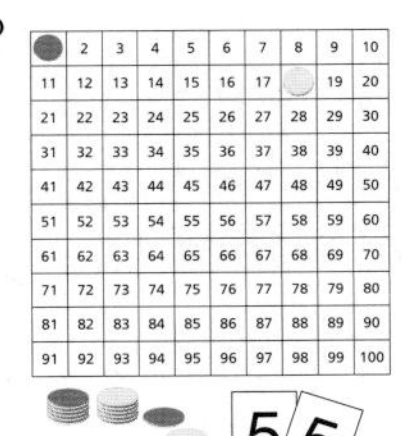

	2	3	4	5	6	7	8	9	10
11	12	13	14	15	16	17		19	20
21	22	23	24	25	26	27	28	29	30
31	32	33	34	35	36	37	38	39	40
41	42	43	44	45	46	47	48	49	50
51	52	53	54	55	56	57	58	59	60
61	62	63	64	65	66	67	68	69	70
71	72	73	74	75	76	77	78	79	80
81	82	83	84	85	86	87	88	89	90
91	92	93	94	95	96	97	98	99	100

Extension, Lesson 11

Activity Note Provide students with the Hundred Chart (TRB M34).

Math Writing Prompt

More Than One Way There are 24 students in Ms. Santiago's class. Ms. Santiago wants the students to work on a group project. Describe the number of possible groups that can be formed and how many students would be in each group.

DESTINATION Math® **Software Support**

Course II: Module 2: Unit 3: Meaning of Division

3 Homework

Goal: Additional Practice

Because you may be using this lesson at any time during the year, no Spiral Review is included. Use this Homework page to provide students with additional practice.

E-11 Homework

Name ____ Date ____

Solve using any method.

Show your work. Check students' work.

1. Jude had a package of 25 pencils. He bundled them in 5 groups with a rubber band. How many pencils were in each group? 5 pencils

2. Beverly had 6 vases of flowers. Each vase had 13 flowers in it. How many flowers did she have in all? 78 flowers

3. Hector needs to count how many floor tiles there are in his bathroom. He counts 19 rows of tiles going across and 8 tiles going down one side. How many tiles does he have? 152 floor tiles

Show how to solve problems 1-3 in another way.

Answers will vary. Possible answers shown.

4. 25 − 5 = 20 − 5 = 15 − 5 = 10 − 5 = 5 − 5 = 0

5. 13 × 6 = 78

6. 20 × 8 = 160 − 8 = 152

7. Write and solve your own word problem.

Check student's work.

8. Show how to solve problem 7 in another way.

Check student's work.

EXTENSION LESSON 11 Different Ways to Solve Problems 359

Homework and Remembering page 359

E-11 Homework

Name ____ Date ____

9. Explain how multiplication and division are related.

Possible answer: I can write related multiplication and division equations using the same numbers. One operation undoes the other.

3 × 4 = 12; 12 ÷ 4 = 3

This shows that multiplication and division are related.

360 EXTENSION LESSON 11 Different Ways to Solve Problems

Homework and Remembering page 360

Home or School Activity

Real World Connection

Change a Recipe Discuss with students how a recipe tells how much of each ingredient is needed. Sometimes you might want to double or even triple a recipe. The recipe for one Lime Pie is shown. Have students determine how much of each ingredient they would need to make 3 pies. Have students explain whether they think it would be most efficient to use repeated addition or multiplication to triple the recipe.

Lime Pie

8 ounces cream cheese, softened
1 can sweetened condensed milk
6 ounces limeade concentrate
4 drops green food coloring
8 ounces frozen whipped topping
1 graham cracker crust
1 kiwifruit, peeled and sliced

Line Graphs

Lesson Objectives

- **Analyze function tables and recognize and describe change in quantities.**
- **Represent change over time using a line graph.**

Vocabulary
function table
line graph

The Day at a Glance

Today's Goals	Materials	
1 Teaching the Lesson **A1:** Recognize and describe change in quantities. **A2:** Represent change over time with a line graph.	**Lesson Activities** Student Activity Book pp. 549–550 or Student Hardcover Book pp. 549–550 Homework and Remembering pp. 361–362 Chart paper (optional) Ruler	**Going Further** Activity Cards E-12 Centimeter Grid Paper (TRB M31) Rulers Colored pencils or markers Math Journals
2 Going Further ▸ Differentiated Instruction		
3 Homework		

Use Math Talk today!

Keeping Skills Sharp

Quick Practice (5 MINUTES)	Daily Routines
Because you may be using this lesson at any time during the year, no specific Quick Practice is recommended. Use any Quick Practice activity that meets your students' needs.	**Homework Review** Have students discuss and help each other solve the difficulties and errors from their homework. **Estimation** Each letter Dahlia is mailing needs 7 stamps. How many letters can be mailed if she has 59 stamps? Explain your answer. 8 letters; $7 \times 8 = 56$; So, Dahlia will have 3 stamps left over.

1 Teaching the Lesson

Activity 1

Function Tables

 30 MINUTES

Goal: Recognize and describe change in quantities.

Materials: Student Activity Book and Hardcover Book p. 549

 **NCTM Standards:**
Number and Operations
Algebra
Problem Solving
Data Analysis and Probability

Ask for Ideas Elicit as much information from students as to what they know and remember about function tables. Encourage them to use examples as they are describing what a function table is. At this point, it is okay if students describe a function table that does not represent data changing over time.

For example, students may describe this, which is okay for this part of the activity.

Number of Tricycles	Number of Wheels
1	3
2	6
3	9
4	12

E–12 Class Activity Name Date

▶ Explore Change Over Time

Look at the function table and answer the questions.

Money in Savings Account

Week	Amount of Money
1	\$210
2	\$225
3	\$240
4	\$255
5	\$270

1. What information does this function table show you?
Possible answer: This function table shows the amount of money in a savings account.

2. How does the money amount change in the savings account from week to week?
it increases by \$15.00

3. Predict how much money there would be in the savings account after week 10.
\$345

4. Explain how you found the answer to exercise 3.
Possible explanation. I added 15 dollars to week 5's total which was 270 + 15 = 285 (Week 6). Then I added 285 + 15 = 300 (Week 7). Then I added 300 +15 = 315 (Week 8). Next I added 315 + 15 = 330 (Week 9). Finally I added 330 + 15 = 345 (Week 10).

5. Do you think the same pattern and function rule will continue over time? Explain.
Check students' explanations.

EXTENSION LESSON 12 Line Graphs 549

Student Activity Book page 549

▶ Explore Change Over Time

WHOLE CLASS

Now, show students how data showing change over time can be displayed in a function table. Direct students' attention to the top of Student Activity Book page 549.

Work together through exercises 1–5 and discuss students' thinking.

English Language Learners

Draw a *function table* on the board showing a tree's growth over time.

- **Beginning** Ask: **Does the tree grow every year?** yes **Does the *function table* show how much the tree grows?** yes
- **Intermediate** Say: **This *function table* shows the relationship of change over __.** time
- **Advanced** Have students tell about the relationship shown in the *function table.*

Activity 2

Line Graphs

 30 MINUTES

Goal: Represent change over time with a line graph.

Materials: Student Activity Book and Hardcover Book p. 550, chart paper (optional), ruler

 **NCTM Standards:**

Number and Operations
Measurement
Problem Solving
Data Analysis and Probability

Teaching Note

Math Background A line graph is a graph that uses points connected by a straight or broken line to show changes in data over time.

Ask for Ideas Remind students about the different ways to display data. Ask students to describe what type of data can be displayed in a line graph. Make a list of their ideas on the board or on chart paper. See data examples here:

Plant height changing over time

Temperature changes

Value of money changing over time

Weight change over time

▶ Explore Data Displays WHOLE CLASS

You may want to use this example to point out how similar data can sometimes be displayed in a line graph, while other times it cannot.

Write the following on the board:

Over the course of the week, Barbara drove a total of 200 miles. Rashid drove 300 miles, and Betsy drove 150 miles.

Now write this on the board:

The temperature was 3° F at 11 A.M. It increased 3° every hour until 3 P.M.

 **Math Talk**

Ask students the following questions:

- Which example of data could be displayed in a line graph? the second example because it's showing change (degrees) over time (hours)
- What type of graph could you use to display the data in the first example? bar graph
- Predict what the line graph would look like in Example 2. Would it have a steady increase, decrease? The line graph would begin at 3° and have a constant increase of 3° every hour until 3 P.M.

Activity continued ▶

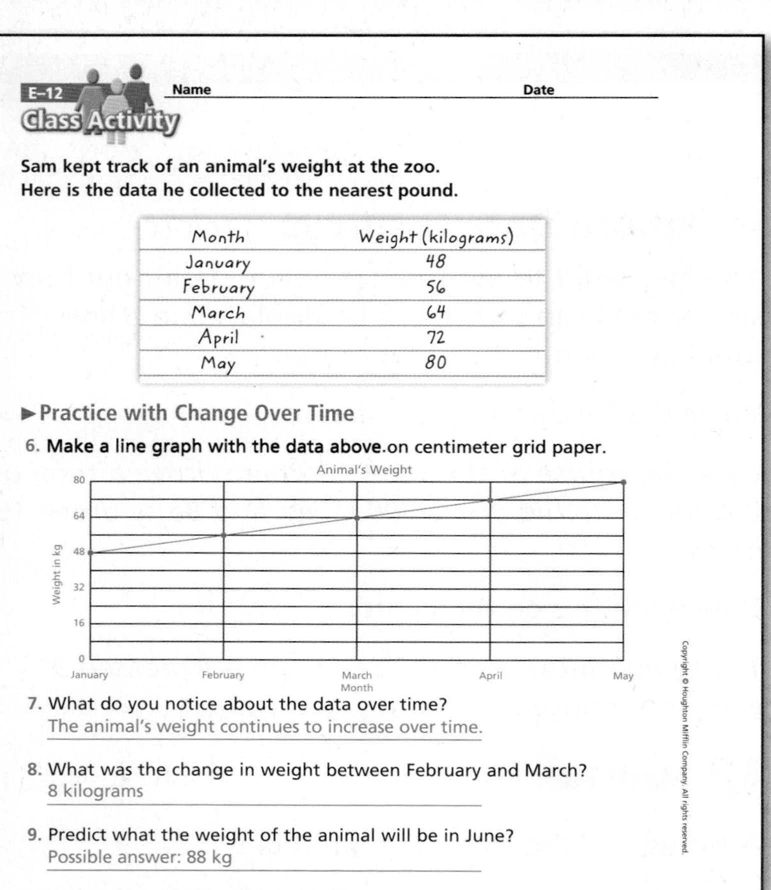

E-12 Class Activity

Name Date

Sam kept track of an animal's weight at the zoo.
Here is the data he collected to the nearest pound.

Month	Weight (kilograms)
January	48
February	56
March	64
April	72
May	80

► Practice with Change Over Time

6. Make a line graph with the data above.on centimeter grid paper.

7. What do you notice about the data over time?
The animal's weight continues to increase over time.

8. What was the change in weight between February and March?
8 kilograms

9. Predict what the weight of the animal will be in June?
Possible answer: 88 kg

10. Explain your thinking for exercise 9.
Possible answer: I predicted the animal's weight would increase since every month before then, the weight increased by about 8 kilograms.

550 EXTENSION LESSON 12 Line Graphs

Student Activity Book page 550

► Practice with Change Over Time

INDIVIDUALS

Direct students' attention to Student Book page 550 and have them independently complete exercises 6–10.

 Math Talk

Once students have completed the page, have volunteers share the results with the class.

Challenge students to describe the data display and make predictions about future data.

 Ongoing Assessment

Draw this table on the board.

Plant	Growth
week 1	3 cm
week 2	4 cm
week 3	2 cm
week 4	5 cm

Ask students to explain how to display this data on a line graph.

2 Going Further

Differentiated Instruction

Intervention

Activity Card E-12

Graph It! Activity Card E-12 ●

Work: On your own

Use:

- TRB M31 (Centimeter Grid Paper)
- Rulers

1. Look at the data about New York City temperatures.
2. Show this data in a line graph.
3. Don't forget to give your graph a title, labels, and a scale.

Temperatures in NY City	
Day	Temperature
1	43° F
2	53° F
3	50° F
4	57° F
5	59° F
6	67° F

Extension, Lesson 12

Activity Note Distribute the Centimeter Grid Paper (TRB M31) to students.

Math Writing Prompt

Make a List Use a list to describe the data that would be best shown on a line graph.

Software Support

Warm Up 58.02

On Level

Activity Card E-12

Change the Scale  Activity Card E-12 ▲

Work: On your own

Use:

- TRB M31 (Centimeter Grid Paper)
- Rulers

1. Look at the data about Deer Population.
2. Remake the line graph, but use an interval of 100,000 on the scale instead of 200,000.
3. **Analyze** Compare the two graphs and analyze if the data looks different or the same.

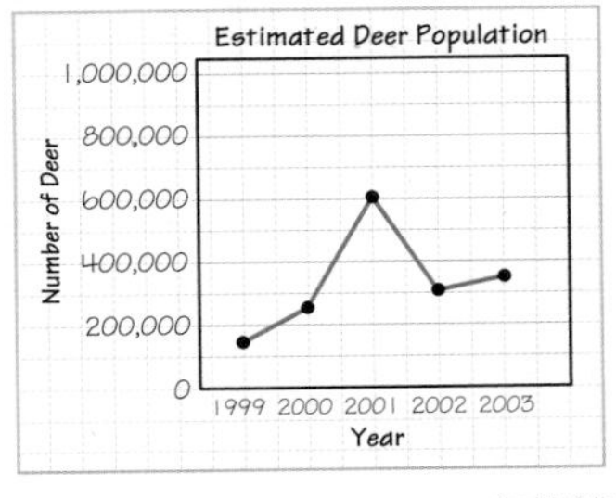

Extension, Lesson 12

Activity Note Distribute the Centimeter Grid Paper (TRB M31) to students.

Math Writing Prompt

Explain Your Thinking Explain how you would choose a scale for a line graph. Use an example.

Software Support

Country Countdown: White Water Graphing, Level K

Challenge

Activity Card E-12

Misleading Line Graph Activity Card E-12 ■

Work: In pairs

Use:

- TRB M31 (Centimeter Grid Paper)
- Rulers
- Colored pencils or markers

1. Look at the data below.
2. Identify three errors on the line graph that make it look misleading. See below for answer.
3. Make a correct version of the graph so it's not misleading.

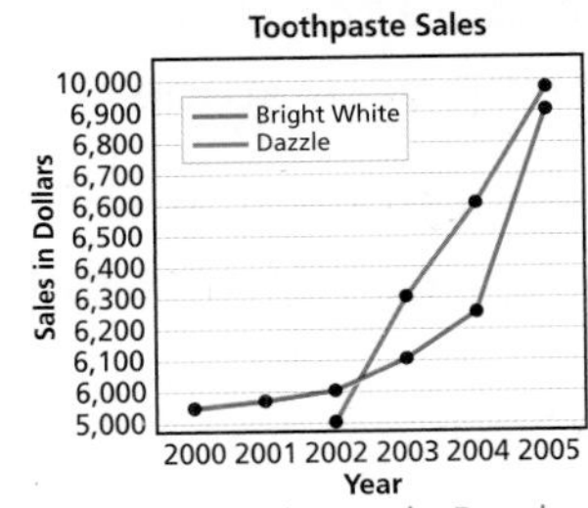

2. Scale doesn't have same intervals; Dazzle doesn't have data in 2000 and in 2001; the scale doesn't start at 0

Extension, Lesson 12

Activity Note You may want to quickly introduce the purpose of a double line graph, and make sure students see the purpose in displaying two sets of data on the line graph.

Math Writing Prompt

Collect Data Pretend you have collected data about the growth of a plant. Create a line graph that could possibly display the data over time.

Software Support

Course II: Module 3: Unit 1: Area

3 Homework

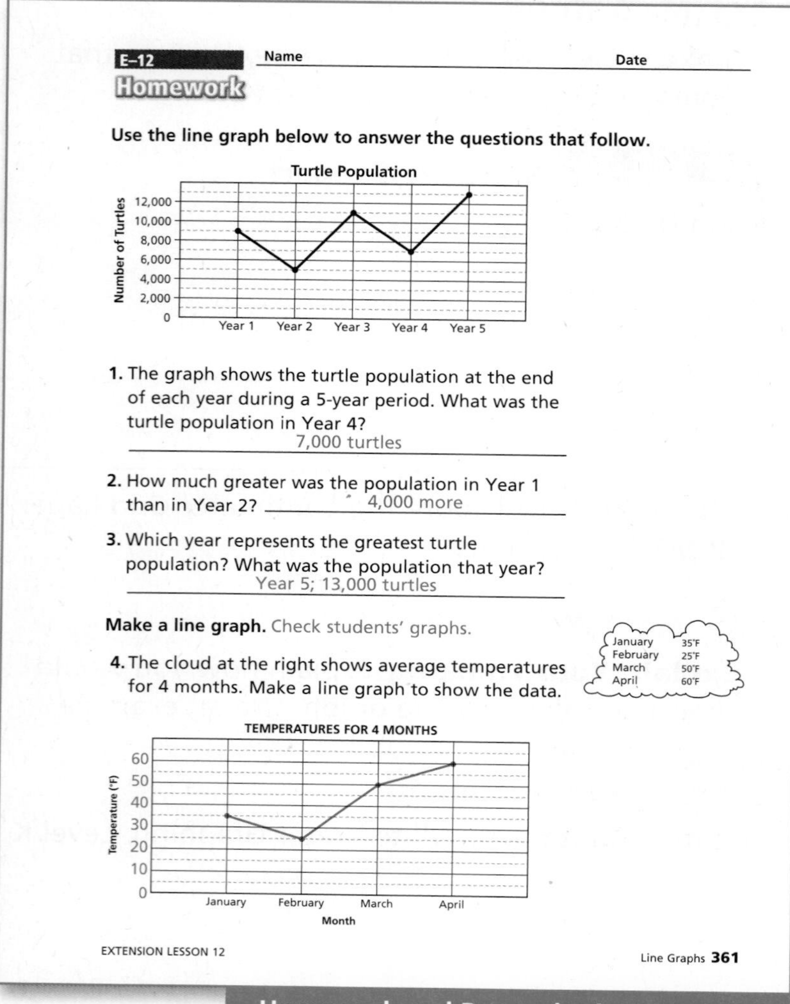

E–12 Homework **Goal:** Additional Practice

Because you may be using this lesson at any time during the year, no Spiral Review is included. Use this Homework page to provide students with additional practice.

Name Date

E-12 Homework

Use the line graph below to answer the questions that follow.

1. The graph shows the turtle population at the end of each year during a 5-year period. What was the turtle population in Year 4? 7,000 turtles
2. How much greater was the population in Year 1 than in Year 2? 4,000 more
3. Which year represents the greatest turtle population? What was the population that year? Year 5; 13,000 turtles

Make a line graph. Check students' graphs.

4. The cloud at the right shows average temperatures for 4 months. Make a line graph to show the data.

EXTENSION LESSON 12 Line Graphs 361

Homework and Remembering page 361

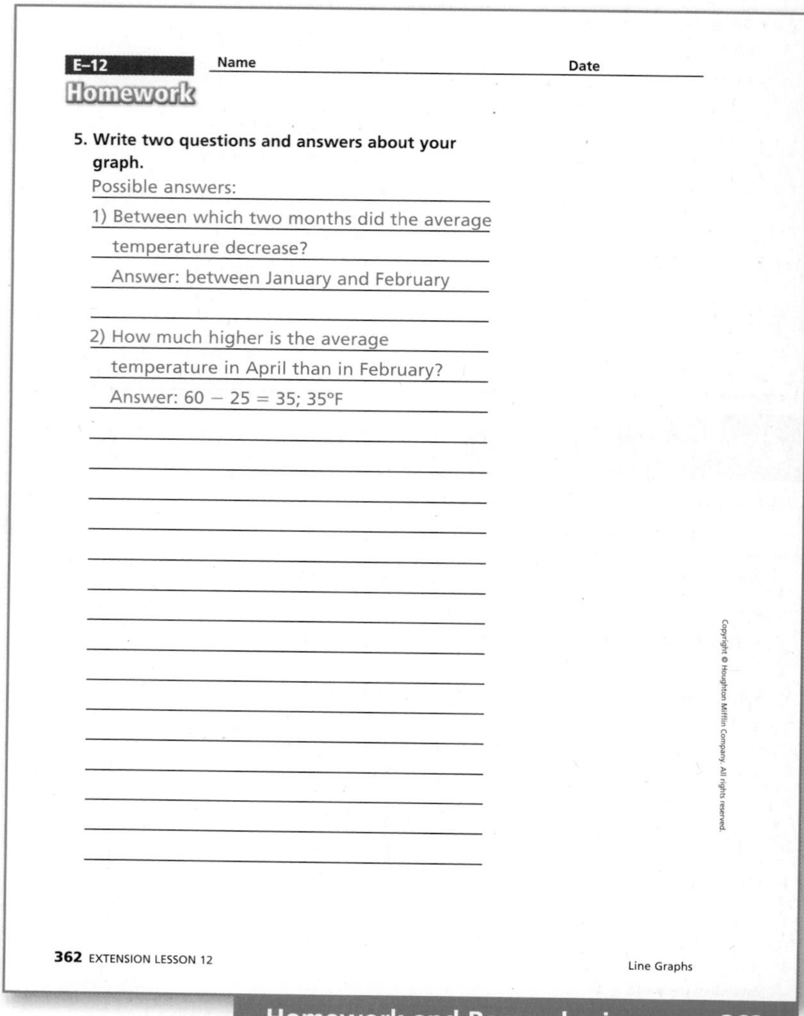

Name Date

E-12 Homework

5. Write two questions and answers about your graph.

Possible answers:

1) Between which two months did the average temperature decrease?
Answer: between January and February

2) How much higher is the average temperature in April than in February?
Answer: 60 − 25 = 35; 35°F

362 EXTENSION LESSON 12 Line Graphs

Homework and Remembering page 362

Home or School Activity

Technology Connection

Computer Graphing There are many kinds of computer software available for making graphs. You may have such software in your school. Graphing software is a good tool for enhancing your students' projects.

Have students do research at the library or on the Internet to find the population of your state for the five past years. Then have them use a computer to make a graph of that data.

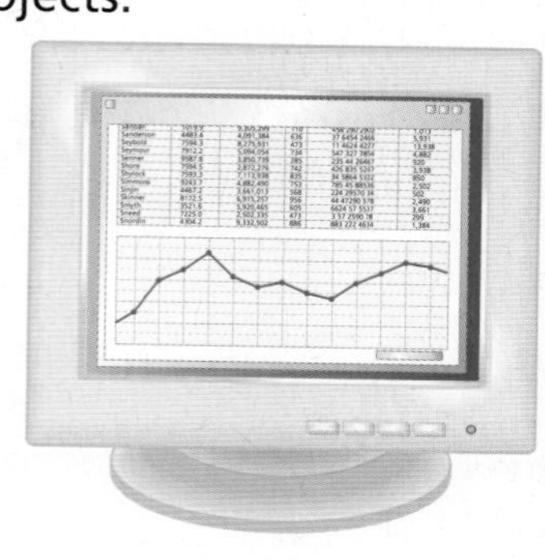

Have students explain:

- the kind of graph they made.
- why they chose that graph for their data.

Student Glossary

Glossary

A

acute angle An angle whose measure is less than 90°.

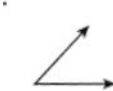

acute triangle A triangle in which the measure of each angle is less than 90°.

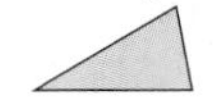

addend A number to be added.

Example: 8 + 4 = 12

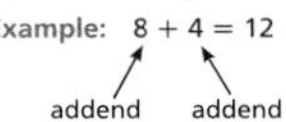

addition A mathematical operation that combines two or more numbers.

Example: 23 + 52 = 75

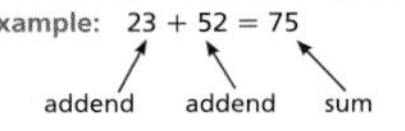

adjacent (sides) Two sides that meet at a point.

Example: Sides *a* and *b* are adjacent.

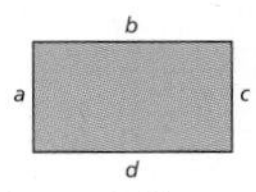

A.M. The time period between midnight and noon.

angle A figure formed by two rays or two line segments that meet at an endpoint.

area The number of square units in a region

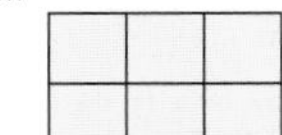

The area of the rectangle is 6 square units.

array An arrangement of objects, pictures, or numbers in columns and rows.

Associative Property of Addition (Grouping Property of Addition) The property which states that changing the way in which addends are grouped does not change the sum.

Example: (2 + 3) + 1 = 2 + (3 + 1)
5 + 1 = 2 + 4
6 = 6

Associative Property of Multiplication (Grouping Property of Multiplication) The property which states that changing the way in which factors are grouped does not change the product.

Example: (2 × 3) × 4 = 2 × (3 × 4)
6 × 4 = 2 × 12
24 = 24

Glossary (Continued)

axis (plural: **axes**) A reference line for a graph. A bar graph has 2 axes; one is horizontal and the other is vertical.

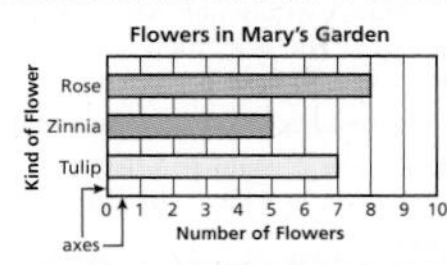

B

bar graph A graph that uses bars to show data. The bars may be horizontal or vertical.

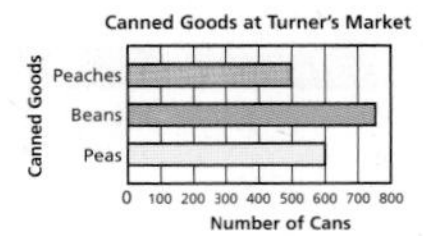

base (of a geometric figure) The bottom side of a 2-D figure or the bottom face of a 3-D figure.

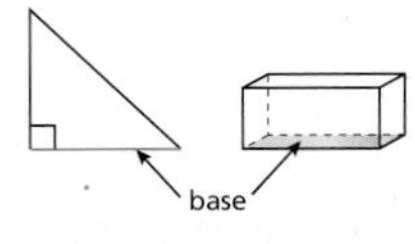

C

calculator A tool used to perform mathematical operations.

capacity The amount a container can hold.

cell A rectangle in a table where a column and row meet.

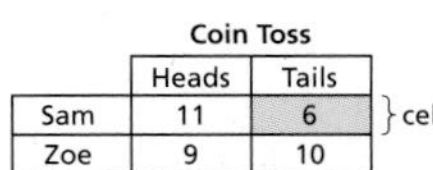

	Heads	Tails
Sam	11	6
Zoe	9	10

centimeter (cm) A metric unit used to measure length.

100 cm = 1 m

circle A plane figure that forms a closed path so that all points on the path are the same distance from a point called the center.

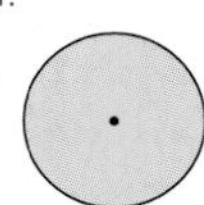

circle graph A graph that represents data as parts of a whole.

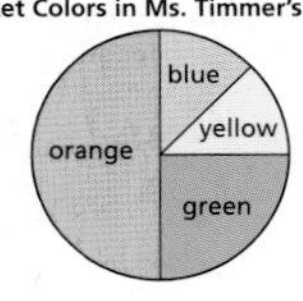

circumference The distance around a circle, about $3\frac{1}{7}$ times the diameter.

column A vertical group of cells in a table.

Coin Toss

	Heads	Tails
Sam	11	6
Zoe	9	10

column

Commutative Property of Addition (Order Property of Addition) The property which states that changing the order of addends does not change the sum.

Example: 3 + 7 = 7 + 3
10 = 10

Commutative Property of Multiplication (Order Property of Multiplication) The property which states that changing the order of factors does not change the product.

Example: 5 × 4 = 4 × 5
20 = 20

comparison bars Bars that represent the larger amount, smaller amount, and difference in a comparison problem.

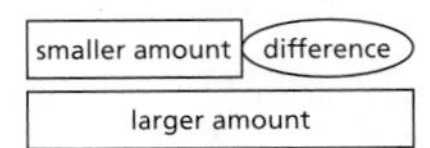

In Volume 2, we use comparison bars for multiplication.

7 [7]
56 [7][7][7][7][7][7][7][7]

cone A solid figure that has a circular base and comes to a point called the vertex.

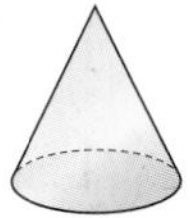

congruent figures Figures that have the same size and shape.

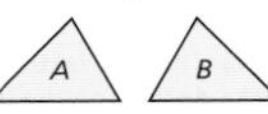

Triangles A and B are congruent.

coordinates The numbers in an ordered pair that locate a point on a coordinate grid. The first number is the distance across and the second number is the distance up.

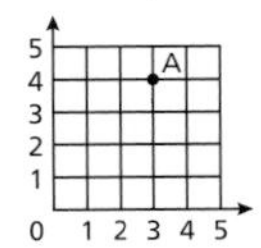

The coordinates 3 and 4 in the ordered pair (3, 4) locate Point *A* on the coordinate grid.

coordinate grid A grid formed by two perpendicular number lines in which every point is assigned an ordered pair of numbers.

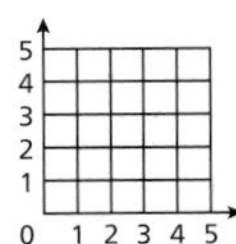

cube A solid figure that has six square faces of equal size.

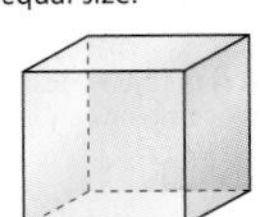

Glossary (Continued)

cup (c) A customary unit of measurement used to measure capacity.

2 cups = 1 pint
4 cups = 1 quart
16 cups = 1 gallon

cylinder A solid figure with two congruent circular or elliptical faces and one curved surface.

D

data Pieces of information.

decimal A number with one or more digits to the right of a decimal point.

Examples: 1.23 and 0.3

decimal point The dot that separates the whole number from the decimal part.

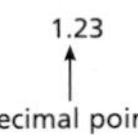

decimeter (dm) A metric unit used to measure length

1 decimeter = 10 centimeters

degree (°) A unit for measuring angles or temperature.

degrees Celsius (°C) The metric unit for measuring temperature.

degrees Fahrenheit (°F) The customary unit of temperature.

denominator The bottom number in a fraction that shows the total number of equal parts in the whole.

Example: $\frac{1}{3}$ ← denominator

diagonal A line segment that connects two corners of a figure and is not a side of the figure.

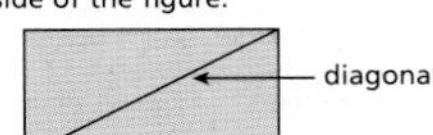

diameter A line segment that connects two points on a circle and also passes through the center of the circle. The term is also used to describe the length of such a line segment.

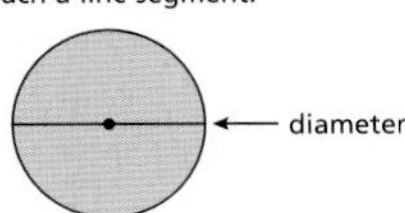

difference The result of subtraction or of comparing.

digit Any of the symbols 0, 1, 2, 3, 4, 5, 6, 7, 8, 9.

dividend The number that is divided in division.

Examples:
12 ÷ 3 = 4 $\quad 3\overline{)12}$ (quotient 4)
dividend $\quad$ dividend

division The mathematical operation that separates an amount into smaller equal groups to find the number of groups or the number in each group.

Example: 12 ÷ 3 = 4 is a division number sentence.

divisor The number that you divide by in division.

Example: 12 ÷ 3 = 4 $\quad 3\overline{)12}$ (quotient 4)

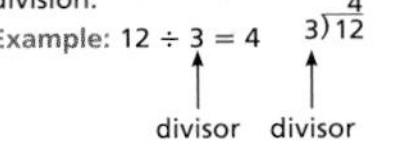

Student Glossary (Continued)

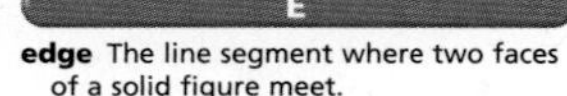

E

edge The line segment where two faces of a solid figure meet.

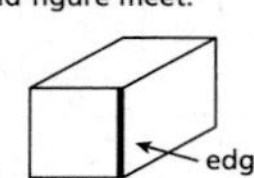

elapsed time The time that passes between the beginning and the end of an activity.

endpoint The point at either end of a line segment or the beginning point of a ray.

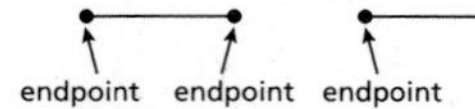

equation A mathematical sentence with an equals sign.

Examples: 11 + 22 = 33
75 − 25 = 50

equilateral triangle A triangle whose sides are all the same length.

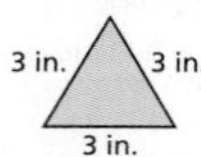

equivalent Equal, or naming the same amount.

equivalent fractions Fractions that name the same amount.

Example: $\frac{1}{2}$ and $\frac{2}{4}$

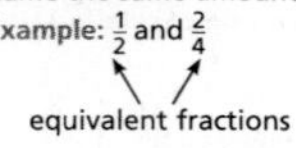

estimate About how many or about how much.

even number A whole number that is a multiple of 2. The ones digit in an even number is 0, 2, 4, 6, or 8.

event In probability, a possible outcome.

expanded form A number written to show the value of each of its digits.

Examples:
347 = 300 + 40 + 7
347 = 3 hundreds + 4 tens + 7 ones

expression A combination of numbers, variables, and/or operation signs. An expression does not have an equals sign.

Examples: 4 + 7 $a - 3$

F

face A flat surface of a solid figure.

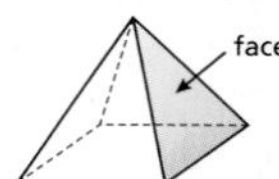

factors Numbers that are multiplied to give a product.

Example: 4 × 5 = 20

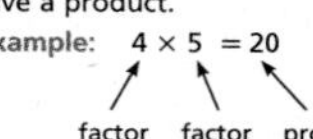

flip To reflect a figure over a line. The size and shape of the figure remain the same.

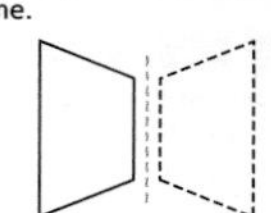

foot (ft) A customary unit used to measure length.

1 foot = 12 inches

Glossary (Continued)

formula An equation with variables that describes a rule.

The formula for the area of a rectangle is:
$A = l \times w$
where A is the area, l is the length, and w is the width.

fraction A number that names part of a whole or part of a set.

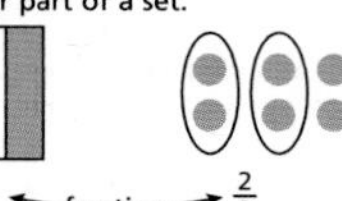

front-end estimation A method of estimating that keeps the largest place value in a number and drops the rest.

Example: 527 → 500
+ 673 → + 600
1,100

The 5 in 527 is the "front end" number
The 6 in 673 is the "front end" number

function table A table of ordered pairs that shows a function.

For every input number, there is only one possible output number.

Rule: add 2	
Input	Output
1	3
2	4
3	5
4	6

G

gallon (gal) A customary unit used to measure capacity.

1 gallon = 4 quarts = 8 pints = 16 cups

gram (g) A metric unit of mass, about 1 paper clip.

1,000 grams = 1 kilogram

greater than (>) A symbol used to compare two numbers.

Example: 6 > 5
6 is greater than 5.

group To combine numbers to form new tens, hundreds, thousands, and so on.

growing pattern A number or geometric pattern that increases.

Examples: 2, 4, 6, 8, 10...
1, 2, 5, 10, 17...

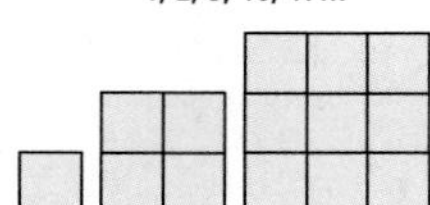

H

height A measurement of vertical length, or how tall something is.

horizontal Extending in two directions, left and right.

horizontal bar graph A bar graph with horizontal bars.

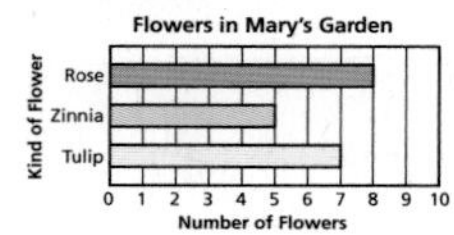

hundredth One of the equal parts when a whole is divided into 100 equal parts.

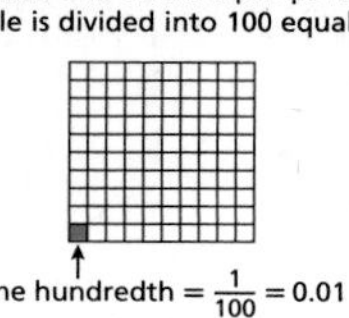

I

improper fraction A fraction in which the numerator is equal to or is greater than the denominator. Improper fractions are equal to or greater than 1.

$\frac{5}{5}$ and $\frac{8}{3}$ are improper fractions.

inch (in.) A customary unit used to measure length.

12 inches = 1 foot

isosceles triangle A triangle that has at least two sides of the same length.

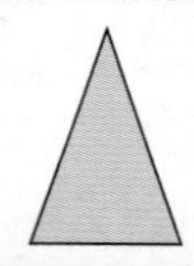

K

key A part of a map, graph, or chart that explains what symbols mean.

kilogram (kg) A metric unit of mass.

1 kilogram = 1,000 grams

kilometer (km) A metric unit of length.

1 kilometer = 1,000 meters

L

less than (<) A symbol used to compare numbers.

Example: 5 < 6
5 is less than 6.

line A straight path that goes on forever in opposite directions.

line graph A graph that uses a straight line or a broken line to show changes in data.

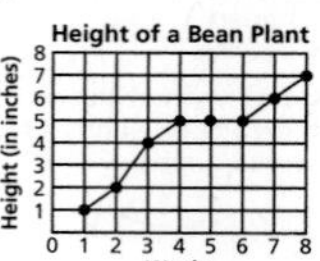

line of symmetry A line on which a figure can be folded so that the two halves match exactly.

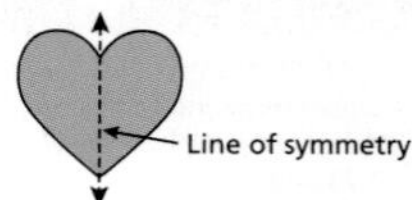

line plot A way to show data using a number line.

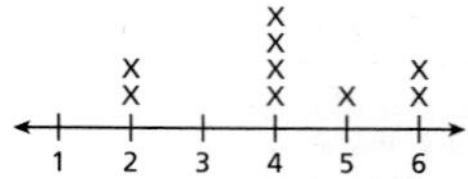

line segment A part of a line. A line segment has two endpoints.

liter (L) A metric unit used to measure capacity.

1 liter = 1,000 milliliters

Glossary (Continued)

M

mass The amount of matter in an object.

mean (average) The sum of the values in a set of data divided by the number of pieces of data in the set.

Example: 3 + 5 + 4 + 8 = 20
20 ÷ 4 = 5 5 is the mean

mental math A way to solve problems without using pencil and paper, or a calculator.

meter (m) A metric unit used to measure length.

1 meter = 100 centimeters

method A procedure, or way, of doing something.

mile (mi) A customary unit of length.

1 mile = 5,280 feet

milliliter (mL) A metric unit used to measure capacity.

1,000 milliliters = 1 liter

mixed number A whole number and a fraction.

$1\frac{3}{4}$ is a mixed number.

mode The number that occurs most often in a set of data.

In this set of numbers {3, 4, 5, 5, 5, 7, 8}, 5 is the mode.

multiple A number that is the product of the given number and another number.

multiplication A mathematical operation that combines equal groups.

Example: 4 × 3 = 12
factor factor product
3 + 3 + 3 + 3 = 12
4 times

N

net A flat pattern that can be folded to make a solid figure.

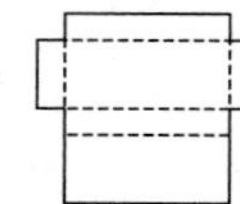

This net can be folded into a rectangular prism.

number line A line on which numbers are assigned to lengths.

numerator The top number in a fraction that shows the number of equal parts counted.

Example: $\frac{1}{3}$ ← numerator

O

obtuse angle An angle that measures more than 90° but less than 180°.

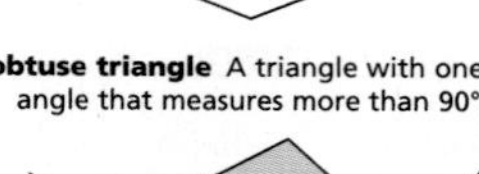

obtuse triangle A triangle with one angle that measures more than 90°.

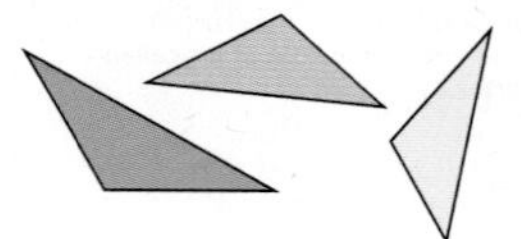

odd number A whole number that is not a multiple of 2. The ones digit in an odd number is 1, 3, 5, 7, or 9.

opposite sides Sides that are across from each other; they do not meet at a point.

Example: Sides *a* and *c* are opposite.

ordered pair A pair of numbers such as (3, 4) in which one number is considered to be first and the other number second. They can name a point on a coordinate grid.

ordinal numbers Numbers used to show order or position.

Example: first, second, fifth

ounce (oz) A customary unit used to measure weight.

16 ounces = 1 pound

P

parallel lines Two lines that are everywhere the same distance apart.

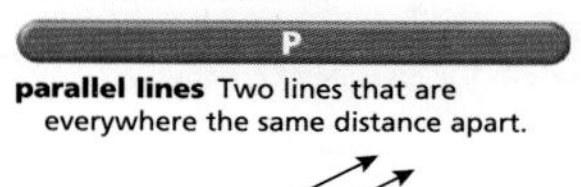

parallelogram A quadrilateral with both pairs of opposite sides parallel.

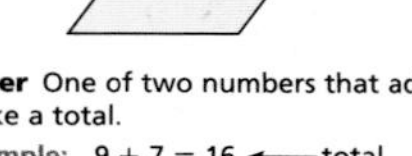

partner One of two numbers that add to make a total.

Example: 9 + 7 = 16 ← total *sum*

partner *addend*, partner *addend*

perimeter The distance around the outside of a figure.

perpendicular Two lines or line segments that cross or meet to form right angles.

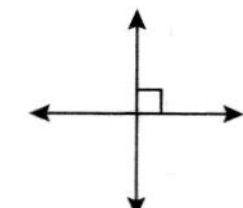

pictograph A graph that uses pictures or symbols to represent data.

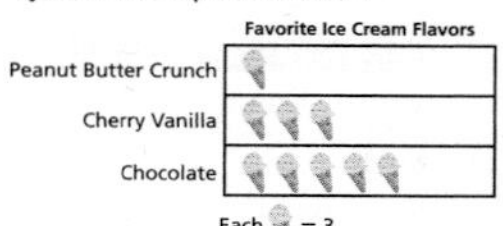

pint (pt) A customary unit used to measure capacity.

1 pint = 2 cups

place value The value assigned to the place that a digit occupies in a number.

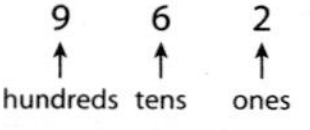

place value drawing A drawing that represents a number. Hundreds are represented by boxes, tens by vertical lines, and ones by small circles.

plane figure A closed figure that has two dimensions.

Glossary (Continued)

P.M. The time period between noon and midnight.

pound (lb) A customary unit used to measure weight.

1 pound = 16 ounces

prism A solid figure with two parallel congruent bases, and rectangles or parallelograms for faces. A prism is named by the shape of its bases.

hexagonal prism

probability The chance of an event occurring.

product The answer when you multiply numbers.

Example: 4 × 7 = 28

factor, factor, product

proof drawing A drawing used to show that an answer is correct.

249 + 386 = 635

pyramid A solid figure with one base and whose other faces are triangles with a common vertex. A pyramid is named by the shape of its base.

square pyramid

Q

quadrilateral A figure with four sides.

quart (qt) A customary unit used to measure capacity.

1 quart = 4 cups

quotient The answer when you divide numbers.

Examples: 35 ÷ 7 = 5 (quotient); $7\overline{)35}$ = 5 ← quotient

R

radius A line segment that connects the center of a circle to any point on the circle. The term is also used to describe the length of such a line segment.

radius

range The difference between the greatest number and the least number in a set of data.

In this set of numbers {12, 15, 18, 19, 20}, the range is 20 − 12 or 8

ray A part of a line that has one endpoint and goes on forever in one direction.

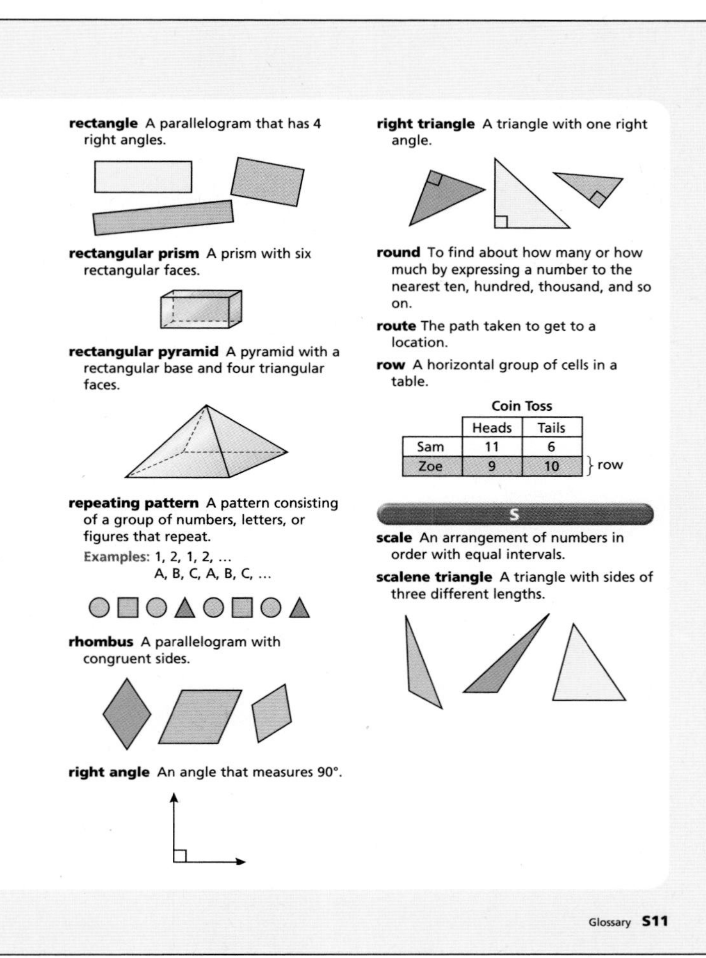

rectangle A parallelogram that has 4 right angles.

rectangular prism A prism with six rectangular faces.

rectangular pyramid A pyramid with a rectangular base and four triangular faces.

repeating pattern A pattern consisting of a group of numbers, letters, or figures that repeat.

Examples: 1, 2, 1, 2, ...
A, B, C, A, B, C, ...

rhombus A parallelogram with congruent sides.

right angle An angle that measures 90°.

right triangle A triangle with one right angle.

round To find about how many or how much by expressing a number to the nearest ten, hundred, thousand, and so on.

route The path taken to get to a location.

row A horizontal group of cells in a table.

Coin Toss

	Heads	Tails
Sam	11	6
Zoe	9	10

} row

S

scale An arrangement of numbers in order with equal intervals.

scalene triangle A triangle with sides of three different lengths.

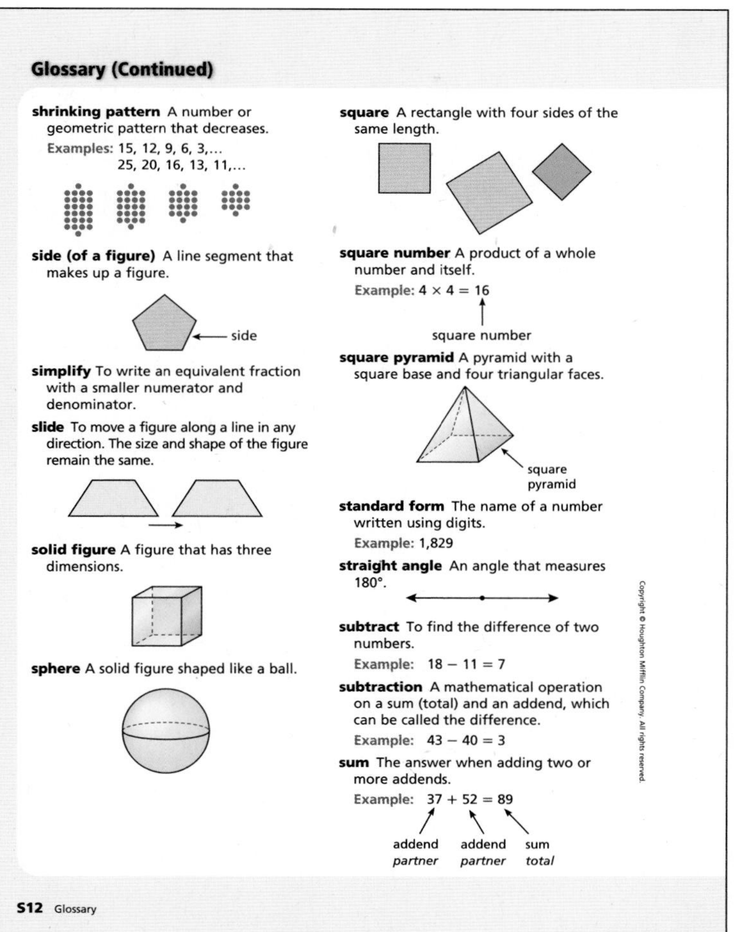

Glossary (Continued)

shrinking pattern A number or geometric pattern that decreases.

Examples: 15, 12, 9, 6, 3,...
25, 20, 16, 13, 11,...

side (of a figure) A line segment that makes up a figure.

side

simplify To write an equivalent fraction with a smaller numerator and denominator.

slide To move a figure along a line in any direction. The size and shape of the figure remain the same.

solid figure A figure that has three dimensions.

sphere A solid figure shaped like a ball.

square A rectangle with four sides of the same length.

square number A product of a whole number and itself.

Example: 4 × 4 = 16

square number

square pyramid A pyramid with a square base and four triangular faces.

square pyramid

standard form The name of a number written using digits.

Example: 1,829

straight angle An angle that measures 180°.

subtract To find the difference of two numbers.

Example: 18 − 11 = 7

subtraction A mathematical operation on a sum (total) and an addend, which can be called the difference.

Example: 43 − 40 = 3

sum The answer when adding two or more addends.

Example: 37 + 52 = 89

addend *partner*, addend *partner*, sum *total*

Student Glossary (Continued)

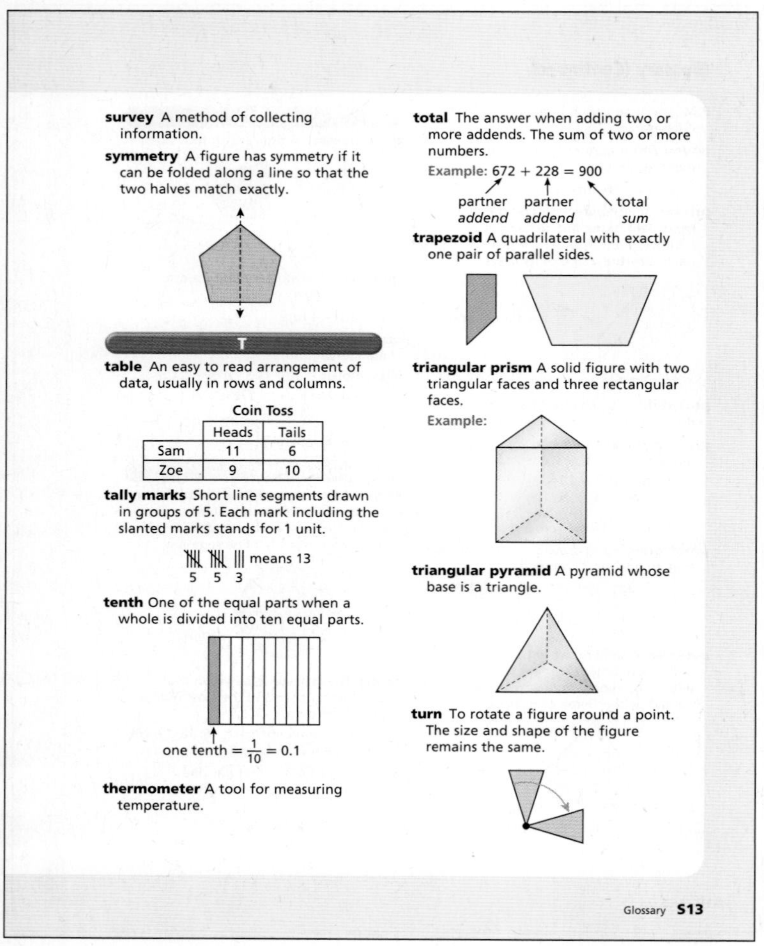

survey A method of collecting information.

symmetry A figure has symmetry if it can be folded along a line so that the two halves match exactly.

T

table An easy to read arrangement of data, usually in rows and columns.

Coin Toss

	Heads	Tails
Sam	11	6
Zoe	9	10

tally marks Short line segments drawn in groups of 5. Each mark including the slanted marks stands for 1 unit.

tenth One of the equal parts when a whole is divided into ten equal parts.

one tenth = $\frac{1}{10}$ = 0.1

thermometer A tool for measuring temperature.

total The answer when adding two or more addends. The sum of two or more numbers.

Example: 672 + 228 = 900

trapezoid A quadrilateral with exactly one pair of parallel sides.

triangular prism A solid figure with two triangular faces and three rectangular faces.

Example:

triangular pyramid A pyramid whose base is a triangle.

turn To rotate a figure around a point. The size and shape of the figure remains the same.

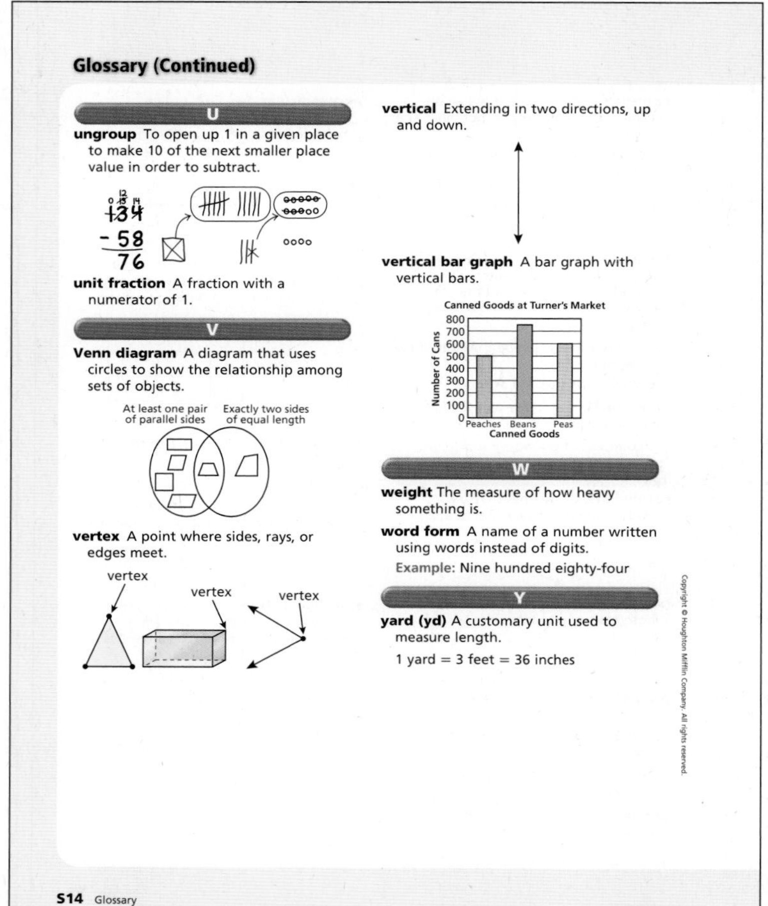

Glossary (Continued)

U

ungroup To open up 1 in a given place to make 10 of the next smaller place value in order to subtract.

unit fraction A fraction with a numerator of 1.

V

Venn diagram A diagram that uses circles to show the relationship among sets of objects.

vertex A point where sides, rays, or edges meet.

vertical Extending in two directions, up and down.

vertical bar graph A bar graph with vertical bars.

W

weight The measure of how heavy something is.

word form A name of a number written using words instead of digits.

Example: Nine hundred eighty-four

Y

yard (yd) A customary unit used to measure length.

1 yard = 3 feet = 36 inches

Teacher Glossary

5s shortcut A strategy for multiplying by numbers larger than 5. For example, to multiply 7×3, students think of the 5 count-by of 3, 15. They then think of the additional count-bys of 3, 18, 21. Therefore, $7 \times 3 = 21$.

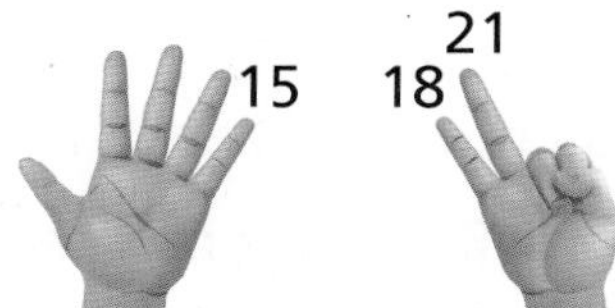

7 times 3 equals 21

A

acute angle An angle whose measure is less than 90°.

acute triangle A triangle in which the measure of each angle is less than 90°.

addend A number to be added. In the equation $8 + 4 = 12$, 8 and 4 are addends.

adjacent (sides) Two sides that meet at a point. In this example, sides *a* and *b* are adjacent.

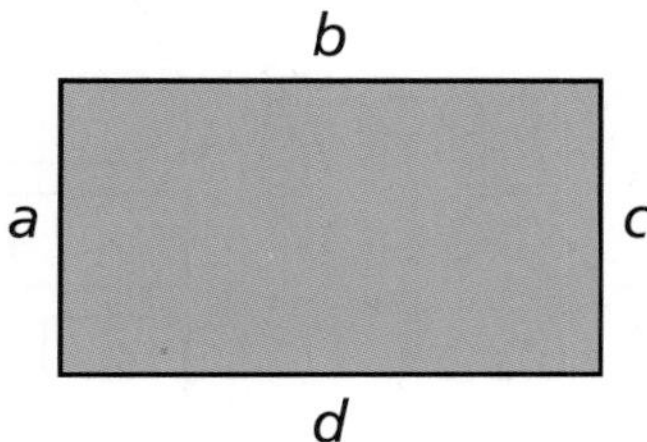

A.M. The abbreviation for *ante meridiem,* Latin for "before noon". Used to indicate a time between midnight and noon.

analog clock A clock with a face, a shorter hand, and a longer hand.

angle A figure formed by two rays or two line segments that meet at an endpoint.

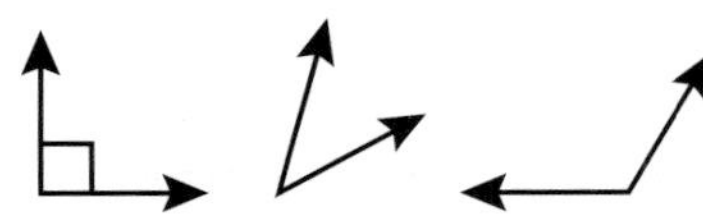

area The number of square units in a region.

area model A model that uses square units to show a multiplication.

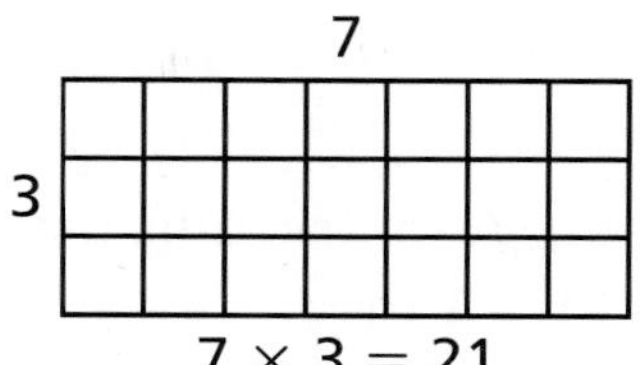

array An arrangement of objects, pictures, or numbers in columns and rows.

Associative Property of Addition Property which states that changing the grouping of addends does not change their sum. For all numbers *a, b,* and *c,* $a + (b + c) = (a + b) + c$.

Associative Property of Multiplication Property which states that changing the grouping of factors does not change their product. For all numbers *a, b* and *c,* $a \times (b \times c) = (a \times b) \times c$.

axis (plural: **axes**) A reference line for a graph. A bar graph has 2 axes; one is horizontal and the other is vertical.

B

bar graph A graph that uses bars to show data. The bars may be horizontal or vertical.

base (of a geometric figure) The bottom side of a 2-D figure or the bottom face of a 3-D figure.

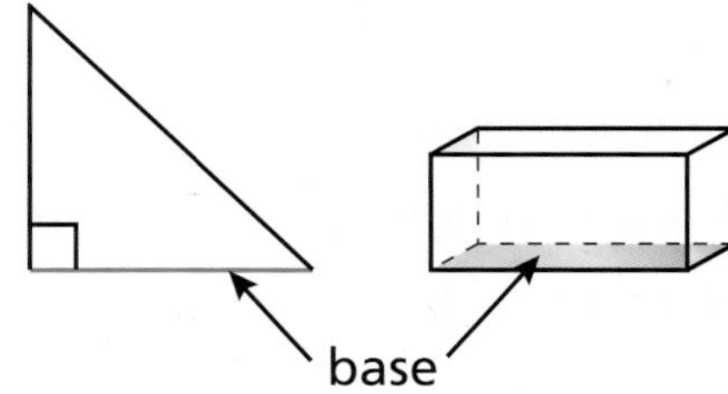

benchmark A reference whose size is familiar to students and approximately equal to a unit of measure. A benchmark helps students visualize the size of the unit. Comparing a known benchmark to an item of unknown size helps students to make a reasonable estimate.

C

capacity The amount a container can hold.

cell A rectangle in a table where a column and row meet.

centimeter (cm) A metric unit used to measure length. 100 cm = 1 m

change minus problem A problem that begins with a given quantity which is then modified by a change—something is subtracted—that results in a new quantity.

Sarah had 12 books. She loaned her friend 9 books. How many books does Sarah have now?

change plus problem A problem that begins with a given quantity which is then modified by a change—something is added—that results in a new quantity.
Alvin had 9 toy cars. He received 3 more for his birthday. How many toy cars does Alvin have now?

circle A plane figure that forms a closed path so that all points on the path are the same distance from a point called the center.

circle graph A graph that represents data as parts of a whole. (Also called a pie graph or pie chart.)

circumference The distance around a circle.

Class Multiplication Table A poster in table form that displays the multiplications for 1–9. Columns of the table are labeled 1–9 and rows are labeled 1–10. The product of the labels is found in the cells where the row and column meet.

clockwise A turn in the same direction as the hands of a clock move.

column A vertical group of cells in a table.

combinations Arrangements of elements

common denominator Any common multiple of the denominators of two or more fractions.

common multiplier The same number that multiplies the numerator and denominator of a fraction so that the resulting fraction is equivalent.

Commutative Property of Addition Property which states that the order in which numbers are added does not change the sum. For all numbers a and b, $a + b = b + a$.

Commutative Property of Multiplication Property which states that the order in which numbers are multiplied does not change the product. For all numbers a and b, $a \times b = b \times a$.

comparison bars Bars that represent the larger amount, smaller amount, and difference in a comparison problem.

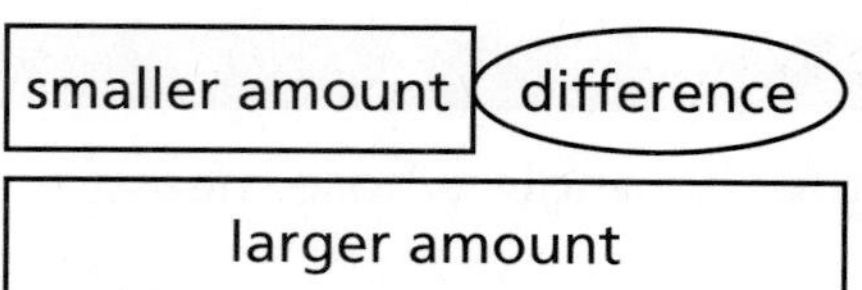

comparison language

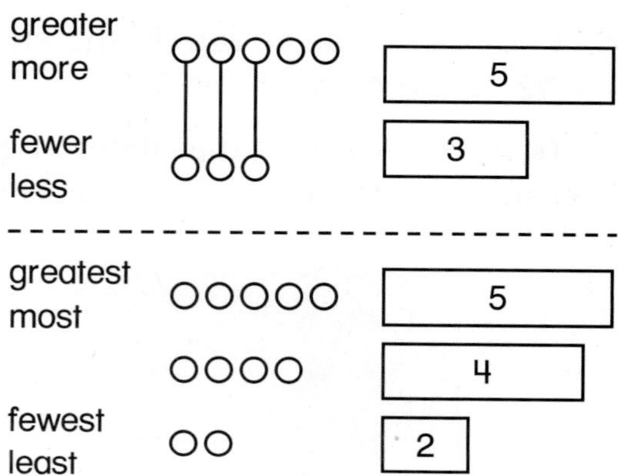

comparison situation A situation in which two amounts are compared by addition or by multiplication. An additive comparison situation compares by asking or telling how much more (how much less) one amount is than another A multiplicative comparison situation compares by asking or telling how many times as many one amount is as another. The multiplicative comparison may also be made using fraction language. For example, you can say, "Sally has one fourth as much as Tom has," instead of saying "Tom has 4 times as much as Sally has."

compatible numbers Numbers that are close to the original numbers and are easy to compute with. The numbers 35 and 80 are compatible numbers for estimating 36 plus 82.

cone A solid figure that has a circular base and comes to a point called the vertex.

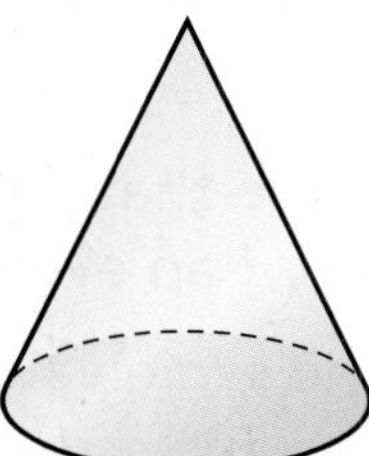

congruent figures Figures that have the same size and shape. In this example triangles A and B are congruent.

coordinate grid A grid formed by two perpendicular number lines in which every point is assigned an ordered pair of numbers.

coordinates The numbers in an ordered pair that locate a point on a coordinate grid. The first number is the distance across and the second number is the distance up. The coordinates 3 and 4 in the ordered pair (3, 4) locate Point A on the coordinate grid.

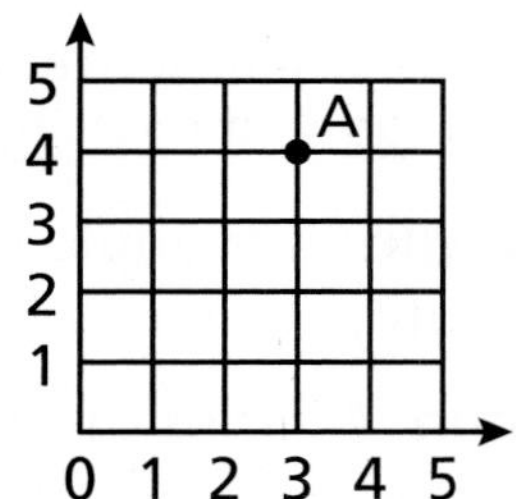

count-bys Products that are found by skip-counting a particular number; 5s count-bys would be 5, 10, 15, 20, 25, and so on; 3s count-bys would be 3, 6, 9, 12, and so on.

counter clockwise A turn in the opposite direction as the hands of a clock move.

count on An addition or subtraction strategy in which children begin with one partner and count on to the total. This strategy can be used to find an unknown partner or an unknown total.

$5 + 3 = \boxed{8}$

$5 + \boxed{3} = 8$

$8 - 5 = \boxed{3}$

Already 5 6 7 8

cube A solid figure that has six square faces of equal size.

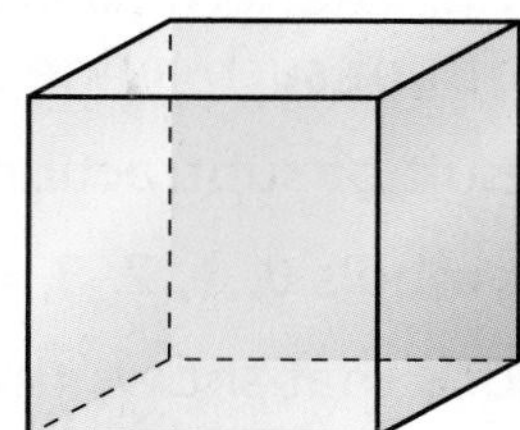

cubic unit A unit for measuring volume such as a cubic inch or cubic centimeter.

cup (c) A customary unit of measurement used to measure capacity. 2 cups = 1 pint
4 cups = 1 quart 16 cups = 1 gallon

cylinder A solid figure with two congruent circular faces and one curved surface.

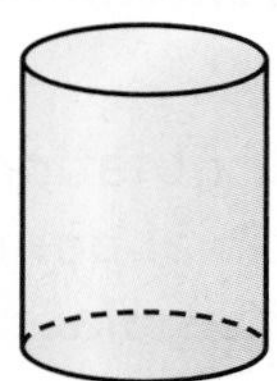

D

data A set of information.

decimal A number with one or more digits to the right of a decimal point. 1.23 and 0.3

decimeter (dm) A metric unit used to measure length. 1 decimeter = 10 centimeters

degree (°) A unit for measuring angles or temperature.

degrees Celsius (°C) The metric unit of temperature.

degrees Fahrenheit (°F) The customary unit of temperature.

Demonstration Secret Code Cards A larger version of the Secret Code Cards for classroom use. (See **Secret Code Cards**.)

denominator The bottom number in a fraction that shows the total number of parts in a whole. In the fraction $\frac{1}{3}$, 3 is the denominator.

diagonal A line segment that connects two corners of a figure and is not a side of the figure.

diameter A line segment that connects two points on a circle and also passes through the center of the circle. The term is also used to describe the length of such a line segment.

difference The result of subtraction.

digit Any of the symbols 0, 1, 2, 3, 4, 5, 6, 7, 8, 9.

digital clock A clock that shows the hour and minutes with digits.

dimension A way to describe how a figure can be measured. A line segment has only length, so it has *one* dimension. A rectangle has length and width, so it has *two* dimensions. A cube has length, width, and height, so it has *three* dimensions.

dimensions The measurements of sides of geometric figures.

dimes place In dollar notation, the first place to the right of the decimal point. In the amount $3.47, 4 is in the dimes place.

Distributive Property of Multiplication The product of a factor and a sum (or difference) equals the sum (or difference) of the products. For all numbers *a, b* and *c,*
$a \times (b + c) = (a \times b) + (a \times c)$

dividend The number that is divided in division. In the equation $12 \div 3 = 4$, 12 is the dividend.

divisible A number is divisible by another number if the quotient is a whole number with no remainder. The number 6 is divisible by 3, but not 4.

divisor The number that you divide by in division. In the equation $12 \div 3 = 4$, 3 is the divisor.

dollars place In dollar notation, the first place to the left of the decimal point. In the amount $3.47, 3 is in the dollars place.

Dot Array An arrangement of dots in rows and columns.

E

edge The line segment where two faces of a solid figure meet.

elapsed time The time that passes between the beginning and end of an event.

equal (=) Having the same value as that of another quantity or expression. $3 + 1 = 4$ is read as 3 plus 1 is equal to 4.

equal groups Concept used in multiplication and division situations. $5 \times 6 = 30$. There are 5 equal groups of 6 items.

Equal Shares drawing A drawing which children create that represents factors and products. It is a numerical form of a Repeated Groups drawing.

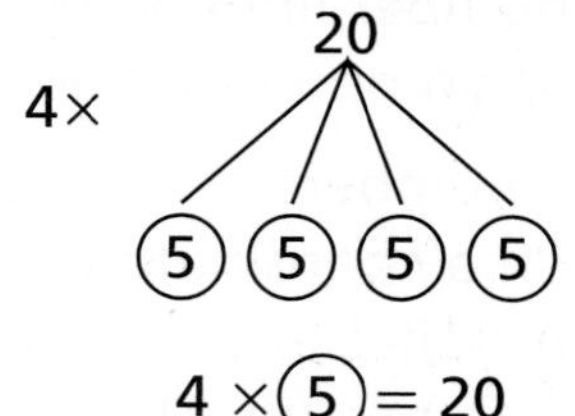

equally likely outcomes In probability, events that have the same chance of occurring.

equation A mathematical sentence with an equals sign. $11 + 22 = 33$ $75 - 25 = 50$

equilateral triangle A triangle whose sides are all the same length.

equivalence chain A series of equivalent fractions connected with equal signs.
$\frac{1}{2} = \frac{2}{4} = \frac{4}{8} = \frac{8}{16}$

equivalent fractions Fractions that name the same amount. $\frac{1}{2}$ and $\frac{2}{4}$ are equivalent fractions.

estimate A number close to an exact amount. About how many or about how much.

evaluate To find the value of a mathematical expression.

even number A whole number that is a multiple of 2. The ones digit in an even number is 0, 2, 4, 6, or 8.

event In probability, a possible outcome.

expanded form A number written to show the value of each of its digits.
Examples: 347 = 300 + 40 + 7
347 = 3 hundreds + 4 tens + 7 ones

expression A combination of numbers and operation signs. 4 + 7

F

face A flat surface of a solid figure.

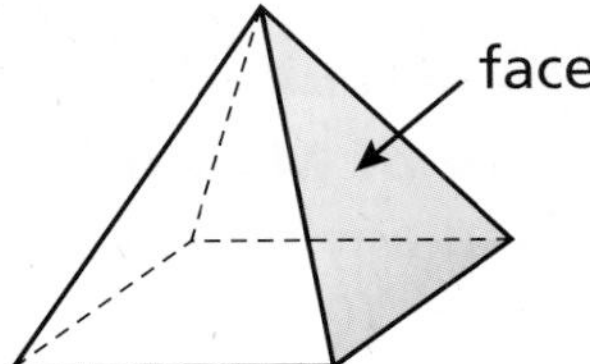

factors Numbers that are multiplied to give a product. In the equation 4 × 5 = 20, 4 and 5 are factors.

Fast-Area drawing A representation of an area model that students can sketch quickly to label the units appropriately on a rectangle.

6 ft, 7 ft, ? 6 ft, 7 ft, 42 sq ft

Fast-Array drawing A representation of an array that shows a missing factor or missing product.

10, 5, 50

fewer Fewer is used to compare two quantities that can be counted. There are fewer red books than blue books. Less is used to compare two quantities that can be measured. There is less water than juice. *See* comparison language.

flip To reflect a figure over a line. The size and shape of the figure remain the same.

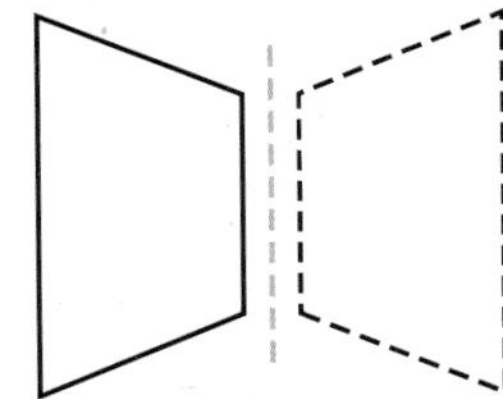

fluid ounce (fl oz) A customary unit of capacity equal to 2 tablespoons.

foot (ft) A customary unit used to measure length. 1 foot = 12 inches

formula An equation with variables that describes a rule. The formula for the area of a rectangle is: $A = l \times w$, where A is the area, l is the length, and w is the width.

fraction A number that names part of a whole or part of a set.

fraction bar A visual representation of a whole divided into equal parts. The fraction bar shown here represents one-third.

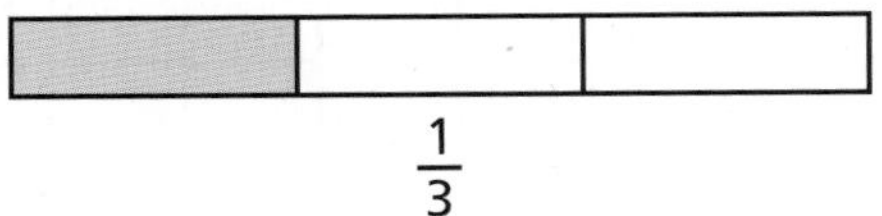

fraction strip Strips of paper divided into equal unit fractional parts that students can fold to explore equivalent fractions.

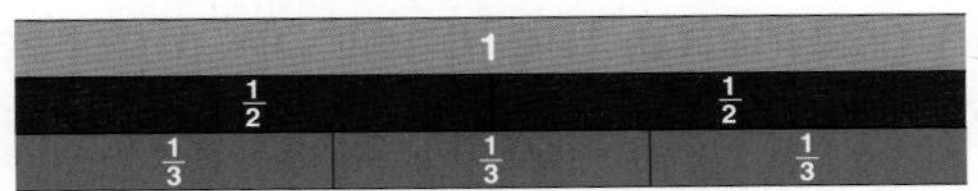

fracture To divide into smaller equal parts.

front-end estimation A method of estimating that uses the largest place value in a number. In the equation 527 + 673 = ☐, you would round 527 to 500 and 673 to 600 for a total of 1,100.

function A set of ordered pairs such that no two ordered pairs have the same first member.

function table A table of ordered pairs that shows a function.

Rule: add 2	
Input	Output
1	3
2	4
3	5
4	6

G

gallon (gal) A customary unit used to measure capacity. 1 gallon = 4 quarts = 16 cups

gram (g) A metric unit of mass.
1,000 grams = 1 kilogram

greater than (>) Having a value that is more than that of another quantity or expression. 6 > 5 is read as 6 is greater than 5.

group To combine numbers to form new tens, hundreds, thousands, and so on.

growing pattern A number or geometric pattern that increases.
Examples: 2, 4, 6, 8, 10 ...
1, 2, 5, 10, 17 ...

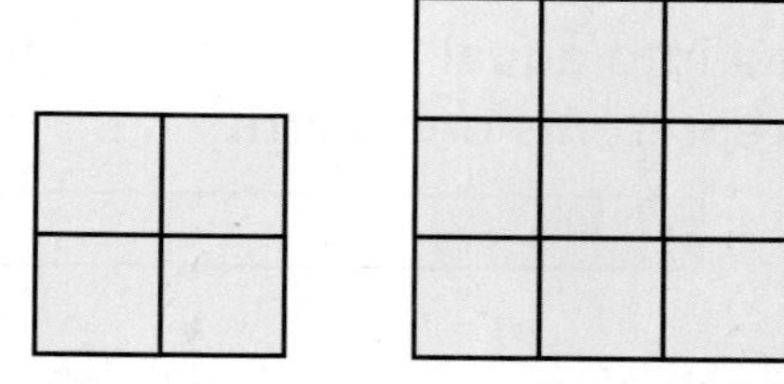

H

half turn A 180° rotation.

height In geometry, the length of a perpendicular line segment from a vertex to the opposite side of a plane figure.

hexagon A six-sided polygon.

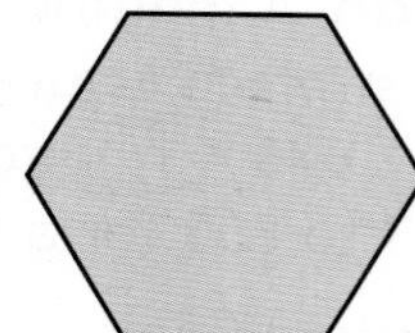

horizontal Extending in two directions, left and right parallel to the horizon.

hundred box In a place value drawing, a square box representing that 10 ten-sticks equal one hundred. A hundred box is a quick way of drawing 100.

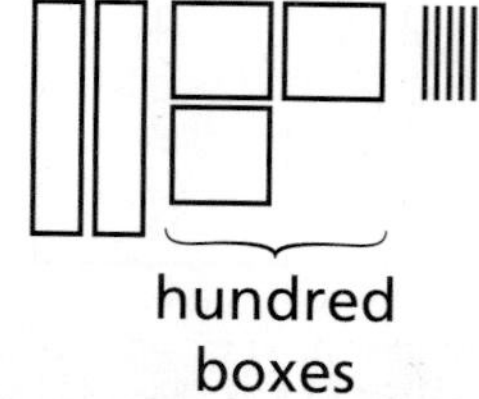

hundredth One of the equal parts when a whole is divided into 100 equal parts.

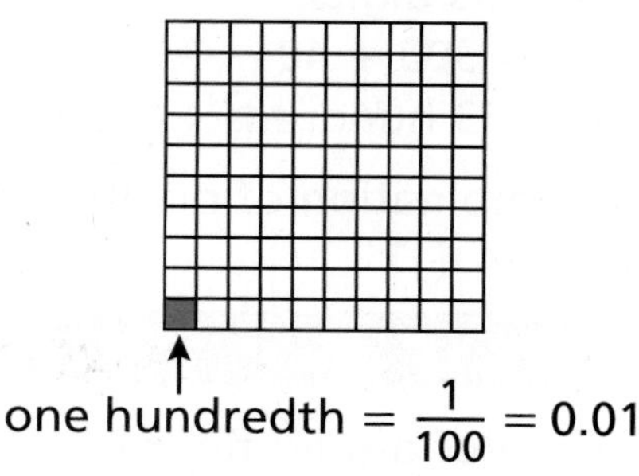

I

Identity Property of Multiplication The product of 1 and any number equals that number. $1 \times 10 = 10$

improper fraction A fraction in which the numerator is equal to or is greater than the denominator. Improper fractions are equal to or greater than 1. $\frac{8}{8}$ and $\frac{8}{3}$ are improper fractions.

inch (in.) A customary unit used to measure length. 12 inches = 1 foot

inequality A statement that two expressions are not equal.

input In a function or rule, the value that is entered into the function or rule to produce an output.

inverse operations Opposite or reverse operations that undo each other. Addition and subtraction are inverse operations. Multiplication and division are inverse operations.

isosceles triangle A triangle that has at least two sides of the same length.

K

key A part of a map, graph, or chart that explains what symbols mean.

kilogram (kg) A metric unit of mass.
1 kilogram = 1,000 grams

kilometer (km) A metric unit of length.
1 kilometer = 1,000 meters

L

less than (<) Having a value that is less than that of another quantity or expression. $5 < 6$ is read as 5 is less than 6.

line A straight path that goes on forever in opposite directions.

line graph A graph that uses a straight line or a broken line to show changes in data.

line of reflection A line around or over which a figure is flipped to produce a mirror image of the figure. Each point of the original figure and flipped figure is the same distance from the line.

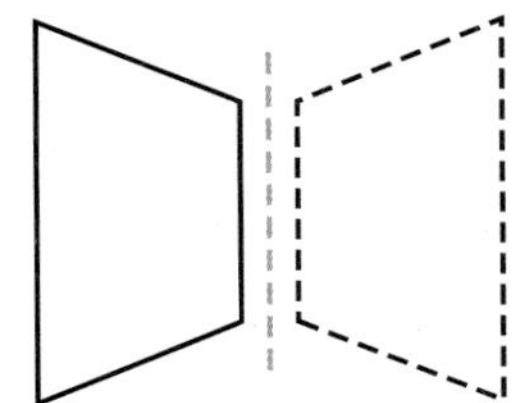

line of symmetry A line on which a figure can be folded so that the two halves match exactly.

line plot A way to show data using a number line.

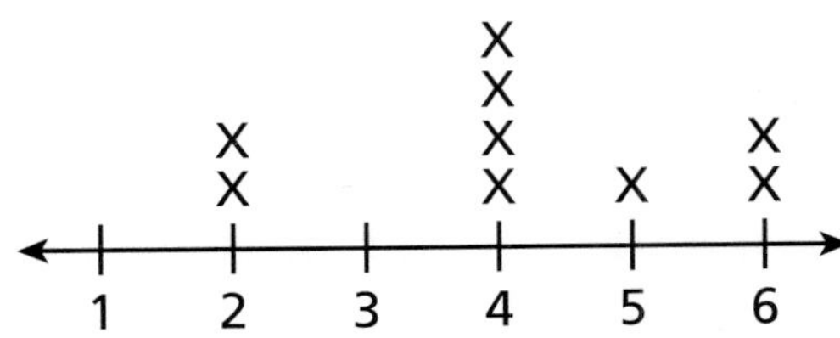

line segment A part of a line. A line segment has two endpoints.

line symmetry A figure has line symmetry if it can be folded along a line so the two halves match exactly.

liter (L) A metric unit used to measure capacity. 1 liter = 1,000 milliliters

M

Make a Hundred Strategy An addition or subtraction strategy in which the student finds the 100-partner of the larger addend and then breaks apart the other addend into that 100-partner and the rest to find the total.
To add $80 + 70$ using the Make a Hundred strategy, the student finds the 100-partner for 80 which is 20, breaks apart 70, the other addend, into $20 + 50$ and then adds the rest, 50, to 100. Thus, $100 + 50 = 150$ so $80 + 70 = 150$.

Make a Ten Strategy An addition strategy in which students find the 10-partner. To add $7 + 9$, the student finds the 10-partner for 9 which is 1, breaks apart 7, the other addend, into $1 + 6$ and then adds the rest, 6, to 10. Thus, $10 + 6 = 16$, so $7 + 9 = 16$.

Make a Thousand Strategy An addition strategy in which the student finds the 1,000-partner of the larger addend and then breaks apart the other addend into that 1,000-partner and the rest to find the total.
To add $800 + 700$ using the Make a Thousand strategy, the student finds the 1,000-partner for 800 which is 200, breaks apart 700, the other addend, into $200 + 500$ and then adds the rest, 500, to 1,000. Thus, $1{,}000 + 500 = 1{,}500$ so $800 + 700 = 1500$.

mass The amount of matter in an object. (Mass is constant; weight varies because weight is the effect of gravity on matter.)

Math Mountain A visual representation of the partners and totals of a number. The total (*sum*) appears at the top and the two partners (*addends*) that are added to produce the total are below to the left and right.

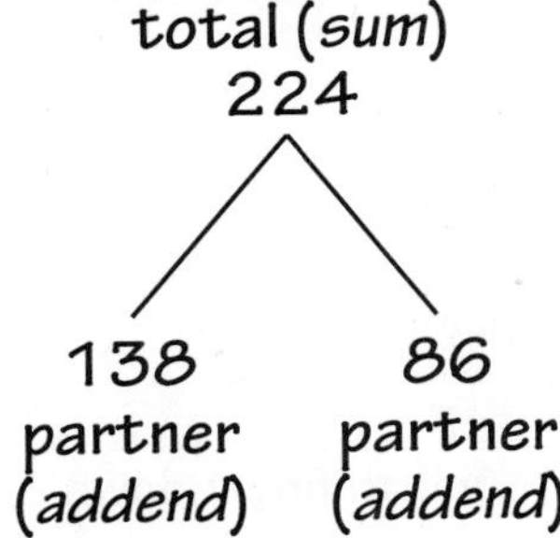

mean (average) The number found by dividing the sum of a group of numbers by the number of addends. For the set of numbers 3, 5, 4, 8: $3 + 5 + 4 + 8 = 20$, $20 \div 4 = 5$, 5 is the mean.

median The middle number when a set of numbers is arranged in order from least to greatest. For an even number of numbers, the median is the average of the two middle numbers.

mental math A way to solve problems without using pencil and paper, or a calculator.

meter (m) A metric unit used to measure length. 1 meter = 100 centimeters

method A procedure, or way of doing something.

mile (mi) A customary unit of length. 1 mile = 5,280 feet

milliliter (mL) A metric unit used to measure capacity. 1,000 milliliters = 1 liter

mixed number A whole number and a fraction. $1\frac{3}{4}$ is a mixed number.

mode The number that occurs most often in a set of data. In this set of numbers {3, 4, 5, 5, 5, 7, 8}, 5 is the mode.

multiple A number that is the product of the given number and another number.

Multiplication Table An array of numbers with rows and columns labeled from 1 through 12. The product of the labels is found in the cell where the row and column intersect.

multiplier One of the factors in a multiplication equation. In the 9s count-bys or multiplications, each of the numbers that 9 is multiplied by, is the multiplier.

multiplier finger Used with the multiplication strategy Quick 9s strategy, the bent finger that indicates the number that 9 is being multiplied by.

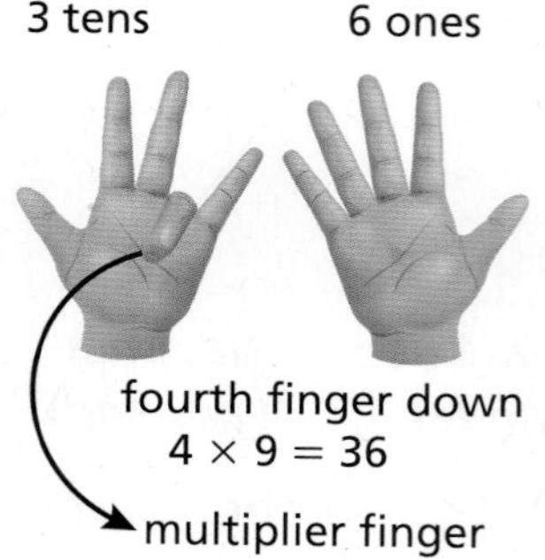

net A flat pattern that can be folded to make a solid figure. This net is for a rectangular prism.

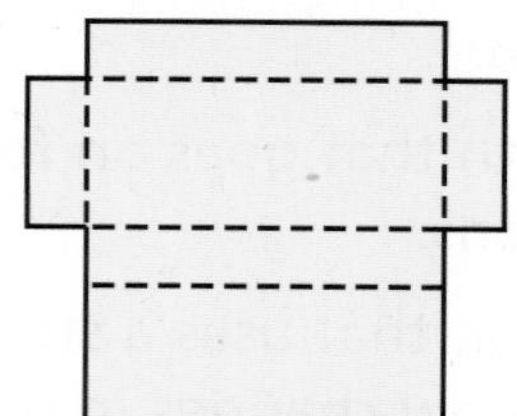

New Groups Above Method A strategy for multi-digit addition. The new groups are placed above the existing groups. This is the current, common method of addition.

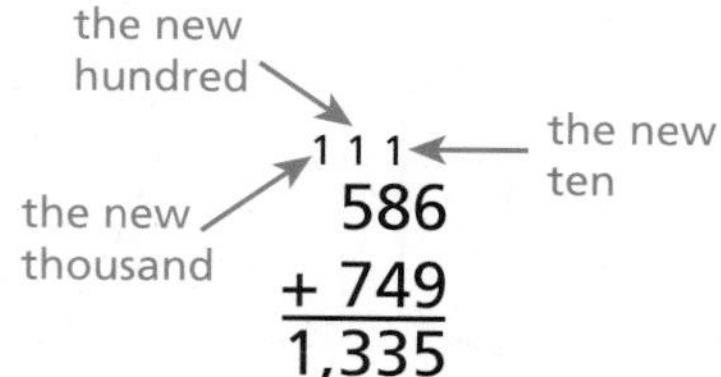

New Groups Below Method A strategy for multi-digit addition. The new groups are placed below the existing groups on the line waiting to be added.

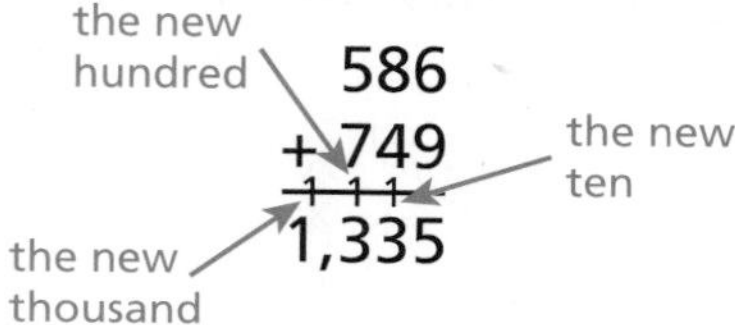

non-standard unit A unit of measure not commonly recognized, such as a paper clip. An inch and a centimeter are standard units of measure.

non-unit fraction A fraction that is built from unit fractions. $\frac{2}{3}$ is a non-unit fraction. It is built from the unit fractions $\frac{1}{3} + \frac{1}{3}$.

number sentence Numbers and expressions related to each other using one of these symbols: =, <, or >.

numerator The top number in a fraction that shows the number of equal parts counted. In the fraction $\frac{1}{3}$, 1 is the numerator.

obtuse angle An angle that measures more than 90° but less than 180°.

obtuse triangle A triangle with one angle that measures more than 90°.

octagon An eight-sided figure

odd number A whole number that is not a multiple of 2. The ones digit in an odd number is 1, 3, 5, 7, or 9.

operation A mathematical process. Addition, subtraction, multiplication, division, and raising a number to a power are operations.

opposite sides Sides that are across from each other; they do not meet at a point. In this example, sides *a* and *c* are opposite.

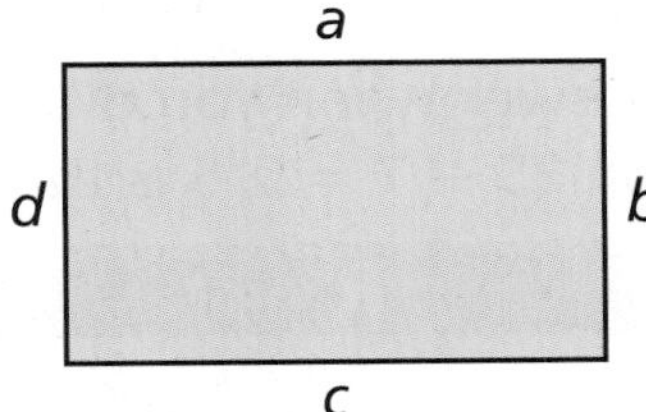

ordered pair A pair of numbers such as (3, 4) in which one number is considered to be first and the other number second. They can name a point on a coordinate grid.

Order of Operations A set of rules that state in which order operations should be performed.
- Compute inside parentheses first
- Multiply and divide in order from left to right
- Add and subtract in order from left to right

ordinal numbers Numbers used to show order or position. For example, first, second, fifth.

ounce (oz) A customary unit used to measure weight. 16 ounces = 1 pound

output In a function table, the value resulting from a specific input and rule.

P

parallel The same distance apart everywhere. This can describe lines, line segments, or faces of a solid figure.

parallelogram A quadrilateral with both pairs of opposite sides parallel.

partner One of two numbers that add to make a total. In the equation 9 + 7 = 16, 9 and 7 are the partners.

pennies place In dollar notation, the second place to the right of the decimal point. In the amount $3.47, the 7 is in the pennies place.

pentagon A five-sided figure.

perimeter The distance around the outside of a figure.

perpendicular Two lines, line segments, or rays that cross or meet to form right angles.

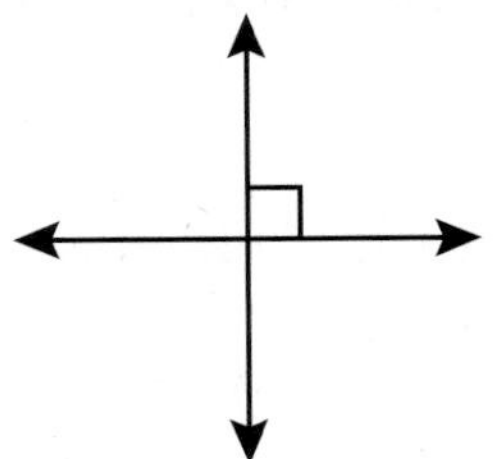

pictograph A graph that uses pictures or symbols to represent data.

pint (pt) A customary unit used to measure capacity. 1 pint = 2 cups

place value The value assigned to the place that a digit occupies in a number.

place value drawing A drawing that represents a number. Thousands are represented by a bar, hundreds are represented by boxes, tens by vertical lines, and ones by small circles.

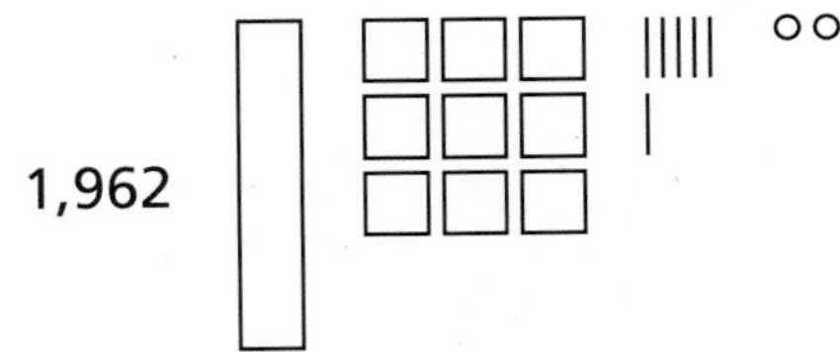

plane A flat surface that extends without end in all directions. It has no thickness.

plane figure A geometric figure that lies entirely in one plane.

P.M. The abbreviation for post meridiem, Latin for after noon. Used to indicate a time after noon.

polygon A closed plane figure make up of line segments.

pound (lb) A customary unit used to measure weight. 1 pound = 16 ounces

prism A solid figure with two parallel congruent bases, and rectangles or parallelograms for faces. A prism is named by the shape of its bases.

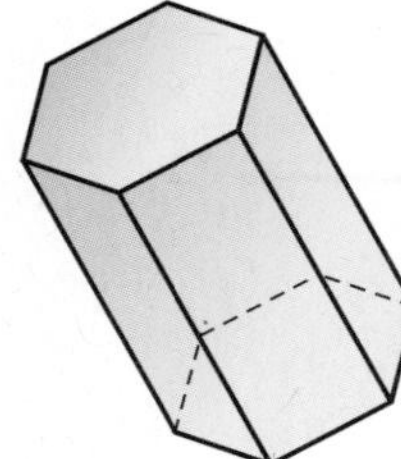

probability The chance of an event occurring.

product The answer when you multiply numbers. In the equation 4 × 7 = 28, 28 is the product.

proof drawing A drawing used to show that an answer is correct.

$$\begin{array}{r} 249 \\ +\ 386 \\ \hline 635 \end{array}$$

put together problem A problem that involves putting together (combining, joining) groups of things to form a total.

pyramid A solid figure with one base and whose other faces are triangles with a common vertex. A pyramid is named by the shape of its base.

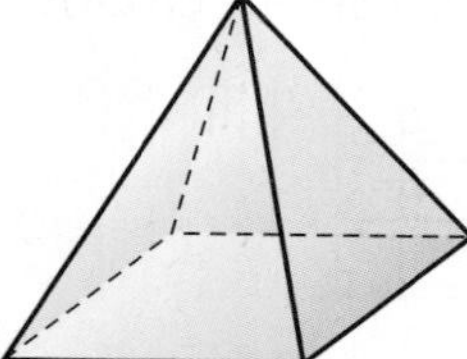

Q

quadrilateral A figure with four sides.

quart (qt) A customary unit used to measure capacity. 1 quart = 4 cups

quarter turn A 90° rotation.

Quick 9s A short-cut for multiplying by 9 in which students bend down one finger to represent the multiplier. The remaining fingers to the left of the bent finger represent the tens digit of the product and the fingers to the right of the bent finger represent the ones digit of the product.

This method works because
3 × 9 = 3 × (10 − 1) = 30 − 3 = 27

quotient The answer when you divide numbers. In the equation 35 ÷ 7 = 5, 5 is the quotient.

R

radius A line segment that connects the center of a circle to any point on the circle. The term is also used to describe the length of such a line segment.

range The difference between the greatest number and the least number in a set of data. In this set of numbers {12, 15, 18, 19, 20}, the range is 20 − 12 or 8.

ray A part of a line that has one endpoint and goes on forever in one direction.

rectangle A parallelogram that has 4 right angles.

reflection (flip) A transformation that involves flipping a figure over a line. The size and shape of the figure remain the same.

reflectional symmetry See **line symmetry**.

remainder In division, the quantity that is left over which is not large enough to make another whole group. In the division example, 32 divided by 6, the quotient is 5 with a remainder of 2. There are 5 groups of 6 and one more group that has only 2 items (the remainder).

repeated addition An introduction to multiplication in which students add the same number (3) several times (4) to show that 3 + 3 + 3 + 3 produces the same result as 4 × 3.

Repeated Groups drawing A drawing which children create that represents factors and products.

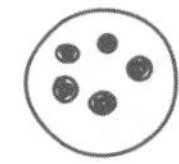 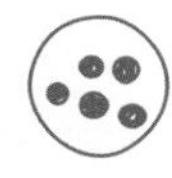 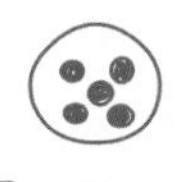 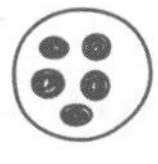

4 × 5 = 20

repeated groups problem A type of multiplication word problem that involves multiple groups with the same number of items in each group.

repeating pattern A pattern consisting of a group of numbers, letters, or figures that repeat.
Examples: 1, 2, 1, 2, ...
A, B, C, A, B, C, ...

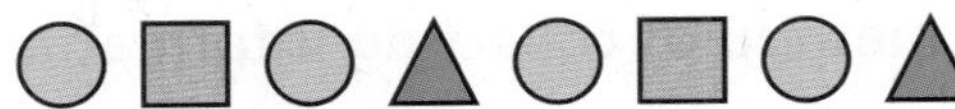

rhombus A parallelogram with congruent sides.

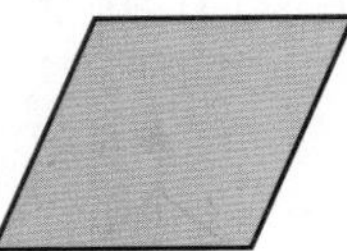

right angle An angle that measures 90°.

right triangle A triangle with one right angle.

rotation (turn) A transformation that involves a turn of a figure about a point. The size and shape of the figure remain the same.

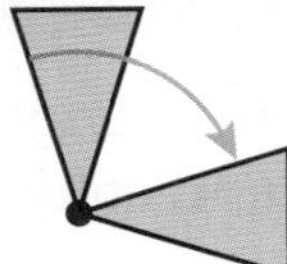

round To find *about* how many or how much by expressing a number to the nearest ten, hundred, thousand, and so on.

route The path taken to get to a location.

row A horizontal group of cells in table.

rule In a pattern such as a function table or number sequence, what is done to the first number to get to the second number and so on. The rule *Add 3* is shown in the function table.

Add 3.	
0	3
1	4
2	5
3	6

The rule $n + 7$ is shown in the number sequence: 2, 9, 16, 23 . . . .

S

scale An arrangement of numbers in order with equal intervals.

scalene triangle A triangle with sides of three different lengths.

Secret Code Cards Cards printed with the digits 0 through 9, multiples of 10 from 10 through 90 and multiples of 100 from 100 through 1,000. The number is represented on the back of the card by dots, sticks, or boxes. The cards are used to teach place value.

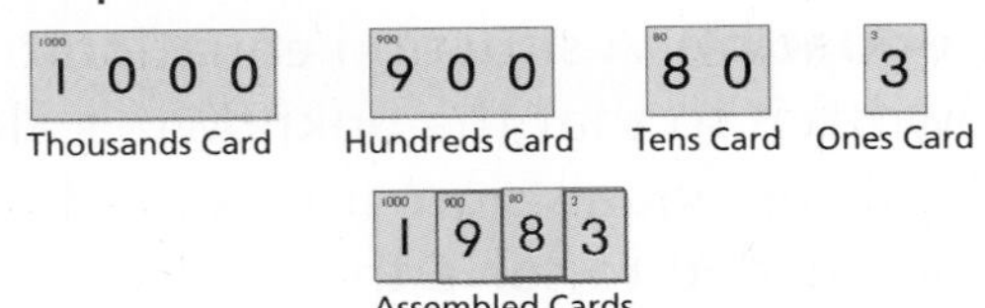

set A group of numbers or other things.

Show All Totals Method A method for finding a total of multi-digit numbers.

```
                586
the new
thousand ---> + 749
              1,200
the new
hundred  --->   120
the new
ten      --->    15
              1,335
```

Teacher Glossary (Continued)

shrinking pattern A number or geometric pattern that decreases.
Example: 15, 12, 9, 6, 3,...
25, 20, 16, 13, 11,...

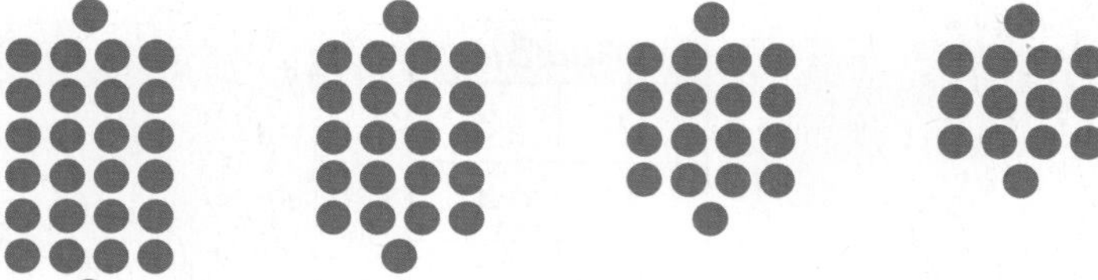

side (of a plane figure) A line segment that makes up a plane figure.

simplify To write an equivalent fraction with a smaller numerator and denominator.

situation equation An equation children write to show a story problem situation. It may or may not have the unknown isolated on one side of the equals sign.

slide To move a figure along a line. The size and shape of the figure remain the same.

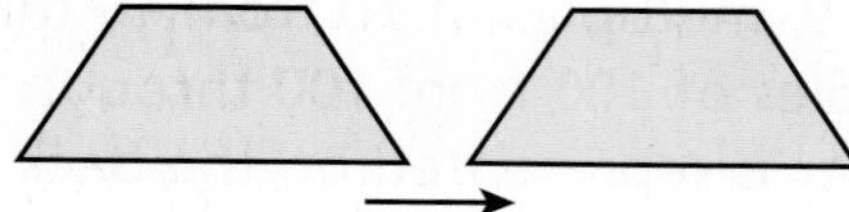

solid figure A figure that has three dimensions.

solution equation A situation equation that has been rewritten so that the unknown is alone on one side of the equals sign. It is related to the operation needed to solve the problem rather than to the actions in the story problem.

sphere A solid figure shaped like a ball.

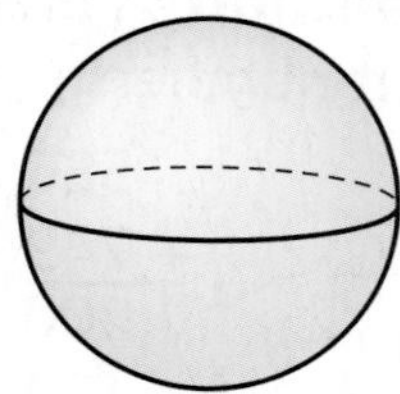

square A rectangle with four sides of the same length.

square number A product of a whole number and itself. $4 \times 4 = 16$, so 16 is a square number.

square unit Unit used to measure area that is 1 unit on each side. A square foot, for example, is a unit that is 1 foot on each side.

standard form The name of a number written using digits. For example, 1,829.

standard unit A recognized unit of measure, such as an inch or centimeter.

straight angle An angle that measures 180°.

strategy cards Cards that display a multiplication or division exercise on one side. The other side shows the answer to the exercise, the count-bys (up to the product) for both factors, and a Fast-Array drawing that shows the product and the two factors.

sum The answer when adding two or more addends. In the equation $37 + 52 = 89$, 89 is the sum.

survey A method of collecting information.

symmetry A figure has symmetry if it can be folded along a line so that the two halves match exactly.

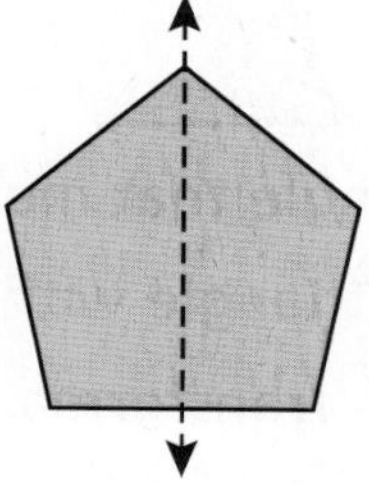

T

table An easy to read arrangement of data, organized in rows and columns.

take apart problem A problem that involves separating a group of objects.

tally marks A group of lines drawn in order to count. Each mark stands for 1 unit.

卌 卌 ||| means 13
5 5 3

ten stick In a place value drawing a vertical line used to represent 10.

tenth One of the equal parts when a whole is divided into ten equal parts.

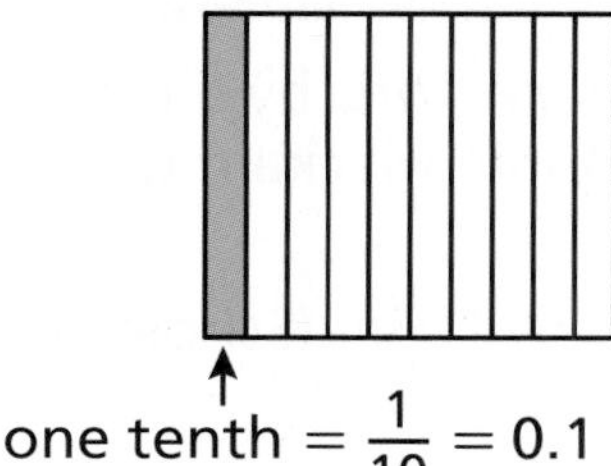

thousand bar In a place value drawing, a bar used to represent 1,000. A thousand bar is a quick way of drawing 1,000.

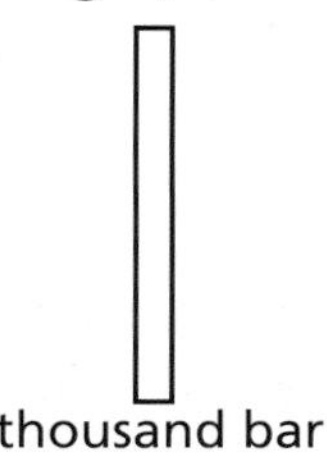

three-dimensional figure A figure with three dimensions.

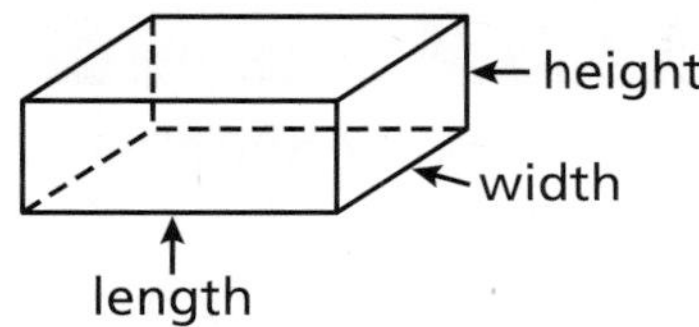

total The sum of two or more numbers. In the equation 672 + 228 = 900, 900 is the total.

transformation One of three basic motions: reflection (flip), rotation (turn), and translation (slide).

translation (slide) A transformation that involves sliding a figure along a line. The size and shape of the figure remain the same.

trapezoid A quadrilateral with exactly one pair of parallel sides.

turn To rotate a figure around a point. The size and shape of the figure remain the same.

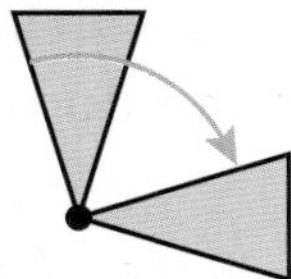

two-dimensional figure A figure with two dimensions.

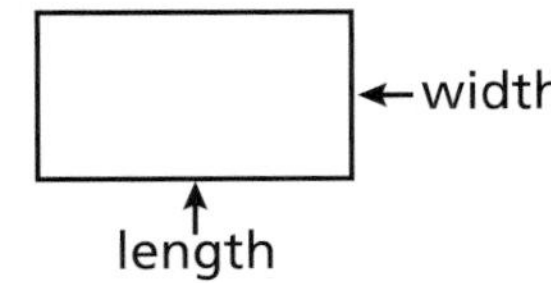

U

ungroup To break into a new group in order to be able to subtract.

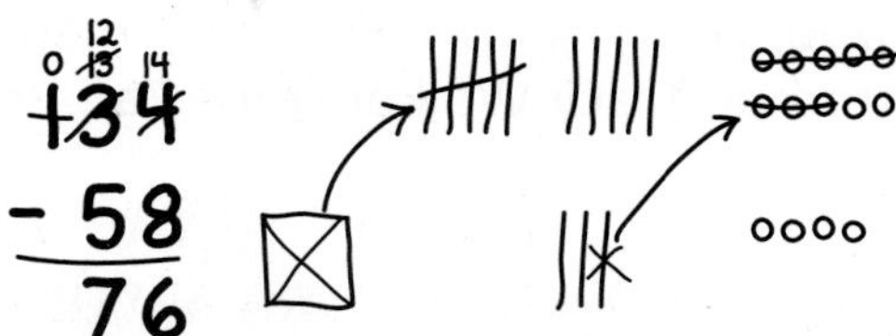

unit fraction A fraction with a numerator of 1.

V

Venn diagram A diagram that uses circles to show the relationship among sets of objects.

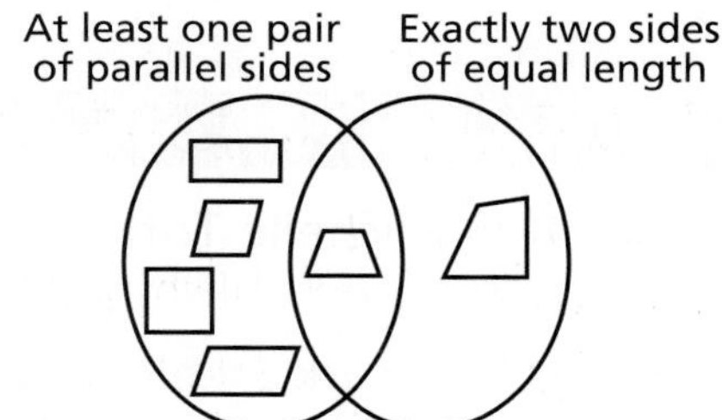

vertex A point where sides, rays, or edges meet.

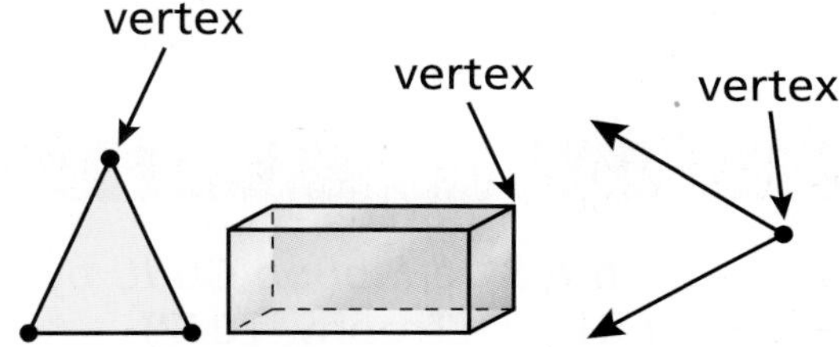

vertical Extending in two directions, up and down.

volume The measure of the amount of space occupied by an object.

W

weight The measure of how heavy something is. (Weight varies because weight is the effect of gravity on matter; mass is constant.)

word form A name of a number written using words instead of digits. For example, nine hundred eighty-four.

Y

yard (yd) A customary unit used to measure length. 1 yard = 3 feet

Recommended Books

Unit 1

How Much, How Many, How Far, How Heavy, How Long, How Tall Is 1000?, by Helen Nolan, illustrated by Tracy Walker (Kids Can Press, 1995)

Unit 2

Grandfather Tang's Story: A Tale Told with Tangrams, by Ann Tompert, illustrated by Robert Andrew Parker (Bantam Doubleday Dell Books for Young Readers, 1997)

Unit 3

One Less Fish, by Kim Michelle Toft and Allen Sheather (Charlesbridge Publishing, 1998)

A Bundle of Beasts, by Mark Steele and Patricia Hooper, illustrated by Mark Steele (Houghton Mifflin, 1987)

Unit 4

Sam Johnson and the Blue Ribbon Quilt, by Lisa Campbell Ernst (HarperTrophy, 2002)

Unit 5

Amanda Bean's Amazing Dream: A Mathematical Story, by Cindy Neuschwander, illustrated by Liza Woodruff, Math Activities by Marilyn Burns (Scholastic Press, 1998)

The Greatest Gymnast of All, by Stuart J. Murphy, illustrated by Cynthia Jabar (HarperTrophy, 1998)

Unit 6

One Hundred Hungry Ants, by Elinor J. Pinczes, illustrated by Bonnie Mackain (Houghton Mifflin Company, 1993)

One Grain of Rice, by Demi (Scholastic Press, 1997)

Unit 7

A Grain of Rice, by Helena Clare Pittman (Yearling, 1995)

Amanda Bean's Amazing Dream: A Mathematical Story, by Cindy Neuschwander, illustrated by Liza Woodruff, Math Activities by Marilyn Burns (Scholastic Press, 1998)

Unit 8

Building with Shapes, by Rebecca Weber (Compass Point Books, 2005)

Spaghetti and Meatballs for All!: A Mathematical Story, by Marilyn Burns, illustrated by Debbie Tilley (Scholastic Press, 1997)

Unit 9

The Doorbell Rang, by Pat Hutchins (Greenwillow Books, 1986)

Sea Squares, by Joy N. Hulme, illustrated by Carol Schwartz (Hyperion Books, 1993)

Unit 10

Jumanji, by Chris Van Allsburg (Houghton Mifflin Company, 1981)

Secret Treasures and Magical Measures: Adventures in Measurement: Temperature, Time, Length, Weight, Volume, Angles, Shapes, and Money, by Chris Kensler (Simon & Schuster, 2003)

Recommended Books (Continued)

Unit 11

Fraction Fun, by David A. Adler, illustrated by Nancy Tobin (Holiday House, 1996)

The Big Orange Splot, by Daniel Manus Pinkwater (Rebound by Sagebrush, 1999)

Jump, Kangaroo, Jump!, by Stuart J. Murphy, illustrated by Kevin O'Malley (HarperTrophy, 1999)

Mega-Fun Fractions, by Martin Lee and Marcia Miller (Teaching Resources, 2002)

The Fraction Family Heads West, by Marti Dryk, Ph.D., illustrated by Trevor Romain, D.M. (Bookaloppy Press, 1997)

Piece = Part = Portion: Fractions = Decimals = Percents, by Scott Gifford, photographs by Shmuel Thaler (Tricycle Press, 2003)

A Remainder of One, by Elinor J. Pinczes, illustrated by Bonnie Mackain (Houghton Mifflin, 1995)

The Great Divide, by Dayle Ann Dodds, illustrated by Tracy Mitchell (Candlewick Press, 2005)

Unit 12

Building with Shapes, by Rebecca Weber (Compass Point Books, 2005)

Unit 13

Penguins at Home: Gentoos of Antartica, by Bruce McMillan (Houghton Mifflin Company, 1993)

Room for Ripley, by Stuart J. Murphy, illustrated by Sylvie Wickstrom (HarperTrophy, 1999)

How Tall, How Short, How Faraway?, by David A. Adler, illustrated by Nancy Tobin (Holiday House, 2000)

Unit 14

Alice Ramsey's Grand Adventure, by Don Brown (Houghton Mifflin Company, 1997)

Index

D

E

F

G

H

I

L

M

Index (Continued)